A PEOPLE & A NATION

A History of the United States

NINTH EDITION

Mary Beth Norton
Cornell University

Carol Sheriff
College of William and Mary

David W. Blight
Yale University

Howard P. Chudacoff
Brown University

Fredrik Logevall
Cornell University

Beth Bailey
Temple University

WADSWORTH
CENGAGE Learning™

Australia • Brazil • Japan • Korea • Mexico • Singapore • Spain • United Kingdom • United States

WADSWORTH
CENGAGE Learning™

A People and A Nation,
Ninth Edition, Advantage Edition
Mary Beth Norton, Carol Sheriff, David W. Blight, Howard P. Chudacoff, Fredrik Logevall, Beth Bailey

Senior Publisher: Suzanne Jeans

Senior Sponsoring Editor: Ann West

Senior Development Editor: Julia Giannotti

Assistant Editor: Megan Chrisman

Editorial Assistant: Patrick Roach

Senior Media Editor: Lisa Ciccolo

Senior Marketing Manager: Katherine Bates

Marketing Coordinator: Lorreen Pelletier

Marketing Communications Manager: Caitlin Green

Project Management: PreMediaGlobal

Senior Art Director: Cate Rickard Barr

Senior Print Buyer: Sandee Milewski

Senior Rights Acquisition Specialist: Shalice Shah-Caldwell

Senior Photo Manager: Jennifer Meyer Dare

Caption: Henri, Robert (1865–1929). The Laundress, c. 1916 (oil on canvas)

Credit: Phoenix Art Museum, Arizona, USA/Gift of Mr. and Mrs. Norman Hirschl/The Bridgeman Art Library

Compositor: PreMediaGlobal

For product information and technology assistance, contact us at **Cengage Learning Customer & Sales Support, 1-800-354-9706**

For permission to use material from this text or product, submit all requests online at **www.cengage.com/permissions.** Further permissions questions can be emailed to **permissionrequest@cengage.com.**

Library of Congress Control Number: 2010941739

ISBN-13: 978-0-495-91624-6

ISBN-10: 0-495-91624-2

Wadsworth
20 Channel Center Street
Boston, MA 02210
USA

Cengage Learning is a leading provider of customized learning solutions with office locations around the globe, including Singapore, the United Kingdom, Australia, Mexico, Brazil and Japan. Locate your local office at **international.cengage.com/region**

Cengage Learning products are represented in Canada by Nelson Education, Ltd.

For your course and learning solutions, visit **www.cengage.com**

Purchase any of our products at your local college store or at our preferred online store **www.cengagebrain.com.**

Instructors: Please visit **login.cengage.com** and log in to access instructor-specific resources.

ted in the United States of America
4 5 6 7 15 14 13 12 11

Brief Contents

Contents

Maps

Preface

In this ninth edition, *A People and A Nation* has undergone significant revisions, while still retaining the narrative strength and focus that have made it so popular with students and teachers alike. In the years since the publication of the eighth edition, new material has been uncovered, novel interpretations advanced, and new themes have come to the forefront of American historical scholarship. All of the authors have incorporated those findings into this text.

Like other teachers and students, we are always re-creating our past, restructuring our memory, and rediscovering the personalities and events that have influenced us, injured us, and bedeviled us. This book represents our continuing rediscovery of America's history—its diverse people and the nation they created and nurtured. As this book demonstrates, there are many different Americans and many different memories. We have sought to present as many of them as possible, in both triumph and tragedy, in both division and unity.

ABOUT A PEOPLE AND A NATION

A People and A Nation, first published in 1982, was the first major textbook in the United States to fully integrate social and political history. From the outset, the authors have been determined to tell the story of *all* the people of the United States. This book's hallmarks have been its melding of social and political history and its movement beyond history's common focus on public figures and events to examine the daily life of America's people. All editions of the book have stressed the interaction of public policy and personal experience, the relationship between domestic concerns and foreign affairs, the various manifestations of popular culture, and the multiple origins of America and Americans. We have consistently built our narrative on a firm foundation in primary sources—on both well-known and obscure letters, diaries, public documents, oral histories, and artifacts of material culture. We have long challenged readers to think about the meaning of American history—not just to memorize facts. Both students and instructors have repeatedly told us how much they appreciate and enjoy our approach to the past.

Numerous maps, tables, graphs, and charts provide readers with the necessary geographical and statistical context for observations in the text. Carefully selected illustrations—many of them unique to this book—offer readers visual insight into the topics under discussion, especially because the authors have written the captions. In this edition, as in all previous ones, we have sought to incorporate up-to-date scholarship, readability, a clear structure, critical thinking, and instructive illustrative material on every page.

THEMES IN THIS BOOK

Several themes and questions stand out in our continuing effort to integrate political, social, and cultural history. We study the many ways that Americans have defined themselves—gender, race, class, region, ethnicity, religion, sexual orientation—and the many subjects that have reflected their multidimensional experiences. We highlight the remarkably diverse everyday lives of the American people—in cities and on farms and ranches, in factories and in corporate headquarters, in neighborhoods and in legislatures, in love relationships and in hate groups, in recreation and in work, in the classroom and in military uniform, in secret national security conferences and in public foreign relations debates, in church and in voluntary associations, in polluted environments and in conservation areas. We pay particular attention to lifestyles, diet and dress, family life and structure, labor conditions, gender roles, migration and mobility, childbearing, and child rearing. We explore how Americans have entertained and informed themselves by discussing their music, sports, theater, print media, film, radio, television, graphic arts, and literature, in both "high" culture and popular culture. We study how technology—such as the internal combustion engine and the computer—has influenced Americans' lives.

Americans' personal lives have always interacted with the public realm of politics and government. To understand how Americans have sought to protect their different ways of life and to work out solutions to thorny problems, we emphasize their expectations of governments at the local, state, and federal levels; governments' role in providing answers; the lobbying of interest groups; the campaigns and outcomes of elections; and the hierarchy of power in any period. Because the United States has long been a major participant in world affairs, we explore America's participation in wars, interventions in other nations, empire-building, immigration patterns, images of foreign peoples, cross-national cultural ties, and international economic trends.

WHAT'S NEW IN THIS EDITION

Planning for the ninth edition began at a two-day authors' meeting at the Cengage offices in Boston. There we discussed the most recent scholarship in the field, the reviews of the eighth edition solicited from instructors, and the findings of our own continuing research. Our author meetings, which we greatly enjoy, are always characterized by intellectual exhilaration and vigorous discussion as we exchange views and ideas.

This edition builds on its predecessors in continuing to enhance the global perspective on American history that has characterized the book since its first edition. From the "Atlantic world" context of European colonies in North and South America to the discussion of international terrorism, the authors have incorporated the most recent globally oriented scholarship throughout the volume. As in the eighth edition, we have worked to strengthen our treatment of the diversity of America's people by examining differences within the broad ethnic categories commonly employed and by paying attention to immigration, cultural, and intellectual infusions from around the world and America's growing religious diversity. We have also stressed the incorporation of different peoples into the United States through territorial acquisition as well as through immigration. At the same time, we have integrated the discussion of such diversity into our narrative so as not to artificially isolate any group from the mainstream.

PRIMARY SOURCES

We believe that students need lots of opportunities to engage in historical thinking around primary sources, and we have provided more opportunities for this type of work in the ninth edition. The new "Visualizing the Past" feature described below helps students engage with visual sources with guided captions and questions. Students will be able to access additional primary sources through links on the student CourseMate web site. Instructors who want a fully integrated online primary source reader to use in conjunction with *A People and A Nation* will find it available as an "Editor's Choice" option inside the new CourseReader for U.S. History (described in the supplements section).

As always, the authors reexamined every sentence, interpretation, map, chart, illustration, and caption, refining the narrative, presenting new examples, and bringing to the text the latest findings of scholars in many areas of history, anthropology, sociology, and political science.

"LINKS TO THE WORLD" AND "VISUALIZING THE PAST"

"Links to the World" features examine both inward and outward ties between America (and Americans) and the rest of the world. The Links appear at appropriate places in certain chapters to explore specific topics at considerable length. Tightly constructed essays detail the often-little-known connections between developments here and abroad. The topics range broadly over economic, political, social, technological, medical, and cultural history, vividly demonstrating that the geographical region that is now the United States has never lived in isolation from other peoples and countries. New to this edition are Links on filibustering, the "back to Africa" movement, study abroad programs and swine flu. Each Link highlights global interconnections with unusual and lively examples that will both intrigue and inform students.

We have a brand-new feature in this edition, "Visualizing the Past," which aims to give students the chance to examine primary source material and engage in critical thinking about it. For certain chapters, the authors have selected one or two visual sources (including cartoons, photographic images, and artwork) that tell a story about the era with captions that help students understand how the careful examination of primary source content can reveal deeper insights into the period under discussion. We have chosen to focus on visual sources for this feature because these are often the hardest for instructors to find and prepare good pedagogy around—and because we have always given visual material a strong role in the text. An example from Chapter 25 includes a photograph of the women's "emergency brigade" demonstration during the 1937 sit-down strike by automobile workers in Flint, Michigan. The caption describes the scene and then asks questions that guide students toward a deeper analysis of the image—and of its historical significance.

SECTION-BY-SECTION CHANGES IN THIS EDITION

Mary Beth Norton, who had primary responsibility for Chapters 1 through 8 and served as coordinating author, augmented the treatment of early European explorations of the Americas (including the publicist Richard Hakluyt) and now explores the use of the calumet (the so-called peace pipe) by Indian nations and Europeans alike. She expanded the discussion of religious diversity in England and its colonies and the religious impulse for colonization and revised the section on the middle passage to give more attention to the experience of enslaved captives on shipboard. To clarify chronology, she moved some material on the French and Spanish colonies in North America from Chapter 3 to Chapter 4 and in the latter greatly increased coverage of the residents of the west in the eighteenth century—Native Americans, Spaniards, and French people alike. New scholarship on the Seven Years' War, the American Revolution, and the Constitutional Convention has been incorporated into Chapters 5 through 7. More information on women's political roles and aims has been added, in conjunction with a considerably expanded treatment of partisanship in the early republic.

Carol Sheriff, responsible for Chapters 9 and 11 through 13, enhanced coverage of the nationalistic culture of the early republic and early New Orleans and revised the discussion of the War of 1812 and Aaron Burr. She has added discussions of the penny press, Henry David Thoreau, science and engineering, women's activities, and penitentiaries. The treatment of politics in general has been reworked, with special attention to political violence, and a new chart detailing the era's presidents has been included. Chapter 13 now contains considerably more information on the southwestern borderlands, includes more quotations from residents of the American West, and deals with anti-expansionism and the abuse of Indians in Catholic missions.

David W. Blight, who had primary responsibility for Chapter 10 and Chapters 14 through 16, has enhanced the discussion of the economic causes of secession and the Civil War and the economic history of the war itself, drawing on extensive new scholarship. He now considers the Union soldiers' ideology and has added material on the effects of the cultural impact of the large numbers of war dead in both North and South. Chapters 15 and 16 both include new treatments of judicial topics, and the latter also discusses scalawags and carpetbaggers at greater length than before.

Howard P. Chudacoff, responsible for Chapters 17 through 21 and Chapter 24, has extensively revised and updated the treatment of technological change in the late nineteenth century and of women's suffrage. He has added discussions of Native peoples in the Southwest, western folk heroes, government and water rights, labor violence in the west, female entertainers (and opposition to them from moralists like Anthony Comstock), Woodrow Wilson's racism, Marcus Garvey, and the Great Migration of African Americans to the North in the twenties. He has also consolidated the analysis of settlement houses in Chapter 21 to avoid repetition.

Fredrik Logevall, with primary responsibility for Chapters 22, 23, 26, and 28, updated the discussions of late nineteenth-century American imperialism and the origins of the Cold War and added new material on nurses and African American soldiers in World War I.

Beth Bailey, primarily responsible for Chapters 25, 27, and 29, incorporated new scholarship on popular culture, the institutional history of the New Deal, the ecological crisis of the thirties, the internment of Japanese citizens and Japanese Americans during World War II, the liberation of Europe, the GI Bill, and the return of veterans in the postwar period. She enhanced the discussion of wartime propaganda and censorship. Parts of Chapter 29 underwent extensive revision and reorganization as well.

Logevall and Bailey shared responsibility for Chapters 30 through 33. These chapters now include expanded consideration of the struggle for civil rights and social justice in the North and the opposition to that struggle in the form of protests against school busing. Chapter 31 has a new section on the freedom and responsibilities of youth and enhanced discussions of popular culture, women in the military, and religious cults. New material has been added on foreign policy and changes in American living patterns. As is always the case, Chapter 33, which covers the recent past, underwent thorough revision and reorganization. It covers the second term of George W. Bush, the election of Barack Obama, the Great Recession, and the Iraq and Afghanistan wars.

TEACHING AND LEARNING AIDS

The supplements listed here accompany the ninth edition of *A People and A Nation*. They have been created with the diverse needs of today's students and instructors in mind.

FOR THE INSTRUCTOR

- *Aplia.* Aplia™ is an online learning solution that helps students take responsibility for their learning by engaging them with course material, honing their critical thinking skills, and preparing them for class. Created by an instructor for other instructors, Aplia prompts history students to read carefully and think critically. For every chapter, text-specific exercises ask students to consider individual details that support larger historical concepts and draw conclusions rather than reciting historical facts. Every chapter includes at least one set of questions based on a map from the text. The assignments also give students experience reading and interpreting primary source documents, images, and other media. The automatically graded assignments include detailed, immediate explanations that ensure students put forth effort on a regular basis. Gradebook analytics help instructors monitor and address student performance on an individual or group basis. For more information, please visit www.aplia. com/cengage.

- *Instructor Companion Site.* Instructors will find here all the tools they need to teach a rich and successful U.S. history survey course. The protected teaching materials include the *Instructor's Resource Manual*, written by George C. Warren of Central Piedmont Community College; a set of customizable Microsoft® PowerPoint® lecture slides, created by Barney Rickman of Valdosta State University; and a set of customizable Microsoft® PowerPoint® slides, including all the images (photos, art, and maps) from the text. The companion web site also provides instructors with access to HistoryFinder and to the Wadsworth American History Resource Center (see descriptions below). Go to www.Cengage.com/history to access this site.

- *PowerLecture CD-ROM with ExamView® and JoinIn®.* This dual-platform, all-in-one multimedia resource includes the *Instructor's Resource Manual*; Test Bank in Word® and PDF formats; customizable Microsoft® PowerPoint® slides of both lecture outlines and images from the text; and *JoinIn®* PowerPoint slides with clicker content. Also included is ExamView®, an easy-to-use assessment and tutorial system that allows instructors to create, deliver, and customize tests in minutes. The test items, written by George C. Warren of Central Piedmont Community College, include multiple-choice, identification, geography, and essay questions.

- *HistoryFinder.* This searchable online database allows instructors to quickly and easily search and download selections from among thousands of assets, including art, photographs, maps, primary sources, and audio/video clips. Each asset downloads directly into a Microsoft® PowerPoint® slide, allowing instructors to easily create exciting PowerPoint presentations for their classrooms.

- *eInstructor's Resource Manual.* Written by George C. Warren of Central Piedmont Community College, this manual contains for each chapter a set of learning objectives, a comprehensive chapter outline, ideas for classroom activities, discussion questions, suggested paper topics, and a lecture supplement. It is available on the instructor's companion web site and in the PowerLecture CD-ROM.

- *WebTutor™ on Blackboard® and WebCT®.* With WebTutor's text-specific, preformatted content and total flexibility, instructors can easily create and manage their own custom course web site. WebTutor's course management tool gives instructors the ability to provide virtual office hours, post syllabi, set up threaded discussions, track student progress with quiz material, and much more. For students, WebTutor offers real-time access to a full array of study tools, including audio chapter summaries, practice quizzes, glossary flashcards, and web links.

- *CourseMate.* Cengage Learning's CourseMate brings course concepts to life with interactive learning, study, and exam preparation tools that support the printed textbook. Watch student comprehension soar as your class works with the printed textbook and the *A People and A Nation* CourseMate web site, with interactive teaching and learning tools, and EngagementTracker, a first-of-its-kind tool that monitors student engagement in the course. Learn more at www.cengagebrain.com.

STUDENT RESOURCES

- *CourseMate.* For students, the CourseMate web site provides an additional source of interactive learning, study, and exam preparation outside the classroom. Students will find outlines and objectives, focus questions, flashcards, quizzes, primary source links, and video clips. The CourseMate site also includes an integrated *A People and A Nation* eBook. Students taking quizzes will be linked directly to relevant sections in the ebook for additional information. The ebook is fully searchable and students can even take notes and save them for later review. In addition, the ebook links to rich media assets such as video and MP3 chapter summaries, primary source documents with critical-thinking questions, and interactive (zoomable) maps. Students can use the ebook as their primary text or as a companion multimedia support. It is available at www.cengagebrain.com.

- *Wadsworth American History Resource Center.* The resource center gives your students access to a "virtual reader" with hundreds of primary sources, including speeches, letters, legal documents and transcripts, poems, maps, simulations, timelines, and additional images that bring history to life, along with interactive assignable exercises. A map feature including Google Earth™ coordinates and exercises will aid in student comprehension of geography and use of maps. Students can compare the traditional textbook map with an aerial view of the location today. It's an ideal resource for study, review, and research. In addition to this map feature, the resource center also provides blank maps for student review and testing. Ask your sales representative for more information on how to bundle access to the HRC with your text.

- *cengagebrain.com.* Save your students time and money. Direct them to www.cengagebrain.com for choice in formats and savings and a better chance to succeed in class. Students have the freedom to purchase à la carte exactly what they need when they need it. There, students can purchase a downloadable ebook or electronic access to the American History Resource Center, the premium study tools and interactive ebook in the *A People and A Nation* CourseMate, or eAudio modules from *The History Handbook*. Students can save 50 percent on the electronic textbook and can pay as little as $1.99 for an individual eChapter.

- *Reader Program.* Cengage Learning publishes a number of readers, some containing exclusively primary sources, others a combination of primary and secondary sources, and many designed to guide students through the process of historical inquiry. Visit Cengage.com/history for a complete list of readers or ask your sales representative to recommend a reader that would work well for your specific needs.

CUSTOM OPTIONS

Nobody knows your students like you, so why not give them a text tailor-fit to their needs? Cengage Learning offers custom solutions for your course—whether it's making a small modification to *A People and A Nation* to match your syllabus or combining multiple sources to create something truly unique. You can pick and choose chapters, include your own material, and add additional map exercises along with the Rand McNally Atlas (including questions developed around the maps in the atlas) to create a text that fits the way you teach. Ensure that your students get the most out of their textbook dollar by giving them exactly what they need. Contact your Cengage Learning representative to explore custom solutions for your course.

- *Rand McNally Atlas of American History, 2e.* This comprehensive atlas features more than 80 maps, with new content covering global perspectives, including events in the Middle East from 1945 to 2005, as well as population trends in the United States mercy and around the world. Additional maps document voyages of discovery; the settling of the colonies; major U.S. military engagements, including the American Revolution and World Wars I and II; and sources of immigrations, ethnic populations, and patterns of economic change.

- *CourseReader.* Cengage Learning's new CourseReader lets instructors create a customized electronic reader in minutes. Instructors can choose exactly what their students will be assigned by searching or browsing Cengage Learning's extensive document database. Sources include hundreds of historical documents, images, and media, plus literary essays that can add additional interest and insight to a primary source assignment. Or instructors can start with the "Editor's Choice" collection created for *A People and A Nation*—and then update it to suit their particular needs. Each source comes with all the pedagogical tools needed to provide a full learning experience, including a descriptive headnote that puts the reading into context as well as critical-thinking and multiple-choice questions designed to reinforce key points. Contact your local Cengage Learning sales representative for more information and packaging options.

ACKNOWLEDGMENTS

The authors would like to thank the following people for their assistance with the preparation of this edition: Philip Daileader, David Farber, Danyel Logevall, Jon Parmenter, Anna Daileader Sheriff, Benjamin Daileader Sheriff, and Selene Sheriff.

At each stage of this revision, a sizable panel of historian reviewers read drafts of our chapters. Their suggestions, corrections, and pleas helped guide us through this momentous revision. We could not include all of their recommendations, but the book is better for our having heeded most of their advice. We heartily thank:

Sara Alpern, *Texas A&M University*
Friederike Baer, *Temple University*
Troy Bickham, *Texas A&M University*
Robert Bionaz, *Chicago State University*
Victoria Bynum, *Texas State University, San Marcos*
Mario Fenyo, *Bowie State University*
Walter Hixson, *University of Akron*
Allison McNeese, *Mount Mercy College*

Steve O'Brien, *Bridgewater State College*
Paul O'Hara, *Xavier University*
John Putman, *San Diego State University*
Thomas Roy, *University of Oklahoma*
Manfred Silva, *El Paso Community College*
Michael Vollbach, *Oakland Community College*

The authors thank the helpful Cengage people who designed, edited, produced, and nourished this book. Many thanks to Ann West, senior sponsoring editor; Julia Giannotti, senior development editor; Jane Lee, content product manager; Debbie Meyer, project editor; Pembroke Herbert, photo researcher; and Charlotte Miller, art editor.

M. B. N.
C. S.
D. B.
H. C.
F. L.
B. B.

About the Authors

MARY BETH NORTON

Born in Ann Arbor, Michigan, Mary Beth Norton received her B.A. from the University of Michigan (1964) and her Ph.D. from Harvard University (1969). She is the Mary Donlon Alger Professor of American History at Cornell University. Her dissertation won the Allan Nevins Prize. She has written *The British-Americans* (1972); *Liberty's Daughters* (1980, 1996); *Founding Mothers & Fathers* (1996), which was one of three finalists for the 1997 Pulitzer Prize in History; and *In the Devil's Snare* (2002), which was one of five finalists for the 2003 *LA Times* Book Prize in History and which won the English-Speaking Union's Ambassador Book Award in American Studies for 2003. She has co-edited three volumes on American women's history. She was also general editor of the *American Historical Association's Guide to Historical Literature* (1995). Her articles have appeared in such journals as the *American Historical Review, William and Mary Quarterly*, and *Journal of Women's History*. Mary Beth has served as president of the Berkshire Conference of Women Historians, as vice president for research of the American Historical Association, and as a presidential appointee to the National Council on the Humanities. She has appeared on Book TV, the History and Discovery Channels, PBS, and NBC as a commentator on Early American history, and she lectures frequently to high school teachers through the Teaching American History program. She has received four honorary degrees and in 1999 was elected a fellow of the American Academy of Arts and Sciences. She has held fellowships from the National Endowment for the Humanities; the Guggenheim, Rockefeller, and Starr Foundations; and the Henry E. Huntington Library. In 2005–2006, she was the Pitt Professor of American History and Institutions at the University of Cambridge and Newnham College.

CAROL SHERIFF

Born in Washington, D.C., and raised in Bethesda, Maryland, Carol Sheriff received her B.A. from Wesleyan University (1985) and her Ph.D. from Yale University (1993). Since 1993, she has taught history at the College of William and Mary, where she has won the Thomas Jefferson Teaching Award, the Alumni Teaching Fellowship Award, and the University Professorship for Teaching Excellence. Her publications include *The Artificial River: The Erie Canal and the Paradox of Progress* (1996), which won the Dixon Ryan Fox Award from the New York State Historical Association and the Award for Excellence in Research from the New York State Archives, and *A People at War: Civilians and Soldiers in America's Civil War, 1854–1877* (with Scott Reynolds Nelson, 2007). Carol has written sections of a teaching manual for the New York State history curriculum, given presentations at

Teaching American History grant projects, consulted on an exhibit for the Rochester Museum and Science Center, and appeared in the History Channel's Modern Marvels show on the Erie Canal, and she is engaged in several public-history projects marking the sesquicentennial of the Civil War. At William and Mary, she teaches the U.S. history survey as well as upper-level classes on the Early Republic, the Civil War Era, and the American West. Most recently, Carol has been named Class of 2013 term distinguished professor in recognition of her teaching, scholarship, and service.

DAVID W. BLIGHT

Born in Flint, Michigan, David W. Blight received his B.A. from Michigan State University (1971) and his Ph.D. from the University of Wisconsin (1985). He is now Class of 1954 Professor of American History and director of the Gilder Lehrman Center for the Study of Slavery, Resistance, and Abolition at Yale University. For the first seven years of his career, David was a public high school teacher in Flint. He has written *Frederick Douglass's Civil War* (1989) and *Race and Reunion: The Civil War in American Memory, 1863–1915* (2001), which received eight awards, including the Bancroft Prize, the Frederick Douglass Prize, and the Abraham Lincoln Prize, as well as four prizes awarded by the Organization of American Historians. His most recent book is *A Slave No More: The Emancipation of John Washington and Wallace Turnage* (2007), which won three prizes. He has edited or co-edited six other books, including editions of W. E. B. DuBois, *The Souls of Black Folk*, and *Narrative of the Life of Frederick Douglass*. David's essays have appeared in the *Journal of American History, Civil War History*, and Gabor Boritt, ed., *Why the Civil War Came* (1996), among others. In 1992–1993, he was senior Fulbright Professor in American Studies at the University of Munich, Germany, and in 2006–2007 he held a fellowship at the Dorothy and Lewis B. Cullman Center, New York Public Library. A consultant to several documentary films, David appeared in the 1998 PBS series, *Africans in America*. He has served on the Council of the American Historical Association. David also teaches summer seminars for secondary school teachers as well as for park rangers and historians of the National Park Service.

HOWARD P. CHUDACOFF

Howard P. Chudacoff, the George L. Littlefield Professor of American History and Professor of Urban Studies at Brown University, was born in Omaha, Nebraska. He earned his A.B. (1965) and Ph.D. (1969) from the University of Chicago. He has written *Mobile Americans* (1972), *How Old Are You?* (1989), *The Age of the Bachelor* (1999), *The Evolution of American Urban Society* (with Judith Smith, 2004), and *Children at Play: An American History* (2007). He has also co-edited with Peter Baldwin *Major Problems in American Urban History* (2004). His articles have appeared in such journals as the *Journal of Family History, Reviews in American History*, and *Journal of American History*. At Brown University, Howard has co-chaired the American Civilization Program and chaired the Department of History, and serves as Brown's faculty representative to the NCAA. He has also served on the board of directors of the Urban History Association. The National Endowment for the Humanities, Ford Foundation, and Rockefeller Foundation have given him awards to advance his scholarship.

FREDRIK LOGEVALL

A native of Stockholm, Sweden, Fredrik Logevall is John S. Knight Professor of International Studies and Professor of History at Cornell University, where he serves as director of the Mario Einaudi Center for International Studies. He received his B. A. from Simon Fraser University (1986) and his Ph.D. from Yale University (1993). His most recent book is *America's Cold War: The Politics of Insecurity* (with Campbell Craig, 2009). His other publications include *Choosing War* (1999), which won three prizes, including the Warren F. Kuehl Book Prize from the Society for Historians of American Foreign Relations (SHAFR); *The Origins of the Vietnam War* (2001); *Terrorism and 9/11: A Reader* (2002); as coeditor, the *Encyclopedia of American Foreign Policy* (2002); and, as co-editor, *The First Vietnam War: Colonial Conflict and Cold War Crisis* (2007). Fred is a past recipient of the Stuart L. Bernath article, book, and lecture prizes from SHAFR and is a member of the SHAFR Council, the Cornell University Press faculty board, and the editorial advisory board of the Presidential Recordings Project at the Miller Center of Public Affairs at the University of Virginia. In 2006–2007, he was Leverhulme Visiting Professor at the University of Nottingham and Mellon Senior Fellow at the University of Cambridge.

BETH BAILEY

Born in Atlanta, Georgia, Beth Bailey received her B.A. from Northwestern University (1979) and her Ph.D. from the University of Chicago (1986). She is now a professor of history at Temple University. Her research and teaching fields include war and society and the U.S. military, American cultural history (nineteenth and twentieth centuries), popular culture, and gender and sexuality. She is the author, most recently, of *America's Army: Making the All-Volunteer Force* (2009). Her other publications include *From Front Porch to Back Seat: Courtship in 20th Century America* (1988), *The First Strange Place: The Alchemy of Race and Sex in WWII Hawaii* (with David Farber, 1992), *Sex in the Heartland* (1999), and *The Columbia Companion to America in the 1960s* (with David Farber, 2001). She is co-editor of *A History of Our Time* (with William Chafe and Harvard Sitkoff, 7th ed., 2007). Beth has served as a consultant and/or on-screen expert for numerous television documentaries developed for PBS and the History Channel. She has received grants or fellowships from the American Council of Learned Societies, the National Endowment for the Humanities, and the Woodrow Wilson International Center for Scholars, and she was named the Ann Whitney Olin scholar at Barnard College, Columbia University, where she was the director of the American Studies Program and Regents Lecturer at the University of New Mexico. She has been a visiting scholar at Saitama University, Japan; at Trinity College at the University of Melbourne; and a senior Fulbright lecturer in Indonesia. She teaches courses on sexuality and gender and war and American culture.

A People & A Nation

1

▼

THREE OLD WORLDS CREATE A NEW
1492–1600

AMERICAN SOCIETIES

Human beings originated on the continent of Africa, where humanlike remains
about 3 million years old have been found in what is now Ethiopia. Over many
millennia, the growing population slowly dispersed to the other continents. Because
the climate was then far colder than it is now, much of the earth's water was concentrated in huge rivers of ice called glaciers. Sea levels were accordingly lower,
and land masses covered a larger proportion of the earth's surface than they do
today. Scholars long believed the earliest inhabitants of the Americas crossed a
land bridge known as Beringia (at the site of the Bering Strait) approximately
twelve thousand to fourteen thousand years ago. Yet striking new archaeological
discoveries in both North and South America suggest that parts of the Americas
may have been settled much earlier, perhaps by seafarers. Some geneticists now
theorize that three successive waves of migrants began at least thirty thousand
years ago. About 12,500 years ago, when the climate warmed and sea levels rose,
Americans were separated from the peoples living on the connected continents of
Asia, Africa, and Europe.

**Ancient
America**
The first Americans are called Paleo-Indians. Nomadic hunters of game and gatherers of wild plants, they spread
throughout North and South America, probably moving as
bands composed of extended families. By about 11,500 years ago, the Paleo-Indians

CHRONOLOGY

12,000–10,000 B.C.E.	Paleo-Indians migrate from Asia to North America across the Beringia land bridge
7000 B.C.E.	Cultivation of food crops begins in America
ca. 2000 B.C.E.	Olmec civilization appears
ca. 300–600 C.E.	Height of influence of Teotihuacán
ca. 600–900 C.E.	Classic Mayan civilization
1000 C.E.	Ancient Pueblos build settlements in modern states of Arizona and New Mexico
1001	Norse establish settlement in "Vinland"
1050–1250	Height of influence of Cahokia
	Prevalence of Mississippian culture in modern midwestern and southeastern United States
14th century	Aztec rise to power
1450s–80s	Portuguese explore and colonize islands in the Mediterranean Atlantic
1477	Marco Polo's *Travels* describes China
1492	Columbus reaches Bahamas
1494	Treaty of Tordesillas divides land claims between Spain and Portugal in Africa, India, and South America
1496	Last Canary Island falls to Spain
1497	Cabot reaches North America
1513	Ponce de León explores Florida
1518–30	Smallpox epidemic devastates Indian population of West Indies and Central and South America
1519	Cortés invades Mexico
1521	Aztec Empire falls to Spaniards
1524	Verrazzano sails along Atlantic coast of United States
1534–35	Cartier explores St. Lawrence River
1534–36	Vaca, Estevan, and two companions walk across North America
1539–42	Soto explores southeastern United States
1540–42	Coronado explores southwestern United States
1587–90	Raleigh's Roanoke colony vanishes
1588	Harriot publishes *A Briefe and True Report of the New Found Land of Virginia*

were making fine stone projectile points, which they attached to wooden spears and used to kill and butcher bison (buffalo), woolly mammoths, and other large mammals then living in the Americas. But as the Ice Age ended and the human population increased, all the large American mammals except the bison disappeared.

Scholars disagree about whether overhunting or the change in climate caused their demise. In either case, deprived of their primary source of meat, Paleo-Indians found new ways to survive.

By approximately nine thousand years ago, the residents of what is now central Mexico began to cultivate food crops, especially maize (corn), squash, beans, avocados, and peppers. In the Andes Mountains of South America, people started to grow potatoes. As knowledge of agricultural techniques improved and spread through the Americas, vegetables and maize proved a more reliable source of food than hunting and gathering. Except for those living in the harshest climates, most Americans started to adopt a more sedentary style of life so that they could tend fields regularly. Some established permanent settlements; others moved several times a year among fixed sites. They cleared forests through the use of controlled burning. The fires not only created cultivable lands by killing trees and fertilizing the soil with ashes but also opened meadows that attracted deer and other wildlife. All the American cultures emphasized producing sufficient food. Although they traded such items as shells, flint, salt, and copper, no society ever became dependent on another group for items vital to its survival.

Wherever agriculture dominated the economy, complex civilizations flourished. Such societies, assured of steady supplies of grains and vegetables, no longer had to devote all their energies to subsistence. Instead, they were able to accumulate wealth, produce ornamental objects, trade with other groups, and create elaborate rituals and ceremonies. In North America, the successful cultivation of nutritious crops, such as maize, beans, and squash, seems to have led to the growth and development of all the major civilizations: first the large city-states of Mesoamerica (modern Mexico and Guatemala) and then the urban clusters known collectively as the Mississippian culture and located in the present-day United States. Each of these societies, historians and archaeologists now believe, reached its height of population and influence only after achieving success in agriculture. Each later declined and collapsed after reaching the limits of its food supply, with dire political and military consequences.

Mesoamerican Civilizations

Archaeologists and historians still know little about the first major Mesoamerican civilization, the Olmecs, who about four thousand years ago lived near the Gulf of Mexico in cities dominated by temple pyramids. The Mayas and Teotihuacán, which developed approximately two thousand years later, are better recorded. Teotihuacán, founded in the Valley of Mexico about 300 B.C.E. (Before the Common Era), eventually became one of the largest urban areas in the world, housing perhaps 100,000 people in the fifth century C.E. (Common Era). Teotihuacán's commercial network extended hundreds of miles in all directions; many peoples prized its obsidian (a green glass), used to make fine knives and mirrors. Pilgrims traveled long distances to visit Teotihuacan's impressive pyramids and the great temple of Quetzalcoatl—the feathered serpent, primary god of central Mexico.

On the Yucatan Peninsula, in today's eastern Mexico, the Mayas built urban centers containing tall pyramids and temples. They studied astronomy and created an elaborate writing system. Their city-states, though, engaged in near-constant warfare with one another. Warfare and an inadequate food supply caused the collapse of the most powerful cities by 900 C.E., thus ending the classic era of Mayan civilization. By the time Spaniards arrived 600 years later, only a few remnants of the once-mighty society remained.

Pueblos and Mississippians   Ancient native societies in what is now the United States learned to grow maize, squash, and beans from Mesoamericans, but the exact nature of the relationship of the various cultures is unknown. (No Mesoamerican artifacts have been found north of the Rio Grande, but some items resembling Mississippian objects have been excavated in northern Mexico.) The Hohokam, Mogollon, and ancient Pueblo peoples of the modern states of Arizona and New Mexico subsisted by combining hunting and gathering with agriculture in an arid region of unpredictable rainfall. Hohokam villagers constructed extensive irrigation systems, but even so, they occasionally had to relocate their settlements when water supplies failed. Between 900 and 1150 C.E. in Chaco Canyon, the Pueblos built fourteen "Great Houses," multistory stone structures averaging two hundred rooms. The canyon, at the juncture of perhaps four hundred miles of roads, served as a major regional trading and processing center for turquoise, used then as now to create beautiful ornamental objects. Yet the aridity eventually caused the Chacoans to migrate to other sites.

At almost the same time, the unrelated Mississippian culture flourished in what is now the midwestern and southeastern United States. Relying largely on maize, squash, nuts, pumpkins, and venison for food, the Mississippians lived in substantial settlements organized hierarchically. The largest of their urban centers was the City of the Sun (now called Cahokia), near modern St. Louis. Located on rich farmland close to the confluence of the Illinois, Missouri, and Mississippi Rivers, Cahokia, like Teotihuacán and Chaco Canyon, served as a focal point for both religion and trade. At its peak (in the eleventh and twelfth centuries C.E.), the City of the Sun covered more than 5 square miles and had a population of about twenty thousand—small by Mesoamerican standards but larger than any other northern community, and larger than London in the same era.

Although the Cahokians never invented a writing system, these sun-worshippers developed an accurate calendar, evidenced by their creation of a woodhenge—a large circle of tall timber posts aligned with the solstices and the equinox. The city's main pyramid (one of 120 of varying sizes), today called Monks Mound, was at the time of its construction the third largest structure of any description in the Western Hemisphere; it remains the largest earthwork ever built anywhere in the Americas. It sat at the northern end of the Grand Plaza, surrounded by seventeen other mounds, some used for burials. Yet following 1250 C.E., the city was abandoned, several decades after a disastrous earthquake. Archaeologists believe that climate change and the degradation of the environment, caused by overpopulation and the destruction of nearby forests, contributed to the city's collapse. Afterwards, warfare increased as large-scale population movements destabilized the region.

Aztecs   Far to the South, the Aztecs (also called Mexicas) migrated into the Valley of Mexico during the twelfth century. The uninhabited ruins of Teotihuacán, which by then had been deserted for at least two hundred years, awed and mystified the migrants. Their chronicles record that their primary deity, Huitzilopochtli—a war god represented by an eagle—directed them to establish their capital on an island where they saw an eagle eating a serpent, the symbol of Quetzalcoatl. That island city became Tenochtitlán, the center of a rigidly stratified society composed of hereditary classes of warriors, merchants, priests, common folk, and slaves.

The Aztecs conquered their neighbors, forcing them to pay tribute in textiles, gold, foodstuffs, and human beings who could be sacrificed to Huitzilopochtli. They also engaged in ritual combat, known as flowery wars, to obtain further sacrificial victims. The war god's taste for blood was not easily quenched. In the Aztec year Ten Rabbit (1502), at the coronation of Motecuhzoma II (the Spaniards could not pronounce his name correctly, so they called him Montezuma), thousands of people were sacrificed by having their still-beating hearts torn from their bodies.

The Aztecs believed they lived in the age of the Fifth Sun. Four times previously, they wrote, the earth and all the people who lived on it had been destroyed. They predicted their own world would end in earthquakes and hunger. In the Aztec year Thirteen Flint, volcanoes erupted, sickness and hunger spread, wild beasts attacked children, and an eclipse of the sun darkened the sky. Did some priest wonder whether the Fifth Sun was approaching its end? In time, the Aztecs learned that Thirteen Flint was called, by Europeans, 1492.

NORTH AMERICA IN 1492

Over the centuries, the Americans who lived north of Mexico adapted their once-similar ways of life to very different climates and terrains, thus creating the diverse culture areas (ways of subsistence) that the Europeans encountered when they arrived (see Map 1.1). Scholars often refer to such culture areas by language group (such as Algonquian or Iroquoian) because neighboring Indian nations commonly spoke related languages. Bands that lived in environments not well suited to agriculture—because of inadequate rainfall or poor soil, for example—followed a nomadic lifestyle. Within the area of the present-day United States, these groups included the Paiutes and Shoshones, who inhabited the Great Basin (now Nevada and Utah). Because of the difficulty of finding sufficient food for more than a few people, such hunter-gatherer bands were small, usually composed of one or more related families. The men hunted small animals, and women gathered seeds and berries. Where large game was more plentiful and food supplies therefore more certain, as in present-day central and western Canada and the Great Plains, bands of hunters were somewhat larger.

In more favorable environments, larger groups combined agriculture with gathering, hunting, and fishing. Those who lived near the seacoasts, like the Chinooks of present-day Washington and Oregon, consumed fish and shellfish in addition to growing crops and gathering seeds and berries. Residents of the interior (for example, the Arikaras of the Missouri River valley) hunted large animals while also cultivating maize, squash, and beans. The peoples of what is now eastern Canada and the northeastern United States also combined hunting, fishing, and agriculture. They regularly used controlled fires both to open land for cultivation and to assist in hunting.

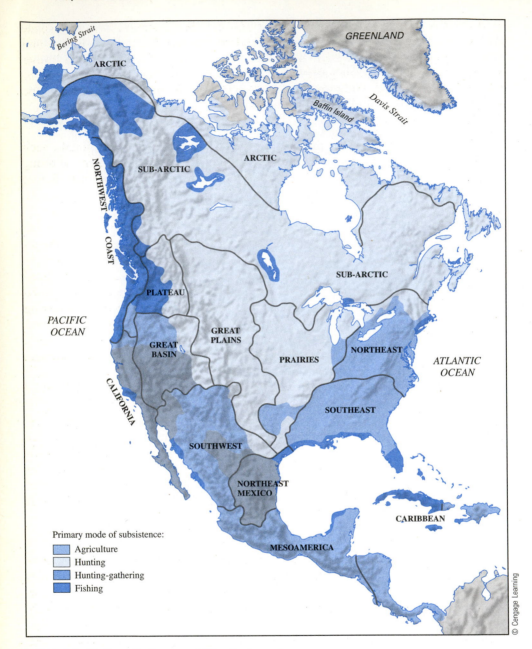

MAP 1.1 Native Cultures of North America

The Natives of the North American continent effectively used the resources of the regions in which they lived. As this map shows, coastal groups relied on fishing, residents of fertile areas engaged in agriculture, and other peoples employed hunting (often combined with gathering) as a primary mode of substenance.

Extensive trade routes linked distant peoples. For instance, hoe and spade blades manufactured from stone mined in modern southern Illinois have been found as far northeast as Lake Erie and as far west as the Plains. Commercial and other interactions among disparate groups speaking different languages were aided by the universally understood symbol of friendship—the calumet, a feathered tobacco pipe offered to strangers at initial encounters.

Gendered Division of Labor

Societies that relied primarily on hunting large animals, such as deer and buffalo, assigned that task to men, allotting food preparation and clothing production to women. Before such nomadic bands acquired horses from the Spaniards, women—occasionally assisted by dogs—also carried the family's belongings whenever the band relocated. Such a sexual division of labor was universal among hunting peoples, regardless of their location. So, too, among seacoast peoples women gathered shellfish along the shore while men fished from boats. Yet agricultural societies assigned work in divergent ways. The Pueblo peoples, who lived in sixty or seventy autonomous villages and spoke five different languages, defined agricultural labor as men's work. In the east, large clusters of peoples speaking Algonquian, Iroquoian, and Muskogean languages allocated most agricultural chores to women, although men cleared the land. In all the farming societies, women gathered wild foods and prepared food for consumption or storage, whereas men were responsible for hunting.

Everywhere in North America, women cared for young children, while older youths learned adult skills from their same-sex parent. Children generally had a great deal of freedom. Young people commonly chose their own marital partners, and in most societies couples could easily divorce if they no longer wished to live together. In contrast to the earlier Mississippian cultures, populations in these societies remained at a level sustainable by existing food supplies, largely because of low birth rates. Infants and toddlers were nursed until the age of two or even longer, and taboos prevented couples from having sexual intercourse during that period.

Social Organization

The southwestern and eastern agricultural peoples had similar social organizations. They lived in villages, sometimes with a thousand or more inhabitants. The Pueblos resided in multistory buildings constructed on terraces along the sides of cliffs or other easily defended sites. Northern Iroquois villages (in modern New York State) were composed of large, rectangular, bark-covered structures, or long houses; the name Haudenosaunee, which the Iroquois called themselves, means "People of the Long House." In the present-day southeastern United States, Muskogeans and southern Algonquians lived in large houses made of thatch. Most of the eastern villages were surrounded by wooden palisades and ditches to aid in fending off attackers.

In all the agricultural societies, each dwelling housed an extended family defined matrilineally (through a female line of descent). Mothers, their married daughters, and their daughters' husbands and children all lived together. Matrilineal descent did not imply matriarchy, or the wielding of power by women, but rather served as a means of reckoning kinship. Matrilineal ties also linked extended families into clans. The nomadic bands of the Prairies and Great Plains, by contrast, were most often related patrilineally (through the male line). They lacked settled villages and defended themselves from attack primarily through their ability to move to safer locations when necessary.

War and Politics   The defensive design of native villages discloses the significance of warfare in pre-Columbian America. Long before Europeans arrived, residents of the continent fought one another for control of the best hunting and fishing territories, the most fertile agricultural lands, or the sources of essential items, such as salt (for preserving meat) and flint (for making knives and arrowheads). Bands of Americans protected by wooden armor battled while standing in ranks facing each other, the better to employ their clubs and throwing spears, which were effective only at close quarters. They began to shoot arrows from behind trees only when they confronted European guns, which rendered their armor useless. People captured by the enemy in such wars were sometimes enslaved and dishonored by losing their previous names and identities, but slavery was never an important source of labor in pre-Columbian America.

American political structures varied considerably. Among Pueblos, the village council, composed of ten to thirty men, was the highest political authority; no government structure connected the villages. Nomadic hunters also lacked formal links among separate bands. The Iroquois, by contrast, had an elaborate political hierarchy incorporating villages into nations and nations into a confederation. A council comprising representatives from each nation made crucial decisions of war and peace for the entire confederacy. In all the North American cultures, civil and war leaders divided political power and wielded authority only so long as they retained the confidence of the people. Autocratic rulers held sway only in southeastern chiefdoms descended from the Mississippians. Women more often assumed leadership roles among agricultural peoples, especially those in which females were the primary cultivators, than among nomadic hunters. Female sachems (rulers) led Algonquian villages in what is now Massachusetts, but women never became heads of hunting bands. Iroquois women did not become chiefs, yet clan matrons exercised political power. The older women of each village chose its chief and could both start wars (by calling for the capture of prisoners to replace dead relatives) and stop them (by refusing to supply warriors with necessary foodstuffs).

Religion   All the American peoples were polytheistic, worshiping a multitude of gods. Each group's most important beliefs and rituals were closely tied to its means of subsistence. The major deities of agricultural peoples like the Pueblos and Muskogeans were associated with cultivation, and their chief festivals centered on planting and harvest. The most important gods of hunters like those living on the Great Plains were associated with animals, and their major festivals were related to hunting. A band's economy and women's role in it helped to determine women's potential as religious leaders. Women held the most prominent positions in those agricultural societies in which they were also the chief food producers, whereas in hunting societies men took the lead in religious as well as political affairs.

A wide variety of cultures, comprising more than 10 million people, thus inhabited America north of Mexico when Europeans arrived. The hierarchical kingdoms of Mesoamerica bore little resemblance to the nomadic hunting societies of the Great Plains or to the agriculturalists of the Northeast or Southwest. The diverse inhabitants of North America spoke well over one thousand different languages. For obvious reasons, they did not consider themselves one people, nor did they think of uniting to repel the European invaders.

AFRICAN SOCIETIES

Fifteenth-century Africa, like fifteenth-century America, housed a variety of cultures adapted to different terrains and climates. Many of these cultures were of great antiquity. In the north, along the Mediterranean Sea, lived the Berbers, who were Muslims, or followers of the Islamic religion founded by the prophet Mohammed in the seventh century C.E. On the east coast of Africa, Muslim city-states engaged in extensive trade with India, the Moluccas (part of modern Indonesia), and China. In these ports, sustained contact and intermarriage among Arabs and Africans created the Swahili language and culture. Through the East African city-states passed the Spice Route, water-borne commerce between the eastern Mediterranean and East Asia; the rest followed the long land route across Central Asia known as the Silk Road.

South of the Mediterranean coast in the African interior lie the great Saharan and Libyan Deserts, vast expanses of nearly waterless terrain crisscrossed by trade routes passing through oases. The introduction of the camel in the fifth century C.E. made long-distance travel possible, and as Islam expanded after the ninth century, commerce controlled by Muslim merchants helped to spread similar religious and cultural ideas throughout the region. Below the deserts, much of the continent is divided between tropical rain forests (along the coasts) and grassy plains (in the interior). People speaking a variety of languages and pursuing different subsistence strategies lived in a wide belt south of the deserts. South of the Gulf of Guinea, the grassy landscape came to be dominated by Bantu-speaking peoples, who left their homeland in modern Nigeria about two thousand years ago and slowly migrated south and east across the continent.

West Africa (Guinea)

West Africa was a land of tropical forests and savanna grasslands where fishing, cattle herding, and agriculture had supported the inhabitants for at least ten thousand years before Europeans set foot there in the fifteenth century. The northern region of West Africa, or Upper Guinea, was heavily influenced by the Islamic culture of the Mediterranean. By the eleventh century C.E., many of the region's inhabitants had become Muslims. Trade via camel caravans between Upper Guinea and the Muslim Mediterranean was sub-Saharan Africa's major connection to Europe and West Asia. Africans sold ivory, gold, and slaves to northern merchants to obtain salt, dates, silk, and cotton cloth.

Upper Guinea runs northeast-southwest from Cape Verde to Cape Palmas. The people of its northernmost region, the so-called Rice Coast (present-day Gambia, Senegal, and Guinea), fished and cultivated rice in coastal swamplands. The Grain Coast, to the south, was thinly populated and not readily accessible from the sea because it had only one good harbor (modern Freetown, Sierra Leone). Its people concentrated on farming and raising livestock.

In Lower Guinea, south and east of Cape Palmas, most Africans were farmers who practiced traditional religions, rather than Islam. Believing that spirits inhabited particular places, they invested those places with special significance. Like the agricultural peoples of the Americas, they developed rituals intended to ensure good harvests. Throughout the region, individual villages composed of kin groups were linked into hierarchical kingdoms. At the time of initial European contact, decentralized political and social authority characterized the region.

Complementary Gender Roles   The societies of West Africa, like those of the Americas, assigned different tasks to men and women. In general, the sexes shared agricultural duties. Men also hunted, managed livestock, and did most of the fishing. Women were responsible for childcare, food preparation, manufacture, and trade. They managed the extensive local and regional networks through which families, villages, and small kingdoms exchanged goods.

Despite their different economies and the rivalries among states, the peoples of Lower Guinea had similar social systems organized on the basis of what anthropologists have called the dual-sex principle. In Lower Guinea, each sex handled its own affairs: just as male political and religious leaders governed men, so females ruled women. In the Dahomean kingdom, for example, every male official had his female counterpart; in the thirty little Akan states on the Gold Coast, chiefs inherited their status through the female line, and each male chief had a female assistant who supervised other women. Many West African societies practiced polygyny (one man's having several wives, each of whom lived separately with her children). Thus, few adults lived permanently in marital households, but the dual-sex system ensured that their actions were subject to scrutiny by members of their own sex.

Throughout Guinea, religious beliefs stressed complementary male and female roles. Both women and men served as heads of the cults and secret societies that directed the spiritual life of the villages. Young women were initiated into the Sandé cult, young men into Poro. Neither cult was allowed to reveal its secrets to the opposite sex. Although West African women (unlike some of their Native American contemporaries) rarely held formal power over men, female religious leaders did govern other members of their sex within the Sandé cult, enforcing conformity to accepted norms of behavior and overseeing their spiritual well-being.

Slavery in Guinea   West African law recognized both individual and communal land ownership, but men seeking to accumulate wealth needed access to labor—wives, children, or slaves—who could work the land. West Africans enslaved for life therefore composed essential elements of the economy. Africans could be enslaved as punishment for crimes, but more often such slaves were enemy captives or people who voluntarily enslaved themselves or their children to pay debts. An African who possessed bondspeople had a right to the products of their labor, although the degree to which slaves were exploited varied greatly, and slave status did not always descend to the next generation. Some slaves were held as chattel; others could engage in trade, retaining a portion of their profits; and still others achieved prominent political or military positions. All, however, found it difficult to overcome the social stigma of enslavement, and they could be traded or sold at the will of their owners.

West Africans, then, were agricultural peoples, skilled at tending livestock, hunting, fishing, and manufacturing cloth from plant fibers and animal skins. Both men and women worked communally, in family groups or alongside others of their own sex. They were accustomed to a relatively egalitarian relationship between the sexes, especially within the context of religion. Carried as captives to the Americas, they became essential to transplanted European societies that used their labor but had little respect for their cultural traditions.

EUROPEAN SOCIETIES

In the fifteenth century, Europeans, too, were agricultural peoples. The daily lives of Europe's rural people had changed little for several hundred years. Split into numerous small, warring countries, Europe was divided linguistically, politically, and economically, yet in social terms Europeans' lives exhibited many similarities. In the hierarchical European societies, a few families wielded autocratic power over the majority of the people. English society in particular was organized as a series of interlocking hierarchies; that is, each person (except those at the very top or bottom) was superior to some, inferior to others. At the base of such hierarchies were people held in various forms of bondage. Although Europeans were not subjected to perpetual slavery, Christian doctrine permitted the enslavement of "heathens" (non-Christians), and some Europeans' freedom was restricted by such conditions as serfdom, which tied them to the land if not to specific owners. In short, Europe's kingdoms resembled those of Africa or Mesoamerica but differed greatly from the more egalitarian societies found in America north of Mexico.

Gender, Work, Politics, and Religion

Most Europeans, like most Africans and Americans, lived in small villages. Only a few cities dotted the landscape, most of them seaports or political capitals. European farmers, called peasants, owned or leased separate landholdings, but they worked the fields communally. Because fields had to lie fallow (unplanted) every second or third year to regain fertility, a family could not ensure itself a regular food supply unless all villagers shared annually the work and the crops. Men did most of the fieldwork; women helped out chiefly at planting and harvest. In some regions men concentrated on herding livestock. Women's duties consisted primarily of childcare and household tasks, including preserving food, milking cows, and caring for poultry. If a woman's husband was a city artisan or storekeeper, she might assist him in business. Because Europeans kept domesticated animals (pigs, goats, sheep, and cattle) for meat, hunting had little economic importance in their cultures. Instead, hunting was primarily a sport for male aristocrats.

Unlike in Africa or America, where women often played prominent roles in politics and religion, men dominated all areas of life in Europe. A few women—notably Queen Elizabeth I of England—achieved status or power by right of birth, but the vast majority were excluded from positions of political authority. European women also generally held inferior social, religious, and economic positions, yet they wielded power in their own households over children and servants. In contrast to the freedom children enjoyed in American families, European children were tightly controlled and subjected to harsh discipline.

Christianity was the dominant European religion. In the West, authority rested in the Catholic Church, based in Rome and led by the pope, who directed a wholly male clergy. Although Europeans were nominally Catholic, many adhered to local belief systems the church deemed heretical and proved unable to extinguish. Kings would ally themselves with the church when it suited their needs but often acted independently. Yet even so, the Christian nations of Europe from the twelfth century on publicly united in a goal of driving nonbelievers (especially Muslims) not only from their own domains but also from the holy city of Jerusalem, which caused the series of wars known as the Crusades. Nevertheless, in the fifteenth century, Muslims dominated the commerce and geography of the Mediterranean world, especially after they conquered Constantinople (capital of the Christian Byzantine empire) in 1453. Few would have predicted that Christian Europeans would ever be able to challenge that dominance.

Effects of Plague and Warfare   When the fifteenth century began, European nations were slowly recovering from the devastating epidemic of plague known as the Black Death, which first struck them in 1346. The Black Death seems to have arrived in Europe from China, traveling with long-distance traders along the Silk Road to the eastern Mediterranean. The disease then recurred with particular severity in the 1360s and 1370s. Although no precise figures are available and the impact of the Black Death varied from region to region, the best estimate is that fully one-third of Europe's people died during those terrible years. A precipitous economic decline followed—in some regions more than half of the workers had died—as did severe social, political, and religious disruption because of the deaths of clergymen and other leading figures.

As plague ravaged the population, England and France waged the Hundred Years' War (1337–1453), initiated because English monarchs had claimed the French throne. The war interrupted overland trade routes connecting England and Antwerp (in modern Belgium) to Venice, a Christian trading center, and thence to India and China. England, on the periphery of the Mediterranean commercial core, exported wool and cloth to Antwerp in exchange for spices and silks from the East. Needing a new way to reach their northern trading partners, eastern Mediterranean merchants forged a maritime route to Antwerp. Using a triangular, or lateen, sail (rather than the then-standard square rigging) improved the maneuverability of ships, enabling vessels to sail out of the Mediterranean and north around the European coast. Other developments of key importance were the acquisition of a Chinese invention, the compass, and the perfection of navigational instruments like the astrolabe and the quadrant, which allowed oceangoing sailors to estimate their position (latitude) by measuring the relationship of the sun, moon, or certain stars to the horizon.

Political and Technological Change

After the Hundred Years' War, European monarchs forcefully consolidated their previously diffuse political power and raised new revenues through increased taxation of an already hard-pressed peasantry. The long military struggle led to new pride in national identity, which eclipsed the prevailing regional and dynastic loyalties. In England, Henry VII in 1485 founded the Tudor dynasty and began uniting a previously divided land. In France, the successors of Charles VII unified the kingdom. Most successful of all were Ferdinand of Aragón and Isabella of Castile, who married in 1469, founding a strongly Catholic Spain. In 1492, they defeated the Muslims who had lived in Spain and Portugal for centuries, thereafter expelling all Jews and Muslims from their domain.

The fifteenth century also brought technological change to Europe. Movable type and the printing press, invented in Germany in the 1450s, made information more accessible than ever before. Printing stimulated the Europeans' curiosity about fabled lands across the seas, lands they could now read about in books. The most important such works were Ptolemy's *Geography*, a description of the known world written in ancient times, first published in 1475 and later updated with new finds; and Marco Polo's *Travels*, published in 1477. The *Travels* recounted a Venetian merchant's adventures in thirteenth-century China and intriguingly described that nation as bordered on the east by an ocean. Polo's account circulated widely among Europe's educated elites, first in manuscript and later in print. The book led many Europeans to believe they could trade directly with China in ocean-going vessels instead of relying on the Silk Road or the Spice Route through East Africa. A transoceanic route, if it existed, would allow northern Europeans to circumvent the Muslim and Venetian merchants who hitherto had controlled their access to Asian goods.

Motives for Exploration

Technological advances and the growing strength of newly powerful national rulers made possible the European explorations of the fifteenth and sixteenth centuries. Each country craved easy access to African and Asian goods—silk, dyes, perfumes, jewels, sugar, gold, and especially spices such as pepper, cloves, cinnamon, and nutmeg. Spices were desirable not only for seasoning food but also because they were believed to have medicinal and magical properties. Their allure stemmed largely from their rarity, their extraordinary cost, and their mysterious origins. They passed through so many hands en route to London or Seville that no European knew exactly where they came from. (Nutmeg, for example, grew only on nine tiny islands in the Moluccas, now eastern Indonesia.) Avoiding intermediaries in Venice and Constantinople, and acquiring such valuable products directly, would improve a nation's income and its standing relative to other countries, in addition to supplying its wealthy leaders with coveted luxury items.

A concern for spreading Christianity around the world supplemented the economic motive. The linking of materialistic and spiritual goals seems contradictory today, but fifteenth-century Europeans saw no necessary conflict between the two. Explorers and colonizers—especially Roman Catholics—honestly sought to convert "heathen" peoples to Christianity. At the same time, they hoped to increase their nation's wealth by establishing direct trade with Africa, China, India, and the Moluccas.

EARLY EUROPEAN EXPLORATIONS

To establish that trade, European mariners first had to explore the oceans. Seafarers needed not just the maneuverable vessels and navigational aids increasingly used in the fourteenth century but also knowledge of the sea, its currents, and especially its winds. Wind would power their ships. But how did the winds run? Where would Atlantic breezes carry their square-rigged ships, which, even with the addition of a triangular sail, needed to run before the wind (that is, to have the wind directly behind the vessel)?

Sailing the Mediterranean Atlantic   Europeans learned the answers to these questions in the region called the Mediterranean Atlantic, the expanse of ocean located south and west of Spain and bounded by the islands of the Azores (on the west) and the Canaries (on the south), with the Madeiras in their midst. Europeans reached all three sets of islands during the fourteenth century—first the Canaries in the 1330s, then the Madeiras and the Azores. The Canaries proved a popular destination for mariners from Iberia, the peninsula that includes Spain and Portugal. Sailing to the Canaries from Europe was easy because strong winds known as the Northeast Trades blow southward along the Iberian and African coastlines. The voyage took about a week, and the volcanic peaks on the islands made them difficult to miss even with imprecise navigational instruments.

The problem was getting back. The Iberian sailor attempting to return home faced a major obstacle: the very winds that had brought him so quickly to the Canaries now blew directly at him. Rowing and tacking back and forth against the wind were similarly tedious and ineffectual. Confronted by contrary winds, mariners had traditionally waited for the wind to change, but the Northeast Trades blew steadily. So they developed a new technique: sailing "around the wind." That meant sailing as directly against the wind as was possible without being forced to change course. In the Mediterranean Atlantic, a mariner would head northwest into the open ocean, until—weeks later—he reached the winds that would carry him home, the so-called Westerlies. Those winds blow (we now know, although the seafarers at first did not) northward along the coast of North America before heading east toward Europe.

This solution must at first have seemed to defy common sense, but it became the key to successful exploration of both the Atlantic and the Pacific Oceans. Once a sailor understood the winds and their allied currents, he no longer feared leaving Europe without being able to return. Faced with a contrary wind, he simply had to sail around it until he found a wind to carry him in the proper direction.

Islands of the Mediterranean Atlantic   During the fifteenth century, armed with knowledge of the winds and currents of the Mediterranean Atlantic, Iberian seamen regularly visited the three island groups, all of which they could reach in two weeks or less. The uninhabited

Azores were soon settled by Portuguese migrants who raised wheat for sale in Europe and sold livestock to passing sailors. The Madeiras also had no native peoples, and by the 1450s Portuguese colonists were employing slaves (probably Jews and Muslims brought from Iberia) to grow large quantities of sugar for export to the mainland. By the 1470s, Madeira had developed a colonial plantation economy. For the first time in world history, a region was settled explicitly to cultivate a valuable crop—sugar—to be sold elsewhere. Moreover, because the work involved in large-scale plantation agriculture was so backbreaking, only a supply of enslaved laborers (who could not opt to quit) could ensure the system's continued success.

The Canaries did have indigenous residents—the Guanche people, who began trading animal skins and dyes with their European visitors. After 1402, the French, Portuguese, and Spanish began sporadically attacking the islands. The Guanches resisted vigorously, even though they were weakened by their susceptibility to alien European diseases. One by one, the seven islands fell to Europeans who then carried off Guanches as slaves to the Madeiras or Iberia. Spain conquered the last island in 1496 and subsequently devoted the land to sugar plantations. Collectively, the Canaries and Madeira became known as the Wine Islands because much of their sugar production was directed to making sweet wines.

Portuguese Trading Posts in Africa

While some Europeans concentrated on exploiting the islands of the Mediterranean Atlantic, others used them as steppingstones to Africa. In 1415, Portugal seized control of Ceuta, a Muslim city in North Africa. Prince Henry the Navigator, son of King John I of Portugal, knew that vast wealth awaited the first European nation to tap the riches of Africa and Asia directly. Repeatedly, he dispatched ships southward along the African coast, attempting to discover an oceanic route to Asia. But not until after Prince Henry's death did Bartholomew Dias round the southern tip of Africa (1488) and Vasco da Gama finally reach India (1498), where at Malabar he located the richest source of peppercorns in the world.

Long before that, Portugal reaped the benefits of its seafarers' voyages. Although West African states successfully resisted European penetration of the interior, they allowed the Portuguese to establish trading posts along their coasts. Charging the traders rent and levying duties on goods they imported, the African kingdoms benefited considerably from their new, easier access to European manufactures. The Portuguese gained, too, for they no longer had to rely on trans-Saharan camel caravans. Their vessels earned immense profits by swiftly transporting African gold, ivory, and slaves to Europe. By bargaining with African masters to purchase their slaves and then carrying those bondspeople to Iberia, the Portuguese introduced black slavery into Europe.

Lessons of Early Colonization

An island off the African coast, previously uninhabited, proved critical to Portuguese success. In the 1480s, they colonized São Tomé, located in the Gulf of Guinea. By that time, Madeira had already reached the limit of its capacity to produce sugar. The soil of São Tomé proved ideal for raising that valuable crop, and plantation agriculture there expanded rapidly. Planters imported large numbers of slaves from the mainland to work in the cane fields, thus creating the first economy based primarily on the bondage of black Africans.

By the 1490s, even before Christopher Columbus set sail to the west, Europeans had learned three key lessons of colonization in the Mediterranean Atlantic. First, they had learned how to transplant their crops and livestock successfully to exotic locations. Second, they had discovered that the native peoples of those lands could be either conquered (like the Guanches) or exploited (like the Africans). Third, they had developed a viable model of plantation slavery and a system for supplying nearly unlimited quantities of such workers. The stage was set for a pivotal moment in world history.

VOYAGES OF COLUMBUS, CABOT, AND THEIR SUCCESSORS

Christopher Columbus was well schooled in the lessons of the Mediterranean Atlantic. Born in 1451 in the Italian city-state of Genoa, this largely self-educated son of a wool merchant was by the 1490s an experienced sailor and mapmaker.

Collection of Mary Beth Norton

A relief carving of a square-rigged vessel, with a lateen sail at the rear for maneuverability. Fittingly, it is found on Vasco da Gama's tomb in the Jéronimos monastery in Belém, Portugal, which is located on the very spot whence he set sail in just such a ship on his voyage to India.

Like many mariners of the day, he was drawn to Portugal and its islands, especially Madeira, where he commanded a merchant vessel. At least once he voyaged to the Portuguese outpost on the Gold Coast. There he became obsessed with gold, and there he came to understand the economic potential of the slave trade.

Like all accomplished seafarers, Columbus knew the world was round. But he differed from other cartographers in his estimate of the earth's size: he thought that China lay only three thousand miles from the southern European coast. Thus, he argued, it would be easier to reach Asia by sailing west than by making the difficult voyage around the southern tip of Africa. Experts scoffed at this crackpot notion, accurately predicting that the two continents lay twelve thousand miles apart. When Columbus in 1484 asked the Portuguese rulers to back his plan to sail west to Asia, they rejected what appeared to be a crazy scheme.

Columbus's Voyage

Ferdinand and Isabella of Spain, jealous of Portugal's successes in Africa, were more receptive to Columbus's ideas. Urged on by some Spanish noblemen and a group of Italian merchants residing in Castile, the monarchs agreed to finance the risky voyage, in part because they hoped the profits would pay for a new expedition to conquer Muslim-held Jerusalem. And so, on August 3, 1492, in command of three ships—the *Pinta*, the *Niña*, and the *Santa Maria*—Columbus set sail from the Spanish port of Palos.

The first part of the journey was familiar, for the ships steered down the Northeast Trades to the Canary Islands. There Columbus refitted his square-rigged ships, adding triangular sails to make them more maneuverable. On September 6, the ships weighed anchor and headed out into the unknown ocean.

Just over a month later, pushed by favorable trade winds, the vessels found land approximately where Columbus thought Cipangu (Japan) was located (see Map 1.2). On October 12, he and his men landed on an island in the Bahamas, which its inhabitants called Guanahaní but which he renamed San Salvador. (Because Columbus's description of his landfall can be variously interpreted, several different places today claim to be his landing site.) Later, he went on to explore the islands now known as Cuba and Hispaniola, which their residents, the Taíno people, called Colba and Bohío. Because he thought he had reached the East Indies (the Spice Islands), Columbus referred to the inhabitants of the region as "Indians." The Taínos thought the Europeans had come from the sky, and wherever Columbus went crowds of curious Taínos gathered to meet and exchange gifts with him.

Columbus's Observations

Three themes predominate in Columbus's log, the major source of information on this first encounter. First, he insistently asked the Taínos where he could find gold, pearls, and spices. Each time, his informants replied (via signs) that such products could be obtained on other islands or on the mainland. Eventually, he came to mistrust such answers, noting, "I am beginning to believe ... they will tell me anything I want to hear."

Second, Columbus wrote repeatedly of the strange and beautiful plants and animals. "Here the fishes are so unlike ours that it is amazing.... The colors are so bright that anyone would marvel," he noted, and again, "The song of the little birds might make a man wish never to leave here. I never tire from looking at

MAP 1.2 European Explorations in America

In the century following Columbus's voyages, European adventurers explored the coasts and parts of the interior of North and South America.

such luxurious vegetation." Yet Columbus's interest was not only aesthetic. "I believe that there are many plants and trees here that could be worth a lot in Spain for use as dyes, spices, and medicines," he observed, adding that he was carrying home to Europe "a sample of everything I can," so that experts could examine them.

Third, Columbus also described the islands' human residents, and he seized some to take back to Spain. The Taínos were, he said, very handsome, gentle, and friendly, though they told him of the fierce Caniba (today called Caribs) who lived on other islands, raided their villages, and ate some captives (hence today's word *cannibal*). Although Columbus feared and distrusted the Caribs, he believed the Taínos to be likely converts to Catholicism, remarking that "if devout religious persons knew the Indian language well, all these people would soon become Christians." But he had more in mind than conversion. The islanders "ought to make good and skilled servants," Columbus declared. It would be easy to "subject everyone and make them do what you wished."

Thus, the records of the first encounter between Europeans and Americans revealed themes that would be of enormous significance for centuries to come. Europeans wanted to extract profits by exploiting American resources, including plants, animals, and peoples alike, and like Columbus others later divided the native peoples into "good" (Taínos) and "bad" (Caribs). Columbus made three more voyages to the west, exploring most of the major Caribbean islands and sailing along the coasts of Central and South America. Until the day he died in 1506 at the age of fifty-five, he believed he had reached Asia. Even before his death, others knew better. Because the Florentine Amerigo Vespucci, who explored the South American coast in 1499, was the first to publish the idea that a new continent had been discovered, Martin Waldseemüller in 1507 labeled the land "America," as is evident in his map. By then, Spain, Portugal, and Pope Alexander VI had signed the Treaty of Tordesillas (1494), confirming Portugal's dominance in Africa—and later Brazil—in exchange for Spanish preeminence in the rest of the Americas.

Norse and Other Northern Voyagers   Five hundred years before Columbus, about the year 1001, a Norse expedition under Leif Ericsson had sailed to North America across the Davis Strait, which separated their villages in Greenland from Baffin Island (located northeast of Hudson Bay; see Map 1.1) by just 200 nautical miles, settling at a site they named "Vinland." Attacks by local residents forced them to depart hurriedly from Vinland after just a few years. In the 1960s, archaeologists determined that the Norse had established an outpost at what is now L'Anse aux Meadows, Newfoundland, but Vinland itself was probably located farther south.

Later Europeans did not know of the Norse explorers, but some historians argue that during the fifteenth century Basque whalers and fishermen (from modern northern France and Spain) located rich fishing grounds off Newfoundland but kept the information secret. Whether or not fishermen crossed the entire Atlantic, they thoroughly explored its northern reaches. Fifteenth-century seafarers voyaged regularly between the European continent, England, Ireland, and Iceland. The mariners who explored the region of North America that was to become the United States and Canada built on their knowledge.

The winds that the northern sailors confronted posed problems on their outbound rather than on their homeward journeys. The same Westerlies that carried Columbus back to Europe blew in the faces of northerners looking west. But mariners soon learned that the strongest winds shifted southward during the winter and that, by departing from northern ports in the spring, they could make adequate headway if they steered northward. Thus, whereas the first landfall of most sailors to the south was somewhere in the Caribbean, those taking the northern route usually reached America along the coast of today's Maine or Canada.

John Cabot's Explorations   The European generally credited with "discovering" North America is Zuan Cabboto, known today as John Cabot. More precisely, Cabot brought to Europe the first formal knowledge of the northern continental coastline and claimed the land for England. Like Columbus, Cabot was a master mariner from the Italian city-state of Genoa; the two men probably knew each other well. Calculating that England—which traded with Asia only through a long series of intermediaries stretching from Antwerp to Venice to the Muslim world—would be eager to sponsor exploratory voyages, he gained financial backing from King Henry VII. He set sail from Bristol in late May 1497 in the *Mathew*, reaching North America about a month later. After exploring the coast of modern Newfoundland for a month,

Cabot rode the Westerlies back to England, arriving just fifteen days after he left North America.

The voyages of Columbus, Cabot, and their successors finally brought the Eastern and Western Hemispheres together. Portuguese explorer Pedro Álvares Cabral reached Brazil in 1500; John Cabot's son Sebastian followed his father to North America in 1507; France financed Giovanni da Verrazzano in 1524 and Jacques Cartier in 1534; and in 1609 and 1610, Henry Hudson explored the North American coast for the Dutch West India Company (see Map 1.2). All were searching primarily for the legendary, nonexistent "Northwest Passage" through the Americas, hoping to find an easy route to the riches of Asia. But in a sign of what was to come, Verrazzano observed that "the [American] countryside is, in fact, full of promise and deserves to be developed for itself. The flora is rich and the fauna abundant."

SPANISH EXPLORATION AND CONQUEST

Only in the areas that Spain explored and claimed did colonization begin immediately. On his second voyage in 1493, Columbus brought to Hispaniola seventeen ships loaded with twelve hundred men, seeds, plants, livestock, chickens, and dogs—along with microbes, rats, and weeds. The settlement named Isabela (in the modern Dominican Republic) and its successors became the staging area for the Spanish invasion of America. On the islands of Cuba and Hispaniola, the Europeans learned to adapt to the new environment as did the horses, cattle, and hogs they imported. When the Spaniards moved on to explore the mainland, they rode island-bred horses and ate island-bred cattle and hogs.

Cortés and Other Explorers   At first, Spanish explorers fanned out around the Caribbean basin. In 1513, Juan Ponce de León reached Florida, and Vasco Núñez de Balboa crossed the Isthmus of Panama to the Pacific Ocean, followed by Pánfilo de Narváez and others who traced the coast of the Gulf of Mexico. In the 1530s and 1540s, conquistadors traveled farther, exploring many regions claimed by the Spanish monarchs: Francisco Vásquez de Coronado journeyed through the southwestern portion of what is now the United States at approximately the same time Hernán de Soto explored the Southeast. Juan Rodríguez Cabrillo sailed along the California coast. Francisco Pizarro, who ventured into western South America, acquired the richest silver mines in the world by conquering the Incas. But the most important conquistador was Hernán Cortés, who in 1521 seized control of the Aztec Empire.

Cortés, an adventurer who first arrived in the Caribbean in 1506, landed a force on the Mexican mainland in 1519 to search for rumored wealthy cities. Near the coast, local Mayas presented him with a group of young enslaved women. One of them, Malinche (whom the Spaniards baptized as a Christian and renamed Doña Marina), had been sold into slavery by the Aztecs and raised by the Mayas. Because she became Cortés's translator, some modern Mexicans regard her as a traitor, but others suggest that she owed no loyalty to people who had enslaved her. In her own day, both Europeans and Aztecs accorded her great respect. Malinche bore Cortés a son, Martín—one of the first *mestizos*, or mixed-blood children—and eventually married one of his officers.

Capture of Tenochtitlán

As he traveled toward the Aztec capital, Cortés, with Malinche's help, cleverly recruited peoples whom the Aztecs had long subjugated. The Spaniards' strange beasts (horses, livestock) and noisy weapons (guns, cannon) awed their new allies. Yet the Spaniards, too, were awed. Years later, Bernal Díaz del Castillo recalled his first sight of Tenochtitlán, situated in the midst of Lake Texcoco: "We were amazed and said that it was like the enchantments ... on account of the great towers and cues [temples] and buildings rising from the water, and all built of masonry." Some soldiers asked, he remembered, "whether the things that we saw were not a dream."

The Spaniards came to Tenochtitlán not only with horses and steel weapons but also with smallpox, bringing an epidemic that had begun on Hispaniola. The disease peaked in 1520, fatally weakening Tenochtitlán's defenders. "It spread over the people as great destruction," an Aztec later remembered. "Some it quite covered [with pustules] on all parts—their faces, their heads, their breasts... There was great havoc. Very many died of it." Largely as a consequence, Tenochtitlán surrendered in 1521, and the Spaniards built Mexico City on its site. Cortes and his men seized a fabulous treasure of gold and silver. Thus, less than three decades after Columbus's first voyage, the Spanish monarchs—who treated the American territories as their personal possessions—controlled the richest, most extensive empire Europe had known since ancient Rome.

Spanish Colonization

Spain established the model of colonization that other countries later attempted to imitate, a model with three major elements. First, the Crown tried to maintain tight control over the colonies, imposing a hierarchical government that allowed little autonomy to American jurisdictions. That control included, for example, carefully vetting prospective emigrants and limiting their number and insisting that the colonies import all their manufactured goods from Spain. In order to encourage social stability, those settlers were then required to live in towns under the authorities' watchful eyes. Roman Catholic priests attempted to ensure the colonists' conformity with orthodox religious views.

Second, men constituted most of the first colonists. Although some Spanish women later immigrated to America, the men took primarily Indian—and, later, African—women as their wives or concubines, a development more often than not encouraged by colonial administrators. They thereby began creating the racially mixed population that characterizes much of Latin America to the present day.

Third, the colonies' wealth was based on the exploitation of both the native population and slaves imported from Africa. The Mesoamerican peoples were accustomed to autocratic rule. Spaniards simply took over the role once assumed by native leaders who had exacted labor and tribute from their subjects. Cortés established the *encomienda* system, which granted Indian villages to individual conquistadors as a reward for their services, thus legalizing slavery in all but name.

In 1542, after cogent criticism from a colonial priest, Bartolomé de las Casas, the monarch formulated a new code of laws to reform the system, forbidding the conquerors from enslaving Indians while still allowing them to collect money and goods from tributary villages. In response to the restrictions and to the declining

Indian population, the *encomenderos*, familiar with slavery in Spain, began to import Africans in order to increase the labor force under their direct control. They employed Indians and Africans primarily in gold and silver mines, on sugar plantations, and on huge horse, cattle, and sheep ranches. African slavery was far more common on the larger Caribbean islands than on the mainland.

Many demoralized residents of Mesoamerica accepted the Christian religion brought to New Spain by Franciscan and Dominican friars—men who had joined religious orders bound by vows of poverty and celibacy. The friars devoted their energies to persuading Mesoamerican people to move into towns and to build Roman Catholic churches. Spaniards leveled existing cities, constructing cathedrals and monasteries on sites once occupied by Aztec, Incan, and Mayan temples. In such towns, Indians were exposed to European customs and religious rituals designed to assimilate Catholic and pagan beliefs. Friars deliberately juxtaposed the cult of the Virgin Mary with that of the corn goddess, and the Indians adeptly melded aspects of their traditional worldview with Christianity, in a process called *syncretism*. Thousands of Indians residing in Spanish territory embraced Catholicism, at least partly because it was the religion of their new rulers and they were accustomed to obedience.

Gold, Silver, and Spain's Decline   The New World's gold and silver, initially a boon, ultimately brought about the decline of Spain as a major power. China, a huge country with silver coinage, insatiably demanded Spanish silver, gobbling up an estimated half of the total output of New World mines while paying twice the price current in Europe. Especially after the Spanish began in the 1570s to dispatch silver-laden galleons annually from Acapulco (on Mexico's west coast) to trade at their new settlement at Manila, in the Philippines, Spaniards acquired easy access to luxury Chinese goods such as silk and Asian spices.

The influx of unprecedented wealth led to rapid inflation, which (among other adverse effects) caused Spanish products to be overpriced in international markets and imported goods to become cheaper in Spain. The once-profitable Spanish textile-manufacturing industry collapsed as did scores of other businesses. The seemingly endless income from American colonies emboldened successive Spanish monarchs to spend lavishly on wars against the Dutch and the English. Several times in the late sixteenth and early seventeenth centuries, the monarchs repudiated the state debt, wreaking havoc on the nation's finances. When the South American gold and silver mines started to give out in the mid-seventeenth century, Spain's economy crumbled, and the nation lost its international importance.

THE COLUMBIAN EXCHANGE

A broad mutual transfer of diseases, plants, and animals (called the Columbian Exchange by historian Alfred Crosby; see Map 1.3) resulted directly from the European voyages of the fifteenth and sixteenth centuries and from Spanish colonization. The Eastern and Western Hemispheres had evolved separately for thousands of years, developing widely different forms of life. Many large mammals, such as cattle and horses, were native to the connected continents of Europe, Asia, and Africa, but the Americas contained no domesticated beasts larger than dogs and llamas. The vegetable crops of the Americas—particularly maize, beans, squash, cassava, and potatoes—were more nutritious and produced higher yields than those of Europe and Africa, such as wheat, millet, and rye. In time, native peoples learned to raise and consume European livestock, and Europeans and Africans became accustomed to planting and eating American crops. The diets of all three peoples were consequently vastly enriched. Partly as a result, the world's population doubled over the next three hundred years. About three-fifths of all crops cultivated in the world today were first grown in the Americas.

Smallpox and Other Diseases   Diseases carried from Europe and Africa, though, had a devastating impact on the Americas. Indians fell victim to microbes that had long infested the other continents and had repeatedly killed hundreds of thousands but had also often left survivors with some measure of immunity. The statistics are staggering. When Columbus landed on Hispaniola in 1492, approximately half a million people resided there. Fifty years later, that island had fewer than two thousand native inhabitants. Within thirty years of the first landfall at Guanahaní, not one Taíno survived in the Bahamas.

MAP 1.3 Major Items in the Columbian Exchange

As European adventurers traversed the world in the fifteenth and sixteenth centuries, they initiated the "Columbian Exchange" of plants, animals, and diseases. These events changed the lives of the peoples of the world forever, bringing new foods and new pestilence to both sides of the Atlantic.

Although measles, typhus, influenza, malaria, and other illnesses severely afflicted the native peoples, as at Tenochtitlán the greatest killer was smallpox, spread primarily by direct human contact. Overall, historians estimate that the long-term effects of the alien microorganisms could have reduced the precontact American population by as much as 90 percent. The epidemics recurred at twenty- to thirty-year intervals, frequently appearing either in tandem or in quick succession, so that weakened survivors of one would be felled by a second or third. Large numbers of deaths also disrupted societies already undergoing severe strains caused by colonization, thus rendering native peoples more vulnerable to droughts, crop failures, or other challenging circumstances.

Even far to the north, where smaller American populations encountered only a few Europeans, disease also ravaged the countryside. A great epidemic, probably viral hepatitis, swept through the villages along the coast north of Cape Cod from 1616 to 1618. Again, the mortality rate may have been as high as 90 percent. An English traveler several years later commented that the people had "died on heapes, as they lay in their houses," and that bones and skulls covered the ruins of villages. Because of this dramatic depopulation of the area, just a few years later English colonists were able to establish settlements virtually unopposed.

The Americans, though, seem to have taken a revenge of sorts. They probably gave the Europeans syphilis, a virulent venereal disease. The first recorded European case of the new ailment occurred in 1493 in Barcelona, Spain, shortly after Columbus's return from the Caribbean. Although less likely than smallpox to cause immediate death, syphilis was dangerous and debilitating. Carried by soldiers, sailors, and prostitutes, it spread quickly through Europe and Asia, reaching China by 1505.

A male effigy dating from 200–800 C.E., found in a burial site in Nayarit, Mexico. The lesions covering the figurine suggest that the person it represents is suffering from syphilis, which, untreated, produces these characteristic markings on the body in its later stages. Such evidence as this pre-Columbian effigy has now convinced most scholars that syphilis originated in the Americas—a hypothesis in dispute for many years.

Sugar, Horses, and Tobacco   The exchange of three commodities had significant impacts on Europe and the Americas. Sugar, first domesticated in the East Indies, was being grown on the islands of the Mediterranean Atlantic by 1450. The ravenous European demand for sugar—which, after initially regarded as a medicine, became a desirable luxury foodstuff—led Columbus to take Canary Island sugar canes to Hispaniola on his 1493 voyage. By the 1520s, plantations in the Greater Antilles worked by African slaves regularly shipped cargoes of sugar to Spain. Half a century later, the Portuguese colony in Brazil (founded 1532) was producing sugar for the European market on an even larger scale, and after 1640, sugar cultivation became the crucial component of English and French colonization in the Caribbean.

Horses—which, like sugar, were brought to America by Columbus in 1493—fell into the hands of North American Indians during the seventeenth century. Through trade and theft, horses spread among the peoples of the Great Plains, reaching most areas by 1750. Lakotas, Comanches, and Crows, among others, came to use horses for transportation and hunting, calculated their wealth in number of horses owned, and waged war primarily on horseback. Women no longer had to carry the band's belongings on their backs. Some groups that previously had cultivated crops abandoned agriculture. Because of the acquisition of horses, a mode of subsistence that had been based on hunting several different animals, in combination with gathering and agriculture, became one focused almost wholly on hunting buffalo.

In America, Europeans encountered tobacco, which at first they believed to have beneficial medicinal effects. Smoking and chewing the "Indian weed" became a fad in Europe after it was planted in Turkey in the sixteenth century. Despite the efforts of such skeptics as King James I of England, who in 1604 pronounced smoking "loathsome to the eye, hatefull to the Nose, harmfull to the brain, [and] dangerous to the Lungs," tobacco's popularity climbed. Its addictive nicotine and its connection to lung cancer were discovered only in the twentieth century.

The European and African invasion of the Americas therefore had a significant biological component, for the invaders carried plants and animals with them. Some creatures, such as livestock, they brought deliberately. Others, including rats (which infested their ships), weeds, and diseases, arrived unexpectedly. And the same process occurred in reverse. When the Europeans returned home, they deliberately took back such crops as maize, potatoes, and tobacco, along with that unanticipated stowaway, syphilis.

EUROPEANS IN NORTH AMERICA

Europeans were initially more interested in exploiting North America's natural resources than in the difficult task of establishing colonies there. John Cabot had reported that fish were extraordinarily plentiful near Newfoundland, so Europeans rushed to take advantage of abundant codfish, which were in great demand in their homelands as an inexpensive source of protein. The French, Spanish, Basques, and Portuguese regularly fished North American waters throughout the sixteenth

LINKS TO THE WORLD

Maize

Maize, to Mesoamericans, was a gift from Quetzalcoatl, the plumed serpent god. Cherokees told of an old woman whose blood produced the prized stalks after her grandson buried her body in a cleared, sunny field. For the Abenakis, the crop began when a beautiful maiden ordered a youth to drag her by the hair through a burned-over field. The long hair of the Cherokee grandmother and the Abenaki maiden turned into silk, the flower on the stalks that Europeans called Indian corn. Both tales' symbolic association of corn and women intriguingly supports archaeologists' recent suggestion that—in eastern North America at least—female plant breeders were responsible for substantial improvements in the productivity of maize.

Sacred to all the Indian peoples who grew it, maize was a major part of their diet. They dried the kernels; ground into meal, maize was cooked as a mush or shaped into baked flat cakes, the forerunners of modern tortillas. Indians also heated the dried kernels of some varieties until they popped open, just as is done today. Although the European invaders of North and South America initially disdained maize, they soon learned it could be cultivated in a wide variety of conditions—from sea level to twelve thousand feet, from regions with abundant rainfall to dry lands with as little as twelve inches of rain a year. Corn was also highly productive, yielding almost twice as many calories per acre as wheat. So Europeans, too, came to rely on corn, growing it not only in their American settlements but also in their homelands.

Maize cultivation spread to Asia and Africa. Today, China is second only to the United States in total corn production, and corn is more widely grown in Africa than any other crop. Still, the United States produces 45 percent of the world's corn—almost half of it in the three states of Illinois, Iowa, and Nebraska—and corn is the nation's single largest crop. More than half of American corn is consumed by livestock. Much of the rest is processed into syrup, which sweetens carbonated beverages and candies, or into ethanol, a gasoline additive that reduces both pollution and dependence on fossil fuels. Corn is an ingredient in light beer and toothpaste. It is used in the manufacture of tires, wallpaper, cat litter, and aspirin. Remarkably, of the ten thousand products in a modern American grocery store, about one-fourth rely to some extent on corn.

Today, this crop bequeathed to the world by ancient American plant breeders provides one-fifth of all the calories consumed by the earth's peoples. The gift of Quetzalcoatl has linked the globe.

century; Verrazzano and Cartier, in 1524 and 1534, respectively, both encountered anonymous vessels already fishing along the American coast. In the early 1570s, after Spain opened its markets to English shipping, the English (who previously had fished near Iceland for home consumption only) eagerly joined the Newfoundland fishery, thereafter selling salt cod to the Spanish in exchange for valuable Asian goods. The English soon became dominant in the region, which by the end of the century was the focal point of a European commerce more valuable than that with the Gulf of Mexico.

Trade Among Indians and Europeans Fishermen quickly realized they could increase their profits by exchanging cloth and metal goods, such as pots and knives, for native trappers' beaver pelts, used to make fashionable hats in Europe. Initially, Europeans traded from ships sailing along the coast, but later they set up outposts on the mainland to centralize and control the traffic in furs. Such outposts were inhabited chiefly by male adventurers, whose major aim was to send as many pelts as possible home to Europe.

The Europeans' demand for furs, especially beaver, was matched by the Indians' desire for European goods that could make their lives easier and establish their superiority over their neighbors. Some bands began to concentrate so completely on trapping for the European market that they abandoned their traditional economies and became partially dependent on others for food. The intensive trade in pelts also had serious ecological consequences. In some regions, beavers were wiped out. The disappearance of their dams led to soil erosion, which increased when European settlers cleared forests for farmland in later decades.

Contest Between Spain and England English merchants and political leaders watched enviously as Spain was enriched by its valuable American possessions. In the mid-sixteenth century, English "sea dogs" like John Hawkins and Sir Francis Drake began to raid Spanish treasure fleets sailing home from the Caribbean. Their actions caused friction between the two countries and helped foment a war that in 1588 culminated in the defeat of a huge invasion force—the Spanish Armada—off the English coast. As part of the contest with Spain, English leaders started to think about planting colonies in the Western Hemisphere, thereby gaining better access to valuable trade goods while simultaneously preventing their enemy from dominating the Americas.

Encouraging the queen and her courtiers in that aim was Richard Hakluyt, a clergyman who became fascinated by tales of exploratory voyages while he was a student in the 1560s. He prepared and published English translations of numerous accounts of discoveries around the globe, repeatedly insisting on England's preeminent claim to the North American continent. In *Divers Voyages* (1582) and especially *Principall Navigations* (1589), he argued unreservedly for the benefits of English colonization in such "fertill and temperate places," contending that "there is none, that of right may be more bolde in this enterprice than the Englishmen."

The first English colonial planners saw Spain's possessions as a model and a challenge. They hoped to reproduce Spanish successes by dispatching to America men who would exploit the native peoples for their own and their nation's benefit. A group that included Sir Walter Raleigh began to promote a scheme to establish outposts that could trade with the Indians and provide bases for attacks on New Spain. Approving the idea, Queen Elizabeth I authorized Raleigh to colonize North America.

Roanoke After two preliminary expeditions, in 1587 Sir Walter Raleigh sent 117 colonists to the territory he named Virginia, after Elizabeth, the "Virgin Queen." They established a settlement on Roanoke

A watercolor by John White, an artist with Raleigh's second preliminary expedition (and who later was governor of the ill-fated 1587 colony). He identified his subjects as the wife and daughter of the chief of Pomeioc, a village near Roanoke. Note the woman's elaborate tattoos and the fact that the daughter carries an Elizabethan doll, obviously given to her by one of the Englishmen.

A cheife Heroroans wyfe of Pomeoc. and her daughter of the age of. 8. or. .10. yeares .

Island, in what is now North Carolina, but in 1590 a resupply ship—delayed in leaving England because of the Spanish Armada—could not find them. The colonists had vanished, leaving only the word *Croatoan* (the name of a nearby island) carved on a tree. Recent tree-ring studies have shown that the North Carolina coast experienced a severe drought between 1587 and 1589, which would have created a subsistence crisis for the settlers and could well have led them to abandon the Roanoke site.

Thus, England's first attempt to plant a permanent settlement on the North American coast failed, as had earlier efforts by Portugal on Cape Breton Island (early 1520s), Spain in modern Georgia (mid-1520s), and France in South Carolina and northern Florida (1560s). All three enterprises collapsed because of the hostility of neighboring peoples and colonists' inability to be self-sustaining in foodstuffs. The Portuguese, the Spanish, the first French settlers, and the English could not maintain friendly relations with local Indians, and Spanish soldiers destroyed the Florida French colony in 1565.

Harriot's *Briefe and True Report*   The explanation for such failings becomes clear in Thomas Harriot's *A Briefe and True Report of the New Found Land of Virginia*, published in 1588 to publicize Raleigh's colony. Harriot, a noted scientist who sailed with the second of the preliminary voyages to Roanoke, described the animals, plants, and people of the region for an English readership. His account revealed that, although the explorers depended on nearby villagers for most of their food, they needlessly antagonized their neighbors by killing some of them for what Harriot admitted were unjustifiable reasons.

The scientist advised later colonizers to deal with the native peoples of America more humanely than his comrades had. But the content of his book suggested why that advice would rarely be followed. *A Briefe and True Report* examined the possibilities for economic development in America. Harriot stressed three points: the availability of commodities familiar to Europeans, such as grapes, iron, copper, and fur-bearing animals; the potential profitability of exotic American products, such as maize, cassava, and tobacco; and the relative ease of manipulating the native population to the Europeans' advantage. Should the Americans attempt to resist the English by force, Harriot asserted, the latter's advantages of disciplined soldiers and superior weaponry would quickly deliver victory.

Harriot's *Briefe and True Report* depicted for his English readers a bountiful land full of opportunities for quick profit. The people residing there would, he thought, "in a short time be brought to civilitie" through conversion to Christianity, admiration for European superiority, or conquest—if they did not die from disease, the ravages of which he witnessed. Thomas Harriot understood the key elements of the story, but his prediction was far off the mark. European dominance of North America would be difficult to achieve. Indeed, it never was fully achieved, in the sense Harriot and his compatriots intended.

SUMMARY

The process of initial contact among Europeans, Africans, and Americans that ended with Thomas Harriot near the close of the sixteenth century began approximately 250 years earlier when Portuguese sailors first set out to explore the Mediterranean Atlantic and the West African coast. Those seamen established commercial ties that brought African slaves first to Iberia and then to the islands the Europeans conquered and settled. The Mediterranean Atlantic and its island sugar plantations nurtured the mariners who, like Christopher Columbus, ventured into previously unknown waters—those who sailed to India and Brazil as well as to the Caribbean and the North American coast. When Columbus first reached the Americas, he thought he had found Asia, his intended destination. Later explorers knew better but, except for the Spanish, regarded the Americas primarily as a barrier that prevented them from reaching their long-sought goal of an oceanic route to the riches of China and the Moluccas. Ordinary European fishermen were the first to realize that the northern coasts had valuable products to offer: fish and furs, both much in demand in their homelands.

The Aztecs had predicted that their Fifth Sun would end in earthquakes and hunger. Hunger they surely experienced after Cortés's invasion, and even if there were no earthquakes, their great temples tumbled to the ground nevertheless, as the Spaniards used their stones (and Indian laborers) to construct cathedrals honoring their God and his son, Jesus, rather than Huitzilopochtli. The conquerors employed, first, American and, later, enslaved African workers to till the fields, mine the precious metals, and herd the livestock that earned immense profits for themselves and their mother country.

The initial impact of Europeans on the Americas proved devastating. Flourishing civilizations were markedly altered in just a few short decades. Europeans' diseases killed millions of the Western Hemisphere's inhabitants; their livestock, along with a wide range of other imported animals and plants, irrevocably modified the American environment. Europe, too, was changed: American foodstuffs like corn and potatoes improved nutrition throughout the continent, and American gold and silver first enriched, then ruined, the Spanish economy.

By the end of the sixteenth century, fewer people resided in North America than had lived there before Columbus's arrival. And the people who did live there—Indian, African, and European—resided in a world that was indeed new—a world engaged in the unprecedented process of combining foods, religions, economies, ways of life, and political systems that had developed separately for millennia. Understandably, conflict and dissension permeated that process.

2

EUROPEANS COLONIZE
NORTH AMERICA 1600–1650

SPANISH, FRENCH, AND DUTCH NORTH AMERICA

Spaniards established the first permanent European settlement within the boundaries of the modern United States, but others had initially attempted that feat. Twice in the 1560s Huguenots (French Protestants), who were seeking to escape persecution, planted colonies on the south Atlantic coast. A passing ship rescued the starving survivors of the first colony, located in present-day South Carolina. The second colony, near modern Jacksonville, Florida, was destroyed in 1565 by a Spanish expedition under the command of Pedro Menéndez de Avilés. To ensure Spanish domination of the strategically important region (located near sea-lanes used by Spanish treasure ships bound for Europe), Menéndez set up a small fortified outpost, which he named St. Augustine—now the oldest continuously inhabited European settlement in the United States.

The local Guale and Timucua nations initially allied themselves with the powerful newcomers and welcomed Franciscan friars into their villages. The relationship did not remain peaceful for long, though, because the natives resisted the imposition of Spanish authority. Still, the Franciscans offered the Indians spiritual solace for the diseases and troubles besetting them after the Europeans' invasion, and eventually they gained numerous converts at missions that stretched westward across Florida and northward into the islands along the Atlantic coast.

New Mexico   More than thirty years passed after the founding of St. Augustine before conquistadors ventured anew into the

CHRONOLOGY

1558	Elizabeth I becomes queen
1565	Founding of St. Augustine (Florida), oldest permanent European settlement in present-day United States
1598	Oñate conquers Pueblos in New Mexico for Spain
1603	James I becomes king
1607	Jamestown founded, first permanent English settlement in North America
1608	Quebec founded by the French
1610	Founding of Santa Fe, New Mexico
1614	Fort Orange (Albany) founded by the Dutch
1619	Virginia House of Burgesses established, first representative assembly in the English colonies
1620	Plymouth colony founded, first permanent English settlement in New England
1622	Powhatan Confederacy attacks Virginia
1624	Dutch settle on Manhattan Island (New Amsterdam)
	English colonize St. Kitts, first island in Lesser Antilles settled by Europeans
	James I revokes Virginia Company's charter
1625	Charles I becomes king
1630	Massachusetts Bay colony founded
1634	Maryland founded
1636	Williams expelled from Massachusetts Bay, founds Providence, Rhode Island
	Connecticut founded
1637	Pequot War in New England
1638	Hutchinson expelled from Massachusetts Bay, goes to Rhode Island
1642	Montreal founded by the French
1646	Treaty ends hostilities between Virginia and Powhatan Confederacy

present-day United States. In 1598, drawn northward by rumors of rich cities, Juan de Oñate, a Mexican-born adventurer whose wife descended from both Cortés and Moctezuma, led a group of about five hundred soldiers and settlers to New Mexico. At first, the Pueblo peoples greeted the newcomers cordially. But when the Spaniards began to use torture, murder, and rape to extort food and clothing from the villagers, the residents of Acoma killed several soldiers, among them Oñate's nephew. The invaders responded ferociously, killing more than eight hundred people and capturing the remainder. All the captives above the age of twelve were ordered enslaved for twenty years, and men older than twenty-five had one foot amputated. Not surprisingly, the other Pueblo villages surrendered.

Yet Oñate's bloody victory proved illusory, for New Mexico held little wealth. It also was too far from the Pacific coast to assist in protecting Spanish sea-lanes, which had been one of Oñate's aims (he, like others, initially believed the continent to be much narrower than it actually is). Many of the Spaniards returned to Mexico, but horses remained, transforming the lives of the indigenous inhabitants. Officials considered abandoning the isolated colony, which lay 800 miles north of the nearest Spanish settlement. Still, for defensive purposes, the authorities decided to maintain a small military outpost and a few Christian missions in the area, with the capital at Santa Fe (founded 1610). As in regions to the south, Spanish leaders were granted *encomiendas,* guaranteeing them control over the labor of Pueblo villagers. But in the absence of mines or fertile agricultural lands, such grants yielded small profit.

Quebec and Montreal

On the Atlantic coast, the French turned their attention northward, to the area that Jacques Cartier had explored in the 1530s. Several times they tried to establish permanent bases along the Canadian coast but failed until 1605, when they founded Port Royal. Then in 1608, Samuel de Champlain set up a trading post at an interior site that the local Iroquois had called Stadacona when Cartier spent the winter there seventy-five years earlier. Champlain renamed it Quebec. He had chosen well: Quebec was the most defensible spot in the entire St. Lawrence River valley, a stronghold that controlled access to the heartland of the continent. In 1642, the French established a second post, Montreal, at the falls of the St. Lawrence (and thus at the end of navigation by oceangoing vessels), a place the Indians called Hochelaga.

Before the founding of these settlements, fishermen served as the major transporters of North American beaver pelts to France, but the new posts quickly took over control of the lucrative trade in furs (see Table 2.1). Only a few Europeans resided in New France; most were men, some of whom married Indian women. The colony's leaders gave land grants along the river to wealthy seigneurs (nobles), who then imported tenants to work their farms. A small number of Frenchmen brought their wives and took up agriculture; even so, more than twenty-five years after Quebec's founding, it had just sixty-four resident families, along with traders and soldiers. With respect to territory occupied and farmed, northern New France never grew much beyond the confines of the river valley between Quebec and Montreal (see Map 2.1). Thus, it differed significantly from New Spain, characterized by scattered cities and direct supervision of Indian laborers.

Jesuit Missions in New France

French missionaries of the Society of Jesus (Jesuits), a Roman Catholic order dedicated to converting nonbelievers to Christianity, also came to New France. First arriving in Quebec in 1625, the Jesuits, whom the Indians called Black Robes, tried to persuade indigenous peoples to live near French settlements and to adopt European agricultural methods. When that effort failed, the Jesuits concluded that they could introduce Catholicism to their new charges without insisting that they fundamentally

VISUALIZING THE PAST

Acoma Pueblo

Today, as in the late sixteenth century when it was besieged and eventually captured by the Spanish conquistador Juan de Oñate, the Acoma Pueblo sits high atop an isolated mesa. Long before the Spaniards arrived in modern New Mexico, the location was selected because it was easily defensible; some structures that date back to the eleventh century are still standing in the middle of the village. Building on a mesa 365 feet high was safer than living on the plains below, but it caused other problems—most notably, with the water supply. To this day there is no source of water in the village. Acoma's residents had to carry water up a steep set of stairs cut into the mesa's

© Kevin Fleming/CORBIS

Acoma Pueblo today. The village is now used primarily for ritual purposes; few people reside there permanently, because all water must be trucked in.

alter their traditional ways of life. Accordingly, the Black Robes learned Indian languages and traveled to remote regions of the interior, where they lived in twos and threes among hundreds of potential converts.

Using a variety of strategies, Jesuits sought to gain the confidence of influential men and to undermine the authority of village shamans, the traditional religious leaders. Trained in rhetoric, Jesuits won admirers with their eloquence. Immune to smallpox (for all had survived the disease already), they explained epidemics among the Indians as God's punishment for sin, their arguments aided by the ineffectiveness of the shamans' traditional remedies against the new pestilence. Drawing on European science, Jesuits predicted solar and lunar eclipses. Perhaps most important, side (today there is an almost equally steep road). The women of Acoma were and are accomplished potters. Some pots, like the one shown here, were designed with a low center of gravity. How would that design help women to reach the top of the mesa with much-needed water? How would they carry such pots?

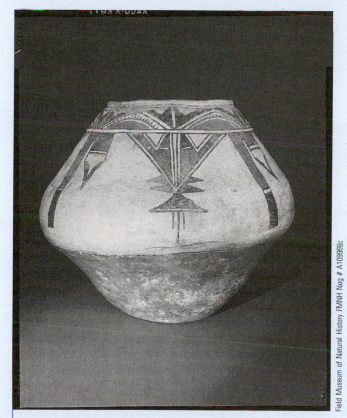

Field Museum of Natural History FMNH Neg # A109989c

A pot designed for carrying water to the top of the mesa.

they amazed villagers by communicating with each other over long distances through marks on paper. The Indians' desire to learn how to harness the extraordinary power of literacy was one of the critical factors that made them receptive to the missionaries' spiritual message.

Although the process took many years, Jesuits slowly gained thousands of converts, some of whom moved to reserves set aside for Christian Indians. Catholicism offered women in particular the inspiring role model of the Virgin Mary, personified in Montreal and Quebec by communities of nuns who taught Indian women and children, and ministered to their needs. Many male and female converts followed Catholic teachings with fervor and piety, altering traditional native customs

TABLE 2.1 | THE FOUNDING OF PERMANENT EUROPEAN COLONIES IN NORTH AMERICA, 1565–1640

Colony	Founder(s)	Date	Basis of Economy
Florida	Pedro Menéndez de Avilés	1565	Farming
New Mexico	Juan de Oñate	1598	Livestock
Virginia	Virginia Co.	1607	Tobacco
New France	France	1608	Fur trading
New Netherland	Dutch West India Co.	1614	Fur trading
Plymouth	Separatists	1620	Farming, fishing
Maine	Sir Ferdinando Gorges	1622	Fishing
St. Kitts, Barbados, et al.	European immigrants	1624	Sugar
Massachusetts Bay	Massachusetts Bay	1630	Farming, fishing, fur trading
Maryland	Cecilius Calvert	1634	Tobacco
Rhode Island	Roger Williams	1636	Farming
Connecticut	Thomas Hooker	1636	Farming, fur trading
New Haven	Massachusetts migrants	1638	Farming
New Hampshire	Massachusetts migrants	1638	Farming, fishing

of allowing premarital sexual relationships and easy divorce, because Catholic doctrine prohibited both. Yet they resisted Jesuits' attempts to have them adopt strict European child-rearing methods, instead retaining their more relaxed practices. Jesuits, unlike Franciscans in New Mexico, recognized that such aspects of native culture could be compatible with Christian beliefs. Their efforts to attract converts were further aided by their lack of interest in labor tribute or land acquisition.

New Netherland Jesuit missionaries faced little competition from other Europeans for native peoples' souls, but French fur traders had to confront a direct challenge. In 1614, only five years after Henry Hudson explored the river that now bears his name, his sponsor, the Dutch West India Company, established an outpost (Fort Orange) on that river at the site of present-day Albany, New York. Like the French, the Dutch sought beaver pelts, and their presence so close to Quebec threatened French domination of the region. The Netherlands, at the time the world's dominant commercial power, aimed primarily at trade rather than at colonization. Thus New Netherland, like New France, remained small, confined largely to a river valley that offered easy access to its settlements. The colony's southern anchor was New Amsterdam, founded in 1624 on Manhattan Island, at the mouth of the Hudson River.

As the Dutch West India Company's colony in North America, New Netherland was a small outpost of a vast commercial empire that extended to Africa, Brazil, the Caribbean, and modern-day Indonesia. Autocratic directors-general ruled the colony

MAP 2.1 European Settlements and Indian Tribes in Eastern North America, 1650

The few European settlements established in the East before 1650 were widely scattered, hugging the shores of the Atlantic Ocean and the banks of its major rivers. By contrast, America's native inhabitants controlled the vast interior expanse of the continent, and Spaniards had begun to move into the West.

for the company; with no elected assembly, settlers felt little loyalty to their nominal leaders. Few migrants arrived. Even an offer in 1629 of large land grants, or patroon-ships, to people who would bring fifty settlers to the province failed to attract takers. (Only one such tract—Rensselaerswyck, near Albany—was ever fully developed.) As late as the mid-1660s, New Netherland had only about five thousand inhabitants. Some were Swedes and Finns who resided in the former colony of New Sweden (founded in 1638 on the Delaware River; see Map 2.1), which was seized by the Dutch in 1655. New Sweden's chief legacy to North American settlement was log cabin construction.

The Indian allies of New France and New Netherland clashed in part because of fur-trade rivalries. In the 1640s the Iroquois, who traded chiefly with the Dutch and lived in modern upstate New York, went to war against the Hurons, who traded primarily with the French and lived in presentday Ontario. The Iroquois wanted to become the major supplier of pelts to Europeans and they wanted to en-sure the security of their hunting territories. They achieved both goals by using guns supplied by the Dutch to virtually exterminate the Hurons, whose population had already been decimated by a smallpox epidemic. The Iroquois thus established themselves as a major force in the region, one that in the future Europeans could ignore only at their peril.

THE CARIBBEAN

In the Caribbean, France, the Netherlands, and England collided repeatedly in the first half of the seventeenth century. The Spanish concentrated their colonization ef-forts on the Greater Antilles—Cuba, Hispaniola, Jamaica, and Puerto Rico. They ignored many smaller islands, partly because of resistance by their Carib inhabi-tants and partly because the mainland offered greater wealth for less effort. But the tiny islands attracted other European powers: they could provide bases from which to attack Spanish vessels loaded with American gold and silver, and they could serve as sources of valuable tropical products such as dyes and fruits.

Warfare and Hurricanes   England was the first northern European nation to establish a permanent foothold in the smaller Caribbean islands (the Lesser Antilles), settling on St. Christopher (St. Kitts) in 1624, then later on other islands, such as Barbados (1627) and Providence (1630). France was able to colonize Guadeloupe and Martinique only by defeating the Caribs, whereas the Dutch more easily gained control of tiny St. Eustatius (strate-gically located near St. Christopher). In addition to indigenous inhabitants, Europeans had to worry about conflicts with Spaniards and with one another. Like Providence Island, many colonies changed hands during the seventeenth century. For example, the English drove the Spanish out of Jamaica in 1655, and the French soon thereafter took over half of Hispaniola, creating the colony of St. Domingue (modern Haiti).

Another danger, too, confronted the new settlers: the great windstorms called by the Taíno people *hurakán*, or, in English, hurricanes. Just nine months after the establishment of the first English outpost on St. Christopher, wrote one colonist, "came a Hericano and blew it away." Two years later, a second storm again devastated the infant colony, leaving the settlers "very miserable," without housing or adequate provisions. Almost every year in the late summer months, one or two islands suffered significant damage from hurricanes. Survivors expressed awe at the destructive force of the storms, which repeatedly forced them to rebuild and replant. To withstand the winds, they designed one- or two-story brick and stone houses with low roofs and heavy wooden shutters over the windows.

Sugar Cultivation   Why did Europeans try to gain and retain control of such imperiled islands? The primary answer is sugar. Europeans loved sugar, which provided a sweet taste and a quick energy boost and greatly enriched those who grew and processed it for international markets. Entering Europe in substantial quantities at approximately the same time as coffee and tea—the stimulating, addictive, and bitter Asian drinks improved by sweetening—sugar quickly became a crucial element of the European diet.

English residents of Barbados, after first experimenting with tobacco, cotton, and indigo, discovered in the early 1640s that the island's soil and climate were ideal for cultivating sugar cane. At the time, the world's supply of sugar came primarily from the Madeiras, the Canaries, SãoTomé, and especially Brazil, where farmers, each with a few servants or slaves, grew much of the crop. Sugar cane needed to be processed within two days of being harvested, or the juice would dry, so Brazilian producers quickly took their cane to central mills where it was crushed, boiled down, and finally refined into brown and white sugars.

Barbadians, several of whom visited northeastern Brazil while it was briefly ruled by the Dutch in the 1630s and 1640s, initially copied both the Brazilians' machinery and their small-scale methods of production, which used an existing work force of servants and slaves. By the mid-1650s, funded by wealthy English merchants and their own profits from raising tobacco and cotton, the more substantial planters expanded their enterprises dramatically. They increased the size of their landholdings, built their own sugar mills, and purchased growing numbers of laborers—first English and Irish servants, then African slaves.

As other Caribbean planters embraced sugarcane cultivation, Barbadians' profit margins were reduced. Even so, sugar remained the most valuable American commodity for more than one hundred years. In the eighteenth century, sugar grown by large gangs of slaves in British Jamaica and French St. Domingue dominated the world market. Yet, in the long run, the future economic importance of the Europeans' American colonies lay on the mainland rather than in the Caribbean.

ENGLISH INTEREST IN COLONIZATION

The failure of Raleigh's Roanoke colony ended English efforts to settle in North America for nearly two decades. When the English decided in 1606 to try once more, they again planned colonies that imitated the Spanish model. Yet greater success came when they abandoned that model and founded settlements very different from those of other European powers. Unlike Spain, France, or the Netherlands, England eventually sent large numbers of men and women to set up agriculturally based colonies on the mainland. Two major developments prompted approximately 200,000 ordinary English men and women to move to North America in the seventeenth century and led their government to encourage their emigration.

Social and Economic Change

The first development was the onset of dramatic social and economic change. In the 150-year period after 1530, largely as a result of the introduction of nutritious American crops, England's population doubled. All those additional people needed food, clothing, and other goods. The competition for goods led to inflation, coupled with a fall in real wages as the number of workers increased. In these new economic and demographic circumstances, some English people—especially those with sizable landholdings that could produce food and clothing fibers for the growing population—substantially improved their lot. Others, particularly landless laborers and those with small amounts of land, fell into poverty. When landowners raised rents, took control of lands that peasants had long been allowed to use in common (enclosure), or decided to combine small holdings into large units, they forced tenants off the land. Consequently, geographical as well as social mobility increased, and the population of the cities swelled. London, for example, more than tripled in size by 1650, when 375,000 residents lived in its crowded buildings.

Wealthy English people reacted with alarm to what they saw as the disappearance of traditional ways of life. Steady streams of the landless and homeless filled the streets and highways. Obsessed with the problem of maintaining order, officials came to believe England was overcrowded. They concluded that colonies established in North America could siphon off England's "surplus population," thus easing social strains at home. For similar reasons, many English people decided they could improve their circumstances by migrating from a small, landscarce, apparently overpopulated island to a large, landrich, apparently empty continent and its nearby islands. Among those attracted by prospects for emigration were younger sons of gentlemen who were excluded from inheriting land by wealthy families' practice of primogeniture, which reserved all real estate for the eldest son. Such economic considerations were rendered even more significant in light of the second development: a major change in English religious practice.

English Reformation

The sixteenth century witnessed a religious transformation that eventually led large numbers of English dissenters to leave their homeland. In 1533 Henry VIII, wanting a male heir and infatuated with Anne Boleyn, asked the pope to annul his marriage to his Spanish-born queen, Catherine of Aragón, despite nearly twenty years of marriage and the birth of a daughter. When the pope refused, Henry left the Roman Catholic Church. He founded the Church of England and—with Parliament's concurrence—proclaimed himself its head. At first, the reformed Church of England differed little from Catholicism in its practices. Under Henry's daughter, Elizabeth I (child of his later marriage to Anne Boleyn), though, new currents of religious belief, which had originated on the European continent early in the sixteenth century, dramatically affected that established church, termed thus because it had the official imprimatur of the government and was supported by tax revenues.

These currents constituted the Protestant Reformation, led by Martin Luther, a German monk, and John Calvin, a French cleric and lawyer. Challenging the Catholic doctrine that priests were intermediaries between laypeople and God, Luther and Calvin insisted that people could interpret the Bible for themselves. That notion stimulated the spread of literacy: to understand and interpret the Bible, people had to learn how to read. Both Luther and Calvin rejected Catholic rituals, denying the need for an elaborate church hierarchy. They also asserted that the key to salvation was faith in God, rather than—as Catholic teaching had it—a combination of faith and good works. Calvin went further than Luther, stressing God's omnipotence and emphasizing the need for people to submit totally to God's will.

Puritans, Separatists, and Presbyterians

Elizabeth I tolerated diverse forms of Christianity as long as her subjects acknowledged her authority as head of the Church of England. During her long reign (1558–1603), Calvin's ideas gained influence in England, Wales, and especially Scotland. (In Ireland, also part of her realm, Catholicism remained dominant.) The Scottish church eventually adopted Presbyterianism, an organizational system that dispensed with bishops and placed religious authority in bodies of clerics and laymen called presbyteries. By the late sixteenth century, though, many Calvinists—including those who came to be called Puritans, because they wanted to purify the church, or Separatists, because they wanted to leave it entirely—believed that reformers in England and Scotland had not gone far enough. Henry had simplified the church hierarchy, and the Scots had altered it; they wanted to abolish it altogether. Henry and the Scots had subordinated the church to the interests of the state; they wanted a church free from political interference. The established churches of England and Scotland, like the Catholic Church or the official Protestant churches of continental European countries, continued to nominally encompass all residents of the realm. Calvinists in England and Scotland preferred a more restricted definition; they wanted to confine church membership to persons they believed "saved"—those God had selected for salvation before birth.

Paradoxically, though, a key article of their faith insisted that people could not know for certain if they were "saved" because mere mortals could not comprehend or affect their predestination to heaven or hell. Thus, pious Calvinists daily confronted serious dilemmas: if the saved (or "elect") could not be identified with certainty, how could proper churches be constituted? If one was predestined and could not alter one's fate, why should one attend church or do good works? Calvinists dealt with the first dilemma by admitting that their judgments as to eligibility for church membership only approximated God's unknowable decisions. They resolved the second by reasoning that God gave the elect the ability to accept salvation and to lead a good life. Therefore, even though one could not earn a place in heaven by piety and good works, such practices could indicate one's place in the ranks of the saved.

Stuart Monarchs

Elizabeth I's Stuart successors, her cousin James I (1603–1625) and his son Charles I (1625–1649), exhibited less tolerance for Calvinists. As Scots, they also had little respect for the traditions of representative government that had developed in England under the Tudors

TABLE 2.2 | TUDOR AND STUART MONARCHS OF ENGLAND, 1509–1649

Monarch	Reign	Relation to Predecessor
Henry VIII	1509–1547	Son
Edward VI	1547–1553	Son
Mary I	1553–1558	Half-sister
Elizabeth I	1558–1603	Half-sister
James I	1603–1625	Cousin
Charles I	1625–1649	Son

and their predecessors (see Table 2.2). The wealthy landowners who sat in Parliament had grown accustomed to having considerable influence on government policies, especially taxation. But James I, taking a position later endorsed by his son, publicly declared his belief in the divine right of kings. The Stuarts insisted that a monarch's power came directly from God and that his subjects had a duty to obey him. They likened the king's absolute authority to a father's authority over his children.

Both James I and Charles I believed their authority included the power to enforce religious conformity. Because Calvinists—and remaining Catholics in England and Scotland—challenged many of the most important precepts of the established churches, the Stuart monarchs authorized the removal of dissenting clergymen from their pulpits. In the 1620s and 1630s, some Puritans, Separatists, Presbyterians, and Catholics decided to move to America where they hoped to put their diverse religious beliefs into practice unhindered by the Stuarts or the church hierarchy. Some fled hurriedly to avoid arrest and imprisonment.

THE FOUNDING OF VIRGINIA

The impetus for England's first permanent colony in the Western Hemisphere was both religious and economic. The newly militant English Protestants were eager to combat "popery" both at home and in the Americas. They concurred with Richard Hakluyt, who remarked that if Spaniards, "in their superstition," had "don so great thinges in so shorte space," surely the adherents of "our true and syncere Religion" could achieve even more remarkable results.

Accordingly, in 1606, a group of merchants and wealthy gentry—some of them aligned with religious reformers—obtained a royal charter for the Virginia Company, organized as a joint-stock company. Such forerunners of modern corporations, initially created for trading voyages and often very profitable, pooled the resources of many small investors through stock sales and spread the risks. Yet the joint-stock company, then as later, proved to be a poor vehicle for establishing colonies because colonies required significant continuing investments of capital. The lack of immediate returns thus generated tension between stockholders and colonists. Although at the outset investors in the Virginia Company anticipated great profits, and neither settlement established by the Virginia Company—one in Maine that collapsed within a year and Jamestown—ever earned much.

Jamestown and Tsenacommacah   In 1607, the company dispatched 104 men and boys to a region near Chesapeake Bay called Tsenacommacah by its native inhabitants. There in May they established the palisaded settlement called Jamestown on a swampy peninsula in a river they also named for their monarch. They quickly constructed small houses and a chapel. Ill-equipped for survival in the unfamiliar environment, the colonists fell victim to dissension and disease as they attempted to maintain traditional English social and political hierarchies. Familiar with Spanish experience, the gentlemen and soldiers at Jamestown expected to rely on local Indians for food and tribute, yet the residents of Tsenacommacah refused to cooperate. Moreover, through sheer bad luck, the settlers arrived in the midst of a severe drought (now known to be the worst in the region for 1,700 years) that persisted until 1612. The lack of rainfall not only made it difficult to cultivate crops but also polluted their drinking water.

The weroance (chief) of Tsenacommacah, Powhatan, had inherited rule over six Algonquian villages and later gained control of some twenty-five others (see Map 2.1). In late 1607 negotiations with Captain John Smith, one of the colony's leaders, the weroance tentatively agreed to an alliance with the Englishmen. In exchange for foodstuffs, Powhatan hoped to acquire guns, hatchets, and swords, which would give him a technological advantage over the enemies of his people. Each side in the alliance wanted to subordinate the other, but neither succeeded.

The fragile relationship soon foundered on mutual mistrust. The wereoance relocated his primary village in early 1609 to a place the newcomers could not access easily. Without Powhatan's assistance, the settlement experienced a "starving time" (winter 1609–1610) when many died and at least one colonist resorted to cannibalism. In spring 1610, the survivors packed up to leave on a newly arrived ship but en route out of the James River encountered a new governor, male and female settlers, and added supplies, so they returned to Jamestown. Sporadic skirmishes ensued as the standoff with the Powhatans continued. To gain the upper hand, the settlers in 1613 kidnapped Powhatan's daughter, Pocahontas, and held her hostage. In captivity, she agreed to convert to Christianity and to marry a colonist, John Rolfe. He had fallen in love with her, but she probably married him for diplomatic reasons; their union initiated a period of peace between the English and her people. Funded by the Virginia Company, she and Rolfe sailed to England to promote interest in the colony. Pocahontas died at Gravesend in 1616, probably of dysentery, leaving an infant son who returned to Virginia as a young adult.

Although their royal charter nominally laid claim to a much wider territory, the Jamestown settlers saw their "Virginia" as essentially corresponding to Tsenacommacah. Powhatan's dominion was bounded on the north by the Potomac, on the south by the Great Dismal Swamp, and on the west by the fall line—the beginning of the upland Piedmont. Beyond those boundaries lay the Powhatans' enemies and (especially in the west) lands the Powhatans feared to enter. English people relied on the Powhatans as guides and interpreters, traveling along rivers and precontact paths in order to trade with the Powhatans' partners. For more than half a century, settlement in "Virginia" was confined to Tsenacommacah.

Algonquian and English Cultural Differences   In Tsenacommacah and elsewhere on the North American coast, English settlers and local Algonquians focused on their cultural differences—not their similarities—although both groups held deep religious beliefs, subsisted primarily through agriculture, accepted social and political hierarchy, and observed well-defined gender roles. From the outset, English men regarded Indian men as lazy because they did not cultivate crops and spent much of their time hunting (a sport, not work, in English eyes). Indian men thought English men effeminate because they did the "woman's work" of cultivation. In the same vein, the English believed Algonquian women were oppressed because they did heavy field labor.

The nature of Algonquian and English hierarchies differed. Among Algonquians like the Powhatans, political power and social status did not necessarily pass directly through the male line, instead commonly flowing through sisters' sons. By contrast, English gentlemen inherited their position from their father. English political and military leaders tended to rule autocratically, whereas Algonquian leaders (even Powhatan) had limited authority over their people. Accustomed to the powerful kings of Europe, the English overestimated the ability of chiefs to make treaties that would bind their people.

Furthermore, Algonquian and English concepts of property differed. Most Algonquian villages held their land communally. Land could not be bought or sold absolutely, although certain rights to use it (for example, for hunting or fishing) could be transferred. Once, most English villagers, too, had used land in common, but because of enclosures in the previous century they had become accustomed to individual farms and to buying and selling land. The English also refused to accept the validity of Indians' claims to traditional hunting territories, insisting that only land intensively cultivated could be regarded as owned or occupied. As one colonist put it, "salvadge peoples" who "rambled" over a region without farming it could claim no "title or propertye" in the land. Ownership of such "unclaimed" property, the English believed, lay with the English monarchy, in whose name John Cabot had laid claim to North America in 1497.

Above all, the English settlers believed unwaveringly in the superiority of their civilization. Although in the early years of colonization they often anticipated living peacefully alongside indigenous peoples, they always assumed that they would dictate the terms of such coexistence. Like Thomas Harriot at Roanoke, they expected native peoples to adopt English customs and to convert to Christianity. They showed little respect for the Indians when they believed English interests were at stake, as was demonstrated by developments in Virginia once the settlers found the salable commodity they sought.

Tobacco Cultivation   That commodity was tobacco, the American crop previously introduced to Europe by the Spanish and subsequently cultivated in Turkey. In 1611, John Rolfe planted seeds of a variety from the Spanish Caribbean, which was superior to the strain grown by Virginia Indians. Nine years later, Virginians exported forty thousand pounds of cured leaves; by the late 1620s, shipments had jumped dramatically to 1.5 million pounds. The great tobacco boom had begun, fueled by high prices and substantial profits for planters as they responded to escalating demand from Europe and Africa. The price later fell almost as sharply as it had risen, fluctuating wildly from year to year in response to increasing supply and international competition. Nevertheless, tobacco made Virginia prosper.

The spread of tobacco cultivation altered life for everyone. Successful tobacco cultivation required abundant land because the crop quickly drained soil of nutrients. Farmers soon learned that a field could produce only about three satisfactory crops before it had to lie fallow for several years to regain its fertility. Thus, the once-small English settlements began to expand rapidly: eager applicants asked the Virginia Company for land grants on both sides of the James River and its tributary streams. Lulled into a false sense of security by years of peace, Virginians established farms at some distance from one another along the riverbanks—a settlement pattern convenient for tobacco cultivation but dangerous for defense.

Indian Assaults

Opechancanough, Powhatan's brother and successor, watched the English colonists' expansion and witnessed their attempts to convert natives to Christianity. Recognizing the danger, the war leader launched coordinated attacks along the James River on March 22, 1622. By the end of the day, 347 colonists (about one-quarter of the total) lay dead, and only a timely warning from two Christian converts saved Jamestown itself from destruction.

Virginia reeled from the blow but did not collapse. Reinforced by new shipments of men and arms from England, the settlers repeatedly attacked Opechancanough's villages. A peace treaty was signed in 1632, but in April 1644 the elderly Opechancanough assaulted the invaders one last time, though he must have known he could not prevail. In 1646, survivors of the Powhatan Confederacy formally subordinated themselves to England. Although they continued to live in the region, their efforts to resist the spread of European settlement ended.

End of Virginia Company

The 1622 assault that failed to destroy the colony did succeed in killing its parent. The Virginia Company never made any profits from the enterprise, for internal corruption and the heavy cost of supporting the settlers offset all its earnings. But before its demise, the company developed two policies that set key precedents. First, to attract settlers, the company in 1617 established the "headright" system. Every new arrival paying his or her own way was promised a land grant of fifty acres; those who financed the passage of others received similar headrights for each person. To ordinary English farmers, many of whom owned little or no land, the headright system offered a powerful incentive to move to Virginia. To wealthy gentry, it promised even more: the possibility of establishing vast agricultural enterprises worked by large numbers of laborers. Two years later, the company introduced a second reform, authorizing the landowning men of the major Virginia settlements to elect representatives to an assembly called the House of Burgesses. English landholders had long been accustomed to electing members of Parliament and controlling their own local governments; therefore, they expected the same privilege in the nation's colonies.

When James I revoked the charter in 1624, transforming Virginia into a royal colony, he continued the company's headright policy. Because he distrusted legislative bodies, though, James abolished the assembly. But Virginians protested so vigorously that by 1629 the House of Burgesses was functioning once again. Only two decades after the first permanent English settlement was planted in North America, the colonists successfully insisted on governing themselves at the local level. Thus, the political structure of England's American possessions came to differ from those of the Spanish, Dutch, and French colonies—all of which were ruled autocratically.

LIFE IN THE CHESAPEAKE

By the 1630s, tobacco was firmly established as the staple crop and chief source of revenue in Virginia. It quickly became just as important in the second English colony planted on Chesapeake Bay: Maryland, given by Charles I to George Calvert, first Lord Baltimore, as a personal possession (proprietorship), which was settled in 1634. (Because Virginia and Maryland both border Chesapeake Bay—see Map 2.1—they often are referred to collectively as "the Chesapeake.") Members of the Calvert family intended the colony to serve as a haven for their persecuted fellow Catholics. Cecilius Calvert, second Lord Baltimore, became the first colonizer to offer freedom of religion to all Christian settlers; he understood that protecting the Protestant majority could also ensure Catholics' rights. Maryland's Act of Religious Toleration codified his policy in 1649.

In everything but religion, the two Chesapeake colonies resembled each other. In Maryland as in Virginia, tobacco planters spread out along the riverbanks, establishing isolated farms instead of towns. The region's deep, wide rivers offered dependable water transportation in an age of few and inadequate roads. Each farm or group of farms had its own wharf, where oceangoing vessels could take on or discharge cargo. Consequently, Virginia and Maryland had few towns, for their residents did not need commercial centers in order to buy and sell goods.

Demand for Laborers   The planting, cultivation, harvesting, and curing of tobacco were repetitive, time-consuming, and labor-intensive tasks. Clearing land for new fields, necessary every few years, also demanded heavy labor. Above all else, then, successful Chesapeake farms required workers. But where and how could they be found? Nearby Indians, their numbers reduced by war and disease, could not supply such needs. Nor were enslaved Africans available: traders could more easily and profitably sell slaves to Caribbean sugar planters. Only a few people of African descent, some of them free, initially trickled into the Chesapeake. By 1650, about three hundred blacks lived in Virginia—a tiny fraction of the population.

Chesapeake tobacco farmers thus looked primarily to England to supply their labor needs. Because of the headright system (which Maryland also adopted in 1640), a tobacco farmer anywhere in the Chesapeake could simultaneously obtain both land and labor by importing workers from England. Good management would make the process self-perpetuating: a farmer could use his profits to pay for the passage of more workers and thereby gain title to more land. Success could even bring movement into the ranks of the planter gentry that began to develop in the region.

Because men did the agricultural work in European societies, colonists assumed that field laborers should be men. Such laborers, along with a few women, immigrated to America as indentured servants—that is, in return for their passage they contracted to work for periods ranging from four to seven years. Indentured servants accounted for 75 to 85 percent of the approximately 130,000 English immigrants to Virginia and Maryland during the seventeenth century. The rest tended to be young couples with one or two children.

Males between the ages of fifteen and twenty-four composed roughly three-quarters of the servants; only one immigrant in five or six was female. Most of these young men came from farming or laboring families, and many originated in regions of England experiencing severe social disruption. Some had already moved several times within England before relocating to America. Often they came from the middling ranks of society—what their contemporaries called the "common sort." Their youth indicated that most probably had not yet established themselves in their homeland.

Conditions of Servitude

For such people, the Chesapeake appeared to offer good prospects. Servants who fulfilled the terms of their indenture earned "freedom dues" consisting of clothes, tools, livestock, casks of corn and tobacco, and sometimes even land. From a distance at least, America seemed to offer chances for advancement unavailable in England. Yet immigrants' lives were difficult. Servants typically worked six days a week, ten to fourteen hours a day, in a climate much warmer than England's. Their masters could discipline or sell them, and they faced severe penalties for running away. Even so, the laws did give them some protection. For example, their masters were supposed to supply them with sufficient food, clothing, and shelter, and they were not to be beaten excessively. Cruelly treated servants could turn to the courts for assistance, sometimes winning verdicts directing that they be transferred to more humane masters or released from their indenture.

Servants and their owners alike contended with epidemic disease. Immigrants first had to survive the process the colonists called "seasoning," a bout with disease (probably malaria) that usually occurred during their first Chesapeake summer. They then often endured recurrences of malaria, along with dysentery, typhoid fever, and other illnesses. Consequently, about 40 percent of male servants did not survive long enough to become freedmen. Even young men of twenty-two who successfully weathered their seasoning could expect to live only another twenty years.

For those who survived, though, the opportunities for advancement were real. Until the last decades of the seventeenth century, former servants often became independent farmers ("freeholders"), thereafter living a modest but comfortable existence. Some even assumed positions of political prominence, such as justice of the peace or militia officer. But in the 1670s, tobacco prices entered a fifty-year period of stagnation and decline. Simultaneously, good land grew increasingly scarce and expensive. In 1681, Maryland dropped its legal requirement that servants receive land as part of their freedom dues, forcing large numbers of freed servants to live for years as wage laborers or tenant farmers. By 1700, the Chesapeake was no longer the land of opportunity it once had been.

Standard of Living   Life in the early Chesapeake was hard for everyone, regardless of sex or status. Farmers (and sometimes their wives) toiled in the fields alongside servants, laboriously clearing land, then planting and harvesting tobacco and corn. Because hogs could forage for themselves in the forests and needed little tending, Chesapeake households subsisted mainly on pork and corn, a filling diet but not sufficiently nutritious. Families supplemented this monotonous fare by eating fish, shellfish, and wildfowl, in addition to vegetables such as lettuce and peas, which they grew in small gardens. The near impossibility of preserving food for safe winter consumption magnified the health problems caused by epidemic disease. Salting, drying, and smoking, the only methods the colonists knew, did not always prevent spoilage.

Few households had many material possessions other than farm implements, bedding, and basic cooking and eating utensils. Chairs, tables, candles, and knives and forks were luxury items. Most people rose and went to bed with the sun, sat on crude benches or storage chests, and held plates or bowls in their hands while eating meat and vegetable stews with spoons. The ramshackle houses commonly had just one or two rooms. Colonists devoted their income to improving their farms, buying livestock, and purchasing more laborers instead of improving their standard of living. Rather than making such items as clothing or tools, families imported necessary manufactured goods from England.

Chesapeake Families   The predominance of males (see Figure 2.1), the incidence of servitude, and the high mortality rates combined to produce unusual patterns of family life. Female servants normally could not marry during their term of indenture because masters did not want pregnancies to deprive them of workers. Many male ex-servants could not marry at all because of the scarcity of women; such men lived alone, in pairs, or as the third member of a household containing a married couple. In contrast, nearly every adult free woman in the Chesapeake married, and widows usually remarried within a few months of a husband's death. Yet because of high infant mortality and because almost all marriages were delayed by servitude or broken by death, Chesapeake women commonly reared only one to three healthy children, in contrast to English women who normally had at least five.

Thus, Chesapeake families were few, small, and short-lived. Youthful immigrants came to America as individuals free of familial control; they commonly died while their children were still young. In one Virginia county, for example, more than three-quarters of the children had lost at least one parent by the time they either married or reached age twenty-one. Those children were put to work as soon as possible on the farms of parents, stepparents, or guardians. Their schooling, if any, was haphazard; whether Chesapeake-born children learned to read or write depended largely on whether their parents were literate and took the time to teach them.

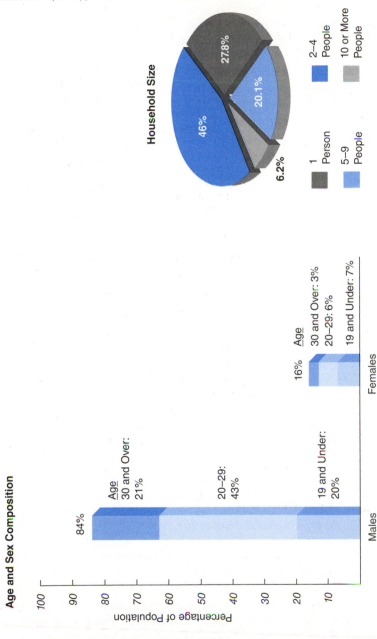

FIGURE 2.1 Population of Virginia, 1625

The only detailed census taken in the English mainland North American colonies during the seventeenth century was prepared in Virginia in 1625. It listed a total of 1,218 people, constituting 309 "households" and living in 278 dwellings—so some houses contained more than one family. The chart shows, on the left, the proportionate age and gender distribution of the 765 individuals for whom full information was recorded, and, on the right, the percentage variation in the sizes of the 309 households. The approximately 42 percent of the residents of the colony who were servants were concentrated in 30 percent of the households. Nearly 70 percent of the households had no servants at all.

Chesapeake Politics

Throughout the seventeenth century, immigrants composed a majority of the Chesapeake population, with important implications for regional political patterns. Most of the members of Virginia's House of Burgesses and Maryland's House of Delegates (established in 1635) were immigrants; they also dominated the governor's council, which simultaneously served as each colony's highest court, part of the legislature, and executive adviser to the governor. A cohesive, native-born ruling elite emerged only in the early eighteenth century.

Representative institutions based on the consent of the governed usually function as a major source of political stability. In the seventeenth-century Chesapeake, most property-owning white males could vote, and such freeholders chose as their legislators (burgesses) the local elites who seemed to be the natural leaders of their respective areas. But because most such men were immigrants lacking strong ties to one another or to the colonies, the assemblies' existence did not create political stability. Unusual demographic patterns thus contributed to the region's contentious politics.

THE FOUNDING OF NEW ENGLAND

The economic and religious motives that prompted English people to move to the Chesapeake also drew men and women to New England, the region known as North Virginia before Captain John Smith renamed it in 1616 after exploring its coast. But because Puritans organized the New England colonies and because of environmental factors, the northern settlements developed very differently from their southern counterparts. The divergence became apparent even as the would-be colonists left England.

Contrasting Regional Demographic Patterns

Hoping to exert control over a migration that appeared disorderly (and which included dissenters seeking to flee the authority of the Church of England), royal bureaucrats in late 1634 ordered port officials in London to collect information on all travelers departing for the colonies. The resulting records for the year 1635 are a treasure trove for historians. They document the departure of fifty-three vessels in that year alone—twenty to Virginia, seventeen to New England, eight to Barbados, five to St. Christopher, two to Bermuda, and one to Providence Island. Almost five thousand people sailed on those ships, with two thousand departing for Virginia, about twelve hundred for New England, and the rest for island destinations. Nearly three-fifths of all the passengers were between fifteen and twenty-four years old, reflecting the predominance of young male servants among migrants to America.

But among those bound for New England, such youths constituted less than one-third of the total; nearly 40 percent were older, and another third were younger. Whereas women made up just 14 percent of those going to Virginia, they composed almost 40 percent of the passengers to New England. Such composite figures show that New England migrants often traveled in family groups. They also brought more goods and livestock with them and tended to travel with other people from the same region. For example, aboard one vessel, more than half came from York; on another, nearly half came from Buckinghamshire. In short, people migrated to New England together with their close associates. Their lives in North America must have been more comfortable and less lonely than those of their southern counterparts.

Contrasting Regional Religious Patterns	Puritan congregations quickly became key institutions in colonial New England, whereas no church had much impact on the early development of the Chesapeake colonies. Spread-out settlement patterns brought great difficulty to anyone who wanted to organize a church.

Catholic and Anglican bishops in England paid little attention to their coreligionists in America, and all Chesapeake congregations languished in the absence of sufficient numbers of ordained clergymen. (For example, in 1665, an observer noted that only ten of the fifty Virginia Church of England parishes had resident clerics.) Not until the 1690s did the Church of England begin to take firmer root in Virginia; by then, it had also replaced Catholicism as the established church in Maryland, and Calvinists were in the minority in both colonies.

In both New England and the Chesapeake, religion affected the lives of pious Calvinists who were expected to reassess the state of their souls regularly. Many devoted themselves to self-examination and Bible study, and families often prayed together each day under the guidance of the husband and father. Yet because even the most pious could never be certain they were numbered among the elect, anxiety about their spiritual state troubled devout Calvinists. This anxiety lent a special intensity to their religious beliefs and to their concern with proper behavior—their own and that of others. During brief periods when they governed Maryland and Virginia, Calvinists attempted to enforce rules of morality Catholics and Anglicans tended to ignore.

Separatists	Separatists who thought the Church of England too corrupt to be salvaged became the first religious dissenters to move

to New England. In 1609, a Separatist congregation relocated to Leiden, in the Netherlands, where they found the freedom of worship denied them in Stuart England. But eventually the Netherlands worried them, for the nation that tolerated them also tolerated religions and behaviors they abhorred. Hoping to isolate themselves and their children from the corrupting influence of worldly temptations, these people, known today as Pilgrims, received permission from the Virginia Company to colonize the northern part of its territory.

In September 1620, more than one hundred people, only thirty of them Separatists, set sail from England on the old and crowded *Mayflower*. Like a few English families that had settled permanently along the coast of Newfoundland during the previous decade, the Pilgrims expected to support their colony through profits from codfishery. In November, they landed on Cape Cod, farther north than they had intended. Still, given the lateness of the season, they decided to stay in the region. They moved across Massachusetts Bay to a fine harbor (named Plymouth by John Smith, who had visited it in 1614) and into the empty dwellings of a Pautuxet village whose inhabitants had died in the epidemic of 1616–1618.

Pilgrims and Pokanokets   Even before they landed, the Pilgrims had to surmount their first challenge—from the "strangers," or non-Separatists, who sailed with them to America. Because they landed outside the jurisdiction of the Virginia Company, some of the strangers questioned the authority of the colony's leaders. In response, the Mayflower Compact, signed in November 1620 on shipboard, established a "Civil Body Politic" as a temporary substitute for a charter. The male settlers elected a governor and initially made all decisions for the colony at town meetings. Later, after more towns had been founded and the population increased, Plymouth, like Virginia and Maryland, created an assembly to which the landowning male settlers elected representatives.

Like the Jamestown settlers before them, the residents of Plymouth were poorly prepared to subsist in the new environment. Only half of the *Mayflower*'s passengers lived to see the spring. That the others survived owed much to the Pokanokets (a branch of the Wampanoags), who controlled the area in which they had settled. Pokanoket villages had suffered terrible losses in the recent epidemic, so to protect themselves from the powerful Narragansetts of the southern New England coast (who had been spared the ravages of the disease), the Pokanokets allied themselves with the newcomers. In the spring of 1621, their leader, Massasoit, agreed to a treaty, and during the colony's first difficult years the Pokanokets supplied the settlers with essential foodstuffs. The colonists also relied on Squanto, a Pautuxet who, like Malinche, served as a conduit between native peoples and Europeans. Captured by fishermen in the early 1610s and taken to Europe, Squanto had learned to speak English. On his return, he discovered that the epidemic had wiped out his village. Squanto became the settlers' interpreter and a major source of information about the environment.

Massachusetts Bay Company   Before the 1620s ended, another group of Puritans (Congregationalists, who hoped to reform the Church of England from within) launched the colonial enterprise that would come to dominate New England and would absorb Plymouth in 1691. Charles I, who became king in 1625, was more hostile to Puritans than his father had been. Under his leadership, the Church of England attempted to suppress Puritan practices, driving clergymen from their pulpits and forcing congregations to worship secretly. Some Congregationalist merchants, concerned about their longterm prospects in England, sent out a body of colonists to Cape Ann (north of Cape Cod) in 1628. The following year, the merchants obtained a royal charter, constituting themselves as the Massachusetts Bay Company.

The new joint-stock company quickly attracted the attention of Puritans who were becoming increasingly convinced that they no longer would be able to practice their religion freely in their homeland. They remained committed to the goal of reforming the Church of England but concluded that they should pursue that aim in America. In a dramatic move, the Congregationalist merchants decided to transfer the Massachusetts Bay Company's headquarters to New England. The settlers would then be answerable to no one in the mother country and would be able to handle their affairs—secular and religious—as they pleased. Like the Plymouth settlers, they expected to profit from the codfishery; they also planned to export timber products.

J. D. Bangs, Courtesy of Leiden American Pilgrim Museum, The Netherlands

Some scholars now believe that this 1638 painting by Dutch artist Adam Willaerts depicts the Plymouth colony about fifteen years after its founding. The shape of the harbor, the wooden gate, and the houses straggling up the hill all coincide with contemporary accounts of the settlement. No one believes that Willaerts himself visited Plymouth, but people returning from the colony to the Netherlands, where the Pilgrims had lived for years before emigrating, could well have described Plymouth to him.

Governor John Winthrop   The most important recruit to the new venture was John Winthrop, a member of the lesser English gentry. In October 1629, the Massachusetts Bay Company elected Winthrop as its governor, and until his death twenty years later, he served the colony continuously in one leadership post or another. Winthrop organized the initial segment of the great Puritan migration to America. In 1630, more than one thousand English men and women moved to Massachusetts—most of them to Boston. By 1643, nearly twenty thousand more had followed.

On board the *Arbella*, en route to New England in 1630, John Winthrop preached a sermon, "A Model of Christian Charity," laying out his expectations for the new colony. Above all, he stressed the communal nature of the endeavor on which he and his fellow settlers had embarked. God, he explained, "hath so disposed of the condition of mankind as in all times some must be rich, some poor, some high and eminent in power and dignity, others mean and in subjection." But differences in status did not imply differences in worth. On the contrary, God had planned the world so that "every man might have need of other, and from hence they might be all knit more nearly together in the bond of brotherly affection." In America, Winthrop asserted, "we shall be as a city upon a hill, the eyes of all people are upon us." If the Puritans failed to carry out their "special commission" from God, "the Lord will surely break out in wrath against us."

Winthrop's was a transcendent vision. He foresaw in Puritan America a true commonwealth, a community in which each person put the good of the whole ahead of his or her private concerns. Although, as in seventeenth-century England, that society would be characterized by social inequality and clear hierarchies of status and power, Winthrop hoped its members would live according to the precepts of Christian love. Of course, such an ideal was beyond human reach. Early Massachusetts and its Caribbean counterpart, Providence Island, had their share of bitter quarrels and unchristian behavior. Remarkably, though, in New England the ideal persisted well into the third and fourth generations of the immigrants' descendants.

Covenant Ideal   The Puritans expressed their communal ideal chiefly in the doctrine of the covenant. They believed God had made a covenant—that is, an agreement or contract—with them when they were chosen for the special mission to America. In turn, they covenanted with one another, promising to work together toward their goals. The founders of churches, towns, and even colonies in Anglo-America often drafted formal documents setting forth the principles on which their institutions would be based. The Pilgrims' Mayflower Compact was a covenant; so, too, was the Fundamental Orders of Connecticut (1639), which laid down the basic law for the settlements established along the Connecticut River valley in 1636 and thereafter.

The leaders of Massachusetts Bay likewise transformed their original joint-stock company charter into the basis for a covenanted community based on mutual consent. Under pressure from landowning male settlers, they gradually changed the General Court—officially the company's small governing body—into a colonial legislature. They also granted the status of freeman, or voting member of the company, to all property-owning adult male church members. Like the Virginians who won the reestablishment of the House of Burgesses after the king had abolished it, the male residents of Massachusetts insisted that their reluctant leaders allow them a greater voice in their government. Less than two decades after the first large group of Puritans arrived in Massachusetts Bay, the colony had a functioning system of self-government composed of a governor and a two-house legislature. The General Court also established a judicial system modeled on England's, although the laws they adopted differed from those of their homeland.

New England Towns   The colony's method of distributing land helped to further the communal ideal. Unlike Virginia and Maryland, where individual applicants acquired headrights and sited their farms separately, in Massachusetts groups of men—often from the same English village—applied together to the General Court for grants of land on which to establish towns (novel governance units that did not exist in England). The men receiving such grants determined how the land would be distributed. Understandably, the grantees copied the villages whence they had come. First, they laid out lots for houses and a church. Then they gave each family parcels of land scattered around the town center: a pasture here, a woodlot there, an arable field elsewhere.

They reserved the best and largest plots for the most distinguished residents, including the minister. People who had low status in England received smaller and less desirable allotments. Still, every man and even a few single women obtained land, thus sharply differentiating these villages from their English counterparts. When migrants began to move beyond the territorial limits of Massachusetts Bay into Connecticut (1636), New Haven (1638), and New Hampshire (1638), the same pattern of land grants and town formation persisted. (Only Maine, with coastal regions thinly populated by fishermen and their families, deviated from the standard practice.)

Town centers developed quickly, evolving in three distinctly different ways. Some, chiefly isolated agricultural settlements in the interior, tried to sustain Winthrop's vision of harmonious community life based on diversified family farms. A second group, the coastal towns like Boston and Salem, became bustling seaports, serving as focal points for trade and places of entry for thousands of new immigrants. The third category, commercialized agricultural towns, grew up in the Connecticut River valley, where easy water transportation made it possible for farmers to sell surplus goods readily. In Springfield, Massachusetts, for example, the merchant-entrepreneur William Pynchon and his son John began as fur traders and ended as large landowners with thousands of acres. Even in New England, then, the entrepreneurial spirit characteristic of the Chesapeake found expression. Yet the plans to profit from timber and fish exports did not materialize quickly or easily; the new settlements lacked the infrastructure necessary to support such enterprises.

Pequot War and Its Aftermath

Migration into the Connecticut valley ended the Puritans' relative freedom from clashes with nearby Indians. The first English people in the valley moved there from Massachusetts Bay under the direction of their minister, Thomas Hooker. Although their new settlements were remote from other English towns, the wide river promised ready access to the ocean. The site had just one problem: it fell within the territory controlled by the powerful Pequots.

The Pequots' dominance stemmed from their role as primary intermediaries in the trade between New England Algonquians and the Dutch in New Netherland. The arrival of English settlers signaled the end of the Pequots' power over such regional trading networks, for previously subordinate bands could now trade directly with Europeans. Clashes between Pequots and English colonists began even before the establishment of settlements in the Connecticut valley, but their founding tipped the balance toward war. The Pequots tried unsuccessfully to enlist other Indians in resisting English expansion. After two English traders were killed (not by Pequots), the English raided a Pequot village. In return, Pequots attacked Wethersfield, Connecticut, in April 1637, killing nine and capturing two. To retaliate, an expedition the following month surrounded and burned the main Pequot town on the Mystic River. The Englishmen and their Narragansett allies slaughtered at least four hundred Pequots, mostly women and children, capturing and enslaving the survivors.

For the next four decades, New England Indians accommodated themselves to the European invasion. They traded with the newcomers and sometimes worked for them, but for the most part they resisted acculturation or incorporation into English society. Native Americans persisted in using traditional farming methods, which did not employ plows or fences, and women rather than men continued to be the chief cultivators. When Indian men learned "European" trades in order to survive, they chose those—like broom making, basket weaving, and shingle splitting—that most nearly accorded with their customary occupations and ensured both independence and income. The one European practice they adopted was keeping livestock, for domesticated animals provided excellent sources of meat once earlier hunting territories had been turned into English farms and wild game had consequently disappeared.

Missionary Activities   Although the official seal of the Massachusetts Bay colony showed an Indian crying, "Come over and help us," most colonists showed little interest in converting the Algonquians to Christianity. Only a few Massachusetts clerics, most notably John Eliot and Thomas Mayhew, seriously undertook missionary work. Eliot insisted that converts reside in towns, farm the land in English fashion, assume English names, wear European-style clothing and shoes, cut their hair, and stop observing a wide range of their own customs. Because Eliot demanded a cultural transformation from his adherents—on the theory that Indians could not be properly Christianized unless they were also "civilized"—he understandably met with little success. At the peak of Eliot's efforts, only eleven hundred Indians (out of many thousands) lived in the fourteen "Praying Towns" he established, and just 10 percent of those town residents had been formally baptized.

Eliot's failure to win many converts contrasted sharply with the successful missions in New France. Puritan services lacked Catholicism's beautiful ceremonies and special appeal for women, and the Calvinist Puritans could not offer pious believers assurances of a heavenly afterlife. Yet on the island of Martha's Vineyard, Thomas Mayhew showed that it was possible to convert substantial numbers of Indians to Calvinist Christianity. He allowed Wampanoag Christians there to lead traditional lives, and he trained men of their own community to minister to them.

What attracted Indians to such religious ideas? Conversion often alienated new Christians (both Catholic and Puritan) from their relatives and traditions—a likely outcome that must have caused many potential converts to hesitate. But surely many hoped to use the Europeans' religion as a means of coping with the dramatic changes the intruders had wrought. The combination of disease, alcohol, new trading patterns, and loss of territory disrupted customary ways of life to an unprecedented extent. Shamans had little success in restoring traditional ways. Many Indians must have concluded that the Europeans' own ideas could provide the key to survival in the new circumstances.

John Winthrop's description of a great smallpox epidemic that swept through southern New England in the early 1630s reveals the relationship among smallpox, conversion to Christianity, and English land claims. "A great mortality among the Indians," he noted in his diary in 1633. "Divers of them, in their sickness, confessed that the Englishmen's God was a good God; and that if they recovered, they would serve him." But most did not recover: in January 1634, an English scout reported that smallpox had spread "as far as any Indian plantation was known to the west." By July, Winthrop observed that most of the Indians within a 300-mile radius of Boston had died of the disease. Therefore, he declared with satisfaction, "the Lord hath cleared our title to what we possess."

LIFE IN NEW ENGLAND

New England's colonizers adopted modes of life that differed from those of both their Algonquian neighbors and their Chesapeake counterparts. Algonquian bands usually moved four or five times each year to take full advantage of their environment. In spring, women planted the fields, but once crops were established, the plants did not need regular attention for several months. Villages then divided into small groups, women gathering wild foods and men hunting and fishing. The villagers returned to their fields for harvest, then separated again for fall hunting. Finally, the people wintered together in a sheltered spot before returning to the fields to start the cycle anew the following spring. Women probably determined the timing of these moves because their activities (gathering wild foods, including shellfish along the shore, and cultivating plants) used the nearby environment more intensively than did men's.

Unlike the mobile Algonquians, English people lived year-round in the same location. And unlike residents of the Chesapeake, New Englanders constructed sturdy dwellings intended to last. (Some survive to this day.) Household furnishings and house sizes resembled those in the Chesapeake, but New Englanders' diets were somewhat more varied. They replowed the same fields, believing it was less arduous to employ manure as fertilizer than to clear new fields every few years. Furthermore, they fenced their croplands to prevent them from being overrun by the cattle, sheep, and hogs that were their chief sources of meat. Animal crowding more than human crowding caused New Englanders to spread out across the countryside; all their livestock constantly needed more pasturage.

New England Families   Because Puritans commonly moved to America in family groups, the age range in early New England was wide; and because many more women migrated to New England than to the tobacco colonies, the population could immediately begin to reproduce itself. Lacking such tropical diseases as malaria, New England was also healthier than the Chesapeake and even the mother country, once settlements had survived the difficult first few years. Adult male migrants to the Chesapeake lost about a decade from their English life expectancy of fifty to fifty-five years; their Massachusetts counterparts gained five or more years.

Consequently, whereas Chesapeake population patterns gave rise to families that were few in number, small in size, and transitory, the demographic characteristics of New England made families there numerous, large, and long-lived. In New England, most men married; immigrant women married young (at age twenty, on the average); and marriages lasted longer and produced more children, who were more likely to live to maturity. If seventeenth-century Chesapeake women could expect to rear one to three healthy children, New England women could anticipate raising five to seven.

The nature of the population had other major implications for family life. The presence of many children combined with Puritans' stress on the importance of reading the Bible led to widespread concern for the education of youth. That people lived in towns meant small schools could be established; girls and boys were taught basic reading by their parents or a school "dame," and boys could then proceed to learn writing and eventually arithmetic and Latin. Further, New England in effect created grandparents because in England people rarely lived long enough to know their children's children. And whereas early Chesapeake parents commonly died before their children married, New England parents exercised a good deal of control over their adult offspring. Young men could not marry without acreage to cultivate, and because of the communal land-grant system, they had to depend on their fathers for that land. Daughters, too, needed a dowry of household goods supplied by their parents. Parents relied on their children's labor and often seemed reluctant to see them marry and start their own households. These needs sometimes led to conflict between the generations. On the whole, though, children seem to have obeyed their parents' wishes, for they had few alternatives.

Impact of Religion   Puritans controlled the governments of Massachusetts Bay, Plymouth, Connecticut, and the other early northern colonies. Congregationalism was the only officially recognized religion; except in Rhode Island members of other sects had no freedom of worship. Some non-Puritans voted in town meetings, but in Massachusetts Bay and New Haven, church membership was a prerequisite for voting in colony elections. All the early colonies, north and south, taxed residents to build churches and pay ministers' salaries, but only New England based provisions of criminal codes on the Old Testament. Massachusetts's first bodies of law (1641 and 1648) incorporated regulations drawn from scriptures; New Haven, Plymouth, New Hampshire, and Connecticut later copied them. All New Englanders were required to attend religious services, whether or not they were church members, and people who expressed contempt for ministers could be punished with fines or whippings.

The Puritan colonies attempted to enforce strict codes of moral conduct. Colonists there could be tried for drunkenness, card playing, dancing, or even idleness—although the frequent prosecutions for such offenses suggest that New Englanders often disobeyed the laws and thoroughly enjoyed such activities. Couples who had sex during their engagement (as revealed by the birth of a baby less than nine months after their wedding) were fined and publicly humiliated. Men, and a handful of women, who engaged in behaviors that today would be called homosexual were seen as especially sinful and reprehensible, and some were executed.

In New England, church and state were thus intertwined to a greater extent than in the Chesapeake, where few such prosecutions occurred. Puritans objected to secular interference in religious affairs but at the same time expected the church to influence the conduct of politics and the affairs of society. They also believed the state was obliged to support and protect the one true church—theirs. Consequently, although they came to America seeking freedom to worship as they pleased, they saw no contradiction in refusing to grant that freedom to those who held different religious beliefs.

Roger Williams   Roger Williams, a Separatist who migrated to Massachusetts Bay in 1631, quickly ran afoul of Puritan orthodoxy. He told his fellow settlers that the king of England had no right to grant them land already occupied by Indians, that church and state should be kept entirely separate, and that Puritans should not impose their ideas on others. Because Puritan leaders placed a heavy emphasis on achieving consensus in both religion and politics, they could not tolerate significant dissent. In October 1635, Massachusetts tried Williams for challenging the validity of the colony's charter and for maintaining that New England Congregationalists had not separated themselves, their churches, or their polity sufficiently from England's corrupt institutions and practices.

Convicted and banished, Williams journeyed in early 1636 to the head of Narragansett Bay, where he founded the town of Providence on land he obtained from the Narragansetts and Wampanoags. Because Williams believed government should not interfere with religion in any way, Providence and other towns in what became Rhode Island adopted a policy of tolerating all religions, including Judaism. Along with Maryland, the tiny colony founded by Williams thus presaged the religious freedom that eventually became one of the hallmarks of the United States.

Anne Hutchinson   A dissenter who presented a more sustained challenge to Massachusetts' leaders was Mistress Anne Hutchinson. (The title *Mistress* revealed her high status.) A skilled medical practitioner popular with the women of Boston, she greatly admired John Cotton, a minister who stressed the covenant of grace, or God's free gift of salvation to unworthy human beings. By contrast, most Massachusetts clerics emphasized the need for Puritans to engage in good works, study, and reflection in preparation for receiving God's grace. (In its most extreme form, such a doctrine could verge on the covenant of works, or the idea that people could earn their salvation.) After spreading her ideas for months in the context of gatherings at childbirths—when no men were present—Mistress Hutchinson began holding women's meetings in her home to discuss Cotton's sermons. Stressing the covenant of grace, she even asserted that the elect could be assured of salvation and communicate directly with God. Such ideas had an immense appeal for Puritans. Anne Hutchinson offered them certainty of salvation instead of a state of constant anxiety. Her approach also lessened the importance of the institutional church and its ministers.

Thus, Mistress Hutchinson's ideas posed a dangerous threat to Puritan orthodoxy. So in November 1637, officials charged her with having maligned the colony's ministers by accusing them of preaching the covenant of works. For two days, she defended herself cleverly, matching scriptural references and wits with John Winthrop himself. But then Anne Hutchinson triumphantly and boldly declared that God had spoken to her directly, explaining that he would curse the Puritans' descendants for generations if they harmed her. That assertion assured her banishment, for what member of the court could acknowledge the legitimacy of such a revelation? After she had also been excommunicated from the church, she and her family, along with some faithful followers, were exiled to Rhode Island in 1638. Several years later, after she moved to New Netherland, she and most of her children were killed by Indians.

The authorities in Massachusetts perceived Anne Hutchinson as doubly dangerous to the existing order: she threatened not only religious orthodoxy but also traditional gender roles. Puritans believed in the equality before God of all souls, but
they considered actual women (as distinct from their spiritual selves) inferior to
men. Christians had long followed Saint Paul's dictum that women should keep silent in church and submit to their husbands. Mistress Hutchinson did neither. The
magistrates' comments during her trial reveal that they were almost as outraged by
her "masculine" behavior as by her religious beliefs. Winthrop charged her with
having set wife against husband because so many of her followers were women. A
clergyman later told her bluntly, "You have stepped out of your place, you have
rather been a Husband than a Wife and a preacher than a Hearer; and a Magistrate
than a Subject."

The New England authorities' reaction to Anne Hutchinson reveals the depth
of their adherence to European gender-role concepts. To them, an orderly society
required the obedience of wives to husbands, subjects to rulers, and ordinary folk
to gentry. English people intended to change many aspects of their lives by coloniz-
ing North America, but not the gendered division of labor, the assumption of male
superiority, or the maintenance of social hierarchies.

SUMMARY

By the middle of the seventeenth century, Europeans had come to North America
and the Caribbean to stay, a fact that signaled major changes for the peoples of
both hemispheres. These newcomers had indelibly altered not only their own lives
but also those of native peoples. Europeans killed Indians with their weapons and
diseases and had varying success in converting them to Christianity. Contacts
with indigenous peoples taught Europeans to eat new foods, speak new languages, and recognize—however reluctantly—the persistence of other cultural
patterns. The prosperity and even survival of many of the European colonies depended heavily on the cultivation of American crops (maize and tobacco) and an
Asian crop (sugar), thus attesting to the importance of post-Columbian ecological
exchange.

Political rivalries once confined to Europe spread around the globe, as England,
Spain, Portugal, France, and the Netherlands vied for control of the peoples and
resources of Asia, Africa, and the Americas. In South America, Spaniards reaped
the benefits of their gold and silver mines, while French people earned their primary
profits from the fur trade (in Canada) and cultivating sugar (in the Caribbean).
Sugar also enriched the Portuguese in Brazil. The Dutch concentrated on commerce,
trading in furs and sugar in North America and the Caribbean.

Although the English colonies, too, at first sought to rely on trade, they quickly took
another form altogether when so many English people of the "middling sort" decided
to migrate to North America. To a greater extent than their European counterparts,
the English transferred the society and politics of their homeland to a new environment. Their sheer numbers, coupled with their need for vast quantities of land on
which to grow their crops and raise their livestock, inevitably brought them into conflict with their Indian neighbors. New England and the Chesapeake differed in the sex
ratio and age range of their immigrant populations, the nature of their developing

economies, their settlement patterns, and the impact of religion. Yet they resembled each other in the internal and external conflicts their expansion engendered. In years to come, both regions would become embroiled in increasingly fierce rivalries besetting the European powers. Those rivalries would continue to affect Americans of all races until after the mid-eighteenth century, when France and England fought the greatest war yet known, and the Anglo-American colonies won their independence.

3

NORTH AMERICA IN THE
ATLANTIC WORLD 1650–1720

THE GROWTH OF ANGLO-AMERICAN SETTLEMENTS

Between 1642 and 1646, civil war between supporters of King Charles I and the Puritan-dominated Parliament engulfed the colonists' English homeland. Parliament triumphed, leading to the execution of the king in 1649 and interim rule by the par-liamentary army's leader, Oliver Cromwell, during the so-called Commonwealth period. But after Cromwell's death, Parliament decided to restore the monarchy if Charles I's son and heir agreed to restrictions on his authority. Charles II did so, and the Stuarts were returned to the throne in 1660 (see Table 3.1). The new king subsequently rewarded nobles and others who had supported him during the Civil War with huge tracts of land on the North American mainland. The colonies thereby established made up six of the thirteen polities that eventually would form the American nation: New York, New Jersey, Pennsylvania (including Delaware), and North and South Carolina (see Map 3.1). Collectively, these became known as the Restoration colonies because they were created by the restored Stuart monarchy. All were proprietorships; in each of them one man or several men held title to the soil and controlled the government.

New York   Charles's younger brother James, the duke of York, benefited quickly. In 1664, Charles II gave James the region between the Connecticut and Delaware Rivers, including the Hudson valley and Long Island. That the Dutch had settled there mattered little; the English and the Dutch

CHRONOLOGY

1642–46	English Civil War
1649	Charles I executed
1651	First Navigation Act passed to regulate colonial trade
1660	Stuarts (Charles II) restored to throne
1663	Carolina chartered
1664	English conquer New Netherland
	New York founded
	New Jersey established
1670s	Marquette, Jolliet, and La Salle explore the Great Lakes and Mississippi valley for France
1675–76	Bacon's Rebellion disrupts Virginia government; Jamestown destroyed
1675–78	King Philip's War devastates New England
1680–1700	Pueblo revolt temporarily drives Spaniards from New Mexico
1681	Pennsylvania chartered
1685	James II becomes king
1686–88	Dominion of New England established, superseding all charters of colonies from Maine to New Jersey
1688–89	James II deposed in Glorious Revolution
	William and Mary ascend throne
1689	Glorious Revolution in America; Massachusetts, New York, and Maryland overthrow colonial governors
1688–99	King William's War fought on northern New England frontier
1691	New Massachusetts charter issued
1692	Witchcraft crisis in Salem; nineteen people hanged
1696	Board of Trade and Plantations established to coordinate English colonial administration
	Vice-admiralty courts established in America
1701	Iroquois adopt neutrality policy toward France and England
1702–13	Queen Anne's War fought by French and English
1711–13	Tuscarora War (North Carolina) leads to capture or migration of most Tuscaroras
1715	Yamasee War nearly destroys South Carolina

were at the time engaged in sporadic warfare, and the English were also attacking other Dutch colonies. In August, James's warships anchored off Manhattan Island, demanding New Netherland's surrender. The colony complied without resistance.

TABLE 3.1 | RESTORED STUART MONARCHS OF ENGLAND, 1660–1714

Monarch	Reign	Relation to Predecessor
Charles II	1660–1685	Son
James II	1685–1688	Brother
Mary	1688–1694	Daughter
William	1688–1702	Son-in-law
Anne	1702–1714	Sister, Sister-in-law

TABLE 3.2 | THE FOUNDING OF ENGLISH COLONIES IN NORTH AMERICA, 1664–1681

Colony	Founder(s)	Date	Basis of Economy
New York (formerly New Netherland)	James, duke of York	1664	Farming, fur trading
New Jersey	Sir George Carteret, John Lord Berkeley	1664	Farming
North Carolina	Carlina proprietors	1665	Tobacco, forest products
South Carolina	Carolina proprietors	1670	Rice, indigo
Pennsylvania (incl. Delaware)	William Penn	1681	Farming

Although in 1672 the Netherlands briefly retook the colony, the Dutch permanently ceded it in 1674.

Thus, James acquired a heterogeneous possession, which he renamed New York (see Table 3.2). In 1664, a significant minority of English people (mostly Puritan New Englanders on Long Island) already lived there, along with the Dutch and sizable numbers of Indians, Africans, Germans, Scandinavians, and a smattering of other European peoples. The Dutch West India Company had imported slaves into the colony, intending some for resale in the Chesapeake. Many, though, remained in New Netherland as laborers; at the time of the English conquest, almost one-fifth of Manhattan's approximately fifteen hundred free and enslaved inhabitants were of African descent. Slaves then made up a higher proportion of New York's urban population than of the Chesapeake's rural people.

Recognizing the population's diversity, James's representatives moved cautiously in their efforts to establish English authority. The Duke's Laws, a legal code proclaimed in 1665, applied solely to the English settlements on Long Island, only later extended to the rest of the colony. James's policies initially maintained Dutch forms of local government, confirmed Dutch land titles, and allowed Dutch residents to maintain customary legal practices. Each town was permitted to decide which church (Dutch Reformed, Congregational, or Church of England) to support

MAP 3.1 The Anglo-American Colonies in the Early Eighteenth Century

By the early eighteenth century, the English colonies nominally dominated the Atlantic coastline of North America. But the colonies' formal boundary lines are deceiving because the western reaches of each colony were still largely unfamiliar to Europeans and because much of the land was still inhabited by Native Americans.

with its tax revenues. Much to the dismay of English residents, the Duke's Laws made no provision for a representative assembly. Like other Stuarts, James distrusted legislative bodies, and not until 1683 did he agree to the colonists' requests for an elected legislature. Before then, an autocratic governor ruled New York.

The English takeover thus had little immediate effect on the colony. The duke did not promote migration, so its population grew slowly, barely reaching eighteen thousand by the time of the first English census in 1698. Until the second decade of the eighteenth century, Manhattan remained a commercial backwater within the orbit of Boston.

New Jersey   The English conquest brought so little change to New York primarily because the duke of York in 1664 regranted the land between the Hudson and Delaware Rivers—East and West Jersey—to his friends Sir George Carteret and John Lord Berkeley. That grant left the duke's own colony hemmed in between Connecticut to the east and the Jerseys to the west and south, depriving it of much fertile land and hindering its economic growth. Meanwhile, the Jersey proprietors acted rapidly to attract settlers, promising generous land grants, limited freedom of religion, and—without authorization from the Crown—a representative assembly. In response, large numbers of Puritan New Englanders migrated southward to the Jerseys, along with some Barbadians, Dutch New Yorkers, and eventually Scots. New Jersey grew quickly; in 1726, at the time of its first census as a united colony, it had 32,500 inhabitants, only eight thousand fewer than New York.

Within twenty years, Berkeley and Carteret sold their interests in the Jerseys to separate groups of investors. The purchasers of all of Carteret's share (West Jersey) and portions of Berkeley's (East Jersey) were members of the Society of Friends, also called Quakers. That small radical sect rejected earthly and religious hierarchies. Quakers believed anyone could directly receive God's "inner light" and all people were equal in God's sight. With no formally trained clergy, Quakers allowed both men and women to speak in meetings and become "public Friends" who traveled to spread God's word. Quakers proselytized throughout the Atlantic world in the 1650s, recruiting followers in all of England's colonies from a base in Barbados. The authorities did not welcome the Quakers' radical egalitarianism, and they encountered persecution everywhere. Mary Dyer—previously a follower of Anne Hutchinson—became a Quaker, returned to Boston as a missionary, and was hanged in 1660 (along with several men) for preaching Quaker doctrines.

Pennsylvania   The Quakers obtained their own colony in 1681, when Charles II granted the region between Maryland and New York to his close friend William Penn, a prominent member of the sect. Penn was then thirty-seven years old; he held the colony as a personal proprietorship, one that earned profits for his descendants until the American Revolution. Even so, Penn, like the Roman Catholic Calverts of Maryland before him, saw his province not merely as a source of revenue but also as a haven for persecuted coreligionists. Penn offered land to all comers on liberal terms, promising toleration of all religions, although only Christian men could vote; guaranteeing English liberties, such as the right to bail and trial by jury; and pledging to establish a representative assembly. He also publicized the ready availability of land in Pennsylvania through widely distributed promotional tracts printed in German, French, and Dutch.

Penn's activities and the Quakers' attraction to his lands gave rise to a migration whose magnitude equaled the Puritan exodus to New England in the 1630s. By mid-1683, more than three thousand people—among them Welsh, Irish, Dutch, and

Germans—had already moved to Pennsylvania, and within five years the population reached twelve thousand. (By contrast, it had taken Virginia more than thirty years to achieve a comparable population.) Philadelphia, carefully sited on the easily navigable Delaware River and planned to be the major city in the province, drew merchants and artisans from throughout the English-speaking world. From mainland and Caribbean colonies alike came Quakers who brought with them years of experience on American soil and well-established trading connections. Pennsylvania's plentiful and fertile lands soon enabled its residents to begin exporting surplus flour and other foodstuffs to the West Indies. Practically overnight Philadelphia acquired more than two thousand citizens and started to challenge Boston's commercial dominance.

A pacifist with egalitarian principles, Penn attempted to treat native peoples fairly. He learned to speak the language of the Delawares (or Lenapes), from whom he purchased tracts of land to sell to European settlers. Penn also established strict regulations for trade and forbade the sale of alcohol to Indians. His policies attracted native peoples who moved to Pennsylvania near the end of the seventeenth century to escape repeated clashes with English colonists in Maryland, Virginia, and North Carolina. Most important were the Tuscaroras, whose experiences are described later in this chapter. Likewise, Shawnees and Miamis moved eastward from the Ohio valley. Ironically, however, the same toleration that attracted Native Americans also brought non-Quaker Europeans who showed little respect for Indian claims to the soil. In effect, Penn's policy was so successful that it caused its own downfall. The Scots-Irish, Germans, and Swiss who settled in Pennsylvania in the first half of the eighteenth century clashed repeatedly over land with Indians who had also recently migrated to the colony.

Carolina   The southernmost proprietary colony, granted by Charles II in 1663, encompassed a huge tract stretching from the southern boundary of Virginia to Spanish Florida. The area had great strategic importance: a successful English settlement there would prevent Spaniards from pushing farther north. The fertile, semitropical land also held forth the promise of producing such exotic and valuable commodities as figs, olives, wines, and silk. The proprietors named their new province Carolina in honor of Charles, whose Latin name was Carolus. The "Fundamental Constitutions of Carolina," which they asked the political philosopher John Locke to draft for them, set forth an elaborate plan for a colony governed by a hierarchy of landholding aristocrats and characterized by a carefully structured distribution of political and economic power.

But Carolina failed to follow the course the proprietors had laid out. Instead, it quickly developed two distinct population centers, which in 1729 split into separate colonies under direct royal rule. Virginia planters settled the Albemarle region that became North Carolina. They established a society much like their own, with an economy based on cultivating tobacco and exporting such forest products as pitch, tar, and timber. Because North Carolina lacked a satisfactory harbor, its planters relied on Virginia's ports and merchants to conduct their trade. The other population center, which eventually formed the core of South Carolina, developed at

Charles Town, founded in 1670 near the juncture of the Ashley and Cooper Rivers. Many of its early residents migrated from overcrowded Barbados. These sugar planters expected to reestablish plantation agriculture and hoped to escape hurricanes. They were disappointed in both respects: they soon learned that sugar would not grow successfully in Carolina, and they experienced a "wonderfully horrid and destructive" hurricane in 1686.

The settlers began to raise corn and herds of cattle, which they sold to Caribbean planters. Like other colonists before them, they also depended on trade with nearby Indians to supply commodities they could sell elsewhere. In Carolina, those items were deerskins, sent to Europe, and enslaved Indians, who were shipped to Caribbean islands and northern colonies. Nearby Indian nations hunted deer with increasing intensity and readily sold captured enemies to the English settlers. During the first decade of the eighteenth century, South Carolina exported an average of 54,000 skins annually, and overseas shipments later peaked at 160,000 a year. Before 1715, Carolinians additionally exported an estimated thirty thousand to fifty thousand Indian slaves.

Chesapeake   The English Civil War retarded the development of the earlier English settlements. In the Chesapeake, struggles between supporters of the king and Parliament caused military clashes in Maryland and political upheavals in Virginia. But once the war ended and immigration resumed, the colonies expanded once again. Some settlers, especially those on Virginia's eastern shore and along that colony's southern border, raised grain, livestock, and flax, which they sold to English and Dutch merchants. Tobacco growers began importing increasing numbers of English indentured servants to work on their farms, which had by then begun to develop into plantations. Freed from concerns about Indian attacks by the final defeat of the Powhatan Confederacy in 1646, they—especially recent immigrants—eagerly sought to enlarge their landholdings.

Although they still depended primarily on English laborers, Chesapeake tobacco planters also started to acquire small numbers of enslaved workers. Almost all came from a population that historian Ira Berlin has termed "Atlantic creoles"— that is, people (perhaps of mixed race) who came from other European settlements in the Atlantic world, primarily from Iberian outposts. Not all the Atlantic creoles who came to the Chesapeake were bondspeople; some were free or indentured. With their arrival, the Chesapeake became what Berlin calls a "society with slaves," or one in which slavery does not dominate the economy but is one of a number of coexisting labor systems.

New England   In New England, migration essentially ceased after the Civil War began in 1642. While Puritans were first challenging the king and then governing England as a commonwealth, they had little incentive to leave their homeland, and few migrated after the Restoration. Yet the Puritan colonies' population continued to grow dramatically because of natural increase. By the 1670s, New England's population had more than tripled to reach approximately seventy thousand. Such a rapid expansion placed great pressure on available land. Colonial settlement spread far into the interior of Massachusetts and Connecticut, and many members of the third and fourth generations migrated—north to New Hampshire or Maine, southwest to New York or New Jersey—to find sufficient farmland for themselves and their children. Others abandoned agriculture and learned such skills as blacksmithing or carpentry to support themselves in the growing towns.

The people who remained behind in the small, yet densely populated older New England communities experienced a new phenomenon after approximately 1650: witchcraft accusations and trials. Other regions largely escaped such incidents, even though most seventeenth-century people believed witches existed. These allies of the Devil were thought to harness invisible spirits for good or evil purposes. For example, a witch might engage in fortunetelling, prepare healing potions or charms, or harm others by causing the death of a child or valuable animals. Yet only New England witnessed many trials of accused witches (about one hundred in all before 1690). Most, though not all, of the accused were middle-aged women who had angered their neighbors. Historians have accordingly concluded that the dynamics of daily interactions in the close-knit communities, where the same families lived nearby for decades, fostered longstanding quarrels that led some colonists to believe others had diabolically caused certain misfortunes. Even so, only a few of the accused were convicted, and fewer still were executed, because judges and juries remained skeptical of such charges.

Colonial Political Structures   That New England courts halted questionable prosecutions suggests the maturity of colonial institutions. By the last quarter of the seventeenth century, almost all the Anglo-American colonies had well-established political and judicial structures. In New England, property-holding men or the legislature elected the governors; in other regions, the king or the proprietor appointed such leaders. A council, either elected or appointed, advised the governor on matters of policy and served as the upper house of the legislature. Each colony had a judiciary with local justices of the peace, county courts, and, usually, an appeals court composed of the councilors.

Local political institutions also developed. In New England, elected selectmen initially governed the towns, but by the end of the seventeenth century, town meetings—held at least annually and attended by most free adult male residents—handled matters of local concern. In the Chesapeake colonies and in both of the Carolinas, appointed magistrates ran local governments. At first, the same was true in Pennsylvania, but by the early eighteenth century, elected county officials began to take over some government functions. And in New York, local elections were the rule even before the establishment of the colonial assembly in 1683.

A DECADE OF IMPERIAL CRISES: THE 1670S

As the Restoration colonies were extending the range of English settlement, the first English colonies and French and Spanish settlements in North America faced crises caused primarily by their changing relationships with America's indigenous peoples. Between 1670 and 1680, New France, New Mexico, New England, and Virginia experienced bitter conflicts as their interests collided with those of America's original inhabitants. All the early colonies changed irrevocably as a result.

New France and   In the mid-1670s Louis de Buade de Frontenac, the governor-
the Iroquois   general of Canada, decided to expand New France's reach
into the south and west, hoping to establish a trade route to
Mexico and to gain direct control of the valuable fur trade on which the prosperity
of the colony rested. Accordingly, he encouraged the explorations of Father Jacques
Marquette, Louis Jolliet, and René-Robert Cavelier de La Salle in the Great Lakes
and Mississippi valley regions. His goal, however, brought him into conflict with
the powerful Iroquois Confederacy, composed of five Indian nations—the
Mohawks, Oneidas, Onondagas, Cayugas, and Senecas. (In 1722, the Tuscaroras
became the sixth.)

Under the terms of a unique defensive alliance forged in the sixteenth century, a
representative council made decisions of war and peace for the entire Iroquois Confederacy, although each nation still retained some autonomy and could not be
forced to comply with a council directive against its will. Before the arrival of
Europeans, the Iroquois waged wars primarily to acquire captives to replenish their
population. Contact with foreign traders brought ravaging disease as early as 1633,
intensifying the need for captives. Simultaneously, the Europeans' presence created
an economic motive for warfare: the desire to dominate the fur trade and to gain
unimpeded access to European goods. The war with the Hurons in the 1640s initiated a series of conflicts with other Indians known as the Beaver Wars, in which the
Iroquois fought to achieve control of the lucrative peltry trade. Iroquois warriors
did not themselves trap beaver; instead, they raided other villages in search of
caches of pelts or attacked Indians from the interior as they carried furs to European
outposts. Then the Iroquois traded that booty for European-made blankets, knives,
guns, alcohol, and other desirable items.

In the mid-1670s, as Iroquois dominance grew, the French intervened, for an
Iroquois triumph would have destroyed France's plans to trade directly with western Indians. Over the next twenty years, the French launched repeated attacks on
Iroquois villages. Although in 1677 New Yorkers and the Iroquois established a
formal alliance known as the Covenant Chain, the English offered little assistance
other than weapons to their trading partners. Without much aid, the confederacy
held its own and even expanded its reach, enabling it in 1701 to negotiate neutrality treaties with France and other Indians. For the next half-century, the Iroquois
nations maintained their power through trade and skillful diplomacy rather than
warfare, forming or abandoning alliances with Indian or European nations to best
achieve their goals.

Pueblo Peoples   In New Mexico, too, events of the 1670s led to a crisis with
and Spaniards   long-term consequences. Over the years under Spanish domination, the Pueblo peoples had added Christianity to their
religious beliefs while still retaining traditional rituals, engaging in syncretic practices as had Mesoamericans. But as decades passed, Franciscans adopted increasingly brutal and violent tactics in order to erase all traces of the native religion.
Priests and secular colonists who held *encomiendas* placed heavy labor demands on
the people who were also suffering from Apache raids and food shortages caused
by a serious drought. In 1680, the Pueblos revolted under the leadership of Popé, a

respected shaman, successfully driving the Spaniards out of New Mexico. Even though Spain managed to restore its authority by 1700, imperial officials had learned their lesson. Afterward, Spanish governors stressed cooperation with the Pueblos, relying on their labor but no longer attempting to violate their cultural integrity. The Pueblo revolt constituted the most successful and longest-sustained Indian resistance movement in colonial North America.

Other native peoples, including those with homelands many miles away from New Mexico, felt the Spanish presence as well. Spanish military outposts (presidios) and Franciscan missions offered some protection to Pueblos, but other Indians' desire to obtain horses and guns led to endemic violence throughout the region. Navajos, Apaches, and Utes attacked each other and the Pueblos in order to obtain captives and hides to trade to the Spanish. Captured Indian men might be sent to Mexican silver mines, whereas Spaniards often retained women and children as domestic laborers. When Comanches migrated west from the Great Plains in the late seventeenth century, Utes allied with them, and after the Pueblo revolt that alliance dominated New Mexico's northern borderlands for several decades.

In the more densely settled English colonies, hostilities developed in the decade of the 1670s, not over religion (as in New Mexico) or trade (as in New France), but over land. Put simply, the rapidly expanding Anglo-American population wanted more of it. In both New England and Virginia—though for different reasons—settlers began to encroach on territories that until then had remained in the hands of Native Americans.

King Philip's War   By the early 1670s, the growing settlements in southern New England surrounded Wampanoag ancestral lands on Narragansett Bay. The local chief, Metacom, or King Philip, was troubled by the loss of territory and concerned about the impact of European culture and Christianity on his people. Philip led his warriors in attacks on nearby communities in June 1675. Other Algonquian peoples, among them Nipmucks and Narragansetts, soon joined King Philip's forces. In the fall, the Indian nations jointly attacked settlements in the northern Connecticut River valley, and the war spread to Maine, too, when the Abenakis entered the conflict. In early 1676, the Indian allies devastated villages like Lancaster, where they captured some settlers and even attacked Plymouth and Providence; later that year, Abenaki assaults forced the abandonment of most settlements in Maine. Altogether, the alliance wholly or partially destroyed twenty-seven of ninety-two towns and attacked forty others, pushing the line of English settlement back toward the east and south.

The tide turned in the south in the summer of 1676. The Indian coalition ran short of food and ammunition, and colonists began to use Christian Indians as guides and scouts. On June 12, the Mohawks—ancient Iroquois enemies of New England Algonquians—devastated a major Wampanoag encampment while most of the warriors were away attacking an English town. After King Philip was killed that August, the southern alliance crumbled. Fighting, though, continued on the Maine frontier for another two years. There the English colonists never defeated the Abenakis; both sides, their resources depleted, simply agreed to end the conflict in 1678.

In addition to the Wampanoags, Nipmucks, Narragansetts, and Abenakis who were captured and sold into slavery, still more died of starvation and disease. New Englanders had broken the power of the southern coastal tribes. Thereafter the southern Indians lived in small clusters, subordinated to the colonists and often working as servants or sailors. Only on the island of Martha's Vineyard did Christian Wampanoags (who had not participated in the war) preserve their cultural identity intact.

The settlers paid a terrible price for their victory: an estimated one-tenth of the able-bodied adult male population was killed or wounded. Proportional to population, it was the most costly conflict in American history. The heavy losses in the war also caused many Puritan colonists to question their earlier confidence that God supported their endeavors; they now wondered if God had turned against them. New Englanders did not fully rebuild abandoned interior towns for another three decades, and not until the American Revolution did the region's per capita income again reach pre-1675 levels.

Bacon's Rebellion   Not coincidentally, conflict simultaneously wracked Virginia. In the early 1670s, ex-servants unable to acquire land greedily eyed the territory reserved by treaty for Virginia's Indians. Governor William Berkeley, the leader of an entrenched coterie of large

Courtesy of Association for the Preservation of Virginia Antiquities

This Virginia mansion, one of only three surviving Jacobean-style great houses in North America or the Caribbean, is known as "Bacon's Castle." Built in 1665, it was captured and fortified by Nathaniel Bacon's men during the rebellion, but Bacon is not known to have visited it. In early 1677, it was one of the last rebel outposts to fall to Sir William Berkeley's forces.

landowners, resisted starting a war to further the aims of settlers who were challenging his authority. Dissatisfied colonists then rallied behind the leadership of a recent immigrant, the gentleman Nathaniel Bacon, who like other new arrivals had found that all the desirable land in settled areas had already been claimed. Using as a pretext the July 1675 killing of an indentured servant by some Doeg Indians, settlers attacked not only the Doegs but also the Susquehannocks, a more powerful nation. In retaliation, Susquehannock bands raided outlying farms early in 1676.

Berkeley and Bacon soon clashed. The governor outlawed Bacon and his men; the rebels then held Berkeley hostage, forcing him to authorize them to attack the Indians. During the chaotic summer of 1676, Bacon alternately pursued Indians and battled the governor. In September, Bacon's forces attacked Jamestown, burning the capital to the ground. But when Bacon died of dysentery the following month, the rebellion began to collapse. Even so, the rebels had made their point. Berkeley was recalled to England, and a new treaty signed in 1677 opened much of the disputed territory to settlement. The end of Bacon's Rebellion thus pushed most of Virginia's Indians farther west, beyond the Appalachians.

The Atlantic Trading System

In the 1670s and 1680s, the prosperity of the Chesapeake rested on tobacco, and successful tobacco cultivation depended, as it always had, on an ample labor supply. But fewer and fewer English men and women proved willing to indenture themselves for long terms of service in Maryland and Virginia. Population pressures had eased in England, and the founding of the Restoration colonies meant that migrants could choose other American destinations. Furthermore, fluctuating tobacco prices in Europe and the growing scarcity of land made the Chesapeake less appealing to potential settlers. That posed a problem for wealthy Chesapeake tobacco growers. Where could they obtain the workers they needed? They found the answer in the Caribbean sugar islands where Dutch, French, English, and Spanish planters were accustomed to purchasing African slaves.

Why African Slavery? Slavery had been practiced in Europe and Islamic lands for centuries. European Christians—both Catholics and Protestants—believed enslaving heathen peoples, especially those of exotic origin, was justifiable in religious terms. Muslims, too, thought infidels could be enslaved, and they imported tens of thousands of black African bondspeople into North Africa and the Middle East. Some Christians argued that holding heathens in bondage would lead to their conversion. Others believed any heathen taken prisoner in wartime could be enslaved. Consequently, when Portuguese mariners reached the sub-Saharan coast and encountered African societies holding slaves, they purchased bondspeople along with gold and other items. Indeed, they initially bought enslaved people in one African nation and sold them in another. From the 1440s on, Portugal imported large numbers of slaves into the Iberian Peninsula; by 1500, enslaved Africans composed about one-tenth of the population of Lisbon and Seville, the chief cities of Portugal and Spain. In 1555, a few of them were taken to England, where—when others followed—residents of London and Bristol in particular became accustomed to seeing black slaves on the streets.

Iberians exported African slavery to their American possessions, New Spain and Brazil. Because the Catholic Church prevented the formal enslavement of Indians in those domains and free laborers saw no reason to work voluntarily in mines or on sugar plantations when they could earn better wages under easier conditions elsewhere, African bondspeople (who had no choice) became mainstays of the Caribbean and Brazilian economies. European planters on all the sugar islands began purchasing slaves—often from the Iberians—soon after they settled in the Caribbean. Accordingly, the first enslaved Africans in the Americas were imported from Angola, Portugal's major early trading partner, and the Portuguese word *Negro* came into use as a common descriptor.

English people had few moral qualms about enslaving other humans. Slavery, after all, was sanctioned in the Bible, and it was widely practiced by their contemporaries. Few at the time questioned the decision to hold Africans and their descendants—or captive Indians from New England or Carolina—in perpetual bondage. Yet their convoluted early attempts to define slave status nevertheless indicate that seventeenth-century English colonists initially lacked clear conceptual categories defining both "race" and "slave." For example, the 1670 Virginia law that first tried to define which people were enslaveable notably failed to employ the racial terminology that would later become commonplace. Instead, awkwardly seeking to single out imported Africans, it declared that "all servants not being christians imported into this colony by shipping shalbe slaves for their lives." Such nonracial phrasing reveals that Anglo-American settlers had not yet fully developed the meaning of *race* and *slave* and that they did so in tandem over time through their experience with the institution of slavery itself.

Atlantic Slave Trade   The planters of the North American mainland could not have obtained the bondspeople they wanted had it not been for the rapid development of an Atlantic trading system, the linchpin of which was the traffic in enslaved human beings. Although this elaborate Atlantic economic system has been called the triangular trade, people and products did not move across the ocean in easily diagrammed patterns. Instead, their movements created a complicated web of exchange that inextricably tied the peoples of the Atlantic world together.

The oceanic slave trade was entirely new, though enslavement was not. The expanding network of commerce between Europe and its colonies was fueled by the sale and transport of slaves, the exchange of commodities produced by slave labor, and the need to feed and clothe so many bound laborers. The European economy, previously oriented toward the Mediterranean and Asia, shifted its emphasis to the Atlantic. By the late seventeenth century, commerce in slaves and the products of slave labor constituted the basis of the European economic system. The irony of Columbus's discoveries thus became complete: seeking the wealth of Asia, Columbus instead found the lands that—along with Africa—ultimately replaced Asia as the source of European prosperity.

The various elements of the trade had different relationships to one another and to the wider web of exchange. Chesapeake tobacco and Caribbean and Brazilian sugar were in great demand in Europe, so planters shipped those products directly to their home countries. The profits paid for both the African laborers who grew their crops and European manufactured goods. The African coastal rulers who ran the entrepôts where European slavers acquired their human cargoes received their payment in European manufactures and East Indian textiles; they had little need for most American products. Europeans purchased slaves from Africa for resale in their colonies and acquired sugar and tobacco from America, in exchange dispatching their manufactures everywhere.

European nations fought bitterly to control the lucrative trade. The Portuguese, who at first dominated the trade, were supplanted by the Dutch in the 1630s. In the Anglo-Dutch wars, the Dutch lost out to the English, who controlled the trade through the Royal African Company, a joint-stock company chartered by Charles II in 1672. Holding a monopoly on all English trade with sub-Saharan Africa, the company built and maintained seventeen forts and trading posts, dispatched to West Africa hundreds of ships carrying English manufactured goods, and transported about 100,000 slaves to England's Caribbean colonies. It paid regular dividends averaging 10 percent yearly, and some of its agents made fortunes. Yet even before the company's monopoly expired in 1712, many individual English and North American traders had illegally entered the market for slaves. By the early eighteenth century, such independent traders carried most of the Africans imported into the colonies, earning huge profits from successful voyages.

By the middle of the eighteenth century, American tobacco had become closely associated with African slavery. An English woodcut advertising tobacco from the York River in Virgina accordingly depicted not a Chesapeake planter but rather an African, shown with a hoe in one hand and a pipe in the other. Usually, of course, slaves would not have smoked the high-quality tobacco produced for export, although they were allowed to cultivate small crops for their own use.

York Tobacco
LONDON

West Africa and   Most of the enslaved people carried to North America origi-
the Slave Trade   nated in West Africa. Some came from the Rice and Grain
                         Coasts, especially the former, but even more had resided in
the Gold and Slave Coasts and the Bight of Biafra (modern Nigeria) and Angola.
Certain coastal rulers—for instance, the Adja kings of the Slave Coast—served as
intermediaries, allowing the establishment of permanent slave-trading posts in their
territories and supplying resident Europeans with slaves to fill ships that stopped
regularly at coastal forts. Such rulers controlled Europeans' access to bound
laborers and simultaneously controlled inland peoples' access to desirable trade
goods, such as textiles, iron bars, alcohol, tobacco, guns, and cowry shells from the
Maldive Islands (in the Indian Ocean), which were widely used as currency.
Through Whydah, Dahomey's major slave-trading port, passed at least 10 percent
of all slaves exported to the Americas, and Whydah's merchants earned substantial
annual profits from the trade. Portugal, England, and France established forts
there; Europeans had to pay fees to Whydah's rulers before they could begin to
acquire cargoes.

The slave trade had varying consequences for the nations of West Africa. The
trade's centralizing tendencies helped to create such powerful eighteenth-century
kingdoms as Dahomey and Asante (formed from the Akan States). Traffic in slaves
destroyed smaller polities and disrupted traditional economic patterns, as goods
once sent north toward the Mediterranean were redirected to the Atlantic and as
local manufactures declined in the face of European competition. Agricultural production intensified, especially in rice-growing areas, because of the need to supply
hundreds of slave ships with foodstuffs for transatlantic voyages. Because prisoners
of war constituted the bulk of the exported slaves, the most active traders were also
the most successful in battle. Some nations even initiated conflicts specifically to acquire valuable captives. For example, the state of Benin sold captive enemies to the
Portuguese in the late fifteenth century, did not do so at the height of its power in
the sixteenth and seventeenth centuries, and renewed the sale of prisoners in the
eighteenth century when its waning power led to conflicts with neighboring states.

The trade therefore affected African regions unevenly. Rulers in parts of Upper
Guinea, especially modern Gambia and Senegal, largely resisted involvement with
the trade; the few slave vessels that departed from that area were much more likely
than others to experience onboard rebellions. Despite planters' preference for male
slaves, women predominated in cargoes originating in the Bight of Biafra. In such
regions as the Gold Coast, the trade had a significant impact on the sex ratio of
the remaining population. There a relative shortage of men increased work demands on women, encouraged polygyny, and opened new opportunities to women
and their children.

New England   New England had the most complex relationship to the
and the   trading system. The region produced only one item England
Caribbean   wanted: tall trees to serve as masts for sailing vessels. To buy
                     English manufactures, New Englanders therefore needed
profits earned elsewhere, especially in the Caribbean. Those islands lacked precisely
the items that New England could produce in abundance: cheap food (primarily

Exotic Beverages

The seventeenth-century colonists developed a taste not only for tea (from China) but also for coffee (from Arabia), chocolate (from Mesoamerica), and rum (distilled from sugar, which also sweetened the bitter taste of the other three). The American and European demand for these once-exotic beverages helped reshape the world economy after the mid-seventeenth century. Indeed, one historian has estimated that approximately two-thirds of the people who migrated across the Atlantic before 1776 were involved in one way or another, primarily as slaves, in the production of tobacco, calico, and these four drinks for the world market. The exotic beverages had a profound impact, too, on custom and culture as they moved swiftly from luxury to necessity.

Each beverage had its own pattern of consumption. Chocolate, brought to Spain from Mexico and enjoyed there for a century before spreading more widely throughout Europe, became the preferred drink of aristocrats, consumed hot at intimate gatherings in palaces and mansions. Coffee, by contrast, became the preeminent morning beverage of English and colonial businessmen, who praised its caffeine for keeping drinkers sober and focused. Coffee was served in new public coffeehouses, patronized only by men, where politics and business were the topics of conversation. The first coffeehouse opened in London in the late 1660s; Boston had several by the 1690s. By the mid-eighteenth century, though, tea had supplanted coffee as the preferred hot, caffeinated beverage in England and

America. It was consumed in the afternoon in private homes at tea tables presided over by women. Tea embodied genteel status and polite conversation. In contrast, rum was the drink of the masses. This inexpensive, potent distilled spirit, made possible by new technology and the increasing production of sugar, was enthusiastically imbibed by free working people everywhere in the Atlantic world.

The American colonies played a vital role in the production, distribution, and consumption of each of these beverages. Chocolate, most obviously, originated in America, and cacao plantations in the South American tropics multiplied in size and number to meet the rising demand. Coffee and tea (particularly the latter) were as avidly consumed in the colonies as in England. And rum involved Americans in every phase of its production and consumption. The sugar grown on French and English Caribbean plantations was transported to the mainland in barrels and ships made from North American wood. There the syrup was turned into rum at 140 distilleries. The Americans themselves drank a substantial share of the distilleries' output—an estimated four gallons per person annually—but exported much of it to Africa. There the rum purchased more slaves to produce more sugar to make still more rum, and the cycle began again.

Thus, new tastes and customs connected to four different beverages linked the colonies to the rest of the world and altered their economic and social development.

---

corn and salt fish) to feed the burgeoning slave population and wood for barrels to hold sugar and molasses. By the late 1640s, decades before the Chesapeake economy became dependent on *production* by slaves, New England's already rested on *consumption* by slaves and their owners. The sale of foodstuffs and wood products to Caribbean sugar planters provided New England farmers and merchants with a major source of income. After the founding of Pennsylvania, New York, and New Jersey, those colonies, too, participated in the lucrative West Indian trade.

Shopkeepers in the interior of New England and the middle colonies bartered with local farmers for grains, livestock, and barrel staves, then traded those items to merchants located in port towns. Such merchants dispatched ships to the Caribbean, where they sailed from island to island, exchanging their cargoes for molasses, sugar, fruit, dyestuffs, and slaves. The system's sole constant was uncertainty, due to the weather, rapid shifts in supply and demand in the small island markets, and the delicate system of credit on which the entire structure depended. Once they had a full load, the ships returned to Boston, Newport, New York, or Philadelphia to dispose of their cargoes (often including enslaved people). Americans began to distill molasses into rum, a crucial aspect of the only part of the trade that could accurately be termed triangular. Rhode Islanders took rum to Africa and traded it for slaves, whom they carried to Caribbean islands to exchange for more molasses to produce still more rum.

Slaving Voyages   Tying the system together was the voyage (commonly called the middle passage) that brought Africans to the Americas, where they cultivated the profitable crops and—on Caribbean islands—consumed foods produced in North America. On shipboard, men were shackled in pairs in the hold except for periods of exercise on deck, whereas during the day women and children were usually free to move around, and to work at such assigned tasks as food preparation and cleaning. At night, men and women were confined to separate quarters. The best evidence of the captives' reaction to their plight comes from accounts of their behavior, since few ever had the chance to record their experiences. Many resisted enslavement by refusing to eat, jumping overboard, or joining in revolts, which rarely succeeded. Their communal singing and drumming, reported by numerous observers, must have simultaneously lifted their spirits and forged a sense of solidarity. But conditions on board were hellish, as captains often packed as many people as possible into holds that were hot, crowded, and reeking with smells from vomit and the "necessary tubs."

The traumatic voyage unsurprisingly brought heavy fatalities to captives and crew alike. An average of 10 to 20 percent of the newly enslaved died en route; on long or disease-ridden voyages, mortality rates could be much higher. In addition, another 20 percent or so died either before the ships left Africa or shortly after their arrival in the Americas. Sailors also died at high rates, chiefly through exposure to such diseases as yellow fever and malaria, which were endemic to Africa. One in every four or five died on voyages, and just 10 percent of the men sent to run the Royal African Company's forts in Lower Guinea lived to return home to England. Sailors signed on to slaving voyages reluctantly; indeed, many had to be coerced or tricked, because conditions on shipboard were difficult for the crew as well as the human cargo. Slave merchants were notoriously greedy and captains notoriously brutal—to sailors as well as to the captives in the hold. Some crew members were themselves slaves or freedmen. Unfortunately, the sailors, often the subject of abuse, in turn frequently abused the bondspeople in their charge. Yet at the same time, through intimate contact with the enslaved, they learned the value of freedom, and sailors became well known throughout the Atlantic world for their fierce attachment to personal independence.

SLAVERY IN NORTH AMERICA AND THE CARIBBEAN

Barbados, America's first "slave society" (an economy wholly dependent on enslavement, as opposed to a "society with slaves"), spawned many others. As the island's population expanded and large planters consolidated their landholdings, about 40 percent of the early English residents dispersed to other colonies. The migrants carried their laws, commercial contacts, and slaveholding practices with them; the Barbados slave code of 1661, for example, served as the model for later codes in Jamaica, Antigua, Virginia, and South Carolina. Moreover, a large proportion of the first Africans imported into North America came via Barbados. In addition to the many Barbadians who settled in Carolina, others moved to the southern regions of Virginia (where they specialized in selling foodstuffs and livestock to their former island home), New Jersey, and New England, where they already had slave-trading partners.

African Enslavement in the Chesapeake   Newly arrived Africans in the Chesapeake tended to be assigned to outlying parts of plantations (called quarters), at least until they learned some English and the routines of American tobacco cultivation. The crop that originated in the Americas was also grown in various locations in West Africa, so Chesapeake planters, who in the late seventeenth century were still experimenting with curing and processing techniques, could well have drawn on their laborers' expertise. Such Africans—the vast majority of them men—lived in quarters composed of ten to fifteen workers housed together in one or two buildings and supervised by an Anglo-American overseer. Each man was expected to cultivate about two acres of tobacco a year. Their lives must have been filled with toil and loneliness, for few spoke the same language, and all were expected to work for their owners six days a week. On Sundays, planters allowed them a day off. Many used that time to cultivate their own gardens or to hunt or fish to supplement their meager diet. Only rarely could they form families because of the scarcity of women.

Slaves usually cost about two and a half times as much as indentured servants, but they could repay the greater investment with a lifetime of service, assuming they survived—which large numbers did not, having been weakened by the voyage and sickened by exposure to new diseases. Those with enough money could take the chance and acquire slaves, accumulate greater wealth, and establish large plantations worked by tens, if not hundreds, of bondspeople, whereas the less affluent could not even afford to purchase indentured servants, whose price rose because of scarcity. As time passed, Anglo-American society in the Chesapeake thus became increasingly stratified—that is, the gap between rich and poor planters steadily widened. The introduction of large numbers of Africans into the Chesapeake accordingly had a significant impact on the shape of Anglo-American society, in addition to reshaping the population as a whole.

So many Africans were imported into Virginia and Maryland so rapidly that, as early as 1690, those colonies contained more slaves than English indentured servants. By 1710, people of African descent composed one-fifth of the region's population. Even so, and despite sizable continuing imports, a decade later American-born slaves already outnumbered their African-born counterparts in the Chesapeake, and the native-born proportion of the slave population continued to increase thereafter.

African Enslavement in South Carolina

Africans who had lived in the Caribbean came with their masters to South Carolina from Barbados in 1670, composing one-quarter to one-third of the early population. The Barbadian slaveowners quickly discovered that African-born slaves had a variety of skills well suited to the semitropical environment of South Carolina. African-style dugout canoes became the chief means of transportation in the colony, which was crossed by rivers and included large islands just off shore. Fishing nets copied from African models proved more efficient than those of English origin. Baskets that enslaved laborers wove and gourds they hollowed out came into general use as containers for food and drink. Africans' skill at killing crocodiles equipped them to handle alligators. And, finally, Africans adapted their traditional techniques of cattle herding for use in America. Because meat and hides numbered among the colony's chief exports in its earliest years, Africans contributed significantly to South Carolina's prosperity.

In 1693, as slavery was taking firm root in South Carolina, officials in Spanish Florida began offering freedom to runaways who would convert to Catholicism. Over the years, hundreds of South Carolina fugitives took advantage of the offer, although not all won their liberty. Many settled in a town founded for them near St. Augustine, Gracia Real de Santa Teresa de Mose, headed by a former slave, Francisco Menendez.

After 1700, South Carolinians started to import slaves directly from Africa. From about 1710 until midcentury, the African-born constituted a majority of the enslaved population in the colony, and, bondspeople by 1750 composed a majority of its residents. The similarity of the South Carolinian and West African environments, coupled with the substantial African-born population, ensured the survival of more aspects of West African culture than elsewhere on the North American mainland. Only in South Carolina did enslaved parents continue to give their children African names; only there did a dialect develop that combined English words with African terms. (Known as Gullah, it has survived to the present day in isolated areas.) African skills remained useful, so techniques lost in other regions when the migrant generation died were instead passed down to the migrants' children. And in South Carolina, African women became the primary petty traders, dominating the markets of Charles Town as they did those of Guinea.

Rice and Indigo

The importation of Africans coincided with the successful introduction of rice in South Carolina. English people knew nothing about the techniques of growing and processing rice, but people from Africa's Rice Coast had spent their lives working with the crop. Although the evidence is circumstantial, the Africans' expertise may well have assisted their English masters in cultivating rice profitably. Productive rice-growing techniques known in West Africa, especially cultivation in inland swamps and tidal rivers, both of which involved substantial water-control projects, were widely adopted and combined with European technologies. In West Africa, women played a crucial role in cultivating and processing rice, and they did so in South Carolina as well. Enslaved men dug the ditches and prepared the fields for planting, but women were responsible for sowing and weeding the crop as well as for pounding harvested rice with a mortar and pestle to remove the hulls and bran, then winnowing to separate the grains from the chaff. Because English grindstones damaged rice kernels (not until the late eighteenth century were new processes developed), South Carolinians continued to utilize the West African system of pounding rice by hand; planters assigned men as well as women to that task.

Every field worker on rice plantations, which were far larger than Chesapeake tobacco quarters, was expected to cultivate three to four acres of rice a year. Most of those field workers were female because many enslaved men were assigned to jobs like blacksmithing or carpentry, which were not given to women. To cut expenses, planters also expected slaves to grow part of their own food. A universally adopted "task" system of predefined work assignments provided that, after bondspeople had finished their set tasks for the day, they could then rest or work in their own garden plots or on other projects. Experienced laborers could often complete their tasks by early afternoon; after that, as on Sundays, their masters had no legitimate claim on their time. One scholar has suggested that the unique task system, which gave bondspeople more freedom than gang labor, and which was used in South Carolina by the early eighteenth century, resulted from negotiations between slaves familiar with rice cultivation and masters who needed their expertise.

Although this rice basket dates from nineteenth-century South Carolina, it is woven in traditional West African style. Enslaved women winnowed rice in such baskets, tossing the grains into the air after they had been pounded, so that the lighter pieces of hull would be blown away by the wind.

Developers of South Carolina's second cash crop also used the task system and drew on slaves' specialized skills. Indigo, the only source of blue dye for the growing English textile industry, was much prized. Eliza Lucas, a young woman managing her father's plantations, began to experiment with indigo cultivation during the early 1740s. Drawing on the knowledge of slaves and overseers from the Caribbean, she developed the planting and processing techniques later adopted throughout the colony. Indigo grew on high ground, and rice was planted in low-lying regions; rice and indigo also had different growing seasons. Thus, the two crops complemented each other. South Carolina indigo never matched the quality of that from the Caribbean, but indigo plantations flourished because the crop was so valuable that Parliament offered Carolinians a bounty on every pound exported to Great Britain.

Indian Enslavement in North and South Carolina

Among the enslaved people in both Carolinas were Indian captives who had been retained rather than exported. In 1708, such Indians composed as much as 14 percent of the South Carolina population. The widespread and lucrative traffic in Indian slaves significantly affected South Carolina's relationship with its indigenous neighbors. Native Americans knew they could always find a ready market for captive enemies in Charles Town, so they took that means of ridding themselves of real or potential rivals. Yet Indian nations soon learned that Carolinians could not be trusted. As settlers and traders shifted their priorities, first one set of former allies, then another, found themselves the enslaved rather than the enslavers.

The trade in Indian slaves began when the Westos (originally known as the Eries), migrated south from the Great Lakes region in the mid-1650s, fleeing their Iroquois enemies after the Beaver Wars. Expert in the use of European firearms, the Westos began raiding Spain's lightly defended Florida missions and selling the resulting Indian captives to Virginians. With the establishment of Carolina, the proprietors took for themselves a monopoly of trade with the Westos, which infuriated local settlers shut out of the profitable commerce in slaves and deerskins. The planters secretly financed attacks on the Westos, essentially wiping them out by 1682. Southeastern Indians reacted to such slave raids—continued by other native peoples after the defeat of the Westos—by trying to protect themselves either through subordination to the English or Spanish, or by coalescing into new, larger political units, such as those known later as Creeks, Chickasaws, or Cherokees.

At first, the Carolinians did not engage directly in conflicts with neighboring Indians. But in 1711 the Tuscaroras, an Iroquoian people, attacked a Swiss-German settlement at New Bern, North Carolina, which had expropriated their lands. South Carolinians and their Indian allies then combined to defeat the Tuscaroras in a bloody war. Afterward, more than a thousand Tuscaroras were enslaved, and the remainder drifted northward, where they joined the Iroquois Confederacy but were not allotted a seat on the council, instead being represented by the Oneidas.

Four years later, the Yamasees, who had helped to overcome the Tuscaroras, turned on their onetime English allies. In what seems to have been long-planned retaliation for multiple abuses by traders as well as threats to their own lands, the Yamasees enlisted the Creeks and other Muskogean peoples in coordinated attacks on outlying English settlements. In the spring and summer of 1715, English and African refugees by the hundreds streamed into Charles Town. The Yamasee-Creek offensive was eventually thwarted when reinforcements arrived from the north, colonists hastily armed their African slaves, and Cherokees joined the fight against the Creeks. After the war, Carolinian involvement in the Indian slave trade ceased, because all their native neighbors moved away for self-protection: Creeks migrated west, Yamasees went south, and other groups moved north. The abuses of the Carolina slave trade thus in effect caused its own destruction. And in the war's aftermath, the native peoples of the Carolinas were able to regroup and rebuild their strength, for they were no longer subjected to slavers' raids.

Enslavement in the North

Atlantic creoles from the Caribbean and native peoples from the Carolinas and Florida, along with local Indians sentenced to slavery for crime or debt, composed the diverse group of bound laborers in the northern mainland colonies. The intricate involvement of northerners in the web of commerce surrounding the slave trade ensured that many people of African descent lived in America north of Virginia and that "Spanish Indians" became an identifiable component of the New England population. Some bondspeople resided in urban areas, especially New York, which in 1700 had a larger black population than any other mainland city. Women tended to work as domestic servants, men as unskilled laborers on the docks. At the end of the seventeenth century, three-quarters of wealthy Philadelphia households included one or two slaves.

Yet even in the North most bondspeople worked in the countryside, the majority at agricultural tasks. Dutch farmers in the Hudson valley and northern New Jersey were especially likely to rely on enslaved Africans, as were the owners of large landholdings in the Narragansett region of Rhode Island. Some bondsmen toiled in new rural enterprises, such as ironworks, working alongside hired laborers and indentured servants at forges and foundries. Although relatively few northern colonists owned slaves, those who did relied heavily on their labor. Therefore, even though slavery overall did not make a substantial contribution to the northern economy, certain individual slaveholders benefited greatly from the institution and had good reason to want to preserve it.

Slave Resistance

As slavery became an integral part of the North American and Caribbean landscapes, so too did slaves' resistance to their masters. Most commonly, that resistance took the form of malingering or running away, but occasionally bondspeople planned rebellions. Seven times before 1713, the English Caribbean experienced major revolts involving at least fifty slaves and causing the deaths of both whites and blacks. Twice, in 1675 and 1692, Barbados authorities thwarted plots shortly before they were to be implemented, afterward executing more than sixty convicted conspirators.

The first slave revolt in the mainland colonies took place in New York in 1712, at a time when enslaved people constituted about 15 percent of the population. The rebels, primarily recent arrivals from the Akan States of the Gold Coast, set a fire and then ambushed those who tried to put it out, killing eight and wounding another twelve. Some rebels committed suicide to avoid capture; of those caught and tried, eighteen were executed. Their decapitated bodies were left to rot outdoors as a warning to others.

IMPERIAL REORGANIZATION AND THE WITCHCRAFT CRISIS

English officials seeking new sources of revenue decided to tap into the profits of the expanding Atlantic trading system in slaves and the products of slave labor. Chesapeake tobacco and Caribbean sugar had obvious value, but other colonial products also had considerable potential. Parliament and the Stuart monarchs accordingly drafted laws designed to harness the proceeds of the trade for the primary benefit of the mother country.

Colonial Autonomy Challenged Like other European nations, England based its commercial policy on a series of assumptions about the operations of the world's economic system, collectively called *mercantilism*. The theory viewed the economic world as a collection of national states whose governments competed for shares of a finite amount of wealth. What one nation gained, another nation lost. Each nation sought to become as economically self-sufficient as possible while maintaining a favorable balance of trade with other countries by exporting more than it imported. Colonies played an important role, supplying the mother country with valuable raw materials to be consumed at home or sent abroad and serving as a market for the mother country's manufactured goods.

Parliament's Navigation Acts—passed between 1651 and 1673—established three main principles that accorded with mercantilist theory. First, only English or colonial merchants and ships could legally trade in the colonies. Second, certain valuable American products could be sold only in the mother country or in other English colonies. At first, these "enumerated" goods included wool, sugar, tobacco, indigo, ginger, and dyes; later acts added rice, naval stores (masts, spars, pitch, tar, and turpentine), copper, and furs to the list. Third, all foreign goods destined for sale in the colonies had to be shipped through England, paying English import duties. Some years later, new laws established a fourth principle: the colonies could not export items (such as wool clothing, hats, or iron) that competed with English products.

These laws adversely affected some colonies, like those in the Chesapeake, because planters there could not seek foreign markets for their staple crops. The statutes initially helped the sugar producers of the English Caribbean by driving Brazilian sugar out of the home market, but later prevented those English planters from selling their sugar elsewhere. In some places, the impact was minimal or even positive. Builders and owners of ships benefited from the monopoly on American trade given to English and colonial merchants; the laws stimulated the creation of a lucrative colonial shipbuilding industry, especially in New England. And the northern and middle colonies produced many unenumerated goods—for example, fish, flour, meat and livestock, and barrel staves. Such products could be traded directly to the French, Spanish, or Dutch Caribbean islands as long as they were carried in English or American ships.

Mercantilism and Navigation Acts   The English authorities soon learned that writing mercantilist legislation was far easier than enforcing it. The many harbors of the American coast provided ready havens for smugglers, and colonial officials often looked the other way when illegally imported goods were offered for sale. In Dutch Caribbean ports like St. Eustatius, American merchants could easily dispose of enumerated goods and purchase foreign items on which duty had not been paid. Because American juries tended to favor local smugglers over customs officers (a colonial customs service was instituted in 1671), Parliament in 1696 established several American vice-admiralty courts, which operated without juries and adjudicated violations of the Navigation Acts.

The Navigation Acts imposed regulations on Americans' international trade, but by the early 1680s mainland governments and their residents had become accustomed to a considerable degree of political autonomy. The tradition of local rule was especially firmly established in New England, where Massachusetts, Plymouth, Connecticut, and Rhode Island operated essentially as independent entities, subject neither to the direct authority of the king nor to a proprietor. Whereas Virginia was a royal colony and New Hampshire (1679) and New York (1685) gained that status, all other mainland settlements were proprietorships, over which the nation exercised little control. Everywhere in the English colonies, free adult men who owned more than a minimum amount of property expected to have an influential voice in their governments, especially in decisions concerning taxation.

After James II became king in 1685, such expectations clashed with those of the monarch. The new king and his successors sought to bring order to the apparently chaotic state of colonial administration by tightening the reins of government and by reducing the colonies' political autonomy. Most significantly, colonial administrators targeted New England. Reports from America convinced English officials that New England was a hotbed of smuggling. Moreover, Puritans refused to allow freedom of religion to non-Congregationalists and insisted on maintaining laws incompatible with English practice. New England thus seemed an appropriate place to exert English authority with greater vigor. The charters of all the colonies from New Jersey to Maine were revoked, and a Dominion of New England was established in 1686. (For the boundaries of the Dominion, see Map 3.1.) Sir Edmund Andros, the governor, had immense power: Parliament dissolved all the assemblies, and Andros needed only the consent of an appointed council to make laws and levy taxes.

Glorious Revolution in America   New Englanders endured Andros's autocratic rule for more than two years. Then they learned that James II's hold on power was crumbling. James had angered his subjects by levying taxes without parliamentary approval and by announcing his conversion to Catholicism. In April 1689, Boston's leaders jailed Andros and his associates. The following month, they received definite news of the bloodless coup known as the Glorious Revolution, in which James was replaced on the throne in late 1688 by his daughter Mary and her husband, the Dutch prince William of Orange. When Parliament offered the throne to the Protestants William and Mary, the Glorious Revolution affirmed the supremacy of both Parliament and Protestantism.

In other colonies, too, the Glorious Revolution emboldened people for revolt. In Maryland, the Protestant Association overturned the government of the Catholic proprietor, and in New York a militia officer of German origin, Jacob Leisler, assumed control of the government. Bostonians, Marylanders, and New Yorkers alike allied themselves with the supporters of William and Mary. They saw themselves as carrying out the colonial phase of the English revolt against Stuart absolutism.

But like James II, William and Mary believed England should exercise tighter control over its unruly American possessions. Consequently, only the Maryland rebellion received royal sanction, primarily because of its anti-Catholic thrust. In New York, Leisler was hanged for treason, and Massachusetts (incorporating the formerly independent Plymouth) became a royal colony with an appointed governor. The province retained its town meeting system of local government and continued to elect its council, but the new 1691 charter eliminated the traditional religious test for voting and office holding. A parish of the Church of England appeared in the heart of Boston. The "city upon a hill," as John Winthrop had envisioned it, had ended.

King William's War   A war with the French and their Algonquian allies compounded New England's difficulties. King Louis XIV of France allied himself with the deposed James II, and England declared war on France in 1689. (This war is today known as the Nine Years' War, but the colonists called it King William's War.) Even before war broke out in Europe, Anglo-Americans and Abenakis clashed over the English settlements in Maine that had been reoccupied after the 1678 truce and were once again expanding. Attacks wholly or partially destroyed a number of towns, including Schenectady, New York, and such Maine communities as Falmouth (now Portland) and York. Expeditions organized by the colonies against Montreal and Quebec in 1690 failed miserably, and throughout the rest of the conflict New England found itself on the defensive. Even the Peace of Ryswick (1697), which formally ended the war in Europe, failed to bring much respite from warfare to the northern frontiers. Maine could not be resettled for several decades because of the continuing conflict.

The 1692 Witchcraft Crisis   During the hostilities, New Englanders understandably feared a repetition of the devastation of King Philip's War. For eight months in 1692, witchcraft accusations spread like wildfire through the rural communities of Essex County, Massachusetts—a heavily populated area directly threatened by the Indian attacks in neighboring southern Maine and New Hampshire. Earlier incidents in which personal disputes occasionally led to isolated witchcraft charges bore little relationship to the witch fears that convulsed the region in 1692 while the war raged just to the north. Before the crisis ended, fourteen women and five men were hanged, one man was pressed to death with heavy stones, fifty-four people confessed to being witches, and more than 140 people were jailed, some for many months.

The crisis began in late February when several children and young women in Salem Village (an outlying precinct of the bustling port of Salem) formally charged some older female neighbors with having tortured them in spectral form. Soon, other accusers and confessors chimed in, some of them female domestic servants who had been orphaned in the Maine war. One had lost her grandparents in King Philip's War and other relatives in King William's War. These young women, perhaps the most powerless people in a region apparently powerless to affect its fate, offered their fellow New Englanders a compelling explanation for the seemingly endless chain of troubles afflicting them: their province was under direct assault not only by the Indians and their French allies but also by the Devil and his allied witches.

The so-called afflicted girls accused not just the older women commonly suspected of such offenses but also prominent men from the Maine frontier who had traded with or failed to defeat the Indians. The leader of the witch conspiracy, accusers and confessors alike declared, was the Reverend George Burroughs, a Harvard graduate who had ministered in both Maine and Salem Village and was charged with bewitching the soldiers sent to combat the Abenakis. The colony's magistrates, who were also its political and military leaders, were all too willing to believe such accusations, because, if the Devil had caused New England's current troubles, they personally bore no responsibility for the terrible losses on the frontier.

In October, the worst phase of the crisis ended when the governor dissolved the special court established to try the suspects. He and several prominent clergymen began to regard the descriptions of spectral torturers as "the Devil's testimony"— and everyone knew the Devil could not be trusted. Most critics of the trials did not think the afflicted were faking, nor did they conclude that witches did not exist or that confessions were false. Rather, they questioned whether the guilt of the accused could be legally established by the evidence presented in court. Accordingly, during the final trials (ending in May 1693) in regular courts, almost all the defendants were acquitted, and the governor quickly reprieved the few found guilty.

New Imperial Measures

In 1696, England took a major step in colonial administration by creating the fifteen-member Board of Trade and Plantations, which thereafter served as the chief organ of government concerned with the American colonies. The board gathered information, reviewed Crown appointments in America, scrutinized legislation passed by colonial assemblies, supervised trade policies, and advised successive ministries on colonial issues. Still, the Board of Trade did not have any direct powers of enforcement. It also shared jurisdiction over American affairs not only with the customs service and the navy but also with a member of the ministry. Although this reform improved the quality of colonial administration, supervision of the American provinces remained decentralized and haphazard.

That surely made it easier for Massachusetts and the rest of the English colonies in America to accommodate themselves to the new imperial order. Most colonists resented alien officials who arrived in America determined to implement the policies of king and Parliament, but they adjusted to their demands and to the trade restrictions imposed by the Navigation Acts. They fought another of Europe's wars—the War of the Spanish Succession, called Queen Anne's War in the colonies—from 1702 to 1713, without enduring the stresses of the first war, despite the heavy economic burdens the conflict imposed. Colonists who allied themselves with the royal government received patronage in the form of offices and land grants, and composed "court parties" that supported English officials. Others, who were either less fortunate in their friends or more principled in defense of colonial autonomy, made up the opposition, or "country" interest. By the end of the first quarter of the eighteenth century, most men in both groups had been born in America. They were members of elite families whose wealth derived in the South from staple-crop production and in the North from commerce.

SUMMARY

The seventy years from 1650 to 1720 established the basic economic and political patterns that were to structure subsequent changes in mainland colonial society. In 1650, just two isolated centers of English population, New England and the Chesapeake, existed along the seaboard, along with the tiny Dutch colony of New Netherland. In 1720, nearly the entire East Coast of North America was in English hands, and Indian control east of the Appalachian Mountains had largely been broken by the outcomes of King Philip's War, Bacon's Rebellion, the Yamasee and Tuscarora wars, and Queen Anne's War. To the west of the mountains, though, Iroquois power reigned supreme. What had been an immigrant population was now mostly American-born, except for the many African-born people in South Carolina and the Chesapeake; economies originally based on trade in fur and skins had become far more complex and more closely linked with the mother country; and a wide variety of political structures had been reshaped into a more uniform pattern. Yet at the same time the adoption of large-scale slavery in the Chesapeake and the Carolinas differentiated their societies from those of the colonies to the north. The production of tobacco, rice, and indigo for international markets distinguished the southern regional economies. They had become true slave societies, heavily reliant on a system of perpetual servitude, not societies with slaves, in which a few bondspeople mingled with indentured servants and free wage laborers.

Even the economies of the northern colonies, though, rested on profits derived from the Atlantic trading system, the key element of which was traffic in enslaved humans, primarily Africans but also including Indians. New England sold corn, salt fish, and wood products to the West Indies, where slaves consumed the foodstuffs and whence planters shipped sugar and molasses in barrels made from staves crafted by northern farmers. Pennsylvania and New York, too, found in the Caribbean islands a ready market for their livestock, grains, and wheat flour. The rapid growth of enslavement drove all the English colonial economies in these years.

Meanwhile, in America north of Mexico Spanish settlements remained largely centered on Florida missions and on New Mexican presidios and missions. The French had explored the Mississippi valley from their base on the St. Lawrence between Montreal and Quebec, but had not yet planted many settlements in the Great

Lakes or the west. Both nations' colonists depended on indigenous people's labor and goodwill. The Spanish could not fully control their Indian allies, and the French did not even try. Yet the extensive Spanish and French presence to the south and west of the English settlements meant that future conflicts among the European powers in North America were nearly inevitable.

By 1720, the essential elements of the imperial administrative structure that would govern the English colonies until 1775 had been put firmly in place. The regional economic systems originating in the late seventeenth and early eighteenth centuries also continued to dominate North American life for another century—until after independence had been won. And Anglo-Americans had developed the commitment to autonomous local government that later would lead them into conflict with Parliament and the king.

4

AMERICAN SOCIETY TRANSFORMED
1720–1770

GEOGRAPHIC EXPANSION AND ETHNIC DIVERSITY

Europe's North American possessions expanded both geographically and demographically during the middle decades of the eighteenth century. The most striking development was the dramatic population growth of the British mainland colonies. Only about 250,000 European-Americans and African Americans resided in the colonies in 1700. Thirty years later, that number had more than doubled; by 1775, it had become 2.5 million.

Although migration from Africa, Scotland, Ireland, England, and Germany accounted for a considerable share of the growth, most of the gain resulted from natural increase. Once the difficult early decades of settlement had passed, the American population doubled approximately every twenty-five years. Such a rate of growth, unparalleled in human history until very recent times, had a variety of causes, chief among them women's youthful age at the onset of childbearing (early twenties for European-Americans, late teens for African Americans). Because married women became pregnant every two or three years, women normally bore five to ten children. Since the colonies, especially those north of Virginia, were relatively healthful places to live, a large proportion of children who survived infancy reached maturity and began families of their own. Consequently, about half of the population of Anglo America was under sixteen years old in 1775. (By contrast, less than one-quarter of the United States population is currently under sixteen.)

CHRONOLOGY

1690	Locke's *Essay Concerning Human Understanding* published, a key example of Enlightenment thought
1718	New Orleans founded in French Louisiana
1721–22	Smallpox epidemic in Boston leads to first widespread adoption of inoculation in America
1732	Founding of Georgia
1733	John Peter Zenger is tried for and acquitted of "seditious libel" in New York
1739	Stono Rebellion (South Carolina) leads to increased white fears of slave revolts
	George Whitefield arrives in America; Great Awakening broadens
1739–48	King George's War affects American economies
1740s	Black population of the Chesapeake begins to grow by natural increase, contributing to rise of large plantations
1741	New York City "conspiracy" reflects whites' continuing fears of slave revolts
1751	Franklin's *Experiments and Observations on Electricity* published, important American contribution to Enlightenment science
1760–75	Peak of eighteenth-century European and African migration to English colonies
1765–66	Hudson River land riots pit tenants and squatters against large landlords
1767–69	Regulator movement (South Carolina) tries to establish order in backcountry
1771	North Carolina Regulators defeated by eastern militia at Battle of Alamance

Spanish and French Territorial Expansion

That rapidly expanding population of British North America was largely sandwiched between the Appalachian Mountains (on the west) and the Atlantic coast (on the east). By contrast, Spanish and French territories expanded across much of North America while their populations increased only modestly. At the end of the eighteenth century, Texas had only about three thousand Spanish residents and California less than one thousand; the largest Spanish colony, New Mexico, included twenty thousand or so. The total European population of the mainland French colonies increased from approximately fifteen thousand in 1700 to about seventy thousand in the 1760s, but those colonists clustered in only a few widely scattered locations. That geographic expansion of French and Spanish settlements had far-reaching effects on native peoples.

The French by water and the Spanish by land ventured separately into the Mississippi valley in the early eighteenth century. There they encountered powerful

Indian nations like the Quapaws, Osages, and Caddos. A few Europeans—priests, soldiers, farmers, traders, ranchers—found themselves surrounded by native peoples who wanted access to manufactured goods, and who accordingly sought friendly relations with the newcomers. The Spanish and French invaders of these territories had to accommodate themselves to Indian diplomatic and cultural practices in order to achieve their objectives. French officials, for example, often complained of being forced to endure lengthy calumet ceremonies; Spaniards, unaccustomed to involving women in diplomacy, had to accede to Texas Indians' use of female representatives. The European nations established neighboring outposts in the lower Mississippi region in 1716—the French at Natchitoches (west of the Mississippi), the Spaniards at Los Adaes, 12 miles further southwest (see Map 4.1). France had already founded a settlement on Biloxi Bay (in the modern state of Mississippi) in 1699 and later strengthened its presence near the Gulf of Mexico by establishing New Orleans in 1718, a move the Spanish could not counter because of the overland distance from Santa Fe.

Instead, Spaniards focused their attention first on Texas (for instance, establishing San Antonio in 1718), then later on the region they called Alta (upper) California. After learning that Russians who hunted sea otters along the coast of northwestern North America were planning to colonize the region, they sent expeditions north from their missions in Baja California. From a base at San Diego where the Franciscan Junipero Serra set up the first mission in Alta California in July 1769, they traveled north by land and sea to Monterey Bay. Here, in April 1770, they formally claimed Alta California for Spain. Over the next decades, they established presidios and missions along the coast from modern San Francisco south to San Diego. In those centers, Franciscan friars from Spain and a few settlers from Mexico lived amid thousands of Indians who had converted to Christianity.

France and the Mississippi   Along the Mississippi, French posts north of New Orleans served as the glue of empire. *Coureurs de bois* (literally, "forest runners") used the rivers and lakes of the American interior to carry goods between Quebec and the new Louisiana territory. At such sites as Michilimackinac (at the junction of Lakes Michigan and Huron) and Kaskaskia (in present-day Illinois), Indians traded furs and hides for guns, ammunition, and other valuable items. The Osages were so eager to acquire firearms that they became, in effect, commercial hunters; witnesses reported that their women were sometimes so fully occupied processing hides that older men prepared the communities' meals. The largest French settlements in the region, known collectively as *le pays de Illinois* ("the Illinois country"), never totaled much above three thousand in population. Located along the Mississippi south of modern St. Louis, the settlements produced wheat for export to New Orleans. In such French outposts, the shortage of European women led to interracial unions between French men and Indian women, and to the creation of mixed-race people known as *metís*. French expansion contributed to the reshaping of native alliances far from the Mississippi. For example, the equestrian Comanches of the Plains, who were now able to trade with the French through Indian intermediaries, no longer needed Spanish goods—or their previous allies, the Utes. Deprived of such powerful partners, the Utes negotiated peace with New Mexico in 1752 and began to attend

MAP 4.1 Louisiana, ca. 1720

By 1720, French forts and settlements dotted the Mississippi River and its tributaries in the interior of North America. Two isolated Spanish outposts were situated near the Gulf of Mexico.

annual Spanish trade fairs. Once commonly enslaved by Spaniards, Utes instead became the enslavers of Paiutes and other nonequestrian peoples who lived to the north and west of the colony. They exchanged hides and slaves—mostly young women—for horses and metal goods. That commercial relationship endured until the end of Spanish rule in the region.

In French officials' minds, Louisiana's chief function was supportive and defensive: its paramount goals were protection of the valuable Caribbean islands and prevention of Spanish and British expansion. They accordingly did not focus their attention on Louisiana's economic development, but the profit-seeking farmers and Indian traders from Canada who settled there soon demanded that the French government supply them with slaves. In 1719 officials acquiesced, dispatching more than six thousand Africans, mostly from Senegal, over the next decade. But residents failed to develop a successful plantation economy. They did raise some tobacco and indigo, which, along with skins and hides obtained from the Indians, composed Louisiana's major exports for most of the eighteenth century. Some enslaved Africans were carried north to the Illinois country, where as farm laborers and domestic servants they made up nearly 40 percent of the population in the 1730s.

Involuntary Migrants from Africa   Louisiana's expansion angered the Natchez Indians, whose lands it had usurped. In 1729, the Natchez, assisted by newly arrived slaves, attacked northern reaches of the colony, killing more than 10 percent of its European people. The French struck back, slaughtering the Natchez and their enslaved allies, but Louisiana remained a fragile and neglected colony as long as French rule continued.

Elsewhere in the Americas, slavery took hold more firmly during the eighteenth century. In all, more Africans than Europeans came to the Americas, the overwhelming majority of them as slaves and about half between 1700 and 1800. Most were transported to Brazil or the Caribbean, primarily in British or Portuguese vessels. Of at least 11 million enslaved people brought to the Americas during the existence of slavery, only about 260,000 were imported by 1775 into the region that became the United States. Rice, indigo, tobacco, and sugar plantations all expanded rapidly in these years, steadily increasing the demand for bondspeople. In the slaveholding societies of South America and the Caribbean, a surplus of males over females and appallingly high mortality rates meant that only a large, continuing influx of slaves could maintain the work force at constant levels. On the mainland of North America, only South Carolina, where rice cultivation was difficult and unhealthful (chiefly because malaria-carrying mosquitoes bred in the rice swamps), similarly required an inflow of Africans to sustain as well as expand its labor force.

The involuntary migrants came from many different ethnic groups and regions of Africa (see Map 4.2). More than 40 percent embarked from West Central Africa (modern Congo and Angola), nearly 20 percent from the Bight of Benin (modern Togo, Benin, and southwestern Nigeria), about 13 percent from the Bight of Biafra (today's Cameroon, Gabon, and southeastern Nigeria), and approximately 9 percent from the Gold Coast (modern Ghana and neighboring countries). Smaller proportions came from East Africa and the Windward and Rice Coasts (modern Senegal, Gambia, and Sierra Leone).

Standard slave-trading practice, in which a vessel loaded an entire cargo at one port and likewise sold them in one place, meant that people from the same area (enemies as well as allies) tended to be taken to the Americas together. That tendency was heightened by planter partiality for slaves of particular ethnic groups. Virginians, for example, purchased primarily Igbos from the Bight of Biafra, whereas South Carolinians and Georgians selected Senegambians and people from West Central Africa. Louisiana planters first chose slaves from the Bight of Benin

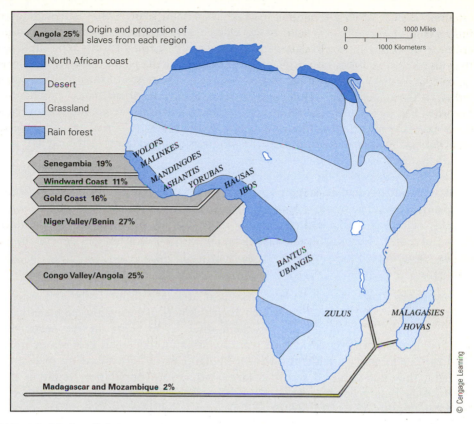

Origin and proportion of slaves from each region

Angola 25%

North African coast

Desert

Grassland

Rain forest

0   1000 Miles

0   1000 Kilometers

WOLOFS
MALINKES
MANDINGOES
ASHANTIS   YORUBAS
HAUSAS
IBOS

Senegambia 19%

Windward Coast 11%

Gold Coast 16%

Niger Valley/Benin 27%

Congo Valley/Angola 25%

BANTUS
UBANGIS

ZULUS   MALAGASIES
HOVAS

Madagascar and Mozambique 2%

© Cengage Learning

MAP 4.2 Major Origins and Destinations of Africans Enslaved in the Americas

As this schematic map shows, enslaved Africans were drawn from many regions of western Africa (with some coming from the interior of the continent) and were shipped to areas throughout the Americas.

but later bought many from West Central Africa. Rice planters' desire to purchase Senegambians, who had cultivated rice in their homeland, is easily explained, but historians disagree about the reasons for the other preferences.

Thousands, possibly tens of thousands, of these enslaved Africans were Muslims. Some were literate in Arabic, and several came from aristocratic families. The discovery of noble birth could lead to slaves' being freed to return home. Job Ben Solomon, for example, arrived in Maryland in 1732. A slave trader from Senegal, he had been captured by raiders while selling bondspeople in Gambia. A letter he wrote in Arabic so impressed his owners that he was liberated the next year. Abd al-Rahman, brought to Louisiana in 1788, was less fortunate. Known to his master as "Prince" because of his aristocratic origins, he was not freed until 1829 through the assistance of a European he had befriended in West Africa.

Despite the approximately 260,000 slaves brought to the mainland, American-born people of African descent came to dominate the enslaved population numerically because of high levels of natural increase, especially after 1740. Although about 40 percent of the Africans were male, women and children together composed a majority of slave imports; the girls and women were valued for their reproductive as well as productive capacities. A planter who owned adult female slaves could watch the size of his labor force expand steadily—through the births of their children, designated as slaves in all the colonies—without making additional major purchases of workers. The slaveholder Thomas Jefferson later pointed up the connections when he observed, "I consider a woman who brings a child every two years more profitable than the best man of the farm. What she produces is an addition to the capital, while his labors disappear in mere consumption."

In the Chesapeake, the number of bondspeople grew rapidly because the imports were added to an enslaved population that had begun to sustain itself through natural increase. The work routines involved in cultivating tobacco, coupled with a roughly equal sex ratio, reduced slave mortality and increased fertility. Even in unhealthful South Carolina, where substantial imports continued, American-born slaves outnumbered the African-born as early as 1750.

Newcomers from Europe   In addition to the new Africans, about 500,000 Europeans moved to British North America during the eighteenth century, most of them after 1730. Late in the seventeenth century, English officials decided to recruit German and French Protestants to prevent further large-scale emigration from England itself. Influenced by mercantilist thought, they had come to regard a large, industrious population at home as an asset rather than a liability. Thus, they ordered the deportation to the colonies of such "undesirables" as vagabonds and Jacobite rebels (supporters of the deposed Stuart monarchs) but otherwise discouraged emigration. They offered foreign Protestants free lands and religious toleration, even financing the passage of some groups. After 1740, they relaxed citizenship (naturalization) requirements, insisting on only the payment of a small fee, seven years' residence, Protestantism, and an oath of allegiance to the king. Such policies created an ethnic diversity found only in Britain's American colonies.

Early arrivals wrote home, urging others to come; those contacts created chains of migration from particular regions. The most successful migrants came well prepared, having learned from their American correspondents that land and resources were abundant, especially in the inland areas known as the backcountry, but that they would need capital to take full advantage of the new opportunities. People who arrived penniless did less well; approximately 40 percent of the newcomers fell into that category, for they immigrated as bound laborers of some sort.

Worst off were the fifty thousand or so migrants who came as criminals convicted of such offenses as theft and murder and sentenced to transportation for two to fourteen years instead of execution. Many unskilled and perhaps one-third female, they were dispatched most often to Maryland, where they were employed in the tobacco fields, or as ironworkers or household servants. Little is known about the ultimate fate of most, but some who committed further crimes in the colonies became notorious on both sides of the Atlantic, thanks to newspaper accounts of their exploits.

In December 1729, probably in New York's Hudson Valley, an unknown artist portrayed J. M. Stolle, son of a Palatine immigrant who came to North America from Germany in 1709. The young man's fancy clothing and the column and balustrade in the background suggest that the artist wanted to convey an image of the family's economic success, though whether that image was accurate is unknown.

National Gallery of Art, Washington, D.C. Gift of Edgar William and Bernice Chrysler Garbisch

Scots-Irish, Scots, and Germans

One of the largest groups of immigrants—over 150,000—came from Ireland or Scotland, largely in family units. About seventy thousand Scots-Irish descendants of Presbyterian Scots who had settled in the north of Ireland during the seventeenth century joined some 35,000 people who came directly to America from Scotland (see Table 4.1). Another 45,000, both Protestants and Catholics, migrated from southern Ireland (often as individuals). High rents, poor harvests, and religious discrimination (in Ireland) combined to push people from lands their families had long occupied. Many of the Irish migrants had supported themselves in Ireland by weaving linen cloth, but linen prices declined significantly in the late 1710s. Because the flax used for weaving was imported from Pennsylvania and flaxseed was exported to the same place, vessels with plenty of room for passengers regularly sailed from Ireland to Pennsylvania. By the 1720s, the migration route was well established, fueled by positive reports of prospects for advancement in North America.

Such immigrants usually landed in Philadelphia or New Castle, Delaware. They moved into the backcountry of western Pennsylvania along the Susquehanna River where the colonial government created a county named Donegal for them. Later migrants moved farther west and south to the backcountry of Maryland, Virginia, and the Carolinas. Frequently unable to afford any acreage, they lived illegally on land belonging to Indians, land speculators, or colonial governments. In the frontier setting, they gained a reputation for lawlessness, hard drinking, and ferocious fighting among themselves and with neighboring Indians.

TABLE 4.1 | WHO MOVED TO AMERICA FROM ENGLAND AND SCOTLAND IN THE EARLY 1770S, AND WHY?

	English Emigrants	Scottish Emigrants	Free American Population
Destination			
13 British colonies	81.1%	92.7%	—
Canada	12.1	4.2	—
West Indies	6.8	3.1	—
Age Distribution			
Under 21	26.8	45.3	56.8%
21–25	37.1	19.9	9.7
26–44	33.3	29.5	20.4
45 and over	2.7	5.3	13.1
Sex Distribution			
Male	83.8	59.9	—
Female	16.2	40.1	—
Unknown	4.2	13.5	—
Traveling Alone or with Families			
In families	20.0	48.0	—
Alone	80.0	52.0	—
Known Occupation or Status			
Gentry	2.5	1.2	—
Merchandising	5.2	5.2	—
Agriculture	17.8	24.0	—
Artisanry	54.2	37.7	—
Laborer	20.3	31.9	—
Why They Left			
Positive reasons (e.g., desire to better one's position)	90.0	36.0	—
Negative reasons (e.g., poverty, unemployment)	10.0	64.0	—

Note: Between December 1773 and March 1776, the British government questioned individuals and families leaving ports in Scotland and England for the American colonies to learn who they were, where they were going, and why they were leaving. This table summarizes just a few of the findings of the official inquiries, which revealed a number of significant differences between the Scottish and English emigrants.

Source: Bernard Bailyn, *Voyagers to the West* (New York: Knopf, 1986), Tables 4.1, 5.2, 5.4, 5.7, 5.23, and 6.1.

Migrants from Germany and German-speaking areas of Switzerland numbered about 85,000, most of them emigrating from the Rhineland between 1730 and 1755. They, too, usually came in family groups and landed in Philadelphia. Many, like the English indentured servants of the previous century, contracted to work as servants for a specified period of years to pay for their passage. When free to do so, Germans tended to settle together; they composed up to half of the population of some counties. Many Germans moved west into Pennsylvania and then south into the backcountry of Maryland and Virginia. Others landed in Charles Town and settled in the southern interior. The Germans belonged to a wide variety of Protestant sects—primarily Lutheran, German Reformed, and Moravian—and therefore added to the already substantial religious diversity of Pennsylvania. Late in the century, they and their descendants accounted for one-third of Pennsylvania's residents. Benjamin Franklin, for one, feared as early as 1751 that they would "Germanize" Pennsylvania. They "will never adopt our Language or Customs," he predicted inaccurately.

The most concentrated period of immigration to the colonies fell between 1760 and 1775. Tough economic times in Germany and the British Isles led many to decide to seek a better life in America; simultaneously, the slave trade burgeoned. In those fifteen years alone, more than 220,000 free and enslaved people arrived—nearly 10 percent of the entire population of British North America in 1775. Late-arriving free immigrants had little choice but to remain in the cities or move to the edges of settlement; land elsewhere was fully occupied (see Map 4.3). In the peripheries they became the tenants of, or bought property from, land speculators who had purchased giant tracts in the (usually vain) hope of making a fortune.

Maintaining Ethnic and Religious Identities   Because of these migration patterns and the concentration of slaveholding in the South, half of the colonial population south of New England had non-English origins by 1775. Whether the migrants assimilated readily into Anglo-American culture depended on patterns of settlement, the size of the group, and the strength of the migrants' ties to their common culture. For example, in the late seventeenth century, the French Protestants (Huguenots) who migrated to Charles Town or New York City were unable to sustain either their language or their religious practices for more than two generations. Yet the Huguenots who created the rural communities of New Paltz and New Rochelle in the Hudson Valley remained recognizably French and Calvinist for a century. By contrast, the equally small group of colonial Jews maintained a distinct identity regardless of where they settled. Most were Sephardic, descended from persecuted Spanish and Portuguese Jews who had first fled to the Netherlands or its American colonies, then later migrated into English territory. In places like New York and Newport, Rhode Island, they established synagogues and worked actively to preserve their religion (for instance, by observing dietary laws and by trying to prevent their children from marrying Christians).

Members of the larger groups of migrants (Germans, Irish, and Scots) found it easier to sustain European ways. Some ethnic groups dominated certain localities. Near Frederick, Maryland, a visitor would have heard more German than English;

Largest Proportion

African		German
Dutch		Scots-Irish
English and Welsh		Scottish

CREEK Indian lands

✡ Jewish synagogues

— Area settled by whites by 1755

© Cengage Learning

MAP 4.3 Non-English Ethnic Groups in the British Colonies, ca. 1775

Non-African immigrants arriving in the years after 1720 were pushed to the peripheries of settlement, as is shown by these maps. Scottish, Scots-Irish, French, and German new-comers had to move to the frontiers. The Dutch remained where they had originally set-tled in the seventeenth century. Africans were concentrated in coastal plantation regions.

in Anson and Cumberland Counties, North Carolina, the same visitor might have thought she was in Scotland. Where migrants from different countries settled in the same region, ethnic antagonisms often surfaced. One German clergyman in Pennsylvania, for example, claimed that Scots-Irish migrants were "lazy, dissipated and poor" and that "it is very seldom that German and English blood is happily united in wedlock." Anglo-American elites fostered such antagonisms in order to fracture opposition and maintain their political and economic power, and they frequently subverted the colonies' generous naturalization laws, thus depriving even long-resident immigrants of a voice in government.

The elites probably would have preferred to ignore the British colonies' growing racial and ethnic diversity, but ultimately they could not do so. When they moved toward revolution in the 1770s, they recognized that they needed the support of non-English Americans. Quite deliberately, they began to speak of "the rights of man," rather than "English liberties," when they sought recruits for their cause.

ECONOMIC GROWTH AND DEVELOPMENT IN BRITISH AMERICA

The dramatic increase in the population of Anglo America caused colonial economies to grow, despite the vagaries of international markets. A comparison with French and Spanish America reveals significant differences. The population and economy of New Spain's northern Borderlands stagnated, for the isolated settlements produced few items for export. French Canada exported large quantities of furs and fish, but the government's monopoly of trade ensured that most of the profits ended up in the home country instead of the colony. The Louisiana colony required substantial government subsidies to survive, and so—of France's American possessions—only the Caribbean islands flourished economically.

Commerce and Manufacturing   In British North America, by contrast, each year the rising population generated ever-greater demands for goods and services, leading to the development of smallscale colonial manufacturing and a complex network of internal trade. Roads, bridges, mills, and stores were built to serve the many new settlements. A lively coastal trade developed; by the late 1760s, more than half of the vessels leaving Boston harbor sailed to other mainland colonies. Such ships not only collected goods for export and distributed imports but also sold items made in America. The colonies no longer wholly depended on European manufactured goods. For the first time, the American population generated sufficient demand to support local manufacturing.

Iron making became the largest industry. Ironworks in the Chesapeake and middle colonies required sizable investments and the coordination of substantial workforces—usually indentured servants, convicts, and slaves—who dug the ore, chopped trees for charcoal production, and finally smelted and refined the ore into iron bars using that charcoal. Because the work was dirty, dangerous, and difficult, convicts and servants often tried to flee, but it offered enslaved men new avenues to learn valuable skills and accumulate property when they were compensated for doing more than their assigned tasks. By 1775, Anglo America's iron production surpassed England's.

Foreign trade nevertheless constituted the major influence on the economy. Colonial prosperity depended heavily on overseas demand for American products like tobacco, rice, indigo, fish, and timber products. The sale of such items earned the colonists the credit they needed to purchase English and European imports. If demand for American exports slowed, the colonists' income dropped, as did their ability to buy imported goods. Merchants were particularly vulnerable to economic downswings, and bankruptcies were common.

Wealth and Poverty

Despite fluctuations, the American economy slowly grew during the eighteenth century. That growth, which resulted partly from higher earnings from exports, in turn produced better standards of living for all property-owning Americans. Early in the century, as the price of British manufactures fell in relation to Americans' incomes, households began to acquire amenities such as chairs and earthenware dishes. Diet also improved as trading networks brought access to more varied foodstuffs. After 1750, luxury items could be found in the homes of the wealthy, and the "middling sort" started to purchase imported English ceramics and teapots. Even the poorest property owners had more and better household goods. The differences lay not so much in *what* items people owned, but rather in the quality and quantity of those possessions.

Yet the benefits of economic growth were unevenly distributed: wealthy Americans improved their position relative to other colonists. The native-born elite families who dominated American political, economic, and social life by 1750 had begun the century with sufficient capital to take advantage of the changes caused by population growth. They were the urban merchants who exported staples and imported luxury goods, the large landowners who rented small farms to immigrant tenants, the slave traders who supplied wealthy planters with their bondspeople, and the owners of rum distilleries. The rise of this group of moneyed families helped to make the social and economic structure of mid-eighteenth-century America more stratified than before.

New arrivals did not have the opportunities for advancement that had greeted their predecessors. Even so, few free settlers in rural areas (where about 95 percent of the colonists lived) appear to have been truly poor; at least two-thirds of rural householders owned their own land by 1750. But in the cities, families of urban laborers lived on the edge of destitution, and everywhere landless workers were available for hire. By the 1760s, applicants for assistance overwhelmed public urban poor-relief systems, and some cities began to build workhouses or almshouses to shelter growing numbers of elderly and infirm people along with widows and their children.

Regional Economies

Within this overall picture, varying regional patterns emerged, in part because of King George's War, also called the War of the Austrian Succession (1739–1748).

New England's export economy rested on trade with the Caribbean: northern forests supplied the timber for building the ships that carried salt fish to feed the slaves on island sugar plantations. The outbreak of war created strong demand for

New England's ships and sailors, thus invigorating the economy, but New Englanders suffered major losses of men and materiel in Caribbean battles and in their successful attack on the fortress of Louisbourg (in modern Nova Scotia), which guarded the sea-lanes leading to New France. When the shipbuilding boom ended with the war, the economy stagnated, and widows and orphans crowded relief rolls. Britain even returned Louisbourg to France in the Treaty of Aix-la-Chapelle (1748).

By contrast, King George's War and its aftermath brought prosperity to the middle colonies and the Chesapeake because the fertile soil and longer growing season in both regions readily produced an abundance of grain. After 1748, when a series of poor harvests in Europe caused flour prices to rise rapidly, Philadelphia and New York took the lead in the foodstuffs trade. Some Chesapeake planters began to convert tobacco fields to wheat and corn. Tobacco remained the largest single export from the mainland colonies, yet the beginnings of grain cultivation caused a significant change in Chesapeake settlement patterns by encouraging the development of port towns (like Baltimore) where merchants and shipbuilders established businesses to handle the new trade.

That South Carolina's staple crop was rice determined its distinctive economic pattern as did its location in the path of Atlantic hurricanes. The colony's rice and indigo crops—like sugar cane in the Caribbean—were periodically devastated by violent storms, causing hardship and bankruptcies. Yet after Parliament in 1730 removed rice from the list of enumerated products, South Carolinians prospered by trading directly with continental Europe. The outbreak of war disrupted that trade, and the colony entered a depression that did not end until the 1760s brought renewed European demand. Overall, though, South Carolina experienced more rapid economic growth than did other British colonies, and it had the highest average wealth per freeholder in mainland Anglo America by the time of the American Revolution.

Closely linked to South Carolina was the newest British settlement, Georgia, chartered in 1732 as a haven for English debtors released from prison so they could emigrate. Its founder, James Oglethorpe, envisioned Georgia as a garrison province peopled by sturdy farmers who would defend the southern flank of English settlement against Spanish Florida. Accordingly, its charter prohibited slavery to ensure that all adult men in the colony could be its protectors. But Carolina rice planters won the removal of the restriction in 1751. Thereafter, they essentially invaded Georgia, which—despite remaining politically independent and becoming a royal colony in 1752—developed into a rice-planting slave society resembling South Carolina.

King George's War initially helped New England and hurt South Carolina and Georgia, but in the long run those effects were reversed. In the Chesapeake and the middle colonies, the war ushered in a long period of prosperity. Such variations highlight the British mainland colonies' disparate experiences within the empire. Despite increasing coastal trade, the colonies' economic fortunes depended not on their North American neighbors but rather on the shifting markets of Europe and the Caribbean. Had it not been for an unprecedented crisis in the British imperial system (discussed in Chapter 5), it is hard to see how they could have been persuaded to join in a common endeavor. Even with that impetus, they found unity difficult to maintain.

COLONIAL CULTURES

By 1750, the population of Britain's American possessions was not only denser and more diverse than it had been a half-century earlier but also marked by new extremes of wealth and poverty, especially visible in the growing cities. Native-born colonial elites sought to distinguish themselves from ordinary folk in a variety of ways as they consolidated their hold on the local economy and political power.

Genteel Culture   One historian has termed these processes "the refinement of America." Colonists who acquired wealth through trade, agriculture, or manufacturing spent their money ostentatiously, dressing fashionably, traveling in horse-drawn carriages driven by uniformed servants, and entertaining one another at lavish parties. Most notably, they built large houses containing rooms designed for such forms of socializing as dancing, cardplaying, or drinking tea. Sufficiently well-off to enjoy "leisure" time (a first for North America), they attended concerts and the theater, gambled at horse races, and played billiards and other games. They also cultivated polite manners, adopting stylized forms of address and paying attention to "proper" ways of behaving. Although the effects of accumulated wealth were most pronounced in Anglo America, elite families in New Mexico, Louisiana, and Quebec set themselves off from the "lesser sort." Together, these wealthy families deliberately constructed a genteel culture quite different from ordinary colonists.

Men from such families prided themselves not only on their possessions and on their positions in the colonial political, social, and economic hierarchy, but also on their level of education and their intellectual connections to Europe. Many had been tutored by private teachers hired by their families; some even attended college in Europe or America. (Harvard, the first colonial college, founded in 1636, was joined by William and Mary in 1693, Yale in 1701, and later by several others, including Princeton in 1747.) In the seventeenth century, only aspiring clergymen attended college, studying a curriculum based on ancient languages and theology. But by the mid-eighteenth century, colleges broadened their curricula to include mathematics, the natural sciences, law, and medicine. Accordingly, a minuscule number of young men from elite or upwardly mobile families enrolled in college to study for careers other than the ministry. American women were mostly excluded from advanced education, with the exception of some who joined nunneries in Canada or Louisiana and could engage in sustained study within convent walls.

The Enlightenment   The intellectual current known as the Enlightenment deeply affected the learned clergymen who headed colonial colleges and their students. Around 1650, some European thinkers began to analyze nature in order to determine the laws governing the universe. They employed experimentation and abstract reasoning to discover general principles behind phenomena like the motions of planets and stars, the behavior of falling objects, and the characteristics of light and sound. Above all, Enlightenment philosophers emphasized acquiring knowledge through reason, taking particular delight in challenging previously unquestioned assumptions. John Locke's

Essay Concerning Human Understanding (1690), for example, disputed the notion that human beings are born already imprinted with innate ideas. All knowledge, Locke asserted, derives from one's observations of the external world. Belief in witchcraft and astrology, among other similar phenomena, thus came under attack.

The Enlightenment had an enormous impact on educated, well-to-do people in Europe and America. It supplied them with a common vocabulary and a unified view of the world, one that insisted the enlightened eighteenth century was better, and wiser, than all previous ages. It joined them in a common endeavor, the effort to make sense of God's orderly creation. Thus, American naturalists like John and William Bartram supplied European scientists with information about New World plants and animals for newly formulated universal classification systems. So, too, Americans interested in astronomy took part in an international effort to learn about the solar system by studying a rare occurrence, the transit of Venus across the face of the sun in 1769. A prime example of America's participation in the Enlightenment was Benjamin Franklin, who retired from a successful printing business in 1748 when he was just forty-two, thereafter devoting himself to scientific experimentation and public service. His *Experiments and Observations on Electricity* (1751) established the terminology and basic theory of electricity still used today.

Enlightenment rationalism affected politics as well as science. Locke's *Two Treatises of Government* (1691) and other works by French and Scottish philosophers challenged previous concepts of a divinely sanctioned, hierarchical political order originating in the power of fathers over families. Men created governments and so could alter them, Locke declared. A ruler who broke the social contract and failed to protect people's rights could legitimately be ousted from power by peaceful—or even violent—means. Government should aim at the good of the people, Enlightenment theorists proclaimed. A proper political order could prevent the rise of tyrants; God's natural laws governed even the power of monarchs.

Oral Cultures

The world in which such ideas were discussed was that of the few, not the many. Most residents of North America were illiterate. Even those who could read—a small proportion in French or Spanish America, about two-thirds of Anglo-Americans—often could not write. Books were scarce until the 1750s, and colonial newspapers did not begin publication until the 1720s. Parents, older siblings, or local widows who needed extra income usually taught youngsters to read; several years later, the more fortunate boys (and genteel girls after the 1750s) might learn to write in private schools. Few Americans other than some Church of England missionaries in the South tried to instruct enslaved children. And only the most zealous Indian converts learned Europeans' literacy skills.

Thus, the cultures of colonial North America were primarily oral, communal, and—at least through the first half of the eighteenth century—intensely local. Face-to-face conversation served as the major means of communication. Information tended to travel slowly and within relatively confined regions. Different locales developed divergent cultural traditions, and racial and ethnic variations heightened those differences. Public rituals served as the chief means through which the colonists forged their cultural identities.

LINKS TO THE WORLD

Smallpox Inoculation

Smallpox, the world's greatest killer of human beings, repeatedly ravaged the population of North America, colonists and Indians alike. Thus, when the vessel *Seahorse* arrived in Boston from the Caribbean in April 1721 with smallpox-infected people on board, New Englanders feared the worst. The authorities ordered the ship and its passengers quarantined, but it was too late: smallpox escaped into the city, and by June several dozen people had caught the dread disease.

Yet there was perhaps some hope. The Reverend Cotton Mather, a member of London's Royal Society (an organization promoting Enlightenment approaches to science), had read in its journal several years earlier two accounts by physicians—one in Constantinople and one in Smyrna—of a medical technique previously unknown to Europeans but widely employed in North Africa and the Middle East. Called inoculation, it involved taking pus from the pustules (or poxes) of an infected person and inserting it into a small cut on the arm of a healthy individual. With luck, that person would experience a mild case of smallpox, thereafter gaining lifetime immunity from the disease. Mather's interest in inoculation was further piqued by his slave, Onesimus, a North African who had been inoculated as a youth and who described the procedure in detail to his master.

With the disease coursing through the city, Mather circulated a manuscript among the local medical community, promoting inoculation as a solution to the current epidemic. But nearly all the city's doctors ridiculed his ideas, challenging his sources—and especially denigrating his reliance on information from Onesimus. Mather won only one major convert, Zabdiel Boylston, a physician and apothecary. The two men inoculated their own children and about two hundred others, despite bitter opposition, which included an attempt to bomb Mather's house. Yet after the epidemic ended, Bostonians could clearly see the results: of those inoculated, just 3 percent had died; among the thousands who took the disease "in the natural way," mortality was 15 percent. Even Mather's most vocal opponents were convinced, thereafter supporting inoculation as a remedy for the disease. Mather wrote reports for the Royal Society, and following their publication even Britain's royal family was inoculated.

Thus, through transatlantic links forged by the Enlightenment and enslavement, American colonists learned how to combat the deadliest disease of all. Today, thanks to a successful campaign by the World Health Organization, smallpox has been wholly eradicated.

Religious and Civic Rituals   Attendance at church was perhaps the most important such ritual. In Congregational (Puritan) churches, church leaders assigned seating to reflect standing in the community. In early New England, men and women sat on opposite sides of a central aisle, arranged in ranks according to age, wealth, and whether or not they had formally become church members. By the mid-eighteenth century, wealthy men and their wives sat in privately owned pews; their children, servants, slaves, and the less fortunate still sat in sex-segregated fashion at the rear, sides, or balcony of the church. In eighteenth-century Virginia, seating in Church of England parishes also conformed to the local status hierarchy. Planter families purchased their own pews, and in some parishes landed

An Hiſtorical

ACCOUNT

OF THE

SMALL-POX

INOCULATED

IN

NEW ENGLAND,

Upon all Sorts of Perſons, *Whites, Blacks,*
and of all Ages and Conſtitutions.

With ſome Account of the Nature of the Infection
in the NATURAL and INOCULATED Way, and their
different Effects on HUMAN BODIES.

With ſome ſhort DIRECTIONS to the UNEXPERIENCED
in this Method of Practice.

Humbly dedicated to her Royal Highneſs the Princeſs of
WALES, by *Zabdiel Boylſton,* Phyſician.

LONDON:
Printed for S. CHANDLER, *at the* Croſs-Keys *in the* Poultry.
M. DCC. XXVI.

Several years after he and Cotton Mather combated a Boston smallpox epidemic by employing inoculation, Zabdiel Boylston published this pamphlet in London to spread the news of their success. The dedication to the Princess of Wales was designed to indicate the royal family's support of the procedure.

gentlemen customarily strode into church as a group just before the service, deliberately drawing attention to their exalted position. In Quebec City, formal processions of men into the parish church celebrated Catholic feast days; each participant's rank determined his place in the procession. By contrast, Quaker meetinghouses in Pennsylvania and elsewhere used an egalitarian but sex-segregated seating system. The varying rituals surrounding people's entrance into and seating in colonial churches thus symbolized their place in society and the values of the local community.

Communal culture also centered on the civic sphere. In New England, governments proclaimed official days of thanksgiving (for good harvests, military victories, and so forth) and days of fasting and prayer (when the colony was experiencing such difficulties as droughts or epidemics). Everyone was expected to participate in the public rituals held in churches on such occasions. Because all able-bodied men between the ages of sixteen and sixty were required to serve in local militias—the only military forces in the colonies—monthly musters also brought the community together.

In the Chesapeake, important rituals occurred on court and election days. When the county court met, men came to file lawsuits, appear as witnesses, or serve as jurors. Attendance at court functioned as a method of civic education; from watching the proceedings, men learned what behavior their neighbors expected of them. Elections served the same purpose, for property-holding men voted in public. An election official, often flanked by the candidates for office, would call each man forward to declare his preference. The voter would then be thanked politely by the gentleman for whom he had cast his oral ballot. Traditionally, the candidates afterward treated their supporters to rum at nearby taverns.

Everywhere in colonial North America, the public punishment of criminals served not just to humiliate the offender but also to remind the community of proper behavioral standards. Public hangings and whippings, along with orders to sit in the stocks, expressed the community's outrage about crimes and restored harmony to its ranks. Judges often assigned penalties that shamed miscreants in especially appropriate ways. In San Antonio, Texas, for example, one cattle thief was sentenced to be led through the town's streets "with the entrails hanging from his neck"; and when a New Mexico man assaulted his father-in-law, he was directed not merely to pay medical expenses but also to kneel before him and beg his forgiveness publicly. New Englanders reprieved after being convicted of capital offenses did not thereby escape public humiliation: frequently, they were ordered to wear a noose around their neck for years, as a constant reminder to themselves, their families, and their neighbors of their heinous violation of community norms.

Rituals of Consumption

By 1770, Anglo-American households on average allocated one-quarter of their spending to purchasing consumer goods, which fostered new rituals centered on consumption. Such purchases established novel links among the various residents of North America, creating what historians have termed "an empire of goods." First came the acquisition of desirable items. In the seventeenth century, settlers acquired necessities by bartering with neighbors or ordering products from a home-country merchant. By the middle of the eighteenth century, specialized shops selling nonessentials had proliferated in cities like Philadelphia and New Orleans. In 1770, Boston alone had more than five hundred stores, which offered consumers a vast selection of millinery, sewing supplies, tobacco, gloves, tableware, and the like. Even small towns had one or two retail establishments. Colonists would set aside time to "go shopping," a novel and pleasurable leisure activity. The purchase of an object—for example, a ceramic bowl, a mirror, or a length of beautiful fabric—initiated the consumption rituals.

Consumers would deploy their purchases in an appropriate manner: hanging the mirror prominently on a wall, displaying the bowl on a table or sideboard, turning the fabric into a special piece of clothing. Colonists took pleasure in owning lovely objects, but they also proudly displayed their acquisitions (and thus their wealth and good taste) publicly to kin and neighbors. A rich man might hire an artist to paint his family using the objects and wearing the clothing, thereby creating a pictorial record that also would be displayed for admiration.

Poor, rural people also participated in the new trends, taking obvious pleasure even in inexpensive purchases. The accounts kept by a backcountry storekeeper in eighteenth-century Virginia, for instance, show that he accepted bartered goods from customers who lacked cash. One woman traded hens and chickens for a pewter dish; another, yards of hand-woven cloth for fancy fabric, ribbons, and a necklace. Local slaves exchanged cotton they had grown in their free time for colorful ribbons and and hats they must have worn with pride. Some also purchased mirrors so they could see themselves bedecked in their acquisitions.

Tea and Madeira

Tea drinking, a consumption ritual dominated and controlled by women, played an important role throughout rural and urban Anglo America alike. Households with aspirations to genteel status sought to acquire the items necessary for the proper consumption of tea: not just pots and cups but also strainers, sugar tongs, bowls, and even special tables. Tea provided a focal point for socializing and, because of its cost, served as a crucial marker of status. Wealthy women regularly entertained their male and female friends at afternoon tea parties. A hot and mildly stimulating drink, tea also appeared healthful. Thus, even poor households consumed tea, although they could not afford the fancy equipment used by their better-off neighbors. Some Mohawk Indians adopted the custom, much to the surprise of a traveler from Sweden, who observed them drinking tea in the late 1740s.

Another drink with connotations of gentility was Madeira wine, imported from the Portuguese islands by merchants with extensive transatlantic familial connections. By 1770, Madeira had become the favored drink of the elite, expensive to purchase and consume properly. Opening the bottle, letting it breathe, decanting and serving it with appropriate glassware were all accomplished with elaborate ceremony. Colonial consumers in different regions had varying tastes to which producers and merchants responded; mainlanders tended to like their Madeira liberally laced with brandy, whereas residents of the Caribbean preferred sweeter and darker wines without added spirits. From the 1750s on, urban dwellers could buy such wines at specialized stores. And much of what they drank must have been smuggled because more wines were advertised for sale than were recorded in customs records.

Rituals on the "Middle Ground"

Other sorts of rituals allowed the disparate cultures of colonial North America to interact with one another. Particularly important rituals developed on what the historian Richard White has termed the "middle ground"—that is, the psychological and geographical space in which Indians and Europeans encountered each other. Most of those cultural encounters occurred in the context of trade or warfare.

When Europeans sought to trade with Indians, they encountered an indigenous system of exchange that stressed gift giving rather than formalized buying and selling. Successful bargaining required French and English traders to present Indians with gifts (cloth, rum, gunpowder, and other items) before negotiating with them for pelts and skins. Eventually, those gifts would be reciprocated, after which formal trading could take place. And that commerce often responded to the native peoples' preferences. For example, Indians in northeastern North America wanted heavy cloths called strouds. Because British manufacturers produced such material in response to natives' demands, British traders acquired an important advantage over their French competitors. To the detriment of Indian societies, rum became a crucial component of many trading rituals. Traders concluded that drunken Indians would sell their furs more cheaply, and some Indians refused to hunt or trade unless they first received rum. Alcohol abuse hastened the deterioration of villages already devastated by disease and dislocation.

Intercultural rituals also developed to deal with murders. Indians and Europeans both believed that murders required a compensatory act but differed over what that act should be. Europeans sought primarily to identify and punish the murderer. To Indians, such "eye for an eye" revenge was just one of many possible responses to murder. Compensation could also be accomplished by capturing another Indian or a colonist who could take the dead person's place, or by "covering the dead"—that is, by providing the family of the deceased with compensatory goods, a crucial strategy for maintaining peace on the frontiers. Eventually, the French and the Algonquians evolved an elaborate ritual for handling frontier murders that encompassed elements of both societies' traditions: murders were investigated and murderers identified, but by mutual agreement deaths were usually "covered" by trade goods rather than by blood revenge.

COLONIAL FAMILIES

Families (rather than individuals) constituted the basic units of colonial society; never-married adults were rare. People living together as families, commonly under the direction of a marital pair, everywhere constituted the chief mechanisms for both production and consumption. Yet family forms and structures varied widely in the mainland colonies.

Indian and Mixed-Race Families   As Europeans consolidated their hold on North America, Indians had to adapt to novel circumstances. Bands reduced in numbers by disease and warfare recombined into new units; for example, the Catawbas emerged in the 1730s in the western Carolinas from the coalescence of several earlier peoples, including Yamasees and Guales. Likewise, European secular and religious authorities reshaped Indian family forms. Whereas many Indian societies had permitted easy divorce, European missionaries frowned on such practices; societies that had allowed polygynous marriages (including New England Algonquians) redefined such relationships, designating one wife as "legitimate" and others as "concubines."

Continued high mortality rates created Indian societies in which extended kin took on new importance, for when parents died, other relatives—even occasionally nonkin—assumed child-rearing responsibilities. Furthermore, once Europeans established dominance in any region, Indians there could no longer pursue traditional modes of subsistence. That led to unusual family structures as well as to a variety of economic strategies. In New England, for instance, Algonquian husbands and wives often could not live together for adults supported themselves by working separately (perhaps wives as domestic servants, husbands as sailors). Some native women married African American men, unions encouraged by sexual imbalances in both populations. And in New Mexico, detribalized Navajos, Pueblos, Paiutes, and Apaches employed as servants by Spanish settlers clustered in the small towns of the Borderlands. Known collectively as *genizaros,* they lost contact with Indian cultures, instead living on the fringes of Latino society.

Wherever the population contained relatively few European women, sexual liaisons (both inside and outside marriage) occurred between European men and Indian women. The resulting mixed-race population of *mestizos* and *métis* worked as a familial "middle ground" to ease other cultural interactions. In New France and the Anglo-American backcountry, such families frequently resided in Indian villages and were enmeshed in trading networks. Often, children of these unions became prominent leaders of Native American societies. For example, Peter Chartier, son of a Shawnee mother and a French father, led a pro-French Shawnee band in western Pennsylvania in the 1740s. By contrast, in the Spanish Borderlands, the offspring of Europeans and *genizaros* were treated as degraded individuals. Largely denied the privilege of legal marriage, they bore generations of "illegitimate" children of various racial mixtures, giving rise in Latino society to a wide range of labels describing degrees of skin color with a precision unknown in English or French America.

European American Families

Eighteenth-century Anglo-Americans used the word *family* to mean all the people who occupied one household (including any resident servants or slaves). The many European migrants to North America had more stable family lives than did Indian and *mestizo* peoples. European men or their widows headed households considerably larger than American families today. In 1790, the average home in the United States contained 5.7 free people; few such households included extended kin, such as grandparents. Family members—bound by ties of blood or servitude—worked together to produce goods for consumption or sale. The head of the household represented it to the outside world, voting in elections, managing the finances, and holding legal authority over the rest of the family—his wife, his children, and his servants or slaves.

In English, French, and Spanish America, the vast majority of European families supported themselves through agriculture by cultivating crops and raising livestock. The scale and nature of the work varied: the production of indigo in Louisiana or tobacco in the Chesapeake required different sorts of labor from subsistence farming in New England or cattle ranching in New Mexico and Texas. Still, just as in the European, African, and Indian societies discussed in Chapter 1, household tasks were allocated by sex. The master, his sons, and his male servants or slaves performed one set of chores; the mistress, her daughters, and her female servants or slaves, a different set.

The mistress took responsibility for what Anglo-Americans called "indoor affairs." She and her female helpers prepared food, cleaned the house, did laundry,

and often made clothing. Preparing food involved planting and cultivating a garden, harvesting and preserving vegetables, salting and smoking meat, drying apples
and pressing cider, milking cows and making butter and cheese, not to mention
cooking and baking. The head of the household and his male helpers, responsible
for "outdoor affairs," also had heavy workloads. They planted and cultivated the
fields, built fences, chopped wood for the fireplace, harvested and marketed crops,
cared for livestock, and butchered cattle and hogs to provide the household with
meat. So extensive was the work involved in maintaining a farm household that a
married couple could not do it alone. If they had no children to help them, they
turned to servants or slaves.

**African
American
Families**
Most African American families lived as components of
European American households—sometimes on plantations
that masters perceived as one large family. More than
95 percent of colonial African Americans were held in per-
petual bondage. Although many lived on farms with only one or two other slaves,
others had the experience of living and working in a largely black setting. In South
Carolina, a majority of the population was of African origin; in Georgia, about
half; and in the Chesapeake, 40 percent. Portions of the Carolina low country were
nearly 90 percent African American by 1790.

The setting in which African Americans lived determined the shape of their families, yet wherever possible slaves established family structures in which youngsters
carried relatives' names or—in South Carolina—followed African naming patterns.

William L. Breton's watercolor of "The Old London Coffee House" in eighteenth-century
Philadelphia shows a slave auction taking place on its porch. That such a scene could have
occurred in front of such a prominent and popular meeting place serves as a reminder of the
ubiquity of slavery in the colonies, north as well as south.

In the North, the scarcity of other blacks often made it difficult for bondspeople to form stable households. In the Chesapeake, men and women who regarded themselves as married (slaves could not legally wed) frequently lived on different quarters or even on different plantations. Children generally resided with their mother, seeing their father only on Sundays. Simultaneously, the natural increase of the population created wide American-born kinship networks among Chesapeake slaves. On large Carolina and Georgia rice plantations, enslaved couples not only usually lived together with their children but also accumulated property through working for themselves after they had completed their daily "tasks." Some Georgia slaves sold their surplus produce at the market in Savannah, thereby earning money to buy nice clothing or such luxuries as tobacco or jewelry, but rarely enough to purchase their freedom.

Forms of Resistance   Because all the British colonies legally permitted slavery, bondspeople had few options for escaping servitude other than fleeing to Florida, where the Spanish offered protection. Some recently arrived Africans stole boats to try to return home or ran off in groups to frontier regions, to join the Indians or establish independent communities. Among American-born slaves, family ties strongly affected such decisions. South Carolina planters soon learned, as one wrote, that slaves "love their families dearly and none runs away from the other," so many owners sought to keep families together for practical reasons. In the Chesapeake, where family members often lived separately, affectionate ties could cause slaves to run away, especially if a family member had been sold or moved to a distant quarter.

Although colonial slaves rarely rebelled collectively, they often resisted enslavement in other ways. Bondspeople uniformly rejected attempts by their owners to commandeer their labor on Sundays without compensation. Extended-kin groups protested excessive punishment of relatives and sought to live near one another. The links that developed among African American families who had lived on the same plantation for several generations served as insurance against the uncertainties of existence under slavery. If parents and children were separated by sale, other relatives could help with child rearing. Among African Americans, just as among Indians, the extended family thus served a more important function than it did among European-Americans.

Most slave families managed to carve out a small measure of autonomy, especially in their working and spiritual lives, and particularly in the Lower South. Enslaved Muslims often clung to their Islamic faith, a pattern especially evident in Louisiana and Georgia. Some African Americans preserved traditional beliefs, and others converted to Christianity (often retaining some African elements), finding comfort in the assurances of their new religion that all people would be free and equal in heaven. Slaves in South Carolina and Georgia jealously guarded their customary ability to control their own time after completing their "tasks." Even on Chesapeake tobacco plantations, slaves planted their own gardens, trapped, or fished to supplement the minimal diet their masters supplied. Late in the century, some Chesapeake planters with a surplus of laborers began to hire slaves out to others, often allowing the workers to keep a small part of their earnings. Such accumulated property could buy desired goods or serve as a legacy for children.

City Life   Just as African Americans and European Americans resided together on plantations, so too they lived side by side in urban neighborhoods. (In 1760s Philadelphia, one-fifth of the work force was enslaved, and by 1775 blacks composed nearly 15 percent of the population of New York City.) Such cities were nothing but medium-sized towns by today's standards. In 1750, the largest, Boston and Philadelphia, had just seventeen thousand and thirteen thousand inhabitants, respectively. Life in the cities nonetheless differed considerably from that on northern farms, southern plantations, or southwestern ranches. City dwellers everywhere purchased food and wood in the markets. Urban residents lived by the clock rather than the sun, and men's jobs frequently took them away from their household. City people also had much more contact with the world beyond their own homes than did their rural counterparts.

By the 1750s, most major cities had at least one weekly newspaper, and some had two or three. Anglo-American newspapers printed the latest "advices from London" (usually two to three months old) and news from other colonies, as well as local reports. Newspapers were available (and often read aloud) at taverns and coffeehouses, so people who could not afford them, even illiterates, could learn the news. Contact with the outside world, however, had its drawbacks. Sailors sometimes brought deadly diseases into port. Boston, New York, Philadelphia, and New Orleans endured terrible epidemics of smallpox and yellow fever, which Europeans and Africans in the countryside largely escaped.

POLITICS: STABILITY AND CRISIS IN BRITISH AMERICA

Early in the eighteenth century, Anglo-American political life exhibited a new stability. Despite substantial migration from overseas, most residents of the mainland had been born in America. Men from genteel families dominated the political structures in each province, for voters (free male property holders) tended to defer to their well-educated "betters" on election days.

Colonial   Throughout the Anglo-American colonies, political leaders
Assemblies   sought to increase the powers of elected assemblies relative to the powers of the governors and other appointed officials. Assemblies began to claim privileges associated with the British House of Commons, such as the rights to initiate all tax legislation and to control the militia. The assemblies also developed effective ways of influencing British appointees, especially by threatening to withhold their salaries. In some colonies (Virginia and South Carolina, for example), elite members of the assemblies usually presented a united front to royal officials, but in others (such as New York), they fought among themselves long and bitterly. To win hotly contested elections, New York's genteel leaders began to appeal to "the people," competing openly for votes. Yet in 1735, the New York government imprisoned a newspaper editor, John Peter Zenger, who had too vigorously criticized its actions. Defending Zenger against the charge of "seditious libel," his lawyer argued that the truth could not be defamatory, thus helping to establish a free-press principle now found in American law.

Assemblymen saw themselves as acting defensively to prevent encroachments on colonists' liberties—for example, by preventing governors from imposing oppressive taxes. By midcentury, they were comparing the structure of their governments to Britain's balanced polity, reputedly a combination of monarchy, aristocracy, and democracy of the sort admired since the days of ancient Greece and Rome. Drawing rough analogies, political leaders equated their governors with the monarch, their councils with the aristocracy, and their assemblies with the House of Commons. All three were believed essential to good government, but Anglo-Americans did not regard them with the same degree of approval. They viewed governors and appointed councils as representatives of Britain who posed potential threats to customary colonial ways of life. Many colonists saw the assemblies, however, as the people's protectors. And in turn, the assemblies regarded themselves as representatives of the people.

Yet such beliefs should not be equated with modern practice. The assemblies, many controlled by dominant families whose members were reelected year after year, rarely responded to the concerns of their poorer constituents. Although settlements continually expanded, assemblies failed to reapportion themselves, which led to serious grievances among backcountry dwellers, especially those from non-English ethnic groups. The colonial ideal of the assembly as the representative defender of liberty must therefore be distinguished from the colonial reality: the most dearly defended and ably represented were wealthy male colonists, particularly the assembly members themselves.

At midcentury, the political structures that had stabilized in a period of relative calm confronted a series of crises. None affected all the mainland colonies, but no colony escaped untouched. The crises of various descriptions—ethnic, racial, economic, regional—exposed internal tensions building in the pluralistic American society, foreshadowing the greater disorder of the revolutionary era. Significantly, they demonstrated that the political accommodations arrived at in the aftermath of the Glorious Revolution were no longer adequate to govern Britain's American empire. Once again, changes appeared necessary, and imminent.

Slave Rebellions in South Carolina and New York   One of the first crises occurred in South Carolina. Early on Sunday, September 9, 1739, about twenty enslaved men, most likely Catholics from Kongo, gathered near the Stono River south of Charles Town. September fell in the midst of the rice harvest (and thus at a time of great pressure for male Africans, less accustomed than women to rice cultivation), and September 8 was, to Catholics, the birthday of the Virgin Mary, venerated in Kongo with special fervor. Seizing guns and ammunition, the slaves killed storekeepers and nearby planter families. Then, joined by other local bondsmen, they headed toward Florida in hopes of finding refuge. By midday, however, the alarm had been sounded among slaveowners in the district. That afternoon a troop of militia attacked the fugitives, who then numbered about a hundred, killing some and dispersing the rest. More than a week later, most of the remaining conspirators were captured. The colony quickly executed the survivors, but for over two years rumors about escaped renegades haunted the colony.

The Stono Rebellion shocked slaveholding Carolinians as well as residents of other colonies. Throughout British America, laws governing the behavior of African

Americans were stiffened. The most striking response came in New York City, the site of the first mainland slave revolt in 1712. There, the news from the South, coupled with fears of Spain generated by the outbreak of King George's War, set off a reign of terror in the summer of 1741. Colonial authorities suspected a biracial gang of thieves and arsonists of conspiring to foment a slave uprising under the guidance of a European thought to be a priest in the pay of Spain. By summer's end, thirty-one blacks and four whites had been executed for participating in the alleged plot. The Stono Rebellion and the New York "conspiracy" not only exposed and confirmed Anglo-Americans' deepest fears about the dangers of slaveholding but also revealed the assemblies' inability to prevent serious internal disorder. Events of the next two decades confirmed that pattern.

Rioters and Regulators   By midcentury, most of the fertile land east of the Appalachians had been purchased or occupied. Consequently, conflicts over land titles and conditions of landholding grew in number and frequency. In 1746, for example, some New Jersey farmers clashed violently with agents of the East Jersey proprietors. The proprietors claimed the farmers' land and demanded annual payments, called quit-rents, for the use of the property. Similar violence occurred in the 1760s in the region that later became Vermont. There, farmers holding land grants issued by New Hampshire battled with speculators claiming title to the area through New York grants.

The most serious land riots took place along the Hudson River in 1765–1766. Late in the seventeenth century, the governor of New York had granted huge tracts in the lower Hudson Valley to prominent families. The proprietors in turn divided these estates into small farms, which they rented chiefly to poor Dutch and German migrants who regarded tenancy as a step on the road to independent freeholder status. By the 1750s, some proprietors had earned large sums annually from quit-rents and other fees.

After 1740, though, increasing migration from New England and Europe brought conflict to the great New York estates. Newcomers resisted the tenancy system. Many squatted on vacant portions of the manors, rejecting all attempts at eviction. In the mid-1760s, the Philipse family sued farmers who had lived on Philipse land for two decades. New York courts upheld the Philipse claim, ordering squatters to make way for tenants with valid leases. Instead of complying, a diverse group of farmers rebelled, terrorizing proprietors and loyal tenants, freeing their friends from jail, and on one occasion battling a county sheriff and his posse. The rebellion lasted nearly a year, ending only when British troops finally captured its leaders.

Violent conflicts of a different sort soon erupted in the Carolinas as well. The Regulator movements of the late 1760s (South Carolina) and early 1770s (North Carolina) pitted backcountry farmers against wealthy eastern planters who controlled the colonial governments. In South Carolina, Scots-Irish settlers protested their lack of an adequate voice in colonial political affairs. For months, they policed the countryside in vigilante bands known as Regulators, complaining of lax and biased law enforcement. North Carolina Regulators who objected primarily to heavy taxation fought and lost a battle with eastern militiamen at Alamance in 1771. Regional, ethnic, and economic tensions thus combined to create these disturbances, which ultimately arose from frontier people's dissatisfaction with the Carolina governments.

A Crisis in Anglo-American Religion

The most widespread crisis, though, was religious. From the mid-1730s through the 1760s, waves of religious revivalism—today known collectively as the First Great Awakening—swept over various colonies, primarily New England (1735–1745) and Virginia (1750s–1760s). Orthodox Calvinists sought to combat Enlightenment rationalism, which denied innate human depravity. Simultaneously, the economic and political uncertainty accompanying King George's War made colonists receptive to evangelists' spiritual messages. Moreover, many recent immigrants and residents of the backcountry had no prior religious affiliation, thus presenting evangelists with many potential converts.

The Great Awakening began in New England, where descendants of the Puritan founding generation composed the membership of Congregational churches. Whether in full or "halfway" communion—the latter, a category established in 1662 to ensure that people who had not experienced saving faith would still be subject to church discipline—such members were predominantly female. From the beginnings of the Awakening, though, men and women responded with equal fervor. In the mid-1730s, the Reverend Jonathan Edwards, a noted preacher and theologian, noticed a remarkable reaction among the youthful members of his church in Northampton, Massachusetts, to a message based squarely on Calvinist principles. Individuals could attain salvation, Edwards contended, only through recognition of their own depraved nature and the need to surrender completely to God's will. Such surrender brought to Congregationalists of both sexes an intensely emotional release from sin, coming to be seen as a single identifiable moment of conversion.

George Whitefield   The effects of such conversions remained isolated until 1739, when George Whitefield, a Church of England clergyman already celebrated for leading revivals in England, arrived in America. For fifteen months, he toured the British colonies, preaching to large audiences from Georgia to New England and concentrating his efforts in the major cities: Boston, New York, Philadelphia, Charles Town, and Savannah. A gripping orator, Whitefield in effect generated the Great Awakening. One historian has termed him "the first modern celebrity" because of his skillful self-promotion and clever manipulation of both his listeners and the newspapers. Everywhere he traveled, his fame preceded him. Readers snapped up books by and about him, the first colonial bestsellers. Thousands of free and enslaved folk turned out to listen—and to experience conversion. Whitefield's journey, the first such ever undertaken, created new interconnections among the previously distinct colonies.

Regular clerics initially welcomed Whitefield and the American-born itinerant evangelist preachers who imitated him. Soon, however, many clergymen began to realize that, although "revived" religion filled their churches, it ran counter to their own approach to doctrine and matters of faith. They disliked the emotional style of the revivalists, whose itinerancy also disrupted normal patterns of church attendance because it took churchgoers away from the services they usually attended. Particularly troublesome to the orthodox were the dozens of female exhorters who took to streets and pulpits, proclaiming their right (even duty) to expound God's word.

Impact of the Awakening   Opposition to the Awakening heightened rapidly, causing congregations to splinter. "Old Lights"—traditional clerics and their followers—engaged in bitter disputes with the "New Light" evangelicals. Already characterized by numerous sects, American Protestantism fragmented even further as Congregationalists and Presbyterians split into Old Light and New Light factions and as new evangelical sects—Methodists and Baptists—gained adherents. After 1771, Methodists sent "circuit riders" (preachers on horseback) to the far reaches of settlement where they achieved widespread success in converting frontier dwellers. Paradoxically, the angry fights and the rapid rise in the number of distinct denominations eventually led to an American willingness to tolerate religious diversity. No single sect could make an unequivocal claim to orthodoxy, so they had to coexist if they were to exist at all.

Most significantly, the Awakening challenged traditional modes of thought, for the revivalists' message directly contested the colonial tradition of deference. Itinerant preachers, only a few of whom were ordained clergymen, claimed they understood the will of God better than did elite college-educated clerics. Moreover, they and their followers divided the world into two groups—the saved and the damned—without respect to gender, age, or status, the previously dominant social categories. The revivalists' emphasis on emotion rather than learning undermined the validity of received wisdom, and New Lights questioned not only religious but also social and political orthodoxy. For example, New Lights began to defend the rights of groups and individuals to dissent from a community consensus, thereby challenging one of the fundamental tenets of colonial political life. The egalitarian themes of the Awakening simultaneously attracted ordinary folk and repelled the elite.

Virginia Baptists   Nowhere was this trend more evident than in Virginia, where tax money supported the established Church of England, and the plantation gentry and their ostentatious lifestyle dominated society. By the 1760s, Baptists had gained a secure foothold in Virginia; inevitably, their beliefs and behavior clashed with the way most genteel families lived. They rejected as sinful the horseracing, gambling, and dancing that occupied much of the gentry's leisure time. They dressed plainly, in contrast to the gentry's fashionable opulence. They addressed one another as "Brother" and "Sister" regardless of social status, and they elected the leaders of their congregations—more than ninety of them by 1776. Their monthly "great meetings," which attracted hundreds of people, introduced new public rituals that rivaled the weekly Anglican services.

Strikingly, almost all the Virginia Baptist congregations included both free and enslaved members. At the founding of the Dan River Baptist Church in 1760, for example, eleven of seventy-four members were African Americans, and some congregations had African American majorities. Church rules applied equally to all members; interracial sexual relationships, divorce, and adultery were forbidden to all. In addition, congregations forbade masters' breaking up slave couples through sale. Biracial committees investigated complaints about church members' misbehavior. Churches excommunicated slaves for stealing from their masters, but they also excommunicated masters for physically abusing their slaves. One such slaveowner so dismissed in 1772 experienced a true conversion. Penalized for "burning" one of his slaves, Charles Cook apologized to the congregation and became a preacher in a largely African American church.

By injecting an egalitarian strain into Anglo-American life at midcentury, the Great Awakening had important social and political consequences, calling into question habitual modes of behavior in the secular as well as the religious realm.

SUMMARY

Over the half-century before 1770, North America was transformed. French and Spanish settlements expanded their geographic reach dramatically, and in the British colonies newcomers from Germany, Scotland, Ireland, and Africa brought their languages, customs, and religions with them. European immigrants settled throughout the English colonies but were concentrated in the growing cities and the backcountry. By contrast, enslaved migrants from Africa lived and worked primarily within one hundred miles of the Atlantic coast. In many areas of the colonial South, 50 to 90 percent of the population was of African origin.

The economic life of Europe's North American colonies proceeded simultaneously on two levels. On the farms, plantations, and ranches on which most colonists resided, the daily, weekly, monthly, and yearly rounds of chores for men, women, and children dominated people's lives while providing the goods consumed by households and sold in markets. Simultaneously, an intricate international trade network affected the economies of the British, French, and Spanish colonies. The bitter wars fought by European nations during the eighteenth century inevitably involved the colonists by creating new opportunities for overseas sales or by disrupting their traditional markets. The volatile colonial economy fluctuated for reasons beyond Americans' control. Those fortunate few who—through skill, control of essential resources, or luck—reaped the profits of international commerce made up the wealthy class of merchants and landowners who dominated colonial political, intellectual, and social life. At the other end of the economic scale, poor colonists, especially city dwellers, struggled to make ends meet.

A century and a half after European peoples first settled in North America, the colonies mixed diverse European, American, and African traditions into a novel cultural blend that owed much to Europe but just as much, if not more, to North America itself. Europeans who interacted regularly with peoples of African and American origin—and with Europeans who came from nations other than their own—had to develop new methods of accommodating intercultural differences in addition to creating ties within their own potentially fragmenting communities. Yet at the same time, the dominant colonists continued to identify themselves as French, Spanish, or British rather than as Americans. That did not change in Canada, Louisiana, or Spanish territory, but in the 1760s some Anglo-Americans began to realize that their interests did not necessarily coincide with those of Great Britain or its monarch. For the first time, they offered a direct challenge to British authority.

5

SEVERING THE BONDS OF EMPIRE
1754–1774

RENEWED WARFARE AMONG EUROPEANS AND INDIANS

In the mid-eighteenth century, the British colonies along the Atlantic seaboard were surrounded by hostile, or potentially hostile, neighbors: Indians everywhere, the Spanish in Florida and along the coast of the Gulf of Mexico, the French along the great inland system of rivers and lakes that stretched from the St. Lawrence to the Mississippi. The Spanish outposts posed little direct threat, for Spain's days as a major power had passed. The French were another matter. Their long chain of forts and settlements dominated the North American interior, facilitating trading partnerships and alliances with the Indians. In none of the three Anglo-French wars fought between 1689 and 1748 was Britain able to shake France's hold on the American frontier. Under the Peace of Utrecht, which ended Queen Anne's War in 1713, the English won control of such peripheral northern areas as Newfoundland, Hudson's Bay, and Acadia (Nova Scotia) and gained access to the Great Lakes region, previously dominated by France. But Britain made no territorial gains in King George's War (see Table 5.1 and Map 5.2).

Iroquois Neutrality During both Queen Anne's War and King George's War, the Iroquois Confederacy maintained the policy of neutrality that it first developed in 1701. While British and French forces vied for nominal control of the North American continent, the confederacy skillfully manipulated the Europeans, refusing to commit warriors fully to either side despite being showered with gifts by both. The Iroquois continued a

CHRONOLOGY

1754	Albany Congress meets to try to forge colonial unity
	Washington defeated at Fort Necessity, Great Meadows, Pennsylvania
1755	Braddock's army defeated in Pennsylvania
1756	Britain declares war on France; Seven Years' War officially begins
1759	British forces take Quebec
1760	American phase of war ends with fall of Montreal to British troops
	George III becomes king
1763	Treaty of Paris ends Seven Years' War
	Pontiac's allies attack forts and settlements in West
	Proclamation of 1763 attempts to close land west of Appalachians to settlement
1764	Sugar Act lays new duties on molasses, tightens customs regulations
	Currency Act outlaws paper money issued by the colonies
1765	Stamp Act requires stamps on all printed materials in colonies
	Sons of Liberty formed
1766	Stamp Act repealed
	Declaratory Act insists that Parliament can tax the colonies
1767	Townshend Acts lay duties on trade within the empire, send new officials to America
1768	Fort Stanwix treaty opens Kentucky to Anglo-American settlement
1768–70	Townshend duties resisted; boycotts and public demonstrations divide merchants and urban artisans
1770	Lord North becomes prime minister
	Townshend duties repealed, except for tea tax
	Boston Massacre kills five colonial rioters
1772	Boston Committee of Correspondence formed
1773	Tea Act aids East India Company
	Bostonians protest the Tea Act
1774	Coercive Acts punish Boston and Massachusetts as a whole
	Quebec Act reforms government of Quebec
	First Continental Congress called

long-standing conflict with Cherokees and Catawbas in the South, thus giving their young warriors combat experience and allowing the replacement of population

TABLE 5.1 | THE COLONIAL WARS, 1689–1763

American Name	European Name	Dates	Participants	American Sites	Dispute
King William's War	Nine Years' War	1689–97	England, Holland versus France, Spain	New England, New York, Canada	French power
Queen Anne's War	War of Spanish Succession	1702–13	England, Holland, Austria versus France, Spain	Florida, New England	Throne of Spain
King George's War	War of Austrian Succession	1739–48	England, Holland, Austria versus France, Spain, Prussia	West Indies, New England, Canada	Throne of Austria
French and Indian War	Seven Years' War	1756–63	England versus France, Spain	Ohio country, Canada	Possession of Ohio country

losses by acquiring new captives. They also cultivated peaceful relationships with Pennsylvania and Virginia, in part to obtain the colonists' imprimatur for their domination of the Shawnees and Delawares. And they forged friendly ties with Algonquians of the Great Lakes region, thereby thwarting potential assaults from those allies of the French and simultaneously making themselves indispensable go-betweens for commerce and communication between the Atlantic coast and the West. Thus, the Iroquois consolidated their control over the entire American interior north of Virginia and south of the Great Lakes.

But even the Iroquois could not prevent the region inhabited by the Shawnees and Delawares (now western Pennsylvania and Virginia, and eastern Ohio) from providing the spark that set off a major war. In a significant reversal of previous patterns, that conflict spread from America to Europe, decisively resolving the contest for North America.

As early as the late 1730s, trouble began brewing east of the Mississippi as British traders pushed west from the Carolinas and Virginia, challenging French power beyond the Appalachians. The French had difficulty supplying their settlements and native allies during a successful British naval blockade of the St. Lawrence during King George's War, which heightened French colonial officials' fear of British incursions, especially when in the 1740s Iroquois negotiators, claiming to speak for the Delawares and Shawnees, ceded large tracts of land to Pennsylvania officials. Squatters (mainly Scots-Irish and Germans) had already moved into parts of the region and had negotiated agreements with the Delawares for rights to settle there; some even paid rent to native "landlords." All resided on isolated farms in Delaware territory, coexisting peacefully with their native neighbors. But the agreements reached by the Penn family's agents and the Iroquois ignored both the local Indians and the squatters, all of whom were told to move. Disgruntled Delawares and Shawnees migrated west, where they joined other displaced eastern Indians and nursed their grievances.

The region to which they moved, claimed by both Virginia and Pennsylvania, was coveted by wealthy Virginians, who, organized as the Ohio Company, received a huge land grant in 1749. The company's agents established trading posts that aimed to dominate the crucial area where the Allegheny and Monongahela Rivers join to form the Ohio (see Map 5.1). But that "Ohio country" was also vital to the French. Because the Ohio River offered direct access by water to French posts on the Mississippi, permanent British presence in the Ohio country would further challenge France's prominence along the western rivers. Thus, in the early 1750s, Pennsylvania fur traders, Ohio Company representatives, the French military, squatters, Iroquois, Delawares, and Shawnees all jostled for position in the region. A 1752 raid by the French and their native allies on a trading outpost sited at modern Cleveland rid the region of Pennsylvanians, but the Virginians posed a more serious challenge. Accordingly, in 1753, the French pushed southward from Lake Erie, building fortified outposts at strategic points.

Albany Congress   In response to the French threat, delegates from seven northern and middle colonies gathered in Albany, New York, in June 1754. With the backing of London officials, they sought two goals: to persuade the Iroquois to abandon their traditional neutrality and to coordinate plans for defense. They succeeded in neither. The Iroquois listened politely to the colonists' arguments but saw no reason to change a policy that had served them well for half a century. And, although the Albany Congress delegates adopted a Plan of Union (which would have established an elected intercolonial legislature with the power to tax), their provincial governments uniformly rejected the plan because those governments feared a loss of autonomy.

While the Albany Congress delegates deliberated, the war for which they sought to prepare was already beginning. Governor Robert Dinwiddie of Virginia sent a small militia troop to build a palisade at the forks of the Ohio, then dispatched reinforcements. When a substantial French force arrived at the forks, the first contingent of Virginia militia surrendered, peacefully abandoning the strategic site. The French began to construct the larger and more elaborate Fort Duquesne. Upon learning of the confrontation, the inexperienced young officer who commanded the Virginia reinforcements pressed onward instead of awaiting further instructions. He encountered a French detachment, and Tanaghrisson, the leader of his Ohio Indian scouts, viciously killed the French commander, leading the Indians to slaughter other wounded French soldiers. Tanaghrisson hoped to start a war that would force the British to defend the Ohio Country against the French, and he succeeded. The Virginians were trapped by pursuing French troops in a crudely built Fort Necessity at Great Meadows, Pennsylvania. After a day-long battle (on July 3, 1754), during which more than one-third of his men were killed or wounded, twenty-two-year-old George Washington surrendered. He and his men were allowed to return to Virginia.

MAP 5.1 European Settlements and Indians, 1754

By 1754, Europeans had expanded the limits of the English colonies to the eastern slopes of the Appalachian Mountains. Few independent Indian nations still existed in the East, but beyond the mountains they controlled the countryside. Only a few widely scattered English and French forts maintained the Europeans' presence there.

Seven Years' War   Washington's blunder and Tanaghrisson's aggression helped ignite a war that eventually encompassed nearly the entire world. In July 1755, a few miles south of Fort Duquesne, a combined force of French and Indians attacked British and colonial troops readying a renewed assault on the fort. In the devastating defeat, General Edward Braddock was killed, and his surviving soldiers were demoralized. Many Ohio Indians subsequently joined the French, believing that the British could not protect them. The Pennsylvania frontier bore the brunt of repeated attacks by Delawares for two more years; over a thousand residents were killed. Settlers felt betrayed because the Indians attacking them had once been (an observer noted) "allmost dayly familiars at their houses eat drank cursed and swore together were even intimate play mates."

After news of the debacle reached London, Britain declared war on France in 1756, thus formally beginning the Seven Years' War. Even before then, Britain, poised for renewed conflict with old enemies, took a fateful step. Britons and New Englanders feared that France would try to retake Nova Scotia, where most of the population was descended from seventeenth-century French settlers who had intermarried with local M'ikmaqs. Afraid that in the event of an attack the approximately twelve thousand French Nova Scotians would abandon the policy of neutrality they had followed since the early years of the century, British commanders in 1755 forced about seven thousand of them from their homeland—the first large-scale modern deportation, now called ethnic cleansing. Ships crammed with Acadians sailed to each of the mainland colonies, where the exiles encountered hostility and discrimination as they were dispersed into widely scattered communities. Many families were separated, some forever. After 1763, the survivors relocated: some returned to Canada, others traveled to France or its Caribbean islands, and many eventually settled in Louisiana, where they became known as Cajuns (derived from *Acadian*).

For three years, one disaster followed another. British officers tried without much success to coerce the colonies into supplying men and materiel to the army. Then, led by William Pitt, the civilian official placed in charge of the war effort in 1757, Britain finally pursued a successful military strategy. Pitt agreed to reimburse the colonies for their wartime expenditures and placed recruitment in local hands, thereby gaining greater American support for the war. (Even so, Virginia burgesses appropriated more funds to defend against possible slave insurrections than to fight the French and Indians.) Large numbers of colonial militiamen served alongside equally large numbers of red-coated regulars sent to North America from Britain; the two groups nevertheless had an antagonistic relationship, lacking mutual respect.

Adding to the tensions were the actions of Anglo-American merchants. During the war, firms in Boston, Philadelphia, and New York continued trading with the French West Indies. Seeking markets for their fish, flour, timber, and other products, they bribed customs officers to look the other way while cargoes nominally bound for such neutral ports as Dutch St. Eustatius or Spanish Monte Cristi (on Hispaniola) actually ended up in the French Caribbean, and they acquired valuable French sugar in return. British officials tried but failed to stop the illicit commerce, some of which was conducted under the guise of exchanging prisoners of war using flags of truce. North American merchants in fact supplied not only the French Caribbean but also France itself with vital materiel during the war.

Nevertheless, in July 1758, British forces recaptured the fortress at Louisbourg, winning control of the entrance to the St. Lawrence River and cutting the major French supply route. In the fall, the Delawares and Shawnees accepted British peace overtures, and the French abandoned Fort Duquesne. Then, in a stunning attack in September 1759, General James Wolfe's regulars defeated the French on the Plains of Abraham and took Quebec. Sensing a British victory, the Iroquois abandoned their traditional neutrality, hoping to gain a postwar advantage by allying themselves with Britain. A year later, the British captured Montreal, the last French stronghold on the continent, and the American phase of the war ended.

In the Treaty of Paris (1763), France ceded its major North American holdings to Britain. Spain, an ally of France toward the end of the war, gave Florida to the victors. France, meanwhile, ceded Louisiana west of the Mississippi to Spain, in partial compensation for its ally's losses elsewhere. The British thus gained control of the continent's fur trade. No longer would the English seacoast colonies have to worry about the threat to their existence posed by France's extensive North American territories (see Map 5.2).

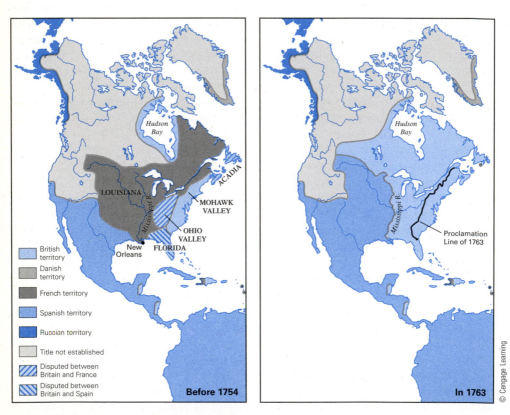

Before 1754

In 1763

British territory

Danish territory

French territory

Spanish territory

Russian territory

Title not established

Disputed between Britain and France

Disputed between Britain and Spain

© Cengage Learning

MAP 5.2 European Claims in North America

The dramatic results of the British victory in the Seven Years' (French and Indian) War are vividly demonstrated in these maps, which depict the abandonment of French claims to the mainland after the Treaty of Paris in 1763.

The overwhelming British triumph stimulated some Americans to think expansively. Men like Benjamin Franklin, who had long touted the colonies' wealth and potential, predicted a glorious new future for British North America—a future that included not just geographical expansion but also economic development and population growth. Such men were to lead the resistance to British measures in the years after 1763. They uniformly opposed any laws that would retard America's growth and persistently supported steps to increase Americans' control over their own destiny. Many of them also speculated in western lands.

1763: A TURNING POINT

The great victory over France had an irreversible impact on North America, felt first by the indigenous peoples of the interior. With France excluded from the continent altogether and Spanish territory now confined to west of the Mississippi, the diplomatic strategy of playing Europeans off against one another, which the Indians had long adopted, became obsolete. The consequences were immediate and devastating.

Even before the Treaty of Paris, southern Indians had to adjust to new circumstances. After Britain gained the upper hand in the American war in 1758, Creeks and Cherokees lost their ability to force concessions by threatening to turn instead to France or Spain. In desperation, and in retaliation for British atrocities, Cherokees attacked the Carolina and Virginia frontiers in 1760. Though initially victorious, the Indians were defeated the following year by a force of British regulars and colonial militia. Late in 1761, the two sides concluded a treaty under which the Cherokees allowed the construction of British forts in their territories and opened a large tract to European settlement.

Neolin and Pontiac
The fate of the Cherokees in the South portended events in the Ohio country. There, the Ottawas, Chippewas, and Potawatomis reacted angrily when Great Britain, no longer facing French competition, raised the price of trade goods and ended traditional gift-giving practices. Settlers rapidly moved into the Monongahela and Susquehanna valleys. A shaman named Neolin (also known as the Delaware Prophet) urged Indians to oppose the incursion on their lands and European influence on their culture. For the first time since King Philip in 1675, an influential native leader called for the unity of all tribes in the face of an Anglo-American threat. Contending that Indian peoples were destroying themselves by dependence on European goods (especially alcohol), Neolin advocated resistance, both peaceful and armed. If all Indians west of the mountains united to reject the invaders, Neolin declared, the Master of Life would replenish the depleted deer herds and once again look kindly upon his people. Ironically, Neolin's call for a return to native traditions itself revealed European origins; his reference to a single Master of Life showed the influence on his thinking of a syncretic Christianity.

Pontiac, war chief of an Ottawa village near Detroit, became the leader of a movement based on Neolin's precepts. In spring 1763, Pontiac forged an unprecedented alliance among Hurons, Chippewas, Potawatomis, Delawares, Shawnees, and Mingoes (Pennsylvania Iroquois). Pontiac besieged Fort Detroit while war parties attacked other British outposts in the Great Lakes. Detroit withstood the siege, but by late June all the other forts west of Niagara and north of Fort Pitt (formerly Fort Duquesne) had fallen to the alliance. Indians then raided the Virginia and Pennsylvania frontiers throughout the summer, slaying at least two thousand settlers. They carried off many enslaved African Americans, frightening planters, who feared an Indian-black alliance. Still, they could not take Niagara, Fort Pitt, or Detroit. In early August, colonial militiamen soundly defeated a combined Indian force at Bushy Run, Pennsylvania. Conflict ceased when Pontiac broke off the siege of Detroit in late October. A treaty ending the war was finally negotiated three years later.

The warfare on the Pennsylvania frontier in 1755–1757 and 1763 ended what had once been a uniquely peaceful relationship between European settlers and Indians in that province. For nearly eighty years, the residents of "Penn's Woods" had avoided major conflicts with each other. But first the Indian attacks and then the settlers' response—especially the massacre of several families of defenseless Conestoga Indians in December 1763 by fifty Scots-Irish men known as the Paxton Boys—revealed that violence in the region would subsequently become endemic.

Benjamin West, the first well-known American artist, engraved this picture of a prisoner exchange at the end of Pontiac's Uprising, with Colonel Henry Bouquet supervising the return of settlers abducted during the war. In the foreground, a child resists leaving the Indian parents he had grown to love. Many colonists were fascinated by the phenomenon West depicted—the reluctance of captives to abandon their adoptive Indian families.

Collection of Mary Beth Norton

Proclamation of 1763

Pontiac's war demonstrated that the huge territory Britain had acquired from France would be difficult to govern. London officials had no experience managing such a vast area, particularly one inhabited by restive peoples: the remaining French settlers along the St. Lawrence and the many Indian communities. In October, the ministry issued the Proclamation of 1763, which designated the headwaters of rivers flowing into the Atlantic from the Appalachians as the temporary western boundary for colonial settlement (see Map 5.1). Its promulgators expected the proclamation to prevent clashes by forbidding colonists to move onto Indian lands until land cessions had been negotiated. But it infuriated two distinct groups of colonists: those who had already squatted west of the line (among them many Scots-Irish immigrants) and land speculation companies from Pennsylvania and Virginia.

In the years after 1763, the latter groups (which included such men as George Washington, Thomas Jefferson, Patrick Henry, and Benjamin Franklin) lobbied vigorously to have their claims validated by colonial governments and London administrators. At a treaty conference in 1768 at Fort Stanwix, New York, they negotiated with Iroquois representatives to push the boundary line farther west and south, opening Kentucky to their speculations. The Iroquois, still claiming to speak for the Delawares and the Shawnees—who used Kentucky as their hunting grounds—agreed to the deal, which brought them valuable trade goods and did not affect their own territories. Yet even though the Virginia land companies eventually gained the support of the House of Burgesses for their claims, they never made any headway where it really mattered—in London—because administrators there realized that significant western expansion would require the expenditure of funds they did not have.

George III

The hard-won victory in the Seven Years' War had cost Britain millions of pounds and created an immense war debt. The problem of paying it, and of finding the money to defend the newly acquired territories, bedeviled King George III, who in 1760 succeeded his grandfather, George II. The twenty-two-year-old monarch, an intelligent, passionate man with a mediocre education, was unfortunately an erratic judge of character. During the crucial years between 1763 and 1770, when the rift with the colonies grew ever wider and a series of political crises beset England, the king replaced ministries with bewildering rapidity. Although determined to assert the power of the monarchy, George III was immature and unsure of himself. He stubbornly regarded adherence to the status quo as the hallmark of patriotism.

The man he selected as prime minister in 1763, George Grenville, believed the American colonies could be more tightly administered. Grenville confronted a financial crisis: England's burden of indebtedness had nearly doubled since 1754, from £73 million to £137 million. Annual expenditures before the war had amounted to no more than £8 million; now the yearly interest on the debt alone came to £5 million. Grenville's ministry had to find new sources of funds, and the British people themselves were already heavily taxed. Because the colonists had benefited greatly from wartime expenditures, Grenville concluded that Anglo-Americans should be asked to pay a larger share of the cost of running the empire.

Theories of Representation Grenville did not question Great Britain's right to levy taxes on the colonies. Like all his countrymen, he believed that government's legitimacy derived ultimately from the consent of the people, but he defined consent differently than the colonists. Americans had come to believe that they could be represented only by men who lived nearby and for whom they or their property-holding neighbors actually voted; otherwise, they could not count on legislators to represent their interests properly. Grenville and his English contemporaries, however, believed that Parliament—king, lords, and commons acting together—by definition represented all British subjects, wherever they resided (even overseas) and whether or not they could vote.

Parliament saw itself as collectively representing the entire nation; the particular constituency that chose a member of the House of Commons had no special claim on that member's vote, nor did the member have to live near his constituents. According to this theory, called virtual representation, all Britons—including colonists—were represented in Parliament. Thus, their consent to acts of Parliament could be presumed. In the colonies, by contrast, members of the lower houses of the assemblies were viewed as specifically representing the regions that had elected them. Before Grenville proposed to tax the colonists, the two notions coexisted because no conflict exposed the central contradiction. But events of the 1760s revealed the incompatibility of the two definitions of representation.

Real Whigs The same events threw into sharp relief Americans' attitudes toward political power. The colonists had become accustomed to a central government that wielded limited authority over them, affecting their daily lives very little. Consequently, they believed a good government was one that largely left them alone, a view in keeping with the theories of a group of British writers known as the Real Whigs. Drawing on a tradition of dissenting thought that reached back to John Locke and even to the English Civil War, the Real Whigs stressed the dangers inherent in a powerful government, particularly one headed by a monarch. Some of them even favored republicanism, which proposed to eliminate monarchs altogether and rest political power more directly on the people. Real Whigs warned the people to guard constantly against government's attempts to encroach on their liberty and seize their property. Political power was always to be feared, wrote John Trenchard and Thomas Gordon in their essay series *Cato's Letters* (originally published in London in 1720–1723 and reprinted many times thereafter in the colonies). The people had to exercise perpetual vigilance to prevent rulers' attempts to corrupt and oppress them.

Britain's efforts to tighten the reins of government and to raise revenues from the colonies in the 1760s and early 1770s convinced many Americans that the Real Whigs' reasoning applied to their circumstances, especially because of the link between liberty and property rights. Excessive and unjust taxation, they believed, could destroy their freedoms. They eventually interpreted British measures in light of the Real Whigs' warnings and saw oppressive designs behind the actions of Grenville and his successors. Historians disagree over the extent to which those perceptions were correct, but by 1775 a large number of colonists believed they were. In the mid-1760s, however, colonial leaders did not immediately accuse Grenville of conspiring to oppress them. Rather, they questioned the wisdom of the laws he proposed.

Sugar and Currency Acts   Parliament passed the first such measures, the Sugar and Currency Acts, in 1764. The Sugar Act (also known as the Revenue Act) revised existing customs regulations and laid new duties on some foreign imports into the colonies. Its key provisions, strongly advocated in London by influential Caribbean sugar planters, aimed at discouraging American rum distillers from smuggling French West Indian molasses. It also established a vice-admiralty court at Halifax, Nova Scotia, to adjudicate violations of the law. Although the Sugar Act appeared to resemble the Navigation Acts, which the colonies had long accepted as legitimate, it broke with tradition in being explicitly designed to raise revenue, not to channel American trade through Britain. The Currency Act effectively outlawed most colonial paper money because British merchants had long complained that Americans were paying their debts in inflated local currencies. Americans could accumulate little sterling because they imported more than they exported; colonists complained that the act deprived them of a useful medium of exchange.

The Sugar and Currency Acts were imposed on an economy already in the midst of depression. A business boom accompanied the Seven Years' War, but the brief spell of prosperity ended abruptly in 1760 when the war shifted overseas. Urban merchants found few buyers for imported goods, and the loss of the military's demand for foodstuffs hurt American farmers. The bottom dropped out of the European tobacco market, threatening the livelihood of Chesapeake planters. Sailors were thrown out of work, and artisans had few customers. In such circumstances, the prospect of increased import duties and inadequate supplies of currency aroused merchants' hostility.

Individual American essayists and incensed colonial governments protested the new policies. But lacking any precedent for a united campaign against acts of Parliament, Americans in 1764 took only hesitant and uncoordinated steps. Eight colonial legislatures sent separate petitions to Parliament requesting the Sugar Act's repeal. They argued that its commercial restrictions would hurt Britain as well as the colonies and that they had not consented to its passage. The protests had no effect. The law remained in force, and Grenville proceeded with another revenue plan.

THE STAMP ACT CRISIS

The Stamp Act (1765), Grenville's most important proposal, was modeled on a law that had been in effect in Britain for almost a century. It touched nearly every colonist by requiring tax stamps on most printed materials, but it placed the heaviest burden on merchants and other members of the colonial elite, who used printed matter more frequently than did ordinary folk. Anyone who purchased a newspaper or pamphlet, made a will, transferred land, bought dice or playing cards, applied for a liquor license, accepted a government appointment, or borrowed money would have to pay the tax, which was doubled for foreign-language newspapers. Never before had a revenue measure of such scope been proposed for the colonies. The act also required that tax stamps be purchased with scarce sterling coin. Violators would be tried by vice-admiralty courts, in which judges alone rendered decisions, leading Americans to fear the loss of their right to trial by jury. Finally, such a law would break decisively with the colonial tradition of self-imposed taxation.

James Otis's Rights of the British Colonies   The most important colonial pamphlet protesting the Sugar Act and the proposed Stamp Act was *The Rights of the British Colonies Asserted and Proved*, by James Otis Jr., a brilliant young Massachusetts attorney. Otis starkly exposed the dilemma that confounded the colonists for the next decade. How could they justify their opposition to certain acts of Parliament without questioning Parliament's authority over them? On the one hand, Otis asserted, Americans were "entitled to all the natural, essential, inherent, and inseparable rights" of Britons, including the right not to be taxed without their consent. "No man or body of men … can take [those rights] away," he declared. On the other hand, Otis admitted that, under the British system established after the Glorious Revolution, "the power of parliament is uncontrollable but by themselves, and we must obey … Let the parliament lay what burthens they please on us, we must, it is our duty to submit and patiently bear them, till they will be pleased to relieve us."

Otis's first contention, drawing on colonial notions of representation, implied that Parliament could not constitutionally tax the colonies because Americans were not represented in its ranks. Yet his second point both acknowledged political reality and accepted the prevailing theory of British government: that Parliament was the sole, supreme authority in the empire. Even unconstitutional laws enacted by Parliament had to be obeyed until Parliament decided to repeal them.

To resolve the dilemma, Otis proposed colonial representation in Parliament, but his idea was never taken seriously on either side of the Atlantic. The British believed colonists were already virtually represented in Parliament, and Anglo-Americans knew that a handful of colonial delegates to London would easily be outvoted. Otis published his pamphlet before the Stamp Act was passed. When Americans first learned of the act's adoption in the spring of 1765, they reacted indecisively. Few colonists—even appointed government officials—publicly favored the law. But colonial petitions had already failed to prevent its adoption, and further lobbying appeared futile. Perhaps Otis was correct: the only course open to Americans was to pay the stamp tax, reluctantly but loyally. Acting on that assumption, colonial agents in London sought the appointment of their American friends as stamp distributors so that the law would at least be enforced equitably.

Patrick Henry and the Virginia Stamp Act Resolves   Not all the colonists resigned themselves to paying the new tax. A twenty-nine-year-old lawyer serving his first term in the Virginia House of Burgesses was appalled by his fellow legislators' complacency. Patrick Henry later recalled that he was "young, inexperienced, unacquainted with the forms of the house and the members that composed it"—but he decided to act. "Alone, unadvised, and unassisted, on a blank leaf of an old law book," he wrote the Virginia Stamp Act Resolves.

Little in Henry's earlier life foreshadowed his success in the political arena that he entered so dramatically. The son of a prosperous Scots immigrant to western Virginia, Henry had little formal education. After marrying at eighteen, he failed at both farming and storekeeping before turning to the law as a means of supporting his wife and their six children. Henry lacked legal training, but his oratorical skills made him an effective advocate, first for his clients and later for his political beliefs. A prominent Virginia lawyer observed, "He is by far the most powerful speaker I ever heard. Every word he says not only engages, but commands the attention."

Patrick Henry introduced his seven proposals near the end of the legislative session, when many burgesses had already departed for home. Henry's fiery speech led the Speaker of the House to accuse him of treason, which Henry denied. The few burgesses remaining in Williamsburg adopted five of Henry's resolutions by a bare majority. Although they repealed the most radical of the five the next day, their action had far-reaching effects. Some colonial newspapers printed Henry's seven original resolutions as if they had been uniformly passed by the House, even though one was rescinded and two others were never debated or voted on at all.

The four propositions adopted by the burgesses repeated Otis's arguments, asserting that colonists had never forfeited the rights of British subjects, among which was consent to taxation. The other three resolutions went much further. The repealed resolution claimed for the burgesses "the only exclusive right" to tax Virginians, and the final two (those never considered) asserted that Virginians need not obey tax laws passed by other legislative bodies (namely, Parliament), terming any opponent of that opinion "an Enemy to this his Majesty's Colony."

Continuing Loyalty to Britain   The burgesses' decision to accept only the first four of Henry's resolutions anticipated the position most Americans would adopt throughout the following decade. Though willing to contend for their rights, the colonists did not seek independence. The Maryland lawyer Daniel Dulany, whose *Considerations on the Propriety of Imposing Taxes on the British Colonies* was the most widely read pamphlet of 1765, expressed the consensus: "The colonies are dependent upon Great Britain, and the supreme authority vested in the king, lords, and commons, may justly be exercised to secure, or preserve their dependence." But, warned Dulany, a superior did not have the right "to seize the property of his inferior when he pleases"; there was a crucial distinction between a condition of "dependence and inferiority" and one of "absolute vassalage and slavery."

Over the next ten years, America's political leaders searched for a formula that would enable them to control their internal affairs, especially taxation, but remain under British rule. The chief difficulty lay in British officials' inability to compromise on the issue of parliamentary power. The notion that Parliament could exercise absolute authority over all colonial possessions inhered in the British theory of government. Even the harshest British critics of the ministries of the 1760s and 1770s questioned only the wisdom of specific policies, not the principles on which they rested. In effect, the Americans wanted British leaders to revise their funda-mental understanding of the workings of their government. That was simply too much to expect.

The ultimate effectiveness of Americans' opposition to the Stamp Act rested on more than ideological arguments over parliamentary power. The decisive and in-ventive actions of some colonists during the late summer and fall of 1765 gave the resistance its primary force.

Anti–Stamp Act Demonstrations   In August, the Loyal Nine, a Boston artisans' social club, organized a demonstration against the Stamp Act. Hoping to show that people of all ranks opposed the act, they ap-proached the leaders of the city's rival laborers' associations, based in Boston's North End and South End neighborhoods. The two groups, composed of unskilled workers and poor tradesmen, often battled each other, but the Loyal Nine con-vinced them to lay aside their differences to participate in the demonstration. All colonists, not just affluent ones, would have to pay the stamp taxes.

Early on August 14, the demonstrators hung an effigy of Andrew Oliver, the province's stamp distributor, from a tree on Boston Common. That night a large crowd led by a group of about fifty well-dressed tradesmen paraded the effigy around the city. The crowd built a bonfire near Oliver's house and added the effigy to the flames. Demonstrators broke most of Oliver's windows and threw stones at officials who tried to disperse them. In the midst of the melee, the North End and South End leaders drank a toast to their successful union. The Loyal Nine achieved success when Oliver publicly promised not to fulfill the duties of his office. One Bostonian jubilantly wrote to a relative, "I believe people never was more Univer-sally pleased not so much one could I hear say he was sorry, but a smile sat on al-most every ones countinance."

But another crowd action twelve days later, aimed this time at Oliver's brother-in-law, Lieutenant Governor Thomas Hutchinson, drew no praise from Boston's re-spectable citizens. On the night of August 26, a mob reportedly led by the South End leader Ebenezer MacIntosh attacked the homes of several customs officers. The crowd then destroyed Hutchinson's elaborately furnished townhouse in one of Boston's most fashionable districts. The lieutenant governor reported that by the next morning "one of the best finished houses in the Province had nothing remain-ing but the bare walls and floors." His trees and garden were ruined, his valuable library lost, and the mob "emptied the house of every thing whatsoever except a part of the kitchen furniture." But Hutchinson took some comfort in the fact that "the encouragers of the first mob never intended matters should go this length and the people in general express the utmost detestation of this unparalleled outrage."

Americans' Divergent Interests   The differences between the two Boston mobs of August 1765 exposed divisions that would continue to characterize subsequent colonial protests. Few colonists sided with Britain during the 1760s, but various colonial groups had divergent goals. The skilled craftsmen who composed the Loyal Nine and merchants, law-yers, and other members of the educated elite preferred orderly demonstrations confined to political issues. For the city's laborers, by contrast, economic grievances may have been paramount. Certainly, their "hellish Fury" as they wrecked Hutchinson's house suggests resentment against his ostentatious display of wealth.

Colonists, like Britons, had a long tradition of crowd action in which disfranchised people took to the streets to redress deeply felt local grievances. But the Stamp Act controversy for the first time drew ordinary urban folk into transatlantic politics, including recent non-English-speaking immigrants targeted by the double taxation of foreign-language newspapers. Matters that previously had been of concern only to the gentry or to members of colonial legislatures were now discussed on every street corner and in every tavern. Benjamin Franklin's daughter observed as much when she informed her father, then serving as a colonial agent in London, that "nothing else is talked of, the Dutch [Germans] talk of the stompt act the Negroes of the tamp, in short every body has something to say."

The entry of unskilled workers, slaves, and women into the realm of imperial politics both threatened and aided the elite men who wanted to mount effective opposition to British measures. On the one hand, crowd action could have a stunning impact. Anti–Stamp Act demonstrations occurred in cities and towns stretching from Halifax in the north to the Caribbean island of Antigua in the south. They were so successful that, by November 1, when the law was scheduled to take effect, not one stamp distributor was willing to carry out his duties. Thus, the act could not be enforced. On the other hand, wealthy men recognized that mobs composed of the formerly powerless—whose goals were not always identical to theirs (as the Boston experience showed)—could endanger their own dominance of the society. What would happen, they wondered, if the "hellish Fury" of the crowd turned against them?

Sons of Liberty   They therefore attempted to channel resistance into acceptable forms by creating an intercolonial association, the Sons of Liberty. New Yorkers organized the first such group in early November, and branches spread rapidly through the coastal cities. Composed of merchants, lawyers, and prosperous tradesmen, the Sons of Liberty by early 1766 linked protest leaders from Charleston, South Carolina, to Portsmouth, New Hampshire. Not surprisingly, in light of the central role of taverns as settings for the exchange of news and opinions, a considerable number of members were tavern owners.

The Sons of Liberty could influence events but not control them. In Charleston (formerly Charles Town) in October 1765, a crowd shouting, "Liberty Liberty and stamp'd paper" forced the resignation of the South Carolina stamp distributor. The victory celebration a few days later—the largest demonstration the city had ever known—featured a British flag with the word "Liberty" emblazoned on it. But the new Charleston chapter of the Sons of Liberty was horrified when in January 1766 local slaves paraded through the streets similarly crying, "Liberty!" Freedom from slavery was not the sort of liberty elite slaveowners had in mind. In Virginia, plantation owners likewise expressed concern about the possibility that their slaves might make common cause with the Indian nations that had recently raided their frontiers.

In Philadelphia, too, resistance leaders were dismayed when an angry mob threatened to attack Benjamin Franklin's house. The city's laborers believed Franklin to be partly responsible for the Stamp Act because he had obtained the post of stamp distributor for a close friend. But Philadelphia's artisans—the backbone of the opposition movement there and elsewhere—were fiercely loyal to Franklin, one of their own who had made good. They gathered to protect his home and family from the crowd. The house was saved, but the resulting split between Philadelphia's better-off tradesmen and common laborers prevented the establishment of an alliance as successful as Boston's.

Opposition and Repeal   During the fall and winter of 1765–1766, opponents of the Stamp Act pursued several different strategies. Colonial legislatures petitioned Parliament to repeal the hated law, and courts closed because they could not obtain the stamps now required for all legal documents. In October, nine colonies sent delegates to a general congress, the first since 1754. The Stamp Act Congress met in New York to draft a protest that stressed the law's adverse economic effects. At the same time, the Sons of Liberty held mass meetings, attempting to rally public support for the resistance movement. Finally, American merchants organized nonimportation associations to pressure British exporters. By the 1760s, one-quarter of all British exports went to the colonies, and American merchants reasoned that London merchants whose sales suffered severely would lobby for repeal. Because times were bad and American merchants were finding few customers for imported goods anyway, a general moratorium on future purchases would also help to reduce their bloated inventories.

In March 1766, Parliament repealed the Stamp Act. The nonimportation agreements had had the anticipated effect, creating allies for the colonies among wealthy London merchants. But boycotts, formal protests, and crowd actions were less important in winning repeal than was the appointment of a new prime minister, chosen by George III for reasons unrelated to colonial politics. Lord Rockingham, who replaced Grenville in the summer of 1765, had opposed the Stamp Act, not because he believed Parliament lacked power to tax the colonies, but because he thought the law unwise and divisive. Thus, although Rockingham proposed repeal, he linked it to passage of a Declaratory Act, which asserted Parliament's authority to tax and legislate for Britain's American possessions "in all cases whatsoever."

News of the repeal arrived in Newport, Rhode Island, in May, and the Sons of Liberty quickly dispatched messengers to carry the welcome tidings throughout the colonies. They organized celebrations commemorating the glorious event and Americans' loyalty to Britain. Their goal achieved, the Sons of Liberty dissolved. Few colonists saw the ominous implications of the Declaratory Act.

RESISTANCE TO THE TOWNSHEND ACTS

The colonists had accomplished their immediate aim, but the long-term prospects were unclear. In the summer of 1766, another change in the ministry in London revealed how fragile their victory had been. The new prime minister, William Pitt, had fostered cooperation between the colonies and Britain during the Seven Years' War. But Pitt fell ill, and another man, Charles Townshend, became the dominant force in the ministry. An ally of Grenville and a supporter of colonial taxation, Townshend decided to renew the attempt to obtain additional funds from Britain's American possessions (see Table 5.2).

The duties Townshend proposed in 1767 were to be levied on trade goods like paper, glass, and tea; thus they seemed to extend the existing Navigation Acts. But the Townshend duties differed from previous customs levies in two ways. First, they applied to items imported into the colonies from Britain, not to those from foreign countries. Accordingly, they violated mercantilist theory. Second, the revenues would be used to pay some colonial officials. Assemblies would no longer be able to threaten to withhold salaries in order to win those officials' cooperation. Additionally, Townshend's scheme established an American Board of Customs Commissioners and vice-admiralty courts at Boston, Philadelphia, and Charleston. Both moves angered merchants, whose profits would be threatened by more vigorous enforcement of the Navigation Acts.

John Dickinson's In 1765, months passed before the colonists protested the
Farmer's Letters Stamp Act. The passage of the Townshend Acts, however, drew a quick response. One series of essays in particular, *Letters from a Farmer in Pennsylvania*, by the prominent lawyer John Dickinson, expressed a broad consensus. Eventually, all but four colonial newspapers printed Dickinson's essays; in pamphlet form, they went through seven American editions. Dickinson contended that Parliament could regulate colonial trade but could not exercise that power to raise revenue. By distinguishing between trade regulation and unacceptable commercial taxation, Dickinson avoided the sticky issues of consent and the colonies' relationship to Parliament. But his argument created a different, and equally knotty, problem. In effect, it obligated the colonies to assess Parliament's motives in passing any law pertaining to trade before deciding whether to obey it. That was unworkable in the long run.

TABLE 5.2 | BRITISH MINISTRIES AND THEIR AMERICAN POLICIES

Head of Ministry	Major Acts
George Grenville	Sugar Act (1764) Currency Act (1764) Stamp Act (1765)
Lord Rockingham	Stamp Act repealed (1766) Declaratory Act (1766)
William Pitt/ Charles Townshend	Townshend Acts (1767)
Lord North	Townshend duties (except for the tea tax) repealed (1770) Tea Act (1773) Coercive Acts (1774) Quebec Act (1774)

The Massachusetts assembly responded to the Townshend Acts by drafting a letter to the other colonial legislatures, suggesting a joint protest petition. Not the letter itself but the ministry's reaction to it united the colonies. When Lord Hillsborough, recently named to the new post of secretary of state for America, learned of the Massachusetts circular letter, he ordered the colony's Governor Francis Bernard to insist that the assembly recall it. He also directed other governors to prevent their assemblies from discussing the letter. Hillsborough's order gave colonial assemblies an incentive to join forces to oppose this new threat to their prerogatives. In late 1768, the Massachusetts legislature met, debated, and resoundingly rejected recall by a vote of 92 to 17. Bernard immediately dissolved the assembly, and other governors followed suit when their legislatures debated the circular letter.

Rituals of Resistance

The number of votes cast against recalling the circular letter—92—assumed ritual significance for the supporters of resistance. The number 45 already had symbolic meaning because John Wilkes, a radical Londoner sympathetic to the American cause, had been jailed for publishing an essay entitled *The North Briton*, No. 45. In Boston, the silversmith Paul Revere made a punchbowl weighing 45 ounces that held 45 gills (half-cups) and was engraved with the names of opposition legislators; James Otis, John Adams, and others publicly drank 45 toasts from it. In Charleston, the city's tradesmen decorated a tree with 45 lights and set off 45 rockets. Carrying 45 candles, they adjourned to a tavern where 45 tables were set with 45 bowls of wine, 45 bowls of punch, and 92 glasses.

Such public rituals served important unifying and educational functions. Just as the pamphlets by Otis, Dulany, Dickinson, and others acquainted literate colonists with the issues raised by British actions, so public rituals taught illiterate Americans about the reasons for resistance and familiarized them with the terms of the argument. When Boston's revived Sons of Liberty invited hundreds of city residents to dine with them each August 14 to commemorate the first Stamp Act demonstration, and the Charleston Sons of Liberty held their meetings in public, crowds gathered to watch and listen. Likewise, the public singing of songs supporting the American cause helped to spread the word. The participants in such events openly expressed their commitment to the cause of resistance and encouraged others to join them.

The Sons of Liberty and other American leaders made a deliberate effort to involve ordinary folk in the campaign against the Townshend duties. Most important, they urged colonists of all ranks and both sexes to sign agreements not to purchase or consume British products. The new consumerism that previously had linked colonists economically now linked them politically as well, supplying them with a ready method of displaying their allegiance. As "A Tradesman" wrote in a Philadelphia paper in 1770, it was essential "for the Good of the Whole, to strengthen the Hands of the Patriotic Majority, by agreeing not to purchase British Goods."

Daughters of Liberty

As the primary purchasers of textiles and household goods, women played a central role in the nonconsumption movement. More than three hundred Boston matrons publicly promised not to buy or drink tea, "Sickness excepted." The women of Wilmington, North Carolina, burned their tea after walking through town in a solemn procession. Women throughout the colonies exchanged recipes for tea substitutes or drank coffee instead. The best known of the protests, the so-called Edenton Ladies Tea Party, had little to do with tea. It was a meeting of prominent North Carolina women who pledged formally to work for the public good and to support resistance to British measures.

Women also encouraged home manufacturing. In many towns, young women calling themselves Daughters of Liberty met to spin in public squares to try to persuade other women to make homespun and to encourage colonists to wear homespun clothing, thereby ending the colonies' dependence on British cloth. These symbolic displays of patriotism—publicized by newspapers and broadsides—served the same purpose as the male rituals involving the numbers 45 and 92. When young ladies from well-to-do families sat outdoors at spinning wheels all day, eating only American food, drinking local herbal tea, and listening to patriotic sermons, they served as political instructors. Many women took great satisfaction in their newfound role. When a satirist hinted that women discussed only "such trifling subjects as Dress, Scandal and Detraction" during their spinning bees, three Boston women replied angrily, "Inferior in abusive sarcasm, in personal invective, in low wit, we glory to be, but inferior in veracity, sincerity, love of virtue, of liberty and of our country, we would not willingly be to any."

Divided Opinion over Boycotts

But the colonists were by no means united in support of nonimportation and nonconsumption. If the Stamp Act protests had occasionally (as in Boston and Philadelphia) revealed a division between artisans and merchants on the one side and common laborers on the other, resistance to the Townshend Acts exposed new splits in American ranks. The most significant—which arose from a change in economic circumstances—divided urban artisans and merchants, allies in 1765.

The Stamp Act boycotts had helped to revive a depressed economy by creating a demand for local products and reducing merchants' inventories. But in 1768 and 1769, merchants were enjoying boom times and had no financial incentive to support a boycott. Consequently, merchants signed the agreements reluctantly and sometimes secretly violated them. In contrast, artisans supported nonimportation enthusiastically, recognizing that the absence of British goods would create a ready market for their own manufactures. Thus, tradesmen formed the core of the crowds that coerced both importers and their customers by picketing stores, publicizing offenders' names, and sometimes destroying property.

Such tactics were effective: colonial imports from England dropped dramatically in 1769, especially in New York, New England, and Pennsylvania. But the tactics also aroused heated opposition, dividing opinion in another way. Some Americans who supported resistance to British measures began to question the use of violence to force others to join the boycott. In addition, the threat to private property inherent in the campaign frightened wealthier and more conservative men and women. Political activism by ordinary colonists challenged the ruling elite's domination, just as its members had feared in 1765.

The Revolutionary Symbolism of Female Spinners

By the 1760s, middling and well-to-do urban colonists purchased fabric and ordered clothing from tailors and dressmakers. Only the poorer residents of rural America continued to spin wool or flax into yarn, then wove that yarn into cloth and made their own wearing apparel. Urban dwellers, accustomed for decades to following the latest English fashions, had long looked down on rustics who wore homespun—and yet the

A Boston poet in 1769 produced this broadside verse to praise spinners who had gathered in the North End of the city.

A

VERSE,

Occasioned by seeing the North-Spinning, in *BOSTON*.

BOSTON, behold the pretty Spinners here,
    And see how gay the pretty Sparks appear :
See Rich and Poor all turn the Spinning-Wheel,
All who Compassion for their Country feel,
All who do love to see Industry live,
And see Frugality in *Boston* thrive.

  Britain, behold thy Trade stole from thy Hand,
And carried on in *Boston's* distant Land :
See now thy Trade and Tradesmen, all expire,
And see them all cut short of their Desire,
Th' Desire they had that *Boston's* Trade should spoil,
That they might reap the Fruit of all our Toil ;
That they might take what we'he been slaving for,
And rule us by the Parlimental Law :
But thanks to GOD, their ill Designs are cropt,
And their Tirannical Designs are stopt.

  Now they have run their Chain's extended Length,
And exhausted all their once encourag'd Strength :
Now have their ill Designs all found an end,
Now they have made a Foe of every Friend :
Now let them starve and die the Death of those,
Who do the Interest of their King oppose.

    BOSTON: Printed and Sold   1769.

Massachusetts Historical Society/Bridgeman Art Library Ltd.

ability to spin was still seen as a quintessentially feminine occupation, with many young girls being taught that skill. One wealthy Philadelphia poet wrote that working at her wheel reminded her of "a train of Female Hands / Chearful uniting in Industrious Bands." And so when colonists joined to boycott British goods, one of the key ways in which women could publicize their support for American resistance was to bring their wheels to a public location. What message does the poem convey about the spinners' aims and impact? What was the importance of women undertaking in public a task usually performed in their own homes, if at all?

National Museum of American History, Smithsonian Institution, Behring Center

An eighteenth-century American flax wheel of the sort that would have been used in a public spinning demonstration. Wheels for spinning wool were too large to move easily.

Disclosures that leading merchants had violated the nonimportation agreement caused dissension in the ranks of the boycotters, so Americans were relieved when news arrived in April 1770 that the Townshend duties had been repealed, with the exception of the tea tax. A new prime minister, Lord North, persuaded Parliament that duties on trade within the empire were ill-advised. Although some colonial leaders argued that nonimportation should continue until the tea tax was repealed, merchants quickly resumed importing. The other Townshend Acts remained in force, but repealing the duties made the provisions for paying officials' salaries and tightening customs enforcement appear less objectionable.

CONFRONTATIONS IN BOSTON

Initially, the new ministry did nothing to antagonize the colonists. Yet on the very day Lord North proposed repeal of the Townshend duties, a confrontation between civilians and soldiers in Boston led to five Americans' deaths. The origins of the event that patriots called the Boston Massacre lay in repeated clashes between customs officers and the people of Massachusetts. The decision to base the American Board of Customs Commissioners in Boston ultimately caused the confrontation.

Mobs targeted the customs commissioners from the day they arrived in November 1767. In June 1768, their seizure of the patriot leader John Hancock's sloop *Liberty* on suspicion of smuggling caused a riot in which customs officers' property was destroyed. The riot in turn helped to convince the ministry that troops were needed to maintain order in the unruly port. The assignment of two regiments of regulars to their city confirmed Bostonians' worst fears; the redcoats constantly reminded city dwellers of the oppressive potential of British power. Guards on Boston Neck, the entrance to the city, checked all travelers and their goods. Redcoat patrols roamed the city day and night, questioning and sometimes harassing passersby. Military parades on Boston Common were accompanied by martial music and often the public whipping of deserters and other violators of army rules. Parents began to fear for the safety of their daughters, who were subjected to soldiers' coarse sexual insults. But the greatest potential for violence lay in the uneasy relationship between the soldiers and Boston laborers. Many redcoats sought employment in their off-duty hours, competing for unskilled jobs with the city's workingmen. Members of the two groups brawled repeatedly in taverns and on the streets.

Boston Massacre   Early on the evening of March 5, 1770, a crowd of laborers began throwing hard-packed snowballs at soldiers guarding the Customs House. Goaded beyond endurance, the sentries acted against express orders and fired on the crowd, killing four and wounding eight, one of whom died a few days later. Reportedly, the first to die was Crispus Attucks, a sailor of mixed Nipmuck and African origins. Resistance leaders idealized Attucks and the other dead rioters as martyrs for the cause of liberty, holding a solemn funeral and later commemorating March 5 annually with patriotic orations. Paul Revere's engraving of the massacre was part of the propaganda campaign.

Leading patriots wanted to ensure that the soldiers did not become martyrs as well. Despite the political benefits the patriots derived from the massacre, they probably did not approve of the crowd action that provoked it. Ever since the destruction of Hutchinson's house in August 1765, men allied with the Sons of Liberty had supported orderly demonstrations and expressed distaste at such uncontrolled riots as the one that provoked the Boston Massacre. Thus, when the soldiers were tried for the killings in November, John Adams and Josiah Quincy Jr., both unwavering patriots, acted as their defense attorneys. Almost all the accused were acquitted, and the two men convicted were released after being branded on the thumb. Undoubtedly, the favorable outcome of the trials persuaded London officials not to retaliate against the city.

A British Plot?   For more than two years after the Boston Massacre and the repeal of the Townshend duties, a superficial calm descended on the colonies. In June 1772, Rhode Islanders, angry with overzealous customs enforcement by the British naval schooner *Gaspée*, attacked and burned it as it lay aground at low tide in Narragansett Bay near Providence, but because a subsequent investigation failed to identify the perpetrators, no adverse consequences followed for the colonists. The most outspoken newspapers, such as the *Boston Gazette*, the *Pennsylvania Journal*, and the *South Carolina Gazette*, published essays drawing on Real Whig ideology and accusing Great Britain of deliberately scheming to oppress the colonies. After the Stamp Act's repeal, the protest leaders had praised Parliament; following repeal of the Townshend duties, they warned of impending tyranny. What had seemed to be an isolated mistake, a single ill-chosen stamp tax, now appeared to be part of a plot against American liberties. Essayists pointed to Parliament's persecution of the British radical John Wilkes, the stationing of troops in Boston, and the growing number of vice-admiralty courts as evidence of plans to enslave the colonists. Indeed, patriot writers played repeatedly on the word *enslavement*. Most free colonists had direct knowledge of slavery (either as slaveholders themselves or as neighbors of slaveowners), and the threat of enslavement by Britain must have hit them with peculiar force.

Still, no one yet advocated independence from the mother country. Although some colonists were becoming increasingly convinced that they should seek freedom from parliamentary authority, they continued to acknowledge their British identity and allegiance to George III. They began, therefore, to envision a system that would enable them to be ruled by their own elected legislatures while remaining subordinate to the king. But any such scheme violated Britons' conception of the nature of their government, which posited that Parliament wielded sole, undivided sovereignty over the empire. Furthermore, in the British mind, Parliament encompassed the king as well as lords and commons, so separating the monarch from the legislature was impossible.

Then, in the fall of 1772, the North ministry began to implement the Townshend Act that provided for governors and judges to be paid from customs revenues. In early November, voters at a Boston town meeting established a Committee of Correspondence to publicize the decision by exchanging letters with other Massachusetts towns. Heading the committee was Samuel Adams, who had proposed its formation.

Samuel Adams and Committees of Correspondence Fifty-one in 1772, Samuel Adams was about a decade older than the other leaders of American resistance, including his distant cousin John. He had been a Boston tax collector, a member and clerk of the Massachusetts assembly, an ally of the Loyal Nine, and one of the Sons of Liberty. Unswerving in his devotion to the American cause, Adams drew a sharp contrast between a corrupt, vice-ridden Britain and the colonies, peopled by simple, liberty-loving folk. An experienced political organizer, Adams continually stressed the necessity of prudent collective action in speeches in the Boston town meeting. His Committee of Correspondence thus undertook the task of creating an informed consensus among the residents of Massachusetts.

Such committees, which were eventually established throughout the colonies, represented the next logical step in the organization of American resistance. Until 1772, the protest movement was confined largely to the seacoast and primarily to major cities and towns. Adams realized the time had come to widen the movement's geographic scope, to attempt to involve more colonists in the struggle. Accordingly, the Boston town meeting directed the Committee of Correspondence "to state the Rights of the Colonists and of this Province in particular"; to list "the Infringements and Violations thereof that have been, or from time to time may be made"; and to send copies to the other towns in the province. In return, Boston requested "a free communication of their Sentiments on this Subject."

The statement of colonial rights prepared by the Bostonians declared that Americans had absolute rights to life, liberty, and property. The idea that "a British house of commons, should have a right, at pleasure, to give and grant the property of the colonists" was "irreconcileable" with "the first principles of natural law and Justice … and of the British Constitution in particular." The list of grievances complained of taxation without representation, the presence of unnecessary troops and customs officers on American soil, the use of imperial revenues to pay colonial officials, the expanded jurisdiction of vice-admiralty courts, and even the nature of the instructions given to American governors by their superiors in London.

The entire document, which was printed as a pamphlet for distribution to the towns, exhibited none of the hesitation that had characterized colonial claims against Parliament in the 1760s. No longer were resistance leaders—at least in Boston—preoccupied with defining the precise limits of parliamentary authority. No longer did they mention the necessity of obedience to Parliament. They were committed to a course that placed American rights first, loyalty to Great Britain a distant second.

The response of the Massachusetts towns to the committee's pamphlet must have caused Samuel Adams to rejoice. Some towns disagreed with Boston's assessment of the state of affairs, but most aligned themselves with the city. From Braintree came the assertion that "all civil officers are or ought to be Servants to the people and dependent upon them for their official Support, and every instance to the Contrary from the Governor downwards tends to crush and destroy civil liberty." The town of Holden declared that "the People of New England have never given the People of Britain any Right of Jurisdiction over us." The citizens of Petersham commented that resistance to tyranny was "the first and highest social Duty of this people." And Pownallborough warned, "Allegiance is a relative Term and like Kingdoms and commonwealths is local and has its bounds." Beliefs like these made the next crisis in Anglo-American affairs the last.

Tea and Turmoil

The tea tax was the only Townshend duty still in effect by 1773. In the years after 1770, some Americans continued to boycott English tea, while others resumed drinking it either openly or in secret. Tea figured prominently in both the colonists' diet and their social lives, so observing the boycott required them not only to forgo a favorite beverage but also to alter habitual forms of socializing. Tea thus retained an explosively symbolic character even though the boycott began to disintegrate after 1770.

Reactions to the Tea Act   In May 1773, Parliament passed an act designed to save the East India Company from bankruptcy. The company, which held a monopoly on British trade with the East Indies, was critically important to the British economy and to the financial well-being of many prominent British politicians who had invested in its stock. According to the Tea Act, legal tea would henceforth be sold in America only by the East India Company's designated agents, which would enable the company to avoid intermediaries in both Britain and the colonies, and to price its tea competitively with that offered by smugglers. The net result would be cheaper tea for American consumers. Resistance leaders, however, interpreted the new measure as a pernicious device to make them admit Parliament's right to tax them, for the less expensive tea would still be taxed under the Townshend law. Others saw the Tea Act as the first step in the establishment of an East India Company monopoly on all colonial trade. Residents of the four cities designated to receive the first shipments of tea accordingly prepared to respond to what they perceived as a new threat to their freedom.

In New York City, tea ships never arrived. In Philadelphia, Pennsylvania's governor persuaded the captain to sail back to Britain. In Charleston, the tea was unloaded and stored; some was destroyed, the rest sold in 1776 by the new state government. The only confrontation occurred in Boston, where both sides—the town meeting, including participants from nearby towns, and Governor Thomas Hutchinson, two of whose sons were tea agents—rejected compromise.

The first of three tea ships, the *Dartmouth*, entered Boston harbor on November 28. The customs laws required cargo to be landed and the appropriate duty paid by its owners within twenty days of a ship's arrival; otherwise, the cargo would be seized by customs officers and sold at auction. After a series of mass meetings, Bostonians voted to post guards on the wharf to prevent the tea from being unloaded. Hutchinson refused to permit the vessels to leave the harbor.

On December 16, one day before the cargo would have been confiscated, more than five thousand people (nearly a third of the city's population) crowded into Old South Church. The meeting, chaired by Samuel Adams, made a final attempt to convince Hutchinson to send the tea back to England. But the governor remained adamant. In the early evening Adams reportedly announced "that he could think of nothing further to be done—that they had now done all they could for the

Salvation of their Country." Cries then rang out from the back of the crowd: "Boston harbor a tea-pot tonight! The Mohawks are come!" Small groups pushed their way out of the meeting. Within a few minutes, about sixty men crudely disguised as Indians assembled at the wharf, boarded the three ships, and dumped the cargo into the harbor. By 9 P.M., their work was done: 342 chests of tea worth approximately £10,000 floated in splinters on the water.

Among the "Indians" were many representatives of Boston's artisans, including the silversmith Paul Revere. Five masons, eleven carpenters and builders, three leatherworkers, a blacksmith, two barbers, a coachmaker, a shoemaker, and twelve apprentices have been identified as participants. That their ranks also included four farmers from outside Boston, ten merchants, two doctors, a teacher, and a bookseller illustrated the widespread support for the resistance movement. The next day John Adams exulted in his diary that the protest was "so bold, so daring, so firm, intrepid and inflexible" that "I can't but consider it as an Epocha in history."

Coercive and Quebec Acts   The North administration reacted with considerably less enthusiasm when it learned of the events in Boston. In March 1774, Parliament adopted the first of four laws that became known as the Coercive, or Intolerable, Acts. It ordered the port of Boston closed until the tea was paid for, prohibiting all but coastal trade in food and firewood. Later in the spring, Parliament passed three other punitive measures. The Massachusetts Government Act altered the province's charter, substituting an appointed council for the elected one, increasing the governor's powers, and forbidding most town meetings. The Justice Act provided that a person accused of committing murder in the course of suppressing a riot or enforcing the laws could be tried outside the colony where the incident had occurred. Finally, the Quartering Act allowed military officers to commandeer privately owned buildings to house their troops. Thus, the Coercive Acts punished not only Boston but also Massachusetts as a whole, alerting other colonies to the possibility that their residents, too, could be subject to retaliation if they opposed British authority.

After passing the last of the Coercive Acts, Parliament turned its attention to much-needed reforms in the government of Quebec. The Quebec Act thereby became linked with the Coercive Acts in the minds of the patriots. Intended to ease strains that had arisen since the British conquest of the formerly French colony, the Quebec Act granted greater religious freedom to Catholics—alarming Protestant colonists, who equated Roman Catholicism with religious and political despotism. It also reinstated French civil law, which had been replaced by British procedures in 1763, and it established an appointed council (rather than an elected legislature) as the governing body of the colony. Finally, in an attempt to provide northern Indians with some protection against Anglo-American settlement, the act annexed to Quebec the area west of the Appalachians, east of the Mississippi River, and north of the Ohio River. That region, still with few European inhabitants, was thus removed from the jurisdiction of the seacoast colonies. The wealthy colonists who hoped to develop the Ohio country to attract additional settlers now faced the prospect of dealing with officials in Quebec.

Members of Parliament who voted for the punitive legislation believed at long last they had solved the problem posed by the troublesome Americans. But resistance leaders showed little inclination to bow to Parliament's authority. In their eyes, the Coercive Acts and the Quebec Act proved what they had feared since 1768: that Britain had embarked on a deliberate plan to oppress them. If the port of Boston could be closed, why not the ports of Philadelphia or New York? If the royal charter of Massachusetts could be changed, why not the charter of South Carolina? If certain people could be transferred to distant locations for trial, why not any violator of any law? If troops could be forcibly quartered in private houses, did that not portend the occupation of all America? If the Catholic Church could receive favored status in Quebec, why not everywhere? It seemed as though the full dimensions of the plot against American rights and liberties had at last been revealed.

The Boston Committee of Correspondence urged all colonies to join an immediate boycott of British goods. But other provinces hesitated to take such a drastic step. Rhode Island, Virginia, and Pennsylvania each suggested another intercolonial congress be convened to consider an appropriate response, and in mid-June 1774 Massachusetts acquiesced. Few people wanted to take hasty action; even the most ardent patriots remained loyal Britons and hoped for reconciliation. Despite their objections to British policy, they continued to see themselves as part of the empire. Americans were approaching the brink of confrontation, but they had not committed themselves to an irrevocable break. So the colonies agreed to send delegates to Philadelphia in September to attend a Continental Congress.

SUMMARY

Just twenty years earlier, at the outbreak of the Seven Years' War in the wilderness of western Pennsylvania, no one could have predicted the future would bring such swift and dramatic change to Britain's mainland colonies. Yet that conflict simultaneously removed France from North America and created a huge debt that Britain had to find means to pay, developments with major implications for the imperial relationship.

In the years after the war ended in 1763, momentous changes occurred in the ways colonists thought about themselves and their allegiances. The number of colonists who defined themselves as political actors increased substantially. Once linked unquestioningly to Great Britain, they began to develop a sense of their own identity as Americans, including a recognition of the cultural and social gulf that separated them from Britons. They started to realize that their concept of the political process differed from that held by people in the mother country. Most important, they held a different definition of what constituted representation and appropriate consent to government actions. They also came to understand that their economic interests did not necessarily coincide with those of Great Britain. Colonial political leaders reached such conclusions only after a long train of events, some of them violent, had altered their understanding of their relationship with the mother country. Parliamentary acts such as the Stamp Act and the Townshend Acts elicited colonial responses—both ideological and practical—that produced further responses from Britain. Tensions escalated until they climaxed when Bostonians destroyed the East India Company's tea.

In the late summer of 1774, Americans were committed to resistance but not to independence. Even so, they had started to sever the bonds of empire. During the next decade, they would forge the bonds of a new American nationality to replace those rejected Anglo-American ties.

6

A REVOLUTION, INDEED 1774–1783

GOVERNMENT BY CONGRESS AND COMMITTEE

When the fifty-five delegates to the First Continental Congress convened in Philadelphia in September 1774, they knew any measures they adopted were likely to enjoy widespread support. That summer, well-publicized open meetings held throughout the colonies had endorsed the idea of another nonimportation pact. Participants in many such meetings promised (like some North Carolina men) to "strictly adhere to, and abide by, such Regulations and Restrictions as the Members of the said General Congress shall agree to." Most of the congressional delegates were selected by extralegal provincial conventions whose members were chosen at local gatherings because governors had forbidden regular assemblies to conduct formal elections. Thus the very act of designating delegates to attend the Congress involved Americans in open defiance of British authority.

First Continental Congress   The colonies' leading political figures—most of them lawyers, merchants, and planters representing every colony but Georgia—attended the Philadelphia Congress. The Massachusetts delegation included Samuel Adams, the experienced organizer of Boston resistance, and his younger cousin John, an ambitious lawyer. Among others, New York sent John Jay, a talented young attorney. From Pennsylvania came the conservative Joseph Galloway and his long-time rival, John Dickinson. Virginia elected Richard Henry Lee and Patrick Henry, both noted for their patriotic zeal, as well as George Washington. Most of these men had never met, but in the weeks, months, and years that followed they became the chief architects of the new nation.

CHRONOLOGY

1774	First Continental Congress meets in Philadelphia, adopts Declaration of Rights and Grievances
	Continental Association implements economic boycott of Britain; committees of observation established to oversee boycott
1774–75	Provincial conventions replace collapsing colonial governments
1775	Battles of Lexington and Concord; first shots of war fired
	Second Continental Congress begins
	Washington named commander-in-chief
	Dunmore's proclamation offers freedom to patriots' slaves who join British forces
1776	Paine publishes *Common Sense,* advocating independence
	British evacuate Boston
	Declaration of Independence adopted
	New York City falls to British
1777	British take Philadelphia
	Burgoyne surrenders at Saratoga
1778	French alliance brings vital assistance to America
	British evacuate Philadelphia
1779	Sullivan expedition destroys Iroquois villages
1780	British take Charleston
1781	Cornwallis surrenders at Yorktown
1782	Peace negotiations begin
1783	Treaty of Paris signed, granting independence to the United States

The congressmen faced three tasks when they convened at Carpenters' Hall on September 5. The first two were explicit: defining American grievances and developing a plan for resistance. The third—articulating their constitutional relationship with Great Britain—was less clear-cut and proved troublesome. The most radical congressmen, like Lee of Virginia, argued that colonists owed allegiance only to George III and that Parliament had no legitimate authority over the colonies. The conservatives—Joseph Galloway and his allies—proposed a formal plan of union that would have required Parliament and a new American legislature to consent jointly to all laws pertaining to the colonies. After heated debate, delegates narrowly rejected Galloway's proposal, but they were not prepared to embrace the radicals' position either.

Finally, they accepted wording proposed by John Adams. The crucial clauses in the Congress's Declaration of Rights and Grievances declared that Americans would obey Parliament, but only voluntarily, and that they would resist all taxes in disguise, like the Townshend duties. Remarkably, such a position—which only a few years before would have been regarded as radical—represented a compromise in the fall of 1774. The Americans had come a long way since their first hesitant protests against the Sugar Act ten years earlier.

Continental
Association

With the constitutional issue resolved, the delegates readily agreed on the laws they wanted repealed (notably the Coercive Acts) and decided to implement an economic boycott while petitioning the king for relief. They adopted the Continental Association, which called for nonimportation of British goods (effective December 1, 1774), nonconsumption of British products (effective March 1, 1775), and nonexportation of American goods to Britain and the British West Indies (effective September 10, 1775).

The provisions of the Association—far more comprehensive than any previous economic measure adopted by the colonies—were carefully designed to appeal to different groups and regions. For example, the inclusive language of the nonimportation agreement banned commerce in slaves as well as manufactures, which accorded with a long-standing desire of the Virginia gentry to halt, or at least to slow, the arrival of enslaved Africans on their shores. (Leading Virginians believed that continuing slave importations had discouraged the immigration to their colony of free Europeans with useful skills.) Delaying nonconsumption until three months after implementing nonimportation allowed northern urban merchants time to sell items they had acquired legally before December 1. And both the novel tactic of nonexportation and its postponement for nearly a year served other interests. In 1773, many Virginians had vowed to stop exporting tobacco, to raise prices in a then-glutted market. So they enthusiastically welcomed an Association that banned exportation while also permitting them to profit from higher prices for their 1774 crop, which needed to be dried and cured before shipment. Postponing the nonexportation agreement also benefited the northern exporters of wood and foodstuffs to the Caribbean, giving them a final season of sales before the embargo began.

Committees of
Observation

To enforce the Continental Association, Congress recommended the election of committees of observation and inspection in every American locality. By specifying that committee members be chosen by all men qualified to vote for members of the lower houses of assembly, Congress guaranteed the committees a broad popular base. The seven to eight thousand committeemen—some experienced officeholders, some new to politics—became the local leaders of American resistance.

Such committees were officially charged only with overseeing implementation of the boycott, but during the next six months they became de facto governments. They examined merchants' records, publicizing those who continued to import British goods. They promoted home manufactures, encouraging Americans to adopt simple modes of dress and behavior to symbolize their commitment to liberty and virtuous conduct. Because expensive leisure-time activities were believed to reflect vice and corruption, Congress (as Janet Schaw learned) urged Americans to forgo dancing, gambling, horseracing, cardplaying, cockfighting, and other forms of "extravagance and dissipation." Some committees extracted apologies from people caught gambling, drinking to excess, or racing. Thus, private activities acquired public significance.

In 1775, a British cartoonist demonstrated his contempt for the pronouncements of the Continental Congress by setting his satire in a privy, or "necessary house," and showing a politician who has used a torn congressional resolution as toilet paper. The person at right is poring over a political pamphlet while portraits of John Wilkes and a man who has been tarred and feathered decorate the walls.

Library of Congress

The committees gradually extended their authority over many aspects of American life. They attempted to identify opponents of American resistance, developing elaborate spy networks, circulating copies of the Continental Association for signatures, and investigating reports of questionable remarks and activities. Suspected dissenters were urged to support the colonial cause publicly; if they refused, the committees had them watched, restricted their movements, or tried to force them into exile. People engaging in casual political exchanges with friends one day could find themselves charged with "treasonable conversation" the next. One Massachusetts man, for example, was called before his local committee for maligning the Congress as "a Pack or Parcell of Fools" that was "as tyrannical as Lord North and ought to be opposed & resisted." When he refused to recant, the committee put him under surveillance.

Provincial Conventions   While the committees of observation were expanding their power during the winter and early spring of 1775, the regular colonial governments were collapsing. Only a few legislatures continued to meet without encountering challenges to their authority. In most colonies, popularly elected provincial conventions took over the task of running the government, sometimes entirely replacing the legislatures and at other times holding concurrent sessions. In late 1774 and early 1775, these conventions approved the Continental Association, elected delegates to the Second Continental Congress (scheduled for May), organized militia units, and gathered arms and ammunition. Unable to stem the tide of resistance, the British-appointed governors and councils watched helplessly as their authority crumbled.

Royal officials suffered humiliation after humiliation. Courts were prevented from meeting, taxes were paid to the conventions' agents rather than to provincial tax collectors, sheriffs' powers were challenged, and militiamen would muster only when committees ordered. In short, during the six months preceding the battles at Lexington and Concord, independence was being won at the local level, but without formal acknowledgment and for the most part without bloodshed. Not many Americans fully realized what was happening. The vast majority still proclaimed their loyalty to Great Britain, denying that they sought to leave the empire.

CONTEST IN THE BACKCOUNTRY

While the committees of observation were consolidating their authority in the East, some colonists were heading west. Ignoring the Proclamation of 1763, pronouncements by colonial governors, and the threat of Indian attacks, land-hungry folk—many of them recent immigrants from Ireland and soldiers who demobilized in North America after the Seven Years War—swarmed onto lands along the Ohio River and its tributaries after the mid-1760s. Sometimes, they purchased property from opportunists with grants of dubious origin; often, they simply surveyed and claimed land, squatting on it in hopes that their titles would eventually be honored. Britain's 1771 decision to abandon (and raze) Fort Pitt removed the final restraints on settlement in the region for the withdrawal rendered the Proclamation of 1763 unenforceable. By late 1775, thousands of new homesteads dotted the landscape of the backcountry from western Pennsylvania south through Virginia and eastern Kentucky into western North Carolina.

Distrust and Warfare   Few of the backcountry folk viewed the region's native peoples positively. (Rare exceptions were the Moravian missionaries who settled with their Indian converts in three, small frontier communities in the upper Ohio valley.) The frontier dwellers had little interest in the small-scale trade that had once helped to sustain an uneasy peace in the region; they wanted only land on which to grow crops and pasture their livestock.

In 1774 Virginia, headed by a new governor, Lord Dunmore, moved vigorously to assert its title to the rapidly developing backcountry. During the spring and early summer, tensions mounted as Virginians surveyed land in Kentucky on the south side of the Ohio River—territory claimed by the Shawnees, who rejected the Fort Stanwix treaty of 1768. "Lord Dunmore's war" consisted of one large-scale confrontation between Virginia militia and some Shawnee warriors. Neither side won a clear-cut victory, but in the immediate aftermath thousands of settlers—including Daniel Boone and his associates—flooded across the mountains.

When war began just as large numbers of people were migrating into Kentucky, the loyalties of Indians and settlers in the backcountry remained, like Boone's, fluid and uncertain. They were hostile to each other, but which side should either take in the imperial struggle? The answer might well depend on which could better serve their interests. Understanding that, the Continental Congress moved to reoccupy the site of Fort Pitt and to establish other garrisons in the Ohio country. Relying on such protection, as many as twenty thousand settlers poured into Kentucky and western Pennsylvania by 1780. Yet frontier affiliations were not clear: the growing town of Pittsburgh, for example, harbored many active loyalists.

The native peoples' grievances against the European American newcomers predisposed many toward an alliance with Great Britain. Yet some chiefs urged caution: after all, the British abandonment of Fort Pitt (and them) suggested that Britain lacked the will and ability to protect them in the future. Furthermore, Britain hesitated to make full, immediate use of its potential native allies. Officials on the scene understood that neither the Indians' style of fighting nor their war aims necessarily coincided with British goals and methods. Accordingly, they at first sought from Indians only a promise of neutrality.

Recognizing their poor standing with native peoples, patriots also sought Indians' neutrality. In 1775, the Second Continental Congress sent a general message to Indian communities, describing the war as "a family quarrel between us and Old England" and requesting that they "not join on either side" because "you Indians are not concerned in it." The Iroquois responded with a pledge of neutrality. But a group of Cherokees led by Chief Dragging Canoe decided to take advantage of the "family quarrel" to regain some land. In summer 1776, they attacked settlements in western Virginia and the Carolinas. After a militia campaign destroyed many Cherokee towns, along with crops and supplies, Dragging Canoe and his die-hard followers fled to the West, establishing new villages. Other Cherokees agreed to a treaty that ceded still more of their land.

Frontier Hostilities   Bands of Shawnees and Cherokees continued to attack settlements in the backcountry throughout the war, but dissent in their own ranks crippled their efforts. The British victory over France in 1763 had destroyed the Indian nations' most effective means of maintaining their independence: playing European powers off against one another. Successful strategies were difficult to envision under these new circumstances, and Indian leaders no longer concurred on a unified course of action. Communities split asunder as older and younger men, or civil and war leaders, disagreed vehemently over what policy to adopt. Only a few communities (among them the Stockbridge Indians of New England and the Oneidas in New York) unwaveringly supported the American revolt; most other native villages either tried to remain neutral or sporadically aligned themselves with the British. And the settlers fought back: in 1778 and early 1779, a frontier militia force under George Rogers Clark captured British posts in modern Illinois (Kaskaskia) and Indiana (Vincennes). Still, the revolutionaries could never mount an effective attack against the redcoats' major stronghold at Detroit.

Warfare between settlers and Indians persisted in the backcountry long after fighting between patriot and redcoat armies had ceased. Indeed, the Revolutionary War itself constituted a brief chapter in the ongoing struggle for control of the region west of the Appalachians, which began in 1763 and continued into the next century.

CHOOSING SIDES

In 1765, protests against the Stamp Act had won the support of most colonists in the Caribbean and Nova Scotia as well as in the future United States. Demonstrations occurred in Halifax, Nova Scotia, St. Christopher, and Nevis as well as in Boston, New York, Charleston, and other mainland towns. When the Stamp Act went into effect, though, Caribbean islanders loyally paid the stamp duties until repeal. In Nova Scotia and the Caribbean, many colonists came to question both the aims and the tactics of the resistance movement, in large part because of their heavy military and economic dependence on Great Britain.

Nova Scotia and the Caribbean   Despite the overwhelming British victory in the Seven Years War, the northern mainland and the southern island colonies believed themselves vulnerable to French counterattack and eagerly sought regular troops and naval vessels stationed within their borders. Additionally, sugar planters—on some islands outnumbered by their bondspeople twenty-five to one—feared the potential for slave revolts in the absence of British troops. Neither region had a large population of European descent, nor were local political structures very strong. Fewer people lived in Halifax in 1775 than in the late 1750s, and the sugar islands had only a few resident planters to provide leadership because successful men headed to England to buy great manors, leaving supervision of their property to hired managers.

Both Nova Scotians and West Indians had major economic reasons for ultimately choosing to support the mother country. In the mid-1770s, the northerners finally broke into the Caribbean market with their cargoes of dried, salted fish. They reduced New England's domination of the northern coastal trade, and once the shooting started they benefited greatly from Britain's retaliatory measures against the rebels' commerce. British sugar producers relied for their profits primarily on their monopoly of trade within the empire, for more efficient French planters were able to sell their sugar for one-third less. Further, the British planters' effective lobbyists in London won the islands' exclusion from some provisions of the Townshend Acts. Accordingly, sugar producers logically concluded that their interests could be adequately protected within the empire. In short, neither islanders nor Nova Scotians had reason to believe they would be better off independent.

Patriots   Many residents of the thirteen colonies—especially members of the groups that dominated colonial society numerically or politically—reached different conclusions, choosing to support resistance, then independence. Active revolutionaries accounted for about two-fifths of the European American population. Among them were small and middling farmers, members of dominant Protestant sects (both Old and New Lights), Chesapeake gentry, merchants handling American commodities, city artisans, elected officeholders, and people of English descent. Wives usually, but not always, agreed with their husbands about politics. Although such patriots supported the Revolution, they pursued divergent goals within the broader coalition, as they had in the 1760s. Some sought limited political reform; others, extensive political change; and still others, social and economic reforms. (The ways their concerns interacted are discussed in Chapter 7.)

Some colonists, though, could not endorse independence. Like their more radical counterparts, most objected to parliamentary policies, but they preferred the remedy of imperial constitutional reform. The events of the crucial year between the passage of the Coercive Acts and the outbreak of fighting in Massachusetts crystallized their thinking. Their objections to violent protest, their desire to uphold legally constituted government, and their fears of anarchy combined to make them sensitive to the dangers of resistance.

Loyalists   About one-fifth of the European American population remained loyal to Great Britain, firmly rejecting independence. Most loyalists had long opposed the men who became patriot leaders, though for varying reasons. British-appointed government officials; Anglican clergy everywhere and lay Anglicans in the North, where their denomination was in the minority; tenant farmers, particularly those whose landlords sided with the patriots; members of persecuted religious sects; many of the backcountry southerners who had rebelled against eastern rule in the late 1760s and early 1770s; and non-English ethnic minorities, especially Scots—all these groups feared the power wielded by those who controlled the colonial assemblies and who had shown little concern for their welfare in the past. Joined by merchants whose trade depended on imperial connections and by former officers and enlisted men from the British army who had settled in America after 1763, they formed a loyalist core that remained true to a self-conception that revolutionaries proved willing to abandon.

During the war, loyalists congregated in cities held by the British army. When those posts were evacuated at war's end, loyalists scattered to different parts of the British Empire—Britain, the Bahamas, and especially Canada. In the provinces of Nova Scotia, New Brunswick, and Ontario they re-created their lives as colonists, laying the foundations of British Canada. All told, perhaps as many as seventy thousand Americans preferred exile to life in a nation independent of British rule.

Neutrals

Between the patriots and the loyalists, there remained in the middle perhaps two-fifths of the European American population. Some who tried to avoid taking sides were sincere pacifists, such as Quakers. Others opportunistically shifted their allegiance to whatever side currently happened to be winning. Still others simply wanted to be left alone; they cared little about politics and usually obeyed whoever was in power. Such colonists also resisted British and Americans alike when the demands on them seemed too heavy—when taxes became too high or when calls for militia service came too often. Their attitude might best be summed up as "a plague on both your houses." Such people made up an especially large proportion of the population in the backcountry (including Boone's Kentucky), where Scots-Irish settlers had little love for either the patriot gentry or the English authorities.

To patriots, apathy or neutrality was as heinous as loyalism: those who were not for them were surely against them. By the winter of 1775–1776, the Second Continental Congress was recommending that all "disaffected" persons be disarmed and arrested. State legislatures passed laws prescribing severe penalties for suspected loyalists or neutrals. Many began to require all voters (or, in some cases, all free adult men) to take oaths of allegiance; the penalty for refusal was usually banishment to England or extra taxes. After 1777, many states confiscated the property of banished persons, using the proceeds for the war effort.

The patriots' policies helped to ensure that their scattered and persecuted opponents could not band together to threaten the revolutionary cause. But loyalists and neutrals were not the patriots' only worry, for revolutionaries could not assume that enslaved people would support them.

African Americans

In New England, with few resident bondspeople, revolutionary fervor was widespread, and free African Americans enlisted in local patriot militias. The middle colonies, where bondspeople constituted a small but substantial proportion of the population, were more divided but still largely revolutionary. In Virginia and Maryland, where free people constituted a slender majority, the potential for slave revolts raised occasional but not disabling fears. By contrast, South Carolina and Georgia, where slaves composed more than half of the population, were noticeably less enthusiastic about resistance to Britain. Georgia sent no delegates to the First Continental Congress and reminded its representatives at the second one to consider its circumstances, "with our blacks and tories [loyalists] within us," when voting on the question of independence. On the mainland as well as in the Caribbean islands, therefore, colonists feared the potential enemy in their midst.

Bondspeople themselves faced a dilemma during the Revolution. Above all, their goal was *personal* independence. But how best could they escape from slavery? Should they fight with or against their masters? African Americans made different decisions, but to most slaves, supporting the British appeared more promising. In late 1774 and early 1775, groups of bondsmen began to offer to assist the British army in return for freedom. The most serious incident occurred in 1775 in Charleston, where Thomas Jeremiah, a free black harbor pilot, was brutally executed after convicted of attempting to foment a slave revolt.

The slaveowners' worst fears were realized in November 1775, when Virginia's royal governor, Lord Dunmore, offered to free any slaves and indentured servants who would leave their patriot masters to join the British forces. Dunmore hoped to use African Americans in his fight against the revolutionaries and to disrupt the economy by depriving planters of their labor force. About one thousand African Americans initially rallied to the British standard; although many of them perished in a smallpox epidemic, three hundred survived to reach occupied New York City under British protection. Because other commanders later renewed Dunmore's proclamation, tens of thousands of runaways eventually joined the British, and at the end of the war at least nine thousand left with the redcoats.

Although bondspeople did not pose a serious threat to the revolutionary cause in its early years, patriots turned rumors of slave uprisings to their own advantage. In South Carolina, resistance leaders argued that unity under the Continental Association would protect masters from their slaves at a time when royal government was unable to muster adequate defense forces. Undoubtedly, many wavering Carolinians were drawn into the revolutionary camp by fear that an overt division among the colony's free people would encourage rebellion by the bondspeople.

Patriots could never completely ignore the threats posed by loyalists, neutrals, slaves, and Indians as well, but only rarely did fear of these groups seriously hamper the revolutionary movement. Occasionally, backcountry militiamen refused to turn out for duty on the seacoast because they feared Indians would attack at home in their absence. Sometimes southern troops refused to serve in the North because they (and their political leaders) were unwilling to leave their regions unprotected against a slave insurrection. But the practical impossibility of a large-scale slave revolt, coupled with dissension in Indian communities and the patriots' successful campaign to disarm and neutralize loyalists, ensured that the revolutionaries would by and large remain firmly in control of the countryside as they fought for independence.

New Nations

The American Revolution not only created the United States but led directly to the formation of three other nations: English-dominated Canada, Sierra Leone, and Australia.

In modern Canada before the Revolution, only Nova Scotia had a sizable number of English-speaking settlers. Those people, largely New Englanders, had been recruited after 1758 to repopulate the region forcibly taken from the exiled Acadians. During and after the Revolution, many loyalist families, especially those from the northern and middle colonies, moved to the region that is now Canada, which remained under British rule. The provinces of New Brunswick and Upper Canada (later Ontario) were established to accommodate them, and some exiles settled in Quebec as well. In just a few years, the loyalist refugees transformed the sparsely populated former French colony, laying the foundation of the modern bilingual (but majority English-speaking) Canadian nation.

Sierra Leone, too, was founded by colonial exiles—African Americans who had fled to the British army during the war, many of whom ended up in London. Seeing the refugees' poverty, a group of charitable merchants—calling themselves the Committee for Relief of the Black Poor —developed a plan to resettle the African Americans elsewhere. After the refugees refused to be sent to the Bahamas, fearing that in the Caribbean they would be reenslaved, they concurred in a scheme to return them to the land of their ancestors. In early 1787, vessels carrying about four hundred settlers reached Sierra Leone in

West Africa, where representatives of the Black Poor Committee acquired land from local rulers. The first years of the new colony were difficult, and many of the newcomers died of disease and deprivation. But in 1792 they were joined by several thousand other loyalist African Americans who had originally moved to Nova Scotia. The influx ensured the colony's survival; it remained a part of the British Empire until achieving its independence in 1961.

While the Sierra Leone migrants were preparing to sail from London in late 1786, the first prison ships were simultaneously being readied for Australia. At the Paris peace negotiations in 1782, American diplomats adamantly rejected British suggestions that the United States continue to serve as a dumping ground for convicts, as had been true throughout the eighteenth century. Britain thus needed another destination for the convicts sentenced in its courts to transportation for crimes such as theft, assault, and manslaughter. It decided to send them halfway around the world, to the continent Captain James Cook had explored and claimed in 1770. Britain continued to dispatch convicts to some parts of Australia until 1868, but long before then voluntary migrants had also begun to arrive. The modern nation was created from a federation of separate colonial governments on January 1, 1901.

Thus, the founding event in the history of the United States links the nation to the formation of its northern neighbor and to new nations in West Africa and the Asian Pacific.

WAR AND INDEPENDENCE

On January 27, 1775, Lord Dartmouth, secretary of state for America, addressed a fateful letter to General Thomas Gage in Boston, urging him to take a decisive step. Opposition could not be "very formidable," Dartmouth wrote, and even if it were, "it will surely be better that the Conflict should be brought on, upon such ground, than in a riper state of Rebellion."

Battles of Lexington and Concord

After Gage received Dartmouth's letter on April 14, he sent an expedition to confiscate colonial military supplies stockpiled at Concord. Bostonians dispatched two messengers, William Dawes and Paul Revere (later joined by Dr. Samuel Prescott), to rouse the countryside. So, when the British vanguard of several hundred men approached Lexington at dawn on April 19, they found a ragtag group of seventy militiamen—about half of the adult male population of the town—mustered on the common. Realizing they could not halt the redcoats' advance, the Americans' commander ordered his men to withdraw. But as they began to disperse, a shot rang out; the British soldiers then fired several volleys. When they stopped, eight Americans lay dead, and another ten had been wounded. The British moved on to Concord, 5 miles away.

There the contingents of militia were larger, Concord residents having been joined by groups of men from nearby towns. An exchange of gunfire at the North Bridge spilled the first British blood of the Revolution: three men were killed and nine wounded. Thousands of militiamen then fired from houses and from behind trees and bushes at the British forces as they retreated to Boston. By the end of the day, the redcoats had suffered 272 casualties, including seventy deaths. Only the arrival of reinforcements and the American militia's lack of coordination prevented much heavier British losses. The patriots suffered just ninety-three casualties.

First Year of War

By the evening of April 20, thousands of American militiamen had gathered around Boston, summoned by local committees that spread the alarm across the countryside. Many did not stay long (they went home for spring planting), but those who remained, along with newer recruits, were organized into formal units. Officers under the command of General Artemas Ward of the Massachusetts militia ordered that latrines be dug, the water supply protected, supplies purchased, military discipline enforced, regular drills held, and defensive fortifications constructed.

For nearly a year, the two armies sat and stared at each other across those siege lines. The redcoats attacked their besiegers only once, on June 17, when they drove the Americans from trenches atop Breed's Hill in Charlestown. In that misnamed Battle of Bunker Hill, the British incurred their greatest losses of the entire war: more than eight hundred wounded and 228 killed. The Americans, though forced to abandon their position, lost less than half that number.

During the same eleven-month period, patriots captured Fort Ticonderoga, a British fort on Lake Champlain, acquiring much-needed cannon. Trying to bring Canada into the war on the American side, they also mounted a northern campaign that ended in disaster at Quebec in early 1776 after their troops were ravaged by smallpox. But the chief significance of the war's first year lay in the long lull in fighting between the main armies at Boston. The delay gave both sides a chance to regroup, organize, and plan their strategies.

British Strategy   Lord North and his new American secretary, Lord George Germain, made three central assumptions about the war they faced. First, they concluded that patriot forces could not withstand the assaults of trained British regulars. They and their generals were convinced that the 1776 campaign would decide the war. Accordingly, they dispatched to America the largest force Great Britain had ever assembled anywhere: 370 transport ships carrying 32,000 troops and tons of supplies, accompanied by seventy-three naval vessels and thirteen thousand sailors. Such an extraordinary effort, they thought, would ensure a quick victory. Among the troops were thousands of professional German soldiers (many from the state of Hesse); the rulers of their principalities had hired them out to Britain.

Second, British officials and army officers treated this war as comparable to conflicts in Europe. They adopted a conventional strategy of capturing major American cities and defeating the rebel army decisively without suffering serious casualties themselves. Third, they assumed a clear-cut military victory would achieve their goal of retaining the colonies' allegiance.

All three assumptions proved false. North and Germain vastly underestimated Americans' commitment to armed resistance. Battlefield defeats did not lead patriots to abandon their political aims and sue for peace. London officials also failed to recognize the significance of the American population's dispersal over an area 1,500 miles long and more than 100 miles wide. Although Britain would control each of the largest American ports at some time during the war, less than 5 percent of the population lived in those cities. Furthermore, the coast offered so many excellent harbors that essential commerce was easily rerouted. In other words, the loss of cities did little to damage the American cause, while British generals repeatedly squandered their resources to capture such ports.

Most of all, London officials did not initially understand that military triumph would not necessarily bring political victory. Securing the colonies permanently would require hundreds of thousands of Americans to return to their original allegiance. After 1778, the ministry adopted a strategy designed to achieve that goal through the expanded use of loyalist forces and the restoration of civilian authority in occupied areas. But the new policy came too late. Britain's leaders never fully realized they were fighting, not a conventional European war, but an entirely new kind of conflict: the first modern war of national liberation.

Second Continental Congress   At least Britain had a bureaucracy ready to supervise the war effort. The Americans had only the Second Continental Congress, originally intended to consider the ministry's response to the Continental Association. Instead, the delegates who convened in Philadelphia on May 10, 1775, had to assume the mantle of intercolonial government. "Such a vast Multitude of objects, civil, political, commercial and military, press and crowd upon us so fast, that we know not what to do first," John Adams wrote a close friend early in the session. Yet as the summer passed, Congress slowly organized the colonies for war. It authorized the printing of money with which to purchase necessary goods, established a committee to supervise relations with foreign countries, took steps to strengthen the militia, and ordered that thirteen frigates be built for a new Continental Navy (eventually, it comprised forty-seven vessels). Most important, it created the Continental Army and appointed its generals.

Until Congress met, the Massachusetts provincial congress supervised Ward and the militiamen encamped at Boston. But that army, composed of men from all over New England, constituted a heavy drain on limited local resources. Consequently, Massachusetts asked the Continental Congress to assume the task of directing the army. Initially, Congress had to choose a commander-in-chief, and many delegates recognized the importance of naming someone who was not a New Englander. John Adams later recalled that in mid-June he proposed the appointment of a Virginian "whose Skill and Experience as an Officer, whose independent fortune, great Talents and excellent universal Character, would command the Approbation of all America": George Washington. The Congress unanimously concurred.

George Washington

Neither fiery radical nor reflective political thinker, Washington had not participated prominently in the pre-revolutionary agitation. Devoted to the American cause, he was dignified, conservative, and respectable—a man of unimpeachable integrity. The younger son of a Virginia planter, Washington did not expect to inherit substantial property and planned to work as a surveyor. But the early death of his older brother and his marriage to the wealthy widow Martha Custis made George Washington one of the largest slaveholders in Virginia. Though an aristocrat, he was unswervingly committed to representative government. After his mistakes at the beginning of the Seven Years War, he had repaired his reputation by rallying the troops and maintaining a calm demeanor under fire during Braddock's defeat in 1755.

Washington also had remarkable stamina. In over eight years of war, he never had a serious illness and took only one brief leave of absence. Moreover, he both looked and acted like a leader. More than six feet tall in an era when most men were five inches shorter, he displayed a stately and commanding presence. Other patriots praised his judgment, steadiness, and discretion, and even a loyalist admitted that Washington could "atone for many demerits by the extraordinary coolness and caution which distinguish his character."

British Evacuate Boston

Washington needed all the coolness and caution he could muster when he took command of the army surrounding Boston in July 1775. The new general continued Ward's efforts to organize and sustain those troops. By March 1776, when the arrival of cannon from Ticonderoga finally enabled him to put direct pressure on the redcoats in the city, the army was prepared to act. Yet an assault on Boston proved unnecessary. Sir William Howe, the new commander, had been considering an evacuation; he wanted to transfer his men to New York City. The patriots' cannon decided the matter. On March 17, the British and more than a thousand of their loyalist allies abandoned Boston forever.

That spring of 1776, as the British fleet left Boston for the temporary haven of Halifax, the colonies were moving inexorably toward independence. Although they had been at war for months, American leaders denied seeking a break with Great Britain until a pamphlet published in January 1776 advocated such a step.

Common Sense   Thomas Paine's *Common Sense* exploded on the American scene, quickly selling tens of thousands of copies. The author, a radical English printer who had lived in America only since 1774, called stridently for independence. Paine also challenged many common American assumptions about government and the colonies' relationship to Britain. Rejecting the notion that only a balance of monarchy, aristocracy, and democracy could preserve freedom, he advocated the establishment of a republic, a government by the people with no king or nobility. Instead of acknowledging the benefits of links to the mother country, Paine insisted that Britain had exploited the colonies unmercifully. And for the frequently heard assertion that an independent America would be weak and divided, he substituted an unlimited confidence in America's strength once freed from European control.

He expressed these striking sentiments in equally striking prose. Scorning the rational style of most other pamphleteers, Paine adopted an enraged tone, describing the king as a "royal brute," a "wretch" unconcerned for the colonists' welfare. His pamphlet reflected the oral culture of ordinary folk. Couched in everyday language, its primary source of authority was the Bible, the only book familiar to most Americans. No wonder the pamphlet had a wider distribution than any other political publication of its day.

It is unclear how many people were converted to the cause of independence by reading *Common Sense*. But by late spring, independence had become inevitable. On May 10, the Second Continental Congress formally recommended that individual colonies form new governments, replacing their colonial charters with state constitutions. Perceiving the trend, the few loyalists still connected with Congress severed their ties to that body.

Then on June 7 came confirmation of the movement toward independence. Richard Henry Lee of Virginia, seconded by John Adams, introduced the crucial resolution: "that these United Colonies are, and of right ought to be, free and independent States, that they are absolved of all allegiance to the British Crown, and that all political connection between them and the State of Great Britain is, and ought to be, totally dissolved." Congress debated but did not immediately adopt Lee's resolution. Instead, it postponed a vote until early July, to allow time for consultation and public reaction. In the meantime, a five-man committee—including Thomas Jefferson, John Adams, and Benjamin Franklin—was directed to draft a declaration of independence.

The committee assigned primary responsibility for writing the declaration to Jefferson, who was well known for his eloquent style. Years later, Adams recalled that Jefferson had modestly protested his selection, suggesting that Adams prepare the initial draft. The Massachusetts revolutionary recorded his frank response: "You can write ten times better than I can."

Jefferson and the Declaration of Independence   Thirty-four-year-old Thomas Jefferson, a Virginia lawyer, had been educated at the College of William and Mary and in the law offices of a prominent attorney. A member of the House of Burgesses, he had read widely in history and political theory. That broad knowledge was evident not only in the declaration but also in his draft of the Virginia state constitution, completed just a few days before his appointment to the committee. Jefferson, an intensely private man, loved his home and family deeply. This early stage of his political career was marked by his beloved wife Martha's repeated difficulties in childbearing. While he wrote and debated in Philadelphia, she suffered a miscarriage at their home, Monticello. Not until after her death in 1782, from complications following the birth of their sixth (but only third surviving) child in ten years of marriage, did Jefferson fully commit himself to public service.

The draft of the declaration was laid before Congress on June 28, 1776. The delegates officially voted for independence four days later, then debated the wording of the declaration for two more days, adopting it with some changes on July 4. Since Americans had long ago ceased to see themselves as legitimate subjects of Parliament, the Declaration of Independence (see appendix) concentrated on George III, who provided an identifiable villain. The document accused the king of attempting to destroy representative government in the colonies and of oppressing Americans through the unjustified use of excessive force.

The declaration's chief long-term importance, however, did not lie in its lengthy catalogue of grievances against George III (including, in a section deleted by Congress, Jefferson's charge that the British monarchy had forced slavery on America). It lay instead in the ringing statements of principle that have served ever since as the ideal to which Americans aspire: "We hold these truths to be self-evident: That all men are created equal; that they are endowed by their Creator with certain unalienable rights; that among these are life, liberty and the pursuit of happiness; that, to secure these rights, governments are instituted among men, deriving their just powers from the consent of the governed; that whenever any form of government becomes destructive of these ends, it is the right of the people to alter or to abolish it, and to institute new government." These phrases have echoed down through American history like no others.

The delegates in Philadelphia who voted to accept the Declaration of Independence could not predict the consequences of their audacious act. When they adopted the declaration, they were committing treason. Therefore, when they concluded with the assertion that they "mutually pledge[d] to each other our lives, our fortunes, and our sacred honor," they spoke no less than the truth. The real struggle still lay before them, and few had Thomas Paine's boundless confidence in success.

THE STRUGGLE IN THE NORTH

In late June 1776, the first ships carrying Sir William Howe's troops from Halifax appeared off the coast of New York (see Map 6.1). On July 2, the day Congress voted for independence, redcoats landed on Staten Island, but Howe waited until more troops arrived from England before attacking. Washington therefore had time to march his army of seventeen thousand south from Boston to defend Manhattan.

New York and New Jersey   But Washington and his men, still inexperienced in fighting and maneuvering, made major mistakes, losing battles at Brooklyn Heights and on Manhattan Island. The city fell to the British, who captured nearly three thousand American soldiers. (Those men

MAP 6.1   The War in the North, 1775–1778

The early phase of the Revolutionary War was dominated by British troop movements in the Boston area, the redcoats' evacuation to Nova Scotia in the spring of 1776, and the subsequent British invasion of New York and New Jersey.

spent most of the rest of the war on British prison ships anchored in New York harbor, where many died of smallpox and other diseases.) Washington slowly retreated across New Jersey into Pennsylvania, and British forces took control of most of New Jersey. Occupying troops met little opposition; the revolutionary cause appeared to be in disarray. "These are the times that try men's souls," wrote Thomas Paine in his pamphlet *The Crisis.* "The summer soldier and the sunshine patriot will, in this crisis, shrink from the service of his country; ... yet we have this consolation with us, that the harder the conflict, the more glorious the triumph."

The British then forfeited their advantage as redcoats stationed in New Jersey went on a rampage of rape and plunder. Washington determined to strike back. Moving quickly, he crossed the Delaware River at night to attack a Hessian encampment at Trenton early on the morning of December 26, while the Germans were still recuperating from celebrating Christmas. The patriots captured more than nine hundred Hessians and killed another thirty; only three Americans were wounded. A few days later, Washington attacked again at Princeton. Having gained command of the field and buoyed American spirits with the two swift victories, Washington set up winter quarters at Morristown, New Jersey.

Campaign of 1777

British strategy for 1777, sketched in London over the winter, aimed to cut New England off from the other colonies. General John Burgoyne, a subordinate of Howe and one of the planners, would lead an invading force of redcoats and Indians down the Hudson River from Canada to rendezvous near Albany with a similar force that would move east along the Mohawk River valley. The combined forces would then presumably link up with Howe's troops in New York City. But in New York, Howe simultaneously prepared his own plan to capture Philadelphia. Consequently, in 1777 the British armies in America would operate independently; the result would be disaster.

Howe took Philadelphia, but he did so in inexplicable fashion, delaying for months before beginning the campaign, then taking six weeks to transport his troops by sea instead of marching them overland. Incredibly, at the end of the

Joseph Brant, the Iroquois leader who helped to persuade the Mohawks, Senecas, and Cayugas to support the British in the latter stages of the Revolution, as painted by Charles Willson Peale in 1797.

Independence National Historic Park Collection

lengthy voyage, he ended up only 40 miles closer to Philadelphia than when he started. By the time Howe advanced on Philadelphia, Washington had had time to prepare its defenses. Twice, at Brandywine Creek and again at Germantown, the two armies clashed near the patriot capital. Although the British won both engagements, the Americans handled themselves well. The redcoats captured Philadelphia in late September, but to little effect. The campaign season was nearly over; the revolutionary army had gained confidence in itself and its leaders; and far to the north, Burgoyne was going down to defeat.

Burgoyne and his men had set out from Montreal in mid-June, traveling first by boat on Lake Champlain, then later marching overland toward the Hudson, hampered by having to clear giant trees felled across their path by patriot militiamen. An easy triumph at Fort Ticonderoga in July was followed in August by two setbacks—the redcoats and Indians marching east along the Mohawk River turned back after a battle at Oriskany, New York; and in a clash near Bennington, Vermont, American militiamen nearly wiped out eight hundred of Burgoyne's German mercenaries. Burgoyne's sluggish progress had given American troops time to prepare for his arrival. After several skirmishes with an American army commanded by General Horatio Gates, Burgoyne was surrounded near Saratoga, New York. On October 17, 1777, he surrendered his entire force of more than six thousand men.

Iroquois Confederacy Splinters   The August 1777 battle at Oriskany divided the Iroquois Confederacy. Although the Six Nations had formally pledged to remain neutral in the war, two influential Mohawk leaders, the siblings Mary and Joseph Brant, believed the Iroquois should ally themselves with the British to protect their territory from land-hungry colonists. The Brants won over the Senecas, Cayugas, and Mohawks, all of whom contributed warriors to the 1777 expedition. But the Oneidas—who had been converted to Christianity by Protestant missionaries—preferred the American side and brought the Tuscaroras with them. The Onondagas split into three factions, one on each side and one supporting neutrality. At Oriskany, some Oneidas and Tuscaroras joined patriot militiamen in fighting their Iroquois brethren, shattering a three-hundred-year-old league of friendship.

The collapse of Iroquois unity and the confederacy's abandonment of neutrality had significant consequences. In 1778, British-allied warriors raided frontier villages in Pennsylvania and New York. To retaliate, the following summer the Americans dispatched an expedition under General John Sullivan to burn Iroquois crops, orchards, and settlements. The resulting devastation led many bands to seek food and shelter north of the Great Lakes during the winter of 1779–1780. A large number of Iroquois people never returned to New York but settled permanently in Canada.

Burgoyne's surrender at Saratoga brought joy to patriots, discouragement to loyalists and Britons. In exile in London, Thomas Hutchinson wrote of "universal dejection" among loyalists there. "Everybody in a gloom," he commented, "most of us expect to lay our bones here." The disaster prompted Lord North to authorize a peace commission to offer the Americans what they had requested in 1774—in effect, a return to the imperial system of 1763. That proposal came far too late: the patriots rejected the overture, and the peace commission sailed back to England empty-handed in mid-1778.

Most important, the American victory at Saratoga drew France formally into the conflict. Since 1763, the French had sought to avenge their defeat in the Seven Years' War, and the American Revolution gave them that opportunity. Even before Benjamin Franklin arrived in Paris in late 1776, France covertly supplied the revolutionaries with military necessities. Indeed, 90 percent of the gunpowder used by the Americans during the war's first two years came from France, transported via the French Caribbean island of Martinique.

Franco-American Alliance of 1778   Benjamin Franklin worked tirelessly to strengthen ties between the two nations. He adopted a plain style of dress that made him conspicuous amid the luxury of the court of King Louis XVI. Presenting himself as a representative of American simplicity, Franklin played on the French image of Americans as virtuous farmers. His efforts culminated in 1778 when the countries signed two treaties. In the Treaty of Amity and Commerce, France recognized American independence, establishing trade ties with the new nation. In the Treaty of Alliance, France and the United States promised—assuming that France would declare war on Britain, which it soon did—that neither would negotiate peace with the enemy without consulting the other. France also formally abandoned any claim to Canada and to North American territory east of the Mississippi River. In the years that followed, the most visible symbol of Franco-American cooperation was the Marquis de Lafayette, a young nobleman who volunteered for service with George Washington in 1777 and fought with American forces until the conflict ended.

The French alliance had two major benefits for the patriot cause. First, France began to aid the Americans openly, sending troops and naval vessels in addition to arms, ammunition, clothing, and blankets. Second, Britain could no longer focus solely on the American mainland, for it had to fight France in the Caribbean and elsewhere. Spain's entry into the war in 1779 as an ally of France (but not of the United States) magnified Britain's problems, for the Revolution then became a global war. French, British, and American ships clashed in the West Indies, along the Atlantic coast of North America, and even in Britain's home waters. The French aided the Americans throughout the conflict, but in its last years that assistance proved vital.

LIFE IN THE ARMY AND ON THE HOME FRONT

Only in the first months of the war was the revolutionaries' army manned primarily by the semi-mythical "citizen-soldier," the militiaman who exchanged his plow for a gun to defend his homeland. After a few months or at most a year, the early arrivals went home. They reenlisted only briefly and only if the contending armies neared their farms and towns. In such militia units, elected officers and the soldiers who chose them reflected existing social hierarchies in their regions of origin, yet also retained a freedom and flexibility absent from the Continental Army, composed of men in formally organized statewide units led by appointed officers.

Continental Army — Continental soldiers, unlike militiamen, were primarily young, single, or propertyless men who enlisted for long periods or for the war's duration, in part to earn monetary bonuses or allotments of land after the war. They responded to calls for "manly resistance" to Britain, seeing in military service an opportunity to protect homes and families, assert their masculine identity, and claim postwar citizenship and property-owning rights. As the fighting dragged on, the bonuses grew larger and more enticing. To meet their quotas, towns and states eagerly recruited everyone they could. Regiments from the middle states contained an especially large proportion of recent immigrants; about 45 percent of Pennsylvania soldiers were of Irish origin, and about 13 percent were German, some serving in German-speaking regiments.

Dunmore's proclamation led Congress in January 1776 to modify an earlier policy that had prohibited the enlistment of African Americans in the regular American army, and recruiters in northern states turned increasingly to bondsmen, who were often promised freedom after the war. Enslaved substitutes for their masters constituted about 10 percent of eastern Connecticut enlistees, for example, along with another 5 percent identified as free blacks, who earned enlistment bounties. Southern states initially resisted the trend, but later all except Georgia and South Carolina also enlisted black soldiers. Approximately five thousand African Americans eventually served in the Continental Army. They commonly served in racially integrated units but were assigned tasks that others shunned, such as burying the dead, foraging for food, and driving wagons. Overall, at any given time they composed about 10 percent of the regular army, but they seldom served in militia units.

Also attached to the American forces were a number of women, the wives and widows of poor soldiers, who came to the army with their menfolk because they were too impoverished to survive alone. Such camp followers—estimated to be about 3 percent of the total number of troops—worked as cooks, nurses, and launderers in return for rations and low wages. The women, along with civilian commissaries and militiamen who floated in and out of camp at irregular intervals, made up an unwieldy assemblage that officers found difficult to manage, especially because none of them could be subjected to the same military discipline as regular soldiers. Yet the army's shapelessness also reflected its greatest strength: an almost unlimited reservoir of manpower and womanpower.

Officer Corps — The officers of the Continental Army developed an intense sense of pride and commitment to the revolutionary cause. The hardships they endured, the battles they fought, the difficulties they overcame all helped to forge an esprit de corps that outlasted the war. The realities of warfare were often dirty, messy, and corrupt, but the officers drew strength from a developing image of themselves as professionals who sacrificed personal gain for the good of the entire nation. When Benedict Arnold, an officer who fought heroically for the patriot cause early in the war, defected to the British, they made his name a metaphor for villainy. "How black, how despised, loved by none, and hated by all," wrote one officer.

The officers' wives, too, prided themselves on their and their husbands' service to the nation. Unlike poor women, they did not travel with the army but instead came for extended visits while the troops were in camp (usually during the winters). Martha Washington and other officers' wives, for example, lived at Valley Forge in the winter of 1777–1778. They brought with them food, clothing, and household furnishings to make their stay more comfortable, and they entertained each other and their menfolk at teas, dinners, and dances. Socializing and discussing current events created friendships later renewed in civilian life when some of their husbands became the new nation's leaders.

Hardship and Disease

Life in the American army was difficult for everyone, although ordinary soldiers endured more hardships than their officers. Wages were low, and often the army could not meet the payroll. Rations (a daily standard allotment of bread, meat, vegetables, milk, and beer) did not always appear, and men had to forage for their own food. Clothing and shoes the army supplied were often of poor quality; soldiers had to make do or find their own. While in camp, soldiers occasionally hired themselves out as laborers to nearby farmers to augment their meager rations or earnings. When conditions deteriorated, troops threatened mutiny (though only a few carried out that threat) or, more often, simply deserted. Punishments for desertion or other offenses such as theft and assault were harsh; convicted soldiers were sentenced to hundreds of lashes, whereas officers were publicly humiliated, deprived of their commission, and discharged in disgrace.

Endemic disease in the camps—especially dysentery, various fevers, and, early in the war, smallpox—made matters worse, sometimes discouraging recruiting. Most native-born colonists had neither been exposed to smallpox nor inoculated against the disease, so soldiers and civilians were vulnerable when smallpox spread through the northern countryside after the early months of 1774. The disease ravaged residents of Boston during the British occupation, the troops attacking Quebec in 1775–1776, and the African Americans who fled to join Lord Dunmore (1775) or Lord Cornwallis (1781). Because most British soldiers had already survived smallpox (which was endemic in Europe), it did not pose a significant threat to redcoat troops.

Washington recognized that smallpox could potentially decimate the revolutionaries' ranks, especially after it helped cause the failure of the 1775 Quebec expedition. Thus, in Morristown in early 1777, he ordered that entire regular army and all new recruits be inoculated, although some would die from the risky procedure and survivors would be incapacitated for weeks. Those dramatic measures, coupled with the increasing numbers of foreign-born (and mostly immune) men who enlisted, helped to protect Continental soldiers later in the war, contributing significantly to the eventual American victory.

American soldiers and sailors unfortunate enough to be captured by the British endured great suffering, especially those held in makeshift prisons or on prison ships (known as hulks) in or near Manhattan. Because Britain refused to recognize the legitimacy of the American government, redcoat officers regarded the patriots as rebellious traitors rather than as prisoners of war with a right to decent treatment. The meager rations and crowded, unsanitary conditions of their confinement meant that half to two-thirds of the prisoners eventually fell victim to disease, especially dysentery. Particularly notorious was the hulk *Jersey*; survivors reported fighting

The Jersey prison hulk, shown here in an eighteenth-century print, was anchored in New York harbor. The stripped British vessel housed hundreds of American prisoners of war in appallingly bad conditions. The Jersey, just one of many such prisons, came to symbolize for Americans the mistreatment of their captured soldiers.

Picture Research Consultants & Archives

over scraps of disgusting food, being covered with "bloody and loathesome filth," and each day having to remove the bodies of five to ten of their dead comrades.

Home Front   Men who enlisted in the army, served in Congress, or were captured by the enemy were absent for long periods of time. Their womenfolk, who previously had handled only the "indoor affairs" of the household, thus shouldered the responsibility for "outdoor affairs" as well. As the wife of a Connecticut soldier later recalled, her husband "was out more or less during the remainder of the war [after 1777], so much so as to be unable to do anything on our farm. What was done, was done by myself." Similarly, John and Abigail Adams took great pride in Abigail's developing skills as a "farmeress." She stopped calling the farm "yours" in letters to her husband and began referring to it as "ours"—a revealing change of pronoun. Most women, like Abigail, did not work in the fields themselves, but they supervised field workers and managed their families' finances. Ever resourceful, Abigail sold small items (like handkerchiefs) that John sent her from Europe at her request, and she used the resulting profits to speculate successfully in state bonds, although John urged her to buy more land instead.

Wartime disruptions affected the lives of all Americans. Even far from the battlefields, people suffered from shortages of necessities like salt, soap, and flour. Small luxuries like new clothing or even ribbons or gloves were essentially unavailable. Severe inflation added to the country's woes, eroding the value of any income. For those who lived near the armies' camps or lines of march, difficulties were compounded. Soldiers of both sides plundered farms and houses, looking for food or salable items; they burned fence rails in their fires and took horses and oxen to transport their wagons. Moreover, they carried smallpox and other diseases with them wherever they went. In such circumstances and in their husbands' absence, women had to make the momentous decision whether to deliberately risk their children's lives by inoculating them with smallpox or to take the chance of the youngsters' contracting the disease "in the natural way," with its even greater risk of death. Many, including Abigail Adams, chose the former course of action and were relieved when their children survived.

VICTORY IN THE SOUTH

In early 1778, in the wake of the Saratoga disaster, Lord George Germain and British military leaders reassessed their strategy. The loyalist exiles in London persuaded them to shift the field of battle southward, contending that loyal southerners would welcome the redcoat army as liberators. Southern colonies that had been pacified and returned to friendly civilian control could serve as bases for again attacking the middle and northern states.

South Carolina and the Caribbean   Sir Henry Clinton, who replaced Sir William Howe, oversaw the regrouping of British forces in America. He ordered the evacuation of Philadelphia in June 1778 and sent a convoy that successfully captured the French Caribbean island of St. Lucia, which thereafter served as a key base for Britain. He also dispatched a small expedition to Georgia at the end of the year. When Savannah and then Augusta fell easily into British hands, Clinton became convinced that a southern strategy would succeed. In late 1779, he sailed down the coast from New York to besiege Charleston, the most important city in the South (see Map 6.2). Although afflicted by smallpox, the Americans trapped in the city held out for months. Still, on May 12, 1780, General Benjamin Lincoln was forced to surrender the entire southern army—5,500 men—to the invaders. In the following weeks, the redcoats spread through South Carolina, establishing garrisons at key points in the interior. Hundreds of South Carolinians renounced allegiance to the United States, proclaiming their renewed loyalty to the Crown. Clinton organized loyalist regiments, and the process of pacification began.

Yet the triumph was less complete than it appeared. The success of the southern campaign depended on control of the seas, for the British armies were so widely dispersed and travel by land was so difficult that only through British naval vessels could the armies coordinate their efforts. For the moment, the Royal Navy safely dominated the American coastline, but French naval power posed a threat to the entire southern enterprise. American privateers infested Caribbean waters, seizing valuable cargoes bound to and from the British islands. Furthermore, after late 1778, France picked off those islands one by one, including Grenada—second only to Jamaica in sugar production—and, in 1781, St. Christopher as well. Even though in early 1781 the British captured and plundered St. Eustatius (the Dutch island that, after French entry into the war, served as the main conduit for the movement of military supplies from Europe to America), the victory did them little good. Indeed, it might well have cost them the war, for Admiral Sir George Rodney, determined to secure the victory (and his personal profits from the plunder), failed to pursue the French fleet under Admiral François de Grasse when it subsequently sailed from the Caribbean to Virginia, where it played a major role in the battle at Yorktown.

Then, too, the redcoats never managed to establish full control of the areas they seized in South Carolina or Georgia. Patriot bands operated freely, and loyalists could not be adequately protected. The fall of Charleston failed to dishearten the patriots; instead, it spurred them to greater exertions. As one Marylander declared confidently, "The Fate of America is not to be decided by the Loss of a Town or

Legend:
- American and allied forces
- British forces
- ✷ American victory
- ✹ British victory

PENNSYLVANIA

N.Y.
New York
N.J.

York • Philadelphia •

Washington and Rochambeau Aug. 1781

Graves and Hood 1781

Barras (from Newport) 1781

MD.
Mount Vernon

DEL.

Wayne

Lafayette

James R.

Richmond

VIRGINIA

Roanoke R.

Yorktown
Oct. 19, 1781

Battle of the Capes
Sept. 5, 1781

Greene 1781

Cornwallis May 1781

Guilford Courthouse
Mar. 15, 1781

Kings Mountain
Oct. 7, 1780

Cornwallis

N. C.

Charlotte

Cape Fear R.

Wilmington

ATLANTIC
OCEAN

Cowpens
Jan. 17, 1781

Tarleton

Gates 1780

Camden
Aug. 16, 1780

De Grasse (from West Indies) 1781

Winnsboro

Pee Dee R.

S. C.

Santee R.

Clinton and Cornwallis 1780

Campbell 1778

Savannah R.

Charles Town
May 12, 1780

Lincoln 1779

GEORGIA

Savannah
Dec. 29, 1778

0   100   200 Miles
0   100   200 Kilometers

© Cengage Learning

MAP 6.2 The War in the South

The southern war—after the British invasion of Georgia in late 1778—was characterized by a series of British thrusts into the interior, leading to battles with American defenders in both North and South Carolina. Finally, after promising beginnings, Cornwallis's foray into Virginia ended with disaster at Yorktown in October 1781.

Two." Patriot women in four states formed the Ladies Association, which collected money to purchase shirts for needy soldiers. Recruiting efforts were stepped up.

Nevertheless, the war in South Carolina went badly for the patriots throughout most of 1780. At Camden in August, forces under Lord Cornwallis, the new British commander in the South, crushingly defeated a reorganized southern army led by Horatio Gates. Thousands of enslaved African Americans joined the redcoats, seeking the freedom promised by Lord Dunmore and later by Sir Henry Clinton. Running away from their patriot masters individually and as families, they seriously disrupted planting and harvesting in the Carolinas and Georgia in 1780 and 1781.

Tens of thousands of slaves were lost to their owners as a result of the war. Not all of them joined the British or won their freedom if they did, but their flight had exactly the effect the British sought. Many served the redcoats as scouts and guides, or as laborers in camps or occupied cities like New York.

Greene and the Southern Campaign   After the Camden defeat, Washington (who had to remain in the North to contain the British army occupying New York) appointed General Nathanael Greene to command the southern campaign. Appalled by conditions in South Carolina, Greene told a friend that "the word difficulty when applied to the state of things here … is almost without meaning, it falls so far short" of reality. His troops needed clothing, blankets, and food, but "a great part of this country is already laid waste and in the utmost danger of becoming a desert." Incessant guerrilla warfare had, he commented, "so corrupted the principles of the people that they think of nothing but plundering one another."

In such dire circumstances, Greene had to move cautiously. He adopted a conciliatory policy toward the many Americans who had switched sides, an advantageous move in a region in which people could well have altered their allegiance up to seven times in less than two years. He also ordered his troops to treat captives fairly and not to loot loyalist property. Recognizing that the patriots needed to convince a war-weary populace that they could bring stability to the region, he helped the shattered provincial congresses of Georgia and South Carolina to reestablish civilian authority in the interior—a goal the British were never able to accomplish. Because he had so few regulars (only sixteen hundred when he took command), Greene had to rely on western volunteers and could not afford to have frontier militia companies occupied in defending their homes from Indian attack. He accordingly pursued diplomacy aimed at keeping the Indians out of the war. Although royal officials cooperating with the redcoat invaders initially won some Indian allies, Greene's careful maneuvers eventually proved successful. By war's end, only the Creeks remained allied with Great Britain.

Even before Greene took command of the southern army in December 1780, the tide had begun to turn. In October, at King's Mountain, a force from the backcountry defeated a large party of redcoats and loyalists. Then in January 1781, Greene's trusted aide Daniel Morgan brilliantly routed the British regiment Tarleton's Legion at Cowpens. Greene himself confronted the main body of British troops under Lord Cornwallis at Guilford Court House, North Carolina, in March. Although Cornwallis controlled the field at the end of the day, most of his army had been destroyed. He had to retreat to Wilmington, on the coast, to receive supplies and fresh troops from New York by sea. Meanwhile, Greene returned to South Carolina, where, in a series of swift strikes, he forced the redcoats to abandon their interior posts and retire to Charleston.

Surrender at Yorktown   Cornwallis headed north into Virginia, where he joined forces with a detachment of redcoats commanded by the American traitor Benedict Arnold. Instead of acting decisively with his new army of 7,200 men, Cornwallis withdrew to the peninsula between the York and James Rivers, where he fortified Yorktown and awaited supplies and reinforcements. Seizing the opportunity, Washington quickly moved more than seven thousand French and American troops south from New York City. When De Grasse's fleet arrived from the Caribbean just in time to defeat the Royal Navy vessels sent to relieve Cornwallis, the British general was trapped. On October 19, 1781, Cornwallis surrendered.

When news of the defeat reached London, Lord North's ministry fell. Parliament voted to cease offensive operations in America, authorizing peace negotiations. Washington returned with the main army to the environs of New York, where his underpaid—and, they thought, underappreciated—officers grew restive. In March 1783, they threatened to mutiny unless Congress guaranteed them adequate compensation for their services. Washington, warned in advance of the so-called Newburgh Conspiracy, met the challenge brilliantly. Summoning his officers, he defused the crisis with a well-reasoned but emotional speech drawing on their patriotism. How could they, he asked, "open the flood Gates of Civil discord, and deluge our rising Empire in Blood"? When at one point he fumbled for glasses, remarking in passing that "I have grown gray in your service and now find myself growing blind," eyewitnesses reported that many of the rebellious officers began to cry. At the end of the year, he stood before Congress and formally resigned his commission as commander-in-chief. Through such actions at the end of the conflict, Washington established an enduring precedent: civilian control of the American military.

The war had been won, but at terrible cost. More than 35,000 American men died in the war, only about one-quarter of them from wounds suffered in battle and fully one-half while prisoners of the British. In the South, years of guerrilla warfare and the loss of thousands of runaway slaves shattered the economy. Indebtedness soared, and local governments were crippled for lack of funds, as few people could afford to pay their taxes. In the 1780s in Charles County, Maryland, for example, men commonly refused to serve in elective or appointive office because their personal estates would become liable for any taxes or fines they were unable to collect. Many of the county's formerly wealthy planters descended into insolvency, and in the 1790s a traveler observed that the countryside "wears a most dreary aspect," remarking on the "old dilapidated mansions" that had once housed well-to-do slaveowners.

Treaty of Paris   Yet Charles County residents and Americans in general rejoiced when they learned of the signing of the preliminary peace treaty at Paris in November 1782. The American diplomats—Benjamin Franklin, John Jay, and John Adams—ignored their instructions from Congress to be guided by France and instead negotiated directly with Great Britain. Their instincts were sound: the French government was more an enemy to Britain than a friend to the United States. In fact, French ministers worked secretly behind the scenes to try to prevent the establishment of a strong, unified government in America. Spain's desire to lay claim to the region between the Appalachian Mountains and the Mississippi River further complicated the negotiations. But the American delegates proved adept at power politics, achieving their main goal: independence as a united nation. Weary of war, the new British ministry, headed by

Lord Shelburne (formerly an outspoken critic of Lord North's American policies), made numerous concessions—so many, in fact, that Parliament ousted the ministry shortly after peace terms were approved.

The treaty, signed formally on September 3, 1783, granted unconditional independence to a nation named "the United States of America." Generous boundaries delineated that new nation: to the north, approximately the present-day boundary with Canada; to the south, the 31st parallel (about the modern northern border of Florida); to the west, the Mississippi River. Florida, which Britain had acquired in 1763, reverted to Spain (see Map 7.2). The Americans also gained unlimited fishing rights off Newfoundland. In ceding so much land to the United States, Britain ignored the territorial rights of its Indian allies, sacrificing their interests to the demands of European politics. British diplomats also poorly served loyalists and British merchants. The treaty's ambiguously worded clauses pertaining to the payment of prewar debts and the postwar treatment of loyalists caused trouble for years to come, proving impossible to enforce.

SUMMARY

The long war finally over, the victorious Americans could look back on their achievement with satisfaction and awe. Having unified the disparate mainland colonies, they had claimed their place in the family of nations and forged a successful alliance with France. With an inexperienced army composed of militia and regulars, they had defeated the professional soldiers of the greatest military power in the world. They accomplished their goal more through persistence and commitment than through brilliance on the battlefield, a persistence that involved wives and families on the home front as well as soldiers. They had won only a few actual victories—most notably, at Trenton, Saratoga, and Yorktown—but their army always survived defeats to fight again, even after the devastating losses at Manhattan and Charleston. Ultimately, the Americans wore their enemy down.

In winning the war, the Americans reshaped the physical and mental landscapes in which they lived. They abandoned the British identity once so important to them, excluding from their new nation their loyalist neighbors who were unwilling to make a break with the mother country. They established republican governments at state and national levels. In the families of Continental Army soldiers in particular they began the process of creating new national loyalties. They also laid claim to most of the territory east of the Mississippi River and south of the Great Lakes, thereby greatly expanding the land potentially open to their settlements and threatening the traditional Indian dominance of the continent's interior.

In achieving independence, Americans surmounted formidable challenges. But in the future they faced perhaps an even greater one: ensuring the survival of their republic in a world dominated by the bitter rivalries among Britain, France, and Spain.

7

FORGING A NATIONAL REPUBLIC
1776–1789

CREATING A VIRTUOUS REPUBLIC

When the colonies declared independence, John Dickinson recalled many years later, "there was no question concerning forms of Government, no enquiry whether a Republic or a limited Monarchy was best.... We knew that the people of this country must unite themselves under some form of Government and that this could be no other than the republican form"—in short, self-government by the people. But how should that goal be implemented?

Varieties of Republicanism Three different definitions of republicanism emerged in the new United States. Ancient history and political theory informed the first, held chiefly by members of the educated elite (such as the Adamses of Massachusetts). The histories of popular governments in Greece and Rome suggested that republics could succeed only if they were small in size and homogeneous in population. Unless a republic's citizens were willing to sacrifice their own private interests for the good of the whole, the government would collapse. A truly virtuous man, classical republican theory insisted, had to forgo personal profit and work solely for the best interests of the nation. In return for sacrifices, though, a republic offered its citizens equality of opportunity. Under such a government, rank would be based on merit rather than on inherited wealth and status. Society would be governed by members of a "natural aristocracy," men

CHRONOLOGY

1776	Second Continental Congress directs states to draft constitutions
	Abigail Adams advises her husband to "Remember the Ladies"
1777	Articles of Confederation sent to states for ratification
	Vermont becomes first jurisdiction to abolish slavery
1781	Articles of Confederation ratified
1783	Treaty of Paris signed, formalizing American independence
1784	Diplomats sign treaty with Iroquois at Fort Stanwix, but Iroquois repudiate it two years later
1785	Land Ordinance of 1785 provides for surveying and sale of national lands in Northwest Territory
1785–86	United States negotiates treaties at Hopewell, South Carolina, with Choctaws, Chickasaws, and Cherokees
1786	Annapolis Convention meets, discusses reforming government
1786–87	Shays's Rebellion in western Massachusetts raises questions about future of the republic
1787	Royall Tyler's *The Contrast*, first successful American play, performed
	Northwest Ordinance organizes territory north of Ohio River and east of Mississippi River
	Constitutional Convention drafts new form of government
1788	Hamilton, Jay, and Madison write *The Federalist* to urge ratification of the Constitution by New York
	Constitution ratified
1789	William Hill Brown publishes *The Power of Sympathy*, first American novel
	Massachusetts orders towns to support public schools
1800	Weems publishes his *Life of Washington*

whose talent had elevated them from what might have been humble beginnings to positions of power and privilege. Rank would not be abolished but instead would be founded on merit.

A second definition, advanced by other members of the elite but also by some skilled craftsmen, drew more on economic theory than on political thought. Instead of perceiving the nation as an organic whole composed of people nobly sacrificing for the common good, this version of republicanism followed the Scottish theorist Adam Smith in emphasizing individuals' pursuit of rational self-interest. The huge profits some men reaped from patriotism by selling supplies to the army underscored such an approach. The nation could only benefit from aggressive economic expansion, argued men such as Alexander Hamilton. When republican men sought to improve their own economic and social circumstances, the entire nation would benefit. Republican virtue would be achieved through the pursuit of private interests, rather than through subordination to communal ideals. Such thinking decisively abandoned the old notion of the Puritan covenant, which the first definition perpetuated in its emphasis on consensus, though not in its stress on an aristocracy of talent rather than birth.

The third notion of republicanism was less influential but more egalitarian than the other two, both of which contained considerable potential for inequality. Many of its illiterate or barely literate proponents could write little to promote their beliefs. Men who advanced the third version of republicanism, most prominently Thomas Paine, called for widening men's participation in the political process. They also wanted government to respond directly to the needs of ordinary folk, rejecting any notion that the "lesser sort" should automatically defer to their "betters." They were, indeed, democrats in more or less the modern sense. For them, the untutored wisdom of the people embodied republican virtue.

Despite the differences, the three strands of republicanism shared many of the same assumptions. All three contrasted the industrious virtue of America with the corruption of Britain and Europe. In the first version, that virtue manifested itself in frugality and self-sacrifice; in the second, it would prevent self-interest from becoming vice; in the third, it was the justification for including propertyless free men in the ranks of voters. "Virtue, Virtue alone … is the basis of a republic," asserted Dr. Benjamin Rush of Philadelphia, an ardent patriot, in 1778. His fellow Americans concurred, even if they defined virtue differently. Most agreed that a virtuous country would be composed of hard-working citizens who would dress simply and live plainly, elect wise leaders to public office, and forgo the conspicuous consumption of luxury goods.

Virtue and the Arts

As citizens of the United States set out to construct their republic, they believed they were embarking on an unprecedented enterprise. With great pride in their new nation, they expected to replace the vices of monarchical Europe—immorality, selfishness, and lack of public spirit—with the sober virtues of republican America. They sought to embody republican principles not only in their governments but also in their society and culture, expecting painting, literature, drama, and architecture to convey messages of nationalism and virtue to the public.

Americans faced a crucial contradiction at the outset of their efforts. To some republicans, fine arts were manifestations of vice. Their presence in a virtuous society, many contended, signaled the existence of luxury and corruption. Why did a frugal farmer need a painting or a novel? Why should anyone spend hard-earned wages to see a play in a lavishly decorated theater? The first American artists, playwrights, and authors confronted an impossible dilemma. They wanted to produce works embodying virtue, but many viewed those very works as corrupting, regardless of their content.

Still, authors and artists tried. William Hill Brown's *The Power of Sympathy* (1789), the first novel written in the United States, related a lurid tale of seduction as a warning to young women. In Royall Tyler's *The Contrast* (1787), the first successful American play, the virtuous conduct of Colonel Manly was contrasted (hence the title) with the reprehensible behavior of the fop Billy Dimple. The most popular book of the era, Mason Locke Weems's *Life of Washington*, published in 1800 shortly after George Washington's death, was intended by its author to "hold up his great Virtues ... to the imitation of Our Youth." Weems could hardly be accused of subtlety. The famous tale he invented—six-year-old George bravely admitting cutting down his father's favorite cherry tree—ended with George's father exclaiming, "Run to my arms, you dearest boy.... Such an act of heroism in my son, is worth more than a thousand trees, though blossomed with silver, and their fruit of purest gold."

Painting and architecture, too, were expected to exemplify high moral standards. Two of the most prominent artists of the period, Gilbert Stuart and Charles Willson Peale, painted innumerable portraits of upstanding republican citizens. John Trumbull's vast canvases depicted such milestones of American history as the Battle of Bunker Hill and Cornwallis's surrender at Yorktown. Such portraits and historical scenes were intended to instill patriotic sentiments in their viewers. Architects likewise hoped to convey in their buildings a sense of the young republic's ideals. When the Virginia government asked Thomas Jefferson, then minister to France, for advice on the design of the state capitol in Richmond, Jefferson unhesitatingly recommended copying a Roman building, the Maison Carrée at Nîmes. "It is very simple," he explained, "but it is noble beyond expression." Jefferson set forth ideals that would guide American architecture for a generation to come: simplicity of line, harmonious proportions, a feeling of grandeur.

Despite the artists' efforts (or, some would have said, because of them), some Americans began to detect signs of luxury and corruption by the mid-1780s. The resumption of European trade after the war brought a return to up-to-date imported fashions for both men and women. Elite families again attended balls and concerts. Parties no longer seemed complete without gambling and cardplaying. Social clubs for young people multiplied; Samuel Adams worried in print about the opportunities for corruption lurking behind plans for tea drinking and genteel conversation among Boston youths. Especially alarming to fervent republicans was the establishment in 1783 of the Society of the Cincinnati, a hereditary association for Revolutionary War officers and their firstborn male descendants. Although the organizers hoped to advance the notion of the citizen-soldier, opponents feared the group would become the nucleus of a native-born aristocracy. All these developments directly challenged the United States' self-image as a virtuous republic.

Educational Reform

Americans' deep-seated concern for the future of the infant republic focused their attention on children, the "rising generation." Education had previously been seen as a private means to personal advancement, the concern of individual families. Now schooling would serve a public purpose. If young people were to resist the temptations of vice and become useful citizens prepared for self-government, they would need a good education. In fact, the very survival of the nation depended on it. The 1780s and 1790s thus witnessed two major changes in educational practice.

First, some northern states began to use tax money to support public elementary schools. In 1789, Massachusetts became one of the first states to require towns

Depicting Virtue

In the 1780s, American printers began publishing magazines that became important vehicles for promoting their notions of virtue. For monthly or bi-monthly magazines filled with locally written poems and essays publishers needed illustrations—something not required by weekly newspapers. One of the most important and longest lasting of these publications was the *Columbian Magazine*, published in Philadelphia from 1786 to 1792. Seen here are two of the many illustrations its printer commissioned from local artists. *Venerate* *the Plow* celebrated American agriculture, with the female figure symbolizing America (note the thirteen stars in a circle over her head) holding a sheaf of grain. In the other, Columbia presents a girl and a boy (the "rising race") to Minerva (goddess of wisdom), who leans on a pedestal lauding independence as "the reward of wisdom, fortitude, and perseverance." In the background, a farmer plows his field and ships ply the ocean. What future did Americans see for themselves, as represented in these pictures?

Columbian Magazine, 1786

Columbian Magazine, 1787

to offer their citizens free public elementary education. Second, schooling for girls was improved. Recognizing the importance of the rising generation led Americans to conclude that mothers would have to be properly educated if they were to instruct their children adequately. Therefore, Massachusetts insisted that town elementary schools teach girls as well as boys. Throughout the United States, private academies were founded to give teenage girls from well-to-do families an opportunity for advanced schooling. No one yet proposed opening colleges to women, but a few fortunate girls could study history, geography, rhetoric, and mathematics. The academies also trained female students in fancy needlework—the only artistic endeavor considered appropriate for genteel women.

Judith Sargent Murray   Judith Sargent Murray of Gloucester, Massachusetts, became the chief theorist of women's education in the early republic. Murray argued in several essays that women and men had equal intellectual capacities, although women's inadequate education might make them seem less intelligent. "We can only reason from what we know," she declared, "and if an opportunity of acquiring knowledge hath been denied us, the inferiority of our sex cannot fairly be deduced from thence." Therefore, concluded Murray, boys and girls should be offered equivalent schooling. She further contended that girls should be taught to support themselves by their own efforts: "Independence should be placed within their grasp."

Murray's direct challenge to the traditional colonial belief that, as one man put it, girls "knew quite enough if they could make a shirt and a pudding" was part of a general rethinking of women's position that occurred as a result of the Revolution. Both men and women realized that female patriots had made vitally important contributions to the American independence movement. Consequently, Americans began to develop new ideas about the roles women should play in a republican society.

Women and the Republic   The best-known expression of those new ideas appeared in a letter Abigail Adams addressed to her husband in March 1776. "In the new Code of Laws which I suppose it will be necessary for you to make I desire you would Remember the Ladies," she wrote. "Remember all Men would be tyrants if they could.... If perticuliar care and attention is not paid to the Laidies [sic] we are determined to foment a Rebelion, and will not hold ourselves bound by any Laws in which we have no voice, or Representation." With these words, Abigail Adams took a step that would be duplicated by other disfranchised Americans. She deliberately applied the ideology developed to combat parliamentary supremacy to purposes revolutionary leaders had never intended. They assumed that wives had no interests different from those of their husbands. Yet Abigail Adams argued that, because men were "Naturally Tyrannical," the United States should reform colonial marriage laws, which subordinated wives to their husbands, giving men control of family property and denying wives the right to independent legal action.

Abigail Adams did not ask for woman suffrage, but others claimed that right, and some male and female authors began to discuss and define the "rights of women" in general terms. The drafters of the New Jersey state constitution in 1776 defined voters carelessly as "all free inhabitants" who met certain property qualifications. They thereby unintentionally gave the vote to property-holding white spinsters and widows as well as to free black landowners. Qualified women and African Americans, politicized by their experiences during the Revolution, regularly voted in New Jersey's local and congressional elections until 1807, when they were disfranchised by the state legislature, which falsely charged them with widespread vote fraud. That women chose to vote was evidence of their altered perception of their place in the political life of the country.

Such dramatic episodes were unusual. After the war, most European-Americans still viewed women in traditional terms, affirming that women's primary function was to be good wives, mothers, and mistresses of households. They perceived significant differences between male and female character, which eventually enabled a resolution of the conflict between the two most influential strands of republican thought and led to new roles for some women. Because wives could not own property or participate directly in economic life, women came to be seen as the embodiment of self-sacrificing, disinterested republicanism. Through new female-run charitable associations founded after the war, better-off women assumed public responsibilities, in particular through caring for poor widows and orphaned children. Thus, men were freed from the naggings of conscience as they pursued their economic self-interest (that other republican virtue), secure in the knowledge that their wives and daughters were fulfilling the family's obligation to the common good. The ideal republican man, therefore, was an individualist, seeking advancement for himself and his family. The ideal republican woman, by contrast, always put the well-being of others ahead of her own.

Together, European American men and women established the context for the creation of a virtuous republic. But nearly 20 percent of the American population was of African descent. How did approximately 700,000 African Americans fit into the developing national plan?

THE FIRST EMANCIPATION AND THE GROWTH OF RACISM

Revolutionary ideology exposed one of the primary contradictions in American society. Both European-Americans and African Americans saw the irony in slaveholders' claims that they sought to prevent Britain from "enslaving" them. Many revolutionary leaders voiced the theme. In 1773, Dr. Benjamin Rush called slavery "a vice which degrades human nature," warning ominously that "the plant of liberty is of so tender a nature that it cannot thrive long in the neighborhood of slavery." Common folk also pointed out the contradiction. When Josiah Atkins, a Connecticut soldier, saw Washington's plantation, he observed in his journal: "Alas! That persons who pretend to stand for the rights of mankind for the liberties of society, can delight in oppression, & that even of the worst kind!"

African Americans did not need revolutionary ideology to tell them that slavery was wrong, but they quickly took advantage of that ideology. In 1779, a group of slaves from Portsmouth, New Hampshire, asked the state legislature "from what authority [our masters] assume to dispose of our lives, freedom and property," pleading "that the name of slave may not more be heard in a land gloriously contending for the sweets of freedom." The same year, several bondsmen in Fairfield, Connecticut, petitioned the legislature for their freedom, characterizing slavery as a "dreadful Evil" and "flagrant Injustice." How could men who were "nobly contending in the Cause of Liberty," they asked, continue "this detestable Practice"?

Emancipation and Manumission   Both legislatures responded negatively, but the postwar years witnessed the gradual abolition of slavery in the North, a process that has become known as "the first emancipation." Vermont, still an independent jurisdiction, banned slavery in its 1777 constitution. Responding to lawsuits filed by enslaved men and women, Massachusetts courts decided in 1783 that the state constitution prohibited slavery. Other states adopted gradual emancipation laws between 1780 (Pennsylvania) and 1804 (New Jersey). New Hampshire did not formally abolish slavery, but only eight slaves were reported on the 1800 census and none in 1810. Although no southern state adopted general emancipation laws, the legislatures of Virginia (1782), Delaware (1787), and Maryland (1790 and 1796) altered laws that earlier had restricted slaveowners' ability to free their bondspeople. Yet South Carolina and Georgia never considered adopting such acts, and North Carolina insisted that all manumissions (emancipations of individual slaves) be approved by county courts.

Revolutionary ideology thus had limited impact on the well-entrenched economic interests of large slaveholders. Only in the northern states—societies with slaves, not slave societies—could state legislatures vote to abolish slavery. Even there, legislators' concern for the *property* rights of owners of human chattel—the Revolution, after all, was fought for property as well as for life and liberty—led them to favor gradual emancipation over immediate abolition. For example, New York's law freed children born into slavery after July 4, 1799, but only after they had reached their mid-twenties (by then having through their labor more than paid back the cost of their upbringing). The laws failed to emancipate the existing slave population, thereby leaving the owners' current human property largely intact. For decades, then, African Americans in the North lived in an intermediate stage between slavery and freedom. Although the emancipation laws forbade the sale of slaves to jurisdictions in which the institution remained legal, slaveowners regularly circumvented such provisions. The 1840 census recorded the presence of slaves in several northern states; not until later that decade did Rhode Island and Connecticut, for instance, abolish all vestiges of slavery.

Growth of Free Black Population   Despite the slow progress of abolition, the number of free people of African descent in the United States grew dramatically in the first years after the Revolution. Before the war, they had been few in number; in 1755, for example, only 4 percent of African Americans in Maryland were free. Most slaves emancipated before the war were mulattos, born of unions between bondswomen and their masters, who then manumitted the children. But wartime disruptions radically augmented the freed population. Wartime escapees from plantations, slaves who had served in the American army, and still others who had been emancipated by their owners or by state laws were now free. By 1790, nearly sixty thousand free people of color lived in the United States; ten years later, they numbered more than 108,000, nearly 11 percent of the total African American population.

In the Chesapeake, manumissions were speeded by economic changes, such as declining soil fertility and the shift from tobacco to grain production, as well as by the rising influence of antislavery Baptists and Methodists. One prominent Baptist convert, the immensely wealthy planter Robert Carter, manumitted all of his bondspeople after he became convinced that slaveowning was sinful. Because grain cultivation was less labor-intensive than tobacco growing, planters began to complain about "excess" slaves. They occasionally solved that problem by freeing some of their less productive or more favored bondspeople. The enslaved also seized the opportunity to negotiate agreements with their owners allowing them to live and work independently until they could purchase themselves with their accumulated earnings. The free black population of Virginia more than doubled between 1790 and 1810; by the latter year, nearly one-quarter of Maryland's African American population was no longer in legal bondage.

Freedpeople's Lives   In the 1780s and thereafter, freedpeople from rural areas often made their way to northern port cities, such as Boston and Philadelphia. Women outnumbered men among the migrants by a margin of three to two, for they had better employment opportunities in the cities, especially in domestic service. Some freedmen also worked in domestic service, but larger numbers were employed as unskilled laborers and sailors. A few of the women and a sizable proportion of men (nearly one-third of those in Philadelphia in 1795) were skilled workers or retailers. These people chose new names for themselves, exchanging the surnames of former masters for names like Newman or Brown, and as soon as possible they established independent two-parent families instead of continuing to live in their employers' households. They also began to occupy distinct neighborhoods, probably as a result of discrimination.

Emancipation did not bring equality. Even whites who recognized African Americans' right to freedom were unwilling to accept them as equals. Laws discriminated against freedpeople as they had against slaves. Several states—among them Delaware, Maryland, and South Carolina—quickly adopted laws denying property-owning black men the vote. South Carolina forbade free blacks from testifying against whites in court. New Englanders used indenture contracts to control freed youths, who were also often denied education in public schools. Freedmen found it difficult to purchase property and find good jobs. And though in many areas African Americans were accepted as members—even ministers—of evangelical churches, they were rarely allowed an equal voice in church affairs.

Gradually, freedpeople developed their own institutions, often based in their own neighborhoods. In Charleston, mulattos formed the Brown Fellowship Society, which provided insurance coverage for its members, financed a school, and helped to support orphans. In 1794, former slaves in Philadelphia and Baltimore, led by the Reverend Richard Allen, founded societies that eventually formed the African Methodist Episcopal (AME) denomination. AME churches later sponsored schools and—along with African Baptist, African Episcopal, and African Presbyterian churches—became cultural centers of the free black community. Freedpeople quickly learned that, to survive and prosper, they had to rely on collective effort rather than on the goodwill of their white compatriots.

Development of Racist Theory   Their endeavors were all the more important because the postrevolutionary years witnessed the development of formal racist theory in the United States. European-Americans had long regarded their slaves as inferior, but the most influential writers attributed that inferiority to environmental factors. They argued that African slaves' seemingly debased character derived from their enslavement, rather than enslavement's being the consequence of inherited inferiority. In the Revolution's aftermath, though, slaveowners needed to defend holding other human beings in bondage against the proposition that "all men are created equal." Consequently, they began to argue that people of African descent were less than fully human and that the principles of republican equality applied only to European-Americans. In other words, to avoid having to confront the contradiction between their practice and the egalitarian implications of revolutionary theory, they redefined the theory so that it would not apply to African Americans.

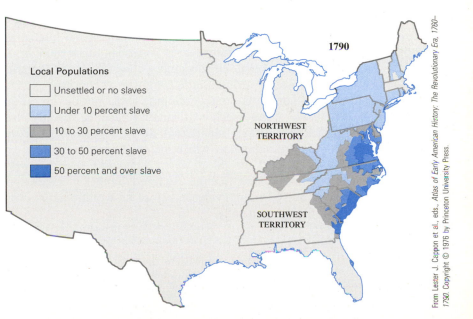

Local Populations

- ☐ Unsettled or no slaves
- ☐ Under 10 percent slave
- ☐ 10 to 30 percent slave
- ☐ 30 to 50 percent slave
- ☐ 50 percent and over slave

NORTHWEST TERRITORY

SOUTHWEST TERRITORY

1790

From Lester J. Cappon et al., eds., *Atlas of Early American History: The Revolutionary Era, 1760–1790.* Copyright © 1976 by Princeton University Press.

MAP 7.1 African American Population, 1790: Proportion of Total Population

The first census clearly indicated that the African American population was heavily concentrated in just a few areas of the United States, most notably in coastal regions of South Carolina, Georgia, and Virginia. Although there were growing numbers of blacks in the backcountry—presumably taken there by migrating slaveowners—most parts of the North and East, with the exception of the immediate vicinity of New York City, had few African American residents.

Simultaneously, the very notion of "race" appeared in coherent form applied to groups defined by skin color as "whites," "reds," and "blacks." The rise of egalitarian thinking among European-Americans both downplayed status distinctions within their own group and differentiated all "whites" from people of color—Indians and African Americans. (That differentiation soon manifested itself in new miscegenation laws adopted in both northern and southern states to forbid intermarriage between whites and blacks or Indians.) Indians from disparate nations, especially in the southeastern United States, had decades earlier begun to refer to themselves as "red." Meanwhile, experience as slaves on American soil forged the identity "African" or "black" from the various ethnic and national affiliations of people who had survived the transatlantic crossing. Strikingly, among the first to term themselves "Africans" were oceanic sailors—men whose wide-ranging contacts with Europeans caused them to construct a unified (and separate) identity for themselves. Thus in the revolutionary era "whiteness," "redness," and "blackness"—along with the superiority of the first, the inferiority of the latter two—developed in tandem as contrasting terms.

Such racism had several intertwined elements. First came the assertion that, as Thomas Jefferson insisted in 1781, blacks were "inferior to the whites in the endowments both of body and mind." (He was less certain about the inferiority of Indians.) There followed the belief that blacks were congenitally lazy and disorderly. Even though owners had often argued, conversely, that slaves were "natural" workers, no one seemed to notice the inherent contradiction. Third was the notion that all blacks were sexually promiscuous and that African American men lusted after European American women. The specter of interracial sexual intercourse involving black men and white women haunted early American racist thought. Significantly, the more common reverse circumstance—the sexual exploitation of enslaved women by their masters—aroused little comment or concern.

African Americans did not allow these developing racist notions to go unchallenged. Benjamin Banneker, a free black mathematical genius, directly disputed Thomas Jefferson's belief in Africans' intellectual inferiority. In 1791, Banneker sent Jefferson a copy of his latest almanac (which included his astronomical calculations) as an example of blacks' mental powers. Jefferson's response admitted Banneker's intelligence but indicated that he regarded Banneker as exceptional; Jefferson insisted that he needed more evidence before he would change his mind about people of African descent generally.

A White Men's Republic   At its birth, then, its leaders defined the republic as a white male enterprise. Even though men of African descent served with honor in the Continental Army, laws from the 1770s on linked "whiteness" and male citizenship rights. Indeed, some historians have argued that the subjugation of blacks, Indians, and women was a necessary precondition for theoretical equality among white men. They have pointed out that identifying common racial antagonists helped to create white solidarity and to lessen the threat to gentry power posed by the enfranchisement of poorer men. Moreover, excluding women from the political realm reserved all power for men, specifically those of the "better sort." That was perhaps one reason why after the Revolution the division of American society between slave and free was transformed into a division between blacks—some of whom were free—and whites. The white male wielders of power ensured their continued dominance in part by substituting race for enslavement as the primary determinant of African Americans' status.

DESIGNING REPUBLICAN GOVERNMENTS

In May 1776, even before adoption of the Declaration of Independence, the Second Continental Congress directed states to devise new republican governments to replace the popularly elected provincial conventions and committees that had met since colonial governments collapsed in 1774 and 1775. Thus, American men initially concentrated on drafting state constitutions and devoted little attention to their national government—an oversight they later had to remedy.

State Constitutions   At the state level, political leaders immediately faced the problem of defining a "constitution." Americans wanted to create tangible documents specifying the fundamental structures of government, but at first legislators could not decide how to accomplish that goal. States eventually concluded that regular legislative bodies should not draft their constitutions. Following the lead established by Vermont in 1777 and Massachusetts in 1780, they began to elect conventions for the sole purpose of drafting constitutions. Thus, states sought direct authorization from the people—the theoretical sovereigns in a republic—before establishing new governments. After preparing new constitutions, delegates submitted them to voters for ratification.

The framers of state constitutions concerned themselves primarily with outlining the distribution of and limitations on government power—both crucial to the survival of republics. If authority was not confined within reasonable limits, the states might become tyrannical, as Britain had. Americans' experience with British rule permeated every provision of their new constitutions. States experimented with different solutions to the problems the framers perceived, and the early constitutions varied considerably in specifics while remaining broadly comparable in outline.

Under their colonial charters, Americans had learned to fear the power of the governor—usually the appointed agent of the king or proprietor—and to see the legislature as their defender. Accordingly, the first state constitutions typically provided for the governor to be elected annually (commonly by the legislature), limited the number of terms he could serve, and gave him little independent authority. Simultaneously, the constitutions expanded the legislature's powers. Every state except Pennsylvania and Vermont retained a two-house structure, with members of the upper house having longer terms and required to meet higher property-holding standards than members of the lower house. But they also redrew electoral districts to more accurately reflect population patterns, and they increased the number of members in both houses. Finally, most states lowered property qualifications for voting. As a result, the legislatures came to include some members who before the war would not have been eligible to vote. Thus, the revolutionary era witnessed the first deliberate attempt to broaden the base of American government, a process that has continued to the present day.

Limiting State Governments But the state constitutions' authors knew that governments designed to be responsive to the people would not necessarily provide sufficient protection if tyrants were elected to office. They consequently included explicit limitations on government authority in the documents they composed, attempting to protect what they regarded as the inalienable rights of individual citizens. Seven constitutions contained formal bills of rights, and others had similar clauses. Most guaranteed citizens freedom of the press, rights to fair trials and to consent to taxation, and protection against general search warrants. An independent judiciary was charged with upholding such rights. Most states also guaranteed freedom of religion, but with restrictions. For example, seven states required that all officeholders be Christians, and some continued to support churches with tax money. (Not until 1833 did Massachusetts become the last state to remove all vestiges of a religious establishment.)

In general, the constitution makers put greater emphasis on preventing state governments from becoming tyrannical than on making them effective wielders of political authority. Their approach to shaping governments was understandable, given the American experience with Great Britain. But establishing such weak political units, especially in wartime, practically ensured that the constitutions would need revision. Soon, some states began to rewrite constitutions they had drafted in 1776 and 1777.

Revising State Constitutions Invariably, the revised versions increased the powers of the governor and reduced the scope of the legislature's authority. By the mid-1780s, some American political leaders had concluded that the best way to limit government power was to balance legislative, executive, and judicial powers, a design called checks and balances. The national Constitution they drafted in 1787 also embodied that principle.

Yet the constitutional theories that Americans applied at the state level did not immediately influence their conception of national government. Because American officials initially focused on organizing the military struggle against Britain, the powers and structure of the Continental Congress evolved by default. Not until late 1777 did Congress send the Articles of Confederation—the document outlining a national government—to the states for ratification, and those Articles simply wrote into law the unplanned arrangements of the Continental Congress.

Articles of Confederation The chief organ of national government was a unicameral (one-house) legislature in which each state had one vote. Its powers included conducting foreign relations, mediating interstate disputes, controlling maritime affairs, regulating Indian trade, and valuing state and national coinage. The Articles did not give the national government the ability to raise revenue effectively or to enforce a uniform commercial policy. The United States of America was described as "a firm league of friendship" in which each state "retains its sovereignty, freedom and independence, and every Power, Jurisdiction and right, which is not by this confederation expressly delegated to the United States, in Congress assembled."

The Articles required unanimous consent of state legislatures for ratification or amendment, and a clause concerning western lands proved troublesome. The draft accepted by Congress allowed states to retain all land claims derived from their original charters. But states with definite western boundaries in their charters (such as Maryland and New Jersey) wanted other states to cede to the national government their landholdings west of the Appalachian Mountains. Otherwise, they feared, states with large claims could expand and overpower their smaller neighbors. Maryland refused to accept the Articles until 1781, when Virginia finally promised to surrender its western holdings to national jurisdiction. Other states followed suit, establishing the principle that unorganized lands would be held by the nation as a whole.

The capacity of a single state to delay ratification for three years portended the fate of American government under the Articles of Confederation. The unicameral legislature, whether it was called the Second Continental Congress (until 1781) or the Confederation Congress (thereafter), was too inefficient and unwieldy to govern

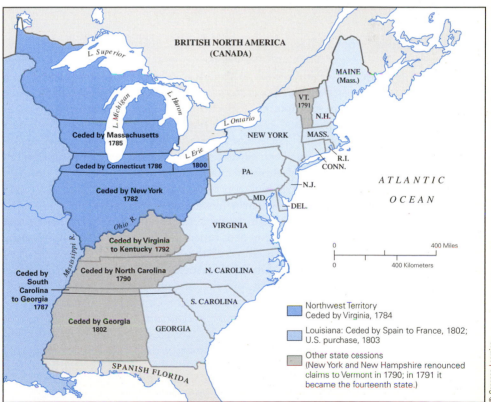

MAP 7.2 Western Land Claims and Cessions, 1782–1802

After the United States achieved independence, states competed with one another for control of valuable lands to which they had possible claims under their original charters. That competition led to a series of compromises among the states or between individual states and the new nation, indicated on this map.

effectively. The Articles' authors had not given adequate thought to the distribution of power within the national government or to the relationship between the Confederation and the states. The Congress they created was simultaneously a legislative body and a collective executive (there was no judiciary), but it had no independent income and no authority to compel the states to accept its rulings. Under the Articles, national government lurched from crisis to crisis.

TRIALS OF THE CONFEDERATION

Finance posed the most persistent problem faced by both state and national governments. Because legislators at all levels levied taxes only reluctantly, both Congress and the states at first tried to finance the war simply by printing currency. Even though the money was backed only by good faith, it circulated freely and without excessive depreciation during 1775 and most of 1776. Demand for military supplies and civilian goods was high, stimulating trade (especially with France) and local production. Indeed, the amount of money issued in those years was probably no more than what a healthy economy required as a medium of exchange.

Financial Affairs   But in late 1776, as the American army suffered reverses in New York and New Jersey, prices began to rise, and inflation set in. The currency's value rested on Americans' faith in their government, a faith that was sorely tested in the years that followed, especially during the dark days of British triumphs in the South (1779 and 1780). State governments fought inflation by controlling wages and prices and requiring acceptance of paper currency on an equal footing with specie (coins). States also borrowed funds, established lotteries, and levied taxes. Their efforts were futile. So, too, was Congress's attempt to stop printing currency altogether and to rely solely on money contributed by the states. By early 1780, it took forty paper dollars to purchase one silver dollar. Soon, Continental currency was worthless.

In 1781, faced with total collapse of the monetary system, Congress undertook ambitious reforms. After establishing a department of finance under the wealthy Philadelphia merchant Robert Morris, it asked the states to amend the Articles of Confederation to allow a national duty of 5 percent on imported goods. Morris put national finances on a solid footing, but the customs duty was never adopted. First Rhode Island and then New York refused to agree to the tax. The states' resistance reflected fear of a too-powerful central government. As one worried citizen wrote in 1783, "If permanent Funds are given to Congress, the aristocratical Influence, which predominates in more than a major part of the United States, will fully establish an arbitrary Government."

Foreign Affairs   Because the Articles denied Congress the power to establish a national commercial policy, the realm of foreign trade also exposed the new government's weaknesses. Immediately after the war, Britain, France, and Spain restricted American trade with their colonies. Americans, who had hoped independence would bring about trade with all nations, were outraged but could do little to change matters. Members of Congress watched helplessly as

British manufactured goods flooded the United States while American produce could no longer be sold in the British West Indies, once its prime market. Although Americans reopened commerce with other European countries and started a profitable trade with China in 1784, neither substituted for access to closer and larger markets.

Congress furthermore had difficulty dealing with the Spanish presence on the nation's southern and western borders. Determined to prevent the republic's expansion, Spain in 1784 closed the Mississippi River to American navigation, thereby depriving the growing settlements west of the Appalachians of access to the Gulf of Mexico. Congress, through its Department of Foreign Affairs, opened negotiations with Spain in 1785, but even John Jay, one of the nation's most experienced diplomats, could not win the necessary concessions. The talks collapsed the following year after Congress divided sharply: southerners and westerners insisted on navigation rights on the Mississippi, whereas northerners were willing to abandon that claim in order to win commercial concessions in the West Indies. The impasse made some congressmen question the possibility of a national consensus on foreign affairs.

Peace Treaty Provisions   Provisions of the 1783 Treaty of Paris, too, caused serious problems. Article Four, which promised payment of prewar debts (most of them owed by Americans to British merchants), and Article Five, which recommended that states allow loyalists to recover their confiscated property, aroused considerable opposition. States passed laws denying British subjects the right to sue for recovery of debts or property in American courts, and town meetings decried the loyalists' return. As residents of Norwalk, Connecticut, put it, few Americans wanted to permit the "Tory Villains" to return "while filial Tears are fresh upon our Cheeks and our Murdered Brethren scarcely cold in their Graves." State governments also had reason to oppose enforcement of the treaty. Sales of loyalists' land, houses, and other possessions had helped finance the war. Because many purchasers were prominent patriots, states hesitated to raise questions about the legitimacy of their property titles.

The refusal of state and local governments to comply with Articles Four and Five gave Britain an excuse to maintain military posts on the Great Lakes long after its troops were supposed to have withdrawn. Furthermore, Congress's inability to convince states to implement the treaty disclosed its lack of power, even in an area—foreign affairs—in which it had authority under the Articles. Concerned nationalists argued publicly that failure to enforce the treaty, however unpopular, challenged the republic's credibility. "Will foreign nations be willing to undertake anything with us or for us," asked Alexander Hamilton, "when they find that the nature of our governments will allow no dependence to be placed on our engagements?"

ORDER AND DISORDER IN THE WEST

Congressmen also confronted knotty problems when they considered the status of land beyond the Appalachians. Although British and American diplomats did not discuss tribal claims, the United States assumed the Treaty of Paris cleared its title to all land east of the Mississippi except the area still held by Spain.

From Lester J. Cappon et al., eds., Atlas of Early American History: The Revolutionary Era, 1760–1790. Copyright © 1976 by Princeton University Press.

MAP 7.3 Cession of Tribal Lands to the United States, 1775–1790

The land claims of the United States meant little as long as Indian nations still controlled vast territories within the new country's formal boundaries. A series of treaties in the 1780s and 1790s opened some lands to white settlement.

Still, recognizing that land cessions should be obtained from the most powerful tribes, Congress initiated negotiations with both northern and southern Indians. (see Map 7.3)

Indian Relations   At Fort Stanwix, New York, in 1784, American diplomats negotiated a treaty with chiefs who claimed to represent the Iroquois; and at Hopewell, South Carolina, in late 1785 and early 1786, they did the same with emissaries from the Choctaw, Chickasaw, and Cherokee nations. In 1786, the Iroquois formally repudiated the Fort Stanwix treaty, denying that the men who attended the negotiations had been authorized to speak for the Six Nations. The confederacy threatened new attacks on frontier settlements, but everyone knew the threat was empty; the flawed treaty stood by default. At intervals until the end of the decade, New York purchased large tracts of land from individual Iroquois nations. By 1790, the once-dominant confederacy was confined to a few scattered reservations. In the South, too, the United States took the treaties as confirmation of its sovereignty, authorizing settlers to move onto the territories in question. European-Americans poured over the southern Appalachians, provoking the Creeks—who had not agreed to the Hopewell treaties—to defend their territory by declaring war. Only in 1790 did they come to terms with the United States.

Western nations, such as the Shawnees, Chippewas, Ottawas, and Potawatomis, had already started to reject Iroquois hegemony as early as the 1750s. After the collapse of Iroquois power, they formed their own confederacy and demanded direct negotiations with the United States. They intended to present a united front to avoid the piecemeal surrender of land by individual bands and villages. But they faced a difficult task. In the postwar world, Indian nations could no longer pursue the diplomatic strategy that had worked so well for so long—playing off European and American powers against one another. France was gone; Spanish territory lay far to the west and south; and British power was confined to Canada, north of the Great Lakes. Only the United States remained.

Ordinance of 1785

At first, the national government ignored the western confederacy. Shortly after state land cessions were completed, Congress began to organize the Northwest Territory, bounded by the Mississippi River, the Great Lakes, and the Ohio River (see Map 7.2). Ordinances passed in 1784, 1785, and 1787 outlined the process through which the land could be sold to settlers and formal governments organized.

To ensure orderly development, Congress in 1785 directed that the land be surveyed into townships 6 miles square, each divided into thirty-six sections of 640 acres (1 square mile). Revenue from the sale of the sixteenth section of each township was to be reserved for the support of public schools—the first instance of federal aid to education in American history. One dollar was the minimum price per acre; the minimum sale was one section. Thus Congress showed little concern for the small farmer: the resulting minimum outlay, $640, lay beyond the reach of ordinary Americans, except those veterans who received part of their army pay in land warrants. Proceeds from western land sales constituted the first independent revenues available to the national government.

Northwest Ordinance

The most important of the three land policies—the Northwest Ordinance of 1787—contained a bill of rights guaranteeing settlers freedom of religion and the right to a jury trial, forbidding cruel and unusual punishments, and nominally prohibiting slavery. Eventually, that prohibition became an important symbol for antislavery northerners, but at the time it had little effect. Some residents of the territory already held slaves, and Congress did not intend to deprive them of their property. Moreover, the ordinance also contained a provision allowing slaveowners to "lawfully reclaim" runaway bondspeople who took refuge in the territory—the first national fugitive slave law. The ordinance prevented slavery from taking deep root by discouraging slaveholders from moving into the territory with their human chattel, but not until 1848 was enslavement abolished throughout the region, known as the Old Northwest. And by omission Congress implied that slavery was legal in the territories south of the Ohio River.

The ordinance of 1787 also specified the process by which territorial residents could organize state governments and seek admission to the Union "on an equal footing with the original States." Early in the nation's history, therefore, Congress laid down a policy of admitting new states on the same basis as the old and assuring residents of the territories the same rights held by citizens of the original states. Having suffered under the rule of a colonial power, congressmen understood the importance of preparing the new nation's first "colony" for eventual self-government. Nineteenth- and twentieth-century Americans were to be less generous in their attitudes toward residents of later territories, many of whom were non-European or non-Protestant. But the nation never fully lost sight of the egalitarian principles of the Northwest Ordinance.

In a sense, though, in 1787 the ordinance was purely theoretical. Miamis, Shawnees, and Delawares in the region refused to acknowledge American sovereignty. They opposed settlement violently, attacking unwary pioneers who ventured too far north of the Ohio River. In 1788, the Ohio Company, to which Congress had sold a large tract of land at reduced rates, established the town of Marietta at the juncture of the Ohio and Muskingum Rivers. But Indians prevented the company from extending settlement very far into the interior.

The problems the United States encountered in ensuring safe settlement of the Northwest Territory revealed the basic weakness of the Confederation government. Not until after the Articles of Confederation were replaced with a new constitution could the United States muster sufficient force to implement the Northwest Ordinance. Thus, although the ordinance is often viewed as one of the few lasting accomplishments of the Confederation Congress, it must be seen within a context of political impotence.

FROM CRISIS TO THE CONSTITUTION

Americans involved in finance, overseas trade, and foreign affairs became acutely aware of the inadequacies of the Articles of Confederation. Congress could not levy taxes, nor could it impose its will on the states to establish a uniform commercial policy or ensure the enforcement of treaties. Partly as a result, the American economy slid into a depression less than a year after war's end. Exporters of staple crops (especially tobacco and rice) and importers of manufactured goods suffered from the postwar restrictions that European powers imposed on American commerce. Although recovery began by 1786, the war's effects proved impossible to erase, particularly in the Lower South. Some estimates suggest that between 1775 and 1790 America's per capita gross national product declined by nearly 50 percent.

Taxation and the Economy   The war wrought permanent change in the American economy. The near-total cessation of foreign commerce in nonmilitary items during the war stimulated domestic manufacturing. Consequently, despite the influx of European goods after 1783, the postwar period witnessed the stirrings of American industrial development. For example, the first American textile mill began production in Pawtucket, Rhode Island, in 1793. Because of continuing population growth, the domestic market assumed greater relative importance in the overall economy. Moreover, foreign trade patterns shifted from Europe and toward the West Indies, continuing a trend that had begun before the war. Foodstuffs shipped to the French and Dutch Caribbean islands became America's largest single export, replacing tobacco (and thus accelerating the Chesapeake's conversion from tobacco to grain production). South Carolina resumed importing slaves on a large scale, as planters sought to replace workers lost to wartime disruptions. Yet without British subsidies, American indigo could not compete with that produced in the Caribbean, and even rice planters struggled to find new markets.

Recognizing the Confederation Congress's inability to deal with commercial matters, representatives of Virginia and Maryland met at Mt. Vernon (George Washington's plantation) in March 1785 to negotiate an agreement about trade on the Potomac River, which divided the two states for much of its length. The successful meeting led to an invitation to other states to discuss trade policy generally at a convention in Annapolis, Maryland. Although nine states named representatives to the meeting in September 1786, only five delegations attended. Those present realized that so few people could not have any significant impact on the political system. They issued a call for another convention, to be held in Philadelphia nine months later, "to devise such further provisions as shall … appear necessary to render the constitution of the federal government adequate to the exigencies of the Union."

At first, few other states responded. But the nation's economic problems also caused taxation woes. The states had run up huge debts to finance the war, issuing securities to soldiers in lieu of pay and to others in return for supplies and loans. During the hard times of the early 1780s, many veterans and other creditors sold those securities to speculators, who then stood to gain when states enacted taxes on the citizenry to pay them off. In 1785, Congress requisitioned still more taxes from the states to pay foreign and domestic holders of national war bonds. Most states tried to comply with the request, but succeeded primarily in arousing popular protests that led the legislatures to adopt laws relieving taxpayers of at least some of the obligations previously enacted. The most dramatic response came in Massachusetts, where the state legislature levied heavy taxes to pay the securities (plus interest) at full price in specie before the end of the decade. Farmers with little prospect of obtaining specie without selling their land responded furiously when the state moved to collect the new taxes. The actions of men from the state's western counties, many of them veterans from leading families, convinced doubters that reform was needed.

Shays's Rebellion   Daniel Shays, a former officer in the Continental Army, assumed nominal leadership of the disgruntled westerners. On January 25, 1787, he led about fifteen hundred troops in an assault on the federal armory at Springfield, attempting to capture the military stores housed there. The militiamen mustered to defend the armory fired on their former comrades-in-arms, who withdrew after suffering twenty-four casualties.

Some (including Shays) fled the state, never to return; two were hanged; and most escaped punishment by paying small fines and taking oaths of allegiance to Massachusetts. The state legislature, for its part, soon dramatically reduced the burden on landowners by enacting new import duties and by easing tax collections.

Even so, the words of the Shaysites reverberated around the new nation. Terming Massachusetts "tyrannical" and styling themselves "Regulators" (like backcountry Carolinians in the 1760s), they had insisted that "whenever any encroachments are made either upon the liberties or properties of the people, if redress cannot be had without, it is virtue in them to disturb government." Thus they linked their rebellion to the earlier independence struggle.

Constitutional Convention   Such explosive assertions convinced many political leaders that the nation's problems extended far beyond trade and tax policies. To some, the rebellion confirmed the need for a much stronger federal government. After most of the states had already appointed delegates, the Confederation Congress belatedly endorsed the proposed convention, "for the sole and express purpose of revising the Articles of Confederation." In mid-May 1787, fifty-five men, representing all the states but Rhode Island, assembled in Philadelphia to begin deliberations.

The vast majority of delegates to the Constitutional Convention were substantial men of property. They all favored reform; otherwise, they would not have come to Philadelphia. Most wanted to give the national government new authority over taxation and foreign commerce. Yet simultaneously they sought to advance their states' interests. Many had been state legislators, and some had helped to draft state constitutions. Their understanding of the success or failure of those constitutions influenced their Philadelphia deliberations. Their ranks included merchants, planters, physicians, generals, governors, and especially lawyers—twenty-three had studied the law. Most had been born in America; many came from families that had arrived a century earlier. Most were Congregationalists, Presbyterians, or Anglicans. In an era when only a tiny handful of men had advanced education, more than half had attended college. A few had been educated in Britain, but most had graduated from American institutions: Princeton, with ten, counted the most alumni participants. The youngest delegate was twenty-six, the oldest—Benjamin Franklin—eighty-one. Like George Washington, whom they elected their presiding officer, most were in their vigorous middle years. A dozen men did the bulk of the convention's work. Of those, James Madison of Virginia most fully deserves the title "Father of the Constitution."

Madison and the Constitution   The frail, shy James Madison was thirty-six years old in 1787. A Princeton graduate raised in western Virginia, he served on the local Committee of Safety and was elected successively to the provincial convention, the state's lower and upper houses, and the Continental Congress (1780–1783). Although Madison returned to Virginia to serve in the state legislature in 1784, he remained in touch with national politics, partly through continuing correspondence with his close friend Thomas Jefferson.

James Madison (1751–1836), the youthful scholar and skilled politician who earned the title "Father of the Consistution."

A promoter of the Annapolis Convention, he strongly supported its call for further reform.

Madison stood out among the delegates for his systematic preparation for the Philadelphia meeting. Through Jefferson, in Paris he bought more than two hundred books on history and government, carefully analyzing their accounts of past confederacies and republics. A month before the Constitutional Convention began, he summed up the results of his research in a lengthy paper entitled "Vices of the Political System of the United States." After listing the flaws he perceived in the current structure of the government (among them "encroachments by the states on the federal authority" and lack of unity "in matters where common interest requires it"), Madison revealed the conclusion that would guide his actions over the next few months. What the government most needed, he declared, was "such a modification of the sovereignty as will render it sufficiently neutral between the different interests and factions, to controul one part of the society from invading the rights of another, and at the same time sufficiently controuled itself, from setting up an interest adverse to that of the whole Society."

Madison thus believed government had to be constructed in such a way that it could not become tyrannical or fall wholly under the influence of a particular faction. He regarded the large size of a potential national republic as an advantage in that respect. Rejecting the common assertion that republics had to be small to survive, Madison asserted that a large, diverse republic should be preferred. Because the nation would include many different factions, no one of them would be able to control the government. Political stability would result from compromises among the contending parties.

Virginia and New Jersey Plans
The so-called Virginia Plan, introduced on May 29 by Edmund Randolph, embodied Madison's conception of national government. The plan provided for a two-house legislature, the lower house elected directly by the people and the upper house selected by the lower; representation in both houses proportional to property or population; an executive elected by Congress; a national judiciary; and congressional veto over state laws. The Virginia Plan gave Congress the broad power to legislate "in all cases to which the separate states are incompetent." Had it been adopted intact, it would have created a government in which national authority reigned unchallenged and state power was greatly diminished. Proportional representation in both houses (however reckoned) would also have given large states a dominant voice in the national government.

The convention included many delegates who recognized the need for change but believed the Virginia Plan went too far in the direction of national consolidation. After two weeks of debate on Randolph's proposal, disaffected delegates— particularly those from small states—united under the leadership of William Paterson of New Jersey. On June 15, Paterson presented an alternative scheme, the New Jersey Plan, calling for strengthening the Articles rather than completely overhauling the government. Paterson proposed retaining a unicameral Congress in which each state had an equal vote, but giving Congress new powers of taxation and trade regulation. Earlier, Paterson had made his position clear in debate. Asserting that the Articles were "the proper basis of all the proceedings of the convention," he contended that the delegates' proper task was "to mark the orbits of the states with due precision and provide for the use of coercion" by the national government. Although the convention initially rejected Paterson's position, he and his allies won a number of victories in the months that followed.

Debates over Congress
The delegates began their work by discussing the structure and functions of Congress. They readily agreed that the new national government should have a two-house (bicameral) legislature. Further, in accordance with Americans' long-standing opposition to virtual representation, they concurred that "the people" (however that term was defined) should be directly represented in at least one house of Congress. But they discovered that they differed widely in their answers to three key questions: Should representation in both houses of Congress be proportional to population? How was representation in either or both houses to be apportioned among the states? And, finally, how were the members of the two houses to be elected?

The last issue proved the easiest to resolve. To quote John Dickinson, the delegates thought it "essential" that members of the lower branch of Congress be elected directly by the people and "expedient" that members of the upper house be chosen by state legislatures. Because legislatures had selected delegates to the Confederation Congress, they would expect a similar privilege in the new government. If the convention had not agreed to allow state legislatures to elect senators, the Constitution would have run into significant opposition among state political leaders. The plan also had the virtue of placing the election of one house of Congress one step removed from the "lesser sort," whose judgment the wealthy convention delegates did not wholly trust.

The possibility of representation proportional to population in the Senate caused considerably greater disagreement. The delegates accepted without much debate the principle of proportional representation in the House of Representatives. But small states, through their spokesman Luther Martin of Maryland, argued for equal representation in the Senate. Such a scheme, they rightly supposed, would give them relatively more power at the national level. Large states, on the other hand, supported a proportional plan, for they would then be allotted more votes in the upper house. For weeks, the convention deadlocked, neither side able to obtain a majority. A committee appointed to work out a compromise recommended equal representation in the Senate, coupled with a proviso that all appropriation bills originate in the lower house. But only the absence of several opponents of the compromise at the time of the decisive vote averted a breakdown.

Slavery and the Constitution

The remaining critical question divided the nation along sectional lines rather than by size of state: how was representation in the lower house to be apportioned among states? Delegates concurred that a census should be conducted every ten years to determine the nation's population, and they agreed that Indians who paid no taxes should be excluded for purposes of representation. Delegates from states with large numbers of slaves wanted African and European inhabitants to be counted equally; delegates from states with few slaves wanted only free people counted. Slavery thus became inextricably linked to the foundation of the new government. Delegates resolved the dispute by using a formula developed by the Confederation Congress in 1783 to allocate financial assessments among states: three-fifths of slaves would be included in population totals. (The formula reflected delegates' judgment that slaves were less efficient producers of wealth than free people, not that they were 60 percent human and 40 percent property.) The three-fifths compromise on representation won unanimous approval. Only two delegates, Gouverneur Morris of New York and George Mason of Virginia, later spoke out against the institution of slavery.

Although the words *slave* and *slavery* do not appear in the Constitution (the framers used such euphemisms as "other persons"), the document contained both direct and indirect protections for slavery. The three-fifths clause, for example, assured white southern male voters not only congressional representation out of proportion to their numbers but also a disproportionate influence on the selection of the president because the number of each state's votes in the electoral college (see next section) was determined by the size of its congressional delegation. In return for southerners' agreement that commercial regulations could be adopted by a simple majority vote in Congress (rather than two-thirds), New Englanders agreed that Congress could not end the importation of slaves for at least twenty years. Further, the fugitive slave clause required all states to return runaways to their masters. By guaranteeing that the national government would aid any states threatened with

"domestic violence," the Constitution promised aid in putting down future slave revolts, as well as incidents like Shays's Rebellion.

Congressional and Presidential Powers   Once delegates agreed on the knotty, conjoined problems of slavery and representation, they achieved consensus on the other issues confronting them, aided by informal conversations at the taverns and boardinghouses where they lived
that summer. All concurred that the national government needed the authority to
tax and to regulate foreign and interstate commerce. But instead of giving Congress
the nearly unlimited scope proposed in the Virginia Plan, delegates enumerated
congressional powers and then provided for flexibility by granting it all authority
"necessary and proper" to carry out those powers. Discarding the congressional
veto contained in the Virginia Plan, the convention implied but did not explicitly
authorize a national judicial veto of state laws. The Constitution plus national laws
and treaties would constitute "the supreme law of the land; and the judges in every
state shall be bound thereby," Article VI declared ambiguously. As another means
of circumscribing state powers, delegates drafted a long list of actions forbidden to
states, including impairing contractual obligations—in other words, preventing the
relief of debtors. And—contrary to many state constitutions—they provided that
religious tests could never be required of U.S. officeholders.

The convention placed primary responsibility for conducting foreign affairs in
the hands of a new official, the president, who was also designated commander-
in-chief of the armed forces. That decision raised the question, left unspecified in the
Constitution's text, of whether the president or Congress acquired special powers in
times of war. With the Senate's consent, the president could appoint judges and other
federal officers. To select the president, delegates established an elaborate mechanism,
the electoral college, whose members would be chosen in each state by legislatures or
qualified voters. If a majority of electors failed to unite behind one candidate, the
House of Representatives (voting as states, not as individuals) would choose the president. Delegates also agreed that the chief executive would serve for four years but be
eligible for reelection, rejecting proposals that he serve one longer term.

The final document showed signs of its origins in the Virginia Plan, but compromises created a system of government less powerful at the national level than Madison and Randolph had envisioned. The key to the Constitution was the distribution
of political authority—that is, separation of powers among executive, legislative, and
judicial branches of the national government, and division of powers between states
and nation (called *federalism*). Two-thirds of Congress and three-fourths of the states,
for example, had to concur on amendments. The branches balanced one another,
their powers deliberately entwined to prevent each from acting independently. The
president could veto congressional legislation, but that veto could be overridden by
two-thirds majorities in both houses, and his treaties and major appointments required the Senate's consent. Congress could impeach the president and federal judges,
but courts appeared to have the final say on interpreting the Constitution. These
checks and balances would make it difficult for the government to become tyrannical.
At the same time, though, the elaborate system would sometimes prevent the government from acting quickly and decisively. Furthermore, the Constitution drew such a

vague line between state and national powers that the United States fought a civil war in the next century over that very issue.

The convention held its last session on September 17, 1787. Of the forty-two delegates present (others had returned home weeks earlier), only three refused to sign the Constitution, two of them in part because of the lack of a bill of rights. Benjamin Franklin had written a speech calling for unity; because his weak voice could not be heard, another delegate read it for him. "I confess that there are several parts of this constitution which I do not at present approve," Franklin admitted. Yet he urged its acceptance "because I expect no better, and because I am not sure, that it is not the best." Only then was the Constitution made public. The convention's proceedings had been entirely secret—and remained so until the delegates' private notes were published in the nineteenth century. (See the appendix for the full text of the Constitution.)

OPPOSITION AND RATIFICATION

Later the same month, the Confederation Congress submitted the Constitution to the states. The ratification clause provided for the new system to take effect once it was approved by special conventions in at least nine states, with delegates elected by qualified voters. Thus, the national Constitution, unlike the Articles of Confederation, would rest directly on popular authority (and the presumably hostile state legislatures would be circumvented).

As states began to elect delegates to the special conventions, discussion of the proposed government grew more heated. Newspaper essays and pamphlets vigorously defended or attacked the Philadelphia convention's decisions. The extent of the debate was unprecedented. Every newspaper in the country printed the full text of the Constitution, and most supported its adoption. It quickly became apparent, though, that disputes within the Constitutional Convention had been mild compared to divisions of opinion within the populace as a whole. Although most citizens concurred that the national government should have more power over taxation and foreign and interstate commerce, some believed the proposed government held the potential for tyranny. The vigorous debate between the two sides frequently spilled out into the streets.

Federalists and Antifederalists   Those supporting the proposed Constitution called themselves Federalists. They built on the notions of classical republicanism, holding forth a vision of a virtuous, collectivist, self-sacrificing republic vigorously led by a manly aristocracy of talent. Claiming the nation did not need to fear centralized authority when good men drawn from the elite were in charge, they argued that the carefully structured government would preclude the possibility of tyranny. A republic could be large, they declared, if the government's design prevented any one group from controlling it. The separation of powers among legislative, executive, and judicial branches, and the division of powers between states and nation, would accomplish that goal. Thus people did not need to be protected in a formal way from the powers of the new government. Instead, their liberties would be guarded by "distinguished worthies"—men of the "better sort" whose only goal (said George Washington) was "to merit the approbation of good and virtuous men."

The Federalists termed those who opposed the Constitution Antifederalists, thus casting them in a negative light. Antifederalists, while recognizing the need for a national source of revenue, feared a too-powerful central government. They saw the states as the chief protectors of individual rights; consequently, weakening the states could bring the onset of arbitrary power. Antifederalist arguments against the Constitution often consisted of lists of potential abuses of government authority.

Heirs of the Real Whig ideology of the late 1760s and early 1770s, Antifederalists stressed the need for constant popular vigilance to avert oppression. Indeed, some of the Antifederalists had originally promulgated those ideas—Samuel Adams, Patrick Henry, and Richard Henry Lee led the opposition to the Constitution. Such older Americans, whose political opinions had been shaped prior to the centralizing, nationalistic Revolution, peopled the Antifederalist ranks. Joining them were small farmers preoccupied with guarding their property against excessive taxation, backcountry Baptists and Presbyterians, and ambitious, upwardly mobile men who would benefit from an economic and political system less tightly controlled than that the Constitution envisioned. Federalists denigrated such men as disorderly, licentious, and even "unmanly" and "boyish" because they would not follow the elites' lead in supporting the Constitution.

Bill of Rights   As public debate continued, Antifederalists focused on the Constitution's lack of a bill of rights. Even if the new system weakened the states, critics believed, people could still be protected from tyranny by specific guarantees of rights. The Constitution did contain some prohibitions on congressional power. For example, the writ of habeas corpus, which prevented arbitrary imprisonment, could not be suspended except in "cases of rebellion or invasion." But Antifederalists found such constitutional provisions to be few and inadequate. Nor were they reassured by Federalist assertions that the new government could not violate people's rights because it had only limited powers. Opponents wanted the national governing document to incorporate a bill of rights, as had most state constitutions.

Letters of a Federal Farmer, perhaps the most widely read Antifederalist pamphlet, listed the rights that should be protected: freedom of the press and religion, trial by jury, and guarantees against unreasonable searches. From Paris, Thomas Jefferson added his voice to the chorus. Replying to Madison's letter conveying a copy of the Constitution, Jefferson declared, "I like much the general idea" but not "the omission of a bill of rights.... A bill of rights is what the people are entitled to against every government on earth, general or particular, and what no just government should refuse, or rest on inference."

Ratification   As state conventions considered ratification, delegates tended to put state and local interests first. Thus, many were persuaded when Federalists argued that the establishment of a national government with the power to tax foreign commerce would lessen the financial burdens that had prompted Shays's Rebellion and localized protests in other states. Yet the lack of a bill of rights loomed ever larger as a flaw in the proposed government. Four of the first five states to ratify did so unanimously, but serious disagreements then surfaced. Massachusetts, in which Antifederalist forces had been bolstered by a backlash against the state government's heavy-handed treatment of the Shays rebels, ratified by a majority of only nineteen votes out of 355 cast and recommended amendments identifying rights. In June 1788, when New Hampshire ratified, the requirement of nine states was satisfied. But New York and Virginia had not yet voted, and everyone realized the new Constitution could not succeed unless those key states accepted it.

Despite a valiant effort by Antifederalist Patrick Henry, pro-Constitution forces won by 10 votes in the Virginia convention, which likewise recommended the addition of specifications of rights. In New York, James Madison, John Jay, and Alexander Hamilton, writing collectively as "Publius," published *The Federalist*, a series of eighty-five political essays explaining the theory behind the Constitution and masterfully answering its critics. Their reasoned arguments, coupled with Federalists' promise to add a bill of rights to the Constitution, helped win the battle. On July 26, 1788, New York ratified the Constitution by the slim margin of 3 votes. Although the last states—North Carolina and Rhode Island—did not join the Union until November 1789 and May 1790, respectively, the new government was a reality.

Celebrating Ratification   Americans in many cities celebrated ratification (somewhat prematurely) with a series of parades on July 4, 1788, ritualistically linking the acceptance of the Constitution to the formal adoption of the Declaration of Independence. The carefully planned processions dramatized the history and symbolized the unity of the new nation, seeking to counteract memories of the dissent that had so recently engulfed many towns. Like pre-Revolution protest meetings, the parades served as political lessons for literate and illiterate Americans alike. The processions aimed to educate men and women about the significance of the new Constitution and to instruct them about political leaders' hopes for industry and frugality on the part of a virtuous American public.

Symbols expressing those goals filled the Philadelphia parade, planned by artist Charles Willson Peale. About five thousand people participated in the procession, which featured floats portraying such themes as "The Grand Federal Edifice" and stretched for a mile and a half. Marchers representing the first pioneers and Revolutionary War troops paraded with groups of farmers and artisans dramatizing their work. More than forty groups of tradesmen, including barbers, hatters, printers, cloth manufacturers, and clockmakers, sponsored floats. Lawyers, doctors, clergymen of all denominations, and congressmen followed the artisans. A final group of marchers symbolized the nation's future: students from the University of Pennsylvania and other city schools bore a flag labeled "The Rising Generation."

SUMMARY

During the 1770s and 1780s, the nation took shape as a political union. It began to develop an economy independent of the British Empire and attempted to chart its own course in the world in order to protect the national interest, defend the country's borders, and promote beneficial trade. Some Americans prescribed guidelines for the cultural and intellectual life they thought appropriate for a republic, outlining artistic and educational goals for a properly virtuous people. An integral part of the formation of the Union was the systematic formulation of American racist thought. Emphasizing race (rather than status as slave or free) as a determinant of African Americans' standing in the nation allowed men who now termed themselves "white" to define republicanism to exclude most men but themselves and to ensure that they would dominate the country for the foreseeable future. White women, viewed primarily as household dependents, had a limited role to play in the republic, as mothers of the next generation and as selfless contributors to the nation's welfare.

The experience of fighting a war and struggling for survival as an independent nation altered the political context of American life in the 1780s. In 1775, most Americans believed "that government which governs best governs least," but, by the late 1780s, many had changed their minds. They were the drafters and supporters of the Constitution, who concluded from the republic's vicissitudes under the Articles of Confederation that a more powerful central government was needed. During ratification debates, they contended that their proposals were just as "republican" in conception as (if not more so than) the Articles.

Both sides concurred in a general adherence to republican principles, but they emphasized different views of republicanism. Federalists advanced a position based on the principles of classical republicanism, stressing the community over the individual. Antifederalists, fearing that elected leaders would not subordinate personal gain to the good of the whole, wanted a weak central government, formal protection of individual rights, and a loosely regulated economy. The Federalists won their point when the Constitution was adopted, however narrowly. The process of consolidating the states into a national whole was thereby formalized. The 1790s, the first decade of government under the Constitution, would witness hesitant steps toward the creation of a true nation, the United States of America.

8

THE EARLY REPUBLIC: CONFLICTS AT HOME AND ABROAD 1789–1800

BUILDING A WORKABLE GOVERNMENT

At first, consensus appeared possible. Only a few Antifederalists ran for office in the congressional elections held late in 1788, and even fewer were elected. Thus, most members of the First Congress supported a strong national government. The drafters of the Constitution had deliberately left many key issues undecided, so the nationalists' domination of Congress meant that their views quickly prevailed.

First Congress   Congress faced four immediate tasks when it convened in April 1789: raising revenue to support the government, responding to states' calls for a bill of rights, setting up executive departments, and organizing the federal judiciary. The last task was especially important. The Constitution established a Supreme Court but left it to Congress to decide whether to have other federal courts.

James Madison, representing Virginia in the House of Representatives, soon became as influential in Congress as he had been at the Constitutional Convention. A few months into the first session, he persuaded Congress to adopt the Revenue Act of 1789, imposing a 5 percent tariff on certain imports. Therefore, the First Congress quickly achieved what the Confederation Congress never had: an effective national tax law. The new government would have problems in its first years, but lack of revenue would not be one of them.

CHRONOLOGY

1789	Washington inaugurated as first president
	Judiciary Act organizes federal court system
	French Revolution begins
1790	Hamilton's *Report on Public Credit* proposes assumption of state debts
1791	First ten amendments (Bill of Rights) ratified
	First national bank chartered
1793	France declares war on Britain, Spain, and the Netherlands
	Washington's neutrality proclamation keeps the United States out of war
	Democratic societies founded, the first grassroots political organizations
1794	Wayne defeats Miami Confederacy at Fallen Timbers
	Whiskey Rebellion in western Pennsylvania protests taxation
1795	Jay Treaty with England resolves issues remaining from the Revolution
	Pinckney's Treaty with Spain establishes southern boundary of the United States
	Treaty of Greenville with Miami Confederacy opens Ohio to settlement
1796	First contested presidential election: Adams elected president, Jefferson vice president
1798	XYZ affair arouses American opinion against France
	Sedition Act penalizes dissent
	Virginia and Kentucky Resolutions protest suppression of dissent
1798–99	Quasi-War with France
	Fries's Rebellion in Pennsylvania protests taxation
1800	Franco-American Convention ends Quasi-War
	Gabriel's Rebellion threatens Virginia slaveowners
1801	Thomas Jefferson elected president by the House of Representatives after stalemate in electoral college

Bill of Rights   Madison also took the lead with respect to constitutional amendments. During the convention, he had opposed additional restrictions on the national government, believing that its limited powers made a Bill of Rights unnecessary. But Madison subsequently changed his mind, observing to a friend that "in every Gov[ernmen]t power may oppress." When introducing nineteen proposed amendments in June, he told his fellow congressmen they needed to respond to the people's will as expressed in the state conventions, noting in particular that North Carolina had vowed not to ratify the Constitution without a Bill of Rights. Many initially resisted his arguments, yet after lengthy, heated debates, Congress approved twelve amendments. The states formally ratified ten, which officially became part of the Constitution on December 15, 1791 (see the appendix for the Constitution and all amendments, including the Twenty-seventh, which was one of the twelve). As Madison had predicted, their adoption defused Antifederalist opposition and rallied support for the new government.

The First Amendment prohibited Congress from passing any law restricting the right to freedom of religion, speech, press, peaceable assembly, or petition. The next two amendments arose directly from the former colonists' fear of standing armies. The Second Amendment guaranteed the right "to keep and bear arms" because of the need for a "well-regulated Militia." The Third Amendment limited the conditions under which troops could be quartered in private homes. The next five pertained to judicial procedures. The Fourth Amendment prohibited "unreasonable searches and seizures," the Fifth and Sixth established the rights of accused persons, the Seventh specified the conditions for jury trials in civil (as opposed to criminal) cases, and the Eighth forbade "cruel and unusual punishments." The Ninth and Tenth Amendments reserved to the people and the states other unspecified rights and powers. In short, the amendments' authors insisted that, in listing some rights, they did not mean to preclude the exercise of others.

Executive and Judiciary

While debating proposed amendments, Congress also considered the organization of the executive branch. It readily agreed to continue the three administrative departments established under the Articles of Confederation: War, Foreign Affairs (renamed State), and Treasury. Congress instituted two lesser posts: the attorney general—the nation's official lawyer—and the postmaster general. Controversy arose over whether the president alone could dismiss officials whom he had originally appointed with the Senate's consent. After some debate, the House and Senate agreed he had such authority, which established the important principle that the heads of executive departments are accountable solely to the president.

The First Congress's most far-reaching law, the Judiciary Act of 1789, defined the jurisdiction of the federal judiciary and established a six-member Supreme Court, thirteen district courts, and three appellate courts. Its most important provision, Section 25, allowed appeals from state to federal courts when cases raised certain constitutional questions. The act presumed that Article VI of the Constitution, which stated that federal statutes and treaties were considered "the supreme Law of the Land," implied the right of appeal from state to federal courts, yet the Constitution did not explicitly permit such actions. In the nineteenth century, judges and legislators committed to states' rights would challenge the constitutionality of Section 25.

During its first decade, the Supreme Court handled few cases of any importance, and several members resigned. (John Jay, the first chief justice, served only six years.) But in a significant 1796 decision, *Ware v. Hylton*, the Court for the first time declared a state law unconstitutional. That same year, it also reviewed the constitutionality of an act of Congress, upholding its validity in the case of *Hylton v. U.S.* The most important case of the decade, *Chisholm v. Georgia* (1793), established that states could be sued in federal courts by citizens of other states. Five years later, the Eleventh Amendment to the Constitution overturned that decision, which was unpopular with state governments.

Debate over Slavery   Despite the constitutional provisions forbidding Congress from prohibiting the importation of slaves for twenty years, in early 1790 three groups of Quakers submitted petitions to Congress favoring abolition and calling for an end to slave importations. In the ensuing debates, the nation's first political leaders directly addressed the questions they had suppressed in euphemisms in the Constitution. Southerners vigorously asserted that Congress should not even discuss the petitions. Had southern states thought that the federal government would consider interfering with the institution of slavery, such congressmen argued, they would never have ratified the Constitution. The legislators developed a positive defense of slavery that forecast most of the arguments offered on the subject during the next seven decades. They insisted that slavery was integral to the Union and that abolition would cause more problems than it solved, primarily by confronting the nation with the question of how to deal with a sizable population of freed people.

Some northern congressmen, and, in his last published essay, Benjamin Franklin, contested the southerners' position, but a consensus soon emerged to quash such discussions in the future. Congress accepted a committee report denying it the power either to halt slave importations before 1808 or to emancipate slaves at any time, that authority "remaining with the several States alone." The precedent that Congress could not abolish slavery held until the Civil War.

DOMESTIC POLICY UNDER WASHINGTON AND HAMILTON

George Washington did not seek the presidency. In 1783, he returned to Mount Vernon eager for the peaceful life of a Virginia planter. But his fellow countrymen never regarded Washington as just another private citizen. Unanimously elected to preside at the Constitutional Convention, he did not participate in debates but consistently voted for a strong national government. After the adoption of the new governmental structure, Americans concurred that only George Washington had sufficient stature to serve as the republic's first president, an office designed largely with him in mind. The unanimous vote of the electoral college merely formalized that consensus.

Reluctant to return to public life, George Washington nevertheless knew he could not ignore his country's call. Awaiting the summons to New York City, the nation's capital, he wrote to an old friend, "My movements to the chair of Government will be accompanied by feelings not unlike those of a culprit who is going to the place of his execution.... I am sensible, that I am embarking the voice of my Countrymen and a good name of my own, on this voyage, but what returns will be made for them, Heaven alone can foretell." Symbolically, he donned a suit of homespun for the inaugural ceremony.

Washington's First Steps

Washington acted cautiously during his first months in office in 1789, knowing that whatever he did would set precedents for the future. When the title by which he should be addressed aroused controversy (Vice President John Adams favored "His Highness, the President of the United States of America, and Protector of their Liberties"), Washington said nothing. The accepted title soon became a plain "Mr. President." By using the heads of the executive departments collectively as his chief advisers, he created the cabinet. As the Constitution required, he sent Congress an annual State of the Union message. Washington also concluded that he should exercise his veto power over congressional legislation sparingly—only, indeed, if he became convinced a bill was unconstitutional.

Early in his term, Washington undertook elaborately organized journeys to all the states. At each stop, he was ritually welcomed by uniformed militia units, young women strewing flowers in his path, local leaders, groups of Revolutionary War veterans, and respectable citizens who presented him with formal addresses reaffirming their loyalty to the United States. The president thus personally came to embody national unity, simultaneously drawing ordinary folk into the sphere of national politics.

Washington's first major task as president was to choose the heads of the executive departments. For the War Department, he selected an old comrade-in-arms, Henry Knox of Massachusetts, who had been his reliable artillery general during the war. His choice for the State Department was fellow Virginian Thomas Jefferson, who had just returned to the United States from his post as minister to France. And for the crucial position of secretary of the treasury, the president chose the brilliant, intensely ambitious Alexander Hamilton.

Alexander Hamilton

The illegitimate son of a Scottish aristocrat and a woman whose husband had divorced her for adultery and desertion, Hamilton was born in the British West Indies in 1757. His early years were spent in poverty; after his mother's death when he was eleven, he worked as a clerk for a mercantile firm. In 1773, with financial support from friends, Hamilton enrolled at King's College (later Columbia University). Only eighteen months later, the precocious seventeen-year-old contributed a pamphlet to the prerevolutionary publication wars. Devoted to the patriot cause, Hamilton volunteered for service in the American army, where he came to Washington's attention. In 1777, Washington appointed the young man as one of his aides, and the two developed great mutual affection.

The general's patronage helped the poor youth of dubious background to marry well. At twenty-three, he wed Elizabeth Schuyler, daughter of a wealthy New York family. After the war, Hamilton practiced law in New York City and served as a delegate to the Annapolis Convention and later the Constitutional Convention. Although he exerted little influence at either gathering, his contributions to *The Federalist* in 1788 revealed him as one of the chief political thinkers in the republic.

In his dual role as treasury secretary and presidential adviser, Hamilton exhibited two traits distinguishing him from most of his contemporaries. First, his primary loyalty lay with the nation. Caribbean-born, Hamilton had no natal ties to

any state; he neither sympathized with nor fully understood demands for local autonomy. His fiscal policies always aimed at consolidating national power. Hamilton
never feared the exercise of centralized executive authority, as did older compatriots
who had clashed repeatedly with colonial governors, and he openly favored maintaining close political and economic ties with Britain.

Second, Hamilton regarded his fellow humans with unvarnished cynicism. Perhaps because of his difficult early life and his own overriding ambition, Hamilton
believed people to be motivated primarily by economic self-interest. He placed no
reliance on people's capacity for virtuous, self-sacrificing behavior. This outlook
set him apart from those Americans who foresaw a rosy future in which public-
spirited citizens would pursue the common good rather than their own private
advantage. Although other Americans (for instance, James Madison) also stressed
the role of private interests in a republic, Hamilton went further in his emphasis on
self-interest as the major motivator of human behavior. Those beliefs significantly
influenced the way he tackled the monumental task before him: straightening out
the new nation's tangled finances.

**National and
State Debts**   Congress ordered the new secretary of the treasury to assess
the public debt and to submit recommendations for sup-
porting the government's credit. Hamilton found that the
country's remaining war debts fell into three categories: those owed by the nation
to foreign governments and investors, mostly to France (about $11 million); those
owed by the national government to merchants, former soldiers, holders of revolutionary bonds, and the like (about $27 million); and, finally, similar debts owed
by state governments (roughly $25 million). With respect to the national debt, few
disagreed: Americans recognized that, if their new government was to succeed, it
would have to repay at full face value those financial obligations the nation had
incurred while winning independence.

The state debts were another matter. Some states—notably, Virginia, Maryland, North Carolina, and Georgia—had already paid off most of their war debts
by levying taxes and handing out land grants in lieu of monetary payments. They
would oppose the national government's assumption of responsibility for other
states' debts because their citizens would be taxed to pay such obligations. Massachusetts, Connecticut, and South Carolina, by contrast, still had sizable unpaid
debts and would welcome a system of national assumption. The possible assumption of state debts also had political implications. Consolidating the debt in the
hands of the national government would help to concentrate economic and political
power at the national level. A contrary policy would reserve greater independence
of action for the states.

**Hamilton's
Financial Plan**   Hamilton's first *Report on Public Credit*, sent to Congress in
January 1790, stimulated lively debate. The treasury secre-
tary proposed that Congress assume outstanding state debts,
combine them with national obligations, and issue new securities covering both
principal and accumulated unpaid interest. Hamilton thereby hoped to ensure that
holders of the public debt—many of them wealthy merchants and speculators—had

a significant financial stake in the new government's survival. The opposition coalesced around James Madison, who opposed the assumption of state debts for two reasons. First, his state of Virginia had already paid off most of its obligations, and second, he wanted to avoid rewarding wealthy speculators who had purchased state and national debt certificates at a small fraction of their face value from needy veterans and farmers.

Prompted in part by Madison, the House initially rejected the assumption of state debts. The Senate, however, adopted Hamilton's plan largely intact. A series of compromises followed, in which the assumption bill became linked to the other major controversial issue of that congressional session: the location of the permanent national capital. Several related political deals were struck. A southern site on the Potomac River (favored by Washington and close to Mount Vernon) was selected for the capital, and the first part of Hamilton's financial program became law in August 1790.

First Bank of the United States

Four months later, Hamilton submitted to Congress a second report on public credit, recommending the chartering of a national bank modeled on the Bank of England. This proposal, too, aroused much opposition, primarily after Congress had already voted to establish the bank.

The Bank of the United States, to be chartered for twenty years, was to be capitalized at $10 million. Just $2 million would come from public funds, while private investors supplied the rest. The bank would act as collecting and disbursing agent for the Treasury, and its notes would circulate as the nation's currency. Most political leaders recognized that such an institution would be beneficial, especially because it would solve the problem of America's perpetual shortage of an acceptable medium of exchange. But another issue loomed large: did the Constitution give Congress the power to establish such a bank?

Interpreting the Constitution

James Madison answered that question with a resounding no. He pointed out that Constitutional Convention delegates had specifically rejected a clause authorizing Congress to issue corporate charters. Consequently, he argued, that power could not be inferred from other parts of the Constitution. Madison's contention disturbed President Washington, who decided to request other opinions before signing the bill into law. Edmund Randolph, the attorney general, and Thomas Jefferson, the secretary of state, agreed with Madison that the bank was unconstitutional. Jefferson referred to Article I, Section 8, of the Constitution, which gave Congress the power "to make all Laws which shall be necessary and proper for carrying into Execution the foregoing Powers." The key word, Jefferson argued, was *necessary*: Congress could do what was needed, but without specific constitutional authorization could not do what was merely desirable. Thus, Jefferson formulated the strict-constructionist interpretation of the Constitution.

Washington asked Hamilton to reply to the negative assessments of his proposal. Hamilton's *Defense of the Constitutionality of the Bank*, presented to the president in February 1791, brilliantly expounded a broad-constructionist view of the Constitution. Hamilton argued forcefully that Congress could choose any means not specifically prohibited by the Constitution to achieve a constitutional end. He reasoned thus: if the end was constitutional and the means was not *un*constitutional, then the means was constitutional.

Washington concurred, and the bill became law. The bank proved successful, as did the scheme for funding the national debt and assuming the states' debts. The new nation's securities became desirable investments for its own citizens and for wealthy foreigners, especially those in the Netherlands, who rushed to purchase American debt certificates. The influx of new capital, coupled with the high prices that American grain now commanded in European markets, eased farmers' debt burdens and contributed to a new prosperity. But two other aspects of Alexander Hamilton's wide-ranging financial scheme did not fare so well.

Report on Manufactures   In December 1791, Hamilton presented to Congress his *Report on Manufactures*, the third and last of his prescriptions for the American economy. It outlined an ambitious plan for encouraging and protecting the United States' infant industries, such as shoemaking and textile manufacturing. Hamilton argued that the nation could never be truly independent as long as it relied heavily on Europe for manufactured goods. He urged Congress to promote the immigration of technicians and laborers and to support industrial development through a limited use of protective tariffs. Many of Hamilton's ideas were implemented in later decades, but few congressmen in 1791 could see much merit in his proposals. They firmly believed America's future lay in

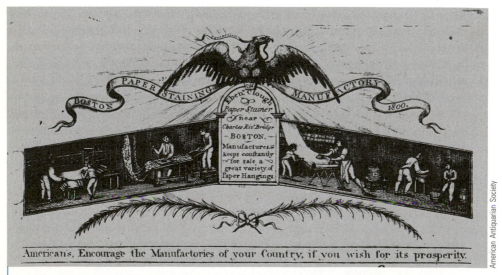

American Antiquarian Society

Although Congress did not react positively to the arguments in Hamilton's Report on Manufactures, *the owners of America's burgeoning industries recognized the importance of the policy Hamilton advocated. Ebenezer Clough, a Boston maker of wallpaper, incorporated into his letterhead the exhortation "Americans, Encourage the Manufactories of your Country, if you wish for its prosperity."*

agriculture and the carrying trade and that the mainstay of the republic was the yeoman farmer. Congress therefore rejected the report.

That same year, Congress accepted another feature of Hamilton's financial program, levying an excise tax on whiskey distilled within the United States. Although proceeds from the Revenue Act of 1789 covered the interest on the national debt, the decision to fund state debts meant that the national government required additional income. A tax on whiskey affected relatively few westerners—the farmers who grew corn and the small and large distillers who turned that corn into whiskey—and might also reduce the consumption of whiskey. (Eighteenth-century Americans, notorious for their heavy drinking, consumed about twice as much alcohol per capita as today's rate.) Moreover, Hamilton knew that those western farmers and distillers were Jefferson's supporters, and he saw the benefits of taxing them rather than the merchants who favored his own policies.

Whiskey Rebellion News of the tax set off protests in the west, where residents were dissatisfied with the army's defense of their region from threats of Indian attack. To their minds, the same government that protected them inadequately was now proposing to tax them disproportionately. Unrest continued for two years on the frontiers of Pennsylvania, Maryland, and Virginia. Large groups of men drafted petitions protesting the tax, deliberately imitated crowd actions of the 1760s, and occasionally harassed tax collectors.

President Washington responded with restraint until violence erupted in July 1794, when western Pennsylvania farmers resisted two excisemen trying to collect the tax. About seven thousand rebels convened on August 1 to plot the destruction of Pittsburgh but decided not to face the heavy guns of the fort guarding the town. Washington then took decisive action to prevent a crisis reminiscent of Shays's Rebellion. On August 7, he called on the insurgents to disperse and summoned nearly thirteen thousand militiamen. By the time federal forces marched westward in October and November (led at times by Washington himself), the disturbances had ceased. The troops met no resistance and arrested only twenty suspects. Two men were convicted of treason, but—continuing his policy of restraint—Washington pardoned both. The leaderless and unorganized rebellion ended with little bloodshed.

The importance of the Whiskey Rebellion lay not in military victory over the rebels—for there was none—but in the forceful message it conveyed to the American people. The national government, Washington had demonstrated, would not allow violent resistance to its laws. In the republic, change would be effected peacefully, by legal means. People dissatisfied with the law should try to amend or repeal it, not take extralegal action as they had during the colonial era.

THE FRENCH REVOLUTION AND THE DEVELOPMENT OF PARTISAN POLITICS

By 1794, some Americans were already beginning to seek change systematically through electoral politics, even though traditional political theory regarded organized opposition—especially in a republic—as illegitimate. In a monarchy, formal opposition groups, commonly called factions, were to be expected. In a government of the people, by contrast, sustained factional disagreement was taken as a sign of corruption and subversion. Such negative judgments, though widely held, did not halt the growth of partisan sentiment.

Republicans and Federalists   Jefferson and Madison became convinced as early as 1792 that Hamilton's policies of favoring wealthy commercial interests at the expense of agriculture would eventually impose a corrupt government on the United States. Characterizing themselves as the true heirs of the Revolution, they charged Hamilton with plotting to subvert republican principles. To dramatize their point, Jefferson, Madison, and their followers in Congress began calling themselves Republicans. Hamilton in turn accused Jefferson and Madison of the same offense: attempting to destroy the republic. Hamilton and his supporters began calling themselves Federalists to legitimize their claims and link themselves with the Constitution. Each group accused the other of being an illicit faction working to sabotage the republican principles of the Revolution. Newspapers aligned with the two sides fanned the flames of partisanship, publishing virulent attacks on political opponents. Indeed, before parties fully coalesced, such newspapers not only provided a means of communication but also served as the very foundation of political identity.

At first, President Washington tried to remain aloof from the political dispute that divided Hamilton and Jefferson, his chief advisers. The growing controversy did help persuade him to promote political unity by seeking office again in 1792. But in 1793 and thereafter, developments in foreign affairs magnified the disagreements, for France (America's wartime ally) and Great Britain (America's most important trading partner) resumed the periodic hostilities that had originated a century earlier.

French Revolution   In 1789, many American men and women welcomed the news of the French Revolution. The French people's success in overthrowing an oppressive monarchy seemed to vindicate the United States' own revolution. Americans saw themselves as the vanguard of an inevitable historical trend that would reshape the world in a republican mold. Dinners, public ceremonies, and balls celebrated the French revolutionaries; women adorned their hats or clothing with revolutionary symbols; and some men began terming themselves "citizen" in the French manner, while women became "citizeness" or "citess." Yet one critical newspaper editor railed against "these fiery frenchified dames" whom he regarded as "monsters in human shape."

By 1793, the reports from France had become disquieting. Outbreaks of violence continued, and political leaders succeeded each other with bewildering rapidity. Executions mounted; the king himself was beheaded early that year. Although many Americans, including Jefferson and Madison, retained sympathy for the revolution, others—among them Alexander Hamilton—began to cite France as a prime example of the perversion of republicanism.

Debates within the United States intensified when the newly republican France became enmeshed in conflict with other European nations. Both because French leaders feared that neighboring monarchies would intervene to crush the revolution and because they sought to spread the republican gospel throughout the continent, they declared war first on Austria and then, in 1793, on Britain, Spain, and Holland. That confronted the Americans with a dilemma. The 1778 Treaty of Alliance with France bound them to that nation "forever," and a mutual commitment to republicanism created ideological bonds. Yet the United States was connected to Great Britain as well. In addition to their shared history and language, America and Britain had again become important economic partners. Americans still purchased most of their manufactured goods from Great Britain. Indeed, because the revenues of the United States depended heavily on import tariffs, the nation's economic health in effect required uninterrupted trade with the former mother country.

Edmond Genêt   The political and diplomatic climate grew even more complicated in April 1793, when Edmond Genêt, a representative of the French government, arrived in Charleston, South Carolina. Genêt's arrival raised troubling questions for President Washington. Should he receive Genêt, thus officially recognizing the French revolutionary government? Should he acknowledge an obligation to aid France under the terms of the 1778 Treaty of Alliance? Or should he proclaim American neutrality?

Washington resolved his dilemma by receiving Genêt but also issuing a proclamation informing the world that the United States would adopt "a conduct friendly and impartial toward the belligerent powers." Federalist newspapers vociferously defended the proclamation, and partisan leaders organized rallies to praise the president's action. Republicans who favored assisting France reluctantly accepted the neutrality policy, which had overwhelming popular support.

Genêt's faction fell from power in Paris, and he subsequently sought political asylum in the United States. But his disappearance from the diplomatic scene did not diminish the impact of the French Revolution in America. The domestic divisions Genêt helped to widen were perpetuated by clubs called Democratic societies, formed by Americans sympathetic to the French Revolution and worried about the policies of the Washington administration. Such societies reflected a growing grassroots concern about the same developments that troubled Jefferson and Madison.

Democratic Societies   More than forty Democratic societies organized between 1793 and 1800. Their members saw themselves as seeking the same goal as the 1760s resistance movement: protecting people's liberties against encroachments by corrupt and self-serving rulers. To that end, they publicly protested government fiscal and foreign policy, repeatedly proclaiming their belief in "the equal rights of man," particularly the rights to free speech, free press, and assembly. Like the Sons of Liberty, the Democratic societies comprised chiefly artisans and craftsmen, although professionals, farmers, and merchants also joined. Although locally based, they communicated effectively through a network of newspapers and allied themselves nationally with congressional Republicans.

The rapid spread of such citizens' groups, outspokenly critical of the administration, disturbed Hamilton and Washington. Federalist writers charged that the organizations were dangerously subversive because elected officials, not "self-created societies," should formulate public policy. The groups' "real design," a newspaper asserted, was "to involve the country in war, to assume the reins of government and tyrannize over the people." The counterattack climaxed in the fall of 1794 when Washington accused the societies of fomenting the Whiskey Rebellion. Republican leaders and newspaper editors responded by defending the societies but condemning the insurgents.

In retrospect, Washington and Hamilton's reaction to the Democratic societies seems disproportionately hostile. But factional disputes were believed to endanger the survival of republics. As the first organized political dissenters in the United States, the Democratic societies alarmed administration officials, who had not yet accepted the idea that one component of a free government was an organized loyal opposition.

PARTISAN POLITICS AND RELATIONS WITH GREAT BRITAIN

In 1794, George Washington dispatched Chief Justice John Jay to London to negotiate several unresolved questions in Anglo-American relations. The British had recently seized some American merchant ships trading in the French West Indies. The United States wanted to establish the countervailing principle of freedom of the seas and to assert its right, as a neutral nation, to trade freely with both combatants. Further, Great Britain still held posts in the American Northwest, thus violating the 1783 peace treaty. Settlers there believed that the British were responsible for renewed warfare with neighboring Indians, and they wanted that threat removed. The Americans also hoped for a commercial treaty and sought compensation for the slaves who left with the British army at the end of the war.

Jay Treaty Debate   The negotiations in London proved difficult because Jay had little to offer in exchange for the concessions he sought. Britain did agree to evacuate the western forts and ease restrictions on American trade to England and the Caribbean. (Some limitations were retained, however, violating the Americans' desire for open commerce.) The treaty established two arbitration commissions—one to deal with prewar debts Americans owed to British creditors and the other to hear claims for captured American merchant ships—but Britain adamantly refused slaveowners compensation for their lost bondspeople. Under the circumstances, Jay had probably done the best he could. Nevertheless, most Americans, including the president, at first expressed dissatisfaction with at least some clauses of the treaty.

The Senate debated the Jay Treaty in secret. Not until after ratification in late June 1795 (by 20 to 10, the exact two-thirds the Constitution required) did members of the public learn its provisions in the pages of the chief Republican newspaper, Benjamin Franklin Bache's *Aurora*. Bache organized the protests that followed, encouraging both publications and popular gatherings urging Washington to reject the treaty. Especially vehement opposition arose in the South, as planters criticized the lack of compensation for runaway slaves and objected to the commission on prewar debts, which might make them pay off obligations to British merchants dating back to the 1760s. But Federalists countered with meetings and essays of their own, contending that the Jay Treaty would prove preferable to the alternative—no treaty at all. The president, displeased by the Republicans' organized vocal opposition and convinced by pro-treaty arguments, signed the pact in mid-August. Just one opportunity remained to prevent it from going into effect: Congress had to appropriate funds to carry out the treaty, and, according to the Constitution, appropriation bills had to originate in the House of Representatives.

Washington delayed submitting the treaty to the House until March 1796, futilely hoping that by then the opposition would have dissipated. During the debate, Republicans argued against approving the appropriations, and they won a vote asking Washington to submit to the House all documents pertinent to the negotiations. In successfully resisting the request, Washington established a power still used today—executive privilege, in which the president may withhold information from Congress if he deems it necessary.

The treaty's opponents initially commanded a congressional majority, but pressure for appropriating the necessary funds built as time passed, fostered by an especially vigorous Federalist campaign of publications and petitions targeting middlestate congressmen whose districts would benefit from approval. Constituent petitions contended that failure to fund the treaty would lead to war with Britain, thus endangering Pennsylvania frontier settlements and New York and New Jersey commercial interests alike. Further, Federalists successfully linked the Jay Treaty with another, more popular pact. In 1795, Thomas Pinckney of South Carolina had negotiated a treaty with Spain giving the United States navigation privileges on the Mississippi River and the right to land and store goods at New Orleans tax free, thus boosting the nation's economy. The overwhelming support for Pinckney's Treaty (the Senate ratified it unanimously) helped to overcome opposition to the Jay Treaty. In late April, the House appropriated the money by the narrow margin of 51 to 48. The vote divided along partisan and regional lines: all but two southerners opposed the treaty, all but three congressional Federalists supported it, and a majority of middle-state representatives voted yes.

The Federalists' campaign to sway public opinion ironically violated their fundamental philosophy of government. They believed ordinary people should defer to the judgment of elected leaders, yet in order to persuade the House to follow the president's lead, they actively engaged in grassroots politicking. Even Federalist women became involved by presenting patriotic banners to militia companies or by taking formal roles in July fourth celebrations. The Federalists had won the battle, but in the long run they lost the war, for Republicans ultimately proved far more effective in appealing to the citizenry at large.

Bases of
Partisanship
To describe the growing partisanship in Congress and the nation is easier than to explain such divisions in the electorate. The terms used by Jefferson and Madison (the people versus aristocrats) or by Hamilton and Washington (true patriots versus subversive rabble) do not adequately explain the growing divisions. Simple economic differences between agrarian and commercial interests do not provide the answer either, as more than 90 percent of Americans still lived in rural areas. Moreover, Jefferson's vision of a prosperous agrarian America rested on commercial farming, not rural self-sufficiency. Nor did the divisions in the 1790s simply repeat the

Federalist-Antifederalist debate of 1787–1788. Even though most Antifederalists became Republicans, the party's leaders, Madison and Jefferson, had supported the Constitution.

Yet certain distinctions can be made. Republicans, especially prominent in the southern and middle states, tended to be self-assured, confident, and optimistic about both politics and the economy. Southern planters, in control of their region and dominating a class of enslaved laborers, foresaw a prosperous future based partly on continued westward expansion, a movement they expected to dominate. Republicans employed democratic rhetoric to win the allegiance of small farmers south of New England. Members of non-English ethnic groups—especially Irish, Scots, and Germans—found Republicans' words attractive. Artisans also joined the coalition; they saw themselves as the urban equivalent of small farmers, cherishing their independence from domineering bosses. Republicans of all descriptions emphasized developing America's own resources, worrying less than Federalists about the nation's place in the world. Republicans also remained sympathetic to France in international affairs.

By contrast, Federalists, concentrated among the commercial interests of New England, came mostly from English stock. Insecure, they stressed the need for order, hierarchy, and obedience to political authority. Wealthy New England merchants aligned themselves with the Federalists, but so, too, did the region's farmers who, prevented from expanding agricultural production because of New England's poor soil, gravitated toward the more conservative party. Federalists, like Republicans, assumed that southern and middle-state interests would dominate western lands, so they had little incentive to work actively to develop that potentially rich territory. In Federalist eyes, potential enemies—both internal and external—threatened the nation, necessitating a protective alliance with Great Britain. Given the dangers posed to the nation by European warfare, Federalists' vision of international affairs may have been accurate, but it was also unappealing. Because Federalists held out little hope of a better future to the voters of any region, it is not surprising that the Republicans prevailed in the end.

Washington's Farewell Address   After the treaty debate, wearied by the criticism to which he had been subjected, George Washington decided to retire. (Presidents had not yet been limited to two terms, as they have been since the adoption of the Twenty-second Amendment in 1951.) In September, Washington published his Farewell Address, most of which had been written by Hamilton. In it, Washington outlined two principles that guided American foreign policy at least until the late 1940s: to maintain commercial but not political ties to other nations and to enter no permanent alliances. He also drew sharp distinctions between the United States and Europe, stressing America's uniqueness—its exceptionalism—and the need for independent action in foreign affairs, today called unilateralism.

Washington lamented the existence of factional divisions among his countrymen. Some interpret his desire for an end to partisan strife as a call for politicians to consider only the good of the whole nation. But in the context of the impending presidential election, the Farewell Address appears rather as an attack on the legitimacy of the Republican opposition. Washington advocated unity behind the

Federalist banner, which he viewed as the only proper political stance. The Federalists (like the Republicans) continued to see themselves as the sole guardians of the truth and the only true heirs of the Revolution. Both sides perceived their opponents as misguided, unpatriotic troublemakers who sought to undermine revolutionary ideals.

Election of 1796   The two organized groups actively contending for office made the presidential election of 1796 the first serious contest for the position. To succeed Washington, the Federalists in Congress put forward Vice President John Adams, with the diplomat Thomas Pinckney as his running mate. Congressional Republicans chose Thomas Jefferson as their presidential candidate; the lawyer, Revolutionary War veteran, and active Republican politician Aaron Burr of New York agreed to run for vice president.

The election was contested, but not decided by popular vote. Most state legislatures appointed electors. Moreover, the method of voting in the electoral college did not take into account the possibility of party slates. The Constitution's drafters had not foreseen the development of competing national political organizations, so the Constitution provided no way to express support for one person for president and another for vice president. The electors simply voted for two people. The man with the highest total became president; the second highest, vice president.

That procedure proved to be the Federalists' undoing. Adams won the presidency with 71 votes, but a number of Federalist electors (especially those from New England) failed to cast ballots for Pinckney. Jefferson won 68 votes, 9 more than Pinckney, to become vice president. The incoming administration was thus politically divided. During the next four years, the new president and vice president, once allies and close friends, became bitter enemies.

JOHN ADAMS AND POLITICAL DISSENT

John Adams took over the presidency peculiarly blind to the partisan developments of the previous four years. As president, he never abandoned an outdated notion discarded by George Washington as early as 1794: that the president should be above politics, an independent and dignified figure who did not seek factional advantage. Thus, Adams kept Washington's cabinet intact, despite its key members' allegiance to his chief Federalist rival, Alexander Hamilton. Adams often adopted a passive posture, letting others (usually Hamilton) take the lead when the president should have acted decisively. As a result, his administration gained a reputation for inconsistency. But Adams's detachment from Hamilton's maneuverings did enable him to weather the greatest international crisis the republic had yet faced: the Quasi-War with France.

XYZ Affair   The Jay Treaty improved America's relationship with Great Britain, but it provoked France to retaliate by ordering its ships to seize American vessels carrying British goods. In response, Congress increased military spending, authorizing the building of ships and the stockpiling of weapons and ammunition. President Adams also sent three commissioners to Paris to negotiate a settlement. For months, the American commissioners sought talks with Talleyrand, the French foreign minister, but Talleyrand's agents demanded a bribe of $250,000 before negotiations could begin. The Americans retorted, "No, no; not a sixpence" and reported the incident in dispatches the president received in early March 1798. Adams informed Congress of the impasse and recommended further increases in defense appropriations.

Convinced that Adams had deliberately sabotaged the negotiations, congressional Republicans insisted that the dispatches be turned over to Congress. Adams complied, aware that releasing the reports would work to his advantage. He withheld only the names of the French agents, referring to them as X, Y, and Z. The revelation that the Americans had been treated with contempt stimulated a wave of anti-French sentiment in the United States. A journalist's version of the commissioners' reply, "Millions for defense, but not a cent for tribute," became the national slogan. Cries for war filled the air. Congress formally abrogated the Treaty of Alliance and authorized American ships to seize French vessels.

Quasi-War with France   Thus began an undeclared war with France fought in Caribbean waters between warships of the U.S. Navy and French privateers. Although Americans initially suffered heavy losses of merchant shipping, by early 1799 the U.S. Navy had established its superiority. Its ships captured eight French privateers and naval vessels, easing the threat to America's vital Caribbean trade.

The Republicans, who opposed war and continued to sympathize with France, could do little to stem the tide of anti-French feelings. Because Agent Y had boasted of the existence of a "French party in America," Federalists flatly accused Republicans of traitorous designs. A New York newspaper declared that anyone who remained "lukewarm" after reading the XYZ dispatches was a "criminal—and the man who does not warmly reprobate the conduct of the French must have a soul black enough to be fit for treason Strategems and spoils." John Adams wavered between calling the Republicans traitors and acknowledging their right to oppose administration measures. His wife was less tolerant. "Those whom the French boast of as their Partizans," Abigail Adams declared, should be "adjudged traitors to their country." If Jefferson had been president, she added, "we should all have been sold to the French."

Alien and Sedition Acts   Federalists saw this climate of opinion as an opportunity to deal a death blow to their Republican opponents. Now that the country seemed to see the truth of what they had been saying ever since the Whiskey Rebellion in 1794—that Republicans were subversive foreign agents—Federalists sought to codify that belief into law. In 1798, the Federalist-controlled Congress adopted a set of four laws known as the Alien and Sedition Acts, intended to suppress dissent and to prevent further growth of the Republican faction.

Three of the acts targeted recently arrived immigrants, whom Federalists accurately suspected of sympathizing with Republicans. The Naturalization Act lengthened the residency period required for citizenship and ordered all resident aliens to register with the federal government. The two Alien Acts, though not immediately implemented, provided for the detention of enemy aliens in time of war and gave the president authority to deport any alien he deemed dangerous to the nation's security.

The fourth statute, the Sedition Act, sought to control both citizens and aliens. It outlawed conspiracies to prevent the enforcement of federal laws, setting the maximum punishment for such offenses at five years in prison and a $5,000 fine. The act also tried to control speech. Writing, printing, or uttering "false, scandalous and malicious" statements against the government or the president "with intent to defame ... or to bring them or either of them, into contempt or disrepute" became a crime punishable by as much as two years' imprisonment and a fine of $2,000. Today, a law punishing speech alone would be unconstitutional. But in the eighteenth century, when any organized political opposition was suspect, many Americans supported the Sedition Act's restrictions on free speech.

The Sedition Act led to fifteen indictments and ten guilty verdicts. Among those convicted were a congressman and former newspaper editor, Matthew Lyon of Vermont; and James Callender, a Scots immigrant and scandalmonger, whose exposés forced Alexander Hamilton to acknowledge an extramarital affair. After turning his attention to President Adams, Callender was convicted, fined, and jailed for nine months. Growing numbers of Republican newspaper editors nevertheless continued their relentless criticisms of Federalists, energized rather than quashed by the persecution. One of the most outspoken, William Duane—successor to Bache as the *Aurora's* editor—ignored a Sedition Act indictment, prosecutions in state and federal courts for other purported offenses, and even a vicious beating by Federalists thugs, to persist in partisan attacks. He and other Republicans created an informal network of newspapers that exchanged information and spread opposition ideas throughout the country.

Virginia and Kentucky Resolutions   Jefferson and Madison combated the acts in another way. Petitioning the Federalist-controlled Congress to repeal the laws would clearly fail, and Federalist judges refused to allow accused individuals to question the Sedition Act's constitutionality. Accordingly, the Republican leaders turned to the only other forum available for formal protest: state legislatures. Carefully concealing their own role— the vice president and congressman wanted to avoid being indicted for sedition— Jefferson and Madison drafted sets of resolutions that were introduced into the Kentucky and Virginia legislatures, respectively, in the fall of 1798. Because a compact among the states had created the Constitution, the resolutions contended, people speaking through their states had a legitimate right to judge the constitutionality of actions taken by the federal government. Both pronounced the Alien and Sedition Acts unconstitutional, and thus (declared Kentucky) "void and of no force," advancing the doctrine later known as nullification.

Although no other state endorsed them, the Virginia and Kentucky Resolutions nevertheless had considerable short- and long-term influence. First, they placed the opposition party squarely in the revolutionary tradition of resistance to tyrannical authority. Second, their theory of union inspired the Hartford Convention of 1814 and southern states' rights advocates in the 1830s and thereafter. Jefferson and Madison had identified a key constitutional issue: How far could states go in opposing the national government? How could a conflict between the two be resolved? These questions would not be definitively answered until the Civil War.

Convention of 1800   Just as the Sedition Act was being implemented and northern legislatures were rejecting the Virginia and Kentucky Resolutions, Federalists split over the course of action the United States should take toward France. Hamilton and his supporters called for a declaration legitimizing the undeclared naval war. Adams, though, received a number of private signals that the French government regretted its treatment of the American commissioners.

Acting on such assurances, Adams dispatched William Vans Murray to Paris to negotiate with Napoleon Bonaparte, France's new leader, who was consolidating his hold on the country and eager to end messy foreign conflicts. The United States sought two goals: compensation for ships the French had seized since 1793 and abrogation of the treaty of 1778. The Convention of 1800, which ended the Quasi-War, provided for the latter but not the former. Still, it freed the United States from its only permanent alliance, thus allowing it to follow the independent diplomatic course George Washington had urged in his Farewell Address.

THE WEST IN THE NEW NATION

By the end of the eighteenth century, the nation had added three states (Vermont, Kentucky, and Tennessee) to the original thirteen and more than 1 million people to the nearly 4 million counted by the 1790 census. It also nominally controlled all the land east of the Mississippi River and north of Spanish Florida, divided by the Ohio

Chicago History Museum

Independence National Historic Park

The two chief antagonists at the Battle of Fallen Timbers and negotiators of the Treaty of Greenville (1795). On the left, Little Turtle, the leader of the Miami Confederacy; on the right, General Anthony Wayne. Little Turtle, in a copy of a portrait painted two years later, appears to be wearing a miniature of Wayne on a bear-claw necklace.

River. Control of the land north of the Ohio was achieved only after considerable bloodshed, for initially the land was dominated by a powerful western confederacy of eight Indian nations led by the Miamis.

War in the Northwest Territory   General Arthur St. Clair, first governor of the Northwest Territory, futilely tried to open more land to settlement through failed treaty negotiations with the western confederacy in early 1789. Sub-sequently, Little Turtle, the confederacy's able war chief, defeated forces led by General Josiah Harmar (1790) and by St. Clair himself (1791) in major battles near the present border between Indiana and Ohio. More than six hundred of St. Clair's men died, and scores more were wounded, in the United States' worst defeat in the entire history of the American frontier.

In 1793, the Miami Confederacy declared that peace could be achieved only if the United States recognized the Ohio River as its northwestern boundary. But the national government refused to relinquish its claims in the region. A reorganized and newly invigorated army under the command of General Anthony Wayne, a Revolutionary War hero, attacked and defeated the confederacy in August 1794 at the Battle of Fallen Timbers (near present-day Toledo, Ohio. Negotiating successfully with the confederacy was crucial for the new nation because without a treaty, warfare would continue indefinitely as American settlers—whom the government regarded as "white savages"—continued to push west. The United States lacked the will and the resources for a prolonged frontier conflict, so Wayne respectfully treated the confederacy's leaders, whom he saw as "red gentlemen." He reached agreement with them in August 1795.

The resulting Treaty of Greenville gave each side a portion of what it wanted. The United States gained the right to settle much of what was to become Ohio, the indigenous peoples retaining only the northwest corner of the region. Indians, though, received the acknowledgment they had long sought: American recognition of their rights to the soil. At Greenville, the United States formally accepted the principle of Indian sovereignty, by virtue of residence, over all lands the native peoples had not ceded. Never again would the U.S. government claim that it had acquired Indian territory solely through negotiation with a European or North American country.

South of the Ohio, Pinckney's Treaty with Spain that same year established the 31st parallel as the boundary between the United States and Florida. Nevertheless, Spanish influence in the Old Southwest continued to raise questions about the loyalty of American settlers in the region, much of it still unceded and occupied by Creeks, Cherokees, and other Indian nations. A Southwest Ordinance (1790) attempted to organize the territory; by permitting slavery, it made the region attractive to slaveholders.

"Civilizing" the Indians   Increasingly, even Indian peoples who lived independent of federal authority came within the orbit of U.S. influence. The nation's stated goal was to "civilize" them. "Instead of exterminating a part of the human race," Henry Knox, Washington's secretary of war, contended in 1789, the government should "impart our knowledge of cultivation and the arts to the aboriginals of the country." The first step in such a project, Knox suggested, should be to introduce to Indian peoples "a love for exclusive property"; to that end, he proposed that the government give livestock to individual Indians. Four years later, the Indian Trade and Intercourse Act of 1793 codified Knox's plan, promising that the federal government would supply Indians with animals and agricultural implements, and also provide appropriate instructors.

The well-intentioned plan reflected federal officials' blindness to the realities of native peoples' lives. Not only did it incorrectly posit that the Indians' traditional commitment to communal notions of landowning could easily be overcome, it also ignored the centuries-long agricultural experience of eastern Indian peoples. The policymakers focused only on Indian men: because they hunted, male Indians were "savages" who had to be "civilized" by being taught to farm. That in these societies women traditionally did the farming was irrelevant because, in the eyes of the officials, Indian women—like those of European descent—should properly confine themselves to child rearing, household chores, and home manufacturing.

Iroquois and Cherokees   Indian nations at first responded cautiously to the "civilizing" plan. The Iroquois Confederacy had been devastated by the war; its people in the 1790s lived in what one historian has called "slums in the wilderness." Restricted to small reservations increasingly surroundedby Anglo-American farmlands, men could no longer hunt and often spent their days in idle carousing. Quaker missionaries started a demonstration farm among the Senecas, intending to teach men to plow, but they quickly learned that women showed greater interest in their message. The same was true among the Cherokees of Georgia, where Indian agents found that women eagerly sought to learn both new farming methods and textile-manufacturing skills. As their southern hunting territories were reduced, Cherokee men did begin to raise cattle and hogs, but they startled the reformers by treating livestock like wild game, allowing the animals to run free in the woods and simply shooting them when needed, in the same way they had once killed deer. Men also started to plow the fields, although Cherokee women continued to bear primary responsibility for cultivation and harvest.

Iroquois men became more receptive to the Quakers' lessons after the spring of 1799, when a Seneca named Handsome Lake experienced a remarkable series of visions. Like other prophets stretching back to Neolin in the 1760s, Handsome Lake preached that Indian peoples should renounce alcohol, gambling, and other destructive European customs. Even though he directed his followers to reorient men's and women's work assignments as the Quakers advocated, Handsome Lake aimed above all to preserve Iroquois culture. He recognized that, because men could no longer obtain meat through hunting, only by adopting the European sexual division of labor could the Iroquois retain an autonomous existence.

"REVOLUTIONS" AT THE END OF THE CENTURY

Three events in the last two years of the eighteenth century can be deemed real or potential revolutions: Fries's Rebellion, Gabriel's Rebellion, and the election of Thomas Jefferson. Although they differed significantly, these events mirrored the tensions and uncertainties of the young republic. The Fries rebels resisted national authority to tax. Gabriel and his followers directly challenged the slave system so crucial to the Chesapeake economy. And the venomous, hard-fought presidential election of 1800 exposed a structural flaw in the Constitution that would have to be corrected by amendment.

Fries's Rebellion   The tax resistance movement known by the name of one of its prominent leaders—militia captain and Revolutionary War veteran John Fries—arose among German American farmers in Pennsylvania's Lehigh Valley in 1798–1799. To finance the Quasi-War, Congress enacted taxes on land, houses, and legal documents. German Americans, imbued with revolutionary ideals (at least two-fifths were veterans), saw in the taxes a threat to their liberties and livelihoods as well as an echo of the hated Stamp Act of 1765. Asserting a right of resistance to unconstitutional laws, they raised liberty poles, signed petitions to Congress, and nonviolently prevented assessors from evaluating their homes. They voiced repeated threats but harmed no one.

Even so, a federal judge ordered the arrest of twenty resisters. In response, in March 1799 Fries led a troop of 120 militiamen to Bethlehem where they surrounded a tavern temporarily housing the prisoners. Lengthy negotiations failed to win their release, but eventually, fearing a violent confrontation, a federal marshal let the men go. President Adams described the militiamen's actions as "treason, being overt acts of levying war against the United States." Fries and many of his neighbors were arrested and tried; he and two others were convicted of treason; thirty-two more, of violating the Sedition Act. Although Fries and the other "traitors" were sentenced to hang, Adams pardoned them (and all the others) just two days before their scheduled execution. Despite clemency from a Federalist president, the region's residents became, and remained, Republican partisans.

Gabriel's Rebellion   Like their white compatriots in the Lehigh Valley and elsewhere, African Americans both slave and free became familiar with concepts of liberty and equality during the Revolution. They, too, witnessed the benefits of fighting collectively for freedom, rather than resisting individually or running away—a message reinforced by the dramatic news of the successful slave revolt in St. Domingue in 1793. Gabriel, an enslaved Virginia blacksmith who planned the second end-of-the-century revolution, drew on both Haitian and American experiences as well as his religious beliefs.

For months, often accompanied by his preacher brother, Martin, Gabriel visited Sunday services at black Baptist and Methodist congregations where bondspeople gathered free of the watchful eyes of their owners. Gabriel first recruited to his cause other skilled African Americans who like himself lived in semi-freedom under minimal supervision. Next, he enlisted rural slaves. The rebels planned to attack Richmond on the night of August 30, 1800; set fire to the city; seize the state capitol; and capture the governor, James Monroe. At that point, Gabriel believed, other slaves and perhaps poor whites would join in.

The plan showed considerable political sophistication, but heavy rain forced a postponement. Several planters then learned of the plot from informers and spread

LINKS TO THE WORLD

Haitian Refugees

Although many European-Americans initially welcomed the news of the French Revolution in 1789, few expressed similar sentiments about the slave rebellion that broke out soon thereafter in the French colony of St. Domingue (later Haiti), which shared the island of Hispaniola with Spanish Santo Domingo. The large number of refugees who soon flowed into the new United States from that nearby revolt brought with them consequences deemed undesirable by most political leaders. Less than a decade after winning independence, the new nation confronted its first immigration crisis.

Among the approximately 600,000 residents of St. Domingue in the early 1790s were about 100,000 free people, almost all of them slaveowners; half were whites, the rest mulattos. When in the wake of the French Revolution those free mulattos split the slaveholding population by seeking greater social and political equality, the slaves seized the opportunity to revolt. By 1793, they had triumphed under the leadership of a former slave, Toussaint L'Ouverture, and in 1804 they finally ousted the French, thereafter establishing the republic of Haiti. Thousands of whites and mulattos, accompanied by as many slaves as they could readily transport, sought asylum in the United States during those turbulent years.

Although willing to offer shelter to refugees from the violence, American political leaders nonetheless feared the consequences of their arrival. Southern plantation owners shuddered at the thought that slaves so familiar with ideas of freedom

and equality would mingle with their own bondspeople. Many were uncomfortable with the immigration of numerous free people of color, even though the immigrants were part of the slaveholding class. Most of the southern states adopted laws forbidding the entry of Haitian slaves and free mulattos, but the laws were difficult if not impossible to enforce, as was a later congressional act to the same effect. So, more than fifteen thousand refugees—white, black, and of mixed-race origins—flooded into the United States and Spanish Louisiana. Many ended up in Virginia (which did not pass an exclusion law) or the cities of Charleston, Savannah, and New Orleans.

There they had a considerable impact on the existing population. In both New Orleans and Charleston, the influx of mulattos gave rise to a heightened color consciousness that placed light-skinned people at the top of a hierarchy of people of color. Not coincidentally, the Charleston Brown Fellowship Society, composed exclusively of free mulattos, was founded in 1793. After the United States purchased Louisiana in 1803, the number of free people of color in the territory almost doubled in three years, largely because of a final surge of immigration from the new Haitian republic. And, in Virginia, stories of the successful revolt helped to inspire local slaves in 1800 when they planned the action that has become known as Gabriel's Rebellion.

The Haitian refugees thus linked both European-Americans and African Americans to current events in the West Indies, indelibly affecting both groups of people.

the alarm. Gabriel avoided arrest for weeks, but militia troops quickly apprehended and interrogated most of the other leaders of the rebellion. Twenty-six rebels, including Gabriel himself, were hanged. Ironically, only those slaves who betrayed their fellows won freedom as a result of the rebellion.

At his trial, one of Gabriel's followers made explicit the links that so frightened Chesapeake slaveholders. He told his judges that, like George Washington, "I have adventured my life in endeavouring to obtain the liberty of my countrymen, and am a willing sacrifice in their cause." Southern state legislatures responded to such claims by increasing the severity of the laws regulating slavery. Before long, all talk of emancipation ceased in the South, and slavery became even more firmly entrenched as an economic institution and way of life.

Election of 1800   The third end-of-the-century revolution was a Republican "takeover"—the election of Thomas Jefferson as president and a Congress dominated by Republicans—and the culmination of a decade of increasing partisanship. Prior to November 1800, Federalists and Republicans not only campaigned for congressional seats but also maneuvered furiously to control the outcome in the electoral college. Each side feared victory by the other, and both wanted to avoid reproducing the divided results of 1796. Republicans again nominated Thomas Jefferson and Aaron Burr; Federalists named John Adams, with Charles Cotesworth Pinckney of South Carolina as vice president. The network of Republican newspapers forged in the fires of Sedition Act prosecutions vigorously promoted the Jeffersonian cause. When the votes were counted, Jefferson and Burr had tied with seventy-three (no Republican elector wanted to chance omitting Burr's name from his ballot), while Adams had sixty-four and Pinckney sixty-three. Under the Constitution, the election had to be decided in the existing House of Representatives; the newly elected Jeffersonians would not take office until the president did.

Balloting continued for six days and thirty-five ballots, with Federalists uniformly supporting Burr, whereas Republicans held firm for Jefferson. Finally, James Bayard, a Federalist and the sole congressman from Delaware, concluded (perhaps correctly) that "we must risk the Constitution and a civil war or take Mr. Jefferson." He brokered a deal that gave the Virginian the presidency on the thirty-sixth ballot. A crucial consequence of the election was the adoption of the Twelfth Amendment, which provided that electors would henceforth cast separate ballots for president and vice president.

The defeated Federalists turned to strengthening their hold on the judiciary while they could. President Adams named his secretary of state, John Marshall, chief justice; Marshall would serve for thirty-four years, leaving a lasting imprint on constitutional interpretation. Adams spent his last hours in office on March 3, 1801, appointing so-called midnight justices to new positions created in the hastily adopted Judiciary Act of 1801, which also reduced the number of Supreme Court justices from six to five. The fiercely partisan Federalists thus hoped to prevent Jefferson from exerting immediate influence on the judicial branch, despite Republican control of the presidency and Congress.

SUMMARY

As the nineteenth century began, inhabitants of the United States faced changed lives in the new republic. Indian peoples east of the Mississippi River found that they had to surrender some aspects of their traditional culture to preserve others. Some African Americans struggled unsuccessfully to free themselves from the inhuman bonds of slavery, then subsequently confronted more constraints than ever because of increasingly restrictive laws.

European-Americans, too, adjusted to changed circumstances. The first eleven years of government under the Constitution established many enduring precedents for congressional, presidential, and judicial action—among them establishment of the cabinet, interpretations of key clauses of the Constitution, and stirrings of judicial review of state and federal legislation. Building on successful negotiations with Spain (Pinckney's Treaty), Britain (the Jay Treaty), and France (the Convention of 1800), the United States developed its diplomatic independence, striving to avoid entanglement with European countries and their continental wars.

Yet especially after 1793 internal political consensus proved elusive. The 1790s spawned vigorous debates over foreign and domestic policy and saw the beginnings of a system of organized factionalism and grassroots politicking involving both men and women, if not yet formal parties. The Whiskey and Fries Rebellions showed that regional conflicts persisted even under the new government. The waging of an undeclared war against France proved extremely contentious, splitting one faction and energizing another. In 1801, after more than a decade of struggle, the Jeffersonian view of the future of agrarian, decentralized republicanism prevailed over Alexander Hamilton's vision of a powerful centralized economy and a strong national government.

9

DEFINING THE NATION 1801–1823

POLITICAL VISIONS

In his inaugural address, Jefferson appealed to his opponents. Standing in the Senate chamber, the Capitol's only completed part, he addressed the electorate not as party members but as citizens with common beliefs: "We are all republicans, we are all federalists." Nearly a thousand people strained to hear his vision of a restored republicanism: "A wise and frugal government, which shall restrain men from injuring one another, which shall leave them free to regulate their pursuits of industry and improvement, and shall not take from the mouth of labor the bread it had earned. This is the sum of good government."

But outgoing president John Adams did not hear Jefferson's call for unity, having left Washington before dawn. He and Jefferson, once close friends, now disliked each other intensely. Despite the spirit of Jefferson's inaugural address, the Democratic-Republicans—as the Republicans of the 1790s now called themselves, after the Democratic societies of the 1790s—and the Federalists remained bitter opponents. These parties held different visions of how society and government should be organized. The Federalists advocated a strong national government with centralized authority to promote economic development. The Democratic-Republicans sought to restrain the national government, believing that limited government would foster republican virtue, which derived from agricultural endeavors. Nearly two decades later, Jefferson would call his election "the revolution of 1800," which was "as real a revolution in the principles of our government as that of 1776 was in its form."

Separation of Church and State

A group of Baptist farmers from Cheshire, Massachusetts sent Jefferson a mammoth (weighing more than twelve hundred pounds) cheese on the first New Year's Day of his

CHRONOLOGY

1801	Marshall becomes chief justice
	Jefferson inaugurated as president
1801–05	United States defeats Barbary pirates
1803	*Marbury v. Madison*
	Louisiana Purchase
1804	Jefferson reelected president, Clinton vice President
1804–06	Lewis and Clark expedition
1805	Tenskwatawa emerges as Shawnee leader
1807	*Chesapeake* affair
	Embargo Act
1808	Congress bans slave importation
	Madison elected president
1808–13	Tenskwatawa and Tecumseh organize Indian resistance
1811	National Road begun
1812	Madison reelected president
1812–15	War of 1812
1813	Tecumseh's death
	Boston Manufacturing Company starts textile mill in Waltham, Massachusetts
1814	Treaty of Ghent
1814–15	Hartford Convention
1815	Battle of New Orleans
1817	Regular steamboat travel begins on Mississippi
1817–25	Erie Canal constructed
1819	*McCulloch v. Maryland*
	Adams-Onis Treaty
1819– early 1820s	First major depression
1820–21	Missouri Compromise
1823	Monroe Doctrine

presidency to express gratitude for his commitment to the separation of church and state. On the very day he received the overripe cheese, Jefferson reciprocated by penning a letter to the Baptist association in Danbury, Connecticut, proclaiming that the Constitution's First Amendment supported a "wall of separation between church and state." Jefferson's letter articulated a core component of his vision of limited government. The president declared that "religion is a matter which lies solely between Man & his God." It lay beyond the government's purview. New England Baptists hailed Jefferson as a hero, but New England Federalists believed their worst fears were confirmed. During the election of 1800, Federalists had waged a venomous campaign against Jefferson, incorrectly labeling him an atheist. Their rhetoric proved so effective that, after Jefferson's election, some New England women hid their Bibles in their gardens and wells to foil Democratic-Republicans allegedly bent on confiscating them. Jefferson's letter to the Danbury Baptists seemingly vindicated such hysteria.

Jefferson became president during a period of religious revivalism, particularly among Methodists and Baptists, whose democratic preaching—all humans, they said, were equal in God's eyes—encouraged a growing democratic political culture. Emboldened by secular and religious ideologies about human equality, society's nonelites articulated their own political visions. Rather than simply taking stands in debates defined by social and political betters, they worked to reshape the debates. When the Cheshire Baptists sent their cheese to President Jefferson, for example, they pointedly informed the Virginia planter that it had been made "without a single slave to assist."

Political Mobilization

The revolution of 1800, which gave the Democratic-Republicans majorities in both houses of Congress in addition to the presidency, resulted from an electorate limited largely, but not exclusively, to property-holding men. The Constitution left the regulation of voting to the individual states. In no state but New Jersey could women vote even when meeting property qualifications, and in New Jersey that right was granted inadvertently and later revoked in 1807. In 1800, free black men meeting property qualifications could vote in all states but Delaware, Georgia, South Carolina, and Virginia, but local custom often kept them from exercising that right. Nonetheless, partisan politics captured nearly all Americans' imaginations, and politicians actively courted nonvoters along with voters. Most political mobilization took place locally, where partisans rallied popular support for candidates and their ideologies on militia training grounds, in taverns and churches, at court gatherings, and during holiday celebrations. Voters and nonvoters alike expressed their views by marching in parades, signing petitions, singing songs, and debating politically charged sermons. Perhaps most important, they devoured a growing print culture of pamphlets, broadsides (posters), almanacs, and—especially—newspapers.

The Partisan Press

Newspapers provided a forum for sustained political conversation. Read aloud in taverns, artisans' workshops, and homes, newspapers gave national importance to local events. Without newspaper publicity, Cheshire's mammoth cheese would have been little more than a massive hunk of curdled milk. With it, a cheese became worthy of presidential response. In 1800, the nation had 260 newspapers; by 1810, it had 396—virtually all of them unabashedly partisan.

The parties adopted official organs. Shortly after his election, Jefferson persuaded the *National Intelligencer* to move from Philadelphia to the new capital of

Washington, where it became the Democratic-Republicans' voice. In 1801, Alexander Hamilton launched the *New York Evening Post* as the Federalist vehicle. It boosted Federalists while frequently calling Jefferson a liar and depicting him as the head of a slave harem. The party organs—published six or seven times a week, year in and year out—ensured that the growing American obsession with partisan politics extended beyond electoral campaigns.

Limited Government
Jefferson needed public servants as well as supporters. To bring into his administration men sharing his vision of individual liberty, an agrarian republic, and limited government, Jefferson refused to recognize appointments made by Adams in his presidency's last days and dismissed Federalist customs collectors. He awarded vacant treasury and judicial offices to Republicans. Federalists accused Jefferson of "hunting the Federalists like wild beasts" and abandoning his inaugural address' peaceful overtures. Jeffersonians worked to make the government leaner. If Alexander Hamilton had viewed the national debt as the engine of economic growth, Jefferson deemed it the source of government corruption. Secretary of the Treasury Albert Gallatin cut the army budget in half and reduced the 1802 navy budget by two-thirds. He moved to reduce the national debt from $83 million to $57 million, hoping to retire it altogether by 1817. Austerity motivated Jefferson to close two of the nation's five diplomatic missions abroad, at The Hague and in Berlin. Jeffersonians attacked taxes as well as spending: the Democratic-Republican–controlled Congress oversaw the repeal of all internal taxes, including the despised whiskey tax of 1791.

Ideas of liberty also distinguished Democratic-Republicans from Federalists. The Alien and Sedition Acts of 1798 had helped unite the Republicans in opposition. Jefferson now declined to use the acts against his opponents, instead pardoning those already convicted of violating them.

Congress let the Sedition Act expire in 1801 and the Alien Act in 1802, and repealed the Naturalization Act of 1798, which had required fourteen years of residency for citizenship. The 1802 act that replaced it, while stipulating the registration of aliens, required of would-be citizens only five years of residency, loyalty to the Constitution, and the forsaking of foreign allegiances and titles. The new act remained the basis of naturalized American citizenship into the twentieth century.

Judicial Politics
To many Democratic-Republicans, the judiciary represented a centralizing and undemocratic force, especially because judges were appointed, not elected, and served for life. Partisan Democratic-Republicans thus targeted opposition judges. At Jefferson's prompting, the House impeached (indicted) and the Senate convicted Federal District Judge John Pickering of New Hampshire. Allegedly deranged and alcoholic, Pickering made an easy mark. On the same day in 1803 that Pickering was ousted from office, the House impeached Supreme Court Justice Samuel Chase for judicial misconduct. A staunch Federalist, Chase had pushed for prosecutions under the Sedition Act, had actively campaigned for Adams in 1800, and had repeatedly denounced Jefferson's administration from the bench. But in the Senate, the Democratic-Republicans failed to muster the two-thirds majority necessary for conviction. The failure to remove Chase preserved the

Court's independence and established the precedent that criminal actions, not political disagreements, justified removal from office.

The Marshall Court Although Jefferson appointed three new Supreme Court justices during his two administrations, the Court remained a Federalist stronghold under the leadership of his distant cousin John Marshall. Marshall adopted some outward trappings of Republicanism—opting for a plain black gown over the more colorful academic robes of his fellow justices—but adhered steadfastly to Federalist ideology. Even after the Democratic-Republicans achieved a majority of Court seats in 1811, Marshall remained extremely influential as chief justice. Under the Marshall Court (1801–1835), the Supreme Court consistently upheld federal supremacy over the states while protecting the interests of commerce and capital.

Marshall made the Court an equal branch of the government in practice as well as theory. Previously regarded lightly, judicial service became a coveted honor for ambitious and talented men. Marshall, moreover, strengthened the Court by having it speak with a more unified voice; rather than issuing a host of individual concurring judgments, the justices now issued joint majority opinions. Marshall became the voice of the majority: from 1801 through 1805, he wrote twenty-four of the Court's twenty-six decisions; through 1810, he wrote 85 percent of the opinions, including every important one.

Judicial Review One of the most important involved Adams's midnight appointments. In his last hours in office, Adams had named Federalist William Marbury a justice of the peace in the District of Columbia. But Jefferson's secretary of state, James Madison, declined to certify the appointment, allowing the new president to appoint a Democratic-Republican instead. Marbury sued, requesting a writ of mandamus (a court order forcing the president to appoint him). *Marbury v. Madison* presented a political dilemma. If the Supreme Court ruled in Marbury's favor, the president probably would not comply with the writ, and the Court could not force him to do so. Yet by refusing to issue the writ, the Federalist-dominated bench would hand the Democratic-Republicans a victory.

To avoid both pitfalls, Marshall brilliantly recast the issue. Writing for the Court, he ruled that Marbury had a right to his appointment but that the Supreme Court could not compel Madison to honor the appointment because the Constitution did not grant the Court power to issue a writ of mandamus. In the absence of any specific mention in the Constitution, Marshall wrote, the section of the Judiciary Act of 1789 authorizing the Court to issue writs was unconstitutional. Thus, the Supreme Court denied itself the power to issue writs of mandamus but established its far greater power to judge the constitutionality of laws passed by Congress. In doing so, Marshall fashioned the theory of judicial review. Because the Constitution was "the supreme law of the land," Marshall wrote, any federal or state act contrary to the Constitution must be null and void. The Supreme Court, whose duty it was to uphold the law, would decide whether a legislative act contradicted the Constitution. "It is emphatically the province and duty of the judicial department," Marshall ruled, "to say what the law is." This power of the Supreme

Court to determine the constitutionality of legislation and presidential acts permanently enhanced the independence of the judiciary and breathed life into the Constitution. "Marshall found the Constitution paper and made it power," President James A. Garfield later observed.

Election of 1804   In the first election after the Twelfth Amendment's ratification, Jefferson took no chances: he dropped Burr as his running mate and, in keeping with the already established convention of having a North-South balance on the ticket, chose George Clinton of New York. They swamped their opponents—South Carolinian Charles Cotesworth Pinckney and New Yorker Rufus King—in the electoral college by 162 votes to 14, carrying fifteen of the seventeen states. That 1804 election escalated the long-standing animosity between Burr and Hamilton, who supported Burr's rival in the New York gubernatorial election. When Hamilton called Burr a liar, Burr challenged Hamilton to a duel. Believing his honor was at stake, Hamilton accepted the challenge even though his son Philip had died in 1801 from dueling wounds. Because New York had outlawed dueling, the encounter took place across the Hudson River in New Jersey. Details of the duel itself remain hazy—did Hamilton withhold his fire, as he claimed he would?—but the outcome was clear: Hamilton died the following day, after being shot by Burr. In New York and New Jersey, prosecutors indicted Burr for murder.

Facing arrest if he returned to either state and with his political career in ruins, Burr fled to the West. While historians disagree about his motives, the "Burr Conspiracy" was understood at the time to involve a scheme with Brigadier General James Wilkinson to create a new empire by using military force to acquire what is now Texas and by persuading already existing western territories to leave the United States and join the new empire. Brought to trial for treason in 1807, Burr faced a prosecution aided by President Jefferson but overseen by Jefferson's political rival Chief Justice Marshall. (At the time, Supreme Court justices presided over circuit courts.) Prompted by Marshall to interpret treason narrowly, the jury acquitted Burr, who fled to Europe.

Nationalism and Culture   As statesmen bickered over how to realize the nation's potential, other Americans touted their own nationalist visions with paintbrushes and pens. Nearly three decades after the Constitution's ratification, painters continued to memorialize great birth scenes of American nationhood, such as the Declaration of Independence's signing, Revolutionary War battle scenes, and the Constitutional Convention. Four of John Trumbull's revolutionary scenes, commissioned in 1817, still hang on the rotunda of the Capitol building in Washington.

With architecture, Americans self-consciously constructed a new, independent nation. Designed by Major Pierre Charles L'Enfant, a French-born engineer who served under George Washington during the Revolution, the city of Washington was meant to embody a "reciprocity of sight": Each of the government's three branches—the legislative, judicial, and executive—should keep an eye on one another at all times. But nationalism could be easier to envision than to construct. Beset by pragmatic difficulties, L'Enfant's plan took nearly a century to implement. A French visitor in 1851 noted that Washington had "streets without houses," "houses without streets," and was "striking proof of this truth, that one cannot create a great city at will." In Washington and elsewhere, wealthier Americans commissioned homes in the "federal" style, which imitated classical architecture in its economy of decoration and which made use of indigenous, rather than imported, building materials.

The era's best-selling book was Noah Webster's spelling book, which proposed making English more "republican." By some estimates, the book sold nearly 100 million copies by the end of the nineteenth century. Webster believed Americans should speak and spell like one another—they should bind together by speaking a national language—but unlike "King's English," their language should not require elite training to master. Words should be spelled as they sound—for example, "honor" should replace "honour." A shared language would unite an increasingly farflung population.

NATIONAL EXPANSION WESTWARD

Little excited Jeffersonians' nationalistic imaginations more than the West and its seeming abundance of unoccupied land ripe for agrarian expansion. Federalists, though, often urged caution, fearing uncontrolled expansion would impede commercial development and federal oversight.

By 1800, hundreds of thousands of white Americans had settled in the rich Ohio River and Mississippi River valleys, intruding on Indian lands. In the Northwest they raised foodstuffs, primarily wheat, and in the Southwest they cultivated cotton. At the time of the American Revolution, cotton production was profitable only for the Sea Island planters in South Carolina and Georgia, who grew the long-staple variety. Short-staple cotton, which grew readily in the interior and in all kinds of soil, was unmarketable because its sticky seeds could be removed only by hand. After a young New England inventor named Eli Whitney designed a cotton gin (short for "engine") in 1793, allowing one person to remove the same number of seeds that previously required fifty people working by hand, the cultivation of short-staple cotton spread rapidly westward into the fertile lands of Louisiana, Mississippi, Alabama, Arkansas, and Tennessee. By exponentially increasing the efficiency with which cotton fiber could be extracted from raw cotton, the cotton gin greatly increased the demand for slaves who seeded, tended, and harvested cotton fields.

Whatever crops they marketed, American settlers depended on free access to the Mississippi River and its Gulf port, New Orleans. "The Mississippi," wrote Secretary of State James Madison, "is to them [western settlers] everything. It is the Hudson, the Delaware, the Potomac and all navigable rivers of the Atlantic States formed into one stream." Whoever controlled the port of New Orleans had a hand on the American economy's throat.

New Orleans   Spain, which had acquired France's territory west of the Mississippi in the settlement of the Seven Years' War (1763), secretly transferred it back to France in 1800 and 1801. American officials learned of the transfer only in 1802, when Napoleon seemed poised to rebuild a French empire in the New World. "Every eye in the United States is now focused on the affairs of Louisiana," Jefferson wrote to Robert R. Livingston, the American minister in Paris. American concerns intensified when Spanish officials, on the eve of ceding control to the French, violated Pinckney's treaty by denying Americans the privilege of storing their products (or exercising their "right of deposit") at New Orleans prior to transshipment to foreign markets. Western farmers and eastern merchants, who traded through New Orleans, thought a devious Napoleon had closed the port; they talked war.

To relieve the pressure for war and win western farmers' support, Jefferson urged Congress to authorize the call-up of eighty thousand militiamen but at the same time sent Virginia Governor James Monroe to join Robert Livingston in France with instructions to buy the port of New Orleans and as much of the Mississippi valley as possible. Arriving in Paris in April 1803, Monroe learned with astonishment that France had already offered to sell all 827,000 square miles of Louisiana to the United States for a mere $15 million. With St. Domingue torn from French control by revolution and slave revolt, Napoleon gave up dreams of a New World empire and no longer needed Louisiana as its breadbasket. His more urgent need was for money to wage war against Britain. On April 30, Monroe and Livingston signed a treaty buying the vast territory whose exact borders and land remained uncharted (see Map 9.1).

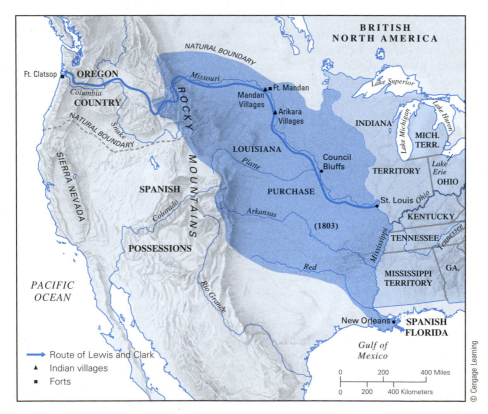

MAP 9.1 Louisiana Purchase

The Louisiana Purchase (1803) doubled the area of the United States and opened the trans-Mississippi West for American settlement.

Louisiana Purchase The Louisiana Purchase appealed to Americans with divergent ideas about how best to achieve national greatness and personal prosperity. The purchase ensured that the United States would control the Mississippi's mouth, giving peace of mind to western settlers who relied on the river to market their goods. It also inspired the commercial visions of those who imagined the United States as the nexus of international trade networks reaching between Europe and Asia. Louisiana promised to fulfill the dreams of easterners seeking cheap, fertile lands. Its vast expanse meant, too, that land could be set aside for Indians displaced by the incursion of white settlers and their black slaves, soothing the consciences of those white Americans who preferred to "civilize" rather than to exterminate the continent's first settlers. The purchase had its critics, though: some doubted its constitutionality (even Jefferson agonized over it); others worried that it belied the Democratic-Republicans' commitment to debt reduction; some New England Federalists complained that it undermined their commercial interests and threatened the sustainability of the republic by spreading the population beyond where it could be properly controlled. Overall, though, the Louisiana Purchase was the most popular achievement of Jefferson's presidency.

Louisiana was not, however, the "vast wilderness" that some Federalists lamented and most Republicans coveted. When the United States acquired the territory, hundreds of thousands of people who had not been party to the agreement became American subjects. These included Native Americans from scores of nations who made their homes within the enormous territory, as well as people of European and African descent—or, often, a complex mixture of the two—who congregated primarily along the Gulf Coast. Around New Orleans, Louisiana's colonial heritage was reflected in its people: creoles of French and Spanish descent, slaves of African descent, free people of color, and Acadians, or Cajuns (descendants of French settlers in eastern Canada), as well as some Germans, Irish, and English. The 1810 census, the first taken after the purchase, reported that 97,000 non-Indians lived in the Louisiana Purchase area, of whom the great majority (77,000) lived in what is now the state of Louisiana. Not all these new Americans welcomed their new national identity. Although Jefferson imagined the West as an "empire of liberty," free people of color soon discovered their exclusion from the Louisiana Purchase treaty's provision that "the inhabitants of the ceded territory" would be accorded the rights of American citizenship. Denied the right to vote and serve on juries, New Orleans' people of color fought to retain their rights to form families and to bequeath as they pleased, and—with the help of sympathetic Anglos serving on juries, as justices, or as legislators—some of them succeeded.

Lewis and Clark Expedition Jefferson had a long-standing interest in the trans-Mississippi West, envisioning it as punctuated with volcanoes and mountains of pure salt, where llamas and mammoths roamed and Welshmen settled. He felt an urgent need to explore it, fearing that, if Americans did not claim it as their own, the British, who still controlled the northern reaches of the continent (in present-day Canada) and parts of the Pacific Northwest, surely would. He lost no time in launching a military-style mission that would chart the region's commercial possibilities—its water passages to the Pacific as well as its trading opportunities with Indians—while cataloguing its geography, peoples, flora, and fauna.

The expedition, headed by Meriwether Lewis and William Clark, began in May 1804 and lasted for more than two years; it traveled up the Missouri River, across the Rockies, and then down the Columbia to the Pacific Ocean—and back. Along the way, the expedition's members "discovered" (as they saw it) dozens of previously unknown Indian tribes, many of whom had long before discovered Europeans. Lewis and Clark found the Mandans and Hidatsas already well supplied with European trade goods, such as knives, corduroy trousers, and rings. Although the Corps of Discovery, as the expedition came to be called, expected to find Indians and prepared for possible conflict, its goal was peaceable: to foster trade relations, win political allies, and take advantage of Indians' knowledge of the landscape. Accordingly, Lewis and Clark brought with them twenty-one bags of gifts for Native American leaders, both to establish goodwill and to stimulate interest in trading for American manufactured goods. Most of the corps' interactions with native peoples were cordial, but when Indians failed to be impressed by Lewis and Clark's gifts, tensions arose. After an encounter with the Lakota (or Sioux), Lewis denounced them as "the vilest miscreants of the savage race."

Although military in style, the Corps of Discovery proved unusually democratic in seating enlisted men on courts-martial and allowing Clark's black slave York as well as the expedition's female guide and translator Sacagawea to vote on where to locate winter quarters in 1805. But unlike the expedition's other members, neither York nor Sacagawea drew wages, and when York later demanded his freedom for his services, Clark repaid him instead with—in Clark's own words—"a severe trouncing."

Lewis and Clark failed to discover a Northwest Passage to the Pacific, and the route they mapped across the Rockies proved more perilous than practical, but their explorations contributed to nationalist visions of American expansion. Fossils and Native American artifacts collected during the expedition were displayed in Charles Willson Peale's museum at Independence Hall in Philadelphia, an institution emphasizing the uniqueness of America's geography and, especially, its republican experiment; in addition to housing natural and human "curiosities," Peale's museum displayed his own renowned portraits of Revolutionary heroes. Nationalists generally overlooked Indians' claims to American lands. Although Jefferson had more sympathy for Indians than did many of his contemporaries—he took interest in their cultures and believed Indians to be intellectually equal to whites—he nonetheless lobbied, unsuccessfully, for a constitutional amendment that would transport them west of the Mississippi into the newly acquired Louisiana Territory. He became personally involved in efforts to pressure the Chickasaws to sell their land, and in the event that legal methods for removing Indians should fail, he advocated trickery. Traders, he suggested, might run the "good and influential individuals" into debt, which they would have to repay "by a cessation of lands."

Divisions Among Indian Peoples   Some Indian nations decided to deal with white intruders by adopting white customs as a means of survival and often agreeing to sell their lands and move west. These "accommodationists" (or "progressives") were opposed by "traditionalists," who urged adherence to native ways and refused to relinquish their lands. Distinctions between accommodationists and traditionalists were not always so clear-cut, however, as the Seneca Handsome Lake had demonstrated just a few years before.

In the early 1800s, two Shawnee brothers, Tenskwatawa (1775–1837) and Tecumseh (1768–1813), led a traditionalist revolt against American encroachment by fostering a pan-Indian federation that centered in the Old Northwest and reached into parts of the South. During the two brothers' lifetimes, the Shawnees had lost most of their Ohio land; by the 1800s, they occupied only scattered sites in Ohio and in the Michigan and Louisiana territories. Despondent, Lalawethika—as Tenskwatawa had been called as a youth—had turned to a combination of European remedies (particularly whiskey) and Native American ones, becoming a shaman in 1804. But when European diseases ravaged his village, he despaired.

Tenskwatawa and Tecumseh   Lalawethika emerged from his own battle with illness in 1805 as a new man, renamed Tenskwatawa ("the Open Door") or—by whites—"the Prophet." Claiming to have died and been resurrected, he traveled widely in the Ohio River valley as a religious leader, attacking the decline of moral values among Native Americans, warning against whiskey, condemning intertribal battles, and stressing harmony and respect for elders. He urged Indians to return to the old ways and to abandon white ways: to hunt with bows and arrows, not guns; to stop wearing hats; and to give up bread for corn and beans. Tenskwatawa was building a religious movement that offered hope to the Shawnees, Potawatomis, and other displaced western Indians.

By 1808, Tenskwatawa and his older brother Tecumseh talked less about spiritual renewal and more about resisting American aggression. They invited Indians from all nations to settle in pan-Indian towns in Indiana, first at Greenville (1806–1808) and then at Prophetstown (1808–1812), near modern-day Lafayette. The new towns challenged the treaty-making process by denying the claims of Indians who had been guaranteed the same land as part of the Treaty of Greenville of 1795 in exchange for enormous cessions. Younger Indians, in particular, flocked to Tecumseh, the more politically oriented of the two brothers.

Convinced that only an Indian federation could stop the advance of white settlement, Tecumseh sought to unify northern and southern Indians by preaching Indian resistance across a wide swath of territory, ranging from Canada to Georgia. Among southern Indians, only one faction of the Creek nation welcomed him, but his efforts to spread his message southward nonetheless alarmed white settlers and government officials. In November 1811, while Tecumseh was in the South, Indiana governor William Henry Harrison moved against Tenskwatawa and his followers. During the battle of Tippecanoe, the army burned their town; as they fled, the Indians exacted revenge on white settlers. "What other course is left for us to pursue," asked Harrison, "but to make a war of extirpation upon them." With the stakes raised, Tecumseh entered a formal alliance with the British, who maintained forts in southern Ontario. This alliance in the West, combined with issues over American neutral rights on the high seas, were propelling the United States toward war with Britain.

THE NATION IN THE ORBIT OF EUROPE

A decade earlier, in 1801, when Jefferson had sought to set a new course for the nation, he tried to put tensions with France to rest. "Peace, commerce, and honest friendship with all nations, entangling alliances with none," he had proclaimed in his first inaugural address. Yet the economy of the early republic relied heavily on both fishing and the carrying trade, in which the American merchant marine transported commodities between nations. Merchants in Boston, Salem, and Philadelphia traded with China, sending cloth and metal to swap for furs with Chinook Indians on the Oregon coast, and then sailing to China to trade for porcelain, tea, and silk. The slave trade lured American ships to Africa. America's commercial interests were clearly focused on the seas, and not long after Jefferson's first inaugural address, the United States was at war with Tripoli—a state along the Barbary Coast of North Africa—over a principle that would long be a cornerstone of American foreign policy: freedom of the seas. In other words, outside national territorial waters, the high seas should be open for free transit of all vessels.

First Barbary War   In 1801, the bashaw (pasha) of Tripoli declared war on the United States for its refusal to pay tribute for safe passage of its ships, sailors, and passengers through the Mediterranean. Jefferson deployed a naval squadron to protect American ships. After two years of stalemate, Jefferson declared a blockade of Tripoli, but when the American frigate *Philadelphia* ran aground in the harbor, its three hundred officers and sailors were imprisoned. Jefferson refused to ransom them, and a small American force accompanied by Arab, Greek, and African mercenaries marched from Egypt to the "shores of Tripoli" (memorialized to this day in the Marine Corps anthem) to seize the port of Derne. A treaty ended the war in 1805, but the United States continued to pay tribute to the three other Barbary states—Algiers, Morocco, and Tunis—until 1815. In the intervening years, the United States became embroiled in European conflicts.

At first, Jefferson managed to distance the nation from the turmoil in Europe in the wake of the French Revolution. After the Senate ratified the Jay Treaty in 1795, the United States and Great Britain appeared to reconcile their differences. Britain withdrew from its western forts on American soil (while still retaining those in Canada and the Pacific Northwest) and interfered less in American trade with France. Then, in May 1803, two weeks after Napoleon sold Louisiana to the United States, France was at war against Britain and, later, Britain's continental allies, Prussia, Austria, and Russia. The Napoleonic wars again trapped the United States between belligerents on the high seas. But at first the United States—as the world's largest neutral shipping carrier—actually benefited from the conflict, and American merchants gained control of most of the West Indian trade. After 1805, however, when Britain defeated the French and Spanish fleets at Trafalgar, Britain's Royal Navy tightened its control of the oceans. Two months later, Napoleon crushed the Russian and Austrian armies at Austerlitz. Stalemated, France and Britain launched a commercial war, blockading each other's trade. As a trading partner of both countries, the United States paid a high price.

Threats to American Sovereignty

One British tactic in particular threatened American sovereignty. To replenish their supply of sailors, British vessels stopped American ships and impressed (forcibly recruited) British deserters, British-born naturalized American seamen, and other sailors suspected of being British. Perhaps six to eight thousand Americans were impressed between 1803 and 1812. Moreover, alleged deserters—many of them American citizens—faced British courts-martial. Americans saw the principle of "once a British subject, always a British subject" as a mockery of U.S. citizenship and an assault on their national sovereignty. Americans also resented the British interfering with their West Indian trade as well as their searching and seizing American vessels within U.S. territorial waters.

In April 1806, Congress responded with the Non- Importation Act, barring British manufactured goods from entering American ports. Because the act exempted most cloth and metal articles, it had little impact on British trade; instead, it warned the British what to expect if they continued to violate American neutral rights. In November, Jefferson suspended the act temporarily while William Pinkney, a Baltimore lawyer, joined James Monroe in London to negotiate a settlement. But the treaty they carried home violated Jefferson's instructions—it did not so much as mention impressment—and the president never submitted it to the Senate for ratification.

Anglo-American relations steadily deteriorated, coming to a head in June 1807 when the USS *Chesapeake*, sailing out of Norfolk for the Mediterranean, was stopped by the British frigate *Leopard*, whose officers demanded to search the ship for British deserters. Refused, the *Leopard* opened fire, killing three Americans and wounding eighteen others, including the captain. The British then seized four deserters, three of whom held American citizenship; one of them was hanged. The *Chesapeake* affair outraged Americans while also exposing American military weakness.

The Embargo of 1807

Had the United States been better prepared militarily, public indignation might have resulted in a declaration of war. Instead, Jefferson opted for what he called "peaceable coercion." In July, the president closed American waters to British warships and soon thereafter increased military and naval expenditures. In December 1807, Jefferson again put economic pressure on Great Britain by invoking the Non-Importation Act, followed eight days later by a new restriction, the Embargo Act. Jefferson and his congressional supporters saw the embargo, which forbade all exports from the United States to any country, as a short-term measure to avoid war by pressuring Britain and France to respect American rights and by preventing confrontation between American merchant vessels and European warships.

The embargo's biggest economic impact, however, fell on the United States. Exports declined by 80 percent in 1808, squeezing New England shippers and their workers as economic depression set in. Manufacturers, by contrast, received a boost, as the domestic market became theirs exclusively, and merchants began to shift their capital from shipping to manufacturing. In 1807, there were twenty cotton and woolen mills in New England; by 1813, there were more than two hundred. Meanwhile, merchants who were willing to engage in smuggling profited enormously.

International Slave Trade   They had only to look at the vibrant slave trade to see how scarcity bred demand. With Jefferson's encouragement, Congress had voted in 1807 to abolish the international slave trade as of January 1, 1808—the earliest date permissible under the Constitution. South Carolina alone still allowed the legal importation of slaves, but most of the state's influential planters favored a ban on the trade, nervous (having seen what happened in St. Domingue) about adding to the black population of a state in which whites were already outnumbered. Congressional debate focused not on whether it was a good idea to abolish the trade but on what should become of any Africans imported illegally after the ban took effect. The final bill provided that smuggled slaves would be sold in accordance with the laws of the state or territory in which they arrived. It underscored, in other words, that slaves (even illegal ones) were property. Had the bill not done so, threatened one Georgia congressman, the result might have been "resistance to the authority of the Government," even civil war. Although the debate over the slave trade did not fall along strictly sectional (or regional) lines, sectional tensions never lay far beneath the surface in this era of heated partisan conflict.

In anticipation of the higher prices that their human property would fetch once the law took effect, traders temporarily withheld their slaves from the market in the months after the law's passage. During the last four months of 1807 alone, sixteen thousand African slaves arrived at Gadsden Wharf in Charleston, where they were detained by merchants eager to wait out the January 1 deadline. Although many of these slaves—hundreds, if not thousands—died in the cramped, disease-ridden holding pens before they could be sold, merchants calculated that the increased value of those who survived until the ban took effect would outweigh the losses. Not that January 1, 1808, brought an end to the international slave trade; a brisk—and profitable—illegal trade took over. As Justice Joseph Story noted in 1819, the slave trade "is still carried on with all the implacable ferocity and insatiable rapacity of former times. Avarice has grown more subtle in its evasions; and watches and seizes its prey with an appetite quickened rather than suppressed by its guilty vigils." In 1819, Congress passed a law authorizing the president to use force to intercept slave ships along the African coast, but the small American navy could not halt the illicit trade in human beings.

Election of 1808   As discussion of the international slave trade subsided, debate over the embargo heated up, especially with the approach of the 1808 presidential election. Democratic Republicans suffered from factional dissent and dissatisfaction in seaboard states hobbled by the trade restrictions. Although nine state legislatures passed resolutions urging Jefferson to run again, the president followed George Washington's lead in declining a third term. He supported James Madison, his secretary of state, as the Democratic-Republican standard-bearer. For the first time, however, the Democratic-Republican nomination was contested. Madison won the endorsement of the party's congressional caucus, but Virginia Democratic-Republicans put forth James Monroe, who later withdrew, and some easterners supported Vice President George Clinton. Madison and Clinton headed the ticket. Charles Cotesworth Pinckney and Rufus King again ran on the Federalist ticket, but with new vigor.

The younger Federalists made the most of the widespread disaffection with Democratic-Republican policy, especially the embargo. Pinckney received only 47 electoral votes to Madison's 122, but he carried all of New England except Vermont, won Delaware, and carried some electoral votes in two other states. Federalists also gained seats in Congress and captured the New York State legislature. Although the Federalist future looked promising, the transition from one Democratic-Republican administration to the next went smoothly.

Women and Politics

This transition was eased, in part, by the wives of elected and appointed officials in the new capital, who encouraged political and diplomatic negotiation. Such negotiations often took place in social settings, even private homes, where people with divergent interests could bridge their ideological divides through personal relationships. Women played crucial roles, fostering conversation, providing an ear or a voice for unofficial messages, and—in the case of international affairs—standing as surrogates for their nation. Elite women hosted events that muted domestic partisan rivalries, events at which Federalists and Democratic-Republicans could find common ground in civility, if not always politics. Political wives' interactions among themselves served political purposes, too: when First Lady Dolley Madison visited congressmen's wives, she cultivated goodwill for her husband while collecting recipes that allowed her to serve regionally diverse cuisine at White House functions. Mrs. Madison hoped her menus would help keep simmering sectional tensions from reaching a boiling point.

But it was women's buying power that may have proved most influential in the era of the embargo. Recalling women's support of revolutionary-era boycotts, Jeffersonians appealed directly for women's support of their embargo. Sympathetic women responded by spurning imported fabric and making (or directing their slaves to make) homespun clothing for themselves and their families. Federalists, however, encouraged women to "keep commerce alive," and sympathetic women bought smuggled goods.

Failed Policies

Under the pressure of domestic opposition, the embargo eventually collapsed. In its place, the Non-Intercourse Act of 1809 reopened trade with all nations except Britain and France, and authorized the president to resume trade with those two nations once they respected American neutral rights. In June 1809, President Madison reopened trade with Britain after its minister to the United States offered assurances that Britain would repeal restrictions on American trade. But his Majesty's government in London repudiated the minister's assurances, leading Madison to revert to nonintercourse.

When the Non-Intercourse Act expired in 1810, Congress substituted Macon's Bill Number 2, reopening trade with both Great Britain and France but providing that, when either nation stopped violating American commercial rights, the president would suspend American commerce with the other. When Napoleon accepted the offer, Madison declared nonintercourse on Great Britain in 1811. Although the French continued to seize American ships, Britain became the main focus of American hostility because its Royal Navy dominated the seas.

In spring 1812, the British admiralty ordered its ships not to stop, search, or seize American warships, and in June Britain reopened the seas to American shipping. But before word of the change in British policy reached American shores, Congress declared war.

Mr. Madison's War   The vote was sharply divided. The House voted 79 to 49 for war; the Senate, 19 to 13. Democratic-Republicans favored war by a vote of 98 to 23; Federalists opposed it 39 to 0. Those who favored war, including President Madison, pointed to assaults on American sovereignty and honor: impressment, violation of neutral trading rights, and British alliances with western Indians. Others saw an opportunity to conquer and annex British Canada. Most militant were land-hungry southerners and westerners—the "War Hawks"—led by John C. Calhoun of South Carolina and first-term congressman and House Speaker Henry Clay of Kentucky. John Randolph of Virginia, an opponent of war, charged angrily, "Agrarian cupidity, not maritime rights, urges war!" He heard "but one word" in Congress: "Canada! Canada! Canada!" Most representatives from the coastal states, and especially from the Northeast, feared disruption to commerce and opposed what they called "Mr. Madison's War."

Initially, the Federalists benefited from antiwar sentiment. They joined renegade Democratic-Republicans in supporting New York City mayor DeWitt Clinton for president in the election of 1812. Clinton lost to President Madison by 128 to 89 electoral votes—a respectable showing against a wartime president—and the Federalists gained some congressional seats and carried many local elections. But the South and the West—areas that favored the war—remained solidly Democratic-Republican.

THE WAR OF 1812

Lasting from 1812 to 1815, the war unfolded in a series of scuffles and skirmishes for which the U.S. armed forces, kept lean by Jeffersonian fiscal policies, were ill prepared. With few experienced army officers—the U.S. Military Academy at West Point, founded in 1802, had produced only eighty-nine regular officers—campaigns were executed poorly. Although the U.S. Navy had a corps of experienced officers, it proved no match for the Royal Navy.

Nor did the United States succeed at enlisting sufficient forces. The government's efforts to lure recruits—with sign-up bonuses, and promises of three months' pay and rights to purchase 160 acres of western land upon discharge—met with mixed success. At first, recruitment went well among westerners, who were motivated by civic spirit, desire for land, strong anti-Indian sentiment, and fears of Tecumseh's pan-Indian organization. But after word spread of delays in pay, as well as inadequate supplies and rations, recruitment dwindled. In New England, raising an army was even more difficult. Federalists discouraged enlistments, and even some New England Democratic-Republicans declined to raise volunteer companies. Others promised their men that they would serve only in defensive roles, as in Maine, where they would guard the coastline. Militias in New England and New York often refused to fight outside their own states. Desperate for soldiers, New York offered freedom to slaves who enlisted, and compensation to their owners, and the U.S. Army made the same offer to slaves in the Old Northwest and in

Canada. In Philadelphia, black leaders formed a "Black Brigade" to defend the city. But in the Deep South, fear of arming slaves kept them out of the military except in New Orleans, where a free black militia dated back to Spanish control of Louisiana. The British, on the other hand, recruited slaves by promising freedom in exchange for service. In the end, British forces—made up of British regulars, their Indian allies, fugitive slaves, and Canadians, many of whom were loyalists who had fled during the American Revolution—outnumbered the Americans overall.

Invasion of Canada   Despite their recruitment problems, Americans expected to take Canada easily. Canada's population was sparse, its army small, and the Great Lakes inaccessible to the Royal Navy in the Atlantic. Americans hoped, too, that French Canadians might welcome U.S. forces.

American strategy aimed to split Canadian forces and isolate pro-British Indians, especially Tecumseh, whom the British had promised an Indian nation in the Great Lakes region. In July 1812, U.S. general William Hull, territorial governor of Michigan, marched his troops, who outnumbered those of the British and their allies, into Upper Canada (modern Ontario), hoping to conquer Montreal. But by abandoning Mackinac Island and Fort Dearborn, and by surrendering Fort Detroit, he left the entire Midwest exposed to the enemy. Captain Zachary Taylor provided the only bright spot, giving the Americans a land victory with his September 1812 defense of Fort Harrison in Indiana Territory. But by the winter of 1812–1813, the British controlled about half of the Old Northwest. The United States had no greater success on the Niagara Front, where New York borders Canada, in large part because New York militiamen refused to leave their state to join the invasion of Canada.

Naval Battles   Despite victories on the Atlantic by the USS *Constitution* (nicknamed "Old Ironsides" after its rout of the HMS *Guerrière*), the USS *Wasp*, and the USS *United States*, the American navy—which began the war with just seventeen ships—could not match the powerful Royal Navy. The Royal Navy blockaded the Chesapeake and Delaware Bays in December 1812, and by 1814 the blockade covered nearly all American ports along the Atlantic and Gulf coasts. After 1811, American trade overseas declined by nearly 90 percent, and the decline in revenue from customs duties threatened to bankrupt the federal government and prostrate New England.

The contest for control of the Great Lakes, the key to the war in the Northwest, evolved as a shipbuilding race. Under Master Commandant Oliver Hazard Perry and shipbuilder Noah Brown, the United States outbuilt the British on Lake Erie and defeated them at the bloody Battle of Put-in-Bay on September 10, 1813, gaining control of Lake Erie.

Burning Capitals   General William Henry Harrison then began what would be among the United States' most successful land campaigns. A ragged group of Kentucky militia volunteers, armed only with swords and knives, marched 20 to 30 miles a day to join Harrison's forces in Ohio. Now 4,500 strong, Harrison's forces attacked and took Detroit before

VISUALIZING THE PAST

Selling War

The War of 1812 was not always a popular war, but in its aftermath many Americans trumpeted the war's successes. On the left, we see a recruitment poster from 1812, in which General William Henry Harrison seeks additional cavalrymen. Hampered in part by transportation difficulties, Harrison is unable to offer

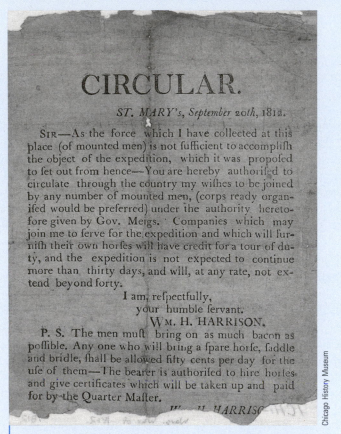

Chicago History Museum

With a tiny regular army, the United States often had to rely on short-term recruits to wage war on the British.

crossing into Canada, where at the Battle of the Thames they defeated British, Shawnee, and Chippewa forces in October 1813. Among the dead was Tecumseh. The Americans then razed the Canadian capital of York (now Toronto), looting and burning the Parliament building before withdrawing.

much—soldiers are even requested to supply their own bacon as well as their own horses—but he does promise that the expedition will be short, undoubtedly a concern to men eager to return to the fall harvest. On the right, we see a handkerchief made in 1815, after the Treaty of Ghent and the Battle of New Orleans; it features the United States' victories against the world's greatest naval power, Great Britain. Made with a decorative border, the kerchief may have been for display. What similar values do we see promoted in the two images, and what factors—such as their intended audiences, their purposes, and when they were created—might account for any differences between them?

© Collection of the New-York Historical Society, USA/Bridgeman Art Library Ltd.

Made in 1815 from cotton textiles—whose domestic production soared during the War of 1812, with trade cut off from Britain—this handkerchief helps promote American "liberty and independence."

After defeating Napoleon in Europe in April 1814, the British launched a land counteroffensive against the United States, concentrating on the Chesapeake Bay region. In retaliation for the burning of York—and to divert American troops from Lake Champlain, where the British planned a new offensive—royal troops occupied

Washington, D.C., in August and set it ablaze, leaving the presidential mansion and parts of the city burning all night. Chaos ruled. The president and cabinet fled. Dolley Madison stayed long enough to oversee the removal of cabinet documents and, famously, to save a Gilbert Stuart portrait of George Washington.

The British intended the attack on Washington only as a diversion. The major battle occurred in September 1814 at Baltimore, where the Americans held firm. Francis Scott Key, detained on a British ship, watched the bombardment of Fort McHenry from Baltimore harbor and the next morning wrote the verses of "The Star-Spangled Banner" (which became the national anthem in 1931). Although the British inflicted heavy damage, they achieved little militarily; their offensive on Lake Champlain proved equally unsuccessful. The war had reached a stalemate.

War in the South   To the south, two wars were happening simultaneously. In what one historian calls "the other War of 1812" (or the Patriots War), a private army of Americans, with secret support from the Madison administration, tried to seize East Florida from Spain's control. What started as a settlers' rebellion along the Georgia-Florida border—in an effort to grab more land, strike at the Spaniards' Indian allies, and later to protest the Spaniards' arming of black soldiers (increasing white settlers' fears of slave rebellion)—turned into a war, with the Patriots receiving support from U.S. regular forces (land and naval) and Georgia militia units. Federalists condemned the invasion of a neutral territory, and the Senate refused twice (in 1812 and 1813) to support a military seizure of Florida. Politically embarrassed, Madison withdrew his support, and the movement collapsed in May 1814. Historians disagree about whether the Patriots War ultimately helped or hindered American efforts to win Florida from the Spanish.

In the war with Britain, the southern theater proved much more successful. The war's final campaign began with an American attack on the Red Stick Creeks along the Gulf of Mexico and the British around New Orleans, and it ended with Americans gaining new territory for white settlement. The Red Sticks had responded to Tecumseh's call (his mother was a Creek) to resist U.S. expansion. Some had died in Indiana Territory, when General Harrison's troops routed Shawnee forces at Tippecanoe in 1811. In 1813, the Red Sticks attacked Fort Mims, about 40 miles from Mobile, killing hundreds of white men, women, and children seeking protection there. Looking for revenge, General Andrew Jackson of Tennessee rallied his militiamen as well as Indian opponents of the Red Sticks (including other Creeks favoring accommodation with whites) and crushed the Red Sticks at Horseshoe Bend (in present-day Alabama) in March 1814, leading to the Treaty of Fort Jackson, in which the Creeks ceded 23 million acres of their land, or about half of their holdings, and withdrew to the southern and western part of Mississippi Territory.

Jackson became a major general in the regular army and continued south toward the Gulf of Mexico, with his eye on New Orleans. After seizing Pensacola (in Spanish Florida) and then securing Mobile, Jackson's forces marched to New Orleans, where for three weeks they played a game of cat-and-mouse with the British soldiers. Finally, on January 8, 1815, the two forces met head-on. In fortified positions, Jackson's poorly trained army held its ground against two British frontal assaults.

At day's end, more than two thousand British soldiers lay dead or wounded (a casualty rate of nearly one-third), while the Americans suffered only twenty-one casualties.

The Battle of New Orleans took place two weeks after the war's official conclusion: word had not yet reached America that British and United States diplomats had signed the Treaty of Ghent on December 24, 1814. Although militarily unnecessary, the Battle of New Orleans catapulted General Andrew Jackson to national political prominence, and the victory over a formidable foe inspired a sense of national pride.

Treaty of Ghent   The Treaty of Ghent essentially restored the prewar status quo. It provided for an end to hostilities with the British and with Native Americans, release of prisoners, restoration of conquered territory, and arbitration of boundary disputes. But the United States received no satisfaction on impressment, blockades, or other maritime rights for neutrals, and the British demands for territorial cessions from Maine to Minnesota went unmet. The British dropped their promise to Tecumseh of an independent Indian nation.

Why did the negotiators settle for so little? Napoleon's defeat allowed the United States to discard its prewar demands because peace in Europe made impressment and interference with American commerce moot issues. Similarly, war-weary Britain—its treasury nearly depleted—stopped pressing for military victory.

Private Collection/Picture Research Consultants & Archives

Americans rejoiced that the War of 1812 had reaffirmed their independence from the British monarchy. The sailor's foot here steps on the crown while broken chains of bondage lie nearby.

**American
Sovereignty
Reasserted**
Yet the War of 1812 had significant consequences for America's status in the world. It affirmed the independence of the American republic and ensured Canada's independence from the United States. Trade and territorial disputes with Great Britain continued, but they never again led to war. Americans strengthened their resolve to steer clear of European politics.

The return of peace allowed the United States to again focus on the Barbary Coast, where the dey (governor) of Algiers had taken advantage of the American preoccupation with British forces to declare his own war on the United States. In the Second Barbary War, U.S. forces captured and detained hundreds of Algerians while negotiating a treaty in the summer of 1815 that forever freed the United States from paying tributes for passage in the Mediterranean. The Second Barbary War reaffirmed America's sovereignty and its commitment to the principle of freedom of the seas.

**Domestic
Consequences**
The War of 1812 had profound domestic consequences. The Federalists' hopes of returning to national prominence all but evaporated with the Hartford Convention, when delegates from New England—frustrated by the stalemated war and the shattered New England economy—met in Hartford, Connecticut, for three weeks in the winter of 1814–1815 to discuss revising the national compact or pulling out of the republic. Although moderates prevented a resolution of secession—a resolution to withdraw from the Union—the delegates condemned the war and the embargo while endorsing constitutional changes that would weaken the South's power vis-à-vis the North and make it harder to declare war. When news arrived in upcoming weeks of, first, Jackson's victory in New Orleans and, then, the Treaty of Ghent, the Hartford Convention made the Federalists look wrong-headed, even treasonous. Federalists survived in a handful of states until the 1820s, but the party faded from the national scene.

With Tecumseh's death, midwestern Indians lost their most powerful leader; with the withdrawal of the British, they lost their strongest ally. In the South, the Red Sticks had ceded vast tracts of fertile land. The war did not bring disaster to all Indians—some accommodationists, such as the Cherokees, temporarily flourished—but it effectively disarmed traditionalists bent on resisting American expansion. Although the Treaty of Ghent pledged the United States to end hostilities with Indians and to restore their prewar "possessions, rights, and privileges," Indians could not make the United States adhere to the agreement.

For American farmers, the war opened vast tracts of formerly Indian land for cultivating cotton in the Old Southwest and wheat in the Old Northwest. For young industries, the war also ultimately proved a stimulant, as Americans could no longer rely on overseas imports of manufactured goods, particularly textiles. The War of 1812 thus fueled demand for raw cotton, and the newly acquired lands in the Southwest beckoned southerners who migrated there with their slaves, or with expectations of someday owning slaves. The war's conclusion accelerated three trends that would dominate U.S. history for upcoming decades: westward expansion, industrial takeoff, and slavery's entrenchment.

THE NATIONALIST PROGRAM

In his final year as president, James Madison and the Democratic-Republicans embraced a nationalist agenda, absorbing the Federalist idea that the federal government should encourage economic growth. In his December 1815 message to Congress, Madison recommended economic development and military expansion. His agenda, which Henry Clay later called the American System, included a national bank, improved transportation, and a protective tariff—a tax on imported goods that was designed to protect American manufacturers from foreign competition. Yet Madison did not stray entirely from his Jeffersonian roots; only a constitutional amendment, he argued, could authorize the federal government to build local roads and canals.

American System

Clay and other congressional leaders, such as Calhoun of South Carolina, believed the American System would ease sectional divides in the expanding nation. The tariff would stimulate New England industry. New England manufactured goods would find markets in the South and West. At the same time, the South's and West's agricultural products—cotton and foodstuffs—would feed New England mills and their workers. Manufactured goods and agricultural products would move in all directions along roads and canals—what contemporaries called internal improvements—which tariff revenues would fund. A national bank would handle the transactions.

In the Madison administration's last year, the Democratic-Republican Congress enacted much of the nationalist program. In 1816, it chartered the Second Bank of the United States (the charter on the first bank had expired in 1811) to serve as a depository for federal funds and to issue currency, collect taxes, and pay the government's debts. The Second Bank of the United States would also oversee state and local banks, ensuring that their paper money had backing in specie (precious metals). Like its predecessor, the bank mixed public and private ownership; the government provided one-fifth of the bank's capital and appointed one-fifth of its directors.

Congress also passed a protective tariff to aid industries that flourished during the War of 1812 but that now were threatened by the resumption of overseas trade. The Tariff of 1816 levied taxes on imported woolens and cottons as well as on iron, leather, hats, paper, and sugar. Foreshadowing a growing trend, though, the tariff did more to divide than to unify the nation. New England as well as the western and Middle Atlantic states stood to benefit from it and thus applauded it, whereas many southerners objected that it raised the price of consumer goods while opening the possibility that Britain would retaliate with a tariff on cotton.

Some southerners did press for internal improvements. Calhoun vocally promoted roads and canals to "bind the republic together." However, on March 3, 1817, the day before leaving office, President Madison, citing constitutional scruples, stunned Congress by vetoing Calhoun's "Bonus Bill," which would have authorized federal funding for such public works.

Early Internal Improvements

Constitutional scruples aside, Federalists and Democratic-Republicans agreed that the nation's prosperity depended on improved transportation. For Federalists, roads and canals were necessary for commercial development; for Jeffersonians, they would spur western expansion and agrarian growth. In 1806, Congress had passed (and Jefferson had signed) a bill authorizing funding for the Cumberland Road (later, the National Road), running 130 miles between Cumberland, Maryland, and Wheeling, Virginia (now West Virginia). Construction began in 1811 and was completed in 1818. Two years later, Congress authorized a survey of the National Road to Columbus, Ohio, a project funded in 1825 and completed in 1833; the road would ultimately extend into Indiana.

After President Madison's veto of the Bonus Bill, though, most transportation initiatives received funding from states, private investors, or a combination of the two. Between 1817 and 1825, the State of New York constructed the Erie Canal, linking the Great Lakes to the Atlantic seaboard. Although southern states constructed modest canals, the South's trade depended on rivergoing steamboats after 1817, when steamboats began traveling regularly upriver on the Mississippi. With canals and steamboats, western agricultural products could travel to market much more quickly and inexpensively, fueling the nation's westward expansion. Unlike steamboats, though, canals expanded commercial networks into regions without natural waterways. Although the Mississippi provided the great commercial highway of the Early Republic, canals began to reorient midwestern commerce through the North.

The Era of Good Feelings   James Monroe, Madison's successor, continued Madison's domestic program, supporting tariffs and vetoing the Cumberland Road Bill (for repairs) in 1822. Monroe was the last president to have attended the Constitutional Convention and the third Virginian elected president since 1801. A former senator and twice governor of Virginia, he had served under Madison as secretary of state and of war and had used his close association with Jefferson and Madison to attain the presidency. In 1816, he and his running mate, Daniel Tompkins, trounced the last Federalist presidential nominee, Rufus King, garnering all the electoral votes except those of the Federalist strongholds of Massachusetts, Connecticut, and Delaware. A Boston newspaper dubbed this one-party period the "Era of Good Feelings."

Led by Federalist chief justice John Marshall, the Supreme Court became the bulwark of the nationalist agenda. In *McCulloch v. Maryland* (1819), the Court struck down a Maryland law taxing banks within the state that were not chartered by its legislature—a law aimed at hindering the Baltimore branch of the federally chartered Second Bank of the United States. The bank refused to pay the tax and sued. At issue was state versus federal jurisdiction. Writing for a unanimous Court, Marshall asserted the supremacy of the federal government over the states. "The Constitution and the laws thereof are supreme," he declared. "They control the constitution and laws of the respective states and cannot be controlled by them." The Court ruled, too, that Congress had the power to charter banks under the Constitution's clause endowing it with the authority to pass "all laws which shall be necessary and proper for carrying into execution" the enumerated powers of government. The Marshall Court thus supported the Federalist view that the federal government could promote interstate commerce.

Government Promotion of Market Expansion

Later Supreme Court cases validated government promotion of economic development and encouraged business enterprise and risk taking. In *Gibbons v. Ogden* (1824), the Supreme Court overturned the New York law that had given Robert Fulton and Robert Livingston (and their successor, Aaron Ogden) a monopoly on the New York–New Jersey steamboat trade. Chief Justice Marshall ruled that the federal power to license new enterprises took precedence over New York's grant of monopoly rights and declared that Congress's power under the commerce clause of the Constitution extended to "every species of commercial intercourse," including transportation. The *Gibbons v. Ogden* ruling built on earlier Marshall Court decisions, such as those in *Dartmouth College v. Woodward* (1819), which protected the sanctity of contracts against state interference, and *Fletcher v. Peck* (1810), which voided a Georgia law that violated individuals' rights to make contracts. Within two years of *Gibbons v. Ogden*, the number of steamboats operating in New York increased from six to forty-three. A later ruling under Chief Justice Roger Taney, *Charles River Bridge v. Warren Bridge* (1837), encouraged new enterprises and technologies by favoring competition over monopoly, and the public interest over implied privileges in old contracts.

Federal and state courts, in conjunction with state legislatures, encouraged the proliferation of corporations—organizations entitled to hold property and transact business as if they were individuals. Corporation owners, called shareholders, were granted limited liability, or freedom from personal responsibility for the company's debts beyond their original investment. Limited liability encouraged investors to back new business ventures.

The federal government assisted the development of a commercial economy in other ways. The U.S. Post Office fostered the circulation of information, a critical element of the market economy. The number of post offices grew from three thousand in 1815 to fourteen thousand in 1845. To promote individual creativity and economic growth, the government protected inventions through patent laws and domestic industries through tariffs on foreign imports.

Boundary Settlements

Monroe's secretary of state, John Quincy Adams, matched the Marshall Court in assertiveness and nationalism. Adams, the son of John and Abigail Adams, managed the nation's foreign policy from 1817 to 1825, pushing for expansion (through negotiations, not war), fishing rights for Americans in Atlantic waters, political distance from Europe, and peace. Under Adams's leadership, the United States settled points of conflict with both Britain and Spain. In 1817, the United States and Great Britain signed the Rush-Bagot Treaty limiting their naval forces to one ship each on Lake Champlain and Lake Ontario and to two ships each on the four other Great Lakes. This first disarmament treaty of modern times demilitarized the border between the United States and Canada. Adams then pushed for the Convention of 1818, which fixed the U.S.-Canadian border from Lake of the Woods in Minnesota westward to the Rockies along the 49th parallel. When they could not agree on the boundary west of the Rockies, Britain and the United

States settled on joint occupation of Oregon for ten years (renewed indefinitely in 1827).

Adams's negotiations resulted in the Adams-Onís Treaty, in which the United States gained Florida, already occupied by General Andrew Jackson under pretext of suppressing Seminole raids against American settlements across the border during the First Seminole War of 1817–1818. Although the Louisiana Purchase had omitted reference to Spanish-ruled West Florida, the United States claimed the territory as far east as the Perdido River (the present-day Florida-Alabama border). During the War of 1812, the United States had seized Mobile and the remainder of West Florida, and after the war—with Spain preoccupied with its own domestic and colonial troubles—Adams had laid claim to East Florida. In 1819, Don Luís de Onís, the Spanish minister to the United States, agreed to cede Florida to the United States without payment if the United States renounced its dubious claims to northern Mexico (Texas) and assumed $5 million of claims by American citizens against Spain. The Adams-Onís (or Transcontinental) Treaty also defined the southwestern boundary of the Louisiana Purchase and set the line between Spanish Mexico and Oregon Country at the 42nd parallel.

Monroe Doctrine

John Quincy Adams's desire to insulate the United States and the Western Hemisphere from European conflict brought about his greatest achievement: the Monroe Doctrine. The immediate issue was recognition of new governments in Latin America. Between 1808 and 1822, the United Provinces of Río de la Plata (present-day northern Argentina, Paraguay, and Uruguay), Chile, Peru, Colombia, and Mexico all broke free from Spain. In 1822, shortly after the ratification of the Adams-Onís Treaty, the United States became the first nation outside Latin America to recognize the new states, including Mexico. But in Europe, reactionary regimes were ascending, and with France now occupying Spain to suppress a liberal rebellion, the United States feared that continental powers would attempt to return the new Latin American states to colonial rule. Having withdrawn from an alliance with continental nations, Britain proposed a joint declaration with the United States against European intervention in the Western Hemisphere. Adams rejected Britain's offer as just the kind of entanglement he sought to avoid, despite clear advantages to allying with the British and their powerful navy.

Monroe presented to Congress in December 1823 what became known as the Monroe Doctrine. His message announced that the American continents "are henceforth not to be considered subjects for future colonization by any European power." This principle addressed American anxiety not only about Latin America but also about Russian expansion beyond Alaska and its settlements in California. Monroe demanded nonintervention by Europe in the affairs of independent New World nations, and he pledged noninterference by the United States in European affairs, including those of Europe's existing New World colonies. Although Monroe's words carried no force—European nations stayed out of New World affairs because they feared the Royal Navy, not the United States' proclamations—they proved popular at home, tapping American nationalism as well as anti-British and anti-European feelings.

SECTIONALISM EXPOSED

The embargo, the War of 1812, and the postwar spurt of internal improvements encouraged the southern and northern economies to develop in different but inter-related ways. While the South became more dependent on cotton, the North underwent an accelerated industrial development, whose groundwork had been laid two decades earlier. With their commitment to frugal government and an agrarian nation, Jeffersonians did not promote industry, but a small number of entrepreneurs did.

Early Industrial Development   Despite their efforts to define themselves as a separate nation, Americans relied on British technology to bring together the many steps of textile manufacturing—carding (or disentangling) fibers, spinning yarn, and weaving cloth—under one factory roof. The first American water-powered spinning mill was established in 1790 by Samuel Slater, a British immigrant who reconstructed from memory the complex machines he had used while working in a British cotton-spinning factory. But Slater's mill only carded and spun yarn; the yarn still needed to be hand-woven into cloth, work often done by farm women seeking to earn cash. In 1810, Bostonian Francis Cabot Lowell, determined to introduce water-powered mechanical weaving in the United States, visited the British textile center of Manchester, where he toured factories, later sketching from memory what he had seen. In 1813, he and his business associates, calling themselves the Boston Manufacturing Company, brought together all phases of textile manufacturing under one roof in Waltham, Massachusetts. A decade later, the Boston Manufacturing Company established what it saw as a model industrial village—named for its now-deceased founder—along the banks of the Merrimack River. At Lowell, Massachusetts, there would be boarding houses for workers, a healthy alternative to the tenements and slums of Manchester. American industrialists envisioned America industrializing without the poverty and degradation associated with European industrialization.

The American textile factory had been born in the midst of the War of 1812. When the British began flooding the American market with cheap textiles after the Treaty of Ghent, Lowell realized the market now needed to be protected. He lobbied hard for the inclusion of cotton textiles in the Tariff of 1816, playing a crucial role in persuading reluctant South Carolinians to support the provision.

Early industrialization, primarily in the northern states, was inextricably linked to slavery. Much of the capital came from merchants who made their fortunes at least in part through the trade in African slaves, and two of the most prominent industries—textiles and shoes—expanded in tandem with a growing southern cotton economy. Southern cotton fed northern textile mills, and northern shoe factories sold their "Negro brogans" (work shoes) to southern planters. Even in an older form of northern industrial labor which took place in private homes—out-work—the connections to the slave South were strong: New England farm girls wove palm-leaf hats for merchants who sold them to southern planters for their slaves.

Panic of 1819   Immediately after the war, the American economy boomed. The international demand for (and price of) American commodities reached new heights. Poor weather in Europe led to crop failures, increasing demand for northern foodstuffs and Southern cotton, which, in turn, touched off western land speculation. Speculators raced to buy large tracts of land at modest, government-established prices and then to resell it at a hefty profit to would-be settlers. This expansion was built on easy credit. With easily obtained loans and paper money, farmers and speculators bought land, while manufacturers established new enterprises or enlarged existing ones.

Prosperity proved short-lived. Now recovered from war as well as weather, by the late 1810s Europeans could grow their own food, and Britain's new Corn Laws established a high tariff on imported foodstuffs, further lessening demand for American agricultural exports. Cotton prices fell in England. Wars in Latin America interfered with mining and reduced the supply of precious metals, leading European nations to hoard specie; in response, American banks furiously printed paper money and expanded credit even further. Fearful of inflation, the Second Bank of the United States, which had itself issued more loans than it could back in hard currency, demanded in 1819 that state banks repay loans in specie. State banks in turn called in the loans and mortgages they had made to individuals and companies. The falling prices of commodities meant that farmers could not pay their mortgages, and the decline of land values—from 50 to 75 percent in portions of the West—meant they could not meet their debts even by selling their farms. The nation's banking system collapsed. The 1819 financial panic reminded Americans all too starkly that they still lived within the economic orbit of Europe.

Hard times came to countryside and city alike. Foreclosures soared. Unemployment skyrocketed, even in older manufacturing areas that had focused on industries like iron making and tobacco processing. In Philadelphia, unemployment reached 75 percent. The contraction devastated workers and their families. As a Baltimore physician noted in 1819, working people felt hard times "a thousand fold more than the merchants." They could not build up savings during boom times to get them through the hard times; often, they could not make it through the winter without drawing on charity for food, clothing, and firewood.

The depression sent tremors throughout American society. Americans from all regions contemplated the virtues and hazards of rapid market expansion, disagreeing most intensely on where to place the blame for its shortcomings. Westerners blamed easterners; farmers and workers blamed bankers. Even as the nation's economy began to rebound in the early 1820s amid a flurry of internal improvement projects, no one could predict with confidence where—in what region, in what sector—the nation's economic and political fortunes would lie.

Missouri   Just as financial panic struck the nation in 1819, so, too, did
Compromise   political crisis. The issue was slavery's westward expansion. Although economic connections abounded between North and South, slavery had long been politically explosive. Since the drafting of the Constitution, Congress had tried to avoid the issue; the one exception had been debates over the international slave trade. In 1819, however, slavery once again

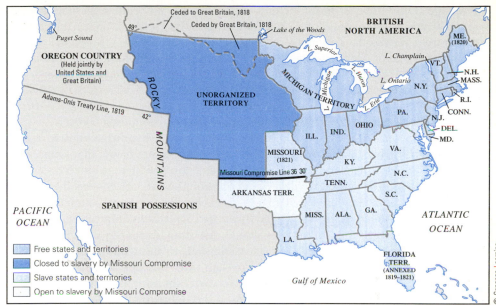

The following labels appear on the map:

Ceded to Great Britain, 1818
Ceded by Great Britain, 1818
49°
Lake of the Woods
Puget Sound
BRITISH NORTH AMERICA
ME. (1820)
L. Superior
OREGON COUNTRY (Held jointly by United States and Great Britain)
L. Champlain
VT.
N.H.
MASS.
MICHIGAN TERRITORY
L. Michigan
Huron
L. Ontario
N.Y.
Adams-Onis Treaty Line, 1819
ROCKY MOUNTAINS
42°
UNORGANIZED TERRITORY
L. Erie
PA.
R.I.
CONN.
N.J.
DEL.
MD.
OHIO
ILL.
IND.
VA.
MISSOURI (1821)
KY.
Missouri Compromise Line 36 30'
N.C.
TENN.
ARKANSAS TERR.
S.C.
PACIFIC OCEAN
SPANISH POSSESSIONS
MISS.
ALA.
GA.
ATLANTIC OCEAN
LA.
FLORIDA TERR. (ANNEXED 1819–1821)
Gulf of Mexico

Legend:
- Free states and territories
- Closed to slavery by Missouri Compromise
- Slave states and territories
- Open to slavery by Missouri Compromise

© Cengage Learning

MAP 9.2 Missouri Compromise and the State of the Union, 1820

The compromise worked out by House Speaker Henry Clay established a formula that avoided debate over whether new states would allow or prohibit slavery. In the process, it divided the United States into northern and southern regions.

burst onto the national political agenda when residents of the Missouri Territory—carved out of the Louisiana Territory—petitioned Congress for admission to the Union with a constitution permitting slavery. At stake was more than the future of slavery in an individual state. Missouri's admission to the Union would give the slaveholding states a two-vote majority in the Senate, and what happened in Missouri would set a precedent for all the new western states created from the vast Louisiana Purchase. "This momentous question," wrote former President Jefferson, fearful for the life of the Union, "like a fire bell in the night, awakened and filled me with terror."

Following the Louisiana Purchase and especially after the end of the War of 1812, the American population had surged westward, leading five new states to join the Union: Louisiana (1812), Indiana (1816), Mississippi (1817), Illinois (1818), and Alabama (1819). Of these, Louisiana, Mississippi, and Alabama permitted slavery. Because Missouri was on the same latitude as free Illinois, Indiana, and Ohio (a state since 1803), its admission as a slave state would thrust slavery not just westward but also northward, as well as tilt the uneasy balance in the Senate.

For two and a half years the issue dominated Congress, with the fiery debate transcending the immediate issue of slavery in Missouri. When Representative James Tallmadge Jr. of New York proposed gradual emancipation in Missouri, some southerners accused the North of threatening to destroy the Union. "If you persist, the Union will be dissolved," Thomas W. Cobb of Georgia shouted at

Tallmadge. Only "seas of blood" could extinguish the fire Tallmadge had ignited, warned Cobb. "Let it come," retorted Tallmadge. The House, which had a northern majority, passed the Tallmadge Amendment, but the Senate rejected it.

House Speaker Henry Clay—himself a western slaveholder—put forward a compromise in 1820. Maine, carved out of Massachusetts, would enter as a free state, followed by Missouri as a slave state, maintaining the balance between slave and free states, at twelve to twelve. In the rest of the Louisiana Territory north of Missouri's southern border of 36°30′, slavery would be prohibited forever.

The compromise carried but almost unraveled when Missouri submitted a constitution barring free blacks from entering the state, a provision that opponents contended would violate the federal constitutional provision that citizens of each state were "entitled to all privileges and immunities of citizens in the several States." Proponents countered that many states, North and South, already barred free blacks from entering. In 1821, Clay proposed a second compromise: Missouri would guarantee that none of its laws would discriminate against citizens of other states. (The compromise carried, but once admitted to the Union, Missouri twice adopted laws barring free blacks.) For more than three decades, the Missouri Compromise would govern congressional policy toward admitting new slave states. But the compromise masked rather than suppressed the simmering political conflict over slavery's westward expansion.

SUMMARY

The partisanship of the 1790s, though alarming to the nation's political leaders, captured Americans' imaginations, making the early republic a period of pervasive and vigorous political engagement. Troubled by vicious partisanship, President Jefferson sought both to unify the nation and to solidify Democratic-Republican control of the government. With a vision of an agrarian nation that protected individual liberty, Jeffersonians promoted a limited national government—one that stayed out of religious affairs and spent little on military forces, diplomatic missions, and economic initiatives. The rival Federalists, who exerted most of their influence through the judiciary, declared federal supremacy over the states even as the judiciary affirmed its own supremacy over other branches of the government. Federalists hoped a strengthened federal government would promote commerce and industry.

Despite his belief in limited government, Jefferson considered the acquisition of the Louisiana Territory and the commissioning of the Corps of Discovery among his most significant presidential accomplishments. The enormous expanse of fertile lands fueled the Jeffersonian dream of an agrarian republic: Americans soon streamed into the Louisiana Territory. Even more would have done so had it not been for the Indians (and their British allies) who stood in their way and for poorly developed transportation routes.

Jefferson's vision rested, too, on American disentanglement from foreign affairs. But with its economy so focused on international shipping, the United States soon faced its greatest threats from abroad, not from partisan or sectional divisions. In its wars with the Barbary states, the United States sought to guard its commerce and ships on the high seas. The second war with Britain—the War of 1812—was fought for similar reasons but against a much more formidable power. Although a military stalemate, the war inspired a new sense of nationalism and launched a new era of American development.

The Treaty of Ghent reaffirmed American independence; thereafter, the nation was able to settle disputes with Great Britain at the bargaining table. The war also dealt a serious blow to Indian resistance in the Midwest and Southwest. At the same time, embargoes and war accelerated the pace of American industrial growth. Because the Federalists' opposition to the war undermined their political credibility, their party all but disappeared from the national political scene by 1820. The absence of well-organized partisan conflict created what contemporaries called an Era of Good Feelings.

Although overt tension was muted in the heady postwar years, competing visions of America's route to prosperity and greatness endured. Under Chief Justice John Marshall, the Supreme Court supported the Federalist agenda, issuing rulings that stimulated commerce and industry through economic nationalism. The Democratic-Republicans looked, instead, toward the South and West, the vast and fertile Louisiana Territory. Whether they supported agrarian or industrial development, almost all Americans could agree on the need for improved transportation, though most internal improvements took place in the North.

During the first quarter of the nineteenth century, the United States vastly expanded its territorial reach, not just through the Louisiana Purchase but also with the acquisition of Florida. Fearful of European intentions to reassert influence in the Americas and emboldened by the nation's expanding boundaries, President Monroe proclaimed that the United States would not tolerate European intervention in American affairs. But even as its expanding boundaries strengthened the United States' international presence, that same territorial expansion would threaten the nation's newfound political unity at home.

That threat became most apparent in 1819, when the postwar economic boom came to a grinding halt and when congressmen predicted dire consequences could result from the dispute over whether to admit Missouri as a slave state. Henry Clay's compromise removed the issue of slavery's expansion from political center stage, but—by addressing only those territories already owned by the United States—it did not permanently settle the issue.

10

THE RISE OF THE SOUTH 1815–1860

THE "DISTINCTIVE" SOUTH

Not until the first half of the 1800s did the region of slaveholding states from the Chesapeake and Virginia to Missouri, and from Florida across to Texas, come to be designated as the South. Today, many still consider it America's most distinctive region. Historians have long examined how the Old South was like and unlike the rest of the nation. Because of its unique history, has the South, in the words of poet Allen Tate, always been "Uncle Sam's other province"? Or as southern writer W. J. Cash said in 1940, is the South "a tree with many age rings, with its limbs and trunk bent and twisted by all the winds of the years, but with its tap root in the Old South?" Analyzing just why the South seems more religious, more conservative, or more tragic than other regions of America has been an enduring practice in American culture and politics.

Certain American values, such as materialism, individualism, and faith in progress, have been associated with the North and values such as tradition, honor, and family loyalty, with the South. The South, so the stereotype has it, was static, even "backward," and the North was dynamic in the decades leading up to the Civil War. There are many measures of just how different South was from North in the antebellum era. At the same time, there were many Souths: low-country rice and cotton regions with dense slave populations; mountainous regions of small farmers and subsistence agriculture; semitropical wetlands in the Southeast; plantation culture in the Cotton Belt and especially the Mississippi valley; Texas grasslands; tobacco- and wheat-growing regions in Virginia and North Carolina; cities with bustling ports; wilderness areas with only the rare homestead of hillfolk.

CHRONOLOGY

1810–20	137,000 slaves are forced to move from the Upper South to Alabama, Mississippi, and other western regions
1822	Vesey's insurrection plot is discovered in South Carolina
1830s	Vast majority of African American slaves are native-born in America
1830s–40s	Cotton trade grows into largest source of commercial wealth and America's leading export
1831	Turner leads a violent slave rebellion in Virginia
1832	Virginia holds the last debate in the South about the future of slavery; gradual abolition is voted down
	Publication of Dew's proslavery tract *Abolition of Negro Slavery*
1836	Arkansas gains admission to the Union as a slave state
1839	Mississippi's Married Women's Property Act gives married women some property rights
1845	Florida and Texas gain admission to the Union as slave states
	Publication of Douglass's *Narrative of the Life of Frederick Douglass, an American Slave, Written by Himself*
1850	Planters' share of agricultural wealth in the South is 90 to 95 percent
1850–60	Of some 300,000 slaves who migrate from the Upper to the Lower South, 60 to 70 percent go by outright sale
1857	Publication of Hinton R. Helper's *The Impending Crisis*, denouncing the slave system
	Publication of George Fitzhugh's *Southern Thought*, an aggressive defense of slavery
1860	405,751 mulattos in the United States, 12.5 percent of the African American population
	Three-quarters of all southern white families own no slaves
	South produces largest cotton crop ever

South-North Similarity   The South was distinctive because of its commitment to slavery, but it also shared much in common with the rest of the nation. The geographic sizes of the South and the North were roughly the same. In 1815, white southerners shared with their fellow free citizens in the North a heritage of heroes and ideology from the era of the American Revolution and the War of 1812. With varying accents, southerners spoke the same language and worshiped the same Protestant God as northerners. Southerners lived under the same Constitution as northerners, and they shared a common mixture of nationalism and localism in their attitudes toward government. Down to the 1840s, northerners and southerners invoked with nearly equal frequency the doctrine of states' rights against federal authority. A sense of American mission and dreams inspired by the westward movement were as much a part of southern as of northern experience.

Indeed, some of the most eloquent visions of America as a land of yeomen—independent, self-sufficient farmers—expanding westward had come from a southerner, Thomas Jefferson. Jefferson believed that "virtue" rested in those who tilled the soil, that farmers made the best citizens. In 1804, Jefferson declared his "moral and physical preference of the agricultural over the manufacturing man." But as slavery and the plantation economy expanded (see Map 10.1), the South did not become a land of individual opportunity in the same manner as the North.

During the forty-five years before the Civil War, the South shared in the nation's economic booms and busts. Research has shown that, despite its enormous cruelties, slavery was a profitable labor system for planters. Southerners and northerners shared an expanding capitalist economy. As it grew, the slave-based economy of money-crop agriculture reflected the rational choices of planters. More land and more slaves generally converted into more wealth.

By the eve of the Civil War in 1860, the distribution of wealth and property in the two sections was almost identical: 50 percent of free adult males owned only 1 percent of real and personal property, and the richest 1 percent owned 27 percent of the wealth. One study comparing Texas and Wisconsin in 1850 shows that the richest 2 percent of families in each state owned 31 to 32 percent of the wealth. So both North and South had ruling classes, even if their wealth was invested in different kinds of property. Entrepreneurs in both sections, whether forging plantations out of Mississippi Delta land or shoe factories and textile mills in New England river towns, sought their fortunes in an expanding market economy. The southern "master class" was, in fact, more likely than propertied northerners to move west to make a profit.

South-North Dissimilarity   There were important differences between the North and the South. The South's climate and longer growing season gave it an unmistakably rural and agricultural destiny. Many great rivers provided rich soil and transportation routes to market. The South's people, white and black, developed an intense attachment to place, to the ways people were related to the land and to one another. The South developed as a biracial society of brutal inequality, where the liberty of one race depended directly on the enslavement of another. White wealth was built on highly valued black labor.

Cotton growers spread out over as large an area as possible to maximize production and income. As a result, population density in the South was low; by 1860, there were only 2.3 people per square mile in vast and largely unsettled Texas, 15.6 in Louisiana, and 18.0 in Georgia. By contrast, population density in the nonslaveholding states east of the Mississippi River was almost three times higher. The Northeast had an average of 65.4 people per square mile. Massachusetts had 153.1 people per square mile, and New York City compressed 86,400 people into each square mile. When, in the 1850s, young Frederick Law Olmsted of Connecticut, later renowned as a landscape architect, toured the South as a journalist, he traveled

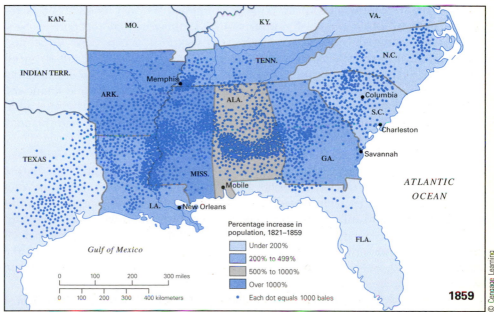

MAP 10.1 Cotton Production in the South

These two maps reveal the rapid westward expansion of cotton production and its importance to the antebellum South.

mostly on horseback along primitive trails. Between Columbus, Georgia, and Montgomery, Alabama, Olmsted found "a hilly wilderness, with a few dreary villages, and many isolated cotton farms." For one who would design Central Park in New York City, this was just too much ruralness.

Where people were scarce, it was difficult to finance and operate schools, churches, libraries, and even inns and restaurants. Similarly, the rural character of the South and the significance of the plantation as a self-sufficient social unit meant that the section put few resources into improving disease control and public health. Southerners were strongly committed to their churches, and some believed in the importance of universities, but all such institutions were far less developed than those in the North. Factories were rare because planters invested most of their capital in slaves. A few southerners did invest in iron or textiles on a small scale. But the largest southern "industry" was lumbering, and the largest factories used slave labor to make cigars. More decisively, the South was slower than the North to develop a unified market economy and a regional transportation network. Despite concerted efforts, the South had only 35 percent of the nation's railroad mileage in 1860.

The Old South never developed its own banking and shipping capacity to any degree. If it had, its effort to be an international cartel might have succeeded longer. Most southern bank deposits were in the North, and southern cotton planters became ever more dependent on New York for shipping. As early as 1822, one-sixth of all southern cotton cleared for Liverpool or Le Havre from the port of New York and constituted two-fifths of all that city's exports. Many New York merchants and bankers developed deep interests in the fate of slavery and cotton prices. In a series of economic conventions held from 1837 to 1839, southern delegates debated the nature of foreign trade, dependence on northern importers and financiers, and other alleged threats to their commercial independence and security. But nothing, save rhetoric, came of these conventions; it was the last time southern planters would organize to break from their Yankee middlemen and shippers.

The South lagged far behind the North in nearly any measure of industrial growth. Its urban centers were mostly ports like New Orleans and Charleston, which became crossroads of commerce and small-scale manufacturing. In the interior were small market towns dependent on agricultural trade—"urbanization without cities," as one historian has said. Slavery slowed urban growth. As a system of racial control, slavery did not work well in cities. Likewise, because of a lack of manufacturing jobs, the South did not attract immigrants as readily as did the North. By 1860, only 13 percent of the nation's foreign-born population lived in the slave states.

Like most northerners, antebellum southerners were adherents to evangelical Christianity. Americans from all regions held in common a faith in a personal God and in conversion and piety as the means to salvation. But southern evangelicalism was distinct from its northern practice. In the South, Baptists and Methodists concentrated on personal rather than social improvement. By the 1830s in the North, evangelicalism was a major wellspring of reform movements (see Chapter 9); but in states where blacks were so numerous and unfree, and where the very social structure received increasingly aggressive attacks from abolitionists, religion, as one scholar has written, preached "a hands-off policy concerning slavery."

Although slaves began to convert to Christianity in the early-nineteenth-century South, many southern whites feared a reform impulse that would foster what one historian has called an "interracial communion" in their churches. Moreover, those women who may have been reform minded were prevented from developing frequent associations with other reformers because of distance and sparse population. The only reform movements that did take hold in the emerging Bible Belt of the South, such as that for temperance, focused on personal behavior, not social reform.

The slave system made it inevitable that the interests and social structures of the North and the South would diverge after 1815. Because of its inherently conservative social structure, antebellum southern law restricted the authority of the courts, reinforcing a tradition of planter control. Penitentiaries tended to house only whites, as most blacks were under the authority of personal masters. Lawbreaking in the South tended to involve crimes of violence rather than crimes against property.

A Southern World-View and the Proslavery Argument

Perhaps in no way was the South more distinctive than in its embrace of a particular world-view, a system of thought and meaning held especially by the planter class, but also influencing the entire society. Like those of all people, southerners' justifications for slavery were not so different from those of any other civilization trying to defend the institutions it inherits. But at the heart of the proslavery argument was a deep and abiding racism. The persistence of modern racism in all sections of the United States is all the more reason to comprehend antebellum southerners' rationalizations for human slavery.

In the wake of the American Revolution, the Enlightenment ideas of natural rights and equality did stimulate antislavery sentiment in the Upper South, produced a brief flurry of manumissions, and led to considerable hope for gradual emancipation. In 1796, Virginian St. George Tucker argued that "slavery not only violates the laws of nature and of civil society, it also wounds the best forms of government." But confidence that the exercise of reason among gentlemen might end such a profitable system as slavery waned in the new nation. As slavery spread, southerners soon vigorously defended it. In 1816, George Bourne, a Presbyterian minister exiled from Virginia for his antislavery sermons and for expulsion of slaveholders from his church, charged that, whenever southerners were challenged on slavery, "they were fast choked, for they had a Negro stuck fast in their throats." After walking home with South Carolina statesman and proslavery advocate John C. Calhoun from an 1820 cabinet meeting, John Quincy Adams confided to his diary that too many southerners "writhe in agonies of fear at the very mention of human rights as applicable to men of color."

By the 1820s, white southerners went on the offensive, actively justifying slavery as a "positive good" and not merely a "necessary evil." They used the antiquity of slavery, as well as the Bible's many references to slaveholding, to foster a historical argument for bondage. Slavery, they deemed, was the natural status of blacks. Whites were the more intellectual race, and blacks the race more inherently physical and therefore destined for labor. Whites were the creators of civilizations, blacks the appointed hewers of wood and drawers of water. Proslavery writers did not mince words. In a proslavery tract written in 1851, John Campbell confidently declared that "there is as much difference between the lowest tribe of negroes and the white Frenchman, Englishman, or American, as there is between the monkey and the negro."

Some southerners defended slavery in practical terms; they simply saw their bondsmen as economic necessities and symbols of their quest for prosperity. In 1845, James Henry Hammond of South Carolina argued that slaveholding was essentially a matter of property rights. Unwilling to "deal in abstractions" about the "right and wrong" of slavery, Hammond considered property sacred and protected by the Constitution, because slaves were legal property—end of argument. The deepest root of the proslavery argument was a hierarchical view of the social order as slavery's defenders believed God or nature had prescribed it. Southerners cherished tradition, duty, and honor, believing social change should come only in slow increments, if at all. As the Virginia legislature debated the gradual abolition of slavery in 1831–1832, in the wake of Nat Turner's rebellion, Thomas R. Dew, a slaveholder and professor of law and history at the College of William and Mary, contended that "that which is the growth of *ages* may require ages to remove." Dew's widely read work *Abolition of Negro Slavery* (1832) ushered in an outpouring of proslavery writing that would intensify over the next thirty years. Until Turner's bloody rebellion, Dew admitted, emancipation in the South had "never been seriously discussed." But as slavery expanded westward and fueled national prosperity, Dew cautioned southerners that any degree of gradual abolition threatened the whole region's "irremediable ruin." Dew declared black slavery part of the "order of nature," an indispensable part of the "deep and solid foundations of society" and the basis of the "well-ordered, well-established liberty" of white Americans. Dew's well-ordered society also included his conception of the proper division of men and women into separate spheres and functions.

Proslavery advocates held views very different from those of northern reformers on the concepts of freedom, progress, and equality. They turned natural-law doctrine to their favor, arguing that the natural state of humankind was inequality of ability and condition, not equality. A former U.S. senator in South Carolina, William Harper, charged in 1837 that Jefferson's famous dictum about equality in the Declaration of Independence was no more than a "sentimental phrase." "Is it not palpably nearer the truth to say that no man was ever born free," Harper argued, "and that no two men were ever born equal?" Proslavery writers believed that people were born to certain stations in life; they stressed dependence over autonomy and duty over rights as the human condition. As Virginia writer George Fitzhugh put it in 1854, "Men are not born entitled to equal rights. It would be far nearer the truth to say, that some were born with saddles on their backs, and others booted and spurred to ride them."

Many slaveholders believed their ownership of people bound them to a set of paternal obligations as guardians of a familial relationship between masters and slaves. Although contradicted by countless examples of slave resistance and escape, as well as by slave sales, planters needed to believe in and exerted great energy in constructing the idea of the contented slave. The slaveholders who promoted their own freedom and pursued personal profits through the bondage of blacks had to justify themselves endlessly.

A Slave Society   Slavery and race affected everything in the Old South. Whites and blacks alike grew up, were socialized, married, reared children, worked, conceived of property, and honed their most basic habits of behavior under the influence of slavery. This was true of slaveholding and non-slaveholding whites as well as of blacks who were slave and free. Slavery shaped the social structure of the South, fueled almost anything meaningful in its economy, and came to dominate its politics. Rudolphe Lucien Desdunes, a Louisiana sugar planter, remembered growing up in a society where "slavery was the pivot around which everything revolved."

The South was interdependent with the North, the West, and even with Europe in a growing capitalist market system. To keep the cotton trade flowing, southerners relied on northern banks, on northern steamship companies working the great western rivers, and on northern merchants. But there were elements of this system that southerners increasingly rejected during the antebellum era, especially urbanism, the wage labor system, a broadening right to vote, and any threat to their racial and class order.

In the antebellum era, as later, there were many Souths, but Americans have always been determined to define what one historian called the "Dixie difference." "The South is both American and something different," writes another historian, "at times a mirror or magnifier of national traits and at other times a counterculture." This was most acutely true in the decades before the Civil War.

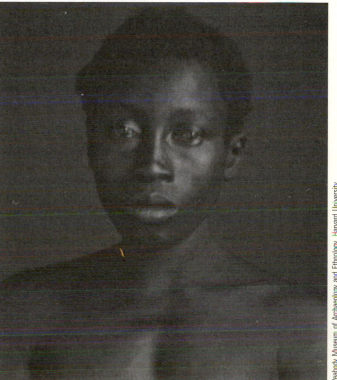

Delia, a slave on the Edgehill plantation, near Columbia, South Carolina, photographed in 1850 by daguerrotypist, Joseph Zealy, for natural scientist, Louis Agassiz. Delia was among seven people Agassiz had photographed nude in an effort to investigate the alleged inferior physiogamy of Africans and African Americans. Delia's tearful gaze haunts the tragic process by which the "racial sciences" tried to categorize and rank human beings in the service of proslavery arguments.

Peabody Museum of Archaeology and Ethnology, Harvard University

Culturally, the South developed a proclivity to tell its own story. Its ruralness and its sense of tradition may have given southerners a special habit of telling tales. "Southerners ... love a good tale," said Mississippi writer Eudora Welty. "They are born reciters, great memory retainers, diary keepers, letter exchangers, and letter savers, history tracers, and debaters, and—outstaying all the rest—great talkers." The South's story is both distinctive and national, and it begins in what we have come to call the Old South, a term only conceivable after the eviction of native peoples from the region.

SOUTHERN EXPANSION, INDIAN RESISTANCE AND REMOVAL

Americans were a restless, moving people when the trans-Appalachian frontier opened in the wake of the War of 1812. Some 5 to 10 percent of the booming population moved each year, usually westward. In the first two decades of the century, they poured into the Ohio valley; by the 1820s, after the death of the Shawnee chief Tecumseh and the collapse of the pan-Indian federation, they were migrating into the Mississippi River valley and beyond. By 1850, two-thirds of Americans lived west of the Appalachians.

A Southern Westward Movement As much as in any other region, this surging westward movement was a southern phenomenon. After 1820, the heart of cotton cultivation and the slave-based plantation system shifted from the coastal states to Alabama and the newly settled Mississippi valley—Tennessee, Louisiana, Arkansas, and Mississippi. Southern slaveholders forced slaves to move with them to the newer areas of the South, and yeoman farmers followed, also hoping for new wealth through cheap land and the ownership of other people.

A wave of migration was evident everywhere in the Southeast. As early as 1817, Georgian Samuel McDonald observed a "disease prevalent" in his region. "The patient," he said, first exhibited a "great love" of talking about "the new country" to the west. Then he tried to "make sale of his stock" and "lastly ... to sell his plantation." Once attacked by this "Alabama fever," most never recovered and were carried "off to the westward." That same year, a Charleston, South Carolina, newspaper reported with alarm that migration out of that state had already reached "unprecedented proportions." Indeed, almost half of the white people born in South Carolina after 1800 left the state, most for the Southwest. And by 1833, Tyrone Power, an Irish actor riding a stagecoach from Georgia into Alabama, encountered many "camps of immigrants" and found the roads "covered" by such pilgrims.

The way to wealth for seaboard planters in the South was to go west to grow cotton for the booming world markets, by purchasing ever more land and slaves. The population of Mississippi soared from 73,000 in 1820 to 607,000 in 1850, with African American slaves in the majority. Across the Mississippi River, the population of Arkansas went from fourteen thousand in 1820 to 210,000 in 1850. By 1835, the American immigrant population in Texas reached 35,000, including three thousand slaves, and outnumbering Mexicans two to one. Aggressive American settlers declared Texas's independence from Mexico in 1836, spurring further American immigration into the region. By 1845, "Texas fever" had boosted the Anglo population to 125,000. Statehood that year opened the floodgates to more immigrants from the east and to a confrontation with Mexico that would lead to war.

As the cotton kingdom grew to what southern political leaders dreamed would be national and world dominion, this westward migration, fueled at first by an optimistic nationalism, ultimately made migrant planters more sectional and more southern. In 1817, Congressman John C. Calhoun embraced national expansion as the means to "bind the Republic together," as he provided the process its unquestioned assumption: "Let us conquer space." In time, political dominance in the South migrated westward into the Cotton Belt as well. By the 1840s and 1850s, these energetic capitalist planters, ever mindful of world markets and fearful that their slave-based economy was under attack, sought to protect and expand their system. Increasingly, they saw themselves, as one historian has written, less as "landowners who happened to own slaves" than as "slaveholders who happened to own land."

Before all this expansion could take place, other, older groups of Americans already occupied much of this land. Before 1830, large swaths of upper Georgia belonged to the Cherokees, and huge regions of Alabama and Mississippi were either Creek, Choctaw, or Chickasaw land. Indians were also on the move, but in forced migrations. The indigenous cultures of the eastern and southern woodlands had to be uprooted to make way for white expansion. For the vast majority of white Americans, the Indians were in the way of their growing empire. Taking Indian land, so the reasoning went, merely reflected the natural course of history: the "civilizers" had to displace the "children of the forest" in the name of progress. National leaders provided all the rhetoric and justification needed. "Nothing," said General Andrew Jackson as early as 1816, "can promote the welfare of the United States, and particularly the southwestern frontier so much as bringing into market … the whole of this fertile country." As president in 1830, Jackson spoke with certainty about why the Indians must go. "What good man would prefer a country," he asked, "covered with forests and ranged by a few thousand savages to our extensive Republic, studded with cities, towns, and prosperous farms?"

Indian Treaty Making   In theory, under the U.S. Constitution, the federal government recognized Indian sovereignty and treated Indian peoples as foreign nations. Indeed, the United States received Indian delegations with pomp and ceremony, exchanging gifts as tokens of friendship. Agreements between Indian nations and the United States were signed, sealed, and ratified like other international treaties. In practice, however, swindle and fraud dominated the government's approach to treaty making and Indian sovereignty. The United States imposed conditions on Indian representatives, and as the country expanded, new treaties replaced old ones, shrinking Indian landholdings.

Although Indian resistance persisted against such pressure after the War of 1812, it only slowed the process. In the 1820s, native peoples in the middle West, Ohio valley, Mississippi valley, and other parts of the cotton South ceded lands totaling 200 million acres for a pittance.

The Amistad Case

In April 1839, a Spanish slave ship, *Tecora*, sailed from Lomboko, the region of West Africa that became Sierre Leone. On board were Mende people, captured and sold by their African enemies. In June, they arrived in Havana, Cuba, a Spanish colony. Two Spaniards purchased fifty-three of the Mende and set sail aboard *La Amistad* for their plantations elsewhere in Cuba. After three days at sea, the Africans revolted. Led by a man the Spaniards called Joseph Cinque, they killed the captain and seized control of the vessel. They ordered the two Spaniard owners to take them back to Africa, but the slaveholders sailed east by day and north by night, trying to reach the shores of the American South. Far off course, *La Amistad* was seized by the USS *Washington* in Long Island Sound and brought ashore in Connecticut.

The "Amistad Africans" were soon a celebrated moral and legal cause for abolitionists and slaveholders, as well as in U.S.–Spanish relations. The Africans were imprisoned in New Haven, and a prolonged dispute ensued around many questions: Were they slaves and murderers, and the property of their Cuban owners, or were they free people exercising their natural rights? Were they Spanish property, seized on the high seas in violation of a 1795 treaty? If a northern state could "free" captive Africans, what did it mean for enslaved African Americans in the South? Connecticut abolitionists immediately went to court, where a U.S. circuit court judge dismissed the charges of mutiny and murder but refused to release the Africans because their Spanish owners claimed them as property.

Meanwhile, the Mende were desperate to tell their own story. A Yale professor of ancient languages, Josiah Gibbs, visited the captives and learned their words for numbers. In New York, he walked up and down the docks repeating the Mende words until an African seaman,

Indian Accommodation

Increasingly, Indian nations east of the Mississippi sought to survive through accommodation. In the first three decades of the century, the Choctaw, Creek, and Chickasaw peoples in the lower Mississippi became suppliers and traders in the nation's expanding market economy. Under treaty provisions, Indian commerce took place through trading posts and stores that provided Indians with supplies, and purchased or bartered Indian-produced goods. The trading posts extended credit to chiefs, who increasingly fell into debt that they could pay off to the federal government only by selling their land.

By 1822, the Choctaw nation had sold 13 million acres but still carried a debt of $13,000. The Indians struggled to adjust, increasing agricultural production and hunting, working as farmhands and craftsmen, and selling produce at market stalls in Natchez and New Orleans. As the United States expanded westward, white Americans promoted their assimilation, through education and conversion to Christianity, with renewed urgency. "Put into the hand of [Indian] children the primer and the hoe," the House Committee on Indian Affairs recommended in 1818, "and they will naturally, in time, take hold of the plough; and, as their minds

James Covey, responded. Covey journeyed to New Haven, conversed with the jubilant Africans, and soon their harrowing tale garnered sympathy all over Yankee New England.

In a new trial, the judge ruled that the Africans were illegally enslaved and ordered them returned to their homeland. Although slavery might be legal in Cuba, the slave trade between Africa and the Americas had been outlawed in a treaty between Spain and Great Britain. Spain's lawyers demanded the return of their "merchandise." In need of southern votes to win reelection, President Martin Van Buren supported the Spanish claims and advocated the Africans' return to a likely death in Cuba.

The administration appealed the case to the Supreme Court in February 1841. Arguing the abolitionists' case, former president John Quincy Adams famously pointed to a copy of the Declaration of Independence on the wall of the court chambers, invoked the natural rights to life and liberty, and chastised the Van Buren administration for its "immense array of power...on the side of injustice." In a 7-to-1 decision, the Court ruled that the Africans were "freeborn" with the right of self-defense, while remaining silent on slavery's legality in the United States.

Fund-raising and speaking tours featuring Cinque made the return voyage possible. On November 27, 1841, thirty-five survivors and five American missionaries disembarked for Africa. They arrived in Sierre Leone on January 15, 1842, whereupon Cinque wrote a letter to the Amistad Committee. "I thank all 'merican people," he said, "I shall never forget 'merican people." But the international meanings of the Amistad case would endure. Sarah Magru, one of the child captives on *La Amistad*, stayed in America to attend Oberlin College and later returned to work at the Mende mission in Sierre Leone.

The Amistad case showed how intertwined slavery was with freedom, and the United States with the world. It poisoned diplomatic relations between America and Spain for a generation, and stimulated Christian mission work in Africa.

become enlightened and expand, the Bible will be their book, and they will grow up in habits of morality and industry." In 1819, in response to missionary lobbying, Congress appropriated $10,000 annually for "civilization of the tribes adjoining the frontier settlements." Protestant missionaries administered the "civilizing fund" and established mission schools.

Within five years, thirty-two boarding schools enrolled Indian students. They substituted English for American Indian languages and taught agriculture alongside the Christian gospel. But this emphasis on agriculture and the value of private property did not deter settlers eyeing Indian land. Wherever native peoples lived, illegal settlers disrupted their lives. The federal government only halfheartedly enforced the integrity of treaties, as legitimate Indian land rights gave way to the advance of white civilization.

Over time, however, the Indians could not prevent the spread of the cotton economy that arose all around them. With loss of land came dependency. The Choctaws came to rely on white Americans not only for manufactured goods but even for food. Dependency, coupled with disease, facilitated removal of American Indian peoples to western lands. While the population of other groups increased rapidly, the Indian population fell, some nations declining by 50 percent in only three decades. The French traveler and author Alexis de Tocqueville noticed the contrast. "Not only have these wild tribes receded, but they are destroyed," Tocqueville concluded, after personally observing the tragedy of forced removal in 1831, "and as they give way or perish, an immense and increasing people fill their place. There is no instance upon record of so prodigious a growth or so rapid a destruction." As many as 100,000 eastern and southern Indian peoples were removed between 1820 and 1850; about thirty thousand died in the process.

The wanderings of the Shawnees, the people of the Prophet and Tecumseh, illustrate the uprooting of Indian peoples. After giving up 17 million acres in Ohio in a 1795 treaty, the Shawnees scattered to Indiana and eastern Missouri. After the War of 1812, some Shawnees sought protection from either the British in Canada or from Mexico. Yet another group moved to the Kansas territory in 1825. By 1854, Kansas was open to white settlement, and the Shawnees had to cede seven-eighths of their land, or 1.4 million acres.

Removal had a profound impact on all Shawnees. The men lost their traditional role as providers; their skills hunting woodland animals were useless on the prairies of Kansas. As grain became the tribe's dietary staple, Shawnee women played a greater role as providers, supplemented by government aid under treaty provisions. Remarkably, the Shawnees preserved their language and culture in the face of these devastating dislocations.

Indian Removal as Federal Policy   Much of the land of the southeastern tribes—Cherokees, Creeks, Choctaws, Chickasaws, and Seminoles—had remained intact after the War of 1812, and they had aggressively resisted white encroachment. In his last annual message to Congress in late 1824, President James Monroe proposed that all Indians be moved beyond the Mississippi River. Monroe described his proposal as an "honorable" one that would protect Indians from invasion and provide them with independence for "improvement and civilization." He believed force would be unnecessary.

But all four tribes unanimously rejected Monroe's proposition. Between 1789 and 1825, the four nations had negotiated thirty treaties with the United States, and they had reached their limit. Most wished to remain on what little was left of their ancestral land.

Pressure from Georgia had prompted Monroe's policy. In the 1820s, the state had accused the federal government of not fulfilling its 1802 promise to remove the Cherokees and Creeks from northwestern Georgia in return for the state's renunciation of its claim to western lands. In 1826, under federal pressure, the Creek nation ceded all but a small strip of its Georgia acreage, but Georgians remained unmoved. Only the complete removal of the Georgia Creeks to the West could resolve the conflict between the state and the federal government.

For the Creeks, the outcome was devastating. In an ultimately unsuccessful attempt to hold fast to the remainder of their traditional lands, which were in Alabama, they radically altered their political structure. In 1829, at the expense of traditional village autonomy, they centralized tribal authority and forbade any chief from ceding land.

In 1830, after extensive debate and a narrow vote in both houses, Congress passed the Indian Removal Act, authorizing the president to negotiate treaties of removal with all tribes living east of the Mississippi. The bill, which provided federal funds for such relocations, would likely not have passed the House without the additional representation afforded slave states due to the three-fifths clause in the Constitution.

Cherokees   Adapting to American ways seemed no more successful than resistance in forestalling removal. No people met the challenge of assimilating to American standards more thoroughly than the Cherokees, whose traditional home centered on eastern Tennessee and northern Alabama and Georgia. Between 1819 and 1829, the tribe became economically self-sufficient and politically self-governing; during this Cherokee renaissance the nearly fifteen thousand adult Cherokees came to think of themselves as a nation, not a collection of villages. In 1821 and 1822, Sequoyah, a self-educated Cherokee, devised an eighty-six-character phonetic alphabet that made possible a Cherokee-language Bible and a bilingual tribal newspaper, *Cherokee Phoenix* (1828). Between 1820 and 1823, the Cherokees created a formal government with a bicameral legislature, a court system, and a salaried bureaucracy. In 1827, they adopted a written constitution modeled after that of the United States. They transformed their economy from hunting, gathering, and subsistence agriculture to commodity trade based on barter, cash, and credit.

Cherokee land laws, however, differed from U.S. law. The nation collectively owned all Cherokee land and forbade land sales to outsiders. Nonetheless, economic change paralleled political adaptation. Many became individual farmers and slaveholders; by 1833, they held fifteen hundred black slaves, and over time Cherokee racial identity became very complex. Both before and after removal to the west, the designations of "mixed bloods" and "full bloods" were woven into the fabric of tribal society, and conflicts over membership as well as the legacy of Cherokee slaveholding still permeate the group today. But these Cherokee transformations failed to win respect or acceptance from white southerners. In the 1820s, Georgia pressed them to sell the 7,200 square miles of land they held in the state. Congress appropriated $30,000 in 1822 to buy the Cherokee land in Georgia, but the Cherokees resisted. Impatient with their refusals to negotiate cession, Georgia annulled the Cherokees' constitution, extended the state's sovereignty over them, prohibited the Cherokee National Council from meeting except to cede land, and ordered their lands seized. Then, the discovery of gold on Cherokee land in 1829 further whetted Georgia's appetite for Cherokee territory.

Cherokee Nation   Backed by sympathetic whites but not by President Andrew
v. Georgia   Jackson, the Cherokees under Chief John Ross turned to the federal courts to defend their treaty with the United States. Their legal strategy reflected their growing political sophistication. In *Cherokee Nation v. Georgia* (1831), Chief Justice John Marshall ruled that under the federal Constitution an Indian tribe was neither a foreign nation nor a state and therefore had no standing in federal courts. Indians' relationship with the United States was

"marked," said Marshall, "by cardinal and peculiar distinctions which exist nowhere else." They were deemed "domestic, dependent nations." Legally, they were in but not of the United States. Nonetheless, said Marshall, the Indians had an unquestionable right to their lands; they could lose title only by voluntarily giving it up.

A year later, in *Worcester v. Georgia*, Marshall defined the Cherokee position more clearly. The Indian nation was, he declared, a distinct political community in which "the laws of Georgia can have no force" and into which Georgians could not enter without permission or treaty privilege. The Cherokees celebrated. *Phoenix* editor Elias Boudinot called the decision "glorious news." Jackson, however, whose reputation had been built as an Indian fighter, did his best to usurp the Court's action. Newspapers widely reported that Jackson had said, "John Marshall has made his decision: now let him enforce it." Keen to open up new lands for settlement, Jackson favored expelling the Cherokees.

Georgians, too, refused to comply; they would not tolerate a sovereign Cherokee nation within their borders, and they refused to hear the pleas of Indian people to share their American dream. A Cherokee census indicated that they owned thirty-three grist mills, thirteen sawmills, one powder mill, sixty-nine blacksmith shops, two tanneries, 762 looms, 2,486 spinning wheels, 172 wagons, 2,923 plows, 7,683 horses, 22,531 cattle, 46,732 pigs, and 2,566 sheep. "You asked us to throw off the hunter and warrior state," declared the Cherokee leader, John Ridge, in 1832. "We did so—you asked us to form a republican government: We did so—adopting your own as a model. You asked us to cultivate the earth, and learn the mechanic arts: We did so. You asked us to learn to read: We did so. You asked us to cast away our idols, and worship your God: We did so." But neither the plow nor the Bible earned the Cherokees respect in the face of the economic, imperial, and racial quests of their fellow southerners (see Map 10.2).

Trail of Tears   The Choctaws went first; they made the forced journey from Mississippi and Alabama to the West in the winter of 1831 and 1832. Alexis de Tocqueville was visiting Memphis when they passed through: "The wounded, the sick, newborn babies, and the old men on the point of death.... I saw them embark to cross the great river," he wrote, "and the sight will never fade from my memory. Neither sob nor complaint rose from that silent assembly. Their afflictions were of long standing, and they felt them to be irremediable." Other tribes soon joined the forced march. The Creeks in Alabama resisted removal until 1836, when the army pushed them westward. A year later, the Chickasaws followed.

Having fought removal in the courts, the Cherokees were divided. Some believed that further resistance was hopeless and accepted removal as the only chance to preserve their civilization. The leaders of this minority agreed in 1835 to exchange their southern home for western land, in the Treaty of New Echota. Most, though, wanted to stand firm. John Ross, with petitions signed by fifteen thousand Cherokees, lobbied the Senate against ratification of the treaty. He lost. But when the time for evacuation came in 1838, most Cherokees refused to move. President Martin Van Buren sent federal troops to round them up. About twenty thousand

MAP 10.2 Removal of Native Americans from the South, 1820–1840

Over a twenty-year period, the federal government and southern states forced Native Americans to exchange their traditional homes for western land. Some tribal groups remained in the South, but most settled in the alien western environment.

Cherokees were evicted, held in detention camps, and marched under military escort to Indian Territory in present-day Oklahoma. Nearly one-quarter of them died of disease and exhaustion on what came to be known as the Trail of Tears.

When the forced march to the West ended, the Indians had traded about 100 million acres east of the Mississippi for 32 million acres west of the river plus $68 million. Only a few scattered remnants, among them the Seminoles in Florida and the Cherokees in the southern Appalachian Mountains, remained east of the Mississippi River.

Forced removal had a disastrous impact on the Cherokees and other displaced Indian nations. In the West, they encountered an alien environment. Unable to live off the land, many became dependent on government payments for survival. Removal also brought new internal conflicts. The Cherokees in particular struggled over their tribal government. In 1839, followers of John Ross assassinated the leaders of the protreaty faction. Violence continued sporadically until a new treaty in 1846 imposed a temporary truce. In time, the Cherokees managed to reestablish their political institutions and a governing body in Tahlequah, in northeastern Oklahoma.

Seminole Wars   In Florida, a small band of Seminoles continued to resist. Some Seminole leaders agreed in the 1832 Treaty of Payne's Landing to relocate to the West within three years, but others opposed the treaty, and some probably did not know it existed. A minority under Osceola, a charismatic leader, refused to vacate their homes and fought the protreaty group. When federal troops were sent to impose removal in 1835, Osceola waged a fierce guerrilla war against them.

The Florida Indians were a varied group that included many Creeks and mixed Indian–African Americans (ex-slaves or descendants of runaway slaves). The U.S. Army, however, considered them all Seminoles, subject to removal. General Thomas Jesup believed that the runaway slave population was the key to the war. "This, you may be assured, is a Negro, not an Indian war," he wrote a friend in 1836, "and if it be not speedily put down, the South will feel the effects of it on their slave population before the end of the next season."

Osceola was captured under a white flag of truce and died in an army prison in 1838, but the Seminoles fought on under Chief Coacoochee (Wild Cat) and other leaders. In 1842, the United States abandoned the removal effort. Most of Osceola's followers agreed to move west to Indian Territory after another war in 1858, but some Seminoles remained in the Florida Everglades.

SOCIAL PYRAMID IN THE OLD SOUTH

As Indians increasingly were forced westward, their lands were now open to restless and mobile white settlers. A large majority of white southern families (three-quarters in 1860) owned no slaves. Most were yeoman farmers who owned their own land and grew their own food. The social distance between poorer whites and the planter class could be great, although the line between slaveholder and non-slaveholder was fluid. Still greater was the distance between whites and blacks with free status. White yeomen, landless whites, and free blacks occupied the broad base of the social pyramid in the Old South.

Yeoman
Farmers   Many of the white farmers who pioneered the southern wilderness, moving into undeveloped regions or Indian land after removal, owned no slaves. After the War of 1812, they moved in successive waves down the southern Appalachians into the Gulf lands or through the Cumberland Gap into Kentucky and Tennessee. In large sections of the South, especially inland from the coast and away from large rivers, small, self-sufficient farms were the norm. Lured by stories of good land, many men repeatedly uprooted their wives and children. So many shared the excitement over new lands that one North Carolinian wrote in alarm, "The Alabama Fever rages here with great violence.... I am apprehensive if it continues to spread as it has done, it will almost depopulate the country."

These farmers were individualistic and hard working. Unlike their northern counterparts, their lives were not transformed by improvements in transportation. They could be independent thinkers as well, but their status as a numerical majority did not mean they set the political or economic direction of the larger society.

Self-reliant and often isolated, absorbed in the work of their farms, they operated both apart from and within the slave-based staple-crop economy.

On the southern frontier, men cleared fields, built log cabins, and established farms while their wives labored in the household economy and patiently re-created the social ties—to relatives, neighbors, fellow churchgoers—that enriched everyone's experience. Women seldom shared the men's excitement about moving. They dreaded the isolation and loneliness of the frontier. "We have been [moving] all our lives," lamented one woman. "As soon as ever we get comfortably settled, it is time to be off to something new."

Some yeomen acquired large tracts of level land, purchased slaves, and became planters. They forged part of the new wealth of the cotton boom states of Mississippi and Louisiana, where mobility into the slaveowning class was possible. Others clung to familiar mountainous areas or sought self-sufficiency because, as one frontiersman put it, they disliked "seeing the nose of my neighbor sticking out between the trees." As one historian has written, though they owned no slaves, yeomen were jealous of their independence, and "the household grounded their own claims to masterhood." Whatever the size of their property, they wanted control over their economic and domestic lives.

Yeoman Folk Culture

The yeomen enjoyed a folk culture based on family, church, and local region. Their speech patterns and inflections recalled their Scots-Irish and Irish backgrounds. They flocked to religious revivals called camp meetings, and in between they got together for house-raisings, logrollings, quilting bees, corn-shuckings, and hunting for both food and sport. Such occasions combined work with fun and fellowship, offering food and liquor in abundance.

A demanding round of work and family responsibilities shaped women's lives in the home. They worked in the fields to an extent that astonished travelers like Frederick Law Olmsted and British writer Frances Trollope, who believed yeomen had rendered their wives "slaves of the soil." Throughout the year, the care and preparation of food consumed much of women's time. Household tasks continued during frequent pregnancies and childcare. Primary nursing and medical care also fell to mothers, who often relied on folk wisdom. Women, too, wanted to be masters of their household, the only space and power over which they could claim domain, although it came at the price of their health.

Yeomen's Livelihoods

Among the men, many aspired to wealth, eager to join the scramble for slaves and cotton profits. North Carolinian John F. Flintoff kept a diary of his struggle for success. At age eighteen in 1841, Flintoff went to Mississippi to seek his fortune. Like other aspiring yeomen, he worked as an overseer of slaves but often found it impossible to please his employers. At one point, he gave up and returned to North Carolina, where he married and lived for a while in his parents' house. But Flintoff was "impatient to get along in the world," so he tried Louisiana next and then Mississippi again.

Flintoff's health suffered in the Gulf region and, routinely, "first rate employment" alternated with "very low wages." Moreover, as a young man working on isolated plantations, Flintoff often felt lonely. Even at a revival meeting in 1844 he felt "little warm feeling." His employers found fault with his work, and in 1846 Flintoff concluded in despair that "managing negroes and large farms is soul destroying."

But a desire to succeed kept him going. At twenty-six, even before he owned any land, Flintoff bought his first slave, "a negro boy 7 years old." Soon he had purchased two more children, the cheapest slaves available. Conscious of his status as a slaveowner, Flintoff resented the low wages he was paid. In 1853, with nine young slaves and a growing family, Flintoff faced "the most unhappy time of my life." Fired by his uncle, he returned to North Carolina, sold some of his slaves, and purchased 124 acres with help from his in-laws. As he began to pay off his debts, he looked forward to freeing his wife from labor and possibly sending his sons to college. Although Flintoff demonstrated that a farmer could move in and out of the slaveholding class, he never achieved the cotton planter status (owning roughly twenty or more slaves) that he desired.

Probably more typical of the southern yeoman was Ferdinand L. Steel, who as a young man moved from North Carolina to Tennessee to work as a river boatman but eventually took up farming in Mississippi. Steel rose every day at 5 a.m. and worked until sundown. He and his family raised corn and wheat, though cotton was his cash product: he sold five or six bales (about two thousand pounds) a year to obtain money for sugar, coffee, salt, calico, gunpowder, and a few other store-bought goods.

Thus, Steel entered the market economy as a small farmer, but with mixed results. He picked his own cotton and complained that it was brutal work and not profitable. He felt like a serf in cotton's kingdom. When cotton prices fell, a small grower like Steel could be driven into debt and lose his farm.

Cincinnati Museum of Art, Gift of the Proctor & Gamble Company. Accession #. 2003.52

North Carolina Emigrants: Poor White Folks, oil on canvas, 1845, by James Henry Beard. This depicts a yeoman family, their belongings all on one hungry horse, as they migrate westward in search of new land and livelihood.

Steel's life in Mississippi in the 1840s retained much of the flavor of the frontier, and he survived on a household economy. He made all the family's shoes; his wife and sister sewed dresses, shirts, and "pantaloons." The Steel women also rendered their own soap and spun and wove cotton into cloth; the men hunted game. Steel doctored his illnesses with boneset tea and other herbs. As the nation fell deeper into crisis over the future of free or slave labor, this independent southern farmer never came close to owning a slave.

The focus of Steel's life was family and religion. Family members prayed together daily, and he studied Scripture for an hour after lunch. "My Faith increases, & I enjoy much of that peace which the world cannot give," he wrote in 1841. Seeking to prepare himself for Judgment Day, Steel borrowed histories, Latin and Greek grammars, and religious books from his church. Eventually, he became a traveling Methodist minister. "My life is one of toil," he reflected, "but blessed be God that it is as well with me as it is."

Landless Whites   Toil with even less security was the lot of two other groups of free southerners: landless whites and free blacks. A sizable minority of white southern workers—from 25 to 40 percent, depending on the state—were hired hands who owned no land and worked for others in the countryside and towns. Their property consisted of a few household items and some animals—usually pigs—that could feed themselves on the open range. The landless included some immigrants, especially Irish, who did heavy and dangerous work, such as building railroads and digging ditches.

In the countryside, white farm laborers struggled to purchase land in the face of low wages or, if they rented, unpredictable market prices for their crops. By scrimping, saving, and finding odd jobs, some managed to climb into the ranks of yeomen. When James and Nancy Bennitt of North Carolina succeeded in their ten-year struggle to buy land, they decided to avoid the unstable market in cotton; thereafter they raised extra corn and wheat as sources of cash. People like the Bennitts were both participants in and victims of an economy dominated by cotton producers who relied on slave labor.

Herdsmen with pigs and other livestock had a desperate struggle to succeed. By 1860, as the South anticipated war to preserve its society, between 300,000 and 400,000 white people in the four states of Virginia, North and South Carolina, and Georgia—approximately one-fifth of the total white population—lived in genuine poverty. Their lives were harsh. An early antebellum traveler in central South Carolina described the white folk he encountered in the countryside: they "looked yellow, poor, and sickly. Some of them lived the most miserably I ever saw any poor people live." Land and slaves determined wealth in the Old South, and many whites possessed neither.

Yeomen's Demands and White Class Relations   Class tensions emerged in the western, nonslaveholding parts of the seaboard states by the 1830s. There, yeoman farmers resented their underrepresentation in state legislatures and the corruption in local government. After vigorous debate, the reformers won many battles. Voters in the more recently settled states of the Old Southwest adopted white manhood suffrage and other electoral reforms, including popular election of governors, legislative apportionment based on white population only, and locally chosen county government. Slaveowners with new wealth, however, knew that a more open government structure could permit troubling class conflicts and were determined to hold the ultimate reins of power.

Given such tensions, it was perhaps remarkable that slaveholders and nonslaveholders did not experience more overt conflict. Historians have offered several explanations. One of the most important factors was race. The South's racial ideology stressed the superiority of all whites to blacks. Thus, slavery became the basis of equality among whites, and white privilege inflated the status of poor whites and gave them a common interest with the rich. At the same time, the dream of upward mobility blunted some class conflict.

Most important, before the Civil War many yeomen were able to pursue their independent lifestyle largely unhindered by slaveholding planters. They worked their farms, avoided debt, and marked progress for their families in rural habitats of their own making. Likewise, slaveholders pursued their goals quite independently of yeomen. Planters farmed for the market but also for themselves. Suppression of dissent also played an increasing role. After 1830, white southerners who criticized the slave system out of moral conviction or class resentment were intimidated, attacked, or rendered politically powerless in a society held together in part by white racial solidarity.

Still, there were signs of class conflict in the late antebellum period. As cotton lands filled up, nonslaveholders faced narrower economic prospects; meanwhile, wealthy planters enjoyed expanding profits. The risks of entering cotton production were becoming too great and the cost of slaves too high for many yeomen to rise in society. From 1830 to 1860, the percentage of white southern families holding slaves declined steadily from 36 to 25 percent. Although slaveowners were a distinct minority in the white population, planters' share of the South's agricultural wealth remained between 90 and 95 percent.

Anticipating possible secession, slaveowners stood secure. In the 1850s, they occupied from 50 to 85 percent of the seats in state legislatures and a similarly high percentage of the South's congressional seats. And planters' interests controlled all the other major social institutions, such as churches and colleges.

Free Blacks

The nearly quarter-million free blacks in the South in 1860 also yearned for mobility. But their condition was generally worse than the yeoman's and often little better than the slave's. The free blacks of the Upper South were usually descendants of men and women manumitted by their owners in the 1780s and 1790s. A remarkable number of slaveholders in Virginia and the Chesapeake region had freed their slaves because of religious principles and revolutionary ideals in the wake of American independence (see Chapter 7). Many free blacks also became free as runaways, especially by the 1830s, disappearing into the southern population; a few made their way northward.

White southerners were increasingly desperate to restrict this growing free black presence in their midst. "It seems the number of free Negroes," complained a Virginia slaveholder, "always exceeds the number of Negroes freed." Some free blacks worked in towns or cities, but most lived in rural areas and struggled to survive. They usually did not own land and had to labor in someone else's fields, often beside slaves. By law, free blacks could not own a gun, buy liquor, violate curfew, assemble except in church, testify in court, or (throughout the South after 1835) vote. Despite these obstacles, a minority bought land, and others found jobs as skilled craftsmen, especially in cities.

A few free blacks prospered and bought slaves. In 1830, there were 3,775 free black slaveholders in the South; 80 percent lived in the four states of Louisiana, South Carolina, Virginia, and Maryland, and approximately half of the total lived in the two cities of New Orleans and Charleston. Most of them purchased their own wives and children, whom they nevertheless could not free because laws required newly emancipated blacks to leave their state. In order to free family members whom they had purchased, hundreds of black slaveholders petitioned for exemption from the antimanumission laws passed in most southern states. At the same time, a few mulattos in New Orleans were active slave traders in its booming market. The complex world of southern free blacks received new attention through Edward P. Jones's *The Known World*, a hugely successful novel published in 2003 about a Virginia family that rises from slavery to slaveownership. Although rare in the United States, the greed and the tragic quest for power that lay at the root of slavery could cross any racial or ethnic barrier.

Free Black Communities   In the Cotton Belt and Gulf regions, a large proportion of free blacks were mulattos, the privileged offspring of wealthy white planters. Not all planters freed their mixed-race offspring, but those who did often recognized the moral obligation of giving their children a good education and financial backing. In a few cities like New Orleans, Charleston, and Mobile, extensive interracial sex, as well as migrations from the Caribbean, had produced a mulatto population that was recognized as a distinct class.

In many southern cities by the 1840s, free black communities formed, especially around an expanding number of churches. By the late 1850s, Baltimore had fifteen churches, Louisville nine, and Nashville and St. Louis four each—most of them African Methodist Episcopal. Class and race distinctions were important to southern free blacks, but outside a few cities, which developed fraternal orders of skilled craftsmen and fellowships of light-skinned people, most mulattos experienced hardship. In the United States, "one drop" of black "blood" (any observable racial mixture to white people's eyes) made them black, and potentially enslaveable.

THE PLANTERS' WORLD

At the top of the southern social pyramid were slaveholding planters. As a group they lived well, but most lived in comfortable farmhouses, not on the opulent scale that legend suggests. The grand plantation mansions, with fabulous gardens and long rows of outlying slave quarters, are an enduring symbol of the Old South. But in 1850, 50 percent of southern slaveholders had fewer than five slaves;

72 percent had fewer than ten; 88 percent had fewer than twenty. Thus, the average slaveholder was not a wealthy aristocrat but an aspiring farmer.

The Newly Rich   Louisiana cotton planter Bennet Barrow, a newly rich planter of the 1840s, was preoccupied with moneymaking. He worried constantly over his cotton crop, filling his diary with weather reports and gloomy predictions of his yields. Yet Barrow also strove to appear above such worries. He hunted frequently and had a passion for racing horses and raising hounds. He could report the loss of a slave without feeling, but emotion broke through his laconic manner when illness afflicted his sporting animals. "Never was a person more unlucky than I am," he mourned. "My favorite pup never lives." His strongest feelings surfaced when his horse Jos Bell—equal to "the best Horse in the South"—"broke down running a mile … ruined for Ever." The same day, the distraught Barrow gave his human property a "general Whipping." In 1841 diary entries, he worried about a rumored slave insurrection. He gave a "severe whipping" to several of his slaves when they disobediently killed a hog. And when a slave named Ginney Jerry "sherked" his cotton-picking duties and was rumored "about to run off," Barrow whipped him one day and the next, recorded matter-of-factly: "took my gun found him in the Bayou behind the Quarter, shot him in his thigh—etc. raining all around."

The richest planters used their wealth to model genteel sophistication. Extended visits, parties, and balls to which women wore the latest fashions provided opportunities for friendship, courtship, and display. Such parties were held during the Christmas holidays, but also on such occasions as molasses stewing, a bachelors' ball, a horserace, or the crowning of the May queen. These entertainments were especially important as diversions for plantation women, and at the same time they sustained a rigidly gendered society. Young women relished social events to break the monotony of their domestic lives. In 1826, a Virginia girl was ecstatic about the "week … I was in Town.… There were five beaux and as many belles in the house constantly," she declared, and all she and her companions did was "eat, visit, romp, and sleep."

Most of the planters in the cotton-boom states of Alabama and Mississippi were newly rich by the 1840s. As one historian put it, "a number of men mounted from log cabin to plantation mansion on a stairway of cotton bales, accumulating slaves as they climbed." And many did not live like rich men. They put their new wealth into cotton acreage and slaves even as they sought refinement and high social status.

William Faulkner immortalized the new wealthy planter in a fictional character, Thomas Sutpen, in his novel *Absalom, Absalom!* (1936). After a huge win at riverboat gambling, Sutpen arrives in a Mississippi county in the 1830s, buys a huge plantation he calls Sutpen's Hundred, and with his troop of slaves converts it into a wealthy enterprise. Sutpen marries a local woman, and although he is always viewed as a mysterious outsider by earlier residents of the county, he becomes a pillar of the slaveholding class, eventually an officer in the Confederate Army. But Sutpen is a self-made man of indomitable will and slave-based wealth. Although his ambition is ultimately his undoing, one of the earliest lessons he learns about success in the South is that "you got to have land and niggers and a fine house."

The cotton boom in the Mississippi valley created one-generation aristocrats. A nonfictional case in point is Greenwood Leflore, a Chocktaw chieftain who owned a plantation in Mississippi with four hundred slaves. After selling his cotton on the world market, he spent $10,000 in France to furnish a single room of his mansion with handwoven carpets, furniture upholstered with gold leaf, tables and cabinets ornamented with tortoise-shell inlay, a variety of mirrors and paintings, and a clock and candelabra of brass and ebony.

Social Status and Planters' Values

Slave ownership was the main determinant of wealth in the South. Slaves were a commodity and an investment, much like gold; people bought them on speculation, hoping for a steady rise in their market value. Many slaveholders took out mortgages on their slaves and used them as collateral. Especially in the growing states, people who could not pay cash for slaves would ask the sellers to purchase the mortgage, just as banks give mortgages on houses today. The slaveholder would pay back the loan in installments with interest. Slaveholders and the people who lent them money put their faith in this "human collateral," believing it would increase in value. Hundreds of thousands of slaves were thus mortgaged, many several times and with full awareness of their masters' financial methods. In St. Landry's Parish, Louisiana, between 1833 and 1837, an eight-year-old slave boy named Jacques was mortgaged three times, sold twice, and converted into what one historian has called a "human cash machine and an investment vehicle" before the age of twelve.

Slavery's influence spread throughout the social system, until even the values and mores of nonslaveholders bore its imprint. The availability of slave labor tended to devalue free labor: where strenuous work under supervision was reserved for an enslaved race, few free people relished it. When Alexis de Tocqueville crossed from Ohio into Kentucky in his travels of 1831, he observed "the effect that slavery produces on society. On the right bank of the Ohio [River] everything is activity, industry; labor is honoured; there are no slaves. Pass to the left bank and the scene changes so suddenly that you think yourself on the other side of the world; the enterprising spirit is gone. There, work is not only painful; it is shameful." Tocqueville's own class impulses found a home in the South, however. There he found a "veritable aristocracy which ... combines many prejudices with high sentiments and instincts."

The values of the aristocrat—lineage, privilege, pride, honor, and refinement of person and manner—commanded respect throughout the South. Many of those qualities were in short supply, however, in the recently settled portions of the cotton kingdom, where frontier values of courage and self-reliance ruled during the 1820s and 1830s. By the 1850s, a settled aristocratic group of planters did rule, however, in much of the Mississippi valley. In this geographically mobile society, independence and codes of honor motivated both planter and frontier farmer alike.

Instead of gradually disappearing, as it did in the North, the Code Duello, which required men to defend their honor through violence, lasted much longer in the South. In North Carolina in 1851, wealthy planter Samuel Fleming sought to settle disputes with lawyer William Waightstill Avery by "cowhiding" him on a public street. According to the code, Avery had two choices: to redeem his honor violently or to brand himself a coward through inaction. Three weeks later, he shot Fleming dead at point-blank range during a session of the Burke County Superior Court. A jury took only ten minutes to find Avery not guilty, and the spectators gave him a standing ovation.

In their pride, aristocratic planters expected not only to wield power but also to receive deference from poorer whites. But the sternly independent yeoman class resented infringements of their rights, and many belonged to evangelical faiths that exalted values of simplicity and condemned the planters' love of wealth. Much of the planters' political power and their claims to leadership, after all, were built on their assumption of a monopoly on world cotton and on a foundation of black slave labor.

King Cotton in a Global Economy

Planters always had their eyes on the international growth of the cotton markets. Cash crops such as cotton were for export; the planters' fate depended on world trade, especially with Europe. The American South so dominated the world's supply of cotton that southern planters gained enormous confidence that the cotton boom was permanent and that the industrializing nations of England and France in particular would always bow to King Cotton.

Made possible in part by the Eli Whitney's invention of the cotton gin in 1793, a device for cleaning the short staple variety of the crop that the British textile industry craved, American cotton production doubled in yield each decade after 1800 and provided three-fourths of the world's supply by the 1840s. Gins, which took on the scale of whole buildings with time, revolutionized cotton production and Southern wealth invested in land and slaves. In the first decade of the nineteenth century in South Carolina alone, wrote one planter, cotton "trebled the price of land suitable to its growth" and "doubled" the annual income of growers. Southern staple crops were fully three-fifths of all American exports by 1850, and one of every seven workers in England depended on American cotton for his job. Indeed, cotton production made slaves the single most valuable financial asset in the United States—greater in dollar value than all of America's banks, railroads, and manufacturing combined. In 1860 dollars, the slaves' total value as property came to an estimated $3.5 billion. In early-twenty-first-century dollars, that would be approximately $70 billion.

"Cotton is King," the *Southern Cultivator* declared in 1859, "and wields an astonishing influence over the world's commerce." Until 1840, the cotton trade furnished much of the export capital to finance northern economic growth. After that date, however, the northern economy expanded without dependence on cotton profits. Nevertheless, southern planters and politicians continued to boast of King Cotton's supremacy. "Our cotton is the most wonderful talisman in the world," announced a planter in 1853. "By its power we are transmuting whatever we choose into whatever we want." "No power on earth dares … to make war on cotton," James Hammond lectured the U.S. Senate in 1858; "Cotton is king." Although the South produced 4.5 million bales in 1861, its greatest cotton crop ever, such world dominance was about to collapse. Thereafter, cotton was more a shackle to the South than a king.

Paternalism   Slaveholding men often embraced a paternalistic ideology that justified their dominance over both black slaves and white women. Instead of stressing the profitable aspects of commercial agriculture, they stressed their obligations, viewing themselves as custodians of the welfare of society in general, and of the black families they owned in particular. The paternalistic planter saw himself not as an oppressor but as the benevolent guardian of an inferior race.

Paul Carrington Cameron, North Carolina's largest slaveholder, exemplifies this mentality. After a period of sickness among his one thousand North Carolina slaves (he had hundreds more in Alabama and Mississippi), Cameron wrote, "I fear the Negroes have suffered much from the want of proper attention and kindness under this late distemper no love of lucre shall ever induce me to be cruel." On another occasion, he described to his sister the sense of responsibility he felt: "Do you remember a cold & frosty morning, during [our mother's] illness, when she said to me Paul my son the people ought to be shod' this is ever in my ears, whenever I see any ones shoes in bad order; and in my ears it will be, so long as I am master."

It was comforting to rich planters to see themselves in this way, and slaves—accommodating to the realities of power—encouraged their masters to think that their benevolence was appreciated. Paternalism also served as a defense against abolitionist criticism. Still, paternalism was often a matter of self-delusion, a means of avoiding some harsh dimensions of slave treatment. In reality, paternalism grew as a give-and-take relationship between masters and slaves, each extracting from the other what they desired—owners took labor from the bondsmen, while slaves obligated masters to provide them a measure of autonomy and living space. As one historian has argued, paternalism "grew out of the necessity to discipline and morally justify a system of exploitation,... a fragile bridge across the intolerable contradictions inherent" in a slave society dependent on "the willing reproduction and productivity of its victims."

Even Paul Cameron's benevolence vanished with changed circumstances. After the Civil War, he bristled at African Americans' efforts to be free and made sweeping economic decisions without regard for their welfare. Writing on Christmas Day 1865, Cameron showed little Christian charity (but a healthy profit motive) when he declared, "I am convinced that the people who gets rid of the free negro first will be the first to advance in improved agriculture. Have made no effort to retain any of mine." With that, he turned off his land nearly a thousand black people, rented his fields to several white farmers, and invested in industry.

Relations between men and women in the planter class were similarly defined by paternalism. The upper-class southern woman was raised and educated to be a wife, mother, and subordinate companion to men. South Carolina's Mary Boykin Chesnut wrote of her husband, "He is master of the house. To hear is to obey.... All the comfort of my life depends upon his being in a good humor." In a social system based on the coercion of an entire race, women found it very difficult to challenge society's rules on sexual or racial relations.

Planters' daughters usually attended one of the South's rapidly multiplying boarding schools. There, they formed friendships with other girls and received an education. Typically, the young woman could entertain suitors whom her parents approved. But very soon she had to choose a husband and commit herself for life to a man whom she generally had known for only a brief time. Young women were often alienated and emotionally unfulfilled. They had to follow the wishes of their family, especially their father. "It was for me best that I yielded to the wishes of papa," wrote a young North Carolinian in 1823. "I wonder when my best will cease to be painful and when I shall begin to enjoy life instead of enduring it."

Upon marriage, a planter-class woman ceded to her husband most of her legal rights, becoming part of his family. Most of the year she was isolated on a large plantation, where she had to oversee the cooking and preserving of food, manage the house, supervise care of the children, and attend sick slaves. All these realities were more rigid and confining on the frontier, where isolation was even greater. Women sought refuge in their extended family and associations with other women. In 1821, a Georgia woman wrote to her brother of the distress of a cousin's wife: "They are living ... in the frontiers of the state and [a] perfectly uncivilized place. Cousin W. gets a good practice [the husband] but she is almost crazy to get to Alabama where one of her sisters is living." Men on plantations could occasionally escape into the public realm—to town, business, or politics. Women could retreat from rural plantation culture only into kinship.

Marriage and Family Among Planters   It is not surprising that a perceptive young white woman sometimes approached marriage with anxiety. Women could hardly help viewing their wedding day, as one put it in 1832, as "the day to fix my fate." Lucy Breckinridge, a wealthy Virginia girl of twenty, lamented the autonomy she surrendered at the altar. In her diary, she recorded this unvarnished observation on marriage: "If [husbands] care for their wives at all it is only as a sort of servant, a being made to attend to their comforts and to keep the children out of the way. A woman's life after she is married, unless there is an immense amount of love, is nothing but suffering and hard work."

Lucy loved young children but knew that childbearing often involved grief, poor health, and death. In 1840, the birth rate for white southern women in their childbearing years was almost 30 percent higher than the national average. The average southern white woman could expect to bear eight children in 1800; by 1860, the figure had decreased to only six, with one or more miscarriages likely. Complications of childbirth were a major cause of death, occurring twice as often in the hot, humid South as in the Northeast.

Sexual relations between planters and slaves were another source of problems that white women had to endure but were not supposed to notice. "Violations of the moral law ... made mulattos as common as blackberries," protested a woman in Georgia, but wives had to play "the ostrich game." "A magnate who runs a hideous black harem," wrote Mrs. Chesnut, " ... poses as the model of all human virtues to these poor women whom God and the laws have given him." Such habits and dalliances produced a very large mixed race population by the 1850s and a strained use of the term "family" across the South.

Southern men tolerated little discussion by women of the slavery issue. In the 1840s and 1850s, as abolitionist attacks on slavery increased, southern men published a barrage of articles stressing that women should restrict their concerns to the home. The *Southern Quarterly Review* declared, "The proper place for a woman is at home. One of her highest privileges, to be politically merged in the existence of her husband."

But some southern women were beginning to seek a larger role. A study of women in Petersburg, Virginia, a large tobacco-manufacturing town, revealed behavior that valued financial autonomy. Over several decades before 1860, the proportion of women who never married, or did not remarry after the death of a spouse, grew to exceed 33 percent. Likewise, the number of women who worked for wages, controlled their own property, and ran dressmaking businesses increased markedly.

Planters forged a society around their domestic lives and local mores. But they did so through the energies and lives of generations of enslaved African Americans who helped them extract great wealth from southern soil.

SLAVE LIFE AND LABOR

For African Americans, slavery was a burden that destroyed some people and forced others to develop modes of survival. Slaves knew a life of poverty, coercion, toil, and resentment. They provided the physical strength, and much of the know-how, to build an agricultural empire. But their daily lives embodied the nation's most basic contradiction: in the world's model republic, they were on the wrong side of a brutally unequal power relationship.

Slaves' Everyday Conditions   Southern slaves enjoyed few material comforts beyond the bare necessities. Although they generally had enough to eat, their diet was monotonous and nonnutritious. Clothing, too, was plain, coarse, and inexpensive. Few slaves received more than one or two changes of clothing for hot and cold seasons, and one blanket each winter. Children of both sexes ran naked in hot weather and wore long cotton shirts in winter. Many slaves had to go without shoes until December, even as far north as Virginia. The bare feet of slaves were often symbolic of their status and one reason why, after freedom, many black parents were so concerned with providing their children with shoes. These conditions were generally better in cities, where slaves frequently lived in the same dwelling as their owners and were hired out to employers on a regular basis, enabling them to accumulate their own money.

Some of the richer plantations provided substantial houses, but the average slave lived in a crude, one-room cabin. The gravest drawback of slave cabins was not lack of comfort but unhealthfulness. Each dwelling housed one or two entire families. Crowding and lack of sanitation fostered the spread of infection and such contagious diseases as typhoid fever, malaria, and dysentery. White plantation doctors were hired to care for sick slaves on a regular basis, but some "slave doctors" attained a degree of power in the quarters and with masters by practicing health care and healing through herbalism and spiritualism.

Slave Work Routines   Hard work was the central fact of slaves' existence. The long hours and large work gangs that characterized Gulf Coast cotton districts operated almost like factories in the field.

Overseers rang the morning bell before dawn, and black people of varying ages, tools in hand, walked toward the fields. Slaves who cultivated tobacco in the Upper South worked long hours picking the sticky, sometimes noxious, leaves under harsh discipline. And as one woman recalled when interviewed in the 1930s, "it was way after sundown fore they could stop that field work. Then they had to hustle to finish their night work [such as watering livestock or cleaning cotton] in time for supper, or go to bed without it."

Working "from sun to sun" became a norm in much of the South. As one planter put it, slaves were the best labor because "you could command them and make them do what was right." Profit took precedence over paternalism. Slave women did heavy fieldwork, often as much as the men and even during pregnancy. Old people were kept busy caring for young children, doing light chores, or carding, ginning, and spinning cotton. The black abolitionist orator Frances Ellen Watkins captured the grinding economic reality of slavery in an 1857 speech, charging that slaveholders had "found out a fearful alchemy by which ... blood can be transformed into gold. Instead of listening to the cry of agony, they listen to the ring of dollars and stoop down to pick up the coin."

By the 1830s, slaveowners found that labor could be similarly motivated by the clock. Incentives had to be part of the labor regime and the master-slave relationship as well. Planters in the South Carolina and Georgia low country used a task system whereby slaves were assigned measured amounts of work to be performed in a given amount of time. So much cotton on a daily basis was to be picked from a designated field, so many rows hoed or plowed in a particular slave's specified section. When their tasks were finished, slaves' time was their own for working garden plots, tending hogs, even hiring out their own extra labor. From this experience and personal space, many slaves developed their own sense of property ownership. When the task system worked best, slaves and masters alike embraced it, fostering a degree of reciprocal trust.

Slave children were the future of the system and widely valued as potential labor. Of the 1860 population of 4 million slaves, fully half were under the age of sixteen. "A child raised every two years," wrote Thomas Jefferson, "is of more profit than the crop of the best laboring man." And in 1858, a slaveowner writing in an agricultural magazine calculated that a slave girl he purchased in 1827 for $400 had borne three sons now worth $3,000 as his working field hands. Slave children gathered kindling, carried water to the fields, swept the yard, lifted cut sugar-cane stalks into carts, stacked wheat, chased birds away from sprouting rice plants, and labored at many levels of cotton and tobacco production. "Work," wrote one historian, "can be rightly called the thief who stole the childhood of youthful bond servants."

As slave children matured, they faced many psychological traumas. They faced a feeling of powerlessness as they became aware that their parents ultimately could not protect them. They had to muster strategies to fight internalizing what whites assumed was their inferiority. Thomas Jones, who grew up in North Carolina, remembered that his greatest struggle with the sense of "suffering and shame" as he "was made to feel ... degraded." Many former slaves resented foremost their denial of education. "There is one sin that slavery committed against me which I will never forgive," recollected the minister James Pennington. "It robbed me of my education." And for girls reaching maturity, the potential trauma of sexual abuse loomed over their lives.

Violence and Intimidation Against Slaves   Slaves could not demand much autonomy, of course, because the owner enjoyed a monopoly on force and violence. Whites throughout the South believed that slaves "can't be governed except with the whip." One South Carolinian frankly explained to a northern journalist that he whipped his slaves regularly, "say once a fortnight; … the fear of the lash kept them in good order." Evidence suggests that whippings were less frequent on small farms than on large plantations. But beatings symbolized authority to the master and tyranny to the slaves, who made them a benchmark for evaluating a master. In the words of former slaves, a good owner was one who did not "whip too much," whereas a bad owner "whipped till he's bloodied you and blistered you."

As these reports suggest, terrible abuses could and did occur. The master wielded virtually absolute authority on his plantation, and courts did not recognize the word of chattel. Slaveholders rarely had to answer to the law or to the state. Pregnant women were whipped, and there were burnings, mutilation, torture, and murder. Yet physical cruelty may have been less prevalent in the United States than in other slaveholding parts of the New World. Especially in some of the sugar islands of the Caribbean, treatment was so poor and death rates so high that the heavily male slave population shrank in size. In the United States, by contrast, the slave population experienced a steady natural increase, as births exceeded deaths and each generation grew larger.

The worst evil of American slavery was not its physical cruelty but the nature of slavery itself: coercion, belonging to another person, virtually no hope for mobility or change. Recalling their time in bondage, some former slaves emphasized the physical abuse, or the "bullwhip days," as one woman described her past. But memories of physical punishment focused on the tyranny of whipping as much as the pain. Delia Garlic made the essential point: "It's bad to belong to folks that own you soul an' body. I could tell you 'bout it all day, but even then you couldn't guess the awfulness of it." Thomas Lewis put it this way: "There was no such thing as being good to slaves. Many people were better than others, but a slave belonged to his master and there was no way to get out of it." To be a slave was to be the object of another person's will and material gain, to be owned, as the saying went, "from the cradle to the grave."

Most American slaves retained their mental independence and self-respect despite their bondage. Contrary to popular belief at the time, they were not loyal partners in their own oppression. They had to be subservient and speak honeyed words to their masters, but they talked and behaved quite differently among themselves. In *Narrative of the Life of Frederick Douglass, an American Slave, Written by Himself* (1845), Douglass wrote that most slaves, when asked about "their condition and the character of their masters, almost universally say they are contented, and that their masters are kind." Slaves did this, said Douglass, because they were governed by the maxim that "a still tongue makes a wise head," especially in the presence of unfamiliar people. Because they were "part of the human family," slaves often

quarreled over who had the best master. But at the end of the day, Douglass remarked, when one had a bad master, he sought a better master; and when he had
a better one, he wanted to "be his own master."

Slave-Master Some former slaves remembered warm feelings between mas-
Relationships ters and slaves, and some "special" bondsmen, such as highly
skilled jockeys for planters who were great horsemen, enjoyed
autonomy, privilege, and even fame. But the prevailing attitudes were distrust and
antagonism. Slaves saw through acts of kindness. One woman said her mistress was
"a mighty good somebody to belong to" but only "'cause she was raisin' us to work
for her." A man recalled that his owners took good care of their slaves, "and
Grandma Maria say, 'Why shouldn't they—it was their money.'" Slaves also resented
being used as beasts of burden. One man observed that his master "fed us reg'lar on
good, 'stantial food, just like you'd tend to your horse, if you had a real good one."

Slaves were alert to the thousand daily signs of their degraded status. One man
recalled the general rule that slaves ate cornbread and owners ate biscuits. If blacks
did get biscuits, "the flour that we made the biscuits out of was the third-grade
sorts." A former slave recalled, "Us catch lots of 'possums," but "the white folks
at [ate] 'em." If the owner took his slaves' garden produce to town and sold it for
them, the slaves often suspected him of pocketing part of the profits.

Suspicion often grew into hatred. When a yellow fever epidemic struck in 1852,
many slaves saw it as God's retribution. An elderly ex-slave named Minnie Fulkes
cherished the conviction that God was going to punish white people for their cruelty to blacks. She described the whippings that her mother had to endure, and then
she exclaimed, "Lord, Lord, I hate white people and the flood waters goin' to
drown some more." On the plantation, of course, slaves had to keep such thoughts
to themselves. Often they expressed one feeling to whites, another within their own
household. In their daily lives, slaves created many ways to survive and to sustain
their humanity in this world of repression.

SLAVE CULTURE AND RESISTANCE

A people is always "more than the sum of its brutalization," wrote African American
novelist Ralph Ellison in 1967. What people create in the face of hard luck and
oppression is what provides hope. The resource that enabled slaves to maintain
such defiance was their culture: a body of beliefs, values, and practices born of their
past and maintained in the present. As best they could, they built a community
knitted together by stories, music, a religious world-view, leadership, the smells of
their cooking, the sounds of their own voices, and the tapping of their feet. "The
values expressed in folklore," wrote African American poet Sterling Brown, provided
a "wellspring to which slaves ... could return in times of doubt to be refreshed."

African Cultural Slave culture changed significantly after 1808, when Con-
Survival gress banned further importation of slaves and the genera-
tions born in Africa died out. For a few years, South
Carolina illegally reopened the international slave trade, but by the 1830s, the vast

majority of slaves in the South were native-born Americans. Many blacks, in fact, can trace their American ancestry back further than most white Americans.

Yet African influences remained strong, despite lack of firsthand memory, especially in appearance and forms of expression. Some slave men plaited their hair into rows and fancy designs; slave women often wore their hair "in string"—tied in small bunches secured by a string or piece of cloth. A few men and many women wrapped their heads in kerchiefs of the styles and colors of West Africa. In burial practices, slaves used jars and other glass objects to decorate graves, following similar African traditions.

Music, religion, and folktales were parts of daily life for most slaves. Borrowing partly from their African background, as well as forging new American folkways, they developed what scholars have called a sacred world-view, which affected all aspects of work, leisure, and self-understanding. Slaves made musical instruments with carved motifs that resembled African stringed instruments. Their drumming and dancing followed African patterns that made whites marvel. One visitor to Georgia in the 1860s described a ritual dance of African origin: "A ring of singers is formed.... They then utter a kind of melodious chant, which gradually increases in strength, and in noise, until it fairly shakes the house, and it can be heard for a long distance." This observer of the "ring shout" also noted the agility of the dancers and the African call-and-response pattern in their chanting.

Many slaves continued to believe in spirit possession. Whites, too, believed in ghosts and charms, but the slaves' belief resembled the African concept of the living dead—the idea that deceased relatives visit the earth for many years until the process of dying is complete. Slaves also practiced conjuration and quasi-magical root medicine. By the 1850s, the most notable conjurers and root doctors were reputed to live in South Carolina, Georgia, Louisiana, and other isolated coastal areas with high slave populations.

These cultural survivals provided slaves with a sense of their separate past. Such practices and beliefs were not static "Africanisms" or mere "retentions." They were cultural adaptations, living traditions re-formed in the Americas in response to new experience. African American slaves in the Old South were a people forged by two centuries of cultural mixture in the Atlantic world, and the South itself was a melding of many African and European cultural forces.

As they became African Americans, slaves also developed a sense of racial identity. In the colonial period, Africans had arrived in America from many different states and kingdoms, represented in distinctive languages, body markings, and traditions. Planters had used ethnic differences to create occupational hierarchies. By the early antebellum period, however, old ethnic identities gave way as American slaves increasingly saw themselves as a single group unified by race. Africans had arrived in the New World with virtually no concept of "race"; by the antebellum era, their descendants had learned through bitter experience that race was now the defining feature of their lives. They were a transplanted and transformed people.

Slaves' Religion and Music   As African culture gave way to a maturing African American culture, more and more slaves adopted Christianity. But they fashioned Christianity into an instrument of support and resistance. Theirs was a religion of justice and deliverance, quite unlike their masters' religious propaganda directed at them as a means of control. "You ought to have heard that preachin'," said one man. "'Obey your master and mistress, don't steal chickens and eggs and meat,' but nary a word about havin' a soul to save." Slaves believed that Jesus cared about their souls and their plight. In their interpretations of biblical stories, as one historian has said, they were "literally willing themselves reborn."

For slaves, Christianity was a religion of personal and group salvation. Devout men and women worshiped every day, "in the field or by the side of the road" or in special "prayer grounds" that afforded privacy. Some slaves held fervent secret prayer meetings that lasted far into the night. Many slaves nurtured an unshakable belief that God would enter history and end their bondage. This faith—and the joy and emotional release that accompanied worship—sustained them.

Slaves also adapted Christianity to African practices. In West African belief, devotees are possessed by a god so thoroughly that the god's own personality replaces the human personality. In the late antebellum era, Christian slaves experienced possession by the Protestant "Holy Spirit." The combination of shouting, singing, and dancing that seemed to overtake black worshipers formed the heart of their religious faith. "The old meeting house caught fire," recalled an ex-slave preacher. "The spirit was there.... God saw our need and came to us. I used to wonder what made people shout but now I don't. There is a joy on the inside and it wells

Abby Aldrich Rockefeller Folk Art Collection, Colonial Williamsburg Foundation

Drawing by Lewis Miller of a Lynchburg Negro Dance, Lynchburg, Virginia, August 18, 1853. This work of art shows the slaves' use of elaborate costumes, string instruments, and "the bones"—folk percussion instruments of African origin, held between the fingers and used as clappers.

up so strong that we can't keep still. It is fire in the bones. Any time that fire touches a man, he will jump." Out in brush arbors or in meetinghouses, slaves took in the presence of God, thrust their arms to heaven, made music with their feet, and sang away their woes. Some travelers observed "bands" of "Fist and Heel Worshippers." Many postslavery black choirs could not perform properly without a good wooden floor to use as their "drum."

Rhythm and physical movement were crucial to slaves' religious experience. In black preachers' chanted sermons, which reached out to gather the sinner into a narrative of meanings and cadences along the way to conversion, an American tradition was born. The chanted sermon was both a message from Scripture and a patterned form that required audience response punctuated by "yes sirs!" and "amens!" But it was in song that the slaves left their most sublime gift to American culture.

Through the spirituals, slaves tried to impose order on the chaos of their lives. Many themes run through the lyrics of slave songs. Often referred to later as the "sorrow songs," they also anticipate imminent rebirth. Sadness could immediately give way to joy: "Did you ever stan' on a mountain, wash yo hands in a cloud?" Rebirth was at the heart as well of the famous hymn "Oh, Freedom": "Oh, Oh, Freedom / Oh, Oh, Freedom over me— / But before I'll be a slave, / I'll be buried in my grave, / And go home to my Lord, / And Be Free!"

This tension and sudden change between sorrow and joy animates many songs: "Sometimes I feel like a motherless chile … / Sometimes I feel like an eagle in the air, / … Spread my wings and fly, fly, fly!" Many songs also express a sense of intimacy and closeness with God. Some songs display an unmistakable rebelliousness, such as the enduring "He said, and if I had my way / If I had my way, if I had my way, / I'd tear this building down!" And some spirituals reached for a collective sense of hope in the black community as a whole.

> O, gracious Lord! When shall it be,
> That we poor souls shall all be free;
> Lord, break them slavery powers—
> Will you go along with me?
> Lord break them slavery powers,
> Go sound the jubilee!

In many ways, American slaves converted the Christian God to themselves. They sought an alternative world to live in—a home other than the one fate had given them on earth. In a thousand variations on the Br'er Rabbit folktales—in which the weak survive by wit and power is reversed—and in the countless refrains of their songs, they fashioned survival out of their own cultural imagination.

The Black Family in Slavery   American slaves clung tenaciously to the personal relationships that gave meaning to life. Although American law did not recognize slave families, masters permitted them; in fact, slaveowners *expected* slaves to form families and have children. As a result, even along the rapidly expanding edge of the cotton kingdom, there was a normal ratio of men to women, young to old. On some of the largest cotton plantations of South Carolina, when masters allowed their slaves increased autonomy through work on the task system, the property accumulation in livestock, tools, and garden produce thus fostered led to more stable and healthier families.

Following African kinship traditions, African Americans avoided marriage be-tween cousins (commonplace among aristocratic slaveowners). By naming their children after relatives of past generations, African Americans emphasized their family histories. Kinship networks and broadly extended families are what held life together in many slave communities.

For slave women, sexual abuse and rape by white masters were ever-present threats to themselves and their family life. By 1860, there were 405,751 mulattos in the United States, comprising 12.5 percent of the African American population. White planters were sometimes open with their behavior toward slave women, but not in the way they talked about it. As Mary Chesnut remarked, sex between slave-holding men and their slave women was "the thing we can't name." Buying slaves for sex was all too common at the New Orleans slave market. In what was called the "fancy trade" (a "fancy" was a young, attractive slave girl or woman), females were often sold for prices as much as 300 percent higher than the average. At such auctions for young women, slaveholders exhibited some of the ugliest values at the heart of the slave system—patriarchal dominance demonstrated by paying $3,000 to $5,000 for female "companions."

Slave women had to negotiate this confused world of desire, threat, and shame. Harriet Jacobs, who spent much of her youth and early adult years dodging her owner's relentless sexual pursuit, described this circumstance as "the war of my life." In recollecting her desperate effort to protect her children and help them find a way north to freedom, Jacobs asked a haunting question that many slave women carried with them to their graves: "Why does the slave ever love? Why allow the tendrils of the heart to twine around objects which may at any moment be wrenched away by the hand of violence?"

The Domestic Slave Trade

Separation by violence from those they loved, sexual appro-priation, and sale were what slave families most feared and hated. Many struggled for years to keep their children to-gether and, after emancipation, to reestablish contact with loved ones lost by forced migration and sale. Between 1820 and 1860, an estimated 2 million slaves were moved into the region extending from western Georgia to eastern Texas. When the Union Army registered thousands of black marriages in Mississippi and Louisiana in 1864 and 1865, fully 25 percent of the men over the age of forty re-ported that they had been forcibly separated from a previous wife. Thousands of black families were disrupted every year to serve the needs of the expanding cotton economy.

Many antebellum white southerners made their living from the slave trade. In South Carolina alone by the 1850s, there were more than one hundred slave-trading firms selling an annual average of approximately 6,500 slaves to southwest-ern states. Although southerners often denied it, vast numbers of slaves moved west by outright sale and not by migrating with their owners. A typical trader's adver-tisement read, "NEGROES WANTED. I am paying the highest cash prices for young and likely NEGROES, those having good front teeth and being otherwise sound." One estimate from 1858 indicated that slave sales in Richmond, Virginia, netted $4 million that year alone. A market guide to slave sales that same year in Richmond listed average prices for "likely ploughboys," ages twelve to fourteen, at $850 to $1,050; "extra number 1 fieldgirls" at $1,300 to $1,350; and "extra number 1 men" at $1,500.

Slave traders were practical, roving businessmen. They were sometimes considered degraded by white planters, but many slaveowners did business with them. Market forces drove this commerce in humanity. At slave "pens" in cities like New Orleans, traders promoted "a large and commodious showroom ... prepared to accommodate over 200 Negroes for sale." Traders did their utmost to make their slaves appear young, healthy, and happy, cutting gray whiskers off men, using paddles as discipline so as not to scar their merchandise, and forcing people to dance and sing as buyers arrived for an auction. When transported to the southwestern markets, slaves were often chained together in "coffles," which made journeys of 500 miles or more on foot.

The complacent mixture of racism and business among traders is evident in their own language. "I refused a girl 20 year[s] old at 700 yesterday," one trader wrote to another in 1853. "If you think best to take her at 700 I can still get her. She is very badly whipped but good teeth." Some sales were transacted at owners' requests, often for tragically inhumane reasons. "Bought a cook yesterday that was to go out of state," wrote a trader; "she just made the people mad that was all." Some traders demonstrated how deeply slavery and racism were intertwined. "I have bought the boy Isaac for 1100," wrote a trader in 1854 to his partner. "I think him very prime.... He is a ... house servant ... first rate cook ... and splendid carriage driver. He is also a fine painter and varnisher and ... says he can make a fine panel door.... Also he performs well on the violin.... He is a genius and its strange to say I think he is smarter than I am."

Strategies of Resistance

Slaves brought to their efforts at resistance the same common sense and determination that characterized their struggle to secure their family lives. The scales weighed heavily against overt revolution, and they knew it. But they seized opportunities to alter their work conditions. They sometimes slacked off when they were not being watched. Thus, owners complained that slaves "never would lay out their strength freely."

Daily discontent and desperation were also manifest in sabotage of equipment; in wanton carelessness about work; in theft of food, livestock, or crops; or in getting drunk on stolen liquor. Some slaves who were hired out hoarded their earnings. Or they might just fall into recalcitrance. "I have a boy in my employ called Jim Archer," complained a Vicksburg, Mississippi, slaveholder in 1843. "Jim does not want to be under anyones control and says ... he wants to go home this summer." A woman named Ellen, hired as a cook in Tennessee in 1856, quietly put mercury poison into a roasted apple for her unsuspecting mistress. And some slave women resisted as best they could by trying to control their own pregnancy, either by avoiding it or by seeking it as a way to improve their physical conditions.

Many male, and some female, slaves acted out their defiance by violently attacking overseers or even their owners. Southern court records and newspapers contain accounts of these resistant slaves who gave the lie to the image of the docile bondsman. The price they paid was high. Such lonely rebels were customarily secured and flogged, sold away, or hanged.

Many individual slaves attempted to run away to the North, and some received assistance from the loose network known as the Underground Railroad. But it was more common for slaves to run off temporarily to hide in the woods. Approximately 80 percent of runaways were male; women simply could not flee as readily because of their responsibility for children. Fear, disgruntlement over treatment, or family separation might motivate slaves to risk all in flight. Only a minority of those who tried such escapes ever made it to freedom in the North or Canada, but these fugitives made slavery a very insecure institution by the 1850s.

But American slavery also produced some fearless revolutionaries. Gabriel's Rebellion involved as many as a thousand slaves when it was discovered in 1800, just before it would have exploded in Richmond, Virginia. According to controversial court testimony, a similar conspiracy existed in Charleston in 1822, led by a free black named Denmark Vesey. Born a slave in the Caribbean, Vesey won a lottery of $1,500 in 1799, bought his own freedom, and became a religious leader in the black community. According to one long-argued interpretation, Vesey was a heroic revolutionary determined to free his people or die trying. But in a recent challenge, historian Michael Johnson points out that the court testimony is the only reliable source on the alleged insurrection. Might the testimony reveal less of reality than of white South Carolina's fears of slave rebellion? The court, says Johnson, built its case on rumors and intimidated witnesses, and "conjured into being" an insurrection that was not about to occur in reality. Whatever the facts, when the arrests and trials were over, thirty-seven "conspirators" were executed, and more than three dozen others were banished from the state.

Nat Turner's Insurrection   The most famous rebel of all, Nat Turner, struck for freedom in Southampton County, Virginia, in 1831. The son of an African woman who passionately hated her enslavement, Nat Turner was a precocious child who learned to read when he was very young. Encouraged by his first owner to study the Bible, he enjoyed certain privileges but also endured hard work and changes of masters. His father successfully escaped to freedom.

Young Nat eventually became a preacher with a reputation for eloquence and mysticism. After nurturing his plan for several years, Turner led a band of rebels from farm to farm in the predawn darkness of August 22, 1831. The group severed limbs and crushed skulls with axes or killed their victims with guns. Before alarmed planters stopped them, Nat Turner and his followers had in forty-eight hours slaughtered sixty whites of both sexes and all ages. The rebellion was soon put down, and in retaliation whites killed slaves at random all over the region, including in adjoining states. Turner was eventually caught and then hanged. As many as two hundred African Americans, including innocent victims of marauding whites, lost their lives as a result of the rebellion.

Nat Turner remains one of the most haunting symbols in America's unresolved history with racial slavery and discrimination. While in jail awaiting execution,

Turner was interviewed by a Virginia lawyer and slaveholder, Thomas R. Gray. Their intriguing creation, *The Confessions of Nat Turner*, became a bestseller within a month of Turner's hanging. Turner told of his early childhood, his religious visions, his zeal to be free; Gray called the rebel a "gloomy fanatic," but in a manner that made him fascinating and produced one of the most remarkable documents in the annals of American slavery. In the wake of Turner's insurrection, many states passed stiffened legal codes against black education and religious practice.

Most important, in 1832 the state of Virginia, shocked to its core, held a full-scale legislative and public debate over gradual emancipation as a means of ridding itself of slavery and of blacks. The plan debated would not have freed any slaves until 1858, and it provided that eventually all blacks would be colonized outside Virginia. But when the House of Delegates voted, gradual abolition lost, 73 to 58. In the end, Virginia opted to do nothing except reinforce its own moral and economic defenses of slavery. It was the last time white southerners would debate any kind of emancipation until war forced their hand.

SUMMARY

During the four decades before the Civil War, the South grew in land, wealth, and power along with the rest of the country. Although the southern states were deeply enmeshed in the nation's heritage and political economy, they also developed as a distinctive region, ideologically and economically, because of slavery. Far more than the North, the antebellum South was a biracial society; whites grew up directly influenced by black folkways and culture; and blacks, the vast majority of whom were slaves, became predominantly native-born Americans and the cobuilders with whites of a rural, agricultural society. From the Old South until modern times, white and black southerners have always shared a tragic mutual history, and many are blood relatives.

With the cotton boom, as well as state and federal policies of Indian Removal, the South grew into a huge slave society. The coercive influence of slavery affected virtually every element of southern life and politics, and increasingly produced a leadership determined to preserve a conservative, hierarchical social and racial order. Despite the white supremacy that united them, the democratic values of yeomen often clashed with the profit motives of aristocratic planters. The benevolent self-image and paternalistic ideology of slaveholders ultimately had to stand the test of the slaves' own judgments. African American slaves responded by fashioning over time a rich, expressive folk culture and a religion of personal and group deliverance. Their experiences could be profoundly different from one region and kind of labor to another. Some blacks were crushed by bondage; many others transcended it in an epic of survival and resistance.

By 1850, through their own wits and on the backs of African labor, white southerners had aggressively built one of the last profitable, expanding slave societies on earth. North of them and deeply intertwined with them in the same nation, economy, constitutional system, and history, a different kind of society had grown even faster—driven by industrialism and free labor. The clash of these two deeply connected—yet mutually fearful and divided societies—would soon explode in political storms over the nation's future.

11

THE RESTLESS NORTH 1815–1860

OR IS IT THE NORTH THAT WAS DISTINCTIVE?

Historian James McPherson has proposed a new twist to the old question of southern distinctiveness: perhaps it was the North—New England, the Middle Atlantic,
and the Old Northwest—that diverged from the norm. At the republic's birth, the
two regions had much in common, with some similarities persisting for decades:
slavery, ethnic homogeneity, an overwhelming proportion of the population
engaged in agricultural pursuits, a small urban population. As late as the War of
1812, the regions were more similar than dissimilar. But all that started to change
with postwar economic development. Although often couched in nationalist terms,
such development was undertaken mostly by state and local governments as well as
private entrepreneurs, and it took place much more extensively and rapidly in the
North. As the North embraced economic progress, it—rather than the South—
diverged from the international norm. The North, writes McPherson, "hurtled forward toward a future that many Southerners found distasteful if not frightening."
With its continual quest for improvement, the North—much more so than the
South—embodied what Frenchman Alexis de Tocqueville, who toured the United
States in 1831–1832, called the nation's "restless spirit."

While the South expanded as a slave society, the North changed rapidly and
profoundly. It transformed, as one historian has put it, from a society with markets
to a market society. In the colonial era, settlers lived in a society with markets, one
in which they engaged in long-distance trade—selling their surpluses to merchants,
who in turn sent raw materials to Europe, using the proceeds to purchase finished
goods for resale—but in which most settlers remained self-sufficient. During and
after the War of 1812, the North became more solidly a market society, one in
which participation in long-distance commerce fundamentally altered individuals'

CHRONOLOGY

1824	*Gibbons v. Ogden* prohibits steamboat monopolies
1825	Erie Canal completed
1827	Construction begins on Baltimore and Ohio (B&O) Railroad
1830	First locomotive runs on B&O Railroad
1830s	Penny press emerges
1830s–50s	Urban riots commonplace
1834	Women workers strike at Lowell
1835	Arkansas passes first women's property law
1836	Second Bank of the United States closes
1837	Panic of 1837 begins economic downturn
1839–43	Economic depression
1840s	Female mill workers' publications appear
1842	*Commonwealth v. Hunt* declares strikes lawful
1844	Federal government sponsors first telegraph line
	Lowell Female Reform Association formed
1845	Massive Irish immigration begins

aspirations and activities. With European trade largely halted during the war, entrepreneurs invested in domestic factories, setting off a series of changes in the organization of daily life. More men, women, and children began working for others in exchange for wages—rather than for themselves on a family farm—making the domestic demand for foodstuffs soar. The result was a transformation of agriculture itself. Farming became commercialized, with individual farmers abandoning self-sufficiency and specializing instead in crops that would yield cash on the market. With the cash that farmers earned when things went well, they now bought goods they had once made for themselves, such as cloth, candles, and soap as well as some luxuries. Unlike the typical southern yeoman, they were not self-reliant, and isolation was rare. In the North, market expansion altered, sometimes dramatically, virtually every aspect of life. Some historians see these rapid and pervasive changes as a market revolution.

Preindustrial Farms   At the beginning of the nineteenth century, few yeoman farmers, North or South, were entirely independent. Most practiced what is called mixed agriculture: they raised a variety of crops and livestock. Their goal was to procure what they called a "competence": everyday comforts and economic opportunities for their children. When they produced more than they needed, they traded the surplus with neighbors or sold it to local storekeepers. Such transactions often took place without money; farmers might trade eggs for shoes, or they might labor in their neighbor's fields in exchange for bales of hay. Even farmers whose main goals were to secure their own independence and seek opportunities for their children engaged in long-distance market exchange. They did not simply trade their farm goods with neighbors but rather sold them for cash to merchants, who then sent the goods on their way to people whom they would never meet, living perhaps hundreds of miles away.

The main source of farm labor was family members, though some yeoman farmers, North and South, also relied on slaves or indentured servants. Work generally divided along gender lines. Men and boys worked in the fields, herded livestock, chopped firewood, fished, and hunted. Women and girls tended gardens, milked cows, spun and wove, processed and preserved food, prepared meals, washed clothes, and looked after infants and toddlers.

In their quest for independence, farmers cooperated with one another. They lent each other farm tools, harvested each other's fields, bartered goods, and raised their neighbors' barns and husked their corn. Little cash exchanged hands, in large part because money was in short supply. Still, New England farmers often kept elaborate account books in which they recorded what they owed and were owed (without assigning monetary value), whereas most farmers in the South rejected such formalities and simply made mental notes of debts. In both regions, years might pass without debts repaid, and when they were, they were not always repaid directly. A farmer who owed a neighbor two days' labor might bring the local storekeeper his eggs, to be credited to the neighbor's account.

Many farmers engaged simultaneously in this local economy and in long-distance trade. In the local economy—where they exchanged goods with people whom they knew—a system of "just price" prevailed, in which neighbors calculated value in terms of how much labor was involved in producing a good or providing a service. When the same farmers engaged in long-distance trade—when they sold their goods to merchants who resold it to other merchants before the goods eventually traveled as far away as coastal cities or even Europe—they set prices based on what the market would bear. In the long-distance market, credit and debt were reckoned in monetary value.

Preindustrial Artisans

Farmers who lived near towns or villages often purchased crafted goods from local cobblers, saddlers, blacksmiths, gunsmiths, silversmiths, and tailors. Most artisans, though, lived in the nation's seaports, where master craftsmen (independent businessmen who owned their own shops and tools) oversaw workshops employing apprentices and journeymen. Although the vast majority of craftsmen, North and South, were white, free blacks were well represented in some cities' urban trades, such as tailoring and carpentry in Charleston, South Carolina. Teenage apprentices lived with their masters, who taught them a craft, lodged and fed them, and offered parental oversight in exchange for labor. The master's wife, assisted by her daughters, cooked, cleaned, and sewed for her husband's workers. The relationship between a master craftsmen and his workers was often familial in nature, if not always harmonious. When the term of their apprenticeship expired, apprentices became journeymen who earned wages, usually with an eye toward saving money to open their own shops. The workplace had little division of labor or specialization. A tailor measured, designed, and sewed an entire suit; a cobbler did the same with shoes.

Men, women, and children worked long days on farms and in workshops, but the pace of work was generally uneven and unregimented. During busy periods, they worked dawn to dusk; the pace of work slowed after the harvest or after a large order had been completed. Market and court days were as much about exchanging gossip and offering toasts as exchanging goods and watching justice unfold. Husking bees and barn raisings brought people together not only to shuck corn and raise buildings, but also to eat, drink, dance, and flirt. Busy periods did not stop artisans from punctuating the day with grog breaks or from taking turns reading the newspaper aloud; they might even close their shops entirely to attend a political meeting. Nor did each workday adhere to a rigid schedule; journeymen craftsmen often staggered in late on Monday mornings, if they showed up at all, after a long night of carousing on their day off. Although the master craftsman was the boss, his workers exerted a good deal of influence over the workplace.

Early Industrialization   By the War of 1812, preindustrial habits had already changed, more noticeably in some places than in others. Early industry in the United States reorganized daily work routines and market relationships. Women and children had long made the clothing, hats, soap, candles, and other goods on which their families relied. In the late eighteenth and early nineteenth centuries, a "putting-out" system—similar to one existing in parts of western Europe—developed in the Northeast, particularly in Massachusetts, New Jersey, and Pennsylvania. Women and children continued to produce goods as they always had but now did so in much greater quantities and for the consumption of people beyond their own families and communities. A merchant supplied them with raw materials, paid them a wage (usually a price for each piece they produced), and sold their wares in distant markets, pocketing the profit for himself. "Outwork," as it is sometimes called, appealed to women eager to earn cash, whether to secure some economic independence or to save money for additional land on which their children might establish their own farms. Particularly in New England—where population density, small farms, and tired soil conspired to constrict farming opportunities and thus to create a surplus labor pool—the putting-out system provided opportunities to earn money with which to buy cheaper, more fertile western lands without requiring that family members seek employment away from home.

Drawing on technology imported from Europe, the earliest factories grew up in tandem with the putting-out system. When Samuel Slater helped set up the first American water-powered spinning mill in Rhode Island in 1790—using children to card and spin raw cotton into thread—he sent the spun thread to nearby farm families who wove it into cloth before sending it back to Slater, from whom they received a wage. Early shoe factories relied on a similar system: factory workers cut cowhide into uppers and bottoms that were sent to rural homes. There, women sewed the uppers while men lasted (or shaped) and pegged the bottoms, a process that also sometimes took place in small workshops. The change was subtle but significant: although the work remained familiar, women now operated their looms for wages and produced cloth for the market, not primarily for their families, while male cobblers made shoes for feet that would never walk into their shops or homes.

THE TRANSPORTATION REVOLUTION

In order to market goods at substantial distances from where they were produced, internal improvements were needed. Before the War of 1812, natural waterways provided the most readily available and cheapest transportation routes for people and goods, but their limitations were readily apparent. Boatmen poled bateaux (cargo boats) down shallow rivers or floated flatboats down deep ones. Cargo generally moved in one direction only—downstream—and most boats were broken up for lumber once they reached their destination. On portions of a few rivers, including the Mississippi and the Hudson, sailing ships could tack their way upstream under the right wind conditions, but upstream commerce was very limited.

Roads   Overland transport was limited, too. Although some roads had been built during the colonial and revolutionary eras, they often became obstructed by fallen trees, soaked by mud, or clouded in dust. To reduce mud and dust, some turnpike companies built "corduroy" roads, whose tightly lined-up logs resembled the ribbed cotton fabric. But passengers complained of nausea from being continually jolted, and merchants remained wary of transporting fragile wares by wagon. Land transportation was slow and expensive, demanding a good deal of human and animal power. In 1800, according to a report commissioned by the federal government, it cost as much to ship a ton of goods 30 miles into the country's interior as to ship the same goods from New York to England. The lack of cheap, quick transportation impeded the westward expansion of the population as well as industrial growth.

After the American Revolution, some northern states chartered private stock companies to build turnpikes (toll roads). These roads expanded commercial possibilities in southern New England and the Middle Atlantic, but during the War of 1812 the nation's lack of a road system in its more northerly and southerly reaches impeded the movement of troops and supplies, prompting renewed interest—in the name of defense—in building roads. Aside from the National Road, the financing fell on the states and private investors, and generally the enthusiasm for building turnpikes greatly outpaced the money and manpower expended. Turnpike companies sometimes adopted improvements, such as laying hard surfaces made of crushed stone and gravel, but many of the newly built roads suffered from old problems. With natural water routes unpredictable and roads predictably bad, an urgent need arose not just for more, but also for better transportation.

Steamboats   The first major innovation was the steamboat. In 1807, Robert Fulton's *Clermont* traveled between New York and Albany on the Hudson River in thirty-two hours, demonstrating the feasibility of using steam engines to power boats. After the Supreme Court's ruling against steamboat monopolies in *Gibbons v. Ogden* (1824), steamboat companies flourished on eastern rivers and, to a lesser extent, on the Great Lakes. These boats carried more passengers than freight, transporting settlers to the Midwest, where they would grow grain and raise pigs that fed northeastern factory workers. Along western rivers like the Mississippi and the Ohio, steamboats played a more direct commercial role, carrying midwestern timber and grain and southern cotton to New Orleans, where they were transferred to oceangoing vessels destined for northern and international ports. In the 1850s, steamboats began plying rivers as far west as California and Washington Territory. Privately owned and operated, steamboats became subject to federal regulations after frequent and deadly accidents in which boilers exploded, fires ignited, and boats collided.

To travel between Ohio and New Orleans by flatboat in 1815 took several months; in 1840, the same trip by steamboat took just ten days. But the steamboat did not supplant the flatboat. Rather, the number of flatboats traveling downstream to New Orleans more than doubled between 1816 and 1846. Now that flatboat crews could return upstream by steamboat rather than by foot, the greatest investment in flatboat travel—time—had been greatly reduced.

Canals

In the late eighteenth and early nineteenth centuries, private companies (sometimes with state subsidies) built small canals to transport goods and produce to and from interior locations previously accessible only by difficult-to-navigate rivers or by poorly maintained roads. These projects rarely reaped substantial profits, making it difficult to court investors for other projects. In 1815, only three canals in the United States measured more than 2 miles long; the longest was 27 miles. After Madison's veto of the Bonus Bill dashed commercially minded New Yorkers' hopes for a canal connecting Lake Erie to the port of New York, Governor DeWitt Clinton pushed hard and successfully for a state-sponsored initiative. What later became known as the Erie Canal was to run 363 miles between Buffalo and Albany, and was to be 4 feet deep. Skeptics derided it as "Clinton's Big Ditch."

But the optimists prevailed. Construction began—amid much symbolism and fanfare—on July 4, 1817. The canal, its promoters emphasized, would help fulfill the nation's revolutionary promise by demonstrating how American ingenuity and hard work could overcome any obstacle, including imposing natural ones, such as the combined ascent and descent of 680 feet between Buffalo and Albany. By so doing, it would help unify the nation and secure its commercial independence from Europe.

Over the next eight years, nearly nine thousand laborers felled forests, shoveled and piled dirt, picked at tree roots, blasted rock, heaved and hauled boulders, re-channeled streams, and molded the canal bed. Stonemasons and carpenters built aqueducts and locks. The work was dangerous. Much of it took place in malaria- and rattlesnake-infested swamps. Where the landscape was rock-solid, gunpowder explosions blew up some workers along with the rock. Collapsing canal beds smothered yet others, while some fell to their death from aqueducts and locks.

The canal's promoters celebrated the waterway as the work of "republican free men," a tribute to the nation's republican heritage. But few of those involved in the canal's construction would have perceived their work as fulfilling Jefferson's notion of republican freedom. Although farmers and artisans provided important labor, unskilled laborers—including many immigrants and some convicts—outnumbered them. Once completed, the Erie Canal relied on the labor of children. Boys led the horses who pulled the canal boats between the canal's eighty-three locks, while girls cooked and cleaned on the boats. When the canal froze shut in winter, many canal workers found themselves with neither employment nor shelter. Some tried, success-fully, to get themselves imprisoned as vagrants; many others experienced destitution.

The Erie Canal's completion in November 1825 brought immediate commercial success. Horse-drawn boats, stacked with bushels of wheat, barrels of oats, and piles of logs, streamed steadily eastward from western New York and Buffalo, where longshoreman transferred shipments from all around Lake Erie to canal boats. Tens of thousands of passengers—forty thousand in 1825 alone—traveled on the new waterway each year. The canal shortened the journey between Buffalo and New York City from twenty to six days and reduced freight charges by nearly 95 percent—thus securing New York City's position as the nation's preeminent port. Goods that previously had not been readily available in the nation's interior now could be had easily and cheaply. Home production of cloth, for example, fell sharply after canal boats began carrying factory-made fabric from the eastern sea-board to central New York.

Other states rushed to construct their own canals. By 1840, canals crisscrossed the Northeast and Midwest, and total canal mileage reached 3,300. Because the South had easily navigable rivers, fewer canals were dug there. None of the new canals, North or South, enjoyed the Erie's financial success. As the high cost of con-struction combined with an economic contraction, investment in canals slumped in the 1830s. Several midwestern states could not repay their canal loans, leading them to bankruptcy or near-bankruptcy. By mid-century, more miles were aban-doned than built. The canal era had ended, though the Erie Canal (by then twice enlarged and rerouted) continued to prosper, remaining in commercial operation until the late twentieth century.

Railroads

The future belonged to railroads. Trains moved faster than canal boats and operated year-round. Railroads did not need to be built near natural sources of water and could therefore connect even the most remote locations to national and international markets. By 1860, the United States had 60,000 miles of track, most of it in the North, and railroads had dramatically reduced the cost and the time involved in shipping goods, exciting the popular imagination in the process.

The railroad era in the United States began in 1830 when Peter Cooper's loco-motive, Tom Thumb, first steamed along 13 miles of Baltimore & Ohio Railroad track. In 1833, the nation's second railroad ran 136 miles from Charleston to Hamburg in South Carolina. Not until the 1850s, though, did railroads offer long-distance service at reasonable rates. Even then, the lack of a common standard for the width of track thwarted development of a national system. Pennsylvania and Ohio railroads, for example, had no fewer than seven different track widths. A journey from Philadelphia to Charleston involved eight different gauges, requir-ing passengers and freight to change trains seven times. Only at Bowling Green, Kentucky, did northern and southern railroads connect to one another. Although northerners and southerners alike raced to construct internal improvements, the na-tion's canals and railroads did little to unite the regions and promote nationalism, as the earliest proponents of government-sponsored internal improvements had hoped.

Railroads, introduced in the 1830s, soon surpassed canals. Easier, quicker, and cheaper to build than canals, they moved goods and people faster. David Matthews, the engineer of the Mohawk & Hudson's John Bull, drew this picture of his early locomotive. The Mohawk & Hudson offered competition to the slower Erie Canal boats.

Government Promotion of Internal Improvements

Northern state and local governments and private investors spent substantially more on internal improvements than did southerners. Pennsylvania and New York together accounted for half of all state monies invested. Southern states did invest in railroads, but—with smaller free populations—they collected fewer taxes, leaving them with less to spend.

For capitalists seeking dividends, southern railroads often seemed a poor bet. To be both profitable for investors and affordable for shippers, trains could not ship only one way; if they took agricultural products to market, their cars had to be filled with manufactured or finished goods for the return trip. But slaves and cash-strapped farmers did not provide much of a consumer base. Although planters bought northern ready-made clothes and shoes for their slaves, such purchases—made on an annual basis—did not constitute a regular source of incoming freight. Because the wealthiest men lived along rivers and could send their cotton to market on steamboats, they sometimes saw little need for railroads. Many reinvested in land and slaves, believing them a surer bet than risky railroad ventures.

The North and South laid roughly the same amount of railroad track per person before the Civil War, but when measured in terms of overall mileage, the more populous North had a web of tracks that stretched considerably farther, forming an integrated system of local lines branching off major trunk lines. In the South, railroads remained local in nature, leaving Southern travelers to patch together trips on railroads, stagecoaches, and boats. Neither people nor goods moved easily across the South, unless they traveled via steamboat or flatboat along the Mississippi River system—and even then, flooded banks disrupted passage for weeks at a time.

Regional Connections

Unlike southern investments in river improvements and steamboats, which disproportionately benefited planters whose lands bordered the region's riverbanks, the North's frenzy of canal and railroad building expanded transportation networks far into the hinterlands, proving not only more democratic but also more unifying. In 1815, nearly all the produce from the Old Northwest floated down the Mississippi to New Orleans, tying that region's fortunes to the South. By the 1850s, though, canals and railroads had strengthened the economic, cultural, and political links between the Old Northwest—particularly the more densely populated northern regions—and the Northeast. (see Map 11.1)

Internal improvements hastened the population's westward migration. They eased the journey itself while also making western settlement more appealing by providing easy access to eastern markets and familiar comforts. News, visitors, and luxuries now traveled regularly to previously remote areas of the Northeast and Midwest.

Samuel F. B. Morse's invention of the telegraph in 1844 made the compression of distance and time even starker. News traveled almost instantaneously along telegraph wires. By 1852, more than 23,000 miles of lines had been strung nation-wide. The telegraph enabled the birth of modern business practices involving the

MAP 11.1 Major Roads, Canals, and Railroads, 1850

A transportation network linked the seaboard to the interior. Settlers followed those routes westward, and they sent back grain, grain products, and cotton to the port cities.

coordination of market conditions, production, and supply across great distances. Together, internal improvements and the telegraph allowed people in previously isolated areas to proclaim themselves—as did one western New Yorker—a "citizen of the world."

Ambivalence Toward Progress Many northerners hailed internal improvements as symbols of progress. Northerners proclaimed that, by building canals and railroads, they had completed God's design for the North American continent. On a more practical level, canals and railroads allowed them to seek opportunities in the West.

But people who welcomed such opportunities could find much to lament. Some decried the enormous numbers of Irish canal diggers and railroad track layers, whom they deemed depraved and racially inferior. Still others worried that, by promoting urban growth, transportation innovations fostered social ills.

The degradation of the natural world proved worrisome, too. When streams were rerouted, swamps drained, and forests felled, natural habitats were disturbed, even destroyed. Humans soon felt the consequences. Deprived of water power, mills no longer ran. Without forests to sustain them, wild animals—on which many rural people (Native American and European American) had relied for protein—sought homes elsewhere. Fishermen, too, found their sources of protein (and cash) dried up when natural waterways were dammed or rerouted to feed canals. If many northerners embraced progress, they also regretted its costs.

Henry David Thoreau, the prominent Transcendentalist (see Chapter 12), offered eloquent expressions of ambivalence toward progress. Even as he denounced the "devilish iron horse" (the railroad) for its shrieks and environmental degradation, he also recognized its awesome nature as a tribute to human inventiveness.

FACTORIES AND INDUSTRIALIZATION

By dramatically lowering transportation costs, internal improvements made possible the Northeast's rapid manufacturing and commercial expansion. After canals and railroads opened the trans-Appalachian West for wide-scale settlement, western farmers supplied raw materials and foodstuffs for northeastern factories and their workers. They also created a larger domestic market for goods manufactured in the Northeast. With most of their time devoted to cultivating their lands, western settlers preferred to buy rather than make cloth, shoes, and other goods. They needed northeastern iron, too—for farm implements (plows, pitchforks, scythes), for nails (to build houses and other buildings, particularly in the Midwest's rapidly burgeoning cities), and for railroad tracks.

One of the oldest industries in North America, iron production was centered in the Middle Atlantic states, especially Pennsylvania, but stretched as far south as Richmond and as far north as Albany. Iron forges flourished wherever ore deposits lay and sources of fuel abounded. During the 1840s, ironworks, which previously heated their furnaces with charcoal, turned increasingly to coal and then steam. But production methods in iron making changed little, with smaller firms remaining more efficient than larger ones. Although the industry expanded, daily work stayed largely the same.

Factory Work   In many other industries, daily life changed dramatically. Much early industrialization involved processing raw materials— milling flour, turning hogs into packaged meat, sawing lumber—and the pork-packing industry illustrates strikingly how specialization turned skilled craftsmen into laborers. Traditionally, each butcher cut up an entire pig. Under the new industrial organization, each worker was assigned a particular task—such as cutting off the right front leg or scooping out the entrails—as the pig made its way down a "disassembly line."

The impersonal nature and formal rules of factory work contrasted sharply with the informal atmosphere of artisan shops and farm households. The bell, the steam whistle, or the clock governed the flow of work. In large factories, laborers never saw owners, working instead under paid supervisors, nor did they see the final product of their labor. Factory workers lost their sense of autonomy in the face of impersonal market forces. Competition from cheaper, less-skilled workers— particularly after European immigration soared in the 1840s—created job insecurity, while opportunities for advancement were virtually nonexistent.

Machinery made mass production possible in some industries. Although at first Americans imported machines or copied British designs, they soon built their own. The American System of manufacturing, as the British called it, used precision machinery to produce interchangeable parts that did not require individual adjust-ment to fit. Eli Whitney, the cotton gin's inventor, promoted the idea of interchange-able parts in 1798, when he contracted with the federal government to make ten thousand rifles in twenty-eight months. In the 1820s, the United States Ordnance Department contracted with private firms to introduce machine-made interchange-able parts for firearms. The American System quickly produced the machine-tool industry—the manufacture of machines for the purpose of mass production. The new system permitted large-scale production at low costs: Waltham watches, Yale locks, and other goods became inexpensive but high-quality household items.

Textile Mills   Mechanization was most dramatic in textiles, with produc-tion centered in New England, near sources of water to power spinning machines and looms. After 1815, New England's rudimentary cot-ton mills developed into modern factories in which machines mass-produced goods. Cotton cloth production rose from 4 million yards in 1817 to 323 million in 1840. Mechanization did not make workers obsolete; rather, more workers were needed to monitor the machines. In the mid-1840s, the cotton mills employed approxi-mately eighty thousand "operatives," more than half of them women. Mill owners employed a resident manager to run the mills, thus separating ownership from management. Workers received wages, and the cloth they produced was sold throughout the United States.

Unable to find enough laborers in the vicinity of their mills, managers recruited New England farm daughters, whom they paid wages and housed in dormitories and boarding houses in what became known as the Waltham or Lowell plan of industrialization. People who made their living off the land often harbored suspi-cions of those who did not—particularly in the young United States, where an agrarian lifestyle was often associated with virtue itself—causing some rural parents to hesitate from sending their daughters to textile mills. To ease such concerns, mill owners offered paternalistic oversight to the mill girls; they enforced curfews, prohibited alcohol, and required church attendance. Despite its restrictions, the system in Waltham offered farm girls opportunities to socialize with women of the same age and to gain a sense of independence that came from living away from home and earning wages. Workers wrote literary pieces for the owner-subsidized *Lowell Offering* and attended educational lectures in the evenings.

Most women imagined their factory stints as temporary, and the conditions of the work itself—the deafening roar of the power looms, the long hours, the regimentation—made few change their minds. Yet they welcomed the social and cultural opportunities as well as the wages, which they used to help their families buy land or send a brother to college, to save for their own dowries or education, or to spend on personal items, such as fashionable clothing. The average girl arrived at sixteen and stayed five years, usually leaving to get married—often to men they met in town rather than to farm boys at home. When they left the mills, younger women took their places.

Although the Waltham plan drew international attention for its novelty, more common was the Rhode Island (or Fall River) plan employed by Samuel Slater, among others. Mills hired entire families, lodging them in company boarding houses. Men often worked farm plots near the factories while their wives and children worked in the mills, though as the system developed, men were more likely to work in the factories full-time, directly supervising the labor of their wives and children in small, family-based work units.

Labor Protests

Mill life got harder over time, especially during the depression of 1837 to 1843, when demand for cloth declined, causing most mills to run part-time. To increase productivity, managers sped up machines and required each worker to operate more machines. Between 1836 and 1850, the number of spindles and looms in Lowell increased 150 and 140 percent, respectively, whereas the number of workers increased by only 50 percent. In the race for profits, owners lengthened hours, cut wages, tightened discipline, and packed the boarding houses.

Workers organized, accusing their bosses of treating them like wage slaves. In 1834, in reaction to a 25 percent wage cut, they unsuccessfully "turned out" (struck) against the Lowell mills. Two years later, when boarding house fees increased, they again turned out, unsuccessfully. With conditions worsening and strikes failing, workers resisted in new ways. In 1844, Massachusetts mill women formed the Lowell Female Reform Association and joined forces with other workers to press, unsuccessfully, for state legislation mandating a ten-hour day—as opposed to the fourteen-hour days that some workers endured.

Women aired their complaints in worker-run newspapers: in 1842, the *Factory Girl* appeared in New Hampshire, the *Wampanoag and Operatives' Journal* in Massachusetts. Two years later, mill workers founded the *Factory Girl's Garland* and the *Voice of Industry*, nicknamed "the factory girl's voice." Even the *Lowell Offering*, the owner-sponsored paper that was the pride of mill workers and managers alike, became embroiled in controversy when workers charged its editors with suppressing articles criticizing working conditions.

Worker turnover weakened organizational efforts. Few militant native-born mill workers stayed to fight the managers and owners, and gradually, fewer New England daughters entered the mills. In the 1850s, Irish immigrant women replaced them. Technological improvements made the work less skilled and more routine, enabling mills to hire unskilled laborers, who could be paid less. Male workers, too, protested changes wrought by the market economy and factories. But, unlike women, they could vote. Labor political parties first formed in Pennsylvania, New York, and Massachusetts in the 1820s, and then spread elsewhere; they advocated free public education and an end to imprisonment for debt, and opposed banks and monopolies. Some advocated for free homesteads, a reminder that most early industrial workers still aspired to land ownership.

Labor Unions   The courts provided organized labor's greatest victory: protection from conspiracy laws. When journeyman shoemakers organized during the century's first decade, their employers accused them of criminal conspiracy. The cordwainers' (shoemakers') cases between 1806 and 1815 left labor organizations in an uncertain position. Although the courts acknowledged the journeymen's right to organize, judges viewed strikes as illegal until a Massachusetts case, *Commonwealth v. Hunt* (1842), ruled that Boston journeyman bootmakers could strike "in such manner as best to subserve their own interests."

The first unions arose among urban journeymen in printing, woodworking, shoemaking, and tailoring. Tending to be local, the strongest resembled medieval guilds, with members seeking protection against competition from inferior workmen by regulating apprenticeships and establishing minimum wages. Umbrella organizations composed of individual craft unions, like the National Trade Union (1834), arose in several cities in the 1820s and 1830s. But the movement disintegrated amid wage reductions and unemployment in the hard times of 1839–1843.

Permanent labor organizations were difficult to sustain. Skilled craftsmen disdained less skilled workers. Moreover, workers divided along ethnic, religious, racial, and gender lines.

CONSUMPTION AND COMMERCIALIZATION

By producing inexpensive cloth, New England mills spawned the ready-made clothing industry. Before the 1820s, women sewed most clothing at home, and some people purchased used clothing. Tailors and seamstresses made wealthy men's and women's clothing to order. By the 1820s and 1830s, much clothing was mass-produced for sale in retail clothing stores. The process often involved little more than the reorganization of work; tailors no longer performed every task involved in making an article of clothing, from measuring to finishing work. Standard sizes replaced measuring, and a division of labor took hold: One worker cut patterns all day, another sewed hems, another affixed buttons, still another attached collars. The sewing machine's invention in 1846 sped the process along, especially with its wide availability in the 1850s. Many farm families still made their own clothing, yet bought clothes when they could afford to do so, creating more time for raising both crops and children.

The Garment Industry

Market expansion created a demand for mass-produced clothing. Rural girls who left farms for factories no longer had time to sew clothes. Young immigrant men—often separated by thousands of miles from mothers and sisters—bought the crudely made, loose-fitting clothing. But the biggest market for ready-made clothes, at least initially, was in the cotton South. With the textile industry's success driving up the demand and price for raw cotton, planters in the cotton kingdom bought ready-made shoes and clothes for slaves, in whose hands they would rather place a hoe than a needle and thread. Doing so made good economic sense.

Retailers often bought goods wholesale, though many manufactured shirts and trousers in their own factories. Lewis and Hanford of New York City boasted of cutting more than 100,000 garments in the winter of 1848–1849. The New York firm did business mostly in the South and owned its own retail outlet in New Orleans. Paul Tulane, a New Orleans competitor, owned a New York factory that made goods for his Louisiana store. In the Midwest, Cincinnati became the center of the men's clothing industry. But although southerners and westerners engaged in the clothing trade, its center remained in New York.

Specialization of Commerce

Commerce expanded with manufacturing. Commercial specialization transformed some traders in big cities, especially New York, into virtual merchant princes. After the Erie Canal opened, New York City became a stop on every major trade route from Europe, southern ports, and the West. New York traders were the intermediaries for southern cotton and western grain. Merchants in other cities played a similar role. Traders in turn sometimes invested their profits in factories, further stimulating urban manufacturing. Some cities specialized: Rochester became a milling center ("The Flour City"), and Cincinnati ("Porkopolis") became the first meatpacking center.

Merchants who engaged in complex commercial transactions required large office staffs, mostly all male. At the bottom of the hierarchy were messenger boys, often preteens, who delivered documents. Above them were copyists, who hand-copied documents. Clerks processed documents and shipping papers, and did translations. Above them were the bookkeeper and the confidential chief clerk. Those seeking employment in such an office, called a counting house, often took a course from a writing master to acquire a "good hand." All hoped to rise some day to the status of partner, although their chances of success grew increasingly slim.

The specialization of commerce came more quickly to cities than to small towns, where merchants continued to exchange some goods with local farm women—trading flour or pots and pans for eggs and other produce. Local craftsmen continued to sell their own finished goods, such as shoes and clothing. In some rural areas, particularly newly settled ones, peddlers acted as general merchants. But as transportation improved and towns grew, small-town merchants increasingly specialized.

Commercial Farming

Even amid the manufacturing and commercial booms, agriculture remained the northern economy's backbone. But the transportation revolution and market expansion transformed formerly semisubsistence farms into commercial enterprises. Many families stopped

VISUALIZING THE PAST

Images of Boom and Bust

The growth of the commercial economy, which saw the mass production of consumer items, also fostered economic boom and bust. Below, we see an advertisement from the *Boston Directory* of 1848–1849 for readymade shirts, and to the right we see how *Harper's Weekly* portrayed New York City, the heart of the garment industry, in the heat of the financial panic of 1857, less than a decade

Warshaw Collection of Business Americana, Smithsonian Institution, Washington, D.C.

Although F. B. Locke continued to make shirts to order, he adapted to the new market for ready-made clothing by becoming a manufacturer, wholesaler, and retailer of men's shirts.

practicing mixed agriculture and began to specialize in cash crops. Although most northerners continued to farm, their daily lives and relationships often looked very different from those of their parents and grandparents.

By the 1820s, eastern farmers had cultivated nearly all the available land, and their small farms, often with uneven terrains, were not suited for the labor-saving farm implements introduced in the 1830s, such as mechanical sowers, reapers, and threshers. Many northern farmers thus either moved west or quit farming for jobs in merchants' houses and factories. Those farmers who remained, however, proved as adaptable on the farm as were their children working at water-powered looms or in countinghouses. State governments energetically promoted agricultural innovation. Massachusetts in 1817 and New York in 1819 began to subsidize agricultural prizes and county fairs. To spread innovation, New York published the winners' essays about how they grew their prize crops.

later. To what values does F. B. Locke appeal in his choice of imagery for his advertisement? Why does *Harper's Weekly* refer to the discounted goods, and the scramble to purchase them, as an "epidemic"? What is the significance, on the image's left side, of the police officer escorting two children out of the store? What does it indicate about how *Harper's* saw the consequences of the "epidemic"? What else does the picture imply about the social consequences of financial collapse? Do the two images suggest that American values shifted in the intervening decade? Why or why not?

As the nation experienced a serious financial contraction in 1857, prices fell as business languished. But the availability of bargains did not compensate for widespread unemployment and falling wages.

In 1820, about one-third of all northern produce was intended for the market, but by 1850 the amount surpassed 50 percent. As farmers shifted toward specialization and market-oriented production, they often invested in additional land (buying the farms of neighbors who moved west), new farming equipment (such as improved iron and steel plows), and new sources of labor (hired hands). Many New England and Middle Atlantic farm families faced steep competition from midwestern farmers after the opening of the Erie Canal, and began abandoning wheat and corn production. Instead, they raised livestock, especially cattle, and specialized in vegetable and fruit production. Much of what they produced ended up in the stomachs of the North's rapidly growing urban and manufacturing populations.

Farmers financed innovations through land sales and debts. Indeed, increasing land values, not the sale of agricultural products, promised the greatest profit. Farm families who owned their own land flourished, but it became harder to take up farming in the first place. By the 1840s, it took more than ten years for a rural laborer in the Northeast to save enough money to buy a farm. The number of tenant farmers and hired hands increased, providing labor to drive commercial expansion. Farmers who had previously employed unpaid family members and enslaved workers now leased portions of their farms or hired waged labor to raise their livestock and crops.

Farm Women's Changing Labor   As the commercial economy expanded, rural women assumed additional responsibilities, increasing their already substantial farm and domestic work. Some did outwork. Many increased their production of eggs, dairy products, and garden produce for sale; others raised bees or silkworms.

With the New England textile mills producing more and more finished cloth, farm women and children often abandoned time-consuming spinning and weaving, bought factory-produced cloth, and dedicated the saved time to producing additional products, such as butter and cheese, for the market. Women had always made butter and cheese; now they produced them in large quantities with intentions of profiting from their sale. Some mixed-agriculture farms converted entirely to dairy production, with men taking over formerly female tasks. Canals and railroads carried cheese to eastern ports, where wholesalers sold it around the world, shipping it to California, England, and China. In 1844, Britain imported more than 5 million pounds of cheese from the United States.

Rural Communities   Although agricultural journals and societies exhorted farmers to manage their farms like time-efficient businesses, not all farmers abandoned the old practices of gathering at market, general stores, taverns, and church. They did not forgo barn raisings and husking bees, but by the 1830s there were fewer young people at such events to dance and flirt. Many young women had left for textile mills, and young men often worked as clerks or factory hands. Those who stayed behind were more likely to come dressed in store-bought clothing and to consume pies made with store-bought flour.

Even as they continued to swap labor and socialize with neighbors, farmers became more likely to reckon debts in dollars. They kept tighter accounts and watched national and international markets more closely. When financial panics hit, cash shortages almost halted business activity, casting many farmers further into debt, sometimes to the point of bankruptcy. Faced with the possibility of losing their land, farmers did what many would have considered unthinkable before: they called in debts with their neighbors, sometimes causing fissures in long-established relationships.

Cycles of Boom and Bust   The market economy's expansion led to cycles of boom and bust. Prosperity stimulated demand for finished goods, such as clothing and furniture. Increased demand in turn led not only to higher prices and still higher production, but also, because of business optimism and expectations of higher prices, to land speculation. Investment money was plentiful as Americans saved and foreign, mostly British, investors bought U.S. bonds and securities. Then production surpassed demand, causing prices and wages to fall; in response, land and stock values collapsed, and investment money flowed out of the United States. This boom-and-bust cycle influenced every corner of the country, but particularly the Northeast, where even the smallest localities became enmeshed in regional and national markets.

Although the 1820s and 1830s were boom times, financial panic triggered a bust cycle in 1837, the year after the Second Bank of the United States closed. Economic contraction remained severe through 1843. Internal savings and foreign investments declined sharply. Many banks could not repay their depositors, and states, facing deficits because of the economy's decline, defaulted on their bonds. European, especially British, investors became suspicious of all U.S. loans and withdrew money from the United States.

Hard times had come. Philadelphia took on an eerie aura. "The streets seemed deserted," Sidney George Fisher observed in 1842. "The largest [merchant] houses are shut up and to rent, there is no business … no money, no confidence." New York countinghouses closed their doors. Former New York mayor Philip Hone later observed, "A deadly calm pervades this lately flourishing city. No goods are selling, no businesses stirring." The hungry formed lines in front of soup societies, and beggars crowded the sidewalks. Some workers looted. Crowds of laborers demanding their deposits gathered at closed banks. Sheriffs sold seized property at one-quarter of pre-hard-time prices. In smaller cities like Lynn, Massachusetts, shoemakers weathered the hard times by fishing and tending gardens, while laborers became scavengers, digging for clams and harvesting dandelions. Once-prosperous businessmen—some victims of the market, others of their own recklessness—lost nearly everything, prompting Congress to pass the Federal Bankruptcy Law of 1841; by the time the law was repealed two years later, 41,000 bankrupts had sought protection under its provisions.

FAMILIES IN FLUX

Anxieties about economic fluctuations reverberated beyond factories and countinghouses into northern homes. Sweeping changes in the household economy, rural as well as urban, led to new family ideals. In the preindustrial era, the family had been primarily an economic unit; now it became a moral and cultural institution, though in reality few families could live up to the new ideal.

The "Ideal" Family

In the North, the market economy increasingly separated the home from the workplace, leading to a new middle-class ideal in which men functioned in the public sphere, while women oversaw the private or domestic sphere. The home became, in theory, an emotional retreat from the competitive, selfish world of business, where men increasingly focused on their work, eager to prosper yet fearful of failure in the unpredictable market economy. At the home's center was a couple that married for love rather than for economic convenience or advantage. Men provided and protected, while women nurtured and guarded the family's morality, making sure that capitalism's excesses did not invade the private sphere. Childhood focused more on education than on work, and the definition of childhood itself expanded: children were to remain at home until their late teens or early twenties. This ideal came to be known as separate-sphere ideology, or sometimes the cult of domesticity or the cult of true womanhood. Although it rigidly separated the male and female spheres, this ideology gave new standing to domestic responsibilities. In her widely read *Treatise on Domestic Economy* (1841), Catharine Beecher approached housekeeping as a science even as she trumpeted mothers' role as their family's moral guardian. Although Beecher advocated the employment of young, single women as teachers, she believed that, once married, women belonged at home. She maintained that women's natural superiority as moral, nurturing caregivers made them especially suited for teaching (when single) and parenting (once married). Although Beecher saw the public sphere as a male domain, she insisted that the private sphere be elevated to the same status as the public.

Shrinking Families   These new domestic ideals depended on smaller families in which parents, particularly mothers, could give children more attention, better education, and more financial help. With the market economy, parents could afford to have fewer children because children no longer played a vital economic role. Urban families produced fewer household goods, and commercial farmers, unlike self-sufficient ones, did not need large numbers of workers year-round, turning instead to hired laborers during peak work periods. Although smaller families resulted in part from first marriages' taking place at a later age—shortening the period of potential childbearing—they also resulted from planning, made easier when cheap rubber condoms became available in the 1850s. Some women chose, too, to end accidental pregnancies with abortion.

In 1800, American women bore seven or eight children; by 1860, the figure had dropped to five or six. This decline occurred even though many immigrants with large-family traditions were settling in the United States; thus, the birth rate among native-born women declined even more sharply. Although rural families remained larger than urban ones, birth rates among both groups declined comparably.

Yet even as birth rates fell, few northern women could fulfill the middle-class ideal of separate spheres. Most wage-earning women provided essential income for their families and could not stay home. They often saw domestic ideals as oppressive, as middle-class reformers mistook poverty for immorality, condemning working mothers for letting their children work or scavenge rather than attend school. Although most middle-class women could stay home, new standards of cleanliness and comfort weighed heavily on their time. These women's contributions to their families were generally assessed in moral terms, even though their economic contributions were significant. When they worked inside their homes, they provided, without remuneration, the labor for which wealthier women paid when they hired domestic servants to perform daily chores. Without servants, moreover, women could not devote themselves primarily to their children's upbringing, placing the ideals of the cult of domesticity beyond the reach of many middle-class families.

Women's Paid Labor   In working-class families, women left their parental home as early as age twelve, earning wages most of their lives, with only short respites for bearing and rearing children.

Unmarried girls and women worked primarily as domestic servants or in factories; married and widowed women worked as laundresses, seamstresses, and cooks. Some hawked food and wares on city streets; other did piecework at home, earning wages in the putting-out system; and some became prostitutes. Few of these occupations enabled women to support themselves or a family at a comfortable level.

Middle-class Americans sought to keep women closer to home. If young girls left the home to work—in New England's textile mills, in new urban stores as clerks—it was only for a brief interval before marriage. Otherwise, teaching was the only occupation consistent with genteel notions of femininity. In 1823, the Beecher sisters, Catharine and Mary, established the Hartford Female Seminary and offered history and science in addition to the traditional women's curriculum of domestic arts and religion. A decade later, Catharine Beecher successfully campaigned for teacher-training schools for women. She argued in part for women's moral superiority and in part for their economic value; because these women would be single, she contended, they need not earn as much as their male counterparts, whom she presumed to be married, though not all were. Unmarried women earned about half the salary of male teachers. By 1850, schoolteaching had become a woman's profession. Many women worked as teachers, usually for two to five years.

The proportion of single women in the population increased significantly in the nineteenth century. In the East, some single women would have preferred to marry but found market and geographic expansion working against them: more and more young men headed west in search of opportunity, leaving some eastern communities with a disproportionate number of young women. But other women chose to remain independent, seeking opportunities opened by the market economy and urban expansion. Because women's work generally paid poorly, those who forswore marriage faced serious challenges, leaving many single women to rely on charitable or family assistance.

THE GROWTH OF CITIES

To many contemporary observers, cities came to symbolize what market expansion had wrought—for better or for worse—on northern society. No period in American history saw more rapid urbanization than the years between 1820 and 1860. The percentage of people living in urban areas (defined as a place with a population of 2,500 or more) grew from just over 7 percent in 1820 to nearly 20 percent in 1860. Most of this growth took place in the Northeast and the Midwest. Although most northerners continued to live on farms or in small villages, the population of individual cities boomed. Many of those residents were temporary—soon moving on to another city or the countryside—and many came from foreign shores.

Urban Boom   Even as new cities sprang up, existing cities grew tremendously (see Map 11.2). In 1820, the United States had thirteen places with a population of ten thousand or more; in 1860, it had ninety-three. New York City, already the nation's largest city in 1820, saw its population grow from 123,709 people in that year to 813,669 in 1860—a growth factor of six and a half times. Philadelphia, the nation's second-largest city in both 1820 and 1860, saw the

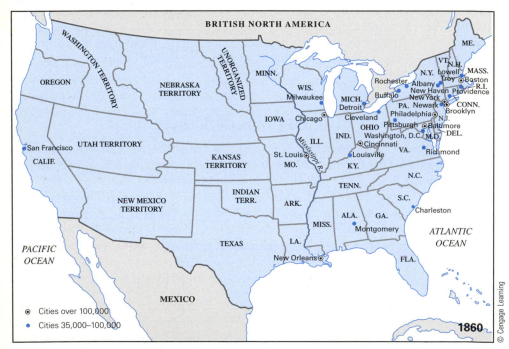

MAP 11.2 Major American Cities in 1820 and 1860

The number of Americans who lived in cities increased rapidly between 1820 and 1860, and the number of large cities grew as well. In 1820, only New York City had a population exceeding 100,000; forty years later, eight more cities had surpassed that level.

size of its population multiply ninefold during that same forty-year period. In 1815, Rochester, New York, had a population of just 300 persons. By 1830, the Erie Canal had turned the sleepy agricultural town into a bustling manufacturing center; it was now the nation's twenty-fifth-largest city, with a population of just over 9,000. Its population continued to multiply at fantastic rates, even doubling in a single decade. By 1860, it had more than 50,000 residents.

Cities experienced geographic expansion as well. New York City, for example, burst its boundaries around 1830. Until then, New Yorkers could walk from one end of the city to the other in an hour. In 1825, Fourteenth Street was the city's northern boundary. By 1860, 400,000 people lived above that divide, and Forty-second Street was the city's northern limit. Gone were the cow pastures, kitchen gardens, and orchards. Public transit made city expansion possible. Horse-drawn omnibuses appeared in New York in 1827, and the Harlem Railroad, completed in 1832, ran the length of Manhattan. By the 1850s, all big cities had horse-drawn streetcars, allowing wealthier residents who could afford the fare to settle on larger plots of land on the cities' outskirts.

Market-Related Development   Cities helped sustain the North's market revolution by serving as transportation hubs, commercial centers, and—in some cases—manufacturing sites. Some cities grew up with manufacturing. The Boston Manufacturing Company selected the site for Lowell, Massachusetts, because of its proximity to the Merrimack River, whose rapidly flowing waters could power its textile mill. Incorporated in 1826, by the 1850s Lowell was the second-largest city in New England. Although most early manufacturing took place in rural areas, some commercial cities, such as New York, experienced what historians sometimes call metropolitan industrialization, a form relying not on mechanization but on reorganization of labor, similar to the earlier putting-out system. Much of the early production of ready-made clothing, for example, took place in tenements throughout New York City, where women performed an urban form of outwork, spending hour after hour sewing on buttons for a piece of ready-made clothing, while others sewed hem after hem. In 1860, 25,000 women worked in manufacturing jobs in New York City, where they constituted a quarter of the waged labor force. Two-thirds of them worked in the garment industry.

The North urbanized more quickly than the South, but what was most striking about northern urbanization was where it took place. With only a few exceptions, southern cities were seaports, whereas the period between 1820 and 1860 saw the creation of many inland cities in the North—usually places that sprang to life with the creation of transportation lines or manufacturing establishments.

Northern cities developed elaborate systems of municipal services but lacked adequate taxing power to provide services for all. At best, they could tax property adjoining new sewers, paved streets, and water mains. New services and basic sanitation depended on residents' ability to pay. Another solution was to charter private companies to sell basic services, such as providing gas for lights. Baltimore first chartered a private gas company in 1816. By mid-century, every major city had done so. Private firms lacked the capital to build adequate water systems, though, and they laid pipe only in commercial and well-to-do residential areas, bypassing the poor. The task of supplying water ultimately fell on city governments.

Extremes of Wealth   Throughout the United States, wealth was concentrating in the hands of a relatively small number of people. By 1860, the top 5 percent of American families owned more than half of the nation's wealth, and the top 10 percent owned nearly three-quarters. In the South, the extremes of wealth were most apparent on rural plantations, but in the North, cities provided the starkest evidence of economic inequities.

Despite the optimistic forecasts of early textile manufacturers that American industrialization need not engender the poverty and degradation associated with European industrialization, America's industrial cities soon resembled European ones. A number of factors contributed to widespread poverty: poor wages, the inability of many workers to secure full-time employment, and the increasingly widespread employment of women and children, which further drove down wages for everyone. Women and children, employers rationalized, did not need a living wage because they were—in the employers' way of thinking—dependent by nature, meaning that they relied on men to support them and did not need to earn a wage that allowed self-sufficiency. In reality, though, not all women or children had men to support them, nor were men's wages always adequate to support a family comfortably.

New York provides a striking example of the extremes of wealth accompanying industrialization. Where workers lived, conditions were crowded, unhealthy, and dangerous. Houses built for two families often held four; tenements built for six families held twelve. Some of those families took in lodgers to pay the rent, adding to the unbearably crowded conditions that encouraged poorer New Yorkers to spend as much time as possible outdoors. But streets in poor neighborhoods were filthy. Excess sewage from outhouses drained into ditches that carried urine and fecal matter into the streets. People piled garbage into gutters or left it to accumulate in backyards or alleys. Pigs, geese, dogs, and vultures scavenged the streets, while enormous rats roamed under cities' wooden sidewalks and through large buildings. Disease thrived. Typhoid, dysentery, malaria, and tuberculosis regularly visited the poorer sections of cities. Epidemics of cholera struck in 1831, 1849, and again in 1866, claiming thousands of victims.

But within walking distance of poverty-stricken neighborhoods were lavish mansions, whose residents could escape to their country estates during the summer's brutal heat or during epidemics. Much of this wealth was inherited. For every John Jacob Astor, who became a millionaire in the western fur trade after beginning life in humble circumstances, ten others had inherited or married money. These rich New Yorkers were not idle, though; they worked at increasing their fortunes and power by investing in commerce and manufacturing.

Between the two extremes of wealth sat a distinct middle class, larger than the wealthy elite but substantially smaller than the working classes. They were businessmen, traders, and professionals, and the rapid turn toward industrialization and commercial specialization made them a much larger presence in northern cities than in southern ones. Middle-class families enjoyed new consumer items: wool carpeting, fine wallpaper, and rooms full of furniture replaced the bare floors, whitewashed walls, and relative sparseness of eighteenth-century homes. Houses were large, from four to six rooms. Middle-class children slept one to a bed, and by the 1840s and 1850s, middle-class families used indoor toilets that were mechanical, though not yet flushing. Middle-class families formed the backbone of urban clubs and societies, filled the family pews in church, and sent their sons to college. They were as distinct from the world of John Jacob Astor as they were from the milieu of the working class and the poor.

Immigration

Many of the urban poor were immigrants. The 5 million immigrants who came to the United States between 1830 and 1860 outnumbered the country's entire population in 1790. The vast majority were Europeans, primarily from Ireland and the German states (see Figure 11.1).

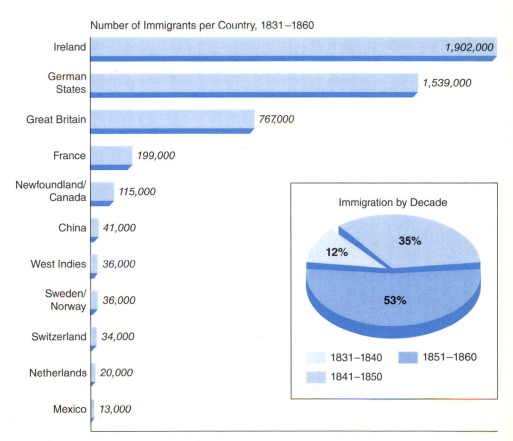

Number of Immigrants per Country, 1831–1860

Country	Number
Ireland	1,902,000
German States	1,539,000
Great Britain	767,000
France	199,000
Newfoundland/Canada	115,000
China	41,000
West Indies	36,000
Sweden/Norway	36,000
Switzerland	34,000
Netherlands	20,000
Mexico	13,000

Immigration by Decade

35% • 12% • 53%

1831–1840   1851–1860
1841–1850

FIGURE 11.1 Major Sources of Immigration to the United States, 1831–1860

Most immigrants came from two areas: Great Britain, of which Ireland was a part, and the German states. These two areas sent more immigrants between 1830 and 1860 than the inhabitants of the United States enumerated at the first census in 1790. By 1860, 15 percent of the white population was of foreign birth.

Source: Data from Stephan Thernstrom, ed., Harvard Encyclopedia of American Ethnic Groups [Cambridge, Mass., and London: Harvard University Press, 1980], 1047.

During the peak period of pre–Civil War immigra-tion (1847–1857), 3.3 million immigrants entered the United States, including 1.3 million Irish and 1.1 million Germans. By 1860, 15 percent of the white population was foreign-born, with 90 percent of immigrants living in northern states. Not all planned to stay perma-nently, and many, like the Irish, saw themselves as exiles from their homeland.

A combination of factors "pushed" Europeans from their homes and "pulled" them to the northern United States. In Ireland, the potato famine (1845–1850)—a period of widespread starvation caused by a diseased potato crop—drove millions from their homeland. Although economic conditions pushed most Germans as well, some were political refugees—liberals, freethinkers, Socialists, communists, and anarchists—who fled after the abortive revolutions of 1848. Europeans' awareness of the United States grew as employers, states, and shipping companies promoted opportunities across the Atlantic. Often the message was stark: work and prosper in America, where everyone could aspire to be an independent farmer, or starve in Europe. Although boosters promised immigrants a land of milk and honey, many soon became disillusioned; hundreds of thousands returned home.

Many early immigrants lived or worked in rural areas. A few settled immedi-ately on farms and eventually bought land. Others, unable to afford even a modest down payment on a farm, worked as hired farm hands, canal diggers, or railroad track layers—often hoping to buy land later. Pádraig Cúndún was among the lucky. The Irishman used his earnings as a canal laborer to buy land in western New York, proclaiming proudly in 1834 that "I have a fine farm of land now, which I own outright. No one can demand rent from me. My family and I can eat our fill of bread and meat, butter and milk any day we like throughout the year, so I think being here is better than staying in Ireland, landless and powerless, without food or clothing." By the 1840s and 1850s—when the steady stream of immigration turned into a flood—the prospects of buying land became more remote.

By 1860, most immigrants settled in cities, often the port at which they arrived. The most destitute could not afford the canal or railroad fare to places farther in-land. Others arrived with resources but fell victim to swindlers who preyed on newly arrived immigrants. Others liked the cities' ethnic flair. In 1855, 52 percent of New York's 623,000 inhabitants were immigrants, 28 percent from Ireland and 16 percent from the German states. Boston, another major entry port, took on a European tone; throughout the 1850s, the city was about 35 percent foreign-born, of whom more than two-thirds were Irish.

Most of the new immigrants from Ireland were young, poor, from rural districts, and Roman Catholic. Women found work as domestic servants or mill hands, while men worked in construction or transportation. Very few Germans settled in New England; most of them came with enough resources to head to the upper Mississippi and Ohio valleys, to states such as Ohio, Illinois, Wisconsin, and Missouri. Although some southern cities like Charleston and Savannah had significant numbers of Irish immigrants, the vast majority of European immigrants, many of whom arrived with aversions to slavery and to semitropical heat, settled in the Northeast or Midwest.

Ethnic Tensions   Tension—often resulting from anxieties over the era's eco-nomic changes—characterized the relationship between native-born Americans and immigrants, particularly Irish Catholics. Native-born workers blamed immigrants for scarce job opportunities and low wages. Middle-class whites blamed them for poverty and crime. As they saw it, immigrants' moral depravity—not poor wages—led to poverty.

Native-born Americans often associated the Irish with another group whom they deemed morally inferior: African Americans. White northerners often portrayed Irish immigrants as nonwhite, as African in appearance. But Irish and African Americans did not develop a sense of solidarity. Instead, some of the era's most virulent riots erupted between Irish immigrants and African Americans.

Closely related to racial stereotyping was anti-Catholicism, which became strident in the 1830s. In Boston, anti-Catholic riots occurred frequently. Nearby Charlestown, Massachusetts, saw a mob burn a convent in 1834. In Philadelphia, a crowd attacked priests and nuns, and vandalized churches in 1844, and in Lawrence, Massachusetts, a mob leveled the Irish neighborhood in 1854. Anti-Catholic violence spread beyond urban areas—riots between native-born and Irish workers erupted along the nation's canals and railroads—but urban riots usually attracted more newspaper attention, fueling fears that cities were violent, depraved places.

German immigrants, at least the majority who were Protestants, mostly fared better than the Irish. In part because Germans generally arrived with some resources and skills, Americans stereotyped them as hard working, self-reliant, and intelligent. But non-Protestant Germans—Catholics and Jews (whom white Americans considered a separate race) frequently encountered hostility fed by racial and religious prejudice.

Immigrants often lived in ethnic enclaves. Intolerance between Protestants and Catholics ran both ways, and Irish Catholics tended to live in their own neighborhoods, where they established Catholic churches and schools. In larger cities, immigrants from the same German states clustered together. Immigrants set up social clubs and mutual-aid societies, such as the Hibernian Society and Sons of Erin (Irish), and B'nai B'rith (Jewish).

People of Color   African Americans also forged their own communities and culture. As late as the 1830s, significant numbers of them remained enslaved in New York and New Jersey, but the numbers of free African Americans grew steadily, and by 1860 nearly 250,000 (many of them refugees from southern slavery) lived in the urban North. Despite differences in status, occupation, wealth, education, and religion, African Americans often felt a sense of racial solidarity. African Methodist Episcopal churches and preachers helped forge communities. Chapels and social halls functioned as town halls and school buildings. Ministers were political leaders, and their halls housed political forums, conventions, and protest meetings.

But white racism impinged on every aspect of northern African Americans' lives. Streetcars, hotels, restaurants, and theaters could turn away African Americans with no legal penalty. City laws barred African Americans from entering public buildings. Even where laws were more liberal, popular attitudes among whites constrained African Americans' opportunities. In Massachusetts, for example, African Americans enjoyed more legal rights than anywhere else in the country. Yet laws protecting civil and political rights could not make whites shop at black businesses. "Colored men in business in Massachusetts receive more respect, and less patronage than in any place I know of," proclaimed a prominent African American lawyer.

African Americans were excluded from factory and clerical jobs. Women worked as house servants, cooks, washerwomen, and child nurses. Most African American men worked as construction workers, porters, longshoremen, or day laborers—all jobs subject to frequent periods of unemployment. Others found employment in the lower-paying but more stable service industry, working as servants, waiters, cooks, barbers, and janitors. Many African American men became sailors and merchant seamen, as commercial sailing offered regular employment and opportunities for advancement, though not protection from racial taunts.

In the growing cities, African Americans turned service occupations into businesses, opening their own restaurants, taverns, hotels, barber shops, and employment agencies for domestic servants. Some became caterers. Others sold used clothing or were junk dealers or small-job contractors. A few became wealthy, invested in real estate, and loaned money. With professionals—ministers, teachers, physicians, dentists, lawyers, and newspaper editors—they formed a small but growing African American middle class.

In cities large and small, African Americans became targets of urban violence. White rioters clubbed and stoned African Americans, destroying their houses, churches, and businesses—and sent African Americans fleeing for their lives. Philadelphia experienced the most violence, with five major riots in the 1830s and 1840s, and major riots occurred in Providence and New York, where in July of 1834 more than sixty buildings were vandalized or destroyed during a three-day riot. By 1860, many hundreds of African Americans had died in urban riots.

Urban Culture   Living in cramped, squalid conditions, working-class families— white and black, immigrant and native-born—spent little time indoors. In the 1840s, a working-class youth culture developed on the Bowery, one of New York's entertainment strips. The lamp-lit promenade, lined with theaters, dance halls, and cafés, became an urban midway. Older and more elite New Yorkers often feared the "Bowery boys and gals." The Bowery boys' greased hair, distinctive clothing, and swaggering gait frightened many middle-class New Yorkers, as did the Bowery girls' colorful costumes and ornate hats, which contrasted with genteel ladies' own modest veils and bonnets. Equally scandalous to an older generation were the middle-class clerks who succumbed to the city's temptations, most notably prostitution.

Gangs of garishly dressed young men and women—flaunting their sexuality, using foul language, sometimes speaking in foreign tongues, and drinking to excess—drove self-styled respectable citizenry to establish private clubs and associations. Some joined the Masonic order, which offered everything the bustling, chaotic city did not: an elaborate hierarchy, an older code of deference between ranks, harmony, and shared values. Although the Masons admitted men only, women organized their own associations, including literary clubs and benevolent societies.

Increasingly, urban recreation and sports became formal commodities to be purchased. One had to buy a ticket to go to the theater, the circus, P. T. Barnum's American Museum in New York City, the racetrack, or the ballpark. Horseracing, walking races, and, in the 1850s, baseball attracted large urban male crowds. Start-ing in 1831, enthusiasts could read the all-sports newspaper, *Spirit of the Times*. A group of Wall Street office workers formed the Knickerbocker Club in 1842 and in 1845 drew up rules for the game of baseball. By 1849, news of boxing was so much in demand that a round-by-round account of a Maryland boxing match was telegraphed throughout the East.

A theater was often the second public building constructed in a town, after a church. Large cities boasted two or more theaters catering to different classes. Some plays cut across class lines—Shakespeare was performed so often and appre-ciated so widely that even illiterate theatergoers knew his plays well—yet the same taste in plays did not soothe class tensions. In 1849, a dispute between an American and a British actor about how to properly stage Shakespeare's *Macbeth* escalated into a working-class riot at New York City's elitist Astor Place Opera House, which hosted the British actor. It was, as one observer explained, "the rich against the poor—the aristocracy against the people." As the disorder escalated, bringing thou-sands into the streets, militia fired into the working-class crowd, killing at least twenty-seven and injuring about 150.

In the 1840s, singing groups, theater troupes, and circuses traveled from city to city. Minstrel shows were particularly popular, featuring white men (often Irish) in burnt-cork makeup imitating African Americans in song, dance, and patter. In the early 1830s, Thomas D. Rice of New York became famous for his role as Jim Crow, an old southern slave. In ill-fitting patched clothing and torn shoes, the blackface Rice shuffled, danced, and sang. Minstrel performers told jokes mocking economic and political elites, and evoked nostalgia for preindustrial work habits and morality, as supposedly embodied by carefree black men. At the same time, the antics of blackface actors encouraged a racist stereotyping of African Americans as sensual and lazy.

The Penny Press

Accounts of urban culture peppered the penny press, a new journalistic form that emerged in the 1830s, soon sweeping northern cities, particularly the ports of New York, Boston, Philadelphia, and Baltimore. Made possible by technological advances—the advent of the steam-powered press, improved methods for producing paper, and trans-portation innovations—the penny press (each newspaper cost one cent) contrasted in fundamental ways to the established six-cent newspapers. The older papers cov-ered mostly commercial news and identified strongly with a political party; politi-cians themselves supplied much of the content, often reprinting their speeches. The penny press, by contrast, proclaimed political independence and dispersed paid reporters to cover local, national, and even international stories. Unlike six-cent newspapers, which relied primarily on mail subscriptions and contributions from political parties for their revenue, penny newspapers were sold by newsboys on the street, earned money by selling advertising, and circulated in much greater numbers to a more economically diverse readership. For the first time, working-class people could afford to buy newspapers regularly.

Penny newspapers focused on daily life, what today would be called "human in-terest stories," giving individuals of one social class the opportunity to peer into the lives of different classes, ethnicities, and races. Working- and middle-class readers, for example, could read about high society—its balls, its horse-racing, its excesses of various sorts. Wealthy and middle-class readers encountered stories about life in poorer neighborhoods—its crime, poverty, and insalubrious conditions. The penny press often sensationalized or slanted the news, and, in the process, influenced urban dwellers' views of one another, and of cities themselves.

Cities as Symbols of Progress   Many northerners saw cities—with their mixtures of people, rapid growth, municipal improvements, and violence—as symbolizing at once progress and decay. On the one hand, cities represented economic advancement; new ones grew at the crossroads of transportation and commerce. Cities nurtured churches, schools, civil governments, and museums—all signs of civilization and culture. As canals and railroads opened the West for mass settlement, many white northerners applauded the appearance of what they called "civilization"—church steeples, public buildings—in areas that had recently been what they called "savage wilderness"; that is, territory controlled by Native Americans. One Methodist newspaper remarked in 1846 that the nation's rapid expansion westward would outpace "our means of moral and intellectual improvement." But the remedies, the editor noted, were evident: bring churches, schools, and moral reform societies to the West. "Cities, civilization, religion, mark our progress," he declared. To many nineteenth-century white Americans, cities represented the moral triumph of civilization over savagery and heathenism.

Yet some of the same Americans deplored the everyday character of the nation's largest cities, which they saw as havens of disease, poverty, crime, and vice. To many middle-class observers, disease combined with crime to represent moral decline. They considered epidemics to be divine scourges, striking primarily those who were filthy, intemperate, and immoral. Many middle-class and wealthy people believed epidemics resulted from the urban poor's moral degradation. Theft and prostitution provided evidence of moral vice, and wealthy observers perceived these crimes not as by-products of poverty but as signs of individual failing. They responded by pressing for laws against vagrancy and disturbing the peace, and by pushing city officials to establish the nation's first police forces. Boston hired daytime policemen in 1838 to supplement its part-time night watchmen and constables, and New York formed its own police force, modeled on London's, in 1845.

How did northerners reconcile urban vice and depravity with their view of cities as symbols of progress? Middle-class reformers focused on purifying cities of disease and vice. If disease was a divine punishment—rather than an offshoot of cramped conditions engendered by economic change—then it was within Americans' power to fix things. Middle-class reformers took to the streets and back alleys, trying to convince the urban working classes that life would improve if they gave up alcohol, worked even harder, and prayed frequently. They talked about how the northern working poor—unlike southern slaves—could improve their condition through hard work and virtuous habits. This belief in upward mobility became central to many northerners' ideas about progress.

Belief in upward mobility related to the idea of free labor, the concept that, in a competitive marketplace, those who worked hard and lived virtuous lives could improve their status. Free-labor ideology appealed especially to manufacturers and merchants eager to believe that their own success emerged from hard work and moral virtue—and eager as well to encourage their factory hands and clerks to work hard and live virtuously, to remain optimistic despite current hardships. Many laborers initially rejected free-labor ideology, seeing it as a veiled attempt to tout industrial work habits, to rationalize poor wages, and to quell worker protest. But by the 1850s, when the question of slavery's westward expansion returned to the political foreground, more and more northerners would embrace free-labor ideology and come to see slavery as antithetical to the free-labor ideology of the North. It was this way of thinking, perhaps more than anything else, that made the North distinctive.

SUMMARY

During the first half of the nineteenth century, the North became rapidly enmeshed in a commercial culture. Northern states and capitalists invested heavily in internal improvements, helping to propel the North down a new development track. Most northerners now turned either toward commercial farming or, in smaller numbers, toward industrial wage labor. Farmers gave up mixed agriculture and specialized in cash crops, while their children often went to work in factories or countinghouses.

To many northerners, the market economy symbolized progress, in which they found much to celebrate: easier access to cheap western lands, employment for surplus farm laborers, and the ready commercial availability of goods that had once been time-consuming to produce. At the same time, though, the market economy led to increased specialization, a less personal workplace, complex market relationships, more regimentation, a sharper divide between work and leisure, and a degradation of natural resources. Northerners' involvement in the market economy also tied them more directly to fluctuating national and international markets, and during economic downturns, many northern families experienced destitution.

With parents relying less directly on children's labor, northerners began producing smaller families. Even as working-class children continued to work as canal drivers and factory hands (or to scavenge urban streets), middle-class families created a sheltered model of childhood in which they tried to shield children from the perceived dangers of the world outside the family. Their mothers, in theory, became moral guardians of the household, keeping the home safe from the encroachment of the new economy's competitiveness and selfishness. Few women, though, had the luxury to devote themselves entirely to nurturing their children and husbands.

Immigrants and free African Americans performed much of the lowest-paying work in the expanding economy, and many native-born whites blamed them for the problems that accompanied the era's rapid economic changes. Anti-immigrant (especially anti-Catholic) and antiblack riots became commonplace. At the same time, immigrants and African Americans worked to form their own communities.

Cities came to symbolize for many Americans both the possibilities and the limits of market expansion. Urban areas were marked by extremes of wealth, and they fostered vibrant working-class cultures even as they encouraged poverty, crime, and mob violence. To reconcile the seeming contradictions of progress—the coexistence, for example, of abundance and destitution—middle-class northerners articulated an ideology of free labor, touting the possibility for upward mobility in a competitive marketplace. This ideology would become increasingly central to northern regional identity.

12

REFORM AND POLITICS 1824–1845

FROM REVIVAL TO REFORM

A series of religious revivals in the late eighteenth and early nineteenth centuries—sometimes called the Second Great Awakening for their resemblance to revivals of the Great Awakening of the eighteenth century—raised people's hopes for the Second Coming of the Christian messiah and the establishment of the Kingdom of God on earth. Revivalists resolved to speed the millennium, or the thousand years of peace on earth that would accompany Christ's Second Coming, by combating sin. Some believed the United States had a special mission in God's design and a special role in eliminating evil. If sin and evil could be eliminated, individuals and society could be perfected. Revivalists called on individuals to renounce personal sins, such as drinking, swearing, and licentiousness. They also called on individuals to combat social evils, including—most prominently—slavery, but also dueling and desecration of the Sabbath. Not until all Americans had been converted, and all social evils suppressed, would Christ make his Second Coming.

Because it was not enough for an individual to embrace God and godliness, revivalists strove for large-scale conversions. Rural women, men, and children traveled long distances to camp meetings, where they listened to fiery sermons preached day and night from hastily constructed platforms and tents in forests or open fields. In cities, women in particular attended daily church services and prayer meetings, sometimes for months on end. Converts renounced personal sin, vowed to live sanctified lives, and committed themselves to helping others see the light.

CHRONOLOGY

1790s–1840s	Second Great Awakening
1820s	Model penitentiaries established
1820s–40s	Utopian communities founded
1824	No electoral-college majority in presidential election
1825	House of Representatives elects Adams president
1826	American Society for the Promotion of Temperance founded
1828	Tariff of Abominations passed
	Jackson elected president
1830	Joseph Smith organizes Mormon Church
1830s–40s	Democratic-Whig competition gels in second party system
1831	Garrison first publishes *The Liberator*
	Antimasons hold first national political convention
1832	Jackson vetoes rechartering Second Bank of the United States
	Jackson reelected president
1832–33	Nullification Crisis
1836	Specie Circular
	Van Buren elected president
1837	*Caroline* affair
	Financial panic ends boom of the 1830s
1837–42	Croton Aqueduct constructed
1838–39	United States and Canada mobilize militias over border dispute
1839–43	Hard times spread unemployment and deflation
1840	Whigs win presidency under Harrison
1841	Tyler assumes presidency after Harrison's death
1846	Smithsonian Institution founded
1848	Seneca Falls Woman's Rights Convention
	American Association for the Advancement of Science established

Revivals   The most famous revival was at Cane Ridge, Kentucky, in August 1801. One report estimated 25,000 people attended, including men and women, free and enslaved, at a time when Kentucky's largest city, Lexington, had fewer than two thousand inhabitants. The call to personal repentance and conversion invigorated southern Protestantism, giving churches an evangelical base. Although laws often restricted or outlawed black churches and preachers, particularly after Nat Turner's bloody revolt in 1831, in practice black and mixed churches often flourished on the local level, with black and white evangelicals forging a united front against their profane neighbors. During the 1840s and 1850s, though, as the slavery issue increasingly entered public debate, southern Presbyterian, Baptist, and Methodist churches seceded from their denominations' national conferences. For the white leaders of these secessionist churches, slavery did not impede human perfectibility but rather ensured it; the paternal guidance of benevolent masters, they reasoned, would bring Africans to Christ.

All revivalists shared a belief in individual self-improvement, but northern revivalists also emphasized communal improvement, becoming missionaries for both individual salvation and social reform. Northern evangelists generated new religious groups and voluntary reform societies. Preachers like Lyman Beecher, who made his base in New England before moving to Cincinnati, and Charles Finney, who traveled the canals and roads linking the Northeast to the Midwest, argued that evil was avoidable, that Christians were not doomed by original sin, and that anyone could achieve salvation. In everyday language, Finney—a former lawyer—preached that "God has made man a moral free agent." Finney's brand of revivalism transcended sects, class, and race. At first a Presbyterian, he eventually became a Methodist. Revivalism thrived among Methodists and Baptists, whose denominational structures maximized democratic participation and drew ministers from ordinary folk.

Finney achieved his greatest successes in the area of western New York that had experienced rapid changes in transportation and industrialization—in what he called the "Burned-Over District" because of the region's intense evangelical fires. Rapid change raised fears of social disorder—family dissolution, drinking, swearing, and prostitution. Many individuals worried, too, whether their status would improve or decline in an economy cycling through booms and busts.

When northern revivalist preachers emphasized the importance of good works—good deeds and piety—they helped ignite many of the era's social reform movements,

Old Sturbridge Village

Often attracting worshippers in the thousands, revivalist meetings became known as "camp meetings" because the faithful camped out for days at a time to hear charismatic preachers, who offered sermons day and night.

which began in the Burned-Over District and spread eastward to New England and the Middle Atlantic and westward to the upper Midwest. Evangelically inspired reform associations together constituted what historians call the "benevolent empire." While advocating for distinct causes, these associations shared a commitment to human perfectibility, and they often turned to the same wealthy men for financial resources and advice.

Moral Reform   Those resources enabled them to make good use of the era's new technologies—steam presses and railroads—to spread the evangelical word. By mass-producing pamphlets and newspapers for distribution far into the country's interior, reformers spread their message throughout the Northeast and Midwest, strengthening cultural connections between regions increasingly tied together economically. With canals and railroads making travel easier, reformers could attend annual conventions and contact like-minded people personally, and local reform societies could host speakers from distant places. Most reform organizations, like political parties, sponsored weekly newspapers, creating a virtual community of reformers.

While industrialists and merchants provided financial resources for evangelical reform, their wives and daughters solicited new members and circulated petitions. The cult of domesticity, which arose in tandem with industrialization and the revivals, assigned women the role of moral guardianship of their families; reformers expanded that role beyond the domestic sphere into the public realm. Women undertook to do more than provide moral guidance to their own children; they would help run reformatories for wayward youth or establish asylums for orphans. Participation in reform movements thus allowed women to exercise moral authority outside the household, giving them a new sense of influence. They might both improve people's lives and hasten the millennium. Women also enjoyed the friendships and intellectual comraderie with other women that participation in benevolent societies fostered. Although some elite women in Upper South cities formed and joined reform societies, moral reform was primarily a northeastern and midwestern phenomenon.

Many female reformers had attended a female academy or seminary, where the curriculum included arts of "refinement"—music, dance, penmanship—but focused on science and literature. Based on the notion that women were men's intellectual equals, the curriculum was modeled on that of men's colleges, and by 1820, approximately the same number of men and women attended institutions of higher education. At the female academies and seminaries, and at the hundreds of reading circles and literary societies in which their alumnae participated, women honed their intellectual and persuasive skills, preparing themselves to influence public opinion even as many of them maintained substantial domestic responsibilities. A few of these women became prominent editors and writers, but most influenced society as educators and, especially, reformers.

For women and some men, reform represented their primary form of political influence at a time when the vote was restricted to property-owning men. The aftermath of an 1830 exposé of prostitution in New York City illustrates how reform led to political action. Even as female reformers organized a shelter for the city's prostitutes and tried to secure respectable employment for them, they publicized the names of brothel clients to shame the men contributing to the women's waywardness. The New York women organized themselves into the Female Moral Reform Society, expanding their geographic scope and activities. By 1840, it had 555 affiliated chapters across the nation. In the next few years, it entered the political sphere by lobbying successfully for criminal sanctions in New York State against men who seduced women into prostitution. If only prostitutes could be freed from the corrupting reach of the men who preyed on them, reformers believed, so-called fallen women might be morally uplifted.

Penitentiaries and Asylums

A similar belief in perfectibility led reformers to establish penitentiaries for criminals and delinquents that aimed not simply to punish, as jails did, but to transform criminals into productive members of society through disciplined regimens. Under the "Auburn System," prisoners worked together in the daytime but were isolated at night, while under the "Philadelphia System," utter silence and isolation prevailed day and night. Isolation and silence were meant to enable reflection and redemption—to provide opportunities for penitence—within individual prisoners. When Frenchman Alexis de Tocqueville came to America in 1831 to study its prisons, he noted that the Philadelphia system made him feel as if he "had traversed catacombs; there were a thousand living beings, and yet it was desert solitude."

Other reformers sought to improve treatment of the mentally ill, who were frequently imprisoned, often alongside criminals, and put in cages or dark dungeons, chained to walls, brutalized, or held in solitary confinement. Dorothea Dix, the movement's leader, exemplifies the early-nineteenth-century reformer who started with a religious belief in individual self-improvement and human perfectibility, and moved into social action by advocating collective responsibility. Investigating asylums, petitioning the Massachusetts legislature, and lobbying other states and Congress, Dix moved from reform to politics and helped create a new public role for women. In response to Dix's efforts, twenty-eight of thirty-three states built public institutions for the mentally ill by 1860.

Temperance

Temperance advocates, who pushed for either partial or full abstinence from alcoholic beverages, likewise crossed from the personal into the political sphere. Drinking was widespread in the early nineteenth century, when men gathered in public houses and rural inns to drink whiskey, rum, and hard cider while they gossiped, talked politics, and played cards. Contracts were sealed, celebrations commemorated, and harvests toasted with liquor. "Respectable" women did not drink in public, but many tippled alcohol-based patent medicines promoted as cure-alls.

Evangelicals considered drinking sinful, and in many denominations, forsaking alcohol was part of conversion. Preachers condemned alcohol for violating the Sabbath—the only day workers had off, which some spent at the public house. Factory owners condemned alcohol for making workers unreliable. Civic leaders connected alcohol with crime. Middleclass reformers, often women, condemned it for squandering wages, diverting men from their family responsibilities, and fostering abusive behavior at home. In the early 1840s, thousands of ordinary women formed Martha Washington societies to protect families by reforming alcoholics, raising children as teetotalers, and spreading the temperance message. Abstinence from alcohol, reformers believed, would foster both religious perfectibility and secular progress. They hoped to quash the raucous drinking culture.

As the temperance movement gained momentum, its goal shifted from moderation to voluntary abstinence and finally to prohibition. By the mid-1830s, five thousand state and local temperance societies touted teetotalism, and more than a million people had taken the pledge of abstinence, including several hundred thousand children who enlisted in the Cold Water Army. Per capita consumption of alcohol fell from five gallons per year in 1800 to below two gallons in the 1840s. The American Society for the Promotion of Temperance, organized in 1826 to promote pledges of abstinence, became a pressure group for legislation to end alcohol manufacture and sale. In 1851, Maine became the first state to ban alcohol except for medicinal purposes; by 1855, similar laws had been enacted throughout New England and in New York, Pennsylvania, and the Midwest.

The temperance campaign had a nativist—or anti-immigrant and anti-Catholic—strain to it. The Irish and Germans, complained the *American Protestant Magazine* in 1849, "bring the grog shops like the frogs of Egypt upon us." Along the nation's canals, reformers lamented the hundreds of taverns catering to the largely Irish work force, and in the cities, they expressed outrage at the Sunday tradition of urban German families' gathering at beer gardens to eat and drink, to dance and sing, and sometimes to play cards. Some Catholics heeded the message, pledging abstinence and forming their own organizations, such as the St. Mary's Mutual Benevolence Total Abstinence Society in Boston.

But temperance spawned strong opposition, too. Many workers—Protestants as well as Catholics—rejected what they saw as reformers' efforts to impose middle-class values on people whose lives they did not understand, and they steadfastly defended their right to drink whatever they pleased. Workers agreed that poverty and crime were problems but believed that poor wages, not drinking habits, were responsible. Even some who abstained from alcohol opposed prohibition, believing that drinking should be a matter of self-control, not state coercion.

Public Schools   Protestants and Catholics often quarreled over education as well. Public education usually included religious education, but when teachers taught Protestant beliefs and used the King James version of the Bible, Catholics established their own schools, which taught Catholic doctrines. Some Protestants began to fear that Catholics would never assimilate into American culture, and some charged Catholics with being exclusionists, plotting to undermine the republic and impose papal control. Yet even as these conflicts brewed, public education touched the lives of more Americans than did any other reform movement.

The movement's leader was Horace Mann, a Massachusetts lawyer and reformer from humble beginnings. Mann advocated free, tax-supported education to replace church schools and the private schools set up by untrained, itinerant young men. Universal education, Mann proposed, would end misery and crime, and would help Americanize immigrants. "If we do not prepare children to become good citizens," he argued, "if we do not develop their capacities, imbue their hearts with the love of truth and duty, and a reverence for all things sacred and holy, then our republic must go down to destruction."

During Mann's tenure as secretary of the Massachusetts Board of Education from 1837 to 1848, Massachusetts led the "common school" movement, establishing schools for training teachers (the "normal school," modeled on the French *école normale*, and the forerunner of teacher-training colleges); lengthening the school year; and raising teachers' salaries to make the profession more attractive. In keeping with the era's notions that women had special claims to morality and that they could be paid less because they were by nature dependents, Mann envisioned a system in which women would prepare future clerks, farmers, and workers with a practical curriculum that deemphasized classics in favor of geography, arithmetic, and science. Like other reform movements, educational reform rested on the notions of progress and perfectibility; given the proper guidance, individuals could educate themselves out of their material and moral circumstances.

Thanks in part to expanding public education, by 1850 the vast majority of native-born white Americans were literate. Newspapers and magazines proliferated, and bookstores spread. Power printing presses and better transportation made possible wide distribution of books and periodicals. The religious press—of both traditional sects and revivalists—produced pamphlets, hymnals, Bibles, and religious newspapers. Secular newspapers and magazines—political organs, the penny press, and literary journals—also abounded from the 1830s on.

Engineering and Science   Public education's emphasis on science reflected a broader tendency to look not just to moral reform but also to engineering and science to remedy the nation's problems. Not everyone blamed epidemics on immorality, for example; scientists and doctors saw unclean, stagnant water as the culprit. With its Fairmount Water Works, constructed between 1819 and 1822, Philadelphia took the lead in building municipal waterworks. After the devastating cholera epidemic of 1832, New York City planned its own massive waterworks: Between 1837 and 1842, it built the 41-mile Croton Aqueduct, an elaborate system of iron pipes encased in brick masonry that brought water from upstate New York to Manhattan.

Science became increasingly important nationally, too, with the founding of institutions that still exist today. After James Smithson, a wealthy British scientist, left his estate to the United States government, Congress established the Smithsonian Institution (1846), which acquired and disseminated scientific knowledge. The Smithsonian's director was Joseph Henry, one of the nation's most talented scientists; his experiments in electromagnetism helped make possible both the telegraph and, later in the century, the telephone. In 1848, Henry helped found the American Association for the Advancement of Science to promote scientific collaboration and, thus, advancement. That Henry was a devoutly religious man did not deter him from seeking scientific knowledge. For many nineteenth-century Americans, particularly those in nonrevivalist sects, religious devotion and scientific inquiry were compatible. They saw scientific discoveries as signs of progress, reassuring them that the millennium was approaching. God had created the natural world, they believed, and it was their Christian duty to perfect it in preparation for God's return.

The Croton Aqueduct, shown here near Harlem, New York, was an engineering marvel of its time. It brought fresh water to New York City.

UTOPIAN EXPERIMENTS

Some idealists dreamed of an entirely new social order. They established dozens of utopian communities—ideal communities designed as models for broader society—based on either religious principles, a desire to resist what they deemed the market economy's excessive individualism, or both. Some groups, like the Mormons, arose during the Second Great Awakening, while others, like the Shakers, had originated in eighteenth-century Europe. Utopian communities attempted to recapture what they perceived as the past's more communal nature, even as they offered sometimes-radical departures from established practices of marriage and child rearing.

Mormons

No utopian experiment had a more lasting influence than the Church of Jesus Christ of Latter-day Saints, whose members were known as the Mormons. During the religious ferment of the 1820s in western New York, Joseph Smith, a young farmer, reported that an angel called Moroni had given him divinely engraved gold plates. Smith published his revelations as the *Book of Mormon* and organized a church in 1830. The next year, the community moved west to Ohio to build a "New Jerusalem" and await the Second Coming of Jesus.

After angry mobs drove the Mormons from Ohio, they settled in Missouri. Anti-Mormons charged that Mormonism was a scam by Joseph Smith, and feared Mormon economic and political power. In 1838, Missouri's governor charged Smith with fomenting insurrection and worked to indict him and other leaders for treason.

Smith and his followers left for Nauvoo, Illinois. The state legislature gave them a city charter making them self-governing and authorized a local militia. But again the Mormons met antagonism, especially after Smith introduced the practice of polygamy in 1841, allowing men to have several wives at once. The next year, Smith became mayor, and this consolidation of religious and political power, as well as Nauvoo's petition to the federal government to be a self-governing territory, further antagonized opponents, now including some former Mormons. In 1844, after Smith and his brother were charged with treason and jailed, and then murdered, the Mormons left Illinois to seek security in the western wilderness. Under the leadership of Brigham Young, they established a cooperative community in the Great Salt Lake valley.

There, the Mormons distributed agricultural land according to family size. An extensive irrigation system, constructed by men who contributed their labor in proportion to the quantity of land they received and the amount of water they expected to use, transformed the arid valley into a rich oasis. As the colony developed, the church elders gained control of water, trade, industry, and eventually the territorial government of Utah.

Shakers

The Shakers, the largest communal utopian experiment, reached their peak between 1820 and 1860, with six thousand members in twenty settlements in eight states. Shaker communities emphasized agriculture and handcrafts, selling their products beyond their own community; most became self-sufficient and profitable enterprises. The community's craft tradition contrasted with the new factory regime. But the Shakers were essentially a spiritual community. Founded in England in 1772 by Mother Ann Lee, their name derived from their worship service, which included shaking their entire bodies, singing, dancing, and shouting. Ann Lee's children had died in infancy, and she saw their deaths as retribution for her sin of intercourse; thus, she advocated celibacy. After imprisonment in England in 1773–1774, she settled in America.

In religious practice and social relations, Shakers offered an alternative to the era's rapid changes. Shakers lived communally, with men and women in separate quarters; individual families were abolished. Men and women shared leadership equally. Many Shaker settlements became temporary refuges for orphans, widows, runaways, abused wives, and laid-off workers. Their settlements depended on new recruits, not only because the practice of celibacy meant no reproduction, but also because some members left, unsuited to either communal living or the Shakers' spiritual message.

Oneidans, Owenites, and Fourierists

Other utopian communities joined in resisting the social changes accompanying industrialism. John Humphrey Noyes, a lawyer converted by Finney's revivals, established two perfectionist communities: first in Putney, Vermont, in 1835, and then—after being indicted for adultery—in Oneida, New York, in 1848. Noyes decried individualism, advocating instead communal property ownership, communal child rearing, and "complex marriage," in which all the community's men were married to all its women, but in which a woman could accept or reject a sexual proposition. The Oneida Colony forbade exclusive sexual relationships and required men to practice "male continence," or intercourse without ejaculation, in order to promote relationships built on more than sexual fulfillment. Pregnancies were to be planned; couples applied to Noyes for permission to have a child, or Noyes assigned two people to reproduce with each other. Robert Dale Owen's community in New Harmony, Indiana (1825–1828), also abolished private property and advocated communal child rearing. The Fourierists, named after French philosopher Charles Fourier, established more than two dozen communities in the Northeast and Midwest; these communities, too, resisted individualism and promoted equality between the sexes.

The most famous Fourier community was Brook Farm, in West Roxbury, Massachusetts, near Boston. Inspired by transcendentalism—the belief that the physical world is secondary to the spiritual realm, which human beings can reach not by custom and experience but only by intuition—Brook Farm's members rejected materialism. Their rural communalism combined spirituality, manual labor, intellectual life, and play. Originally founded in 1841 by the Unitarian minister George Ripley, Brook Farm attracted farmers, craftsmen, and writers, among them the novelist Nathaniel Hawthorne. Brook Farm residents contributed regularly to the *Dial*, the leading Transcendentalist journal. Although Unitarians were not evangelicals, their largely middle- and upper-class followers had a long-standing "devotion to progress," as one of their most influential ministers put it. In 1845, Brook Farm's one hundred members organized themselves into phalanxes (working-living units), following a model suggested by Fourier. As rigid regimentation replaced individualism, membership dropped. A year after a disastrous fire in 1846, the experiment collapsed.

After visiting Brook Farm in 1843, Transcendentalist Henry David Thoreau decided that organized utopian communities did not suit him: "As for these communities, I think I had rather keep bachelor's hall in hell than go to board in heaven." Two years later, Thoreau constructed his own one-man utopia in a small cabin along the shores of Walden Pond, in Massachusetts, where he mediated and wrote about nature, morality, spirituality, progress, society, and government.

American Renaissance

Thoreau joined a literary outpouring known today as the American Renaissance. Ralph Waldo Emerson, a pillar of the transcendental movement, was its prime inspiration. After quitting his Boston Unitarian ministry in 1831, followed by a two-year sojourn in Europe, Emerson returned to lecture and write, preaching individualism and self-reliance. Widely admired, he influenced Hawthorne, *Dial* editor Margaret Fuller, Herman Melville, and Thoreau, among many others. In philosophical intensity and moral idealism, the American Renaissance was both distinctively American and an outgrowth of the European romantic movement. It addressed universal themes using American settings and characters. Hawthorne, for instance, used Puritan New England as a backdrop, and Melville wrote of great spiritual quests as seafaring adventures.

Perhaps more than any other American Renaissance author, Thoreau emphasized individualism and its practical applications. In his 1849 essay on "Resistance to Civil Government" (known after his death as "Civil Disobedience"), Thoreau advocated individual resistance to a government engaged in immoral acts. Thoreau had already put into practice what he preached: In the midst of the War with Mexico (see Chapter 14), Thoreau refused to pay his taxes, believing they would aid an immoral war to expand slavery, and was briefly jailed. "I cannot for an instant recognize that political organization as my government which is the *slave's* government also," Thoreau wrote. Later, in defiance of federal law, Thoreau aided escaped slaves on their way to freedom.

ABOLITIONISM

Thoreau joined evangelical abolitionists in trying to eradicate slavery, which they deemed both an individual and a communal sin suffusing American society. Their efforts built on an earlier generation of antislavery activism.

Early Abolitionism and Colonization   From the nation's earliest days—in places like Philadelphia, New York, Albany, Boston, and Nantucket—free blacks formed societies to petition legislatures, seek judicial redress, stage public marches, and, especially, publish tracts chronicling slavery's horrors. African American abolitionists wrote about slavery's devastating impact on both black and white families, advocated slavery's immediate termination, assisted escaped slaves, and promoted legal equality for free blacks. By 1830, the nation had fifty African American abolitionist societies. But more than anything else, David Walker's words captured white Americans' attention. In his *Appeal … to the Colored Citizens* (1829), Walker—a southern-born free African American—advocated slavery's violent overthrow, igniting fear throughout the white South and much of the North.

Violent overthrow did not figure in the goals of white abolitionists who, after the American Revolution, had come together in places like Boston and, especially, Philadelphia, with its large population of Quakers, whose religious beliefs emphasized human equality. These early antislavery advocates pressed for slavery's gradual abolition and an end to the international slave trade. Although they aided African Americans seeking freedom through judicial decisions, their assumptions about blacks' racial inferiority kept them from advocating for equal rights. Early white abolitionists tended to be wealthy, socially prominent men whose societies excluded women, African Americans, and less elite white men.

More often, elites supported the colonization movement, which crystallized in 1816 with the organization of the American Colonization Society. Its members planned to purchase and relocate American slaves, as well as free blacks, to Africa or the Caribbean. Among its supporters were Thomas Jefferson, James Madison, James Monroe, and Henry Clay, as well as many lesser-known men and women from the North and, especially, the Upper South. In 1824, the society founded Liberia, on Africa's west coast, and began a settlement for African Americans who were willing to go. The society had resettled nearly twelve thousand people in Liberia by 1860. Some colonizationists aimed to strengthen slavery by ridding the South of troublesome slaves or to purge the North of African Americans altogether. Others hoped colonization would improve African Americans' conditions. Although some African Americans supported the movement, black abolitionists generally denounced it.

In the early 1830s, a new group of more radical white abolitionists—most prominently, William Lloyd Garrison—rejected both the violent overthrow advocated by David Walker and the gradual approaches of white legal reformers and colonizationists. Instead, they demanded immediate, complete, and uncompensated emancipation. In the first issue of *The Liberator*, which he began publishing in 1831, Garrison declared, "I am in earnest—I will not equivocate—I will not excuse—I will not retreat a single inch—and *I will be heard.*" Two years later, he founded the American Antislavery Society, which became the era's largest abolitionist organization.

Immediatism

Immediatists, as they came to be called, believed slavery was an absolute sin needing urgent eradication. They were influenced by African American abolitionist societies and by evangelicals' notion that humans, not God, determined their own spiritual fate by deciding whether to choose good or evil. In that sense, all were equal before God's eyes. When all humans had chosen good over evil, the millennium would come. Slavery, however, denied enslaved men and women the ability to make such choices, the ability to act as what Finney called "moral free agents." For every day that slavery continued, the millennium was postponed.

Because the millennium depended on *all* hearts being won over to Christ, because it depended on the perfectibility of everyone, including slaveowners, Garrison advocated "moral suasion." He and his followers hoped to bring about emancipation not through coercion, but by winning the hearts of slaveowners as well as others who supported or tolerated slavery. Evangelical abolitionism depended, then, on large numbers of ministers and laypeople spreading the evangelical message all across the nation.

The Lane Debates

In 1829, Congregationalists and Presbyterians founded the Lane Seminary in Cincinnati to train ministers who would carry the evangelical message westward. With Lyman Beecher as president, it drew northern and southern students, and encouraged "people of color" to apply. Not long after Theodore Weld, one of Charles Finney's most faithful converts, arrived at the Lane Seminary in 1833, he organized what became known as the Lane Debates, eighteen days of discussion among the school's students and faculty about the relative merits of colonization and immediatism. Immediatism won.

Led by Weld, the Lane students and faculty next founded an antislavery society, and expanded their efforts to reach Cincinnati's growing African American population, which in 1829 had been brutally attacked by white people. Fearful of renewed disorder, white business leaders protested against the antislavery society. Lane's trustees, with Beecher's sanction, clamped down, barring further antislavery activities. The "Lane Rebels" publicly broke from the seminary and enrolled in a new seminary at Oberlin, a town in northern Ohio founded as a Christian perfectionist settlement. The new seminary, dedicated to immediatism, became the first college to admit women and one of the first to admit African Americans. Weld declined a faculty post at Oberlin, preferring instead to carry the abolitionist message directly into the western countryside as an agent for the American Antislavery Society.

The American Antislavery Society

By 1838, at its peak, the society had two thousand local affiliates and a membership of over 300,000. Unlike earlier white abolitionist societies, the immediatist organizations welcomed men and women of all racial and class backgrounds. Lydia Maria Child, Maria Chapman, and Lucretia Mott served on its executive committee; Child edited its official paper, the *National Anti-Slavery Standard*, from 1841 to 1843, and Chapman coedited it from 1844 until 1848. The society sponsored black and female speakers, and women undertook most of the day-to-day conversion efforts.

In rural and small-town northern and midwestern communities, women addressed mail, collected signatures, raised money, organized boycotts of textiles made from slave-grown cotton, and increased public awareness. With the "great postal campaign," launched in 1835, the society's membership flooded the mails with antislavery tracts. Women went door to door collecting signatures on antislavery petitions; by 1838, more than 400,000 petitions, each with numerous signatures, had been sent to Congress. Abolitionist-minded women met in "sewing circles," making clothes for escaped slaves while organizing future activities, such as antislavery fairs at which they sold goods—often items they had made themselves—whose proceeds they donated to antislavery causes. These fairs increased their cause's visibility and drew more Americans into direct contact with abolitionists and their ideas.

African American Abolitionists

Even as white abolitionist societies opened membership to African Americans and sponsored speaking tours by former slaves, African Americans continued into the 1840s and 1850s their independent efforts to end slavery and to improve the status of free African Americans. Former slaves—most famously, Frederick Douglass, Henry Bibb, Harriet Tubman, and Sojourner Truth—dedicated their lives to ending slavery through their speeches, publications, and participation in a secret network known as the Underground Railroad, which spirited enslaved men, women, and children to freedom. By the thousands, less famous African Americans continued the work of the postrevolutionary generation and established their churches, founded moral reform societies, published newspapers, created schools and orphanages for African American children, and held conventions to consider tactics for improving African Americans' status within the free states.

Although genuine friendships emerged among white and black abolitionists, many white abolitionists treated blacks as inferiors, driving some African Americans to reject white antislavery organizations and to form their own. Others lacked the patience for the supposed immediatism of William Lloyd Garrison; they did not object to moral suasion, but they sought even more immediate solutions, such as legislation, to African Americans' problems in both the South and the North. African American abolitionists nonetheless took heart in the immediatists' success at winning converts.

Opposition to Abolitionism

But that very success gave rise to a virulent, even violent, opposition. In the South, mobs blocked the distribution of antislavery tracts. In South Carolina, officials intercepted and burned abolitionist literature; in 1835, proslavery assailants killed four abolitionists

LINKS TO THE WORLD

The International Antislavery Movement

The heart of the international antislavery movement had been in Great Britain, but in the 1830s many of Britain's local antislavery societies thought they had accomplished their mission and disbanded. Over the previous three decades, the international slave trade had greatly diminished, and in 1833 Parliament ended slavery in the British Empire. At the same time, however, abolitionism in the United States was on the rise, and now American abolitionists extended their work across the Atlantic. They revived the international movement to end slavery where it still existed—in Spanish possessions like Cuba, in independent and colonial South America, in Africa and Asia, and in the United States.

American abolitionism in the 1830s was invigorated by the militancy of black abolitionists and by the conversion of William Lloyd Garrison to immediatism. Seeking to raise money and to put international pressure on the United States to abolish slavery, African American abolitionists in the 1840s toured Britain regularly. On the lecture circuit and in published narratives, they appealed for support. Especially effective were ex-slaves, who recounted their firsthand experiences of slavery and bared their scarred bodies.

Black abolitionists spoke in small towns and villages, and in Britain's industrial centers. After fugitive slave Moses Gandy toured England, he published his autobiography, the first of dozens of slave narratives published in London. The next year, 1845, Frederick Douglass began a nineteen-month tour, giving three hundred lectures in Britain.

In 1849, black abolitionists William Wells Brown, Alexander Crummell, and J. W. C. Pennington were among the twenty American delegates at the international Paris Peace Conference. There, Brown likened war to slavery, telling the eight hundred delegates from western Europe and the United States that "it is impossible to maintain slavery without maintaining war." His scheduled brief lecture tour in Britain turned into a five-year exile because, after passage of the 1850 Fugitive Slave Law, he feared being seized and sent back to slavery if he returned to the United States. In 1854, he became free when British abolitionists purchased his freedom from his former master.

Gandy, Douglass, Brown, and dozens of other former slaves helped revive abolitionism as an international issue. They energized the British and Foreign Anti-Slavery Society, founded in 1839, and hundreds of more militant local societies. By the early 1850s, national abolitionist movements succeeded in abolishing slavery in Colombia, Argentina, Venezuela, and Peru. Although the United States continued to resist internal and international pressure, its black abolitionists were instrumental not only in reviving the worldwide antislavery movement, but also, as advocates of women's rights, international peace, temperance, and other reforms, in linking Americans to reform movements around the world.

in South Carolina and Louisiana as well as forty people allegedly plotting a slave rebellion in Mississippi and Louisiana.

White northerners had their own reasons for opposing abolition: they recognized cotton's vital economic role, and they feared emancipation would prompt an enormous influx of freed slaves into their own region. Like many southerners, they questioned the institution's morality but not its practicality: They believed blacks to be inherently inferior and incapable of acquiring the attributes—virtue and diligence—required of freedom and citizenship. Some northerners, too, objected to white women's involvement in abolitionism, believing that women's proper role lay within the home.

The North experienced its own anti-abolitionist violence. In Boston, David Walker died under mysterious circumstances in 1830. Among those northerners who most despised abolitionists were "gentlemen of property and standing"—a nineteenth-century term for commercial and political elites—who often had strong economic connections to the southern cotton economy and political connections to leading southerners. Northern gentlemen incited anti-abolitionist riots. In Utica, New York, in 1835 merchants and professionals broke up the state Anti-Slavery Convention, which had welcomed blacks and women. Mob violence peaked that year, with more than fifty riots aimed at abolitionists or African Americans. In 1837, in Alton, Illinois, a mob murdered white abolitionist editor Elijah P. Lovejoy, and rioters sacked his printing office. The following year, rioters in Philadelphia hurled stones and insults at three thousand black and white women attending the Anti-Slavery Convention of American Women in the brand-new Pennsylvania Hall, a building constructed to house abolitionist meetings and an abolitionist bookstore. The following day, a mob burned the building to the ground, three days after its dedication.

Moral Suasion Versus Political Action   Such violence made some immediatists question whether moral suasion was a realistic tactic. Men like James G. Birney, the son of a Kentucky slaveowner, embraced immediatism but believed abolition could be effected only in the male sphere of politics. Involving women violated the natural order of things and detracted from the ultimate goal: freedom for slaves. Thus, when William Lloyd Garrison, an ardent supporter of women's rights, endorsed Abby Kelly's appointment to the American Antislavery Society's business committee, in 1840, he provoked an irreparable split in the abolitionist movement. Arthur Tappan and Theodore Weld led a dissident group that established the American and Foreign Anti-Slavery Society. That society in turn formed a new political party: the Liberty Party, which nominated Birney for president in 1840 and 1844.

Although committed to immediate abolitionism, the Liberty Party doubted the federal government's authority to abolish slavery where it already existed. States, not the federal government, had the jurisdiction to determine slavery's legality within their bounds. Where the federal government could act was in the western territories, and the party demanded that all new territories prohibit slavery. Some prominent black abolitionists, including Frederick Douglass, endorsed the party, whose leaders emphasized, too, the need to combat northern prejudice.

WOMEN'S RIGHTS

Some female abolitionists, frustrated by their treatment, took the lead in advocating women's rights. At the first World Anti-Slavery Convention in London in 1840, abolitionists Lucretia Mott and Elizabeth Cady Stanton first met, united in their dismay that female abolitionists were denied seats in the convention's main hall; eight years later, the two would help organize the first American women's rights convention. Angelina and Sarah Grimké came from a slaveholding family but moved north and became active abolitionists. After critics attacked them for speaking to audiences that included men, they rejected claims that women should not lecture, but rather obey men, and they became vocal advocates for women's legal and social equality.

For many lesser-known women, too, their political consciousness developed from abolitionist activities, particularly petitioning campaigns. In the 1830s, women's petitions to Congress employed humbling language, with petitioners "praying" their political leaders to consider their grievances about slavery. After Congress voted to automatically table antislavery petitions in 1836, women defended their right to have their petitions considered. Women began employing more demanding language in their petitions, which now offered specific legislative advice. Female petitioners increasingly saw themselves as citizens and less as political subjects.

Religious revivalism and reform movements also led women to reexamine their positions in society. Revivals helped women to see themselves as inherently equal to men, and reform movements brought middle-class women outside the home and into the public sphere. Female reformers' lobbying helped to effect legal change, making some think the next step was obvious: full citizenship rights for women.

Legal Rights

A great many legal obstacles had to be overcome. After independence, American states carried over traditional English marriage law, giving husbands absolute control over the family. Men owned their wives' personal property, were their children's legal guardians, and owned whatever family members produced or earned. A father could legally oppose his daughter's choice of husband, though by 1800 most American women chose their own marriage partner.

Married women made modest gains in property and spousal rights from the 1830s on. Arkansas in 1835 passed the first married women's property law, and by 1860 sixteen more states had followed with laws allowing women—single, married, or divorced—to own and convey property. When a wife inherited property, it was hers, not her husband's, though money earned or acquired in some other way continued to belong to her husband. Women could also write wills. Such laws were particularly popular among wealthy Americans, South and North, hoping to protect their family fortunes during periods of economic boom and bust; property in a woman's name was safe from her husband's creditors. In the 1830s, states also liberalized divorce laws, adding cruelty and desertion as grounds for divorce, but divorce remained rare.

A few radical reformers still argued that marriage constituted a form of bondage. Among the most outspoken was Lucy Stone, who finally consented to marry fellow abolitionist Henry Blackwell, but only under the condition that she not take a vow of obedience and that she keep her own surname. The term "Lucy Stoner" entered common parlance as a reference to married women who did not adopt their husband's name.

Political Rights   By the time Lucy Stone and Harry Blackwell married in 1855, both were active in the organized movement to secure women's political rights. That movement had been launched in July 1848, when Elizabeth Cady Stanton, Lucretia Mott, Mary Ann McClintock, Martha Wright, and Jane Hunt—all abolitionists and all, except Stanton, Quakers—organized the first Woman's Rights Convention at Seneca Falls, New York. Those at Seneca Falls were not the first women's rights activists: Radical reformers, such as Fanny Wright, had trumpeted the cause for decades, and two years earlier, in 1846, six rural New York women demanded—unsuccessfully but with little public outcry—their state's new constitution return to "true democratic principles" by guaranteeing women equal political and civil rights. But the Seneca Falls convention addressed national, not just state, citizenship, and it drew more attention—and rancor.

At Seneca Falls, three hundred women and men demanded women's social and economic equality, and some advocated political equality, too. They protested women's legal disabilities and their social restrictions, such as exclusion from many occupations. Their Declaration of Sentiments, modeled on the Declaration of Independence, broadcast the injustices suffered by women and launched the women's rights movement. "All men and women are created equal," the declaration proclaimed. The similar premises of abolitionism and women's rights led many reformers, including former slaves like Sojourner Truth, to work simultaneously for both movements in the 1850s. Even among those supporting the movement's general aims, though, the question of female suffrage became divisive. William Lloyd Garrison and Frederick Douglass supported women's right to vote, but most men actively opposed it. At Seneca Falls, the resolution on woman suffrage passed only after Douglass passionately endorsed it, but some participants still refused to sign. In 1851, Elizabeth Cady Stanton joined with Susan B. Anthony, a temperance advocate, to become the most vocal and persistent activists for woman suffrage. They won relatively few converts and many critics.

JACKSONIANISM AND PARTY POLITICS

No less than reformers, politicians sought to control the direction of change in the expanding nation. They reframed their political visions to appeal to an increasingly broad-based electorate. Hotly contested elections helped make politics the great nineteenth-century American pastime, drawing the interest and participation of voters and nonvoters alike. But intense interest also fueled bitter, even deadly, rivalries.

Expanding   Property restrictions for voters, which states began abandon-
Political   ing during the 1810s, remained in only seven of twenty-six
Participation   states by 1840. Some states even allowed foreign nationals
who had officially declared their intention of becoming American citizens to vote. The net effect was a sharply higher number of votes cast in presidential elections. Between 1824 and 1828, that number increased threefold, from 360,000 to over 1.1 million. In 1840, 2.4 million men cast votes. The proportion of eligible voters who cast ballots also grew, from about 27 percent in 1824 to more than 80 percent in 1840.

At the same time, the method of choosing presidential electors became more democratic. Previously, a caucus of party leaders had done so in most states, but by 1824 eighteen out of twenty-four states chose electors by popular vote, compared to just five of sixteen in 1800. As a result, politicians augmented their direct appeals to voters, and the election of 1824 saw the end of the congressional caucus, when House and Senate members of the same political party came together to select their candidate.

Election of 1824   As a result, five candidates, all of whom identified as Democratic-Republicans, came forward to run for president in 1824. The poorly attended Republican caucus chose William H. Crawford of Georgia, secretary of the treasury, as its presidential candidate. But other Democratic-Republicans boycotted the caucus as undemocratic, ending Congress's role in nominating presidential candidates. Instead, state legislatures nominated candidates, offering the expanded electorate a slate of sectional candidates. John Quincy Adams drew support from New England, while westerners backed House Speaker Henry Clay of Kentucky. Some southerners at first supported Secretary of War John C. Calhoun, who later dropped his bid for the presidency and ran for the vice presidency instead. The Tennessee legislature nominated Andrew Jackson, a military hero with unknown political views.

Among the four candidates remaining in the race until the election, Jackson led in both electoral and popular votes, but no candidate received an electoral college majority. Adams finished second; Crawford and Clay trailed far behind. Under the Constitution, the House of Representatives, voting by state delegation, one vote to a state, would select the next president from among the three leaders in electoral votes. Clay, with the fewest votes, was dropped, and the three others courted his support, hoping he would influence his electors to vote for them. Crawford, disabled from a stroke suffered before the election, never received serious consideration. Clay backed Adams, who won with thirteen of the twenty-four state delegations and thus became president. Adams named Clay to the cabinet position of secretary of state, the traditional steppingstone to the presidency.

Angry Jacksonians denounced the election's outcome as a "corrupt bargain," claiming Adams had stolen the election from their candidate by offering Clay a cabinet position in exchange for his votes. Jackson's bitterness fueled his later emphasis on the people's will. The Republican Party split. The Adams wing emerged as the National Republicans, and the Jacksonians became the Democrats; they immediately began planning for 1828.

As president, Adams proposed a strong nationalist policy incorporating Henry Clay's American System, a program of protective tariffs, a national bank, and internal improvements. Adams believed the federal government's active role should extend to education, science, and the arts, and he proposed a national university in Washington, D.C. Brilliant as a diplomat and secretary of state, Adams fared less well as chief executive. He underestimated the lingering effects of the Panic of 1819 and the resulting staunch opposition to a national bank and a protective tariff.

Election of 1828   The 1828 election pitted Adams against Jackson in a rowdy campaign. Nicknamed "Old Hickory" after the toughest of American hardwood, Andrew Jackson was a rough-and-tumble, ambitious man. Born in South Carolina in 1767, he rose from humble beginnings to become a wealthy Tennessee planter and slaveholder. After leading the Tennessee militia campaign to remove Creeks from the Alabama and Georgia frontier, Jackson burst onto the national scene in 1815 as the hero of the Battle of New Orleans; in 1818, he enhanced his glory in an expedition against Seminoles in Spanish Florida. Jackson served as a congressman and senator from Tennessee and as the first territorial governor of Florida (1821), before running for president in 1824.

Both voters and nonvoters displayed enthusiasm for Jackson with badges, medals, and other campaign paraphernalia, mass-produced for the first time. In an intensely personal contest, Jackson's supporters accused Adams of stealing the 1824 election and, when he was envoy to Russia, of having secured prostitutes for the czar. Anti-Jacksonians countered with reports that Jackson's wife, Rachel, had married Jackson before her divorce from her first husband was final, making her an adulterer and a bigamist. In 1806 Jackson, attempting to defend Rachel's integrity, had killed a man during a duel, and the cry of "murderer!" was revived in the election.

Although Adams kept the states he had won in 1824, his opposition now unified behind a single candidate, and Jackson swamped him, polling 56 percent of the popular vote and winning in the electoral college by 178 to 83 votes. Jacksonians believed the people's will had finally prevailed. Through a lavishly financed coalition of state parties, political leaders, and newspaper editors, a popular movement had elected the president. The Democratic Party became the nation's first well-organized national party, and tight party organization became the hallmark of nineteenth-century American politics.

Democrats   The Democrats represented a wide range of views but shared a fundamental commitment to the Jeffersonian concept of an agrarian society. They viewed a strong central government as antithetical to individual liberty, and they condemned government intervention in the economy as favoring the rich at the expense of the artisan and the ordinary farmer. When it came to westward expansion, though, Jacksonians called for federal intervention, with Jackson initiating Indian removal despite protests from northeastern reformers.

Like Jefferson, Jackson strengthened the government's executive branch even as he advocated limited government. In combining the roles of party leader and chief of state, he centralized power in the White House. He relied on political friends, his "Kitchen Cabinet," for advice, rarely consulting his official cabinet. Jackson commanded enormous loyalty and rewarded his followers handsomely. Rotating officeholders, Jackson claimed, made government more responsive to the public will, and he appointed loyal Democrats to office, a practice his critics called the spoils system, in which the victor gives the spoils of victory to his supporters. Although not the first president to do so—Jefferson had replaced many of Adams's appointees—Jackson's own outcry against corrupt bargains made him an easy target for inflammatory rhetoric. The spoils system, opponents charged, corrupted the government because it based appointments on loyalty, not competency.

King Andrew   Opponents mocked Jackson as "King Andrew I," charging him with abuse of power by ignoring the Supreme Court's ruling on Cherokee rights, by sidestepping his cabinet, and by replacing office-holders with his own political cronies. They rejected his claim of restoring republican virtue and accused him of recklessly destroying the economy.

Perhaps nothing rankled Jackson's critics more than his frequent use of the veto, which he employed to promote his vision of a limited government. In 1830, he vetoed the Maysville Road bill, which would have funded construction of a 60-mile turnpike from Maysville to Lexington, Kentucky. Constitutionally, he insisted, states not the federal government bore responsibility for funding internal improvements confined to a single state. The veto undermined Henry Clay's American System and personally embarrassed Clay because the project was in his home district.

From George Washington to John Quincy Adams, the first six presidents had vetoed nine bills; Jackson alone vetoed twelve. Previous presidents believed vetoes were justified only on constitutional grounds, but Jackson considered policy

Whigs, who named themselves after the loyal opposition in Britain, delighted in portraying Andrew Jackson as a power-hungry leader eager to turn a republic into a monarchy.

disagreements legitimate grounds as well. He made the veto an effective weapon for controlling Congress, which had to weigh the possibility of a presidential veto as it deliberated.

FEDERALISM AT ISSUE: THE NULLIFICATION AND BANK CONTROVERSIES

Soon after the Maysville Road veto, Jackson directly faced the question of state versus federal power. The slave South feared federal power and no state more so than South Carolina, where the planter class was the strongest and slavery the most concentrated. Southerners also resented protectionist tariffs, one of the foundations of Clay's American System, which in 1824 and 1828 protected manufactures by imposing import duties on manufactured cloth and iron. In protecting northern factories, the tariff raised the costs of manufactured goods to southerners, who quickly labeled the high tariff of 1828 the Tariff of Abominations.

Nullification   South Carolina's political leaders rejected the 1828 tariff, invoking the doctrine of nullification, which held that a state had the right to overrule, or nullify, federal legislation. Nullification drew from the idea expressed in the Virginia and Kentucky Resolutions of 1798—that the states, representing the people, have a right to judge the constitutionality of federal actions. Jackson's vice president, John C. Calhoun of South Carolina, argued in his unsigned *Exposition and Protest* that, in any disagreement between the federal government and a state, a special state convention—like the conventions called to ratify the Constitution—should decide the conflict by either nullifying or affirming the federal law. Only the power of nullification, Calhoun asserted, could protect the minority against the majority's tyranny.

As Jackson's running mate in 1828, Calhoun had avoided endorsing nullification and thus embarrassing the Democratic ticket; he also hoped to win Jackson's support as the Democratic presidential heir apparent. Thus, in early 1830, Calhoun presided silently over the Senate and its packed galleries when Senator Daniel Webster of Massachusetts and Senator Robert Y. Hayne of South Carolina debated states' rights. The debate started over a resolution to restrict western land sales, soon turned to the tariff, and from there focused on the nature of the Union, with nullification a subtext. Hayne charged the North with threatening to bring disunity. For two days, Webster eloquently defended New England and the republic, keeping supporters of nullification on the defensive. Although debating Hayne, he aimed his remarks at Calhoun. At the debate's climax, Webster invoked two powerful images. One was the outcome of nullification: "states dissevered, discordant, belligerent; on a land rent with civil feuds, or drenched … in fraternal blood!" The other was a patriotic vision of a great nation flourishing under the motto "Liberty and Union, now and forever, one and inseparable."

Though sympathetic to states' rights and distrustful of the federal government, Jackson rejected the idea of state sovereignty. He strongly believed sovereignty rested with the people. Believing deeply in the Union, he shared Webster's dread of nullification. Soon after the Webster-Hayne debate, the president made his position clear at a Jefferson Day dinner with the toast "Our Federal Union, it must and shall be preserved." Vice President Calhoun, when his turn came, toasted "The Federal Union—next to our liberty the most dear," revealing his adherence to states' rights. Calhoun and Jackson grew apart, and Jackson looked to Secretary of State Martin Van Buren, not Calhoun, as his successor.

Tension resumed when Congress passed a new tariff in 1832, reducing some duties but retaining high taxes on imported iron, cottons, and woolens. Although a majority of southern representatives supported the new tariff, South Carolinians did not, insisting that the constitutional right to control their own destiny had been sacrificed to northern industrialists' demands. They feared the act could set a precedent for congressional legislation on slavery. In November 1832, a South Carolina state convention nullified both the 1828 and the 1832 tariffs, declaring it unlawful for federal officials to collect duties in the state.

The Force Act   Privately, Jackson threatened to invade South Carolina and hang Vice President Calhoun; publicly, he took measured steps. In December, Jackson issued a proclamation opposing nullification. He moved troops to federal forts in South Carolina and prepared U.S. marshals to collect the required duties. At Jackson's request, Congress passed the Force Act, authorizing the president to call up troops but also offering a way to avoid force by collecting duties before foreign ships reached Charleston's harbor. Jackson also extended an olive branch by recommending tariff reductions.

Calhoun, disturbed by South Carolina's drift toward separatism, resigned as vice president and soon won election to the U.S. Senate, where he worked with Henry Clay to draw up the compromise Tariff of 1833. Quickly passed by Congress and signed by the president, the new tariff lengthened the list of duty-free items and reduced duties over nine years. Satisfied, South Carolina's convention repealed its nullification law. In a final salvo, it also nullified Jackson's Force Act. Jackson ignored the gesture.

Nullification offered a genuine debate on the nature and principles of the republic. Each side believed it was upholding the Constitution and opposing subversion of republican values. South Carolina's leaders opposed the tyranny of the federal government and manufacturing interests. Jackson fought the tyranny of South Carolina, whose refusal to bow to federal authority threatened to split the republic. Neither side won a clear victory, though both claimed to have done so. It took another crisis, over a central bank, to define the powers of the federal government more clearly.

Second Bank of the United States   At stake was survival of the Second Bank of the United States, whose twenty-year charter would expire in 1836. The bank served as a depository for federal funds and provided credit for businesses. Its bank notes circulated as currency throughout the country; they could be readily exchanged for gold, and the federal government accepted them as payment in all transactions, including land sales. Through its twenty-five branch offices, the Second Bank acted as a clearing-house for state banks, refusing to accept bank notes of any state bank lacking sufficient gold reserves. Most state banks resented the central bank's police role, which they saw as potentially ruinous. Moreover, state banks were unable to compete equally with the Second Bank, which had more money in reserve.

Many state governments regarded the national bank as unresponsive to local needs, and many western settlers and urban workers remembered with bitterness the bank's conservative credit policies during the Panic of 1819. As a private, profit-making institution, its policies reflected the interest of its owners, especially its president, Nicholas Biddle, who controlled the bank completely. An eastern patrician, Biddle symbolized all that westerners found wrong with the bank, and all that eastern workers found wrong with the commercial elite.

Political Violence

Controversy over the Second Bank inflamed longstanding political animosities, bringing violence to the streets. Elections often involved fraud, and with no secret ballot, political parties employed operatives to intimidate voters. New York City was home to the most powerful political machine, the Democrats' Tammany Hall, and thus while the bank controversy exacerbated tensions nationwide, New York's mayoral election of 1834 led to mayhem.

Three days of rioting began when Democratic operatives attacked Whig headquarters in the sixth ward. After beating some Whigs unconscious, the Democrats turned their fists and clubs against police, who tried to restore order; eight of them suffered severe wounds, and even the mayor was injured in the fray. Vowing revenge, more than five hundred Whigs stole weapons from the armory, but before they could use them, the state militia arrived to restore order.

A few months later, an election-day riot in Philadelphia left two dead and five substantial buildings burned to the ground. Although these two riots stood out for their proportions and intensity, voter intimidation and fraud—initiated by both Democrats and Whigs—characterized the second party system.

Antimasonry

Violence was a catalyst for the formation of the Antimason Party, which had started in upstate New York in the mid-1820s as a grassroots movement against Freemasonry, a secret male fraternity that attracted middle- and upper-class men prominent in commerce and civic affairs. Opponents of Masonry claimed the fraternity to be unrepublican; Masons colluded to bestow business and political favors on each other, and—in the incident that sparked the organized Antimasonry movement—Masons had obstructed justice in the investigation of the 1826 disappearance and presumed murder of a disgruntled former member who had written an exposé of the society. Evangelicals denounced Masonry, claiming its members neglected their families for alcohol and ribald entertainment. Antimasonry soon developed into a vibrant political movement in the Northeast and parts of the Midwest. In the 1828 presidential election, the Antimasons opposed Jackson, himself a Mason. With their confidence bolstered by strong showings in gubernatorial elections in 1830, the Antimasons held the first national political convention in Baltimore in 1831, nominating William Wirt of Maryland for president and Amos Ellmaker of Pennsylvania for vice president.

Election of 1832   Following the Antimasons' lead, the Democrats and National Republicans held their own conventions. The Democrats reaffirmed the choice of Jackson, who had already been nominated by state legislatures, for president and nominated Martin Van Buren of New York for vice president. The National Republican convention selected Clay and John Sergeant of Pennsylvania. The Independent Democrats ran John Floyd and Henry Lee of Virginia; as governor of Virginia, Floyd had supported nullification, winning him support from many South Carolinians.

The Bank of the United States became the election's main issue. Jacksonians denounced the bank as a vehicle for special privilege and economic power, while the Republicans supported it as a pillar of their plan for economic nationalism. The bank's charter was valid until 1836, but as part of his campaign strategy, Clay persuaded Biddle to ask Congress to approve an early rechartering. If Jackson signed the rechartering bill, then Clay could attack the president's inconsistency on the issue. If he vetoed it, then—Clay reasoned—the voters would give Clay the nod. The plan backfired. The president vetoed the bill and issued a pointed veto message appealing to voters who feared that the era's rapid economic development spread its advantages undemocratically. Jackson acknowledged that prosperity could never be evenly dispersed, but he took a strong stand against special interests that tried to use the government to their own unfair advantage. "It is to be regretted," he wrote, "that the rich and powerful too often bend the acts of government to their selfish purposes." The message proved powerful and successful. Jackson won 54 percent of the popular vote to Clay's 37 percent, and he captured 76 percent of the electoral college. Although the Antimasons won just one state, Vermont, they nonetheless helped galvanize the anti-Jackson opposition.

Jackson's Second Term   After a sweeping victory and second inauguration, Jackson began in 1833 dismantling the Second Bank and depositing federal funds in state-chartered banks (termed "pet banks" by critics). Without federal money, the Second Bank shriveled. When its federal charter expired in 1836, it became just another Pennsylvania-chartered private bank. Five years later, it closed its doors.

As Congress allowed the Bank of the United States to die, it passed the Deposit Act of 1836, authorizing the secretary of the treasury to designate one bank in each state and territory to provide services formerly performed by the Bank of the United States. The act also provided that the federal surplus in excess of $5 million—income derived from the sale of public lands to speculators, who bought large quantities of land to re-parcel and sell, they hoped, at a profit—be distributed to the states as interest-free loans (or "deposits") beginning in 1837. (The loans were understood to be forgiven and, in fact, they were never repaid.) Eager to use the money for state-funded internal improvements, Democrats joined Whigs in supporting the measure overwhelmingly. Fearing that the act would fuel speculation, promote inflation, and thus undermine farmers' interests, Jackson opposed the bill. Because support was strong enough to override a veto, Jackson signed the bill but first insisted on a provision prohibiting state banks from issuing or accepting small-denomination paper money. Jackson hoped that by encouraging the use of coins, the provision would prevent unscrupulous businessmen from defrauding workers by paying them in devalued paper bills.

Specie Circular   The president then ordered Treasury Secretary Levi Wood-bury to issue the Specie Circular, which provided that, after August 1836, only settlers could use paper money to buy land; speculators would have to use specie (gold or silver). The policy proved disastrous, significantly reducing public-land sales, which in turn reduced the federal government's surplus and its loans to the states.

Meanwhile, a banking crisis emerged. One western banker remarked that people "appear to distrust all Banks, they think Govt. has no confidence in them." Fearful that their banknotes would lose value, people sought to redeem them for specie, creating a shortage that forced the banks to suspend payment, further reducing confidence.

Jackson's opponents were irate, largely because the Senate, fearing such consequences, had defeated a bill similar to the Specie Circular just three months earlier. Now "King Andrew" had used presidential powers to defy legislative will, and with disastrous consequences. In the waning days of Jackson's administration, Congress repealed the circular, but the president pocket-vetoed the bill by holding it unsigned until Congress adjourned. Finally, in May 1838, after Jackson had left office, a joint resolution of Congress overturned the circular.

THE WHIG CHALLENGE AND THE SECOND PARTY SYSTEM

In the 1830s, opponents of the Democrats, including remnants of the National Republican and Antimason parties, joined together to become the Whig Party. Resentful of Jackson's domination of Congress, the Whigs borrowed the name of the eighteenth-century British party that opposed the Hanoverian monarchs' tyranny. They, too, were the loyal opposition. From 1834 through the 1840s, the Whigs and the Democrats competed on nearly equal footing, and each drew supporters from all regions. The era's political competition—the second party system—was more intense and better organized than what scholars have labeled as the first party system of Democratic-Republicans versus Federalists.

Whigs and Reformers   Whigs favored economic expansion through an activist government. They supported corporate charters, a national bank, and paper currency; Democrats opposed all three. Whigs generally professed a strong belief in progress and perfectibility, and they favored social reforms, including public schools, prison and asylum reform, and temperance. Jacksonians criticized reform associations for undermining the people's will by giving undue influence to political minorities; Whigs countered they served the common good. Nor did Whigs object to helping special interests if doing so promoted the general welfare. The chartering of corporations, they argued, expanded economic opportunity for everyone, laborers and farmers alike. Democrats, distrustful of concentrated economic power and of moral and economic coercion, held fast to the Jeffersonian principle of limited government.

Whigs stressed a "harmony of interests" among all classes and interests. Their philosophy was one of equal opportunity. Democrats tended to see society as divided into the "haves" and the "have nots," and they embraced a motto of "equal rights." They championed "heroic artisans" whereas Whigs remained wary of the "excesses of democracy" and preferred to see society ruled from the top down. Whigs believed in free-labor ideology and thought that society's wealthy and powerful had risen by their own merits. Democrats alleged that, instead, their political opponents had benefited from special favors.

But religion and ethnicity, as much as class, influenced party affiliation. The Whigs' support for energetic government and moral reform won the favor of evangelical Protestants. Methodists and Baptists were overwhelmingly Whigs, as were the small number of free black voters. In many locales, the membership rolls of reform societies overlapped those of the party. Indeed, Whigs practiced a kind of political revivalism. Their rallies resembled camp meetings; their speeches employed pulpit rhetoric; their programs embodied reformers' perfectionist beliefs.

By appealing to evangelicals, Whigs alienated members of other faiths. The evangelicals' ideal Christian state had no room for nonevangelical Protestants, Catholics, Mormons, or religious freethinkers. Those groups opposed Sabbath laws and temperance legislation in particular, and state interference in moral and religious questions in general. In fact, they preferred to keep religion and politics separate. As a result, more than 95 percent of Irish Catholics, 90 percent of Reformed Dutch, and 80 percent of German Catholics voted Democratic.

The parties' platforms thus attracted what might seem to be an odd coalition of voters. Favoring government-sponsored commercial development and fearful of social disorder, the Whigs wanted a slower, more controlled settlement of western lands; later, they opposed slavery's westward expansion. Groups as diverse as black New Englanders and well-settled slave owners, especially in the Upper South, found these ideas appealing; the former, to undercut slavery itself, and the latter to protect their own investments from cheap western competition. Democrats' promises to open additional lands for settlement attracted yeoman farmers, wage earners, frontier slaveowners, and immigrants. With such broad coalitions of voters, there was room within each party for a broad spectrum of beliefs, particularly when it came to slavery.

Politicians recognized, however, the potentially divisive nature of slavery, and some went to extremes to keep it out of national political debate. In response to the American Antislavery Society's petitioning campaign, the House of Representatives in 1836 adopted what abolitionists labeled the "gag rule," which automatically tabled abolitionist petitions, effectively preventing debate on them. Former president John Quincy Adams, now a representative from Massachusetts, dramatically defended the right to petition and took to the floor many times to speak against the gag rule, which was ultimately repealed in 1844.

Election of 1836

Vice President Martin Van Buren, handpicked by Jackson, headed the Democratic ticket in the 1836 presidential election. A career politician, Van Buren had built a political machine—the Albany Regency—in New York and then left to join Jackson's cabinet in 1829, first as secretary of state and then as American minister to Great Britain.

Because the Whigs in 1836 had not yet coalesced into a national party, they entered three sectional candidates: Daniel Webster (New England), Hugh White (the South), and William Henry Harrison (the West). By splintering the vote, they hoped to throw the election into the House of Representatives. Van Buren, however, comfortably captured the electoral college even though he had only a 25,000-vote edge out of a total of 1.5 million votes cast. No vice-presidential candidate received a majority of electoral votes, and for the only time in American history, the Senate decided a vice-presidential race, selecting Democratic candidate Richard M. Johnson of Kentucky.

Van Buren and Hard Times   Van Buren took office just weeks before the American credit system collapsed. With banks refusing to redeem paper currency with gold in response to the Specie Circular, a downward economic spiral began, curtailing bank loans and strangling business confidence. Credit contraction made things worse. After a brief recovery, hard times persisted from 1839 until 1843.

Van Buren followed Jackson's hard-money policies. He cut federal spending, causing prices to drop further, and opposed a national bank, which would have expanded credit. The president proposed a new regional treasury system for government deposits. The proposed treasury branches would accept and disperse only gold and silver coin; they would not accept paper currency or checks drawn on state banks. Van Buren's independent treasury bill became law in 1840. By increasing the demand for hard coin, it deprived banks of gold and accelerated price deflation. These issues dominated state elections. Whigs favored new banks, more paper currency, and readily available corporate and bank charters. As the party of hard money, Democrats favored eliminating paper currency altogether. Increasingly, the Democrats became distrustful even of state banks; by the mid-1840s, a majority favored eliminating all bank corporations.

Anglo-American Tensions   Amid hard times came a renewal of Anglo-American tensions. One of the most troublesome disputes arose from the *Caroline* affair. After the privately owned steamer *Caroline* carried supplies to aid an unsuccessful Canadian uprising against Great Britain, a group of British loyalists burned the ship, killing an American citizen in the process. Britain refused to apologize, and American newspapers called for revenge. Fearing that popular support for the Canadian rebels would ignite war, President Van Buren posted troops under General Winfield Scott at the border to discourage Americans from seeking vigilante retaliation. Tensions subsided in late 1840 when New York authorities arrested a Canadian deemed responsible for the American's death aboard the *Caroline*. The alleged murderer was acquitted. Had the verdict gone otherwise, Lord Palmerston, the British foreign minister, might have sought war.

At almost the same time, an old border dispute between Maine and New Brunswick disrupted Anglo-American relations. Great Britain had accepted an 1831 arbitration decision fixing a new boundary, but the U.S. Senate rejected it. Thus, when Canadian lumbermen cut trees in the disputed region in the winter of 1838–1839, a posse of Maine citizens assembled to expel them. The lumbermen captured the posse, both sides mobilized their militias, and Congress authorized a call-up of fifty thousand men. General Scott was dispatched to Aroostook, Maine, where he arranged a truce. The Webster-Ashburton Treaty (1842) settled the boundaries between Maine and New Brunswick, and along the Great Lakes, but left unresolved the still-disputed northern boundary of Oregon, joint occupancy of which had been renewed in 1827.

William Henry Harrison and the Election of 1840

With the nation gripped by hard times, the Whigs confidently approached the election of 1840. Their strategy was simple: maintain loyal supporters and court independents by blaming hard times on the Democrats. The Whigs rallied behind a military hero, General William Henry Harrison, conqueror of the Shawnees at Tippecanoe Creek in 1811. The Democrats renominated President Van Buren, and the newly formed Liberty Party ran James Birney.

Harrison, or "Old Tippecanoe," and his running mate, John Tyler of Virginia, ran a "log cabin and hard cider" campaign—a people's crusade—against the aristocratic president in "the Palace." Although descended from a Virginia plantation family, Harrison presented himself as an ordinary farmer. While party hacks blamed Democrats for hard times, Harrison remained silent, earning the nickname "General Mum." Whigs wooed voters with huge rallies, parades, songs, posters, campaign mementos, and a party newspaper, The Log Cabin. They appealed to voters as well as nonvoters, including women, who attended their rallies and speeches, and women actively promoted the Whig cause; one Virginia woman, for example, published two pamphlets backing Harrison's candidacy. In a huge turnout, 80 percent of eligible voters cast ballots. Winning the popular vote by a narrow margin, Harrison swept the electoral college, 234 to 60.

Immediately after taking office in 1841, President Harrison convened Congress in special session to pass the Whig program: repeal of the independent treasury system, a new national bank, and a higher protective tariff. But the sixty-eight-year-old Harrison caught pneumonia and died within a month of his inauguration. His vice president, John Tyler, who had left the Democratic Party to protest Jackson's nullification proclamation, now became the first vice president whose president had died in office. The Constitution did not stipulate what should happen, but Tyler quickly took full possession of executive powers, setting a crucial precedent that would not be codified in the Constitution until 1967 with the Twenty-fifth Amendment's ratification.

President Tyler

In office, Tyler became more a Democrat than a Whig. He repeatedly vetoed Clay's protective tariffs, internal improvements, and bills to revive the Bank of the United States. Two days after Tyler's second veto of a bank bill, the entire cabinet except Secretary of State Daniel Webster resigned; Webster, once done negotiating the Webster-Ashburton treaty, followed. Tyler became a president without a party, and the Whigs lost the presidency without losing an election. Disgusted Whigs referred to Tyler as "His Accidency."

Like Jackson, Tyler expanded presidential powers and emphasized westward expansion. His expansionist vision contained Whig elements, though: he eyed commercial markets in Hawaii and China. During his presidency, the United States negotiated its first treaties with China, and Tyler expanded the Monroe Doctrine to include Hawaii (or the Sandwich Islands). But Tyler's vision for the nation's path to greatness fixed mostly on Texas and the westward expansion of slavery.

SUMMARY

Religion and reform shaped politics from 1824 through the 1840s. Driven by a belief in human perfectibility, many evangelicals, especially women, worked tirelessly to right the wrongs of American society. They hoped to trigger the millennium, the thousand years of earthly peace accompanying Christ's return. Reformers battled the evils of prostitution and alcohol, and they sought to reform criminals and delinquents, improve insane asylums, and establish public schools. Some rejected the possibility of reforming American society from within and instead joined experimental communities that modeled radical alternatives to the social and economic order. Abolitionists combined the reformers' and utopians' approaches; they worked to perfect American society from within but through radical means—the eradication of slavery. As women entered the public sphere as advocates of reform and, especially, abolitionism, some of them turned toward the equally radical proposition of full legal and political rights for women.

Reform remade politics, and politicians reshaped public discourse to appeal to the broadening electorate. As did reformers, President John Quincy Adams raised expectations about an expanded governmental role. The struggles between the National Republicans and the Democrats, then between the Democrats and the Whigs, stimulated even greater interest in campaigns and political issues. The Democrats and Whigs competed almost equally for voter loyalty by building strong organizations that faced off in national and local elections often characterized by fraud, and sometimes by violence. Both parties favored economic development but by different means: The Whigs advocated centralized government initiative to spur commercial growth, whereas Democrats advocated limited government and sought agricultural expansion. Jackson did not hesitate, however, to use presidential authority; his opponents dubbed him King Andrew. The controversies over the Second Bank of the United States and nullification exposed different interpretations of the nation's founding principles.

The late 1830s and early 1840s brought uncertainty: The economy once again cycled through a period of bust; tensions with the British resurfaced; and—for the first time—a president died in office. As John Tyler, derided by his critics as "His Accidency," took office, he tenaciously articulated a vision of American greatness that depended on its westward expansion.

13

THE CONTESTED WEST 1815–1860

CHAPTER OUTLINE

• The West in the American Imagination • Expansion and Resistance in the Trans-Appalachian West • The Federal Government and Westward Expansion • *LINKS TO THE WORLD Gold in California* • The Southwestern Borderlands • Cultural Frontiers in the Far West • The Politics of Territorial Expansion • Summary

---

THE WEST IN THE AMERICAN IMAGINATION

For historian Frederick Jackson Turner, writing in the late nineteenth century, it was the West, not the South or the North, that was distinctive. With its abundance of free land, the western frontier—what he saw as the "meeting point between savagery and civilization"—bred American democracy, shaped the American character, and made the United States exceptional among nations. Modern historians generally eschew the notion of American exceptionalism, stressing instead the deep and complex connections between the United States and the rest of the world. Although today's scholars also reject the racialist assumptions of Turner's definition of *frontier*, some see continued value in using the term to signify a meeting place of different cultures. Others see the West as fundamentally a place, not a process, though they disagree over what delineates it.

Defining the West
For early-nineteenth-century Americans of European descent, the West included anything west of the Appalachian Mountains. But it was, first and foremost, a place representing the future—a place offering economic and social betterment for themselves and their children. For many, betterment entailed land ownership; the West's seeming abundance of land meant that anyone could hope to own a farm and achieve economic and political independence. Men who already owned land, like Pettis Perkinson, looked westward for cheaper, bigger, and more fertile landholdings. With the discovery of gold in California in 1848, the West became a place to strike it rich before returning home to live in increased comfort or even opulence.

CHRONOLOGY

1812	General Land Office established
1820	Price lowered on public lands
1821	Santa Fe Trail charted
	Mexico's independence
1823	Mexico allows Stephen Austin to settle U.S. citizens
1824	Congressional General Survey Act
	Jedediah Smith's South Pass publicized
	Indian Office established
1825–32	*Empresario* contracts signed
1826	Fredonia rebellion fails
1830	Indian Removal Act (see Chapter 10)
1832	Black Hawk War
1834	McCormick reaper patented
1836	Lone Star Republic founded
	U.S. Army Corps of Topographical Engineers established
1840–60	250,000 to 500,000 migrants travel overland
1841	Log Cabin Bill
1844	Presidential campaign features Texas annexation
1845	"Manifest destiny" coined
	Texas annexed (March 1) and becomes twenty-eighth state (December 29)
1846–48	War with Mexico (see Chapter 14)
1847	Mormons settle Great Salt Lake valley
1848	California gold discovered
1849–50s	Migrants stream into Great Plains and Far West
1855	Ash Hollow Massacre
1857–58	Mormons and U.S. Army in armed conflict
1862	Homestead Act

Many people arrived in the West under the threat of force. These included enslaved men, women, and children whose owners moved them, often against their will, as well as Indians removed from their eastern homelands by the U.S. military under provisions of the Indian Removal Act of 1830.

To others, the very notion of the West would have been baffling. Emigrants from Mexico and Central or South America traveled north to get to what European-Americans called the West. Chinese nationals traveled eastward to California. Many Indians simply considered the West home. Other Indians and French Canadians journeyed southward to the West. All these people, much like European-Americans, arrived in the western portion of the North American continent because of a combination of factors pushing and pulling them.

**Frontier
Literature**

For European-Americans, Daniel Boone became the archetypical frontiersman, a man whose daring individualism opened the Eden-like West for virtuous and hard-working freedom lovers. Through biographies published by John Filson during Boone's lifetime and by Timothy Flint after Boone's death (in 1784 and 1833, respectively), Boone became a familiar figure in American and European households. The mythical Boone lived in the wilderness, became "natural" himself, and shrank from society, feeling compelled to relocate upon seeing smoke billowing from a neighboring cabin. He single-handedly overpowered bears and Indians. Even as he adopted wilderness ways, according to legend, Boone became the pathfinder for civilization. As a friend wrote, Boone "has been the instrument of opening the road to millions of the human family from the pressure of sterility and want, to a Land flowing with milk and honey." By borrowing biblical language—the land of milk and honey denoting the Promised Land, the idyllic place that God promised to the beleaguered Israelites—Boone's friend suggested that Boone was Moses-like, leading his people to a land of abundance.

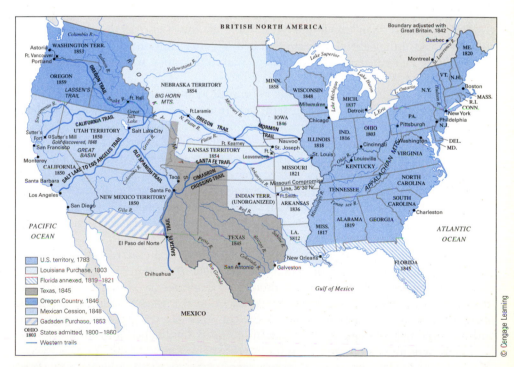

MAP 13.1 Westward Expansion, 1800–1860

Through exploration, purchase, war, and treaty, the United States became a continental nation, stretching from the Atlantic to the Pacific.

Such stories mythologized not only Boone, but the West itself. The Indian-fighting Boone, according to Flint's bestselling biography, had wrested for civilized society "the great west—the garden of the earth." Little matter that the real Boone regretted having killed Indians and often struggled to support his family. When Boone became the heroic model for James Fenimore Cooper's *Leatherstocking Tales* (1823–1841)—set on the frontier of western New York—he came to symbol-ize not only American adventure but also individualism and freedom.

With the invention of the steam press in the early 1830s, western adventure stories became cheap and widely read. Davy Crockett, another real-life figure turned into mythical hero, was featured in many of them. In real life, Crockett had first fought the Creeks under Andrew Jackson but later championed Indian rights, rebuking the removal bill. After losing his life defending the Alamo mission during Texas's fight for independence (1836), though, Crockett often appeared in stories portraying the West as violent, a place where one escaped civilized society and fought Indians and Mexicans. But even in this version of the western myth, the American West symbolized what white Americans saw as their nation's core value: freedom.

Western Art   Inspired partly by such literature, many easterners yearned to see the West and its native peoples, and artists hastened to accommodate them. Yet the images they produced often revealed more about white Americans' ideals than about the West itself. In these portrayals, the West was sometimes an untamed wilderness inhabited by savages (noble or otherwise), and sometimes a cultivated garden, a land of milk and honey where the Jeffersonian agrarian dream was realized.

The first Anglo-American artists to travel west were Samuel Seymour and Titian Ramsay Peale, whom the federal government hired to accompany explorer Stephen H. Long on his 1820 expedition to the Rocky Mountains. They pioneered an influential art genre: facsimiles in government reports. Between 1840 and 1860, Congress published nearly sixty works on western exploration, featuring hundreds of lithographs and engravings of plants, animals, and people. Some reports became bestsellers. The most popular was the twelve-volume Pacific Railway Survey (1855–1860), chronicling expeditions to explore four possible railroad routes. The government distributed more than 53,000 copies, helping easterners visualize for themselves the continent's western reaches.

Although government reports often faithfully reproduced original paintings, they sometimes made telling alterations. When Richard Kern accompanied explorer James H. Simpson in 1849 to the Southwest, for example, he painted a Navajo man in a submissive pose. The painting's reproduction for general distribution trans-formed the man's pose into a rebellious one. In other cases, the government reports transformed artists' depictions of Indian-occupied landscapes into empty terrain seemingly free for the taking.

Yet the original artwork did not necessarily offer an accurate view of the West either. Artists' own cultural assumptions colored their portrayals, and commercial artists produced what they thought the public craved. When George Catlin traveled west in the early 1830s, he may have genuinely hoped to paint what he saw as the

Indians' vanishing way of life. But he also aimed to attract a paying public of east-erners to his exhibitions. Traveling and painting immediately following the Indian Removal Act of 1830, Catlin painted the West with a moral in mind. Indians came in two varieties—those who preserved their original, almost noble qualities, characterized by freedom and moderation, and those who, after coming in contact with whites, had become "dissolute." Indians, he implied, benefited from removal from white Americans' corrupting influence.

Western artwork became widely viewed as facsimiles appeared in magazines and books and even on banknotes. Such images nurtured easterners' curiosities and fantasies—and sometimes their itch to move westward.

Countering the Myths   But western realities often clashed with promoters' promises, and disappointed settlers sometimes tried to clarify matters for future migrants. From Philadelphia in the 1850s came a song parodying the familiar call of "to the West":

> At the west they told me there was wealth to be won,
> The forest to clear, was the work to be done;
> I tried it—couldn't do it—gave it up in despair,
> And just see if you'll ever again catch me there.
> The little snug farm I expected to buy,
> I quickly discovered was just all in my eye,
> I came back like a streak—you may go—but I'm bless'd
> If you'll ever again, sirs, catch me at the west.

Rebecca Burlend, an English immigrant in Illinois, encountered hardships aplenty—intemperate weather, difficult working conditions, swindlers—and with her son wrote an autobiographical account, *A True Picture of Emigration* (1831), alerting her countrymen to what awaited them in the American West. The Burlends had been lured to Illinois by an Englishman's letters extolling "a land flowing with milk and honey." Burlend reckoned that he must have "gathered his honey rather from thorns than flowers." Her account sought not to discourage emigration, but to substitute a realistic for a rosy description.

EXPANSION AND RESISTANCE IN THE TRANS-APPALACHIAN WEST

Americans had always been highly mobile, but never to the extent following the War of 1812, which weakened Indian resistance and set off a flurry of transporta-tion projects. In the 1820s and 1830s, settlers streamed west of the Appalachian Mountains into the Old Northwest and the Old Southwest. They traveled by foot, horseback, wagon, canal boat, steamboat, or—often—by some combination of means. Many people, like Pettis Perkinson and his slaves, moved several times, looking for better opportunities, and when opportunities failed to materialize, some returned home.

Both the Old Northwest and the Old Southwest saw population explosions during the early nineteenth century. But while the Old Southwest grew by an im-pressive 50 percent each decade, the Northwest's population grew exponentially.

In 1790, the region's white population numbered just a few hundred people. By 1860, nearly 7 million people called the region home. Between 1810 and 1830, the population of Ohio more than quadrupled, while Indiana and Illinois grew fourteenfold and thirteenfold, respectively. Michigan's population multiplied by fifty times in the thirty years between 1820 and 1850. Migration rather than birth rates accounted for most of this growth, and once in the Old Northwest, people did not stay put. By the 1840s, more people left Ohio than moved into it. Geographic mobility, the search for more and better opportunities, and connections to the market economy defined the region that became known as the Midwest following the acquisition of U.S. territory farther west. This region came to symbolize, for many northerners, the heart of American values: freedom and upward mobility, both of which could be achieved (for white Americans and European immigrants) through hard work and virtuous behavior.

Deciding Where to Move   The decision to move west—and then to move again—could be difficult, even heart-wrenching. Moving west meant leaving behind worn-out soil and settled areas with little land available for purchase, but it also meant leaving behind family, friends, and communities. One woman remembered how on the evening before her departure for the West, her entire family gathered together for the last time "looking as if we were all going to our graves the next morning." The journey promised to be arduous and expensive, as did the backbreaking labor of clearing new lands. The West was a land of opportunity but also of uncertainty. What if the soil proved less fertile than anticipated? What if neighbors—white as well as Indian—proved unfriendly, or worse? What if homesickness became unbearable?

Given all that western settlers risked, they tried to control as many variables as possible. Like Pettis Perkinson, people often relocated to communities where they had relatives or friends, and they often traveled with acquaintances from home. They moved to climates similar to those they left behind. Massachusetts farmers headed to western New York or Ohio, Virginians and North Carolinians went to Missouri, Georgians populated Mississippi and Texas, and Europeans—mostly Germans and Irish—headed to the Old Northwest in much larger numbers than to the Old Southwest. Migrants settled in ethnic communities or with people of similar religious values and affiliations. As a result, the Midwest was—in the words of two of its historians—"more like an ethnic and cultural checkerboard than the proverbial melting pot."

When westward-bound Americans fixed on particular destinations, their decisions often rested on slavery's status there. Some white southerners, tired of the planter elite's social and political power, sought homes in areas free from slavery— or at least where there were few plantations. Many others, though, went west to improve their chances of owning slaves, or of purchasing additional slaves. White northerners also resented elite slaveowners' economic and political power and hoped to distance themselves from slavery as well as from free blacks. In the 1850s, many midwestern states passed "black laws" prohibiting African Americans, free or enslaved, from living within their boundaries. (Oregon passed a similar law.) Ironically, many free blacks migrated west to free themselves from eastern prejudice.

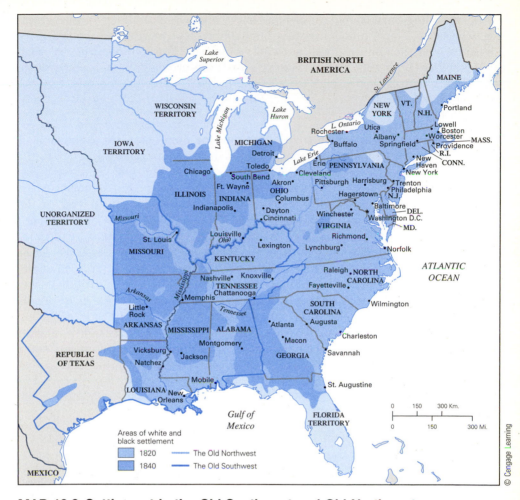

MAP 13.2 Settlement in the Old Southwest and Old Northwest, 1820 and 1840

Removal of Indians and a growing transportation network opened up land to white and black settlers in the regions known as the Old Southwest and the Old Northwest, as the U.S. population grew from 9.6 million in 1820 to 17.1 million in 1840.

Between 1815 and 1860, few western migrants settled on the Great Plains, a region reserved for Indians until the 1850s, and relatively few easterners risked the overland journey to California and Oregon before the transcontinental railroad's completion in 1869. Although at first the Southwest seemed to hold the edge in attracting new settlers, the Midwest—with its better-developed transportation routes, its more democratic access to economic markets, its smaller African American population, its smaller and cheaper average landholding, and its climatic similarity to New England and northern Europe—proved considerably more attractive in the decades after 1820. The Old Northwest's thriving transportation hubs also made good first stops for western migrants lacking cash to purchase land. They found work unloading canal boats, planting and harvesting wheat on nearby farms, grinding wheat into flour, or sawing trees into lumber—or, more often, cobbling together a combination of these seasonal jobs. The South offered fewer such opportunities. With the Old Northwest's population growing more quickly, white southerners worried increasingly about congressional representation and laws regarding slavery.

Indian Removal and Resistance   In both the Midwest and the Southwest, the expansion of white settlement depended on Indian removal. Even as the U.S. Army escorted Indians from the Old Southwest (see Chapter 10), the federal government arranged treaties in which northeastern Indian nations relinquished their land titles in exchange for lands west of the Mississippi River. Between 1829 and 1851, the U.S. government and northern Indian tribes signed eighty-six such treaties. Some northern Indians evaded removal, including the Miamis in Indiana, the Ottawas and Chippewas in the upper Midwest, and the Winnebagos in southern Wisconsin. In 1840, for example, Miami chiefs had acceded to pressure to exchange 500,000 acres in Indiana for equivalent acreage in Indian Country. Under the treaty's terms, their people had five years to move. When they did not, federal troops arrived to escort them. But about half of the Miami nation dodged the soldiers—and many of those who did trek to Indian Country later returned unauthorized. In Wisconsin, some Winnebagos similarly eluded removal or returned to Wisconsin after being escorted west by soldiers.

Black Hawk War   The Sauks (or "Sacs") and Fox fared much less well. In a series of treaties between 1804 and 1830, their leaders exchanged lands in northwestern Illinois and south-western Wisconsin for lands across the Mississippi River in Iowa Territory. Black Hawk, a Sauk warrior who had sided with the British during the War of 1812, disputed the treaties' validity and vowed his people would return to their ancestral lands. In 1832, he led a group of Sauk and Fox families to Illinois, causing panic among white settlers. The state's governor activated the militia, who were later joined by militia from surrounding states and territories as well as by U.S. Army regular soldiers. Over the next several months, hundreds of Indians and dozens of whites died under often-gruesome circumstances in what is known as the Black Hawk War. As the Sauks and Fox tried to flee across the Mississippi River, American soldiers on steamboats and on land fired indiscriminately. Those men, women, and children who survived the river crossing met gunfire on the western shore from Lakota (Sioux), their longtime enemies now allied with the Americans.

Black Hawk survived to surrender, and U.S. officials undertook to impress on him and the uprising's other leaders the futility of resistance. After being imprisoned, then sent to Washington, D.C., along a route meant to underscore the United States' immense size and population, and then imprisoned again, the Indians were returned to their homes. The Black Hawk War marked the end of militant Indian uprisings in the Old Northwest, adding to the region's appeal to white settlers.

Selling the West   Land speculators, developers of "paper towns" (ones existing on paper only), steamboat companies, and manufacturers of farming implements all promoted the Midwest as a tranquil place of unbounded opportunity. Land proprietors emphasized the region's connections to eastern customs and markets. They knew that, when families uprooted themselves and headed west, they did not—the mythical Daniel Boone and Davy Crockett aside—seek to escape civilization. When Michael D. Row, the proprietor of Rowsburg in northern Ohio, sought to sell town lots in 1835, he emphasized that Rowsburg was in a "thickly settled" area, stood at the crossroads of public transportation leading in every direction, and had established mills and tanning yards.

Western settlement generally followed rather than preceded connections to national and international markets. Eastern farmers, looking to escape tired soil or tenancy, sought fertile lands for growing commercial crops. Labor-saving devices, such as Cyrus McCormick's reaper (1834) and John Deere's steel plow (1837), made the West more alluring. McCormick, a Virginia inventor, patented a horse-drawn reaper that allowed two men to harvest the same number of acres of wheat that previously required between four and sixteen men, depending on which hand-held tool they wielded. Because the reaper's efficiency achieved its greatest payoffs on the prairies, where tracts of land were larger and flatter than in the Shenandoah valley, McCormick relocated his factory to Chicago in 1847 and began a dogged campaign to sell his reaper—which at $100 was an expensive investment for the average farmer—and, along with it, the West itself. Without John Deere's steel plow, which unlike wooden and iron plows could break through tough grass and roots and did not require constant cleaning, "breaking the plains" might not have been possible at all.

Clearing the Land   Most white migrants intended to farm. After locating a suitable land claim, they immediately constructed a rudimentary cabin if none already existed. Time did not permit more elaborate structures, for—contrary to McCormick reaper ads—few settlers found plowed fields awaiting them. First they had to clear the land.

For those settling in wooded areas, the quickest and easiest way to get crops in the ground was to girdle, or to cut deep notches with an ax around a tree's base, cutting off the flow of sap. A few weeks later, the trees would lose their leaves, which farmers burned for fertilizer. As soon as enough light came through, settlers planted corn—a durable and nutritious crop. Eventually the dead trees fell and were chopped for firewood and fences, leaving stumps whose removal was a backbreaking task. At the rate of five to ten acres a year, depending on a family's size, the average family needed ten years to fully clear a farm, assuming they did not relocate sooner. Prairie land took less time. Throughout the 1850s, though, many farmers dismissed lands free of timber as equivalent to deserts, unfit for cultivation.

Whereas farming attracted families, lumbering and mining appealed mostly to single young men. By the 1840s, the nation's timber industry centered around the Great Lakes. As eastern forests became depleted, northeastern lumber companies and their laborers migrated to Wisconsin, Michigan, and Minnesota. Recently arrived Scandinavians and French Canadians also worked in the booming lumber industry, which provided construction materials for growing cities and wooden ties for expanding railroads. As the Great Lakes forests thinned, lumbermen moved again—some to the Gulf States' pine forests, some to Canada, and some to the Far West, where Mexicans in California and British in Canada had already established flourishing lumber industries. With the rapid growth of California's cities following the Gold Rush of 1849, timber's demand soared, drawing midwestern lumbermen farther west.

The Midwest's own cities nurtured the surrounding countryside's settlement. Steamboats turned river settlements like Louisville and Cincinnati into vibrant commercial centers, while Chicago, Detroit, and Cleveland grew up on the Great Lakes' banks. By the mid-nineteenth century, Chicago, with its railroads, stockyards, and grain elevators, dominated the region's economy; western farmers transported livestock and grain by rail to that city, where pigs became packed meat and grain became flour before being shipped east. The promise of future flour and future pigs gave rise to commodities markets. Some of the world's most sophisticated and speculative economic practices took place in Chicago.

THE FEDERAL GOVERNMENT AND WESTWARD EXPANSION

Few white Americans considered settling in the West before the region had been explored, surveyed, secured, and "civilized," by which they meant not only the removal of native populations but also the establishment of churches, businesses, and American legal structures. Although some individuals headed west in advance of European civilization, wide-scale settlement depended on the federal government's sponsorship.

The Fur Trade

No figure better represents the mythical westerner than the mountain man: the loner who wandered the mountains, trapping beaver, living off the land, casting off all semblance of civilization, and daring to go where no white person had ever trod. Fur trappers were, in fact, among the first white Americans in the trans-Appalachian West, but in reality, their lives bore faint resemblance to the myth. Although many had little contact with American society, they interacted regularly with the West's native peoples. Fur trappers lived among Indians, became multilingual, and often married Indian women. Indian women transformed animal carcasses into finished pelts, and they also smoothed trade relations between their husbands and their own native communities. The offspring of such marriages—métis or mestizos (people of mixed Indian and European heritage)—often entered the fur trade and added to the West's cultural complexity.

The fur trade was an international business, with pelts from deep in the American interior finding their way to Europe and Asia. Until the 1820s, British companies dominated the trade, but American ventures prospered in the 1820s and 1830s. The American Fur Company made John Jacob Astor the nation's wealthiest man. While Astor lived lavishly in his New York City mansion, his business employed hundreds of trappers and traders who lived and worked among native peoples in the Great Lakes and Pacific Northwest regions. From its base in Astoria on the Columbia River,

MAP 13.3 Western Indians and Routes of Exploration

Although western explorers believed they were discovering new routes and places, Indians had long lived in most of the areas through which explorers traveled.

just a few miles from the Pacific Ocean in present-day Oregon, the American Fur Company made millions by sending furs to China.

Even for the great majority of trappers who never made it to Astoria, the fur trade had an international dimension. Beginning in the 1820s, they came together annually for a "rendezvous"—a multiday gathering where they traded fur for guns, tobacco, and beads that they could later exchange with Indians. They also shared stories and alcohol, and gambled. Modeled on similar Indian gatherings that had occurred for generations, the rendezvous brought together Americans, Indians, Mexicans, and people of mixed heritage from all over the West—as far north as Canada and as far south as Mexico. Rendezvous took place in remote mountain locations but were cosmopolitan affairs.

By the 1840s, the American fur trade was declining. Beavers had been over-hunted and fashions had shifted, with silk supplanting beaver fur as the preferred material for hats. The traders' legacy includes setting a pattern of resource extraction and depletion (and boom and bust), introducing native peoples to devastating diseases, and developing trails across the trans-Mississippi West.

Transcontinental Exploration   A desire for quicker and safer routes for transporting goods to trading posts drove much early exploration. William Becknell, an enterprising merchant, helped in 1821 to chart the Santa Fe Trail running between Missouri and Santa Fe, New Mexico, where it connected to the Chihuahua Trail running southward into Mexico, allowing American and Mexican merchants to develop a vibrant exchange of American manufactured goods for furs and other items. Fur trader Jedediah Smith redis-covered in 1824 the South Pass; this 20-mile break in the Rocky Mountains in present-day Wyoming had previously been known only to Native Americans and a handful of fur trappers from the Pacific Fur Company who had passed through in 1812. The South Pass became the route followed by most overland travelers to California and Oregon. Less well-known traders, trappers, missionaries, and gold seekers, often assisted by Native American guides, also discovered traveling routes throughout the West, and some—most famously, mountain man Kit Carson—aided government expeditions.

Lewis and Clark's Corps of Discovery was only the first of many federally sponsored expeditions to chart the trans-Mississippi West. These expeditions often had diplomatic goals, aiming to establish cordial relations with Indian groups with whom Americans might trade or enter military alliances. Some had scientific mis-sions, charged with recording information about the region's native inhabitants, flora, and fauna. But they were always also commercial in purpose. Just as Lewis and Clark had hoped to find what proved to be an elusive Northwest Passage to the Pacific, so, too, did later explorers hope to locate land, water, and rail routes that would allow American businessmen and farmers to trade nationally and internationally.

In 1805, the U.S. Army dispatched Zebulon Pike to find the Mississippi River's source and a navigable route west. He was instructed to collect information on nat-ural resources and native peoples, and foster diplomatic relationships with Indian leaders. He was also to purchase land from Indians; before the Supreme Court ru-led in *Johnson v. M'Intosh* (1823) that Indians did not own land but rather had only a "right of occupancy," government officials instructed Pike and other ex-plorers to identify and purchase lands suitable for military garrisons.

Although Pike failed to identify the Mississippi's source and had limited success in cultivating relationships and purchasing land, he nonetheless gathered important information. Shortly after returning from present-day Minnesota, he left for what are now Missouri, Nebraska, Kansas, and Colorado. After Pike and his men wan-dered into Spanish territory to the south, military officials held Pike captive for sev-eral months in Mexico, inadvertently giving him a tour of areas that he might not have otherwise explored. After his release, Pike wrote an account of his experiences describing a potential market in southwestern cities as well as bountiful furs and precious metals. The province of Tejas (Texas), with its fertile soil and rich grasslands, enchanted him. At the same time, Pike dismissed the other northern provinces of Mexico, whose boundaries stretched to the northern borders of present-day Nevada and Utah, as unsuitable for human habitation. Although nomadic Indians might sustain themselves there, he explained, the region was unfit for cultivation by civilized people.

Stephen Long, another army explorer, similarly declared in 1820 that the region comprising modern-day Oklahoma, Kansas, and Nebraska was "the Great American Desert," incapable of cultivation. Until the 1850s, when a transcontinental railroad was planned, this "desert" was reserved for Indian settlement, and most army-sponsored exploration focused elsewhere. In 1838, Congress established the U.S. Army Corps of Topographical Engineers to systematically explore the West in advance of widespread settlement. As a second lieutenant in that corps, John C. Frémont undertook three expeditions to the region between the upper Mississippi and Missouri rivers, the Rockies, the Great Basin, Oregon, and California. He helped survey the Oregon Trail. With the assistance of his wife, Jessie Benton Frémont, Frémont published bestselling accounts of his explorations, earning him the nickname "The Pathfinder" and paving the way for a political career. The Corps of Topographical Engineers' most significant contributions came in the 1850s with its surveying of possible routes for a transcontinental railroad.

The federal government spent millions publicizing the results of its explorations, much more than it allotted for exploration itself. Westward migrants often carried two books with them: the Bible and Frémont's account of his army explorations.

A Military Presence

The army did more than explore. It also helped ready the West for settlement. With the General Survey Act of 1824, Congress empowered the military to chart transportation improvements deemed vital to the nation's military protection or commercial growth. In addition to working on federally funded projects, army engineers helped design state- and privately sponsored roads, canals, and railroads, and its soldiers cleared forests and lay roadbeds. A related bill, also in 1824, authorized the army to improve the Ohio and Mississippi rivers; a later amendment did the same for the Missouri.

By the 1850s, 90 percent of the U.S. military was stationed west of the Mississippi River. When Indians refused to relinquish their lands, the army escorted them westward; when they inflicted harm on whites or their property, the army waged war. The army sometimes destroyed the crops and buildings of white squatters refusing to vacate lands settled without legal title. But, primarily, the army assisted overland migration. Army forts on the periphery of Indian Country intimidated Indians, defended settlers and migrants from Indian attacks, and supplied information and provisions. In theory, the army was also supposed to protect Indians by driving settlers off Indian lands and enforcing laws prohibiting the sale of alcohol to Indians. Yet even when officers were disposed to enforce such policies, the army's small size relative to the territory it regulated made it virtually impossible to do so.

LINKS TO THE WORLD

Gold in California

When James Marshall discovered gold in Sutter's Mill, California, in January 1848, word spread quickly—and quite literally around the world. Within a year, tens of thousands of adventurers from other countries rushed to California, making it the most cosmopolitan place in North America, and perhaps the entire world.

In an era before the telegraph crossed the oceans, the news traveled surprisingly fast. Mexicans heard first. Next, word spread to Chile, Peru, and throughout South America; then across the Pacific to Hawai'i, China, and Australia; and then to Europe—Ireland, France, and the German states. How did the news travel? Overland travelers brought the news south to Baja California and Sonora in Mexico. By spring 1849, some six thousand Mexicans were panning for gold around the newly established town of Sonora, California. Many of the Mexicans came north seasonally to seek gold, spreading news of California on every trip home.

Sailing ships brought news of California gold to Hawai'i. The newspaper *Honolulu Polynesian* announced it in the kingdom on June 24, 1848. "Honolulu has never before witnessed such an excitement as the gold fever has created," the *Polynesian* reported later that summer. Gold seekers and merchants sailed from Hawai'i to California, and their letters home recruited

The Center for American History, The University of Texas at Austin

Charles Koppel portrayed the Colorado Desert and Signal Mountain for the Pacific Railway Reports *(1853). The desert appears vast and unlimited, and those who travel through it seem to be advancing into the unknown.*

others. The constant traffic led to regular steamship service between Hawai'i and California as early as 1853.

A ship brought news of California gold discoveries to Valparaiso, Chile, in August 1848. More dramatically, a few weeks later, another sailing vessel landed with $2,500 in gold dust aboard. Although Chilean newspapers initially ignored the discovery, people in Chile's cities talked feverishly about gold. By November, newspapers reported rumors of California's overnight riches. Before year's end, two thousand Chileans had left for California, and many Chilean merchants opened branch stores in San Francisco.

Word of gold and California reached Australia in December 1848. Gold seekers quickly made travel arrangements, and by 1850 every ship in Sydney Harbour was destined for California. News had already reached China in mid-1848. A San Francisco merchant headed for the gold fields, Chum Ming, had written a cousin about his hopes for wealth. Four months later, the cousin arrived in San Francisco —with fellow villagers. Widespread poverty and gold's allure prompted many other Chinese to follow. By the mid-1850s, one in five gold miners was Chinese.

Californians, new and old, foreign and native-born, expressed amazement at the ethnic variety. One described it as "the most curious Babel of a place imaginable." In 1850, the new state of California had nearly 40 percent foreign-born inhabitants, the majority non-European. Through word of mouth, rumor, letters home, and newspaper reports, the discovery of gold in 1848 linked California to millions of ordinary people around the globe.

The Office of Indian Affairs handled the government's other Indian interactions, including treaty negotiations, school management, and trade oversight. Created in 1824 as part of the War Department, the Indian Office cooperated with the military in removing Indians from lands that stood in the way of American expansion and in protecting those citizens who staked their future in the West. In 1849 the Indian Office became part of the newly established Department of the Interior, and soon shifted its focus from removal to civilization, through a reservation system. Whereas some Indians accepted reservations as the best protection from white incursion, others rejected them, sometimes setting off deadly intratribal disagreements.

Public Lands   The federal government controlled vast tracts of land, procured either from the states' cessions of their western claims after the Revolution or through treaties with foreign powers, including Indian nations. The General Land Office, established in 1812 as part of the Treasury Department, handled those lands' distribution. Its earliest policies, designed to raise revenue, divided western lands into 640-acre tracts to be sold at public auction at a minimum price of $2 an acre. These policies favored speculators over individual, cash-poor farmers. Speculators bought up millions of acres of land. Unable to afford federal lands, many settlers became squatters, prompting Congress in 1820 to lower the price of land to $1.25 per acre and to make available tracts as small as 80 acres. Twelve years later, it began selling forty-acre tracts. Yet it demanded that the land be bought outright, and in a cash-poor society (particularly in the aftermath of the Panic of 1819), few would-be western settlers had enough cash to purchase government land. Because speculators sold land on credit, many small-time farmers bought from them instead, but at inflated prices.

Farmers pressed for a federal policy of preemption—that is, the right to settle on land without obtaining title, to improve it, and to buy it later at the minimum price ($1.25 an acre) established by law. Although some states offered lands through preemption, and although Congress authorized preemption of federal lands in particular instances in the 1820s and 1830s, the first general preemption law, the so-called Log Cabin Bill, came in 1841, and even then, it applied only to surveyed land. The right of preemption extended to unsurveyed lands with the Homestead Act of 1862, which provided that land would be provided free to any U.S. citizen (or foreigner who had declared the intention of becoming a citizen), provided he or she resided on it for five years and improved it. Alternatively, settlers could buy the land outright at $1.25 an acre after six months of residency, an arrangement that allowed them to use the land as collateral for loans to purchase additional land, farming supplies, or machinery. By the time of the Homestead Act, though, much of the remaining federal land was arid, and 160 acres was not always enough for an independent farm. Most of the best land, moreover, ended up in speculators' hands.

THE SOUTHWESTERN BORDERLANDS

Along the Louisiana Territory's southwestern border lay vast provinces controlled mostly by the Comanches and other Indians but claimed first by Spain and then—after 1821—by the newly independent nation of Mexico. New Mexico, with its bustling commercial centers of Albuquerque and Santa Fe, remained under Mexican federal control until the United States conquered the territory during its War with Mexico. Texas, by contrast, had a much more attenuated relationship with the Mexican government; in 1824, it became an autonomous state, giving it substantially more political independence from federal authorities than New Mexico enjoyed. This situation fostered Texas's struggle for national independence and then annexation to the United States, which in turn returned the divisive issue of slavery to the forefront of American political debate.

Southwestern Slavery   By the time Anglo-Americans became interested in Mexico's northern reaches, slavery in the Southwest was centuries-old. Yet as practiced by indigenous peoples—Comanches, Apaches, Kiowas, Navajos, Utes, and Pueblos—and by Spaniards, slavery differed from the chattel slavery of Africans and African Americans in the American South. Southwestern slavery was no less violent, but it centered on capturing women and children, who were then assimilated into their captors' communities, where they provided labor and status while fostering economic and diplomatic exchanges with the communities from which they had been captured.

This system of "captives and cousins," as one scholar terms it, was built on racial mixing—a practice anathema to most white Americans. As white slaveholders from the Southeast pushed their way into Mexican territory during the 1820s and

1830s, they often justified their conquest in racial terms. Even the region's Hispanic settlers, they reasoned, had been rendered lazy and barbarous by racial intermixing and were thus destined to be supplanted, whether peaceably or otherwise.

The New Mexican Frontier When Mexico gained independence from Spain in 1821, the Hispanic population of New Mexico outnumbered the indigenous Pueblo peoples by three to one. There were 28,000 Hispanics, including people born in Spain and, especially, criollos, people born in New Spain to parents of Spanish descent. Whether Spanish, Indian, criollo, or mestizo, most New Mexicans engaged in irrigated agriculture. To the north of Santa Fe, they farmed small plots, but to the south, larger farms and ranches predominated. Rancheros' wealth came from selling their wool and corn in distant markets, and from relying on unpaid laborers: farm hands, often their own relatives, bound to the rancheros by debt. United by a threat from the province's raiding Indian tribes—Apaches, Utes, Navajos, and Comanches—Hispanics, Pueblos, and mestizos sometimes united in common defense. But relations among Hispanics and the sedentary Pueblos were not always peaceful. Their numerical superiority allowed Hispanics to seize many of the Pueblos' villages and lands in the rich northern river valleys of an otherwise arid region.

The Santa Fe Trail caused a commercial explosion in New Mexico, doubling the value of imports in just two years. Whereas the Spanish had tried to keep foreigners out, the Mexican government offered enormous land grants to Anglo-American and French entrepreneurs, sometimes in partnership with the region's Hispanic residents, hoping they would develop the region's industry and agriculture, and strengthen commercial ties with the United States.

Although commercial ties did strengthen, very few Americans settled permanently in New Mexico during the 1820s and 1830s. Most of the best lands had already been taken by Indians and Hispanics. And Americans in search of cheap, fertile land did not need to travel that far west; they could find what they were looking for in Texas.

The Texas Frontier That they would do so, however, was not evident at the time of Mexican independence. Unlike in New Mexico, indigenous Indians remained the dominant group in Texas in 1821, though the population also included Hispanics, Anglos, mestizos, and immigrant Indians. Of the thirty thousand indigenous people, most were Comanches, but there were also Jumanos, Coahuiltecans, Tonkawas, Karankawas, Apaches, Caddos, and Wichitas. Texas was part of what one historian has called the Comanche Empire, an enormous territory spreading from northern Mexico to Louisiana that the Comanches dominated through a combination of kinship ties, trade, diplomacy, and violence. People of European heritage were a relatively small presence in Texas in 1821. Hispanic peoples had been there since the 1500s, establishing missions and presidios, but by 1820, they numbered only five thousand. Most raised livestock on ranches, while others made their living from trading with Indians. Living so distant from the Spanish colonial capital in Mexico City, they

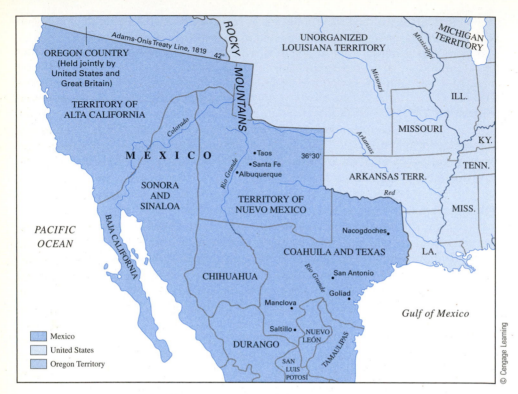

MAP 13.4 Mexico's Far North

What is now considered the American Southwest was made up of the northern provinces of Mexico until the United States conquered the territory during the Mexican War (1846–1848).

formed a distinctive identity, seeing themselves as Tejanos (or Texans) rather than as Spaniards. Many intermarried with Indians.

After the War of 1812, Anglo-Americans had begun entering Texas, where they sought furs, silver, or adventure. They traded manufactured goods—such as guns, ammunition, and kettles—for animal hides, horses, and mules; soon they largely supplanted the Tejanos as the Indians' trading partners. Although some Anglos settled in Texas, often living among Indians, most simply traveled the Santa Fe and Chihuahua trails without settling. They were deterred in part by the region's violence.

The Comanche Empire   As Indians competed with one another for resources, the southwestern borderlands experienced intermittent but often brutal violence. Mounted on horses, the Comanches hunted bison, took captives, and stole horses, livestock, and crops from their enemies, among whom were the Pawnees, Arapahos, Cheyennes, and Osage. Other, smaller Indian groups, such as the Wichitas and Caddos, mostly farmed, growing enough corn, beans, squash, and pumpkin to feed themselves and to trade with the more mobile Comanches. When crops failed, farmers often turned to bison hunting as well, sometimes causing conflict with the Comanches.

Tensions increased around the time of Mexican independence, when another ten thousand Indians began migrating into the region. From the Old Northwest came Shawnees and Kickapoos—former members of Tecumseh's confederacy—who after their defeat during the War of 1812 had headed north to Canada before heading back southward into Kansas, Indian Territory, and then Texas. From the Old Southwest came Cherokees, Creeks, Choctaws, Chickasaws, and Seminoles, some with African American slaves. Indian newcomers often clashed with indigenous Indians, with whom they vied for land and animals. The conflict was cultural, too: Some immigrant Indians, having adopted Anglo clothing and racial ideologies, dismissed as "savage" the indigenous Indians who hunted buffalo, wore skins, and did not value land as a commodity.

Because such violence threatened the viability of southeastern Indian removal and disrupted trade, the U.S. government brokered a treaty in 1835: The Comanches agreed to allow immigrants onto their lands in exchange for trade opportunities. Before long, trade boomed. Immigrant Indians swapped agricultural products and manufactured goods, such as rifles and ammunition, for the Comanches' meats, robes, and horses. The Comanches also traded human captives, seized in Texas or northern Mexico. That same year, the Comanches ended more than a century of war with the Osages. As peace returned, so too did American traders, who now built permanent trading posts. Meanwhile, the U.S. government's Indian removal continued apace, fueling Americans' commitment to cotton cultivation and expansionism. Mexican officials feared for the region's future.

American Empresarios

More than a decade earlier, before Mexican independence, the Spanish had worried about the security of Texas, which they saw as a buffer between hostile Indians, particularly Comanches, and the United States. Their solution was to populate the region. Thus when Moses Austin, a miner and trader from Missouri, approached Spanish authorities in Mexico City in January 1821 about settling Americans in Texas, they were willing to make a deal as long as Austin brought with him Americans willing to assimilate into Texas society. In exchange for promising to bring three hundred Catholic families—and no slaves—Austin would receive an enormous land grant of approximately 200,000 acres along the Brazos River. Before Austin could act, though, he died, and Mexico won its independence from Spain in September 1821.

Austin's son, Stephen, pursued his father's scheme, pressing the new Mexican government to honor the grant, which it did in 1823, provided that the younger Austin renounce his American citizenship and become a Mexican national. By 1825, Stephen Austin had settled three hundred families (two thousand white people) and, despite the promise of no slaves, four hundred "contract laborers" of African descent. With contracts that ran for ninety-nine years, these African Americans were essentially slaves. Still, Austin's success at luring settlers to Texas encouraged the Mexican government to sign three more contracts granting Austin land in exchange for his bringing nine hundred additional families.

Generally satisfied with the Austin experiment, in 1824 Mexico passed a Colonization Law providing land and tax incentives to future foreign settlers and leaving the details of colonization to the individual Mexican states. Coahuila y Texas specified that the head of a family could obtain as much as 4,428 acres of grazing land or 177 acres of farming land. The land was cheap, and—unlike land in the United States—could be paid for in installments over six years, with no money due until the fourth year. To be eligible, foreigners had to be upstanding Christians with "good habits," and they had to establish permanent residency. As an incentive for these new settlers to assimilate into Mexican society, the Coahuila y Texas government provided additional land to those who married Mexican women.

Most U.S. citizens who settled in Mexico did so under the auspices of an *empresario,* or immigration agent, who took responsibility for selecting "moral" colonists, distributing lands, and enforcing regulations. In exchange, he received nearly 25,000 acres of grazing land and 1,000 acres of farming land for every hundred families that he settled. Between 1825 and 1832, approximately twenty-four *empresario* contracts (seventeen of which went to Anglo-Americans) had been signed, with the *empresarios* agreeing to bring eight thousand families total. The land grants were so vast that together they covered almost all of present-day Texas.

During the 1820s, Anglo-Americans emigrated, with their slaves, to Texas, motivated by a combination of push and pull factors. Some felt pushed by the hard times following the Panic of 1819; at the same time, they were drawn by cheap land and, especially, generous credit terms. Despite Mexican efforts to encourage assimilation, these Americans tended to settle in separate communities and to interact little with the Tejanos. Even more troubling to the Mexican government, the Anglo-Americans outnumbered the Tejanos two to one. Authorities worried that the transplanted Americans would try to make Texas part of the United States.

Texas Politics   In 1826, their fears seemed to materialize when an *empresario* named Haden Edwards called for an independent Texas, the "Fredonia Republic." Other *empresarios,* reasoning that they had more to gain than to lose from peaceful relations with the Mexican government, resisted Edwards's secessionist movement. Austin even sent militia to help quash the rebellion. Although the Fredonia revolt failed, Mexican authorities dreaded what it might foreshadow.

The answer to the secessionist threat, Mexican authorities thought, was to weaken the American presence in Texas. In 1830, they terminated legal immigration from the United States while simultaneously encouraging immigration from Europe and other parts of Mexico in order to dilute the American influence. They prohibited American slaves from entering Texas, a provision that brought Texas in line with the rest of Mexico—where slavery had been outlawed the previous year— and that was meant to repel American slaveholders. Yet these laws did little to discourage Americans and their slaves from coming; soon they controlled most of the Texas coastline and its border with the United States. Mexican authorities repealed the anti-immigration law in 1833, reasoning that it discouraged upstanding settlers but did nothing to stem the influx of undesirable settlers. By 1835, the non-Indian population of Texas was nearly thirty thousand, with Americans outnumbering Tejanos seven to one.

White Texans divided into two main factions. There were those, like Stephen Austin, who favored staying in Mexico but demanding more autonomy, the legalization of slavery, and free trade with the United States. Others pushed for Texas secession from Mexico and asked to be annexed to the United States. In 1835, the secessionists overtook a Mexican military installation charged with collecting taxes at Galveston Bay. Austin advocated a peaceful resolution to the crisis, but Mexican authorities nonetheless considered him suspicious and jailed him for eighteen months, an act that helped convert him to the independence cause. But it would be Sam Houston and Davy Crockett—newly arrived Americans—who would lead the movement.

The Lone Star Republic

With discontent over Texas increasing throughout Mexico, Mexican president General Santa Anna declared himself dictator and marched his army toward Texas. Fearing Santa Anna would free their slaves, and citing similarities between their own cause and that of the American colonies in the 1770s, Texans staged an armed rebellion. After initial defeats at the Alamo mission in San Antonio and at Goliad in March 1836, the Texans easily triumphed by year's end. They declared themselves the Lone Star Republic and elected Sam Houston as president. Their constitution legalized slavery and banned free blacks from living within Texas.

Texas then faced the challenge of nation building, which to its leaders involved Indian removal. When the Indians refused to leave, Mirabeau Lamar, the nation's second president, mobilized the Texas Rangers—mounted nonuniformed militia—to drive them out through terror. Sanctioned by the Texas government, but sometimes acting on their own, the Rangers raided Indian villages, where they robbed, raped, and murdered. Although some Texas officials tried to negotiate with the Indians and Tejanos, it was what one historian has called "ethnic cleansing" that cleared the land of its native settlers to make room for white Americans and their African American slaves. Before long, the surviving Comanches would face starvation and depopulation—weakened by European disease, drought, and over-hunting—but not before fighting back with devastating raids on northern Mexico, ravaging its inhabitants and countryside, and inadvertently paving the way for American conquest.

Wartime Losses and Profits

After annexing Texas in 1845, the United States, seeking to further expand its territorial reach, waged war against Mexico from 1846 to 1848 (see Chapter 14). In the borderlands, as in Mexico itself, civilians—Indians, tejanos, californios, and Mexicans—got caught in the fray. Some lost their lives, and many more, precariously caught between the two sides, suffered wartime depredations. If they aided the Mexicans, the U.S. Army destroyed their homes; if they refused aid to the Mexicans, then the Mexicans destroyed their homes. A U.S. army report in 1847 acknowledged that its "wild volunteers ... committed ... all sorts of atrocities on the persons and property of Mexicans." Many civilians fled. Even once the war ended in the borderlands, violence did not stop. From 1847 to 1848, Texas Rangers slaughtered Indians. "They think that the death of an Indian is a fair offsett [sic] to the loss of a horse," wrote one Anglo American.

Yet some civilians profited from the war. Farmers sold provisions and mules to the armies, peddlers sold alcohol and food to soldiers, and others set up gambling and prostitution businesses near army camps. Even still, tension generally characterized the relationship between civilians and soldiers, largely because of the American soldiers' racial attitudes.

CULTURAL FRONTIERS IN THE FAR WEST

Even before the United States seized tremendous amounts of new territory during the War with Mexico, some Americans took the gamble of a lifetime and moved to the Far West, often to places—such as California and Utah—that Mexico controlled. Some sought religious freedom or to convert others to Christianity, but most wanted fertile farmland. Whatever their reasons for moving west, they often encountered people from different cultures. Such encounters sometimes led to cooperation, but more often to tension or open conflict.

Western Missionaries   Catholic missionaries maintained a strong presence in the Far West. In the Spanish missions, priests treated Indians as "spiritual children," introducing them to Catholic sacraments; holding them to a rigid system of prayer, sexual conduct, and work; and treating them as legal minors. When they failed to live up to priests' or soldiers' expectations, they were subject to corporeal punishment. When they ran away, they were forcibly returned. With no political voice and few other choices, Indians often responded to abusive practices with armed uprisings, in the process helping to weaken the mission system itself.

A Mexican law secularized the California missions in 1833, removing them from ecclesiastical control and using them primarily to organize Indian labor. Some Indians stayed at the missions, others left to farm their own land or to find employment elsewhere, but for almost all, secularization brought enhanced personal freedom despite persistent limitations to their legal rights.

Even after the missions' secularization, Catholic missionaries—Americans, Europeans, and converted Indians—continued ministering to immigrants, working to convert Indians, and encouraging specifically Roman Catholic colonies. Missionaries founded schools and colleges, introduced medical services, and even aided in railroad explorations.

In the Pacific Northwest, Catholics vied directly with Protestants for Indian souls. Although evangelicals focused on the Midwest, a few hoped to bring Christianity to the Indians of the Far West. Under the auspices of the American Board of Commissioners for Foreign Missions, two missionary couples—generally credited as being the first white migrants along the Oregon Trail—traveled to the Pacific Northwest in 1836. Narcissa and Marcus Whitman built a meetinghouse for Cayuse Indians in Waiilatpu, near present-day Walla Walla, Washington, while Eliza and Henry Spalding worked to convert the Nez Percé at Lapwai, in what is now Idaho. With their air of cultural superiority, the Whitmans did little to endear themselves to the Cayuses, none of whom converted. The Whitmans redirected their efforts toward the ever-increasing stream of white migrants flowing into Oregon beginning in the 1840s.

These migrants' arrival escalated tensions with the Cayuses, and when a devastating measles epidemic struck in 1847, the Cayuses saw it as a calculated assault. They retaliated by murdering the Whitmans and twelve other missionaries. After the Whitmans' violent deaths, the Spaldings abandoned their own, more successful mission; blamed Catholics for inciting the massacre; and became farmers in Oregon, not returning to Lapwai for another fifteen years.

Mormons   The Mormons, who had been persecuted in Missouri and Illinois, sought religious sanctuary in the West. In 1847, Brigham Young led them to their "Promised Land" in the Great Salt Lake valley, still under Mexican control but soon to become part of the unorganized U.S. territory of Utah. As non-Mormons began to settle in Utah, Brigham Young tried to dilute their influence by attracting new Mormon settlers to what he called the state of Deseret. In 1849, Young and his associates established the Perpetual Emigration Fund, which sponsored "handcart companies" of poor migrants, particularly from Europe, who pushed all their belongings to Utah in small handcarts.

The Mormon's arrival in the Great Basin complicated the region's already complex relations among Indians. The Utes, for example, had long traded in stolen goods and captured people, particularly Paiutes. After Mormons tried to curtail the slave trade, Ute slavers tortured their Paiute captives, particularly children, calculating that Mormons would buy them. The ploy often worked; when it did not, Ute slavers sometimes killed the children, in one case dangling them by their feet and thrashing them against stones. The purchased children often worked as servants in Mormon homes, which encouraged their distraught families, eager for proximity to their children, to settle near Mormon villages. Although the Mormons tried to bring the Paiutes into their religious fold, they—much like Catholic missionaries in California—treated adult Indians as children, causing friction, even violence, when the Paiutes sought to secure their autonomy. Sharing the Utes as a common enemy, the Mormons and Paiutes nonetheless formed an uneasy alliance in the early 1850s.

With their slave trade threatened and their economy in shambles, the Utes attacked Mormon and Paiute settlements to steal livestock and horses for resale, and then to vandalize their crops and property in an effort to drive away the Mormons. War erupted in 1853, and although an uneasy truce was reached in 1854, tensions continued between the Mormons and their Indian neighbors.

And between Mormons and their white neighbors. Although Mormons prospered from providing services, such as ferries, and supplies to tens of thousands of California-bound settlers and miners passing by their settlements, Young discouraged "gentiles" (his term for non-Mormons) from settling in Deseret and advocated boycotts of gentile businesses. When in 1852 the Mormons openly sanctioned polygamy, which some of its followers had practiced for more than a decade, anti-Mormon sentiment increased throughout the nation. After some young Mormons vandalized federal offices in Utah, President James Buchanan—hoping to divert Americans' attention from the increasingly divisive slavery issue—dispatched 2,500 federal troops in June 1857 to suppress an alleged Mormon rebellion.

Anxious over their own safety, a group of Mormons joined some Paiutes in attacking a passing wagon train of non-Mormon migrants. Approximately 120 men, women, and children died in the so-called Mountain Meadows Massacre in August 1857. In the next two years, the U.S. Army and the Mormons engaged in armed conflict, resulting in much property destruction but no fatalities. As the Mormons' relationships with their neighbors and passersby indicate, western violence often emerged from complex interactions and alliances which did not simply pit natives against newcomers.

Oregon and California Trails   Nor were all encounters between natives and newcomers violent. From 1840 until 1860, between 250,000 and 500,000 people, including many children, walked across much of the continent, a a trek that took seven months on average. Although they traveled armed for conflict, most of their encounters with Indians were peaceful, if tense.

The overland journeys began at one of the so-called jumping-off points—towns such as Independence, St. Joseph, and Westport Landing—along the Missouri River, where migrants bought supplies for the 2,000-mile trip still ahead of them. After cramming supplies into wagons already overflowing with household possessions, they set out either in organized wagon trains or on their own. While miners frequently traveled alone or in groups of fortune-seeking young men, farmers—including many women migrating only at their husbands' insistence—often traveled with relatives, neighbors, church members, and other acquaintances.

They timed their departures to be late enough that they could find forage grass for their oxen and livestock, but not so late that they would encounter the treacherous snows that came early to the Rockies and the Sierra Nevada. Not all were successful. From 1846 to 1847, the Donner Party took a wrong turn, got caught in a blizzard, and resorted to cannibalism. More fortunate overland migrants trudged alongside their wagons, beginning their days well before dawn, pausing only for a short midday break, and walking until late afternoon. They covered on average 15 miles a day, in weather ranging from freezing cold to blistering heat. In wagon trains composed of families, men generally tended livestock during the day, while women—after an energy-draining day on the trail—set up camp, prepared meals, and tended small children. Many women gave birth on the trail, where an always-difficult experience could become excruciating. "Her sufferings were so great," one woman wrote about her sister. "It all seems like a jumble of jolting wagon, crying baby, dust, sagebrush and the never ceasing pain." Even under normal circumstances, trail life was exhausting, both physically and emotionally. Overlanders worried about Indian attack, getting lost, running out of provisions or water, and losing loved ones, who would have to be buried along the trail, in graves never again to be visited. But for most adults, trail life did not prove particularly dangerous, with Indian attacks rare and death rates approximating those of society at large. Children, though, had a greater risk than adults of being crushed by wagon wheels or drowning during river crossings.

Indians were usually peaceful, if cautious. Particularly during the trails' early days, Indians provided food and information or ferried migrants across rivers; in exchange, migrants offered wool blankets, knives, metal pots, tobacco, ornamental

This rare stereocard shows an emigrant train, including two women and possibly a child, dwarfed by the natural landscape in Strawberry Valley, California, in the 1860s.

Library of Congress

beads, and other items in short supply in Indian societies. When exchanges went bad—when one of the parties misunderstood the other's cultural practices or tried to swindle the other—relationships grew tense, not just between the particular persons involved, but between Indians and migrants more generally. Indians grew suspicious of all white people, just as migrants failed to distinguish different native bands or tribes.

A persistent aggravation among migrants was the theft of livestock, which they usually blamed on Indians even though white thieves stole livestock, too. Indians who took livestock often did so when whites failed to offer gifts in exchange for grazing rights. One such incident, the so-called Mormon Cow Incident (or the Grattan Massacre), resulted in human bloodshed, forever altering relationships along the Oregon Trail.

In August 1854, a Lakota in present-day Wyoming slaughtered a cow that had strayed from a nearby Mormon camp. When Lakota leaders offered compensation, U.S. Army Lieutenant John Grattan, intent on making a point, refused the offer. Tempers flared, Grattan ordered his men to shoot, and after a Lakota chief fell dead, the Indians returned the fire, killing Grattan and all twenty-nine of his men. In retaliation, the following year General William Harney led six hundred soldiers to a village near Ash Hollow, where migrants and Indians had traded peaceably for many years. When Indian leaders refused to surrender any of their people to Harney, the general ordered his men to fire. Thirty minutes later, eighty-seven Indians lay dead, and seventy women and children had been taken prisoner. The event disrupted peaceful exchange along the trail and laid the groundwork for nearly two decades of warfare between the Lakotas and the U.S. Army.

Indian Treaties   Even as the U.S. Army became embroiled in armed conflict, the Indian Office worked to negotiate treaties to keep Indians—and their intertribal conflicts—from interfering with western migration and commerce. The Fort Laramie Treaty of 1851 (or the Horse Creek Council Treaty) was signed by the United States and eight northern Plains tribes—the Lakotas, Cheyennes, Arapahos, Crows, Assiniboines, Gros-Ventres, Mandans, and Arrickaras—who occupied the Platte River valley through which the three great overland routes westward—the Oregon, California, and Mormon Trails—all passed. Two years later, in 1853, the United States signed a treaty with three southwestern nations, the Comanches, Kiowas, and Apaches, who lived in the vicinity of the Sante Fe Trail. Under the terms of both treaties, the Indians agreed to maintain peace among themselves, to recognize government-delineated tribal boundaries, to allow the United States to construct roads and forts within those boundaries, to refrain from depredations against western migrants, and to issue restitution for any depredations nonetheless committed. In return, they would receive annual allotments from the U.S. government for ten years, to be paid with provisions, domestic animals, and agricultural implements. These allotments could be renewed for another five years at the discretion of the president of the United States.

But these treaties often meant different things to their Indian signatories and to the U.S. officials who brokered them. Contrary to U.S. expectations, Indian chiefs did not see such treaties as perpetually binding. Government officials, meanwhile, promised allotments but did little to ensure their timely arrival, often leaving Indians starving and freezing. The treaties did not end intratribal warfare, nor did they fully secure the overlanders' safety. But they did represent the U.S. government's efforts to promote expansion and to protect those citizens who caught the western fever.

Ecological Consequences of Cultural Contact   Armed conflict took relatively few lives compared to cholera, smallpox, and other maladies. The trails' jumping-off points, where migrants camped in close quarters while preparing for their journeys, bred disease, which migrants inadvertently carried to the Indians with whom they traded. Fearful of infection, Indians and migrants increasingly shied away from trading.

The disappearance of the buffalo (American bison) from the trails' environs further inflamed tensions. The buffalo not only provided protein to Plains Indians; they also held great spiritual significance. Many Native Americans blamed the migrants for the buffalo's disappearance, even though most overlanders never laid eyes on a buffalo. By the time the overland migration reached its peak in the late 1840s and 1850s, the herds had already been overhunted, in part by Native Americans eager to trade their hides. As traffic increased along the trail, the surviving buffalo scattered to where the grass was safe from the voracious appetites, and trampling feet, of the overlanders' livestock. But on those rare occasions when wagon trains did stumble upon bison herds, men rushed to fulfill their frontier fantasies—nurtured by the literature they had read—and shot the animals; such buffalo chases provided diversions from the trail's drudgery. Overlanders hunted other animals for sport, too, leaving behind rotting carcasses of antelopes, wolves, bears, and birds—animals that held spiritual significance for many Native Americans.

Overland migrants also sparked prairie fires. Indians had long used fire to clear farm land, to stimulate the growth of grasslands, and to create barren zones that would discourage bison from roaming into a rival nation's territory. But now emigrants—accustomed to stoves, not open fires—accidentally started fires that raged across the prairies, killing animals and the vegetation on which they survived. On rarer occasions, Indians started fires in the hope of capturing the migrants' fleeing livestock. Stories about intentionally lit fires exaggerated their extent, but they, too, contributed to increasing hostility between Indians and overlanders.

Gold Rush

Nowhere did migrants intrude more deeply on Indian life than near the California gold strikes. In January 1848, John Wilson Marshall discovered gold on John Sutter's property along a shallow tributary to the American River near present-day Sacramento, California. During the next year, tens of thousands of "forty-niners" rushed to California, where they practiced what is called placer mining, panning and dredging for gold in the hope of instant riches.

Some did indeed make fortunes. Peter Brown, a black man from Ste. Genevieve, Missouri, wrote his wife in 1851 that "California is the best country in the world to make money. It is also the best place for black folks on the globe." But not everyone reveled in the gold strikes. John Sutter complained that gold "destroyed" his milling and tanning businesses, as his Indians and Mormon workers left him for the mines and vandals stole his property. Most forty-niners never found enough gold to pay their expenses. "The stories you hear frequently in the States," one gold seeker wrote home, "are the most extravagant lies imaginable—the mines are a humbug." With their dreams dashed—and too poor or embarrassed to return home—many forty-niners took wage-paying jobs with large mining companies that used dangerous machinery to cut deep into the earth's surface to reach mineral veins.

The discovery of gold changed the face of California. (See Map 13.5.) As a remote Mexican province, California had a chain of small settlements surrounded by military forts (presidios) and missions, and it was inhabited mostly by Indians, along with a small number of Mexican rancheros, who raised cattle and sheep on enormous landholdings worked by coerced Indian laborers. As word spread of gold strikes, new migrants—from South America, Asia, Australia, and Europe—rushed to California. Although a California Supreme Court ruling—*People v. Hall* (1854)— made it virtually impossible to prevent violence against Chinese immigrants, Chinese citizens continued to seek their fortunes in California; by 1859, approximately 35,000 of them worked in the goldfields.

MAP 13.5 The California Gold Rush

Gold was discovered at Sutter's Mill in 1848, sparking the California gold rush that took place mostly along the western foothills of the Sierra Nevada mountains.

With so many hungry gold miners to feed, California experienced an agricultural boom. Although the immediate vicinity of mines became barren, when hydraulic mining washed away surface soil to expose buried lodes, California agriculture thrived overall, with wheat becoming the preferred crop: it required minimal investment, was easily planted, and had a relatively short growing season. In contrast to the Midwest's and Oregon's family farms, though, California's large-scale wheat farming depended on bonded Indian laborers.

Mining Settlements   Mining brought commercial and industrial boom, too, as enterprising merchants rushed to supply, feed, and clothe the new settlers. Among them was Levi Strauss, a German Jewish immigrant, whose tough mining pants found a ready market among the prospectors. Because men greatly outnumbered women, women's skills (and company) were in great demand. Even as men set up all-male households and performed tasks that bent prevailing notions of gender propriety, women received high fees for cooking, laundering, and sewing. Women also ran boarding houses, hotels, and brothels.

Cities sprang up. In 1848, San Francisco had been a small mission settlement of about 1,000 Mexicans, Anglos, soldiers, friars, and Indians. With the gold rush, it became an instant city, ballooning to 35,000 people in 1850. It was the West Coast gateway to the interior, and ships bringing people and supplies jammed the harbor. A French visitor in that year wrote, "At San Francisco, where fifteen months ago one found only a half-dozen large cabins, one finds today a stock exchange, a theater, churches of all Christian cults, and a large number of quite beautiful homes."

Yet as the Anglo-American, European, Hispanic, Asian, and African American populations swelled, the Indian population experienced devastation. Although California was admitted into the Union as a free state in 1850, its legislature soon passed "An Act for the Government and Protection of Indians" that essentially legalized Indians' enslavement. The practice of using enslaved Indians in the mines between 1849 and 1851 ended only when newly arrived miners brutally attacked the Indian workers, believing they degraded white labor and gave an unfair advantage to established miners. Those slaves who survived the violence were sent to work instead as field workers and house servants. Between 1821 and 1860, the Indian population of California fell from 200,000 to 30,000, as Indians died from disease, starvation, and violence. Because masters separated male and female workers, even Indians who survived failed to reproduce in large numbers.

THE POLITICS OF TERRITORIAL EXPANSION

With the population's westward movement shifting the locus of political power, Democratic and Whig politicians tried to keep the slavery issue out of the politics of territorial expansion. But they could not. Westward expansion was central to Democratic ideology, which saw the West's fertile and abundant lands as essential for creating a society in which white men could establish independent livelihoods and receive equal rights, freed from the undue influence of established slaveholders or urban elites. Whigs were more suspicious of rapid westward expansion, though they welcomed the commercial opportunities it might bring. Instead, they pushed harder for industrial and commercial development within the nation's current boundaries. Henry Clay, a leading Whig, explained that it "is much more important that we unite, harmonize, and improve what we have than attempt to acquire more."

The Texas issue, however, made it impossible to disentangle westward expansion and slavery. Soon after establishing the Lone Star Republic, Sam Houston approached American authorities to propose annexation as a state. But a new slave state would upset the balance of slave and free states in the Senate, a balance maintained since before the Missouri Compromise. Neither Whigs nor Democrats, wary of causing sectional divisions within their ranks, were inclined to confront the issue. In the 1830s, Democratic presidents Andrew Jackson and Martin Van Buren—one a strong proponent of slavery, the other a mild opponent—sidestepped the issue. But by the mid-1840s—with cotton cultivation expanding rapidly—some Democratic politicians began to equate the annexation of Texas with the nation's manifest destiny.

Manifest Destiny

The belief that American expansion westward and southward was inevitable, just, and divinely ordained dated to the nation's founding but was first labeled "manifest destiny" in 1845, by John L. O'Sullivan, editor of the *United States Magazine and Democratic Review*. O'Sullivan claimed that Texas annexation would be "the fulfillment of our manifest destiny to overspread the continent allotted by Providence for the free development of our yearly multiplying millions." The nation's destiny, he and others believed, was to encompass the continent. Manifest destiny implied that Americans had a God-given right, perhaps even an obligation, to expand their republican and Christian institutions to less fortunate and less civilized peoples. Manifest destiny motivated few Americans to pack their wagons and head westward. It did, however, provide a political rationale for territorial expansion.

Implicit in the idea of manifest destiny was the belief that American Indians and Hispanics, much like people of African descent, were inferior peoples best controlled or conquered. White racial theorists believed that, unlike white people, pure-blooded Indians and blacks were not capable of self-improvement. Nor, according to these racial theorists, were Hispanics because intermarriage with Indians had left them incapable of improvement. Lansford Hastings, an Ohio native who ventured west and authored *The Emigrants' Guide to Oregon and California* (1845) noted that a *Californio* (a Mexican living in California) was "scarcely a visible grade, in the scale of intelligence, above the barbarous tribes by whom he is surrounded." Hastings hoped that, if enough Anglo-Saxons migrated to California, they could conquer the Mexicans with sheer numbers. And if they did so, they could congratulate themselves for carrying out God's will. Others, however, felt that an expanding American empire defied God's will. During debates over Texas annexation, Transcendentalist William Ellery Channing argued that the United States should expand its empire by example not conquest: It should "assume the role of sublime moral empire, with a mission to diffuse freedom by manifesting its fruits, not to plunder, crush, and destroy."

In June 1846, impatient expansionists, including John C. Frémont, staged an armed rebellion against Mexican authorities and declared California an independent republic. Because the U.S. military soon conquered California in its War with Mexico, the "Bear Flag Rebellion"—so named for the symbol on the revolutionaries' flag—was short-lived but further inflamed racial tensions in California.

Fifty-Four Forty or Fight

To the north, Britain and the United States had jointly occupied the disputed Oregon Territory since 1818. Beginning with John Quincy Adams's administration, the United States had tried to fix the boundary at the 49th parallel, but Britain was determined to maintain access to Puget Sound and the Columbia River. As migrants streamed into Oregon in the early 1840s, expansionists demanded the entire Oregon Country for the United States, up to its northernmost border at latitude 54° 40′. Soon "fifty-four forty or fight" became their rallying cry.

President Tyler wanted both Oregon and Texas, but was obsessed with Texas. He argued that there was little to fear from slavery's expansion, for it would spread the nation's black population more thinly, causing the institution's gradual demise. But when word leaked out that Secretary of State John Calhoun had written to the British minister in Washington to justify Texas annexation as a way of protecting slavery—"a political institution essential to the peace, safety, and prosperity of those States in which it exists"—the Senate rejected annexation in 1844 by a vote of 35 to 16.

Polk and the Election of 1844   Worried southern Democrats persuaded their party's 1844 convention to adopt a rule requiring that the presidential nominee receive two-thirds of the convention votes, effectively giving the southern states a veto and allowing them to block the nomination of Martin Van Buren, an opponent of annexation. Instead, the party ran "Young Hickory," House Speaker James K. Polk, an avid expansionist and slaveholding cotton planter from Tennessee. The Democratic platform, designed to appeal to voters across regional lines, called for occupation of the entire Oregon Territory and annexation of Texas. The Whigs, who ran Henry Clay, argued that the Democrats' belligerent nationalism would lead to war with Great Britain or Mexico or both. Clay favored expansion through negotiation, whereas many northern Whigs opposed annexation altogether, fearful it would lead to additional slave states and strained relations with vital trading partners.

Polk and the Democrats won the election by 170 electoral votes to 105, though with a margin of just 38,000 out of 2.7 million votes cast. Polk won New York's 36 electoral votes by just 6,000 popular votes. Abolitionist James G. Birney, the Liberty Party candidate, had drawn almost 16,000 votes away from Clay by running on a Free-Soil platform. Without Birney, Clay might have won New York,

This 1845 portrayal of Oregon City, the western terminus of the Oregon Trail, was provided by a British army officer sent to investigate the influence of large-scale American immigration into a territory jointly occupied by Great Britain and the United States. After the Oregon Treaty (1846) drew the boundary between British and American territory at the forty-ninth parallel, Oregon City became the capital of the Oregon Territory from 1848 to 1851.

giving him an edge of 141 to 134 in the electoral college. Abolitionist forces thus unwittingly helped elect a slaveholder as president.

Annexation of Texas   Interpreting Polk's victory as a mandate for annexation, President Tyler proposed that Texas be admitted by joint resolution of Congress. The usual method of annexation, by treaty negotiation, required a two-thirds vote in the Senate—which expansionists did not have because there were sufficient opponents to slavery who stood against annexation. Joint resolution required only a simple majority in each house. On March 1, 1845, the resolution passed the House by 120 to 98 and the Senate by 27 to 25. Three days before leaving office, Tyler signed the measure. Mexico, which had never recognized Texas independence, immediately broke relations with the United States. In October, the citizens of Texas ratified annexation, and Texas joined the Union, with a constitution permitting slavery, in December 1845. The nation was on the brink of war with Mexico. That conflict—like none other before it—would lay bare the inextricable relationships among westward expansion, slavery, and sectional discord.

SUMMARY

Encouraged by literary and artistic images of the frontier, easterners often viewed the West as a place of natural abundance, where hard-working individuals could seek security, freedom, and perhaps even fortune. By the millions they poured into the Old Southwest and Old Northwest in the early decades of the nineteenth century. Although the federal government promoted westward expansion—in the form of support for transportation improvements, surveying, cheap land, and protection from Indians—western migrants did not make the decision to head west lightly. Nor did they always find what they were looking for. Some returned home, some moved to new locations, and some—too poor or too embarrassed— stayed in the West, where they reluctantly abandoned their dreams of economic independence. Others found what they were looking for in the West, though often the road to success proved much slower and more circuitous than they had anticipated.

Not everyone who went west did so voluntarily, nor did everyone in the West think of it as an expanding region. African American slaves were moved westward by their owners in enormous numbers in the years between 1820 and 1860. Native Americans saw their lands and their livelihoods constrict, and their environments so altered that their economic and spiritual lives were threatened. Some Indians responded to the white incursion through accommodation and peaceful overtures; others resisted, sometimes forcefully. If their first strategy failed, then they tried another. But the sheer force of numbers favored whites. For Indians in Texas and California, white incursions brought devastation.

Although their belief in Native Americans' inferiority allowed many white Americans to rationalize the Indians' fate, it was white attitudes toward black people and slavery that drove their decisions about where to locate in the West. Those who believed that slavery degraded white labor headed along a northern trajectory, whereas those who dreamed of slave ownership headed southward, where they clashed with yet another group of people whom they deemed racially inferior: Mexicans. When American settlers in Texas achieved their independence from Mexico, legalized slavery, and applied for annexation by the United States, they brought the divisive issue of slavery's westward expansion to the surface of American politics. Although Democratic politicians at first tried to maintain a geographic equilibrium by proposing an ambitious territorial agenda in Oregon as well, it would be Texas annexation that set the stage for military conflict, the addition of vast territories in the Southwest, and reinvigorated sectional conflict.

14

SLAVERY AND AMERICA'S FUTURE:
THE ROAD TO WAR 1845–1861

THE WAR WITH MEXICO AND ITS CONSEQUENCES

In the 1840s, territorial expansion surged forward under the leadership of President James K. Polk of North Carolina. The annexation of Texas just before his inauguration did not necessarily make war with Mexico inevitable, but through a series of calculated decisions, Polk brought the conflict on. Mexico broke off relations with the United States, and during the annexation process, Polk urged Texans to seize all land to the Rio Grande and claim the river as their southern and western border. Mexico held that the Nueces River was the border; hence, the stage was set for conflict. Nothing could weaken Polk's determination to fulfill the nation's manifest destiny to rule the continent. He wanted Mexico's territory all the way to the Pacific, and all of Oregon Country as well. He and his expansionist cabinet achieved their goals but were largely unaware of the price in domestic harmony that expansion would exact.

Oregon   During the 1844 campaign, Polk's supporters had threatened war with Great Britain to gain all of Oregon. As president, however, Polk turned first to diplomacy. Not wanting to fight Mexico and Great Britain at the same time, he tried to avoid bloodshed in the Northwest, where America and Britain had since 1819 jointly occupied disputed territory. Dropping the demand for a boundary at latitude 54°40', he pressured the British to accept the 49th parallel. In 1846, Great Britain agreed. The Oregon Treaty gave the United

CHRONOLOGY

1846	War with Mexico begins
	Oregon Treaty negotiated
	Wilmot Proviso inflames sectional divisions
1847	Cass proposes idea of popular sovereignty
1848	Treaty of Guadalupe Hidalgo gives United States new territory in the Southwest
	Free-Soil Party formed
	Taylor elected president
	Gold discovered in California, which later applies for admission to Union as free state
1850	Compromise of 1850 passes, containing controversial Fugitive Slave Act
1852	Stowe publishes *Uncle Tom's Cabin*
	Pierce elected president
1854	Publication of "Appeal of the Independent Democrats"
	Kansas-Nebraska Act wins approval and ignites controversy
	Republican Party formed
	Return of fugitive Burns to slavery in Virginia
1856	Bleeding Kansas troubles nation
	Brooks attacks Sumner in Senate chamber
	Buchanan elected president, but Republican Frémont wins most northern states
1857	*Dred Scott v. Sanford* endorses southern views on black citizenship and slavery in territories
	Economic panic and widespread unemployment begin
1858	Kansas voters reject Lecompton Constitution
	Lincoln-Douglas debates attract attention
	Douglas contends popular sovereignty prevails over Dred Scott decision in territories
1859	Brown raids Harpers Ferry
1860	Democratic Party splits in two; southern Democrats demand constitutional guarantee for the territories
	Lincoln elected president in divided, sectional election
	Crittenden Compromise fails
	South Carolina secedes from Union
1861	Six more Deep South states secede
	Confederacy established at Montgomery, Alabama
	Attack on Fort Sumter begins Civil War
	Four states in the Upper South join the Confederacy

States all of present-day Oregon, Washington, and Idaho, and parts of Wyoming and Montana. Thus, a new era of land acquisition and conquest had begun under the eleventh president of the United States, the sixth to be a slaveholder and one who, through an agent, secretly bought and sold slaves from the White House.

"Mr. Polk's War"   Toward Mexico, Polk was more aggressive. In early 1846, he ordered American troops under "Old Rough and Ready," General Zachary Taylor, to march south and defend the contested border of the Rio Grande across from the town of Matamoros, Mexico (see Map 14.1). Polk especially desired California as the prize in his expansionist strategy, and he attempted to buy from Mexico a huge tract of land extending to the Pacific. When that effort failed, Polk waited for war. Negotiations between troops on the Rio Grande were awkwardly conducted in French because no American officer spoke Spanish and no Mexican spoke English. After a three-week standoff, the tense

MAP 14.1 The War with Mexico

This map shows the territory disputed between the United States and Mexico. After U.S. gains in northeastern Mexico, in New Mexico, and in California, General Winfield Scott captured Mexico City in the decisive campaign of the war.

situation came to a head. On April 24, 1846, Mexican cavalry ambushed a U.S. cavalry unit on the north side of the river; eleven Americans were killed, and sixty-three were taken captive. On April 26, Taylor sent a dispatch overland to Washington, D.C., which took two weeks to arrive, announcing, "Hostilities may now be considered as commenced."

Polk now drafted a message to Congress: Mexico had "passed the boundary of the United States, had invaded our territory and shed American blood on American soil." In the bill accompanying the war message, Polk deceptively declared that "war exists by the act of Mexico itself" and summoned the nation to arms. Two days later, on May 13, the House recognized a state of war with Mexico by a vote of 174 to 14, and the Senate, by 40 to 2, with numerous abstentions. Some antislavery Whigs had tried to oppose the war in Congress but were barely allowed to speak. Because Polk withheld key facts, the full reality of what had happened on the distant Rio Grande was not known. But the theory and practice of manifest destiny had launched the United States into its first major war on foreign territory.

Foreign War and the Popular Imagination

The idea of war unleashed great public celebrations. Huge crowds gathered in southern cities, such as Richmond and Louisville, to voice support for the war effort. Twenty thousand Philadelphians and even more New Yorkers rallied in the same spirit. After news came of General Taylor's first two battlefield victories at Palo Alto and Resaca de la Palma, volunteers swarmed recruiting stations. From his home in Lansingburgh, New York, writer Herman Melville remarked that "the people here are all in a state of delirium.... A military ardor pervades all ranks.... Nothing is talked of but the Halls of the Montezumas." Publishers rushed books about Mexican geography into print; "Palo Alto" hats and root beer went on sale. And new daily newspapers, now printed on rotary presses, boosted their sales by giving the war a romantic appeal.

Here was an adventurous war of conquest in a far-off, exotic land. Here was the fulfillment of an Anglo-Saxon–Christian destiny to expand and possess the North American continent and to take civilization to the "semi-Indian" Mexicans. For many, racism fueled the expansionist spirit. In 1846, an Illinois newspaper justified the war on the basis that Mexicans were "reptiles in the path of progressive democracy." For those who read newspapers, the War with Mexico became the first national event experienced with immediacy. The battles south of the border were reported by war correspondents. From Vera Cruz on the Gulf Coast of Mexico, ships carried news dispatches to New Orleans, whose nine daily newspapers ran a faster steamer out to meet them. With stories set in type before they even reached shore, riders carried the news to the North. Near the end of the war, news traveled by telegraph in only three days from New Orleans to Washington, D.C.

The war spawned an outpouring of poetry, song, drama, travel literature, and lithographs that captured the popular imagination and glorified the conflict. New lyrics to the tune of "Yankee Doodle" proclaimed: "They attacked our men upon our land / and crossed our river too sir / now show them all with sword in hand / what yankee boys can do sir." Most of the war-inspired flowering of the popular arts was patriotic. But not everyone cheered. Abolitionist James Russell Lowell considered the war a "national crime committed in behoof of slavery, our common sin."

Ralph Waldo Emerson confided to his journals in 1847, "The United States will conquer Mexico, but it will be as the man swallows arsenic, which brings him down in turn. Mexico will poison us." Even proslavery spokesman John C. Calhoun saw the perils of expansionism. Mexico, he said, was "the forbidden fruit; the penalty of eating it would be to subject our institutions to political death."

Conquest

The troops proved unruly and undisciplined, and their politically ambitious commanders often quarreled among themselves. Nevertheless, early in the war, U.S. forces made significant gains. In May 1846, Polk ordered Colonel Stephen Kearny and a small detachment to invade the remote and thinly populated provinces of New Mexico and California. Taking Santa Fe largely without opposition, Kearny pushed into California, where he joined forces with two U.S. naval units and rebellious American settlers led by Captain John C. Férmont. General Zachary Taylor's forces attacked and occupied Monterrey, which surrendered in September, securing northeastern Mexico (see Map 14.1).

New Mexico did not prove easy for U.S. forces to subdue, however. In January 1847, in Taos, northwest of Santa Fe, Hispanics and Indians led by Pablo Montoya and Tomas Romero rebelled against the Americans and killed numerous government officials. In what came to be known as the Taos Revolt, some 500 Mexican and Indian insurgents laid siege to a mill in Arroyo Hondo, outside Taos. The U.S. command acted swiftly to suppress the revolt with 300 heavily armed troops. The growing band of insurgents eventually retreated to Taos Pueblo and held out in a thick-walled church. With cannon, the U.S. Army succeeded in killing some 150 and capturing 400 of the rebels. After many arrests, approximately 28 insurgent leaders were hanged in the Taos plaza, ending the bloody resistance to U.S. occupation of lands still claimed by Mexican and Indian peoples.

Before the end of 1846, American forces had also established dominion over California. Because losses on the periphery of their large country had not broken Mexican resistance, General Winfield Scott carried the war to the enemy's heartland. Landing at Veracruz, he led fourteen thousand men toward Mexico City. This daring invasion proved the decisive campaign of the war. Scott's men, outnumbered and threatened by yellow fever, encountered a series of formidable Mexican defenses, but engineers repeatedly discovered flanking routes around their foes. After a series of hard-fought battles, U.S. troops captured the Mexican capital.

Treaty of Guadalupe Hidalgo

Representatives of both countries signed the Treaty of Guadalupe Hidalgo in February 1848. The United States gained California and New Mexico (including present-day Nevada, Utah, and Arizona, and parts of Colorado and Wyoming), and recognition of the Rio Grande as the southern boundary of Texas. In return, the American government agreed to settle the claims of its citizens (mostly Texans) against Mexico ($3.2 million) and to pay Mexico a mere $15 million. On the day Polk received the treaty from the Senate, a mob in Paris forced Louis Philippe to abdicate the throne of France, and a German writer, Karl Marx, published a pamphlet, *The Communist Manifesto*, in London. The enormous influence of Marx's work would be many years away, but as the 1848 nationalistic revolutions against monarchy spread to Italy, Austria, Hungary, and Germany, republican America seized a western empire.

The costs of the war included the deaths of thirteen thousand Americans (mostly from disease) and fifty thousand Mexicans. Moreover, enmity between Mexico and the United States endured into the twentieth century. The domestic cost to the United States was even higher. Public opinion was sharply divided. Southwesterners were enthusiastic about the war, as were most southern planters; New Englanders strenuously opposed it. Whigs in Congress charged that Polk, a Democrat, had "provoked" an unnecessary war and "usurped the power of Congress." The aged John Quincy Adams denounced the war, and an Illinois Whig named Abraham Lincoln called Polk's justifications the "half insane mumbling of a fever-dream." Abolitionists and a small minority of antislavery Whigs charged that the war was a plot to extend slavery. Congressman Joshua Giddings of Ohio charged that Polk's purpose was "to render slavery secure in Texas" and to extend slavery's dominion over the West.

"Slave Power Conspiracy"   These charges fed northern fear of the "Slave Power." Abolitionists had long warned of a slaveholding oligarchy that intended to dominate the nation through its hold on federal power. Slaveholders had gained control of the South by suppressing dissent. They had forced the gag rule on Congress in 1836 and threatened northern liberties. To many white northerners, even those who saw nothing wrong with slavery, it was the battle over free speech that first made the idea of a Slave Power credible. The War with Mexico deepened such fears. Had this questionable war, asked antislavery northerners, not been launched for vast, new slave territory?

Northern opinion on slavery's expansion began to shift, but the impact of the war on southern opinion was even more dramatic. At first, some southern Whigs attacked the Democratic president for causing the war, and few southern congressmen saw slavery as the paramount issue. Many whites in both North and South feared that large land seizures would bring thousands of nonwhite Mexicans into the United States and upset the racial order. An Indiana politician did not want "any mixed races in our Union, nor men of any color except white, unless they be slaves." And the *Charleston* (South Carolina) *Mercury* asked if the nation expected "to melt into our population eight millions of men, at war with us by race, by language, by religion, manners and laws." Yet, despite their racism and such numerical exaggerations, many statesmen soon saw other prospects in the outcomes of a war of conquest in the Southwest.

Wilmot Proviso   In August 1846, David Wilmot, a Pennsylvania Democrat, proposed an amendment, or proviso, to a military tary appropriations bill: that "neither slavery nor involuntary servitude shall ever exist" in any territory gained from Mexico. Although the proviso never passed both houses of Congress, its repeated introduction by northerners transformed the debate over the expansion of slavery. Southerners suddenly circled their wagons to protect the future of a slave society. Alexander H. Stephens, only recently "no defender of slavery," now declared that slavery was based on the Bible and above moral criticism, and John C. Calhoun took an aggressive stand. The territories, Calhoun insisted, belonged to all the states, and the federal government could do nothing to limit the spread of slavery there. Southern slaveholders had a constitutional right rooted in the Fifth Amendment, Calhoun claimed, to take their slaves (as property) anywhere in the territories.

This position, often called "state sovereignty," which quickly became a test of orthodoxy among southern politicians, was a radical reversal of history. In 1787, the Confederation Congress had discouraged if not fully excluded slavery from the Northwest Territory; Article IV of the U.S. Constitution had authorized Congress to make "all needful rules and regulations" for the territories; and the Missouri Compromise had barred slavery from most of the Louisiana Purchase. Now, however, southern leaders demanded future guarantees for slavery.

In the North, the Wilmot Proviso became a rallying cry for abolitionists. Eventually the legislatures of fourteen northern states endorsed it—and not because all of its supporters were abolitionists. David Wilmot, significantly, was neither an abolitionist nor an antislavery Whig. He denied having any "squeamish sensitiveness upon the subject of slavery" or "morbid sympathy for the slave." Instead, his goal was to defend "the rights of white freemen" and to obtain California "for free white labor." Wilmot's involvement in antislavery controversy is a measure of the remarkable ability of the territorial issue to alarm northerners of many viewpoints.

As Wilmot demonstrated, it was possible, however, to be both a racist and an opponent of slavery. The vast majority of white northerners were not active abolitionists, and their desire to keep the West free from slavery was often matched by their desire to keep blacks from settling there. Fear of the Slave Power was thus building a potent antislavery movement that united abolitionists and antiblack voters. At stake was an abiding version of the American Dream: the free individual's access to social mobility through acquisition of land in the West. This sacred ideal of free labor, and its dread of concentrated power, fueled a new political persuasion in America. A man's ownership and sale of his own labor, wrote British economist Adam Smith, was "the most sacred and inviolable foundation of all property." Slave labor, thousands of northerners had come to believe, would degrade the honest toil of free men and render them unemployable. The West must therefore be kept free of slaves.

The Election of 1848 and Popular Sovereignty

The divisive slavery question now infested national politics. After Polk renounced a second term as president, the Democrats nominated Senator Lewis Cass of Michigan for president and General William Butler of Kentucky for vice president. Cass, a party loyalist who had served in Jackson's cabinet, had devised in 1847 the idea of "popular sovereignty"—letting residents in the western territories decide the question of slavery for themselves. His party's platform declared that Congress lacked the power to interfere with slavery's expansion. The Whigs nominated General Zachary Taylor, a southern slaveholder and war hero; Congressman Millard Fillmore of New York was his running mate. The Whig convention similarly refused to assert that Congress had power over slavery in the territories.

But the issue could not be avoided. Many southern Democrats distrusted Cass and eventually voted for Taylor because he was a slaveholder. Among northerners, concern over slavery led to the formation of a new party. New York Democrats committed to the Wilmot Proviso rebelled against Cass and nominated former

TABLE 14.1 | NEW POLITICAL PARTIES

Party	Period of Influence	Area of Influence	Outcome
Liberty Party	1839–1848	North	Merged with other antislavery groups to form Free-Soil Party
Free-Soil Party	1848–1854	North	Merged with Republican Party
Know-Nothings (American Party)	1853–1856	Nationwide	Disappeared, freeing most to join Republican Party
Republican Party	1854–present	North (later nationwide)	Became rival of Democratic Party and won presidency in 1860

president Martin Van Buren. Antislavery Whigs and former supporters of the Liberty Party then joined them to organize the Free-Soil Party, with Van Buren as its candidate (see Table 14.1). This party, which sought to restrict slavery expansion to any western territories and whose slogan was "Free Soil, Free Speech, Free Labor, and Free Men," won almost 300,000 northern votes. For a new third party to win 10 percent of the national vote was unprecedented. Taylor polled 1.4 million votes to Cass's 1.2 million and won the White House, but the results were more ominous than decisive.

American politics had split along sectional lines as never before. Religious denominations, too, severed into northern and southern wings. As the 1850s dawned, the legacies of the War with Mexico and the conflicts of 1848 dominated national life and threatened the nature of the Union itself.

1850: COMPROMISE OR ARMISTICE?

The first sectional battle of the new decade involved California. More than eighty thousand Americans flooded into California during the gold rush of 1849. With Congress unable to agree on a formula to govern the territories, President Taylor urged these settlers to apply directly for admission to the Union. They promptly did so, proposing a state constitution that did not allow for slavery. Because California's admission as a free state would upset the sectional balance of power in the Senate (the ratio of slave to free states was fifteen to fifteen), southern politicians wanted to postpone admission and make California a slave territory, or at least extend the Missouri Compromise line west to the Pacific.

Debate over Slavery in the Territories   Henry Clay, the venerable Whig leader, sensed that the Union was in peril. Twice before—in 1820 and 1833—Clay, the "Great Pacificator," had taken the lead in shaping sectional compromise; now he struggled one last time to preserve the nation. To hushed Senate galleries Clay presented a series of compromise measures in the winter of 1850. At one point, he held up what he claimed was a piece of George Washington's coffin as a means of inspiring unity. Over the weeks that followed, he and Senator Stephen A. Douglas of Illinois steered their compromise package through debate and amendment.

The problems to be solved were numerous and difficult. Would California, or part of it, become a free state? How should the territory acquired from Mexico be organized? Texas, which allowed slavery, claimed large portions of the new land as far west as Santa Fe. Southerners complained that fugitive slaves were not returned as the Constitution required, and northerners objected to slave auctions held in the nation's capital. Eight years earlier, in *Prigg v. Pennsylvania* (1842), the Supreme Court had ruled that enforcement of the fugitive slave clause in the Constitution was a federal, not a state, obligation, buttressing long-standing southern desires to bring this issue to a head. Most troublesome of all, however, was the status of slavery in the territories.

Clay and Douglas hoped to avoid a specific formula, and in the idea of popular sovereignty they discovered what one historian called a "charm of ambiguity." Ultimately Congress would have to approve statehood for a territory, but "in the meantime," said Lewis Cass, it should allow the people living there "to regulate their own concerns in their own way."

Those simple words proved all but unenforceable. When could settlers prohibit slavery? To avoid dissension within their party, northern and southern Democrats explained Cass's statement to their constituents in two incompatible ways. Southerners claimed that neither Congress nor a territorial legislature could bar slavery. Only late in the territorial process, when settlers were ready to draft a state constitution, could they take that step, thus allowing time for slavery to take root. Northerners, however, insisted that Americans living in a territory were entitled to local self-government and thus could outlaw slavery at any time.

The cause of compromise gained a powerful supporter when Senator Daniel Webster committed his prestige and eloquence to Clay's bill. "I wish to speak today," Webster declaimed on March 7 in a scene of high drama, "not as a Massachusetts man, nor as a Northern man, but as an American. I speak today for the preservation of the Union." Abandoning his earlier support for the Wilmot Proviso, Webster urged northerners not to "taunt or reproach" the South with antislavery measures. To southern firebrands, he issued a warning that disunion inevitably would cause violence and destruction. For his efforts at compromise, Webster was condemned by many former abolitionist friends in New England who accused him of going over to the "devil."

Only three days earlier, with equal drama, Calhoun had been carried from his sickbed to deliver a speech opposing the compromise. As Calhoun was unable to stand and speak, Senator James Mason of Virginia read his address for him. Grizzled and dying, the South's intellectual defender warned that the "cords which bind these states" were "already greatly weakened." Calhoun did not address the specific measures in the bill; he predicted disunion if southern demands were not met, thereby frightening some into support of compromise.

With Clay sick and absent from Washington, Douglas reintroduced the compromise measures one at a time. Although there was no majority for compromise, Douglas shrewdly realized that different majorities might be created for the separate measures. Because southerners favored some bills and northerners the rest, a small majority for compromise could be achieved on each distinct issue. The strategy worked, and Douglas's resourcefulness alleviated the crisis as the Compromise of 1850 became law.

Compromise of 1850

The compromise had five essential measures:

1. California became a free state.
2. The Texas boundary was set at its present limits (see Map 14.2 later in the chapter), and the United States paid Texas $10 million in compensation for the loss of New Mexico Territory.
3. The territories of New Mexico and Utah were organized on a basis of popular sovereignty.
4. The fugitive slave law was strengthened.
5. The slave trade was abolished in the District of Columbia.

Jubilation greeted passage of the compromise; crowds in Washington and other cities celebrated the happy news. "On one glorious night," records a modern historian, "the word went abroad that it was the duty of every patriot to get drunk. Before the next morning many a citizen had proved his patriotism."

In reality, there was less cause for celebration than people hoped. At best, the Compromise of 1850 was an artful evasion. As one historian has argued, the legislation was more an "armistice," delaying greater conflict, than a compromise. Douglas had found a way to pass the five proposals without convincing northerners and southerners to agree on fundamentals. The compromise bought time for the nation, but it did not provide a real settlement of the territorial questions.

Furthermore, the compromise had two basic flaws. The first concerned the ambiguity of popular sovereignty. Southerners insisted there would be no prohibition of slavery during the territorial stage, and northerners declared that settlers could bar slavery whenever they wished. The compromise even allowed for the appeal of a territorial legislature's action to the Supreme Court. One witty politician remarked that the legislators had enacted a lawsuit instead of a law.

Fugitive Slave Act

The second flaw lay in the Fugitive Slave Act, which gave new—and controversial—protection to slavery. The law empowered slaveowners to go into court in their own states to present evidence that a slave who owed them service had escaped. The resulting transcript and a description of the fugitive would then serve as legal proof of a person's slave status, even in free states and territories. Specially appointed court officials adjudicated the identity of the person described, not whether he or she was indeed a slave. Penalties made it a felony to harbor fugitives, and the law stated that northern citizens could be summoned to hunt fugitives. The fees paid to U.S. marshals favored slaveholders: $10 if the alleged fugitive was returned to the slaveowner, $5 if not returned.

Abolitionist newspapers quickly attacked the Fugitive Slave Act as a violation of fundamental American rights. Why were alleged fugitives denied a trial by jury? Why were they given no chance to present evidence or cross-examine witnesses? Why did the law give authorities a financial incentive to send suspected fugitives into bondage, and why would northerners now be arrested if they harbored run-aways? These arguments convinced some northerners that all free blacks were vulnerable to kidnapping and enslavement. The "free" states were no longer a safe haven for black folk, whatever their origins; an estimated twenty thousand fled to Canada in the wake of the Fugitive Slave Act.

Between 1850 and 1854, protests and violent resistance to slave catchers occurred in dozens of northern towns. Sometimes a captured fugitive was broken out of jail or from the clutches of slave agents by abolitionists, as in the 1851 Boston case of Shadrach Minkins, who was spirited by a series of wagons and trains across Massachusetts, up through Vermont, to Montreal, Canada. Also in 1851, a fugitive named Jerry McHenry was freed by an abolitionist mob in Syracuse, New York, and hurried to Canadian freedom. That same year as well, the small black community in Lancaster County, Pennsylvania, rose up in arms to defend four escaped slaves from a federal posse charged with reenslaving them. At this "Christiana riot," the fugitives shot and killed Edward Gorsuch, the Maryland slaveowner who sought the return of his "property." Amid increasing border warfare over fugitive slaves, a headline reporting the Christiana affair screamed, "Civil War, The First Blow Struck!"

Many abolitionists became convinced by their experience of resisting the Fugitive Slave Act that violence was a legitimate means of opposing slavery. In an 1854 column entitled "Is It Right and Wise to Kill a Kidnapper?" Frederick Douglass said that the only way to make the fugitive slave law "dead letter" was to make a "few dead slave catchers."

Uncle Tom's Cabin   At this point, a novel portrayed the humanity and suffering of slaves in a way that touched millions of northerners. Harriet Beecher Stowe, whose New England family had produced many prominent ministers, wrote *Uncle Tom's Cabin* out of deep moral conviction. Her story, serialized in 1851 and published as a book in 1852, conveyed the agonies faced by slave families and described a mother's dash to freedom with her child across the frozen Ohio River. Stowe also portrayed slavery's evil effects on slaveholders, indicting the institution itself more harshly than she indicted the southerners caught in its web. Moreover, Stowe exposed northern racism and complicity with slavery by making the worst slaveholder a man of New England birth and a visiting relative on a plantation a squeamish Vermont woman who could hardly cope with the near presence of blacks.

In nine months, the book sold over 300,000 copies and by mid-1853 over 1 million. Countless people saw *Uncle Tom's Cabin* performed as a stage play, heard the story in dramatic readings, or read similar novels inspired by it. Stowe brought home the evil of slavery to many who had never given it much thought. Indeed, for generations, the characters in *Uncle Tom's Cabin*—Eliza, Little Eva, Simon Legree, and Uncle Tom himself—entered the American imagination as symbols of slavery and its demise.

The popularity of *Uncle Tom's Cabin* alarmed anxious southern whites. In politics and now in popular literature they saw threats to their way of life. Behind the South's aggressive claims about territorial rights lay the fear that, if nearby areas outlawed slavery, they would be used as bases from which to spread abolitionism into the slave states. To most white southerners, a moral condemnation of slaveholding anywhere meant the same thing everywhere.

To protect slavery in the arena of ideas, southerners needed to counter indictments of the institution as a moral wrong. Accordingly, some fifteen to twenty proslavery novels were published in the 1850s as responses to *Uncle Tom's Cabin*. Most of these paled in comparison to Mrs. Stowe's masterpiece, but southern writers continued to defend their system as more humane than wage labor, and they blamed the slave trade on the "outside interference" of Yankee speculators. In awkward stories, such as J. W. Page's *Uncle Robin in His Cabin and Tom Without One in Boston*, slaves were induced to run away by visiting abolitionists, and then all but starved in northern cities.

The Underground Railroad In reality, slaveholders were especially disturbed by the 1850s over what was widely called the Underground Railroad. This loose, illegal network of civil disobedience, spiriting runaways to freedom, had never been very organized. Thousands of slaves did escape by these routes, but largely through their own wits and courage, and through the assistance of blacks in some northern cities. Lewis Hayden in Boston, David Ruggles in New York, William Still in Philadelphia, John Parker in Ripley, Ohio, and Jacob Gibbs in Washington, D.C., were only some of the many black abolitionists who managed fugitive slave escapes through their regions.

Moreover, Harriet Tubman, herself an escapee in 1848, returned to her native Maryland and to Virginia at least a dozen times, and through clandestine measures helped possibly as many as three hundred slaves, some of them her own family members, to freedom. Maryland planters were so outraged at her heroic success that they offered a $40,000 reward for her capture.

In Ohio, numerous white abolitionists, often Quakers, joined with blacks as agents of slave liberation at various points along the river border between slavery and freedom. The Underground Railroad also had numerous maritime routes, as coastal slaves escaped aboard ship out of Virginia or the Carolinas, or from New Orleans, and ended up in northern port cities, the Caribbean, or England. Many fugitive slaves from the Lower South and Texas escaped to Mexico, which had abolished slavery in 1829. Some slaves escaped by joining the Seminole communities in Florida, where they fought with them against the U.S. Army in the Seminole Wars of 1835–1842 and 1855–1858.

This constant, dangerous flow of humanity was a testament to human courage and the will for freedom. It never reached the scale believed by some angry slaveholders or that of the countless safe houses and hideaways claimed by hundreds of

In Still Life of Harriet Tubman with Bible and Candle, *we see the youthful, calm, determined leader of the Underground Railroad. Appearing gentle, Tubman was in her own way a revolutionary who liberated nearly three hundred of her people.*

Louis Psihoyos/Science Faction

northern towns and local historical societies today. But in reality and in legend, the Underground Railroad applied pressure to the institution of slavery and provided slaves with a focus for hope.

Election of 1852 and the Collapse of Compromise   The 1852 election gave southern leaders hope that slavery would be secure under the administration of a new president. Franklin Pierce, a Democrat from New Hampshire, won an easy victory over the Whig presidential nominee, General Winfield Scott. Southerners hoped that Pierce firmly supported the Compromise of 1850. Because Scott's views on the compromise had been unknown and the Free-Soil candidate, John P. Hale of New Hampshire, had openly rejected it, Pierce's victory suggested widespread support for the compromise.

The Whig party was weak, however, and by 1852 sectional discord had rendered it all but dead. President Pierce's embrace of the compromise appalled many northerners. His vigorous enforcement of the Fugitive Slave Act provoked outrage and fear of the Slave Power, especially in the case of the fugitive slave Anthony Burns, who had fled Virginia by stowing away on a ship in 1852. In Boston, thinking he was safe in a city known for abolitionism, Burns began a new life. But in 1854, federal marshals found and placed him under guard in Boston's courthouse. An interracial crowd of abolitionists attacked the courthouse, killing a jailer in an unsuccessful attempt to free Burns, whose case attracted nationwide attention.

Pierce moved decisively to enforce the Fugitive Slave Act. He telegraphed local officials to "incur any expense to insure the execution of the law" and sent marines, cavalry, and artillery to Boston. U.S. troops marched Burns to Boston harbor through streets that his supporters had draped in black and hung with American flags at half-mast. At a cost of $100,000, a single black man was returned to slavery through the power of federal law.

The national will to sustain the future of slavery was now tested at every turn. This demonstration of federal support for slavery radicalized opinion, even among many conservatives. Textile manufacturer Amos A. Lawrence observed that "we went to bed one night old fashioned, conservative, Compromise Union Whigs & waked up stark mad Abolitionists." Juries refused to convict the abolitionists who had stormed the Boston courthouse, and New England states began to pass personal liberty laws designed to impede or block federal enforcement. In such laws, local judges were absolved from enforcing the Fugitive Slave Act, in effect nullifying federal authority. What northerners now saw as evidence of a dominating Slave Power, outraged slaveholders saw as the legal defense of their rights.

Pierce confronted sectional conflict at every turn. His proposal for a transcontinental railroad derailed when congressmen fought over its location, North or South. His attempts to acquire foreign territory stirred more trouble. An annexation treaty with Hawai'i failed because southern senators would not vote for another free state, and efforts to acquire slaveholding Cuba through the Ostend Manifesto angered northerners. Written after a meeting among the U.S. foreign ministers to Britain, France, and Spain, the document advocated conquest of Cuba if it could not be "purchased." The ministers predicted that Cuba "would be Africanized and become a second St. Domingo, with all its attendant horrors to the white race." Antislavery advocates once again saw schemes of the Slave Power.

Events in the Pacific also caused division at home over just how far American expansion should extend. With two orchestrated landings in the Bay of Tokyo, in 1853 and 1854, Commodore Matthew Perry established U.S. intentions to trade with Japan. Offended and intrigued, the Japanese were impressed with Perry's steam-powered warships, the first such black smoke–belching, floating machines they had seen. Perry's Treaty of Kanagawa in March 1854 negotiated two ports as coaling stations for American ships. The much sought-after trading arrangements were slow in coming, although this did not stop merchants and bankers from lavishing on Perry a hero's honors when he returned to the United States. In his meetings with the Japanese, the pompous Perry had given his hosts, whom he considered an inferior people, a telegraph system, a quarter-scale railroad train, a bound history of the War with Mexico, and one hundred gallons of Kentucky whiskey.

Soon, back home, another territorial bill threw Congress and the nation into even greater turmoil, and the Compromise of 1850 fell into complete collapse.

SLAVERY EXPANSION AND COLLAPSE OF THE PARTY SYSTEM

The new controversy began in a surprising way. Stephen A. Douglas, one of the architects of the Compromise of 1850, introduced a bill to establish the Kansas and Nebraska Territories. Talented and ambitious for the presidency, Douglas was known for compromise, not sectional quarreling. But he did not view slavery as a fundamental problem, and he was willing to risk some controversy to win economic benefits for Illinois, his home state. A transcontinental railroad would encourage settlement of the Great Plains and stimulate the economy of Illinois, but no company would build such a railroad before Congress organized the territories it would cross. Thus, interest in promoting the construction of such a railroad drove Douglas to introduce a bill that inflamed sectional passions.

The Kansas-   The Kansas-Nebraska Act exposed the conflicting inter-
Nebraska Act   pretations of popular sovereignty. Douglas's bill left "all
                     questions pertaining to slavery in the Territories … to the
people residing therein." Northerners and southerners, however, still disagreed violently over what territorial settlers could constitutionally do. Moreover, the Kansas and Nebraska Territories lay within the Louisiana Purchase, and the Missouri Compromise prohibited slavery in all that land from latitude 36°30' north to the Canadian border. If popular sovereignty were to mean anything in Kansas and Nebraska, it had to mean that the Missouri Compromise was no longer in effect and that settlers could establish slavery there.

Southern congressmen, anxious to establish slaveholders' right to take slaves into any territory, pressed Douglas to concede this point. They demanded an explicit repeal of the 36°30' limitation as the price of their support. During a carriage ride with Senator Archibald Dixon of Kentucky, Douglas debated the point at length. Finally, he made an impulsive decision: "By God, Sir, you are right. I will incorporate it in my bill, though I know it will raise a hell of a storm."

Perhaps Douglas underestimated the storm because he believed that conditions of climate and soil would keep slavery out of Kansas and Nebraska. Nevertheless, his bill threw open to slavery land from which it had been prohibited for thirty-four years. Opposition from Free-Soilers and antislavery forces was immediate and enduring; many considered this turn of events a betrayal of a sacred trust. The titanic struggle in Congress lasted three and a half months. Douglas won the support of President Pierce and eventually prevailed: the bill became law in May 1854 by a vote that demonstrated the dangerous sectionalization of American politics (see Map 14.2 and Table 14.2).

But the storm was just beginning. Northern fears of slavery's influence deepened. Opposition to the Fugitive Slave Act grew dramatically; between 1855 and 1859, Connecticut, Rhode Island, Massachusetts, Michigan, Maine, Ohio, and Wisconsin passed personal-liberty laws. These laws enraged southern leaders by providing counsel for alleged fugitives and requiring trial by jury. More important was the devastating impact of the Kansas-Nebraska Act on political parties. The weakened Whig Party broke apart into northern and southern wings that could no longer cooperate nationally. The Democrats survived, but their support in the North fell

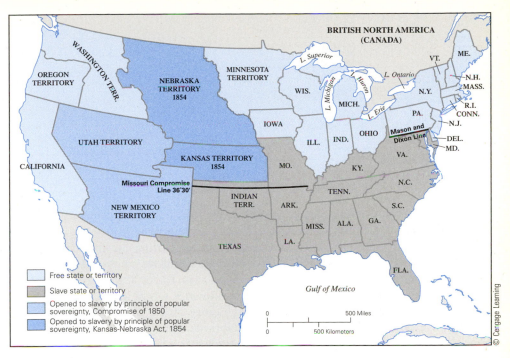

MAP 14.2 The Kansas-Nebraska Act and Slavery Expansion, 1854

The vote on the Kansas-Nebraska Act in the House of Representatives (see also Table 14.2) demonstrates the sectionalization of American politics due to the slavery question.

drastically in the 1854 elections. Northern Democrats lost sixty-six of their ninety-one congressional seats and lost control of all but two free-state legislatures.

Birth of the Republican Party

The beneficiary of northern voters' wrath was a new political party. During debate on the Kansas-Nebraska Act, six congressmen had published an "Appeal of the Independent Democrats." Joshua Giddings, Salmon Chase, and Charles Sumner—the principal authors of this protest—attacked Douglas's legislation as a "gross violation of a sacred pledge" (the Missouri Compromise) and a "criminal betrayal of precious rights" that would make free territory a "dreary region of despotism." Their appeal tapped a reservoir of deep concerns in the North, cogently expressed by Illinois's Abraham Lincoln.

Although Lincoln did not personally condemn southerners—"They are just what we would be in their situation"—he exposed the meaning of the Kansas-Nebraska Act. Lincoln argued that the founders, from love of liberty, had banned slavery from the Northwest Territory, kept the word *slavery* out of the Constitution, and treated it overall as a "cancer" on the republic. Rather than encouraging liberty, the Kansas-Nebraska Act put slavery "on the high road to extension and

TABLE 14.2 | THE VOTE ON THE KANSAS-NEBRASKA ACT

The vote was 113 to 100 in favor	Aye	Nay
Northern Democrats	44	42
Southern Democrats	57	2
Northern Whigs	0	45
Southern Whigs	12	7
Northern Free-Soilers		4

perpetuity," and that constituted a "moral wrong and injustice." America's future, Lincoln warned, was being mortgaged to slavery and all its influences.

Thousands of ordinary white northerners agreed. During the summer and fall of 1854, antislavery Whigs and Democrats, Free-Soilers, and other reformers throughout the Old Northwest met to form the new Republican Party, dedicated to keeping slavery out of the territories. The influence of the Republicans rapidly spread to the East, and they won a stunning victory in the 1854 elections. In their first appearance on the ballot, Republicans captured a majority of northern House seats. Antislavery sentiment had created a new party and caused roughly a quarter of northern Democrats to desert their party.

For the first time, too, a sectional party had gained significant power in the political system. Now the Whigs were gone, and only the Democrats struggled to maintain national membership. The Republicans absorbed the Free-Soil Party and grew rapidly in the North. Indeed, the emergence of the Republican coalition of antislavery interests is the most rapid transformation in party allegiance and voter behavior in American history.

Know-Nothings   Republicans also drew into their coalition a fast-growing nativist movement that called itself the American Party, or Know-Nothings (because its first members kept their purposes secret, answering, "I know nothing" to all questions). This group exploited fear of foreigners and Catholics. Between 1848 and 1860, nearly 3.5 million immigrants entered the United States—proportionally the heaviest inflow of foreigners ever in American history. Democrats courted the votes of these new citizens, but many native-born Anglo-Saxon Protestants believed that Irish and German Catholics would owe primary allegiance to the pope in Rome and not to the American nation.

In 1854, anti-immigrant fears gave the Know-Nothings spectacular success in some northern states. They triumphed especially in Massachusetts, electing 11 congressmen, a governor, all state officers, all state senators, and all but 2 of 378 state representatives. The temperance movement also gained new strength early in the 1850s with its promises to stamp out the evils associated with liquor and immigrants (a particularly anti-Irish campaign). In this context, the Know-Nothings strove to reinforce Protestant morality and to restrict voting and office holding to the native-born. As the Whig Party faded from the scene, the Know-Nothings

Throughout the North, the Kansas-Nebraska Act kindled fires of alarm over the Slave Power's "determination to extend its dominion" and "control the government of the nation." Public meetings like the one announced here, held in West Chester, Pennsylvania, aided the new Republican Party.

American Antiquarian Society

temporarily filled the void. But like the Whigs, the Know-Nothings could not keep their northern and southern wings together in the face of the slavery expansion issue, and they dissolved after 1856. The growing Republican coalition wooed the nativists with temperance ordinances and laws postponing suffrage for naturalized citizens (see Table 14.1).

Party Realignment and the Republicans' Appeal   With nearly half of the old electorate up for grabs, the demise of the Whig Party ensured a major realignment of the political system. The remaining parties made appeals to various segments of the electorate. Immigration, temperance, homestead bills, the tariff, internal improvements—all played important roles in attracting voters during the 1850s. The Republicans appealed strongly to those interested in the economic development of the West. Commercial agriculture was booming in the Ohio–Mississippi–Great Lakes area, but residents of that region desired more canals, roads, and river and harbor improvements. Because credit was scarce, a homestead program—the idea that western land should be free to individuals who would farm it and make a home on it—attracted many voters. The Republicans seized on these political desires.

Partisan ideological appeals became the currency of the realigned political system. As Republicans preached, "Free Soil, Free Labor, Free Men," they captured a self-image of many northerners. These phrases resonated with traditional ideals of equality, liberty, and opportunity under self-government—the heritage of republicanism. Invoking that heritage also undercut charges that the Republican Party was radical and abolitionist.

The northern economy was booming, and thousands of migrants had moved west to establish productive farms and growing communities. Midwesterners multiplied their yields by using new machines, such as mechanical reapers. Railroads were carrying their crops to urban markets. And industry was beginning to perform wonders of production, making available goods that only recently had been beyond the reach of the average person.

Republican Ideology   The key to progress appeared, to many people, to be free labor—the dignity of work and the incentive of opportunity. Any hard-working and virtuous man, it was thought, could improve his condition and achieve economic independence by seizing the main chance. Republicans argued that the South, with little industry and slave labor, was backward by comparison. Their arguments captured the spirit of the age in the North.

Traditional republicanism hailed the virtuous common man as the backbone of the country. In Abraham Lincoln, a man of humble origins who had become a successful lawyer and political leader, Republicans had a symbol of that tradition. They portrayed their party as the guardian of economic opportunity, giving individuals a chance to work, acquire land, and attain success. In the words of an Iowa Republican, the United States was thriving because its "door is thrown open to all, and even the poorest and humblest in the land, may, by industry and application, gain a position which will entitle him to the respect … of his fellow-men."

At stake in the crises of the 1850s were thus two competing definitions of "liberty": southern planters' claims to protection of their liberty in the possession and transport of their slaves anywhere in the land, and northern workers' and farmers' claims to protection of their liberty to seek a new start on free land, unimpeded by a system that defined labor as slave and black.

Opposition to the extension of slavery had brought the Republicans into being, but party members carefully broadened their appeal by adopting the causes of other groups. Their coalition ideology consisted of many elements: resentment of southern political power, devotion to unionism, antislavery based on free-labor arguments, moral revulsion to slavery, and racial prejudice. As *New York Tribune* editor Horace Greeley wrote in 1856, "It is beaten into my bones that the American people are not yet anti-slavery." Four years later, Greeley again observed that "an Anti-Slavery man per se cannot be elected." But, he added, "a Tariff, River-and-Harbor, Pacific Railroad, Free Homestead man, may succeed although he is Anti-Slavery." As these elements placed their hopes in the Republican Party, they also grew to fear slavery even more.

William Walker and Filibustering

Between 1848 and 1861, the United States was officially at peace with foreign nations. But that did not stop private citizens, sometimes with the support of politicians and businessmen, from launching adventurous attempts to take over foreign lands, especially in Mexico, Central America, and the Caribbean. The 1850s was the heyday of "filibustering," defined in this era as private military expeditions designed to destabilize or conquer foreign lands in the name of Manifest Destiny, commerce, the spread of slavery and white supremacy, or masculine daring.

At least a dozen filibustering schemes emerged in this era of expansion and sectional crises, all of them illegal and often opposed by American presidents as blatant violations of a Neutrality Act of 1818 that outlawed the attempted overthrow of foreign "dominions." Such laws did not stop some senators, railroad and shipping entrepreneurs, and especially the self-styled soldier of fortune, William Walker, from flaunting law and seeking the "Southern dream" of a Latin American empire. The law also did not stop several American presidents from engaging in numerous more official attempts to annex Cuba in these years.

Born in Tennessee, Walker traveled and studied in Europe as the 1848 revolutions rocked that continent. After a short stint editing a newspaper in New Orleans, he moved to California, practiced law, and courted conflict by fighting at least three duels. After an ill-fated but determined attempt in 1853 to create by force an American "colony" in Sonora and the Baja peninsula in Mexico, Walker turned his sights to Nicaragua, already of great interest to thousands of Americans using its isthmus as the fastest route to the California gold fields.

With a small army of mercenaries, Walker invaded Nicaragua in 1856, exploited its ongoing civil war, seized its government, declared himself president, and reintroduced slavery into a society that had banned it. Defeated by a coalition of Nicaraguans and British in 1857, Walker returned to the United States and launched a fund-raising and speaking campaign on which he was often treated as a romantic hero. On his return to Nicaragua, he was arrested by a U.S. Navy squadron, brought once again to American soil, tried and acquitted.

In 1860, Walker published an account of his exploits, *War in Nicaragua*. His wide fame was due in part to his swashbuckling character; some saw him as a pirate serving the "Slave Power Conspiracy," and others as the "grey-eyed man of destiny" advancing the causes of slavery and American hegemony. Walker became more aggressively proslavery in Nicaragua when he desperately needed Southern political support to supply his plots. On Walker's third return to Central America in 1860 to pursue his insatiable dream of fame and power, he was arrested by a British captain who turned him over to Honduran authorities who promptly executed him by firing squad. These filibustering adventures fired the imagination of Manifest Destiny and were merely small precursors of a larger Latin American exploitation and conquest by the United States in the century to follow. Walker's legend lives on today in Central America, both heroic and notorious, as well as in two American movies, *Burn* (1969), starring Marlon Brando, and *Walker* (1987), starring Ed Harris. Filibusters were links to the world that gave the United States a difficult legacy to overcome with its neighbors from Cuba to Hawaii.

Southern Democrats   In the South, the disintegration of the Whig Party had left many southerners at loose ends politically; they included a good number of wealthy planters, smaller slaveholders, and urban businessmen. In the increasingly tense atmosphere of sectional crisis, these people were highly susceptible to strong states' rights positions and the defense of slavery. The security of their own communities seemed at stake, and in the 1850s, most formerly Whig slaveholders converted to the Democratic Party.

Since Andrew Jackson's day, however, nonslaveholding yeomen had been the heart of the Democratic Party. Democratic politicians, though often slaveowners themselves, lauded the common man and argued that their policies advanced his interests. According to the southern version of republicanism, white citizens in a slave society enjoyed liberty and social equality because black people were enslaved. As Jefferson Davis put it in 1851, in other societies distinctions were drawn "by property, between the rich and the poor." But in the South, slavery elevated every white person's status and allowed the nonslaveholder to "stand upon the broad level of equality with the rich man." To retain the support of ordinary whites, southern Democrats appealed to racism, warning starkly of the main issue: "shall negroes govern white men, or white men govern negroes?"

Southern leaders also portrayed sectional controversies as matters of injustice and insult to the honor and prestige of the South. The rights of all southern whites were in jeopardy, they argued, because antislavery and Free-Soil forces threatened an institution protected in the Constitution. The stable, well-ordered South was the true defender of constitutional principles; the rapidly changing North, their destroyer.

Racial fears and traditional political loyalties helped keep the volatile political alliance between yeoman farmers and planters largely intact through the 1850s. Across class lines, white southerners joined together in the interest of community security against what they perceived as the Republican Party's capacity to cause slave unrest in their midst. In the South, no viable party emerged to replace the Whigs, and as in the North, political realignment sharpened sectional identities.

Political leaders of both sections used race in their arguments about opportunity, but northerners and southerners saw different futures. The *Montgomery* (Alabama) *Mail* warned southern whites in 1860 that the Republicans intended "to free the negroes and force amalgamation between them and the children of the poor men of the South. The rich will be able to keep out of the way of the contamination." Republicans warned northern workers that, if slavery entered the territories, the great reservoir of opportunity for ordinary citizens would be poisoned.

Bleeding Kansas   The Kansas-Nebraska Act spawned hatred and violence as land-hungry partisans in the sectional struggle clashed repeatedly in Kansas Territory. Abolitionists and religious groups sent in armed Free-Soil settlers; southerners sent in their reinforcements to establish slavery and prevent "northern hordes" from stealing Kansas away. Conflicts led to vicious bloodshed, and soon the whole nation was talking about "Bleeding Kansas."

Politics in the territory resembled war more than democracy. During elections for a territorial legislature in 1855, thousands of proslavery Missourians—known as Border Ruffians—invaded the polls and ran up a large but fraudulent majority for proslavery candidates. They murdered and intimidated free state settlers. At one rally of such ruffians with other southerners, flags flapped in the breeze with the mottoes "Southern Rights," "Supremacy of the White Race," and "Alabama for Kansas." The resulting legislature legalized slavery, and in response Free-Soilers held an unauthorized convention at which they created their own government and constitution. Kansas was a tinderbox. By the spring of 1856, newspapers screamed for violence. "In a fight, let our motto be War to the knife, and knife to the hilt," demanded the proslavery *Squatter Sovereign.* Slavery's advocates taunted their adversaries as cowards and likened "abolitionists" to "infidels" worthy only of "total extermination."

In May, a proslavery posse sent to arrest the Free-Soil leaders sacked the Kansas town of Lawrence, killing several people and destroying a hotel with cannon shot. In revenge, John Brown, a radical abolitionist with a band of followers, murdered five proslavery settlers living along Pottawatomie Creek. The victims were taken in the dark of night from the clutches of their families, their heads and limbs hacked to pieces by heavy broadswords, their bodies heaved into dead brush. Brown himself did not wield the swords, but he did fire a single shot into the head of one senseless foe to assure his death. Soon, armed bands of guerrillas roamed the territory, battling over land claims as well as slavery.

These passions brought violence to the U.S. Senate in May 1856, when Charles Sumner of Massachusetts denounced "the Crime against Kansas." Radical in his anti-slavery views, Sumner bitterly assailed the president, the South, and Senator Andrew P. Butler of South Carolina. Soon thereafter, Butler's cousin, Representative Preston Brooks, approached Sumner at the latter's Senate desk, raised his cane, announced the defense of his kin's honor, and mercilessly beat Sumner on the head. The senator collapsed, bleeding, on the floor while unsympathetic colleagues watched.

Shocked northerners recoiled from what they saw as another case of wanton southern violence and an assault on free speech. William Cullen Bryant, editor of the *New York Evening Post,* asked, "Has it come to this, that we must speak with bated breath in the presence of our southern masters?" As if in reply, the *Richmond Enquirer* denounced "vulgar Abolitionists in the Senate" who "have been suffered to run too long without collars. They must be lashed into submission." Popular opinion in Massachusetts strongly supported Sumner; South Carolina voters re-elected Brooks and sent him dozens of commemorative canes.

Election of 1856   The election of 1856 showed how extreme such polarization had become. For Republicans, "Bleeding Sumner" and "Bleeding Kansas" had become rallying cries. When Democrats met to select a nominee, they shied away from prominent leaders whose views on the territorial question would invite controversy. Instead, they chose James Buchanan of Pennsylvania, whose chief virtue was that for the past four years he had been ambassador to Britain, uninvolved in territorial controversies. Superior party organization helped Buchanan win 1.8

million votes and the election, but he owed his victory to southern support. Hence, he was tagged with the label "a northern man with southern principles."

Eleven of sixteen free states voted against Buchanan, and Democrats did not regain ascendancy in those states for decades. The Republican candidate, John C. Frémont, famous as a western explorer, won those eleven free states and 1.3 million votes; Republicans had become the dominant party in the North after only two years of existence. The Know-Nothing candidate, Millard Fillmore, won almost 1 million votes, but this election was that party's last hurrah. The coming battle would pit a sectional Republican Party against an increasingly divided Democratic Party. With huge voter turnouts, as high as 75 to 80 percent in many states, Americans were about to learn that elections really matter.

SLAVERY AND THE NATION'S FUTURE

For years, the issue of slavery in the territories had convulsed Congress, and Congress had tried to settle the issue with vague formulas. In 1857, the Supreme Court stepped into the fray, took up this emotionally charged subject, and attempted to silence controversy with a definitive verdict.

Dred Scott Case   A Missouri slave named Dred Scott and his wife, Harriet Robinson Scott, had sued for their freedom. Scott based his claim on the fact that his former owner, an army surgeon, had taken him for several years into Illinois, a free state, and to Fort Snelling in the Minnesota Territory, from which slavery had been barred by the Missouri Compromise. Scott first won and then lost his case as it moved on appeal through the state courts into the federal system and, finally, after eleven years, to the Supreme Court.

The impetus for the lawsuit likely came as much from Harriet as from Dred Scott. They were legally married at Fort Snelling (free territory) in 1836 when Dred was forty and Harriet seventeen. She had already lived as a slave on free soil for at least five years and had given birth to four children, also born on free soil: two sons who died in infancy and two daughters, Eliza and Lizzie, who lived. In all likelihood, the quest to achieve "freedom papers" through a lawsuit—begun in 1846 as two separate cases, one in his name and one in hers—came as much from Harriet's desire to sustain her family and protect her two teenage daughters from potential sale and sexual abuse as from the aging and sickly Dred. Indeed, her legal case for freedom may have been even stronger than Dred's, but their lawyers subsumed her case into his during the long appeal process.

Normally, Supreme Court justices were reluctant to inject themselves into major political issues. An 1851 decision had declared that state courts determined the status of blacks who lived within their jurisdictions. The Supreme Court had only to follow this precedent to avoid ruling on substantive, and very controversial, issues: Was a black person like Dred Scott a citizen of the United States and thus eligible to sue in federal court? Had residence in a free state or territory made him free? Did Congress have the power to prohibit or promote slavery in a territory?

After hesitation, the Supreme Court agreed to hear *Dred Scott v. Sanford* and decided to rule on the Missouri Compromise after all. Two northern justices indicated they would dissent from the assigned opinion and argue for Scott's freedom and the constitutionality of the Missouri Compromise. Their decision emboldened southerners on the Court, who were growing eager to declare the 1820 geographical restriction on slavery unconstitutional. Southern sympathizers in Washington were pressing for a proslavery verdict, and several justices felt they should simply try to resolve sectional strife once and for all.

In March 1857, Chief Justice Roger B. Taney of Maryland delivered the majority opinion of a divided Court (the vote was 7 to 2). Taney declared that Scott was not a citizen of either the United States or Missouri, that residence in free territory did not make Scott free, and that Congress had no power to bar slavery from any territory. The decision not only overturned a sectional compromise that had been honored for thirty-seven years, it also invalidated the basic ideas of the Wilmot Proviso and popular sovereignty.

The Slave Power seemed to have won a major constitutional victory. African Americans were especially dismayed, for Taney's decision asserted that the founders had never intended for black people to be citizens. At the nation's founding, the chief justice wrote, blacks had been regarded "as beings of an inferior order" with "no rights which the white man was bound to respect." Taney was mistaken, however. African Americans had been citizens in several of the original states and had in fact voted.

Nevertheless, the ruling seemed to shut the door permanently on black hopes for justice. After 1857, African Americans lived in the land of the *Dred Scott* decision. In northern black communities, rage and despair prevailed. Many who were still fugitive slaves sought refuge in Canada; others considered emigration to the Caribbean or even to Africa. Mary Ann Shadd Cary, who was free and the leader of an emigration movement to Canada, advised her fellow blacks, "Your national ship is rotten and sinking, why not leave it?" Another black abolitionist said that the *Dred Scott* decision had made slavery "the supreme law of the land and all descendants of the African race denationalized." In this state of social dislocation and fear, blacks contemplated whether they had any future in the United States.

Northern whites who rejected the decision's content were suspicious of the circumstances that had produced it. Five of the nine justices were southerners; three of the northern justices actively dissented or refused to concur in parts of the decision. The only northerner who supported Taney's opinion, Justice Robert Grier of Pennsylvania, was known to be close to President Buchanan. In fact, Buchanan had secretly brought to bear improper but effective influence.

A storm of angry reaction broke in the North. The decision seemed to confirm every charge against the aggressive Slave Power. "There is such a thing as the slave power," warned the *Cincinnati Daily Commercial*. "It has marched over and annihilated the boundaries of the states. We are now one great homogenous slaveholding community." The *Cincinnati Freeman* asked, "What security have the Germans and the Irish that their children will not, within a hundred years, be reduced to slavery in this land of their adoption?" Poet James Russell Lowell expressed the racial and economic anxieties of poor northern whites when he had his Yankee character Ezekiel Biglow say, in the language of the day,

> Wy, it's just ez clear ez figgers,
> Clear ez one an' one make two,
> Chaps thet make black slaves o' niggers,
> Want to make wite slaves o' you.

Abraham Lincoln and the Slave Power

Republican politicians used these fears to strengthen their antislavery coalition. Abraham Lincoln stressed that the territorial question affected every citizen. "The whole nation," he had declared as early as 1854, "is interested that the best use shall be made of these Territories. We want them for homes of free white people. This they cannot be, to any considerable extent, if slavery shall be planted within them." The territories must be reserved, he insisted, "as an outlet for free white people everywhere" so that immigrants could come to America and "find new homes and better their condition in life."

More important, Lincoln warned of slavery's increasing control over the nation. The founders had created a government dedicated to freedom, Lincoln insisted. Admittedly they had recognized slavery's existence, but the public mind, he argued in the "House Divided" speech of 1858, had always rested in the belief that slavery would die either naturally or by legislation. The next step in the unfolding Slave Power conspiracy, Lincoln alleged, would be a Supreme Court decision "declaring that the Constitution does not permit a State to exclude slavery from its limits…. We shall lie down pleasantly, dreaming that the people of Missouri are on the verge of making their State free; and we shall awake to the reality instead, that the Supreme Court has made Illinois a slave State." This charge was not hyperbole, for lawsuits soon challenged state laws that freed slaves brought within their borders. Countless northerners heeded Lincoln's warnings, as events convinced them that slaveholders were intent on making slavery a national institution. Southerners, fatefully, never forgot Lincoln's use of the direct words "ultimate extinction."

Politically, Republicans were now locked in conflict with the *Dred Scott* decision. By endorsing the South's doctrine of state sovereignty, the Court had in effect declared that the central position of the Republican Party—no extension of slavery— was unconstitutional. Republicans could only repudiate the decision, appealing to a "higher law," or hope to change the personnel of the Court. They did both and gained politically as fear of the Slave Power grew. But fear also deepened among free blacks. Frederick Douglass continued to try to fashion hope among his people but concluded a speech in the wake of the *Dred Scott* decision bleakly: "I walk by faith, not by sight."

The Lecompton Constitution and Disharmony Among Democrats

For northern Democrats like Stephen Douglas, the Court's decision posed an awful dilemma. Northern voters were alarmed by the prospect that the territories would be opened to slavery. To retain their support, Douglas had to find some way to reassure these voters. Yet given his presidential ambitions, Douglas could not afford to alienate southern Democrats.

Douglas chose to stand by his principle of popular sovereignty, even if the result angered southerners. In 1857, Kansans voted on a proslavery constitution that had been drafted at Lecompton. It was defeated by more than ten thousand votes in a referendum boycotted by most proslavery voters. The evidence was overwhelming that Kansans did not want slavery, yet President Buchanan tried to force the Lecompton Constitution through Congress in an effort to hastily organize the territory.

Never had the Slave Power's influence over the government seemed more blatant; the Buchanan administration and southerners demanded a proslavery outcome, contrary to the majority will in Kansas. Breaking with the administration, Douglas threw his weight against the Lecompton Constitution. But his action infuriated southern Democrats. After the *Dred Scott* decision, southerners like Senator Albert G. Brown of Mississippi believed slavery was protected in the territories: "The Constitution as expounded by the Supreme Court awards it. We demand it; we mean to have it." Increasingly, though, many southerners believed their sectional rights and slavery would be safe only in a separate nation. And northern Democrats, led by Douglas, found it harder to support the territorial protection for slavery that southern Democrats insisted was theirs as a constitutional right. Thus, in North and South, the issue of slavery in the territories continued to destroy moderation and promote militancy.

DISUNION

It is worth remembering that, in the late 1850s, most Americans were not always caught up daily in the slavery crisis. They were preoccupied with personal affairs, especially coping with the effects of the economic panic that had begun in the spring of 1857. They were worried about widespread unemployment, the plummeting price of wheat, the declining wages at a textile mill, or sons who needed land. In the Midwest, clerks, mechanics, domestics, railroad hands, and lumber camp workers lost jobs by the thousands. Bankers were at a loss for what to do about a weak credit system caused by frenzied western land speculation that began early in the decade. In parts of the South, such as Georgia, the panic intensified class divisions between upcountry yeomen and coastal slaveholding planters. Farmers blamed the tight money policies of Georgia's budding commercial banking system on wealthy planters who controlled the state's Democratic Party.

The panic had been caused by several shortcomings of the unregulated American banking system, by frenzies of speculation in western lands and railroads, and by a weak and overburdened credit system. By 1858, Philadelphia had 40,000 unemployed workers and New York City, nearly 100,000. Fear of bread riots and class warfare gripped many cities in the North. True to form, blame for such economic woe became sectionalized, as southerners saw their system justified by the temporary collapse of industrial prosperity and northerners feared even more the incursions of the Slave Power on an insecure future.

John Brown's Raid on Harpers Ferry   Soon, however, the entire nation's focus would be drawn to a new dimension of the slavery question—armed rebellion, led by the abolitionist who had killed proslavery settlers along Pottawatomie Creek in "Bleeding Kansas." Born in Connecticut in 1800, John Brown had been raised by staunchly religious antislavery parents. Between 1820 and 1855, he engaged in some twenty business ventures, including farming, nearly all of them failures. But Brown had a distinctive vision of abolitionism. He relied on an Old Testament conception of justice—"an eye for an eye"—and he had a puritanical obsession with the wickedness of others, especially southern slaveowners. Brown believed that slavery was an "unjustifiable" state of war conducted by one group of people against another. He also believed violence in a righteous cause was a holy act, even a rite of purification for those who engaged in it. To Brown, the destruction of slavery in America required revolutionary ideology and revolutionary acts.

On October 16, 1859, Brown led a small band of eighteen whites and blacks in an attack on the federal arsenal at Harpers Ferry, Virginia. Hoping to trigger a slave rebellion, Brown failed miserably and was quickly captured. In a celebrated trial in November and a widely publicized execution in December, in Charles Town, Virginia, Brown became one of the most enduring martyrs, as well as villains, of American history. His attempted insurrection struck fear into the South.

Then it became known that Brown had received financial backing from several prominent abolitionists. When such northern intellectuals as Ralph Waldo Emerson

Ohio Historical Society

The earliest known photograph of John Brown, probably taken in 1846 in Massachusetts, shows him pledging his devotion to an unidentified flag, possibly an abolitionist banner. Already Brown was aiding runaway slaves and pondering ways to strike at slavery.

and Henry David Thoreau praised Brown as a holy warrior who "would make the gallows as glorious as the cross," white southerners' outrage intensified. The South almost universally interpreted Brown's attack at Harpers Ferry as an act of midnight terrorism, as the fulfillment of their long-stated dread of "abolition emissaries" who would infiltrate the region to incite slave rebellion.

Perhaps most telling of all was the fact that the pivotal election of 1860 was less than a year away when Brown went so eagerly to the gallows, handing a note to his jailer with the famous prediction "I John Brown am now quite certain that the crimes of this guilty land will never be purged away, but with blood." Most troubling to southerners, perhaps, was their awareness that, though Republican politicians condemned Brown's crimes, they did so in a way that deflected attention onto the still-greater crime of slavery.

Election of 1860

Many Americans believed the election of 1860 would decide the fate of the Union. The Democratic Party was the only party that was truly national in scope. "One after another," wrote a Mississippi editor, "the links which have bound the North and South together, have been severed … [but] the Democratic party looms gradually up … and waves the olive branch over the troubled waters of politics." But, fatefully, at its 1860 convention in Charleston, South Carolina, the Democratic Party split.

Stephen Douglas wanted his party's presidential nomination, but he could not afford to alienate northern voters by accepting the southern position on the territories. Southern Democrats, however, insisted on recognition of their rights—as the *Dred Scott* decision had defined them—and they moved to block Douglas's nomination. When Douglas obtained a majority for his version of the platform, delegates from the Deep South walked out of the convention. After efforts at compromise failed, the Democrats presented two nominees: Douglas for the northern wing, and Vice President John C. Breckinridge of Kentucky for the southern.

The Republicans nominated Abraham Lincoln at a rousing convention in Chicago. The choice of Lincoln reflected the growing power of the Midwest, and he was perceived as more moderate on slavery than the early front runner, Senator William H. Seward of New York. A Constitutional Union Party, formed to preserve the nation but strong only in the Upper South, nominated John Bell of Tennessee.

Bell's only issue in the ensuing campaign was the urgency of preserving the Union; Constitutional Unionists hoped to appeal to history, sentiment, and moderation to hold the country together. Douglas desperately sought to unite his northern and southern supporters, while Breckinridge quickly backed away from the appearance of extremism, and his supporters in several states stressed his unionism. Although Lincoln and the Republicans denied any intent to interfere with slavery in the states where it existed, they stood firm against the extension of slavery into the territories.

The election of 1860 was sectional in character, and the only one in American history in which the losers refused to accept the result. Lincoln won, but Douglas, Breckinridge, and Bell together received a majority of the votes. Douglas had broad-based support but won few states. Breckinridge carried nine southern states, all in the Deep South. Bell won pluralities in Virginia, Kentucky, and Tennessee. Lincoln prevailed in the North, but in the four slave states that ultimately remained loyal to the Union (Missouri, Kentucky, Maryland, and Delaware—the border states) he

TABLE 14.3 | PRESIDENTIAL VOTE IN 1860 (BY STATE)

Lincoln (Republican)*	Carried all northern states and all electoral votes except 3 in New Jersey
Breckinridge (Southern Democrat)	Carried all slave states except Virginia, Kentucky, Tennessee, Missouri
Bell (Constitutional Union)	Carried Virginia, Kentucky, Tennessee
Douglas (Northern Democrat)	Carried only Missouri

*Lincoln received only 26,000 votes in the entire South and was not even on the ballot in ten slave states. Breckinridge was not on the ballot in three northern states.

gained only a plurality, not a majority (see Table 14.3). Lincoln's victory was won in the electoral college. He polled only 40 percent of the total vote and was not even on the ballot in ten slave states.

Opposition to slavery's extension was the core issue for Lincoln and the Republican Party. Moreover, abolitionists and Free-Soil supporters in the North worked to keep the Republicans from compromising on their territorial stand. Meanwhile, in the South, proslavery advocates and secessionists whipped up public opinion and demanded that state conventions assemble to consider secession.

Lincoln made the crucial decision not to soften his party's position on the territories. He wrote of the necessity of maintaining the bond of faith between voter and candidate and of declining to set "the minority over the majority." Although many conservative Republicans—eastern businessmen and former Whigs who did not feel strongly about slavery—hoped for a compromise, the original and most committed Republicans—old Free-Soilers and antislavery Whigs—held the line on slavery expansion.

In the winter of 1860–1861, Senator John J. Crittenden of Kentucky tried to craft a late-hour compromise. Hoping to don the mantle of Henry Clay and avert disunion, Crittenden proposed that the two sections divide the territories between them at the Missouri Compromise line, 36°30'. But this well-worn and controversial idea did not work. When Lincoln ruled out concessions on the territorial issue, Crittenden's peacemaking effort, based on discredited measures, collapsed.

Secession and the Confederate States of America

Meanwhile, on December 20, 1860, South Carolina passed an ordinance of secession amid jubilation and cheering. Secession strategists concentrated their efforts on the most extreme proslavery state, hoping that South Carolina's bold act would create momentum and induce other states to follow.

By reclaiming its independence, South Carolina raised the stakes in the sectional confrontation. No longer was secession an unthinkable step; the Union was broken. Secessionists now argued that other states should follow South Carolina and that those who favored compromise could make a better deal outside the Union than in it. Moderates from regions with fewer slaves and more diversified economies than the cotton belt, fearing economic chaos and arguing for "resistance short of secession," still felt deep affection for the Union and had family ties in the

North; secession was by no means inevitable or widely popular in upper South states like Virginia or Tennessee.

Southern extremists soon got their way in the Deep South. Overwhelming their opposition, they called separate state conventions and passed secession ordinances in Mississippi, Florida, Alabama, Georgia, Louisiana, and Texas. By February 1861, these states had joined South Carolina to form a new government in Montgomery, Alabama: the Confederate States of America. The delegates at Montgomery chose Jefferson Davis of Mississippi as their president, and the Confederacy began to function independently of the United States.

This apparent unanimity of action was deceiving. Confused and dissatisfied with the alternatives, many southerners—perhaps as much as 40 percent even in the deep South—opposed immediate secession. In some state conventions, the secession vote was close and decided by overrepresentation of plantation districts. In Georgia, where more than three in five voters were nonslaveholders, the secession convention voted 166–130 to secede after a bitterly divided debate. Four states in the Upper South where wheat production and commerical ties to the North had grown steadily in the 1850s—Virginia, North Carolina, Tennessee, and Arkansas—flatly rejected secession and did not join the Confederacy until after fighting had begun. In Augusta County, Virginia, in the Shenandoah Valley, where one-fifth of households held slaves, the majority steadfastly sought

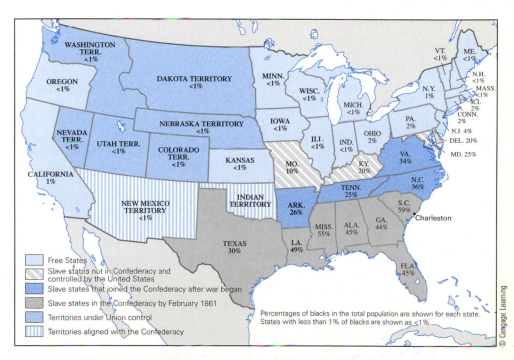

MAP 14.3 The Divided Nation—Slave and Free Areas, 1861

After fighting began, the Upper South joined the Deep South in the Confederacy. How does the nation's pattern of division correspond to the distribution of slavery and the percentage of blacks in the population?

alternatives to secession until after Fort Sumter. In the border states, popular sentiment was deeply divided; minorities in Kentucky and Missouri tried to secede, but these slave states ultimately came under Union control, along with Maryland and Delaware (see Map 14.3).

Such misgivings were not surprising. Secession posed new and troubling issues for southerners. Analysis of election returns from 1860 and 1861 indicates that slaveholders and nonslaveholders were beginning to part company politically. Heavily slaveholding counties strongly supported secession. But nonslaveholding areas that had favored Breckinridge in the presidential election proved far less willing to support secession: economic interests and fear of war on their own soil provided a potent, negative reaction to abstractions such as "state rights" (see Figure 14.1). With war on the horizon, yeomen were beginning to consider their class interests and to ask themselves how far they would go to support slavery and slaveowners.

As for why the Deep South bolted, we need look no further than the speeches and writings of the secession commissioners sent out by the seven seceded states to try to convince the other slave states to join them. Repeatedly, they stressed independence as the only way to preserve white racial security and the slave system against the hostile Republicans. Upon "slavery," said the Alabama commissioner, Stephen Hale, to the Kentucky legislature, rested "not only the wealth and prosperity of the southern people, but their very existence as a political community." Only

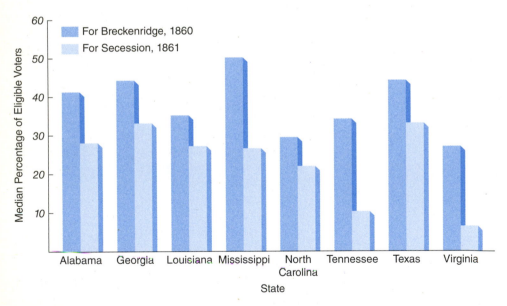

FIGURE 14.1 Voting Returns of Counties with Few Slaveholders, Eight Southern States, 1860 and 1861

This graph depicts voting in counties whose percentage of slaveholders ranked them among the lower half of the counties in their state. How does voters' support for secession in 1861 compare with support for John Breckinridge, the southern Democratic candidate in 1860? Why was their support for secession so weak? At this time counties with many slaveholders were giving increased support to secession.

secession, Hale contended, could sustain the "heaven-ordained superiority of the white over the black race." This combination of economic interests and beliefs fueled the tragedy about to happen.

Fort Sumter and Outbreak of War The dilemma facing President Lincoln on inauguration day in March 1861 was how to maintain the authority of the federal government without provoking war. Proceeding cautiously, he sought only to hold onto forts in the states that had left the Union, reasoning that in this way he could assert federal sovereignty while waiting for a restoration. But Jefferson Davis, who could not claim to lead a sovereign nation if the Confederate ports were under foreign (that is, U.S.) control, was unwilling to be so patient. A collision soon came.

It arrived in the early morning hours of April 12, 1861, at Fort Sumter in Charleston harbor. A federal garrison there ran low on food, and Lincoln notified the South Carolinians that he was sending a ship to resupply the fort. For the Montgomery government, the alternatives were to attack the fort or to acquiesce to Lincoln's authority. After the Confederate cabinet met, the secretary of war ordered local commanders to obtain a surrender or attack the fort. After two days of heavy bombardment, the federal garrison finally surrendered. No one died in battle, though an accident during post-battle ceremonies killed two Union soldiers. Confederates permitted the U.S. troops to sail away on unarmed vessels while Charlestonians celebrated wildly. The Civil War—the bloodiest war in America's history—had begun.

Causation Historians have long debated the immediate and long-term roots of the Civil War. Some have interpreted it as an "irrepressible conflict," the clash of two civilizations on divergent trajectories of history. Another group saw the war as "needless," the result of a "blundering generation" of irrational politicians and activists who trumped up an avoidable conflict. But the issues dividing Americans in 1861 were fundamental to the future of the republic. The logic of Republican ideology tended in the direction of abolishing slavery, even though Republicans denied any such intention. The logic of southern arguments led to establishing slavery everywhere, though southern leaders, too, denied such a motive. Republicans were devoted to promoting the North's free labor economy, burgeoning in the Great Lakes region through homesteading, internal improvements, and protective tariffs. The lords of the cotton kingdom, owners of $3 billion in slave property and the largest single asset in the American economy, were determined to protect and expand their "way of life." Small investors in land and large investors in slaves were on a collision course.

Lincoln put these facts succinctly. In a postelection letter to his old congressional colleague, Alexander Stephens of Georgia, soon to be vice president of the Confederacy, Lincoln offered assurance that Republicans would not attack slavery in the states where it existed. But Lincoln continued, "You think slavery is right and ought to be expanded; while we think it is wrong and ought to be restricted. That I suppose is the rub." Frederick Douglass demonstrated that he understood this in a postwar speech in which he declared that the "fight" had not been between "rapacious birds and ferocious beasts, a mere display of brute courage… but it was a war between men of thought, as well as of action, and in dead earnest for something beyond the battlefield."

Directly or indirectly, as a matter of *interests* and *morality*, Douglass's "something" had to do with slavery. Without slavery, there would have been no war. Many Americans still hold to a belief that the war was about states' rights, the theory and practice of the proper relationship of state to federal authority. But the significance of states' rights, then as now, is always in the cause in which it is employed. If secession was an exercise in states' rights—to what end? To borrow from Douglass, it is the meaning within the fight that we must understand.

SUMMARY

Events often seem inevitable after they have occurred. We should never fall into the trap of seeing big events in history only through a lens of inevitability. The events and ideas that Americans clashed over were links in a chain leading to conflict; humans made choices all along the way and to go to war.

The War with Mexico fostered massive land acquisition, which in turn forced an open debate about slavery in the West. The Compromise of 1850 attempted to settle the dispute but only added fuel to the fires of sectional contention, leading to the fateful Kansas-Nebraska Act of 1854, which tore asunder the political party system and gave birth to a genuine antislavery coalition. With Bleeding Kansas and the *Dred Scott* decision by 1857, Americans North and South faced clear and dangerous choices about the future of labor and the meaning of liberty in an ambitious and expanding society. And finally, by 1859, when radical abolitionist John Brown attacked Harpers Ferry to foment a slave insurrection, southerners and northerners came to see each other in conspiratorial terms. Meanwhile, African Americans, slave and free, fled from slave catchers in unprecedented numbers and grew to expect violent if uncertain resolutions to their dreams of freedom in America. No one knew the future, but all knew the issues and conflicts were real.

Throughout the 1840s and 1850s, many able leaders had worked to avert the outcome of disunion. As late as 1858, even Jefferson Davis had declared, "This great country will continue united." Secession dismayed northern editors and voters, and it also plunged some planters into depression. Paul Cameron, the largest slaveowner in North Carolina, confessed that he was "very unhappy. I love the Union." Many blacks, however, shared Frederick Douglass's outlook. "The contest must now be decided," he wrote in March 1861, "and decided forever, which of the two, Freedom or Slavery, shall give law to this Republic. Let the conflict come."

Why had war broken out? Why had all efforts to prevent it failed? The emotions bound up in attacking and defending slavery's future were too powerful, and the interests it affected too vital for a final compromise. Advocates of compromise anticipated that the tradition of conciliation and sectional adjustment would yet again save the Union in 1860, but their hopes were dashed.

During the 1850s, every southern victory in territorial expansion increased fear of the Slave Power, and each new expression of Free-Soil sentiment prompted slaveholders to harden their demands. In the profoundest sense, slavery was the root of the war. But as the fighting began, the fate of the war's central issue was shrouded in confusion. As a people and a nation, Americans had reached the most fateful turning point in their history. Answers would now come from the battlefield and from the mobilization of two societies to wage war on a scale they had not imagined.

15

TRANSFORMING FIRE: THE CIVIL WAR 1861–1865

CHAPTER OUTLINE

• America Goes to War, 1861–1862 • War Transforms the South • Wartime Northern Economy and Society • The Advent of Emancipation • The Soldiers' War • 1863: The Tide of Battle Turns • Disunity: South, North, and West • 1864–1865: The Final Test of Wills • *LINKS TO THE WORLD The Civil War in Britain* • Summary

AMERICA GOES TO WAR, 1861–1862

Few Americans understood what they were getting into when the war began. The onset of hostilities sparked patriotic sentiments, optimistic speeches, and joyous ceremonies in both North and South. Northern communities raised companies of volunteers eager to save the Union and sent them off with fanfare. In the South, confident recruits boasted of whipping the Yankees and returning home before Christmas. Southern women sewed dashing uniforms for men who would soon be lucky to wear drab gray or butternut homespun. Americans went to war in 1861 with decidedly romantic notions of what they would experience.

First Battle of Bull Run   Through the spring of 1861, both sides scrambled to organize and train their undisciplined armies. On July 21, 1861, the first battle took place outside Manassas Junction, Virginia, near a stream called Bull Run. General Irvin McDowell and thirty thousand Union troops attacked General P. G. T. Beauregard's twenty-two thousand southerners. As raw recruits struggled amid the confusion of their first battle, federal forces began to gain ground. Then they ran into a line of Virginia troops under General Thomas Jackson. "There is Jackson standing like a stone wall," shouted one Confederate. "Stonewall" Jackson's line held, and the arrival of nine thousand Confederate reinforcements by train won the day for the South. Union troops fled

CHRONOLOGY

1861   Battle of Bull Run

McClellan organizes Union Army

Union blockade begins

U.S. Congress passes first confiscation act

Trent affair

1862   Union captures Fort Henry and Fort Donelson

U.S. Navy captures New Orleans

Battle of Shiloh shows the war's destructiveness

Confederacy enacts conscription

McClellan's peninsula campaign fails to take Richmond

U.S. Congress passes second confiscation act, initiating emancipation

Confederacy mounts offensive in Maryland and Kentucky

Battle of Antietam ends Lee's drive into Maryland in September

British intervention in the war on Confederate side is averted

1863   Emancipation Proclamation takes effect

U.S. Congress passes National Banking Act

Union enacts conscription

African American soldiers join Union Army

Food riots occur in southern cities

Battle of Chancellorsville ends in Confederate victory but Jackson's death

Union wins key victories at Vicksburg and Gettysburg

Draft riots take place in New York City

1864   Battles of the Wilderness and Spotsylvania produce heavy casualties on both sides

Battle of Cold Harbor continues carnage in Virginia

Sherman captures Atlanta

Confederacy begins to collapse on home front

Lincoln wins reelection, eliminating any Confederate hopes for negotiated end to war

Jefferson Davis proposes arming slaves

Sherman marches through Georgia to the sea

1865   Sherman marches through Carolinas

U.S. Congress approves Thirteenth Amendment

Lee abandons Richmond and Petersburg

Lee surrenders at Appomattox Court House

Lincoln assassinated

Death toll in war reaches 620,000

back to Washington, observed by shocked northern congressmen and spectators who had watched the battle; a few sightseers were actually captured for their folly.

The unexpected rout at Bull Run gave northerners their first hint of the nature of the war to come. Although the United States enjoyed an enormous advantage in resources, victory would not be easy. Pro-Union feeling was growing in western Virginia, and loyalties were divided in the four border slave states—Missouri, Kentucky, Maryland, and Delaware. But the rest of the Upper South—the states of North Carolina, Virginia, Tennessee, and Arkansas—had joined the Confederacy in the wake of the attack on Fort Sumter. Moved by an outpouring of regional loyalty, half a million southerners volunteered to fight—so many that the Confederate government could hardly arm them all. The United States therefore undertook a massive mobilization of troops around Washington, D.C.

Lincoln gave command of the army to General George B. McClellan, an officer who proved better at organization and training than at fighting. McClellan put his growing army into camp and devoted the fall and winter of 1861 to readying a formidable force of a quarter-million men whose mission would be to take Richmond, established as the Confederate capital by July 1861. "The vast preparation of the enemy," wrote one southern soldier, produced a "feeling of despondency" in the South for the first time. But southern morale remained high early in the war. Most Americans still possessed a rather romantic conception of the war looming on their horizon.

Grand Strategy

While McClellan prepared, the Union began to implement other parts of its overall strategy, which called for a blockade of southern ports and eventual capture of the Mississippi River. Like a constricting snake, this "Anaconda plan" would strangle the Confederacy. At first, the Union Navy had too few ships to patrol 3,550 miles of coastline and block the Confederacy's avenues of supply. Gradually, however, the navy increased the blockade's effectiveness, though it never stopped southern commerce completely.

The Confederate strategy was essentially defensive. A defensive posture was not only consistent with the South's claim of independence, but also reasonable in light of the North's advantage in resources (see Figure 15.1). But Jefferson Davis called the southern strategy an "offensive defensive," taking advantage of opportunities to attack and using its interior lines of transportation to concentrate troops at crucial points. In its war aims, the Confederacy did not need to conquer the North; the Union effort, however, as time would tell, required conquest of the South.

Strategic thinking on both sides slighted the importance of the West, that vast expanse of territory between Virginia and the Mississippi River and beyond. Guerrilla warfare broke out in 1861 in the politically divided state of Missouri, and key locations along the Mississippi and other major western rivers would prove crucial prizes in the North's eventual victory. Beyond the Mississippi River, the Confederacy hoped to gain an advantage by negotiating treaties with the Creeks, Choctaws, Chickasaws, Cherokees, Seminoles, and smaller groups of Plains Indians. Meanwhile, the Republican U.S. Congress carved the West into territories in anticipation of state making. For most Indians west of the Mississippi, what began during the Civil War was nearly three decades of offensive warfare against them, an enveloping strategy of conquest, relocation, and slaughter.

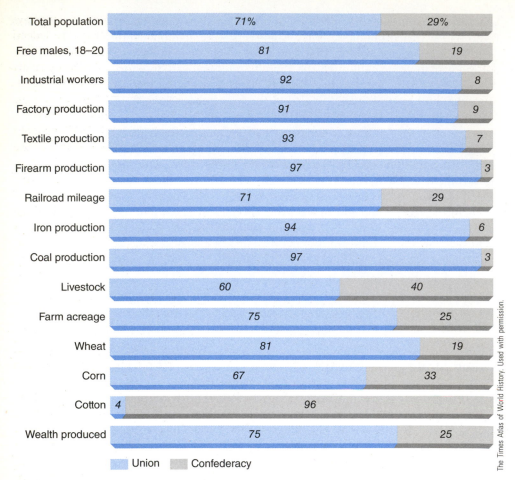

	Union	Confederacy
Total population	71%	29%
Free males, 18–20	81	19
Industrial workers	92	8
Factory production	91	9
Textile production	93	7
Firearm production	97	3
Railroad mileage	71	29
Iron production	94	6
Coal production	97	3
Livestock	60	40
Farm acreage	75	25
Wheat	81	19
Corn	67	33
Cotton	4	96
Wealth produced	75	25

The Times Atlas of World History. Used with permission.

FIGURE 15.1 Comparative Resources, Union and Confederate States, 1861

The North had vastly superior resources. Although the North's advantages in manpower and industrial capacity proved very important, the South still had to be conquered, its society and its will crushed.

Union Naval Campaign

The last half of 1861 brought no major land battles, but the North made gains by sea. Late in the summer, Union naval forces captured Cape Hatteras and then Hilton Head, one of the Sea Islands off Port Royal, South Carolina. A few months later, similar operations secured vital coastal points in North Carolina as well as Fort Pulaski, which defended Savannah. Federal naval operations established significant beachheads along the Confederate coastline.

The coastal victories off South Carolina foreshadowed a revolution in slave society. At the federal gunboats' approach, planters abandoned their land and fled. For a while, Confederate cavalry tried to round up slaves and move them to the interior as well. But thousands of slaves greeted what they hoped to be freedom with rejoicing and broke the hated cotton gins. Some entered their masters' homes and took clothing and furniture, which they conspicuously displayed. A growing stream of runaways poured into Union lines. Unwilling at first to wage a war against slavery, the federal government did not acknowledge the slaves' freedom—though it began to use their labor in the Union cause. This swelling tide of emancipated slaves, defined by many Union officers as "contraband" of war (confiscated enemy property), forced first a bitter and confused debate within the Union Army and government over how to treat the freedmen, and then a forthright attempt to harness their labor and military power.

The coastal incursions worried southerners, but the spring of 1862 brought even stronger evidence of the war's gravity. In March, two ironclad ships—the *Monitor* (a Union warship) and the *Merrimack* (a Union ship seized by the Confederacy)—fought each other for the first time off the coast of Virginia. Their battle, though indecisive, ushered in a new era in naval design. In April, Union ships commanded by Admiral David Farragut smashed through log booms blocking the Mississippi River and fought their way upstream to capture New Orleans. The city at the mouth of the Mississippi, the South's greatest seaport and slave-trading center, was now in federal hands.

War in the Far West

Farther west, three full Confederate regiments were organized, mostly of Cherokees, from Indian Territory, but a Union victory at Elkhorn Tavern, Arkansas, shattered southern control of the region. Thereafter, dissension within Native American groups and a Union victory the following year at Honey Springs, Arkansas, reduced Confederate operations in Indian Territory to guerrilla raids.

In the westernmost campaign of the war, from February to May 1862, some three thousand Confederate and four thousand Union forces fought for control of New Mexico Territory. The military significance of the New Mexico campaign was limited, but the Confederate invasion had grander aims: access to the trade riches of the Santa Fe Trail and possession of gold mines in Colorado and California. If the campaign had endured long enough, the Confederacy would have been much stronger with a western empire. But Colorado and New Mexico Unionists fought for their region, and in a series of battles at Glorieta Pass, 20 miles east of Santa Fe, on March 26 through 28, they blocked the Confederate invasion. By May 1, Confederate forces straggled down the Rio Grande River back into Texas, ending their effort to take New Mexico.

Grant's Tennessee Campaign and the Battle of Shiloh

Meanwhile, in February 1862, land and river forces in northern Tennessee won significant victories for the Union. A Union commander named Ulysses S. Grant saw the strategic importance of Fort Henry and Fort Donelson, the Confederate outposts guarding the Tennessee and Cumberland Rivers. If federal troops could capture these forts, Grant realized, they would open two prime routes into the heartland of the Confederacy. In just ten days, he seized the forts—completely cutting off the Confederates and demanding "unconditional surrender" of Fort Donelson. A path into Tennessee, Alabama, and Mississippi now lay open before the Union Army. Grant's achievement of such a surrender from his former West Point roommate, Confederate commander Simon Bolivar Buckner, inspired northern public opinion.

Grant moved on into southern Tennessee and the first of the war's shockingly bloody encounters, the Battle of Shiloh. On April 6, Confederate general Albert Sidney Johnston caught federal troops with their backs to the water awaiting reinforcements along the Tennessee River. The Confederates attacked early in the morning and inflicted heavy damage all day. Close to victory, General Johnston was shot from his horse and killed. Southern forces almost achieved a breakthrough, but Union reinforcements arrived that night. The next day, the tide of battle turned and, after ten hours of terrible combat, Grant's men forced the Confederates to withdraw.

Neither side won a decisive victory at Shiloh, yet the losses were staggering, and the Confederates were forced to retreat into northern Mississippi. Northern troops lost thirteen thousand men (killed, wounded, or captured) out of sixty-three thousand; southerners sacrificed eleven thousand out of forty thousand. Total casualties in this single battle exceeded those in all three of America's previous wars combined. Now both sides were beginning to sense the true nature of the war. "I saw an open field," Grant recalled, "over which Confederates had made repeated charges ... so covered with dead that it would have been possible to walk across the clearing, in any direction, stepping on dead bodies, without a foot touching the ground." Shiloh utterly changed Grant's thinking about the war. He had hoped that southerners would soon be "heartily tired" of the conflict. After Shiloh, "I gave up all idea of saving the Union except by complete conquest." Memories of the Shiloh battlefield, and many others to come, would haunt the soldiers who survived for the rest of their lives. Herman Melville's "Shiloh, A Requiem" captures the pathos of that spring day when armies learned the truth about war:

Skimming lightly, wheeling still,
The swallows fly low
Over the field in clouded days,
The forest-field of Shiloh—
Over the field where April rain
Solaced the parched ones stretched in pain
Through the pause of night
That followed the Sunday fight
Around the church of Shiloh—
The church so lone, the log-built one,
That echoed to many a parting groan
And natural prayer
Of dying foemen mingled there—
Foemen at morn, but friends at eve—
Fame or country least their care:
(What like a bullet can undeceive!)
But now they lie low,
While over them the swallows skim,
And all is hushed at Shiloh.

McClellan and the Peninsula Campaign

On the Virginia front, President Lincoln had a different problem. General McClellan was slow to move. Only thirty-six, McClellan had already achieved notable success as an army officer and railroad president. Habitually overestimating the size of enemy forces, he called repeatedly for reinforcements and ignored Lincoln's directions to advance. McClellan advocated war of limited aims that would lead to a quick reunion. He intended neither disruption of slavery nor war on noncombatants. McClellan's conservative vision of the war was practically outdated before he even moved his army into Virginia. Finally, he chose to move by a water route, sailing his troops down the Chesapeake, landing them on the peninsula between the York and James Rivers, and advancing on Richmond from the east.

After a bloody but indecisive battle at Fair Oaks on May 31 through June 1, the federal armies moved to within 7 miles of the Confederate capital. They could see the spires on Richmond churches. The Confederate commanding general, Joseph E. Johnston, was badly wounded at Fair Oaks, and President Jefferson Davis placed his chief military adviser, Robert E. Lee, in command. The fifty-five-year-old Lee was an aristocratic Virginian, a lifelong military officer, and a veteran of distinction from the War with Mexico. Although he initially opposed secession, Lee loyally gave his allegiance to his state and became a staunch Confederate nationalist. He soon foiled McClellan's legions.

First, Lee sent Stonewall Jackson's corps of seventeen thousand northwest into the Shenandoah valley behind Union forces, where they threatened Washington, D.C., and with rapid-strike mobility drew some federal troops away from Richmond to protect their own capital. Further, in mid-June, in an extraordinary four-day ride around the entire Union Army, Confederate cavalry under J. E. B. Stuart, a self-styled Virginia cavalier with red cape and plumed hat, confirmed the exposed position of a major portion of McClellan's army north of the rain-swollen Chickahominy River. Then, in a series of engagements known as the Seven Days Battles, from June 26 through July 1, Lee struck at McClellan's army. Lee never managed to close his pincers around the retreating Union forces, but the daring move of taking the majority of his army northeast and attacking the Union right flank, while leaving only a small force to defend Richmond, forced McClellan (always believing he was outnumbered) to retreat toward the James River.

During the sustained fighting of the Seven Days, the Union forces suffered 20,614 casualties and the Confederates, 15,849. After repeated rebel assaults against entrenched positions on high ground at Malvern Hill, an officer concluded, "It was not war, it was murder." By August 3, McClellan withdrew his army back to the Potomac and the environs of Washington. Richmond remained safe for almost two more years.

Confederate Offensive in Maryland and Kentucky

Buoyed by these results, Jefferson Davis conceived an ambitious plan to turn the tide of the war and gain recognition of the Confederacy by European nations. He ordered a general offensive, sending Lee north into Maryland and Generals Kirby Smith and Braxton Bragg into Kentucky. Calling on residents of Maryland and Kentucky, still slave states, to make a separate peace with his government, Davis also invited northwestern states like Indiana, which sent much of their trade down the Mississippi to New Orleans, to leave the Union. This was a coordinated effort to take the war to the North and to try to force both a military and a political turning point.

The plan was promising, but in the end the offensive failed. Lee's forces achieved a striking success at the battle of Second Bull Run, August 29 through 30,

Library of Congress

In October 1862 in New York City, photographer Mathew Brady opened an exhibition of photographs from the Battle of Antietam. Although few knew it, Brady's vision was very poor, and this photograph of Confederate dead was actually made by his assistants, Alexander Gardner and James F. Gibson.

just southwest of Washington, D.C. On the same killing fields along Bull Run Creek where federal troops had been defeated the previous summer, an entire Union army was sent in retreat back into the federal capital. Thousands of wounded occupied schools and churches, and two thousand suffered on cots in the rotunda of the U.S. Capitol.

But in the bloodiest day of the entire war, September 17, 1862, McClellan turned Lee back from Sharpsburg, Maryland. In this Battle of Antietam, five thousand men died, and another eighteen thousand were wounded. Lee was lucky to escape destruction, for McClellan had intercepted a lost battle order, wrapped around cigars for each Confederate corps commander and inadvertently dropped by a courier. But McClellan moved slowly, failed to use his larger forces in simultaneous attacks, and allowed Lee's stricken army to retreat to safety across the Potomac. In the wake of Antietam, Lincoln removed McClellan from command.

In Kentucky, Generals Smith and Bragg secured Lexington and Frankfort, but their effort to force the Yankees back to the Ohio River was stopped at the Battle of Perryville on October 8. Bragg's army retreated back into Tennessee, where—from December 31, 1862, to January 2, 1863—they fought an indecisive but much bloodier battle at Murfreesboro. Casualties exceeded even those of Shiloh, and many lives were sacrificed on a bitter winter landscape.

Confederate leaders marshaled all their strength for a breakthrough but failed. Outnumbered and disadvantaged in resources, the South could not continue the offensive. Profoundly disappointed, Davis admitted to a committee of Confederate representatives that southerners were entering "the darkest and most dangerous period we have yet had."

But 1862 also brought painful lessons to the North. Confederate general J. E. B. Stuart executed a daring cavalry raid into Pennsylvania in October. Then, on December 13, Union general Ambrose Burnside, now in command of the Army of the Potomac, unwisely ordered his soldiers to attack Lee's army, which held fortified positions on high ground at Fredericksburg, Virginia. Lee's men performed so efficiently in killing northerners that Lee was moved to say, "It is well that war is so terrible. We should grow too fond of it." Burnside's repeated assaults up Marye's Heights shocked even the opponents. "The Federals had fallen like the steady dripping of rain from the eaves of a house," remarked Confederate general James Longstreet. And a Union officer observed of the carnage of thirteen hundred dead and ninety-six hundred wounded Union soldiers, "The whole plain was covered with men, prostrate and dropping.... I had never before seen fighting like that ... the next brigade coming up in succession would do its duty, and melt like snow coming down on warm ground." The scale of carnage now challenged people on both sides to search deeply for the meaning of such a war. At the front some soldiers lost their sense of humanity in the face of the challenge. In the wake of Antietam's death toll, one Union burial crew, exhausted and perhaps inebriated, threw fifty-eight Confederate bodies down the well of a local farmer.

WAR TRANSFORMS THE SOUTH

The war caused tremendous disruptions in civilian life and altered southern society beyond all expectations. One of the first traditions to fall was the southern preference for local and limited government. States' rights had been a formative ideology for the Confederacy, but state governments were weak operations. To withstand the massive power of the North, the South needed to centralize; like the colonial revolutionaries, southerners faced a choice of joining together or dying separately.

The Confederacy and Centralization   Jefferson Davis moved promptly to bring all arms, supplies, and troops under centralized control. But by early 1862, the scope and duration of the conflict required something more. Tens of thousands of Confederate soldiers had volunteered for just one year's service, planning to return home in the spring to plant their crops. More recruits were needed constantly to keep southern armies in the field. However, as one official admitted, "the spirit of volunteering had died out." Finally, faced with a critical shortage of troops, in April 1862 the Confederate government enacted the first national conscription (draft) law in American history. Thus, the war forced unprecedented change on states that had seceded out of fear of change.

Davis adopted a firm leadership role toward the Confederate Congress, which raised taxes and later passed a tax-in-kind—paid in farm products. Nearly forty-five hundred agents dispersed to collect the tax. Where opposition arose, the government suspended the writ of habeas corpus (which prevented individuals from being held without trial) and imposed martial law. Despite Davis's unyielding stance, this tax system proved inadequate for the South's war effort.

To replace the food that men in uniform would have grown, Davis exhorted state governments to require farmers to switch from cash crops to food crops. But the army remained short of food and labor. The War Department resorted to impressing slaves to work on fortifications, and after 1861 the government relied heavily on confiscation of food to feed the troops. Officers swooped down on farms in the line of march and carted away grain, meat, wagons, and draft animals. Such raids caused increased hardship and resentment for women managing farms in the absence of husbands and sons.

Soon, the Confederate administration in Richmond gained virtually complete control over the southern economy. The Confederate Congress also gave the central government almost complete control of the railroads. A large bureaucracy sprang up to administer these operations: over seventy thousand civilians staffed the Confederate administration. By war's end, the southern bureaucracy was larger in proportion to population than its northern counterpart.

Confederate Nationalism

Historians have long argued over whether the Confederacy itself was a "rebellion," a "revolution," or the creation of a genuine "nation." Whatever label we apply, Confederates created a culture and an ideology of nationalism. Southerners immediately tried to forge their own national symbols and identity. In flags, songs, language, seals, school readers, and other national characteristics, Confederates created their own story.

In its conservative crusade to preserve states' rights, the social order, and racial slavery, southerners believed the Confederacy was the true legacy of the American Revolution—a bulwark against centralized power in keeping with the war for independence. In this view, southern "liberty" was no less a holy cause than that of the patriots of 1776. To southerners, theirs was a continuing revolution against the excesses of Yankee democracy, and George Washington (a Virginian) on horseback formed the center of the official seal of the Confederacy.

Also central to Confederate nationalism was a refurbished defense of slavery as a benign, protective institution. In wartime schoolbooks, children were instructed in the divinely inspired, paternalistic character of slavery. And the idea of the "faithful slave" was key to southerners' nationalist cause. A poem popular among whites captured an old slave's rejection of the Emancipation Proclamation:

Now, Massa, dis is berry fine, dese words
You've spoke to me,
No doubt you mean it kindly, but ole Dinah
Won't be free …
Ole Massa's berry good to me—and though I am
His slave,
He treats me like I'se kin to him—and I would
Rather have
A home in Massa's cabin, and eat his black
Bread too,
Dan leave ole Massa's children and go and
Lib wid you.

In the face of defeat and devastation, this and other forms of Confederate nationalism collapsed in the final year of the war. But much of the spirit and substance of Confederate nationalism would revive in the postwar period in a new ideology of the Lost Cause.

Southern Cities and Industry

Clerks and subordinate officials crowded the towns and cities where Confederate departments set up their offices. Clerks had always been males, but now "government girls" staffed the Confederate bureaucracy. The sudden urban migration that resulted overwhelmed the housing supply and stimulated new construction. The pressure was especially great in Richmond, whose population increased 250 percent. Mobile's population jumped from twenty-nine thousand to forty-one thousand; Atlanta, too, began to grow; and ten thousand people poured into war-related industries in little Selma, Alabama.

As the Union blockade disrupted imports of manufactured products, the traditionally agricultural South forged new industries. Many planters shared Davis's hope that industrialization would bring "deliverance, full and unrestricted, from all commercial dependence" on the North or the world. Indeed, beginning almost from scratch, the Confederacy achieved tremendous feats of industrial development. Chief of Ordnance Josiah Gorgas increased the capacity of Richmond's Tredegar Iron Works and other factories to the point that by 1865, his Ordnance Bureau was supplying all Confederate small arms and ammunition. Meanwhile, the government constructed new railroad lines and ironworks, and much of the labor consisted of slaves relocated from farms and plantations.

Changing Roles of Women

White women, restricted to narrow roles in antebellum society, gained substantial new responsibilities in wartime. The wives and mothers of soldiers now headed households and performed men's work, including raising crops and tending animals. Women in nonslaveowning families cultivated fields themselves, while wealthier women suddenly had to perform as overseers and manage field work. In the cities, white women—who had been largely excluded from the labor force—found a limited number of respectable paying jobs, often in the Confederate bureaucracy, where some found clerks' jobs as "government girls." And female schoolteachers appeared in the South for the first time.

Women experienced both confidence and agony from their new responsibilities. Among them was Janie Smith, a young North Carolinian. Raised in a rural area by prosperous parents, she now faced grim realities as the war reached her farm and troops turned her home into a hospital. "It makes me shudder when I think of the awful sights I witnessed that morning," she wrote to a friend. "Ambulance after ambulance drove up with our wounded.... Under every shed and tree, the tables were carried for amputating the limbs.... The blood lay in puddles in the grove; the groans of the dying ... were horrible." But Janie Smith learned to cope with crisis. She ended her account with the proud words "I can dress amputated limbs now and do most anything in the way of nursing wounded soldiers."

Patriotic sacrifice appealed to some women, but others resented their new burdens. A Texas woman who had struggled to discipline slaves pronounced herself "sick of trying to do a man's business." Others grew angry over shortages and resented cooking and unfamiliar contact with lower-class women. Some women grew scornful of the war and demanded that their men return to help provide for their families.

Human Suffering, Hoarding, and Inflation

For millions of ordinary southerners, the war brought privation and suffering. Mass poverty descended for the first time on a large minority of the white population. Many yeoman families had lost their breadwinners to the army. As a South Carolina newspaper put it, "The duties of war have called away from home the sole supports of many, many families.... Help must be given, or the poor will suffer." Women on their own sought help from relatives, neighbors, friends, anyone. Sometimes they pleaded their case to the Confederate government. "In the name of humanity," begged one woman, "discharge my husband he is not able to do your government much good and he might do his children some good ... my poor children have no home nor no Father." To the extent that the South eventually lost the will to fight in the face of defeat, women played a role in demanding an end to the war.

The South was in many places so sparsely populated that the conscription of one skilled craftsman could wreak hardship on the people of an entire county. Often, they begged in unison for the exemption or discharge of the local miller, or the neighborhood tanner or wheelwright. Physicians were also in short supply. Most serious, however, was the loss of a blacksmith. As a petition from Alabama explained, "Our Section of County [is] left entirely Destitute of any man that is able to keep in order any kind of Farming Tules."

The blockade of Confederate shipping created shortages of important supplies— salt, sugar, coffee, nails—and speculation and hoarding made the shortages worse. Greedy businessmen cornered the supply of some commodities; prosperous citizens stocked up on food. The *Richmond Enquirer* criticized a planter who purchased so many wagonloads of supplies that his "lawn and paths looked like a wharf covered with a ship's loads." North Carolina's Governor Zebulon Vance worried about "the cry of distress ... from the poor wives and children of our soldiers.... What will become of them?"

Inflation raged out of control, fueled by the Confederate government's heavy borrowing and inadequate taxes, until prices had increased almost 7,000 percent. Inflation particularly imperiled urban dwellers without their own sources of food. As early as 1861 and 1862, newspapers reported that "want and starvation are staring thousands in the face," and troubled officials predicted that "women and children are bound to come to suffering if not starvation." Hoarding continued to cause local conflict, and a rudimentary relief program organized by the Confederacy failed to meet the need.

Inequities of the Confederate Draft

As their fortunes declined, people of once-modest means looked around and found abundant evidence that all classes were not sacrificing equally. The Confederate government enacted policies that decidedly favored the upper class. Until the last year of the war, for example, prosperous southerners could avoid military service by hiring substitutes. Prices for substitutes skyrocketed until it cost a man $5,000 or $6,000 to send someone to the front in his place. Well over fifty thousand upper-class southerners purchased such substitutes. Mary Boykin Chesnut knew of one young aristocrat who "spent a fortune in substitutes.... He is at the end of his row now, for all able-bodied men are ordered to the front. I hear he is going as some general's courier."

Anger at such discrimination exploded in October 1862, when the Confederate Congress exempted from military duty anyone who was supervising at least twenty slaves. "Never did a law meet with more universal odium," observed one representative. "Its influence upon the poor is most calamitous." Protests poured in from every corner of the Confederacy, and North Carolina's legislators formally condemned the law. Its defenders argued, however, that the exemption preserved order and aided food production, and the statute remained on the books.

This "twenty Negro" law is indicative of the racial fears many Confederates felt as the war threatened to overturn southern society. But it also fueled desertion and stimulated new levels of overt Unionism in nonslaveholding regions of the South. In Jones County, Mississippi, an area of piney woods and few slaves or plantations, Newt Knight, a Confederate soldier, led a band of renegades who took over the county, declared their allegiance to the Union, and called their district the "Free State of Jones." They held out for the remainder of the war as an enclave of independent Union sympathizers.

The bitterness of letters to Confederate officials suggests the depth of the dissension and class anger. "If I and my little children suffer [and] die while there Father is in service," threatened one woman, "I invoke God Almighty that our blood rest upon the South." Another woman swore to the secretary of war that, unless help was provided to poverty-stricken wives and mothers, "an allwise god ... will send down his fury ... [on] those that are in power." War magnified existing social tensions in the Confederacy, and created a few new ones.

WARTIME NORTHERN ECONOMY AND SOCIETY

With the onset of war, a tidal wave of change rolled over the North as well. Factories and citizens' associations geared up to support the war, and the federal government and its executive branch gained new powers. The energies of an industrializing society were harnessed to serve the cause of the Union. Idealism and greed flourished together, and the northern economy proved its awesome productivity.

Northern Business, Industry, and Agriculture At first, the war was a shock to business. Northern firms lost their southern markets, and many companies had to change their products and find new customers. Southern debts became uncollectible, jeopardizing not only northern merchants but also many western banks. Farm families struggled with a shortage of labor caused by army enlistments. A few enterprises never pulled out of the tailspin caused by the war. Cotton mills lacked cotton; construction declined; and shoe manufacturers sold few of the cheap shoes that planters had bought for their slaves.

But certain entrepreneurs, such as wool producers, benefited from shortages of competing products, and soaring demand for war-related goods swept some businesses to new success. To feed the hungry war machine, the federal government pumped unprecedented sums into the economy. The Treasury issued $3.2 billion in bonds and paper money called "greenbacks," and the War Department spent over $360 million in revenues from new taxes, including the nation's first income tax.

War-related spending revived business in many northern states. In 1863, a merchants' magazine examined the effects of the war in Massachusetts: "Seldom, if ever, has the business of Massachusetts been more active or profitable than during the past year.... In every department of labor the government has been, directly or indirectly, the chief employer and paymaster." Government contracts saved Massachusetts shoe manufacturers, as well as many firms in other states, from ruin.

The northern economy also grew because of a complementary relationship between agriculture and industry. Mechanization of agriculture had begun before the war. Wartime recruitment and conscription, however, gave western farmers an added incentive to purchase labor-saving machinery. The shift from human labor to machines created new markets for industry and expanded the food supply for the urban industrial work force. The boom in the sale of agricultural tools was tremendous. Cyrus and William McCormick built an industrial empire in Chicago from the sale of their reapers. Between 1862 and 1864, the manufacture of mowers and reapers doubled to 70,000 yearly; by war's end, 375,000 reapers were in use, triple the number in 1861. Thus northern farm families whose breadwinners went to war did not suffer as much as did their counterparts in the South. "We have seen," one magazine observed, "a stout matron whose sons are in the army, cutting hay with her team ... and she cut seven acres with ease in a day, riding leisurely upon her cutter." Northern farms, generally not ravaged by foraging armies and devastation, thrived during wartime.

The Quartermaster and Military-Government Mobilization   This government-business marriage emerged from a greatly empowered Quartermaster Department, which as a bureaucracy grew to be the single largest employer in the United States, issuing thousands of manufacturing contracts to hundreds of firms. The 100,000 civilian employees of the Quartermaster Department labored throughout a network of procurement centers, especially in the cities of Washington, D.C., Phildelphia, New York, Cincinnati, and St. Louis. Many of the senior military officers in the department had considerable prewar experience, especially in the West.

A portion of Secretary of War Edwin M. Stanton's list of the weapons supplies alone needed by the Ordnance Department indicates the scope of the demand for government and business cooperation: "7,892 cannon, 11,787 artillery carriages, 4,022,130 small-arms, ... 1,022,176,474 cartridges for small-arms, 1,220,555,435 percussion caps, ... 26,440,054 pounds of gunpowder, ... and 90,416,295 pounds of lead." In an unprecedented military mobilization, the government also purchased huge quantities of uniforms, boots, food, camp equipment, saddles, horses, ships, and other necessities. By 1865, the government had purchased some 640,000 horses and 300,000 mules at a cost well over $100 million.

Two-thirds of all U.S. war spending went to supply the forces in the field and, to command that process, President Lincoln appointed the talented West Point–trained engineer, Montgomery Meigs. Meigs, whose experience included overseeing the building of the Capitol dome, insisted on issuing government contracts only with competitive bidding. He spent $1.8 billion of the public's money to wage the war, a figure larger than all previous U.S. government expenditures combined since independence. His efforts, argued one historian, made the Union army "the best fed, most lavishly supplied army that had ever existed." Many historians consider

Meigs the "unsung hero of Northern victory," a claim hard to deny, although he benefitted from his corps of Quartermaster officers who won the war one contract at a time. The success of such military mobilization left an indelible mark on American political-economic history and provided perhaps the oldest root of the modern American military-industrial state.

Nothing illustrated the wartime partnership between business and government better than the work of Jay Cooke, a wealthy New York financier. Cooke threw himself into the marketing of government bonds to finance the war effort. With imagination and energy, he convinced both large investors and ordinary citizens to invest enormous sums, in the process earning hefty commissions for himself. But the financier's profit served the Union cause, as the interests of capitalism and government merged in American history's first era of "big government."

Northern Workers' Militancy   Northern industrial and urban workers did not fare as well as many of the companies for which they labored. After the initial slump, jobs became plentiful, but inflation ate up much of a worker's paycheck. The price of coffee had tripled; rice and sugar had doubled; and clothing, fuel, and rent had all climbed. Between 1860 and 1864, consumer prices rose at least 76 percent, while daily wages rose only 42 percent. Workers' families consequently suffered a substantial decline in their standard of living.

As their real wages shrank, industrial workers lost job security. To increase production, some employers replaced workers with labor-saving machines. Other employers urged the government to promote immigration to secure cheap labor. Workers responded by forming unions and sometimes by striking. Skilled craftsmen organized to combat the loss of their jobs and status to machines; women and unskilled workers, who were excluded by the craftsmen, formed their own unions. Indeed, thirteen occupational groups—including tailors, coal miners, and railway engineers—formed national unions during the Civil War, and the number of strikes climbed steadily.

Employers reacted with hostility to this new labor independence. Manufacturers viewed labor activism as a threat to their freedom of action and accordingly formed statewide or craft-based associations to cooperate and pool information. These employers shared blacklists of union members and required new workers to sign "yellow dog" contracts (promises not to join a union). To put down strikes, they hired strikebreakers from among blacks, immigrants, and women, and sometimes used federal troops to break the unions' will.

Labor militancy, however, prevented employers neither from making profits nor from profiteering on government contracts. Unscrupulous businessmen took advantage of the suddenly immense demand for army supplies by selling clothing and blankets made of "shoddy"—wool fibers reclaimed from rags or worn cloth. Shoddy goods often came apart in the rain; most of the shoes purchased in the early months of the war were worthless. Contractors sold inferior guns for double the usual price and passed off tainted meat as good. Corruption was so widespread that it led to a year-long investigation by the House of Representatives. These realities of everyday economic life eroded the early romance for war among many Americans.

Economic Nationalism and Government-Business Partnership

Legitimate enterprises also made healthy profits. The output of woolen mills increased so dramatically that dividends in the industry nearly tripled. Some cotton mills made record profits on what they sold, even though they reduced their output. Brokerage houses worked until midnight and earned unheard-of commissions. Railroads carried immense quantities of freight and passengers, increasing their business to the point that railroad stocks skyrocketed in value.

Railroads were also a leading beneficiary of government largesse. With southern representatives absent from Congress, the northern route of the transcontinental railroad quickly prevailed. In 1862 and 1864, Congress chartered two corporations—the Union Pacific Railroad and the Central Pacific Railroad—and assisted them financially in connecting Omaha, Nebraska, with Sacramento, California. For each mile of track laid, the railroads received a loan of from $16,000 to $48,000 in government bonds plus 20 square miles of land along a free 400-foot-wide right of way. Overall, the two corporations gained approximately 20 million acres of land and nearly $60 million in loans.

Other businessmen benefited handsomely from the Morrill Land Grant Act (1862). To promote public education in agriculture, engineering, and military science, Congress granted each state thirty thousand acres of federal land for each of its congressional districts. The law eventually fostered sixty-nine colleges and universities as it also enriched a few prominent speculators. At the same time, the Homestead Act of 1862 offered cheap, and sometimes free, land to people who would settle the West and improve their property.

Before the war, adequate national banking, taxation, and currency did not exist. Banks operating under state charters issued no fewer than seven thousand different kinds of notes. During the war, Congress and the Treasury Department established a national banking system empowered to issue national bank notes and, by 1865, most state banks were forced by a prohibitive tax to join the national system. This process created sounder currency but also inflexibility in the money supply and an eastern-oriented financial structure that, later in the century, pushed farmers in need of credit and cash to revolt.

Republican economic policies expanded the scope of government and bonded people to the nation as never before. Yet ostentation coexisted with idealism. In the excitement of wartime moneymaking, an eagerness to display one's wealth flourished in the largest cities. *Harper's Monthly* reported that "the suddenly enriched contractors, speculators, and stock-jobbers ... are spending money with a profusion never before witnessed in our country.... The men button their waistcoats with diamonds ... and the women powder their hair with gold and silver dust." The *New York Herald* summarized that city's atmosphere: "This war has entirely changed the American character.... The individual who makes the most money—no matter how—and spends the most—no matter for what—is considered the greatest man."

The Union Cause

In thousands of self-governing towns and communities, northern citizens felt a personal connection to representative government. Secession threatened to destroy their system, and northerners rallied to its defense. In the first two years of the war, northern morale remained remarkably high for a cause that today may seem abstract—the Union—but at the time meant the preservation of a social and political order that people cherished.

Secular and church leaders supported the cause, and even ministers who preferred to separate politics and pulpit denounced "the iniquity of causeless rebellion. Abolitionists campaigned to turn the war into a crusade against slavery." Free black communities and churches, both black and white, responded to the needs of slaves who flocked to the Union lines, sending clothing, ministers, and teachers to aid the freedpeople. Indeed, northern blacks gave wholehearted support to the war, volunteering by the thousands at first and in spite of the initial rejection they received from the Lincoln administration.

Thus, northern society embraced strangely contradictory tendencies. Materialism and greed flourished alongside idealism, religious conviction, and self-sacrifice. In decades to come, Americans would commemorate and build monuments to soldiers' sacrifice and idealism, not to opportunism and sometimes not even to the causes for which they fought, which was a way of forgetting the deeper nature of the conflict.

Northern Women on Home Front and Battlefront

Northern women, like their southern counterparts, took on new roles. Those who stayed home organized over ten thousand soldiers' aid societies, rolled bandages, and raised $3 million to aid injured troops. Women were instrumental in pressing for the first trained ambulance corps in the Union Army, and they formed the backbone of the U.S. Sanitary Commission, a civilian agency officially recognized by the War Department in 1861. The Sanitary Commission provided crucial nutritional and medical aid to soldiers. Although most of its officers were men, the bulk of the volunteers who ran its seven thousand auxiliaries were women. Women organized elaborate "Sanitary Fairs" to raise money and awareness for soldiers' health and hygiene.

Approximately thirty-two hundred women also served as nurses in frontline hospitals. Yet women had to fight for a chance to serve at all; the professionalization of medicine since the Revolution had created a medical system dominated by men, and many male physicians did not want women's aid. Even Clara Barton, famous for her persistence in working in the worst hospitals at the front, was ousted from her post in 1863. But along with Barton, women such as the stern Dorothea Dix, well known for her efforts to reform asylums for the insane, and an Illinois widow, Mary Ann Bickerdyke, who served tirelessly in Sherman's army in the West, established a heroic tradition for Civil War nurses. They also advanced the professionalization of nursing, as several schools of nursing were established in northern cities during or after the war.

Women also wrote popular fiction about the war. In sentimental war poetry, short stories, and novels, and in printed war songs that reached thousands of readers, women produced a commercial literature in illustrated weeklies, monthly periodicals, and special "story papers." In many stories, female characters seek recognition for their loyalty and service to the Union, while others probe the suffering and death of loved ones at the front. One woman writer was Louisa May Alcott, arrived at her job as a nurse in Washington, D.C., just after the horrific Union defeat at Fredericksburg, in December 1862, and later immortalized her experience in

Hospital Sketches (1863), a popular book in which she described shattered men, "riddled with shot and shell," who had "borne suffering for which we have no name." Alcott provided northern readers a clear-eyed view of the hospitals in which so many of their loved ones agonized and perished.

At its heart, in what one historian has called a "feminized war literature," woman writers explored the relationship between individual and national needs, between home and "the cause." And by 1863, many women found the liberation of slaves an inspiring subject, as Julia Ward Howe did in her immortal "Battle Hymn of the Republic":

> As He died to make men holy
> Let us die to make men free.

Walt Whitman's War   The poet Walt Whitman also left a record of his experiences as a volunteer nurse in Washington, D.C. As he dressed wounds and tried to comfort suffering and lonely men, Whitman found "the marrow of the tragedy concentrated in those Army Hospitals." But despite "indescribably horrid wounds," he also found inspiration in such suffering and a deepening faith in American democracy. Whitman celebrated the "incredible dauntlessness" and sacrifice of the common soldier who fought for the Union. As he had written in the preface to his great work *Leaves of Grass* (1855), "The genius of the United States is not best or most in its executives or legislatures, but always most in the common people." Whitman worked this idealization of the common man into his poetry, which also explored homoerotic themes and rejected the lofty meter and rhyme of European verse to strive for a "genuineness" that would appeal to the masses.

In "The Wound Dresser," Whitman meditated unforgettably on the deaths he had witnessed on both sides:

> On, on I go, (open doors of time! open hospital doors!)
> The crush'd head I dress, (poor crazed hand tear not the bandage away,)
> The neck of the cavalry-man with the bullet through and through I
>   examine,
> Hard the breathing rattles, quite glazed already the eye, yet life struggles
>   hard, (Come sweet death! be persuaded O beautiful death!
> In mercy come quickly.)

Whitman mused for millions in the war who suffered the death of a husband, brother, father, or friend. Indeed, the scale of death in this war shocked many Americans into believing that the conflict had to be for purposes larger than themselves.

THE ADVENT OF EMANCIPATION

Despite the sense of loyalty to cause that animated soldiers and civilians on both sides, the governments of the United States and the Confederacy lacked clarity about the purpose of the war. Throughout the first several months of the struggle, both Davis and Lincoln studiously avoided references to slavery. Davis realized that emphasis on the issue could increase class conflict in the South. To avoid identifying the Confederacy only with the interests of slaveholders, he articulated a broader, traditional ideology. Davis told southerners they were fighting for constitutional liberty: northerners had betrayed the founders' legacy, and southerners had seceded to preserve it. As long as Lincoln also avoided making slavery an issue, Davis's strategy seemed to work.

Lincoln had his own reasons for avoiding slavery. It was crucial at first not to antagonize the Union's border slave states, whose loyalty was tenuous. Also, for many months Lincoln hoped that a pro-Union majority would assert itself in the South. It might be possible, he thought, to coax the South back into the Union and stop the fighting, short of what he later called "the result so fundamental and astounding"—emancipation. Raising the slavery issue would severely undermine both goals. Powerful political considerations also dictated Lincoln's reticence. The Republican Party was a young and unwieldy coalition. Some Republicans burned with moral outrage over slavery; others were frankly racist, dedicated to protecting free whites from the Slave Power and the competition of cheap slave labor. No Republican, or even northern, consensus on what to do about slavery existed early in the war.

Lincoln and Emancipation

The president's hesitancy ran counter to some of his personal feelings. Lincoln's compassion, humility, and moral anguish during the war were evident in his speeches and writings. But as a politician, Lincoln distinguished between his own moral convictions and his official acts. His political positions were studied and complex, calculated for maximum advantage.

Many blacks attacked Lincoln furiously during the first year of the war for his refusal to convert the struggle into an "abolition war." When Lincoln

A group of "contrabands" (liberated slaves), photographed at Cumberland Landing, Virginia, May 14, 1862, at a sensitive point in the war when their legal status was still not fully determined. The faces and generations of the women, men, and children represent the human drama of emancipation.

countermanded General John C. Frémont's order of liberation for slaves owned by disloyal masters in Missouri in September 1861, the *Anglo-African* declared that the president, by his actions, "hurls back into the hell of slavery thousands … rightfully set free." As late as July 1862, Frederick Douglass condemned Lincoln as a "miserable tool of traitors and rebels," and characterized administration policy as reconstruction of "the old union on the old and corrupting basis of compromise, by which slavery shall retain all the power that it ever had." Douglass wanted the old Union destroyed and a new one created in the crucible of a war that would destroy slavery and rewrite the Constitution in the name of human equality. To the black leader's own amazement, within a year, just such a profound result began to take place.

Lincoln first broached the subject of slavery in a substantive way in March 1862, when he proposed that the states consider emancipation on their own. He asked Congress to promise aid to any state that decided to emancipate, appealing especially to border state representatives. What Lincoln proposed was gradual emancipation, with compensation for slaveholders and colonization of the freed slaves outside the United States. To a delegation of free blacks in August 1862, he explained that "it is better for us both … to be separated."

Until well into 1864, Lincoln's administration promoted an impractical scheme to colonize blacks in Central America or the Caribbean. Lincoln saw colonization as one option among others in dealing with the impending freedom of America's 4.2 million slaves. He was as yet unconvinced that America had any prospect as a biracial society, and he desperately feared that white northerners might not support a war for black freedom. Led by Frederick Douglass, black abolitionists vehemently opposed these machinations by the Lincoln administration.

Other politicians had much greater plans for a struggle against slavery. A group of Republicans in Congress, known as the Radicals and led by men such as George Julian, Charles Sumner, and Thaddeus Stevens, dedicated themselves to a war for emancipation. They were instrumental in creating a special House-Senate committee on the conduct of the war, which investigated Union reverses, sought to make the war effort more efficient, and prodded the president to take stronger measures against slavery.

Confiscation Acts

In August 1861, at the Radicals' instigation, Congress passed its first confiscation act. Designed to punish the Confederates, the law confiscated all property used for "insurrectionary purposes." Thus, if the South used slaves in a hostile action, those slaves were seized and liberated as "contraband" of war. A second confiscation act (July 1862) went much further: it confiscated the property of anyone who supported the rebellion, even those who merely resided in the South and paid Confederate taxes. Their slaves were declared "forever free of their servitude." These acts stemmed from the logic that, in order to crush the southern rebellion, the government had to use extraordinary powers.

Lincoln refused to adopt that view in the summer of 1862. He stood by his proposal of voluntary gradual emancipation by the states and made no effort at first to enforce the second confiscation act. His stance provoked a public protest from Horace Greeley, editor of the powerful *New York Tribune*. In an open letter to the president entitled "The Prayer of Twenty Millions," Greeley pleaded with Lincoln to "execute the laws" and declared, "On the face of this wide earth, Mr. President, there is not one ... intelligent champion of the Union cause who does not feel that all attempts to put down the Rebellion and at the same time uphold its inciting cause are preposterous and futile." Lincoln's reply was an explicit statement of his calculated approach to the question. He disagreed, he said, with all those who would make slavery the paramount issue of the war. "I would save the Union," announced Lincoln. "If I could save the Union without freeing any slave I would do it, and if I could save it by freeing all the slaves I would do it; and if I could save it by freeing some and leaving others alone I would also do that. What I do about slavery, and the colored race, I do because I believe it helps to save the Union." Lincoln closed with a personal disclaimer: "I have here stated my purpose according to my view of official duty; and I intend no modification of my oft-expressed personal wish that all men everywhere could be free."

When he wrote those words, Lincoln had already decided to boldly issue a presidential Emancipation Proclamation. He was waiting, however, for a Union victory so that it would not appear to be an act of desperation. Yet the letter to Greeley represents Lincoln's concern with conditioning public opinion as best he could for the coming social revolution, and he needed to delicately consider international opinion as well.

Emancipation Proclamations

On September 22, 1862, shortly after Union success at the Battle of Antietam, Lincoln issued the first part of his two-part proclamation. Invoking his powers as commander-in-chief of the armed forces, he announced that on January 1, 1863, he would emancipate the slaves in the states "in rebellion." Lincoln made plain that he would judge a state to be in rebellion in January if it lacked legitimate representatives in the U.S. Congress. Thus, his September 1862 proclamation was less a declaration of the right of slaves to be free than a threat to southerners: unless they put down their arms and returned to Congress, they would lose their slaves. "Knowing the value that was set on the slaves by the rebels," said Garrison Frazier, a black Georgia minister, "the President thought that his proclamation would stimulate them to lay down their arms ... and their not doing so has now made the freedom of the slaves a part of the war." Lincoln had little expectation that southerners would give up their effort, but he was determined to make them reply.

In the fateful January 1, 1863, proclamation, Lincoln declared that "all persons held as slaves" in areas in rebellion "shall be then, thenceforward, and forever free." But he excepted (as areas in rebellion) every Confederate county or city that had fallen under Union control. Those areas, he declared, "are, for the present, left precisely as if this proclamation were not issued." Nor did Lincoln liberate slaves in the border slave states that remained in the Union. "The President has purposely made the proclamation inoperative in all places where ... the slaves [are] accessible," charged the anti-administration *New York World*. "He has proclaimed emancipation only where he has notoriously no power to execute it." Partisanship aside, even Secretary of State Seward said sarcastically, "We show our sympathy with slavery by emancipating slaves where we cannot reach them and holding them in bondage where we can set them free."

But Lincoln was worried about the constitutionality of his acts, and he anticipated that after the war southerners might sue in court for restoration of their "property." Making the liberation of the slaves "a fit and necessary war measure" raised a variety of legal questions: How long did a war measure remain in force? Did it expire with the suppression of a rebellion? The proclamation did little to clarify the status or citizenship of the freed slaves, although it did open the possibility of military service for blacks. How, indeed, would this change the character and purpose of the war?

Thus the Emancipation Proclamation was legally an ambiguous document. But as a moral and political document it had great meaning. Because the proclamation defined the war as a war against slavery, congressional Radicals could applaud it. Yet at the same time, it protected Lincoln's position with conservatives, leaving him room to retreat if he chose and forcing no immediate changes on the border slave states. It was a delicate balancing act, but one from which there was no real turning back.

Most important, though, thousands of slaves had already reached Union lines in various sections of the South. They had "voted with their feet" for emancipation, as many said, well before the proclamation. And now, every advance of federal forces into slave society was a liberating step.

Across the North and in Union-occupied sections of the South, blacks and their white allies celebrated the Emancipation Proclamation with unprecedented fervor. Full of praise songs, these celebrations demonstrated that, whatever the fine print of the proclamation, black folks knew they had lived to see a new day. At a large "contraband camp" in Washington, D.C., some six hundred black men, women, and children gathered at the superintendent's headquarters on New Year's Eve and sang through the night. In chorus after chorus of "Go Down, Moses" they announced the magnitude of their painful but beautiful exodus. One newly supplied verse concluded with "Go down, Abraham, away down in Dixie's land, tell Jeff Davis to let my people go!"

African American Recruits The need for men soon convinced the administration to recruit northern and southern blacks for the Union Army. By the spring of 1863, African American troops were answering the call of a dozen or more black recruiters barnstorming the cities and towns of the North. Lincoln came to see black soldiers as "the great available and yet unavailed of force for restoring the Union."

African American leaders hoped that military service would secure equal rights for their people. Once the black soldier had fought for the Union, wrote Frederick Douglass, "there is no power on earth which can deny that he has earned the right of citizenship in the United States." If black soldiers turned the tide, asked another man, "would the nation refuse us our rights?"

In June 1864, with thousands of black former slaves in blue uniforms, Lincoln gave his support to a constitutional ban on slavery. On the eve of the Republican national convention, Lincoln called on the party to "put into the platform as the keystone, the amendment of the Constitution abolishing and prohibiting slavery forever." The party promptly called for the Thirteenth Amendment. Republican delegates probably would have adopted such a plank without his urging, but Lincoln demonstrated his commitment by lobbying Congress for quick approval of the measure. The proposed amendment passed in early 1865 and was sent to the states for ratification. The war to save the Union had also become the war to free the slaves.

Who Freed the Slaves? It has long been debated whether Abraham Lincoln deserved the label (one he never claimed for himself) of "Great Emancipator." Was Lincoln ultimately a reluctant emancipator, following rather than leading Congress and public opinion? Or did Lincoln give essential presidential leadership to the most transformative and sensitive aspect of the war by going slow on emancipation but, once moving, never backpedaling on black freedom? Once he had realized the total character of the war and decided to prosecute it to the unconditional surrender of the Confederates, Lincoln made the destruction of slavery central to the war's purpose.

Others have argued, however, that the slaves themselves are the central story in the achievement of their own freedom. When they were in proximity to the war zones or had opportunities as traveling laborers, slaves fled for their freedom by the thousands. Some worked as camp laborers for the Union armies, and eventually more than 180,000 black men served in the Union Army and Navy. Sometimes freedom came as a combination of confusion, fear, and joy in the rural hinterlands of the South. Some found freedom as individuals in 1861, and some not until 1865, as members of trains of refugees trekking great distances to reach contraband camps.

However freedom came to individuals, emancipation was a historical confluence of two essential forces: one, a policy directed by and dependent on the military authority of the president in his effort to win the war; and the other, the will and courage necessary for acts of self-emancipation. Emancipation could result from both a slave's own extraordinary heroism and the liberating actions of the Union forces. Most blacks comprehended their freedom as both given and taken, but also as their human right. "I now dreaded the gun and handcuffs ... no more," remembered Wallace Turnage, a former slave, of his liberation. "Nor the blowing of horns and running of hounds, nor the threats of death from rebels' authority." He was free in body and mind. "I could now speak my opinion" Turnage concluded, "to men of all grades and colors."

A Confederate Plan of Emancipation Before the war was over, the Confederacy, too, addressed the issue of emancipation. Late in the war, Jefferson Davis himself was willing to sacrifice slavery to achieve independence. He proposed that the Confederate government purchase forty thousand slaves to work for the army as laborers, with a promise of freedom at the end of their service. Soon Davis upgraded the idea, calling for the recruitment and arming of slaves as soldiers, who likewise would gain their freedom at war's end. The wives and children of these soldiers, he made plain, must also receive freedom from the states. Davis and his advisers envisioned an "intermediate" status for ex-slaves of "serfage or peonage." Thus, at the bitter end, a few southerners were willing to sacrifice some of the racial, if not class, destiny for which they had launched their revolution.

Bitter debate over Davis's plan resounded through the Confederacy. When the Confederate Congress finally approved slave enlistments in March 1865, owners had to comply only on a "voluntary" basis. In sheer desperation for manpower, General Lee also supported the idea of slave soldiers. Against the reality all around them of slaves fleeing to Union lines, some southern leaders mistakenly hoped that they could still count on the "loyalty" of their bondsmen. Most Confederate slaveholders and editors vehemently opposed the enlistment plan; those who did support it acknowledged that the war had already freed some portion of the slave population. Their aim was to fight to a stalemate, achieve independence, and control the postwar racial order through their limited wartime emancipation schemes. It was too late. As a Mississippi planter wrote to his state's governor, the plan seemed "like a drowning man catching at straws."

By contrast, Lincoln's Emancipation Proclamation stimulated a vital infusion of forces into the Union armies. Before the war was over, 134,000 former slaves (and 52,000 free blacks) had fought for freedom and the Union. Their participation was pivotal for northern victory. As both policy and process, emancipation had profound practical and moral implications for the new nation to be born out of the war.

THE SOLDIERS' WAR

The intricacies of policymaking and social revolutions were often far from the minds of most ordinary soldiers. Military service completely altered their lives. Enlistment took young men from their homes and submerged them in large organizations whose military discipline ignored their individuality. Army life meant tedium, physical hardship, and separation from loved ones. Yet the military experience had powerful attractions as well.

Ordinary Soldiers and Ideology   Most common soldiers, according to recent studies, were also committed to the ideological purposes of the war on both sides and not merely pawns caught up in a struggle they did not comprehend. The thousands of soldiers' letters, as well as regimental newspapers, indicate a deep awareness, if varying degrees of resolve, about slavery as the principle reason for the war.

The old idea that Civil War soldiers fought largely because of unit cohesion and the devotion of the men next to them is no longer an adequate explanation of why so many endured so much hardship for so long. Comradeship, duty, and honor were all powerful motivators for the men of the line. So were "union," "home," "the government," "freedom," "flag," "liberty," and "states' rights." But multitudes of literate soldiers left testimony of how much they saw slavery at the heart of the matter. In typical phrasing, members of the Thirteenth Wisconsin Infantry declared the conflict "a war of, by and for Slavery … as plain as the noon day sun." And their foes in Morgan's Confederate Brigade from Virginia agreed with different intentions: "any man who pretends to believe that this is not a war for the emancipation of the blacks … is either a fool or a liar."

Hospitals and Camp Life   The soldiers' lot was often misery. They benefited from certain new products, such as canned condensed milk, but blankets, clothing, and arms were often of poor quality. Hospitals were badly managed at first. Rules of hygiene in large camps were scarcely enforced; latrines were poorly made or carelessly used. One investigation turned up "an area of over three acres, encircling the camp as a broad belt, on which is deposited an almost perfect layer of human excrement." Water supplies were unsafe and typhoid epidemics common. About 57,000 men died from dysentery and diarrhea; in fact, 224,000 Union troops died from disease or accidents, far more than the 110,100 who died as a result of battle. Confederate troops were less well supplied, especially in the latter part of the war, and they had no sanitary commission. Still, an extensive network of hospitals, aided by many white female volunteers and black woman slaves, sprang up to aid the sick and wounded.

On both sides, troops quickly learned that soldiering was far from glorious. "The dirt of a camp life knocks all its poetry into a cocked hat," wrote a North Carolina volunteer in 1862. One year later, he marveled at his earlier innocence. Fighting had taught him "the realities of a soldier's life. We had no tents after the 6th of August, but slept on the ground, in the woods or open fields…. I learned to eat fat bacon raw, and to like it…. Without time to wash our clothes or our persons … the whole army became lousy more or less with body lice." Union troops "skirmished" against lice by boiling their clothes, but, reported one soldier, "I find some on me in spite of all I can do."

Few had seen violent death before, but war soon exposed them to the blasted bodies of their friends and comrades. "Any one who goes over a battlefield after a battle," wrote one Confederate, "never cares to go over another…. It is a sad sight to see the dead and if possible more sad to see the wounded—shot in every possible way you can imagine." Many men died gallantly; there were innumerable striking displays of courage. But often soldiers gave up their lives in mass sacrifice, in tactics that made little sense.

Still, Civil War soldiers developed deep commitments to each other and to their task. As campaigns dragged on, most soldiers who did not desert grew determined to see the struggle through. "We now, like true Soldiers go determined not to yield one inch," wrote a New York corporal. When at last the war was over, "it seemed like breaking up a family to separate," one man observed. Another admitted, "We shook hands all around, and laughed and seemed to make merry, while our hearts were heavy and our eyes ready to shed tears."

The Rifled Musket

Advances in technology made the Civil War particularly deadly. By far the most important were the rifle and the "minie ball." Bullets fired from a smoothbore musket tumbled and wobbled as they flew through the air, and thus were not accurate at distances over eighty yards. Cutting spiraled grooves inside the barrel gave the projectile a spin and much greater accuracy, but rifles remained difficult to load and use until Frenchman Claude Minie and American James Burton developed a new kind of bullet. Civil War bullets were lead slugs with a cavity at the bottom that expanded on firing so that the bullet "took" the rifling and flew accurately. With these bullets, rifles were deadly at four hundred yards.

This meant, of course, that soldiers assaulting a position defended by riflemen were in greater peril than ever before; the defense thus gained a significant advantage. While artillery now fired from a safe distance, there was no substitute for the infantry assault or the popular turning movements aimed at an enemy's flank. Thus, advancing soldiers had to expose themselves repeatedly to accurate rifle fire. Because medical knowledge was rudimentary, even minor wounds often led to amputation and death through infection. Never before in Europe or America had such massive forces pummeled each other with weapons of such destructive power. As losses mounted, many citizens wondered at what Union soldier (and future Supreme Court justice) Oliver Wendell Holmes Jr. called "the butcher's bill."

The Black Soldier's Fight for Manhood   At the outset of the war, racism in the Union Army was strong. Most white soldiers wanted nothing to do with black people and regarded them as inferior. "I never came out here for to free the black devils," wrote one soldier, and another objected to fighting beside African Americans because "we are a too superior race for that." For many, acceptance of black troops grew only because they could do heavy labor and "stop Bullets as well as white people." A popular song celebrated "Sambo's Right to Be Kilt" as the only justification for black enlistments.

But among some, a change occurred. While recruiting black troops in Virginia in late 1864, Massachusetts soldier Charles Brewster sometimes denigrated the very men he sought to enlist. But he was delighted at the sight of a black cavalry unit because it made the local "secesh" furious, and he praised black soldiers who "fought nobly" and filled hospitals with "their wounded and mangled bodies." White officers who volunteered to lead segregated black units only to gain promotion found that experience altered their opinions. After just one month with black troops, a white captain informed his wife, "I have a more elevated opinion of their abilities than I ever had before. I know that many of them are vastly the superiors of those … who would condemn them all to a life of brutal degradation." One general reported that his "colored regiments" possessed "remarkable aptitude for military training."

Black troops created this change through their own dedication. They had a mission to destroy slavery and demonstrate their equality. "When Rebellion is crushed," wrote a black volunteer from Connecticut, "who will be more proud than I to say, I was one of the first of the despised race to leave the free North with a rifle on my shoulder, and give the lie to the old story that the black man will not fight." Corporal James Henry Gooding of Massachusetts's black Fifty-fourth Regiment explained that his unit intended "to live down all prejudice against its color, by a determination to do well in any position it is put." After an engagement, he was proud that "a regiment of white men gave us three cheers as we were passing them" because "it shows that we did our duty as men should."

Through such experience under fire, the blacks and whites of the Fifty-fourth Massachusetts forged deep bonds. Just before the regiment launched its costly assault on Fort Wagner in Charleston harbor, in July 1863, a black soldier called out to abolitionist Colonel Robert Gould Shaw, who would perish that day, "Colonel, I will stay by you till I die." "And he kept his word," noted a survivor of the attack. "He has never been seen since." Indeed, the heroic assault on Fort Wagner was celebrated for demonstrating the valor of black men. This bloody chapter in the history of American racism proved many things, not least of which that black men had to die in battle to be acknowledged as men.

Such valor emerged despite persistent discrimination. The Union government paid white privates $13 per month plus a clothing allowance of $3.50, whereas black privates earned only $10 per month less $3 for clothing. Outraged by this injustice, several regiments refused to accept any pay whatsoever, and Congress eventually remedied the inequity. In this instance at least, the majority of legislators agreed with a white private that black troops had "proved their title to manhood on many a bloody field fighting freedom's battles."

1863: THE TIDE OF BATTLE TURNS

The fighting in the spring and summer of 1863 did not settle the war, but it began to suggest the outcome. The campaigns began in a deceptively positive way for Confederates, as Lee's army performed brilliantly in battles in central Virginia.

Battle of Chancellorsville For once, a large Civil War army was not slow and cumbersome, but executed tactics with speed and precision. On May 2 and 3, west of Fredericksburg, Virginia, some 130,000 members of the Union Army of the Potomac bore down on fewer than 60,000 Confederates. Boldly, Lee and Stonewall Jackson divided their forces, ordering 30,000 men under Jackson on a day-long march westward to prepare a flank attack.

This classic turning movement was carried out in the face of great numerical disadvantage. Arriving at their position late in the afternoon, Jackson's seasoned "foot cavalry" found unprepared Union troops laughing, smoking, and playing cards. The Union soldiers had no idea they were under attack until frightened deer and rabbits bounded out of the forest, followed by gray-clad troops. The Confederate attack drove the entire right side of the Union Army back in confusion. Eager to press his advantage, Jackson rode forward with a few officers to study the ground. As they returned at twilight, southern troops mistook them for federals and fired, fatally wounding their commander. The next day, Union forces left in defeat. Chancellorsville was a remarkable southern victory, but costly because of the loss of Stonewall Jackson, who would forever remain a legend in Confederate memory.

Siege of Vicksburg July brought crushing defeats for the Confederacy in two critical battles—Vicksburg and Gettysburg—that severely damaged Confed-erate hopes for independence. Vicksburg was a vital western citadel, the last major fortification on the Mississippi River in southern hands. After months of searching through swamps and bayous, General Ulysses S. Grant found an advantageous approach to the city. He laid siege to Vicksburg in May, bottling up the defending army of General John Pemberton. If Vicksburg fell, Union forces would control the river, cutting the Confederacy in two and gaining an open path into its interior. To stave off such a result, Jefferson Davis gave command of all other forces in the area to General Joseph E. Johnston and beseeched him to go to Pemberton's aid. Meanwhile, at a council of war in Richmond, General Robert E. Lee proposed a Confederate invasion of the North. Although such an offensive would not relieve Vicksburg directly, it could stun and dismay the North and, if successful, possibly even lead to peace. By invading the North a second time, Lee hoped to take the war out of war-weary Virginia, garner civilian support in Maryland, win a major victory on northern soil, threaten major cities, and thereby force a Union capitulation on his terms.

As Lee's emboldened army advanced through western Maryland and into Pennsylvania, Confederate prospects to the south along the Mississippi darkened. Davis repeatedly wired General Johnston, urging him to concentrate his forces and attack Grant's army. Johnston, however, did little, telegraphing back: "I consider saving Vicksburg hopeless." Grant's men, meanwhile, were supplying themselves from the abundant crops of the Mississippi River valley and could continue their siege indefinitely. Their rich meat-and-vegetable diet became so tiresome, in fact, that one day, as Grant rode by, a private looked up and muttered, "Hardtack," referring to the dry biscuits that were the usual staple of soldiers' diets. Soon a line of soldiers was shouting, "Hardtack! Hardtack!" demanding respite from turkey and sweet potatoes.

Battle of Gettysburg

In such circumstances, the fall of Vicksburg was inevitable, and on July 4, 1863, its commander surrendered. The same day, a battle that had been raging for three days concluded at Gettysburg, Pennsylvania (see Map 15.1).On July 1, Confederate forces hunting for a supply of shoes had collided with part of the Union Army. Heavy fighting on the second day over two steep hills left federal forces in possession of high ground along Cemetery Ridge, running more than a mile south of the town. There, they enjoyed the protection of a stone wall and a clear view of their foe across almost a mile of open field.

Undaunted, Lee believed his reinforced troops could break the Union line and, on July 3, he ordered a direct assault. Full of foreboding, General James Longstreet warned Lee that "no 15,000 men ever arrayed for battle can take that position." But Lee stuck to his plan. Virginians under General George E. Pickett and North Carolinians under General James Pettigrew methodically marched up the slope in a doomed assault known as Pickett's Charge. For a moment, a few hundred Confederates breached the enemy's line, but most fell in heavy slaughter. On July 4, Lee had to withdraw, having suffered almost four thousand dead and about twenty-four thousand missing and wounded. The Confederate general reported to President Davis that "I am alone to blame" and offered to resign. Davis replied that to find a more capable commander was "an impossibility." The Confederacy had reached what many consider its "high water mark" on that ridge at Gettysburg.

Southern troops displayed unforgettable courage and dedication at Gettysburg, and under General George G. Meade, the Union Army, which suffered twenty-three thousand casualties (nearly one-quarter of the force), exhibited the same bravery in stopping the Confederate invasion. But the results there and at Vicksburg were disastrous for the South. The Confederacy was split in two; west of the Mississippi, General E. Kirby Smith had to operate on his own, virtually independent of Richmond. Moreover, the heartland of Louisiana, Tennessee, and Mississippi lay exposed to invasion. Far to the north, Lee's defeat spelled the end of major southern offensive actions. Too weak to prevail in attack, the Confederacy henceforth would have to conserve its limited resources and rely on a prolonged defense. By refusing to be beaten and by wearing down northern morale, the South might yet win, but its prospects were darker than before.

MAP 15.1 Battle of Gettysburg

In the war's greatest battle, fought around a small market town in southern Pennsylvania, Lee's invasion of the North was repulsed. Union forces had the advantage of the high ground, shorter lines, and superior numbers. The casualties for the two armies—dead, wounded, and missing—exceeded 50,000 men.

© Cengage Learning

DISUNITY: SOUTH, NORTH, AND WEST

Both northern and southern governments waged the final two years of the war in the face of increasing opposition at home. Dissatisfactions that had surfaced earlier grew more intense and sometimes violent. The gigantic costs of a civil war that neither side seemed able to win fed the unrest. But protest also arose from fundamental stresses in the social structures of North and South.

Union Occupation Zones Wherever Union forces invaded, they imposed a military occupation consisting roughly of three zones: garrisoned towns, with large numbers of troops in control of civilian and economic life; the Confederate frontier, areas still under southern control but also with some federal military penetration; and "no man's land," the land between the two armies, beyond Confederate authority and under frequent Union patrols.

As many as one hundred southern towns were garrisoned during the war, causing severe disruption to the social landscape. Large regions of Tennessee, Virginia, Louisiana, Mississippi, and Georgia fell under this pattern of occupation and suffered food shortages, crop and property destruction, disease, roadway banditry, guerrilla warfare, summary executions, and the random flow of escaped slaves. After two years of occupation, a southern white woman wrote to a kinsman about their native Clarksville, Tennessee. "You would scarcely know the place," she lamented, "it is nothing but a dirty hole filled ... with niggers and Yankees."

Disintegration of Confederate Unity   Vastly disadvantaged in industrial capacity, natural resources, and labor, southerners felt the cost of the war more directly and more painfully than northerners. But even more fundamental were the Confederacy's internal problems; the southern class system threatened the Confederate cause.

One ominous development was the planters' increasing opposition to their own government. Along with new taxation, Confederate military authorities also impressed slaves to build fortifications. And when Union forces advanced on plantation areas, Confederate commanders burned stores of cotton that lay in the enemy's path. Many planters bitterly complained about such interference with their agricultural production and financial interests.

Nor were the centralizing policies of the Davis administration popular. In fact, the Confederate constitution had granted substantial powers to the central government, especially in time of war. But many planters took the position articulated by R. B. Rhett, editor of the *Charleston Mercury*, that the Confederate constitution "leaves the States untouched in their Sovereignty, and commits to the Confederate Government only a few simple objects, and a few simple powers to enforce them." Governor Joseph E. Brown of Georgia took a similar states' rights position, occasionally prohibiting supplies and that state's soldiers from leaving its borders.

Years of opposition to the federal government within the Union had frozen southerners in a defensive posture. Now they erected the barrier of states' rights as a defense against change, hiding behind it while their capacity for creative statesmanship atrophied. Planters sought, above all, a guarantee that their plantations and their lives would remain untouched. As secession revolutionized their world and hard war took so many lives, some could never fully commit to the cause.

Confused and embittered planters struck out at Jefferson Davis. Conscription, thundered Governor Brown, was "subversive of [Georgia's] sovereignty, and at war with all the principles for the support of which Georgia entered into this revolution." Searching for ways to frustrate the law, Brown ordered local enrollment officials not to cooperate with the Confederacy. The *Charleston Mercury* told readers that "conscription ... is ... the very embodiment of Lincolnism, which our gallant armies are today fighting." In a gesture of stubborn selfishness, Robert Toombs of Georgia, a former U.S. senator, refused to switch from cotton to food crops, defying the wishes of the government, the newspapers, and his neighbors' petitions.

The southern courts ultimately upheld Davis's power to conscript. Davis was deeply devoted to southern independence, but some of his actions earned him the hatred of influential and elite citizens.

Food Riots in Southern Cities   Meanwhile, for ordinary southerners, the dire predictions of hunger and suffering were becoming a reality. Food riots occurred in the spring of 1863 in Atlanta, Macon,

Columbus, and Augusta, Georgia, and in Salisbury and High Point, North Carolina. On April 2, a crowd assembled in Richmond to demand relief. A passerby, noticing the excitement, asked a young girl, "Is there some celebration?" "We celebrate our right to live," replied the girl. "We are starving. As soon as enough of us get together we are going to the bakeries and each of us will take a loaf of bread." Soon they did just that, sparking a riot that Davis ordered quelled at gunpoint.

Throughout the rural South, ordinary people resisted more quietly—by refusing to cooperate with conscription, tax collection, and impressments of food. "In all the States impressments are evaded by every means which ingenuity can suggest, and in some openly resisted," wrote a commissary officer. Farmers who did provide food for the army refused to accept payment in certificates of credit or government bonds, as required by law. Conscription officers increasingly found no one to draft. "The disposition to avoid military service is general," observed one of Georgia's senators in 1864. In some areas, tax agents were killed in the line of duty.

Jefferson Davis was ill-equipped to deal with such discontent. Austere and private by nature, he failed to communicate with the masses. His class perspective also distanced him from the sufferings of the common people. While his social circle in Richmond dined on duck and oysters, ordinary southerners recovered salt from the drippings on their smokehouse floors and went hungry.

Desertions from the Confederate Army   Such discontent was certain to affect the Confederate armies. "What man is there that would stay in the army and no that his family is sufring at home?" an angry citizen wrote anonymously to the secretary of war. Worried about their loved ones and resentful of what they saw as a rich man's war, large numbers of men did indeed leave the armies. Their friends and neighbors gave them support. Mary Chesnut observed a man being dragged back to the army as his wife looked on. "Desert agin, Jake!" she cried openly. "You desert agin, quick as you kin. Come back to your wife and children."

Desertion did not become a serious problem for the Confederacy until mid-1862, and stiffer policing solved the problem that year. But from 1863 on, the number of men on duty fell rapidly. By mid-1863, John A. Campbell, the South's assistant secretary of war, wondered whether "so general a habit" as desertion could be considered a crime. Campbell estimated that 40,000 to 50,000 troops were absent without leave and that 100,000 were evading duty in some way. Furloughs, amnesty proclamations, and appeals to return had little effect; by November 1863, Secretary of War James Seddon admitted that one-third of the army could not be accounted for.

The defeats at Gettysburg and Vicksburg dealt a heavy blow to Confederate morale. When the news reached Josiah Gorgas, the genius of Confederate ordnance operations, he confided to his diary, "Today absolute ruin seems our portion. The Confederacy totters to its destruction." In desperation, President Davis and several state governors resorted to threats and racial scare tactics to drive southern whites to further sacrifice. Defeat, Davis warned, would mean "extermination of yourselves, your wives, and children." Governor Charles Clark of Mississippi predicted "elevation of the black race to a position of equality—aye, of superiority, that will make them your masters and rulers."

From this point on, the internal disintegration of the Confederacy quickened. A few newspapers began to call openly for peace. "We are for peace," admitted the *Raleigh* (North Carolina) *Daily Progress*, "because there has been enough of blood and carnage, enough of widows and orphans." Confederate leaders began to realize they were losing the support of the common people. It is, indeed, remarkable how long and how effectively the Confederacy sustained a military effort in the face of such internal division.

Antiwar Sentiment, South and North   In North Carolina, a peace movement grew under the leadership of William W. Holden, a popular Democratic politician and editor. He and his followers convened over one hundred public meetings in support of peace negotiations, which took place during the summer of 1863. In Georgia early in 1864, Governor Brown and Alexander H. Stephens, vice president of the Confederacy, led a similar effort. Ultimately, however, these movements came to naught. The lack of a two-party system threw into question the legitimacy of any criticism of the government; even Holden and Brown could not entirely escape the taint of dishonor and disloyalty.

The results of the 1863 congressional elections strengthened dissent in the Confederacy. Everywhere, secessionists and supporters of the administration lost seats to men not identified with the government. In the last years of the war, Davis's support in the Confederate Congress dwindled. Some newspaper editors and a core of courageous, determined soldiers, especially in Lee's Army of Northern Virginia, kept the Confederacy alive in spite of disintegrating popular support.

By 1864, much of the opposition to the war had moved entirely outside the political sphere. Southerners were simply giving up the struggle. Deserters dominated some whole towns and counties. Active dissent was particularly common in upland and mountain regions, where support for the Union had always been genuine. "The condition of things in the mountain districts of North Carolina, South Carolina, Georgia, and Alabama," admitted Assistant Secretary of War Campbell, "menaces the existence of the Confederacy as fatally as either of the armies of the United States."

Opposition to the war, though less severe, existed in the North as well. Alarm intensified over the growing centralization of government and, by 1863, war-weariness was widespread. Resentment of the draft sparked protest, especially among poor citizens, and the Union Army, too, struggled with a troubling desertion rate. But the Union was so much richer than the South in human resources that none of these problems ever threatened the effectiveness of the government.

Moreover, Lincoln possessed a talent that Davis lacked: he knew how to stay in touch with the ordinary citizen. Through public letters to newspapers and private ones to soldiers' families, he reached the common people. The battlefield carnage, the tortuous political problems, and the ceaseless criticism weighed heavily on him, but his administration never lost control of the federal war effort.

Peace Democrats   Much of the wartime protest in the North was political in origin. The Democratic Party fought to regain power by blaming Lincoln for the war's death toll, the expansion of federal powers, inflation and the high tariff, and the emancipation of blacks.

In the Union government's conscription system, a draftee could hire a "substitute" to replace him in the army, lending credence to the claim by some that the conflict became a "rich man's war but a poor man's fight." Less than 7 percent of all Union soldiers were draftees, but this practice caused problems in northern morale.

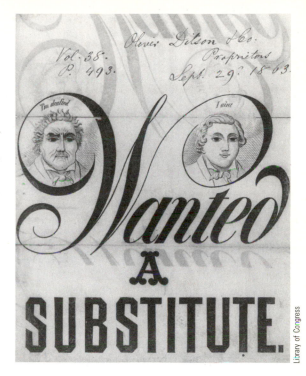

Library of Congress

Appealing to tradition, its leaders called for an end to the war and reunion on the basis of "the Constitution as it is and the Union as it was." The Democrats denounced conscription and martial law, and defended states' rights. They charged repeatedly that Republican policies were designed to flood the North with blacks, threatening white men's privileges. In the 1862 congressional elections, the Democrats made a strong comeback, with peace Democrats wielding influence in New York State and majorities in the legislatures of Illinois and Indiana.

Led by outspoken men like Representative Clement L. Vallandigham of Ohio, the peace Democrats became highly visible. Vallandigham criticized Lincoln as a "dictator" who had suspended the writ of habeas corpus without congressional authority, arrested thousands of innocent citizens, and shut down opposition newspapers (which was true). He condemned both conscription and emancipation, and urged voters to use their power at the polls to depose "King Abraham." Vallandigham stayed carefully within legal bounds, but his attacks seemed so damaging to the war effort that military authorities arrested him for treason. Lincoln wisely decided against punishment—and martyr's status—for the Ohioan and exiled him to the Confederacy. Vallandigham eventually returned to the North through Canada.

Some antiwar Democrats did encourage draft resistance, discourage enlistment, sabotage communications, and generally plot to aid the Confederacy. Likening such groups to a poisonous snake, Republicans sometimes branded them—and by extension the peace Democrats—as "Copperheads." Although some Confederate agents were active in the North and Canada, they never genuinely threatened the Union war effort and their suppression remains a vexing legal legacy.

New York City
Draft Riots

More violent opposition to the government arose from ordinary citizens facing the draft, which became law in 1863. Although many soldiers risked their lives willingly out of a desire to preserve the Union or extend freedom, others openly sought to avoid service. Under the law, a draftee could stay at home by providing a substitute or paying a $300 commutation fee. Many wealthy men chose these options and—in response to popular demand—clubs, cities, and states provided the money for others to escape conscription. In all, 118,000 substitutes were provided and 87,000 commutations paid before Congress ended the commutation system in 1864.

The urban poor and immigrants in strongly Democratic areas were especially hostile to conscription. Federal enrolling officers made up the lists of eligibles, a procedure open to personal favoritism and prejudice. The North's poor viewed the system as discriminatory, and many immigrants suspected (wrongly, on the whole) that they were called in disproportionate numbers. (Approximately 200,000 men born in Germany and 150,000 born in Ireland served in the Union Army.)

As a result, there were scores of disturbances. Enrolling officers received rough treatment in many parts of the North, and riots occurred in New Jersey, Ohio, Indiana, Pennsylvania, Illinois, and Wisconsin. By far, the most serious outbreak of violence occurred in New York City in July 1863. The war was unpopular in that Democratic stronghold, and racial, ethnic, and class tensions ran high. Shippers had recently broken a longshoremen's strike by hiring black strikebreakers to work under police protection. Working-class New Yorkers feared an inflow of black labor from the South and regarded blacks as the cause of the war. Poor Irish workers resented being forced to serve in the place of others who could afford to avoid the draft.

Military police officers came under attack first, and then mobs crying, "Down with the rich" looted wealthy homes and stores. But blacks became the special target. The mob rampaged through African American neighborhoods, beating and murdering people in the streets, and burning an orphan asylum. At least seventy-four people died in the violence, which raged out of control for three days. Only the dispatch of army units directly from Gettysburg ended this tragic episode of racism and class resentment.

War Against
Indians in the
Far West

East and West, over race, land, and culture, America was a deeply divided country. A civil war of another kind raged on the Great Plains and in the Southwest. By 1864, U.S. troops under the command of Colonel John Chivington waged full-scale war against the Sioux, Arapahos, and Cheyennes in order to eradicate Indian title to all of eastern Colorado. Indian chiefs sought peace, but American commanders had orders to "burn villages and kill Cheyennes whenever and wherever found." A Cheyenne chief, Lean Bear, was shot from his horse as he rode toward U.S. troops, holding in his hand papers given him by President Lincoln during a visit to Washington, D.C. Another chief, Black Kettle, was told by the U.S. command that, by moving his people to Sand Creek, Colorado, they would find a safe haven. But on November 29, 1864, 700 cavalrymen, many drunk, attacked the Cheyenne village. With most of the men absent hunting, the slaughter included 105

Cheyenne women and children and 28 men. American soldiers scalped and mutilated their victims, carrying women's body parts on their saddles or hats back to Denver. The Sand Creek Massacre, and the retaliation against white ranches and stagecoaches by Indians in 1865, would live in western historical memory forever.

In New Mexico and Arizona Territories, an authoritarian and brutal commander, General James Carleton, waged war on the Apaches and the Navajos. Both tribes had engaged for generations in raiding the Pueblo and Hispanic peoples of the region to maintain their security and economy. During the Civil War years, Anglo-American farms also became Indian targets. In 1863, the New Mexico Volunteers, commanded in the field by former mountain man Kit Carson, defeated the Mescalero Apaches and forced them onto a reservation at Bosque Redondo in the Pecos River valley.

But the Navajos, who lived in a vast region of canyons and high deserts, resisted. In a "scorched earth" campaign, Carson destroyed the Navajos' livestock, orchards, and crops. On the run, starving and demoralized, the Navajos began to surrender for food in January 1864. Three-quarters of the twelve thousand Navajos were rounded up and forced to march 400 miles (the "Long Walk") to the Bosque Redondo Reservation, suffering malnutrition and death along the way. When General William T. Sherman visited the reservation in 1868, he found the Navajos "sunk into a condition of absolute poverty and despair." Permitted to return to a fraction of their homelands later that year, the Navajos carried with them searing memories of the federal government's ruthless policies of both removal and eradication of Indian peoples.

Election of 1864

Back east, war-weariness reached a peak in the summer of 1864, when the Democratic Party nominated the popular general George B. McClellan for president and inserted a peace plank into its platform. The plank, written by Vallandigham, called for an armistice and spoke vaguely about preserving the Union. The Democrats made racist appeals to white insecurity, calling Lincoln "Abe the nigger-lover" and "Abe the widow-maker." Lincoln concluded that it was "exceedingly probable that this Administration will not be reelected." No incumbent president had been reelected since 1832, and no nation had ever held a general election in the midst of all-out civil war. Some Republicans worked to dump Lincoln from their ticket in favor of either Salmon P. Chase or John C. Frémont, although little came of either effort. Even a relatively unified Republican Party, declaring itself for "unconditional surrender" of the Confederacy and a constitutional amendment abolishing slavery, had to contend with the horrible casualty lists and the battlefield stalemate of the summer of 1864.

The fortunes of war soon changed the electoral situation. With the fall of Atlanta and Union victories in the Shenandoah Valley by early September, Lincoln's prospects rose. Decisive in the election was that eighteen states allowed troops to vote at the front; Lincoln won an extraordinary 78 percent of the soldier vote. In taking 55 percent of the total popular vote, Lincoln's reelection—a referendum on the war and emancipation—had a devastating impact on southern morale. Without such a political outcome in 1864, a Union military victory and a redefined nation might never have been possible.

1864–1865: The Final Test of Wills

During the final year of the war, the Confederates could still have won their version of victory if military stalemate and northern antiwar sentiment had forced a negotiated settlement. But events and northern determination prevailed, as Americans endured the bloodiest nightmare in their history.

Northern Diplomatic Strategy

The North's long-term diplomatic strategy succeeded in 1864. From the outset, the North had pursued one paramount goal: to prevent recognition of the Confederacy by European nations. Foreign recognition would belie Lincoln's claim that the United States was fighting an illegal rebellion and would open the way to the financial and military aid that could ensure Confederate independence. Both England and France stood to benefit from a divided and weakened America. Thus, to achieve their goal, Lincoln and Secretary of State Seward needed to avoid both serious military defeats and controversies with the European powers.

Aware that the textile industry employed one-fifth of the British population directly or indirectly, southerners banked on British recognition of the Confederacy. But at the beginning of the war, British mills had a 50 percent surplus of cotton on hand, and they later found new sources of supply in India, Egypt, and Brazil. And throughout the war, some southern cotton continued to reach Europe, despite the Confederacy's embargo on cotton production, an ill-fated policy aimed at securing British support. The British government flirted with recognition of the Confederacy but awaited battlefield demonstrations of southern success. France, though sympathetic to the South, was unwilling to act independently of Britain. Confederate agents managed to purchase valuable arms and supplies in Europe and obtained loans from European financiers, but they never achieved a diplomatic breakthrough.

More than once, the Union strategy nearly broke down. An acute crisis occurred in 1861 when the overzealous commander of an American frigate stopped the British steamer *Trent* and removed two Confederate ambassadors, James Mason and John Slidell, sailing to Britain. When they were imprisoned in Boston, northerners cheered, but the British interpreted the capture as a violation of freedom of the seas and demanded the prisoners' release. Lincoln and Seward waited until northern public opinion cooled and then released the two southerners. The incident strained U.S.-British relations.

Then the sale to the Confederacy of warships constructed in England sparked vigorous protest from U.S. ambassador Charles Francis Adams. A few English-built ships, notably the *Alabama,* reached open water to serve the South. Over a period of twenty-two months, without entering a southern port (because of the Union blockade), the *Alabama* destroyed or captured more than sixty U.S. ships, leaving a bitter legal legacy to be settled in the postwar period.

Battlefield Stalemate and a Union Strategy for Victory

On the battlefield, northern victory was far from won in 1864. General Nathaniel Banks's Red River campaign, designed to capture more of Louisiana and Texas, fell apart, and the capture of Mobile Bay in August did not cause the fall of Mobile. Union general William Tecumseh Sherman

LINKS TO THE WORLD

The Civil War in Britain

So engaged was the British public with America's disunion and war that an unemployed weaver, John Ward, frequently trekked many miles from Britain's Low Moor to Clitheroe just to read newspaper accounts of the strife.

Because of the direct reliance of the British textile industry on southern cotton (cut off by the war) as well as the many ideological and familial ties between the two nations, the American war was significant in Britain's economy and domestic politics. The British aristocracy and most cotton mill owners were solidly pro-Confederate and proslavery, whereas a combination of clergymen, shopkeepers, artisans, and radical politicians worked for the causes of Union and emancipation. Most British workers saw their future at stake in a war for slave emancipation. "Freedom" to the huge British working class (who could not vote) meant basic political and civil rights as well as the bread and butter of secure jobs in an industrializing economy, now damaged by a "cotton famine" that threw millhands out of work.

English aristocrats saw Americans as untutored, wayward cousins and took satisfaction in America's troubles. Conservatives believed in the superiority of the British system of government and looked askance at America's leveling tendencies. And some aristocratic British Liberals also saw Americans through their class bias and sympathized with the Confederacy's demand for "order" and independence. English racism also intensified in these years, exemplified by the popularity of minstrelsy and the employment of science in the service of racial theory.

The intensity of the British propaganda war over the American conflict is evident in the methods of their debate: public meetings organized by both sides were huge affairs, with cheering and jeering, competing banners, carts and floats, orators and resolutions. In a press war, the British argued over when rebellion is justified, whether secession was right or legal, whether slavery was at the heart of the conflict, and especially over the democratic image of America itself. This bitter debate about America's trial became a test of reform in Britain: those eager for a broadened franchise and increased democracy were pro-Union, and those who preferred to preserve Britain's class-ridden political system favored the Confederacy.

The nature of the internal British debate was no better symbolized than by the dozens of African Americans who served as pro-Union agents in England. The most popular was William Andrew Jackson, Confederate president Jefferson Davis's former coachman, who had escaped from Richmond in September 1862. Jackson's articulate presence at British public meetings countered pro-Confederate arguments that the war was not about slavery.

In the end, the British government did not recognize the Confederacy and, by 1864, English cotton lords had found new sources of the crop in Egypt and India. But in this link between America and its English roots at its time of greatest travail, we can see that the Civil War was a transformation of international significance.

commented that the North had to "keep the war South until they are not only ruined, exhausted, but humbled in pride and spirit." Sherman soon brought total war to the southern heartland. On the eastern front during the winter of 1863–1864, the two armies in Virginia settled into a stalemate awaiting yet another spring offensive by the North.

Military authorities throughout history have agreed that deep invasion is very risky: the farther an army penetrates enemy territory, the more vulnerable are its own communications and supply lines. Moreover, observed the Prussian expert Karl von Clausewitz, if the invader encounters a "truly national" resistance, his troops will be "everywhere exposed to attacks by an insurgent population." The South's vast size and a determined resistance could yet make a northern victory elusive.

General Grant, by now in command of all the federal armies, decided to test southern will with a strategic innovation of his own: raids on a massive scale. Less tied to tradition and textbook maneuver than most other Union commanders, Grant proposed to use armies to destroy Confederate railroads, thus ruining the enemy's transportation and economy. Abandoning their lines of support, Union troops would live off the land while laying waste all resources useful to the military and to the civilian population of the Confederacy. After General George H. Thomas's troops won the Battle of Chattanooga in November 1863, the heartland of Georgia lay open. Grant entrusted General Sherman with 100,000 men for an invasion deep into the South, toward the rail center of Atlanta.

Fall of Atlanta   Jefferson Davis countered by positioning the army of General Joseph E. Johnston in Sherman's path. Davis's entire political strategy for 1864 was based on demonstrating Confederate military strength and successfully defending Atlanta. Davis hoped that southern resolve would lead to the political defeat of Lincoln and the election of a president who would sue for peace. When General Johnston slowly but steadily fell back toward Atlanta, Davis grew anxious and sought assurances that Atlanta would be held. From a purely military point of view, Johnston maneuvered skillfully. But when Johnston fell silent and continued to retreat, Davis replaced him with the one-legged General John Hood, who knew his job was to fight. "Our all depends on that army at Atlanta," wrote Mary Chesnut. "If that fails us, the game is up."

For southern morale, the game *was* up. Hood attacked but was beaten, and Sherman's army occupied Atlanta on September 2, 1864. The victory buoyed northern spirits and ensured Lincoln's reelection. A government clerk in Richmond wrote, "Our fondly-cherished visions of peace have vanished like a mirage of the desert." Davis exhorted southerners to fight on and win new victories before the federal elections, but he had to admit that "two-thirds of our men are absent ... without leave." In a desperate diversion, Hood's army marched north to cut Sherman's supply lines and force him to withdraw, but Sherman began to march sixty thousand of his marauding men straight to the sea, destroying Confederate resources as he went (see Map 15.2).

Sherman's March   Sherman's army was an unusually formidable force, com-
to the Sea   posed almost entirely of battle-tested veterans and officers who had risen through the ranks from the midwestern states. Before the march began, army doctors weeded out any men who were weak or sick. Weathered, bearded, and tough, the remaining veterans were determined, as one put it, "to Conquer this Rebelien or Die." They believed "the South are to blame for this war" and were ready to make the South pay. Although many harbored racist attitudes, most had come to support emancipation because, as one said, "Slavery stands

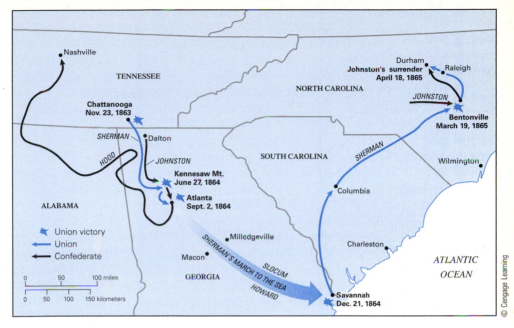

© Cengage Learning

MAP 15.2 Sherman's March to the Sea

The Deep South proved a decisive theater at the end of the war. From Chattanooga, Union forces drove into Georgia, capturing Atlanta. Following the fall of Atlanta, General Sherman embarked on his march of destruction through Georgia to the coast and then northward through the Carolinas.

in the way of putting down the rebellion." Confederate General Johnston later commented, "There has been no such army since the days of Julius Caesar."

As Sherman's men moved across Georgia, they cut a path 50 to 60 miles wide and more than 200 miles long. The totality of the destruction they caused was awesome; indeed, it was Sherman's campaign that later prompted many historians to deem this the first modern "total war." A Georgia woman described the "Burnt Country" this way: "The fields were trampled down and the road was lined with carcasses of horses, hogs, and cattle that the invaders, unable either to consume or to carry with them, had wantonly shot down to starve our people…. The stench in some places was unbearable." Such devastation diminished the South's material resources and sapped its will to resist.

After reaching Savannah in December, Sherman marched his armies north into the Carolinas. To his soldiers, South Carolina was "the root of secession." They burned and destroyed as they marched, encountering little resistance. The opposing army of General Johnston was small, but Sherman's men should have been prime targets for guerrilla raids and harassing attacks by local defense units. The absence of both led South Carolina's James Chesnut Jr. (a politician and the husband of Mary Chesnut) to write that his state "was shamefully and unnecessarily lost…. We had time, opportunity and means to destroy him. But there was wholly wanting the energy and ability required." Southerners had lost the will to continue the struggle.

Sherman's march drew additional human resources to the Union cause. In Georgia alone, as many as nineteen thousand slaves gladly embraced emancipation and followed the marauding Union troops. Others remained on the plantations to await the end of the war because of either an ingrained wariness of whites or negative experiences with federal soldiers. The destruction of food harmed slaves as well as white rebels, and many blacks lost livestock, clothing, crops, and other valuables to their liberators. In fact, the brutality of Sherman's troops shocked some liberated slaves. "I've seen them cut the hams off of a live pig or ox and go off leavin' the animal groanin,'" recalled one man. "The master had 'em kilt then, but it was awful."

Virginia's Bloody Soil   It was awful, too, in Virginia, where the path to victory proved protracted and ghastly. Throughout the spring and summer of 1864, intent on capturing Richmond, Grant hurled his troops at Lee's army and suffered appalling losses: almost eighteen thousand casualties in the Battle of the Wilderness, where skeletons poked out of the shallow graves dug one year before; more than eight thousand at Spotsylvania; and twelve thousand in the space of a few hours at Cold Harbor.

Before the assault at Cold Harbor (which Grant later admitted was a grave mistake), Union troops pinned scraps of paper bearing their names and addresses to their backs, certain they would be mowed down as they rushed Lee's trenches. In four weeks in May and June, Grant lost as many men as were enrolled in Lee's entire army. From early May until July, when Union forces had marched and fought all the way from forests west of Fredericksburg to Petersburg, south of Richmond, which they besieged, the two armies engaged each other nearly every day. The war had reached a horribly modern scale. Wagon trains carrying thousands of Union wounded crawled back toward Washington. "It was as if war," wrote historian Bruce Catton, "the great clumsy machine for maiming people, had at last been perfected. Instead of turning out its grist spasmodically, with long waits between each delivery, it was at last able to produce every day, without any gaps at all."

Undaunted, Grant kept up the pressure, saying, "I propose to fight it out along this line if it takes all summer." Although costly, and testing northern morale to its limits, these battles prepared the way for eventual victory: Lee's army shrank until offensive action was no longer possible, while Grant's army kept replenishing its forces with new recruits. The siege of Petersburg, with the armies facing each other in miles of trenches, lasted throughout the winter of 1864–1865.

Surrender at Appomattox   The end finally came in the spring of 1865. Grant kept battering Lee, who tried but failed to break through the Union line. With the numerical superiority of Grant's army now greater than two to one, Confederate defeat was inevitable. On April 2, Lee abandoned Richmond and Petersburg. On April 9, hemmed in by Union troops, short of rations, and with fewer than thirty thousand men left, he surrendered at Appomattox Court House. Grant treated his rival with respect and paroled the defeated troops, allowing cavalrymen to keep their horses and take them home. The war was over at last. Within weeks, Confederate forces under Johnston surrendered to Sherman in North Carolina, and Davis, who had fled Richmond but wanted the war to continue, was captured in Georgia. The North rejoiced, and most southerners fell into despair, expecting waves of punishment. In the profound relief and stillness of the surrender field at Appomattox, no one could know the harrowing tasks of healing and justice that lay ahead.

With Lee's surrender, Lincoln knew the Union had been preserved, yet he lived to see but a few days of war's aftermath. On the evening of Good Friday, April 14, he accompanied his wife to Ford's Theatre in Washington to enjoy a popular comedy. There John Wilkes Booth, an embittered southern sympathizer, shot the president in the head at point-blank range. Lincoln died the next day. Twelve days later, troops tracked down and killed Booth. The Union had lost its wartime leader, and millions publicly mourned the martyred chief executive along the route of the funeral train that took his body home to Illinois. Relief at the war's end mingled hauntingly with a renewed sense of loss and anxiety about the future. Millions never forgot where they were and how they felt at the news of Lincoln's assassination.

Financial Tally   Property damage and financial costs were enormous, though difficult to tally. U.S. loans and taxes during the conflict totaled almost $3 billion, and interest on the war debt was $2.8 billion. The Confederacy borrowed over $2 billion but lost far more in the destruction of homes, crops, livestock, and other property. In southern war zones, the landscape was desolated. Over wide regions, fences and crops were destroyed; houses, barns, and bridges burned; and fields abandoned and left to erode. Union troops had looted factories and put two-thirds of the South's railroad system out of service.

Estimates of the total cost of the war exceed $20 billion—five times the total expenditures of the federal government from its creation until 1861. By 1865, the federal government's spending had soared to twenty times the prewar level and accounted for over 26 percent of the gross national product. Many of these changes were more or less permanent, as wartime measures left the government more deeply involved in manufacturing, banking, and transportation.

Death Toll and   The human costs of the Civil War were especially staggering.
Its Impact   The total number of military casualties on both sides exceeded 1 million—a frightful toll for a nation of 31 million people. Approximately 360,000 Union soldiers died, the majority from disease. Another 275,175 Union soldiers were wounded but survived. On the Confederate side, an estimated 260,000 lost their lives, and almost as many suffered wounds. More men died in the Civil War than in all other American wars combined until Vietnam. Not all died on the battlefield: 30,218 northerners died in southern prisons, and 25,976 Confederates died in Union prisons.

The scale and the anonymous nature of death overwhelmed American culture and led to the establishment of national cemeteries, where the large majority of the fallen were buried without identification. This prompted desperate efforts by families to find their loved ones, usually in vain. In a Christian culture believing in the "good death," where the deceased is surrounded by family and a clear narrative of the final hours could be remembered, mass death and dismembered bodies strewn on war-ravaged landscapes violated the values of a romantic age. On the mass private level, countless Americans, soldiers, and family members alike never psychologically recovered or found true consolation from the war's personal loss. The age's earlier belief that suffering was always purposeful underwent fundamental shock. The desperate urge to memorialize individual soldiers in this war, writes historian Drew Faust, stemmed from "the anguish of wives, parents, siblings, and children who found undocumented, unconfirmed, and unrecognizable loss intolerable." For some, the magnitude of death meant living could never be the same.

These unprecedented losses (approximately 620,000 total dead) flowed from fundamental strife over the nature of the Union and the liberty of black people. Both sides saw vital interests in the struggle but lost control of its scope. As Julia Ward Howe wrote in her famous "Battle Hymn of the Republic," they had heard "the trumpet that shall never call retreat." And so the war took its horrifying course.

SUMMARY

The Civil War altered American society forever. The first great legacy of the war in the lives of its survivors was, therefore, death itself. Although precise figures on enlistments are unavailable, it appears that 700,000 to 800,000 men served in the Confederate armies. Far more, possibly 2.3 million, served in the Union armies. All of these men were taken from home, family, and personal goals; their lives, if they survived, were disrupted in ways that were never repaired. During the war, in both North and South, women, too, took on new roles as they struggled to manage the hardships of the home front, to grieve, and to support the war effort.

Industrialization and economic enterprises grew exponentially in tandem with the war. Ordinary citizens found that their futures were increasingly tied to huge organizations. The character and extent of government power, too, changed markedly. Under Republican leadership, the federal government expanded its power not only to preserve the Union but also to extend freedom. A social revolution and government authority emancipated the slaves. A republic desperately divided against itself had survived, but in new constitutional forms yet to take shape during Reconstruction.

It was unclear at the end of the war how or whether the nation would use its power to protect the rights of the former slaves. Secession was dead, but whether Americans would continue to embrace a centralized nationalism remained to be seen. The war ended decisively after tremendous sacrifice, but it left many unanswered questions: How would white southerners, embittered and impoverished, respond to efforts to reconstruct the nation? How would the country care for the maimed, the orphans, the farming women without men to work their land, and all the dead who had to be found and properly buried? What would be the place of black men and women in American life?

In the West, two civil wars had raged: one between Union and Confederate forces and the other resulting in a conquest of southwestern Indians by U.S. troops and land-hungry settlers. On the diplomatic front, the Union government had delicately managed to keep Great Britain and other foreign powers out of the war. Dissent flourished in both North and South, playing a crucial role in the ultimate collapse of the Confederacy.

In the Civil War, Americans had undergone an epic of destruction and survival—a transformation like nothing else in their history. White southerners had experienced defeat that few other Americans had ever faced. Blacks were moving proudly but anxiously from slavery to freedom. White northerners were, by and large, self-conscious victors in a massive war for the nation's existence and for new definitions of freedom. The war, with all of its drama, sacrifice, and social and political change, would leave a compelling memory in American hearts and minds for generations.

16

RECONSTRUCTION: AN UNFINISHED
REVOLUTION 1865–1877

WARTIME RECONSTRUCTION

Civil wars leave immense challenges of healing, justice, and physical rebuilding. Anticipating that process, reconstruction of the Union was an issue as early as 1863, well before the war ended. Many key questions loomed on the horizon when and if the North succeeded on the battlefield: How would the nation be restored? How would southern states and leaders be treated—as errant brothers or as traitors? What was the constitutional basis for readmission of states to the Union, and where, if anywhere, could American statesmen look for precedence or guidance? More specifically, four vexing problems compelled early thinking and would haunt the Reconstruction era throughout. One, who would rule in the South once it was defeated? Two, who would rule in the federal government—Congress or the president? Three, what were the dimensions of black freedom, and what rights under law would the freedmen enjoy? And four, would Reconstruction be a preservation of the old republic or a second Revolution, a reinvention of a new republic?

Lincoln's 10 Percent Plan   Abraham Lincoln had never been antisouthern, though he had become the leader of an antislavery war. He lost three brothers-in-law, killed in the war on the Confederate side. His worst fear was that the war would collapse at the end into guerrilla warfare across the South, with surviving bands of Confederates carrying on resistance. Lincoln insisted that his generals give lenient terms to southern soldiers once they

CHRONOLOGY

1865	Johnson begins rapid and lenient Reconstruction
	White southern governments pass restrictive black codes
	Congress refuses to seat southern representatives
	Thirteenth Amendment ratified, abolishing slavery
1866	Congress passes Civil Rights Act and renewal of Freedmen's Bureau over Johnson's veto
	Congress approves Fourteenth Amendment
	In *Ex parte Milligan*, the Supreme Court reasserts its influence
1867	Congress passes First Reconstruction Act and Tenure of Office Act
	Constitutional conventions called in southern states
1868	House impeaches and Senate acquits Johnson
	Most southern states readmitted to Union under Radical plan
	Fourteenth Amendment ratified
	Grant elected president
1869	Congress approves Fifteenth Amendment (ratified in 1870)
1871	Congress passes second Enforcement Act and Ku Klux Klan Act
	Treaty with England settles Alabama claims
1872	Amnesty Act frees almost all remaining Confederates from restrictions on holding office
	Grant reelected
1873	*Slaughter-House* cases limit power of Fourteenth Amendment
	Panic of 1873 leads to widespread unemployment and labor strife
1874	Democrats win majority in House of Representatives
1875	Several Grant appointees indicted for corruption
	Congress passes weak Civil Rights Act
	Democratic Party increases control of southern states with white supremacy campaigns
1876	*U.S. v. Cruikshank* further weakens Fourteenth Amendment
	Presidential election disputed
1877	Congress elects Hayes president

surrendered. In his Second Inaugural Address, delivered only a month before his assassination, Lincoln promised "malice toward none; with charity for all," as Americans strove to "bind up the nation's wounds."

Lincoln planned early for a swift and moderate Reconstruction process. In his "Proclamation of Amnesty and Reconstruction," issued in December 1863, he proposed to replace majority rule with "loyal rule" as a means of reconstructing southern state governments. He proposed pardons to all ex-Confederates except the highest-ranking military and civilian officers. Then, as soon as 10 percent of the voting population in the 1860 general election in a given state had taken an oath to the United States and established a government, the new state would be recognized. Lincoln did not consult Congress in these plans, and "loyal" assemblies (known as "Lincoln governments") were created in Louisiana, Tennessee, and Arkansas in 1864, states largely occupied by Union troops. These governments were weak and dependent on northern armies for survival.

Congress and the Wade-Davis Bill

Congress responded with great hostility to Lincoln's moves to readmit southern states in what seemed such a premature manner. Many Radical Republicans, strong proponents of emancipation and of aggressive prosecution of the war against the South, considered the 10 percent plan a "mere mockery" of democracy. Led by Thaddeus Stevens of Pennsylvania in the House and Charles Sumner of Massachusetts in the Senate, congressional Republicans locked horns with Lincoln and proposed a longer and harsher approach to Reconstruction. Stevens advocated a "conquered provinces" theory, arguing that southerners had organized as a foreign nation to make war on the United States and, by secession, had destroyed their status as states. They therefore must be treated as "conquered foreign lands" and returned to the status of "unorganized territories" before any process of readmission could be entertained by Congress.

In July 1864, the Wade-Davis bill, named for its sponsors, Senator Benjamin Wade of Ohio and Congressman Henry W. Davis of Maryland, emerged from Congress with three specific conditions for southern readmission.

1. It demanded a "majority" of white male citizens participating in the creation of a new government.
2. To vote or be a delegate to constitutional conventions, men had to take an "ironclad" oath (declaring that they had never aided the Confederate war effort).
3. All officers above the rank of lieutenant and all civil officials in the Confederacy would be disfranchised and deemed "not a citizen of the United States."

The Confederate states were to be defined as "conquered enemies," said Davis, and the process of readmission was to be harsh and slow. Lincoln, ever the adroit politician, pocket-vetoed the bill and issued a conciliatory proclamation of his own, announcing that he would not be inflexibly committed to any "one plan" of Reconstruction.

This exchange came during Grant's bloody campaign against Lee in Virginia, when the outcome of the war and Lincoln's reelection were still in doubt. On August 5, Radical Republicans issued the "Wade-Davis Manifesto" to newspapers. An unprecedented attack on a sitting president by members of his own party, it accused Lincoln of usurpation of presidential powers and disgraceful leniency toward an eventually conquered South. What emerged in 1864–1865 was a clear debate and a potential constitutional crisis. Lincoln saw Reconstruction as a means of weakening the Confederacy and winning the war; the Radicals saw it as a longer-term transformation of the political and racial order of the country.

Thirteenth Amendment

In early 1865, Congress and Lincoln joined in two important measures that recognized slavery's centrality to the war. On January 31, with strong administration backing, Congress passed the Thirteenth Amendment, which had two provisions: first, it abolished involuntary servitude everywhere in the United States; second, it declared that

Congress shall have the power to enforce this outcome by "appropriate legislation." When the measure passed by 119 to 56, a mere 2 votes more than the necessary two-thirds, rejoicing broke out in Congress. A Republican recorded in his diary, "Members joined in the shouting and kept it up for some minutes. Some embraced one another, others wept like children. I have felt ever since the vote, as if I were in a new country."

But the Thirteenth Amendment had emerged from a long congressional debate and considerable petitioning and public advocacy. One of the first and most remarkable petitions for a constitutional amendment abolishing slavery was submitted early in 1864 by Elizabeth Cady Stanton, Susan B. Anthony, and the Women's Loyal National League. Women throughout the Union accumulated thousands of signatures, even venturing into staunchly pro-Confederate regions of Kentucky and Missouri to secure supporters. It was a long road from the Emancipation Proclamation to the Thirteenth Amendment—through treacherous constitutional theory about individual "property rights," a bedrock of belief that the sacred document ought never to be altered, and partisan politics. But the logic of winning the war by crushing slavery, and of securing a new beginning under law for the nation that so many had died to save, won the day.

Freedmen's Bureau

Potentially as significant, on March 3, 1865, Congress created the Bureau of Refugees, Freedmen, and Abandoned Lands— the Freedmen's Bureau, an unprecedented agency of social uplift necessitated by the ravages of the war. Americans had never engaged in federal aid to citizens on such a scale. With thousands of refugees, white and black, displaced in the South, the government continued what private freedmen's aid societies had started as early as 1862. In the mere four years of its existence, the Freedmen's Bureau supplied food and medical services, built several thousand schools and some colleges, negotiated several hundred thousand employment contracts between freedmen and their former masters, and tried to manage confiscated land.

The Bureau would be a controversial aspect of Reconstruction—within the South, where whites generally hated it, and within the federal government, where politicians divided over its constitutionality. Some bureau agents were devoted to freedmen's rights, whereas others were opportunists who exploited the chaos of the postwar South. The war had forced into the open an eternal question of republics: what are the social welfare obligations of the state toward its people, and what do people owe their governments in return? Apart from their conquest and displacement of the eastern Indians, Americans were relatively inexperienced at the Freedmen's Bureau's task—social reform through military occupation.

Ruins and Enmity

In 1865, due to the devastation of the war, America was now a land with ruins. Like the countries of Europe, it now seemed an older, more historic landscape. It had torn itself asunder—physically, politically, spiritually. Some of its cities lay in rubble, large stretches of the southern countryside were depopulated and defoliated, and thousands of people, white and black, were refugees. Some of this would in time seem romantic to northern travelers in the postwar South.

Thousands of yeoman farmer-soldiers, some paroled by surrenders and others who had abandoned Confederate ranks earlier, walked home too late in the season to plant a crop in a collapsed economy. Many white refugees faced genuine starvation. Of the approximately 18,300,000 rations distributed across the South in the first three years of the Freedmen's Bureau, 5,230,000 went to whites. In early 1866, in a proud agricultural society, the legislature of South Carolina issued $300,000 in state bonds to purchase corn for the destitute.

In October 1865, just after a five-month imprisonment in Boston, former Confederate Vice President Alexander H. Stephens rode a slow train southward. In Virginia he found "the desolation of the country ... was horrible to behold." When Stephens reached northern Georgia, his native state, his shock ran over: "War has left a terrible impression.... Fences gone, fields all a-waste, houses burnt." A northern journalist visiting Richmond that same fall observed a city "mourning for her sins ... in dust and ashes." The "burnt district" was a "bed of cinders ... broken and blackened walls, impassable streets deluged with debris." Above all, every northern traveler encountered a wall of hatred among white southerners for their conquerors. An innkeeper in North Carolina told a journalist that Yankees had killed his sons in the war, burned his house, and stolen his slaves. "They left me one inestimable privilege," he said, "to hate 'em. I git up at half-past four in the morning, and sit up 'til twelve at night, to hate 'em."

THE MEANINGS OF FREEDOM

Black southerners entered into life after slavery with hope and circumspection. A Texas man recalled his father's telling him, even before the war was over, "Our forever was going to be spent living among the Southerners, after they got licked." Freed men and women tried to gain as much as they could from their new circumstances. Often the changes they valued the most were personal—alterations in location, employer, or living arrangements.

The Feel of Freedom   For America's former slaves, Reconstruction had one paramount meaning: a chance to explore freedom. A southern white woman admitted in her diary that the black people "showed a natural and exultant joy at being free." Former slaves remembered singing far into the night after federal troops, who confirmed rumors of their emancipation, reached their plantations. The slaves on a Texas plantation shouted for joy, their leader proclaiming, "We is free—no more whippings and beatings." A few people gave in to the natural desire to do what had been impossible before. One angry grandmother dropped her hoe and ran to confront her mistress. "I'm free!" she yelled. "Yes, I'm free! Ain't got to work for you no more! You can't put me in your pocket now!" Another man recalled that he and others "started on the move," either to search for family members or just to exercise the human right of mobility.

Many freed men and women reacted more cautiously and shrewdly, taking care to test the boundaries of their new condition. "After the war was over," explained one man, "we was afraid to move. Just like terrapins or turtles after emancipation. Just stick our heads out to see how the land lay." As slaves, they had learned to expect hostility from white people, and they did not presume it would instantly disappear. Life in freedom might still be a matter of what was possible, not what was right. Many freedpeople evaluated potential employers with shrewd caution. "Most all the Negroes that had good owners stayed with 'em, but the others left. Some of 'em come back and some didn't," explained one man. After considerable wandering in search of better circumstances, a majority of blacks eventually settled as agricultural workers back on their former farms or plantations. But they relocated their houses and did their utmost to control the conditions of their labor.

Reunion of African American Families   Throughout the South, former slaves devoted themselves to reuniting their families, separated during slavery by sale or hardship, and during the war by dislocation and the emancipation process. With only shreds of information to guide them, thousands of freedpeople embarked on odysseys in search of a husband, wife, child, or parent. By relying on the black community for help and information, and by placing ads that continued to appear in black newspapers well into the 1880s, some succeeded in their quest, while others searched in vain.

Husbands and wives who had belonged to different masters established homes together for the first time, and, as they had tried under slavery, parents asserted the right to raise their own children. A mother bristled when her old master claimed a right to whip her children. She informed him that "he warn't goin' to brush none of her chilluns no more." The freed men and women were too much at risk to act recklessly, but, as one man put it, they were tired of punishment and "sure didn't take no more foolishment off of white folks."

Blacks' Search for Independence   Many black people wanted to minimize contact with whites because, as Reverend Garrison Frazier told General Sherman in January 1865, "There is a prejudice against us ... that will take years to get over." To avoid contact with overbearing whites who were used to supervising them, blacks abandoned the slave quarters and fanned out to distant corners of the land they worked. "After the war my stepfather come," recalled Annie Young, "and got my mother and we moved out in the piney woods." Others described moving "across the creek" or building a "saplin house ... back in the woods." Some rural dwellers established small, all-black settlements that still exist along the back roads of the South.

Even once-privileged slaves desired such independence and social separation. One man turned down his master's offer of the overseer's house and moved instead to a shack in "Freetown." He also declined to let the former owner grind his grain for free because it "make him feel like a free man to pay for things just like anyone else."

Freedpeople's Desire for Land   In addition to a fair employer, what freed men and women most wanted was the ownership of land. Land represented self-sufficiency and a chance to gain compensation for generations of bondage. General Sherman's special Field Order Number 15, issued in February 1865, set aside 400,000 acres of land in the Sea Islands region for the exclusive settlement of freedpeople. Hope swelled among ex-slaves as forty-acre plots, mules, and "possessary titles" were promised to them. But President Johnson ordered them removed in October and the land returned to its original owners under army enforcement. A northern observer noted that slaves freed in the Sea Islands of South Carolina and Georgia made "plain, straight-forward" inquiries as they settled on new land. They wanted to be sure the land "would be theirs after they had improved it." Everywhere, blacks young and old thirsted for homes of their own.

But most members of both political parties opposed genuine land redistribution to the freedmen. Even northern reformers who had administered the Sea Islands during the war showed little sympathy for black aspirations. The former Sea Island slaves wanted to establish small, self-sufficient farms. Northern soldiers, officials, and missionaries of both races brought education and aid to the freedmen but also insisted that they grow cotton for competitive market.

"The Yankees preach nothing but cotton, cotton!" complained one Sea Island black. "We wants land," wrote another, but tax officials "make the lots too big, and cut we out." Indeed, the U.S. government eventually sold thousands of acres in the Sea Islands, 90 percent of which went to wealthy investors from the North. At a protest against evictions from a contraband camp in Virginia in 1866, freedman Bayley Wyatt made black desires and claims clear: "We has a right to the land where we are located. For why? I tell you. Our wives, our children, our husbands, has been sold over and over again to purchase the lands we now locates upon; for that reason we have a divine right to the land."

Black Embrace of Education   Ex-slaves everywhere reached out for education. Blacks of all ages hungered for the knowledge in books that had been permitted only to whites. With freedom, they started schools and filled classrooms both day and night. On log seats and dirt floors, freed men and women studied their letters in old almanacs and in discarded dictionaries. Young children brought infants to school with them, and adults attended at night or after "the crops were laid by." Many a teacher had "to make herself heard over three other classes reciting in concert" in a small room. The desire to escape slavery's ignorance was so great that, despite their poverty, many blacks paid tuition, typically $1 or $1.50 a month. These small amounts constituted major portions of a person's agricultural wages and added up to more than $1 million by 1870.

The federal government and northern reformers of both races assisted this pursuit of education. In its brief life, the Freedmen's Bureau founded over four thousand schools, and idealistic men and women from the North established others funded by private philanthropy. The Yankee schoolmarm—dedicated, selfless, and religious—became an agent of progress in many southern communities. Thus did African Americans seek a break from their past through learning. More than 600,000 were enrolled in elementary school by 1877.

Blacks and their white allies also saw the need for colleges and universities. The American Missionary Association founded seven colleges, including Fisk and Atlanta Universities, between 1866 and 1869. The Freedmen's Bureau helped to establish Howard University in Washington, D.C., and northern religious groups, such as the Methodists, Baptists, and Congregationalists, supported dozens of seminaries and teachers' colleges.

During Reconstruction, African American leaders often were highly educated individuals; many were from the prewar elite of free people of color. Francis Cardozo, who held various offices in South Carolina, had attended universities in Scotland and England. P. B. S. Pinchback, who became lieutenant governor of Louisiana, was the son of a planter who had sent him to school in Cincinnati. Both of the two black senators from Mississippi, Blanche K. Bruce and Hiram Revels, possessed privileged educations. Bruce was the son of a planter who had

African Americans of all ages eagerly pursued the opportunity to gain an education in freedom. This young woman in Mt. Meigs, Alabama, is helping her mother learn to read.

Smithsonian Institution, photo by Rudolf Eickemeyer

provided tutoring at home; Revels was the son of free North Carolina blacks who had sent him to Knox College in Illinois. These men and many self-educated former slaves brought to political office not only fervor but education.

Growth of Black Churches   Freed from the restrictions and regulations of slavery, blacks could build their own institutions as they saw fit. The secret churches of slavery came into the open; in countless communities throughout the South, ex-slaves "started a brush arbor." A brush arbor was merely "a sort of ... shelter with leaves for a roof," but the freed men and women worshiped in it enthusiastically. "Preachin' and shouting sometimes lasted all day," they recalled, for the opportunity to worship together freely meant "glorious times."

Within a few years, independent branches of the Methodist and Baptist denominations had attracted the great majority of black Christians in the South. By 1877, in South Carolina alone, the African Methodist Episcopal (A.M.E.) Church had a thousand ministers, forty-four thousand members, and its own school of theology, while the A.M.E. Zion Church had forty-five thousand members. In the rapid growth of churches, some of which became the wealthiest and most autonomous institutions in black life, the freedpeople demonstrated their most secure claim on freedom and created enduring communities.

Rise of the Sharecropping System   The desire to gain as much independence as possible also shaped the former slaves' economic arrangements. Since most of them lacked money to buy land, they preferred the next best thing: renting the land they worked. But the South had a cash-poor economy with few sources of credit, and few whites would consider renting land to blacks. Most blacks had no means to get cash before the harvest, so other alternatives had to be tried.

Black farmers and white landowners therefore turned to sharecropping, a system in which farmers kept part of their crop and gave the rest to the landowner while living on his property. The landlord or a merchant "furnished" food and supplies, such as draft animals and seed, needed before the harvest, and he received payment from the crop. White landowners and black farmers bargained with one another; sharecroppers would hold out, or move and try to switch employers from one year to another. As the system matured during the 1870s and 1880s, most sharecroppers worked "on halves"—half for the owner and half for themselves.

The sharecropping system, which materialized as early as 1868 in parts of the South, originated as a desirable compromise between former slaves and landowners. It eased landowners' problems with cash and credit, and provided them a permanent, dependent labor force; blacks accepted it because it gave them freedom from daily supervision. Instead of working in the hated gangs under a white overseer, as in slavery, they farmed their own plots of land in family groups. But sharecropping later proved to be a disaster. Owners and merchants developed a monopoly of control over the agricultural economy, as sharecroppers found themselves riveted in ever-increasing debt.

The fundamental problem, however, was that southern farmers as a whole still concentrated on cotton. In freedom, black women often chose to stay away from the fields and cotton picking, to concentrate on domestic chores. Given the diminishing incentives of the system, they placed greater value on independent choices about gender roles and family organization than on reaching higher levels of production. The South did recover its prewar share of British cotton purchases, but the rewards diminished. Cotton prices began a long decline, as world demand fell off.

Thus, southern agriculture slipped deeper and deeper into depression. Black sharecroppers struggled under a growing burden of debt which reduced their independence and bound them to landowners and to furnishing merchants almost as oppressively as slavery had bound them to their masters. Many white farmers became debtors, too, gradually lost their land, and joined the ranks of sharecroppers. By the end of Reconstruction, over one-third of all southern farms were worked by sharecropping tenants, white and black. This economic transformation took place as the nation struggled to put its political house back in order.

JOHNSON'S RECONSTRUCTION PLAN

When Reconstruction began under President Andrew Johnson, many expected his policies to be harsh. Throughout his career in Tennessee, he had criticized the wealthy planters and championed the small farmers. When an assassin's bullet thrust Johnson into the presidency, many former slaveowners shared the dismay of a North Carolina woman who wrote, "Think of Andy Johnson [as] the president! What will become of us—'the aristocrats of the South' as we are termed?" Northern Radicals also had reason to believe that Johnson would deal sternly with the South. When one of them suggested the exile or execution of ten or twelve leading rebels to set an example, Johnson replied, "How are you going to pick out so small a number? ... Treason is a crime; and crime must be punished."

Andrew Johnson of Tennessee   Like his martyred predecessor, Johnson followed a path in antebellum politics from obscurity to power. With no formal education, he became a tailor's apprentice. But from 1829, while in his early twenties, he held nearly every office in Tennessee politics: alderman, state representative, congressman, two terms as governor, and U.S. senator by 1857. Although elected as a southern Democrat, Johnson was the only senator from a seceded state who refused to follow his state out of the Union. Lincoln appointed him war governor of Tennessee in 1862; hence his symbolic place on the ticket in the president's bid for reelection in 1864.

Although a Unionist, Johnson's political beliefs made him an old Jacksonian Democrat. And as they said in the mountainous region of east Tennessee, where Johnson established a reputation as a stump speaker, "Old Andy never went back on his raisin.'" Johnson was also an ardent states' rightist. Before the war, he had supported tax-funded public schools and homestead legislation, fashioning himself as a champion of the common man. Although he vehemently opposed secession, Johnson advocated limited government. He shared none of the Radicals' expansive conception of federal power. His philosophy toward Reconstruction may be summed up in the slogan he adopted: "The Constitution as it is, and the Union as it was."

Through 1865, Johnson alone controlled Reconstruction policy, for Congress recessed shortly before he became president and did not reconvene until December. In the following eight months, Johnson formed new state governments in the South by using his power to grant pardons. He advanced Lincoln's leniency by extending even easier terms to former Confederates.

Johnson's Racial Views   Johnson had owned house slaves, although he had never been a planter. He accepted emancipation as a result of the war, but he did not favor black civil and political rights. Johnson believed that black suffrage could never be imposed on a southern state by the federal government, and that set him on a collision course with the Radicals. When it came to race, Johnson was a thoroughgoing white supremacist. He held what one politician called "unconquerable prejudices against the African race." In perhaps the most blatantly racist official statement ever delivered by an American president, Johnson declared in his annual message of 1867 that blacks possessed less "capacity for government than any other race of people. No independent government of any form has ever been successful in their hands; … wherever they have been left to their own devices they have shown a constant tendency to relapse into barbarism."

Such racial views had an enduring effect on Johnson's policies. Where whites were concerned, however, Johnson seemed to be pursuing changes in class relations. He proposed rules that would keep the wealthy planter class at least temporarily out of power.

Johnson's Pardon Policy   White southerners were required to swear an oath of loyalty as a condition of gaining amnesty or pardon, but Johnson barred several categories of people from taking the oath: former federal officials, high-ranking Confederate officers, and political leaders or graduates of West Point or Annapolis who joined the Confederacy. To this list, Johnson added another important group: all ex-Confederates whose taxable property was worth more than $20,000. These individuals had to apply personally to the president for pardon and

Combative and inflexible, President Andrew Johnson contributed greatly to the failure of his own Reconstruction program.

Library of Congress

restoration of their political rights. The president, it seemed, meant to take revenge on the old planter elite and thereby promote a new leadership of deserving yeomen.

Johnson appointed provisional governors, who began the Reconstruction process by calling state constitutional conventions. The delegates chosen for these conventions had to draft new constitutions that eliminated slavery and invalidated secession. After ratification of these constitutions, new governments could be elected, and the states would be restored to the Union with full congressional representation. But only those southerners who had taken the oath of amnesty and had been eligible to vote on the day the state seceded could participate in this process. Thus unpardoned whites and former slaves were not eligible.

Presidential Reconstruction   If Johnson intended to strip former aristocrats of their power, he did not hold to his plan. The old white leadership proved resilient and influential; prominent Confederates won elections and turned up in various appointive offices. Then Johnson started pardoning planters and leading rebels. He hired additional clerks to prepare the necessary documents and then began to issue pardons to large categories of people. By September 1865, hundreds were issued in a single day. These pardons, plus the rapid return of planters' abandoned lands, restored the old elite to power and quickly gave Johnson an image as the South's champion.

Why did Johnson allow the planters to regain power? Personal vanity may have played a role, as he turned proud planters into pardon seekers. He was also determined to achieve a rapid Reconstruction in order to deny the Radicals any opportunity for the more thorough racial and political changes they desired in the South. And Johnson needed southern support in the 1866 elections; hence, he declared Reconstruction complete only eight months after Appomattox. Thus, in

December 1865, many Confederate congressmen traveled to Washington to claim seats in the U.S. Congress. Even Alexander Stephens, vice president of the Confederacy, returned to Capitol Hill as a senator-elect from Georgia.

The election of such prominent rebels troubled many northerners. Some of the state conventions were slow to repudiate secession; others admitted only grudgingly that slavery was dead and wrote new laws to show it.

Black Codes   Furthermore, to define the status of freed men and women and control their labor, some legislatures merely revised large sections of the slave codes by substituting the word *freedmen* for *slaves*. The new black codes compelled former slaves to carry passes, observe a curfew, live in housing provided by a landowner, and give up hope of entering many desirable occupations. Stiff vagrancy laws and restrictive labor contracts bound freedpeople to plantations, and "anti-enticement" laws punished anyone who tried to lure these workers to other employment. State-supported schools and orphanages excluded blacks entirely.

It seemed to northerners that the South was intent on returning African Americans to servility and that Johnson's Reconstruction policy held no one responsible for the terrible war. But memories of the war—not yet even a year over—were still raw and would dominate political behavior for several elections to come. Thus, the Republican majority in Congress decided to call a halt to the results of Johnson's plan. On reconvening, the House and Senate considered the credentials of the newly elected southern representatives and decided not to admit them. Instead, they bluntly challenged the president's authority and established a joint committee to study and investigate a new direction for Reconstruction.

THE CONGRESSIONAL RECONSTRUCTION PLAN

Northern congressmen were hardly unified, but they did not doubt their right to shape Reconstruction policy. The Constitution mentioned neither secession nor reunion, but it gave Congress the primary role in the admission of states. Moreover, the Constitution declared that the United States shall guarantee to each state a "republican form of government." This provision, legislators believed, gave them the authority to devise policies for Reconstruction.

They soon found that other constitutional questions affected their policies. What, for example, had rebellion done to the relationship between southern states and the Union? Lincoln had always believed secession impossible—the Confederate states had engaged in an "insurrection" within the Union in his view. Congressmen who favored vigorous Reconstruction measures argued that the war had broken the Union and that the South was subject to the victor's will. Moderate congressmen held that the states had forfeited their rights through rebellion and thus had come under congressional supervision.

The Radicals   These theories mirrored the diversity of Congress itself. Northern Democrats, weakened by their opposition to the war in its final year, denounced any idea of racial equality and supported Johnson's policies. Conservative Republicans, despite their party loyalty, favored a limited federal role in Reconstruction. The Radical Republicans, led by Thaddeus Stevens, Charles Sumner, and George Julian, wanted to transform the South. Although a minority in their party, they had the advantage of clearly defined goals. They believed it was essential to democratize the South, establish public education, and ensure the rights of the freedpeople. They favored black suffrage, supported some land confiscation and redistribution, and were willing to exclude the South from the Union for several years if necessary to achieve their goals.

Born of the war and its outcome, the Radicals brought a new civic vision to American life; they wanted to create an activist federal government and the beginnings of racial equality. A large group of moderate Republicans, led by Lyman Trumbull, opposed Johnson's leniency but wanted to restrain the Radicals. Trumbull and the moderates were, however, committed to federalizing the enforcement of civil, if not political, rights for the freedmen.

One overwhelming political reality faced all four groups: the 1866 elections. Ironically, Johnson and the Democrats sabotaged the possibility of a conservative coalition. They refused to cooperate with conservative or moderate Republicans and insisted that Reconstruction was over, that the new state governments were legitimate, and that southern representatives should be admitted to Congress. Among the Republicans, the Radicals' influence grew in proportion to Johnson's intransigence and outright provocation.

Congress Versus Johnson

Trying to work with Johnson, Republicans believed a compromise had been reached in the spring of 1866. Under its terms, Johnson would agree to two modifications of his program: extension of the Freedmen's Bureau for another year and passage of a civil rights bill to counteract the black codes. This bill would force southern courts to practice equality under the ultimate scrutiny of the federal judiciary. Its provisions applied to public, not private, acts of discrimination. The Civil Rights Bill of 1866 was the first statutory definition of the rights of American citizens and is still on the books today.

Johnson destroyed the compromise, however, by vetoing both bills (they later became law when Congress overrode the president's veto). Denouncing any change in his program, the president condemned Congress's action and revealed his own racism. Because the civil rights bill defined U.S. citizens as native-born persons who were taxed, Johnson claimed it discriminated against "large numbers of intelligent, worthy, and patriotic foreigners … in favor of the negro." The bill, he said, operated "in favor of the colored and against the white race."

All hope of presidential-congressional cooperation was now dead. In 1866, newspapers reported daily violations of blacks' rights in the South and carried alarming accounts of antiblack violence—notably in Memphis and New Orleans, where police aided brutal mobs in their attacks. In Memphis, forty blacks were killed and twelve schools burned by white mobs, and in New Orleans, the toll was thirty-four African Americans dead and two hundred wounded. Such violence convinced Republicans, and the northern public, that more needed to be done. A new Republican plan took the form of the Fourteenth Amendment to the Constitution.

Fourteenth Amendment

Of the five sections of the Fourteenth Amendment, the first would have the greatest legal significance in later years. It conferred citizenship on "all persons born or naturalized in the United States" and prohibited states from abridging their constitutional "privileges and immunities" (see the Appendix for the Constitution and all amendments). It also barred any state from taking a person's life, liberty, or property "without due process of law" and from denying "equal protection of the laws." These resounding phrases have become powerful guarantees of African Americans' civil rights—indeed, of the rights of all citizens, except for Indians, who were not granted citizenship rights until 1924.

Nearly universal agreement emerged among Republicans on the amendment's second and third sections. The fourth declared the Confederate debt null and void, and guaranteed the war debt of the United States. Northerners rejected the notion of paying taxes to reimburse those who had financed a rebellion, and business groups agreed on the necessity of upholding the credit of the U.S. government. The second and third sections barred Confederate leaders from holding state and federal office. Only Congress, by a two-thirds vote of each house, could remove the penalty. The amendment thus guaranteed a degree of punishment for the leaders of the Confederacy.

The second section of the amendment also dealt with representation and embodied the compromises that produced the document. Northerners disagreed about whether blacks should have the right to vote. As a citizen of Indiana wrote to a southern relative, "[a]lthough there is a great deal [of] profession among us for the relief of the darkey yet I think much of it is far from being cincere. I guess we want to compell you to do right by them while we are not willing ourselves to do so." Those arched words are indicative not only of how revolutionary Reconstruction had become, but also of how far the public will, North and South, lagged behind the enactments that became new constitutional cornerstones. Many northern states still maintained black disfranchisement laws during Reconstruction.

Emancipation finally ended the three-fifths clause for the purpose of counting blacks, which would increase southern representation. Thus, the postwar South stood to gain power in Congress, and if white southerners did not allow blacks to vote, former secessionists would derive the political benefit from emancipation. That was more irony than most northerners could bear. So Republicans determined that, if a southern state did not grant black men the vote, their representation would be reduced proportionally. If they did enfranchise black men, their representation would be increased proportionally. This compromise avoided a direct enactment of black suffrage but would deliver future black southern voters to the Republican Party.

The Fourteenth Amendment specified for the first time that voters were "male" and ignored female citizens, black and white. For this reason, it provoked a strong reaction from the women's rights movement. Advocates of women's equality had worked with abolitionists for decades, often subordinating their cause to that of the slaves. During the drafting of the Fourteenth Amendment, however, female activists demanded to be heard. Prominent leaders, such as Elizabeth Cady Stanton and Susan B. Anthony, ended their alliance with abolitionists and fought for women, while others remained committed to the idea that it was "the Negro's hour." Thus, the amendment infused new life into the women's rights movement and caused considerable strife among old allies. Many male former abolitionists, white and black, were willing to delay the day of woman suffrage in favor of securing freedmen the right to vote in the South.

The South's and Johnson's Defiance   In 1866, however, the major question in Reconstruction politics was how the public would respond to the congressional initiative. Johnson did his best to block the Fourteenth Amendment in both North and South. Condemning Congress for its refusal to seat southern representatives, the president urged state legislatures in the

South to vote against ratification. Every southern legislature, except Tennessee's, rejected the amendment by a wide margin.

To present his case to northerners, Johnson organized a National Union Convention and took to the stump himself. In an age when active personal campaigning was rare for a president, Johnson boarded a special train for a "swing around the circle" that carried his message into the Northeast, the Midwest, and then back to Washington. In city after city, he criticized the Republicans in a ranting, undignified style. Increasingly, audiences rejected his views, hooting and jeering at him. In this whistle-stop tour, Johnson began to hand out American flags with thirty-six rather than twenty-five stars, declaring the Union already restored. At many towns, he likened himself to a "persecuted" Jesus who might now be martyred "upon the cross" for his magnanimity toward the South. And, repeatedly, he labeled the Radicals "traitors" for their efforts to take over Reconstruction.

The elections of 1866 were a resounding victory for Republicans in Congress. Radicals and moderates whom Johnson had denounced won reelection by large margins, and the Republican majority grew to two-thirds of both houses of Congress. The North had spoken clearly: Johnson's official policies of states' rights and white supremacy were prematurely giving the advantage to rebels and traitors. Although the Radicals may have been out ahead of public opinion, most northerners feared Johnson's approach more. Thus, Republican congressional leaders won a mandate to pursue their Reconstruction plan.

But Johnson and southern intransigence had brought the plan to an impasse. Nothing could be accomplished as long as the "Johnson governments" existed and the southern electorate remained exclusively white. Republicans resolved to form new state governments in the South and enfranchise the freedmen.

Reconstruction Acts of 1867–1868   After some embittered debate in which Republicans and the remaining Democrats in Congress argued over the meaning and memory of the Civil War itself, the First Reconstruction Act passed in March 1867. This plan, under which the southern states were actually readmitted to the Union, incorporated only a part of the Radical program. Union generals, commanding small garrisons of troops and charged with supervising elections, assumed control in five military districts in the South (see Map 16.1). Confederate leaders designated in the Fourteenth Amendment were barred from voting until new state constitutions were ratified. The act guaranteed freedmen the right to vote in elections as well as serve in state constitutional conventions and in subsequent elections. In addition, each southern state was required to ratify the Fourteenth Amendment, to ratify its new constitution by majority vote, and to submit it to Congress for approval (see Table 16.1).

Thus, African Americans gained an opportunity to fight for a better life through the political process, and ex-Confederates were given what they interpreted as a bitter pill to swallow in order to return to the Union. The Second, Third, and Fourth Reconstruction Acts, passed between March 1867 and March 1868, provided the details of operation for voter registration boards, the adoption of constitutions, and the administration of "good faith" oaths on the part of white southerners.

Failure of Land Redistribution   In the words of one historian, the Radicals succeeded in "clipping Johnson's wings." But they had hoped Congress

TABLE 16.1 | PLANS FOR RECONSTRUCTION COMPARED

	Johnson's Plan	Radicals' Plan	Fourteenth Amendment	Reconstruction Act of 1867
Voting	Whites only; high-ranking Confederate leaders must seek pardons	Give vote to black males	Southern whites may decide but can lose representation if they deny black suffrage	Black men gain vote; whites barred from office by Fourteenth Amendment cannot vote while new state governments are being formed
Officeholding	Many prominent Confederates regain power	Only loyal white and black males eligible	Confederate leaders barred until Congress votes amnesty	Fourteenth Amendment in effect
Time out of Union	Brief	Several years; until South is thoroughly democratized	Brief	3–5 years after war
Other change in southern society	Little; gain of power by yeomen not realized; emancipation grudgingly accepted, but no black civil or political rights	Expand public education; confiscate land and provide farms for freedmen; expansion of activist federal government	Probably slight, depending on enforcement	Considerable, depending on action of new state governments

could do much more. Thaddeus Stevens, for example, argued that economic opportunity was essential to the freedmen. "If we do not furnish them with homesteads from forfeited and rebel property," Stevens declared, "and hedge them around with protective laws ... we had better left them in bondage." Stevens therefore drew up a plan for extensive confiscation and redistribution of land, but it was never realized.

Racial fears among whites and an American obsession with the sanctity of private property made land redistribution unpopular. Northerners were accustomed to a limited role for government, and the business community staunchly opposed any interference with private-property rights, even for former Confederates. Thus, black farmers were forced to seek work in a hostile environment in which landowners opposed their acquisition of land.

Constitutional Crisis   Congress's quarrels with Andrew Johnson grew still worse. To restrict Johnson's influence and safeguard its plan,

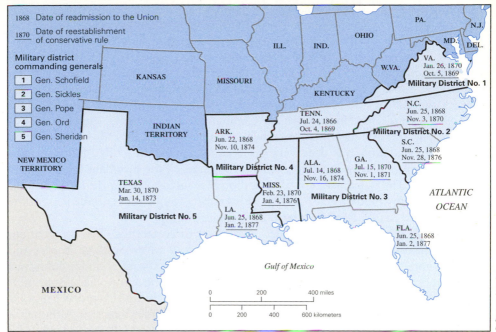

MAP 16.1 The Reconstruction

This map shows the five military districts established when Congress passed the Reconstruction Act of 1867. As the dates within each state indicate, conservative Democratic forces quickly regained control of government in four southern states. So-called Radical Reconstruction was curtailed in most of the others as factions within the weakened Republican Party began to cooperate with conservative Democrats.

Congress passed a number of controversial laws. First, it limited Johnson's power over the army by requiring the president to issue military orders through the General of the Army, Ulysses S. Grant, who could not be dismissed without the Senate's consent. Then Congress passed the Tenure of Office Act, which gave the Senate power to approve changes in the president's cabinet. Designed to protect Secretary of War Stanton, who sympathized with the Radicals, this law violated the tradition that a president controlled appointments to his own cabinet.

All of these measures, as well as each of the Reconstruction Acts, were passed by a two-thirds override of presidential vetoes. The situation led some to believe that the federal government had reached a stage of "congressional tyranny" and others to conclude that Johnson had become an obstacle to the legitimate will of the people in reconstructing the nation on a just and permanent basis.

Johnson took several belligerent steps of his own. He issued orders to military commanders in the South, limiting their powers and increasing the powers of the civil governments he had created in 1865. Then he removed military officers who were conscientiously enforcing Congress's new law, preferring commanders who allowed disqualified Confederates to vote. Finally, he tried to remove Secretary of War Stanton. With that attempt, the confrontation reached its climax.

Impeachment of President Johnson

Impeachment is a political procedure provided for in the Constitution as a remedy for crimes or serious abuses of power by presidents, federal judges, and other high government officials. Those impeached (judged or politically indicted) in the House are then tried in the Senate. Historically, this power has generally not been used as a means to investigate and judge the private lives of presidents, although in recent times it was used in this manner in the case of President Bill Clinton.

Twice in 1867, the House Judiciary Committee had considered impeachment of Johnson, rejecting the idea once and then recommending it by only a 5-to-4 vote. That recommendation was decisively defeated by the House. After Johnson tried to remove Stanton, however, a third attempt to impeach the president carried easily in early 1868. The indictment concentrated on his violation of the Tenure of Office Act, though many modern scholars regard his efforts to obstruct enforcement of the Reconstruction Act of 1867 as a far more serious offense.

Johnson's trial in the Senate lasted more than three months. The prosecution, led by Radicals, attempted to prove that Johnson was guilty of "high crimes and misdemeanors." But they also argued that the trial was a means to judge Johnson's performance, not a judicial determination of guilt or innocence. The Senate ultimately rejected such reasoning, which could have made removal from office a political weapon against any chief executive who disagreed with Congress. Although a majority of senators voted to convict Johnson, the prosecution fell one vote short of the necessary two-thirds majority. Johnson remained in office, politically weakened and with less than a year left in his term. Some Republicans backed away from impeachment because they had their eyes on the 1868 election and did not want to hurt their prospects of regaining the White House.

Election of 1868

In the 1868 presidential election, Ulysses S. Grant, running as a Republican, defeated Horatio Seymour, a New York Democrat. Grant was not a Radical, but his platform supported congressional Reconstruction and endorsed black suffrage in the South. (Significantly, Republicans stopped short of endorsing black suffrage in the North.) The Democrats, meanwhile, vigorously denounced Reconstruction and preached white supremacy. Indeed, in the 1868 election, the Democrats conducted the most openly racist campaign to that point in American history. Both sides waved the "bloody shirt," accusing each other as the villains of the war's sacrifices. By associating themselves with rebellion and with Johnson's repudiated program, the Democrats went down to defeat in all but eight states, though the popular vote was fairly close. Participating in their first presidential election ever on a wide scale, blacks decisively voted en masse for General Grant.

In office, Grant acted as an administrator of Reconstruction but not as its enthusiastic advocate. He vacillated in his dealings with the southern states, sometimes defending Republican regimes and sometimes currying favor with Democrats. On occasion, Grant called out federal troops to stop violence or enforce acts of Congress. But he never imposed a true military occupation on the South. Rapid demobilization had reduced a federal army of more than 1 million to 57,000 within a year of the surrender at Appomattox. Thereafter, the number of troops in the South continued to fall, until in 1874 there were only 4,000 in the southern states outside Texas. The later legend of "military rule," so important to southern claims of victimization during Reconstruction, was steeped in myth.

Fifteenth Amendment

In 1869, the Radicals pushed through the Fifteenth Amendment, the final major measure in the constitutional revolution of Reconstruction. This measure forbade states to deny the right to vote "on account of race, color, or previous condition of servitude." Such wording did not guarantee the right to vote. It deliberately left states free to restrict suffrage on other grounds so that northern states could continue to deny suffrage to women and certain groups of men—Chinese immigrants, illiterates, and those too poor to pay poll taxes.

Although several states outside the South refused to ratify, three-fourths of the states approved the measure, and the Fifteenth Amendment became law in 1870. It, too, had been a political compromise, and though African Americans rejoiced all across the land at its enactment, it left open the possibility for states to create countless qualification tests to obstruct voting in the future.

With passage of the Fifteenth Amendment, many Americans, especially supportive northerners, considered Reconstruction essentially completed. "Let us have done with Reconstruction," pleaded the *New York Tribune* in April 1870. "The country is tired and sick of it.... Let us have Peace!" But some northerners, like abolitionist Wendell Phillips, worried. "Our day," he warned, "is fast slipping away. Once let public thought float off from the great issue of the war, and it will take ... more than a generation to bring it back again."

POLITICS AND RECONSTRUCTION IN THE SOUTH

From the start, Reconstruction encountered the resistance of white southerners. In the black codes and in private attitudes, many whites stubbornly opposed emancipation, and the former planter class proved especially unbending because of their tremendous financial loss in slaves. In 1866, a Georgia newspaper frankly observed that "most of the white citizens believe that the institution of slavery was right, and ... they will believe that the condition, which comes nearest to slavery, that can now be established will be the best." And for many poor whites who had never owned slaves and yet had sacrificed enormously in the war, destitution, plummeting agricultural prices, disease, and the uncertainties of a growing urban industrialization drove them off land, toward cities, and into hatred of the very idea of black equality.

White Resistance

Fearing loss of control over their slaves, some planters attempted to postpone freedom by denying or misrepresenting events. Former slaves reported that their owners "didn't tell them it was freedom" or "wouldn't let [them] go." Agents of the Freedmen's Bureau reported that "the old system of slavery [is] working with even more rigor than formerly at a few miles distant from any point where U.S. troops are stationed." To hold onto their workers, some landowners claimed control over black children and used guardianship and apprentice laws to bind black families to the plantation.

Whites also blocked blacks from acquiring land. A few planters divided up plots among their slaves, but most condemned the idea of making blacks landowners. A Georgia woman whose family was known for its support of religious education for slaves was outraged that two property owners planned to "rent their lands to the Negroes!" Such action was, she declared, "injurious to the best interest of the community."

Adamant resistance by whites soon manifested itself in other ways, including violence. In one North Carolina town, a local magistrate clubbed a black man on a public street, and in several states bands of "Regulators" terrorized blacks who displayed any independence. Amid their defeat, many planters believed, as a South Carolinian put it, that blacks "can't be governed except with the whip." And after President Johnson encouraged the South to resist congressional Reconstruction, many white conservatives worked hard to capture the new state governments while others boycotted the polls in an attempt to defeat Congress's plans.

Black Voters and the Southern Republican Party   Very few black men stayed away from the polls. Enthusiastically and hopefully, they voted Republican. Most agreed with one man who felt he should "stick to the end with the party that freed me." Illiteracy did not prohibit blacks (or uneducated whites) from making intelligent choices. Although Mississippi's William Henry could read only "a little," he testified that he and his friends had no difficulty selecting the Republican ballot. "We stood around and watched," he explained. "We saw D. Sledge vote; he owned half the county. We knowed he voted Democratic so we voted the other ticket so it would be Republican." Women, who could not vote, encouraged their husbands and sons, and preachers exhorted their congregations to use the franchise. Zeal for voting spread through entire black communities.

Thanks to a large black turnout and the restrictions on prominent Confederates, a new southern Republican Party came to power in the constitutional conventions of 1868–1870. Republican delegates consisted of a sizable contingent of blacks (265 out of the total of just over 1,000 delegates throughout the South), some northerners who had moved to the South, and native southern whites who favored change. The new constitutions drafted by this Republican coalition were more democratic than anything previously adopted in the history of the South. They eliminated property qualifications for voting and holding office, and they turned many appointed offices into elective posts. They provided for public schools and institutions to care for the mentally ill, the blind, the deaf, the destitute, and the orphaned.

Southern blacks attempting to vote are halted by White Leaguers in this engraving by J. H. Wares. The black man doffing his cap holds a "Republican ticket" but it will not get him to the ballot box, guarded by the election judge with a loaded pistol.

Granger Collection

The conventions broadened women's rights in property holding and divorce. Usually, the goal was not to make women equal with men but to provide relief to thousands of suffering debtors. In white families left poverty-stricken by the war and weighed down by debt, it was usually the husband who had contracted the debts. Thus, giving women legal control over their own property provided some protection to their families.

Triumph of Republican Governments   Under these new constitutions, the southern states elected Republican-controlled governments. For the first time, the ranks of state legislators in 1868 included black southerners. It remained to be seen now how much social change these new governments would foster. Contrary to what white southerners would later claim, the Republican state governments did not disfranchise ex-Confederates as a group. James Lynch, a leading black politician from Mississippi, explained why African Americans shunned the "folly" of disfranchising whites. Unlike northerners who "can leave when it becomes too uncomfortable," landless former slaves "must be in friendly relations with the great body of the whites in the state. Otherwise ... peace can be maintained only by a standing army." Despised and lacking material or social power, southern Republicans strove for acceptance, legitimacy, and safe ways to gain a foothold in a depressed economy.

Far from being vindictive toward the race that had enslaved them, most southern blacks treated leading rebels with generosity and appealed to white southerners to adopt a spirit of fairness. In this way, the South's Republican Party condemned itself to defeat if white voters would not cooperate. Within a few years, most of the fledgling Republican parties in the southern states would be struggling for survival against violent white hostility. But for a time, some propertied whites accepted congressional Reconstruction as a reality.

Industrialization and Mill Towns   Reflecting northern ideals and southern necessity, the Reconstruction governments enthusiastically promoted industry. Accordingly, Reconstruction legislatures encouraged investment with loans, subsidies, and short-term exemptions from taxation. The southern railroad system was rebuilt and expanded, and coal and iron mining made possible Birmingham's steel plants. Between 1860 and 1880, the number of manufacturing establishments in the South nearly doubled.

This emphasis on big business, however, produced higher state debts and taxes, drew money away from schools and other programs, and multiplied possibilities for corruption in state legislatures. The alliance between business and government took firm hold, often at the expense of the needs of common farmers and laborers. It also locked Republicans into a conservative strategy and doomed them to failure in building support among poorer whites.

Poverty remained the lot of vast numbers of southern whites. On a daily basis during the Reconstruction years, they had to subordinate politics to the struggle for livelihood. The war had caused a massive one-time loss of income-producing wealth, such as livestock, and a steep decline in land values. From 1860 to 1880, the South's share of per capita income fell from nearly equal to only 51 percent of the national average. In many regions, the old planter class still ruled the best land and access to credit or markets.

As many poor whites and blacks found farming less tenable, they moved to cities and new mill towns. Industrialization did not sweep the South as it did the North, but it certainly laid deep roots. Attracting textile mills to southern towns became a competitive crusade. "Next to God," shouted a North Carolina evangelist, "what this town needs is a cotton mill!" In 1860, the South counted some 10,000 mill workers; by 1880, the number grew to 16,741 and by the end of the century, to 97,559. In thousands of human dramas, poor southerners began the multigenerational journey from farmer to mill worker and other forms of low-income urban wage earner.

Republicans and Racial Equality   Policies appealing to African American voters never went beyond equality before the law. In fact, the whites who controlled the southern Republican Party were reluctant to allow blacks a share of offices proportionate to their electoral strength. Aware of their weakness, black leaders did not push very far for revolutionary economic or social change. In every southern state, they led efforts to establish public schools, although they did not press for integrated facilities. In 1870, South Carolina passed the first comprehensive school law in the South. By 1875, 50 percent of black school-age children in that state were enrolled in school, and approximately one-third of the three thousand teachers were black.

Some African American politicians did fight for civil rights and integration. Many were from cities such as New Orleans or Mobile, where large populations of light-skinned free blacks had existed before the war. Their experience in such communities had made them sensitive to issues of status, and they spoke out for open and equal public accommodations. Laws requiring equal accommodations won passage, but they often went unenforced.

The vexing questions of land reform and enforcement of racial equality, however, all but overwhelmed the Republican governments. Land reform largely failed because in most states whites were in the majority, and former slaveowners controlled the best land and other sources of economic power. Economic progress was uppermost in the minds of most freedpeople. Black southerners needed land, and much land did fall into state hands for nonpayment of taxes. Such land was offered for sale in small lots. But most freedmen had too little cash to bid against investors or speculators. South Carolina established a land commission, but it could help only those with money to buy. Any widespread redistribution of land had to arise from Congress, which never supported such action.

Myth of "Negro Rule"   Within a few years, as centrists in both parties met with failure, white hostility to congressional Reconstruction began to dominate. Some conservatives had always wanted to fight Reconstruction through pressure and racist propaganda. They put economic and social pressure on blacks: one black Republican reported that "my neighbors will not employ me, nor sell me a farthing's worth of anything." Charging that the South had been turned over to ignorant blacks, conservatives deplored "black domination," which became a rallying cry for a return to white supremacy.

Such attacks were inflammatory propaganda and part of the growing myth of "Negro rule," which would serve as a central theme in battles over the memory of Reconstruction. African Americans participated in politics but hardly dominated or controlled events. They were a majority in only two out of ten state constitutional writing conventions (transplanted northerners were a majority in one). In the state legislatures, only in the lower house in South Carolina did blacks ever constitute a majority. Sixteen blacks won seats in Congress before Reconstruction was over, but none was ever elected governor. Only eighteen served in a high state office, such as lieutenant governor, treasurer, superintendent of education, or secretary of state.

In all, some four hundred blacks served in political office during the Reconstruction era, a signal achievement by any standard. Although they never dominated the process, they established a rich tradition of government service and civic activism. Elected officials, such as Robert Smalls in South Carolina, labored tirelessly for cheaper land prices, better healthcare, access to schools, and the enforcement of civil rights for black people. For too long, the black politicians of Reconstruction were the forgotten heroes of this seedtime of America's long civil rights movement.

Carpetbaggers and Scalawags

Conservatives also assailed the allies of black Republicans. Their propaganda denounced whites from the North as "carpetbaggers," greedy crooks planning to pour stolen tax revenues into their sturdy luggage made of carpet material. Immigrants from the North, who held the largest share of Republican offices, were all tarred with this rhetorical brush.

In fact, most northerners who settled in the South had come seeking business opportunities, as schoolteachers, or to find a warmer climate; most never entered politics. Those who did enter politics generally wanted to democratize the South and to introduce northern ways, such as industry and public education. Carpetbaggers' ideals were tested by hard times and ostracism by white southerners.

Carpetbaggers' real actions never matched the sensational stereotypes, although by the mid-1870s even some northerners who soured on Reconstruction or despaired over southern violence endorsed the images. Thomas Wentworth Higginson, a Union officer and commander of an African-American regiment during the Civil War, suggested that any Yankee politician who remained in the South by 1874 was, more likely than not, a "mean man," a "scoundrel," and "like Shakespeare's Shylock." And that same year, the African-American editors of the *Christian Recorder* distanced themselves from carpetbaggers. The "corrupt political vampires who rob and cheat and prey upon the prejudices of our people" and "feed upon the political carcass of a prostrate state," the paper insisted, were not black folks' allies. The white southern counterrevolutionaries seemed to be winning the propaganda war.

Conservatives also invented the term *scalawag* to discredit any native white southerner who cooperated with the Republicans. A substantial number of southerners did so, including some wealthy and prominent men. Most scalawags, however, were yeoman farmers, men from mountain areas and nonslaveholding districts who had been Unionists under the Confederacy. They saw that they could benefit from the education and opportunities promoted by Republicans. Sometimes banding together with freedmen, they pursued common class interests and hoped to make headway against the power of long-dominant planters. In the long run, however, the hope of such black-white coalitions floundered in the quicksand of racism.

Tax Policy and Corruption as Political Wedges

Taxation was a major problem for the Reconstruction governments. Republicans wanted to repair the war's destruction, stimulate industry, and support such new ventures as public schools. But the Civil War had destroyed much of the South's tax base. One category of valuable property—slaves—had disappeared entirely. And hundreds of thousands of citizens had lost much of the rest of their property— money, livestock, fences, and buildings—to the war. Thus, an increase in taxes (sales, excise, and property) was necessary even to maintain traditional services. Inevitably, Republican tax policies aroused strong opposition, especially among the yeomen.

Corruption was another serious charge levied against the Republicans. Unfortunately, it was often true. Many carpetbaggers and black politicians engaged in fraudulent schemes, sold their votes, or padded expenses, taking part in what scholars recognize was a nationwide surge of corruption in an age ruled by "spoilsmen". Corruption carried no party label, but the Democrats successfully pinned the blame on unqualified blacks and greedy carpetbaggers among southern Republicans.

Ku Klux Klan

All these problems hurt the Republicans, whose leaders also allowed factionalism along racial and class lines to undermine party unity. But in many southern states, the deathblow came through violence. The Ku Klux Klan (its members altered the Greek word for "circle," *kuklos*), a secret veterans' club that began in Tennessee in 1866, spread through the South, and rapidly evolved into a terrorist organization. Violence against African Americans occurred from the first days of Reconstruction but became far more organized and purposeful after 1867. Klansmen sought to frustrate Reconstruction and keep the freedmen in subjection. Nighttime harassment, whippings, beatings, rapes, and murders became common, as terrorism dominated some counties and regions.

Although the Klan tormented blacks who stood up for their rights as laborers or individuals, its main purpose was political. Lawless nightriders made active Republicans the target of their attacks. Leading white and black Republicans were killed in several states. After freedmen who worked for a South Carolina scalawag started voting, terrorists visited the plantation and, in the words of one victim, "whipped every … [black] man they could lay their hands on." Klansmen also attacked Union League clubs—Republican organizations that mobilized the black vote—and schoolteachers who were aiding the freedmen.

Klan violence was not a spontaneous outburst of racism; very specific social forces shaped and directed it. In North Carolina, for example, Alamance and Caswell Counties were the sites of the worst Klan violence. Slim Republican majorities there rested on cooperation between black voters and white yeomen, particularly those whose Unionism or discontent with the Confederacy had turned them against local Democratic officials. Together, these black and white Republicans had ousted officials long entrenched in power. The wealthy and powerful men in Alamance and Caswell who had lost their accustomed political control were the Klan's county officers and local chieftains. They organized a deliberate campaign of terror, recruiting members and planning atrocities. By intimidation and murder, the Klan weakened the Republican coalition and restored a Democratic majority.

Klan violence injured Republicans across the South. One of every ten black leaders who had been delegates to the 1867–1868 state constitutional conventions was attacked, seven fatally. In one judicial district of North Carolina, the Ku Klux Klan was responsible for twelve murders, over seven hundred beatings, and other acts of violence, including rape and arson. A single attack on Alabama Republicans in the town of Eutaw left four blacks dead and fifty-four wounded. In South Carolina, five hundred masked Klansmen lynched eight black prisoners at the Union County jail, and in nearby York County, the Klan committed at least eleven murders and hundreds of whippings. According to historian Eric Foner, the Klan "made it virtually impossible for Republicans to campaign or vote in large parts of Georgia."

Thus, a combination of difficult fiscal problems, Republican mistakes, racial hostility, and terror brought down the Republican regimes. In most southern states, Radical Reconstruction lasted only a few years (see Map 16.1). The most enduring failure of Reconstruction, however, was not political; it was social and economic. Reconstruction failed to alter the South's social structure or its distribution of wealth and power.

RETREAT FROM RECONSTRUCTION

During the 1870s, northerners increasingly lost the political will to sustain Reconstruction in the South as a vast economic and social transformation occurred in their own region as well as in the West. Radical Republicans like Albion Tourgée, a former Union soldier who moved to North Carolina and was elected a judge, condemned Congress's timidity. Turning the freedman out on his own without protection, said Tourgée, constituted "cheap philanthropy." Indeed, many African Americans believed that, during Reconstruction, the North "threw all the Negroes on the world without any way of getting along." As the North underwent its own transformations and lost interest in the South's dilemmas, Reconstruction collapsed.

Political Implications of Klan Terrorism   In one southern state after another, Democrats regained control, and they threatened to defeat Republicans in the North as well. Whites in the old Confederacy referred to this decline of Reconstruction as "southern redemption," and during the 1870s, "redeemer" Democrats claimed to be the saviors of the South from alleged "black domination" and "carpetbag rule." And for one of only a few times in American history, violence and terror emerged as a tactic in normal politics.

In 1870 and 1871, the violent campaigns of the Ku Klux Klan forced Congress to pass two Enforcement Acts and an anti-Klan law. These laws made actions by individuals against the civil and political rights of others a federal criminal offense for the first time. They also provided for election supervisors and permitted martial law and suspension of the writ of habeas corpus to combat murders, beatings, and threats by the Klan. Federal prosecutors used the laws rather selectively. In 1872 and 1873, Mississippi and the Carolinas saw many prosecutions; but in other states where violence flourished, the laws were virtually ignored. Southern juries sometimes refused to convict Klansmen; out of a total of 3,310 cases, only 1,143 ended in convictions. Although many Klansmen (roughly 2,000 in South Carolina alone) fled their state to avoid prosecution, and the Klan officially disbanded, the threat of violence did not end. Paramilitary organizations known as Rifle Clubs and Red Shirts often took the Klan's place.

Klan terrorism openly defied Congress, yet even on this issue there were ominous signs that the North's commitment to racial justice was fading. Some conservative but influential Republicans opposed the anti-Klan laws. Rejecting other Republicans' arguments that the Thirteenth, Fourteenth, and Fifteenth Amendments had made the federal government the protector of the rights of citizens, these dissenters echoed an old Democratic charge that Congress was infringing on states' rights. Senator Lyman Trumbull of Illinois declared that the states remained "the depositories of the rights of the individual." If Congress could punish crimes like assault or murder, he asked, "what is the need of the State governments?" For years, Democrats had complained of "centralization and consolidation"; now some Republicans seemed to agree with them. This opposition foreshadowed a more general revolt within Republican ranks in 1872.

Industrial Expansion and Reconstruction in the North   Both immigration and industrialization surged in the North. Between 1865 and 1873, 3 million immigrants entered the country, most settling in the industrial cities of the North and West. Within only eight years, postwar industrial production increased by 75 percent. For the first time, nonagricultural workers outnumbered farmers, and wage earners outnumbered independent craftsmen. And by 1873, only Britain's industrial output was greater than that of the United States. Government financial policies did much to bring about this rapid growth. Low taxes on investment and high tariffs on manufactured goods aided the growth of a new class of powerful industrialists, especially railroad entrepreneurs.

Railroads became the symbol of and the stimulus for the American age of capital. From 1865 to 1873, thirty-five thousand miles of new track were laid, a total exceeding the entire national rail network of 1860. Railroad building fueled the banking industry and made Wall Street the center of American capitalism. Eastern railroad magnates, such as Thomas Scott of the Pennsylvania Railroad, the largest corporation of its time, created economic empires with the assistance of huge government subsidies of cash and land. Railroad corporations also bought up mining operations, granaries, and lumber companies. In Congress and in every state legislature, big business now employed lobbyists to curry favor with government. Corruption ran rampant; some congressmen and legislators were paid annual retainers by major companies.

This soaring capitalist-political alliance led as well to an intensified struggle between labor and capital. As captains of industry amassed unprecedented fortunes in an age with no income tax, gross economic inequality polarized American society. The work force, worried a prominent Massachusetts business leader, was in a "transition state … living in boarding houses" and becoming a "permanent factory population." In Cincinnati, three large factories employed as many workers as the city's thousands of small shops. In New York or Philadelphia, workers increasingly lived in dark, unhealthy tenement housing. Thousands would list themselves on the census as "common laborer" or "general jobber." Many of the free labor maxims of the Republican Party were now under great duress. Did the individual work ethic guarantee social mobility in America or erode, under the pressure of profit making, into a world of unsafe factories, child labor, and declining wages? In 1868, the Republicans managed to pass an eight-hour workday bill in Congress that applied to federal workers. The "labor question" (see Chapter 18) now preoccupied northerners far more than the "southern" or the "freedmen" question.

Then, the Panic of 1873 ushered in over five years of economic contraction. Three million people lost their jobs as class attitudes diverged, especially in large cities. Debtors and the unemployed sought easy-money policies to spur economic expansion (workers and farmers desperately needed cash). Businessmen, disturbed by the widespread strikes and industrial violence that accompanied the panic, fiercely defended property rights and demanded "sound money" policies. The chasm between farmers and workers on the one hand, and wealthy industrialists on the other, grew ever wider.

Liberal Republican Revolt   Disenchanted with Reconstruction, a largely northern group calling itself the Liberal Republicans bolted the party in 1872 and nominated Horace Greeley, the famous editor of the *New York Tribune*, for president. The Liberal Republicans were a varied group, including foes of corruption and advocates of a lower tariff. Normally such disparate elements would not cooperate with one another, but two popular and widespread attitudes united them: distaste for federal intervention in the South and an elitist desire to let market forces and the "best men" determine policy and events.

The Democrats also gave their nomination to Greeley in 1872. The combination was not enough to defeat Grant, who won reelection, but it reinforced Grant's desire to avoid confrontation with white southerners. Greeley's campaign for North-South reunion, for "clasping hands across the bloody chasm," was a bit premature to win at the polls but was a harbinger of the future in American politics. Organized Blue-Gray fraternalism (gatherings of Union and Confederate veterans) began as early as 1874. Grant continued to use military force sparingly and in 1875 refused a desperate request from the governor of Mississippi for troops to quell racial and political terrorism in that state.

Dissatisfaction with Grant's administration grew during his second term. Strong-willed but politically naive, Grant made a series of poor appointments. His secretary of war, his private secretary, and officials in the Treasury and Navy Departments were involved in bribery or tax-cheating scandals. Instead of exposing the corruption, Grant defended the culprits. In 1874, as Grant's popularity and his party's prestige declined, the Democrats recaptured the House of Representatives, signaling the end of the Radical Republican vision of Reconstruction.

General Amnesty   The effect of Democratic gains in Congress was to weaken legislative resolve on southern issues. Congress had already lifted the political disabilities of the Fourteenth Amendment from many former Confederates. In 1872, it had adopted a sweeping Amnesty Act, which pardoned most of the remaining rebels and left only five hundred barred from political office holding. In 1875, Congress passed a Civil Rights Act, partly as a tribute to the recently deceased Charles Sumner, purporting to guarantee black people equal accommodations in public places, such as inns and theaters, but the bill was watered down and contained no effective provisions for enforcement. (The Supreme Court later struck down this law.)

Democrats regained control of four state governments before 1872 and a total of eight by the end of January 1876 (see Map 16.1). In the North, Democrats successfully stressed the failure and scandals of Reconstruction governments. As opinion shifted, many Republicans sensed that their constituents were tiring of southern issues and the legacies of the war. Sectional reconciliation now seemed crucial for commerce. The nation was expanding westward rapidly, and the South was a new frontier for investment.

The West, Race, and Reconstruction   Nowhere did the new complexity and violence of American race relations play out so vividly as in the West. As the Fourteenth Amendment and other enactments granted to blacks the beginnings of citizenship, other nonwhite peoples faced continued persecution. Across the West, the federal government pursued a policy of containment against Native Americans. In California, where white farmers and ranchers often forced Indians into captive labor, some civilians practiced a more violent form of "Indian hunting." By 1880, thirty years of such violence left an estimated forty-five hundred California Indians dead at the hands of white settlers.

In Texas and the Southwest, the rhetoric of national expansion still deemed Mexicans and other mixed-race Hispanics to be debased, "lazy," and incapable of self-government. And in California and other states of the Far West, thousands of Chinese immigrants became the victims of brutal violence. Few whites had objected to the Chinese who did the dangerous work of building railroads through the Rocky Mountains. But when the Chinese began to compete for urban, industrial jobs, great conflict emerged. Anticoolie clubs appeared in California in the 1870s, seeking laws against Chinese labor, fanning the flames of racism, and organizing vigilante attacks on Chinese workers and the factories that employed them. Western politicians sought white votes by pandering to prejudice, and in 1879 the new California constitution denied the vote to Chinese.

If we view America from coast to coast, and not merely on the North-South axis, the Civil War and Reconstruction years both dismantled racial slavery and fostered a volatile new racial complexity, especially in the West. During the same age when early anthropologists employed elaborate theories of "scientific" racism to determine a hierarchy of racial types, the West was a vast region of racial mixing and conflict. Some African Americans, despite generations of mixture with Native Americans, asserted that they were more like whites than the nomadic, "uncivilized" Indians, while others, like the Creek freedmen of Indian Territory, sought an Indian identity. In Texas, whites, Indians, blacks, and Hispanics had mixed for decades, and by the 1870s forced reconsideration in law and custom of who was white and who was not.

During Reconstruction, America was undergoing what one historian has called a reconstruction of the very idea of race itself. As it did so, tumbling into some of the darkest years of American race relations, the turbulence of the expanding West reinforced the new nationalism and the reconciliation of North and South based on a resurgent white supremacy.

Foreign Expansion Following the Civil War, pressure for expansion reemerged (see Chapter 22), and in 1867 Secretary of State William H. Seward arranged a vast addition of territory to the national domain through the purchase of Alaska from Russia. Opponents ridiculed Seward's $7.2 million venture, calling Alaska "Frigidia," "the Polar Bear Garden," and "Walrussia." But Seward convinced important congressmen of Alaska's economic potential, and other lawmakers favored the dawning of friendship with Russia.

Also in 1867, the United States took control of the Midway Islands, a thousand miles northwest of Hawai'i. And in 1870, President Grant tried unsuccessfully to annex the Dominican Republic. Seward and his successor, Hamilton Fish, also resolved troubling Civil War grievances against Great Britain. Through diplomacy they arranged a financial settlement of claims on Britain for damage done by the *Alabama* and other cruisers built in England and sold to the Confederacy. They recognized that sectional reconciliation in Reconstruction America would serve new ambitions for world commerce and expansion.

Judicial Retreat from Reconstruction Meanwhile, the Supreme Court played its part in the northern retreat from Reconstruction. During the Civil War, the Court had been cautious and inactive. Reaction to the *Dred Scott*

LINKS TO THE WORLD

The "Back to Africa" Movement

In the wake of the Civil War, and especially after the despairing end of Reconstruction, some African Americans sought to leave the South for the American West or North, but also to relocate to Africa. Liberia had been founded in the 1820s by the white-led American Colonization Society (ACS), an organization dedicated to relocating blacks "back" in Africa. Some eleven thousand African Americans had emigrated voluntarily to Liberia by 1860, with largely disastrous results. Many died of disease, and others felt disoriented in the strange new land and ultimately returned to the United States.

Reconstruction reinvigorated the emigration impulse, especially in cotton-growing districts where blacks had achieved political power before 1870 but were crushed by violence and intimidation in the following decade. When blacks felt confident in their future, the idea of leaving America fell quiet; but when threatened or under assault, whole black communities dreamed of a place where they could become an independent "race," a "people," or a "nation" as their appeals often announced. Often that dream, more imagined than realized, lay in West Africa.

Before the Civil War, most blacks had denounced the ACS for its racism and its hostility to their sense of American birthright. But letters of inquiry flooded into the organization's headquarters after 1875. Wherever blacks felt the reversal of the promise of emancipation the keenest, they formed local groups such as the Liberia Exodus Association of Pinesville, Florida; or the Liberian Exodus Arkansas Colony; and many others.

At emigration conventions, and especially in churches, blacks penned letters to the ACS asking for maps or any information about a new African homeland. Some local organizers would announce eighty or a hundred recruits "widawake for Liberia," although such enthusiasm rarely converted into an Atlantic voyage. The impulse was genuine, however. "We wants to be a People," wrote the leader of a Mississippi emigration committee; "we can't be it heare and find that we ar compel to leve this Cuntry." Henry Adams, a former Louisiana slave, Union soldier, and itinerant emigration organizer, advocated Liberia, but also supported "Kansas fever" with both Biblical and natural rights agruments. "God ... has a place and a land for all his people," he wrote in 1879. "It is not that we think the soil climate or temperature" elsewhere is "more congenial to us— but it is the idea that pervades our breast 'that at last we will be free,' free from oppression, free from tyranny, free from bulldozing, murderous southern whites."

By the 1890s, Henry McNeal Turner, a free-born former Georgia Reconstruction politician, and now Bishop of the African Methodist Episcopal Church, made three trips to Africa and vigorously campaigned through press and pulpit for blacks to "Christianize" and "civilize" Africa. Two shiploads of African Americans sailed to Liberia, although most returned disillusioned or ill. Turner's plan of "Africa for the Africans" was as much a religious vision as an emigration system, but like all such efforts then and since, it reflected the despair of racial conditions in America more than realities in Africa. The numbers do not tell the tale of the depth of the impulse in this link to the world: in 1879–1880, approximately twenty-five thousand southern blacks moved to Kansas, whereas from 1865 to 1900, just under four thousand emigrated to West Africa.

decision (1857) had been so vehement, and the Union's wartime emergency so great, that the Court had avoided interference with government actions. The justices breathed a collective sigh of relief, for example, when legal technicalities prevented them from reviewing the case of Clement Vallandigham, a Democratic opponent of

Lincoln's war effort who had been convicted by a military tribunal of aiding the enemy. But in 1866, a similar case, *Ex parte Milligan*, reached the Court.

Lambdin P. Milligan of Indiana had plotted to free Confederate prisoners of war and overthrow state governments. For these acts, a military court sentenced Milligan, a civilian, to death. Milligan challenged the authority of the military tribunal, claiming he had a right to a civil trial. Reasserting its authority, the Supreme Court declared that military trials were illegal when civil courts were open and functioning.

In the 1870s, the Court successfully renewed its challenge to Congress's actions when it narrowed the meaning and effectiveness of the Fourteenth Amendment. The *Slaughter-House* cases (1873) began in 1869, when the Louisiana legislature granted one company a monopoly on the slaughtering of livestock in New Orleans. Rival butchers in the city promptly sued. Their attorney, former Supreme Court justice John A. Campbell, argued that Louisiana had violated the rights of some of its citizens in favor of others. The Fourteenth Amendment, Campbell contended, had revolutionized the constitutional system by bringing individual rights under federal protection, safeguarding them from state interference.

But in the *Slaughter-House* decision, the Supreme Court dealt a stunning blow to the scope of the Fourteenth Amendment. The Court declared state citizenship and national citizenship separate. National citizenship involved only matters such as the right to travel freely from state to state, and only such narrow rights, held the Court, were protected by the Fourteenth Amendment.

The Supreme Court also concluded that the butchers who sued had not been deprived of their rights or property in violation of the due-process clause of the amendment. Shrinking from a role as "perpetual censor" for civil rights, the Court's majority declared that the framers of the recent amendments had not intended to "destroy" the federal system, in which the states exercised "powers for domestic and local government, including the regulation of civil rights." Thus, the justices severely limited the amendment's potential for securing and protecting the rights of black citizens—its original intent.

The next day, the Court decided *Bradwell v. Illinois*, a case in which Myra Bradwell, a female attorney, had been denied the right to practice law in Illinois because she was a married woman, and hence not considered a free agent. Pointing to the Fourteenth Amendment, Bradwell's attorneys contended the state had unconstitutionally abridged her "privileges and immunities" as a citizen. The Supreme Court rejected her claim, declaring a woman's "paramount destiny ... to fulfill the noble and benign offices of wife and mother."

In 1876, the Court weakened the Reconstruction era amendments even further by emasculating the enforcement clause of the Fourteenth Amendment and revealing deficiencies inherent in the Fifteenth Amendment. In *U.S. v. Cruikshank,* the Court overruled the conviction under the 1870 Enforcement Act of Louisiana whites who had attacked a meeting of blacks and conspired to deprive them of their rights. The justices ruled that the Fourteenth Amendment did not give the federal government power to act against these whites who had murdered possibly as many as one hundred blacks. The duty of protecting citizens' equal rights, the Court said, "rests alone with the States." Such judicial conservatism, practiced by justices, all of whom had been appointed by Republican presidents Lincoln and Grant, left a profound imprint down through the next century, blunting the revolutionary potential in the Civil War amendments.

Disputed Election of 1876 and Compromise of 1877

As the 1876 elections approached, most political observers saw that the nation was increasingly focused on economic issues and that the North was no longer willing to pursue the goals of Reconstruction. The results of a disputed presidential election confirmed this fact. Samuel J. Tilden, the Democratic governor of New York, ran strongly in the South and needed only one more electoral vote to triumph over Rutherford B. Hayes, the Republican nominee. Nineteen electoral votes from Louisiana, South Carolina, and Florida (the only southern states not yet under Democratic rule) were disputed; both Democrats and Republicans claimed to have won in those states despite fraud committed by their opponents (see Map 16.2).

To resolve this unprecedented situation, Congress established a fifteen-member electoral commission. Membership on the commission was to be balanced between Democrats and Republicans. Because the Republicans held the majority in Congress, they prevailed, 8 to 7, on every attempt to count the returns, with commission members voting along strict party lines. Hayes would become president if Congress accepted the commission's findings.

Congressional acceptance was not certain. Democrats controlled the House and could filibuster to block action on the vote. Many citizens worried that the nation would slip once again into civil war, as some southerners vowed, "Tilden or Fight!" The crisis was resolved when Democrats acquiesced in the election of Hayes based on a "deal" cut in a Washington hotel between Hayes's supporters and southerners who wanted federal aid to railroads, internal improvements, federal patronage, and removal of troops from southern states. Northern and southern Democrats simply decided not to contest the election of a Republican who was not going to continue Reconstruction policies in the South. Thus, Hayes became president, inaugurated

MAP 16.2 Presidential Election of 1876 and the Compromise of 1877

In 1876, a combination of solid southern support and Democratic gains in the North gave Samuel Tilden the majority of popular votes, but Rutherford B. Hayes won the disputed election in the electoral college, after a deal satisfied Democratic wishes for an end to Reconstruction.

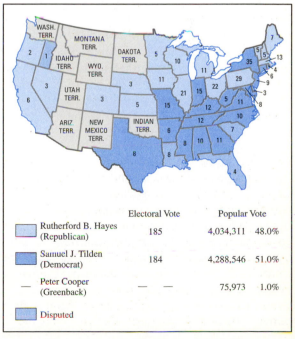

	Electoral Vote	Popular Vote	
Rutherford B. Hayes (Republican)	185	4,034,311	48.0%
Samuel J. Tilden (Democrat)	184	4,288,546	51.0%
Peter Cooper (Greenback)	— —	75,973	1.0%
Disputed			

© Cengage Learning

privately inside the White House to avoid any threat of violence. Southerners re-lished their promises of economic aid, and Reconstruction was unmistakably over.

Southern Democrats rejoiced, but African Americans grieved over the betrayal of their hopes for equality. The Civil War had brought emancipation, and Recon-struction had guaranteed their rights under law. But events and attitudes in larger white America were foreboding. In a Fourth of July speech in Washington, D.C., in 1875, Frederick Douglass anticipated this predicament. He reflected anxiously on the American centennial to be celebrated the following year. The nation, Douglass feared, would "lift to the sky its million voices in one grand Centennial hosanna of peace and good will to all the white race … from gulf to lakes and from sea to sea." Douglass looked back on fifteen years of unparalleled change for his people and worried about the hold of white supremacy on America's historical memory: "If war among the whites brought peace and liberty to the blacks, what will peace among the whites bring?" Dou-glass's question would echo down through American political culture for decades.

SUMMARY

Reconstruction left a contradictory record. It was an era of tragic aspirations and failures but also of unprecedented legal, political, and social change. The Union vic-tory brought about an increase in federal power, stronger nationalism, sweeping federal intervention in the southern states, and landmark amendments to the Con-stitution. But northern commitment to make these changes endure had eroded, and the revolution remained unfinished. The mystic sense of promise for new lives and liberties among the freedpeople, had eroded if not died.

The North embraced emancipation, black suffrage, and constitutional alterations strengthening the central government. But it did so to defeat the rebellion and se-cure the peace. As the pressure of these crises declined, Americans, especially in the North, retreated from Reconstruction. The American people and the courts maintained a preference for state authority and a distrust of federal power. The ide-ology of free labor dictated that property should be respected and that individuals should be self-reliant. Racism endured and transformed into the even more virulent forms of Klan terror and theories of black degeneration. Concern for the human rights of African Americans and other reforms frequently had less appeal than mon-eymaking in an individualistic, industrializing society.

New challenges began to overwhelm the aims of Reconstruction. How would the country develop its immense resources in an increasingly interconnected national economy? Could farmers, industrial workers, immigrants, and capitalists coexist? Industrialization not only promised prosperity but also wrought increased exploita-tion of labor. Moreover, industry increased the nation's power and laid the founda-tion for an enlarged American role in international affairs. The American imagination again turned to the conquest of new frontiers.

In the wake of the Civil War, Americans faced two profound tasks—the achieve-ment of healing and the dispensing of justice. Both had to occur, but they never de-veloped in historical balance. Making sectional reunion compatible with black freedom and equality overwhelmed the imagination in American political culture, and the nation still faced much of this dilemma more than a century later.

17

$$\blacktriangledown$$

THE DEVELOPMENT OF THE WEST
1865–1900

CHAPTER OUTLINE

• The Economic Activities of Native Peoples • The Transformation of Native Cultures • Life on the Natural Resource Frontier • Irrigation and Transportation • *LINKS TO THE WORLD* *The Australian Frontier* • Farming the Plains • The Ranching Frontier • Summary

---

THE ECONOMIC ACTIVITIES OF NATIVE PEOPLES

Native Americans settled the West long before other Americans migrated there. Neither passive nor powerless in the face of nature, Indians had been shaping their environment—for better and for worse—for centuries. Nevertheless, almost all native economic systems weakened in the late nineteenth century. Several factors explain why and how these declines happened.

Subsistence Cultures

Western Indian communities varied. Some natives inhabited permanent settlements; others lived in a series of temporary camps. Seldom completely isolated, most Indians were both participants and recipients in a flow of goods, culture, language, and disease carried by bands that migrated from one region to another. Regardless of their type of community, all Indians based their economy to differing degrees on four activities: crop growing; livestock raising; hunting, fishing, and gathering; and trading and raiding. Corn was the most common crop; sheep and horses, acquired from Spanish colonizers and from other Indians, were the livestock; and buffalo (American bison) were the primary prey of hunts. Indians raided one another for food, tools, and horses, which in turn they used in trading with other Indians and with whites. They also attacked to avenge wrongs and to oust competitors from hunting grounds. To achieve their standards of living, Indians tried to balance their economic systems. When a buffalo hunt failed, they subsisted on crops. When crops failed, they could still hunt buffalo and steal food and horses in a raid or trade livestock and furs for necessities.

CHRONOLOGY

1862	Homestead Act grants free land to citizens who live on and improve the land
	Morrill Land Grant Act gives states public land to sell in order to finance agricultural and industrial colleges
1864	Chivington's militia massacres Black Kettle's Cheyennes at Sand Creek
1869	First transcontinental railroad completed
1872	Yellowstone becomes first national park
1876	Lakotas and Cheyennes ambush Custer's federal troops at Little Big Horn, Montana
1877	Nez Percé Indians under Young Joseph surrender to U.S. troops
1878	Timber and Stone Act allows citizens to buy timberland cheaply but also enables large companies to acquire huge tracts of forest land
1879	Carlisle School for Indians established in Pennsylvania
1881–82	Chinese Exclusion Acts prohibit Chinese immigration to the United States
1883	National time zones established
1884	U.S. Supreme Court first denies Indians as wards under government protection
1887	Dawes Severalty Act ends communal ownership of Indian lands and grants land allotments to individual native families
1887–88	Devastating winter on Plains destroys countless livestock and forces farmers into economic hardship
1890	Final suppression of Plains Indians by U.S. Army at Wounded Knee
	Census Bureau announces closing of the frontier
	Yosemite National Park established
1892	Muir helps found Sierra Club
1902	Newlands Reclamation Act passed

For Indians on the Great Plains, whether nomads such as the Lakotas ("Sioux") or village dwellers such as the Pawnees, everyday life focused on the buffalo. They cooked and preserved buffalo meat; fashioned hides into clothing, moccasins, and blankets; used sinew for thread and bowstrings; and carved tools from bones and horns. Buffalo were so valuable that Pawnees and Lakotas often fought over access to herds. Plains Indians also depended on horses, which they used for transportation and hunting, and as symbols of wealth. To provide food for their herds, Plains Indians altered the environment by periodically setting fire to tall-grass prairies. The fires burned away dead plants, facilitating growth of new grass in the spring so that horses could feed all summer.

In the Southwest, Indians led varying lifestyles, depending on the environment. For example, among the O'odham of southeastern Arizona and northwest Mexico, whose name translates into "The People," some groups grew irrigated crops in the few river valleys while those who inhabited the mountainous and desert regions followed more of a hunter-gatherer existence. Once foreigners arrived, The People traded for what was useful—tools, cloth, tobacco, livestock—and aided in raids against the Apache, who were enemies of both whites and O'odham. (Significantly, the Apache called themselves Nnee, which also meant "The People.") The Navaho (or Dine', also meaning "The People") were herders, whose sheep, goats, and horses provided status and security.

What buffalo were to Plains Indians and sheep were to southwestern Indians, salmon were to Indians of the Northwest. Before the mid-nineteenth century, the Columbia River and its tributaries supported the densest population of native peoples in North America, all of whom fished for salmon in the summer and stored dried fish for the winter. To harvest fish, the Clatsops, Klamath, and S'Klallams developed technologies of stream diversion, platform construction over the water, and special baskets. Like natives of other regions, many of these Indians traded for horses, buffalo robes, beads, cloth, and knives.

Horses, sometimes numbering more than one hundred, and women and children, usually twenty or thirty, were a liability as well as a help to a Plains Indian camp. The horses competed with buffalo for valuable pasturage, and the women and children made camps vulnerable when white soldiers attacked.

Slaughter of Buffalo

On the Plains and in parts of the Southwest, native worlds began to dissolve after 1850, when white migrants entered and competed with Indians for access to and control over natural resources. Perceiving buffalo and Indians as hindrances to their ambitions, whites endeavored to eliminate both. The U.S. Army refused to enforce treaties that reserved hunting grounds for exclusive Indian use, so railroads sponsored buffalo hunts in which eastern sportsmen shot at the bulky targets from slow-moving trains. Some hunters collected from $1 to $3 from tanneries for hides that were sent east for use mainly as belts to drive industrial machinery; others did not even stop to pick up their kill.

Unbeknownst to both Indians and whites, however, a complex combination of circumstances had already doomed the buffalo before the slaughter of the late 1800s. Natives themselves contributed to the depletion of the herds by increasing their kills, especially to trade hides with whites and other Indians. Also, a period of generally dry years in the 1840s and 1850s had forced Indians to set up camps in river basins, where they competed with buffalo for space and water. As a result, the buffalo were pushed out of nourishing grazing territory and faced threats of starvation. When whites arrived on the Plains, they, too, sought to settle in the same river basin areas, further forcing buffalo away from nutritious grasslands. At the same time, lethal animal diseases, such as anthrax and brucellosis, brought in by white-owned livestock, decimated buffalo already weakened by malnutrition and drought. Increasing numbers of horses, oxen, and sheep, owned by white newcomers as well as by some Indians, also upset the buffalo's grazing patterns by devouring grasses they depended on at certain times of the year. In sum, human and environmental shocks created vulnerability among the buffalo, to which mass killing only struck the final blow. By the 1880s, only a few hundred of the 25 million buffalo estimated on the Plains in 1820 remained.

Decline of Salmon

In the Northwest, the basic wild source of Indian food supply, salmon, suffered a fate similar to that of the buffalo, but for different reasons. White commercial fishermen and canneries moved into the Columbia and Willamette River valleys during the 1860s and 1870s, and they harvested increasing numbers of salmon running upriver to spawn before laying their eggs, so the fish supply was not being replenished. By the 1880s, they had greatly diminished salmon runs on the Columbia, and by the early 1900s, construction of dams on the river and its tributaries further impeded the salmon's ability to reproduce. The U.S. government protected Indian fishing rights, but not the supply of fish on the river. Hatcheries helped restore some of this supply, but dams built to provide power, combined with overfishing and pollution, diminished salmon stocks.

THE TRANSFORMATION OF NATIVE CULTURES

Buffalo slaughter and salmon reduction undermined Indian subsistence, but a unique mix of human demography contributed as well. For most of the nineteenth century, white populations that migrated into western lands inhabited by Indians were overwhelmingly young and male. In 1870, white men outnumbered white women by three to two in California, two to one in Colorado, and two to one in Dakota Territory. By 1900, preponderances of men remained throughout these places. Most of these males were unmarried and in their twenties and thirties, the stage of life when they were most prone to violent behavior. In other words, the whites with whom Indians were most likely to come into contact first were traders, trappers, soldiers, prospectors, and cowboys—almost all of whom owned guns and had few qualms about using their weapons against animals and humans who got in their way.

Western Men   Moreover, these men subscribed to prevailing attitudes that Indians were primitive, lazy, devious, and cruel. Such contempt made exploiting and killing natives all the easier, and whites often justified violence against Indians by claiming preemptive defense of threats to life and property. When Indians raided white settlements, they sometimes mutilated bodies, burned buildings, and kidnapped women, acts that were embellished in campfire stories, pamphlets, and popular fiction—all of which reinforced images of Indians as savages. Inside the bachelor society of saloons and cabins, men boasted of their exploits in Indian fighting and showed off trophies of scalps and other body parts taken from victims.

Indian warriors, too, were young, armed, and prone to violence. Valuing bravery and vengeance, they boasted of fighting white interlopers. But Indian communities contrasted with those of whites in that they contained excesses of women, the elderly, and children, making native bands less mobile and therefore vulnerable to attack. They also were susceptible to bad habits of bachelor white society. Indians copied white males' behavior of bingeing on cheap whiskey and indulging in prostitution. The syphilis and gonorrhea that Indian men contracted from Indian women infected by white men killed many and reduced natives' ability to reproduce, a consequence that their populations, already declining from smallpox and other diseases spread by whites, could not afford. Thus, the age and gender structure of the white frontier population, combined with attitudes of racial contempt, created a further threat to western Indians' existence.

Government Policy and Treaties   Government policy reinforced efforts to remove Indians from the path of white ambitions, but the organization of Indian groups caused confusion. North American natives were organized not so much into tribes, as whites believed, as into countless bands and confederacies in the Plains and villages in the Southwest and Northwest. Some two hundred languages and dialects separated these groups, making it difficult for Indians to unite against white invaders. Although a language group could be defined as a tribe, separate bands and clans within each group had their own leaders, and seldom did a chief hold widespread power. Moreover, bands often spent more time battling among themselves than with white settlers.

Nevertheless, the U.S. government needed some way of categorizing Indians so as to fashion a policy toward them. It did so by imputing more meaning to tribal organization than was warranted. After 1795, American officials considered Indian tribes to be separate nations with which they could make treaties that ensured peace and defined boundaries between Indian and white lands. This was a faulty assumption because chiefs who agreed to a treaty did not always speak for all members of a band and the group would not necessarily abide by an agreement. Moreover, white settlers seldom accepted treaties as guarantees of Indians' land rights. On the Plains, whites assumed they could settle wherever they wished, and they rarely hesitated to commandeer choice farmland along river basins. In the Northwest, whites considered treaties protecting Indians' fishing rights on the Columbia River to be nuisances and ousted Indians from the best locations so that they could use mechanical devices to harvest fish. As white migrants pressed into Indian territories, treaties made one week were violated the next.

Reservation Policy   Prior to the 1880s, the federal government tried to force western Indians onto reservations, where, it was thought, they could be "civilized." Reservations usually consisted of those areas of a group's previous territory that were least desirable to whites. When assigning Indians to such parcels, the government promised protection from white encroachment and agreed to provide food, clothing, and other necessities.

Reservation policy helped make way for the market economy. In the early years of contact in the West, trade had benefited both Indians and whites and had taken place on a nearly equal footing, much as it had between eastern Indians and whites in the preceding century. Indians acquired clothing, guns, and horses from whites in return for furs, jewelry, and, sometimes, military assistance against other Indians. In the West, however, whites' needs and economic power grew disproportionate to Indians' needs and power. Indians became more dependent, and whites increasingly dictated what was to be traded and on what terms. For example, white traders persuaded Navajo weavers in the Southwest to produce heavy rugs suitable for eastern customers and to adopt new designs and colors to boost sales. Meanwhile, Navajos raised fewer crops and were forced to buy food because the market economy undermined their subsistence agriculture. Soon they were selling land and labor to whites as well, and their dependency made it easier to force them onto reservations.

Reservation policy had degrading consequences. First, Indians had no say over their own affairs on reservations. Supreme Court decisions in 1884 and 1886 defined them as wards (falling, like helpless children, under government protection) and denied them the right to become U.S. citizens. Thus, they were unprotected by the Fourteenth and Fifteenth Amendments, which had extended to African Americans the privileges and legal protections of citizenship. Second, pressure from white farmers, miners, and herders who continually sought Indian lands made it difficult for the government to preserve reservations intact. Third, the government ignored native history, even combining on the same reservation Indian bands that habitually had warred against each other. Rather than serving as civilizing communities, reservations weakened every aspect of Indian life, except the resolve to survive.

Native Resistance   Not all Indians succumbed to market forces and reservation restrictions. Apache bands long had raided white settlements in the Southwest and continued their insurgence even after most of their people had been forced onto reservations. Their raiding ended only after the last of their leaders, the Chiricahua chief Geronimo, was captured in 1886. Pawnees in the Midwest resisted the disadvantageous deals that white traders tried to impose on them. In the Northwest, Nez Percé Indians defied being forced onto a reservation by fleeing to Canada in 1877. They successfully eluded U.S. troops and their Crow and Cheyenne scouts over 1,800 miles of rugged terrain, but when they reached Montana, their leader, Young Joseph, decided they could not succeed, and he ended the flight. Sent to a reservation, Joseph repeatedly petitioned the government to return his peoples' ancestral lands, but his appeals went unheeded.

As they had done earlier in the East, whites responded to western Indian defiance with military aggression. The attitude of many resembled that of an Arizona journalist who wrote, "extermination is our only hope, and the sooner the better." In 1860, for example, Navajos, reacting to U.S. military pressure, carried out a destructive raid on Fort Defiance in Arizona Territory. In reprisal, the army eventually attacked and starved the Navajo into submission, destroying their fields, houses, and livestock, and in 1863–1864 forced them on a "Long Walk" from their homelands to a reservation at Bosque Redondo in New Mexico. Also in 1864, in order to eliminate natives who blocked white ambitions in the Sand Creek region of Colorado, a militia commanded by Methodist minister John Chivington attacked a Cheyenne band led by Black Kettle, killing almost every Indian. In 1879, four thousand U.S. soldiers forced a surrender from Utes who already had given up most of their ancestral territory in western Colorado but were resisting further concessions.

The most publicized battle occurred in June 1876, when 2,500 Lakotas and Cheyennes led by Chiefs Rain-in-the-Face, Sitting Bull, and Crazy Horse surrounded and annihilated 256 government troops led by the rash Colonel George A. Custer near the Little Big Horn River in southern Montana. Although Indians consistently demonstrated military skill in such battles, shortages of supplies and relentless pursuit by U.S. soldiers, including African American units of Union Army veterans called Buffalo Soldiers (so named by the Cheyennes and Comanches they fought), eventually overwhelmed armed Indian resistance. Native Americans were not so much conquered in battle as they were harassed and starved into submission.

Reform of Indian Policy   In the 1870s and 1880s, reformers and government officials sought more purposely than in the past to "civilize" and "uplift" natives through landholding and education. This meant changing native identities and outlawing customs deemed to be "savage and barbarous." In this regard, the United States copied imperialist policies of other nations, such as the French, who banned native religious ceremonies in their Pacific island colonies, and the British, who jailed African religious leaders. The American government determined to persuade Indians to abandon their traditional cultures and adopt presumed American values of ambition, thrift, and materialism.

At the same time, other groups argued for sympathetic—and sometimes patronizing—treatment. Reform treatises, such as George Manypenny's *Our Indian*

Wards (1880) and Helen Hunt Jackson's *A Century of Dishonor* (1881), plus unfavorable comparison with Canada's management of Indian affairs aroused the American conscience. Canada had granted native peoples the rights of British subjects and proceeded more slowly than the United States in efforts to acculturate Indians. A high rate of intermarriage between Indians and Canadian whites also promoted smoother relations.

In the United States, the most active Indian reform organizations were the Women's National Indian Association (WNIA) and the Indian Rights Association (IRA). The WNIA sought to use women's domestic skills of nurture and compassion to help people in need and urged gradual assimilation of Indians. The IRA, which was more influential but numbered few Native Americans among its members, advocated citizenship and landholding by individual Indians. Most reformers believed Indians were culturally inferior to whites and assumed Indians could succeed economically only if they embraced middle-class values of diligence and education.

Reformers particularly deplored Indians' sexual division of labor. Native women seemed to do all the work—tending crops, raising children, cooking, curing hides, making tools and clothes—while being servile to men, who hunted but were otherwise idle. Ignoring the fact that white men sometimes mistreated white women, groups such as the WNIA and IRA wanted Indian men to bear more responsibilities; treat Indian women more respectfully; and resemble male heads of white, middle-class households. But when Indian men and women adopted this model of white society, in which women were supposed to be submissive and private, Indian women lost much of the economic independence and power over daily life that they once had.

Zitkala-Sa

Some exceptional Indians managed to use white-controlled education to their advantage. Zitkala-Sa (Red Bird) was a Yankton Sioux born on Pine Ridge reservation in South Dakota in 1876. At age twelve, she was sent to a Quaker boarding school in Indiana and later attended Earlham College and the Boston Conservatory of Music. She became an accomplished orator and violinist, but her major contribution was her writing on behalf of her people's needs and the preservation of their cultures. In 1901, Zitkala-Sa published *Old Indian Legends*, in which she translated Sioux oral tradition into stories. She wrote other pieces for *Harper's* and *Atlantic Monthly* and served in various capacities on the Standing Rock and Ute reservations. In 1902, Zitkala-Sa married a mixed-race army captain who had taken the name Ray Bonnin and became known as Gertrude Bonnin. Subsequently, she was elected the first full-blooded Indian secretary of the Society of American Indians and served as editor of *American Indian Magazine*, all the while advocating for Indian rights.

Dawes Severalty Act

In 1887, Congress reversed its reservation policy and passed the Dawes Severalty Act. The act, supported by reformers, authorized dissolution of community-owned Indian property and granted land allotments to individual Indian families. The government held that land in trust for twenty-five years, so families could not sell their allotments. The law also awarded citizenship to all who accepted allotments (an act of

Congress in 1906 delayed citizenship for those Indians who had not yet taken their allotment). It also entitled the government to sell unallocated land to whites.

Indian policy, as implemented by the Interior Department, now took on two main features, both of which aimed at assimilating Indians into white American culture. First and foremost, as required by the Dawes Act, the government distributed reservation land to individual families in the belief that the American institution of private property would create productive citizens and integrate Indians into the larger society. As one official stated, the goal was to "weaken and destroy [Indians'] tribal relations and individualize them by giving each a separate home and having them subsist by industry." Second, officials believed that Indians would abandon their "barbaric" habits more quickly if their children were educated in boarding schools away from the reservations.

The Dawes Act represented a Euro-American and Christian world-view, an earnest but narrow belief that a society of families headed by men was the most desired model. Government agents and reformers were joined by educators who viewed schools as tools to create a patriotic, industrious citizenry. Using the model of Hampton Institute, founded in Virginia in 1869 to educate newly freed slaves, educators helped establish the Carlisle School in Pennsylvania in 1879, which served as the flagship of the government's Indian school system. In keeping with European American custom, the boarding schools imposed white-defined sex roles: boys were taught farming and carpentry, and girls learned sewing, cleaning, and cooking.

Ghost Dance

In 1890, the government made one last show of force. With active resistance suppressed, some Lakotas and other groups turned to the religion of the Ghost Dance as a spiritual means of preserving native culture. Inspired by a Paiute prophet named Wovoka, the Ghost Dance consisted of movement in a circle until dancers reached a trancelike state and envisioned dead ancestors who, dancers believed, heralded a day when buffalo would return and all elements of white civilization, including guns and whiskey, would be buried. The Ghost Dance expressed this messianic vision in a ritual involving several days of dancing and meditation.

Ghost Dancers forswore violence but appeared threatening when they donned sacred shirts they believed would repel the white man's bullets. As the religion spread, government agents became alarmed about the possibility of renewed Indian uprisings. Charging that the cult was anti-Christian, the army began arresting Ghost Dancers. Late in 1890, the government sent the Seventh Cavalry, Custer's old regiment, to detain Lakotas moving toward Pine Ridge, South Dakota. Although the Indians were starving and seeking shelter, the army assumed they were armed for revolt. Overtaking the band at a creek called Wounded Knee, the troops massacred an estimated three hundred men, women, and children in the snow.

The Losing of the West

Indian wars and the Dawes Act effectively accomplished what whites wanted and Indians feared: it reduced native control over land. Eager speculators induced Indians to sell their newly acquired property, in spite of federal safeguards against such practices.

Between 1887 and the 1930s, native landholdings dwindled from 138 million acres to 52 million. Land-grabbing whites were particularly cruel to the Ojibwas of the northern plains. In 1906, Senator Moses E. Clapp of Minnesota attached to an Indian appropriations bill a rider declaring that mixed-blood adults on the White Earth reservation were "competent" (meaning educated in white ways) enough to sell their land without having to observe the twenty-five-year waiting period stipulated in the Dawes Act. When the bill became law, speculators duped many Ojibwas into signing away their land in return for counterfeit money and worthless merchandise. The Ojibwas lost more than half their original holdings, and economic ruin overtook them.

Government policy had other injurious effects on Indians' ways of life. The boarding-school program enrolled thousands of children and tried to teach them that their inherited customs were inferior, but most returned to their families demoralized rather than ready to assimilate into white society. Polingaysi Qoyawayma, a Hopi woman forced to take the Christian name Elizabeth Q. White, recalled after four years spent at the Sherman Institute in Riverside, California, "As a Hopi, I was misunderstood by the white man; as a convert of the missionaries, I was looked upon with suspicion by the Hopi people."

Ultimately, political and ecological crises overwhelmed most western Indian groups. White violence and military superiority alone did not defeat them. Their economic systems had started to break down before the military campaigns occurred. Buffalo extinction, enemy raids, and disease combined to hobble subsistence culture to the point where Native Americans had no alternative but to yield their lands to market-oriented whites. Believing their culture superior, whites determined to transform Indians into successful farmers by teaching them the value of private property; educating them in American ideals; and eradicating their "backward" languages, lifestyles, and religions. Although Indians tried to retain their culture by adapting to the various demands they faced, by the end of the century they had lost control of the land and were under increasing pressure to shed their group identity. The West was won at their expense, and to this day they remain casualties of an aggressive age.

LIFE ON THE NATURAL RESOURCE FRONTIER

In contrast to Indians, who used natural resources to meet subsistence needs and small-scale trading, most whites who migrated to the West and Great Plains were driven by the desire for material success. To their eyes, the vast stretches of territory lay as untapped sources of wealth that could bring about a better life (see Map 17.1). Extraction of these resources advanced settlement and created new markets at home and abroad; it also fueled revolutions in transportation, agriculture, and industry that swept across the United States in the late nineteenth century. This same extraction of nature's wealth also gave rise to wasteful interaction with the environment and fed habits of racial and sexual oppression.

Mining and Lumbering

In the mid-1800s, eager prospectors began to comb western terrain for gold, silver, copper, and other minerals. The mining frontier advanced rapidly, drawing thousands of

© Cengage Learning

MAP 17.1 The Development and Natural Resources of the West

By 1890, mining, lumbering, and cattle ranching had penetrated many areas west of the Mississippi River, and railroad construction had linked together both the economy and the spread of mechanized agriculture, altered both the economy and the people who were involved in them.

people to Nevada, Idaho, Montana, Utah, and Colorado. California, where a gold rush helped populate a thriving state by 1850, furnished many of the miners, who traveled to nearby states in search of riches. Others seeking mineral riches followed traditional routes, moving from the East and Midwest to western mining regions.

Prospectors tended to be restless optimists, willing to climb mountains and trek across deserts in search of a telltale glint of precious metal. They shot game for food and financed their explorations by convincing merchants to advance credit for equipment in return for a share of the as-yet-undiscovered lode. Unlucky prospectors whose credit ran out took jobs and saved up for another search.

Digging up and transporting minerals was extremely expensive, so prospectors who did discover veins of metal seldom mined them. Instead, they sold their claims to large mining syndicates, such as the Anaconda Copper Company. Financed by eastern capital, these companies brought in engineers, heavy machinery, railroad lines, and work crews, and helped boost populations in cities such as El Paso and Tucson. In doing so, they made western mining corporate, just like eastern manufacturing. Although discoveries of gold and silver sparked national publicity, mining companies usually exploited less romantic but equally lucrative bonanzas of lead, zinc, tin, quartz, and copper.

Unlike mining, cutting trees for lumber to satisfy demands for construction and heating materials required vast tracts of forest land to be profitable. Because tree supplies in the upper Midwest and South had been depleted—aided by such inventions as bandsaws and feeding machines, which quickened the pace of timber cutting—lumber corporations moved into the forests of the Northwest. They often grabbed millions of acres under the Timber and Stone Act, passed by Congress in 1878 to stimulate settlement in California, Nevada, Oregon, and Washington. It allowed private citizens to buy, at a low price, 160-acre plots "unfit for cultivation" and "valuable chiefly for timber." Lumber companies hired seamen from waterfront boarding houses to register claims to timberland and then transfer those claims to the companies. By 1900 private citizens had bought over 3.5 million acres, but most of that land belonged to corporations.

While mining corporations were excavating western mineral deposits and lumber corporations were cutting down Northwest timberlands, oil companies were beginning to drill wells in the Southwest. In 1900, most of the nation's petroleum still came from the Appalachians and the Midwest, but rich oil reserves had been discovered in southern California and eastern Texas, creating not only new wealth but also boosting boom cities, such as Los Angeles and Houston. Although oil and kerosene were still used mostly for lubrication and lighting, oil discovered in the Southwest later became a vital new source of fuel for autos and other machines.

Complex Communities   As the West developed, it became a rich multiracial society, including not only Native Americans and white migrants but also Mexicans, African Americans, and Asians, all involved in a process of community building. A crescent of territory, a borderland stretching from western Texas through New Mexico and Arizona to northern California, but also including Mexico, supported ranchers and sheepherders, descendants of the Spanish who had originally claimed the land. In New Mexico, Spaniards mixed with Indians to form a *mestizo* population of small farmers and ranchers. All along the Southwest frontier, Mexican immigrants moved into American territory to find work. Some returned to Mexico seasonally; others stayed. Although the Treaty of Guadalupe Hidalgo (1848) had guaranteed property rights to Hispanics, "Anglo" (the Mexican name for a white American) miners, speculators, and railroads used fraud and other means to steal much of Hispanic landholdings. As a result, many Mexicanos moved to cities such as San Antonio and Tucson, and became wage laborers.

Before the Chinese Exclusion Act of 1882 prohibited the immigration of Chinese laborers, some 200,000 Chinese—mostly young, single males—entered the United States and built communities in California, Oregon, and Washington. Many came with five-year contracts to work on railroad construction, then return home, presumably with resources for a better life. They also labored in the fields. By the 1870s, Chinese composed half of California's agricultural work force. The state's farms and citrus groves demanded a huge migrant work force, and Chinese laborers moved from one ripening crop to another, working as pickers and packers. In cities such as San Francisco, they labored in textile and cigar factories, and lived in large boarding houses. Few married because Chinese women were scarce.

Like Chinese and Mexicans, Japanese and European immigrants moved from place to place as they worked in mining and agricultural communities. The region consequently developed its own migrant economy, with workers shifting communities within a large geographical area as they took short-term jobs in mining, farming, and railroad construction.

African Americans tended to be more settled, many of them "exodusters" who built all-black western towns. Nicodemus, Kansas, for example, was founded in 1877 by black migrants from Lexington, Kentucky, and grew to six hundred residents within two years. Early experiences were challenging, but eventually the town developed newspapers, shops, churches, a hotel, and a bank. When attempts to obtain railroad connections failed, however, the town declined, as many of its businesses moved across the Solomon River to the town of Bogue, where a Union Pacific Railroad camp was located.

The major exodus occurred in 1879, when some six thousand blacks, many of them former slaves, moved from the South to Kansas, aided by the Kansas Freedmen's Relief Association. Other migrants, encouraged by editors and land speculators, went to Oklahoma Territory. In the 1890s and early 1900s, African American settlers founded thirty-two all-black communities in Oklahoma, and the territory boasted several successful black farmers.

Western Women   Although unmarried men numerically dominated the western natural-resource frontier, many communities contained populations of white women who had come for the same reason as men: to make their fortune. But on the mining frontier as elsewhere, women's independence was limited; they usually accompanied a husband or father and seldom prospected themselves. Even so, many women used their labor as a resource and earned money by cooking and laundering and, in some cases, providing sexual services for miners in houses of prostitution. In the Northwest, they worked in canneries, cleaning and salting the fish their husbands caught. Mexicano women took jobs in cities as laundresses and seamstresses.

A number of white women helped to bolster family and community life as members of the home mission movement. Protestant missions had long sponsored benevolent activities abroad, such as in China, and had aided the settlement of Oregon in the 1830s and 1840s. But in the mid-nineteenth century, some women broke away from male-dominated missionary organizations. Using the slogan "Woman's work for women," they exerted moral authority in the West by establishing missionary societies and aiding women—unmarried mothers, Mormons, Indians, and Chinese—who they believed had fallen prey to men or who had not yet accepted the principles of Christian virtue.

Significance of Race

To control labor and social relations within this complex population, white settlers made race an important distinguishing characteristic. They usually classified people into five races: Caucasians (themselves), Indians, Mexicans (both Mexican Americans, who had originally inhabited western lands, and Mexican immigrants), "Mongolians" (a term applied to Chinese), and "Negroes." In applying these categories, whites imposed racial distinctions on people who, with the possible exception of African Americans, had never before considered themselves a "race." Whites using these categories ascribed demeaning characteristics to others, judging them to be permanently inferior. In 1878, for example, a federal judge in California ruled that Chinese could not become U.S. citizens because they were not "white persons."

Racial minorities in western communities occupied the bottom segment of a two-tiered labor system. Whites dominated the top tier of managerial and skilled labor positions, while Irish, Chinese, Mexican, and African American laborers held unskilled positions. All non-Anglo groups, in addition to the Irish, encountered prejudice, especially as dominant whites tried to reserve for themselves whatever riches the West might yield. Anti-Chinese violence erupted during hard times. When the Union Pacific Railroad tried to replace white workers with lower-waged Chinese in Rock Springs, Wyoming, in 1885, whites invaded and burned down the Chinese part of town, killing twenty-eight. Mexicans, many of whom had been the original owners of the land in California and elsewhere, saw their property claims ignored or stolen by white miners and farmers.

The multiracial quality of western communities, however, also included a cross-racial dimension. Because so many white male migrants were single, intermarriage with Mexican and Indian women was common. Such unions were acceptable for white men, but not for white women, especially where Asian immigrants were involved. Most miscegenation laws passed by western legislatures were intended to prevent Chinese and Japanese men from marrying white women.

Conservation Movement

As whites were wresting ownership of the land from Indian and Mexican inhabitants of the West, questions arose over who should control the nation's animal, mineral, and timber resources. Much of the undeveloped territory west of the Mississippi was in the public domain, and some people believed the federal government, as its owner, should limit its exploitation. Others, however, believed their own and the nation's prosperity depended on unlimited use of the land.

Questions about natural resources caught Americans between a desire for progress and a fear of spoiling nature. After the Civil War, people eager to protect the natural landscape began to organize a conservation movement. Sports hunters, concerned about loss of wildlife, opposed commercial hunting and lobbied state legislatures to pass hunting regulations. Artists and tourists in 1864 persuaded Congress to preserve the beautiful Yosemite Valley by granting it to the state of California, which reserved it for public use. Then, in 1872, Congress designated the Yellowstone River region in Wyoming as the first national park. And in 1891, conservationists, led by naturalist John Muir, pressured Congress to authorize President Benjamin Harrison to create forest reserves—public lands protected from private timber companies.

Such policies met with strong objections from lumber companies, lumber dealers, railroads, and householders accustomed to cutting timber freely for fuel and building material. Despite Muir's activism and efforts by the Sierra Club (which Muir helped found in 1892) and by such corporations as the Southern Pacific Railroad, which supported rational resource development, opposition was loudest in the West, where people remained eager to take advantage of nature's bounty. Ironically, however, by prohibiting trespass in areas such as Yosemite and Yellowstone, conservation policy deprived Indians and white settlers of the wildlife, water, and firewood they had previously taken from federal lands.

Admission of New States   Development of mining and forest regions, as well as of farms and cities, brought western territories to the economic and population threshold of statehood (see Map 17.2). In 1889, Republicans seeking to solidify control of Congress passed an omnibus bill granting statehood to North Dakota, South Dakota, Washington, and Montana. Wyoming and Idaho, both of which allowed women to vote, were admitted the following year. Congress denied statehood to Utah until 1896, wanting assurances from the Mormons, who constituted a majority of the territory's population and controlled its government, that they would prohibit polygamy.

Western states' varied communities spiced American folk culture and fostered a "go-getter" optimism that distinguished the American spirit. The lawlessness and hedonism of places such as Deadwood, in Dakota Territory, and Tombstone, in Arizona Territory, gave their region notoriety and romance. Legends, only partly true, arose about characters whose lives both typified and magnified the western experience, and promoters such as folk character Buffalo Bill enhanced the appeal of western folklore.

Western Folk Heroes   Arizona's mining towns, with their free-flowing cash and loose law enforcement, attracted gamblers, thieves, and opportunists whose names came to stand for the Wild West. Near Tombstone, the infamous Clanton family and their partner John Ringgold (Johnny Ringo) engaged in smuggling and cattle rustling. Inside the town, the Earp brothers—Wyatt, Jim, Morgan, Virgil, and Warren—and their friends William

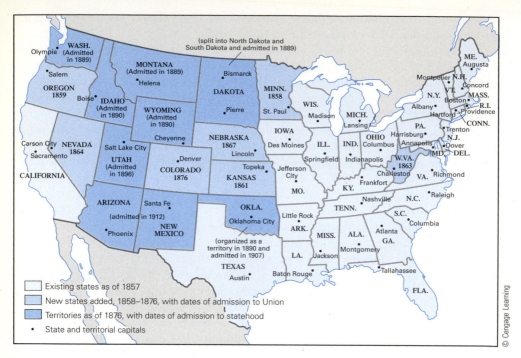

MAP 17.2 The United States, 1876–1912

A wave of admissions between 1889 and 1912 brought remaining territories to statehood and marked the final creation of new states until Alaska and Hawai'i were admitted in the 1950s.

("Bat") Masterson and John Henry ("Doc") Holliday operated on both sides of the law as gunmen, gamblers, and politicians. A feud between the Clantons and Earps climaxed on October 26, 1881, in a shootout at the OK Corral, where three Clantons were killed and Holliday and Morgan Earp were wounded. These characters and their exploits provided material for future novels, movies, and television programs.

Writers Mark Twain, Bret Harte, and others captured the flavor of western life, and characters such as Buffalo Bill, Annie Oakley, and Wild Bill Hickok became western folk heroes. But violence and eccentricity were not widely common. Most miners and lumbermen worked long hours, often for corporations rather than as rugged individuals, and had little time, energy, or money for gambling, carousing, or gunfights. Women worked as long or longer as teachers, laundresses, storekeepers, and housewives. Only a few were sharpshooters or dance-hall queens. For most, western life was a matter of adapting and surviving.

IRRIGATION AND TRANSPORTATION

Glittering gold, tall trees, and gushing oil shaped popular images of the West, but water gave it life. If western lands promised wealth from mining, cutting, and drilling, their agricultural potential promised more—but only if settlers could find a way to

This Nebraska scene reveals the unrelenting treeless landscape that farmer familiess confronted. Using windmills to raise water for their cattle and horses, farmers faced difficulties in obtaining enough water to irrigate their crops unless a river was nearby.

bring water to the arid soil. Western economic development is the story of how public and private interests used technology and organization to utilize the region's sometimes scarce water resources to make it agriculturally productive. Just as control of land was central to western development, so, too, was control of water.

For centuries, Indians irrigated southwestern fields to sustain their subsistence farming. When the Spanish arrived, they began tapping the Rio Grande River to irrigate farms in southwest Texas and New Mexico. Later, they channeled water to California mission communities of San Diego and Los Angeles. The first Americans of northern European ancestry to practice extensive irrigation were the Mormons. After arriving in Utah in 1847, they diverted streams and rivers into networks of canals, whose water enabled them to farm the hard-baked soil. By 1890, Utah boasted over 263,000 irrigated acres supporting more than 200,000 people.

Rights to Water   Efforts at land reclamation through irrigation in Colorado and California sparked conflict over rights to the precious streams that flowed through the West. Americans inherited the English common-law principle of riparian rights, which held that only those who owned land along a river's banks could appropriate from the water's flow. The stream itself, according to riparianism, belonged to God; those who lived near it could take water for normal needs but were not to diminish the river. This principle, intended to protect nature, discouraged economic development because it prohibited each property owner from damming or diverting water at the expense of others who lived downstream.

The Australian Frontier

America's frontier West was not unique. Australia, founded like the United States as a European colony, had a frontier society that resembled the American West in several ways, especially in its mining development, its folk society, and its treatment of indigenous people. Australia experienced a gold rush in 1851, just two years after the United States, and large-scale mining companies quickly moved into its western regions to extract lucrative mineral deposits. In 1897, future U.S. president Herbert Hoover, who at that time was a twenty-two-year-old geology graduate, went to work in Australia and began his successful career as a mining engineer.

Promise of mineral wealth lured thousands of immigrants to Australia in the late nineteenth century. Many of the newcomers arrived from China, and, as in the United States, these immigrants, most of them men, encountered abusive treatment. Anti-Chinese riots erupted in ports in New South Wales in 1861 and 1873, and beginning in 1854, the Australian government passed several laws restricting Chinese immigration. When the country became an independent British federation in 1901, one of its first acts applied a strict literacy test that virtually terminated Chinese immigration for over fifty years.

As in the American West, the Australian frontier bred folk heroes who came to

Americans who settled the West rejected riparianism in favor of prior appropriation, which awarded a river's water to the first person who claimed it. Westerners, taking cues in part from eastern Americans who had diverted waterways to power mills and factories, asserted that water, like timber, minerals, and other natural resources, existed to serve human needs and advance profits. They argued that anyone intending a "reasonable" or "beneficial" (economically productive) use of river water should have the right to appropriation, and the courts generally agreed.

Government Supervision of Water Rights

Under appropriation, those who dammed and diverted water often reduced the flow of water downstream. People disadvantaged by such action could protect their interests either by suing those who deprived them of water or by establishing a public authority to regulate water usage. Thus in 1879, Colorado created several water divisions, each with a commissioner to regulate water rights. In 1890, Wyoming enlarged the concept of government control with a constitutional provision declaring that the state's rivers were public property subject to supervision.

Destined to become the most productive agricultural state, California devised a dramatic response to the problem of water rights, sometimes called the California Solution. In the 1860s, a few individuals controlled huge tracts of land in the fertile Sacramento and San Joaquin River valleys, which they used for speculating in real estate, raising cattle, and growing wheat. But around the edges of the wheat fields lay unoccupied lands that could profitably support vegetable and fruit farming if irrigated properly.

symbolize white masculinity. In a society where men vastly outnumbered women, Australians glorified the tough, aggressive individual who displayed self-reliance and quick judgment that made the Australian backcountry man as idealized as the American cowboy. Australian outlaws (called "bushrangers") such as Ned Kelly, an infamous bandit who was hanged in 1880, achieved the same notoriety as Americans Jesse James and Billy the Kid.

Although Australians immortalized white men who brought a spirit of personal liberty and opportunism to a new country, they also considered indigenous peoples, whom they called "Aborigines," as savages needing to be conquered and civilized. Christian missionaries viewed aborigines as lost in pagan darkness and tried to convert them. In 1869, the government of Victoria Province passed an Aborigine Protection Act that, like American policy toward Indians, encouraged removal of native children from their families so they could learn European customs in schools run by whites. Aborigines adapted in their own ways. They formed cricket teams, and those with light skin sometimes hid their identity by telling census takers they were white. In the end, though, assimilation did not work, and Australians resorted to reservations as a means of "protecting" Aborigines, just as Americans isolated native peoples on reserved land. Like the Americans, white Australians could not find a place for indigenous people in a land of opportunity.

Unlike western states that had favored appropriation rights over riparian rights, California maintained a mixed legal system that upheld riparianism while allowing for some appropriation. This system disadvantaged irrigators and prompted them to seek to change state law. In 1887, the legislature passed a bill permitting farmers to organize into districts that would construct and operate irrigation projects. An irrigation district could use its authority to purchase water rights, seize private property to build irrigation canals, and finance projects through taxation or by issuing bonds. As a result of this legislation, California became the nation's leader in irrigated acreage, with more than 1 million irrigated acres by 1890, making the state's fruit and vegetable agriculture the most profitable in the country.

Newlands Reclamation Act   Although state-supervised irrigation stimulated farming, the federal government still owned most western land in the 1890s, ranging from 64 percent of California to 96 percent of Nevada. Prodded by land-hungry developers, states wanted the federal government to transfer to them at least part of public domain lands. States claimed they could make these lands profitable through reclamation—providing them with irrigated water. Congress generally refused such transfers because of the controversies they raised. If one state sponsored irrigation to develop its own land, who would regulate waterways that flowed through more than one state? If, for example, California assumed control of the Truckee River, which flowed westward out of Lake Tahoe on the California-Nevada border, how would Nevadans be assured that California would give them sufficient water? Only the federal government, it seemed, had the power to regulate regional water development.

In 1902, after years of debates, Congress passed the Newlands Reclamation Act. Named for Nevada congressman Francis Newlands, the law allowed the federal government to sell western public lands to individuals in parcels not to exceed 160 acres and to use proceeds from such sales to finance irrigation projects. The Newlands Act provided for control but not conservation of water because three-fourths of the water used in open-ditch irrigation, the most common form, was lost to evaporation. Thus, the Newlands Reclamation Act fell squarely within the tradition of development of nature for human profit. It represented a decision by the federal government to aid the agricultural and general economic development of the West, just as state and federal subsidies to railroads during the 1850s and 1860s aided western settlement.

Railroad Construction   Between 1865 and 1890, railroad expansion boomed, as total track grew from 35,000 to 200,000 miles, mostly from construction west of the Mississippi River (see Map 17.1). By 1900, the United States contained one-third of all railroad track in the world. A diverse mix of workers made up construction crews. The Central Pacific, built eastward from San Francisco, employed thousands of Chinese; the Union Pacific, extending westward from Omaha, Nebraska, used mainly Irish construction gangs. Workers lived in shacks and tents that were dismantled, loaded on flatcars, and relocated each day.

Railroad construction had powerful economic effects. After 1880, when steel rails began to replace iron rails, railroads helped to boost the nation's steel industry to international leadership. Railroad expansion also spawned related industries, including coal production, passenger- and freight-car manufacture, and depot construction. Influential and essential, railroads also gave important impetus to western urbanization. With their ability to transport large loads of people and freight, lines such as the Union Pacific and the Southern Pacific accelerated the growth of western hubs such as Chicago, Omaha, Kansas City, Cheyenne, Los Angeles, Portland, and Seattle.

Railroad Subsidies   Railroads accomplished these feats with help from some of the largest government subsidies in American history. Promoters argued that because railroads were a public benefit, the government should aid them by giving them land from the public domain, which they could then sell to finance construction. During the Civil War, Congress, dominated by business-minded Republicans and in the absence of representatives from the seceded southern states, was sympathetic, as it had been when it aided steamboat companies earlier in the century. As a result, the federal government granted railroad corporations over 180 million acres, mostly for interstate routes. These grants usually consisted of a right of way, plus alternate sections of land in a strip 20 to 80 miles wide along the right of way. Railroads funded construction by using the land as security for bonds or by selling it for cash. States and localities heaped on further subsidies. State legislators, many of whom had financial interests in a railroad's success, granted some 50 million acres. Cities and towns also assisted, usually by offering loans or by purchasing railroad bonds or stocks.

Government subsidies had mixed effects. Although capitalists often opposed government involvement in the economic affairs of private companies, railroads nevertheless accepted public aid and pressured governments into meeting their needs. The Southern Pacific, for example, threatened to bypass Los Angeles unless the city paid a bonus and built a depot. Localities that could not or would not pay suffered. Without public help, few railroads could have prospered sufficiently to attract private investment, yet such aid was not always salutary. During the 1880s, the policy of generosity haunted communities whose zeal had prompted them to commit too much to railroads that were never built or that defaulted on loans. Some laborers and farmers fought subsidies, arguing that companies such as the Southern Pacific would become too powerful. Many communities boomed, however, because they had linked their fortunes to the iron horse. Moreover, railroads helped attract investment into the West and drew farmers into the market economy.

Standard Gauge,   Railroad construction brought about important technological
Standard Time   and organizational reforms. By the late 1880s, almost all lines had adopted standard-gauge rails so that their tracks could connect with one another. Air brakes, automatic car couplers, and other devices made rail transportation safer and more efficient. The need for gradings, tunnels, and bridges spurred the growth of the American engineering profession. Organizational advances included systems for coordinating passenger and freight schedules, and the adoption of uniform freight-classification systems. Railroads also, however, helped reinforce racial segregation by separating black from white passengers on railroad cars and in stations.

Rail transportation altered conceptions of time and space. First, by surmounting physical barriers by bridging rivers and tunneling through mountains, railroads transformed space into time. Instead of expressing the distance between places in miles, people began to refer to the amount of time it took to travel from one place to another. Second, railroad scheduling required nationwide standardization of time. Before railroads, local clocks struck noon when the sun was directly overhead, and people set clocks and watches accordingly. But because the sun was not overhead at exactly the same moment everywhere, time varied from place to place. Boston's clocks, for instance, differed from those in New York by almost twelve minutes. To impose regularity, railroads created their own time zones. In 1883, without authority from Congress, the nation's railroads agreed to establish four standard time zones for the country. Most communities adjusted accordingly, and railroad time became national time.

FARMING THE PLAINS

While California emerged as the nation's highest-yielding agricultural state, extraordinary development occurred in the Great Plains. There, farming in the late 1800s exemplified two important achievements: the transformation of arid, windswept prairies into arable land that would yield crops to benefit human-kind, and the transformation of agriculture into big business by means of mechanization, long-distance transportation, and scientific cultivation. These feats did not come easily. The region's climate and terrain presented formidable challenges, and overcoming them did not guarantee success. Irrigation and mechanized agriculture enabled farmers to feed the nation's burgeoning population and turned the United States into the world's breadbasket, but the experience also scarred the lives of countless men and women who made that accomplishment possible.

Settlement of the Plains

During the 1870s and 1880s, more acres were put under cultivation in states such as Kansas, Nebraska, and Texas than in the entire country during the previous 250 years. The number of farms tripled between 1860 and 1910, as hundreds of thousands of hopeful farmers streamed into the Plains region. The Homestead Act of 1862 and other measures to encourage western settlement offered cheap or free plots to people who would reside on and improve their property. Railroads that had received land subsidies were especially aggressive, advertising cheap land, arranging credit terms, offering reduced fares, and promising instant success. Railroad agents—often former immigrants—traveled to Denmark, Sweden, Germany, and other European nations to recruit settlers and greeted newcomers at eastern ports.

Most families who settled western farmlands migrated because opportunities there seemed to promise a second chance, a better existence than their previous one. Railroad expansion gave farmers in remote regions a way to ship produce to market, and construction of grain elevators eased problems of storage. As a result of worldwide as well as national population growth, demand for farm products burgeoned, and the prospects for commercial agriculture—growing crops for profit and for shipment to distant, including international, markets—became more favorable than ever.

Hardship on the Plains

Life on the farm, however, was much harder than advertisements and railroad agents insinuated. Migrants often encountered scarcities of essentials they had once taken for granted, and they had to adapt to the environment. Barren prairies contained insufficient lumber for housing and fuel, so pioneer families had to build houses of sod and burn buffalo dung for heat. Water for cooking and cleaning was sometimes scarce also. Machinery for drilling wells was expensive, as were windmills for drawing water to the surface.

Weather was even more formidable than the terrain. The climate between the Missouri River and the Rocky Mountains divides along a line running from Minnesota southwest through Oklahoma, then south, bisecting Texas. West of this line, annual rainfall averages less than twenty-eight inches, not enough for most crops or trees (see Map 17.3), and even that scant life-giving rain was never certain. Heartened by adequate water one year, farmers gagged on dust and broke plows on hardened limestone soil the next.

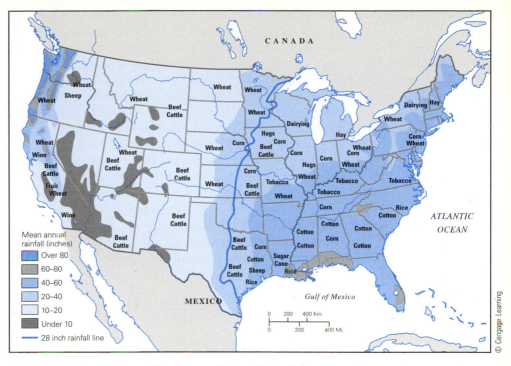

MAP 17.3 Agricultural Regions of the United States, 1890

In the Pacific Northwest and east of the twenty-eight-inch-rainfall line, farmers could grow a greater variety of crops. Territory west of the line was either too mountainous or too arid to support agriculture without irrigation. The grasslands that once fed buffalo herds could now feed beef cattle.

Weather seldom followed predictable cycles. Weeks of torrid summer heat and parching winds suddenly gave way to violent storms that washed away crops and property. Frigid winter blizzards piled up mountainous snowdrifts that halted out-door movement. During the Great Blizzard that struck Nebraska, Wyoming, and Dakota Territory in the winter of 1886–1887, the temperature plunged to 36 degrees below zero. In springtime, melting snow swelled streams and floods threatened millions of acres. In fall, a week without rain turned dry grasslands into tinder, and the slightest spark could ignite a raging prairie fire. Severe drought in Texas between 1884 and 1886 drove many farmers off the land, and a more widespread drought in 1886 struck areas as diverse as Dakota, Wyoming, and California.

Nature could be cruel even under good conditions. Weather favorable for crops was also good for breeding insects. Worms and flying pests ravaged fields. In the 1870s and 1880s, grasshopper swarms virtually ate up entire farms. Heralded only by the din of buzzing wings, a mile-long cloud of insects would smother the land and devour everything: plants, tree bark, and clothing. As one farmer lamented, the "hoppers left behind nothing but the mortgage."

Social Isolation   Settlers also had to cope with social isolation. In New England and Europe, farmers lived in villages and traveled daily to nearby fields. This pattern of community building was rare in the vast expanses of the Plains—and in the Far West and South as well—where peculiarities of land division compelled rural dwellers to live apart from each other. Because most plots were rectangular—usually encompassing 160 acres—at most four families could live near one another, but only if they built homes around their shared four-corner intersection. In practice, farm families usually lived back from their boundary lines, and at least a half-mile separated farmhouses. Men might find escape by working in distant fields and taking occasional trips to town to sell crops or buy supplies. Women were more isolated, confined by domestic chores to the household. They visited and exchanged food and services with neighbor women when they could, but, as one writer observed, a farm woman's life was "a weary, monotonous round of cooking and washing and mending."

Letters that Ed Donnell, a young Nebraska homesteader, wrote to his family in Missouri reveal how time and circumstances could dull optimism. In the fall of 1885, Donnell rejoiced to his mother, "I like Nebr first rate.... I have saw a pretty tuff time a part of the time since I have been out here, but I started out to get a home and I was determined to win or die in the attempt.... Have got a good crop of corn, a floor in my house and got it ceiled overhead." Already, though, Donnell was lonely. He went on, "There is lots of other bachelors here but I am the only one I know who doesn't have kinfolks living handy.... You wanted to know when I was going to get married. Just as quick as I can get money ahead to get a cow."

A year and a half later, Donnell's dreams were dissolving and, still a bachelor, he was beginning to look for a second chance elsewhere. He wrote to his brother, "The rats eat my sod stable down.... I may sell out this summer, land is going up so fast.... If I sell I am going west and grow up with the country." By fall, conditions had worsened. Donnell lamented, "We have been having wet weather for 3 weeks.... My health has been so poor this summer and the wind and the sun hurts my head so. I think if I can sell I will... move to town for I can get $40 a month working in a grist mill and I would not be exposed to the weather." Donnell's doubts and hardships, shared by thousands of other people, fed the cityward migration of farm folk that fueled late-nineteenth-century urban growth (see Chapter 19).

Mail-Order Companies and Rural Free Delivery   Farm families survived by sheer resolve and by organizing churches and clubs where they could socialize a few times a month. By 1900, two developments had brought rural settlers who lived east of the rainfall line into closer contact with modern consumer society. First, mail-order companies, such as Montgomery Ward (founded in 1872) and Sears, Roebuck (founded in 1893), made new products attainable. Emphasizing personal attention to customers, Ward and Sears received letters that often reported family news and sought advice on needs from gifts to childcare. A Washington man wrote to Mr. Ward, "As you advertise everything for sale that a person wants, I thought I would write you, as I am in need of a wife, and see what you could do for me." Another reported, "I suppose you wonder why we haven't ordered anything from you since the fall. The cow kicked my arm and broke it and besides my wife was sick, and there was the doctor bill. But now, thank God, that is paid, and we are all well again, and we have a fine new baby boy, and please send plush bonnet number 29d8077."

Second, after farmers petitioned Congress for extension of the postal service, in 1896 the government made Rural Free Delivery (RFD) widely available. Farmers previously had to go to town to pick up mail. Now they could receive letters, newspapers, and catalogues in a roadside mailbox nearly every day. In 1913, the postal service inaugurated parcel post, which enabled people to receive packages, such as orders from Ward and Sears, more cheaply.

Mechanization of Agriculture

As with industrial production (see Chapter 18), the late-nineteenth-century agricultural revolution was driven by the expanded use of machinery. When the Civil War drew men away from farms in the upper Mississippi River valley, women and older men who remained behind began using reapers and other mechanical implements to grow crops to satisfy demand for food and take advantage of high grain prices. After the war, demand encouraged farmers to continue utilizing machines, and inventors developed new implements to facilitate planting and harvesting. Seeders, combines, binders, mowers, and rotary plows, carried westward by railroads, improved grain growing on the Plains and in California. Technology also aided dairy and poultry farming. The centrifugal cream separator, patented in 1879, sped the process of skimming cream from milk, and a mechanized incubator, invented in 1885, made chicken raising more profitable.

For centuries, the acreage of grain a farmer planted was limited by the amount that could be harvested by hand. Machines—driven first by animals, then by steam—significantly increased productivity. Before mechanization, a farmer working alone could harvest about 7.5 acres of wheat. Using an automatic binder that cut and bundled the grain, the same farmer could harvest 135 acres. Machines dramatically reduced the time and cost of farming other crops as well.

Legislative and Scientific Aids

Meanwhile, Congress and scientists worked to improve existing crops and develop new ones. The 1862 Morrill Land Grant Act gave each state federal lands to sell in order to finance agricultural research at educational institutions. The act prompted establishment of public universities in Wisconsin, Illinois, Minnesota, California, and other states. A second Morrill Act in 1890 aided more schools, including several all-black colleges. The Hatch Act of 1887 provided for agricultural experiment stations in every state, further encouraging the advancement of farming science and technology.

Science also enabled farmers to use the soil more efficiently. Researchers developed dry farming, a technique of plowing and harrowing that minimized evaporation of precious moisture. Botanists perfected varieties of "hard" wheat whose seeds could withstand northern winters, and millers invented a process for grinding the tougher wheat kernels into flour. Agriculturists adapted new varieties of alfalfa from Mongolia, corn from North Africa, and rice from Asia. Horticulturist Luther

TABLE 17.1 | SUMMARY: GOVERNMENT LAND POLICY

Railroad land grants (1850–1871)	Granted 181 million acres to railroads to encourage construction and development
Homestead Act (1862)	Gave 80 million acres to settlers to encourage settlement
Morrill Act (1862)	Granted 11 million acres to states to sell to fund public agricultural colleges
Other grants	Granted 129 million acres to states to sell for other educational and related purposes
Dawes Act (1887)	Allotted some reservation lands to individual Indians to promote private property and weaken tribal values among Indians and offered remaining reservation lands for sale to whites (by 1906, some 75 million acres had been acquired by whites)
Various laws	Permitted direct sales of 100 million acres by the Land Office

Source: Goldfield, David; Abbott, Carl E.; Anderson, Virginia Dejohn; Argersinger, Jo Ann E.; Argersinger, Peter H.; Barney, William.; Weir, Robert M., *American Journey, The*, Volume II, 3rd ed., © 2004. Printed and electronically reproduced by permission of Pearson Education, Inc., Upper Saddle River, New Jersey.

Burbank developed hundreds of new food plants and flowers at a garden laboratory in Sebastopol, California. George Washington Carver, a son of slaves who became a chemist and taught at Alabama's Tuskegee Institute, created hundreds of products from peanuts, soybeans, and sweet potatoes. Other scientists devised means of combating plant and animal diseases. Just as in mining and manufacturing, science and technology provided American farming with means for expanding productivity in the market economy (see Table 17.1).

THE RANCHING FRONTIER

While commercial farming overspread the West, it ran headlong into one of the region's most romantic industries—ranching. Beginning in the sixteenth century, Spanish landholders had engaged in cattle raising in Mexico and what would become the American Southwest. They employed Indian and Mexican cowboys, known as *vaqueros*, who tended the herds and rounded up cattle to be branded and slaughtered. Anglo ranchers moving into Texas and California in the early nineteenth century hired *vaqueros*, who in turn taught their skills in roping, branding, horse training, and saddle making to white and African American cowboys.

By the 1860s, cattle raising became increasingly profitable, as population growth boosted the demand for beef and railroads simplified the transportation of food. By 1870, drovers were herding thousands of Texas cattle northward to Kansas, Missouri, and Wyoming (see Map 17.1). At the northern terminus, the cattle were sold to northern ranches or loaded onto trains bound for Chicago and St. Louis, for slaughter and distribution to national and international markets.

The long drive gave rise to romantic lore of bellowing cattle, buckskin-clad cowboys, and smoky campfires under starry skies, but the process was not very

Nebraska State Historical Society

A group of cowboys prepare for a roundup. Note the presence of African Americans, who, along with Mexicans, made up one-fourth of all cowboys. Though they rarely became trail bosses or ranch owners, black cowboys enjoyed an independence on the trails unavailable to them on tenant farms and city streets.

efficient. Trekking 1,000 miles or more for two to three months made cattle sinewy and tough. Herds traveling through Indian territory and farmers' fields were sometimes shot at and later prohibited from such trespass by state laws. Ranchers adjusted by raising herds nearer to railroad routes. When ranchers discovered that crossing Texas longhorns with heavier Hereford and Angus breeds produced animals better able to survive harsh winters, cattle raising expanded northward, and proliferating herds in Kansas, Nebraska, Colorado, Wyoming, Montana, and Dakota crowded out already declining buffalo populations. Profits were considerable. A rancher could purchase a calf for $5, let it feed on grasslands for a few years, recapture it in a roundup, and sell it at a market price of $40 or $45.

The Open Range   Cattle raisers needed vast pastures to graze their herds while incurring as little expense as possible. Thus, they often bought a few acres bordering a stream and turned their herds loose on adjacent public domain that no one wanted because it lacked water access. By this method, called open-range ranching, a cattle raiser could utilize thousands of acres by owning only a hundred or so. Neighboring ranchers often formed associations and allowed herds to graze together. Owners identified their cattle by burning a brand into each animal's hide. Each ranch had its own brand—a shorthand method for labeling movable property. But as more profit-seeking ranchers flowed into the Plains, cattle began to overrun the range, and other groups challenged ranchers over use of the land.

In California and New Mexico, sheepherders were also using the public domain, sparking territorial clashes. Ranchers complained that sheep ruined grassland by eating down to the roots and that cattle refused to graze where sheep had been. Occasionally ranchers and sheepherders resorted to armed conflict rather than settle disagreements in court, where a judge might discover that both were using public land illegally.

More important, however, the advancing farming frontier was generating new demands for land. Devising a way to organize property resulted in an unheralded but significant change in land management. The problem was fencing. Lacking sufficient timber and stone for traditional fencing, western settlers could not easily define and protect their property. Tensions flared when farmers accused cattle raisers of allowing their herds to trespass on cropland and when herders in turn charged that farmers should fence their property against grazing animals. But ranchers and farmers alike lacked an economical means of enclosing herds and fields.

Barbed Wire   The solution was barbed wire. Invented in 1873 by Joseph F. Glidden, a DeKalb, Illinois, farmer, this fencing consisted of wires held in place by sharp spurs. Mass-produced by the Washburn and Moen Manufacturing Company of Worcester, Massachusetts—80.5 million pounds worth in 1880 alone—barbed wire provided a cheap and durable means of enclosure. It opened the Plains to homesteaders by enabling them to protect their farms from grazing cattle. It also ended open-range ranching and made roundups unnecessary because it enabled large-scale ranchers to enclose their herds within massive stretches of private property. In addition, the development of the round silo for storing and making fodder enabled cattle raisers to feed their herds without grazing them on vast stretches of land.

Ranching as Big Business   By 1890, big businesses were taking over the cattle industry and applying scientific methods of breeding and feeding. Corporations also used technology to squeeze larger returns out of meatpacking. Like buffalo, all parts of a cow had uses. Only about half of it consisted of salable meat. Meatpackers' largest profits came from livestock by-products: hides for leather, blood for fertilizer, hooves for glue, fat for candles and soap, and the rest for sausages. But cattle processing also had a harmful environmental impact. What meatpackers and leather tanners could not sell was dumped into rivers and streams. By the late nineteenth century, the stench from the Chicago River, which flowed past the city's mammoth processing plants, made nearby residents sick.

Open-range ranching made beef a staple of the American diet and created a few fortunes, but it could not survive the rush of history. During the 1880s, overgrazing destroyed nourishing grass supplies on the Plains, and the brutal winter of 1886–1887 destroyed 90 percent of some herds and drove small ranchers out of business. By 1890, large-scale ranchers owned or leased the land they used, though some illegal fencing persisted. Cowboys formed labor organizations and participated in strikes for higher pay. The myth of the cowboy's freedom and individualism lived on, but ranching, like mining and farming, quickly became a corporate business.

SUMMARY

The landscape of the American West exerted lasting influence, through its majesty and its fragility, on the complex mix of people who built communities there. Indians, the original inhabitants, had used, and sometimes abused, the land to support subsistence cultures that included trade and war as well as hunting and farming. Living mostly in small groups, they depended on delicate resources such as buffalo herds and salmon runs. When they came into contact with commerce-minded, migratory European-Americans, their resistance to the market economy, diseases, and violence that whites brought into the West failed. The result was that the story of the American West became the story of the invaders, not that of the natives.

Mexicans, Chinese, African Americans, and Anglos discovered a reciprocal relationship between human activities and the nonhuman world that they had not always anticipated. Miners, timber cutters, farmers, and builders extracted raw minerals to supply eastern factories, used irrigation and machines to bring forth agricultural abundance from the land, filled pastures with cattle and sheep to expand food sources, and constructed railroads to tie the nation together. In doing so, they transformed half of the nation's territory within a few decades. But the environment also exerted its own power over humans, through its climate, its insects and parasites, and its impenetrable hazards and barriers to human movement and agriculture.

The West's settlers, moreover, employed violence and greed that sustained discrimination within a multiracial society, left many farmers feeling cheated and betrayed, provoked contests over use of water and pastures, and sacrificed environmental balance for market profits. The region's raw materials and agricultural products raised living standards and hastened industrial progress, but not without human and environmental costs.

18

THE MACHINE AGE 1877–1920

TECHNOLOGY AND THE TRIUMPH OF INDUSTRIALIZATION

While some people pursued opportunity in the American frontier, others sought new ways of doing things with technology. Thomas Edison was one such person. In 1876, he and his associates opened an "invention factory" in Menlo Park, New Jersey, where they intended to turn out "a minor invention every ten days and a big thing every six months or so." Edison's attitude reflected the spirit that enlivened American inventiveness, which in turn drove industrialization in the late nineteenth century. Activity at the U.S. Patent Office, created by the Constitution to "promote the Progress of science and useful Arts," reflected this spirit. Between 1790 and 1860, the government granted a total of 36,000 patents. In the next seventy-year span, 1860 to 1930, it registered 1.5 million. Inventions often sprang from a marriage between technology and business organization. The harnessing of electricity, internal combustion, and industrial chemistry illustrates how this marriage worked.

Birth of the Electrical Industry

Most of Edison's one thousand inventions used electricity to transmit light, sound, and images. His biggest "big thing" project began in 1878 when he embarked on a search for an efficient means of indoor lighting. After tedious experiments, Edison perfected an incandescent bulb that used tungsten to prevent the filament from burning up when electrical current passed through it. At the same time, his Edison Electric Light Company devised a system of power generation and distribution that could provide electricity conveniently to thousands of customers. To market his ideas, Edison acted as his own publicist. During the 1880 Christmas season, he illuminated Menlo Park; and in 1882, he built a power plant that lighted

CHRONOLOGY

1869	Knights of Labor founded
1873–78	Economy declines
1877	Widespread railroad strikes protest wage cuts
1878	Edison Electric Light Company founded
1879	George's *Poverty and Progress* argues for taxing unearned wealth
1881	First federal trademark law begins spread of brand names
1882	Standard Oil Trust founded
1884–85	Economy declines
1886	Haymarket riot in Chicago protests police brutality against labor demonstrations
	American Federation of Labor (AFL) founded
1890	Sherman Anti-Trust Act outlaws "combinations in restraint of trade"
1892	Homestead (Pennsylvania) steelworkers strike against Carnegie Steel Company
1893–97	Economic depression causes high unemployment and business failures
1894	Workers of Pullman Palace Car Company strike
1895	*U.S. v. E. C. Knight Co.* limits Congress's power to regulate manufacturing
1896	*Holden v. Harcy* upholds law regulating miners' working hours
1903	Women's Trade Union League (WTUL) founded
1905	*Lochner v. New York* overturns law limiting bakery workers' working hours
	Industrial Workers of the World (IWW) founded
1908	*Muller v. Oregon* upholds law limiting women to ten-hour workday
	First Ford Model T built
1911	Triangle Shirtwaist Company fire in New York City leaves 146 workers dead
1913	Ford begins moving assembly-line production
1919	Telephone operators strike in New England

eighty-five buildings on New York's Wall Street. A *New York Times* reporter marveled that working in his office at night now "seemed almost like writing in daylight."

The application of electricity to production and everyday life illustrates the dynamic and flexible quality of American inventiveness and organizational skill in the industrial era. For example, though Edison had applied his genius to inventions that utilized electricity, his system of direct current could transmit electricity only a mile or two because it lost voltage the farther it was transmitted. George Westinghouse, an inventor from Schenectady, New York, who had previously created an air brake for railroad cars, solved the problem. Westinghouse purchased European patent rights to generators that used alternating current and to transformers that reduced high-voltage power to lower voltage levels, thus making long-distance transmission more efficient.

Other entrepreneurs created new practices to market Edison's and Westinghouse's technological breakthroughs. Samuel Insull, formerly Edison's private secretary, organized Edison power plants across the country, amassing an electric utility empire. In the late 1880s and early 1890s, financiers Henry Villard and J. P. Morgan bought up patents in electric lighting and merged small equipment-manufacturing companies into the General Electric Company. Equally important, General Electric and Westinghouse Electric encouraged practical applications of electricity by establishing research laboratories that paid scientists to create electrical products for everyday use.

While corporations organized company labs, independent inventors tried, sometimes successfully and sometimes not, to sell their handiwork and patents to large manufacturers. One such inventor, Granville T. Woods, an engineer sometimes called "the black Edison," patented thirty-five devices vital to electronics and communications. Among his inventions, most of which he sold to companies such as General Electric, were an automatic circuit breaker, an electromagnetic brake, and instruments to aid communications between railroad trains.

Henry Ford and the Automobile Industry   In 1885, German engineer Gottlieb Daimler built a lightweight, internal-combustion motor driven by vaporized gasoline—an invention that inspired one of America's most visionary manufacturers, Henry Ford. In the 1890s, Ford, an electrical engineer in Detroit's Edison Company, experimented in his spare time using Daimler's engine to power a vehicle. George Selden, a Rochester, New York, lawyer, had already been tinkering with such technology, but Ford applied organizational genius to this invention and spawned a massive industry.

Like Edison, Ford had a scheme as well as a product. In 1909, he declared, "I am going to democratize the automobile. When I'm through, everybody will be able to afford one, and about everyone will have one." Ford proposed to reach this goal by mass-producing thousands of identical cars in exactly the same way. Adapting methods of the meatpacking and metalworking industries, Ford engineers set up assembly lines that drastically reduced the time and cost of producing autos. Instead of performing numerous tasks, each worker performed only one task, performed repeatedly, using the same specialized machine. In this way, workers assembled the entire car as it passed by them on a conveyor belt.

In 1913, the Ford Motor Company's first full assembly line began operation in Highland Park outside Detroit, and the next year, Ford sold 248,000 cars. Soon, other manufacturers entered the field. Rising output created more jobs,

Data from U.S. Bureau of the Census, *Fourteenth Census of the United States, 1920*, Vol. IX, Manufacturing (U.S. Government Printing Office Washington, D.C., 1921).

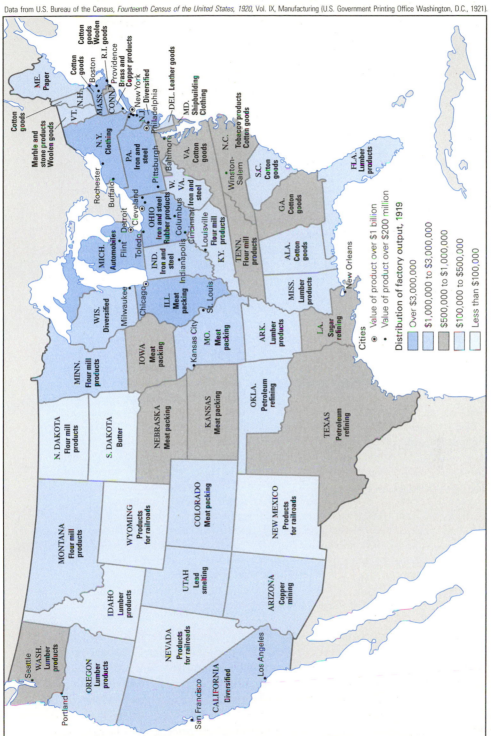

MAP 18.1 Industrial Production, 1919

By the early twentieth century, each state could boast at least one kind of industrial production. Although the value of goods produced was still highest in the Northeast, states such as Minnesota and California had impressive dollar values of outputs.

LINKS TO THE WORLD

The Atlantic Cable

During the late nineteenth century, as American manufacturers expanded their markets overseas, their ability to communicate with customers and investors improved immeasurably because of a telegraph cable laid beneath the Atlantic Ocean. Cyrus Field, the man who thought up the idea to build an undersea cable, was an American. Yet most of the engineers who worked on the Atlantic cable, as well as most of the capitalists involved in the venture, were British. In 1851, a British company laid the first successful undersea telegraph cable from Dover, England, to Calais, France, proving that an insulated wire could carry signals underwater. The benefits of this venture, which connected Reuters news service to the European continent and allowed French investors to receive instantaneous messages from the London Stock Exchange, inspired British and American businessmen to attempt a larger project across the Atlantic.

The first attempts to build a transatlantic cable failed, but in 1866 a British ship, funded by British investors, successfully laid a telegraph wire that operated without interruption. The project was designed by cooperative efforts of American and British electrical engineers. Thereafter, England and the United States grew more closely linked in their diplomatic relations, and citizens of both nations developed greater concern for each other

as a result of their ability to receive international news more quickly. When American president James Garfield was assassinated in 1881, the news traveled almost instantly to Great Britain, and Britons mourned the death more profusely than they had mourned the passing of Abraham Lincoln, whose death was unknown in England until eleven days after it had occurred because transatlantic messages at that time traveled by steamship.

Some people lamented the stresses that near-instant international communications now created. One observer remarked that the telegraph tended "to make every person in a hurry, and I do not believe that with our business it is very desirable that it should be so." But others welcomed the benefits from the cable's link. Rapid availability of stock quotes boomed activity at the New York and London stock exchanges, much to investors' delight. Newspaper readers enjoyed reading about events on the other side of the ocean the next day, instead of a week after they had occurred. And the success of the Atlantic cable inspired similar ventures in the Mediterranean Sea, the Indian Ocean and, eventually, across the Pacific. By 1902, underwater cables circled the globe, and the age of global telecommunications had begun.

---

higher earnings, and greater profits not only for car manufacturers, but also in related industries such as steel, oil, paint, rubber, and glass. Moreover, assembly-line production in these and other industries required new companies to fabricate precision machine tools to create standardized parts. Advances in grinding and cutting technology in this era made production processes accurate to one-thousandth of an inch.

By 1914, a Ford car cost $490, about one-fourth of its price a decade earlier. Yet even $490 was too expensive for many workers, who earned at best $2 a day.

That year, however, Ford tried to spur productivity, prevent high labor turnover, head off unionization, and better enable his workers to buy the cars they produced by offering them the Five-Dollar-Day plan—a combination of wages and profit sharing.

Carnegie and Steel

Many new products, including machines themselves, required strong, hard metal. Steel served the purpose. Though in use for many centuries, steel production was inefficient until a British engineer, Henry Bessemer, developed a process that enabled mass production of inexpensive, high-quality steel from molten iron. In America, industrialist Andrew Carnegie was one of the first to realize the benefits of the Bessemer process. After observing the process during a visit to England in 1872, Carnegie raised money to build a steel plant near Pittsburgh, which he named the Edgar Thompson Steel works after his former boss at the Pennsylvania Railroad. Using funds raised from several investors, Carnegie purchased other steel mills, notably the Homestead Steel Company in 1888, and began selling his steel, which initially had been used primarily to manufacture rails and bridge girders for railroads, to companies that utilized new technologies for plating and pressing steel to make barbed wire, tubing, and other products. In 1892, he combined his assets into the Carnegie Steel Company and by 1900 controlled about 60 percent of the country's steel business. In 1901, Carnegie retired, selling his holdings to a group organized by J. P. Morgan, who formed the huge U.S. Steel Corporation.

The du Ponts and the Chemical Industry

The du Pont family's role in the chemical industry matched that of Edison, Carnegie, and Ford in their respective industries. Eleuthiere Irenee du Pont, a French immigrant, began manufacturing gunpowder in Delaware in the early 1800s. In 1902, fearing antitrust prosecution for the company's near monopoly of the American explosives industry, three cousins, Alfred, Coleman, and Pierre, took over E. I. du Pont de Nemours and Company, and broadened production into fertilizers, dyes, and other chemical products. In 1911, du Pont scientists working in the nation's first corporate research laboratory adapted cellulose to the production of such consumer goods as photographic film, textile fibers, and plastics. The du Pont company also pioneered methods of management, accounting, and reinvestment of earnings, all of which contributed to efficient production, better record-keeping, and higher profits.

Technology and Southern Industry

The South's major staple crops, tobacco and cotton, drew industry to the region after the Civil War, and other forms of production developed as well. Americans first used tobacco mainly for snuff, cigars, and chewing. But in 1876 James Bonsack, an eighteen-year-old Virginian, invented a machine for rolling cigarettes. In 1885, James B. Duke, owner of a North Carolina tobacco company, licensed Bonsack's machine and began mass-production. Like Edison and Ford, Duke marketed what he manufactured. Sales soared when he began enticing consumers with free samples, trading cards, and billboard ads. By 1900, his American Tobacco Company was a global business, dominating sales in England and Japan as well as the United States. Duke's and other cigarette factories employed black and white workers (including women), though in separate locations of the plant.

New technology helped relocate the textile industry to the South, as electricity made New England's water-powered mills obsolete. Factories with electric looms were more efficient because they needed fewer workers with fewer skills, and electric lighting expanded hours of production. Investors built new plants in southern communities, where a cheap labor force was available. By 1900, the South had more than four hundred textile mills. Women and children who worked in these mills earned 50 cents a day for twelve or more hours of work—about half the wages that northern millworkers received. Most mills refused to hire black workers except as janitors. Many companies built villages around their mills, where they controlled housing, stores, schools, and churches. Inside these towns, owners banned criticism of the company and squelched attempts at union organization.

Northern and European as well as the region's own investors financed other southern industries. During the 1880s, northern capitalists developed southern iron and steel manufacturing, much of it in the boom city of Birmingham, Alabama. Between 1890 and 1900, northern lumber syndicates moved into the pine forests of the Gulf states, boosting production 500 percent. Southern wood production not only advanced the construction industry but also prompted the relocation of furniture and paper production from the North to the South.

Encouraged by industrial expansion, boosters heralded the emergence of a New South. A business class of manufacturers, merchants, and financiers made southern cities nerve centers of a new economic order, challenging the power of the planter class. Industrialists believed the South should put the military defeat of the Civil War behind it—though never forget the heroism of Confederate soldiers—and emulate the North's economic growth. Henry Grady, editor of the *Atlanta Constitution* and passionate advocate of southern progress, proclaimed, "We have sowed towns and cities in the place of theories, and put business in place of politics. We have challenged your spinners in Massachusetts and your iron-makers in Pennsylvania.... We have fallen in love with work."

Consequences of Technology   In all regions, the timing of technological innovation varied from one industry to another, but machines broadly altered the economy and everyday life. Telephones and typewriters made face-to-face communication less important and facilitated correspondence and recordkeeping in growing insurance and banking as well as industrial firms. Electric sewing machines made mass-produced clothing available to almost everyone. Refrigeration changed dietary habits by enabling the preservation and shipment of meat, fruit, vegetables, and dairy products. Cash registers and adding machines revamped accounting and created new clerical jobs. At the same time, American universities established programs in engineering, enabling manufacturers such as Edison and the du Ponts to hire new graduates in chemistry and physics.

In many instances, initial advances in technology originated abroad. Europeans were responsible for early discoveries in electricity and internal combustion engines.

Taken at the historic moment of liftoff, this photograph shows the first airplane flight at Kitty Hawk, North Carolina, on December 17, 1903. With Orville Wright lying at the controls and brother Wilbur standing nearby, the plane was airborne only twelve seconds and traveled 120 feet. Even so, the flight marked the beginning of one of the twentieth century's most influential industries.

Library of Congress

The Bessemer process for producing steel was developed in England, and the du Ponts imported both capital and machinery from France for their gunpowder operation. But Americans proved particularly adroit at adapting and advancing these developments. Edison's trial-and-error experiments in electic lighting, Carnegie employees' utilization of the Bessemer steelmaking process, Ford's assembly-line production of automobiles, southern textile owners' use of faster looms, construction companies' development of huge steam shovels—all these and more enabled the United States to surpass other industrializing nations in output by the turn of the century.

Profits resulted from higher production at lower costs. Skilled crafts, such as cabinet making and metalworking, persisted, but as technological innovations made large-scale production more economical, owners replaced small workshops with large factories. Between 1850 and 1900, average capital investment in a manufacturing firm increased by 250 percent. Only large companies could afford to buy complex machines and operate them at full capacity. And large companies could best take advantage of discounts for shipping products in bulk and buying raw materials in quantity. Economists call such advantages economies of scale.

Profitability depended as much on how production was arranged as on the machines in use. Where once workers controlled the methods and timing of production, by the 1890s engineers and managers with "expert" knowledge had assumed this responsibility. They planned every task to increase output. Through standardization, they reduced the need for human skills and judgment, boosting profits at the expense of worker independence.

Frederick W. Taylor and Efficiency

The most influential advocate of efficient production was Frederick W. Taylor. As foreman and engineer for the Midvale Steel Company in the 1880s, Taylor concluded that the best way a company could reduce costs and increase profits was to apply studies of "how quickly the various kinds of work ... ought to be done." The "ought" in Taylor's formulation signified producing more for lower cost per unit, usually by eliminating unnecessary workers. Similarly, "how quickly" meant that time and money were equivalent. He called his scheme "scientific management."

In 1898, Taylor took his stopwatch to the Bethlehem Steel Company to illustrate how his principles worked. His experiments, he explained, required studying workers and devising "a series of motions which can be made quickest and best." Applying this technique to the shoveling of ore, Taylor designed fifteen kinds of shovels and prescribed proper motions for using each one, thereby reducing a crew of 600 men to 140. Soon other companies began applying Taylor's theories to their production lines.

As a result of Taylor's writings and experiments, time, as much as quality, became the measure of acceptable work, and management accumulated knowledge of and power over the ways of doing things. As integral elements of the assembly line, which divided work into specific time-determined tasks, employees feared they were becoming another kind of interchangeable part.

MECHANIZATION AND THE CHANGING STATUS OF LABOR

By 1900, the status of labor had shifted dramatically in just a single generation. Technological innovation and assembly-line production created new jobs, but because most machines were labor saving, fewer workers could produce more in less time. Moreover, workers could no longer be termed producers, as farmers and craftsmen had traditionally thought of themselves. The working class now consisted mainly of employees—people who worked not on their own but when someone hired them. Producers had been paid in accordance with the quality of what they produced; employees received wages for time spent on the job.

Mass Production   By subdividing manufacturing into small tasks, mass production required workers to repeat the same standardized operation all day every day. One investigator found that a worker became

> a mere machine…. Take the proposition of a man operating a machine to nail on 40 to 60 cases of heels in a day. That is 2,400 pairs, 4,800 shoes in a day. One not accustomed to it would wonder how a man could pick up and lay down 4,800 shoes in a day, to say nothing of putting them… into a machine…. That is the driving method of the manufacture of shoes under these minute subdivisions.

Assembly lines and scientific management also deprived employees of their independence. Workers could no longer decide when to begin and end the workday, when to rest, what tools and techniques to use. The clock regulated them. As a Massachusetts factory laborer testified in 1879, "[d]uring working hours the men are not allowed to speak to each other, though working close together, on pain of instant discharge. Men are hired to watch and patrol the shop." And employees now were surrounded by others who labored at the same rate for the same pay.

Workers affected by these changes struggled to retain autonomy and self-respect in the face of employers' ever-increasing power. Artisans such as glass workers and coopers (barrel makers), caught in the transition from hand labor to machine production, fought to preserve their work pace and customs—say, by appointing a fellow worker to read a newspaper aloud while they worked. When immigrants went to work in factories, they tried to persuade foremen to hire their relatives and friends, thus preserving on-the-job family and village ties. Off the job, workers gathered in saloons and parks for such leisure-time activities as social drinking and holiday celebrations, ignoring employers' attempts to control their social lives.

Restructuring of the Work Force

Employers, concerned with efficiency, wanted certain standards of behavior upheld. Ford Motor Company required a worker to satisfy the company's behavior code before becoming eligible for a part of the Five-Dollar-Day plan. To increase worker incentives, some employers established piecework rates, paying laborers an amount per item produced rather than an hourly wage. These efforts to increase productivity and maximize use of machines were intended to make workers perform like the machines they operated.

As machines and assembly lines reduced the need for skilled workers, employers found they could cut labor costs by hiring women and children, and paying them low wages. Between 1880 and 1900, the numbers of employed women soared from 2.6 million to 8.6 million. At the same time, their occupational patterns underwent striking changes (see Figure 18.1). The proportion of women in domestic service (maids, cooks, laundresses)—the most common and lowest-paid form of female employment—dropped as jobs opened in other sectors. In manufacturing, women usually held menial positions in textile mills and food-processing plants that paid as little as $1.56 a week for seventy hours of labor. (Unskilled men received $7 to $10 for a similar workweek.) Although the number of female factory hands tripled between 1880 and 1900, the proportion of women workers in these jobs remained about the same.

Expansion of the clerical and retail sectors, however, greatly boosted the numbers and percentages of women who were typists, bookkeepers, and sales clerks. Previously, men with accounting and letter-writing skills had dominated sales and office positions. New inventions, such as the typewriter, cash register, and adding machine, simplified these tasks, and employers replaced males with lower-paid females, many of whom had taken courses in typing and shorthand in school. By 1920, women filled nearly half of all clerical jobs; in 1880, only 4 percent had been women. An official of a sugar company observed in 1919 that "all the bookkeeping of this company ... is done by three girls and three bookkeeping machines ... one operator takes the place of three men." Although poorly paid, women were attracted to sales jobs because of the respectability, pleasant surroundings, and contact with affluent customers that such positions offered compared with factory and domestic work. Nevertheless, sex discrimination persisted. In department stores, male cashiers handled cash transactions; women seldom were given responsibility for billing or for counting money. Women held some low-level supervisory positions, but males dominated managerial ranks.

Although most children who worked toiled on their parents' farms, the number in nonagricultural occupations tripled between 1870 and 1900. In 1890, over

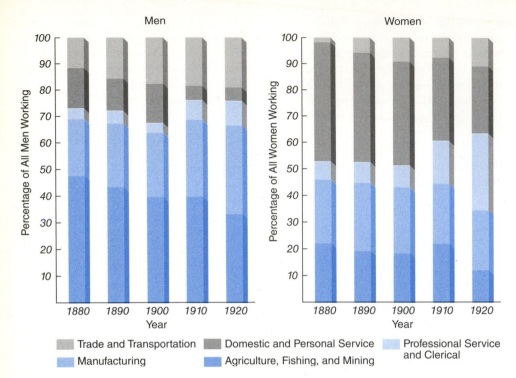

FIGURE 18.1 Distribution of Occupational Categories Among Employed Men and Women, 1880–1920

The changing lengths of the bar segments of each part of this graph represent trends in male and female employment. Over the forty years covered by this graph, the agriculture, fishing, and mining segment for men and the domestic service segment for women declined the most, whereas notable increases occurred in manufacturing for men and professional services (especially store clerks and teachers) for women.

Source: U.S. Bureau of the Census, *Census of the United States, 1880, 1890, 1900, 1910, 1920* (Washington, D.C.: U.S. Government Printing Office).

18 percent of all children between ages ten and fifteen were gainfully employed (see Figure 18.2). Textile and shoe factories in particular employed young workers. Mechanization created numerous light tasks, such as running errands and helping machine operators, which children could handle at a fraction of adult wages. Conditions were especially hard for child laborers in the South, where growing numbers of textile mills needed unskilled hands. Mill owners induced white sharecroppers and tenant farmers, who desperately needed extra income, to bind their children over to factories at miserably low wages.

Several states, especially in the Northeast, passed laws specifying minimum ages and maximum workday hours for child labor. But large companies could evade regulations because such statutes regulated only firms operating within state borders, not those engaged in interstate commerce. Enforcing age requirements proved difficult because many parents, needing income from child labor, lied about their children's ages, and employers rarely asked. After 1900, state laws and automation,

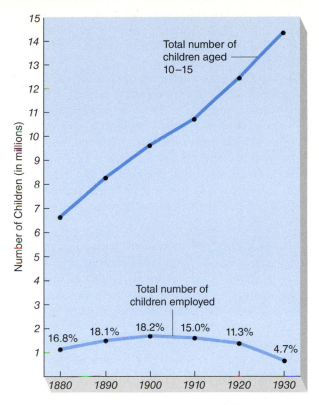

FIGURE 18.2 Children in the Labor Force, 1880–1930

The percentage of children in the labor force peaked around the turn of the century. Thereafter, the passage of state laws requiring children to attend school until age fourteen and limiting the ages at which children could be employed caused child labor to decline.

Source: Data from *The Statistical History of the United States from Colonial Times to the Present* (Stamford, Conn.: Fairfield Publishers, 1965).

along with compulsory school attendance laws, began to reduce the number of children employed in manufacturing, and Progressive era reformers sought federal legislation to restrict child labor (see Chapter 21). Still, many children continued to work at street trades—shining shoes and peddling newspapers and other merchandise—and as helpers in stores. The poorest children also scavenged city streets for pieces of coal and wood, discarded clothing and furniture, and other items their families could use.

Industrial
Accidents
For all workers, industrial labor was dangerous. Repetitive tasks using high-speed machinery dulled concentration, and the slightest mistake could cause serious injury. Industrial accidents rose steadily before 1920, killing or maiming hundreds of thousands of people each year. In 1913, for example, even after factory owners had installed

safety devices, some twenty-five thousand people died in industrial mishaps, and 1 million were injured. For those with mangled limbs, infected cuts, and chronic illnesses, there was no disability insurance to replace lost income, and families stricken by such misfortunes suffered acutely.

Sensational disasters, such as explosions and mine cave-ins, aroused outcries for better safety regulations. The most notorious tragedy was a fire at New York City's Triangle Shirtwaist Company in 1911, which killed 146 workers, most of them teenage immigrant women trapped in locked workrooms. Despite public clamor, prevailing free-market views hampered passage of legislation that would regulate working conditions, and employers denied responsibility for employees' well-being. As one railroad manager declared, "The regular compensation of employees covers all risk or liability to accident. If an employee is disabled by sickness or any other cause, the right to claim compensation is not recognized."

Freedom of Contract   To justify their treatment of workers, employers asserted the principle of "freedom of contract." The relationship between employee and employer, according to this principle, resembled one between a customer and a seller. Like the price of an item for sale, wages and working conditions were the result of a free market in which laws of supply and demand prevailed. In addition, employers asserted, workers entered into a contract with bosses, either explicit or assumed, in which they "sold" their labor. If a worker did not like the contract's provisions, such as the wages and hours, the worker was free to decline and seek another job elsewhere, just as the customer was free to buy a product somewhere else. In practice, however, employers used supply and demand to set wages as low as laborers would accept, causing workers to conclude that the system trapped them. A factory worker told Congress in 1879, "The market is glutted, and we have seasons of dullness; advantage is taken of men's wants, and the pay is cut down; our tasks are increased, and if we remonstrate, we are told our places can be filled. I work harder now than when my pay was twice as high."

Court Rulings on Labor Reform   Reformers and union leaders lobbied Congress for laws to improve working conditions, but the Supreme Court, agreeing with business interests, limited the scope of such legislation by narrowly defining which jobs were dangerous and which workers needed protection. In *Holden v. Hardy* (1896), the Court upheld a law regulating miners' working hours, concluding that an overly long workday would increase the threat of injury. In *Lochner v. New York* (1905), however, the Court voided a law limiting bakery workers to a sixty-hour week and ten-hour day. Offsetting the argument that states had authority to protect workers' health and safety, the Court ruled that baking was not a dangerous enough occupation to justify restricting workers' right to sell their labor freely. Such restriction, according to the Court, violated the Fourteenth Amendment's guarantee that no state could "deprive any person of life, liberty, or property without due process of law."

In *Muller v. Oregon* (1908), the Court used a different rationale to uphold a law limiting women in laundries to a ten-hour workday. In this case, the Court set aside its *Lochner* argument that a state could not interfere with an individual's right of contract, asserting instead that a woman's well-being as the bearer of children "becomes an object of public interest and care in order to preserve the strength and vigor of the race." The case represented a victory for reform groups such as the Consumers' League, which had sought government regulation of women's hours and working conditions. As a result of the *Muller* decision, however, labor laws effectively barred women from occupations, such as in printing and transportation, that required heavy lifting, long hours, or night work, further confining women to low-paying, dead-end jobs.

LABOR VIOLENCE AND THE UNION MOVEMENT

Workers adjusted to mechanization as best they could. Some submitted to the demands of the factory, machine, and time clock. Some tried to blend old ways of working into the new system. Others resisted. Individuals challenged the system by ignoring management's orders, skipping work, or quitting. But anxiety over the loss of independence and desire for better wages, hours, and working conditions drew disgruntled workers into unions. Organized labor was not new in the late nineteenth century. Trade unions for skilled workers in crafts such as printing and iron molding dated from the early 1800s, but their influence was limited. But by the 1870s, the spread of companies with large labor forces and the tightening of management control spurred a unionization response.

Railroad Strikes of 1877   In the economic slump that followed the Panic of 1873, railroad managers cut wages, increased workloads, and laid off workers, especially those who had joined unions. Such actions drove workers to strike and riot. The year 1877 marked a crisis. In July, unionized railroad men organized a series of strikes to oppose wage cuts. Venting pent-up anger, protesters attacked railroad property from Pennsylvania and West Virginia to the Midwest, Texas, and California, derailing trains and burning rail yards. State militias, organized and commanded by employers, broke up picket lines and fired into threatening crowds. In several communities, factory workers, wives, and merchants aided the strikers, while railroads enlisted strikebreakers to replace union men.

The worst violence occurred in Pittsburgh, where on July 21 state troops bayoneted and fired on rock-throwing demonstrators, killing ten and wounding many more. Infuriated, the mob drove the troops into a railroad roundhouse and set fires that destroyed 39 buildings, 104 engines, and 1,245 freight and passenger cars. The next day, the troops shot their way out of the roundhouse and killed twenty more citizens before fleeing the city. After more than a month of further violence, President Rutherford B. Hayes sent in federal soldiers—the first significant use of the army to quell labor unrest. Throughout the strike, emotions ran high. A Pennsylvania militiaman, ordered to break the 1877 strike, recalled, "I talked to all the strikers I could get my hands on, and I could find but one spirit and one purpose among them—that they were justified in resorting to any means to break down the power of the corporations."

Knights of Labor

Although they sometimes spoke for all laborers, railroad workers had struck in 1877 in their own interest. About the same time, however, an organization called the Knights of Labor tried to attract a broad base of laborers. Founded in 1869 by Philadelphia garment cutters, the Knights began recruiting other workers in the 1870s. In 1879, Terence V. Powderly, a machinist and mayor of Scranton, Pennsylvania, was elected grand master. Under his guidance, Knights membership grew rapidly, peaking at 730,000 in 1886. In contrast to most craft unions, Knights welcomed unskilled and semiskilled workers, including women, immigrants, and African Americans (but not Chinese laborers).

The Knights tried to avert the bleak future they believed industrialism portended by building an alternative to profit-oriented industrial capitalism. They intended to eliminate conflict between labor and management by establishing a cooperative society in which workers, not capitalists, owned factories, mines, and railroads. The goal, argued Powderly, was to "eventually make every man his own master—every man his own employer." The cooperative idea, attractive in the abstract, was unattainable because employers held the economic leverage and could outcompete and out-invest laborers who might try to establish their own businesses. Strikes offered one means of achieving immediate goals, but Powderly and other Knights leaders argued that strikes tended to divert attention from the long-term goal of a cooperative society and that workers tended to lose more by striking than they won.

Some Knights, however, supported militant action. In 1886, the Knights demanded higher wages and union recognition from railroads in the Southwest. Railroad magnate Jay Gould refused to negotiate, and a strike began in Texas, then spread to Kansas, Missouri, and Arkansas. As violence increased, Powderly met with Gould and called off the strike, hoping for a settlement. But Gould again rejected concessions, and the Knights gave in. Militant craft unions began to desert the Knights, upset by Powderly's compromise and confident that they could attain more on their own.

After the Haymarket riot (see below), Knights membership dwindled, although the union and its cooperative vision survived in a few small towns, where it made a brief attempt to unite with Populists in the 1890s (see Chapter 20). The special interests of craft unions replaced the Knights' broad-based but often vague appeal, and dreams of labor unity faded.

Haymarket Riot

The same year that Knights struck against railroads in the Southwest, workers both inside and outside unions generated mass strikes in favor of an eight-hour workday. On May 1, 1886, in Chicago, some 100,000 such workers turned out for the largest labor demonstration in the country's history. Their numbers included anarchists who believed in using violence to replace all government with voluntary cooperation. Chicago police, fearing that European radicals were transplanting a tradition of violence to the United States, mobilized to prevent disorder, especially among striking workers at the huge McCormick reaper plant. The day passed calmly, but two days later, police stormed an area near the factory and broke up a battle between unionists and nonunion strikebreakers, killing two unionists and wounding several others.

The Haymarket riot of 1886 was one of the most violent incidents of labor unrest in the late nineteenth century. This drawing, from Frank Leslie's Illustrated Newspaper, *shows workers fleeing while police beat demonstrators with nightsticks. As this clash was occurring, a bomb, allegedly set off by anarchists, exploded, killing both police and workers.*

The next evening, laborers gathered at Haymarket Square near downtown Chicago to protest police brutality. As a police company approached the rally, a bomb exploded, killing seven and injuring sixty-seven. In reaction, authorities made mass arrests of anarchists and unionists. Eventually a court convicted eight anarchists of the bombing, though evidence of their guilt was questionable. Four were executed, and one committed suicide in prison. The remaining three received pardons in 1893 from Illinois governor John P. Altgeld, who believed they had been victims of the jurors' "malicious ferocity." Denounced by capitalists as a friend of anarchy, Altgeld found that his act of conscience ruined his political career.

The Haymarket bombing, like the 1877 railroad strikes, heightened fears of labor discontent and of radicalism. The presence of anarchists and socialists at Haymarket, many of them foreign-born, created a feeling that civic leaders must act swiftly to prevent social turmoil. To protect their interests, private Chicago donors helped to establish a military base near the city. Elsewhere, governments strengthened police forces and armories. Employer associations, coalitions of manufacturers in the same industry, countered labor militancy by circulating blacklists of union activists whom they would not employ and by hiring private detectives to guard company property and suppress strikes.

American Federation of Labor

The American Federation of Labor (AFL) emerged from the upheavals of 1886 as the major workers' organization. An alliance of national craft unions, the AFL had about 140,000 members, most of them skilled workers. Led by Samuel Gompers, former head of the Cigar Makers' Union, the AFL avoided the Knights' and anarchists' idealism to press for concrete goals: higher wages, shorter hours, and the right to bargain collectively. Born in London to German Jewish parents, Gompers developed his commitment to unionism from interactions with émigré socialists, but he was more of a pragmatist than a radical. In contrast to the Knights, Gompers and the AFL accepted capitalism and worked to improve conditions within it.

AFL member unions retained autonomy in their own areas of skill but tried to develop a policy that would suit all members. The national organization required constituent unions to hire organizers to expand membership, and it collected dues for a fund to aid members on strike. The AFL avoided party politics, adhering instead to Gompers's dictum of supporting labor's friends and opposing its enemies, regardless of party.

AFL membership grew to 1 million by 1901 and 2.5 million by 1917, when it consisted of 111 national unions and 27,000 locals. But because member unions organized by craft rather than by workplace, they had little interest in recruiting unskilled workers. Nor did they recruit women. Of 6.3 million employed women in 1910, fewer than 2 percent belonged to unions. Male unionists rationalized women's exclusion by insisting that women should not be employed. According to one labor leader, "Woman is not qualified for the conditions of wage labor…. The mental and physical makeup of woman is in revolt against wage service. She is competing with the man who is her father or husband or is to become her husband." Mostly, unionists worried that, because women were paid less, men's wages would be lowered or they would lose jobs if women invaded the workplace. Moreover, male workers, accustomed to sex segregation in employment, could not imagine working side by side with women.

Organized labor also excluded most immigrants and African Americans. Many white workers feared that such groups would depress wages, but outright nativism and racism also influenced union policies. Only a few trade unions in which foreign-born craftsmen were leaders welcomed immigrants. Blacks were prominent in the coal miners' union and were partially unionized in such trades as construction, barbering, and dock work, which employed numerous African American workers. But they could belong only to segregated local unions in the South, and the majority of northern AFL unions had exclusion policies. Long-held prejudices were reinforced when blacks and immigrants, eager for any work they could get, accepted jobs as strikebreakers to replace striking whites.

Homestead and Pullman Strikes   The AFL and the labor movement suffered setbacks in the early 1890s, when once again labor violence stirred public fears. In July 1892, the AFL-affiliated Amalgamated Association of Iron and Steelworkers refused to accept pay cuts and went on strike in Homestead, Pennsylvania. In response, Henry C. Frick, president of Carnegie Steel Company, closed the plant. Shortly thereafter, Frick hired three hundred guards from the Pinkerton Detective Agency to protect the factory and floated them in by barge under cover of darkness. Lying in wait on the shore of the Monongahela River, angry workers attacked and routed the Pinkertons. State troops intervened, and after five months the strikers gave in. By then, public opinion had turned against the union, after a young anarchist who was not a striker attempted to assassinate Frick.

In 1894, workers at the Pullman Palace (railroad passenger) Car Company walked out in protest over exploitative policies at the company town near Chicago.

The paternalistic owner, George Pullman, provided everything for the twelve thousand residents of the so-called model town named after him. His company controlled all land and buildings, the school, the bank, and the water and gas systems. It paid wages, fixed rents, and spied on disgruntled employees. As one laborer grumbled, "We are born in a Pullman house, fed from the Pullman shop, taught in the Pullman school, catechized in the Pullman church, and when we die we shall be buried in the Pullman cemetery and go to the Pullman hell."

One thing Pullman would not do was negotiate with workers. When hard times hit in 1893, Pullman tried to protect profits and stock dividends by cutting wages 25 to 40 percent while holding firm on rents and prices in the town. Hard-pressed workers sent a committee to Pullman to protest his policies. He reacted by firing three committee members. Enraged workers, most of them from the American Railway Union, called a strike; Pullman retaliated by closing the factory. The union, led by the charismatic Eugene V. Debs, voted to aid strikers by refusing to handle any Pullman cars attached to any trains anywhere. Pullman rejected arbitration. The railroad owners' association then enlisted aid from U.S. Attorney General Richard Olney, a former railroad lawyer, who obtained a court injunction to prevent the union from "obstructing the railways and holding up the mails." President Grover Cleveland ordered federal troops to Chicago, ostensibly to protect rail-carried mail, but in reality to crush the strike. Within a month, strikers gave in, and Debs was imprisoned for defying the court injunction. The Supreme Court upheld Debs's six-month sentence on grounds that the federal government could legally remove obstacles to interstate commerce.

Labor Violence in the West

In the West, unionized miners, led by the Western Federation of Miners (WFM), engaged in some especially violent strikes during the 1890s. In 1894, at Cripple Creek, Colorado, fighting eruped when miners struck after mine owners increased the workday from eight to ten hours without increasing pay. When negotiations broke down, owners organized a private army to protect strikebreaking workers, and miners formed their own fighting force in response. The two sides battled for over a week until state militia, called out by Governor Davis Waite, intervened. Waite obtained a settlement with mine owners agreeing to restore the eight-hour day. As a result, membership in the WFM rose but so, too, did reaction by employers against the union.

In Idaho, federal troops were called out three times to combat striking miners and protect company property during the 1890s. In 1899, after strikers blew up buildings of the Bunker Hill Mining Company in Wardner, Idaho, soldiers arrested every male in the town, and Governor Frank Steunenberg declared martial law. In 1905, Steunenberg, no longer in office, was assassinated outside his home; speculation arose that the WFM had killed him out of revenge. Investigation by Pinkerton Detective James McParland resulted in the arrest of WFM Secretary-Treasurer William "Big Bill" Haywood, a brawny, one-eyed radical, and two other WFM officials. Tried for murder in 1907, Haywood was acquitted after his attorney, the famed Clarence Darrow, subverted testimony of a key witness.

IWW

In 1905, in the wake of these and other events, rebel unionists formed a new, radical labor organization, the Industrial Workers of the World (IWW). Unlike the AFL but like the Knights of Labor, the IWW strove to unite all laborers of all races who were excluded from craft unions. Its motto was "An injury to one is an injury to all," and its goal was "One Big Union." But the "Wobblies," as IWW members were known, exceeded the tactics of the Knights by espousing violence and sabotage. Embracing rhetoric of class conflict and an ideology of socialism, Wobblies believed workers should seize and run the nation's industries. Leaders such as Haywood; Mary "Mother" Jones, an Illinois coalfield union organizer; Elizabeth Gurley Flynn, a fiery orator known as the "Joan of Arc of the labor movement"; Italian radical Carlo Tresca; and Swedish-born organizer and songwriter Joe Hill headed a series of strife-torn strikes. Demonstrations erupted in the steel town of McKees Rocks, Pennsylvania (1907), and in textile mills at Lawrence, Massachusetts (1912), as well as in the western lumber and mining camps. Although the Wobblies' anticapitalist goals and aggressive tactics attracted considerable publicity, the organization collapsed during the First World War when federal prosecution sent many of its leaders to jail and local police forces violently harassed IWW members.

Women Unionists

Despite their general exclusion from unions, some women employees organized and fought employers as strenuously as men did. The "Uprising of the 20,000" in New York City, a 1909 strike by male and female immigrant members of the International Ladies' Garment Workers' Union (ILGWU), was one of the country's largest strikes to that time. Women were also prominent in the 1912 Lawrence, Massachusetts, textile workers' "Bread and Roses" strike. Female trade-union membership grew during the 1910s, but men monopolized national leadership, even in industries with large female work forces, such as garment manufacturing, textiles, and boots and shoes.

Women, however, did dominate one union: the Telephone Operators' Department of the International Brotherhood of Electrical Workers. Organized in Boston in 1912, the union spread throughout the Bell system, the nation's monopolistic telephone company and single largest employer of women. To promote solidarity among their mostly young female members, union leaders organized dances, excursions, and bazaars. They also sponsored educational programs to enhance members' leadership skills. The union focused mainly on workplace issues. Intent on developing pride and independence among telephone operators, the union resisted scientific management techniques and tightening of supervision. In 1919, several militant union branches paralyzed the phone service of five New England states, but the union collapsed after a failed strike, again in New England, in 1923.

A key organization seeking to promote interests of laboring women was the Women's Trade Union League (WTUL), founded in 1903 and patterned after a similar organization in England. The WTUL sought legislation to improve workplace conditions and reduce hours for workers, sponsored educational activities, and campaigned for woman suffrage. It helped telephone operators organize their union, and in 1909 it supported the ILGWU's massive strike against New York City sweatshops. Initially the WTUL's highest offices were held by middle-class women who sympathized with female wage laborers, but control shifted in the 1910s to forceful working-class leaders, notably Agnes Nestor, a glove maker; Rose Schneiderman, a cap maker; and Mary Anderson, a shoe worker. The WTUL advocated opening apprenticeship programs to women so they could enter skilled trades and training female workers to assume leadership roles. It served as a vital link between the labor and women's movements into the 1920s.

The Experience of Wage Work The dramatic labor struggles in the half-century following the Civil War make it easy to forget that only a small fraction of American wage workers belonged to unions. In 1900, about 1 million out of a total of 27.6 million workers were unionized. By 1920, union membership had grown to 5 million, still only 13 percent of the work force. Unionization was strong in construction trades, transportation, communications, and, to a lesser extent, manufacturing. For many workers, getting and keeping a job took priority over bargaining for higher wages and shorter hours. Job instability and the seasonal nature of work seriously hindered union-organizing efforts. Few companies employed a full work force year-round; most employers hired during peak seasons and laid workers off during slack periods. The 1880 census showed that in some communities, 30 percent of adult males had been jobless at some time during the previous year. Moreover, union organizers took no interest in large segments of the industrial labor force and intentionally barred others.

The millions of men, women, and children who were not unionized tried in their own ways to cope with pressures of the machine age. Increasing numbers, both native-born and immigrant, joined fraternal societies, such as the Polish Roman Catholic Union, the African American Colored Brotherhood and Sisterhood of Honor, and the Jewish B'nai B'rith. For small monthly or yearly contributions these organizations, widespread by the early twentieth century, provided members with life insurance, sickness benefits, and burial costs.

For most American workers, then, the machine age had mixed results. Industrial wages, though rarely generous, rose between 1877 and 1914, boosting purchasing power and creating a mass market for standardized goods. Yet in 1900 most employees worked sixty hours a week at wages that averaged 20 cents an hour for skilled work and 10 cents an hour for unskilled. And workers found that, even as wages rose, living costs increased even faster.

STANDARDS OF LIVING

Some Americans distrusted a system that treated them like machines, but few could resist experts' claims that the industrial system was improving everyday life. The expansion of railroad, postal, and telephone service drew even once-isolated communities into the orbit of a consumer society. American ingenuity combined with mass production and mass marketing to make available myriad goods that previously had not existed or had been the exclusive property of the wealthy. As a result, Americans were better fed, better clothed, and better housed than ever before. The new material well-being, symbolized by canned foods, ready-made clothing, and home appliances, had a dual effect. It absorbed Americans into consumer communities defined not by place of residence but by possessions, and it accentuated differences between those who could afford goods and services and those who could not.

Commonplace Luxuries   If a society's affluence is measured by how it converts luxuries into commonplace articles, the United States was indeed becoming affluent between 1880 and 1920. In 1880, only residents of Florida, Texas, and California could enjoy fresh oranges; smokers rolled their own cigarettes; and people made candy and soap at home. By 1899, manufactured goods and perishable foodstuffs had become increasingly available. That year, Americans consumed oranges at the rate of 100 crates for every 1,000 people, bought 2 billion machine-produced cigarettes, and spent averages of $1.08 per person on store-bought candy and 63 cents per person on soap. By 1921, the transformation had advanced further. Americans smoked 43 billion cigarettes that year (403 per person), ate 248 crates of oranges per 1,000 people, and spent $1.66 per person on confectionery goods and $1.40 on soap.

What people can afford obviously depends on their resources and incomes. Data for the period show that incomes rose broadly. At the top of society, the expanding economy spawned massive fortunes and created a new industrial elite. An 1891 magazine article estimated that 120 Americans were worth at least $10 million ($250 million in current dollars). By 1920, the richest 5 percent of the population received almost one-fourth of all earned income. Incomes also rose among the middle class. For example, average pay for clerical workers rose 36 percent between 1890 and 1910 (see Table 18.1). In 1900, employees of the federal executive branch averaged $1,072 a year, and college professors, $1,100 (around $30,000 in modern dollars)—not handsome sums, but much more than manual workers received. With such salaries, the middle class, whose numbers were increasing as a result of new job opportunities, could afford relatively comfortable housing. A six- or seven-room house cost around $3,000 to buy or build (about $70,000 in current dollars) and from $15 to $20 per month ($400 to $500 in current dollars) to rent.

Although hourly wages for industrial employees increased, workers had to expend a disproportionate amount of income on necessities. On average, annual wages of factory laborers rose about 30 percent, from $486 in 1890 (about $12,000 in modern dollars) to $630 in 1910 (about $15,500 in current dollars). In industries with large female work forces, such as shoe manufacturing, hourly pay rates remained lower than in male-dominated industries, such as coal mining and iron production. Regional variations were also wide. Nevertheless, as Table 18.1 shows, most wages moved upward. Income for farm laborers followed the same trend, though wages remained relatively low because farm workers usually received free room and board.

Cost of Living   Wage increases mean little, however, if living costs rise as fast or faster. That is what happened. In few working-class occupations did incomes rise as fast as prices. The weekly cost of living for a typical wage earner's family of four rose over 47 percent between 1889 and 1913.

TABLE 18.1 | AMERICAN LIVING STANDARDS, 1890–1910

	1890	1910
Income and Earnings		
Annual income		
Clerical worker	$848	$1,156
Public school teacher	256	492
Industrial worker	486	630
Farm laborer	233	336
Hourly wage		
Soft-coal miner	0.18*	0.21
Iron worker	0.17*	0.23
Shoe worker	0.14*	0.19
Paper worker	0.12*	0.17
Labor Statistics		
Number of people in labor force	28.5 million	41.7 million**
Average workweek in manufacturing	60 hours	51 hours

*1892
**1920

Thus, a combination of housing, food, and other goods that cost $68 in 1889 increased, after a slight dip in the mid-1890s, to $100 by 1913.

How, then, could working-class Americans afford machine-age goods and services? Many could not. The daughter of a textile worker, recalling her school days, described how "some of the kids would bring bars of chocolate, others an orange.... I suppose they were richer than a family like ours. My father used to buy a bag of candy and a bag of peanuts every payday.... And that's all we'd have until the next payday." Another woman explained how her family coped with high prices and low wages: "My mother made our clothes. People then wore old clothes. My mother would rip them out and make them over."

Supplements to Family Income Still, a family could raise its income and partake modestly in consumer society by sending children and women into the labor market. In a household whose main breadwinner made $600 a year, wages of other family members might lift total family income to $800 or $900. Many families also rented rooms to boarders and lodgers, a practice that could yield up to $200 a year. These means of increasing family income enabled people to purchase important services. Between 1889 and 1901, working-class families markedly increased expenditures for life insurance and funeral policies as well as for new leisure activities (see Chapter 19). Workers were thus able to improve their living standard, but not without sacrifices.

More than ever, American working people lived within a highly developed money economy. Between 1890 and 1920, the labor force increased by 50 percent, from 28 million workers to 42 million. These figures, however, are misleading because they represent a change in the nature of work as much as an increase in the number of available jobs. In rural households that predominated in the nineteenth century, women and children performed tasks crucial to a family's daily existence—cooking, cleaning, planting, and harvesting—but these jobs seldom appeared in employment figures because they earned no wages. As the nation industrialized and the agricultural sector's share of national income declined, paid employment became more common. Jobs in urban industries and commerce were easier to define and easier to count. The proportion of Americans who worked—whether in fields, households, factories, or offices—probably did not increase markedly. Most Americans, male and female, had always worked. What was new was the increase in paid employment, making purchases of consumer goods and services more affordable.

Higher Life Expectancy
Science and technology eased some of life's struggles, and their impact on living standards strengthened after 1900. Medical advances, better diets, and improved housing sharply reduced death rates and extended life. Between 1900 and 1920, life expectancy rose by fully six years, and the death rate dropped by 24 percent. Notable declines occurred in deaths from typhoid, diphtheria, influenza (except for a harsh pandemic in 1918 and 1919), tuberculosis, and intestinal ailments—diseases that had been scourges of earlier generations. There were, however, significantly more deaths from cancer, diabetes, and heart disease, afflictions of an aging population and of new environmental factors such as smoke and chemical pollution. Americans also found more ways to kill one another: although suicide rates remained stable, homicides and automobile-related deaths—effects of a fast-paced urban society—increased dramatically.

Not only were amenities and luxuries more available than in the previous half-century, means to upward mobility seemed more accessible as well. Although inequities that pervaded earlier eras remained in place, and race, gender, religion, and ethnicity still affected access to opportunity, education increasingly became the key to success. Public education, aided by construction of new schools and passage of laws that required children to stay in school to age fourteen, equipped young people to achieve a living standard higher than their parents'. Between 1890 and 1922, the number of students enrolled in public high schools rose dramatically, though by today's standards graduation rates among young people were low— 16.3 percent in 1920, up from 3.5 percent in 1890. The creation of managerial and sales jobs in service industries helped to counter the downward mobility that resulted when mechanization pushed skilled workers out of their crafts. And the resulting goods of mass production meant that even workers found life more convenient.

Flush Toilets and Other Innovations
At the vanguard of a revolution in lifestyles stood the toilet. The chain-pull, washdown water closet, invented in England around 1870, reached the United States in the 1880s. Shortly after 1900, the flush toilet appeared; thanks to mass

production of enamel-coated metal fixtures, it became common in American homes and buildings. Cheap and easy to install, toilets brought about a shift in habits and attitudes. Before 1880, only luxury hotels and wealthy families had private indoor bathrooms. By the 1890s, the germ theory of disease was raising fears about carelessly disposed human waste as a source of infection and water contamination. Much more rapidly than Europeans, middle-class Americans combined a desire for cleanliness with an urge for convenience and began installing modern toilets in their urban houses. By the 1920s, toilets were prevalent in many working-class homes, too. Bodily functions took on an unpleasant image, and the home bathroom became a place of utmost privacy. Edward and Clarence Scott, who manufactured white tissue in perforated rolls, provided Americans a more convenient form of toilet tissue than the rough paper they had previously used. Plumbing advances thus belonged to a broader democratization of convenience that accompanied mass production and consumerism.

The tin can also altered lifestyles. Before the mid-nineteenth century, Americans typically ate only foods that were in season. Drying, smoking, and salting could preserve meat for a short time, but the availability of fresh meat and milk was limited; there was no way to prevent spoilage. A French inventor developed the cooking-and-sealing process of canning around 1810, and in the 1850s an American man named Gail Borden devised a means of condensing and preserving milk. Sales of canned goods and condensed milk increased during the 1860s, but processing some foods was difficult and cans had to be made by hand. In the 1880s, technology solved production problems. Inventors fashioned machines to peel fruits and vegetables as well as stamping and soldering machines to mass-produce cans from tin plate. Now, even people remote from markets, like sailors and cowboys, could readily consume tomatoes, milk, oysters, and other alternatives to previously monotonous diets. Housewives preserved their own fruits and vegetables, "putting up" foods in sealed glass jars.

Other trends and inventions broadened Americans' diets. Growing urban populations created demands that encouraged fruit and vegetable farmers to raise more produce. Railroad refrigerator cars enabled growers and meatpackers to ship perishables greater distances and to preserve them for longer periods. By the 1890s, northern city dwellers could enjoy southern and western strawberries, grapes, and tomatoes for several months of the year. Home iceboxes enabled middle-class families to store perishables. An easy means of producing ice commercially was invented in the 1870s, and by 1900 the nation had two thousand ice plants, most of which made home deliveries.

Dietary Reform   Availability of new foods also inspired health advocates to reform American diets. In the 1870s, John H. Kellogg, nutritionist at the Western Health Reform Institute in Battle Creek, Michigan, began serving patients health foods, including peanut butter and wheat flakes. Several years later, his brother, William K. Kellogg, invented corn flakes, and another nutritionist, Charles W. Post, introduced Grape-Nuts, revolutionizing breakfast by replacing eggs, potatoes, and meat with ready-to-eat cereal, which supposedly was healthier. Like Edison and Ford, Post believed in the power of advertising, and he personally wrote ads for his products. His company became one of the fastest growing in the country.

Other developments affected the ways people prepared and consumed food. Just before the First World War, scientists discovered the dietetic value of vitamins A and B (C and D were discovered later). Growing numbers of cookbooks and the opening of cooking schools reflected heightened interest in food's possibilities for health and enjoyment. Home gardens in urban backyards also became easier to tend, aided by the Burpee Company, founded in 1876, which mailed flower and vegetable seeds to gardeners who bought them through mail-order catalogues—just as they bought goods from Sears, Roebuck.

As in the past, the poorest people still consumed cheap foods, heavy in starches and carbohydrates. Southern textile workers, for example, ate corn mush and fatback (the strip of meat from a hog's back) almost every day. Poor urban families seldom could afford meat. Now, though, many of them could purchase previously unavailable fruits, vegetables, and dairy products. Workers had to spend a high percentage of their income on food—almost half of a breadwinner's wages—but they never suffered the severe malnutrition that plagued other developing nations.

Ready-Made Clothing   Just as cans and iceboxes made many foods more common, the sewing machine and standardized sizes sparked a revolution in clothing. The sewing machine, invented in Europe but refined in the mid-nineteenth century by Americans Elias Howe Jr. and Isaac M. Singer, facilitated clothing and shoe manufacture. Demand for uniforms during the Civil War boosted the ready-made (as opposed to custom-made) clothing industry, and by 1890 annual retail sales of machine-made garments reached $1.5 billion. Mass production enabled manufacturers to turn out good-quality apparel at relatively low cost and to standardize sizes to fit different body shapes. By 1900, only the poorest families could not afford "ready-to-wear" clothes. Tailors and seamstresses were relegated to repair work. Many women continued to make clothing at home, to save money or as a hobby, but commercial dress patterns intended for use with a sewing machine simplified home production and injected another form of standardization into everyday life.

Mass-produced garments altered clothing styles and tastes. Restrictive Victorian designs still dominated female fashion, but women were abandoning the most burdensome features. As women's participation in work and leisure activities became more active, dress designers placed greater emphasis on comfort. In the 1890s, long sleeves and skirt hemlines receded, and high-boned collars disappeared. Women began wearing factory-made tailored blouses called shirtwaists. For comfort, designers used less fabric; by the 1920s, a dress required three yards of material instead of ten. Petite prevailed as the ideal: the most desirable waist measurement was eighteen to twenty inches, and corsets were big sellers. In the early 1900s, long hair tied up behind the neck was the most popular style. By the First World War, when many women worked in hospitals and factories, shorter hairstyles had become acceptable.

Men's clothes, too, became lightweight and stylish. Before 1900, men in the middle and well-off working classes would have owned two suits: one for Sundays and special occasions, and one for everyday wear. After 1900, however, manufacturers began producing inexpensive garments from fabrics of different weights and for different seasons. Men replaced derbies with felt hats, and stiff collars and cuffs with soft ones; somber, dark-blue serge gave way to lighter shades and more intricate weaves. Workingmen still needed durable, inexpensive overalls, shirts, and shoes. But even for males of modest means, clothing was becoming something to be bought instead of made and remade by wives and mothers.

Department and Chain Stores   Department stores and chain stores helped to create and serve this new consumerism. Between 1865 and 1900, Macy's Department Store in New York, Wanamaker's in Philadelphia, Marshall Field in Chicago, and the Emporium in San Francisco became urban landmarks. Previously, working classes bought goods in stores with limited inventories, and wealthier people patronized fancy shops; prices, quality of goods, and social custom discouraged each from shopping at the other's establishments. Now, department stores, with open displays of clothing, housewares, and furniture—available in large quantities to anyone with the purchase price—caused a merchandising revolution. They offered not only variety but also home deliveries, exchange policies, and charge accounts.

Meanwhile, the Great Atlantic Tea Company, founded in 1859, became the first grocery chain. Renamed the Great Atlantic & Pacific Tea Company in 1869 (ultimately known as A&P), the firm bought in volume and sold to the public at low prices. By 1915, there were eighteen hundred A&P stores, and twelve thousand more were built over the next ten years. Other chains, such as Woolworth's dime stores, which sold inexpensive personal items and novelties, grew rapidly during the same period.

Advertising   A society of scarcity does not need advertising: when demand exceeds supply, producers have no trouble selling what they market. But in a society of rising abundance, such as industrial America, supply frequently outstrips demand, necessitating a means to create and increase demand. Advertising assumed this function. In 1865, retailers spent about $9.5 million on advertising; that sum reached $95 million by 1900 and nearly $500 million by 1919.

In the late nineteenth century, companies that mass-produced consumer goods hired advertisers to create "consumption communities," bodies of consumers loyal to a particular brand name. In 1881, Congress passed a trademark law enabling producers to register and protect brand names. Thousands of companies registered products as varied as Hires Root Beer, Uneeda Biscuits, and Carter's Little Liver Pills. Advertising agencies—a service pioneered by N. W. Ayer & Son of Philadelphia—offered expert advice to firms that wished to cultivate brand loyalty. Newspapers served as the prime instrument for advertising. In the mid-nineteenth century, publishers began to pursue higher revenues by selling more ad space. Wanamaker's placed the first full-page ad in 1879, and advertisers began using large print and elaborate illustrations of products. Such attention-getting techniques transformed advertising into news. More than ever before, people read newspapers to find out what was for sale as well as what was happening.

Outdoor billboards and electrical signs rivaled newspapers as important selling devices. Billboards on city buildings, in railroad stations, and alongside roads promoted such products as Gillette razors, Wrigley chewing gum, and Budweiser beer. In the mid-1890s, electric lights made billboards more dynamic and appealing. Commercial districts sparkled under what one observer called "a medium of motion, of action, of *life*, of *light*, of compulsory attraction." The flashing electrical signs on New York City's Broadway—including a forty-five-foot Heinz pickle in green bulbs and dazzling theater marquees—gave the street its label "the Great White Way." Soon, "talking" signs were installed, with words moving along signboards providing news as well as advertising copy in a multitude of colors. Americans now had an enticing variety of inducements to consume.

THE CORPORATE CONSOLIDATION MOVEMENT

Neither new products nor new marketing techniques could mask unsettling factors in the American economy. The huge capital investment needed for new technology required that factories operate at near capacity to recover costs. But the more manufacturers produced, the more they had to expand markets for their products.

Advertising, which developed into a powerful medium in the late nineteenth century, used explicit and implicit domestic images to reinforce a wife's role as homemaker. This ad implies that a devoted wife lovingly assumes such tasks as sewing and mending clothing, guided into her role by a strong and superior husband.

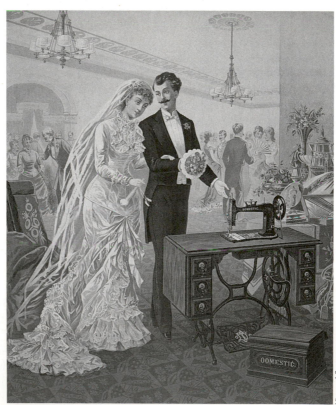

Library of Congress

To sell more and outdo competitors, they had to advertise and reduce prices. To compensate for advertising costs and low prices, they further expanded production and often reduced wages. To expand, they raised capital by selling stock and borrowing money from commercial banks, savings banks, insurance companies, and investment houses. And to repay loans and reward stockholders, they had to produce and sell even more. This spiraling process strangled small firms that could not keep pace and thrust workers into constant uncertainty. Similar cycles also unsettled commerce, banking, and transportation.

In this environment of unregulated expansion, optimism could dissolve at the hint that debtors could not meet their obligations. Economic downturns occurred with painful regularity—1873, 1884, 1893. Business leaders disagreed on what caused these strains. Some blamed overproduction; others pointed to underconsumption; still others blamed lax credit and investment practices. Whatever the explanation, businesspeople began seeking ways to combat the uncertainty of boom-and-bust cycles by creating increasingly tighter and larger forms of centralized organization.

Rise of Corporations

Industrialists never questioned the capitalist system. They sought new ways to enlarge the base that had supported economic growth since the early 1800s, when states liberalized incorporation laws to encourage commerce and industry. Under such laws, almost anyone could start a company and raise money by selling stock. Stockholders (investors) shared in profits without personal risk because laws limited their liability for company debts to the amount of their own investment; the rest of their wealth was protected from creditors should the company fail. Nor did investors need to concern themselves with a firm's day-to-day operation; responsibility for company administration rested with its managers.

Corporations proved the best instruments to raise capital for industrial expansion, and by 1900 two-thirds of all goods manufactured in the United States were produced by corporate firms such as General Electric and the American Tobacco Company. Corporations won judicial protection in the 1880s and 1890s when the Supreme Court ruled that they, like individuals, are protected by the Fourteenth Amendment, meaning that states could not deny corporations equal protection under the law nor deprive them of property rights without due process of law. Such rulings insulated corporations from government interference in their operations.

Pools and Trusts

Between the late 1880s and early 1900s, a number of massive corporate conglomerates formed that have since dominated the nation's economy. At first, such alliances were tentative and informal, consisting mainly of cooperative agreements called *pools* among firms that manufactured the same product or offered the same service. Through these arrangements, competing companies tried to control the market by agreeing how much each should produce and by sharing profits. Such "gentlemen's agreements" worked during good times when there was enough business for all; but during slow periods, desire for profits often tempted pool members to secretly reduce prices or sell more than the agreed quota.

In 1879, one of John D. Rockefeller's lawyers, Samuel Dodd, devised a more reliable means of dominating a market. Dodd suggested adapting a legal device called a *trust*, in which one company could control an industry by luring or forcing stockholders of smaller companies in that industry to yield control of their stock "in trust" to the larger company's board of trustees. This method allowed Rockefeller to achieve *horizontal integration*—the control of similar companies—of the profitable petroleum industry in 1882 by combining his corporation with other refineries.

Holding Companies   In 1888, New Jersey adopted laws allowing corporations chartered there to own property and stock in other corporations in other states. (Trusts provided for trusteeship, not ownership.) This liberalization facilitated creation of the *holding company*, which owned a partial or complete interest in other companies and merged their holdings' assets (buildings, equipment, inventory, and cash) under single management. Under this arrangement, Rockefeller's holding company combined forty formerly independent operations into Standard Oil of New Jersey. By 1898, Standard Oil refined 84 percent of all oil produced in the nation, controlled most pipelines, and engaged in natural-gas production and ownership of oil-producing properties. To dominate their markets, many holding companies sought control over all aspects of the industry, including raw-materials extraction, product manufacture, and distribution. A model of such *vertical integration*, which fused related businesses under unified management, was Gustavus Swift's Chicago meat-processing operation. During the 1880s, Swift invested in livestock, slaughterhouses, refrigerator cars, and marketing to ensure profits from meat sales at prices he could control. With their widespread operations, both Swift & Company and Standard Oil extended economic tentacles to all regions of the nation.

Mergers provided answers to industry's search for orderly profits. Between 1889 and 1903, some three hundred combinations were formed, most of them trusts and holding companies. Other mammoth combinations included Amalgamated Copper Company, American Sugar Refining Company, and U.S. Rubber Company. At the same time, these huge companies ruthlessly put thousands of small firms out of business.

Financiers   The merger movement created a new species of businessman, one whose vocation was financial organizing rather than producing a particular good. Shrewd investors sought opportunities for combination, formed a holding company, raised money by selling stock and borrowing from banks, then persuaded producers to sell their firms to the new company. Their attention ranged widely. W. H. Moore organized the American Tin Plate Company, Diamond Match Company, National Biscuit Company, and the Rock Island Railroad. Elbert H. Gary similarly participated in consolidation of the barbed-wire industry and of U.S. Steel. Investment bankers such as J. P. Morgan and Jacob Schiff piloted the merger movement, inspiring awe with their financial power and organizational skills.

Growth of corporations turned stock and bond exchanges into hubs of activity. In 1886, trading on the New York Stock Exchange passed 1 million shares a day.

By 1914, the number of industrial stocks traded reached 511, compared with 145 in 1869. Between 1870 and 1900, foreign investment in American companies rose from $1.5 billion to $3.5 billion, as the country's economy assumed the image of a safe and lucrative investment. Assets of savings banks, concentrated in the Northeast and on the West Coast, rose by 700 percent between 1875 and 1897. These institutions, along with commercial banks and insurance companies, invested heavily in railroads and industrial enterprises. As one journal, exaggerating capitalists' optimism, proclaimed, "Nearly the whole country (including the typical widow and orphan) is interested in the stock market."

THE GOSPEL OF WEALTH AND ITS CRITICS

Business leaders used corporate consolidation to minimize competition. To justify their tactics, they invoked the doctrine of Social Darwinism. Developed by British philosopher Herbert Spencer and preached in the United States by Yale professor William Graham Sumner, Social Darwinism loosely grafted Charles Darwin's theory of survival of the fittest onto laissez faire, the doctrine that government should not interfere in private economic matters. Social Darwinists reasoned that, in a free-market economy, wealth would flow naturally to those most capable of handling it. Acquisition and possession of property were thus sacred and deserved rights. Civilization depended on this system, explained Sumner. "If we do not like the survival of the fittest," he wrote, "we have only one possible alternative, and that is survival of the unfittest." In this view, large corporations represented the natural accumulation of economic power by those best suited for wielding it.

Social Darwinists reasoned, too, that wealth carried moral responsibilities to provide for those less fortunate or less capable. Steel baron Andrew Carnegie asserted what he called "the Gospel of Wealth," meaning that he and other industrialists, as guardians of society's wealth, had a duty to serve society in humane ways. Over his lifetime, Carnegie donated more than $350 million to libraries, schools, peace initiatives, and the arts. Such philanthropy, however, also implied a right for benefactors such as Rockefeller and Carnegie to define what was good and necessary for society; it did not translate into paying workers decent wages.

Government Assistance to Business

Like western entrepreneurs who lauded rugged individualism while seeking public subsidies in their mining, railroad, and agricultural businesses, leaders in the corporate consolidation movement extolled independent initiative while requesting government assistance. They denounced efforts to legislate maximum working hours or to regulate factory conditions as interference with natural economic laws, but they lobbied forcefully for public subsidies and tax relief to encourage business growth. Grants to railroads (see Chapter 17) were one form of such assistance. Tariffs, which benefited American products by placing taxes on imported products, were another. Since the inception of tariffs in the early nineteenth century, industrialists argued that tariff protection encouraged the development of new products and enterprises. But tariffs also forced consumers to pay artificially high prices for many goods.

Dissenting Voices

While defenders such as Carnegie and Rockefeller insisted that trusts and other forms of big business were natural outcomes of economic development, critics charged that these methods were unnatural because they stifled opportunity and originated from greed. Such charges, emanating from farmers, workers, and intellectuals, reflected a fear of monopoly—the domination of an economic activity (such as oil refining) by one powerful company (such as Standard Oil). Those who feared monopoly believed that large corporations fixed prices, exploited workers, destroyed opportunity by crushing small businesses, and threatened democracy by corrupting politicians—all of which was not only unnatural but immoral.

Critics believed they knew a better, more ethical path to progress. By the mid-1880s, a few intellectuals began to challenge Social Darwinism and laissez-faire economics. Much of their thought derived from the philosophy of pragmatism espoused by philosopher and psychologist William James. Though he accepted Darwin's theory of evolution because it meant that nature was full of change, James believed that human will, independent of the environment, could alter existence. To James, truth was relative; something was true if humans accepted it as true. Such a pragmatic belief meant that social relationships were not fixed by immutable law, as Social Darwinists implied; rather, humans, especially those selected by society, could bring about change.

Sociologist Lester Ward, in his book *Dynamic Sociology* (1883), similarly argued that human control of nature, not natural law, accounted for civilization's advance. A system that guaranteed survival only to the fittest was wasteful and brutal; instead, Ward reasoned, cooperative activity fostered by government intervention was more just. Economists Richard Ely, John R. Commons, and Edward Bemis agreed that natural forces should be harnessed for the public good. They denounced laissez-faire for its "unsound morals" and praised the positive assistance that government could offer to ordinary people.

Whereas academics endorsed intervention in the natural economic order, visionaries such as Henry George and Edward Bellamy questioned why the United States had to have so many poor people while a few became fabulously wealthy. George, a printer with only a seventh-grade education, was an avid reader of economic theory. Alarmed at the poverty among working people like himself, he came to believe that inequality stemmed from the ability of a few to profit from rising land values and the ever-higher rents they charged. Unlike wages paid to workers, wealth from landowning was created without any productive effort. To prevent profiteering, George proposed to replace all taxes with a "single tax" on the "unearned increment"—the rise in property values caused by increased market demand rather than by owners' improvements. George's scheme, argued in *Progress and Poverty* (1879), had great popular appeal and almost won him the mayoralty of New York City in 1886.

Unlike George, who accepted private ownership, novelist Edward Bellamy believed competitive capitalism promoted waste. Instead, he proposed a state in which government owned the means of production. Bellamy outlined his dream in *Looking Backward* (1888). The novel, which sold over a million copies, depicted Boston in the year 2000 as a peaceful community where everyone had a job and a council of benevolent elders managed the economy. In Bellamy's utopia, a "principle of fraternal cooperation" replaced vicious competition and wasteful monopoly. His vision, which he called "Nationalism," sparked formation of Nationalist clubs across the country and kindled appeals for political reform, social welfare measures, and government ownership of railroads and utilities.

Antitrust Legislation   Few people supported the government ownership envisioned by Bellamy, but several states took steps to prohibit monopolies and regulate business. By 1900, twenty-seven states had laws forbidding pools and fifteen had constitutional provisions outlawing trusts. Most were agricultural states in the South and West that were responding to anti-monopolistic pressure from farm organizations (see Chapter 20). But state governments lacked the staff and judicial support for an effective attack on big business, and corporations found ways to evade restrictions. Only national legislation, it seemed, could work.

Congress moved hesitantly toward such legislation but in 1890 passed the Sherman Anti-Trust Act. Introduced by Senator John Sherman of Ohio, the law made illegal "every contract, combination in the form of trust or otherwise, or conspiracy in the restraint of trade." Those found guilty of violating the law faced fines and jail terms, and those wronged by illegal combinations could sue for triple damages. However, the law was left purposely vague and watered down when it was rewritten by pro-business eastern senators. It did not clearly define "restraint of trade" and consigned interpretation of its provisions to the courts, which at the time were allies of business.

Judges used the law's vagueness to blur distinctions between reasonable and unreasonable restraints of trade. When in 1895 the federal government prosecuted the Sugar Trust for owning 98 percent of the nation's sugar-refining capacity, eight of nine Supreme Court justices ruled in *U.S. v. E. C. Knight Co.* that control of manufacturing did not necessarily mean control of trade. According to the Court, the Constitution empowered Congress to regulate interstate commerce, but manufacturing (which in the *Knight* case took place entirely within Pennsylvania) did not fall under congressional control.

Between 1890 and 1900, the federal government prosecuted only eighteen cases under the Sherman Anti-Trust Act. The most successful involved railroads directly involved in interstate commerce. Ironically, the act equipped the government with a tool for breaking up labor unions: courts that did not consider monopolistic production a restraint on trade willingly applied antitrust provisions to boycotts encouraged by striking unions.

SUMMARY

Mechanization and inventions thrust the United States, once just a developing country, into the vanguard of industrial nations. By the early twentieth century, American industrial output surpassed that of Great Britain, France, and Germany combined. Industrial growth transformed the national economy and freed the United States from dependence on European capital and manufactured goods. Imports and foreign investments still flowed into the United States. But by 1900, factories, stores, and banks were converting America from a debtor, agricultural nation into an industrial, financial, and exporting power. In addition, developments in electrical power, steel production, internal-combustion engines, and chemistry immeasurably altered daily life at home and abroad.

But in industry, as in farming and mining, massive size and aggressive consolidation engulfed the individual, changing the nature of work from a singular activity undertaken by skilled producers to mass production undertaken by wage earners. Laborers fought to retain control of their work and struggled to organize unions to meet their needs. The outpouring of products created a mass society based on consumerism and dominated by technology and the communications media.

The problems of enforcing the Sherman Anti-Trust Act reflected the uneven distribution of power. Corporations consolidated to control resources, production, and politics. Laborers and reformers had numbers and ideas but lacked influence. They benefited from material gains that technology and mass production provided, but they accused businesses of acquiring too much influence and profiting at their expense. In factories and homes, some people celebrated the economic transformation, while others struggled with the dilemma of industrialism: whether new accumulations of wealth would undermine the ideal of a republic based on republicanism, democracy, and equality.

The march of industrial expansion proved almost impossible to stop, however, because so many people, powerful and ordinary, were benefiting from it. Moreover, the waves of newcomers pouring into the nation's cities were increasingly furnishing both workers and consumers for America's expanding productive capacity. The dynamo of American vitality now rested in its urban centers.

19

THE VITALITY AND TURMOIL OF URBAN LIFE 1877–1920

GROWTH OF THE MODERN CITY

Although their initial functions had been commercial, cities became the main arenas for industrial development in the late nineteenth century. As centers of labor, transportation, communication, and consumption of goods and services, cities supplied everything factories needed. Thus urban growth and industrialization wound together in a mutually advantageous spiral. The further industrialization advanced, the more opportunities it created for jobs and investment. Increased opportunities in turn drew more people to cities; as workers and as consumers, they fueled yet more industrialization. Urban growth in modern America was a dynamic process involving all groups of Americans, including those already settled and new arrivals from Europe and Asia.

Industrial Development Most cities housed a variety of manufacturing enterprises, but product specialization became common. Mass production of clothing concentrated in New York City, the shoe industry in Philadelphia, and textiles in New England cities such as Lowell. Industries in other cities created goods from surrounding agricultural regions: flour in Minneapolis, cottonseed oil in Memphis, beef and pork in Chicago. Still others processed natural resources: gold and copper in Denver, fish and lumber in Seattle, iron in Pittsburgh and Birmingham, and oil in Houston and Los Angeles. Such activities increased cities' magnetic attraction for people in search of steady employment.

CHRONOLOGY

1867	First law regulating tenements passes in New York State
1870	One-fourth of Americans live in cities
1876	National League of Professional Baseball Clubs founded
1880s	"New" immigrants from eastern and southern Europe begin to arrive in large numbers
1883	Brooklyn Bridge completed
	Pulitzer buys *New York World*, creating major publication for yellow journalism
1885	Safety bicycle invented
1886	First settlement house opens in New York City
1889	Edison invents motion picture and viewing device
1890s	Electric trolleys replace horse-drawn mass transit
1893	Columbian Exposition opens in Chicago
1895	Hearst buys *New York Journal*, which becomes another popular yellow-journalism newspaper
1898	Race riot erupts in Wilmington, North Carolina
1900–10	Immigration reaches peak
1903	Boston beats Pittsburgh in baseball's first World Series
1905	Intercollegiate Athletic Association, forerunner of National Collegiate Athletic Association (NCAA) is formed, restructuring rules of football
1915	Griffith directs *Birth of a Nation*, one of the first major technically sophisticated movies
1919	Race riot erupts in East St. Louis, Illinois
1920	Majority (51.4 percent) of Americans live in cities

At the same time, the compact city of the early nineteenth century—where residences mingled among shops, factories, and warehouses—burst open. From Boston to Los Angeles, the built environment sprawled several miles beyond the original settlement. No longer did walking distance determine a city's size. Instead, cities separated into distinct districts: working- and middle-class neighborhoods, commercial strips, downtown, and a ring of suburbs. Two forces were responsible for this new arrangement. One, mass transportation, was centrifugal, propelling people and enterprises outward. The other, economic change, was centripetal, drawing human and material resources inward.

Mechanization of Mass Transportation

By the 1870s, horse-drawn vehicles began sharing city streets with motor-driven conveyances that moved riders faster and farther. First, many railroads made stops in outlying areas, enabling commuters to ride to and from city centers. In the

1880s, cable cars (carriages that moved by clamping onto a moving underground wire) started operating in Chicago, San Francisco, and other cities. Then, in the 1890s, electric-powered streetcars began replacing horse cars and cable cars. Designed in Montgomery, Alabama, and Richmond, Virginia, electric trolleys spread to nearly every large American city. In a few cities, companies raised track onto trestles, enabling "elevated" vehicles to travel above jammed downtown streets. In Boston, New York, and Philadelphia, transit firms dug underground subway tunnels, also to avoid traffic congestion. Because "els" were extremely expensive to construct, they appeared only in the few cities where companies could amass the necessary capital and where there were enough riders to ensure profits.

Another form of mass transit, the electric interurban railway, linked neighboring cities. Usually built over shorter distances than steam railroads, interurbans operated between cities with growing suburban populations and furthered urban development by making outlying regions attractive for home buyers and businesses. The extensive Pacific Electric Railway network in Southern California, for example, facilitated travel and economic progress in that region.

Urban Sprawl

Mass transit launched urban dwellers into remote neighborhoods and created a commuting public. The resulting expansion benefited urban populations unevenly and was essentially unplanned. Streetcar lines serviced mainly districts that promised the most riders whose fares would increase company revenues. Working-class families, who needed every cent, found streetcars unaffordable. But those of the growing middle class who could afford the fare—usually 5 cents a ride—could escape to quiet, tree-lined neighborhoods on the outskirts; live in bungalows with their own yards; and commute to the inner city for work, shopping, and entertainment. A home several miles from downtown was inconvenient, but benefits outweighed costs. As one suburbanite wrote in 1902, "It may be a little more difficult for us to attend the opera, but the robin in my elm tree struck a higher note and a sweeter one yesterday than any prima donna ever reached."

Streetcars, els, and subways altered commercial as well as residential patterns. When consumers moved outward, businesses followed, locating at trolley-line intersections and near el stations. Branches of department stores and banks joined groceries, theaters, taverns, and shops to create neighborhood shopping centers, forerunners of today's suburban malls. Meanwhile, the urban core became a work zone, where tall buildings loomed over streets clogged with people, horses, and vehicles. Districts such as Chicago's Loop and New Orleans's Canal Street employed thousands in commerce and finance.

Population Growth

Between 1870 and 1920, the total number of Americans living in cities increased from 10 million to 54 million. During this period, the number of cities with more than 100,000 people swelled from fifteen to sixty-eight; those with more than 500,000 rose from two to twelve (see Map 19.1). These figures, dramatic in themselves, represent millions of stories of dreams and frustration, coping and confusion, success and failure.

American urban growth derived not from natural increase (excess of births over deaths) but through the annexation of bordering land and people, and mostly

by net migration (excess of in-migrants over out-migrants). Every city grew territo-
rially. For example, in 1898, New York City, which previously consisted of only
Manhattan and the Bronx, merged with Brooklyn, Staten Island, and part of
Queens, and doubled from 1.5 million to 3 million people. Elsewhere, cities gob-
bled up miles of surrounding area made accessible by mass transportation. Suburbs often desired annexation for the schools, water, fire protection, and sewer
systems that cities could provide. Sometimes annexation preceded settlement, adding vacant land to which new residents could move. In the 1880s, Chicago,
Minneapolis, and Los Angeles incorporated hundreds of undeveloped square miles
into their borders.

**Urban
In-Migration**   In-migration from the countryside and immigration from
abroad made by far the greatest contribution to urban population growth. In fact, movement to cities matched the
massive migration to the West that was occurring at the same time. Urban newcomers arrived from two major sources: the American countryside and Europe.
Asia, Canada, and Latin America also supplied immigrants, though in smaller
numbers.

Despite land rushes in the West, rural populations declined as urban populations burgeoned. Low crop prices and high debts dashed white farmers' hopes
and drove them toward opportunities that cities seemed to offer. Migrants filled
major cities, such as Detroit, Chicago, and San Francisco, but also secondary cities,
such as Indianapolis, Salt Lake City, Nashville, and San Diego. The thrill of city
life beckoned especially to young people. A character in the play *The City* (1920)
spoke for many youths when she exclaimed, "Who wants to smell new-mown hay,
if he can breathe in gasoline on Fifth Avenue instead! Think of the theaters! The
crowds! Think of being able to go out on the street and see someone you didn't
know by sight!" For every four men who migrated cityward, five women did the
same, often to escape an unhappy home life. But like men, young women were
also attracted by the independence—the remaking of themselves—that urban employment offered.

Thousands of rural African Americans also moved cityward, seeking better
employment and fleeing crop liens, ravages of the boll weevil on cotton crops, racial violence, and political oppression. Black migration accelerated after 1915, but
thirty-two cities already had more than ten thousand black residents by 1900.
African American populations rose in southern cities such as Baltimore, Atlanta, and
Birmingham, but northern places, such as New York, Cleveland, and Chicago, also
received thousands of black migrants. These newcomers resembled other migrants
in their rural backgrounds and economic motivations, but they differed in several
important ways. Because few factories would employ African Americans, most
found jobs in the service sector—cleaning, cooking, and driving—rather than in industrial trades. Also, because most service openings were traditionally female jobs,
black women outnumbered black men in most cities. In the South, rural black migrants became an important source of unskilled labor in the region's growing cities.
By 1900, almost 40 percent of the total population of both Atlanta, Georgia, and
Charlotte, North Carolina, was black.

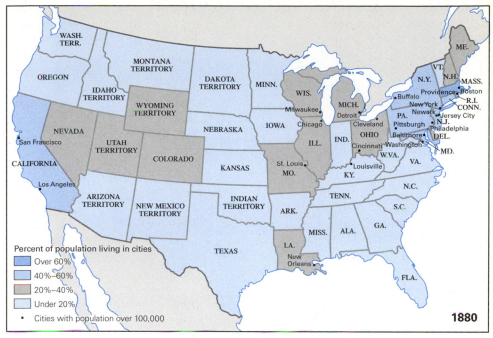

1880

Percent of population living in cities
- Over 60%
- 40%–60%
- 20%–40%
- Under 20%
- Cities with population over 100,000

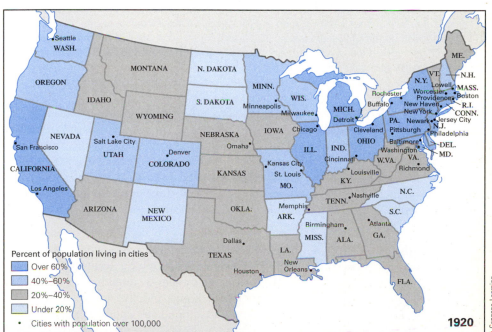

1920

Percent of population living in cities
- Over 60%
- 40%–60%
- 20%–40%
- Under 20%
- Cities with population over 100,000

© Cengage Learning

MAP 19.1 Urbanization, 1880 and 1920

In 1880, the vast majority of states were still heavily rural. By 1920, only a few had less than 20 percent of their population living in cities.

Records of the Public Health Service. (90-G-125-29)/US GOV National Archives

Fresh off the boat and wearing homeland clothing, immigrants pose for a photograph outside the federal immigration station at Ellis Island, offshore from New York City. Situated in the shadow of the Statue of Liberty, Ellis Island immigration officials processed millions of newcomers such as these, asking them questions about their background and examining them for health problems.

In the West, Hispanics—once a predominantly rural population—also moved into cities such as Los Angeles, San Diego, and San Antonio. They took unskilled construction jobs previously held by Chinese laborers who had been driven from Southern California cities by racist measures, and in some Texas cities, native Mexicans (called *Tejanos*) held the majority of unskilled jobs. Mexican men often left home for long periods to take temporary jobs in Los Angeles and other cities, leaving behind female heads of household.

New Foreign Immigration   Most newcomers were foreign immigrants who had fled villages and cities in Europe, Asia, Canada, and Latin America for the United States. Many never intended to stay; they wanted only to make enough money to return home and live in greater comfort and security. For every hundred foreigners who entered the country, around thirty ultimately left. Still, most of the 26 million immigrants who arrived between 1870 and 1920 remained, and the majority settled in cities, where they helped reshape American culture.

New immigration to the United States was part of a worldwide movement pushing people away from traditional means of support and pulling them toward better opportunities. Population pressures, land redistribution, and industrialization induced millions of peasants, small landowners, and craftsmen to leave Europe and Asia for Canada, Australia, Brazil, and Argentina, as well as the United States. Religious persecution, too, particularly the merciless pogroms and military conscription that Jews suffered in eastern Europe, forced people to escape across the Atlantic. Migration has always characterized human history, but in the late nineteenth century, technological advances in communications and transportation spread news of opportunities and made travel cheaper, quicker, and safer.

Immigrants from northern and western Europe—Ireland, Germany, and England—had long made the United States their main destination, but after 1880 economic and demographic changes propelled a second wave of immigrants from other regions who joined and outnumbered them. Increased numbers came from eastern and southern Europe, plus smaller groups from Canada, Mexico, and Japan (see Map 19.2). Between 1900 and 1909, when the new wave peaked, two-thirds of immigrants came from Italy, Austria-Hungary, and Russia. By 1910, arrivals from Mexico outnumbered arrivals from Ireland, and numerous Japanese had moved to the West Coast and Hawai'i. Foreign-born blacks, chiefly from the West Indies, also came.

Many long-settled Americans feared those whom they called "new immigrants," whose folk customs, Catholic and Jewish faiths, and poverty made them seem more alien than previous newcomers. Unlike immigrants from Great Britain and Ireland, new immigrants did not speak English, and more than half worked in low-skill occupations. Yet old and new immigrants closely resembled each other in their strategies for coping. The majority of both groups hailed from societies that made family the focus of all undertakings. Whether and when to emigrate was decided in light of family needs, and family bonds remained tight after immigrants reached America. New arrivals usually knew where they wanted to go and how to get there because they received aid from relatives who had already immigrated. Workers often helped kin obtain jobs, and family members pooled resources to maintain and improve their standard of living.

Geographic and Social Mobility   Once they arrived, in-migrants and immigrants rarely stayed put. Each year millions of families packed up and went elsewhere. Some moved to another neighborhood; others left town. A railroad ticket cost only a few dollars, and many had little to lose by moving. Transience affected every region, every city. From Boston to San Francisco, from Minneapolis to San Antonio, more than half the families residing in a city at any one time were gone ten years later. Even within a city, it was common for a family to live at three or more different addresses over a ten- or fifteen-year period. Overall, one in every three or four families moved each year (today the rate is one in five). Population turnover affected almost every neighborhood and every ethnic and occupational group.

Migration offered one escape to opportunity; remaking oneself occupationally offered another. Advance up the social scale through better jobs was available mostly to white males. Thousands of businesses were needed to supply goods and services to burgeoning urban populations and, as corporations grew and centralized operations, they required new personnel. Capital for a large business was hard to amass, but an aspiring merchant could open a saloon or shop for a few hundred dollars. Knowledge of accounting could qualify one for white-collar jobs with higher incomes than manual labor. Thus, nonmanual jobs and the higher social status and income that tended to accompany them were available.

Such advancement occurred often. To be sure, only a very few could accumulate large fortunes. The vast majority of the era's wealthiest businessmen began their careers with distinct advantages: American birth, Protestant religion, superior education, and relatively affluent parents. Yet considerable movement occurred along the road from poverty to moderate success, from manual to nonmanual work. Successes such as those of Meyer Grossman—a Russian immigrant to Omaha, Nebraska, who worked as a teamster before saving enough to open a successful furniture store—were common.

Rates of upward occupational mobility were slow but steady between 1870 and 1920. In fast-growing cities such as Atlanta and Los Angeles, approximately one in five white manual workers rose to white-collar or owner's positions within ten years—provided they stayed in the city that long. In older cities such as Boston and Philadelphia, upward mobility averaged closer to one in six workers in ten years. Some men slipped from a higher to a lower rung on the occupational ladder, but rates of upward movement usually doubled downward rates. Although patterns varied, immigrants generally experienced less upward and more downward mobility than did the native-born. Still, regardless of birthplace, the chances for a white male to rise occupationally over his lifetime or to hold a higher-status job than his father were relatively good.

What constitutes a better job, however, depends on one's definition of improvement. Many immigrant artisans, such as a German carpenter or an Italian shoemaker, considered an accountant's job unmanly. People with traditions of pride in working with their hands neither desired nonmanual jobs nor encouraged their children to seek them. As one Italian tailor explained, "I learned the tailoring business in the old country. Over here, in America, I never have trouble finding a job because I know my business from the other side [Italy].... I want that my oldest boy learn my trade because I tell him that you could always make at least enough for the family."

Business ownership, moreover, entailed risks. Failure rates were high among saloon owners and other small proprietors in working-class neighborhoods because the low incomes of their customers made profits uncertain. Many manual workers sought security rather than mobility, preferring a steady wage to risks of ownership. A Sicilian who lived in Bridgeport, Connecticut, observed that "the people that come here they afraid to get in business because they don't know how that business goes. In Italy these people don't know much about these things because most of them work on farms or in [their] trade."

Many women held paying jobs and, like men, migrated within and between cities, but they usually went with fathers or husbands whose economic standing defined their social position. Women could rise in status by marrying men with wealth or potential, but other avenues were mostly closed to them. Laws limited what women could inherit, educational institutions blocked their training in such professions as medicine and law, and prevailing assumptions attributed higher aptitude for manual skills and business to men than to women. For African Americans, American Indians, Mexican Americans, and Asian Americans, opportunities were

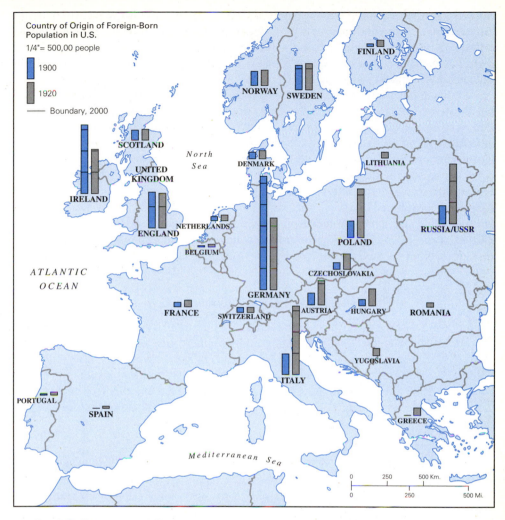

MAP 19.2 Sources of European-Born Population, 1900 and 1920

In just a few decades, the proportion of European immigrants to the United States who came from northern and western Europe decreased (Ireland and Germany) or remained relatively stable (England and Scandinavia), while the proportion from eastern and southern Europe increased dramatically.

Source: Data from U.S. Census Bureau, "Historical Census Statistics on the Foreign-Born Population of the United States: 1850–1990," February 1999, http://www.census.gov/population (accessed February 12, 2000).

even scarcer. Assigned to the lowest-paying occupations by prejudice, they could make few gains.

In addition to advancing occupationally, a person might achieve social mobility by acquiring property, such as building or buying a house. But home ownership was not easy to achieve. Banks and savings-and-loan institutions had strict lending practices, and mortgage loans carried high interest rates and short repayment periods. Thus renting, even of single-family houses, was common, especially in big cities. Nevertheless, some families succeeded in amassing savings, which they could use as down payments on property. Ownership rates varied regionally—higher in western cities, lower in eastern cities—but 36 percent of all urban American families owned their homes in 1900, the highest homeownership rate of any western nation except for Denmark, Norway, and Sweden.

Many, particularly unskilled workers, did not improve their status; they simply floated from one low-paying job to another. Others could not maintain their Old World occupations. Still others, however, did find greener pastures. Studies of Boston, Omaha, Atlanta, and other cities show that most men who rose occupationally or acquired property had migrated from somewhere else. Thus, although cities frustrated the hopes of some, they offered opportunities to others. The possibilities for upward mobility seemed to temper people's dissatisfaction with the stresses of city life. For every story of rags to riches, there were myriad small triumphs. Although the gap between rich and poor widened and discrimination dashed some peoples' hopes, for those in between, the expanding economies of American cities created room.

URBAN NEIGHBORHOODS

Despite the constant turnover that made them dynamic places, American cities were characterized by collections of subcommunities where people, most of whom had migrated from somewhere else, coped with daily challenges to their cultures. Rather than yield completely to pressures to assimilate, migrants and immigrants interacted with the urban environment in a complex way that enabled them to retain their identity while also altering both their own outlook and the social structure of cities themselves.

Cultural Retention and Change In new surroundings—where the English language was a struggle, where the clock regulated their workday, and where housing and employment were uncertain—immigrants first anchored their lives to what they knew best: their culture. Old World customs persisted in immigrant districts of Italians from the same province, Japanese from the same island district, and Russian Jews from the same *shtetl*. Newcomers recreated mutual aid societies they had known in their homeland. For example, in American cities, Japanese recreated *ken* societies, which in Japan sponsored social celebrations and relief services, and Chinese reproduced loan associations, called *whey*, which raised money to help members acquire businesses. Chinese also transplanted village associations called *fongs*, which rented apartments to members; *kung saw*, assistance organizations of people with the same family name regardless of what part of China they came from; and *tongs*, secret societies designed to aid people but that often acted as gangs that extorted protection money from businesses. Southern Italians transplanted the system whereby a *padrone* (boss) found jobs for unskilled workers by negotiating with—and receiving payoffs from—an employer. Newcomers from various sources practiced religion as they always had, held traditional feasts and pageants, married within their group, and pursued long-standing feuds with people from rival villages.

Urban Borderlands In large cities such as Chicago, Philadelphia, and Detroit, European immigrants initially clustered in inner neighborhoods where low-skill jobs and cheap housing were most available. These districts often were multi-ethnic, places historians have called "urban borderlands," where a diversity of people and lifestyles coexisted. Members of the same group often tried to exclude outsiders from their neighborhood space and institutions, but even within districts identified with a certain group, such as Little Italy, Jewtown, Polonia, or Greektown, rapid mobility constantly undermined residential homogeneity as former inhabitants dispersed to other neighborhoods and new inhabitants moved in. Often, a particular area was occupied by several ethnic groups, while local businesses and institutions, such as bakeries, butcher shops, churches, and club headquarters—which usually were operated by and for one ethnic group—gave a neighborhood its identity.

For first- and second-generation immigrants, their neighborhoods acted as havens until individuals were ready to cross from the borderland into the majority society. But borderland experiences often dissolved, sometimes in a generation, sometimes in just a few years. The expansion of mass transportation and outward movement of factories enabled people to move to other neighborhoods, where they interspersed with families of their own socioeconomic class but not necessarily of their own ethnicity. European immigrants did encounter prejudice, such as the exclusion of Jews from certain neighborhoods, professions, and clubs, or the inability of Italians to break into urban politics, but discrimination rarely was systematic or complete. For people of color, however—African Americans, Asians, and Mexicans—borderlands kept a more persistent character that, because of discrimination, became less multiethnic over time.

Racial Segregation and Violence Although the small numbers of African Americans who inhabited American cities in the eighteenth and early nineteenth centuries lived near or interspersed with whites, by the late nineteenth century rigid racial discrimination forced them into relatively permanent, highly segregated ghettos. By 1920 in Chicago, Detroit, Cleveland, and other cities where tens of thousands of blacks now lived, two-thirds or more of the total black population inhabited only 10 percent of the residential area. Within their neighborhoods, African Americans, like other urban dwellers, nurtured institutions that helped them cope with city life: shops, clubs, theaters, dance halls, newspapers, and saloons. Churches, particularly branches of Baptist and African Methodist Episcopal (AME) Protestantism, were especially influential. Pittsburgh blacks boasted twenty-eight such churches in the early 1900s. Membership in Cincinnati's black Baptist churches doubled between 1870 and 1900. In Louisville, blacks pooled resources and built their own theological institute. In virtually all cities, religious activity not only dominated African American life but also represented cooperation across class lines.

Often, the only way blacks could relieve the pressures of crowding that resulted from increasing migration was to expand residential borders into surrounding, previously white neighborhoods, a process that resulted in harassment and attacks by white residents whose intolerant attitudes were intensified by fears that black neighbors would cause property values to decline. The increased presence of African Americans in cities, North and South—as well as their competition with whites for housing, jobs, and political influence—sparked a series of race riots. In 1898, white residents of Wilmington, North Carolina, resenting African Americans' involvement in local government and incensed by an editorial in an African American newspaper accusing white women of loose sexual behavior, rioted and killed dozens of blacks. In the fury's wake, white supremacists overthrew the city government, expelling black and white officeholders, and instituted restrictions to prevent blacks from voting. In Atlanta in 1906, newspaper accounts alleging attacks by black men on white women provoked an outburst of shooting and killing that left twelve blacks dead and seventy injured. An influx of unskilled black strikebreakers into East St. Louis, Illinois, heightened racial tensions in 1917. Rumors that blacks were arming for an assault on whites resulted in numerous attacks by white mobs on black neighborhoods. On July 1, blacks fired back at a car whose occupants they believed had shot into their homes and mistakenly killed two policemen riding in the car. The next day, a full-scale riot erupted that ended only after nine whites and thirty-nine blacks had been killed and three hundred buildings destroyed.

Asians also encountered discrimination and segregation. Although Chinese immigrants often preferred to live apart from Anglos in Chinatowns of San Francisco, Seattle, Los Angeles, and New York City, where they created their own business, government, and social institutions, Anglos made every effort to keep them separated. In San Francisco, anti-Chinese hostility was fomented by Denis Kearney, an Irish immigrant who blamed Chinese for unemployment problems in the late 1870s. Using the slogan "The Chinese must go," Kearney and his followers intimidated employers into refusing to hire Chinese and drove hundreds of Asians out of the city. San Francisco's government prohibited Chinese laundries (which were social centers as well as commercial establishments) from locating in white neighborhoods and banned the wearing of queues, the traditional Chinese hair braid. In 1882, Congress passed the Chinese Exclusion Act, which suspended immigration of Chinese laborers and prohibited naturalization of Chinese already residing in the United States. And in 1892, Congress approved the Geary Act, which extended immigration restriction and required Chinese Americans to carry certificates of residence issued by the Treasury Department. A San Francisco–based organization called the Chinese Six Companies fought the law, but in 1893 the U.S. Supreme Court upheld the Geary Act in *Fong Yue Ting v. United States*. Japanese immigrants, called Issei, most of whom settled in or near Los Angeles, were prevented by law from becoming American citizens and, like the Chinese, developed communities with their own economic and residential character.

Mexican Barrios   Mexicans in southwestern cities experienced somewhat more complex residential patterns. In places such as Los Angeles, Santa Barbara, and Tucson, Mexicans had been the original inhabitants; Anglos were newcomers who overtook the city, pushing Mexicans into adjoining areas. Mexicans became increasingly isolated in residential and commercial districts called *barrios*. Frequently, real-estate covenants, by which property owners pledged not to sell homes to Mexicans (or to African Americans or Jews), kept Mexican families confined in barrios of Los Angeles, Albuquerque, and San Antonio. These areas tended to be located away from central-city multiethnic borderlands housing European immigrants. To a considerable extent, then, racial bias, more than any other factor, made urban experiences of African Americans, Asians, and Mexicans unique and hindered their opportunities to remake their lives.

Cultural Adaptation Virtually everywhere immigrants lived, Old World culture mingled with New World realities. On one hand, people often found their local identities eclipsed by national identities. Although many foreigners identified themselves by their village or region of birth, native-born Americans simplified by categorizing them by nationality. People from County Cork and County Limerick, for example, were merged into Irish; those from Schleswig and Württemberg into Germans; those from Calabria and Campobasso into Italians. Immigrant institutions, such as newspapers and churches, found they had to appeal to the entire nationality in order to survive.

Moreover, the diversity of American cities prompted foreigners to modify their attitudes and habits. With so many people interacting on streets and in workplaces, few newcomers could avoid contact with groups different from themselves, and few could prevent such contacts from altering old ways of life. Although many immigrants tried to preserve their native language, English—taught in schools and needed on the job—soon penetrated nearly every community. Foreigners fashioned garments in homeland styles but had to use American rather than traditional fabrics. Italians went to American doctors but still carried traditional amulets to ward off evil spirits. Unavailability of Asian vegetables and spices forced Chinese American cooks to improvise by using local ingredients in a new dish they called "chop suey." Music especially revealed adaptations. Polka bands entertained at Polish social gatherings, but their repertoires blended American and Polish folk music; Mexican ballads acquired new themes that described adventures of border crossing and hardships of labor in the United States.

The influx of so many immigrants between 1870 and 1920 transformed the United States from a basically Protestant nation into a diverse collection of Protestants, Catholics, Orthodox Christians, Jews, Buddhists, and Muslims. Newcomers from Italy, Hungary, Polish lands, and Slovakia joined Irish and Germans to boost the proportion of Catholics in many cities. In Buffalo, Cleveland, Chicago, and Milwaukee, Catholic immigrants and their offspring approached a majority of the population. Catholic Mexicans constituted over half of the population of El Paso. German and Russian immigrants gave New York City one of the largest Jewish populations in the world.

Partly in response to Protestant charges that their religions prevented them from assimilating, many Catholics and Jews tried to accommodate their faiths to the new environment. Catholic and Jewish leaders from earlier immigrant groups supported liberalizing trends—use of English in services, the phasing out of such Old World rituals as saints' feasts, and a preference for public over religious schools. As long as new immigrants continued to arrive, however, these trends met stiff resistance. Catholics, for example, supported parochial schools and occasionally campaigned for public funding for them. In some cases, Catholic children's attendance at parochial schools prevented public schools from becoming even more crowded than they already were.

Newcomers usually held onto familiar religious practices, whether the folk Catholicism of southern Italy or the Orthodox Judaism of eastern Europe. Because Catholic parishes served distinct geographic areas, immigrants wanted parish priests of their own "kind," in spite of church attempts to make American Catholicism more uniform. Bishops acceded to pressures from predominantly Polish congregations for Polish rather than German-born priests. Eastern European Jews, convinced that Reform Judaism sacrificed too much to American ways, established the Conservative branch, which retained traditional ritual though it abolished the segregation of women in synagogues and allowed English prayers. In addition, the tendency of second-generation Catholics and Jews to marry coreligionists of other ethnic groups—an Italian Catholic marrying a Polish Catholic, for example—kept religious identity strong while undercutting ethnic identity.

Each of the three major migrant groups that peopled American cities—native-born whites, foreigners of various races, and native-born blacks—created the pluralism of modern American culture. The country's cultural diversity prevented domination by a single racial or ethnic majority. The cities nurtured rich cultural variety: American folk music and literature, Italian and Mexican cuisine, Irish comedy, Yiddish theater, African American jazz and dance, and much more. Newcomers in the late nineteenth century changed their environment as much as they were changed by it.

Living Conditions in the Inner City

Although filled with inhabitants rich in varied cultures, the central sections of American cities also seemed to suffer every affliction that plagues modern urban society: poverty, disease, crime, and the tensions that occur when manifold people live close together. City dwellers coped as best they could, and technology, private enterprise, and public authority achieved some remarkable successes. But many of their problems evaded solution.

Inner-City Housing   Scarcity of adequate housing—one of the most persistent shortcomings—has origins in nineteenth-century urban development. In spite of massive construction, population growth outpaced housing supplies. Lack of inexpensive living quarters especially distressed working-class families who, because of low wages, had to rent their homes. As cities grew, landlords exploited shortages in inexpensive rental housing by splitting up existing buildings to house more people, constructing multiple-unit tenements, and hiking rents. Low-income families adapted to high costs and short supply by sharing space and expenses. It became common in many cities for a one-family apartment to be occupied by two or three families, or by one family plus several boarders.

The result was unprecedented crowding. In 1890, New York City's immigrant-packed Lower East Side averaged 702 people per acre, one of the highest population densities in the world. Inner districts acquired distinctive physical appearances in different cities: six- to eight-story barracks-like buildings in New York, dilapidated row houses in Baltimore and Philadelphia, converted slave quarters in Charleston and New Orleans, crumbling two- and three-story frame houses in Seattle and San Francisco. But everywhere crowding was common.

Inside these structures, conditions were harsh. The largest rooms were barely ten feet wide, and interior rooms either lacked windows or opened onto narrow shafts that bred vermin and rotten odors. Describing such a duct, one immigrant housekeeper revealed, "It's damp down there, and the families, they throw out garbage and dirty papers and the insides of chickens, and other unmentionable filth…. I just vomited when I first cleaned up the air shaft." Few buildings had indoor plumbing; residents had to use privies (outdoor toilets) in the back yard or basement. Often, the only source of heat was dangerous, polluting coal-burning stoves.

Housing Reform   Housing problems sparked widespread reform campaigns. New York State took the lead by passing laws in 1867, 1879, and 1901 that established light, ventilation, and safety codes for new tenement buildings. These and similar measures in other states could not remedy ills of existing buildings, but they did impose minimal obligations on landlords. A few reformers, such as journalist Jacob Riis and humanitarian Lawrence Veiller, advocated housing families in "model tenements," with more spacious rooms and better facilities. Model tenements, however, required landlords to limit their profits, a sacrifice few were willing to make. Reformers and public officials opposed government financing of better housing, fearing that such a step would undermine private enterprise. Still, housing codes and regulatory commissions strengthened the power of local government to oversee construction.

New Home Technology   Eventually, technology brought about important changes in home life. Advanced systems of central heating (furnaces), electric lighting, and indoor plumbing created more comfort, first for middle-class households and later for most others. Whereas formerly families had bought coal or chopped wood for cooking and heating, made candles for light, and hauled water for bathing, their homes and apartments increasingly connected to outside pipes and wires for gas, water, and electricity. Central heat and artificial light allowed residents to enjoy a steady, comfortable temperature and to turn night into day, while indoor plumbing removed unpleasant experiences of the outhouse. Moreover, these utilities helped create new attitudes about privacy among those who could afford the technology. Middle-class bedrooms and bathrooms became private retreats. Even children could have their own bedrooms, complete with individualized decoration.

Scientific and technological advances eventually enabled city dwellers and the entire nation to live in greater safety. By the 1880s, doctors had begun to accept the theory that microorganisms (germs) cause disease. In response, cities established more efficient systems of water purification and sewage disposal. Although disease and death rates remained higher in cities than in the countryside, and tuberculosis and other respiratory ills continued to plague inner-city districts, public health regulations as applied to water purity, sewage disposal, and food quality helped to control such dread diseases as cholera, typhoid fever, and diphtheria.

Meanwhile, street paving, modernized firefighting equipment, and electric street lighting spread rapidly across urban America. Steel-frame construction, which supports a building with a metal skeleton rather than with masonry walls, enabled the erection of skyscrapers—and thus more efficient vertical use of scarce and costly urban land. Electric elevators and steam-heating systems serviced these buildings. Steel-cable suspension bridges, developed by John A. Roebling and epitomized by his Brooklyn Bridge (completed in 1883), replaced ferry boats and linked metropolitan sections more closely.

Poverty Relief   None of these improvements, however, lightened the burden of poverty. The urban economy, though generally expanding, advanced erratically. Employment, especially for unskilled workers in manufacturing and construction, rose and fell with business cycles and changing seasons. An ever-increasing number of families lived on the margins of survival.

Since colonial days, Americans have disagreed about how much responsibility the public should assume for poor relief. According to traditional beliefs, still widespread at the beginning of the twentieth century, anyone could escape poverty through hard work and clean living; indigence existed because some people were morally weaker than others. Such reasoning bred fear that aid to poor people would encourage paupers to rely on public support rather than their own efforts. As business cycles fluctuated and poverty increased, this attitude hardened, and city governments discontinued direct grants of food, fuel, and clothing to needy families. Instead, cities provided relief in return for work on public projects and sent special cases to state-run almshouses; orphanages; and homes for the blind, deaf, and mentally ill.

Efforts to rationalize relief fostered some changes in attitude. Between 1877 and 1892, philanthropists in ninety-two cities formed Charity Organization Societies, an attempt to make social welfare (like business) more efficient by merging disparate charity groups into coordinated units. Believing poverty to be caused by personal defects, such as alcoholism and laziness, members of these organizations spent most of their time visiting poor families and encouraging them to be thriftier and more virtuous. These visits were also intended to identify the "deserving" poor.

Close observation of the poor, however, prompted some humanitarians to conclude that people's environments, not personal shortcomings, caused poverty and that society ought to shoulder greater responsibility for improving conditions. These reformers had faith that they could reduce poverty by improving housing, education, sanitation, and job opportunities rather than by admonishing the poor to be more moral. This attitude fueled campaigns for building codes, factory regulations, and public health measures in the Progressive era of the early twentieth century (see Chapter 21). Still, most middle- and upper-class Americans continued to endorse the creed that in a society of abundance only the unfit were poor and that poverty relief should be tolerated but never encouraged. As one charity worker put it, relief "should be surrounded by circumstances that shall … repel every one … from accepting it."

Crime and Violence   Crime and disorder, as much as crowding and poverty, nurtured fears that cities, especially their slums, threatened the nation. The more cities grew, it seemed, the more they shook with violence. While homicide rates declined in industrialized nations such as England and Germany, those in America rose alarmingly: 25 murders per million people in 1881; 107 per million in 1898. In addition, innumerable disruptions, ranging from domestic violence to muggings to gang fights, made cities scenes of constant turbulence. Pickpockets, swindlers, and burglars roamed every city. Urban outlaws, such as Rufus Minor, acquired as much notoriety as western desperadoes. Short, stocky, and bald, Minor resembled a shy clerk, but one police chief labeled him "one of the smartest bank sneaks in America." Minor often grew a beard before holding up a bank, then shaved to avoid identification by eyewitnesses. Minor was implicated in bank heists in New York City, Cleveland, Detroit, Providence, Philadelphia, Albany, Boston, and Baltimore—all between 1878 and 1882.

Despite fears, however, urban crime and violence may simply have become more conspicuous and sensational rather than more prevalent. Undeniably, concentrations of wealth and the mingling of different peoples provided opportunities for larceny, vice, and assault. But urban lawlessness and brutality probably did not exceed that of backwoods mining camps and southern plantations. Nativists were quick to blame immigrants for urban crime, but the law-breaking population included native-born Americans as well as foreigners. One investigation of jails in 1900 concluded that "we have ourselves evolved as cruel and cunning criminals as any that Europe may have foisted upon us."

MANAGING THE CITY

Those concerned with managing cities faced daunting challenges. Burgeoning populations and physical expansion created urgent needs for sewers, police and fire protection, schools, parks, and other services. Such needs strained municipal resources, and city governments were poorly organized to address problems. In addition to a mayor and a city council, governmental responsibilities typically were scattered among independent boards that administered health regulations, public works, poverty relief, and other functions. Philadelphia at one time had thirty such boards. State governments also often interfered in local matters, appointing board members and limiting cities' abilities to levy taxes and borrow money.

Water Supply and Sewage Disposal   Finding sources of clean water and a way to dispose of waste became increasingly pressing challenges. In the early 1800s, urban households used privies to dispose of human excrement, and factories dumped untreated sewage into rivers, lakes, and bays. By the late nineteenth century, most cities had replaced private water companies with public water supplies, but these services did not guarantee pure water. The waste from sewer systems and flush toilets, plus use of water as a coolant in factories, overwhelmed waterways, contaminating drinking-water sources and sending pollution to communities downstream. The stench of rivers was often unbearable, and pollution bred disease. In 1878, nineteen thousand people fled a yellow fever epidemic in Memphis and 80 percent of those left behind caught the disease. By 1900, the Passaic River in northern New Jersey, once a popular recreation and fishing site, had been ruined by discharge from cities along its banks.

Acceptance in the 1880s of the germ theory of disease prompted health officials to take steps to reduce chances that human waste and other pollutants would endanger water supplies, but the task proved difficult. Some states passed laws prohibiting discharge of raw sewage into rivers and streams, and a few cities began the expensive process of chemically treating sewage. Gradually, water managers installed mechanical filters, and cities, led by Jersey City, began purifying water supplies by adding chlorine. These efforts dramatically reduced death rates from typhoid fever.

But waste disposal remained a thorny problem. Experts in 1900 estimated that every New Yorker generated annually some 160 pounds of garbage (food and bones); 1,200 pounds of ashes (from stoves and furnaces); and 100 pounds of rubbish (shoes, furniture, and other discarded items). Europeans of that era produced about half as much trash. Solid waste dumped from factories and businesses included tons of scrap metal and wood. Also, each of the estimated 3.5 million horses in American cities in 1900 daily dropped about 20 pounds of manure and a gallon of urine that rain washed into nearby water sources. In past eras, excrement and trash could be dismissed as nuisances; by the twentieth century, they had become health and safety hazards.

Urban Engineers

Citizens' groups, led by women's organizations, began discussing these dilemmas in the 1880s, and by 1900 urban governments began to hire sanitary engineers, such as George Waring, to design efficient systems to collect garbage and dispose of it in incinerators and landfills. Waring designed a sewer system in Memphis in the wake of the yellow fever epidemic and as New York City's street cleaning commissioner in the 1890s instituted extensive reforms in sanitation and organization. Engineers also made cities more livable in other ways. Street lighting, bridge construction, fire protection, and other vital services required creativity, and in addressing these issues American engineers developed systems and standards of worldwide significance. Elected officials came to rely on the expertise of engineers, who seemed best qualified to supervise a city's expansion. Insulated within bureaucratic agencies away from tumultuous party politics, engineers generally fulfilled their responsibilities efficiently and made some of the most lasting contributions to urban management.

Law Enforcement

After the mid-nineteenth century, urban dwellers increasingly depended on professional police to protect life and property, but law enforcement became complicated and controversial, as various urban groups differed in their views of the law and how it should be enforced. Ethnic and racial minorities were more likely to be arrested than those with economic or political influence. And police officers applied the law less harshly to members of their own ethnic groups and to people who bought exemptions with bribes.

As law enforcers, police, often poorly trained and prone to corruption, were squeezed between demands for swift and severe action on the one hand and for leniency on the other. As urban society diversified, some people clamored for police crackdowns on saloons, gambling halls, and houses of prostitution; at the same time, others who profited from and patronized such customer-oriented criminal establishments favored loose law enforcement. Achieving balance between the idealistic intentions of criminal law and people's desire for personal freedom grew increasingly difficult, and it has remained so to this day.

Political Machines

Out of the apparent confusion surrounding urban management arose political machines, organizations whose main goals were the rewards—money, influence, and prestige—of getting and keeping power. Machine politicians routinely used fraud and bribery to further their ends. But they also provided relief, security, and service to the crowds of newcomers who voted for them and kept them in power. By meeting people's needs, machine politicians accomplished things that other agencies had been unable or unwilling to attempt.

Urban machines bred leaders, called bosses, who built power bases among working classes and especially among immigrants. Most bosses had immigrant backgrounds and had grown up in the inner city, so they knew their constituents' needs firsthand. Bosses held power because they dealt with problems of everyday life. Martin Lomasney, boss of Boston's South End, explained, "There's got to be in every ward somebody that any bloke can come to—no matter what he's done—and get help. Help, you understand, none of your law and justice, but help." In return for votes, bosses provided jobs, built parks and bathhouses, distributed food and clothing to the needy, and helped when someone ran afoul of the law. New York's "Big Tim" Sullivan, for example, gave out shoes and sponsored annual picnics. Such personalized service cultivated mass attachment to the boss; never before had public leaders assumed such responsibility for people in need. Bosses, moreover, made politics a full-time profession. They attended weddings and wakes, joined clubs, and held open houses in saloons where neighborhood folk could speak to them personally. According to George Washington Plunkitt, a neighborhood boss in New York City, "As a rule [the boss] has no business or occupation other than politics. He plays politics every day and night in the year and his headquarters bears the inscription, 'Never closed.'"

To finance their activities and election campaigns, bosses exchanged favors for votes and money. Power over local government enabled machines to control the awarding of public contracts, the granting of utility and streetcar franchises, and the distribution of city jobs. Recipients of city business and jobs were expected to repay the machine with a portion of their profits or salaries and to cast supporting votes on election day. Critics called this process graft; bosses called it gratitude.

Bosses such as Philadelphia's "Duke" Vare, Kansas City's Tom Pendergast, and New York's Richard Croker lived like kings, though their official incomes were slim. Yet machines were rarely as dictatorial or corrupt as critics charged.

Street Cleaning and Urban Reform

As street cleaning became an ever-increasing necessity in burgeoning cities, the numbers of employees of sanitation departments multiplied and the tools they used on their job became more elaborate. As early as 1896, inventors were designing machines and vehicles with brushes to replace the brooms used by past streetcleaning crews and scrapers for clearing snow. One such inventor,

Miriam and Ira D. Wallach Division of Art, Prints and Photographs, The New York Public Library.

Beginning of New York's Street Cleaning Department.   Calling the roll, 1868

As the human and horse populations of cities grew, garbage, litter, and manure became nagging inconveniences and health hazards. In 1868, street sweepers, hired to clean the streets, often consisted of crews hired by political bosses and were required to report to a supervisor for morning roll call.

Rather, several machines, like businesses, evolved into tightly structured operations, such as New York's Tammany Hall organization (named after a society that originally began as a patriotic fraternal club), which blended public accomplishments with personal gain. The system rested on a popular base held together by loyalty and service. A few bosses had no permanent organization; they were freelance opportunists who bargained for power, sometimes winning and sometimes losing. But most machines were coalitions of smaller organizations that derived power directly from inner-city neighborhoods. Bosses also could boast major achievements. Aided by engineers, machine-led governments constructed

Charles Brooks of Newark, New Jersey, not only patented a street-cleaning and snow-removal truck but also designed a receptacle for storing trash and other litter picked up by his machine. But to the minds of engineers and sanitarians, improving the technology of street cleaning was not enough. The process needed to be organized and controlled in what to their minds was a logical way, giving workers a sense of value and professionalism. These two images reveal an important change in the appearance of the New York City street-cleaning force between 1868 and 1920. What reform attitudes do the contrasting images represent? Given the contrasting dress of the two crews, how would the general public have reacted to each?

Astor, Lenox and Tilden Foundations.

This shows the great improvements made by Colonel Waring as Street Commissioner.   Calling the roll in 1920

By the early 1900s, the profession of sanitary engineer became an important one to the urban environment.

the urban infrastructure—public buildings, sewer systems, schools, bridges, and mass-transit lines—and expanded urban services—police, firefighting, and health departments.

Machine politics, however, was rarely neutral or fair. Racial minorities and new immigrant groups, such as Italians and Poles, received only token jobs and nominal favors, if any. And bribes and kickbacks made machine projects and services costly to taxpayers. Cities could not ordinarily raise enough revenue for their construction projects from taxes and fees, so they financed expansion with loans from the public in the form of municipal bonds. Critics charged that these loans were inflated or unnecessary. Necessary or not, municipal bonds caused public debts to soar, and taxes had to be raised to repay their interest and principal. In addition, payoffs from gambling, prostitution, and illicit liquor traffic often became important sources of machine revenue. But in an age of economic individualism, bosses were no more guilty of discrimination and self-interest than were business leaders who exploited workers, spoiled the environment, and manipulated government in pursuit of profits. Sometimes humane and sometimes criminal, bosses acted as brokers between sectors of urban society and an uncertain world.

Civic Reform   While bosses were consolidating their power, others were trying to destroy them. Many middle- and upper-class Americans feared that immigrant-based political machines menaced democracy and that unsavory alliances between bosses and businesses wasted municipal finances. Anxious over the poverty and disorder that accompanied city growth, and convinced that urban services were making taxes too high, civic reformers organized to install more responsible leaders at the helm of government. Civic reform arose in part from the industrial system's emphasis on eliminating inefficiency. Business-minded reformers believed government should run like a company. The way to achieve this goal, they concluded, was to elect officials who would limit costs and prevent corruption.

To implement business principles in government, civic reformers supported structural changes, such as city-manager and commission forms of government, which would place administration in the hands of experts rather than politicians, and nonpartisan citywide rather than neighborhood-based election of officials. Armed with such strategies, reformers believed they could cleanse city government of party politics and weaken bosses' power bases. They rarely realized, however, that bosses succeeded because they used government to meet people's needs. Reformers noticed only the waste and dishonesty that machines bred.

A few reform mayors moved beyond structural changes to address social problems. Hazen S. Pingree of Detroit, Samuel "Golden Rule" Jones of Toledo, and Tom Johnson of Cleveland worked to provide jobs to poor people, reduce charges by streetcar and utility companies, and promote governmental responsibility for the welfare of all citizens. They also supported public ownership of gas, electric, and telephone companies, a quasi-socialist reform that alienated their business allies. But Pingree, Jones, and Johnson were exceptions. Civic reformers could not match the bosses' political savvy; they achieved some successes but rarely held office for very long.

Social Reform   A different type of reform arose outside politics. Driven to improve as well as manage society, social reformers—mostly young and middle class—embarked on campaigns to investigate and solve urban problems. ousing reformers pressed local governments for building codes to ensure safety in tenements. Educational reformers sought to use public schools as a means of preparing immigrant children for citizenship by teaching them American values. Health reformers tried to improve medical care for those who could not afford it. And residents of settlement houses—places located in inner-city neighborhoods with the aim of bridging the gulf between classes—offered vocational classes, lessons in English, and childcare, and they sponsored programs to improve nutrition and housing. Settlement-house workers such as Jane Addams and Florence Kelley of Chicago and Lillian Wald of New York broadened their scope to fight for school nurses, factory safety codes, and public playgrounds; they became reform leaders in cities and in the nation.

The City Beautiful Movement   While female activists tried to assist people in need and revive neighborhoods, a group of male reformers organized the City Beautiful movement to improve cities' physical organization. Inspired by the Columbian Exposition of 1893, a dazzling world's fair built on Chicago's South Side, architects and planners, led by architect Daniel Burnham, urged the construction of civic centers, parks, and boulevards that would make cities economically efficient as well as beautiful. "Make no little plans," Burnham urged. "Make big plans; aim high in hope and work." This attitude spawned beautification projects in the early 1900s in Chicago, San Francisco, and Washington, D.C. Yet most big plans existed mostly as big dreams. Neither government nor private businesses could finance large-scale projects, and planners disagreed among themselves and with social reformers over whether beautification would truly solve urban problems.

Regardless of their focus, urban reformers wanted to save cities, not abandon them. They believed they could improve urban life by achieving cooperation among all citizens. They often failed to realize, however, that cities were places of great diversity and that different people held conflicting views about what reform actually meant. To civic reformers, appointing government workers on the basis of civil service exams rather than party loyalty meant progress, but to working-class men, civil service signified reduced employment opportunities. Moral reformers believed that restricting the sale of alcoholic beverages would prevent working-class breadwinners from squandering wages and ruining their health, but immigrants saw such crusades as interference in their private lives. Planners saw new streets and buildings as modern necessities, but such structures often displaced the poor. Well-meaning humanitarians criticized immigrant mothers for the way they shopped, dressed, did housework, and raised children, without regard for these mothers' inability to afford products that the consumer economy created. Thus urban reform merged idealism with naïveté and insensitivity.

FAMILY LIFE

Although the vast majority of Americans lived within families, this basic social institution suffered strain during the era of urbanization and industrialization. New institutions—schools, social clubs, political organizations, unions—increasingly competed with the family to provide nurture, education, and security. Clergy and journalists warned that the growing separation between home and work, rising divorce rates, entrance of women into the work force, and loss of parental control over children spelled peril for home and family. Yet the family retained its fundamental role as a cushion in a hard, uncertain world.

Family and Household Structures

Throughout modern western history, most people have lived in two overlapping social units: household and family. A household is a group of people, related or unrelated, who share the same residence. A family is a group related by kinship, some members of which typically live together. In the late nineteenth and early twentieth centuries, different patterns characterized the two institutions.

Until recently, when high divorce rates and relatively late age at first marriage have increased the percentage of one-person households, most American households (75 to 80 percent) have consisted of nuclear families—usually a married couple, with or without children. Only a small minority of households consisted of extended families—usually a married couple, their children, and one or more relatives, such as parents of the husband or wife, adult siblings, or other kin, and not many people lived alone.

Several factors explain this pattern. Because immigrants tended to be young, the American population as a whole was young. In 1880, the median age was under twenty-one; by 1920, it was still only twenty-five. (Median age at present is thirty-five.) Moreover, in 1900, the death rate among people aged forty-five to sixty-four was double what it is today. As a result, there were few elderly people: only 4 percent of the population was sixty-five or older, compared with 12 percent today. Thus, few families could form extended three-generation households, and fewer children than today had living grandparents.

Declining Birth Rates

The average size of nuclear families also changed. Most of Europe and North America experienced falling birth rates in the nineteenth century. The decline in the United States began early in the 1800s and accelerated toward the end of the century. In 1880, the birth rate was 40 live births per 1,000 people; by 1900, it had dropped to 32; by 1920, to 28. Although fertility was higher among black, immigrant, and rural women than among white native-born urban females, birth rates of all groups fell.

In part, this decline occurred because, as the United States became more urbanized, the economic value of children lessened. On farms, where children worked at home or in the fields, each child born represented an addition to the family labor force. In the wage-based urban economy, children could not contribute significantly to the family income for many years, and a new child represented a draw on family income. Second, infant mortality fell as diet and medical care improved, and families did not have to bear many children to ensure that some would survive.

Perhaps most importantly, as economic trends changed, attitudes toward children changed. No matter what the era, parents always cherished their children. But as American society industrialized and urbanized, the idea of a child as a pure, innocent being who not only needed shelter from society's corruptions but who also could provide parents with emotional rewards spread, first among the middle class and gradually to the working class as well. A mother's investment of care could be more focused and effective if she had few rather than many children. Such an attitude seems to have stimulated decisions by parents to limit family size—either by abstaining from sex during the wife's fertile period or by using contraception.

Families with six or eight children became rare; three or four became more usual. Birth-control technology—diaphragms and condoms—had been utilized for centuries, but in this era new materials made devices more convenient and dependable. Use of rubber rather than animal membranes for condoms after 1869 inspired British playwright and philosopher George Bernard Shaw to exclaim that new birth-control devices were "the greatest invention of the nineteenth century."

Stages of Life   Although the family remained resilient and adaptable, notable shifts began to occur in individual life patterns. Before the late nineteenth century, stages of life were less distinct than they are today, and generations blended together with relatively little differentiation. Childhood, for instance, had been regarded as a period during which young people prepared for adulthood by gradually assuming more roles and responsibilities. Subdivisions of youth—toddlers, schoolchildren, teenagers, and the like—were not recognized or defined. Because married couples had more children over a longer time span than is common today, active parenthood occupied most of adult life. And because relatively few people lived to advanced age or left work voluntarily, and because old-age homes were rare, older people were not isolated from other age groups. By the late nineteenth century, however, decreasing birth rates shortened the period of parental responsibility, so more middle-aged couples experienced an "empty nest" when all their children had grown up and left home. Longer life expectancy and a tendency by employers to force aged workers to retire separated the old from the young.

New patterns of childhood also emerged. Separation of home and work, especially prevalent in cities, meant that children were less likely than previously to be involved in producing income for the family. To be sure, youngsters in working-class families still helped out—working in factories, scavenging streets for scraps of wood and coal, and peddling newspapers and other goods—but generally youngsters had more time for other activities. As states passed compulsory school attendance laws in the 1870s and 1880s, education occupied more of children's daily time than ever before, keeping them in school nine months of the year until they were teenagers and strengthening peer rather than family influence over their behavior. Also, influenced by the era's scientific spirit, psychologists and educators began studying children to help shape them into moral, productive adults. Researchers such as G. Stanley Hall and Luther H. Gulick advocated that teachers and parents should match education and play activities to the needs that children had at different stages of their development. Anxious that children be protected from city streets, "child-saving" advocates asserted that adult-supervised playgrounds should be established to give children alternatives to dangerous activities and unhealthy contacts.

The Unmarried   Although marriage rates were high, large numbers of city dwellers were unmarried, largely because many people waited to wed until they were in their late twenties. In 1890, almost 42 percent of adult American men and 37 percent of women were single, almost twice as high as figures for 1960 but slightly lower than they are today. About half of all single

As cities grew and became increasingly congested, children in immigrant and working-class neighborhoods used streets and sidewalks as play sites. Activities of youngsters such as these, playing unsupervised in front of a Polish saloon, prompted adults to create playgrounds, clubs, and other places where they could protect children's safety and innocence and where they could ensure that play would be orderly and obedient.

Chicago Historical Society

people still lived in their parents' household, but others inhabited boarding houses or rooms in the homes of strangers. Mostly young, these men and women constituted a separate subculture that helped support institutions such as dance halls, saloons, cafés, and the Young Men's Christian Association (YMCA) and Young Women's Christian Association (YWCA).

Some unmarried people were part of the homosexual populations that especially thrived in large cities such as New York, San Francisco, and Boston. Although numbers are difficult to estimate, gay men had their own subculture of clubs, restaurants, coffeehouses, theaters, and support networks. A number of same-sex couples, especially women, formed lasting marital-type relationships, sometimes called "Boston marriages." People in this subculture were categorized more by how they acted—men acting like women, women acting like men—than by who their sexual partners were. The term *homosexual* was not used. Men who dressed and acted like women were called "fairies," and men who displayed masculine traits could be termed "normal" even though they might have sexual relations with fairies. Gay women remained more hidden, and a lesbian subculture of clubs and commercial establishments did not develop until the 1920s. The gay world, then, was a mostly concealed one that included a variety of relationships and institutions.

Boarding and Lodging

In every city, boarding houses and lodging hotels were common, but families also commonly took in boarders to occupy rooms vacated by grown children and to get additional income. (Boarders usually received meals along with a room; lodgers only rented a room.) By 1900, as many as 50 percent of city residents had lived either as, or with, boarders at some point during their lifetime. Housing reformers charged that boarding and lodging caused overcrowding and loss of privacy. Yet the practice was highly useful. For people on the move, boarding was a transitional stage, providing a quasi-family environment until they set up their own households. Especially in communities where economic hardship or rapid growth made housing expensive or scarce, newlyweds sometimes lived temporarily with one spouse's parents. Families also took in widowed parents or unmarried siblings who otherwise would have lived alone.

Functions of Kinship

At a time when welfare agencies were scarce, the family was the institution to which people could turn in times of need. Even when relatives did not live together, they often resided nearby and aided one another with childcare, meals, advice, and consolation. They also obtained jobs for relatives. Factory foremen who had responsibility for hiring often recruited new workers recommended by their employees. According to one new arrival, "After two days my brother took me to the shop he was working in and his boss saw me and he gave me the job."

But obligations of kinship were not always welcome. Immigrant families pressured last-born female children to stay at home to care for aging parents, a practice that stifled opportunities for education, marriage, and independence. As an aging Italian American father confessed, "One of our daughters is an old maid [and] causes plenty of troubles…. it may be my fault because I always wished her to remain at home and not to marry for she was of great financial help." Tensions also developed between generations, when immigrant parents and American-born children clashed over the abandonment of Old World ways or over the amount of wages that employed children should contribute to the household. Nevertheless, for better or worse, kinship provided a means of coping with stresses caused by urban-industrial society.

Thus, family life and functions were both changing and holding firm. New institutions were assuming tasks formerly performed by the family, and people's roles in school, at home, on the job, and in the community came to be determined by age more than by other characteristics. Schools made education a community responsibility. Employment agencies, personnel offices, and labor unions were taking responsibility for employee recruitment and job security. Age-based peer groups exerted greater influence over people's values and activities. Migration seemed to be splitting families apart. Yet in the face of these pressures, the family adjusted by expanding and contracting to meet temporary needs, and kinship remained a dependable though not always appreciated institution.

Holiday Celebrations Family togetherness became especially visible at holiday celebrations. Thanksgiving, Christmas, and Easter were special times for family reunion and child-centered activities, and female relatives made special efforts to cook and decorate the home. Birthdays, too, took on an increasingly festive quality, both as an important family occasion and as a milestone for how an individual measured what she or he had experienced and accomplished relative to others of the same age. In 1914, President Woodrow Wilson signed a proclamation designating the second Sunday in May as Mother's Day, capping a six-year campaign by Anna Jarvis, a schoolteacher who believed grown children too often neglected their mothers. Ethnic and racial groups made efforts to tailor national celebrations to their cultures, using holidays as occasions for preparing special ethnic foods and engaging in special ceremonies. For many, holiday celebrations were a testimony to the vitality of family life. "As I grew up, living conditions were a bit crowded," one woman reminisced, "but no one minded because we were a family ... thankful we all lived together."

THE NEW LEISURE AND MASS CULTURE

On December 2, 1889, as hundreds of workers paraded through Worcester, Massachusetts, in support of shorter working hours, a group of carpenters hoisted a banner proclaiming "Eight Hours for Work, Eight Hours for Rest, Eight Hours for What We Will." That last phrase was significant, for it laid claim to a special segment of daily life that belonged to the individual. Increasingly, among all urban social classes, leisure activities, doing "what we will," filled this time segment.

Increase in Leisure Time American inventors had long tried to create labor-saving devices, but not until the late 1800s did technology become truly time-saving. Mechanization and assembly-line production cut the average workweek in manufacturing from sixty-six hours in 1860 to sixty in 1890 and forty-seven in 1920. These reductions meant shorter workdays and freer weekends. White-collar employees spent eight to ten hours a day on the job and often worked only half a day or not at all on weekends. Laborers in steel mills and sweatshops still endured twelve- or fourteen-hour shifts and had little time or energy for leisure. But as the economy shifted from one of scarcity and production to one of surplus and consumption, more Americans began to escape into a variety of recreations, and a substantial segment of the economy provided for—and profited from—leisure. By 1900, Americans were enmeshed in the business of play.

Amusement became an organized, commercial activity, as home entertainment expanded. Mass-produced pianos and sheet music became important consumer purchases for middle-class families and made singing of popular songs a common form of home entertainment. The vanguard of new leisure pursuits, however, was sports. Formerly a fashionable indulgence of elites, organized sports became a favored pastime of all classes, attracting countless participants and spectators. Even those who could not play or watch got involved by reading about sports in the newspapers.

Baseball

The most popular sport was baseball. Derived from older bat, ball, and base-circling games, baseball was formalized in 1845 by the Knickerbocker Club of New York, which standardized the rules of play. By 1860, at least fifty baseball clubs existed, and youths played informal games on city lots and rural fields across the nation. In 1869, a professional club, the Cincinnati Red Stockings, went on a national tour, and other teams followed suit. The National League of Professional Baseball Clubs, founded in 1876, gave the sport a stable, businesslike structure. Not all athletes benefited, however; as early as 1867, a "color line" excluded black players from professional teams. Nevertheless, by the 1880s, professional baseball was big business. In 1903, the National League and competing American League (formed in 1901) began a World Series between their championship teams, entrenching baseball as the national pastime. The Boston Red Sox beat the Pittsburgh Pirates in that first series.

Croquet and Cycling

Baseball appealed mostly to men. But croquet, which also swept the nation, attracted both sexes. Middle- and upper-class people held croquet parties and outfitted wickets with candles for night contests. In an era when the departure of paid work from the home had separated men's from women's spheres, croquet increased opportunities for social contact between the sexes.

Meanwhile, cycling achieved a popularity rivaling that of baseball, especially after 1885, when the cumbersome velocipede, with its huge front wheel and tall seat, gave way to safety bicycles with pneumatic tires and wheels of identical size. By 1900, Americans owned 10 million bicycles, and clubs such as the League of American Wheelmen were petitioning state governments to build more paved roads. African American cyclists were allowed to compete as professionals, unlike baseball. One black rider, Major Taylor, achieved success in Europe and the United States between 1892 and 1910. Like croquet, cycling brought men and women together, combining opportunities for exercise and courtship. Moreover, the bicycle played an influential role in freeing women from the constraints of Victorian fashions. In order to ride the dropped-frame female models, women had to wear divided skirts and simple undergarments. As the 1900 census declared, "Few articles ... have created so great a revolution in social conditions as the bicycle."

Football

American football, as an intercollegiate competition, attracted mostly players and spectators wealthy enough to have access to higher education. By the late nineteenth century, however, the game was appealing to a broader audience. The 1893 Princeton-Yale game drew fifty thousand spectators, and informal games were played in yards and playgrounds throughout the country. Soon, however, football became a national scandal because of its violence and use of "tramp athletes," nonstudents whom colleges hired to help their teams win. Critics accused football of mirroring undesirable features of American society. An editor of *The Nation* charged in 1890 that "the spirit of the American Youth, as of the American man, is to win, to get there, by fair means or foul; and the lack of moral scruple which pervades the struggles of the business world meets with temptations equally irresistible in the miniature contests of the football field."

The scandals climaxed in 1905, when 18 players died from game-related injuries and 159 were seriously injured. President Theodore Roosevelt, a strong advocate of athletics, convened a White House conference to discuss ways to eliminate brutality and foul play. The gathering founded the Intercollegiate Athletic Association (renamed the National College Athletic Association—NCAA—in 1910) to police college sports. In 1906, the association altered the game to make it less violent and more open. New rules outlawed "flying-wedge" rushes, extended from five to ten yards the distance needed to earn a first down, legalized the forward pass, and tightened player eligibility requirements.

As more women enrolled in college, they pursued physical activities besides croquet and cycling. Believing that intellectual success required active and healthy bodies, physical educators encouraged college women to participate in such sports as rowing, track, and swimming. Eventually women made basketball their most popular intercollegiate sport. Invented in 1891 as a winter sport for men, basketball received women's rules (which limited dribbling and running, and encouraged passing) from Senda Berenson of Smith College.

Show Business

Going out for commercial entertainment became a popular leisure-time pursuit, and as it did, three branches of American show business—popular drama, musical comedy, and vaudeville—matured. New theatrical performances offered audiences escape into melodrama, adventure, and comedy. Plots were simple, heroes and villains recognizable. For urban people unfamiliar with the frontier, popular plays made the mythical Wild West and Old South come alive through stories of Davy Crockett, Buffalo Bill, and the Civil War. Virtue and honor always triumphed in melodramas such as *Uncle Tom's Cabin* and *The Old Homestead*, reinforcing faith that, in an uncertain and disillusioning world, goodness would prevail.

Musical comedies entertained audiences with song, humor, and dance. The American musical derived from lavishly costumed operettas common in Europe. The introduction of American themes (often involving ethnic groups), folksy humor, and catchy tunes in the late nineteenth century helped these shows spawn the nation's most popular songs and entertainers. George M. Cohan, a singer, dancer, and songwriter born into an Irish family of entertainers, became master of American musical comedy in the early twentieth century. Drawing on patriotism and traditional values in songs such as "Yankee Doodle Boy" and "You're a Grand Old Flag," Cohan helped boost morale during the First World War. Comic opera, too, became popular. Initially, American comic operas imitated European musicals, but by the early 1900s composers such as Victor Herbert were writing for American audiences.

Vaudeville was probably the most popular mass entertainment in early-twentieth-century America because it offered something for everyone. Shows, whose acts followed a fixed schedule just like trains and factory production, included jugglers, magicians, acrobats, comedians, singers, dancers, and specialty acts like magician Harry Houdini's escapes. Around 1900, the number of vaudeville theaters and troupes skyrocketed, and big-time operators such as Tony Pastor (who gave Houdini his first vaudeville job) and the partnership of Benjamin Keith and Edward Albee consolidated theaters and acts under their management in the same manner that other businessmen were consolidating factory production. Marcus Loew, an owner of theaters that attracted working-class audiences, was known as "the Henry Ford of show business." Producer Florenz Ziegfeld brilliantly packaged shows in a stylish format—the Ziegfeld Follies—and gave the nation a new model of femininity, the Ziegfeld Girl, whose graceful dancing and alluring costumes suggested a haunting sensuality.

Opportunities for Women and Minorities   Show business provided economic and social mobility to female, African American, and immigrant performers, but also encouraged stereotyping and exploitation. Comic opera diva Lillian Russell, vaudeville singer-comedienne Fanny Brice, and burlesque queen Eva Tanguay attracted intensely loyal fans, commanded handsome fees, and won respect for their talents. In contrast to the demure Victorian female, they conveyed an image of pluck and independence. There was something both shocking and confident about Eva Tanguay when she moved energetically around the stage singing earthy songs like "It's All Been Done Before but Not the Way I Do It" and "I Don't Care." One news reporter proclaimed, "Eva Tanguay is a mass of nerves quivering, shrieking, undeniable nerves, superbly harnessed to an indestructible ego. Her whole performance is of herself, for herself, by herself." But lesser female performers and showgirls (called "soubrettes") were often exploited by male promoters and theater owners, many of whom wanted only to profit by titillating the public with the sight of scantily clad women.

Before the 1890s, the chief form of commercial entertainment that employed African American performers had been the minstrel show, but vaudeville opened new opportunities to them. As stage settings shifted from the plantation to the city, music shifted from sentimental folk tunes to syncopated rhythms of ragtime. Pandering to prejudices of white audiences, composers ridiculed blacks, and black performers were forced to portray demeaning characters. In songs such as "He's Just a Little Nigger, But He's Mine All Mine" and "You May Be a Hawaiian on Old Broadway, But You're Just Another Nigger to Me," blacks were degraded on stage much as they were in society. Burt Williams, a talented black comedian and dancer who had graduated from high school at a time when most whites did not, achieved success by wearing blackface makeup and playing stereotypical roles of a smiling fool and dandy, but was tormented by the humiliation he had to suffer.

An ethnic flavor gave much of American mass entertainment its uniqueness. Many performers were immigrants, and their stage acts reflected their experiences. Vaudeville in particular utilized ethnic humor and exaggerated dialects. Skits and songs were fast-paced, replicating the tempo of factories, offices, and the streets. Performances reinforced ethnic stereotypes, but such distortions were more self-conscious and sympathetic than those directed at blacks. Ethnic humor often satirized everyday difficulties that immigrants faced. A typical scene involving Italians, for example, highlighted a character's uncertain grasp of English, which caused him to confuse *diploma* with *the plumber* and *pallbearer* with *polar bear*. Other scenes included gags about dealing with modern society. Thus, when a stage doctor required ten dollars for his advice, the patient responded, "Ten dollars is too much. Here's two dollars. Take it, that's *my* advice." Such scenes allowed audiences to laugh with, rather than at, foibles of the human condition.

Movies Shortly after 1900, live entertainment began to yield to a more accessible form of commercial amusement: motion pictures. Perfected by Thomas Edison in the 1880s, movies began as slot-machine peepshows in arcades and billiard parlors. Eventually, images of speeding trains, acrobats, and belly dancers were projected onto a screen so that large audiences could view them, and a new medium was born. Producers, many of them from Jewish immigrant backgrounds, discovered that a film could tell a story in exciting ways and, like vaudeville performers, catered to viewers' desires. Using themes of patriotism and working-class experience, early filmmakers helped shift American culture away from its more straitlaced Victorian values to a more cosmopolitan outlook.

As they expanded from minutes to hours in length, movies presented controversial social messages as well as innovative technology and styles of expression. For example, the film *Birth of a Nation* (1915), by the creative director D. W. Griffith, was a stunning epic film about the Civil War and Reconstruction, but it also fanned racial prejudice by depicting African Americans as threats to white moral values. The National Association for the Advancement of Colored People (NAACP), formed in 1909, led organized protests against it. But the film's ground-breaking techniques—close-ups, fade-outs, and battle scenes—heightened the drama.

Technology and entrepreneurship also made news a mass consumer product. Using high-speed printing presses, cheaply produced paper, and profits from growing advertisement revenues, shrewd publishers created a medium that made people crave news and ads just as they craved amusements. City life and increased leisure time seemed to nurture a fascination with the sensational, and from the 1880s onward popular urban newspapers increasingly whetted that appetite.

Yellow Journalism Joseph Pulitzer, a Hungarian immigrant who bought the *New York World* in 1883, made news a mass commodity. Believing that newspapers should be "dedicated to the cause of the people," Pulitzer filled the *World* with stories of disasters, crimes, and scandals. Screaming headlines, set in large, bold type like that used for advertisements, attracted readers. Pulitzer's journalists not only reported news but also sought it out and created it. *World* reporter Nellie Bly (real name, Elizabeth Cochrane), for example, faked her way into a mental asylum and wrote a brazen exposé of the sordid conditions she found. Other reporters staged stunts and hunted down heart-rending human-interest stories. Pulitzer also popularized comics, and the yellow ink in which they were printed gave rise to the term *yellow journalism* as a synonym for sensationalism.

Pulitzer's strategy was immensely successful. In one year, the *World*'s circulation increased from 20,000 to 100,000, and by the late 1890s it reached 1 million. Other publishers, such as William Randolph Hearst, who bought the *New York Journal* in 1895 and started an empire of mass-circulation newspapers, adopted Pulitzer's techniques. Pulitzer, Hearst, and their rivals boosted circulation further by making sports and women's news a mass commodity. Newspapers had previously reported sporting events, but yellow-journalism papers gave such stories greater prominence by printing separate, expanded sports pages. Sports news re-created a game's drama through narrative and statistics, and promoted sports as a leisure-time attraction. To capture female readers, newspapers also added special sections devoted to household tips, fashion, etiquette, and club news.

Other Mass-Market Publications

By the early twentieth century, mass-circulation magazines overshadowed the expensive elitist journals of earlier eras. Publications such as *McClure's, Saturday Evening Post*, and *Ladies' Home Journal* offered human-interest stories, muckraking exposés, titillating fiction, photographs, colorful covers, and eye-catching ads to a growing mass market. Meanwhile, the number of published books more than quadrupled between 1880 and 1917. Rising consumption of news and books reflected growing literacy. Between 1870 and 1920, the proportion of Americans over age ten who could not read or write fell from 20 percent to 6 percent.

Other forms of communication also expanded. In 1891, there was less than 1 telephone for every 100 people in the United States; by 1901 the number had grown to 2.1, and by 1921 it swelled to 12.6. In 1900, Americans used 4 billion postage stamps; in 1922, they bought 14.3 billion. The term *community* took on new dimensions, as people used the media, mail, and telephone to extend their horizons far beyond their immediate locality.

More than ever before, people in different parts of the country knew about and discussed the same news event, whether it was a sensational murder, sex scandal, or the fortunes of a particular entertainer or athlete. America was becoming a mass society where the same products, the same technology, and the same information dominated everyday life, regardless of region.

Anthony Comstock

All the opening up of leisure and amusement did not go unopposed. Most prominent among reactionary moralists was Anthony Comstock, who made a career out of attempts to censor sexually explicit and suggestive literature and entertainment. In 1873, Comstock created the Society for the Supression of Vice and convinced Congress to pass a law outlawing the distribution of "lewd and lascivious" material. He was able to get an appointment as a postal inspector and worked diligently to ban marriage manuals and birth control literature from the mails. Between the 1870s and his death in 1915, Comstock also carried out constant campaigns against what he believed to be indecent displays and performances, especially in New York City. His targets included not only printed material but also paintings of nude women, an exhibition of physical culture, and a play by noted British author George Bernard Shaw that had prostitution as one of its themes.

But try as they might, crusaders such as Anthony Comstock could not alter the flow of cultural change taking place in cities. Mass culture, perhaps more than any other factor, represented democracy because influences flowed upward from the experiences and desires of ordinary people as much as, if not more than, they were imposed from above by the rich and powerful. The popularity of sports, the themes depicted in movies and on stage, and the content of everyday publications reveal not only that Americans in the urban-industrial era had time to patronize leisure-time activities but also that savvy entrepreneurs understood that what they produced needed to meet the needs of the new consumers. At the same time, producers helped people adapt by providing information about new social and economic conditions and by making some of the disruptive factors more tolerable through drama and humor. The major exception was the portrayal and treatment of African Americans with a viciousness that did not diminish as entertainment expanded.

To some extent, then, cities' new amusements and media had a homogenizing influence, allowing different social groups to share common experiences. Parks, ball fields, vaudeville shows, movies, and the feature sections of newspapers and magazines were nonsectarian and apolitical. Yet different consumer groups adapted them to their own cultural needs. Immigrants, for example, often used parks and amusement areas as sites for special ethnic gatherings. To the dismay of reformers who hoped that public recreation and holidays would assimilate newcomers and teach them habits of restraint, immigrants converted picnics and Fourth of July celebrations into occasions for boisterous drinking and sometimes violent behavior. Young working-class men and women resisted parents' and moralists' warnings, and frequented urban dance halls, where they explored forms of courtship and sexual behavior free from adult oversight. And children often used streets and rooftops to create their own recreation rather than participate in adult-supervised games in parks and playgrounds. Thus, as Americans learned to play, their leisure—like their work and politics—expressed, and was shaped by, the pluralistic forces that thrived in urban life.

SUMMARY

People and technology made the late nineteenth and early twentieth centuries the "age of the city." Flocking cityward, migrants already in America and those coming from foreign parts remade themselves and remade the urban environment as well. Although they may have escaped their previous homelands, they also brought with them cultures that in turn enriched American culture. They also found further escape in new and expanded forms of mass leisure and entertainment. Cities were dynamic places, where everyday life brought new challenges, where politics and reform took on new meanings, and where family life reflected both change and continuity.

Although their governments and neighborhoods may have seemed chaotic, American cities experienced an "unheralded triumph" by the early 1900s. Amid corruption and political conflict, engineers modernized sewer, water, and lighting services, and urban governments made cities safer by expanding professional police and fire departments. When native inventiveness met the traditions of European, African, and Asian cultures, a new kind of society emerged. This society seldom functioned smoothly; there really was no coherent urban community, only a collection of subcommunities. The jumble of social classes, ethnic and racial groups, and political and professional organizations sometimes lived in harmony, sometimes not. Generally, cities managed to thrive because of, rather than in spite of, their diverse fragments.

Optimists had envisioned the American nation as a melting pot, where various nationalities would fuse into a unified people. Instead, many ethnic groups proved unmeltable, preferring—and sometimes forced—to pursue their own ways of acting, and racial minorities got burned on the bottom of the pot. As a result of immigration and urbanization, the United States became a pluralistic society in which cultural influences moved in both directions: imposed from above by people with power and influence, and adopted from below through the traditions and tastes brought to cities by disparate peoples. When the desire to retain one culture met with the need to fit in, often the results were compound identifications: Irish American, Italian American, Polish American, and the like.

By 1920, immigrants and their offspring outnumbered the native-born in many cities, and the national economy depended on these new workers and consumers. Migrants and immigrants transformed the United States into an urban nation. They gave American culture its rich and varied texture just by living their lives but also, by changing the course of entertainment and consumerism, and they laid the foundations for the liberalism that would characterize American politics in the twentieth century.

20

GILDED AGE POLITICS 1877–1900

CHAPTER OUTLINE

- The Nature of Party Politics • Issues of Legislation • Tentative Presidents
- Discrimination, Disfranchisement, and Responses • Agrarian Unrest and
Populism • *LINKS TO THE WORLD* Russian Populism • The Depression and
Protests of the 1890s • The Silver Crusade and the Election of 1896
- Summary

THE NATURE OF PARTY POLITICS

At no other time in the nation's history was public interest in elections more avid than between 1870 and 1896. Consistently, around 80 percent of eligible voters (white and black males in the North, somewhat lower rates among mostly white males in the South) cast ballots in local, state, and national elections. Politics served as a form of recreation, more popular than baseball or circuses. Actual voting provided only the final step in a process that included parades, picnics, and speeches. As one observer remarked, "What the theatre is to the French, or the bull fight . . . to the Spanish . . . [election campaigns] are to our people."

Cultural-Political Alignments Currently, more voters consider themselves independents rather than allying themselves with one political party or another. But in the Gilded Age, party loyalty was vigorous and emotional. With some exceptions, people who opposed government interference in matters of personal liberty identified with the Democratic Party; those who believed government could be an agent of reform identified with the Republican Party. Democrats included foreign-born and second-generation Catholics and Jews, who followed rituals and sacraments to guide personal behavior and prove faith in God. Republicans consisted mostly of native-born Protestants, who believed that salvation was best achieved by purging the world of evil and that legislation could protect people from sin.

There was also a geographic dimension to these divisions. Northern Republicans tried to capitalize on bitter memories of the Civil War by "waving the bloody shirt" at northern and southern Democrats. As one Republican orator scolded in

CHRONOLOGY

1873	Congress ends coinage of silver dollars
1873–78	Economic hard times hit
1877	Georgia passes poll tax, disfranchising most African Americans
1878	Bland-Allison Act requires Treasury to buy between $2 and $4 million in silver each month
1881	Garfield assassinated; Arthur assumes presidency
1883	Pendleton Civil Service Act introduces merit system
	Supreme Court strikes down 1883 Civil Rights Act
1886	*Wabash* case declares that only Congress can limit interstate commerce rates
1887	Farmers' Alliances form
	Interstate Commerce Commission begins regulating rates and practices of interstate shipping
1890	McKinley Tariff raises tariff rates
	Sherman Silver Purchase Act commits Treasury to buying 4.5 million ounces of silver each month
	"Mississippi Plan" uses poll taxes and literacy tests to prevent African Americans from voting
	National Woman Suffrage Association formed
1890s	Jim Crow laws, discriminating against African Americans in legal treatment and public accommodations, passed by southern states
1892	Populist convention in Omaha draws up reform platform
1893	Sherman Silver Purchase Act repealed
1893–97	Major economic depression hits United States
1894	Wilson-Gorman Tariff passes
	Coxey's Army marches on Washington, D.C.
1896	*Plessy v. Ferguson* establishes separate-but-equal doctrine
1898	Louisiana implements "grandfather clause," restricting voting by African Americans
1899	*Cummings v. County Board of Education* applies separate-but-equal doctrine to schools

1876, "Every man that tried to destroy this nation was a Democrat. . . . Soldiers, every scar you have on your heroic bodies was given you by a Democrat." Democrats in the north tended to focus more on urban and economic issues, but southern Democratic candidates waved a different bloody shirt, calling Republicans traitors to white supremacy and states' rights.

At state and local levels, partisan politicians often battled over how much government should control people's lives. The most contentious issues were use of leisure time and celebration of Sunday, the Lord's day. Protestant Republicans tried to

keep the Sabbath holy through legislation that prohibited bars, stores, and commercial amusements from being open on Sundays. Immigrant Democrats, accustomed
to feasting and playing after church, fought saloon closings and other restrictions
on the only day they had free from work. Similar splits developed over public versus parochial schools and over prohibition versus unrestricted availability of liquor.

These issues made politics a personal as well as a community activity. In an
era before media celebrities occupied public attention, people formed emotional
loyalties to individual politicians, loyalties that often overlooked crassness and corruption. James G. Blaine—Maine's flamboyant and powerful Republican congressman, senator, presidential aspirant, and two-time secretary of state—typified this
appeal. Followers called him the "Plumed Knight," composed songs and organized
parades in his honor, and sat mesmerized by his long speeches, while disregarding
his corrupt alliances with businessmen and his animosity toward laborers and
farmers.

Allegiances to national parties and candidates were so evenly divided that no
faction gained control for any sustained period of time. Between 1877 and 1897,
Republicans held the presidency for three terms, Democrats for two. Rarely did
the same party control both the presidency and Congress simultaneously. From
1876 through 1892, presidential elections were extremely close. The outcome often
hinged on votes in a few populous northern states—Connecticut, New York, New
Jersey, Ohio, Indiana, and Illinois. Both parties tried to gain advantages by nominating presidential and vice-presidential candidates from these states (and by committing vote fraud on their candidates' behalf).

Party Factions   Factional quarrels split both the Republican and the Democratic parties. Among Republicans, New York's senator
Roscoe Conkling led one faction, known as "Stalwarts." A physical fitness devotee
labeled "the finest torso in public life," Conkling worked the spoils system to win
government jobs for his supporters. The Stalwarts' rivals were the "Half Breeds,"
led by James G. Blaine, who pursued influence as blatantly as Conkling did.
On the sidelines stood more idealistic Republicans, or "Mugwumps" (supposedly
an Indian term meaning "mug on one side of the fence, wump on the other").
Mugwumps, such as Missouri Senator Carl Schurz, scorned the political roguish-
ness that tainted Republican leaders and believed that only righteous, educated men
like themselves should govern. Republican allies of big business supported the use
of gold as the standard for currency, whereas those from mining regions favored
silver. Democrats subdivided into white-supremacist southerners; working-class,
immigrant-stock supporters of urban political machines; business-oriented advocates of low tariffs and the gold standard; and debtor-oriented advocates of free
silver. Like Republicans, Democrats avidly pursued the spoils of office.

In each state, one party usually dominated, and a few men typically held dictatorial sway. Often the state "boss" was a senator who doled out jobs and parlayed
his clout into national influence. (Until ratification of the Seventeenth Amendment
to the Constitution in 1913, state legislatures elected U.S. senators.) Besides
Conkling and Blaine, senatorial powers included Thomas C. Platt of New York,
Nelson W. Aldrich of Rhode Island, Mark A. Hanna of Ohio, and Matthew S.

Quay of Pennsylvania. These men exercised their power brazenly. Quay once responded to an inquiry about using secret information from a Senate investigation to profit from an investment in the American Sugar Refining Company by pronouncing, "I do not feel that there is anything in my connection with the Senate to interfere with my buying or selling stock when I please, and I propose to do so in the future."

ISSUES OF LEGISLATION

In Congress, issues of sectional controversies, patronage abuses, railroad regulation, tariffs, and currency provoked heated debates and partisan discord. From the end of the Civil War into the 1880s, Congress spent much time discussing soldiers' pensions. The Grand Army of the Republic, an organization of 400,000 Union Army veterans, allied with the Republican Party and cajoled Congress into providing generous pensions for former soldiers and their widows. Many pensions were deserved: Union troops had been poorly paid, and thousands of wives had been widowed. But the war's emotional memories furnished some veterans opportunity to profit at public expense. Although the Union Army spent $2 billion to fight the Civil War, pensions to veterans ultimately cost $8 billion, one of the largest welfare commitments the federal government has ever made. By 1900, soldiers' pensions accounted for roughly 40 percent of the federal budget. Confederate veterans received none of this money, though some southern states funded small pensions and built old-age homes for ex-soldiers.

Civil Service Reform
Few politicians dared oppose pensions, but some attempted to dismantle the spoils system. During the Civil War, the federal government had expanded considerably, and the practice of awarding government jobs to the party faithful regardless of their qualifications, which had taken root before the war, flourished afterward. As the postal service, diplomatic corps, and other government agencies expanded, so did the public payroll. Between 1865 and 1891, the number of federal jobs tripled, from 53,000 to 166,000. (There are 1.3 million today.) Elected officials scrambled to control these jobs as a means to benefit themselves and their party. In return for comparatively short hours and high pay, appointees to federal positions pledged votes and a portion of their earnings to their patrons.

Shocked by such corruption, especially after the revelation of scandals in the Grant administration, some reformers began advocating appointments and promotions based on merit—civil service—rather than on political connections. Support for change accelerated in 1881 with formation of the National Civil Service Reform League, led by editors E. L. Godkin and George W. Curtis. That year, the assassination of President James Garfield by a distraught job seeker hastened the drive for reform. The Pendleton Civil Service Act, passed by Congress in 1882 and signed by President Chester Arthur in 1883, created the Civil Service Commission to oversee competitive examinations for government positions. The act gave the commission jurisdiction over only 10 percent of federal jobs, though the president could expand the list. Because the Constitution barred Congress from interfering in state affairs, civil service at state and local levels developed in a haphazard manner.

Nevertheless, the Pendleton Act marked a beginning and provided a model for further reform.

Veterans' pensions and civil service reform were not the main issues of the Gilded Age, however. Rather, economic policy occupied congressional concerns more than ever. Railroads particularly provoked controversy. As rail networks spread, so did competition. In their quest for customers, railroads reduced rates to outmaneuver rivals, but rate wars hurt profits, and inconsistent freight charges angered shippers and farmers. On noncompetitive routes, railroads often boosted charges as high as possible to compensate for unprofitably low rates on competitive routes, making pricing disproportionate to distance. Per mile charges for short-distance shipments served by only one line could exceed those on long-distance shipments served by competing lines. Railroads also played favorites, reducing rates to large shippers and offering free passenger passes to preferred customers and politicians.

Railroad Regulation   Such favoritism stirred farmers, small merchants, and reform politicians to demand rate regulation. Their efforts succeeded first at the state level. By 1880, fourteen states had established commissions to limit freight and storage charges of state-chartered lines. Using corrupt lobbyists and pressure tactics, railroads fought these measures, arguing that the Fourteenth Amendment to the Constitution guaranteed them freedom to acquire and use property without government restraint. But in 1877, in *Munn v. Illinois*, the Supreme Court upheld the principle of state regulation, declaring that grain warehouses owned by railroads acted in the public interest and therefore must submit to regulation for "the common good."

State legislatures, however, could not regulate interstate lines, a limitation affirmed by the Supreme Court in the *Wabash* case of 1886, in which the Court declared that only Congress could limit rates involving interstate commerce. Reformers thereupon demanded action by the federal government. With support from businessmen who believed that they, like farmers, suffered from discriminatory rates, Congress passed the Interstate Commerce Act in 1887. The law prohibited rebates and rate discrimination, and created the Interstate Commerce Commission (ICC), the nation's first regulatory agency, to investigate railroad rate making, issue cease-and-desist orders against illegal practices, and seek court aid to enforce compliance. The legislation's weak provisions for enforcement, however, left railroads room for evasion, and judges minimized ICC powers. In the *Maximum Freight Rate* case (1897), for example, the Supreme Court ruled that the ICC lacked power to set rates, and in the *Alabama Midlands* case (1897), the Court overturned prohibitions against long-haul/short-haul discrimination. Even so, the principle of regulation—though weakened—remained in force.

Tariff Policy   The issue of tariffs carried strong political implications. From 1789 onward, Congress had created tariffs, which levied duties (taxes) on imported goods, to protect American manufactures and agricultural products from European competition. But tariffs quickly became a tool by which special interests could enhance their profits. By the 1880s, these interests had succeeded in obtaining tariffs on more than four thousand items. A few economists and farmers argued for free trade, but most politicians insisted that tariffs were a necessary form of government assistance to support industry and preserve jobs.

To support economic growth, the Republican Party put protective tariffs at the core of its political agenda. Democrats complained that tariffs made prices artificially high by discouraging imports of less expensive foreign goods, thereby benefiting domestic manufacturers while hurting farmers whose crops were not protected and consumers who wanted to buy manufactured goods. For example, a yard of flannel produced abroad might cost 10 cents, but an 8-cent import duty raised the price to 18 cents. An American manufacturer of a similar yard of flannel, also costing 10 cents, could charge 17 cents, underselling *foreign* competition by 1 cent yet still pocketing a 7-cent profit.

During the Gilded Age, revenues from tariffs and other levies created a surplus in the federal treasury. Most Republicans liked the idea that the government was earning more than it spent and hoped to keep the surplus as a reserve or to spend it on projects such as harbor improvements, which would aid commerce. Democrats, however, asserted that the federal government should not be a profit-making operation. They acknowledged a need for protection of some manufactured goods and raw materials, but they favored lower tariff duties to encourage foreign trade and to reduce the Treasury surplus.

Manufacturers and their congressional allies firmly controlled tariff policy. The McKinley Tariff of 1890 boosted already-high rates by 4 percent. When House

A SENATE FOR REVENUE ONLY.

Federal economic policies such as tariffs sparked heated debates between businesses and their allies in Congress on one side and those who believed these policies benefited only special interests. This cartoon, clearly opposing the McKinley Tariff, depicts Uncle Sam, the symbol for America, bound up and held captive by the tariff and its raucous Senate supporters.

The Granger Collection, New York

Democrats supported by President Grover Cleveland passed a bill to trim tariffs in 1894, Senate Republicans, aided by southern Democrats eager to protect their region's infant textile and steel industries, added six hundred amendments restoring most cuts (the Wilson-Gorman Tariff). In 1897, the Dingley Tariff raised rates further. Attacks on duties, though unsuccessful, made tariffs a symbol of privileged business in the public mind and a continuing target for reformers.

Monetary Policy   Debates over monetary policy inflamed even stronger emotions than tariffs did because they represented conflict between haves and have-nots. When increased industrial and agricultural production caused prices to fall after the Civil War, debtors (have-nots) and creditors (haves) had opposing reactions. Farmers suffered because the prices they received for crops were dropping; however, because high demand for a relatively limited supply of money in circulation raised interest rates on loans, it was costly for them to borrow funds to pay mortgages and other debts. They favored the coinage of silver to increase the amount of currency in circulation, which in turn would reduce interest rates, making their debts less burdensome. Small businessmen, also in need of loans, agreed with farmers. Large merchants, manufacturers, and bankers favored a more stable, limited money supply backed only by gold. They feared that the value of currency not backed by gold would fluctuate; the resulting uncertainty would threaten investors' confidence in the U.S. economy. Arguments over the quantity and quality of money also reflected sectional cleavages: western silver-mining areas and agricultural regions of the South and West against the more conservative industrial Northeast.

Before the 1870s, the federal government had bought both gold and silver to back its paper money (dollars), setting a ratio that made a gold dollar worth sixteen times more than a silver dollar. In theory, a person holding a specific sum of dollar bills could exchange them for one ounce of gold or sixteen ounces of silver. Discovery and mining of gold in the West, however, increased the gold supply and lowered its market price relative to that of silver. Consequently, silver dollars disappeared from circulation—because of their inflated value relative to gold, owners hoarded them—and in 1873 a congressional act stopped the coinage of silver dollars. Through this action, the United States unofficially adopted the gold standard, meaning that its currency was backed chiefly by gold.

But within a few years, new mines in the West began to flood the market with silver, and its price dropped. Because gold now became relatively less plentiful than silver and therefore worth more than sixteen times the value of silver, it became worthwhile for people to spend rather than hoard silver dollars. Silver producers wanted the government to resume buying silver at the old sixteen-to-one ratio because they then could sell silver to the government above its market price. Debtors, hurt by the economic hard times of 1873–1878, saw silver as a means of expanding the currency supply, so they joined silver producers to press for resumption of silver coinage at the old sixteen-to-one ratio.

With both parties split into silver and gold factions, Congress first tried to compromise. The Bland-Allison Act (1878) authorized the Treasury to buy between $2 million and $4 million worth of silver each month, and the Sherman Silver Purchase Act (1890) increased the government's monthly silver purchase by specifying weight (4.5 million ounces) rather than dollars. Neither measure satisfied the different interest groups. Creditors wanted the government to stop buying silver, whereas for debtors, the legislation failed to expand the money supply satisfactorily and still left the impression that the government favored creditors' interests. The issue would become even more emotional during the presidential election of 1896.

Legislative Accomplishments   Members of Congress dealt with such thorny issues as civil service, railroad regulation, and monetary policy under difficult conditions in the Gilded Age. Senators and representatives earned small salaries and usually had the financial burden of maintaining two residences: one in their home district and one in Washington. Most members of Congress had no private office space, only a desk. They worked long hours responding to constituents' requests, wrote their own speeches, and paid for staff out of their own pocket. Though corruption and greed tainted several, most politicians were principled and dedicated. They managed to deal with important issues and pass some significant legislation.

TENTATIVE PRESIDENTS

Operating under the cloud of Andrew Johnson's impeachment, Grant's scandals, and doubts about the legitimacy of the 1876 election (see Chapter 16), American presidents between 1877 and 1900 moved gingerly to restore authority to their office. Proper and honest, Presidents Rutherford Hayes (1877–1881), James Garfield (1881), Chester Arthur (1881–1885), Grover Cleveland (1885–1889 and 1893–1897), Benjamin Harrison (1889–1893), and William McKinley (1897–1901) tried to act as legislative as well as administrative leaders. Like other politicians, they used symbols. Hayes served lemonade at the White House to emphasize that he, unlike his predecessor Ulysses Grant, was no hard drinker. McKinley set aside his cigar in public so photographers would not catch him setting a bad example for youth. More important, each president made cautious attempts to initiate legislation and use vetoes to guide national policy.

Hayes, Garfield, and Arthur   Rutherford B. Hayes had been a Union general and Ohio congressman and governor before his disputed election to the presidency, an event that prompted opponents to label him "Rutherfraud." Although his party expected him to serve business interests, Hayes played a quiet role as conciliator. He emphasized national harmony over sectional rivalry and opposed racial violence. He tried to overhaul the spoils system by appointing civil service reformer Carl Schurz to his cabinet and by battling New York's patronage king, Senator Conkling. (He fired Conkling's protégé Chester Arthur, from the post of New York customs house collector.) Though averse to using government power to aid the oppressed, Hayes believed society should not ignore the needs of the American Chinese and Indians, and after retiring from the presidency, he worked to aid former slaves.

When Hayes declined to run for reelection in 1880, Republicans nominated another Ohio congressman and Civil War hero, James A. Garfield, who defeated

Democrat Winfield Scott Hancock, also a Civil War hero, by 40,000 votes out of 9 million cast. By winning the pivotal states of New York and Indiana, however, Garfield carried the electoral college by a comfortable margin, 214 to 155. Solemn and cautious, Garfield tried to secure an independent position among party potentates. He hoped to reduce the tariff and develop economic relations with Latin America, and he pleased civil service reformers by rebuffing Conkling's patronage demands. But his chance to make lasting contributions ended in July 1881 when Charles Guiteau shot him in a Washington railroad station. Garfield lingered for seventy-nine days with a bullet in his spine, but he succumbed to infection, heart ailments, and pneumonia and died September 19.

Garfield's successor was Vice President Chester A. Arthur, the New York Stalwart whom Hayes had fired. Republicans had nominated Arthur for vice president only to help Garfield win New York State's electoral votes. Although his elevation to the presidency made reformers shudder, Arthur became a dignified and temperate executive. He signed the Pendleton Civil Service Act, urged Congress to modify outdated tariff rates, and supported federal regulation of railroads. He wielded the veto aggressively, killing bills that excessively benefited railroads and corporations. Arthur wanted to run for president in 1884 but Republicans nominated James G. Blaine instead.

To oppose Blaine, Democrats picked New York's governor, Grover Cleveland, a bachelor who admitted during the campaign that he had fathered an out-of-wedlock son. The election reflected the nastiness of partisanship. Alluding to Cleveland's son, Republicans chided him with catcalls of "Ma! Ma! Where's my pa?" to which Democrats replied, "Gone to the White House, Ha! Ha! Ha!" Distaste for Blaine prompted some Mugwump Republicans to desert their party. On election day, Cleveland beat Blaine by only 29,000 popular votes; his tiny margin of 1,149 votes in New York gave him that state's 36 electoral votes, enough for a 219-to-182 victory in the electoral college. Cleveland may have won New York thanks to last-minute remarks of a Protestant minister, who equated Democrats with "rum, Romanism, and rebellion." Democrats eagerly publicized the slur among New York's large Irish-Catholic population, urging voters to protest by supporting Cleveland.

Cleveland and Harrison   Cleveland, the first Democratic president since James Buchanan (1857–1861), tried to exert vigorous leadership. He expanded civil service, vetoed private pension bills, and urged Congress to cut tariff duties. When advisers warned that his actions might weaken his chances for reelection, the president retorted, "What is the use of being elected or reelected, unless you stand for something?" But Senate protectionists killed tariff reform passed by the House in response to Cleveland's wishes, and when Democrats renominated Cleveland for president in 1888, businessmen in the party convinced him to moderate his attacks on high tariffs.

Republicans in 1888 nominated Benjamin Harrison, former senator from Indiana and grandson of President William Henry Harrison (1841). During the campaign, some Republicans manipulated a British diplomat into stating that Cleveland's reelection would be good for England. Irish Democrats, who hated England's colonial rule over Ireland, took offense, as intended, and turned against

Cleveland. Perhaps more beneficial to Harrison were the bribery and multiple voting that helped him win Indiana by 2,300 votes and New York by 14,000. (Democrats also indulged frauds, but Republicans proved more successful at it.) Those states' electoral votes ensured Harrison's victory. Although Cleveland outpolled Harrison by 90,000 popular votes, Harrison carried the electoral college 233 votes to 168.

The first president since 1875 whose party had majorities in both houses of Congress, Harrison used various methods, ranging from threats of vetoes to informal dinners and consultations with politicians, to influence the course of legislation. Partly in response, the Congress of 1889–1891 passed 517 bills, 200 more than the average passed by Congresses between 1875 and 1889. Harrison showed support for civil service by appointing reformer Theodore Roosevelt as civil service commissioner, but neither the president nor Congress could resist pressures from special interests, especially those waving the bloody shirt. Harrison signed the Dependents' Pension Act, which provided pensions for Union veterans who had suffered war-related disabilities and granted aid to their widows and children. The bill doubled the number of welfare recipients from 490,000 to 966,000.

The Pension Act and other appropriations in 1890 pushed the federal budget past $1 billion for the first time in the nation's history. Democrats blamed the "Billion-Dollar Congress" on spendthrift Republicans. Voters reacted by unseating seventy-eight Republicans in the congressional elections of 1890. Seeking to capitalize on voter unrest, Democrats nominated Grover Cleveland to run against Harrison in 1892. This time, Cleveland attracted large contributions from business and beat Harrison by 370,000 popular votes (3 percent of the total), easily winning the electoral vote.

In office again, Cleveland addressed problems of currency, tariffs, and labor unrest, but his actions reflected political weakness. During his campaign, Cleveland had promised sweeping tariff reform but made little effort to line up support in the Senate, where protectionists undercut efforts to reduce rates. In addition, he bowed to requests from railroad interests and sent federal troops to put down the Pullman strike of 1894. In spite of Cleveland's attempts to take the initiative, major events—particularly economic downturn and agrarian ferment—pushed the country in a different direction.

DISCRIMINATION, DISFRANCHISEMENT, AND RESPONSES

Although speechmakers often spoke of freedom and opportunity during the Gilded Age, policies of discrimination and exclusion continued to haunt more than half of the nation's population. Just as before the Civil War, issues of race shaped politics in the South, home to the vast majority of African Americans. Southern white farmers and workers, facing economic insecurity, feared that newly enfranchised African American men would challenge whatever political and social superiority (real and imagined) they enjoyed. Wealthy landowners and merchants fanned these fears, using them to divide the races and to distract poor whites from protesting their own economic subjugation. Even some white feminists, such as Susan B. Anthony, opposed voting and other rights for blacks on the grounds that white women deserved such rights before black men did.

In the North, custom more than law bounded the opportunities of black people. Discrimination in housing; employment; and access to facilities such as parks, hotels, and department stores kept African Americans separate. Whites always were concerned that blacks remained "in their place." Whether it was the wages they received, the return they received for their crops, or the prices they paid for goods, African Americans felt the sting of their imposed inferiority.

Violence Against African Americans   The abolition of slavery altered the legal status of African Americans, but it did not markedly improve their economic opportunities. In 1880, the South was home to the vast majority of blacks, and 90 percent of them depended for a living on farming or personal and domestic service—the same occupations they had held as slaves. Discrimination was rampant. Some communities considered themselves "sundown towns," where only whites were allowed on the streets at night. The New South, moreover, proved as violent for blacks as the Old South. Between 1889 and 1909, more than seventeen hundred African Americans were lynched in the South. Most lynching victims were accused of assault—rarely proved—on a white woman. These acts of terror occurred often, but by no means exclusively, in sparsely populated districts where whites felt threatened by an influx of migrant blacks who had no friends to vouch for them.

Blacks did not suffer such violence silently, however. Their most notable activist at this time was Ida B. Wells, a Memphis schoolteacher. In 1884, Wells was

In the years after Reconstruction, lynchings of African American men occurred with increasing frequency, chiefly in sparsely populated areas where whites looked at strangers, especially black strangers, with fear and suspicion.

© R. P. Kingston/PhotoLibrary

forcibly removed from a railroad car when she refused to surrender her seat to a white man. The incident sparked her career as a forceful and tireless spokesperson against white supremacy and violence. In 1889, Wells became partner of a Memphis newspaper, the *Free Speech and Headlight*, in which she published attacks against white injustice. When three black Memphis grocers were lynched in 1892 after defending themselves against whites who had attacked them, Wells wrote an editorial urging local blacks to migrate to the West. She subsequently toured England and Europe, giving speeches and writing articles drumming up opposition to lynching and discrimination. Unable to return to hostile Memphis, she moved to Chicago where she became a powerful advocate for racial justice.

Disfranchisement

In northern communities, whites sometimes made it uncomfortable for people of color to vote and hold office, but it was mainly in the South that white leaders, eager to reassert authority over people whom they believed to be inferior, instituted measures to prevent blacks from voting. Despite threats and intimidation against them in the wake of Reconstruction's demise, blacks still formed the backbone of the southern Republican Party and won numerous elective positions. In North Carolina, for example, eleven African Americans served in the state Senate and forty-three in the House between 1877 and 1890. Situations like these were unacceptable to many whites and racist politicians tried to eliminate them by depriving blacks of their right to vote. Beginning with Tennessee in 1889 and Arkansas in 1892, southern states levied taxes of $1 to $2 on all citizens wishing to vote. These poll taxes proved prohibitive to most blacks, who were so poor and deeply in debt that they rarely had cash for any purpose. Other schemes disfranchised blacks who could not read.

Disfranchisement was also accomplished in other devious ways. The Supreme Court determined in *U.S. v. Reese* (1876) that Congress had no control over local and state elections other than the explicit provisions of the Fifteenth Amendment, which prohibits states from denying the vote "on account of race, color, or previous condition of servitude." State legislatures found ways to exclude black voters without mentioning race, color, or servitude. For instance, an 1890 state constitutional convention established the "Mississippi Plan," requiring prospective voters to pay a poll tax eight months before each election, present the tax receipt at election time, and prove that they could read and interpret the state constitution. Registration officials applied stiffer standards to blacks than to whites, even declaring black college graduates ineligible on grounds of illiteracy. In 1898, Louisiana enacted the first "grandfather clause," which established literacy and property qualifications for voting but exempted sons and grandsons of those eligible to vote before 1867. Other southern states initiated similar measures.

Such restrictions proved highly effective. In South Carolina, for example, 70 percent of eligible blacks voted in the 1880 election; by 1896, the rate dropped to 11 percent. By the 1900s, African Americans had effectively lost political rights in the South. More importantly, because voting is often considered a common right of citizenship, disfranchisement stripped African American men of their social standing as U.S. citizens. Disfranchisement also affected poor whites, few of whom could meet poll tax, property, and literacy requirements. Consequently, the total number of eligible voters in Mississippi shrank from 257,000 in 1876 to 77,000 in 1892.

Legal Segregation

Racial discrimination also stiffened in areas beyond voting, as existing customs of racial separation were expanded. In all regions of the country, segregation by custom was common, as whites in power sought to keep racial minorities "in their place" by refusing them service and access. But in a series of cases during the 1870s, the Supreme Court opened the door to laws that established racial discrimination by ruling that the Fourteenth Amendment protected citizens' rights only against infringement by state governments, not over what individuals, private businesses, or local governments might do. These rulings climaxed in 1883 when, in the *Civil Rights* cases, the Court struck down the 1875 Civil Rights Act, which prohibited segregation in facilities, such as streetcars, theaters, and parks. Again the Court declared that the federal government could not regulate private behavior in matters of race relations. Thus railroads, such as the Chesapeake & Ohio Railroad, which had forced Ida B. Wells out of her seat, could maintain discriminatory policies.

The Supreme Court also upheld as legal segregation on a "separate-but-equal" basis in the case of *Plessy v. Ferguson* (1896). This case began in 1892 when a New Orleans organization of African Americans chose Homer Plessy, a dark-skinned creole who was only one-eighth black (but still considered black by Louisiana law), as a volunteer to violate a state law by sitting in a whites-only railroad car. As expected, Plessy was arrested, and the appeal of his conviction reached the U.S. Supreme Court in 1896. The Court disappointed Plessy's supporters by affirming that a state law providing for separate facilities for the two races was reasonable because it preserved "public peace and good order." Writing for the Court, Associate Justice Billings Brown said that legislation could not alter prejudice. "If the two races are to meet upon terms of social equality," he wrote, "it must be the result of . . . a voluntary consent of individuals." Thus, believed the Court, a law separating the races did not necessarily "destroy the legal equality of the races." Although the ruling did not specify the phrase "separate but equal," it legalized separate facilities for black and white people as long as they were equal. In 1899, the Court applied the separate-but-equal doctrine to schools in *Cummins v. County Board of Education*, permitting school segregation until it was overturned by *Brown v. Board of Education* in 1954.

Segregation laws—known as Jim Crow laws—multiplied throughout the South, confronting African Americans with daily reminders of inferior status. State and local statutes, most of which were passed in the 1890s, restricted blacks to the rear of streetcars, to separate public drinking fountains and toilets, and to separate sections of hospitals and cemeteries. A Birmingham, Alabama, ordinance required that the races be "distinctly separated . . . by well defined physical barriers" in "any room, hall, theatre, picture house, auditorium, yard, court, ballpark, or other indoor or outdoor place." Mobile, Alabama, passed a curfew requiring blacks to be off the streets by 10 p.m., and Atlanta mandated separate Bibles for the swearing-in of black witnesses in court.

African American Activism

African American women and men challenged injustice in several ways. Some organized boycotts of segregated streetcars and discriminatory businesses; others promoted "Negro enterprise." In 1898, for example, Atlanta University professor John Hope called on blacks to become their own employers and supported formation of Negro Business Men's Leagues. A number of blacks used higher education as a means of elevating their status. In all-black teachers' colleges, young men and women sought to expand opportunities for themselves and their race. Education also seemed to present a way to foster interracial cooperation. But the white supremacy campaigns that Jim Crow laws reflected taught southern blacks that they would have to negotiate in a biracial, rather than an interracial, society.

While disfranchisement pushed African American men—who, in contrast to women, had previously been able to vote—out of public life, African American women used traditional domestic roles as mothers, educators, and moral guardians to uplift the race and seek better services for black communities. Their efforts signified political activity that was more subtle than voting—though they also did fight for the vote. They successfully lobbied southern governments for cleaner city streets, better public health, expanded charity services, and vocational education. In these efforts, black women found ways to join with white women in campaigns to negotiate with the white male power structure to achieve their goals. In many instances, however, white women sympathized with white men in support of racial exclusion.

Women Suffrage

Though some women acquiesced to their own discrimination, others challenged male power structures by seeking the right to vote. Some, such as Frances Willard, founder of the Women's Christian Temperance Union, chose indirect tactics. An intensely religious woman, Willard believed that (Chrstian) faith would empower women to uplift society. She utilized the Christian model of conversion, urging women who joined the Women's Christian Temperance Union to sign a pledge to abstain from alcohol as a first step toward protecting home and family from the evils of drink. But Willard also believed that the WCTU could best do the Lord's work of improving society if women could vote. Thus, at its 1884 convention, the WCTU passed a resolution deploring the "disenfranchisement of 12 million people who are citizens." Willard devised a rationale for women who wanted to justify public activity while avoiding a taint of radicalism. She traversed the country giving inspired speeches on behalf of her cause and became the most well-known woman in America.

The more direct crusade for suffrage was conducted by two organizations: the National Woman Suffrage Association (NWSA) and the American Woman Suffrage Association (AWSA). The NWSA, led by Elizabeth Cady Stanton and Susan B. Anthony, advocated women's rights in courts and workplaces as well as at the ballot box. The two women, both veterans of the women's rights movement of the 1840s, did not always agree. Anthony was less radical, believing that the NWSA should accommodate moderate suffragists. Stanton disdained religiosity and supported birth control, liberalized divorce laws, and property rights for women. She once wrote, "I would rather live under a government of man alone with religious liberty than under a mixed government without it." Nevertheless, Anthony and Stanton remained friends and worked tirelessly on behalf of their cause.

The AWSA, led by former abolitionists Lucy Stone, focused more narrowly on suffrage. Consisting of female and male moderate advocates of free suffrage, the AWSA worked especially at the state level. Personality conflicts, more than ideology, separated the NWSA and AWSA. But in the late 1880s, Stone proposed that the two groups overcome their differences, and they merged in 1890 to form the National American Woman Suffrage Association with Stanton as first president.

Congress failed to heed any suffrage group. Anthony's argument for a constitutional amendment for woman suffrage received little support. On the few occasions when the Senate discussed a bill for the amendment, senators voted it down, claiming that suffrage would interfere with women's family obligations. Moreover, the women's suffrage campaign was tainted by racial intolerance. Many movement leaders espoused the superiority of whites and accommodated racial prejudices of both the North and South in order to retain support from organization members. AWSA and NWSA membership was all white and mostly middle class. Blacks who joined the WCTU did so within a separate Department of Colored Temperance. Also, leaders, such as Anthony and Stanton felt humiliated that the Fifteenth Amendment had enfranchised black men but not women. Such suffragists believed that "educated" white women should vote and that "illiterate" blacks, both men and women, should not have such a privilege.

Women did win partial victories. Between 1870 and 1910, eleven states (mostly in the West) legalized limited woman suffrage. By 1890, nineteen states allowed women to vote on school issues and three granted suffrage on tax and bond issues. The right to vote in national elections awaited a later generation, but the activities of leaders such as Ida B. Wells, Susan B. Anthony, and Lucy Stone proved that women did not have to vote to be politically active. And although their campaigns succeeded only slightly, they helped train a corps of female leaders in political organizing and public speaking.

AGRARIAN UNREST AND POPULISM

While voting and racial segregation concerned those suffering from political exclusion, economic inequity sparked a mass movement that would shake American society. Despite rapid industrialization and urbanization in the Gilded Age, the United States remained an agrarian society. In 1890, 64 percent of the total population lived in rural areas, many of which suffered economic hardship and were primed for protest. The expression of farmers' discontent—a mixture of strident rhetoric, nostalgic dreams, and hard-headed egalitarianism—began in Grange organizations in the early 1870s. It accelerated when Farmers' Alliances formed in Texas in the late 1870s and spread across the South and Great Plains in the 1880s. The Alliance movement flourished chiefly in areas where debt, weather, and insects demoralized struggling farmers. Once under way, the agrarian rebellion inspired visions of a co-operative, democratic society.

Sharecropping and Tenant Farming in the South   Southern agriculture, unlike that of the Midwest, did not benefit much from mechanization. Tobacco and cotton, the principal southern crops, required constant hoeing and weeding by hand. Tobacco needed careful harvesting, because the leaves matured at different rates and because the stems were too fragile for machines. Also, mechanical devices were not precise enough to pick cotton. Thus, in former plantation areas after the Civil War, southern agriculture remained labor-intensive, and laborlords, who had once utilized slaves, were replaced by landlords, who employed sharecroppers and tenant farmers.

Sharecropping and tenant farming—meaning that farmers rented their land rather than owned it—entangled millions of black and white southerners in webs of debt and humiliation, weighed down by the crop lien. Most farmers, too poor to have ready cash, borrowed in order to buy necessities such as seed, tools, and food. They could offer as collateral only what they could grow. A farmer helpless without supplies dealt with a "furnishing merchant," who would exchange provisions for a "lien," or legal claim, on the farmer's forthcoming crop. After the crop was harvested and brought to market, the merchant collected his debt by claiming the portion of the crop that would repay the loan. All too often, however, the debt exceeded the crop's value. The farmer could pay off only part of the debt but still needed food and supplies for the coming year. The only way he could get these supplies was to sink deeper into debt by reborrowing and giving the merchant a lien on his next crop.

Merchants frequently took advantage of farmers' powerlessness by inflating prices and charging excessive interest on the advances farmers received. Suppose, for example, that a cash-poor farmer needed a 20-cent bag of seed or a 20-cent piece of cloth. The furnishing merchant would sell the goods on credit but would boost the price to 28 cents. At year's end, that 28-cent loan would have accumulated interest of 50 percent or more, raising the farmer's debt to 42 cents—more than double the item's original cost. The farmer, having pledged more than his crop's worth against scores of such debts, fell behind in payments and never recovered. If he fell too far behind, he could be evicted.

In the southern backcountry, which in antebellum times had been characterized by small, family-owned farms, few slaves, and diversified agriculture, economic changes compounded crop-lien problems. New spending habits illustrate these changes. In 1884, Jephta Dickson, who farmed land in the northern Georgia hills, bought $55.90 worth of flour, potatoes, peas, meat, corn, and syrup from merchants. Before the Civil War, farmers grew almost all the food they needed and such varied expenditures would have been rare. But after the war, yeomen like Dickson shifted to commercial farming; in the South, that meant raising cotton rather than diversified agriculture. This specialization came about for two reasons: constant debt forced farmers to grow crops that would bring in cash, and railroads enabled them to transport cotton to market more easily than before. As backcountry yeomen devoted more acres to cotton, they raised less of what they needed on a daily basis and found themselves more frequently at the mercy of merchants.

Hardship in the Midwest and West   In the Midwest, as growers cultivated more land, as mechanization boosted productivity, and as foreign competition increased, supplies of agricultural products exceeded national and worldwide demand. Consequently, prices for staple crops dropped steadily. A bushel of wheat that sold for $1.45 in 1866 brought only 80 cents in the mid-1880s and 49 cents by the mid-1890s. Meanwhile, transportation and storage fees remained high. Expenses for seed, fertilizer, manufactured goods, taxes, and mortgage interest trapped many farm families in stressful and sometimes desperate circumstances. In order to buy necessities and pay bills, farmers had to produce more. But the spiral wound ever more tightly: the more farmers produced, the lower crop prices dropped.

The West suffered from special hardships. In Colorado, absentee capitalists seized control of access to transportation and water, and concentration of technology in the hands of large mining companies pushed out small firms. Charges of monopolistic behavior by railroads echoed among farmers, miners, and ranchers in Wyoming and Montana. In California, Washington, and Oregon, wheat and fruit growers found opportunities blocked by railroads' control of transportation and storage rates.

Grange Movement   Even before they felt the full impact of these developments, farmers began to organize. With aid from Oliver H. Kelley, a clerk in the Bureau of Agriculture who wanted to elevate the status of farming, farmers in almost every state during the 1860s and 1870s founded the Patrons of Husbandry, or The Grange, dedicated to improving economic and social conditions. By 1875, the Grange had twenty thousand branches and a million members. Like voluntary organizations throughout the country, Granges had constitutions, elected officers, and membership oaths. Strongest in the Midwest and South, Granges sponsored meetings and educational events to relieve the loneliness of farm life. Family-oriented local Granges welcomed women's participation.

As membership flourished, Granges turned to economic and political action. Many members joined the Greenback Labor Party, formed in 1876 to advocate expanding the money supply by keeping "greenbacks"—the paper money created by the government during the Civil War to help pay costs—in circulation. Local Grange branches formed cooperative associations to buy supplies and market crops and livestock. In a few instances, Grangers operated farm-implement factories and insurance companies. Most enterprises failed, however, because farmers lacked capital for large-scale buying and because competition from large manufacturers and dealers undercut them. For example, the mail-order firm Montgomery Ward could furnish rural customers with cheaper products more conveniently than could Granges.

Granges achieved some political successes in the late 1870s, convincing states to establish agricultural colleges, electing sympathetic legislators, and pressing state legislatures for so-called Granger laws to regulate transportation and storage rates. But these ventures faltered when, in the *Wabash* case of 1886, the U.S. Supreme Court overturned Granger laws by denying states the power to regulate railroad rates. Granges disavowed party politics and thus would not challenge the power of business interests within the two major parties. Their attempts at economic and political influence declined, and today Granges exist mainly as social and service organizations.

The White Hats   In the Southwest, migration of English-speaking ranchers into pastureland used communally by Mexican farmers sparked resistance that sometimes turned violent. In the late 1880s, a group calling itself Las Gorras Blancas, or White Hats, struggled to control grazing areas once held by their ancestors. They burned buildings, destroyed fences that Anglos had erected, and threatened the town of Las Vegas in New Mexico territory. Sounding like the Grangers and Knights of Labor before them and the Populists after them, the White Hats proclaimed in 1889: "Our purpose is to protect the rights and interest of the people in general and especially those of the helpless classes." Their cause, however, could not halt Anglos from legally buying and using public land and, by 1900 many Hispanics had given up farming to work as agricultural laborers or to migrate to cities.

Farmers' Alliances   By 1890, rural activism shifted to the Farmers' Alliances, two networks of organizations—one in the Great Plains, one in the South—that constituted a new mass movement. (The West had small Alliance groups, but they tended to be more closely linked to labor radicals and antimonopoly organizations.) The first Alliances arose in Texas, where hard-pressed farmers rallied against crop liens, merchants, and railroads in particular, and against money power in general. Using traveling lecturers to recruit members, Alliance leaders expanded the movement into other southern states. By 1889, the southern Alliance boasted 2 million members, and a separate Colored Farmers' National Alliance claimed 1 million black members. A similar movement arose in the Plains, which in the late 1880s organized 2 million members in Kansas, Nebraska, and the Dakotas. Like Granges, Farmers' Alliances tried to foster community spirit. Women participated actively in Alliance activities, and members of the Knights of Labor were invited to join the "struggle against monopolistic oppression."

The Alliance remedy for economic woes combined a culture of generosity with government assistance. To bypass corporate power and control markets, Alliances, like the Grange, proposed that farmers form cooperatives, in which they would join as a unified group to sell crops and livestock, and buy supplies and manufactured goods. By pooling resources, Alliances reasoned, farmers could exert far more economic pressure than they could individually, and they could share the benefits of their hard work rather than competing against each other.

To relieve the most serious rural problem, shortages of cash and credit, Alliances proposed a system of government aid called a subtreasury. The plan had two parts. One called for the federal government to construct warehouses where farmers could store nonperishable crops while awaiting higher market prices; the government would then loan farmers Treasury notes amounting to 80 percent of the market price that the stored crops would bring. Farmers could use these notes to pay debts and make purchases. Once the stored crops were sold, farmers would repay the loans plus small interest and storage fees. This provision would enable farmers to avoid the exploitative crop lien system.

The subtreasury plan's second part would provide low-interest government loans to farmers who wanted to buy land. These loans, along with the Treasury notes loaned to farmers who temporarily stored crops in government warehouses, would inject cash into the economy and encourage the kind of inflation that advocates hoped would raise crop prices without raising other prices. If the government subsidized business through tariffs and land grants, reasoned Alliance members, why should it not help farmers earn a decent living, too?

Problems in Achieving Alliance Unity   If Farmers' Alliances had been able to unite politically, they could have wielded formidable power, but racial and sectional differences and personality clashes thwarted early attempts at merging. Racial barriers weakened Alliance voter strength because southern white Democrats had succeeded in creating restrictions that prevented African Americans from voting. In addition, raw racism blocked acceptance of blacks by white Alliances. Some southern leaders, such as Georgia's Senator Tom Watson, tried to unite black and white farmers, realizing that both races suffered from similar burdens. But poor white farmers could not drop their prejudices. Many considered African Americans an inferior people and took comfort in the belief that there always would be people worse off than they were. At an 1889 meeting in St. Louis, white southerners rejected uniting with northern Alliances because such a merger would have abolished their whites-only membership rules.

Differences on regional issues also prevented unity. Northern Alliances declined to unite with southerners, fearing domination by more experienced southern leaders. Northern farmers also favored protective tariffs to keep out foreign grain, whereas white southerners wanted low tariffs to curb costs of imported manufactured goods. Northern and southern Alliances agreed on some issues, however; both favored government regulation of railroads, equitable taxation, currency reform, an end to alleged election frauds that perpetuated special interests in office, and prohibition of landownership by foreign investors.

Rise of Populism   In spite of their initial divisions, growing membership and rising confidence drew Alliances into politics. By 1890, farmers had elected several officeholders sympathetic to their cause, especially in the South, where Alliances controlled four governorships, eight state legislatures, forty-four seats in the House of Representatives, and three in the Senate. In the Midwest, Alliance candidates running on third-party tickets, such as the Greenback Party, won some victories in Kansas, Nebraska, and the Dakotas. Leaders crisscrossed the country organizing meetings to recruit support for a new party. During the summer of 1890, the Kansas Alliance held a "convention of the people" and nominated candidates who swept the state's fall elections. Formation of this People's, or Populist, Party gave a title to Alliance political activism. (Populism, derived from *populus*, the Latin word for "people," is the political doctrine that asserts the rights and powers of common people in their struggle against privileged elite.) The election successes in 1890 energized efforts to unite Alliance groups into a single Populist party. By 1892, southern Alliance members decided to leave the Democratic Party and join northern counterparts in summoning a People's Party convention to draft a platform and nominate a presidential candidate. The gathering met in Omaha, Nebraska, on July 4.

The new party's platform was a sweeping reform document, reflecting goals of moral regeneration, political democracy, and antimonopolism. Its preamble charged that the nation had been "brought to the verge of moral, political, and material ruin. Corruption dominates the ballot box, the legislatures, the Congress, and . . . even the [courts]." Charging that inequality (between white classes) threatened to splinter society, the platform declared, "The fruits of the toil of millions are boldly stolen to build up colossal fortunes for a few," and that "wealth belongs to him that creates it." The document addressed three central sources of rural

LINKS TO THE WORLD

Russian Populism

Before American Populism arose late in the 1890s, a different form of populism took shape in another largely rural country: Russia. Whereas American Populism emerged from the Alliance organizations of farmers, Russian populism was the creation of intellectuals who wanted to educate peasants to agitate for social and economic freedom.

Propelled by reforms imposed by Czar Alexander II, Russian society had begun to modernize in the mid-nineteenth century. Government administration and the judiciary were reformed, town governments were given control of taxation, and education became more widespread. Perhaps most importantly, in 1861 Alexander signed an Edict of Emancipation, freeing Russian serfs (slaves attached to specific lands) and granting them compensation to buy land from their landlords. The reforms were slow to take hold, however, prompting some young, educated Russians, called nihilists because they opposed the czar and feudalism, to press for more radical reforms, including socialism. The reformers became known as *narodniki*, or populists, from *narod*, the Russian term for "peasant."

Narodniki envisioned a society of self-governing village communes, somewhat like the cooperatives proposed by American Farmers' Alliances, and in the 1870s they visited Russian villages and attempted to educate peasants about their ideas. One of their leaders, Peter Lavrov, believed that intellectuals needed to narrow the gap between themselves and the people and help the masses improve their lives. This message, however, included a more radical tone than the American Populists' campaign for democracy because Russian populists believed that only a social revolution, an uprising against the czar, could realize their goals. When Alexander instituted repressive policies against the *narodniki* in the late 1870s, many of them turned to terrorism, a move that resulted in the assassination of Alexander II in 1881.

Russian populism failed in different ways than American Populism. Russian peasants were not receptive to intervention from educated young people, and many peasants remained tied to tradition and could not abandon loyalty to the czar. Arrests and imprisonments after Alexander's assassination discouraged populists' efforts, and the movement declined. Nevertheless, just as many aims of American Populists were adopted by other reformers after the turn of the century, the ideas of Russian populism became the cornerstone of the Russian Revolution of 1917 and of Soviet social and political ideology that followed.

unrest: transportation, land, and money. Frustrated with weak state and federal regulation, Populists demanded government ownership of railroad and telegraph lines. They urged the federal government to reclaim all land owned for speculative purposes by railroads and foreigners. The monetary plank called on the government to expand the currency by making more money available for farm loans and by restoring unlimited coinage of silver. Other planks advocated a graduated income tax, postal savings banks, direct election of U.S. senators, and a shorter workday. As its presidential candidate, the party nominated James B. Weaver of Iowa, a former Union general and supporter of an expanded money supply, who already had run for the presidency when he was the Greenback Party's candidate in 1880.

Populist **Spokespeople** The Populist campaign featured dynamic personalities and rousing rhetoric. The Kansas plains rumbled with speeches by Mary Lease, who could allegedly "recite the multiplication table and set a crowd hooting and harrahing at her will," and by "Sockless Jerry" Simpson, an unschooled but canny rural reformer who got his nickname after he ridiculed silk-stockinged wealthy people, causing a reporter to muse that Simpson probably wore no stockings at all. The South produced equally dynamic leaders, such as Georgia's Tom Watson and North Carolina's Leonidas Polk. Colorado's governor, Davis "Bloody Bridles" Waite, attacked mine owners, and Texas's governor James Hogg battled railroads and other corporations. Minnesota's Ignatius Donnelly, pseudoscientist and writer of apocalyptic novels, became chief visionary of the northern plains and penned the Omaha platform's thunderous language. The campaign also attracted opportunists, such as one-eyed, sharp-tongued South Carolina's Senator "Pitchfork Ben" Tillman, who exploited agrarian resentments for their own political ends.

In the 1892 presidential election, Populist candidate James Weaver garnered 8 percent of the popular vote, majorities in four states, and twenty-two electoral votes. Not since 1856 had a third party done so well in its first national effort. Nevertheless, they had little power. The election had been successful for Populists only in the West. The vote-rich Northeast ignored Weaver, and Alabama was the only southern state that gave Populists as much as one-third of its votes.

Still, Populism gave rural dwellers in the South and West faith in a future of cooperation and democracy. Although Populists were flawed egalitarians—they mistrusted blacks and foreigners—they sought change in order to fulfill their version of American ideals. Amid hardship and desperation, millions of people came to believe that a cooperative democracy in which government would ensure equal opportunity could overcome corporate power. A banner draped above the stage at the Omaha convention captured the movement's spirit: "We do not ask for sympathy or pity. We ask for justice." With this goal, Populists looked ahead to the presidential election of 1896 with hope.

THE DEPRESSION AND PROTESTS OF THE 1890s

Before that election took place, however, the nation suffered a severe economic disruption. In 1893, shortly before Grover Cleveland's second presidency began, the Philadelphia & Reading Railroad, once a thriving and profitable line, went bankrupt. Like other railroads, it had borrowed heavily to lay track and build stations and bridges. But overexpansion cut into profits, and ultimately the company was unable to pay its debts.

The same problem beset manufacturers. For example, output at McCormick farm machinery factories was nine times greater in 1893 than in 1879, but revenues had only tripled. To compensate, the company bought more equipment and squeezed more work out of fewer laborers. This strategy, however, increased debt and unemployment. Jobless workers found themselves in the same plight as employers: they could not pay their bills. Banks suffered, too, when their customers defaulted. The failure of the National Cordage Company in May 1893 sparked a chain reaction of business and bank closings. By year's end, five hundred banks and sixteen hundred businesses had failed. An adviser warned President Cleveland, "We are on the eve of a very dark night." He was right. Between 1893 and 1897, the nation suffered a devastating economic depression.

Personal hardship followed business collapse; nearly 20 percent of the labor force was jobless for a significant time during the depression. Falling demand caused prices to drop between 1892 and 1895, but layoffs and wage cuts more than offset declining living costs. Many people could not afford basic necessities. The New York police estimated that twenty thousand homeless and jobless people roamed the city's streets. Surveying the impact on Boston, Henry Adams wrote, "Men died like flies under the strain, and Boston grew suddenly old, haggard, and thin."

Continuing Currency Problems

As the depression deepened, the currency dilemma reached a crisis. The Sherman Silver Purchase Act of 1890 had committed the government to use Treasury notes (silver certificates) to buy 4.5 million ounces of silver each month. Recipients could redeem these certificates for gold, at the ratio of one ounce of gold for every sixteen ounces' worth of silver. But a western mining boom made silver more plentiful, causing its market value relative to gold to fall and prompting holders of silver certificates and greenback currency issued during the Civil War to cash in their notes in exchange for more valuable gold. As a result, the nation's gold reserve dwindled, falling below $100 million in early 1893.

The $100 million level had psychological importance. If investors believed that the country's gold reserve was disappearing, they would lose confidence in America's economic stability and refrain from investing. British capitalists, for example, owned $4 billion in American stocks and bonds. If dollars were to depreciate because there was too little gold to back them up, the British would stop investing in American economic growth. In fact, the lower the gold reserve dropped, the more people rushed to redeem their money—to get gold before it disappeared. Panic spread, causing more bankruptcies and unemployment.

Vowing to protect the gold reserve, President Cleveland called a special session of Congress to repeal the Sherman Silver Purchase Act. Repeal passed in late 1893, but the run on gold continued. In early 1895, reserves fell to $41 million. In desperation, Cleveland accepted an offer from a banking syndicate led by financier J. P. Morgan to sell the government 3.5 million ounces of gold for $65 million worth of federal bonds. When the bankers resold the bonds to the public, they made a $2 million profit. Cleveland claimed that he had saved the reserves, but discontented farmers, workers, silver miners, and even some of Cleveland's Democratic allies saw only humiliation in the president's deal with big businessmen. "When Judas betrayed Christ," charged Senator Tillman, "his heart was not blacker than this scoundrel, Cleveland, in betraying the [Democratic Party]."

Few people knew what the president was privately enduring. At about the time Cleveland called Congress into special session, doctors discovered a tumor on his palate that required immediate removal. Fearful that publicity of his illness would hasten the run on gold, and intent on preventing Vice President Adlai E. Stevenson, a silver supporter, from gaining influence, Cleveland kept his condition a secret. He announced that he was going sailing, and doctors removed his cancer while the yacht floated outside New York City. Outfitted with a rubber jaw, Cleveland resumed a full schedule five days later, hiding terrible pain to dispel rumors that he was seriously ill. He eventually recovered, but those who knew of his surgery believed it had sapped his vitality.

The deal between Cleveland and Morgan did not end the depression. After improving slightly in 1895, the economy plunged again. Farm income, declining since 1887, slid further; factories closed; banks that remained open restricted withdrawals. The tight money supply depressed housing construction, drying up jobs and discouraging immigration. Cities like Detroit encouraged citizens to cultivate "potato patches" on vacant land to help alleviate food shortages. Each night, urban police stations filled up with homeless persons who had no place to stay.

Consequences of Depression   The depression ultimately ran its course. In the late 1890s, gold discoveries in Alaska, good harvests, and industrial growth brought relief. But the downturn hastened the crumbling of the old economic system and the emergence of a new one. The American economy had expanded well beyond local and sectional bases; the fate of a large business in one part of the country now had repercussions elsewhere. When farmers in the West fell into debt and lost purchasing power, their depressed condition in turn weakened railroads, farm-implement manufacturers, and banks in other regions. Moreover, the trend toward corporate consolidation that characterized the new business system had tempted many companies to expand too rapidly. When contraction occurred, as it did in 1893, their reckless debts dragged them down, and they pulled other industries with them.

At the same time, a new global marketplace was emerging, forcing American farmers to contend not only with discriminatory transportation rates and falling crop prices at home, but also with Canadian and Russian wheat growers, Argentine cattle ranchers, Indian and Egyptian cotton manufacturers, and Australian wool producers. More than ever before, the condition of one country's economy affected the economies of other countries. In addition, the glutted domestic market persuaded American businessmen to seek new markets abroad (see Chapter 22).

Depression-Era Protests   The depression exposed fundamental tensions in the industrial system. Technological and organizational changes had been widening the gap between employees and employers for half a century, and an upsurge of dissent emerged from this gap. The era of labor protest began with the railroad strikes of 1877. The vehemence of those strikes, and the support they drew from working-class people, raised fears that the United States would experience a popular uprising like the one in France in 1871, which had briefly overturned the government and introduced communist principles. The Haymarket riot of 1886, the prolonged strike at the Carnegie Homestead Steel plant in 1892, and the extensive labor violence among miners in the West heightened anxieties (see Chapter 18). To many middle- and upper-class people, it seemed as if worker protests portended an economic and political explosion. In 1894, the year the economy plunged into depression, there were over thirteen hundred strikes and countless riots. Contrary to accusations of business leaders, few protesters were immigrant anarchists or communists come to sabotage American democracy.

Rather, the disaffected included thousands of Americans who believed that in a democracy their voices should be heard.

Socialists   Small numbers of socialists participated in these confrontations. Some socialists believed that workers should control factories and businesses; others supported government ownership. All socialists, however, opposed the private enterprise of capitalism. Their ideas derived from the writings of Karl Marx (1818–1883), the German philosopher and father of communism, who contended that whoever controls the means of production determines how well people live. Marx wrote that industrial capitalism generates profits by paying workers less than the value of their labor and that mechanization and mass production alienate workers from their labor. Thus, Marx contended, capitalists and laborers engage in an inescapable conflict over how much workers should benefit from their efforts. According to Marx, only by abolishing the return on capital—profits—could labor receive its true value, an outcome possible only if workers owned the means of production. Marx predicted that workers worldwide would become so discontented that they would revolt and seize factories, farms, banks, and transportation lines. This revolution would establish a socialist order of justice and equality. Marx's vision appealed to some workers, including many who did not consider themselves socialists, because it promised independence and security. It appealed to some intellectuals as well, because it promised to end class conflict and crass materialism.

In America, socialists disagreed over how to achieve Marx's vision. Much of the movement was influenced by immigrants, first from Germany but also by Russian Jews, Italians, Hungarians, and Poles. Although American socialism splintered into small groups, one of its main factions was the Socialist Labor Party, led by Daniel DeLeon, a fiery editor and lawyer born in Curacao and educated in Germany, who criticized American labor organizations like the AFL as too conservative. Yet as he and other socialist leaders argued points of doctrine, they ignored workers' everyday needs and thus failed to attract the mass of laborers. Nor could they rebut clergy and business leaders who celebrated opportunity, self-improvement, social mobility, and consumerism. Workers hoped they or their children would benefit through education and acquisition of property or by becoming their own boss; most American workers sought individual advancement rather than the betterment of all.

Eugene V. Debs   As the nineteenth century closed, however, a new and inspiring leader invigorated American socialism. Indiana-born Eugene V. Debs headed the newly formed American Railway Union, which had carried out the 1894 strike against the Pullman Company. Jailed for defying the injunction against striking rail workers, Debs read works of Karl Marx in prison. Once released, he flirted briefly with Populism, then became the leading spokesman for American socialism, combining visionary Marxism with Jeffersonian and Populist antimonopolism. Debs captivated audiences with passionate eloquence and indignant attacks on the free-enterprise system. "Many of you think you are competing," he would lecture. "Against whom? Against Rockefeller? About as I would if I had a wheelbarrow and competed with the Santa Fe [railroad] from here to Kansas City." By 1900, the group soon to be called the Socialist Party of America was uniting around Debs. It would make its presence felt more forcefully in the new century.

Coxey's Army   In 1894, not Debs but rather a quiet businessman named Jacob Coxey from Massillon, Ohio, captured public attention with his act of protest. Coxey had a vision. He was convinced that, to aid debtors, the government should issue $500 million of "legal tender" paper money and make low-interest loans to local governments, which would in turn use the funds to pay unemployed men to build roads and other public works. He planned to publicize his scheme by leading a march from Massillon to Washington, D.C., gathering a "petition in boots" of unemployed workers along the way. To emphasize his sincerity, Coxey named his newborn son Legal Tender and proposed that his teenage daughter lead the procession on a white horse.

Coxey's army, about 200 strong, left in March 1894. Hiking across Ohio into Pennsylvania, the marchers received food and housing in depressed industrial towns and rural villages and attracted additional recruits. Elsewhere, a dozen similar processions from places such as Seattle, San Francisco, and Los Angeles also began the trek eastward. Sore feet prompted some marchers to commandeer trains, but most marches were peaceful and law-abiding.

Coxey's band of 500, including women and children, entered Washington on April 30. The next day (May Day, the anniversary of the Haymarket violence), the group, armed with "war clubs of peace," advanced to the Capitol. When Coxey and a few others vaulted a wall surrounding the grounds, mounted police moved in and routed the demonstrators. Coxey tried to speak from the Capitol steps, but police dragged him away. As arrests and clubbings continued, Coxey's dream of a demonstration of 400,000 jobless workers dissolved. Like the strikes, the first people's march on Washington yielded to police muscle.

Unlike socialists, who wished to replace the capitalist system, Coxey's troops merely wanted more jobs and better living standards. Today, in an age of union contracts, regulation of business, and government-sponsored unemployment relief, their goals do not appear radical. The brutal reactions of officials, however, reveal how threatening dissenters like Coxey and Debs seemed to defenders of the existing social order.

THE SILVER CRUSADE AND THE ELECTION OF 1896

Amid the tumult of social protest and economic depression, it appeared that the presidential election of 1896 would be pivotal. Debates over money and power were climaxing, Democrats and Republicans continued their battle over control of Congress and the presidency, and the Populists stood at the center of the political whirlwind. The key question was whether or not voters would abandon old party loyalties for the Populist party.

Free Silver   The Populist crusade against "money power" settled on the issue of silver, which many people saw as a simple solution to the nation's complex ills. To them, coinage of silver symbolized an end to special privileges for the rich and the return of government to the people because it would lift the common people out of debt, increase the amount of cash in circulation, and reduce interest rates. Populists made free coinage of silver their political battle cry.

As the election of 1896 approached, Populists had to decide how to translate their few previous electoral victories into larger success. Should they join with sympathetic factions of the major parties, thus risking a loss of identity, or should they remain an independent third party and settle for minor wins at best? Except in mining areas of the Rocky Mountain states, where free coinage of silver had strong support, Republicans were unlikely allies because their support for the gold standard and their big-business orientation represented what Populists opposed.

In the North and West, alliance with Democrats was more plausible. There, the Democratic Party retained vestiges of antimonopoly ideology and sympathy for a looser currency system, though "gold Democrats," such as President Cleveland and Senator David Hill of New York, held powerful influence. Populists assumed they shared common interests with Democratic urban workers, who they believed suffered the same oppression that beset farmers. In the South, Alliances had previously supported Democratic candidates, but the failure of these candidates to carry out their promises once in office caused southern farmers to feel betrayed. Whichever option they chose, fusion (alliance with Democrats) or independence, Populists ensured that the election campaign of 1896 would be the most issue oriented since 1860.

Nomination of McKinley

As they prepared to nominate their presidential candidate, both parties were divided internally. Republicans were guided by Ohio industrialist Marcus A. Hanna, who for a year had been maneuvering to win the nomination for Ohio's governor, William McKinley. By the time the party convened in St. Louis, Hanna had corralled enough delegates to succeed. "He had advertised McKinley," quipped Theodore Roosevelt, "as if he were a patent medicine." The Republicans' only distress occurred when they adopted a platform supporting the gold standard, rejecting a prosilver stance proposed by Colorado senator Henry M. Teller. Teller, who had been among the party's founders forty years earlier, walked out of the convention in tears, taking a small group of silver Republicans with him.

At the Democratic convention, prosilver delegates wearing silver badges and waving silver banners paraded through the Chicago Amphitheatre. Observing their tumultuous demonstrations, one delegate wrote, "For the first time I can understand the scenes of the French Revolution!" A *New York World* reporter remarked that "all the silverites need is a Moses." They found one in William Jennings Bryan.

William Jennings Bryan

Bryan arrived at the Democratic convention as a member of a contested Nebraska delegation. A former congressman whose support for coinage of silver had annoyed President Cleveland, Bryan found the depression's impact on midwestern farmers distressing. Shortly after the convention seated Bryan and his colleagues instead of a competing faction that supported the gold standard, Bryan joined the party's resolutions

THE LOCKOUT IS ENDED; HE HOLDS THE KEY.

Collection of David J. and Janice L. Frent

During the 1896 presidential campaign, Republicans depicted their candidate, William McKinley, as holding the key to prosperity for both the working man and the white-collar laborer, shown here raising their hats to the candidate. Republicans successfully made this economic theme—rather than the silver crusade of McKinley's unsuccessful opponent, William Jennings Bryan—the difference in the election's outcome.

committee and helped write a platform calling for unlimited coinage of silver. When the committee presented the platform to the full convention, Bryan rose to speak on its behalf. His now-famous closing words ignited the delegates.

> Having behind us the producing masses of this nation and the world, supported by the commercial interests, the laboring interests, and the toilers everywhere, we will answer [the wealthy classes'] demand for a gold standard by saying to them: You shall not press down upon the brow of labor this crown of thorns, you shall not crucify mankind upon a cross of gold.

The speech could not have been better timed. Delegates who backed Bryan for president now began enlisting support. It took five ballots to win the nomination, but the magnetic "Boy Orator" proved irresistible. In accepting the silverite goals of southerners and westerners, and repudiating Cleveland's policies, the Democratic Party became more attractive to discontented farmers. But like the Republicans, it, too, alienated a minority wing. Some gold Democrats withdrew and nominated their own candidate.

Bryan's nomination presented the Populist party convention meeting in St. Louis with a dilemma. Should Populists join Democrats in support of Bryan, or should they nominate their own candidate? Tom Watson, who opposed fusion with Democrats, warned that "the Democratic idea of fusion [is] that we play Jonah while they play whale." Others reasoned that supporting a separate candidate would split the anti-McKinley vote and guarantee a Republican victory. In the end the convention compromised, first naming Watson as its vice-presidential nominee to preserve party identity (Democrats had nominated Maine shipping magnate Arthur Sewall for vice president) and then nominating Bryan for president.

The campaign, as Kansas journalist William Allen White observed, "took the form of religious frenzy . . . as the crusaders of the revolution rode home, praising the people's will as though it were God's will and cursing wealth for its iniquity." Bryan preached that "every great economic question is in reality a great moral question." Republicans countered Bryan's attacks on privilege by predicting chaos if he won. While Bryan raced around the country giving twenty speeches a day, Hanna invited thousands of people to McKinley's home in Canton, Ohio, where the candidate plied them with homilies on moderation and prosperity, promising something for everyone. In an appeal to working-class voters, Republicans stressed the new jobs that a protective tariff would create.

Election Results   The election results revealed that the political standoff had ended. McKinley, symbol of urban and corporate ascendancy, beat Bryan by 600,000 popular votes and won in the electoral college by 271 to 176. It was the most lopsided presidential election since 1872.

Bryan worked hard to rally the nation, but obsession with silver prevented Populists from building the urban-rural coalition that would have expanded their appeal. The silver issue diverted voters from focusing on broader reforms of cooperation and government aid that the Alliance movement and 1892 Omaha platform had proposed. Urban workers, who might have benefited from Populist goals, feared that silver coinage would shrink the value of their wages. Labor leaders, such as the AFL's Samuel Gompers, though partly sympathetic, would not commit themselves fully because they viewed farmers as businessmen, not workers. And socialists like Daniel DeLeon denounced Populists as "retrograde" because they, unlike socialists, believed in free enterprise. Thus, the Populist crusade collapsed. Although Populists and fusion candidates won a few state and congressional elections, the Bryan-Watson ticket of the Populist party polled only 222,600 votes nationwide.

The McKinley Presidency   As president, McKinley reinforced his support of business by signing the Gold Standard Act (1900), requiring that all paper money be backed by gold. A seasoned and personable politician, McKinley was best known for crafting protective tariffs; as a congressman, he had guided passage of record-high tariff rates in 1890. He accordingly supported the Dingley Tariff of 1897, which raised duties even higher. A believer in opening new markets abroad to sustain profits at home, McKinley encouraged imperialistic ventures in Latin America and the Pacific. Domestic tensions subsided as prosperity returned. Better times and victory in the Spanish-American War enabled him to beat Bryan again in 1900.

SUMMARY

Though buffeted by special interests and lingering consequences of the Civil War, Gilded Age politicians succeeded in making many modest, and some major, accomplishments. Guided by well-meaning, generally competent people, much of what occurred in statehouses, the halls of Congress, and the White House prepared the nation for the twentieth century. Laws encouraging economic growth with some principles of regulation, measures expanding government agencies while reducing crass patronage, and federal intervention in trade and currency issues all evolved during the 1870s and 1880s.

Nevertheless, the United States remained a nation of inconsistencies. Those who supported disfranchisement of African Americans and continued discrimination against blacks and women still polluted politics. Neither were blacks nor women united in their goals, and women's quest for suffrage included racial and class-based exclusion. People in power, often representing special-interest groups, could not tolerate radical views like those expressed by socialists, Coxey, or Populists, but many of the ideas raised by these groups continued to find supporters as the new century dawned.

The 1896 election realigned national politics. The Republican Party, founded in the 1850s amid a crusade against slavery and benefiting from northern victory in the Civil War, became the majority party by emphasizing government aid to business, expanding its social base among the urban middle class, and playing down its moralism. The Democratic Party miscalculated on the silver issue but held its support in the South and in urban political machines. At the national level, however, loyalties lacked the potency they once had. Suspicion of party politics increased, and voter participation rates declined. The Populists tried to energize a third-party movement, but their success was fleeting. A new kind of politics was brewing, one in which technical experts and scientific organization would attempt to supplant the backroom deals and favoritism that had characterized the previous age.

Although the silver issue faded, as the twentieth century progressed, many Populist goals were incorporated by the major parties, including regulation of railroads, banks, and utilities; shorter workdays; a variant of the subtreasury plan; a graduated income tax; and direct election of senators. These reforms succeeded because a variety of groups united behind them. Immigration, urbanization, and industrialization had transformed the United States into a pluralistic society in which compromise among interest groups had become a political fact of life. As the Gilded Age ended, business was still ascendant, and large segments of the population were still excluded from political and economic opportunity. But the winds of dissent and reform had begun to blow more strongly.

21

THE PROGRESSIVE ERA 1895–1920

THE VARIED PROGRESSIVE IMPULSE

Progressive reformers addressed vexing issues that had surfaced in the previous half-century, but they did so in a new political climate. After the heated election of 1896, party loyalties eroded and voter turnout declined. In northern states, voter participation in presidential elections dropped from 80 percent of the eligible (male) electorate in the 1880s to under 60 percent. In southern states, where poll taxes and literacy tests prevented most African American and many poor white males from voting, it fell below 30 percent. Parties, it seemed, were losing influence over government policies. At the same time, new interest groups—which championed their own special causes—gained influence, making Progressive reform issue-oriented rather than influenced by party ideologies.

National Associations and Foreign Influences
Many formerly local organizations that had formed around specific interests and issues became nationwide after 1890. These organizations included professional associations, such as the American Bar Association; women's organizations, such as the National American Woman Suffrage Association; issue-oriented groups, such as the National Consumers League; civic-minded clubs, such as the National Municipal League; and minority-group associations, such as the National Negro Business League and the Society of American Indians. Because they usually acted outside established parties, such groups made politics more fragmented and issue-focused than in earlier eras.

CHRONOLOGY

1895	Booker T. Washington gives Atlanta Compromise speech
	National Association of Colored Women founded
1898	*Holden v. Hardy* upholds limits on miners' working hours
1901	McKinley assassinated; T. Roosevelt assumes presidency
1904	*Northern Securities* case dissolves railroad trust
1905	*Lochner v. New York* removes limits on bakers' working hours
1906	Hepburn Act tightens ICC control over railroads
	Meat Inspection Act passed
	Pure Food and Drug Act Passed
1908	*Muller v. Oregon* upholds limits on women's working hours
1909	NAACP founded
1910	Mann-Elkins Act reinforces ICC powers
	White Slave Traffic Act (Mann Act) prohibits transportation of women for "immoral purposes"
	Taft fires Pinchot
1911	Society of American Indians founded
1913	Sixteenth Amendment ratified, legalizing income tax
	Seventeenth Amendment ratified, providing for direct election of senators
	Underwood Tariff institutes income tax
	Federal Reserve Act establishes central banking system
1914	Federal Trade Commission created to investigate unfair trade practices
	Clayton Anti-Trust Act outlaws monopolistic business practices
1919	Eighteenth Amendment ratified, establishing prohibition of alcoholic beverages
1920	Nineteenth Amendment ratified, giving women the vote in federal elections

American reformers also adopted foreign ideas. Some reform plans were introduced by Americans who had encountered them while studying in England, France, and Germany; others, by foreigners visiting the United States. (Europeans also learned from Americans, but the balance of the idea flow tilted toward the United States.) Americans copied from England such schemes as the settlement house, in which reformers went to live among and aid the urban poor, and workers' compensation for victims of industrial accidents. Other reforms, such as old-age insurance, subsidized workers' housing, city planning, and rural reconstruction, also originated abroad and were adopted in America.

Issues and methods arising from a new age distinguished Progressive reform from the preceding Populist movement. Although goals of the rural-based

Populists—moral regeneration, political democracy, and antimonopolism—continued after the movement faded, the Progressive quest for social justice, educational and legal reform, and government streamlining had a largely urban quality. Utilizing advances in mail, telephone, and telegraph communications, urban reformers could exchange information and coordinate efforts more easily than rural reformers could.

The New Middle Class and Muckrakers   Progressive goals—ending abuse of power, protecting the welfare of all classes, reforming institutions, and promoting social efficiency—existed at all levels of society. But a new middle class of men and women in professions of law, medicine, engineering, social service, religion, teaching, and business formed an important reform vanguard. Offended by corruption and immorality in business, government, and human relations, these people determined to apply the rational techniques that they had learned in their professions to problems of the larger society. They also believed they could create a unified nation by transforming immigrants and Indians—"Americanizing" them through education—to conform to middle-class customs and ideals.

Indignation over abuses of power motivated many middle-class reformers. Their views were voiced by journalists whom Theodore Roosevelt dubbed muckrakers (after a character in the Puritan allegory *Pilgrim's Progress*, who, rather than looking heavenward at beauty, looked downward and raked the muck on the floor). Muckrakers fed public tastes for scandal and sensation by exposing social, economic, and political wrongs. Their investigative articles in *McClure's, Cosmopolitan*, and other popular magazines attacked adulterated foods, fraudulent insurance, prostitution, and political corruption. Lincoln Steffens's articles in McClure's, later published as *The Shame of the Cities* (1904), epitomized muckraking style. Steffens hoped his exposés of bosses' misrule would inspire outrage and, ultimately, reform. Other celebrated muckraking works included Upton Sinclair's *The Jungle* (1906), a novel that disclosed outrages of the meatpacking industry; Ida M. Tarbell's disparaging history of Standard Oil (first published in *McClure's*, 1902–1904); Burton J. Hendrick's *Story of Life Insurance* (1907); and David Graham Phillips's *Treason of the Senate* (1906).

To remedy corrupt politics, these Progressives advocated nonpartisan elections to prevent the fraud and bribery bred by party loyalties. To make officeholders more responsible, they urged adoption of the initiative, which permitted voters to propose new laws; the referendum, which enabled voters to accept or reject a law; and the recall, which allowed voters to remove offending officials and judges from office. The goal, like that of the business-consolidation movement, was efficiency: middle-class Progressives would reclaim government by replacing the boss system with accountable managers chosen by a responsible electorate.

Upper-Class Reformers   The Progressive spirit also stirred some male business leaders and wealthy females. Executives like Alexander Cassatt of the Pennsylvania Railroad supported some government regulation and political restructuring to protect their interests from more radical reformers. Others, like E. A. Filene, founder of a Boston department store, and Tom Johnson, a Cleveland streetcar magnate, were humanitarians who worked unselfishly for social justice. Business-dominated organizations like the Municipal Voters League and U.S. Chamber of Commerce thought that running schools, hospitals, and local government like efficient businesses would help stabilize society. Elite women led and gave financial support to organizations like the Young Women's Christian Association (YWCA), which aided unmarried working women, and to settlement houses.

Settlement Houses   Young, educated middle-class women and men bridged the gap between social classes that industrialism seemed to have opened by leaving their comfortable surroundings and living in inner-city outposts called settlement houses. An idea adopted from England, residents envisioned the settlement house as a place where people could learn from each other and mutually mitigate modern problems through education, art, and reform. Between 1886 and 1910, over four hundred settlements were established, mostly in big cities, and they sponsored a wide range of activities ranging from English-language classes, kindergartens and nurseries, health clinics, vocational training, playgrounds, and art exhibits. As first-hand observers of urban poverty and poor housing, settlement house workers focused considerable energy on improving living conditions and marched at the vanguard of progressivism. They backed housing and labor reform, offered meeting space to unions, and served as school nurses, juvenile probation officers, and teachers. They also worked in campaigns of political reformers.

Though several men helped initiate the settlement movement, the most influential participants were women. Jane Addams of Chicago's Hull House settlement, Lillian Wald of New York's Henry Street settlement, Vida Scudder of Boston's Denison House, and Florence Kelley of Hull House were among many strong-minded leaders who not only broadened traditional roles of female service but also used settlement work as a springboard to larger roles in reform. Kelley's investigations into the exploitation of child labor prompted Illinois governor John Altgeld to appoint her state factory inspector; she later founded the National Consumers League. Wald helped make nursing a respected profession and co-founded the NAACP. And Addams had broad political influence, and her efforts on behalf of world peace garnered her the Nobel Peace Prize in 1931.

Working-Class Reformers   Vital elements of what became modern American liberalism derived from working-class urban experiences. By 1900, many urban workers were pressing for government intervention to ensure safety and security. They advocated such "bread-and-butter reforms" as safe factories, shorter workdays, workers' compensation, protection of child and women laborers, better housing, and a more equitable tax structure. Politicians like Senator Robert F. Wagner of New York and Governor Edward F. Dunne of Illinois worked to alleviate hardships that resulted from urban-industrial growth. They trained in the trenches of machine politics, and their constituents

Foreign Universities and Study Abroad

The university as a degree-granting institution of higher education originated during Medieval times in Islamic Morocco and Egypt. Shortly thereafter, universities arose in Italy, France, England, and Spain. By the end of the nineteenth century, the chief models for the modern university existed in German cities and in British institutions at Oxford and Cambridge, where study involving research, seminars, and laboratories replaced a curriculum heavily focused on religion. It was these universities, with their academic freedom and faculties of dynamic scholars, that attracted young Americans traveling abroad and seeking a place for themselves in the modern world. German universities were especially inexpensive; travel costs plus fees at these schools cost Americans only a third as much as they would have to pay at comparable American institutions.

As a result of visits and study at British and European universities, many Americans became inspired with ideas about improving society. The muckraking journalist Lincoln Steffens, for example, graduated with an undergraduate degree from the University of California, where he "got the religion of scholarship and science." He then decided to study at German universities because he wanted to learn from the great minds that his California

professors "quoted and looked up to as their high priests." So he visited campuses in Berlin, Heidleberg, Munich, and Leipzig. Progressive economist Richard Ely also went to Germany, studying philosophy in Halle, and scholar and civil rights activist W. E. B. Du Bois pursued graduate work at the University of Berlin. British universities also proved influential. Progressive historian Charles Beard was moved by his studies at Oxford University, and Edith Abbott, who pioneered social work in America, studied welfare policy at the London School of Economics.

Some American students abroad were exposed to the European ideology of social democracy, a movement related to socialism but one that emphasized reform through politics rather than through revolution. Social democrats aligned themselves with the struggles of the working class and often called themselves "socialists." But they tended to stress moral issues that welded society together rather than pitting one class against another. When these Americans returned to their own country, they brought with them an opposition to the every-man-for-himself implications of laissez faire and an impetus for using the government to unite society for the betterment of all. Thus, foreign study provided important underpinnings to Progressive reform.

were the same people who supported political bosses, supposedly the enemies of reform. Yet bossism was not necessarily incompatible with humanitarianism. When "Big Tim" Sullivan, an influential boss in New York's Tammany Hall political machine, was asked why he supported shorter workdays for women, he explained, "I had seen me sister go out to work when she was only fourteen and I know we ought to help these gals by giving 'em a law which will prevent 'em from being broken down while they're still young." Those who represented working-class interests did not subscribe to all reforms. As protectors of individual liberty, they opposed schemes such as prohibition, Sunday closing laws, civil service, and nonpartisan elections, which conflicted with their constituents' interests. On the other hand, they joined with other reformers to pass laws aiding labor and promoting social welfare.

The Social Gospel   Much of Progressive reform rested on religious underpinnings from which arose new thoughts about how to fortify social relations with moral principles. In particular, a movement known as the Social Gospel, led by Protestant ministers Walter Rauschenbusch, Washington Gladden, and Charles Sheldon, would counter competitive capitalism by interjecting Christian churches into practical, worldly matters, such as arbitrating industrial harmony and improving the conditions of the poor. Believing that service to fellow humans provided the way to securing individual salvation and creating God's kingdom on earth, Social Gospelers actively participated in social reform and governed their lives by asking, "What would Jesus do?"

Others took more secular pathways. Those who believed in service to all people tried to "Americanize" immigrants and Indians by expanding their educational, economic, and cultural opportunities. But at times well-intentioned humanitarians undermined their efforts by imposing their own values on people of different cultures. Working-class Catholic and Jewish immigrants, for example, sometimes rejected the Protestant creed and Americanization efforts of Social Gospelers and resented middle-class reformers' interference in their prerogative to raise their children according to their own beliefs.

Socialists   Some disillusioned people wanted to create a different society altogether. A blend of immigrant intellectuals, industrial workers, former Populists, and women's rights activists, they turned to socialism. Taking a cue from European counterparts—especially in Germany, England, and France, where the government sponsored such socialist goals as low-cost housing, workers' compensation, old-age pensions, public ownership of municipal services, and labor reform—they advocated that the United States adopt similar measures. By 1912, the Socialist Party of America, founded in 1901, claimed 150,000 members, and the socialist newspaper Appeal to Reason achieved the largest circulation— 700,000 subscribers—of any weekly newspaper in the country.

In politics, socialists united behind Eugene V. Debs, the American Railway Union organizer who drew nearly 100,000 votes as Socialist Party candidate in the 1900 presidential election. A spellbinding orator who appealed to urban immigrants and western farmers alike, Debs won 400,000 votes in 1904 and polled 900,000 in 1912, at the pinnacle of his and his party's career. Although Debs and other Socialist leaders, such as Victor Berger of Wisconsin, the first socialist to be elected to the U.S. Congress, and New York labor lawyer Morris Hillquit, did not always agree on tactics, they made compelling overtures to reform-minded people.

Ultimately, American socialism had difficulty sustaining widespread acceptance. Some Progressives joined the Socialist Party, but most reformers favored capitalism too much to want to overthrow it. Municipal ownership of public utilities represented their limit of drastic change. In Wisconsin, where Progressivism was most advanced, reformers refused to ally with Berger's more radical group. In California, Progressives temporarily allied with conservatives to prevent socialists from gaining power in Los Angeles. Although some AFL unions supported socialist goals and candidates, many other unions opposed a reform like unemployment insurance because it would increase taxes on members' wages. Moreover, private real-estate interests opposed any government intervention in housing, and manufacturers tried to suppress socialist activity by blacklisting militant laborers.

Southern and Western Progressivism

In some ways, Progressive reform in the South resembled that in other regions. Essentially urban and middle class in nature, it included the same goals of railroad and utility regulation, factory safety, pure food and drug legislation, and moral reform as existed in the North. The South pioneered some political reforms; the direct primary originated in North Carolina; the city-commission plan arose in Galveston, Texas; and the city-manager plan began in Staunton, Virginia. Progressive governors, such as Braxton Bragg Comer of Alabama and Hoke Smith of Georgia, introduced business regulation, educational expansion, and other reforms that duplicated actions taken by northern counterparts.

In the West, several politicians championed humanitarianism and regulation, putting the region at the forefront of campaigns to expand functions of federal and state governments. Nevada's Progressive Senator Francis Newlands advocated national planning and federal control of water resources. California Governor Hiram Johnson fought for direct primaries, regulation of child and women's labor, workers' compensation, a pure food and drug act, and educational reform. Montana's Senator Thomas J. Walsh fought against corruption and for woman suffrage.

Southern and western women, white and black, made notable contributions to Progressive causes, just as they did in the North and East. In western states, women could vote on state and local matters so that they could participate directly in political reform. But the more effective women's reform efforts in both regions took place outside politics, and their projects remained racially distinct. White women crusaded against child labor, founded social service organizations, and challenged unfair wage rates. African American women, using a nonpolitical guise as homemakers and religious leaders—roles that whites found more acceptable than political activism—served their communities by acting as advocates for street cleaning, better education, and health reforms.

Opponents of Progressivism

It would be a mistake to assume that a Progressive spirit captivated all of American society between 1895 and 1920. Large numbers of people, heavily represented in Congress, disliked government interference in economic affairs and found no fault with existing power structures. Defenders of free enterprise opposed regulatory measures out of fear that government programs undermined the initiative and competition that they believed were basic to a free-market system. "Old-guard" Republicans, such as Senator Nelson W. Aldrich of Rhode Island and House Speaker Joseph

Cannon of Illinois, championed this ideology. Outside Washington, D.C., tycoons like J. P. Morgan and John D. Rockefeller insisted that progress would result only from maintaining the profit incentive and an unfettered economy.

Moreover, prominent Progressives were not "progressive" in every respect. Their attempts to Americanize immigrants reflected prejudice as well as naiveté. As governor, Hiram Johnson promoted discrimination against Japanese Americans, and whether Progressive or not, most southern governors, such as Smith, Comer, Charles B. Aycock of North Carolina, and James K. Vardaman of Mississippi, rested their power on appeals to white supremacy. In the South, the disfranchisement of blacks through poll taxes, literacy requirements, and other means meant that electoral reforms affected only whites—and then only white men with enough cash and schooling to satisfy voting prerequisites. Settlement houses in northern cities kept blacks and whites apart in separate programs and buildings.

Progressive reformers generally occupied the center of the ideological spectrum. Moderate, socially aware, sometimes contradictory, they believed on one hand that laissez faire was obsolete and on the other that a radical departure from free enterprise was dangerous. Like Thomas Jefferson, they expressed faith in the conscience and will of the people; like Alexander Hamilton, they desired strong central government to act in the interest of conscience. Their goals were both idealistic and realistic. As minister-reformer Walter Rauschenbusch wrote, "We shall demand perfection and never expect to get it."

GOVERNMENT AND LEGISLATIVE REFORM

Mistrust of tyranny had traditionally prompted Americans to believe that democratic government should be small, should interfere in private affairs only in unique circumstances, and should withdraw when balance had been restored. But in the late 1800s, this viewpoint weakened when problems resulting from economic change seemed to overwhelm individual effort. Corporations pursued government aid and protection for their enterprises. Discontented farmers sought government regulation of railroads and other monopolistic businesses. And city dwellers, accustomed to favors performed by political machines, came to expect government to act on their behalf. Before 1900, state governments had been concerned largely with railroads and economic growth; the federal government had focused primarily on tariffs and the currency. But after 1900, issues of regulation, both economic and social, demanded attention. More than in the past, public opinion, roused by muckraking media, influenced change.

Restructuring Government   Middle-class Progressive reformers rejected the laissez-faire principle of government. Increasingly aware that a simple, inflexible government was inadequate in a complex industrial age, they reasoned that public authority needed to counteract inefficiency and exploitation. But before activists could effectively use such power, they would have to reclaim government from politicians whose greed they believed had soiled the democratic system. Thus, eliminating corruption from government was one central thrust of Progressive activity.

Prior to the Progressive era, reformers had attacked corruption in city governments through such structural reforms as civil service, nonpartisan elections, and close scrutiny of public expenditures. After 1900, campaigns to make cities run more efficiently resulted in city-manager and commission forms of government, in which urban officials were chosen for professional expertise rather than for political connections. But reforming city management was not sufficient to realize the improvements reformers sought, and they refocused attention on state and federal governments for help.

At the state level, faith in a reform-minded executive prompted Progressives to support a number of skillful and charismatic governors. Perhaps the most dynamic of Progressive governors was Wisconsin's Robert M. La Follette. A small-town lawyer, La Follette rose through the state Republican Party to become governor in 1900. In office, he initiated a multipronged reform program, including direct primaries, more equitable taxes, and regulation of railroads. He also appointed commissions staffed by experts, who supplied him with data that he used in speeches to arouse support for his policies. After three terms as governor, La Follette became a U.S. senator and carried his ideals into national politics. "Battling Bob" displayed a rare ability to approach reform scientifically while still exciting people with moving rhetoric. His goal, he proclaimed, was "not to 'smash' corporations, but to drive

Robert M. La Follette (1855–1925) was one of the most dynamic of Progressive politicians. As governor of Wisconsin, he sponsored a program of politcal reform and business regulation known as the Wisconsin Plan. In 1906 he entered the U.S. Senate and continued to champion Progressive reform. The National Progressive Republican League, which La Follette founded in 1911, became the core of the Progressive Party.

Wisconsin Historical Society #WHi 2390

them out of politics, and then to treat them exactly the same as other people are treated."

Crusades against corrupt politics made the system more democratic. By 1916, all but three states had direct primaries, and many had adopted the initiative, referendum, and recall. Political reformers achieved a major goal in 1913 with adoption of the Seventeenth Amendment to the Constitution, which provided for direct election of U.S. senators, replacing election by state legislatures. Such measures, however, did not always achieve the desired ends. Party bosses, better organized and more experienced than reformers, were still able to control elections, and special-interest groups spent large sums to influence voting. Moreover, courts usually aided rather than reined in entrenched power.

Labor Reform   State laws resulting from Progressive efforts to improve labor conditions had more effect than did political reforms because middle-class and working-class reformers agreed on the need for them. At the instigation of middle-class/working-class coalitions, many states enacted factory inspection laws, and by 1916 nearly two-thirds of states required compensation for victims of industrial accidents. The same alliance induced some legislatures to grant aid to mothers with dependent children. Under pressure from the National Child Labor Committee, nearly every state set a minimum age for employment (varying from twelve to sixteen) and limited hours that employers could make children work. Labor laws did not work perfectly, however. They seldom provided for the close inspection of factories that enforcement required. And families that needed extra income evaded child labor restrictions by falsifying their children's ages for employers.

Several middle- and working-class groups also united behind measures that restricted working hours for women and that aided retirees. After the Supreme Court, in *Muller v. Oregon*, upheld Oregon's ten-hour limit in 1908, more states passed laws protecting female workers. Meanwhile, in 1914, efforts of the American Association for Old Age Security made progress when Arizona established old-age pensions. Judges struck down the law, but demand for pensions continued, and in the 1920s many states enacted laws to provide for needy elderly people.

Prohibition   Increasing government responsibilities and protecting women and children brought together reform coalitions. But when an issue involved regulating behavior such as drinking habits and sexual conduct, differences emerged, especially when reformers used both morality and social control as a basis for their agenda. For example, the Anti-Saloon League, formed in 1893, intensified the long-standing campaign against drunkenness and its costs to society. This organization allied with the Woman's Christian Temperance Union (founded in 1874) to publicize alcoholism's role in causing health problems and family distress. The League was especially successful in shifting attention from the immorality of drunkenness to using law enforcement to break the alleged link between the drinking that saloons encouraged and the accidents, poverty, and poor productivity that resulted.

Against the wishes of many working-class people who valued individual freedom, the war on saloons prompted many states and localities to restrict liquor consumption. By 1900, one-fourth of the nation's population lived in "dry" communities that prohibited the sale of liquor. But consumption of alcohol increased as a result of the influx of immigrants whose cultures included social drinking, convincing prohibitionists that a nationwide ban was the best solution. They enlisted support from such notables as Supreme Court Justice Louis D. Brandeis and former president William Howard Taft, and in 1918 Congress passed the Eighteenth Amendment (ratified in 1919 and implemented in 1920), outlawing the manufacture, sale, and transportation of intoxicating liquors. Not all prohibitionists were Progressive reformers, and not all Progressives were prohibitionists. Nevertheless, the Eighteenth Amendment can be seen as an expression of the Progressive goal to protect family and workplace through reform legislation.

Controlling Prostitution   Moral outrage erupted when muckraking journalists charged that international gangs were kidnapping young women and forcing them into prostitution, a practice called white slavery. Accusations were exaggerated, but they alarmed some moralists who falsely perceived a link between immigration and prostitution, and who feared that prostitutes were producing genetically inferior children. Although some women voluntarily entered "the profession" because it offered much higher income than any other form of work available and other women occasionally performed sexual favors in return for gifts, those fearful about the social consequences of prostitution prodded governments to investigate and pass corrective legislation. The Chicago Vice Commission, for example, undertook a "scientific" survey of dance halls and illicit sex, and published its findings as *The Social Evil in Chicago* in 1911. The report concluded that poverty, gullibility, and desperation drove women into prostitution. Such investigations publicized rising numbers of prostitutes but failed to prove that criminal organizations deliberately lured women into "the trade."

Reformers nonetheless believed they could attack prostitution by punishing both those who promoted it and those who practiced it. In 1910, Congress passed the White Slave Traffic Act (Mann Act), prohibiting interstate and international transportation of a woman for immoral purposes. By 1915, nearly every state had outlawed brothels and solicitation of sex. Such laws ostensibly protected young women from exploitation, but in reality they failed to address the more serious problem of sexual violence that women suffered at the hands of family members, presumed friends, and employers.

Like prohibition, the Mann Act reflected sentiment that government could improve behavior by restricting it. Middle-class reformers believed that the source of evil was neither original sin nor human nature but the social environment. If evil was created by human will, it followed that sin could be eradicated by human effort. Intervention in the form of laws could help create a heaven on earth. The new working classes, however, resented such meddling as unwarranted attempts to control them. Thus, when Chicagoans voted on a referendum to make their city dry shortly before the Eighteenth Amendment was passed, three-fourths of the city's immigrant voters opposed it, and the measure went down to defeat.

NEW IDEAS IN SOCIAL INSTITUTIONS

In addition to legislative paths, Progressive reform opened new vistas in the ways social institutions were organized. Preoccupation with efficiency and scientific management infiltrated the realms of education, law, religion, and social science. Darwin's theory of evolution had challenged traditional beliefs in a God-created world, immigration had created complex social diversity, and technology had made old habits of production obsolete. Thoughtful people in several professions grappled with how to respond to the new era yet preserve what was best from the past.

John Dewey and Progressive Education   Changing attitudes about childhood and increases in school attendance altered approaches to education. As late as 1870, when families needed children at home to do farm work, Americans attended school for an average of only a few months a year for four years. By 1900, however, the urban-industrial economy and its expanding middle class helped to create a more widespread appreciation of childhood as a special life stage requiring that youngsters be sheltered from society's dangers and promoting their physical and emotional growth. Those concerned about children's development believed that youngsters required particular forms of education and activity appropriate to a child's biological and cultural development.

Educators argued that expanded schooling produced better adult citizens and workers. In the 1870s and 1880s, states passed laws that required children to attend school to age fourteen, and swelling populations of immigrant and migrant children jammed schoolrooms. Meanwhile, the number of public high schools grew from five hundred in 1870 to ten thousand in 1910. By 1900, educational reformers, such as psychologist G. Stanley Hall and philosopher John Dewey, asserted that schools needed to prepare children for a modern world. They insisted that personal development should be the focus of the curriculum and that the school be the center of the community.

Progressive education, based on Dewey's *The School and Society* (1899) and *Democracy and Education* (1916), was a uniquely American phenomenon. Dewey believed that learning should involve real-life problems and that children should be taught to use intelligence and ingenuity as instruments for controlling their environments. From kindergarten through high school, Dewey asserted, children needed to learn through direct experience, not by rote memorization. Dewey and his wife, Alice, put these ideas into practice in their own Laboratory School located at the University of Chicago.

Growth of Colleges and Universities   A more practical curriculum also became the driving principle behind reform in higher education. Previously, the purpose of American colleges and universities had resembled that of European counterparts: to train a select few for careers in law, medicine, and religion. But in the late 1800s, institutions of higher learning multiplied as states established their own public universities using federal funds from the Morrill Acts of 1862 and 1890. The number of private institutions also expanded. Between 1870 and 1910, the total of American colleges and universities grew from 563 to nearly 1,000. Curricula broadened as educators sought to make learning more appealing and keep pace with technological and social changes. Harvard University, under President Charles W. Eliot, pioneered in substituting electives for required courses and experimenting with new teaching methods. The University of Wisconsin and other state universities achieved distinction in new areas of study, such as political science, economics, and sociology. Many schools, private and public, considered athletics vital to a student's growth, and men's intercollegiate sports became a permanent feature of student life and source of school pride.

Southern states, in keeping with separate-but-equal policies, created segregated colleges for blacks in addition to institutions for whites. Aided by land-grant funds, such schools as Alabama Agricultural and Mechanical University (A&M), South Carolina State University, and the A&M College for the Colored Race (North Carolina) opened their doors. Separate was a more accurate description of these institutions than equal. African Americans continued to suffer from inferior educational opportunities. Nevertheless, African American men and women found intellectual stimulation in all-black colleges and hoped to use education to promote the uplifting of their race.

As higher education expanded, so did female enrollments. Between 1890 and 1910, the number of women attending colleges and universities swelled from 56,000 to 140,000. Of these, 106,000 attended coeducational institutions (mostly state universities); the rest enrolled in women's colleges, such as Wellesley and Barnard. By 1920, 283,000 women attended college, accounting for 47 percent of total enrollment. But discrimination lingered in admissions and curriculum policies. Women were encouraged (indeed, they usually sought) to take home economics and education courses rather than science and mathematics, and most medical schools refused to admit women or imposed stringent quotas. Separate women's medical schools, such as the Women's Medical College of Philadelphia and Women's Medical College of Chicago, trained female physicians, but most of these schools were absorbed or put out of business by larger institutions dominated by men.

American educators justifiably congratulated themselves for increasing enrollments and making instruction more meaningful. By 1920, 78 percent of children between ages five and seventeen were enrolled in public schools; another 8 percent attended private and parochial schools. These figures represented a huge increase over 1870 attendance rates. There were 600,000 college and graduate students in 1920, compared with only 52,000 in 1870. Yet few people looked beyond the numbers to assess how well schools were doing their job. Critical analysis seldom tested the faith that schools could promote equality as well as personal growth and responsible citizenship.

Progressive Legal Thought   The legal profession also embraced new emphases on experience and scientific principles. Harvard law professor Roscoe Pound and Oliver Wendell Holmes Jr., associate justice of the Supreme Court (1902–1932) led an attack on the traditional view of law as universal and unchanging. "The life of the law," wrote Holmes, sounding like Dewey, "has not been logic; it has been experience." The opinion that law should reflect society's needs challenged the practice of invoking inflexible legal precedents that often obstructed social legislation. Louis D. Brandeis, a lawyer who later joined Holmes on the Supreme Court, insisted that judges' opinions be based on scientifically gathered information about social realities. Using this approach, Brandeis collected extensive data on harmful effects of long working hours to convince the Supreme Court, in *Muller v. Oregon* (1908), to uphold Oregon's ten-hour limit on women's workday.

New legal thinking provoked some resistance. Judges raised on laissez-faire economics and strict interpretation of the Constitution overturned laws that Progressives thought necessary for effective reform. Thus, despite Holmes's forceful dissent, in 1905 the Supreme Court, in *Lochner v. New York*, revoked a state law limiting bakers' working hours. In this and similar cases, the Court's majority argued that the Fourteenth Amendment protected an individual's right to make contracts without government interference. Judges weakened federal regulations by invoking the Tenth Amendment, which prohibited the federal government from interfering in matters reserved to the states.

Courts did uphold some regulatory measures, particularly those intended to safeguard life and limb. A string of decisions, beginning with *Holden v. Hardy* (1898), in which the Supreme Court sustained a Utah law regulating working hours for miners, confirmed the use of state police power to protect health, safety, and morals. Judges also affirmed federal police power and Congress's authority over interstate commerce by upholding legislation, such as the Pure Food and Drug Act, the Meat Inspection Act, and the Mann Act. In these instances citizens' welfare took precedence over the Tenth Amendment.

But the concept of general welfare often conflicted with the principle of equal rights when majorities imposed their will on minorities. Even if one agreed that laws should address society's needs, whose needs should prevail? The United States was (and remains) a mixed nation where interests of gender, race, religion, and ethnicity often conflict. Thus outcries resulted when a native-born Protestant majority imposed Bible reading in public schools (offending Catholics and Jews), required businesses to close on Sundays, limited women's rights, restricted religious practices of Mormons and other groups, prohibited interracial marriage, and enforced racial segregation. Justice Holmes asserted that laws should be made for "people of fundamentally differing views," but fitting such laws to a nation of so many different interest groups has sparked debates that continue to this day.

Social Science   Social science—the study of society and its institutions— experienced changes similar to those affecting education and law. In economics, several scholars used statistics to argue that laws governing economic relationships were not timeless. Instead, they claimed, theory should reflect prevailing social conditions. Richard T. Ely of Johns Hopkins University and the University of Wisconsin, for example, argued that poverty and impersonality resulting from industrialization required intervention by "the united efforts of Church, state, and science." A new breed of sociologists led by Lester Ward, Albion Small, and Edward A. Ross agreed, adding that citizens should actively work to cure social ills rather than passively wait for problems to solve themselves.

Meanwhile, historians Frederick Jackson Turner, Charles A. Beard, and Vernon L. Parrington examined the past to explain present American society. Beard, like other Progressives, believed that the Constitution was a flexible document amenable to growth and change, not a sacred code imposed by wise forefathers. His *Economic Interpretation of the Constitution* (1913) argued that a group of merchants and business-oriented lawyers created the Constitution to defend private property. If the Constitution had served special interests in one age, he argued, it could be changed to serve broader interests in another age.

Public health, organizations such as the National Consumers League (NCL) joined physicians and social scientists to bring about some of the most far-reaching Progressive reforms. Founded by Florence Kelley in 1899, the NCL pursued protection of female and child laborers and elimination of potential health hazards in the marketplace. After aiding in the success of *Muller v. Oregon*, the organization joined reform lawyers Louis Brandeis and Felix Frankfurter in support of further court cases on behalf of women workers. Local NCL branches united with women's clubs to advance consumer protection measures, such as the licensing of food vendors and inspection of dairies. They also urged city governments to fund neighborhood clinics that provided health education and medical care to the poor.

Eugenics

The Social Gospel served as a response to Social Darwinism, the application of biological natural selection and survival of the fittest to human interactions. But another movement that flourished during the Progressive era, eugenics, sought to apply Darwinian principles to society in a more intrusive way. The brainchild of Francis Galton, an English statistician and cousin of Charles Darwin, eugenics was more social philosophy than science. It rested on the belief that human character and habits could be inherited. If good traits could be inherited, so could unwanted traits, such as criminality and mental illness. Just as some Progressives believed that society had an obligation to intervene and erase poverty and injustice, eugenicists believed that society had an obligation to prevent the reproduction of those thought to be mentally defective and criminally inclined, by preventing them from marrying and, in extreme cases, sterilizing them. Such ideas targeted immigrants and people of color. Supported by such American notables as Alexander Graham Bell, Margaret Sanger, and W. E. B. Du Bois, eugenics was discredited, especially after it became a linchpin of Nazi racial policies, but modern genetic engineering has evolved from some of the eugenics legacy.

Some reformers endorsed eugenics, but others saw immigration restriction as a more acceptable way of controlling the composition of American society. A leading restrictionist was Madison Grant, whose *The Passing of the Great Race* (1916) strongly bolstered theories that immigrants from southern and eastern Europe threatened to weaken American society because they were inferior mentally and morally to earlier Nordic immigrants. Such ideas prompted many people, including some Progressives, to conclude that new laws should curtail the influx of Poles, Italians, Jews, and other eastern and southern Europeans, as well as Asians. Efforts to limit immigration reached fruition in the 1920s, when restrictive legislation drastically closed the door to "new" immigrants.

Thus, a new breed of men and women pressed for political reform and institutional change in the two decades before the First World War. Concerned middle-class professionals, confident that new ways of thinking could bring about progress, and representatives of working classes, who experienced social problems first-hand, helped broaden government's role to meet the needs of a mature industrial society. But their questioning of prevailing assumptions also unsettled conventional attitudes toward race and gender.

CHALLENGES TO RACIAL AND SEXUAL DISCRIMINATION

White male reformers of the Progressive era dealt primarily with issues of politics and institutions, and in so doing ignored issues directly affecting former slaves, non-white immigrants, Indians, and women. Yet activists within these groups caught the Progressive spirit, challenged entrenched customs, and made strides toward their own advancement. Their efforts, however, posed a dilemma. Should women and nonwhites aim to imitate white men, with white men's values as well as their rights? Or was there something unique about racial and sexual cultures that they should preserve at the risk of sacrificing broader gains? Both groups fluctuated between attraction to and rejection of the culture that excluded them.

Continued Discrimination for African Americans
In 1900, nine-tenths of African Americans lived in the South, where repressive Jim Crow laws had multiplied in the 1880s and 1890s. Denied legal and voting rights, and officially segregated in almost all walks of life, southern blacks faced constant exclusion as well as relentless violence from lynching and countless acts of intimidation. In 1910, only 8,000 out of 970,000 high-school-age blacks were enrolled in southern high schools. In response, many African Americans moved northward in the 1880s, accelerating their migration after 1900. The conditions they found in places like Chicago, Cleveland, and Detroit represented relative improvement over rural sharecropping, but job discrimination, inferior schools, and segregated housing still prevailed.

African American leaders differed sharply over how—and whether—to pursue assimilation in their new environments. In the wake of emancipation, ex-slave Frederick Douglass urged "ultimate assimilation through self-assertion, and on no other terms." Others favored separation from white society and supported emigration to Africa or the establishment of all-black communities in Oklahoma Territory and Kansas. Others advocated militancy, believing, as one writer stated, "Our people must die to be saved and in dying must take as many along with them as it is possible to do with the aid of firearms and all other weapons."

Booker T. Washington and Self-Help
Most blacks could neither escape nor conquer white society. They sought other routes to economic and social improvement. Self-help, a strategy articulated by educator Booker T. Washington, offered one popular alternative. Born into slavery in Virginia in 1856, Washington obtained an education and in 1881 founded Tuskegee Institute, an all-black vocational school, in Alabama. There he developed

a philosophy that blacks' best hopes for assimilation lay in at least temporarily accommodating whites. Rather than fighting for political rights, Washington counseled African Americans to work hard, acquire property, and prove they were worthy of respect. Washington voiced his views in a speech at the Atlanta Exposition in 1895. "Dignify and glorify common labor," he urged, in what became known as the Atlanta Compromise. "Agitation of questions of racial equality is the extremest folly." Envisioning a society where blacks and whites would remain apart but share similar goals, Washington observed that "in all things that are purely social we can be as separate as the fingers, yet one as the hand in all matters essential to mutual progress."

Whites welcomed Washington's accommodation policy because it advised patience and reminded black people to stay in their place. Because he said what they wanted to hear, white businesspeople, reformers, and politicians chose to regard Washington as representing all African Americans. Although Washington endorsed a separate-but-equal policy, he projected a subtle racial pride that would find more direct expression in black nationalism in the twentieth century, when some African Americans would advocate control of their own businesses and schools. Washington never argued that blacks were inferior; rather, he asserted that they could enhance their dignity through self-improvement.

Some blacks, however, concluded that Washington endorsed second-class citizenship. His southern-based philosophy did not appeal to educated northern African Americans like newspaper editors William Monroe Trotter and T. Thomas Fortune. In 1905, a group of "anti-Bookerites" convened near Niagara Falls and pledged militant pursuit of such rights as unrestricted voting, economic opportunity, integration, and equality before the law. Representing the Niagara movement was W. E. B. Du Bois, an outspoken critic of the Atlanta Compromise.

W. E. B. Du Bois and the "Talented Tenth"   A New Englander and the first black to receive a Ph.D. from Harvard, Du Bois was both a Progressive and a member of the black elite. He first studied at all-black Fisk University then studied in Germany, where he learned about scientific investigation. While a faculty member at Atlanta University, Du Bois compiled fact-filled sociological studies of black urban life and wrote poetically in support of civil rights. He treated Washington politely but could not accept accommodation. "The way for a people to gain their reasonable rights," Du Bois asserted, "is not by voluntarily throwing them away." Instead, blacks must agitate for what was rightfully theirs. Du Bois believed that an intellectual vanguard of cultured, educated blacks, the "Talented Tenth," should lead in the pursuit of racial equality. In 1909, he joined white liberals who also were discontented with Washington's accommodationism to form the National Association for the Advancement of Colored People (NAACP). The organization aimed to end racial discrimination, eradicate lynching, and obtain voting rights through legal redress in the courts. By 1914, the NAACP had fifty branch offices and six thousand members.

Within the NAACP and in other ways, African Americans struggled with questions about their place in white society. Du Bois voiced this dilemma poignantly, observing that "one ever feels his twoness—an American, a Negro, two souls, two thoughts, two unreconciled strivings, two warring ideals in one dark body." Somehow blacks had to reconcile that "twoness" by combining racial pride with national identity. As Du Bois wrote in 1903, a black "would not Africanize America, for America has too much to teach the world and Africa. He would not bleach his Negro soul in a flood of white Americanism, for he knows that Negro blood has a message for the world. He simply wishes to make it possible for a man to be both a Negro and an American." That simple wish would haunt the nation for decades to come.

Society of American Indians

The dilemma of identity vexed American Indians, but had an added tribal dimension. Since the 1880s, most Native American reformers had belonged to white-led organizations. In 1911, however, some middle-class Indians formed their own association, the Society of American Indians (SAI), to work for better education, civil rights, and healthcare. It also sponsored "American Indian Days" to cultivate pride and offset the images of savage peoples promulgated in Wild West shows.

The SAI's emphasis on racial pride, however, was squeezed between pressures for assimilation on one side and tribal allegiance on the other. Its small membership did not fully represent the diverse and unconnected Indian nations, and its attempt to establish a unifying governing body fizzled. Some tribal governments no longer existed to select representatives, and most SAI members simply promoted their self-interest. At the same time, the goal of achieving acceptance in white society proved elusive. Individual hard work was not enough to overcome prejudice and condescension, and attempts to redress grievances through legal action faltered for lack of funds. Ultimately, the SAI had little effect on poverty-stricken Indians who seldom knew that the organization even existed. Torn by internal disputes, the association folded in the early 1920s.

"The Woman Movement"

Challenges to established social assumptions also raised questions of identity among women. The ensuing quandaries resembled those faced by racial minorities: What tactics should women use to achieve rights? What should be women's role in society? Should they try to achieve equality within a male-dominated society? Or should they assert particular female qualities to create a new place for themselves within society?

The answers that women found involved a subtle but important shift in their politics. Before 1910, crusaders for women's rights referred to themselves as "the woman movement." This label applied to middle-class women who strove to move beyond the household into higher education and paid professions. Like African American and Indian leaders, women argued that legal and voting rights were indispensable to such moves. They based their claims on the theory that women's special, even superior, traits as guardians of family and morality would humanize all of society. Settlement-house founder Jane Addams, for example, endorsed woman suffrage by asking, "If women have in any sense been responsible for the gentler side of life which softens and blurs some of its harsher conditions, may not they have a duty to perform in our American cities?"

Women's Clubs   Women's clubs represented a unique dimension of the woman movement. Originating as literary and educational organizations, women's clubs began taking stands on public affairs in the late nineteenth century. Because female activists were generally barred from holding public office (except in a few western states), they asserted traditional female responsibilities for home and family as the rationale for reforming society through an enterprise that historians have called social housekeeping. Rather than advocate reforms like trustbusting and direct primaries, female reformers worked for factory inspection, regulation of children's and women's labor, improved housing, and consumer protection.

Such efforts were not confined to white women. Mostly excluded from white women's clubs, African American women had their own club movement, including the Colored Women's Federation, which sought to establish a training school for "colored girls." Founded in 1895, the National Association of Colored Women was the nation's first African American social service organization; it concentrated on establishing nurseries, kindergartens, and retirement homes. Black women also developed reform organizations within Black Baptist and African Methodist Episcopal churches.

Feminism   Around 1910, some of those concerned with women's place in society began using the term *feminism* to represent their ideas. Whereas the woman movement spoke generally of duty and moral purity, feminists emphasized rights and self-development as key to economic and sexual independence. Charlotte Perkins Gilman, a major figure in the movement, denounced Victorian notions of womanhood and articulated feminist goals in her numerous writings. Her book *Women and Economics* (1898), for example, declared that domesticity and female innocence were obsolete, and attacked men's monopoly on economic opportunity. Arguing that paid employees should handle domestic chores, such as cooking, cleaning, and childcare, Gilman asserted that modern women must have access to jobs in industry and the professions.

Margaret Sanger's Crusade   Feminists also supported a single standard of behavior for men and women, and several feminists joined the birth-control movement led by Margaret Sanger. A former visiting nurse who believed in women's rights to sexual pleasure and to determine when to have a child, Sanger helped reverse state and federal laws that had banned publication and distribution of information about sex and contraception. Her speeches and actions initially aroused opposition from those who saw birth control as a threat to family and morality, and she also was a eugenicist who perceived birth control as a means of limiting the numbers of children born to "inferior" immigrant and nonwhite mothers. Sanger persevered and in 1921 formed the American Birth Control League, enlisting physicians and social workers to convince judges to allow distribution of birth-control information. Most states still prohibited the sale of contraceptives, but Sanger succeeded in introducing the issue into public debate.

Woman Suffrage

A new generation of Progressive feminists, represented by Harriot Stanton Blatch, daughter of nineteenth-century suffragist Elizabeth Cady Stanton, carried on women's battle for the vote. Blatch had broad experience in suffrage activities, having accompanied her mother on speaking tours, and participated in the British women's suffrage movement. In America, Blatch linked voting rights to the improvement of women's working conditions. She joined the Women's Trade Union League and founded the Equality League of Self Supporting Women in 1907. Declaring that every woman worked, whether she performed paid labor or unpaid housework, Blatch believed that all women's efforts contributed to society's betterment. In her view, achievement rather than wealth and refinement was the best criterion for public status. Thus, women should exercise the vote, not to enhance the power of elites, but to promote and protect women's economic roles.

By the early twentieth century, suffragists had achieved some successes. Nine states, all in the West, allowed women to vote in state and local elections by 1912, and women continued to press for national suffrage (see Map 21.1). Their tactics ranged from persistent letter-writing and publications of the National American Woman Suffrage Association, led by Carrie Chapman Catt, to spirited meetings

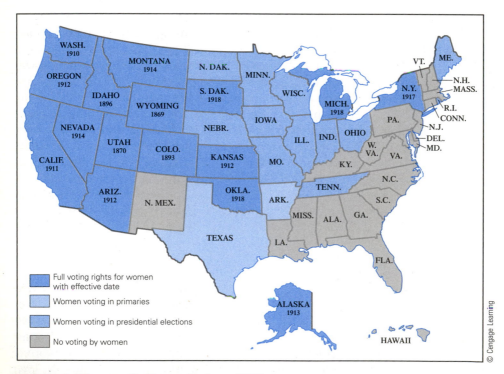

Full voting rights for women with effective date

Women voting in primaries

Women voting in presidential elections

No voting by women

© Cengage Learning

MAP 21.1 Woman Suffrage Before 1920

Before Congress passed and the states ratified the Nineteenth Amendment, woman suffrage already existed, but mainly in the West. Several Midwestern states allowed women to vote in only presidential elections, but legislatures in the South and the Northeast generally refused such rights until forced to do so by constitutional amendment.

and militant marches of the National Woman's Party, led by Alice Paul and Harriot Stanton Blatch. All these activities heightened public awareness. More decisive, however, was women's service during the First World War as factory laborers, medical volunteers, and municipal workers. By convincing legislators that women could shoulder public responsibilities, women's wartime contributions gave final impetus to passage of the national suffrage amendment (the Nineteenth) in 1920.

In spite of these accomplishments, the activities of women's clubs, feminists, and suffragists failed to create an interest group united or powerful enough to overcome men's political, economic, and social power. During the Progressive era, the resolve and energy of leaders like Blatch, Paul, and Catt helped clarify issues that concerned women and finally won women the right to vote, but that victory was only a step, not a conclusion. Discrimination in employment, education, and law continued to shadow women for decades to come. As feminist Crystal Eastman observed in the aftermath of the suffrage crusade: "Men are saying perhaps, 'Thank God, this everlasting women's fight is over!' But women, if I know them, are saying, 'Now at last we can begin.' … Now they can say what they are really after, in common with all the rest of the struggling world, is freedom."

THEODORE ROOSEVELT AND REVIVAL OF THE PRESIDENCY

The Progressive era's theme of reform in politics, institutions, and social relations drew attention to government, especially the federal government, as the foremost agent of change. Although the federal government had notable accomplishments during the preceding Gilded Age, its role had been mainly to support rather than control economic expansion, as when it transferred western public lands and resources to private ownership. Then, in September 1901, the political climate suddenly shifted. The assassination of President William McKinley by anarchist Leon Czolgosz vaulted Theodore Roosevelt, the young vice president (he was forty-two), into the White House. As governor of New York, Roosevelt had angered state Republican bosses by showing sympathy for regulatory legislation, so they rid themselves of him by pushing him into national politics. Little did they anticipate that they provided the steppingstone for the nation's most forceful president since Lincoln, one who bestowed the office with much of its twentieth-century character.

Theodore Roosevelt

As a youth, Roosevelt suffered from asthma and nearsightedness. Driven throughout his life by an obsession to overcome his physical limitations, he exerted what he and his contemporaries called "manliness," meaning a zest for action and display of courage in a "strenuous life." In his teens, he became a marksman and horseman, and later competed on Harvard's boxing and wrestling teams. In the 1880s, he went to live on a Dakota ranch, where he roped cattle and brawled with cowboys. Descended from a Dutch aristocratic family, Roosevelt had the wealth to indulge in such pursuits. But he also inherited a sense of civic responsibility that guided him into a career in public service. He served three terms in the New York legislature, sat on the federal Civil Service Commission, served as New York City's

California Museum of Photography, University of California

Theodore Roosevelt (1858–1919) liked to think of himself as a great outdoorsman. He loved most the rugged countryside and believed that he and his country should serve as examples of "manliness."

police commissioner, and was assistant secretary of the navy. In these offices Roosevelt earned a reputation as a combative, politically crafty leader. In 1898, he thrust himself into the Spanish-American War by organizing a volunteer cavalry brigade, called the Rough Riders, to fight in Cuba. Although his dramatic act had little impact on the war's outcome, it excited public imagination and made him a media hero.

Roosevelt carried his youthful exuberance into the White House. (A British diplomat once quipped, "You must always remember that the president is about 6.") Considering himself a Progressive, he concurred with his allies that a small, uninvolved government would not suffice in the industrial era. Instead, economic progress necessitated a government powerful enough to guide national affairs. "A simple and poor society," he observed, "can exist as a democracy on the basis of sheer individualism. But a rich and complex society cannot so exist." Especially in economic matters, Roosevelt wanted government to act as an umpire, deciding when big business was good and when it was bad. But his brash patriotism and dislike of qualities that he considered effeminate also recalled earlier eras of unbridled expansion, when raw power prevailed in social and economic affairs.

Regulation of Trusts   The federal regulation of business that has since character-ized American history began with Roosevelt's presidency. Roosevelt turned attention first to massive trusts created in previous decades by corporate consolidation. Although labeled a trustbuster, Roosevelt actually considered business consolidation an efficient means to achieve material progress. He believed in distinguishing between good and bad trusts, and preventing bad ones from manipulating markets. Thus, he instructed the Justice Department to use antitrust laws to prosecute railroad, meatpacking, and oil trusts, which he believed unscrupulously exploited the public. Roosevelt's policy tri-umphed in 1904 when the Supreme Court, convinced by the government's argu-ments, ordered the breakup of Northern Securities Company, the huge railroad combination created by J. P. Morgan. Roosevelt chose, however, not to attack other trusts, such as U.S. Steel, another of Morgan's creations.

When prosecution of Northern Securities began, Morgan reportedly collared Roosevelt and offered, "If we have done anything wrong, send your man to my man and they can fix it up." The president refused but was more sympathetic to cooperation between business and government than his rebuff might suggest. Rather than prosecute at every turn, he urged the Bureau of Corporations (part of the newly created Department of Labor and Commerce) to assist companies in merging and expanding. Through investigation and consultation, the administration cajoled busi-nesses to regulate themselves; corporations often cooperated because government reg-ulation helped them operate more efficiently and reduced overproduction.

Roosevelt also supported regulatory legislation, especially after his resounding electoral victory in 1904, in which he won votes from Progressives and businesspeo-ple alike. After a year of wrangling with railroads and their political allies, Roose-velt persuaded Congress to pass the Hepburn Act (1906), which strengthened the Interstate Commerce Commission (ICC) by giving it authority to view railroad financial records and set railroad "just and reasonable" freight rates and extending that authority over ferries, express companies, storage facilities, and oil pipelines. In the Elkins Act of 1903, Congress had already allowed the ICC to levy heavy fines against railroads and their customers involved in rebates on published shipping rates. The Hepburn Act still allowed courts to overturn ICC decisions, but in a break from previous laws, it required shippers to prove they were not in violation of regulations, rather than making the government demonstrate violations.

Pure Food and Drug Laws   Knowing that the political process made it difficult to achieve full business regulation, Roosevelt showed willing-ness to compromise on legislation to ensure the purity of food and drugs. For decades, reformers had been urging government regulation of pro-cessed meat and patent medicines. Public outrage at fraud and adulteration flared in 1906 when Upton Sinclair published *The Jungle,* a fictionalized exposé of Chicago meatpacking plants. Sinclair, a socialist whose objective was to improve working conditions, shocked public sensibilities with vivid descriptions.

> There would be meat stored in great piles in rooms; and the water from the leaky roofs would drip over it, and thousands of rats would race about on it. It was too dark in these storage places to see well, but a man could run his hand over these piles of meat

and sweep off handfuls of dried dung of rats. These rats were a nuisance, and the packers would put poisoned bread out for them; they would die, and then rats, bread, and meat would go into the hoppers together.

After reading the novel, Roosevelt ordered an investigation. Finding Sinclair's descriptions accurate, he supported the Meat Inspection Act, which passed Congress in 1906. Like the Hepburn Act, this law reinforced the principle of government regulation, requiring that government agents monitor the quality of processed meat. But as part of a compromise with meatpackers and their congressional allies, the bill provided that the government, rather than the meatpackers, had to finance inspections, and meatpackers could appeal adverse decisions in court. Nor were companies required to provide date-of-processing information on canned meats. Most large meatpackers welcomed the legislation anyway because it restored foreign confidence in American meat products.

The Pure Food and Drug Act (1906) not only prohibited dangerously adulterated foods but also addressed abuses in the patent medicine industry. Makers of tonics and pills had long been making undue claims about their products' effects and liberally using alcohol and narcotics as ingredients. Ads in popular publications, like one for a "Brain Stimulator and Nerve Tonic" in the Sears, Roebuck catalogue, made wildly exaggerated claims. Although the law did not ban such products, it required that labels list the ingredients—a goal consistent with Progressive confidence that if people knew the facts they would make wiser purchases.

Roosevelt's approach to labor resembled his compromises with business over matters of regulation. When the United Mine Workers struck against Pennsylvania coal-mine owners in 1902 over an eight-hour workday and higher pay, the president urged arbitration between the conflicting parties. Owners, however, refused to recognize the union or to arbitrate grievances. As winter approached and nationwide fuel shortages threatened, Roosevelt roused public opinion. He threatened to use federal troops to reopen the mines, thus forcing management to accept arbitration of the dispute by a special commission. The commission decided in favor of higher wages and reduced hours and required management to deal with grievance committees elected by the miners. But in a compromise with management, it did not mandate recognition of the union. The decision, according to Roosevelt, provided a "square deal" for all. The settlement also embodied Roosevelt's belief that the president or his representatives should determine which labor demands were legitimate and which were not. In Roosevelt's mind, there were good and bad labor organizations (socialists, for example, were bad), just as there were good and bad business combinations.

Race Relations   Although he angered southern congressmen by inviting Booker T. Washington to the White House to discuss racial matters, Roosevelt believed in white superiority and was neutral toward blacks only when it helped him politically. An incident in 1906 illustrates this belief. That year, the army transferred a battalion of African American soldiers from Nebraska to Brownsville, Texas. Anglo and Mexican residents resented their presence and banned them from parks and businesses. They also protested unsuccessfully to

Washington. On August 14, a battle between blacks and whites broke out, and a white man was killed. Brownsville residents blamed the soldiers, but when army investigators asked the troops to identify who had participated in the riot, none of the soldiers cooperated. As a result, Roosevelt discharged 167 black soldiers without a hearing or trial, and prevented them from receiving their pay and pensions even though there was no evidence against them. Black leaders were outraged. Roosevelt, hoping that blacks would support Republican candidates in the 1906 elections, had stalled before doing anything. But after the elections, he signed the discharge papers and offered no support when a bill was introduced in the Senate to allow the soldiers to reenlist.

Conservation

Roosevelt combined the Progressive impulse for efficiency with his love for the outdoors to make lasting contributions to resource conservation. Government involvement in this endeavor, especially the establishment of national parks, had begun in the late nineteenth century. Roosevelt advanced the movement by favoring *conservation* over *preservation*. He not only exercised presidential power to protect such natural wonders as the Olympic Peninsula in Washington and the Grand Canyon in Arizona, as well as such human marvels as the native cliff dwellings in Colorado and Arizona, by declaring them national monuments, but also backed a policy of "wise use" of forests, waterways, and other resources in order to conserve them for future generations. Previously, the government had transferred ownership and control of natural resources on federal land to the states and private interests. Roosevelt, however, believed the most efficient way to use and conserve resources would be for the federal government to retain management over lands that remained in the public domain.

Roosevelt used federal authority over resources in several ways. He created five national parks and fifty-one national bird reservations, protected waterpower sites from sale to private interests, and charged permit fees for users who wanted to produce hydroelectricity. He also supported the Newlands Reclamation Act of 1902, which controlled sale of irrigated federal land in the West, and in 1908 he brought the nation's governors to the White House to discuss the efficient use of resources. During his presidency, Roosevelt tripled the number and acreage of national forests and backed conservationist Gifford Pinchot in creating the U.S. Forest Service.

Gifford Pinchot

As chief forester of the United States and principal advocate of "wise use" policy, Pinchot promoted scientific management of the nation's woodlands. He obtained Roosevelt's support for transferring management of the national forests from the Interior Department to his bureau in the Agriculture Department, arguing that forests were crops grown on "tree farms." Under his guidance, the Forest Service charged fees for grazing livestock within the national forests, supervised bidding for the cutting of timber, and hired university-trained foresters as federal employees.

Pinchot and Roosevelt did not seek to lock up—preserve—resources permanently; rather, they wanted to guarantee—conserve—their efficient use and make those who profited from using public lands pay the government for that use.

Although antigovernment, pro-development attitudes still prevailed in the West, many of those involved in natural-resource exploitation welcomed such a policy because, like regulation of food and drugs, it enabled them to have better control over products, such as when Roosevelt and Pinchot encouraged lumber companies to engage in reforestation. As a result of new federal policies, the West and its resources fell under the Progressive spell of expert management.

Panic of 1907   In 1907, economic crisis forced Roosevelt to compromise his principles and work more closely with big business. That year, a financial panic caused by reckless speculation forced some New York banks to close in order to prevent frightened depositors from withdrawing money. J. P. Morgan helped stem the panic by persuading financiers to stop dumping stocks. In return for Morgan's aid, Roosevelt approved a deal allowing U.S. Steel to absorb the Tennessee Iron and Coal Company—a deal at odds with Roosevelt's trustbusting aims.

But during his last year in office, Roosevelt retreated from the Republican Party's traditional friendliness to big business. He lashed out at irresponsible "malefactors of great wealth" and supported stronger business regulation and heavier taxation of the rich. Having promised that he would not seek reelection, Roosevelt backed his friend, Secretary of War William Howard Taft, for the Republican nomination in 1908, hoping that Taft would continue his initiatives. Democrats nominated William Jennings Bryan for the third time, but the "Great Commoner" lost again. Aided by Roosevelt, who still enjoyed great popularity, Taft won by 1.25 million popular votes and a 2-to-1 margin in the electoral college.

Taft Administration   Early in 1909, Roosevelt traveled to Africa to shoot game, leaving Taft to face political problems that Roosevelt had managed to postpone. Foremost was the tariff; rates had risen to excessive levels. Honoring Taft's pledge to cut tariffs, the House passed a bill sponsored by Representative Sereno E. Payne that provided for numerous reductions. Protectionists in the Senate prepared, as in the past, to amend the bill and revise rates upward. But Senate Progressives, led by La Follette, attacked the tariff for benefiting special interests, trapping Taft between reformers who claimed to be preserving Roosevelt's antitrust campaign and protectionists who still dominated the Republican Party. In the end, Senator Aldrich restored most cuts the Payne bill had made, and Taft—who believed the bill had some positive provisions and understood that extreme cuts were not politically possible—signed what became known as the Payne-Aldrich Tariff (1909). In Progressives' eyes, Taft had failed the test of filling Roosevelt's shoes.

Progressive and conservative wings of the Republican Party openly split. Soon after the tariff controversy, a group of insurgents in the House, led by Nebraska's George Norris, challenged Speaker "Uncle Joe" Cannon of Illinois, whose power over committee assignments and the scheduling of debates could make or break a piece of legislation. Taft first supported, then abandoned, the insurgents, who nevertheless managed to liberalize procedures by enlarging the influential Rules

Committee and removing selection of its members from Cannon's control. In 1910, Taft also angered conservationists by firing Gifford Pinchot, who had protested Secretary of the Interior Richard A. Ballinger's plans to aid private development by selling Alaskan coal lands and reducing federal supervision of western waterpower sites.

In reality, Taft was as sympathetic to reform as Roosevelt was. He prosecuted more trusts than Roosevelt; expanded national forest reserves; signed the Mann-Elkins Act (1910), which bolstered regulatory powers of the ICC; and supported such labor reforms as shorter work hours and mine safety legislation. The Sixteenth Amendment, which legalized the federal income tax as a permanent part of federal power, and the Seventeenth Amendment, which provided for direct election of U.S. senators, were initiated during Taft's presidency (and ratified in 1913). Like Roosevelt, Taft compromised with big business, but unlike Roosevelt, he lacked the ability to manipulate the public with spirited rhetoric. Roosevelt had expanded presidential power and infused the presidency with vitality. "I believe in a strong executive," he once asserted. "I believe in power." Taft, by contrast, believed in the strict restraint of law. He had been a successful lawyer and judge, and returned to the bench as chief justice of the United States between 1921 and 1930. His caution and unwillingness to offend disappointed those accustomed to Roosevelt's magnetism.

Candidates in 1912

In 1910, when Roosevelt returned from Africa, he found his party torn and tormented. Reformers, angered by Taft's apparent insensitivity to their causes, formed the National Progressive Republican League and rallied behind Robert La Follette for president in 1912, though many hoped Roosevelt would run. Another wing of the party remained loyal to Taft. Disappointed by Taft's performance (particularly his firing of Pinchot), Roosevelt began to speak out. He filled speeches with references to "the welfare of the people" and stronger regulation of business. When La Follette became ill early in 1912, Roosevelt, proclaiming himself fit as a "bull moose," threw his hat into the ring for the Republican presidential nomination.

Taft's supporters controlled the Republican convention and nominated him for a second term. In protest, Roosevelt's supporters bolted the convention to form a third party—the Progressive, or Bull Moose, Party—and nominated the fifty-three-year-old former president. Meanwhile, Democrats took forty-six ballots to select their candidate, New Jersey's Progressive governor Woodrow Wilson. Socialists, by now an organized and growing party, again nominated Eugene V. Debs. The ensuing campaign exposed voters to the most thorough debate on the nature of American democracy since 1896.

New Nationalism Versus New Freedom

Central to Theodore Roosevelt's campaign as the Progressive Party's nominee was a scheme called the New Nationalism, a term coined by reform editor Herbert Croly. The New Nationalism envisioned an era of national unity in which government would coordinate and regulate economic activity. Echoing his statements made in the last years of his presidency, Roosevelt asserted that he would establish regulatory commissions of experts who would protect citizens' interests and ensure wise use of economic power. "The effort at prohibiting all combinations has substantially failed," he claimed. "The way out lies ... in completely controlling them."

Wilson offered a more idealistic proposal, the "New Freedom," based on ideas of Progressive lawyer Louis Brandeis. Wilson argued that concentrated economic power threatened individual liberty and that monopolies should be broken up so that the marketplace could become genuinely open. But he would not restore laissez faire. Like Roosevelt, Wilson would enhance government authority to protect and regulate. "Freedom today," he declared, "is something more than being let alone. Without the watchful ... resolute interference of the government, there can be no fair play between individuals and such powerful institutions as the trust." Wilson stopped short, however, of advocating the cooperation between business and government inherent in Roosevelt's New Nationalism.

Roosevelt and Wilson stood closer together than their rhetoric implied. Despite his faith in experts as regulators, Roosevelt's belief in individual freedom was as strong as Wilson's. And Wilson was not completely hostile to concentrated economic power. Both men supported equality of opportunity (chiefly for white males), conservation of natural resources, fair wages, and social betterment. Neither would hesitate to expand government intervention through strong personal leadership and bureaucratic reform.

Amid passionate moral pronouncements from Roosevelt and Wilson, as well as a hard-hitting critique from Debs and a low-key defense of conservatism from Taft, the popular vote was inconclusive. The victorious Wilson won just 42 percent, though he did capture 435 out of 531 electoral votes. Roosevelt received 27 percent of the popular vote. Taft finished third, polling 23 percent and only 8 electoral votes. Debs won 6 percent but no electoral votes. One major outcome was evident, however; three-quarters of the electorate supported some alternative to the view of restrained government that Taft represented. Thus, Wilson could proclaim on inauguration day in 1913, "The Nation has been deeply stirred by a solemn passion.... The feelings with which we face this new age of right and opportunity sweep across our heartstrings like some air out of God's own presence, where justice and mercy are reconciled and the judge and the brother are one."

WOODROW WILSON AND EXTENSION OF PROGRESSIVE REFORM

Woodrow Wilson   The public fondly called Roosevelt "Teddy" and "TR," but Thomas Woodrow Wilson was too aloof to be nicknamed "Woody" or "WW." Born in Virginia in 1856 and raised in the South, Wilson was the son of a Presbyterian minister. He earned a B.A. degree at Princeton University (and served as the university's president from 1902 to 1920), studied law at the University of Virginia, received a Ph.D. degree from Johns Hopkins University, and became a professor of history, jurisprudence, and political economy. Between 1885 and 1908, he published several respected books on American history and government.

Wilson's manner and attitudes reflected his background. On one hand, he was a superb orator who could inspire intense loyalty with religious imagery and eloquent expressions of American ideals. But he harbored strong disdain for African Americans; he wrote that slaves were treated "indulgently," belittled blacks who held office during Reconstruction, had no misgivings about Jim Crow laws, and opposed admitting blacks to Princeton. At Princeton, he upset tradition with curricular reforms and battles against the university's aristocratic elements and earned enough of a reputation as a reformer so that in 1910 New Jersey's Democrats, eager for respectability, nominated Wilson for governor. After winning the election, Wilson repudiated the party bosses and promoted Progressive legislation. A poor administrator, he often lost his temper and stubbornly refused to compromise. His accomplishments nevertheless attracted national attention and won him the Democratic nomination for president in 1912.

Wilson's Policy on Business Regulation   As president, Wilson found it necessary to blend New Freedom competition with New Nationalism regulation; in so doing, he set the direction of future federal economic policy.

Corporate consolidation had made restoration of open competition impossible. Wilson could only try to prevent abuses by expanding government's regulatory powers. He thus supported congressional passage in 1914 of the Clayton Anti-Trust Act and a bill creating the Federal Trade Commission (FTC). The Clayton Act corrected deficiencies of the Sherman Anti-Trust Act of 1890 by outlawing such practices as price discrimination (lowering prices in some regions but not in others) and interlocking directorates (management of two or more competing companies by the same executives). The act also aided labor by exempting unions from its anticombination provision, thereby making peaceful strikes, boycotts, and picketing less vulnerable to government interference. The FTC could investigate companies and issue cease-and-desist orders against unfair practices. Accused companies could appeal FTC orders in court; nevertheless, the FTC represented another step toward consumer protection.

Also under Wilson, the Federal Reserve Act (1913) established the nation's first central banking system since 1836. To break the power that syndicates like that of J. P. Morgan held over the money supply, the act created twelve district banks to hold reserves of member banks throughout the nation. The district banks, supervised by the Federal Reserve Board, would lend money to member banks at a low interest rate called the discount rate. By adjusting this rate (and thus the amount a member bank could afford to borrow), district banks could increase or decrease the amount of money in circulation. In other words, in response to the nation's economic needs, the Federal Reserve Board could loosen or tighten credit, making interest rates fairer, especially for small borrowers.

Tariff and Tax Reform   Wilson and Congress attempted to restore trade competition and aid consumers with the Underwood Tariff of 1913. By reducing or eliminating certain tariff rates, the Underwood Tariff encouraged importation of cheaper foreign materials and manufactured goods. To replace revenues lost because of tariff reductions, the act levied a

Depicted here as a stern Roman consul, Woodrow Wilson was a former professor (his university background is represented here by the scholarly owl at his side) who as president used a stubborn moralism to guide the nation toward his ideals.

EXECVTRIX
AVGVSTA
     MINERVA
LVMINARIA !

SALVE
  O WOODREGINA
ATHENA
      PROLETARIA!
PRINCETONIENSIS
     POPVLIOVE
DEA
     TVTORLARIA
           !

graduated income tax on U.S. residents—an option made possible when the Sixteenth Amendment was ratified earlier that year. The tax was tame by today's standards. Incomes under $4,000 were exempt; thus, almost all factory workers and farmers escaped taxation. Individuals and corporations earning between $4,000 and $20,000 had to pay a 1 percent tax; thereafter rates rose to a maximum of 6 percent on earnings over $500,000.

The outbreak of the First World War (see Chapter 23) and the approaching presidential election campaign prompted Wilson to support stronger reforms in 1916. To aid farmers, the president backed the Federal Farm Loan Act. This measure created twelve federally supported banks (not to be confused with Federal Reserve banks), which could lend money at moderate interest to farmers who belonged to credit institutions—a diluted version of the subtreasury plan that Populists had proposed a generation earlier. To forestall railroad strikes that might disrupt transportation at a time of national emergency, Wilson in 1916 also pushed passage of the Adamson Act, which mandated eight-hour workdays and time-and-a-half overtime pay for railroad laborers. He pleased Progressives by appointing Brandeis, the "people's advocate," to the Supreme Court, though an anti-Semitic backlash almost blocked Senate approval of the Court's first Jewish justice. In addition, Wilson pleased social reformers by backing laws that regulated child labor and provided workers' compensation for federal employees who suffered work-related injuries or illness.

Amid his reforms, however, Wilson never overcame his racism. He fired several black federal officials, and his administration preserved racial separation in restrooms, restaurants, and government office buildings. Wilson responded to protesting blacks that "segregation is not a humiliation but a benefit, and ought to be so regarded by you gentlemen." When the pathbreaking but inflammatory film about the Civil War and Reconstruction, *The Birth of a Nation*, was released in 1915, Wilson allowed a showing at the White House, though he subsequently prohibited it during the First World War.

Election of 1916   In selecting a candidate to oppose Wilson in the presidential election of 1916, Republicans snubbed Theodore Roosevelt in favor of Charles Evans Hughes, Supreme Court justice and former reform governor of New York. Aware of public anxiety over the world war raging in Europe since 1914, Wilson ran on a platform of neutrality and Progressivism, using the slogan "He Kept Us Out of War." Hughes advocated greater military preparedness, but Wilson's peace platform resonated with voters. The election outcome was close. Wilson received 9.1 million votes to Hughes's 8.5 million and barely won in the electoral college, 277 to 254. The Socialist candidate drew only 600,000 votes, down from 901,000 in 1912, largely because Wilson's reforms had won over some Socialists and because the ailing Eugene Debs was no longer the party's standard-bearer.

During Wilson's second term, U.S. involvement in the First World War increased government regulation of the economy. Mobilization and war, he believed, required greater coordination of production and cooperation between the public and private sectors. The War Industries Board exemplified this cooperation: private businesses regulated by the board submitted to its control on condition that their profit motives would continue to be satisfied. After the war, Wilson's administration dropped most cooperative and regulatory measures, including farm price supports, guarantees of collective bargaining, and high taxes. This retreat from regulation, prompted in part by the election of a Republican Congress in 1918, stimulated a new era of business ascendancy in the 1920s.

SUMMARY

By 1920, a quarter-century of reform had wrought momentous changes in government, the economy, and society. In their efforts to achieve goals of ending abuses of power, reforming institutions, and applying scientific and efficient management, Progressives established the principle of public intervention to ensure fairness, health, and safety. Concern over poverty and injustice reached new heights. But reformers could not sustain their efforts indefinitely. Although Progressive values lingered after the First World War, a mass-consumer society began to refocus people's attention away from reform to materialism.

Multiple and sometimes contradictory goals characterized the era. By no means was there a single Progressive movement. Programs on the national level ranged from Roosevelt's faith in big government as a coordinator of big business to Wilson's promise to dissolve economic concentrations and legislate open competition. At state and local levels, reformers pursued causes as varied as neighborhood improvement, government reorganization, public ownership of utilities, and betterment of working conditions. National associations coordinated efforts on specific issues, but reformers with different goals often worked at cross-purposes, sometimes expanding rights but at other times restricting liberty. Women and African Americans developed new consciousness about identity, and although women made some inroads into public life, both groups still found themselves in confined social positions and lacking white male support in their quest for dignity and recognition.

In spite of their successes, the failure of many Progressive initiatives indicates the strength of the opposition as well as weaknesses within the reform movements themselves. As issues such as Americanization, eugenics, prohibition, education, and general moral uplift illustrate, social reform often merged into social control—attempts to impose one group's values on all of society and to regulate behavior of immigrant and nonwhite racial groups. In political matters, courts asserted constitutional and liberty-of-contract doctrines in striking down key Progressive legislation, notably the federal law prohibiting child labor. In states and cities, adoption of the initiative, referendum, and recall did not encourage greater participation in government as had been hoped; those mechanisms either were seldom used or became tools of special interests. Federal regulatory agencies rarely had enough resources for thorough investigations; they had to depend on information from the very companies they policed. Progressives thus failed in many respects to redistribute power. In 1920, as in 1900, government remained under the influence of business, a situation that many people in power considered quite satisfactory.

Yet the reform movements that characterized the Progressive era reshaped the national outlook. Trustbusting, however faulty, made industrialists more sensitive to public opinion, and insurgents in Congress partially diluted the power of dictatorial politicians. Progressive legislation equipped government with tools to protect consumers against price fixing and dangerous products. Social reformers relieved some ills of urban and industrial life. And perhaps most important, Progressives challenged old ways of thinking. Although the questions they raised about the quality of American life remained unresolved, Progressives made the nation acutely aware of its principles and promises.

22

THE QUEST FOR EMPIRE 1865–1914

IMPERIAL DREAMS

Foreign policy assumed a new importance for Americans in the closing years of the nineteenth century. For much of the Gilded Age, they had been preoccupied by internal matters, such as industrialization, the construction of the railroads, and the settlement of the West. Over time, however, increasing numbers of political and business leaders began to look outward, and to advocate a more activist approach to world affairs. The motives of these expansionists were complex and varied, but all of them emphasized the supposed benefits of such an approach to the country's domestic health.

That proponents of overseas expansion stressed the benefits that would accrue at home should come as no surprise, for foreign policy has always sprung from the domestic setting of a nation—its needs and moods, ideology and culture. The leaders who guided America's expansionist foreign relations were the same ones who guided the economic development of the machine age, forged the transcontinental railroad, built America's bustling cities and giant corporations, and shaped a mass culture. They unabashedly espoused the idea that the United States was an exceptional nation, so different from and superior to others because of its Anglo-Saxon heritage and its God-favored and prosperous history.

Exceptionalism was but one in an intertwined set of ideas that figured prominently in the American march toward empire. Nationalism, capitalism, Social Darwinism, and a paternalistic attitude toward foreigners influenced American leaders as well. "They are children and we are men in these deep matters of government," future president Woodrow Wilson announced in 1898. The very words he chose reveal the gender and age bias of American attitudes. Where these attitudes intersected with foreign cultures, there came not only adoption but rejection, not only imitation but clash.

CHRONOLOGY

1861–69	Seward sets expansionist course
1867	United States acquires Alaska and Midway
1876	Pro-U.S. Díaz begins thirty-four-year rule in Mexico
1878	United States gains naval rights in Samoa
1885	Strong's *Our Country* celebrates Anglo-Saxon destiny of dominance
1887	United States gains naval rights to Pearl Harbor, Hawai'i McKinley Tariff hurts Hawaiian sugar exports
1893	Economic crisis leads to business failures and mass unemployment Pro-U.S. interests stage successful coup against Queen Lili'uokalani of Hawai'i
1895	Cuban revolution against Spain begins Japan defeats China in war, annexes Korea and Formosa (Taiwan)
1898	United States formally annexes Hawai'i U.S. battleship *Maine* blows up in Havana harbor United States defeats Spain in Spanish-American War
1899	Treaty of Paris enlarges U.S. empire United Fruit Company forms and becomes influential in Central America Philippine insurrection breaks out, led by Emilio Aguinaldo
1901	McKinley assassinated; Theodore Roosevelt becomes president
1903	Panama grants canal rights to United States Platt Amendment subjugates Cuba
1904	Roosevelt Corollary declares United States a hemispheric "police power"
1905	Portsmouth Conference ends Russo-Japanese War
1906	San Francisco School Board segregates Asian schoolchildren United States invades Cuba to quell revolt
1907	"Great White Fleet" makes world tour
1910	Mexican revolution threatens U.S. interests
1914	U.S. troops invade Mexico First World War begins Panama Canal opens

Foreign Policy Elite   It would take time for most Americans to grasp the changes under way. "The people" may influence domestic policy directly, but the making of foreign policy is usually dominated by what scholars have labeled the "foreign policy elite"—opinion leaders in politics, journalism, business, agriculture, religion, education, and the military. In the post–Civil War era, this small group, whom Secretary of State Walter Q. Gresham called "the thoughtful men of the country," expressed the opinions that counted. Better read and better traveled than most Americans, more cosmopolitan in outlook, and politically active, they believed that U.S. prosperity and security depended on the exertion of U.S. influence abroad. Increasingly in the late nineteenth century, and especially in the 1890s, the expansionist-minded elite urged both formal and informal imperialism. Ambitious and clannish, the imperialists often met in Washington, D.C., at the homes of historian Henry Adams and of writer and diplomat John Hay (who became secretary of state in 1898) or at the Metropolitan Club. They talked about building a bigger navy and digging a canal across Panama, Central America, or Mexico; establishing colonies; and selling surpluses abroad. Theodore Roosevelt, appointed assistant secretary of the navy in 1897, was among them; so were Senator Henry Cabot Lodge, who joined the Foreign Relations Committee in 1896, and corporate lawyer Elihu Root, who later would serve as both secretary of war and secretary of state. Such well-positioned luminaries kept up the drumbeat for empire.

These American leaders believed that selling, buying, and investing in foreign marketplaces were important to the United States. Why? One reason was profits from foreign sales. "It is my dream," declared the governor of Georgia in 1878, to see "in every valley … a cotton factory to convert the raw material of the neighborhood into fabrics which shall warm the limbs of Japanese and Chinese." Fear also helped make the case for foreign trade, as foreign commerce might serve as a safety valve to relieve overproduction, unemployment, economic depression, and the social tension that arose from them. The nation's farms and factories produced more than Americans could consume, all the more so during the 1890s' depression. Surpluses had to be exported, the economist David A. Wells warned, or "we are certain to be smothered in our own grease." Economic ties also permitted political influence to be exerted abroad and helped spread the American way of life, especially capitalism, creating a world more hospitable to Americans. In an era when the most powerful nations in the world were also the greatest traders, vigorous foreign economic expansion symbolized national stature.

Foreign Trade Expansion   Although most business leaders remained focused on the domestic marketplace, foreign trade figured prominently in the tremendous economic growth of the United States after the Civil War. Foreign commerce in turn stimulated the building of a larger protective navy, the professionalization of the foreign service, calls for more colonies, and a more interventionist foreign policy. In 1865, U.S. exports totaled $234 million; by 1900, they had climbed to $1.5 billion. By 1914, at the outbreak of the First World War, exports had reached $2.5 billion, prompting some Europeans to protest an American "invasion" of goods. In 1874, the United States reversed its historically unfavorable balance of trade (importing more than it exported) and began to enjoy a long-term favorable balance (exporting more than it imported)—though the balance of payments remained in the red. Most of America's products went to Britain, continental Europe, and Canada, but increasing amounts flowed to new markets in Latin America and Asia. Meanwhile, direct American investments abroad reached $3.5 billion by 1914, placing the United States among the top four investor countries.

Agricultural goods accounted for about three-fourths of total exports in 1870 and about two-thirds in 1900, with grain, cotton, meat, and dairy products topping the export list that year. More than half of the annual cotton crop was exported each year. Midwestern farmers transported their crops by railroad to seaboard cities and then on to foreign markets. Farmers' livelihoods thus became tied to world-market conditions and the outcomes of foreign wars. Wisconsin cheese*makers shipped to Britain; the Swift and Armour meat companies exported refrigerated beef to Europe. To sell American grain abroad, James J. Hill of the Great Northern Railroad distributed wheat cookbooks translated into several Asian languages.

In 1913, when the United States outranked both Great Britain and Germany in manufacturing production (see Figure 22.1), manufactured goods led U.S. exports for the first time. Substantial proportions of America's steel, copper, and petroleum were sold abroad, making many workers in those industries dependent on American exports. George Westinghouse marketed his air brakes in Europe; almost as many Singer sewing machines were exported as were sold at home; and Cyrus McCormick's "reaper kings" harvested the wheat of Russian fields.

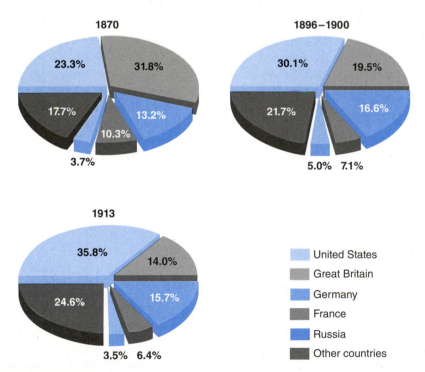

FIGURE 22.1 The Rise of U.S. Economic Power in the World

These pie charts showing percentage shares of world manufacturing production for the major nations of the world demonstrate that the United States came to surpass Great Britain in this significant economic measurement of power.

Source: Friedberg, Aaron L.; *The Weary Titan.* © 1988 Princeton University Press, 1989 paperback edition. Reprinted by permission of Princeton University Press.

Race Thinking and the Male Ethos

In promoting the expansion of U.S. influence overseas, many officials championed a nationalism based on notions of American supremacy. Some, echoing the articulations of European imperialists (who had their own conceptions of national supremacy), found justification for expansionism in racist theories then permeating western thought and politics. For decades, the western scientific establishment had classified humankind by race, and students of physical anthropology drew on phrenology and physiognomy—the analysis of skull size and shape, and the comparison of facial features—to produce a hierarchy of superior and inferior races. One well-known French researcher, for example, claimed that blacks represented a "female race" and "like the woman, the black is deprived of political and scientific intelligence; he has never created a great state ... he has never accomplished anything in industrial mechanics. But on the other hand he has great virtues of sentiment. Like women he also likes jewelry, dancing, and singing."

The language of U.S. leaders was also weighted with words like *manliness* and *weakling*. Congressman Augustus P. Gardner, son-in-law of Senator Lodge and Spanish-American War veteran, extolled the "arena of lust and blood, where true men are to be found." The warrior and president Theodore Roosevelt viewed people of color (or "darkeys," as he called them) as effeminate weaklings who lacked the ability to govern themselves and could not cope with world politics. Americans regularly debased Latin Americans as half-breeds needing close supervision, distressed damsels begging for manly rescue, or children requiring tutelage. The gendered imagery prevalent in U.S. foreign relations joined race thinking to place women, people of color, and nations weaker than the United States in the low ranks of the hierarchy of power and, hence, in a necessarily dependent status justifying U.S. dominance.

Reverend Josiah Strong's popular and influential *Our Country* (1885) celebrated an Anglo-Saxon race destined to lead others. "As America goes, so goes the world," he declared. A few years later, he wrote that "to be a Christian and an Anglo-Saxon and an American ... is to stand at the very mountaintop of privilege." Social Darwinists saw Americans as a superior people certain to overcome all competition. Secretary of State Thomas F. Bayard (1885–1889) applauded the "overflow of our population and capital" into Mexico to "saturate those regions with Americanism." But, he added, "we do not want them" until "they are fit."

Race thinking—popularized in magazine photos and cartoons, world's fairs, postcards, school textbooks, museums, and political orations—reinforced notions of American greatness, influenced the way U.S. leaders dealt with other peoples, and obviated the need to think about the subtle textures of other societies. The magazine *National Geographic*, which published its first issue in 1888, chronicled with photographs America's new overseas involvements in Asia and the Pacific. Even when smiling faces predominated in these shots, the image portrayed was that of strange, exotic, premodern peoples who had not become "Western." Fairs also put so-called uncivilized people of color on display in the "freak" or "midway" section. Dog-eating Filipinos aroused particular comment at the 1904 St. Louis World's Fair. Such racism downgraded diplomacy and justified domination and war because self-proclaimed superiors do not negotiate with people ranked as inferiors.

The same thinking permeated attitudes toward immigrants, whose entry into the United States was first restricted in these years. Although the Burlingame Treaty

LINKS TO THE WORLD

National Geographic

On a winter day in early 1888, thirty-three members of the elite Cosmos Club in Washington, D.C., convened around a mahogany table to consider "the advisability of organizing a society for the increase and diffusion of geographical knowledge."

The result was the National Geographic Society, destined to become the largest nonprofit scientific and educational institution in the world.

At the heart of the enterprise would be a magazine designed to win broad support for

National Geographic had already gone through five different cover formats when Robert Weir Crouch, an English-born Canadian decorative artist, came up with a design that cemented the magazine's visual identity. Singular and immediately recognizable, the oak-and-laurel frame on the cover of the February 1910 issue would remain largely unchanged for nearly half a century.

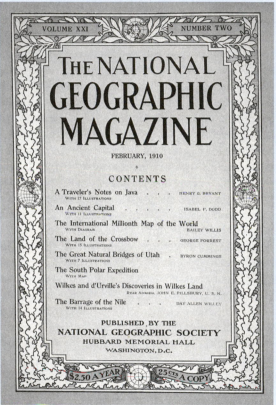

National Geographic Society Image Collection

(1868) had provided for free immigration between the United States and China, riots against Chinese immigrants erupted again and again in the American West—in Los Angeles (1871), San Francisco (1877), Denver (1880), and Seattle (1886). A new treaty in 1880 permitted Congress to suspend Chinese immigration to the United States, and it did so two years later. A violent incident occurred in Rock Springs, Wyoming, in 1885, when white coal miners and railway workers rioted and massacred at least twenty-five Chinese.

the society. *National Geographic Magazine* (later simply *National Geographic*) appeared for the first time in October 1888. Early issues were brief, technical, and visually bland, and sales lagged. In 1898, however, Alexander Graham Bell became president of the society and made two key changes: he shifted emphasis from newsstand sales to society membership, reasoning correctly that armchair travelers would flock to join a distinguished fellowship, and he appointed a talented new editor, Gilbert H. Grosvenor, age twenty-three. Grosvenor commissioned articles of general interest and, in an unprecedented move, filled eleven pages of one issue with photographs.

These and other early photos showed people stiffly posed in their native costumes, displayed as anthropological specimens. But they caused a sensation. By 1908, pictures occupied 50 percent of the magazine's space. In 1910, the first color photographs appeared, in a twenty-four-page spread on Korea and China—at that time the largest collection of color photographs ever published in a single issue of any magazine. In later years, *National Geographic* would have several other photographic firsts, including the first natural-color photos of Arctic life and the undersea world.

The society also used membership dues to sponsor expeditions, such as the 1909 journey to the North Pole by Robert Peary and Matthew Henson and, later, Jacques Cousteau's many oceanic explorations and Jane Goodall's up-close observations of wild chimpanzees. The tales of these adventures then appeared in the magazine's pages, along with stunning photographs. By the end of Grosvenor's tenure as editor, in 1954, circulation had grown to more than 2 million.

Grosvenor's winning formula included less-admirable elements. His editors pressured photographers to provide "pictures of pretty girls" to the point at which, as one photographer recalled, "hundreds of bare-breasted women, all from poorer countries, were published at a time of booming subscription rates." Editors also developed a well-earned reputation for avoiding controversial issues and presenting a rosy view of the world. An article about Berlin published just before the start of World War II, for example, contained no criticism of the Nazi regime and no mention of its persecution of Jews. Recent years have seen the magazine take on more newsworthy items—AIDS, stem cell research, Hurricane Katrina, global warming—but in measured, generally nonpolitical tones.

Throughout, the society has continued to expand its reach, moving into the production of books, atlases, globes, and television documentaries. Targeting overseas readers, the society in 1995 launched a Japanese-language edition and subsequently added twenty-five other foreign editions. *National Geographic*, after a century of linking Americans to faraway places, now went in the other direction, connecting readers in many of those locales to the United States.

In 1906, the San Francisco School Board, reflecting the anti-Asian bias of many West Coast Americans, ordered the segregation of all Chinese, Koreans, and Japanese in special schools. Tokyo protested the discrimination against its citizens. The following year, President Roosevelt quieted the crisis by striking a "gentleman's agreement" with Tokyo restricting the inflow of Japanese immigrants; San Francisco then rescinded its segregation order. Relations with Tokyo were jolted again in 1913 when the California legislature denied Japanese residents the right to own property in the state.

The "Civilizing"
Impulse

With a mixture of self-interest and idealism typical of American thinking on foreign policy, expansionists believed that empire benefited both Americans and those who came under their control. When the United States intervened in other lands or lectured weaker states, Americans claimed that in remaking foreign societies they were extending liberty and prosperity to less fortunate people. William Howard Taft, as civil governor of the Philippines (1901–1904), described the United States' mission in its new colony as lifting Filipinos up "to a point of civilization" that will make them "call the name of the United States blessed." Later, after becoming secretary of war (1904–1908), Taft said about the Chinese that "the more civilized they become ... the wealthier they become, and the better market they become for us." "The world is to be Christianized and civilized," declared Reverend Josiah Strong. "And what is the process of civilizing but the creating of more and higher wants."

Missionaries dispatched to Africa and Asia helped spur the transfer of American culture and power abroad—"the peaceful conquest of the world," as Reverend Frederick Gates put it. One organization, the Student Volunteers for Foreign Missions, began in the 1880s on college campuses and by 1914 had placed some 6,000 missionaries abroad. In 1915 a total of 10,000 American missionaries worked overseas. In China by 1915, more than 2,500 American Protestant missionaries—most of them female—labored to preach the gospel, teach school, and administer medical care.

AMBITIONS AND STRATEGIES

The U.S. empire grew gradually, sometimes haltingly, as American leaders defined guiding principles and built institutions to support overseas ambitions. William H. Seward, one of its chief architects, argued relentlessly for extension of the American frontier as senator from New York (1849–1861) and secretary of state (1861–1869). "There is not in the history of the Roman Empire an ambition for aggrandizement so marked as that which characterizes the American people," he once said. Seward envisioned a large, coordinated U.S. empire encompassing Canada, the Caribbean, Cuba, Central America, Mexico, Hawai'i, Iceland, Greenland, and the Pacific islands. This empire would be built not by war but by a natural process of gravitation toward the United States. Commerce would hurry the process, as would a canal across Central America, a transcontinental American railroad to link up with Asian markets, and a telegraph system to speed communications.

Seward's Quest
for Empire

Most of Seward's grandiose plans did not reach fruition in his own day. In 1867, for example, he signed a treaty with Denmark to buy the Danish West Indies (Virgin Islands), but his domestic political foes in the Senate and a hurricane that wrecked St. Thomas scuttled his effort. The Virgin Islanders, who had voted for annexation, had to wait until 1917 for official U.S. status. Also doomed to failure was Seward's scheme with unscrupulous Dominican Republic leaders to gain a Caribbean naval base at Samaná Bay. The stench of corruption rising over this unsavory deal-making wafted into the Ulysses S. Grant administration and foiled Grant's initiative in 1870 to buy the entire island nation. The Senate rejected annexation.

Anti-imperialism, not just politics, blocked Seward. Opponents of empire such as Senator Carl Schurz and E. L. Godkin, editor of the magazine *The Nation*, argued that the country already had enough unsettled land and that creating a showcase of democracy and prosperity at home would best persuade other peoples to adopt American institutions and principles. Some anti-imperialists, sharing the racism of the times, opposed the annexation of territory populated by dark-skinned people.

Seward did enjoy some successes. In 1866, citing the Monroe Doctrine, he sent troops to the border with Mexico and demanded that France abandon its puppet regime there. Also facing angry Mexican nationalists, Napoleon III abandoned the Maximilian monarchy that he had installed by force three years earlier. In 1867, Seward paid Russia $7.2 million for the 591,000 square miles of Alaska—land twice the size of Texas. Some critics lampooned "Seward's Icebox," but the secretary of state extolled the Russian territory's rich natural resources, and the Senate voted overwhelmingly for the treaty. That same year, Seward laid claim to the Midway Islands (two small islands and a coral atoll northwest of Hawai'i, so named because they are nearly halfway between North America and Asia) in the Pacific Ocean.

International Communications   Seward realized his dream of a world knit together by a giant communications system. In 1866, through the persevering efforts of financier Cyrus Field, an underwater transatlantic cable linked European and American telegraph networks. Backed by J. P. Morgan's capital, communications pioneer James A. Scrymser strung telegraph lines to Latin America, entering Chile in 1890. In 1903, a submarine cable reached across the Pacific to the Philippines; three years later, it extended to Japan and China. Information about markets, crises, and war flowed steadily and quickly. Wire telegraphy—like radio (wireless telegraphy) later—shrank the globe. Drawn closer to one another through improved communications and transportation, nations found that faraway events had more and more impact on their prosperity and security. Because of the communications revolution, "every nation elbows other nations today," observed Amherst College professor Edwin Grosvenor in 1898.

More and more, American diplomats found that they could enter negotiations with their European counterparts on roughly equal terms—a sure sign that the United States had arrived on the international stage. Washington officials, for example, successfully confronted European powers in a contest over Samoa, a group of beautiful South Pacific islands located 4,000 miles from San Francisco on the trade route to Australia. In 1878, the United States gained exclusive right to a coaling station at Samoa's coveted port of Pago Pago. Eyeing the same prize, Britain and Germany began to cultivate ties with Samoan leaders. Year by year tensions grew, as the powers dispatched warships to Samoa and aggravated factionalism among Samoa's chiefs. War seemed possible. At the eleventh hour, however, Britain, Germany, and the United States met in Berlin in 1889 and, without consulting the Samoans, devised a three-part protectorate that limited Samoa's independence. Ten years later, the three powers partitioned Samoa: the United States received Pago Pago through annexation of part of the islands (now called American Samoa and administered by the U.S. Department of the Interior); Germany took what is today independent Western Samoa; and Britain, for renouncing its claims to Samoa, obtained the Gilbert Islands and the Solomon Islands.

Alfred T. Mahan   With eyes on all parts of the world, even on Africa, where
and Navalism   U.S. interests were minimal, ardent expansionists embraced
navalism—the campaign to build an imperial navy. Calling
attention to the naval buildup by the European powers, notably Germany, they
argued for a bigger, modernized navy, adding the "blue water" command of the
seas to its traditional role of "brown water" coastline defense and riverine operations. Captain Alfred Thayer Mahan became a major popularizer for this "New
Navy." Because foreign trade was vital to the United States, he argued, the nation
required an efficient navy to protect its shipping; in turn, a navy required colonies
for bases. "Whether they will or no," Mahan wrote, "Americans must now begin
to look outward. The growing production of the country demands it." Mahan's
lectures at the Naval War College in Newport, Rhode Island, where he served as
president, were published as *The Influence of Sea Power upon History* (1890). This
book sat on every serious expansionist's shelf, and foreign leaders turned its pages.
Theodore Roosevelt and Henry Cabot Lodge eagerly consulted Mahan, sharing his
belief in the links among trade, navy, and colonies, and his growing alarm over
"the aggressive military spirit" of Germany.

Moving toward naval modernization, Congress in 1883 authorized construction of the first steel-hulled warships. American factories went to work to produce
steam engines, high-velocity shells, powerful guns, and precision instruments. The
navy shifted from sail power to steam and from wood construction to steel. Often
named for states and cities to kindle patriotism and local support for naval expansion, New Navy ships, such as the *Maine*, *Oregon*, and *Boston*, thrust the United
States into naval prominence, especially during crises in the 1890s.

CRISES IN THE 1890S: HAWAI'I, VENEZUELA, AND CUBA

In the depression-plagued 1890s, crises in Hawai'i and Cuba gave expansionist
Americans opportunities to act on their zealous arguments for what Senator Lodge
called a "large policy." Belief that the frontier at home had closed accentuated the
expansionist case. In 1893, historian Frederick Jackson Turner postulated that an
ever-expanding continental frontier had shaped the American character. That
"frontier has gone," Turner pronounced, "and with its going has closed the first
period of American history." He did not explicitly say that a new frontier had to
be found overseas in order to sustain the American way of life, but he did claim
that "American energy will continually demand a wider field for its exercise."

Annexation   Hawai'i, the Pacific Ocean archipelago of eight major islands
of Hawai'i   located 2,000 miles from the West Coast of the United States,
emerged as a new frontier for Americans. The Hawaiian Islands
had long commanded American attention—commercial, missionary religious, naval,
and diplomatic. Wide-eyed U.S. expansionists envisioned ships sailing from the eastern
seaboard through a Central American canal to Hawai'i and then on to the fabled China
market. By 1881, Secretary of State James Blaine had already declared the Hawaiian
Islands "essentially a part of the American system." By 1890, Americans owned about
three-quarters of Hawai'i's wealth and subordinated its economy to that of the United
States through sugar exports that entered the U.S. marketplace duty-free.

In Hawaiʻi's multiracial society, Chinese and Japanese nationals far outnumbered Americans, who represented a mere 2.1 percent of the population. Prominent Americans on the islands—lawyers, businessmen, and sugar planters, many of them the sons of missionaries—organized secret clubs and military units to contest the royal government. In 1887, they forced the king to accept a constitution that granted foreigners the right to vote and shifted decision-making authority from the monarchy to the legislature. The same year, Hawaiʻi granted the United States naval rights to Pearl Harbor. Many native Hawaiians (53 percent of the population in 1890) believed that the *haole* (foreigners)—especially Americans—were taking their country from them.

The McKinley Tariff of 1890 created an economic crisis for Hawaiʻi that further undermined the native government. The tariff eliminated the duty-free status of Hawaiian sugar exports in the United States. Suffering declining sugar prices and profits, the American island elite pressed for annexation of the islands by the United States so that their sugar would be classified as domestic rather than foreign. When Princess Liliʻuokalani assumed the throne in 1891, she sought to roll back the political power of the *haole*. The next year, the white oligarchy—questioning her moral rectitude, fearing Hawaiian nationalism, and reeling from the McKinley Tariff—formed the subversive Annexation Club.

The annexationists struck in January 1893 in collusion with John L. Stevens, the chief American diplomat in Hawaiʻi, who dispatched troops from the USS Boston to occupy Honolulu. The queen, arrested and confined, surrendered. However, rather than yield to the new provisional regime, headed by Sanford B. Dole, son of missionaries and a prominent attorney, she relinquished authority to the U.S. government. Up went the American flag. "The Hawaiian pear is now fully ripe and this is the golden hour to pluck it," a triumphant Stevens informed Washington. Against the queen's protests as well as those of Japan, President Benjamin Harrison hurriedly sent an annexation treaty to the Senate.

Sensing foul play, incoming President Grover Cleveland ordered an investigation, which confirmed a conspiracy by the economic elite in league with Stevens and noted that most Hawaiians opposed annexation. Down came the American flag. But when Hawaiʻi gained renewed attention as a strategic and commercial way station to Asia and the Philippines during the Spanish-American War, President William McKinley maneuvered annexation through Congress on July 7, 1898, by means of a majority vote (the Newlands Resolution) rather than by a treaty, which would have required a two-thirds count. Under the Organic Act of June 1900, the people of Hawaiʻi became U.S. citizens with the right to vote in local elections and to send a nonvoting delegate to Congress. Statehood for Hawaiʻi came in 1959.

Venezuelan Boundary Dispute   The Venezuelan crisis of 1895 also saw the United States in an expansive mood. For decades Venezuela and Great Britain had quarreled over the border between Venezuela and British Guiana. The disputed territory contained rich gold deposits and the mouth of the Orinoco River, a commercial gateway to northern South America. Venezuela asked for U.S. help. President Cleveland decided that the "mean and hoggish" British had to be warned away. In July 1895, Secretary of State Richard Olney brashly lectured the British that the Monroe Doctrine prohibited European powers from denying self-government to nations in the Western

Hemisphere. He aimed his spread-eagle words at an international audience, proclaiming the United States "a civilized state" whose "fiat is law" in the Americas. The United States, he declared, is "master of the situation and practically invulnerable as against any or all other powers." The British, seeking international friends to counter intensifying competition from Germany, quietly retreated from the crisis. In 1896, an Anglo-American arbitration board divided the disputed territory between Britain and Venezuela. The Venezuelans were barely consulted. Thus, the United States displayed a trait common to imperialists: disregard for the rights and sensibilities of small nations.

In 1895 came another crisis forced by U.S. policy, this one in Cuba. From 1868 to 1878, the Cubans had battled Spain for their independence. Slavery was abolished but independence denied. While the Cuban economy suffered depression, repressive Spanish rule continued. Insurgents committed to *Cuba libre* waited for another chance, and José Martí, one of the heroes of Cuban history, collected money, arms, and men in the United States.

Revolution in Cuba   American financial support of the Cuban cause was but one of the many ways the lives of Americans and Cubans intersected. Their cultures, for example, melded. Cubans of all classes had settled in Baltimore, New York, Boston, and Philadelphia. Prominent Cubans on the island had sent their children to schools in the United States. When Cuban expatriates returned home, many came in American clothes, spoke English, had American names, played baseball, and had jettisoned Catholicism for Protestant denominations. Struggling with competing identities, Cubans admired American culture but resented U.S. economic hegemony (predominance).

The Cuban and U.S. economies were also intertwined. American investments of $50 million, mostly in sugar plantations, dominated the Caribbean island. More than 90 percent of Cuba's sugar was exported to the United States, and most island imports came from the United States. Havana's famed cigar factories relocated to Key West and Tampa to evade protectionist U.S. tariff laws. Martí, however, feared that "economic union means political union," for "the nation that buys, commands" and "the nation that sells, serves." Watch out, he warned, for a U.S. "conquering policy" that reduced Latin American countries to "dependencies."

Martí's fears were prophetic. In 1894, the Wilson-Gorman Tariff imposed a duty on Cuban sugar, which had been entering the United States duty-free under the McKinley Tariff. The Cuban economy, highly dependent on exports, plunged into deep crisis, hastening the island's revolution against Spain and its further incorporation into "the American system."

In 1895, from American soil, Martí launched a revolution against Spain that mounted in human and material costs. Rebels burned sugar-cane fields and razed mills, conducting an economic war and using guerrilla tactics to avoid head-on clashes with Spanish soldiers. "It is necessary to burn the hive to disperse the swarm," explained insurgent leader Máximo Gómez. U.S. investments went up in smoke, and Cuban-American trade dwindled. To separate the insurgents from their supporters among the Cuban people, Spanish general Valeriano Weyler instituted a policy of "reconcentration." Some 300,000 Cubans were herded into fortified towns and camps, where hunger, starvation, and disease led to tens of thousands of deaths. As reports of atrocity and destruction became headline news in the American yellow press, Americans increasingly sympathized with the insurrectionists. In late 1897, a new government in Madrid modified reconcentration and promised some autonomy for Cuba, but the insurgents continued to gain ground.

Sinking of the *Maine*

President William McKinley had come to office as an imperialist who advocated foreign bases for the New Navy, the export of surplus production, and U.S. supremacy in the Western Hemisphere. Vexed by the turmoil in Cuba, he came to believe that Spain should give up its colony. At one point, he explored the purchase of Cuba by the United States for $300 million. Events in early 1898 caused McKinley to lose faith in Madrid's ability to bring peace to Cuba. In January, when antireform pro-Spanish loyalists and army personnel rioted in Havana, Washington ordered the battleship *Maine* to Havana harbor to demonstrate U.S. concern and to protect American citizens.

On February 15, an explosion ripped the *Maine*, killing 266 of 354 American officers and crew. Just a week earlier, William Randolph Hearst's inflammatory *New York Journal* had published a stolen private letter written by the Spanish minister in Washington, Enrique Dupuy de Lôme, who belittled McKinley as "weak and a bidder for the admiration of the crowd" and suggested that Spain would fight on. Congress soon complied unanimously with McKinley's request for $50 million in defense funds. The naval board investigating the *Maine* disaster then reported that a mine had caused the explosion. Vengeful Americans blamed Spain. (Later, official and unofficial studies attributed the sinking to an accidental internal explosion, most likely caused by spontaneous combustion of inadequately ventilated coal bunkers.)

McKinley's Ultimatum and War Decision

The impact of these events narrowed McKinley's diplomatic options. Though reluctant to go to war, he decided to send Spain an ultimatum. In late March, the United States insisted that Spain accept an armistice, end reconcentration altogether, and designate McKinley as arbiter. Madrid made concessions. It abolished reconcentration and rejected, then accepted, an armistice. The weary president hesitated, but he would no longer tolerate chronic disorder just 90 miles off the U.S. coast. On April 11, McKinley asked Congress for authorization to use force "to secure a full and final termination of hostilities between … Spain and … Cuba, and to secure in the island the establishment of a stable government, capable of maintaining order." American intervention, he said, meant "hostile constraint upon both the parties to the contest."

McKinley listed the reasons for war: the "cause of humanity"; the protection of American life and property; the "very serious injury to the commerce, trade, and business of our people"; and, referring to the destruction of the *Maine*, the "constant menace to our peace." At the end of his message, McKinley mentioned Spain's recent concessions but made little of them. He did not mention another possible motivation: de Lôme's depiction of him as "weak," a charge also leveled by Assistant Secretary of the Navy Theodore Roosevelt. On April 19, Congress declared Cuba free and independent and directed the president to use force to remove Spanish authority from the island. The legislators also passed the Teller Amendment,

The Wadsworth Atheneum Museum of Art, Hartford, Connecticut. Gift of Henry E. Schnakenberg

On July 1, 1898, U.S. troops stormed Spanish positions on San Juan Hill near Santiago, Cuba. Both sides suffered heavy casualties. A Harper's *magazine correspondent reported a "ghastly" scene of hundreds killed and thousands wounded. The American painter William Glackens (1870–1938) put to canvas what he saw. Because Santiago surrendered on July 17, propelling the United States to victory in the war, and because Rough Rider Theodore Roosevelt fought at San Juan Hill and later gave a self-congratulatory account of the experience, the human toll has often gone unnoticed.*

which disclaimed any U.S. intention to annex Cuba or control the island except to ensure its "pacification" (by which they meant the suppression of any actively hostile elements of the population). McKinley beat back a congressional amendment to recognize the rebel government. Believing that the Cubans were not ready for self-government, he argued that they needed a period of American tutoring.

THE SPANISH-AMERICAN WAR AND THE DEBATE OVER EMPIRE

Diplomacy had failed. By the time the Spanish concessions were on the table, events had already pushed the antagonists to the brink. Washington might have been more patient, and Madrid might have faced the fact that its once-grand empire had disintegrated. Still, prospects for compromise appeared dim because the advancing

Cuban insurgents would settle for nothing less than full independence, and no Spanish government could have given up and remained in office. Nor did the United States welcome a truly independent Cuban government that might attempt to reduce U.S. interests. As historian Louis A. Perez Jr. has argued, McKinley's decision for war may have been "directed as much against Cuban independence as it was against Spanish sovereignty." Thus came a war some have titled (awkwardly, but accurately) the "Spanish-American-Cuban-Filipino War" so as to represent all the major participants and identify where the war was fought and whose interests were most at stake.

Motives for War   The motives of Americans who favored war were mixed and complex. McKinley's April message expressed a humanitarian impulse to stop the bloodletting, a concern for commerce and property, and the psychological need to end the nightmarish anxiety once and for all. Republican politicians advised McKinley that their party would lose the upcoming congressional elections unless he solved the Cuba question. Many businesspeople, who had been hesitant before the crisis of early 1898, joined many farmers in the belief that ejecting Spain from Cuba would open new markets for surplus production.

Inveterate imperialists saw the war as an opportunity to fulfill expansionist dreams, while conservatives, alarmed by Populism and violent labor strikes, welcomed war as a national unifier. One senator commented that "internal discord" was disappearing in the "fervent heat of patriotism." Sensationalism also figured in the march to war, with the yellow press exaggerating stories of Spanish misdeeds. Theodore Roosevelt and others too young to remember the bloody Civil War looked on war as adventure and used masculine rhetoric to trumpet the call to arms.

More than 263,000 regulars and volunteers served in the army and another 25,000 in the navy during the war. Most of them never left the United States. The typical volunteer was young (early twenties), white, unmarried, native-born, and working class. Many were southerners, a fact that helped the cause of reconciliation following the bitter divisions of the Civil War era. Deaths numbered 5,462—but only 379 in combat. The rest fell to yellow fever and typhoid, and most died in the United States, especially in camps in Tennessee, Virginia, and Florida, where in July and August a typhoid epidemic devastated the ranks. About 10,000 African American troops, assigned to segregated regiments, found no relief from racism and Jim Crow, even though black troops played a key role in the victorious battle for Santiago de Cuba. For all, food, sanitary conditions, and medical care were bad. Still, Roosevelt could hardly contain himself. Although his Rough Riders, a motley unit of Ivy Leaguers and cowboys, proved undisciplined and often ineffective, they nonetheless received good press largely because of Roosevelt's self-serving publicity efforts.

Dewey in the Philippines   To the surprise of most Americans, the first war news actually came from faraway Asia, from the Spanish colony of the Philippine Islands. Here, too, Madrid faced a rebellion from Filipinos seeking independence. On May 1, 1898, Commodore George Dewey's New Navy ship *Olympia* led an American squadron into Manila Bay and wrecked

The Spanish fleet in the Caribbean was commanded by Admiral Pascual Cervera y Topete. His squadron entered Santiago Bay, Cuba, May 19, 1898, where it was immediately blockaded by Admiral William T. Sampson's fleet. On July 3, Cervera—following orders from Madrid—tried a heroic but unsuccessful escape from the U.S. blockade. This painting by Henry Reuterdahl depicts the destruction of the squadron. Cervera survived and became a prisoner of war.

the outgunned Spanish fleet. Dewey and his sailors had been on alert in Hong Kong since February, when he received orders from imperial-minded Washington to attack the islands if war broke out. Manila ranked with Pearl Harbor and Pago Pago as a choice harbor, and the Philippines sat significantly on the way to China and its potentially huge market.

Facing Americans and rebels in both Cuba and the Philippines, Spanish resistance collapsed rapidly. U.S. ships blockaded Cuban ports to prevent Spain from resupplying its army, which suffered hunger and disease because Cuban insurgents had cut off supplies from the countryside. American troops saw their first ground-war action on June 22, the day several thousand of them landed near Santiago de Cuba and laid siege to the city. On July 3, U.S. warships sank the Spanish Caribbean squadron in Santiago harbor. American forces then assaulted the Spanish colony of Puerto Rico to obtain another Caribbean base for the navy and a strategic site to help protect a Central American canal. Losing on all fronts, Madrid sued for peace.

Treaty of Paris   On August 12, Spain and the United States signed an armistice to end the war. In Paris, in December 1898, American and Spanish negotiators agreed on the peace terms: independence for Cuba from Spain; cession of the Philippines, Puerto Rico, and the Pacific island of Guam to the United States; and American payment of $20 million to Spain for the territories. The U.S. empire now stretched deep into Asia, and the annexation of Wake Island (1898), Hawai'i (1898), and Samoa (1899) gave American traders, missionaries, and naval promoters other steppingstones to China.

During the war with Spain, the *Washington Post* detected "a new appetite, a yearning to show our strength.... The taste of empire is in the mouth of the people." But as the nation debated the Treaty of Paris, anti-imperialists such as author Mark Twain, Nebraska politician William Jennings Bryan, intellectual William Graham Sumner, reformer Jane Addams, industrialist Andrew Carnegie, and Senator George Hoar of Massachusetts argued vigorously against annexation of the Philippines. They were disturbed that a war to free Cuba had led to empire, and they stimulated a momentous debate over the fundamental course in American foreign policy.

Anti-Imperialist Arguments   Imperial control could be imposed either formally (by military occupation, annexation, or colonialism) or informally (by economic domination, political manipulation, or the threat of intervention). Anti-imperialist ire focused mostly on the formal kind of imperial control, involving an overseas territorial empire comprised of people of color living far from the mainland. Some critics appealed to principle, citing the Declaration of Independence and the Constitution: the conquest of people against their wills violated the right of self-determination. Philosopher William James charged that the United States was throwing away its special place among nations; it was, he warned, about to "puke up its heritage."

Other anti-imperialists feared that the American character was being corrupted by imperialist zeal. Jane Addams, seeing children play war games in the streets of Chicago, pointed out that they were not freeing Cubans but rather slaying Spaniards. Hoping to build a distinct foreign policy constituency out of networks of women's clubs and organizations, prominent women like Addams championed peace and an end to imperial conquest.

Some anti-imperialists protested that the United States was practicing a double standard—"offering liberty to the Cubans with one hand, cramming liberty down the throats of the Filipinos with the other, but with both feet planted upon the neck of the negro," as an African American politician from Massachusetts put it. Still other anti-imperialists warned that annexing people of color would undermine Anglo-Saxon purity and supremacy at home.

For Samuel Gompers and other anti-imperialist labor leaders, the issue was jobs: they worried that what Gompers called the "half-breeds and semi-barbaric people" of the new colonies would undercut American labor. Might not the new colonials be imported as cheap contract labor to drive down the wages of American workers? Would not exploitation of the weak abroad become contagious and lead to further exploitation of the weak at home? Would not an overseas empire drain interest and resources from pressing domestic problems, delaying reform?

The anti-imperialists entered the debate with many handicaps and never launched an effective campaign. Although they organized the Anti-Imperialist League in November 1898, they differed so profoundly on domestic issues that they found it difficult to speak with one voice on a foreign question. They also appeared inconsistent: Gompers favored the war but not the postwar annexations; Carnegie would accept colonies if they were not acquired by force; Hoar voted for annexation of Hawai'i but not of the Philippines; Bryan backed the Treaty of Paris but only, he said, to hurry the process toward Philippine independence. Finally, possession of the Philippines was an established fact, very hard to undo.

Imperialist Arguments   The imperialists answered their critics with appeals to patriotism, destiny, and commerce. They sketched a scenario of American greatness: merchant ships plying the waters to boundless Asian markets; naval vessels cruising the Pacific to protect American interests; missionaries uplifting inferior peoples. It was America's duty, they insisted, quoting a then-popular Rudyard Kipling poem, to "take up the white man's burden." Furthermore, Filipino insurgents were beginning to resist U.S. rule, and it seemed cowardly to pull out under fire. Germany and Japan, two powerful international competitors, were nosing around the Philippines, apparently ready to seize them if the United States' grip loosened. National honor dictated that Americans keep what they had shed blood to take. Republican Senator Albert Beveridge of Indiana asked, "Shall [history] say that, called by events to captain and command the proudest, ablest, purest race of history in history's noblest work, we declined that great commission?"

In February 1899, by a 57-to-27 vote (just 1 more than the necessary two-thirds majority), the Senate passed the Treaty of Paris, ending the war with Spain. Most Republicans voted yes and most Democrats no. An amendment promising independence as soon as the Filipinos formed a stable government lost by only the tie-breaking ballot of the vice president. Democratic presidential candidate Bryan carried the anti-imperialist case into the election of 1900, warning that repudiation of self-government in the Philippines would weaken the principle at home. But the victorious McKinley refused to apologize for American imperialism, asserting that his policies had served the nation's interests.

ASIAN ENCOUNTERS: WAR IN THE PHILIPPINES, DIPLOMACY IN CHINA

As McKinley knew, however, the Philippine crisis was far from over. He said he intended to "uplift and civilize" the Filipinos, but they denied that they needed U.S. help. Emilio Aguinaldo, the Philippine nationalist leader who had been battling the Spanish for years, believed that American officials had promised independence for his country. But after the victory over Spain, U.S. officers ordered Aguinaldo out of Manila and isolated him from decisions affecting his nation. In early 1899, feeling betrayed by the Treaty of Paris, he proclaimed an independent Philippine Republic and took up arms. U.S. officials soon set their jaws against the rebellion.

Philippine Insurrection and Pacification   In a war fought viciously by both sides, American soldiers burned crops and villages and tortured captives, while Filipino forces staged hit-and-run ambushes that were often brutally effective. Like guerrillas in many later wars, they would strike suddenly and ferociously, and then melt into the jungle or friendly villages. Americans spoke of the "savage" Filipino; one soldier declared that the Philippines "won't be pacified until the niggers [Filipinos] are killed off like the Indians." U.S. troops introduced a variant of the Spanish reconcentration policy—in the province of Batangas, for instance, U.S. troops forced residents to live in designated zones in an effort to separate the insurgents from local supporters.

Disaster followed. Poor sanitation, starvation, and malaria and cholera killed several thousand people. Outside the secure areas, Americans destroyed food supplies to starve out the rebels. At least one-quarter of the population of Batangas died or fled.

Before the Philippine insurrection was suppressed in 1902, some 20,000 Filipinos had died in combat, and as many as 600,000 had succumbed to starvation and disease. More than 4,000 Americans lay dead. Resistance to U.S. rule, however, did not disappear. The fiercely independent, vehemently anti-Christian, and often violent Muslim Filipinos of Moro Province refused to knuckle under. The U.S. military ordered them to submit or be exterminated. In 1906, the Moros finally met defeat; 600 of them, including many women and children, were slaughtered at the Battle of Bud Dajo. As General Leonard Wood, the Moro provincial governor, wrote the president, "Work of this kind has its disagreeable side."

U.S. officials, with a stern military hand, soon tried to Americanize the Philippines. Architect Daniel Burnham, leader of the City Beautiful movement, planned modern Manila. U.S. authorities instituted a new educational system, with English as the main language of instruction. Thousands of young American educators, many of them motivated by idealism, were recruited to teach in the new schools. The Philippine economy grew while it was an American satellite, and a sedition act silenced critics of U.S. authority by sending them to prison. In 1916, the Jones Act vaguely promised independence once the Philippines established a "stable government." The United States finally ended its rule in 1946 during an intense period of decolonization after the Second World War.

China and the Open Door Policy

In China, McKinley opted for an approach that emphasized negotiations, with greater success. Outsiders had been pecking away at China since the 1840s, but the Japanese onslaught intensified the international scramble. Taking advantage of the Qing (Manchu) dynasty's weakness, the major imperial powers carved out spheres of influence (regions over which the outside powers claimed political control and exclusive commercial privileges): Germany in Shandong, Russia in Manchuria, France in Yunnan and Hainan, Britain in Kowloon and Hong Kong. Then, in 1895, the same year as the outbreak of the Cuban revolution, Japan claimed victory over China in a short war and assumed control of Formosa and Korea as well as parts of China proper (see Map 22.1). American religious and business leaders petitioned Washington to halt the dismemberment of China before they were closed out.

Secretary of State John Hay knew the United States could not force the imperial powers out of China, but he was determined to protect American commerce and missionaries. He knew that missionaries had become targets of Chinese nationalist anger and that American oil and textile companies had been disappointed in the results of their investments in the country. Thus, in September 1899, Hay sent the nations with spheres of influence in China a note asking them to respect the principle of equal trade opportunity—an Open Door. The recipients sent evasive replies, privately complaining that the United States was seeking, for free, the trade rights in China that they had gained at considerable military and administrative cost.

The next year, a Chinese secret society called the Boxers (so named in the western press because some members were martial artists) incited riots that killed foreigners, including missionaries, and laid siege to the foreign legations in Beijing. The Boxers sought ultimately to expel all foreigners from China. The United States, applauded by American merchants and missionaries alike, joined the other imperial powers in sending troops to lift the siege. Hay also sent a second Open Door note in July, which instructed other nations to preserve China's territorial integrity and to honor "equal and impartial trade." Hay's protests notwithstanding, China continued for years to be fertile soil for foreign exploitation, especially by the Japanese.

Although Hay's foray into Asian politics settled little, the Open Door policy became a cornerstone of U.S. diplomacy. The "open door" had actually been a long-standing American principle, for as a trading nation the United States opposed barriers to international commerce and demanded equal access to foreign markets. After 1900, however, when the United States began to emerge as the premier world trader, the Open Door policy became an instrument first to pry open markets and then to dominate them, not just in China but throughout the world. The Open Door also developed as an ideology with several tenets: first, that America's domestic well-being required exports; second, that foreign trade would suffer interruption unless the United States intervened abroad to implant American principles and keep markets open; and third, that the closing of any area to American products, citizens, or ideas threatened the survival of the United States itself.

TR's World

Theodore Roosevelt played an important role in shaping U.S. foreign policy in the McKinley administration. As assistant secretary of the navy (1897–1898), as a Spanish-American War hero, and then as vice president in McKinley's second term, Roosevelt worked tirelessly to make the United States a key member of the great power club. He had long had a fascination with power and its uses. He also relished hunting and killing. After an argument with a girlfriend in his youth, he vented his anger by shooting a neighbor's dog. When he killed his first buffalo in the West, he danced crazily around the carcass as his Indian guide watched in amazement. Roosevelt justified the slaughtering of American Indians, if necessary, and took his Rough Riders to Cuba, desperate to get in on the fighting. He was not disappointed. "Did I tell you," he wrote Henry Cabot Lodge afterward, "that I killed a Spaniard with my own hands?"

Like many other Americans of his day, Roosevelt took for granted the superiority of Protestant Anglo-American culture, and he believed in the importance of using American power to shape world affairs (a conviction he summarized by citing the West African proverb "Speak softly and carry a big stick, and you will go far"). In

MAP 22.1 Imperialism in Asia: Turn of the Century

As seen in the map on the right, China and the Pacific region had become imperialist hunting grounds by the turn of the century. The European powers and Japan controlled more areas than the United States, which nonetheless participated in the imperial race by annexing the Philippines, Wake, Guam, Hawai'i, and Samoa; announcing the Open Door policy; and expanding trade. As the spheres of influence in China demonstrate, that besieged nation succumbed to outsiders despite the Open Door policy.

© Cengage Learning

CANADA

UNITED STATES

San Francisco

2400 miles

ALASKA

Bering Sea

ALEUTIAN IS. (U.S)

KAMCHATKA (RUSS.)

SAKHALIN (RUSS.)

KURILE IS. (Jap.)

PACIFIC OCEAN

HAWAIIAN IS. (U.S.)

MIDWAY IS. (U.S.)

JOHNSTON I. (U.S.)

WAKE I. (U.S.)

5000 miles

MARCUS I. (Jap.)

GILBERT IS. (Br.)

ELLICE IS. (Br.)

SAMOA (Ger./U.S.)

MARSHALL IS. (Ger.)

NAURU (Ger.)

SANTA CRUZ IS. (Br.)

NEW HEBRIDES (Fr./Br.)

FIJI IS. (Br.)

NEW CALEDONIA (Fr.)

Coral Sea

MARIANAS IS. (Ger.)

CAROLINE IS. (Ger.)

Equator

BISMARCK ARCHIPELAGO (Ger.)

SOLOMON IS. (Ger./Br.)

NEW GUINEA (Ger.)

PAPUA (Br.)

BONIN IS. (Jap.)

VOLCANIC IS. (Jap.)

GUAM (U.S.)

PELEW IS. (Ger.)

RUSSIAN EMPIRE

MONGOLIA

MANCHURIA

Mukden

Beijing (Peking)

Vladivostok

JAPAN

Tokyo

KOREA

See Inset

Shanghai

PESCADORES IS. (Jap.)

RYUKYU IS. (Jap.)

FORMOSA (Jap.)

Amoy

Guangzhou (Canton)

Kowloon (Br.)

Hong Kong (Br.)

Macao (Port.)

HAINAN

CHINA

TIBET

BURMA (Br.)

YUNNAN

Hanoi

FRENCH INDO-CHINA

SIAM

Bangkok

MALAY STATES

Singapore

SUMATRA

INDIAN OCEAN

JAVA

Batavia

BRUNEI (Br.)

SARAWAK (Br.)

NO. BORNEO (Br.)

BORNEO

CELEBES

NETHERLANDS EAST INDIES

TIMOR (Port.)

PHILIPPINE ISLANDS (U.S.)

LUZON

Manila

Batangas

LEYTE

MINDANAO

AUSTRALIA

Russian sphere

German sphere

British sphere

French sphere

Japanese sphere

Japanese sphere (after 1905)

Inset:

MANCHURIA

KOREA

Mukden

Liaodong Pen. (Russ.)

Port Arthur (Russ.)

Wei-hai-wei (Br.)

Qingdao (Tsingtao) (Ger.)

Jiaozhou (Kiaochow) (Ger.)

Shandong

Yellow Sea

CHINA

Beijing (Peking)

675

TR's world, there were "civilized" and "uncivilized" nations; the former, primarily white and Anglo-Saxon or Teutonic, had a right and a duty to intervene in the affairs of the latter (generally nonwhite, Latin, or Slavic, and therefore "backward") to preserve order and stability. If violent means had to be used to accomplish this task, so be it.

Presidential Authority   Roosevelt's love of the good fight caused many to rue his ascension to the presidency after McKinley's assassination in September 1901. But there was more to this "cowboy" than mere bluster; he was also an astute analyst of foreign policy and world affairs. TR understood that American power, though growing year by year, remained limited, and that in many parts of the world the United States would have to rely on diplomacy and nonmilitary means to achieve satisfactory outcomes. It would have to work in concert with other powers.

Roosevelt sought to centralize foreign policy in the White House. The president had to take charge of foreign relations, he believed, in the same way he took the lead in formulating domestic priorities of reorganization and reform. Congress was too large and unwieldy. As for public opinion, it was, Roosevelt said, "the voice of the devil, or what is still worse, the voice of the fool." This conviction that the executive branch should be supreme in foreign policy was to be shared by most presidents who followed TR in office, down to the present day.

With this bald assertion of presidential and national power, Roosevelt stepped onto the international stage. His first efforts were focused on Latin America, where U.S. economic and strategic interests and power towered (see Map 22.2), and on Europe, where repeated political and military disputes persuaded Americans to develop friendlier relations with Great Britain while avoiding entrapment in the continent's troubles, many of which Americans blamed on Germany.

As U.S. economic interests expanded in Latin America, so did U.S. political influence. Exports to Latin America, which exceeded $50 million in the 1870s, had risen to more than $120 million when Roosevelt became president in 1901, and then reached $300 million in 1914. Investments by U.S. citizens in Latin America climbed to a commanding $1.26 billion in 1914. In 1899, two large banana importers had merged to form the United Fruit Company. United Fruit owned much of the land in Central America (more than a million acres in 1913), as well as the railroad and steamship lines, and the firm became an influential economic and political force in the region. The company worked to eradicate yellow fever and malaria at the same time it manipulated Central American politics, partly by bankrolling favored officeholders.

Cuba and the Platt Amendment   After the destructive war in Cuba, U.S. citizens and corporations continued to dominate the island's economy, controlling the sugar, mining, tobacco, and utilities industries, and most of the rural lands. Private U.S. investments in Cuba grew from $50 million before the revolution to $220 million by 1913, and U.S. exports to the island rose from $26 million in 1900 to $196 million in 1917. The Teller Amendment outlawed the annexation of Cuba, but officials in Washington

MAP 22.2 in the map area:

- **UNITED STATES**
- N. MEX.
- N.C.
- S.C.
- TEXAS
- **ATLANTIC OCEAN**
- Columbus
- U.S. Expeditionary Force, 1916–1917
- MISS.
- ALA.
- GA.
- LA.
- Houston
- New Orleans
- FLORIDA
- Santa Ysabel
- Parral
- Sinking of *Maine*, 1898
- U.S. troops, 1915–1934 / Financial supervision, 1916–1941
- Revolutions, 1868–1878, 1895–1898 / U.S. troops, 1898–1902, 1906–1909, 1912, 1917–1922 / Platt Amendment, 1903–1934 / U.S. exports to, 1865–1917 = $1.6 billion
- Miami
- BAHAMA IS. (Br.)
- U.S. attempted to buy, 1869 / U.S. troops, 1916–1924 / Financial supervision, 1905–1941
- **MEXICO**
- Purchased from Denmark, 1917
- Havana
- **CUBA**
- Tampico
- Guantánamo
- DOMINICAN REP.
- PUERTO RICO
- GUADELOUPE (Fr.)
- Mexico City
- Vera Cruz
- U.S. attack, 1914
- U.S. naval base, 1903–
- HAITI
- VIRGIN IS.
- BR. HONDURAS
- JAMAICA (Br.)
- U.S. troops, 1924–1925
- U.S. possession after 1898 / Puerto Ricans became U.S. citizens, 1917
- MARTINIQUE (Fr.)
- Revolution, 1910 / Americans controlled 43% of Mexican property, 1910 / U.S. exports to, 1865–1917 = $1.3 billion
- GUATEMALA
- HONDURAS
- BARBADOS (Br.)
- EL SALVADOR
- NICARAGUA
- U.S. leased Corn Is., 1914
- TRINIDAD (Br.)
- United Fruit Co. organized for banana trade, 1899
- COSTA RICA
- Caracas
- U.S. troops, 1909–1910, 1912–1925, 1926–1933 / Financial supervision, 1911–1924 / Canal option, 1916
- PANAMA
- Venezuelan crisis, 1895–1896
- **VENEZUELA**
- U.S. acquired Canal Zone, 1903 / Canal completed, 1914
- *PACIFIC OCEAN*
- Bogotá
- **COLOMBIA**
- **BRAZIL**
- © Cengage Learning

MAP 22.2 Hegemony in the Caribbean and Latin America

Through many interventions, territorial acquisitions, and robust economic expansion, the United States became the predominant power in Latin America in the early twentieth century. The United States often backed up the Roosevelt Corollary's declaration of a "police power" by dispatching troops to Caribbean nations, where they met nationalist opposition.

soon used the document's call for "pacification" to justify U.S. control. American troops remained there until 1902.

Favoring the "better classes," U.S. authorities restricted voting rights largely to propertied Cuban males, excluding two-thirds of adult men and all women. American officials also forced the Cubans to append to their constitution a frank avowal of U.S. hegemony known as the Platt Amendment. This statement prohibited Cuba from making a treaty with another nation that might impair its independence; in practice, this meant that all treaties had to have U.S. approval. Most important, another Platt Amendment provision granted the United States "the right to intervene" to preserve the island's independence and to maintain domestic order. The amendment also required Cuba to lease a naval base to the United States (at Guantánamo Bay, still under U.S. jurisdiction today). Formalized in a 1903 treaty, the amendment governed Cuban-American relations until 1934. "There is, of course, little or no independence left Cuba under the Platt Amendment," General Wood, military governor of the island until 1902, told President Roosevelt.

The Cubans, like the Filipinos, chafed under U.S. mastery. Widespread demonstrations protested the Platt Amendment, and a rebellion against the Cuban government in 1906 prompted Roosevelt to order another invasion of Cuba. The marines stayed until 1909, returned briefly in 1912, and occupied the island again from 1917 to 1922. All the while, U.S. officials helped to develop a transportation system, expand the public school system, found a national army, and increase sugar production. When Dr. Walter Reed's experiments, based on the theory of the Cuban physician Carlos Juan Finlay, proved that mosquitoes transmitted yellow fever, sanitary engineers controlled the insect and eradicated the disease.

Puerto Rico, the Caribbean island taken as a spoil of war in the Treaty of Paris, also developed under U.S. tutelage. Although no Puerto Rican sat at the negotiating table for that treaty, the Puerto Rican elite at first welcomed the United States as an improvement over Spain. But disillusionment soon set in. The condescending U.S. military governor, General Guy V. Henry, regarded Puerto Ricans as naughty, ill-educated children who needed "kindergarten instruction in controlling themselves without allowing them too much liberty." Some residents warned against the "Yankee peril"; others applauded the "Yankee model" and futilely anticipated statehood.

Panama Canal   Panama, meanwhile, became the site of a bold U.S. expansionist venture. In 1869, the world had marveled at the completion of the Suez Canal, a waterway in North-east Africa that greatly facilitated travel between the Indian Ocean and Mediterranean Sea, and enhanced the power of the British Empire. Surely that feat could be duplicated in the Western Hemisphere, possibly in Panama, a province of Colombia. One expansionist, U.S. navy captain, Robert W. Shufeldt, predicted that a new canal would convert "the Gulf of Mexico into an American lake." Business interests joined politicians, diplomats, and navy officers in insisting that the United States control such an interoceanic canal.

To construct such a canal, however, the United States had to overcome daunting obstacles. The Clayton-Bulwer Treaty with Britain (1850) had provided for joint control of a canal. The British, recognizing their diminishing influence in the region and cultivating friendship with the United States as a counterweight to Germany, stepped aside in the Hay-Pauncefote Treaty (1901) to permit a solely U.S.-run canal. When Colombia hesitated to meet Washington's terms, Roosevelt encouraged Panamanian rebels to declare independence and ordered American warships to the isthmus to back them.

In 1903, the new Panama awarded the United States a canal zone and long-term rights to its control. The treaty also guaranteed Panama its independence. (In 1922, the United States paid Colombia $25 million in "conscience money" but did not apologize.) The completion of the Panama Canal in 1914 marked a major technological achievement. During the canal's first year of operation, more than one thousand merchant ships squeezed through its locks.

Roosevelt Corollary   As for the rest of the Caribbean, Theodore Roosevelt resisted challenges to U.S. hegemony. Worried that Latin American nations' defaults on debts owed to European banks were provoking European intervention (England, Germany, and Italy sent warships to

Venezuela in 1902), the president in 1904 issued the Roosevelt Corollary to the Monroe Doctrine. He warned Latin Americans to stabilize their politics and finances. "Chronic wrongdoing," the corollary lectured, might require "intervention by some civilized nation," and "in flagrant cases of such wrongdoing or impotence," the United States would have to assume the role of "an international police power." Laced with presumptions of superiority, Roosevelt's declaration provided the rationale for frequent U.S. interventions in Latin America.

From 1900 to 1917, U.S. presidents ordered American troops to Cuba, Panama, Nicaragua, the Dominican Republic, Mexico, and Haiti to quell civil wars, thwart challenges to U.S. influence, gain ports and bases, and forestall European meddling (see Map 22.2). U.S. authorities ran elections, trained national guards that became politically powerful, and renegotiated foreign debts, shifting them to U.S. banks. They also took over customs houses to control tariff revenues and government budgets (as in the Dominican Republic, from 1905 to 1941).

U.S.-Mexican Relations   U.S. officials focused particular attention on Mexico, where long-time dictator Porfirio Díaz (1876–1910) aggressively recruited foreign investors through tax incentives and land grants. American capitalists came to own Mexico's railroads and mines, and invested heavily in petroleum and banking. By the early 1890s, the United States dominated Mexico's foreign trade. By 1910, Americans controlled 43 percent of Mexican property and produced more than half of the country's oil; in the state of Sonora, 186 of 208 mining companies were American owned. The Mexican revolutionaries who ousted Díaz in 1910, like nationalists elsewhere in Latin America, set out to reclaim their nation's sovereignty by ending their economic dependency on the United States.

The revolution descended into a bloody civil war with strong anti-Yankee overtones, and the Mexican government intended to nationalize extensive American-owned properties. Washington leaders worked to thwart this aim, with President Woodrow Wilson twice ordering troops onto Mexican soil: once in 1914, at Veracruz, to avenge a slight to the U.S. uniform and flag, and to overthrow the nationalistic government of President Victoriano Huerta, who was also trying to import German weapons; and again in 1916, in northern Mexico, where General John J. "Black Jack" Pershing spent months pursuing Pancho Villa after the Mexican rebel had raided an American border town. Having failed to capture Villa and facing another nationalistic government led by Venustiano Carranza, U.S. forces departed in January 1917.

As the United States reaffirmed the Monroe Doctrine against European expansion in the hemisphere and demonstrated the power to enforce it, European nations reluctantly honored U.S. hegemony in Latin America. In turn, the United States held to its tradition of standing outside European embroilments. The balance of power in Europe was precarious, and seldom did an American president involve the United States directly. Theodore Roosevelt did help settle a Franco-German clash over Morocco by mediating a settlement at Algeciras, Spain (1906). But the president drew American criticism for entangling the United States in a European problem. Americans endorsed the ultimately futile Hague peace conferences (1899 and 1907) and negotiated various arbitration treaties, but on the whole stayed outside the European arena, except to profit from extensive trade with it.

Peacemaking
in East Asia
In East Asia, though, both Roosevelt and his successor, William Howard Taft, took an activist approach. Both sought to preserve the Open Door and to contain Japan's rising power in the region. Many race-minded Japanese interpreted the U.S. advance into the Pacific as an attempt by whites to gain ascendancy over Asians. Japanese leaders nonetheless urged their citizens to go to America to study it as a model for industrializing and achieving world power. Although some Americans proudly proclaimed the Japanese the "Yankees of the East," the United States gradually had to make concessions to Japan to protect the vulnerable Philippines and to sustain the Open Door policy. Japan continued to plant interests in China and then smashed the Russians in the Russo-Japanese War (1904–1905). President Roosevelt mediated the negotiations at the Portsmouth Conference in New Hampshire and won the Nobel Peace Prize for this effort to preserve a balance of power in Asia and shrink Japan's "big head."

In 1905, in the Taft-Katsura Agreement, the United States conceded Japanese hegemony over Korea in return for Japan's pledge not to undermine the U.S. position in the Philippines. Three years later, in the Root-Takahira Agreement, Washington recognized Japan's interests in Manchuria, whereas Japan again pledged the security of the Pacific possessions held by the United States and endorsed the Open Door in China. Roosevelt also built up American naval power to deter the Japanese; in late 1907, he sent on a world tour the navy's "Great White Fleet" (so named because the ships were painted white for the voyage). Duly impressed, the Japanese began to build a bigger navy of their own.

Dollar
Diplomacy
President Taft, for his part, thought he might counter Japanese advances in Asia through dollar diplomacy—the use of private funds to serve American diplomatic goals and garner profits for American financiers, and at the same time bring reform to less-developed countries. In this case, Taft induced American bankers to join an international consortium to build a railway in China. Taft's venture, however, seemed only to embolden Japan to solidify and extend its holdings in China, where internal discord continued after the nationalist revolution of 1911 overthrew the Qing dynasty.

In 1914, when the First World War broke out in Europe, Japan seized Shandong and some Pacific islands from the Germans. In 1915, Japan issued its Twenty-One Demands, virtually insisting on hegemony over all of China. The Chinese door was being slammed shut, but the United States lacked adequate countervailing power in Asia to block Japan's imperial thrusts. A new president, Woodrow Wilson, worried about how the "white race" could blunt the rise of "the yellow race."

Anglo-American
Rapprochement
British officials in London shared this concern, though their attention was focused primarily on rising tensions in Europe. A special feature of American-European relations in the TR-Taft years was the flowering of an Anglo-American cooperation that had been growing throughout the late nineteenth century. One outcome of the intense German-British rivalry and the rise of the United States to world power was London's quest for

friendship with Washington. Already prepared by racial ideas of Anglo-Saxon kinship, a common language, and respect for representative government and private-property rights, Americans appreciated British support in the 1898 war and the Hay-Pauncefote Treaty, and London's virtual endorsement of the Roosevelt Corollary and withdrawal of British warships from the Caribbean. As Mark Twain said of the two imperialist powers, "We are kin in sin."

British-American trade and U.S. investment in Britain also secured ties. By 1914, more than 140 American companies operated in Britain, including H. J. Heinz's processed foods and F. W. Woolworth's "penny markets." Many Britons decried an Americanization of British culture. One journalist complained that a Briton "wakes in the morning at the sound of an American alarm clock; rises from his New England sheets, and shaves with … a Yankee safety razor. He … slips his Waterbury watch into his pocket [and] catches an electric train made in New York…. At his office … he sits on a Nebraskan swivel chair, before a Michigan roll-top desk." Such exaggerated fears and the always prickly character of the Anglo-American relationship, however, gave way to cooperation in world affairs, most evident in 1917 when the United States threw its weapons and soldiers into the First World War on the British side against Germany.

SUMMARY

In the years from the Civil War to the First World War, expansionism and imperialism elevated the United States to world power status. By 1914, Americans held extensive economic, strategic, and political interests in a world made smaller by modern technology. The victory over Spain in 1898 was but the most dramatic moment in the long process. The outward reach of U.S. foreign policy from Seward to Wilson sparked opposition from domestic critics, other imperialist nations, and foreign nationalists, but expansionists prevailed, and the trend toward empire endured.

From Asia to Latin America, economic and strategic needs and ideology motivated and justified expansion and empire. The belief that the United States needed foreign markets to absorb surplus production in order to save the domestic economy joined missionary zeal in reforming other societies through the promotion of American products and culture. Notions of racial and male supremacy and appeals to national greatness also fed the appetite for foreign adventure and commitments. The greatly augmented navy became a primary means for satisfying American ideas and wants.

Revealing the great diversity of America's intersection with the world, missionaries, generals like Wood in Cuba, companies like Singer in Africa and Heinz in Britain, and politicians like Taft in the Philippines carried American ways, ideas, guns, and goods abroad to a mixed reception. The conspicuous declarations of Olney, Hay, Roosevelt, and other leaders became the guiding texts for U.S. principles and behavior in world affairs. A world power with far-flung interests to protect, the United States had to face a tough test of its self-proclaimed greatness and reconsider its political isolation from Europe when a world war broke out in August 1914.

23

AMERICANS IN THE GREAT WAR
1914–1920

PRECARIOUS NEUTRALITY

The war that erupted in August 1914 grew from years of European competition over trade, colonies, allies, and armaments. Two powerful alliance systems had formed: the Triple Alliance of Germany, Austria-Hungary, and Italy, and the Triple Entente of Britain, France, and Russia. All had imperial holdings and ambitions for more, but Germany seemed particularly bold, as it rivaled Great Britain for world leadership. Many Americans saw Germany as a threat to U.S. interests in the Western Hemisphere and viewed Germans as an excessively militaristic people who embraced autocracy and spurned democracy.

Outbreak of the First World War Strategists said that Europe enjoyed a balance of power, but crises in the Balkan countries of southeastern Europe triggered a chain of events that shattered the "balance." Slavic nationalists sought to enlarge Serbia, an independent Slavic nation, by annexing regions such as Bosnia, then a province of the Austro-Hungarian Empire (see Map 23.1). On June 28, 1914, Archduke Franz Ferdinand, heir to the Austro-Hungarian throne, was assassinated by a Serbian nationalist while on a state visit to Sarajevo, the capital of Bosnia. Alarmed by the prospect of an engorged Serbia on its border, Austria-Hungary consulted its Triple Alliance partner Germany, which urged toughness. When Serbia called on its Slavic friend Russia for help, Russia in turn looked for backing from its ally France. In late July, Austria-Hungary declared war against Serbia. Russia then began to mobilize its armies.

CHRONOLOGY

1914	First World War begins in Europe
1915	Germans sink *Lusitania* off coast of Ireland
1916	After torpedoing the *Sussex*, Germany pledges not to attack merchant ships without warning
	National Defense Act expands military
1917	Germany declares unrestricted submarine warfare
	Russian Revolution ousts the czar; Bolsheviks later take power
	United States enters First World War
	Selective Service Act creates draft
	Espionage Act limits First Amendment rights
	Race riot breaks out in East St. Louis, Illinois
1918	Wilson announces Fourteen Points for new world order
	Sedition Act further limits free speech
	U.S. troops at Château-Thierry help blunt German offensive
	U.S. troops intervene in Russia against Bolsheviks
	Spanish flu pandemic kills 20 million worldwide
	Armistice ends First World War
1919	Paris Peace Conference punishes Germany and launches League of Nations
	May Day bombings help instigate Red Scare
	American Legion organizes for veterans' benefits and antiradicalism
	Wilson suffers stroke after speaking tour
	Senate rejects Treaty of Versailles and U.S. membership in League of Nations
	Schenck v. U.S. upholds Espionage Act
1920	Palmer Raids round up suspected radicals

Germany—having goaded Austria-Hungary toward war and believing war inevitable—struck first, declaring war against Russia on August 1 and against France two days later. Britain hesitated, but when German forces slashed into neutral Belgium to get at France, London declared war against Germany on August 4. Eventually, Turkey (the Ottoman Empire) joined Germany and Austria-Hungary as the Central Powers, and Italy (switching sides) and Japan teamed up with Britain, France, and Russia as the Allies. Japan took advantage of the European war to seize Shandong, Germany's area of influence in China.

President Wilson at first sought to distance America from the conflagration by issuing a proclamation of neutrality—the traditional U.S. policy toward European wars. He also asked Americans to refrain from taking sides, to exhibit "the dignity of self-control." In private, the president said, "We definitely have to be neutral,

☐ Central Powers (Triple Alliance— except Italy—and allies)	
☐ The Allies (Triple Entente and allies)	
☐ Neutral nations	

1. June 28
Assassination at Sarajevo

2. July 28
Austria-Hungary declares war on Serbia

3. July 30
Russia begins mobilization

4. August 1
Germany declares war on Russia

5. August 3
Germany declares war on France and invades Belgium

6. August 4
Great Britain declares war on Germany

7. August 6
Russia and Austria-Hungary at war

8. August 12
Great Britain declares war on Austria-Hungary

© Cengage Learning

MAP 23.1 Europe Goes to War, Summer 1914

Bound by alliances and stirred by turmoil in the Balkans, where Serbs repeatedly up-ended peace, the nations of Europe descended into war in the summer of 1914. Step by step, a Balkan crisis escalated into the "Great War."

since otherwise our mixed populations would wage war on each other." The United States, he fervently hoped, would stand apart as a sane, civilized nation in a deranged international system.

Taking Sides   Wilson's lofty appeal for American neutrality and unity at home collided with several realities. First, ethnic groups in the United States did take sides. Many German Americans and anti-British Irish Americans (Ireland was then trying to break free from British rule) cheered for the Central Powers. Americans of British and French ancestry, and others with roots in

Allied nations, tended to champion the Allied cause. Germany's attack on Belgium confirmed in many people's minds that Germany had become the archetype of unbridled militarism.

The pro-Allied sympathies of Wilson's administration also weakened the U.S. neutrality proclamation. Honoring Anglo-American rapprochement, Wilson shared the conviction with British leaders that a German victory would destroy free enterprise and government by law. If Germany won the war, he prophesied, "it would change the course of our civilization and make the United States a military nation." Several of Wilson's chief advisers and diplomats—his assistant, Colonel Edward House; ambassador to London Walter Hines Page; and Robert Lansing, a counselor in the State Department who later became secretary of state—held similar anti-German views, which often translated into pro-Allied policies.

U.S. economic links with the Allies also rendered neutrality difficult, if not impossible. England had long been one of the nation's best customers. Now the British flooded America with new orders, especially for arms. Sales to the Allies helped pull the American economy out of its recession. Between 1914 and 1916, American exports to England and France grew 365 percent, from $753 million to $2.75 billion. In the same period, however, largely because of Britain's naval blockade, exports to Germany dropped by more than 90 percent, from $345 million to only $29 million. Loans to Britain and France from private American banks—totaling $2.3 billion during the neutrality period—financed much of U.S. trade with the Allies. Germany received only $27 million in the same period. The Wilson administration, which at first frowned on these transactions, came to see them as necessary to the economic health of the United States.

From Germany's perspective, the links between the American economy and the Allies meant that the United States had become the Allied arsenal and bank. Americans, however, faced a dilemma: cutting their economic ties with Britain would constitute a nonneutral act in favor of Germany. Under international law, Britain—which controlled the seas—could buy both contraband (war-related goods) and noncontraband from neutrals. It was Germany's responsibility, not America's, to stop such trade in ways that international law prescribed—that is, by an effective blockade of the enemy's territory, by the seizure of contraband from neutral (American) ships, or by the confiscation of goods from belligerent (British) ships. Germans, of course, judged the huge U.S. trade with the Allies an act of nonneutrality that had to be stopped.

Wilsonianism   The president and his aides believed, finally, that Wilsonian principles stood a better chance of international acceptance if Britain, rather than the Central Powers, sat astride the postwar world. "Wilsonianism," the cluster of ideas that Wilson espoused, consisted of traditional American principles (such as democracy and the Open Door) and a conviction that the United States was a beacon of freedom to the world. Only the United States could lead the convulsed world into a new, peaceful era of unobstructed commerce, free-market capitalism, democratic politics, and open diplomacy. American Progressivism, it seemed, was to be projected onto the world.

"America had the infinite privilege of fulfilling her destiny and saving the world," Wilson claimed. Empires had to be dismantled to honor the principle of self-determination. Armaments had to be reduced. Critics charged that Wilson often violated his own credos in his eagerness to force them on others—as his military interventions in Mexico in 1914, Haiti in 1915, and the Dominican Republic in 1916 testified. All agreed, though, that such ideals served American commercial purposes; in this way idealism and self-interest were married.

To say that American neutrality was never a real possibility given ethnic loyalties, economic ties, and Wilsonian preferences is not to say that Wilson sought to enter the war. He emphatically wanted to keep the United States out. Time and again, he tried to mediate the crisis to prevent one power from crushing another. In early 1917, the president remarked that "we are the only one of the great white nations that is free from war today, and it would be a crime against civilization for us to go in." But go in the United States finally did. Why?

Violations of Neutral Rights

The short answer is that Americans got caught in the Allied–Central Power crossfire. British naval policy aimed to sever neutral trade with Germany in order to cripple the German economy. The British, "ruling the waves and waiving the rules," declared a blockade of water entrances to Germany and mined the North Sea. They also harassed neutral shipping by seizing cargoes and defining a broad list of contraband (including foodstuffs) that they prohibited neutrals from shipping to Germany. American commerce with Germany dwindled rapidly. Furthermore, to counter German submarines, the British flouted international law by arming their merchant ships and flying neutral (sometimes American) flags. Wilson frequently protested British violations of neutral rights, pointing out that neutrals had the right to sell and ship noncontraband goods to belligerents without interference. But London often deftly defused Washington's criticism by paying for confiscated cargoes, and German provocations made British behavior appear less offensive by comparison.

Unable to win the war on land and determined to lift the blockade and halt American-Allied commerce, Germany looked for victory at sea by using submarines. In February 1915, Berlin declared a war zone around the British Isles, warned neutral vessels to stay out so as not to be attacked by mistake, and advised passengers from neutral nations to stay off Allied ships. President Wilson informed Germany that the United States would hold it to "strict accountability" for any losses of American life and property.

Wilson was interpreting international law in the strictest possible sense. The law that an attacker had to warn a passenger or merchant ship before attacking, so that passengers and crew could disembark safely into lifeboats, predated the submarine. The Germans thought the slender, frail, and sluggish *Unterseebooten* (U-boats) should not be expected to surface to warn ships, for surfacing would cancel out the U-boats' advantage of surprise and leave them vulnerable to attack. Berlin protested that Wilson was denying it the one weapon that could break the British economic stranglehold, disrupt the Allies' substantial connection with U.S. producers and bankers, and win the war. To all concerned—British, Germans, and Americans—naval warfare became a matter of life and death.

THE DECISION FOR WAR

Ultimately, it was the war at sea that doomed the prospects for U.S. neutrality. In the early months of 1915, German U-boats sank ship after ship, most notably the British liner *Lusitania* on May 7. In mid-August, after a lull following Germany's promise to refrain from attacking passenger liners, another British vessel, the *Arabic*, was sunk off Ireland. Three Americans died. The Germans quickly pledged that an unarmed passenger ship would never again be attacked without warning. But the sinking of the *Arabic* fueled debate over American passengers on belligerent vessels. Critics asked: why not require Americans to sail on American craft? From August 1914 to March 1917, after all, only 3 Americans died on an American ship (the tanker *Gulflight*, sunk by a German U-boat in May 1915), whereas about 190 were killed on belligerent ships.

Peace Advocates   In March 1916, a U-boat attack on the Sussex, a French vessel crossing the English Channel, took the United States a step closer to war. Four Americans were injured on that ship, which the U-boat commander mistook for a minelayer. Stop the marauding submarines, Wilson lectured Berlin, or the United States will sever diplomatic relations. Again the Germans retreated, pledging not to attack merchant vessels without warning. At about the same time, U.S. relations with Britain soured. The British crushing of the Easter Rebellion in Ireland and further British restriction of U.S. trade with the Central Powers aroused American anger.

As the United States became more entangled in the Great War, many Americans urged Wilson to keep the nation out. In early 1915, Jane Addams, Carrie Chapman Catt, and other suffragists helped found the Woman's Peace Party, the U.S. section of the Women's International League for Peace and Freedom. "The mother half of humanity," claimed women peace advocates, had a special role as "the guardians of life." Later that same year, some pacifist Progressives—including Oswald Garrison Villard, Paul Kellogg, and Lillian Wald—organized an antiwar coalition, the American Union Against Militarism. Businessman Andrew Carnegie, who in 1910 had established the Carnegie Endowment for International Peace, helped finance peace groups. So did Henry Ford, who in late 1915 traveled on a "peace ship" to Europe to propagandize for a negotiated settlement. Socialists like Eugene Debs added their voices to the peace movement.

Antiwar advocates emphasized several points: that war drained a nation of its youth, resources, and reform impulse; that it fostered repression at home; that it violated Christian morality; and that wartime business barons reaped huge profits at the expense of the people. Militarism and conscription, Addams pointed out, were what millions of immigrants had left behind in Europe. Were they now—in the United States—to be forced into the decadent system they had escaped? Although the peace movement was splintered—some wanted to keep the United States out of the conflict but did not endorse the pacifists' claim that intervention could never be justified—it carried political and intellectual weight that Wilson could not ignore, and it articulated several ideas that he shared. In fact, he campaigned on a peace platform in the 1916 presidential election. After his triumph, Wilson futilely labored once again to bring the belligerents to the conference table. In early 1917, he advised them to temper their acquisitive war aims, appealing for "peace without victory."

Unrestricted Submarine Warfare   In Germany, Wilson's overture went unheeded. Since August 1916, leaders in Berlin had debated whether to resume the unrestricted U-boat campaign. Opponents feared a break with the United States, but proponents claimed there was no choice. Only through an all-out attack on Britain's supply shipping, they argued, could Germany win the war before the British blockade and trench warfare in France had exhausted Germany's ability to keep fighting. If the U-boats could sink 600,000 tons of Allied shipping per month, the German admiralty estimated, Britain would be brought to the brink of starvation. True, the United States might enter the war, but that was a risk worth taking. Victory might be achieved before U.S. troops could be ferried across the Atlantic in sizable numbers. It proved a winning argument. In early February 1917, Germany launched unrestricted submarine warfare. All warships and merchant vessels—belligerent or neutral—would be attacked if sighted in the declared war zone. Wilson quickly broke diplomatic relations with Berlin.

This German challenge to American neutral rights and economic interests was soon followed by a German threat to U.S. security. In late February, British intelligence intercepted and passed to U.S. officials a telegram addressed to the German minister in Mexico from German foreign secretary Arthur Zimmermann. Its message: If Mexico joined a military alliance against the United States, Germany would help Mexico recover the territories it had lost in 1848, including several western states. Zimmermann hoped to "set new enemies on America's neck—enemies which give them plenty to take care of over there."

The Zimmermann telegram stiffened Wilson's resolve. Even though Mexico City rejected Germany's offer, the Wilson administration judged Zimmermann's telegram "a conspiracy against this country." Mexico still might let German agents use Mexican soil to propagandize against the United States, if not sabotage American properties. The prospect of a German-Mexican collaboration helped turn the tide of opinion in the American Southwest, where antiwar sentiment had been strong.

Soon afterward, Wilson asked Congress for "armed neutrality" to defend American lives and commerce. He requested authority to arm American merchant ships and to "employ any other instrumentalities or methods that may be necessary." In the midst of the debate, Wilson released Zimmermann's telegram to the press. Americans were outraged. Still, antiwar senators Robert M. La Follette and George Norris, among others, saw the armed-ship bill as a blank check for the president to move the country to war, and they filibustered it to death. Wilson proceeded to arm America's commercial vessels anyway. The action came too late to prevent the sinking of several American ships. War cries echoed across the nation. In late March, an agonized Wilson called Congress into special session.

War Message and War Declaration   On April 2, 1917, the president stepped before a hushed Congress. Solemnly, he accused the Germans of "warfare against mankind." Passionately and eloquently, Wilson enumerated U.S. grievances: Germany's violation of freedom of the seas, disruption of commerce, interference with Mexico, and breach of human rights by killing innocent Americans. The "Prussian autocracy" had to be punished by "the democracies." Russia was now among the latter, he was pleased to report, because the Russian Revolution had ousted the czar just weeks before. Congress declared war against Germany on April 6 by a vote of 373 to 50 in the House and 82 to 6 in the Senate. (This vote was for war against Germany only; a declaration of war against Austria-Hungary came several months later, on December 7.) Montana's Jeannette Rankin, the first woman ever to sit in Congress, cast a ringing no vote. "Peace is a woman's job," she declared, "because men have a natural fear of being classed as cowards if they oppose war" and because mothers should protect their children from death-dealing weapons.

For principle, for morality, for honor, for commerce, for security, for reform—for all of these reasons, Wilson took the United States into the Great War. The submarine was certainly the culprit that drew a reluctant president and nation into the maelstrom. Yet critics did not attribute the U.S. descent into war to the U-boat alone. They emphasized Wilson's rigid definition of international law, which did not accommodate the submarine's tactics. They faulted his contention that Americans should be entitled to travel anywhere, even on a belligerent ship loaded with contraband. They criticized his policies as nonneutral. But they lost the debate. Most Americans came to accept Wilson's view that the Germans had to be checked to ensure an open, orderly world in which U.S. principles and interests would be safe.

America went to war to reform world politics, not to destroy Germany. Wilson once claimed that the United States was "pure air blowing in world politics, destroying illusions and cleaning places of morbid miasmic gasses." By early 1917, the president concluded that America would not be able to claim a seat at the postwar peace conference unless it became a combatant. At the peace conference, Wilson intended to promote the principles he thought essential to a stable world order, to advance democracy and the Open Door, and to outlaw revolution and aggression. Wilson tried to preserve part of his country's status as a neutral by designating the United States an "Associated" power rather than a full-fledged Allied nation, but this was akin to a hope of being only partly pregnant.

WINNING THE WAR

Even before the U.S. declaration of war, the Wilson administration—encouraged by such groups as the National Security League and the Navy League, and by mounting public outrage against Germany's submarine warfare—had been strengthening the military under the banner of "preparedness." When the pacifist song "I Didn't Raise My Boy to Be a Soldier" became popular, preparedness proponents retorted, "I Didn't Raise My Boy to Be a Coward." The National Defense Act of 1916 provided for increases in the army and National Guard and for summer training camps modeled on the one in Plattsburgh, New York, where a slice of America's social and economic elite had trained in 1915 as "citizen-soldiers." The Navy Act of 1916 started the largest naval expansion in American history.

The Draft and the Soldier   To raise an army after the declaration of war, Congress in May 1917 passed the Selective Service Act, requiring all males between the ages of twenty-one and thirty (later changed to eighteen and forty-five) to register. National service, proponents believed, would not only prepare the nation for battle but also instill patriotism and respect for order, democracy, and personal sacrifice. Critics feared it would lead to the militarization of American life.

On June 5, 1917, more than 9.5 million men signed up for the "great national lottery." By war's end, 24 million men had been registered by local draft boards. Of this number, 4.8 million had served in the armed forces, 2 million of that number in France. Among them were hundreds of thousands who had volunteered before December 1917, when the government prohibited enlistment because the military judged voluntarism too inefficient (many volunteers were more useful in civilian factories than in the army) and too competitive (enlistees got to choose the service they wanted, thus setting off recruiting wars). Millions of laborers received deferments from military duty because they worked in war industries or had dependents.

The typical soldier was a draftee in his early to mid-twenties, white, single, American-born, and poorly educated (most had not attended high school, and perhaps 30 percent could not read or write). Tens of thousands of women enlisted in the army Nurse Corps, served as "hello girls" (volunteer bilingual telephone operators) in the army Signal Corps, and became clerks in the navy and Marine Corps. On college campuses, 150,000 students joined the Student Army Training Corps or similar navy and marine units. At officer training camps, the army turned out "ninety-day wonders."

Some 400,000 African Americans also served in the military. Although many southern politicians feared arming blacks, the army drafted them into segregated units, where they were assigned to menial labor and endured crude abuse and miserable conditions. Ultimately, more than 40,000 African Americans would see combat in Europe, however, and several black units served with distinction in various divisions of the French army. The all-black 369th Infantry Regiment, for example, spent more time in the trenches—191 days—and received more medals than any other American outfit. The French government awarded the entire regiment the Croix de Guerre.

Although French officers had their share of racial prejudice and often treated the soldiers from their own African colonies poorly, black Americans serving with the French reported a degree of respect and cooperation generally lacking in the U.S. army. They also spoke of getting a much warmer reception from French civilians than they were used to in the United States. The irony was not lost on African American leaders, such as W. E. B. Du Bois. Du Bois had endorsed the support of the National Association for the Advancement of Colored People (NAACP) for the war and echoed its call for blacks to volunteer for the fight so that they might help make the world safe for democracy and help blur the color lines at home.

Not everyone eligible for military service was eager to sign up, however. Approximately 3 million men evaded draft registration. Some were arrested, and others fled to Mexico or Canada, but most stayed at home and were never discovered. Another 338,000 men who had registered and been summoned by their draft boards failed to show up for induction. According to arrest records, most of these "deserters" and the more numerous "evaders" were lower-income agricultural and industrial laborers. Some simply felt overwhelmed by the government bureaucracy

Some fifteen thousand Native Americans served in the military in World War I. Most of them were enlistees who sought escape from restrictive Indian schools and lives of poverty, opportunities to develop new skills, and chances to prove their patriotism. This photo shows Fast Fred Horse, a Rosebud Sioux, as he recuperates in a New York hospital after suffering injury and paralysis during the Meuse-Argonne campaign of fall 1918. Unlike African Americans, Native Americans were not assigned to segregated units during the war. Native Americans participated in all major battles against German forces and suffered a high casualty rate in large part because they served as scouts, messengers, and snipers.

William Hammond Mathers Museum, Indiana University

and stayed away; others were members of minority or ethnic groups who felt alienated. Although nearly 65,000 draftees initially applied for conscientious-objector status (refusing to bear arms for religious or pacifist reasons), some changed their minds or, like so many others, failed preinduction examinations. Quakers and Mennonites were numerous among the 4,000 inductees actually classified as conscientious objectors (COs). They did not have it easy. General Leonard Wood called COs "enemies of the Republic," and the military harassed them. COs who refused noncombat service, such as in the medical corps, faced imprisonment.

Trench Warfare   The U.S. troops who shipped out to France would do their fighting under American command. General John J. Pershing, head of the American Expeditionary Forces (AEF), insisted that his "sturdy rookies" remain a separate, independent army. He was not about to turn over his "doughboys" (so termed, apparently, because the large buttons on American uniforms in the 1860s resembled a deep-fried bread of that name) to Allied commanders, who had become wedded to unimaginative and deadly trench warfare, producing a military stalemate and ghastly casualties on the western front. Since the fall of 1914, zigzag trenches fronted by barbed wire and mines stretched across France. Between the muddy, stinking trenches lay "no man's land," denuded by artillery fire. When ordered out, soldiers would charge enemy trenches. If machine gun fire did not greet them, poison gas might.

First used by the Germans in April 1915, chlorine gas stimulated overproduction of fluid in the lungs, leading to death by drowning. One British officer tending to troops who had been gassed reported that "quite 200 men passed through my hands.... Some died with me, others on the way down.... I had to argue with many of them as to whether they were dead or not." Gas in a variety of forms (mustard and phosgene, in addition to chlorine) would continue in use throughout the war, sometimes blistering, sometimes incapacitating, often killing.

The extent of the dying in the trench warfare is hard to comprehend. At the Battle of the Somme in 1916, the British and French suffered 600,000 dead or wounded to earn only 125 square miles; the Germans lost 400,000 men. At Verdun that same year, 336,000 Germans perished, and at Passchendaele in 1917 more than 370,000 British men died to gain about 40 miles of mud and barbed wire. Ambassador Page grew sickened by what Europe had become—"a bankrupt slaughter-house inhabited by unmated women."

Shell Shock   The first American units landed in France on June 26, 1917, marched in a Fourth of July parade in Paris, and then moved by train toward the front. They soon learned about the horrors caused by advanced weaponry. Some suffered shell shock, a form of mental illness also known as war psychosis. Symptoms included a fixed, empty stare; violent tremors; paralyzed limbs; listlessness; jabbering and screaming; and haunting dreams. The illness could strike anyone; even those soldiers who appeared most manly and courageous cracked after days of incessant shelling and inescapable human carnage. "There was a limit to human endurance," one lieutenant explained. Providing some relief were Red Cross canteens, staffed by women volunteers, which gave soldiers way stations in a strange land and offered haircuts, food, and recreation. Some ten thousand Red Cross nurses also cared for the young warriors, while the American Library Association distributed 10 million books and magazines.

In Paris, where forty large houses of prostitution thrived, it became commonplace to hear that the British were drunkards, the French were whoremongers, and the Americans were both. Venereal disease became a serious problem. French prime minister Georges Clemenceau offered licensed, inspected prostitutes in "special houses" to the American army. When the generous Gallic offer reached Washington, Secretary of War Newton Baker gasped, "For God's sake ... don't show this to the President or he'll stop the war." By war's end, about 15 percent of America's soldiers had contracted venereal disease, costing the army $50 million and 7 million days of active duty. Periodic inspections, chemical prophylactic treatments, and the threat of court-martial for infected soldiers kept the problem from being even greater.

American Units in France   The experience of being in Europe enlarged what for many American draftees had been a circumscribed world. Soldiers filled their diaries and letters with descriptions of the local customs and "ancient" architecture, and noted how the grimy and war-torn French countryside bore little resemblance to the groomed landscapes they had seen in paintings. Some felt both admiration for the spirit of endurance they saw in the populace and irritation that the locals were not more grateful for the Americans' arrival. "Life in France for the American soldier meant marching in the dirt and mud, living in cellars in filth, being wet and cold and fighting," the chief of staff of the Fourth Division remarked. "He had come to help France in the hour of distress and he was glad he came but these French people did not seem to appreciate him at all."

The influx of American men and materiel—and the morale blow they delivered to the Central Powers—decided the outcome of the First World War. With both sides exhausted, the Americans tipped the balance toward the Allies. It took time, though, for the weight of the American military machine to make itself felt. From an early point, the U.S. Navy battled submarines and escorted troop carriers, and pilots in the U.S. Air Service, flying mostly British and French aircraft, saw limited action, mostly against German ground troops and transport. American "aces" like Eddie Rickenbacker took on their German counterparts in aerial "dogfights" and became heroes, as much in France as in their own country. But only ground troops could make a decisive difference, and American units actually did not engage in much combat until after the lull in the fighting during the harsh winter of 1917–1918.

The Bolshevik Revolution

By then, the military and diplomatic situation had changed dramatically because of an event that was arguably the most important political development of the twentieth century: the Bolshevik Revolution in Russia. In November 1917, the liberal-democratic government of Aleksander Kerensky, which had led the country since the czar's abdication early in the year, was overthrown by radical socialists led by V. I. Lenin. Lenin seized power vowing to change world politics and end imperial rivalries on terms that challenged Woodrow Wilson's. Lenin saw the war as signaling the impending end of capitalism and looked for a global revolution, carried out by workers, that would sweep away the "imperialist order." For western leaders, the prospect of Bolshevik-style revolutions spreading worldwide was too frightening to contemplate. The ascendancy of the world's laboring classes working in unity would destroy governments everywhere.

In the weeks following their takeover, the Bolsheviks attempted to embarrass the capitalist governments and incite world revolution by publishing several secret agreements among the Allies for dividing up the colonies and other territories of the Central Powers in the event of an Allied victory. Veteran watchers of world affairs found nothing particularly shocking in the documents, and Wilson had known of them, but the disclosures belied the noble rhetoric of Allied war aims. Wilson confided to Colonel House that he really wanted to tell the Bolsheviks to "go to hell," but he accepted the colonel's argument that he would have to address Lenin's claims that there was little to distinguish the two warring sides and that socialism represented the future.

Fourteen Points

The result was the Fourteen Points, unveiled in January 1918, in which Wilson reaffirmed America's commitment to an international system governed by laws and renounced territorial gains as a legitimate war aim. The first five points called for diplomacy "in the public view," freedom of the seas, lower tariffs, reductions in armaments, and the decolonization of empires. The next eight points specified the evacuation of foreign troops from Russia, Belgium, and France, and appealed for self-determination for nationalities in Europe, such as the Poles. For Wilson, the fourteenth point was the most important—the mechanism for achieving all the others: "a general association of nations" or League of Nations.

Wilson's appeal did not impress Lenin, who called for an immediate end to the fighting, the eradication of colonialism, and self-determination for all peoples. Lenin also made a separate peace with Germany—the Treaty of Brest-Litovsk, signed on March 3, 1918. The deal erased centuries of Russian expansion, as Poland, Finland, and the Baltic states were taken from Russia and Ukraine was granted independence. One of Lenin's motives was to allow Russian troops loyal to the Bolsheviks to return home to fight anti-Bolshevik forces, who had launched a civil war to oust the new government.

The emerging feud between Lenin and Wilson contained the seeds of the super-power confrontation that would dominate the international system after 1945. Both men rejected the old diplomacy, which they claimed had created the conditions for the current war; both insisted on the need for a new world order. Although each professed adherence to democratic principles, they defined democracy differently. For Lenin, it meant workers everywhere seizing control from the owners of capital and establishing worker-led governments. For Wilson, it meant independent governments operating within capitalist systems and according to republican political practices.

Americans in Battle   In March 1918, with German troops released from the Russian front and transferred to France, the Germans launched a major offensive. By May, they had pushed to within 50 miles of Paris. Late that month, troops of the U.S. First Division helped blunt the German advance at Cantigny (see Map 23.2). In June, the Third Division and French forces held positions along the Marne River at Château-Thierry, and the Second Division soon attacked the Germans in the Belleau Wood. American soldiers won the battle after three weeks of fighting, but thousands died or were wounded after they made almost sacrificial frontal assaults against German machine guns.

Allied victory in the Second Battle of the Marne in July 1918 stemmed all German advances. In September, French and American forces took St. Mihiel in a ferocious battle in which American gunners fired 100,000 rounds of phosgene gas shells. Then the Allies began their massive Meuse-Argonne offensive. More than 1 million Americans joined British and French troops in weeks of fierce combat; some 26,000 Americans died before the Allies claimed the Argonne Forest on October 10. For Germany—its ground and submarine war stymied, its troops and cities mutinous, its allies Turkey and Austria dropping out, its Kaiser abdicated, and facing the prospect of endless American troop reinforcements—peace became imperative. The Germans accepted a punishing armistice that took effect on the morning of November 11, 1918, at the eleventh hour of the eleventh day of the eleventh month.

MAP 23.2 American Troops at the Western Front, 1918

America's 2 million troops in France met German forces head-on, ensuring the defeat of the Central Powers in 1918.

Casualties   The cost of the war is impossible to compute, but the scale is clear enough: the belligerents counted 10 million soldiers and 6.6 million civilians dead and 21.3 million people wounded. Fifty-three thousand American soldiers died in battle, and another 62,000 died from disease. Many of the latter died from the virulent strain of influenza that ravaged the world in late 1918 and would ultimately claim more victims than the Great War itself. The economic damage was colossal as well, helping to account for the widespread starvation Europe experienced in the winter of 1918–1919. Economic output on the continent dwindled, and transport over any distance was in some countries virtually nonexistent. "We are at the dead season of our fortunes," wrote one British observer. "Never in the lifetime of men now living has the universal element in the soul of man burnt so dimly."

Casualties of the conflagration, the German, Austro-Hungarian, Ottoman, and Russian empires were no more. For a time, it appeared the Bolshevik Revolution might spread westward, as communist uprisings shook Germany and parts of central Europe. Even before the armistice, revolutionaries temporarily took power in the German cities of Bremen, Hamburg, and Lübeck. In Hungary, a government actually held power for several months, while Austria was racked by left-wing demonstrations. In Moscow, meanwhile, the new Soviet state sought to consolidate its power. "We are sitting upon an open powder magazine," Colonel House worried, "and some day a spark may ignite it."

The Influenza Pandemic of 1918

In the summer and fall of 1918, as World War I neared its end, a terrible plague swept the earth. It was a massive outbreak of influenza, and it would kill more than twice as many as the Great War itself—somewhere between 25 and 40 million people. In the United States, 675,000 people died.

The first cases were identified in midwestern military camps in early March. Soldiers complained of flulike symptoms—headache, sore throat, fever—and many did not recover. At Fort Riley, Kansas, 48 men died. But with the war effort in full swing, few in government or the press took notice. Soldiers shipped out to Europe in large numbers (84,000 in March), some unknowingly carrying the virus in their lungs. The illness appeared on the western front in April. By the end of June, an estimated 8 million Spaniards were infected, thereby giving the disease its name, the Spanish flu.

In August, after a midsummer lull, a second, deadlier form of the influenza began spreading. This time, the epidemic erupted simultaneously in three cities on three continents: Freetown, Sierra Leone, in Africa; Brest, France, the port of entry for many American soldiers; and Boston, Massachusetts. In September, the disease swept down the East Coast to New York, Philadelphia, and beyond. That month, 12,000 Americans died.

It was a flu like no other. People could be healthy at the start of the weekend and dead by the end of it. Some experienced a rapid accumulation of fluid in the lungs and would quite literally drown. Others died more slowly, of secondary infections with bacterial pneumonia. Mortality rates were highest for twenty- to twenty-nine-year-olds—the same group dying in huge numbers in the trenches.

In October, the epidemic hit full force. It spread to Japan, India, Africa, and Latin America. In the United States, 200,000 perished. There was a nationwide shortage of caskets and gravediggers, and funerals were limited to fifteen minutes. Bodies were left in gutters or on front porches, to be picked up by trucks that drove the streets. Stores were forbidden to hold sales; schools and cinemas closed. Army surgeon general Victor Vaughan made a frightening calculation: "If the epidemic continues its mathematical rate of acceleration, civilization could easily disappear from the face of the earth within a few weeks."

Then, suddenly, in November, for reasons still unclear, the epidemic eased, though the dying continued into 1919. In England and Wales, the final toll was

MOBILIZING THE HOME FRONT

"It is not an army that we must shape and train for war," declared President Wilson, "it is a nation." The United States was a belligerent for only nineteen months, but the war had a tremendous impact at home. The federal government moved swiftly to expand its power over the economy to meet war needs and intervened in American life as never before. The vastly enlarged Washington bureaucracy managed the economy, labor force, military, public opinion, and more. Federal expenditures increased tremendously as the government spent more than $760 million a month from April 1917 to August 1919. As tax revenues lagged behind, the administration resorted to deficit spending. The total cost of the war was difficult to

200,000. Samoa lost a quarter of its population, while in India the epidemic may have claimed a staggering 20 million. It was, in historian Roy Porter's words, "the greatest single demographic shock mankind has ever experienced."

World War I had helped spread the disease, but so had technological improvements that in previous decades facilitated global travel. The world was a smaller, more intimate place, often for good but sometimes for ill. Americans, accustomed to thinking that two great oceans could isolate them, were reminded that they were immutably linked to humankind.

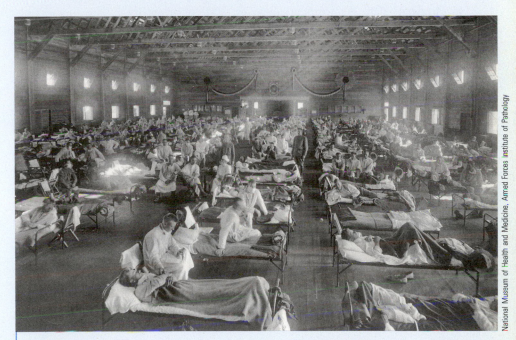

National Museum of Health and Medicine, Armed Forces Institute of Pathology

The influenza pandemic of 1918 perhaps started in earnest here, at Camp Funston, Kansas, in the spring of that year. Soldiers were struck with a debilitating illness they called "knock me down fever."

calculate because future generations would have to pay veterans' benefits and interest on loans. To Progressives of the New Nationalist persuasion, the wartime expansion and centralization of government power were welcome. To others, these changes seemed excessive, leading to concentrated, hence dangerous, federal power.

Business-Government Cooperation

The federal government and private business became partners during the war. So-called dollar-a-year executives flocked to the nation's capital from major companies, retaining their corporate salaries while serving in official administrative and consulting capacities. But evidence of self-interested business-people cashing in on the national interest aroused public protest. The head of the aluminum advisory committee, for example, was also president of the largest aluminum company. The assorted committees were disbanded in July 1917 in favor of a single manager, the War Industries Board. But the federal government continued to work closely with business through trade associations, which grew significantly to two thousand by 1920. The government also suspended antitrust laws and signed cost-plus contracts, which guaranteed companies a healthy profit and a means to pay higher wages to head off labor strikes. Competitive bidding was virtually abandoned. Under such wartime practices, big business grew bigger.

Hundreds of new government agencies, staffed primarily by businesspeople, placed controls on the economy in order to shift the nation's resources to the Allies, the AEF, and war-related production. The Food Administration, led by engineer and investor Herbert Hoover, launched voluntary programs to increase production and conserve food—Americans were urged to grow "victory gardens" and to eat meatless and wheatless meals—but it also set prices and regulated distribution. The Railroad Administration took over the railway industry. The Fuel Administration controlled coal supplies and rationed gasoline. When strikes threatened the telephone and telegraph companies, the federal government seized and ran them.

The largest of the superagencies was the War Industries Board (WIB), headed by financier Bernard Baruch. At one point, this Wall Streeter told Henry Ford frankly that he would dispatch the military to seize his plants if the automaker did not accept WIB limits on car production. Ford relented. Although the WIB seemed all-powerful, in reality it had to conciliate competing interest groups and compromise with the business executives whose advice it so valued. Designed as a clearing-house for coordinating the national economy, the WIB made purchases, allocated supplies, and fixed prices at levels that business requested. The WIB also ordered the standardization of goods to save materials and streamline production. The varieties of automobile tires, for example, were reduced from 287 to 3.

Economic Performance

The performance of the mobilized economy was mixed, but it delivered enough men and materiel to France to ensure the defeat of the Central Powers. About one-quarter of all American production was diverted to war needs. As farmers enjoyed boom years of higher prices, they put more acreage into production and mechanized as never before. From 1915 to 1920, the number of tractors in American fields jumped tenfold. Gross farm income for the period from 1914 to 1919 increased more than 230 percent. Although manufacturing output leveled off in 1918, some industries realized substantial growth because of wartime demand. Steel reached a peak production of 45 million tons in 1917, twice the prewar figure. As U.S. soldiers popularized American brands in Europe, tobacconists profited from a huge increase in cigarette sales: from 26 billion cigarettes in 1916 to 48 billion in 1918. Overall, the gross national product in 1920 stood 237 percent higher than in 1914.

The rush to complete massive assignments caused mistakes to be made. Weapons deliveries fell short of demand; the bloated bureaucracy of the War Shipping Board failed to build enough ships. In the severe winter of 1917–1918, millions of

Americans could not get coal. Coal companies held back on production to raise prices; railroads did not have enough coal cars; and harbors froze, closing out coal barges. People died from pneumonia and freezing. A Brooklyn man went out in the morning to forage for coal and returned to find his two-month-old daughter frozen to death in her crib.

To help pay its wartime bills, the government dramatically increased taxes. The Revenue Act in 1916 started the process by raising the surtax on high incomes and corporate profits, imposing a federal tax on large estates, and significantly increasing the tax on munitions manufacturers. Still, the government financed only one-third of the war through taxes. The other two-thirds came from loans, including Liberty bonds sold to the American people through aggressive campaigns. The War Revenue Act of 1917 provided for a more steeply graduated personal income tax; a corporate income tax; an excess-profits tax; and increased excise taxes on alcoholic beverages, tobacco, and luxury items.

Although these taxes did curb excessive corporate profiteering, there were loopholes. Sometimes companies inflated costs to conceal profits or paid high salaries and bonuses to their executives. Four officers of Bethlehem Steel, for example, divided bonuses of $2.3 million in 1917 and $2.1 million the next year. Corporate net earnings for 1913 totaled $4 billion; in 1917, they reached $7 billion; and in 1918, after the tax bite and the war's end, they still stood at $4.5 billion. Profits and patriotism went hand in hand in America's war experience. The abrupt cancellation of billions of dollars' worth of contracts at the end of the war, however, caused a brief economic downturn, a short boom, and then an intense decline (see Chapter 24).

Labor Shortage

For American workers, the full-employment wartime economy increased earnings and gave many of them time-and-a-half pay for overtime work. With the higher cost of living, however, workers saw minimal improvement in their economic standing. Turnover rates were high as workers switched jobs for higher pay and better conditions. Some employers sought to overcome labor shortages by expanding welfare and social programs, and by establishing personnel departments—"specialized human nature engineers to keep its human machinery frictionless," as General Electric explained.

To meet the labor crisis, the Department of Labor's U.S. Employment Service matched laborers with job vacancies, especially attracting workers from the South and Midwest to war industries in the East. The department also temporarily relaxed the literacy-test and head-tax provisions of immigration law to attract farm labor, miners, and railroad workers from Mexico. Because the labor crisis also generated a housing crisis as workers crammed into cities, the U.S. Housing Corporation and Emergency Fleet Corporation, following British example, built row houses in Newport News, Virginia, and Eddystone, Pennsylvania.

The tight wartime labor market had another consequence: new work opportunities for women. In Connecticut, a special motion picture, Mr. and *Mrs. Hines of Stamford Do Their Bit*, appealed to housewives' patriotism, urging them to take factory jobs. Although the total number of women in the work force increased slightly, the real story was that many changed jobs, sometimes moving into formerly male domains. Some white women left domestic service for factories, shifted from clerking in department stores to stenography and typing, or departed textile mills for employment in firearms plants. At least 20 percent of all workers in the wartime electrical-machinery, airplane, and food industries were women. Some 100,000 women worked in the railroad industry. As white women took advantage of these new opportunities, black women took some of their places in domestic service and in textile factories. For the first time, department stores employed black women as elevator operators and cafeteria waitresses. Most working women were single and remained concentrated in sex-segregated occupations, serving as typists, nurses, teachers, and domestic servants.

Women also participated in the war effort in other ways. As volunteers, they made clothing for refugees and soldiers, served at Red Cross facilities, and taught French to nurses. Some drove ambulances in the war zone. Many worked for the Women's Committee of the Council of National Defense, whose leaders included Ida Tarbell and Carrie Chapman Catt. A vast network of state, county, and town volunteer organizations, the council publicized government mobilization programs, encouraged home gardens, sponsored drives to sell Liberty bonds, and continued the push for social welfare reforms. This patriotic work won praise from men and improved the prospects for passage of the Nineteenth Amendment granting woman suffrage. "We have made partners of women in this war," Wilson said as he endorsed woman suffrage in 1918. "Shall we admit them only to a partnership of suffering and sacrifice … and not to a partnership of privilege and right?"

Among African Americans, war mobilization wrought significant change as southern blacks undertook a great migration to northern cities to work in railroad yards, packing houses, steel mills, shipyards, and coal mines. Between 1910 and 1920, Cleveland's black population swelled by more than 300 percent, Detroit's by more than 600 percent, and Chicago's by 150 percent. Much of the increase occurred between 1916 and 1919. All told, about a half-million African Americans uprooted themselves to move to the North. Families sometimes pooled savings to send one member; others sold their household goods to pay for the journey. Most of the migrants were males—young (in their early twenties), unmarried, and skilled or semiskilled. Wartime jobs in the North provided an escape from low wages, sharecropping, tenancy, crop liens, debt peonage, lynchings, and political disfranchisement. To a friend back in Mississippi, one African American wrote: "I just begin to feel like a man…. I don't have to humble to no one. I have registered. Will vote the next election."

National War Labor Board   To keep factories running smoothly, Wilson instituted the National War Labor Board (NWLB) in early 1918. The NWLB discouraged strikes and lockouts and urged management to negotiate with existing unions. In July, after the Western Union Company fired eight hundred union members for trying to organize the firm's workers and then defied an NWLB request to reinstate the employees, the president nationalized the telegraph lines and put the laborers back to work. That month, too, the NWLB directed General Electric to raise wages and stop discriminating against metal trades union members in Schenectady, New York. On the other hand, in September the NWLB ordered striking Bridgeport, Connecticut, machinists back to munitions factories, threatening to revoke their draft exemptions (granted earlier because they worked in an "essential" industry).

Many labor leaders hoped the war would offer opportunities for recognition and better pay through partnership with government. Samuel Gompers threw the AFL's loyalty to the Wilson administration, promising to deter strikes. He and other moderate labor leaders accepted appointments to federal agencies. The anti-war Socialist Party blasted the AFL for becoming a "fifth wheel on [the] capitalist war chariot," but union membership climbed from roughly 2.5 million in 1916 to more than 4 million in 1919.

The AFL, however, could not curb strikes by the radical Industrial Workers of the World (IWW, also known as "Wobblies") or rebellious AFL locals, especially those controlled by labor activists and socialists. In the nineteen war months, more than six thousand strikes expressed workers' demands for a "living wage" and improved working conditions (many called for an eight-hour workday). Exploiting Wilsonian wartime rhetoric, workers and their unions also sought to create "industrial democracy," a more representative workplace with a role for labor in determining job categories and content, and with workplace representation through shop committees. By 1920, in defiance of the national AFL, labor parties had sprung up in twenty-three states.

CIVIL LIBERTIES UNDER CHALLENGE

Gompers's backing of the call to arms meant a great deal to Wilson and his advisers, and they noted with satisfaction that most newspapers, religious leaders, and public officials were similarly supportive. They were less certain, however, about the attitudes of ordinary Americans. "Woe be to the man that seeks to stand in our way in this day of high resolution," the president warned. An official and unofficial campaign soon began to silence dissenters who questioned Wilson's decision for war or who protested the draft. In the end, the Wilson administration compiled one of the worst civil liberties records in American history.

The targets of governmental and quasi-vigilante repression were the hundreds of thousands of Americans and aliens who refused to support the war: pacifists from all walks of life, conscientious objectors, socialists, radical labor groups, the debt-ridden tenant farmers of Oklahoma who staged the Green Corn Rebellion against the draft, the Non-Partisan League, reformers like Robert La Follette and Jane Addams, and countless others. In the wartime process of debating the question of the right to speak freely in a democracy, the concept of "civil liberties" emerged for the first time in American history as a major public policy issue.

The Committee on Public Information   The centerpiece of the administration's campaign to win support for the war was the Committee on Public Information (CPI), formed in April 1917 and headed by Progressive journalist George Creel. Employing some of the nation's most talented writers and scholars, the CPI used propaganda to shape and mobilize public opinion. Pamphlets and films demonized the Germans, and CPI "Four-Minute Men" spoke at movie theaters, schools, and churches to pump up a patriotic mood. Encouraged by the CPI to promote American participation in the war, film companies and their trade association, the National Association of the Motion Picture Industry, produced documentaries, newsreels, and anti-German movies, such as *The Kaiser, the Beast of Berlin* (1918) and *To Hell with the Kaiser* (1918).

The committee also urged the press to practice "self-censorship" and encouraged people to spy on their neighbors. Ultrapatriotic groups, such as the Sedition Slammers and the American Defense Society, used vigilantism. A German American miner in Illinois was wrapped in a flag and lynched. In Hilger, Montana, citizens burned history texts that mentioned Germany. By the end of the war, sixteen states had banned the teaching of the German language. To avoid trouble, the Kaiser-Kuhn grocery in St. Louis changed its name to Pioneer Grocery. Germantown, Nebraska, became Garland, and the townspeople in Berlin, Iowa, henceforth hailed from Lincoln. The German shepherd became the Alsatian shepherd.

Because towns had Liberty Loan quotas to fill, they sometimes bullied "slackers" into purchasing bonds. Nativist advocates of "100% Americanism" exploited the emotional atmosphere to exhort immigrants to throw off their Old World cultures. Companies offered English language and naturalization classes in their factories and refused jobs and promotions to those who did not make adequate strides toward learning English. Even labor's drive for compulsory health insurance, which before the war had gained advocates in several states, including New York and California, became victimized by the poisoned war atmosphere. Many physicians and insurance companies had for years denounced health insurance as "socialistic"; after the United States entered the war, they discredited it as "Made in Germany."

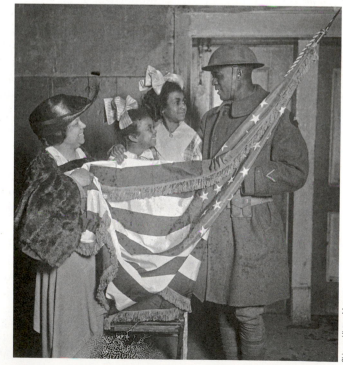

A member of the Eighth Regiment of the Illinois National Guard with his family, circa 1918. Originally organized as a volunteer regiment during the Spanish-American War in 1898, the Eighth Regiment achieved its greatest fame during World War I. The only regiment to be entirely commanded by blacks and headquartered at the only black armory in the U.S., the "Fighting 8th" served with distinction in France, with 143 of its members losing their lives.

Chicago History Museum

Even institutions that had long prided themselves on tolerance became contaminated by the spirit of coercion. Wellesley College economics professor Emily Greene Balch was fired for her pacifist views (she won the Nobel Peace Prize in 1946). Three Columbia University students were apprehended in mid-1917 for circulating an antiwar petition. Columbia also fired Professor J. M. Cattell, a distinguished psychologist, for his antiwar stand. His colleague Charles Beard, a historian with a prowar perspective, resigned in protest, stating, "If we have to suppress everything we don't like to hear, this country is resting on a pretty wobbly basis." In a number of states, local school boards dismissed teachers who questioned the war.

Espionage and Sedition Acts   The Wilson administration also guided through an obliging Congress the Espionage Act (1917) and the Sedition Act (1918). The first statute forbade "false statements" designed to impede the draft or promote military insubordination, and it banned from the mails materials considered treasonous. The Sedition Act made it unlawful to obstruct the sale of war bonds and to use "disloyal, profane, scurrilous, or abusive" language to describe the government, the Constitution, the flag, or the military uniform. These loosely worded laws gave the government wide latitude to crack down on critics. More than two thousand people were prosecuted under the acts, and many others were intimidated into silence.

Progressives and conservatives alike used the war emergency to throttle the Industrial Workers of the World and the Socialist Party. Government agents raided IWW meetings, and the army marched into western mining and lumber regions to put down IWW strikes. By the end of the war, most of the union's leaders were in jail. In summer 1918, with a government stenographer present, Socialist Party leader Eugene V. Debs delivered a spirited oration extolling socialism and freedom of speech—including the freedom to criticize the Wilson administration for taking America into the war. Federal agents arrested him. Debs told the court what many dissenters—and, later, many jurists and scholars—thought of the Espionage Act: it was "a despotic enactment in flagrant conflict with democratic principles and with the spirit of free institutions." Handed a ten-year sentence, Debs remained in prison until late 1921, when he received a pardon.

The Supreme Court endorsed such convictions. In *Schenck v. U.S.* (1919), the Court unanimously upheld the conviction of a Socialist Party member who had mailed pamphlets urging resistance to the draft. In time of war, Justice Oliver Wendell Holmes wrote, the First Amendment could be restricted: "Free speech would not protect a man falsely shouting 'fire' in a theater and causing panic." If, according to Holmes, words "are of such a nature as to create a clear and present danger that they will bring about the substantial evils that Congress has a right to prevent," free speech could be limited.

RED SCARE, RED SUMMER

The line between wartime suppression of dissent and the postwar Red Scare is not easily drawn. In the name of patriotism, both harassed suspected internal enemies and deprived them of their constitutional rights; both had government sanction.

Together, they stabbed at the Bill of Rights and wounded radicalism in America. Yet in at least two respects, the phenomena were different. Whereas in wartime the main fear had been of subversion, after the armistice it was revolution; and whereas in 1917 the target had often been German Americans, in 1919 it was frequently organized labor. The Russian Revolution and the communist uprisings elsewhere in Europe alarmed many Americans, and the fears grew when in 1919 the Soviet leadership announced the formation of the Communist International (or Comintern), whose purpose was to export revolution throughout the world. Terrified conservatives responded by looking for pro-Bolshevik sympathizers (or "Reds," from the red flag used by communists) in the United States, especially in immigrant groups and labor unions.

Labor Strikes

Labor union leaders emerged out of the war determined to secure higher wages for workers, to meet rising prices, and to retain wartime bargaining rights. Employers instead rescinded benefits they had been forced to grant to labor during the war, including recognition of unions. The result was a rash of labor strikes in 1919, which sparked the Red Scare. All told, more than 3,300 strikes involving 4 million laborers jolted the nation that year, including the Seattle general strike in January. On May 1, a day of celebration for workers around the world, bombs were sent through the mails to prominent Americans. Most of the devices were intercepted and dismantled, but police never captured the conspirators. Most people assumed, not unreasonably, that anarchists and others bent on the destruction of the American way of life were responsible. Next came the Boston police strike in September. Some sniffed a Bolshevik conspiracy, but others thought it ridiculous to label Boston's Irish American, Catholic cops "radicals." The conservative governor of Massachusetts, Calvin Coolidge, gained national attention by proclaiming that nobody had the right to strike against the public safety. State guardsmen soon replaced the striking policemen.

Unrest in the steel industry in September stirred more ominous fears. Many steelworkers worked twelve hours a day, seven days a week, and lived in squalid housing. They looked to local steel unions, organized by the National Committee for Organizing Iron and Steel Workers, to help them improve their lives. When postwar unemployment in the industry climbed and the U.S. Steel Corporation refused to meet with committee representatives, some 350,000 workers walked off the job, demanding the right to collective bargaining, a shorter workday, and a living wage. The steel barons hired strikebreakers and sent agents to club strikers. Worried about both the 1919 strikes and Bolshevism, President Wilson warned against "the poison of disorder" and the "poison of revolt." But in the case of steel, the companies won; the strike collapsed in early 1920.

One of the leaders of the steel strike was William Z. Foster, a former IWW member and militant labor organizer who later joined the Communist Party. His presence in a labor movement seeking bread-and-butter goals permitted political and business leaders to dismiss the steel strike as a foreign threat orchestrated by American radicals. There was in fact no conspiracy, and the American left was badly splintered. Two defectors from the Socialist Party, John Reed and Benjamin Gitlow, founded the Communist Labor Party in 1919. The rival Communist Party of the United States of America, composed largely of aliens, was launched the same year. Neither party commanded many followers—their combined membership probably did not exceed seventy thousand—and in 1919 the harassed Socialist Party could muster no more than thirty thousand members.

American Legion

Although divisiveness among radicals actually signified weakness, both Progressives and conservatives interpreted the advent of the new parties as strengthening the radical menace. That is certainly how the American Legion saw the question. Organized in May 1919 to lobby for veterans' benefits, the Legion soon preached an antiradicalism that fueled the Red Scare. By 1920, 843,000 Legion members, mostly middle- and upper-class, had become stalwarts of an impassioned Americanism that demanded conformity.

Wilson's attorney general, A. Mitchell Palmer, also insisted that Americans think alike. A Progressive reformer, Quaker, and ambitious politician, Palmer declared that "revolution" was "eating its way into the homes of the American workmen, licking the altars of the churches, leaping into the belfry of the school bell." Palmer appointed J. Edgar Hoover to head the Radical Division of the Department of Justice. The zealous Hoover compiled index cards bearing the names of allegedly radical individuals and organizations. During 1919, agents jailed IWW members, and Palmer saw to it that 249 alien radicals, including the outspoken anarchist Emma Goldman, were deported to Russia.

Again, state and local governments took their cue from the Wilson administration. States passed peacetime sedition acts under which hundreds of people were arrested. Vigilante groups and mobs flourished once again, their numbers swelled by returning veterans. In November 1919, in Centralia, Washington, American Legionnaires broke from a parade to storm the IWW hall. Several were wounded. A number of Wobblies were soon arrested, and one of them, an ex-soldier, was taken from jail by a mob, then beaten, castrated, and shot. The New York State legislature expelled five duly elected Socialist Party members in early 1920.

Palmer Raids

The Red Scare reached a climax in January 1920 in the Palmer Raids. J. Edgar Hoover planned and directed the operation; government agents in thirty-three cities broke into meeting halls and homes without search warrants. More than four thousand people were jailed and denied counsel. In Boston, some four hundred people were kept in detainment on bitterly cold Deer Island; two died of pneumonia, one leaped to his death, and another went insane. Because of court rulings and the courageous efforts of Assistant Secretary of Labor Louis Post, who deliberately held up paperwork, most of the arrestees were released, although in 1920–1921 nearly six hundred aliens were deported.

Palmer's disregard for elementary civil liberties drew criticism, with many charging that his tactics violated the Constitution. Many of the arrested "communists" had committed no crimes. When Palmer called for a peacetime sedition act, he alarmed both liberal and conservative leaders. His dire prediction that pro-Soviet radicals would incite violence on May Day 1920 proved mistaken—not a single disturbance occurred anywhere in the country. Palmer, who had taken to calling himself the "Fighting Quaker," was jeered as the "Quaking Fighter."

Racial Unrest   Palmer also blamed communists for the racial violence that gripped the nation in these years. Here again, the charge was baseless. African Americans realized well before the end of the war that their participation did little to change discriminatory white attitudes. Segregation remained social custom. The Ku Klux Klan was reviving, and racist films like D.W. Griffith's *The Birth of a Nation* (1915) fed prejudice with its celebration of the Klan and its demeaning depiction of blacks. Lynching statistics exposed the wide gap between wartime declarations of humanity and the American practice of inhumanity at home: between 1914 and 1920, 382 blacks were lynched, some of them in military uniform.

Northern whites who resented "the Negro invasion" vented their anger in riots, as in East St. Louis, Illinois, in July 1917. The next month, in Houston, where African American soldiers faced white harassment and refused to obey segregation laws, whites and blacks exchanged gunfire. Seventeen whites and two African Americans died, and the army sentenced thirteen black soldiers to death and forty-one to life imprisonment for mutiny. During the bloody "Red Summer" of 1919 (so named by black author James Weldon Johnson for the blood that was spilled), race riots rocked two dozen cities and towns. The worst violence occurred in Chicago, a favorite destination for migrating blacks. In the very hot days of July 1919, a black youth swimming at a segregated white beach was hit by a thrown rock and drowned. Rumors spread, tempers flared, and soon blacks and whites were battling each other. Stabbings, burnings, and shootings went on for days until state police restored some calm. Thirty-eight people died, twenty-three African Americans and fifteen whites.

By the time of this tragedy, a disillusioned W. E. B. Du Bois had already concluded that black support for the war had not diminished whites' adherence to inequality and segregation. That spring he vowed a struggle: "We return. We return from fighting. We return fighting." Or as poet Claude McKay put it after the Chicago riot in a poem he titled "If We Must Die,"

> Like men we'll face the murderous cowardly pack. Pressed to the wall, dying, but fighting back.

Black Militancy   The exhortations of Du Bois and McKay reflected a new-found militancy among black veterans and in the growing black communities of the North. Editorials in African American newspapers subjected white politicians, including the president, to increasingly harsh criticism and at the same time implored readers to embrace their own prowess and beauty: "The black man is a power of great potentiality upon whom consciousness of his own strength is about to dawn." The NAACP stepped up its campaign for civil rights and equality, vowing in 1919 to publicize the terrors of the lynch law and to seek legislation to stop "Judge Lynch." Other blacks, doubting the potential for equality, turned instead to a charismatic Jamaican immigrant named Marcus Garvey, who called on African Americans to abandon their hopes for integration and to seek a separate black nation.

The crackdown on laborers and radicals, and the resurgence of racism in 1919, dashed wartime hopes. Although the passage of the Nineteenth Amendment in 1920, guaranteeing women the right to vote, showed that reform could happen, it was the exception to the rule. Unemployment, inflation, racial conflict, labor upheaval, a campaign against free speech—all inspired disillusionment in the immediate postwar years.

The Defeat of Peace

President Wilson seemed focused on confronting the threat of radicalism more abroad than at home. Throughout the final months of the war, he fretted about the Soviet takeover in Russia, and he watched with apprehension the communist uprisings in various parts of central Europe. Months earlier, in mid-1918, Wilson had revealed his ardent anti-Bolshevism when he ordered five thousand American troops to northern Russia and ten thousand more to Siberia, where they joined other Allied contingents in fighting what was now a Russian civil war. They fought on the side of the "Whites" (various counterrevolutionary forces) against the "Reds" (the Bolsheviks). Wilson did not consult Congress. He said the military expeditions would guard Allied supplies and Russian railroads from German seizure and would also rescue a group of Czechs who wished to return home to fight the Germans.

Worried that the Japanese were building influence in Siberia and closing the Open Door, Wilson also hoped to deter Japan from further advances in Asia. Mostly, though, he wanted to smash the infant Bolshevik government, a challenge to his new world order. Thus, he backed an economic blockade of Russia, sent arms to anti-Bolshevik forces, and refused to recognize Lenin's government. The United States also secretly passed military information to anti-Bolshevik forces and used food relief to shore up opponents of the Soviets in the Baltic region. Later, at the Paris Peace Conference, representatives of the new Soviet government were denied a seat. U.S. troops did not leave Russia until spring 1920, after the Bolsheviks had demonstrated their staying power. The actions by Wilson and other Allied leaders in 1918–1920 generated powerful feelings of resentment and suspicion among many Russians.

Wilson faced a monumental task in securing a postwar settlement. When he departed for the Paris Peace Conference in December 1918, he faced obstacles erected by his political enemies, by the Allies, and by himself. Some observers suggested that a cocky Wilson underestimated his task. During the 1918 congressional elections, Wilson committed the blunder of suggesting that patriotism required the election of a Democratic Congress; Republicans had a field day blasting the president for questioning their love of country. The GOP gained control of both houses, and Wilson aggravated his political problems by not naming a senator to his advisory American Peace Commission. He also refused to take any prominent Republicans with him to Paris or to consult with the Senate Foreign Relations Committee before the conference. It did not help that the president denounced his critics as "blind and little provincial people."

Wilson was greeted with huge and adoring crowds in Paris, London, and Rome. Behind closed doors, however, the leaders of these countries—Georges Clemenceau of France, David Lloyd George of Britain, and Vittorio Orlando of Italy (with Wilson, the Big Four)—became formidable adversaries. Clemenceau mused, "God gave man the Ten Commandments, and he broke every one. Wilson has given us Fourteen Points. We shall see." After four years of horrible war, the

Allies were not about to be cheated out of the fruits of victory. Wilson could wax lyrical about a "peace without victory," but the late-arriving Americans had not suffered the way the peoples of France and Great Britain had suffered. Germany would have to pay, and pay big, for the calamity it had caused.

Paris Peace Conference   At the conference, held at the ornate palace of Versailles, the Big Four tried to work out an agreement, mostly behind closed doors. Critics quickly pointed out that Wilson had immediately abandoned the first of his Fourteen Points: diplomacy "in the public view." The victors demanded that Germany (which had not been invited to the proceedings) pay a huge reparations bill. Wilson instead called for a small indemnity, fearing that a resentful and economically hobbled Germany might turn to Bolshevism or disrupt the postwar community in some other way. Unable to moderate the Allied position, the president reluctantly gave way, agreeing to a clause blaming the war on the Germans and to the creation of a commission to determine the amount of reparations (later set at $33 billion). Wilson acknowledged that the peace terms were "hard," but he also came to believe that "the German people must be made to hate war."

As for the breaking up of empires and the principle of self-determination, Wilson could deliver on only some of his goals. To the crushing disappointment of much of the world's nonwhite majority, the imperial system emerged largely unscathed, as the conferees created a League-administered "mandate" system that placed former German and Turkish colonies under the control of other imperial nations. Japan gained authority over Germany's colonies in the Pacific, while France and Britain obtained parts of the Middle East—the French obtained what became Lebanon and Syria, while the British received the three former Ottoman provinces that became Iraq. Britain also secured Palestine, on the condition that it uphold its wartime promise to promote "the establishment in Palestine of a national home for the Jewish people" without prejudice to "the civil and religious rights of existing non-Jewish communities"—the so-called Balfour Declaration of 1917.

In other arrangements, Japan replaced Germany as the imperial overlord of China's Shandong Peninsula, and France was permitted occupation rights in Germany's Rhineland. Elsewhere in Europe, Wilson's prescriptions fared better. Out of Austria-Hungary and Russia came the newly independent states of Austria, Hungary, Yugoslavia, Czechoslovakia, and Poland. Wilson and his colleagues also built a cordon sanitaire (buffer zone) of new westward-looking nations (Finland, Estonia, Latvia, and Lithuania) around Russia, to quarantine the Bolshevik contagion.

League of Nations and Article 10   Wilson worked hardest on the charter for the League of Nations, the centerpiece of his plans for the postwar world. He envisioned the League as having power over all disputes among states, including those that did not arise from the peace agreement; as such, it could transform international relations. Even so, the great powers would have preponderant say: the organization would have an influential council of five permanent members and elected delegates from smaller states, an assembly of all members, and a World Court.

Wilson identified Article 10 as the "kingpin" of the League covenant: "The Members of the League undertake to respect and preserve as against external aggression the territorial integrity and existing political independence of all Members of the League. In case of any such aggression or in case of any threat or danger of such aggression the Council shall advise upon the means by which this obligation shall be fulfilled." This collective-security provision, along with the entire League charter, became part of the peace treaty because Wilson insisted there could be no future peace with Germany without a league to oversee it.

German representatives at first refused to sign the punitive treaty but submitted in June 1919. They gave up 13 percent of Germany's territory, 10 percent of its population, all of its colonies, and a huge portion of its national wealth. Many people wondered how the League could function in the poisoned postwar atmosphere of humiliation and revenge. But Wilson waxed euphoric: "The stage is set, the destiny disclosed. It has come about by no plan of our conceiving, but by the hand of God."

Critics of the Treaty

Critics in the United States were not so sure. In March 1919, thirty-nine senators (enough to deny the treaty the necessary two-thirds vote) had signed a petition stating that the League's structure did not adequately protect U.S. interests. Wilson denounced his critics as "pygmy" minds, but he persuaded the peace conference to exempt the Monroe Doctrine and domestic matters from League jurisdiction. Having made these concessions to senatorial advice, Wilson would budge no more. Compromises with other nations had been necessary to keep the conference going, he insisted, and the League would rectify wrongs. Could his critics not see that membership in the League would give the United States "leadership in the world"?

By summer, criticism intensified: Wilson had bastardized his own principles. He had conceded Shandong to Japan. He had personally killed a provision affirming the racial equality of all peoples. The treaty did not mention freedom of the seas, and tariffs were not reduced. Reparations on Germany promised to be punishing. Senator La Follette and other critics on the left protested that the League would perpetuate empire. Conservative critics feared that the League would limit American freedom of action in world affairs, stymie U.S. expansion, and intrude on domestic questions. And Article 10 raised serious questions: Would the United States be *obligated* to use armed force to ensure collective security? And what about colonial rebellions, such as in Ireland or India? Would the League feel compelled to crush them? "Were a League of Nations in existence in the days when George Washington fought and won," an Irish American editor wrote, "we would still be an English colony."

Henry Cabot Lodge of Massachusetts led the Senate opposition to the League. A Harvard-educated Ph.D. and partisan Republican who also had an intense personal dislike of Wilson, Lodge packed the Foreign Relations Committee with critics and prolonged public hearings. He introduced several reservations to the treaty, the most important of which held that Congress had to approve any obligation under Article 10.

In September 1919, Wilson embarked on a speaking tour of the United States. Growing more exhausted every day, he dismissed his antagonists as "contemptible quitters." Provoked by Irish American and German American hecklers, he lashed out in Red Scare terms: "Any man who carries a hyphen about him carries a dagger which he is ready to plunge into the vitals of the Republic." While doubts about Article 10 multiplied, Wilson tried to highlight neglected features of the League charter—such as the arbitration of disputes and an international conference to abolish child labor. In Colorado, a day after delivering another passionate speech, the president awoke to nausea and uncontrollable facial twitching. "I just feel as if I am going to pieces," he said. A few days later, he suffered a massive stroke that paralyzed his left side. He became peevish and even more stubborn, increasingly unable to conduct presidential business. More and more, his wife Edith had to select issues for his attention and delegate other matters to his cabinet heads. Advised to placate Lodge and other "Reservationist" senatorial critics so the Versailles treaty would have a chance of being approved by Congress, Wilson rejected "dishonorable compromise." From Senate Democrats he demanded utter loyalty—a vote against all reservations.

Senate Rejection of the Treaty and League   Twice in November the Senate rejected the Treaty of Versailles and thus U.S. membership in the League. In the first vote, Democrats joined sixteen "Irreconcilables," mostly Republicans who opposed any treaty whatsoever, to defeat the treaty with reservations (39 for and 55 against). In the second vote, Republicans and Irreconcilables turned down the treaty without reservations (38 for and 53 against). In March 1920, the Senate again voted; this time, a majority (49 for and 35 against) favored the treaty with reservations, but the tally fell short of the two-thirds needed. Had Wilson permitted Democrats to compromise—to accept reservations—he could have achieved his fervent goal of membership in the League, which, despite the U.S. absence, came into being.

At the core of the debate lay a basic issue in American foreign policy: whether the United States would endorse collective security or continue to travel the more solitary path articulated in George Washington's Farewell Address and in the Monroe Doctrine. In a world dominated by imperialist states unwilling to subordinate their strategic ambitions to an international organization, Americans preferred their traditional nonalignment and freedom of choice over binding commitments to collective action. That is why so many of Wilson's critics targeted Article 10. Wilson countered that this argument amounted to embracing the status quo—the European imperialist states are selfish, so the United States should be, too. Acceptance of Article 10 and membership in the League promised something better, he believed, for the United States and for the world; it promised collective security in place of the frail protection of alliances and the instability of a balance of power.

An Unsafe World   In the end, World War I did not make the world safe for democracy. Wilson failed to create a new world order through reform. Still, the United States emerged from the First World War an even greater world power. By 1920, the United States had become the world's leading economic power, producing 40 percent of its coal, 70 percent of its petroleum, and half of its pig iron. It also rose to first rank in world trade. American companies took advantage of the war to nudge the Germans and British out of foreign markets, especially in Latin America. Meanwhile, the United States shifted from a debtor to a creditor nation, becoming the world's leading banker.

After the disappointment of Versailles, appeals for arms control accelerated, and the peace movement revitalized. At the same time, the military became better armed and more professional. The Reserve Officers Training Corps (ROTC) became permanent; military "colleges" provided upper-echelon training; and the Army Industrial College, founded in 1924, pursued business-military cooperation in the area of logistics and planning. The National Research Council, created in 1916 with government money and Carnegie and Rockefeller funds, continued after the war as an alliance of scientists and businesspeople engaged in research relating to national defense. Tanks, quick-firing guns, armor-piercing explosives, and oxygen masks for high-altitude-flying pilots were just some of the technological advances that emerged from the First World War.

The international system born in these years was unstable and fragmented. Espousing decolonization and taking to heart the Wilsonian principle of self-determination, nationalist leaders active during the First World War, such as Ho Chi Minh of Indochina and Mohandas K. Gandhi of India, vowed to achieve independence for their peoples. Communism became a disruptive force in world politics, and the Soviets bore a grudge against those invaders who had tried to thwart their revolution. The new states in central and eastern Europe proved weak, dependent on outsiders for security. Germans bitterly resented the harsh peace settlement, and German war debts and reparations problems dogged international order for many years. As it entered the 1920s, the international system that Woodrow Wilson had vowed to reform was fraught with unresolved problems.

SUMMARY

At the close of the First World War, historian Albert Bushnell Hart observed that "it is easy to see that the United States is a new country." Actually, America came out of the war an unsettled mix of the old and the new. The war years marked the emergence of the United States as a world power, and Americans could take justifiable pride in the contribution they had made to the Allied victory. At the same time, the war exposed deep divisions among Americans: white versus black, nativist versus immigrant, capital versus labor, men versus women, radical versus Progressive and conservative, pacifist versus interventionist, nationalist versus internationalist. It is little wonder that Americans—having experienced race riots, labor strikes, disputes over civil liberties, and the League fight—wanted to escape into what President Warren G. Harding called "normalcy."

During the war, the federal government intervened in the economy and influenced people's everyday lives as never before. Centralization of control in Washington, D.C., and mobilization of the home front served as models for the future. Although the Wilson administration shunned reconstruction or reconversion plans (war housing projects, for example, were sold to private investors) and quickly dismantled the many government agencies, the World War I experience of the activist state served as guidance for 1930s reformers battling the Great Depression (see Chapter 25). The partnership of government and business in managing the wartime economy advanced the development of a mass society through the standardization of products and the promotion of efficiency. Wilsonian wartime policies also nourished the concentration of corporate ownership through the suspension of antitrust laws. Business power dominated the next decade. American labor, by contrast, entered lean years, although new labor management practices, including corporate welfare programs, survived.

Although the disillusionment evident after Versailles did not cause the United States to adopt a policy of isolationist withdrawal (see Chapter 26), skepticism about America's ability to right wrongs abroad marked the postwar American mood. The war was grimy and ugly, far less glorious than Wilson's lofty rhetoric had suggested. People recoiled from photographs of shell-shocked faces and of bodies dangling from barbed wire. American soldiers, tired of idealism, craved the latest baseball scores and their regular jobs. Those Progressives who had believed that entry into the war would deliver the millennium later marveled at their naiveté. Many lost their enthusiasm for crusades, and many others turned away in disgust from the bickering of the victors. Some felt betrayed. Journalist William Allen White angrily wrote to a friend that the Allies "have—those damned vultures—taken the heart out of the peace, taken the joy out of the great enterprise of the war, and have made it a sordid malicious miserable thing like all the other wars in the world."

By 1920, Woodrow Wilson's idealism seemed to many Americans to be a spent force, both at home and abroad. Aware of their country's newfound status as a leading world power, they were unsure what this reality meant for the nation, or for their individual lives. With a mixed legacy from the Great War, and a sense of uneasiness, the country entered the new era of the 1920s.

24

THE NEW ERA 1920–1929

CHAPTER OUTLINE

• Big Business Triumphant • Politics and Government • A Consumer Society • Cities, Migrants, and Suburbs • *VISUALIZING THE PAST Expansion of Suburbs in the 1920s* • New Rhythms of Everyday Life • Lines of Defense • The Age of Play • Cultural Currents • The Election of 1928 and End of the New Era • Summary

---

BIG BUSINESS TRIUMPHANT

The 1920s began with a jolting economic decline. Shortly after the First World War ended, industrial output dropped as wartime orders dried up. As European agriculture recovered from war, American exports contracted and farm incomes plunged. In the West, railroads and the mining industry suffered. When demobilized soldiers flooded the work force, unemployment, around 2 percent in 1919, passed 12 percent in 1921. Layoffs spread through New England as textile companies abandoned outdated factories for the convenient raw materials and cheap labor of the South. The consequence of all these patterns was that consumer spending dwindled, causing more contraction and joblessness.

New Economic Expansion   Aided by electric energy, a recovery began in 1922 and continued unevenly until 1929. Electric motors enabled manufacturers to replace steam engines and to produce goods more cheaply and efficiently. Using new metal alloys, such as aluminum, and synthetic materials, such as rayon, producers could turn out an expanded array of consumer goods, including refrigerators, toasters, vacuum cleaners, and clothing. In addition, most urban households now had electric service, enabling them to utilize new appliances. The expanding economy gave Americans more spending money for these products, as well as for restaurants, beauty salons, and movie theaters. But, more important, installment, or time-payment, plans ("A dollar down and a dollar forever," one critic quipped) drove the new consumerism. Of 3.5 million automobiles sold in 1923, 80 percent were bought on credit.

CHRONOLOGY

1920	Volstead Act implements prohibition (Eighteenth Amendment)
	Nineteenth Amendment ratified, legalizing vote for women in federal elections
	Harding elected president
	KDKA transmits first commercial radio broadcast
1920–21	Postwar deflation and depression
1921	Federal Highway Act funds national highway system
	Emergency Quota Act establishes immigration quotas
	Sacco and Vanzetti convicted
	Sheppard-Towner Act allots funds to states to set up maternity and pediatric clinics
1922	Economic recovery raises standards of living
	Coronado Coal Company v. United Mine Workers rules that strikes may be illegal actions in restraint of trade
	Bailey v. Drexel Furniture Company voids restrictions on child labor
	Federal government ends strikes by railroad shop workers and miners
	Fordney-McCumber Tariff raises rates on imports
1923	Harding dies; Coolidge assumes presidency
	Adkins v. Children's Hospital overturns a minimum wage law affecting women
1923–24	Government scandals (Teapot Dome) exposed
1924	Snyder Act grants citizenship to all Indians not previously citizens
	National Origins Act revises immigration quotas
	Coolidge elected president
1925	Scopes trial highlights battle between religious fundamentalists and modernists
1927	Lindbergh pilots solo transatlantic flight
	The Jazz Singer, first movie with sound, released
1928	Stock market soars
	Hoover elected president
1929	Stock market crashes; Great Depression begins

Economic expansion in the 1920s brought a continuation of the corporate consolidation that had created trusts and holding companies in the late nineteenth century. Although Progressive era trustbusting had achieved some regulation of big business, it had not eliminated oligopoly, the control of an entire industry by one or a few large firms. Now, sprawling companies, such as U.S. Steel and General Electric, dominated basic industries, and oligopolies controlled much of marketing, distribution, and finance as well.

Associations and "New Lobbying"

Business and professional organizations that had arisen around 1900 also expanded in the 1920s. Retailers and manufacturers formed trade associations to swap information and coordinate planning. Farm bureaus promoted scientific agriculture and tried to stabilize markets. Lawyers, engineers, and social scientists expanded their professional societies. These special-interest groups participated in what is called the "new lobbying." In a complex society in which government was playing an increasingly influential role, hundreds of organizations sought to convince federal and state legislators to support their interests. One Washington, D.C., observer contended that "lobbyists were so thick they were constantly falling over one another."

Government policies helped business thrive, and legislators depended on lobbyists' expertise in making decisions. Prodded by lobbyists, Congress cut taxes on corporations and wealthy individuals in 1921, and passed the Fordney-McCumber Tariff Act (1922) to raise tariff rates. Presidents Warren G. Harding, Calvin Coolidge, and Herbert Hoover appointed cabinet officers who were favorable toward business. Regulatory agencies, such as the Federal Trade Commission and the Interstate Commerce Commission, monitored company activities but, under the influence of lobbyists, cooperated with corporations more than they regulated them.

The Supreme Court, led by Chief Justice William Howard Taft, the former president whom Harding nominated to the Court in 1921, protected business and private property as aggressively as in the Gilded Age and abandoned its Progressive era antitrust stance. Key decisions sheltered business from government regulation and hindered organized labor's ability to achieve its ends through strikes and legislation. In *Coronado Coal Company v. United Mine Workers* (1922), Taft ruled that a striking union, like a trust, could be prosecuted for illegal restraint of trade, yet in *Maple Floor Association v. U.S.* (1929), the Court decided that trade associations that distributed anti-union information were not acting in restraint of trade. The Court also voided the federal law restricting child labor (*Bailey v. Drexel Furniture Company*, 1922) because it infringed on state power, and overturned a minimum wage law affecting women because it infringed on liberty of contract (*Adkins v. Children's Hospital*, 1923).

Setbacks for Organized Labor

Organized labor suffered other setbacks during the 1920s. Fearful of communism allegedly brought into the country by radical immigrants, public opinion turned against workers who disrupted everyday life with strikes. Perpetuating tactics used during the Red Scare of 1919, the Harding administration in 1922 obtained a sweeping court injunction to quash a strike by 400,000 railroad shop workers. The same year, the Justice Department helped end a nationwide strike by 650,000 miners. Courts at both the state and federal level issued injunctions to prevent strikes and permitted businesses to sue unions for damages suffered because of labor actions.

Meanwhile, corporations fought unions directly. To prevent labor organization, employers imposed yellow-dog contracts that, as a condition of employment, compelled an employee to agree not to join a union. Companies also countered the appeal of unions by offering pensions, profit sharing, and company-sponsored picnics and sporting events—a policy known as welfare capitalism. State legislators aided employers by prohibiting closed shops (workplaces where unions required that all employees be members of their labor organization) and permitting open shops (in which employers could hire nonunion employees). As a result of court action, welfare capitalism, and ineffective leadership, union membership fell from 5.1 million in 1920 to 3.6 million in 1929.

Languishing Agriculture   Farming was one sector of the national economy that languished during the 1920s. Pressed into competition with growers in other countries and trying to increase productivity by investing in machines, such as harvesters and tractors, American farmers found themselves steeped in hardship. Irrigation and mechanization had created "factories in the fields," making large-scale farming so efficient that fewer farmers could produce more crops than ever before. As a result, crop prices plunged, big agribusinesses took over, and small landholders and tenants could not make a living. Shortly after the end of the First World War, for example, the price that farmers could get for cotton dropped by two-thirds, and that for livestock fell by half. Foreign competition made matters worse. Incomes of small farmers (but not agribusinesses) plummeted, and debts rose.

POLITICS AND GOVERNMENT

A series of Republican presidents extended Theodore Roosevelt's notion of government-business cooperation, but they made government a compliant coordinator rather than the active manager Roosevelt had advocated. A symbol of government's goodwill toward business was President Warren G. Harding, elected in 1920 when the populace no longer desired national or international crusades. Democrats had nominated Ohio's Governor James M. Cox, who supported Woodrow Wilson's fading hope for U.S. membership in the League of Nations. But Cox and running mate Franklin D. Roosevelt, governor of New York, failed to excite voters. Harding, who kept his position on the League vague, captured 16 million popular votes to 9 million for Cox. (The total vote in the 1920 presidential election was 36 percent higher than in 1916, reflecting participation of women voters for the first time.)

Scandals of the Harding Administration   A popular small-town newspaperman and senator from Ohio, Harding appointed some capable assistants who helped promote business growth, notably Secretary of State Charles Evans Hughes, Secretary of Commerce Herbert Hoover, Secretary of the Treasury Andrew Mellon, and Secretary of Agriculture Henry C. Wallace. Harding also backed some reforms. Harding, however, had personal weaknesses. As a senator, he had an extramarital liaison with the wife of an Ohio merchant. In 1917, he began a relationship with Nan Britton, who was thirty-one years his junior and who had been obsessed with Harding since her girlhood. A daughter was born from the affair in 1919, and Britton revealed the secret in a book, *The President's Daughter*, published in 1927. Unlike Grover Cleveland, Harding never acknowledged his illegitimate offspring.

Of more consequence than his sexual escapades, Harding appointed cronies who saw office holding as an invitation to personal gain. Charles Forbes, head of the Veterans Bureau, went to federal prison, convicted of fraud and bribery in connection with government contracts. Attorney General Harry Daugherty resigned after being implicated in a kickback scheme involving bootleggers of illegal liquor; he escaped prosecution by refusing to testify against himself. Most notoriously, a congressional inquiry in 1923–1924 revealed that Secretary of the Interior Albert Fall had accepted bribes to lease government property to private oil companies. For his role in the affair—called the Teapot Dome scandal after a Wyoming oil reserve that he handed to the Mammoth Oil Company—Fall was fined $100,000 and spent a year in jail, the first cabinet member ever to be so disgraced.

By mid-1923, Harding had become disillusioned. Amid rumors of mismanagement and crime, he told a journalist, "My God, this is a hell of a job. I have no trouble with my enemies.... But my friends, my God-damned friends ... they're the ones that keep me walking the floor nights." On a speaking tour that summer, Harding became ill and died in San Francisco on August 2. Although his death preceded revelation of the Teapot Dome scandal, some people speculated that, to avoid impeachment, Harding committed suicide or was poisoned by his wife. Most evidence, however, points to death from natural causes, probably heart disease. Regardless, Harding was widely mourned. A warm, dignified-looking man who relished good jokes and evenings of poker, he seemed suited to a nation recovering from world war and domestic hard times.

Coolidge Prosperity

Vice President Calvin Coolidge, who now became president, was far less outgoing than his predecessor. Journalists nicknamed him "Silent Cal," and one quipped that Coolidge could say nothing in five languages. As governor of Massachusetts, Coolidge had attracted national attention in 1919 when he used the national guard to end a strike by Boston policemen, an action that won him business support and the vice-presidential nomination in 1920. Coolidge's presidency coincided with and assisted business prosperity. Respectful of private enterprise and aided by Andrew Mellon, who was retained as treasury secretary, Coolidge's administration reduced federal debt, lowered income-tax rates (especially for the wealthy), and began construction of a national highway system. But Coolidge refused to apply government power to assist struggling farmers. Responding to farmers' complaints of falling prices, Congress twice passed bills to establish government-backed price supports for staple crops (the McNary-Haugen bills of 1927 and 1928). Resembling the subtreasury scheme that Farmers' Alliances had advocated in the 1890s, these bills proposed to establish a system whereby the government would buy surplus farm products and either hold them until prices rose or sell them abroad. Farmers argued that they deserved as much government protection as manufacturers got. Coolidge, however, vetoed the measures both times as improper government interference in the market economy.

"Coolidge prosperity" was the decisive issue in the 1924 presidential election. Both major parties ran candidates who favored private initiative over government intervention. Republicans nominated Coolidge with little dissent. At their national convention, Democrats first debated whether to denounce the revived Ku Klux Klan, voting 542 to 541 against condemnation. They then endured 103 ballots, deadlocked between southern prohibitionists, who supported former treasury secretary William G. McAdoo, and antiprohibition easterners, who backed New York's governor, Alfred E. Smith. They finally compromised on John W. Davis, a New York corporate lawyer. Remnants of the Progressive movement formed a new Progressive Party and nominated Robert M. La Follette, the aging Wisconsin reformer. The new party stressed previous reform issues: public ownership of railroads and power plants, conservation of natural resources, aid to farmers, rights for organized labor, and regulation of business. The electorate, however, endorsed Coolidge prosperity. Coolidge beat Davis by 15.7 million to 8.4 million popular votes, and 382 to 136 electoral votes. La Follette finished third, receiving 4.8 million popular votes and 13 electoral votes.

Extensions of Progressive Reform   In Congress and the presidency, the urgency for political and economic reform that had moved the generation of Progressive reformers faded in the 1920s. Much reform, however, occurred at state and local levels. Following initiatives begun before the First World War, thirty-four states instituted or expanded workers' compensation laws and public welfare programs in the 1920s. In cities, social workers strove for better housing and poverty relief. By 1926, every major city and many smaller ones had planning and zoning commissions to harness physical growth to the common good. As a result of their efforts, a new generation of reformers who later influenced national affairs acquired valuable experience in statehouses, city halls, and universities.

Indian Affairs and Politics   Disturbed by the federal government's generally apathetic Indian policy, reform organizations such as the Indian Rights Association, the Indian Defense Association, and the General Federation of Women's Clubs worked to obtain justice and social services, including better education and return of tribal lands. But most Americans perceived Indians as no longer a threat to whites' ambitions and expected them to assimilate like other minorities. Such assumption overlooked important drawbacks. Severalty, the federal policy created by the Dawes Act of 1887, allotting land to individuals rather than to tribes, failed to make Indians self-supporting. Indian farmers had to suffer poor soil, unavailable irrigation, and scarce medical care. Deeply attached to their land, they showed little inclination to move to cities. Whites still hoped to convert native peoples into "productive" citizens, but in a way that ignored indigenous cultures. Reformers were especially critical of Indian women, who refused to adopt middle-class homemaking habits and balked at sending their children to boarding schools.

Meanwhile, the federal government struggled to clarify Indians' citizenship status. The Dawes Act had conferred citizenship on all Indians who accepted land allotments, but not on those who remained on reservations. Also, the government retained control over Indians that it did not exercise over others. For example, because of alleged drunkenness on reservations, federal law banned the sale of liquor to Indians even before ratification of prohibition. After several court challenges, Congress finally passed an Indian Citizenship Act (Snyder Act) in 1924, granting full citizenship to all Indians who previously had not received it in hopes that Indians would help Indians to assimilate.

Women and Politics   Even after achieving suffrage in 1920 with ratification of the Nineteenth Amendment, politically active women remained excluded from local and national power structures. But like business associations, women's voluntary organizations used tactics that advanced modern pressure-group politics. Whether the issue was birth control, peace, education, Indian affairs, or opposition to lynching, women in these associations lobbied legislators to support their causes. For example, the League of Women Voters, reorganized out of the National Woman Suffrage Association, encouraged women to run for office and actively lobbied for laws to improve conditions for employed women, the mentally ill, and the urban poor.

In 1921, action by women's groups persuaded Congress to pass the Sheppard-Towner Act, which allotted funds to states to create maternity and pediatric clinics as means of reducing infant mortality. (The measure ended in 1929, when Congress, under pressure from private physicians, canceled funding.) The Cable Act of 1922 reversed the law under which an American woman who married a foreigner lost her American citizenship and had to assume her husband's citizenship. At the state level, too, women achieved rights, such as the ability to serve on juries.

As new voters, however, women faced daunting tasks in achieving their goals and overcoming internal differences. Members of the National Association of Colored Women, for example, fought for the rights of minority women and men without support from either the white dominated National Woman's Party or the newly organized League of Women Voters. Some groups, such as the National Woman's Party, pressed for an equal rights amendment to ensure women's equality with men under the law. But such activity alienated the National Consumers League, the Women's Trade Union League, the League of Women Voters, and other organizations that supported special protective legislation to limit hours and improve conditions for employed women. But like men, women of all types sought participation in the new era's consumerism.

A Consumer Society

Between 1919 and 1929, the gross national product—the total value of all goods and services produced in the United States—swelled by 40 percent. Wages and salaries also grew (though not as drastically), while the cost of living remained relatively stable. People had more purchasing power, and they spent as Americans had never spent (see Table 24.1). Technology's benefits reached more people than ever before. By 1929, two-thirds of all Americans lived in dwellings that had electricity, compared with one-sixth in 1912. In 1929, one-fourth of all families owned vacuum cleaners and one-fifth had toasters. Many could afford these goods plus

TABLE 24.1 | CONSUMERISM IN THE 1920S

1900

2 bicycles	$ 70.00
Wringer and washboard	5.00
Brushes and brooms	5.00
Sewing machine (mechanical)	25.00
TOTAL	$ 105.00

1928

Automobile	$ 700.00
Radio	75.00
Phonograph	50.00
Washing machine	150.00
Vacuum cleaner	50.00
Sewing machine (electric)	60.00
Other electrical equipment	25.00
Telephone (per year)	35.00
TOTAL	$ 1,145.00

Source: From an article in *Survey Magazine* in 1928 reprinted in *Another Part of the Twenties*, by Paul Carter. Copyright 1977 by Columbia University Press. Reprinted with permission of the publisher.

radios, cosmetics, and movie tickets because more than one family member earned wages or because the breadwinner took a second job. Nevertheless, new products and services were available to more than just the rich, especially to people living in cities. For example, indoor plumbing and electricity became more common in private residences, and canned foods and ready-made clothes were more affordable.

Effects of the Automobile

The automobile stood as vanguard of the era's material wonders. During the 1920s, automobile registrations soared from 8 million to 23 million, and by 1929 one in every five Americans had a car. Mass production and competition made cars affordable even to some working-class families. A Ford Model T cost less than $300, and a Chevrolet sold for $700 by 1926—when factory workers earned about $1,300 a year and clerical workers about $2,300. Used cars cost less. At those prices, people could consider the car a necessity rather than a luxury. "There is no such thing as a 'pleasure automobile,'" proclaimed one newspaper ad in 1925. "You might as well talk of 'pleasure fresh air,' or of 'pleasure beef steak.'... The automobile increases length of life, increases happiness, represents above all other achievements the progress and the civilization of our age."

Cars altered American life as much as railroads had seventy-five years earlier. Owners acquired a new "riding habit" and abandoned crowded, inconvenient streetcars. Streets became cleaner as autos replaced the horses that had dumped tons of manure every day. Women drivers achieved newfound independence, taking touring trips with female friends, conquering muddy roads, and making repairs when their vehicles broke down. Families created "homes on wheels," packing food and camping equipment to "get away from it all." By 1927, most autos were enclosed (they previously had open tops), offering young people new private space for courtship and sex. A vast choice of models (108 automobile manufacturers in 1923) and colors allowed owners to express personal tastes. Most important, the car was a social equalizer. As one writer observed in 1924, "It is hard to convince Steve Popovich, or Antonio Branca, or plain John Smith that he is being ground into the dust by Capital when at will he may drive the same highways, view the same scenery, and get as much enjoyment from his trip as the modern Midas."

Americans' passion for driving necessitated extensive road construction and abundant fuel supplies. Since the late 1800s, farmers and bicyclists had been lobbying for improved roads. After the First World War, motorists joined the campaign, and in the 1920s government aid made "automobility" truly feasible. In 1921, Congress passed the Federal Highway Act, providing funds for state roads, and in 1923 the Bureau of Public Roads planned a national highway system. Roadbuilding in turn inspired such technological developments as mechanized graders and concrete mixers. The oil-refining industry, which produced gasoline, became vast and powerful. In 1920, the United States produced about 65 percent of the world's oil. Automobiles also forced public officials to pay more attention to safety and traffic control. General Electric Company produced the first timed stop-and-go traffic light in 1924.

Advertising

Advertising, an essential component of consumerism, acquired new prominence. By 1929, more money was spent on advertising goods and services than on all types of formal education. Blending psychological theory with practical cynicism, advertising theorists confidently asserted that any person's tastes could be manipulated, and marketers developed new techniques to achieve their ends. For example, cosmetics manufacturers like Max Factor, Helena Rubenstein, and African American entrepreneur Madame C. J. Walker used movie stars and beauty advice in magazines to induce women to buy their products. Other advertisers hired baseball star Babe Ruth and football's Red Grange to endorse food and sporting goods.

Radio

Radio became a powerful advertising and entertainment agent. By 1929, 10 million families owned radios, and Americans spent $850 million a year on radio equipment. In the early 1920s, Congress decided that broadcasting should be a private enterprise, not a tax-supported public service as in Great Britain. As a result, American radio programming consisted mainly of entertainment rather than educational content because entertainment attracted larger audiences and higher profits from advertisers. Station KDKA in Pittsburgh, owned by Westinghouse Electric Company, pioneered commercial radio in 1920, broadcasting results of the 1920 presidential election. Then, in 1922, an AT&T-run station in New York City broadcast recurring advertisements—"commercials"—for a real estate developer. Other stations began airing commercials; by the end of 1922, there were 508 such stations. In 1929, the National Broadcasting Company began assembling a network of stations and soon was charging advertisers $10,000 to sponsor an hour-long show.

Like automobiles, radio transformed American society. In 1924, the presidential nominating conventions of both political parties were broadcast, enabling candidates and issues to reach more Americans simultaneously than ever before. And as a result of its mass marketing and standardized programming, radio had the effect of blurring ethnic boundaries and creating—at least in one way—a homogeneous "American" culture, an effect that television and other mass media expanded throughout the twentieth century.

CITIES, MIGRANTS, AND SUBURBS

Consumerism signified not merely an economically mature nation but also an urbanized one. The 1920 federal census revealed that, for the first time, a majority of Americans lived in urban areas (places with 2,500 or more people); the city had become the focus of national experience. In addition to growth in metropolises like Chicago and New York, manufacturing and services helped propel expansion in dozens of regional centers. Industries like steel, oil, and auto production energized Birmingham, Houston, and Detroit; services and retail trades boosted Seattle, Atlanta, and Minneapolis. Explosive growth also occurred in warm-climate cities—notably Miami and San Diego—where promises of comfort and profit attracted thousands of real estate speculators.

As cities grew, the agrarian way of life waned. During the 1920s, 6 million Americans left farms for the city. Young people who felt stifled when they compared their existence with the flashy openness of urban life moved to regional centers like Kansas City and Indianapolis or to the West. Between 1920 and 1930, California's population increased 67 percent, and California became a highly urbanized state while retaining its status as a leader in agricultural production. Meanwhile, streams of rural southerners moved to western industrial cities or rode railroads northward to Chicago and Cleveland.

African American Migration   African Americans, in what has come to be called the Great Migration, made up a sizable portion of people on the move during the 1920s. Pushed from cotton farming by a boll weevil plague and lured by industrial jobs, 1.5 million blacks moved, doubling the African American populations of New York, Chicago, Detroit, and Houston. Black communities also enlarged in Los Angeles, San Francisco, and San Diego. In these cities, they found jobs not much different from those in the South—menial and manual labor as janitors, longshoremen, and domestic servants for whites. But the move northward included psychological release because a parcel of freedom was available in New York and Chicago that did not exist in Charleston or Atlanta. In the North, a black person did not always have to act subordinately to a white. As one migrant wrote back home, "I ... am living well.... Don't have to mister every little boy comes along ... I can ride in the [streetcar] anywhere I can get a seat."

Forced by low wages and discrimination to seek the cheapest housing, black newcomers squeezed into ghettos like Chicago's South Side, New York's Harlem, and Los Angeles's Central Avenue. On the West Coast, however, black home ownership rates were higher than in other regions. Many took advantage of Los Angeles's "bungalow boom," in which they could purchase a small, one-story house for as little as $900. But unlike white migrants, who were free to move away from the inner city when they could afford to, blacks everywhere found better neighborhoods closed to them. They could either crowd further into already densely populated black neighborhoods or spill into nearby white neighborhoods, a process that sparked resistance and violence. Fears of such "invasion" prompted neighborhood associations to adopt restrictive covenants, whereby white homeowners pledged not to sell or rent property to blacks.

Marcus Garvey   In response to discrimination, threats, and violence, thousands of urban blacks joined movements that glorified racial independence. The most influential of these black nationalist groups was the Universal Negro Improvement Association (UNIA), headquartered in Harlem and led by Marcus Garvey, a Jamaican immigrant who believed blacks should separate from corrupt white society. Proclaiming, "I am the equal of any white man," and appealing for pride in African heritage, Garvey spread his message with mass meetings and parades. Unlike the NAACP, which had been formed by elite African American and white liberals, the UNIA was comprised exclusively of blacks, most of whom occupied the lower rungs of the economic hierarchy.

Garvey furthered Booker T. Washington's ideas of economic independence by promoting black-owned businesses that would manufacture and sell products to black consumers, and his proposed Phyllis Wheatley Hotel (named after a notable African American poet) would enable any black person to make a reservation. His newspaper, Negro World, preached black independence, and he founded the Black Star steamship line to transport manufactured goods and raw materials among black businesses in North America, the Caribbean, and Africa. In an era when whites were pouring money into stock market speculations, thousands of hopeful blacks invested their dollars in the Black Star Line.

The UNIA declined in the mid-1920s after mismanagement plagued Garvey's economic plans. In 1923, Garvey was imprisoned for mail fraud involving the bankrupt Black Star Line and then deported to Jamaica in 1927. He had been charged with trying to sell stock in the company by advertising a ship that it did not own. His prosecution, however, was politically motivated. Middle-class black leaders, such as W. E. B. Du Bois, and several clergymen opposed the UNIA, fearing that its extremism would undermine their efforts and influence. Beginning in 1919, the U.S. Bureau of Investigation (BOI), forerunner to the FBI, had been monitoring Garvey's radical activities by infiltrating the UNIA since 1919, and the BOI's deputy head, J. Edgar Hoover, proclaimed Garvey to be one of the most dangerous blacks in American. Du Bois also became incensed when word leaked out in

1922 that Garvey had met secretly with the leader of the Ku Klux Klan, who supported Garvey's idea of enabling blacks to move to Africa. Nevertheless, for several years the UNIA attracted a large following (contemporaries estimated 500,000; Garvey claimed 6 million), and Garvey's speeches instilled in many African Americans a heightened sense of racial pride.

Newcomers from Mexico and Puerto Rico   The newest immigrants came from Mexico and Puerto Rico, where, as in rural North America, declining fortunes pushed people off the land. During the 1910s, Anglo farmers' associations encouraged Mexican immigration as a source of cheap workers; by the 1920s, Mexican migrants constituted three-fourths of farm labor in the American West. Growers treated Mexican laborers as slaves, paying them extremely low wages. Resembling other new immigrant groups, Mexican newcomers generally lacked resources and skills, and men outnumbered women. Although some achieved middle-class status as shopkeepers and professionals, most crowded into low-rent districts in growing cities like Denver, San Antonio, Los Angeles, and Tucson, where they suffered poor sanitation, poor police protection, and poor schools. Both rural and urban Mexicans moved back and forth between their homeland and the United States, seeking jobs and creating a way of life that Mexicans called sin fronteras—without borders.

The 1920s also witnessed an influx of Puerto Ricans to the mainland. Puerto Rico had been a U.S. possession since 1898, and its natives were granted U.S. citizenship in 1916. As a shift in the island's economy from sugar to coffee production created a labor surplus, Puerto Ricans left for New York and other cities, attracted by employers seeking cheap labor. In the cities, they created *barrios* (communities) and found jobs in factories, hotels, restaurants, and domestic service. Puerto Ricans maintained traditional customs and developed businesses—*bodegas* (grocery stores), cafes, boarding houses—and social organizations to help them adapt to American society. As with Mexicans, educated Puerto Rican elites—doctors, lawyers, business owners—became community leaders.

Suburbanization   As urbanization peaked, suburban growth accelerated. Although towns had sprouted around major cities since the nation's earliest years, prosperity and automobile transportation in the 1920s made suburbs more accessible to those wishing to leave urban neighborhoods. Between 1920 and 1930, suburbs of Chicago (such as Oak Park and Evanston), Cleveland (Shaker Heights), and Los Angeles (Burbank and Inglewood) grew five to ten times faster than did the nearby central cities. They sparked an outburst of home construction; Los Angeles builders alone erected 250,000 homes for auto-owning suburbanites. Although some suburbs, such as Highland Park (near Detroit) and East Chicago, were industrial satellites, most were middle- and upper-class bedroom communities.

Increasingly, suburbs resisted annexation to core cities. Suburbanites wanted to escape big-city crime, grime, and taxes, and they fought to preserve control over their own police, schools, and water and gas services. Particularly in the Northeast and Midwest, suburbs' fierce independence choked off expansion by the central cities and prevented them from access to the resources and tax bases of wealthier suburban residents. Suburban expansion had other costs, too, as automobiles and the dispersal of population spread the environmental problems of city life—trash, pollution, noise—across the entire metropolitan area.

Together, cities and suburbs fostered the mass culture that gave the decade its character. Most of the consumers who jammed shops, movie houses, and sporting arenas, and who embraced fads like crossword puzzles and miniature golf, lived in or around cities. In these places, people defied older morals by patronizing speakeasies (illegal saloons during prohibition), wearing outlandish clothes, and dancing to jazz. Yet the ideal of small-town society survived. While millions thronged cityward, Americans reminisced about the simplicity of a world gone by, however mythical that world might have been. This was the dilemma the modern nation faced: how does one anchor oneself in a world of rampant materialism and rapid social change?

New Rhythms of Everyday Life

Amid changes to consumer society, Americans developed new patterns of everyday life. One pattern involved uses of time. People increasingly split their day into distinct time compartments: work, family, and leisure. For many, time on the job shrank as mechanization and higher productivity enabled employers to shorten the workweek for many industrial laborers from six days to five and a half. White-collar employees often worked a forty-hour week, enjoyed a full weekend off, and received annual vacations as a job benefit.

Family time is hard to measure, but certain trends are clear. Family size decreased between 1920 and 1930 as birth control became more widely practiced. Among American women who married in the 1870s and 1880s, over half who survived to age fifty had five or more children; of their counterparts who married in the 1920s, however, just 20 percent had five or more children. Lower birth rates and longer life expectancy meant that adults were devoting a smaller portion of their lives to raising children and having more time for nonfamily activities. Meanwhile, divorce rates rose. In 1920, there was 1 divorce for every 7.5 marriages; by 1929, the national ratio was 1 in 6, and in many cities it was 2 in 7.

Household Management   At home, housewives still worked long hours cleaning, cooking, and raising children, but machines now lightened some tasks and enabled women to use time differently than their forebears had. Especially in middle-class households, electric irons and washing machines simplified some chores. Gas- and oil-powered central heating and hot-water heaters eliminated the hauling of wood, coal, and water, the upkeep of a kitchen fire, and the removal of ashes.

Even as technology and economic change made some tasks simpler, they also created new demands on a mother's time. The pool of those who could help housewives with cleaning, cooking, and childcare shrank because daughters of working-class families stayed in school longer, and alternative forms of employment caused a

VISUALIZING THE PAST

Expansion of Suburbs in the 1920s

An outburst of housing and highway construction made possible the rapid growth of suburbs in the 1920s. The Chicago suburb of Niles Centre, later renamed Niles Center and ultimately called the Village of Skokie, was incorporated in 1888. Aided by the service of commuter railroads, the village began to grow in the early 1900s, and in 1913 the first permanently paved road in Cook County was built in Niles

Skokie Historical Society

In some areas, real estate developers laid out streets and blocks in burgeoning suburbs, enticing offices, stores, and institutions before residences were even built. This photograph of Niles Center, Illinois, taken from an airplane around 1927, reveals how roads and automobiles had become essential to suburban expansion.

shortage of domestic servants. In addition, the availability of washing machines, hot water, vacuum cleaners, and commercial soap put greater pressure on housewives to keep everything clean. Advertisers of these products tried to make women feel guilty for not devoting enough attention to cleaning the home. No longer a producer of food and clothing as her ancestors had been, a housewife instead became the chief shopper, responsible for making sure her family spent money wisely. And the automobile made the wife a family's chief chauffeur. One survey found that

Center. After 1920, a real estate boom began, and by the mid 1920s the village had its own water, sewer, and street lighting services, along with many more paved roads. Wealthy Chicagoans such as utilities and railroad investor Samuel Insull built lavish homes in Niles Center, and soon commercial and office buildings sprang up along the major thoroughfares. Population grew so rapidly that the community boasted that it was "The World's Largest Village." The Great Depression halted the boom in 1929, but significant growth resumed after the Second World War. How do you think daily life changed as a result of the growth of suburbs?

As the 1920s proceeded, suburban housing construction accelerated. These private homes, one still under construction, along Brown Street in Niles Center, Illinois, in 1926 reveal how an open prairie was converted into a residential community. Note the presence of autos, a flatbed truck, and electrical wires, all critical to suburban life.

Skokie Historical Society

urban housewives spent on average seven and one-half hours per week driving to shop and to transport children.

Health and Life Expectancy   Emphasis on nutrition added a scientific dimension to housewives' responsibilities. With the discovery of vitamins between 1915 and 1930, nutritionists began advocating consumption of certain foods to prevent illness. Producers of milk, canned fruits and vegetables, and other foods exploited the vitamin craze with claims about health benefits that were hard to dispute because little was known about these invisible, tasteless ingredients. Welch's Grape Juice, for example, avoided mentioning the excess sugars in its product when it advertised that it was "Rich in Health Values" and "the laxative properties you cannot do without." Even chocolate candy manufacturers plugged their bars as vitamin packed.

Better diets and improved hygiene made Americans generally healthier. Life expectancy at birth increased from fifty-four to sixty years between 1920 and 1930, and infant mortality decreased by two-thirds. Public sanitation and research in bacteriology combined to reduce risks of life-threatening diseases such as tuberculosis and diphtheria. But medical progress did not benefit all groups equally; race and class mattered in health trends as they did in everything else. Infant mortality rates were 50 to 100 percent higher among nonwhites than among whites, and tuberculosis in inner-city slums remained alarmingly common. Moreover, fatalities from car accidents rose 150 percent, and deaths from heart disease and cancer—ailments of old age—increased 15 percent. Nevertheless, Americans in general were living longer: the total population over age sixty-five grew 35 percent between 1920 and 1930, while the rest of the population increased only 15 percent.

Older Americans and Retirement

As numbers of elderly increased, their worsening economic status stirred interest in pensions and other forms of old-age assistance. Industrialism put premiums on youth and agility, pushing older people into poverty from forced retirement and reduced income. Recognizing the needs of aging citizens, most European countries established state-supported pension systems in the early 1900s. Many Americans, however, believed that individuals should prepare for old age by saving in their youth; pensions, they felt, smacked of socialism. As late as 1923, the Pennsylvania Chamber of Commerce labeled old-age assistance "un-American and socialistic ... an entering wedge of communistic propaganda."

Yet conditions were alarming. Most inmates in state poorhouses were older people, and almost one-third of Americans age sixty-five and older depended financially on someone else. Few employers, including the federal government, provided for retired employees. Noting that the government fed retired horses until they died, one postal worker complained, "For the purpose of drawing a pension, it would have been better had I been a horse than a human being." Resistance finally broke at the state level in the 1920s. Led by physician Isaac Max Rubinow and journalist Abraham Epstein, reformers persuaded voluntary associations, labor unions, and legislators to endorse old-age assistance through pensions, insurance, and retirement homes. By 1933, almost every state provided at least minimal support to needy elderly people, and a path had been opened for a national program of old-age insurance.

Social Values

As Americans encountered new ways to use their time, altered habits and values were inevitable. Aided by new fabrics and chemical dyes, clothes became a means of self-expression as women and men wore more casual and gaily colored styles than their parents would have considered. The line between acceptable and inappropriate behavior blurred as smoking, drinking, and frankness about sex became fashionable. Birth control gained a large following in respectable circles. Newspapers, magazines, motion pictures, and popular songs made certain that Americans did not suffer from "sex starvation." A typical movie ad promised "brilliant men, beautiful jazz babies, champagne baths, midnight revels, petting parties in the purple dawn, all ending in one terrific smashing climax that makes you gasp."

Other trends weakened inherited customs. Because state child-labor laws and compulsory-attendance rules kept children in school longer than ever before, peer groups rather than parents played an influential role in socializing youngsters. In earlier eras, different age groups had often shared the same activities: children interacted with adults in fields and kitchens, and young apprentices toiled in workshops beside journeymen and craftsmen. Now, school classes, sports, and clubs constantly brought together children of the same age, separating them from the company and influence of adults.

Furthermore, the ways that young males and females interacted with each other underwent fundamental changes. Between 1890 and the mid-1920s, ritualized middle- and upper-class courtship, consisting of men's formally "calling on" women and of chaperoned social engagements, faded in favor of "dating," without adult supervision, in which a man "asked out" a woman and, usually, spent money on her. The more liberal practice arose from new freedoms and opportunities of urban life and spread from the working class to the middle and upper classes. Unmarried young people, living away from family restraints, eagerly went on dates to new commercial amusements, such as movies and nightclubs, and when automobiles became the major mode of transportation, they made dating even more extensive. A woman's job seldom provided sufficient income for her to afford these entertainments, but she could enjoy them if a man "treated" and escorted her. Companionship, romance, and, at times, sexual exploitation accompanied the practice, especially when a woman was expected to give sexual favors in return for being treated. A date thus ironically weakened a woman's prerogative at the same time that it expanded her opportunities. Under the courtship system, a woman had control over who could "call" on her. But once she entered a system in which a man's money enabled her to fulfill her desire for entertainment and independence, she might find herself faced with difficult moral choices.

Women in the Work Force   The practice of dating burgeoned because, after the First World War, women continued to stream into the labor force. By 1930, 10.8 million women held paying jobs, an increase of 2 million since war's end. Although the proportion of women working in agriculture shrank, proportions in categories of urban jobs grew or held steady (see Figure 24.1). The sex segregation that had long characterized workplaces persisted; most women took jobs that men seldom sought, and vice versa. Thus, over 1 million women held jobs as teachers and nurses. In the clerical category, some 2.2 million women were typists, bookkeepers, and filing clerks, a tenfold increase since 1920. Another 736,000 were store clerks, and growing numbers could be found in the personal service category as waitresses and hairdressers. Although almost 2 million women worked in manufacturing, their numbers grew very little over the decade. Wherever women were employed, their wages seldom exceeded half of those paid to men.

Although women worked outside the home for a variety of reasons, their families' economic needs were paramount. The consumerism of the 1920s tempted working-class and middle-class families to satisfy their wants and needs by living beyond their means or by expanding their income with women's wages. Even though the vast majority of married women did not hold paying jobs (only 12 percent were employed in 1930), married women as a proportion of the work force rose by 30 percent during the 1920s, and the number of employed married women swelled from 1.9 million to 3.1 million. These figures omit countless widowed, divorced, and abandoned women who held jobs and who, like married women, often had children to support.

Employment of Minority Women   The proportion of racial and ethnic minority women in paid labor was double that of white women. Often they entered the workforce because their husbands were unemployed or underemployed. The majority of employed African American women held domestic jobs doing cooking, cleaning, and laundry. The few who held factory jobs, such as in cigarette factories and meatpacking plants, performed the least desirable, lowest-paying tasks. Some opportunities opened for educated black women in social work, teaching, and nursing, but these women also faced discrimination and low incomes. More than white mothers, employed black mothers called on a family network of grandmothers and aunts to help with childcare.

Economic necessity also drew thousands of other minority women into the labor force. Mexican women increasingly entered into wage labor, although their tradition resisted female employment. Exact figures are elusive, but it is certain that many Mexican women in the Southwest worked as domestic servants, operatives in garment factories, and agricultural laborers. Next to black women, Japanese American women were the most likely to hold paying jobs. They worked as field hands and domestics, jobs in which they encountered racial bias and low pay.

Alternative Images of Femininity   Employed or not, some women remade the image of femininity. In contrast to the heavy, floor-length dresses and long hair of previous generations, the short skirts and bobbed hair of the 1920s "flapper" symbolized independence and sexual freedom. Although few women lived the flapper life, the look became fashionable among office workers and store clerks as well as college coeds. As Cecil B. DeMille's movies showed, chaste models of female behavior were eclipsed by movie temptresses, such as Clara Bow, known as the "It Girl," and Gloria Swanson, notorious for torrid love affairs on and off the screen. Many women were asserting new social equality with men. One observer described "the new woman" as intriguingly independent.

> She takes a man's point of view as her mother never could.... She will never make you a hatband or knit you a necktie, but she'll drive you from the station ... in her own little sports car. She'll don knickers and go skiing with you, ... she'll dive as well as you, perhaps better, she'll dance as long as you care to, and she'll take everything you say the way you mean it.

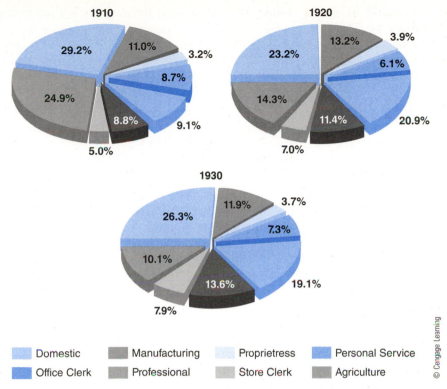

FIGURE 24.1 Changing Dimensions of Paid Female Labor, 1910–1930

These charts reveal the extraordinary growth in clerical and professional occupations among employed women and the accompanying decline in agricultural labor in the early twentieth century. Notice that manufacturing employment peaked in 1920 and that domestic service fluctuated as white immigrant women began to move out of these jobs and were replaced by women of color.

Gay and Lesbian Culture   The era's openness regarding sexuality also enabled the underground homosexual culture to surface a little more than in previous eras. In nontraditional city neighborhoods, such as New York's Greenwich Village and Harlem, cheap rents and an apparent tolerance for alternate lifestyles attracted gay men and lesbians, who patronized dance halls, speakeasies, cafes, and other gathering places. Establishments that catered to gay clientele remained targets for police raids, however, demonstrating that gays and lesbians could not expect acceptance from the rest of society.

These trends represented a break with the more restrained culture of the nineteenth century. But social change rarely proceeds smoothly. As the decade wore on, various groups mobilized to defend older values.

LINES OF DEFENSE

Early in 1920, the leader of a newly formed organization, using a tactic adopted by modern businesses, hired two public relations experts to recruit members. The experts, Edward Clarke and Elizabeth Tyler, canvassed communities in the South, Southwest, and Midwest, where they found countless people eager to pay a $10 membership fee and $6 for a white uniform. Clarke and Tyler pocketed $2.50 from each membership they sold. Their success helped build the organization to 5 million members and four thousand chapters by 1923.

Ku Klux Klan   No ordinary civic club, this was the Ku Klux Klan (KKK), a revived version of the hooded order that terrorized southern communities after the Civil War. Reconstituted in 1915 by William J. Simmons, an Atlanta, Georgia, evangelist and insurance salesman, the Klan adopted the hoods, intimidating tactics, and mystical terminology of its forerunner (its leader was the Imperial Wizard; its book of rituals, the Kloran). But the new Klan had broader objectives than the old. It fanned outward from the Deep South and for a time wielded political power in places as diverse as Oregon, where Portland's mayor was a Klan member, and Indiana, where Klansmen held the governorship and several seats in the legislature. Its membership included many from the urban middle class who were fearful of losing social and economic gains achieved from postwar prosperity and nervous about a new youth culture that seemed to be eluding family control. It included a women's adjunct, Women of the Ku Klux Klan, consisting of an estimated half-million members.

One phrase summed up Klan goals: "Native, white, Protestant supremacy." Native meant no immigration, no "mongrelization" of American culture. According to Imperial Wizard Hiram Wesley Evans, white supremacy was a matter of survival. "The world," he warned, "has been so made so that each race must fight for its life, must conquer, accept slavery, or die. The Klansman believes the whites will not become slaves, and he does not intend to die before his time." Evans praised Protestantism for promoting "unhampered individual development," and he accused the Catholic Church of discouraging assimilation and enslaving people to priests and a foreign pope.

Using threatening assemblies, violence, and political and economic pressure, the Klan menaced many communities in the early 1920s. Klansmen meted out vigilante justice to suspected bootleggers, wife beaters, and adulterers; forced schools to stop teaching the theory of evolution; campaigned against Catholic and Jewish political candidates; pledged members not to buy from merchants who did not share their views; and fueled racial tensions against Mexicans in Texas border cities and against blacks everywhere. Although men firmly controlled Klan activities, women not only joined male members in efforts to promote native white Protestantism but also, with male approval, worked for moral reform and enforcement of prohibition. Because the KKK vowed to protect the "virtue" of women, housewives and other women sometimes appealed to the Klan for help in punishing abusive, immoral, or irresponsible husbands and fathers when legal authorities would not intervene. Rather than an arrest and trial, the Klan's method of justice was flogging.

By 1925, however, the Invisible Empire was weakening, as scandal undermined its moral base. Most notably, in 1925 Indiana grand dragon David Stephenson was convicted of second-degree murder after he kidnapped and raped a woman who later died either from taking poison or from infection caused by bites on her body.

More generally, the Klan's negative, exclusive brand of patriotism and purity could not compete in a pluralistic society.

The KKK had no monopoly on bigotry in the 1920s; intolerance pervaded American society. Nativists had urged an end to free immigration since the 1880s. They charged that Catholic and Jewish immigrants clogged city slums, flouted community norms, and stubbornly embraced alien religious and political beliefs. Fear of immigrant radicals also fueled a dramatic trial in 1921, when two Italian anarchists, Nicola Sacco and Bartolomeo Vanzetti, were convicted of murdering a paymaster and guard in Braintree, Massachusetts. Evidence for their guilt was flimsy, but Judge Webster Thayer openly sided with the prosecution, privately calling the defendants "anarchistic bastards."

Immigration Quotas

Guided by such sentiments, the movement to restrict immigration gathered support. Labor leaders warned that floods of alien workers would depress wages and raise unemployment. Business executives, who formerly had opposed restrictions because they desired cheap immigrant laborers, changed their minds, having realized that they could keep wages low by mechanizing. Even some humanitarian reformers supported restriction as a means of reducing poverty and easing assimilation. Drawing support from such groups, Congress reversed previous policy and, in the Emergency Quota Act of 1921, set yearly immigration allocations for each nationality. Reflecting preference for Anglo-Saxon Protestant immigrants and prejudice against Catholics and Jews from southern and eastern Europe, Congress stipulated that annual immigration of a given nationality could not exceed 3 percent of the number of immigrants from that nation residing in the United States in 1910. The act thereby discriminated against immigrants from southern and eastern Europe, whose numbers were small in 1910 relative to those from northern Europe.

In 1924, Congress replaced the Quota Act with the National Origins Act. This law limited annual immigration to 150,000 people and set quotas at 2 percent of each nationality residing in the United States in 1890, except for Asians, who were banned completely. (Chinese had been excluded by legislation in 1882.) The act further restricted southern and eastern Europeans because even fewer of those groups lived in the United States in 1890 than in 1910. The law did, however, allow foreign-born wives and children of U.S. citizens to enter as nonquota immigrants. In 1927, a revised National Origins Act apportioned new quotas to begin in 1929. It retained the annual limit of 150,000 but redefined quotas to be distributed among European countries in proportion to the "national-origins" (country of birth or descent) of American inhabitants in 1920. People coming from the Western Hemisphere did not fall under the quotas (except for those whom the Labor Department defined as potential paupers), and soon they became the largest immigrant groups (see Figure 24.2).

Fundamentalism

Whereas nativists tried to establish ethnic and racial purity, the pursuit of spiritual purity stirred religious fundamentalists. Millions of Americans sought certainty and salvation from what they perceived

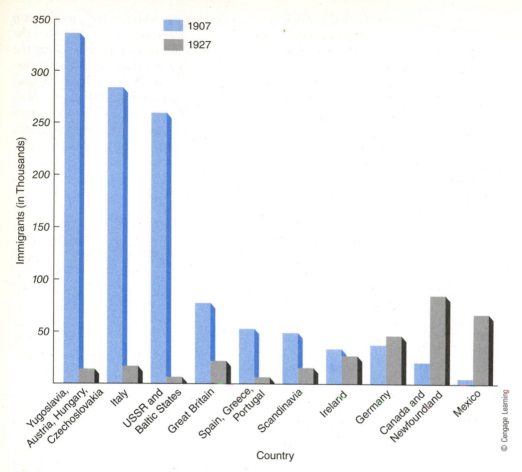

FIGURE 24.2 Sources of Immigration, 1907 and 1927

Immigration peaked in 1907 and 1908, when newcomers from southern and eastern Europe poured into the United States. After immigration restriction laws were passed in the 1920s, the greatest number of immigrants came from the Western Hemisphere (Canada and Mexico), which was exempted from the quotas, and the number coming from eastern and southern Europe shrank.

as society's materialism and hedonism by following Protestant evangelical denominations that interpreted the Bible literally. Resolutely believing that God's miracles created the world and its living creatures, they condemned the theory of evolution as heresy and argued that wherever fundamentalists constituted a majority of a community, as they did in many places, they should be able to determine what would be taught in schools. Their enemies were "modernists," who used reasoning from social sciences, such as psychology and anthropology, to interpret behavior. To modernists, God was important to the study of culture and history, but science was responsible for advancing knowledge.

Scopes Trial   In 1925, Christian fundamentalism clashed with modernism in a celebrated case in Dayton, Tennessee. Early that year, the state legislature passed a law forbidding public school instructors from teaching the theory that humans had evolved from lower forms of life rather than having descended from Adam and Eve. Shortly thereafter, high-school teacher John Thomas Scopes volunteered to serve in a test case and was arrested for violating the law. Scopes's trial that summer became a headline event. William Jennings Bryan, former secretary of state and three-time presidential candidate, argued for the prosecution, and a team of civil liberties lawyers headed by Clarence Darrow represented Scopes. News correspondents crowded into town, and radio stations broadcast the trial.

Although Scopes was convicted—clearly he had broken the law—modernists claimed victory. The testimony, they believed, showed fundamentalism to be illogical. The trial's climax occurred when Bryan took the witness stand as an expert on the Bible. Responding to Darrow's probing, Bryan asserted that Eve really had been created from Adam's rib, that the Tower of Babel was responsible for the diversity of languages, and that Jonah had actually been swallowed by a big fish. Spectators in Dayton cheered Bryan for his declarations, but the liberal press mocked him and his allies. Nevertheless, fundamentalists were not discouraged. For example, the Southern Baptist Convention, the fastest-growing Protestant sect, continued to attract members and, along with other fundamentalist groups, pressured school boards to stop teaching about evolution. Advocates for what they believed to be basic values of family and conduct, these churches created an independent subculture, with their own schools, camps, radio ministries, and missionary societies.

Religious Revivalism   Religious fervor spread wherever people struggling with economic insecurity became nervous about modernism's attack on old-time religion. Cities housed countless Pentecostal churches, which attracted blacks and whites who were swayed by their pageantry and depiction of a personal Savior. Using modern advertising techniques and elaborately staged broadcasts on radio, magnetic "revivalist" preachers—such as the flamboyant Aimee Semple McPherson of Los Angeles; former baseball player Billy Sunday, who preached on nationwide travels; and Father Divine, an African American who amassed an interracial following from his base on Long Island—stirred revivalist fervor.

Revivalism represented only one means of sustaining old-fashioned values and finding comfort in a fast-moving consumer society. Millions who did not belong to the KKK firmly believed that nonwhites and immigrants were inferior people who imperiled national welfare. Clergy and teachers of all faiths condemned dancing, new dress styles, and sex in movies and parked cars. Many urban dwellers supported prohibition, believing that eliminating the temptation of drink would help win the battle against poverty, vice, and corruption. Yet even while mourning a lost past, most Americans sincerely sought some kind of balance as they tried to adjust to the modern order in one way or another. Few refrained from listening to the radio and seeing movies—activities that proved less corrupting than critics feared. More than ever, Americans sought fellowship in civic organizations such as Rotary, Elks, and women's clubs. Perhaps most important, more people were finding release in recreation and new uses of leisure time.

THE AGE OF PLAY

Americans in the 1920s embraced commercial entertainment as never before. In 1919, they spent $2.5 billion on leisure activities; by 1929, such expenditures topped $4.3 billion, a figure not again equaled until after the Second World War. Spectator amusements—movies, music, and sports—accounted for 21 percent of the 1929 total; the rest involved participatory recreation such as games, hobbies, and travel. Entrepreneurs responded to an appetite for fads and spectacles. Early in the 1920s, mahjong, a Chinese tile game, was the craze. In the mid-1920s, devotees popularized crossword puzzles, printed in mass-circulation newspapers and magazines. Next, fun seekers adopted miniature golf as their fad. By 1930, the nation boasted thirty thousand miniature golf courses featuring tiny castles, windmills, and waterfalls. Dances like the Charleston won fans throughout the country, aided by live and recorded music on radio and the growing popularity of jazz.

Movies and Sports   In addition to indulging actively, Americans were avid spectators, particularly of movies and sports. In total capital investment, motion pictures became one of the nation's leading industries. Nearly every community had at least one theater, whether a hundred-seat, small-town establishment or a big-city "picture palace" with ornate lobbies and thousands of cushioned seats. In 1922, movies attracted 40 million viewers weekly; by 1929, the number neared 100 million—at a time when the nation's population was 120 million and total weekly church attendance was 60 million. New technology increased movies' appeal. Between 1922 and 1927, the Technicolor Corporation developed a means of producing movies in color. This process, along with the introduction of sound in *The Jazz Singer* in 1927, made movies even more exciting and realistic.

Responding to tastes of mass audiences, the movie industry produced escapist entertainment. Although DeMille's romantic comedies like *Why Change Your Wife?* explored worldly themes, his most popular films—*The Ten Commandments* (1923) and *The King of Kings* (1927)—were biblical. Lurid dramas like *Souls for Sale* (1923) and *A Woman Who Sinned* (1924) also drew big audiences, as did slapstick comedies starring Harold Lloyd and Charlie Chaplin. Movie content was tame by current standards, however. In 1927, producers, bowing to pressure from legislators and religious leaders, instituted self-censorship, forbidding nudity, rough language, and plots that did not end with justice and morality triumphant. Movies also reproduced social prejudices. Although white actresses and actors played roles as glamour queens and action heroes, what few black actors there were had to take roles as maids and butlers.

Spectator sports also boomed as each year millions packed stadiums and ball-parks. In an age when technology and mass production had robbed experiences and objects of their uniqueness, sports provided some of the unpredictability and drama that people craved. Newspapers and radio magnified this tension, feeding sports news to eager readers and glorifying events with such dramatic narrative that sports promoters did not need to buy advertising.

Baseball's drawn-out suspense, diverse plays, and potential for keeping statistics attracted a huge following. After the "Black Sox scandal" of 1919, when eight members of the Chicago White Sox were banned from the game for allegedly throwing the World Series to the Cincinnati Reds (even though a jury acquitted them), baseball regained respectability by transforming itself. Discovering that home runs excited fans, the leagues redesigned the ball to make it livelier. Game attendance skyrocketed. A record 300,000 people attended the six-game 1921 World Series between the New York Giants and New York Yankees. Millions gathered regularly to watch local teams, and even more listened to professional games on the radio. Although African American ballplayers were prohibited from playing in the major leagues, they formed their own teams, and in 1920 the first successful Negro League was founded in Kansas City, with Andrew "Rube" Foster as its president. The league consisted of eight teams from places such as Chicago, Kansas City, and Indianapolis, and several rival leagues formed in the following years.

Sports Heroes   Sports, movies, and the news created a galaxy of heroes. As technology and mass society made the individual less significant, people clung to heroic personalities as a means of identifying with the unique. Athletes like Bill Tilden in tennis, Gertrude Ederle in swimming (in 1926, she became the first woman to swim across the English Channel), and Bobby Jones in golf had national reputations. The power and action of boxing, football, and baseball produced the most popular sports heroes. Heavyweight champion Jack Dempsey, the "Manassa (Colorado) Mauler," attracted the first of several million-dollar gates in his fight with Frenchman Georges Carpentier in 1921. Harold "Red" Grange, running back for the University of Illinois football team, thrilled fans and sportswriters with his speed and agility.

Baseball's foremost hero was George Herman "Babe" Ruth, who began his career as a pitcher but found he could use his prodigious strength to better advantage hitting home runs. Ruth hit twenty-nine homers in 1919, fifty-four in 1920 (the year the Boston Red Sox traded him to the New York Yankees), fifty-nine in 1921, and sixty in 1927—each year a record. His talent and boyish grin endeared him to millions. Known for overindulgence in food, drink, and sex, he charmed fans into forgiving his excesses by appearing at public events and visiting hospitalized children.

Movie Stars and   Americans also fulfilled their yearning for romance and ad-
Public Heroes   venture through movie idols. The films and personal lives of Douglas Fairbanks, Gloria Swanson, and Charlie Chaplin were discussed in parlors and pool halls across the country. One of the decade's most adored movie personalities was Rudolph Valentino, whose looks and suave manner made women swoon and men imitate his pomaded hairdo and slick sideburns. Valentino's image exploited the era's sexual liberalism and flirtation with wickedness. In his most famous film, Valentino played a passionate sheik who carried away beautiful women to his tent, combining the roles of abductor and seducer. When he died at thirty-one of complications from ulcers and appendicitis, the press turned his funeral into a public extravaganza. Mourners lined up for a mile to file past his coffin.

Picture Research Consultants & Archives

© Underwood

Standing beside his plane, the "Spirit of St. Louis," shortly before takeoff on his solo transatlantic flight, young Charles Lindbergh exhibits the self-reliance and determination that made him one of the most revered heroes of the 1920s. Lindbergh's feat signified a blend of new technology with old-fashioned individual effort.

The era's most celebrated hero, however, was Charles A. Lindbergh, an indomitable aviator who in May 1927 flew a plane solo from New York to Paris. The flight seized the attention of practically every American, as newspaper and telegraph reports followed Lindbergh's progress. After the pilot landed successfully, President Coolidge dispatched a warship to bring "Lucky Lindy" back home. Celebrants sent Lindbergh 55,000 telegrams and dropped 1,800 tons of shredded paper on him during a triumphant homecoming parade. Among countless prizes, Lindbergh received the Distinguished Flying Cross and the Congressional Medal of Honor. Promoters offered him millions of dollars to tour the world and $700,000 for a movie contract. Through it all, Lindbergh, nicknamed "The Lone Eagle," remained dignified, even aloof. Although his flight and its aftermath symbolized the new combination of technology and mass culture of the 1920s, Lindbergh himself epitomized individual achievement, self-reliance, and courage—old-fashioned values that attracted public respect amid the media frenzy.

Prohibition

In their quest for fun and self-expression, some Americans became lawbreakers by refusing to give up drinking. The Eighteenth Amendment (1919), which prohibited the manufacture, sale, and transportation of alcoholic beverages, and the federal law that implemented it (the Volstead Act of 1920) worked well at first. Per capita consumption of liquor dropped, as did arrests for drunkenness, and the price of illegal booze exceeded what average workers could afford. But federal and state authorities for the most part refrained from enforcing the new law. In 1922, Congress gave the Prohibition Bureau only three thousand employees and less than $7 million for nationwide enforcement, and by 1927 most state budgets omitted funds to enforce prohibition.

After 1925, the so-called noble experiment of prohibition faltered as thousands of people made their own wine and gin illegally, and bootleg importers along the country's borders and shorelines easily evaded the few patrols that attempted to intercept them. Moreover, drinking, like gambling and prostitution, was a business with willing customers, and criminal organizations capitalized on public demand. The most notorious of such mobs belonged to Al Capone, a burly tough who seized control of illegal liquor and vice in Chicago, maintaining power over politicians and the vice business through intimidation, bribery, and violence. Capone contended, in a statement revealing of the era, "Prohibition is a business. All I do is supply a public demand." Americans wanted their liquor and beer, and until 1931, when a federal court convicted and imprisoned him for income-tax evasion (the only charge for which authorities could obtain hard evidence), Capone supplied them. Reflecting on contradictions inherent in prohibition, columnist Walter Lippmann wrote in 1931, "The high level of lawlessness is maintained by the fact that Americans desire to do so many things which they also desire to prohibit."

CULTURAL CURRENTS

Along with consumerism enthusiasm, the new era's hardship and crassness spawned unease, and intellectuals like Lippmann were quick to point to persisting hypocrisies. Serious authors and artists felt at odds with society, and their rejection of materialism and conformity was both biting and bitter.

Literature of Alienation   In protest, several writers from the so-called Lost Generation, including novelist Ernest Hemingway and poets Ezra Pound and T. S. Eliot, abandoned the United States for Europe. Others, like novelists William Faulkner and Sinclair Lewis, remained in America but, like the expatriates, expressed disillusionment with the materialism that they witnessed. F. Scott Fitzgerald's novels *This Side of Paradise* (1920) and *The Great Gatsby* (1925); Lewis's *Babbitt* (1922), *Arrowsmith* (1925), and *Elmer Gantry* (1927); and Eugene O'Neill's plays scorned Americans' preoccupation with money. Edith Wharton explored the clash of old and new moralities in novels such as *The Age of Innocence* (1920). Ellen Glasgow, one of the South's leading literary figures, lamented the trend toward impersonality in *Barren Ground* (1925). John Dos Passos's *Three Soldiers* (1921) and Hemingway's *A Farewell to Arms* (1929) interwove antiwar sentiment with critiques of emptiness in modern relationships.

Harlem Renaissance   Discontent quite different from that of white authors inspired a new generation of African American artists. Middle-class, educated, and proud of their African heritage, black writers rejected white culture and exalted the militantly assertive "New Negro." Most of them lived in New York's Harlem; in this "Negro Mecca," black intellectuals and artists, aided by a few white patrons, celebrated black culture during what became known as the Harlem Renaissance.

The 1921 musical comedy *Shuffle Along* is often credited with launching the Harlem Renaissance. The show featured talented black artists, such as lyricist Noble Sissle; composer Eubie Blake; and singers Florence Mills; Josephine Baker, and Mabel Mercer. The Harlem Renaissance also fostered several gifted writers, among them poets Langston Hughes, Countee Cullen, and Claude McKay; novelists Zora Neale Hurston, Jessie Fauset, and Jean Toomer; and essayist Alain Locke. The movement included such visual artists as painter Aaron Douglas and sculptress Augusta Savage. Black writers from other parts of the country also flourished during the decade. They included novelist Sutton E. Griggs of Houston and Memphis and journalist and historian Drusilla Dunjee Houston from Oklahoma.

These artists and intellectuals grappled with notions of identity. Though cherishing their African heritage and the folk culture of the slave South, they realized that blacks had to come to terms with themselves as free Americans. Thus, Alain Locke urged that the New Negro should become "a collaborator and participant in American civilization." But Langston Hughes wrote, "We younger Negro artists who create now intend to express our individual dark-skinned selves without fear or shame. If white people are pleased, we are glad. If they are not, it doesn't matter. We know we are beautiful."

Jazz

The Jazz Age, as the 1920s is sometimes called, owes its name to the music of black culture. Evolving from African and black American folk music, early jazz communicated exuberance, humor, and autonomy that African Americans seldom experienced in their public and political lives. With its emotional rhythms and improvisation, jazz blurred the distinction between composer and performer and created intimacy between performer and audience. As African Americans moved northward and westward, jazz traveled with them, as centers of their music arose in Kansas City, Chicago, and San Diego. Urban dance halls and nightclubs, some of which included interracial audiences of blacks, whites, Latinos, and Asians, featured gifted jazz performers like trumpeter Louis Armstrong, trombonist Kid Ory, and blues singer Bessie Smith. They and others enjoyed wide fame thanks to phonograph records and radio. Music recorded by black artists and aimed at black consumers (sometimes called "race records") gave African Americans a place in commercial culture. More important, jazz endowed America with its own distinctive art form.

In many ways, the 1920s were the most creative years the nation had yet experienced. Painters such as Georgia O'Keeffe, Aaron Douglas, and John Marin forged a uniquely American style of visual art. Composer Henry Cowell pioneered electronic music, and Aaron Copland built orchestral works around native folk motifs. George Gershwin blended jazz rhythms, classical forms, and folk melodies in serious works (*Rhapsody in Blue*, 1924, and Piano Concerto in F, 1925), musical dramas (*Funny Face*, 1927), and hit tunes such as "The Man I Love." In architecture, skyscrapers, including the art deco Chrysler Building of New York designed by William van Allen, drew worldwide attention to American forms. At the beginning of the decade, essayist Harold Stearns had complained that "the most ... pathetic fact in the social life of America today is emotional and aesthetic starvation." By 1929, that contention had been disproved.

THE ELECTION OF 1928 AND END OF THE NEW ERA

Intellectuals' uneasiness about materialism seldom affected the confident rhetoric of politics. Herbert Hoover voiced that confidence when he accepted the Republican nomination for president in 1928. "We in America today," Hoover boasted, "are nearer to the final triumph over poverty than ever before in the history of any land.... We have not yet reached the goal, but, given a chance to go forward with the policies of the last eight years, we shall soon, with the help of God, be in sight of the day when poverty will be banished from this nation."

Herbert Hoover   Hoover was an apt Republican candidate in 1928 (Coolidge chose not to seek reelection) because he fused the traditional value of individual hard work with modern emphasis on corporate action. A Quaker from Iowa, orphaned at age ten, Hoover worked his way through Stanford University and became a wealthy mining engineer. During and after the First World War, he distinguished himself as U.S. food administrator and head of food relief for Europe.

As secretary of commerce under Harding and Coolidge, Hoover promoted what has been called "associationalism." Recognizing the extent to which nationwide associations dominated commerce and industry, Hoover wanted to stimulate a cooperative associational relationship between business and government. He took every opportunity to make the Commerce Department a center for the promotion of business, encouraging the formation of trade associations, holding conferences, and issuing reports, all aimed at improving productivity and profits. His active leadership prompted one observer to quip that Hoover was "Secretary of Commerce and assistant secretary of everything else."

Al Smith   As their candidate, Democrats in 1928 chose New York's governor Alfred E. Smith, whose background contrasted with Hoover's. Hoover had rural, native-born, Protestant, and business roots, and had never run for public office. Smith was an urbane, gregarious politician of Irish stock with a career embedded in New York City's Tammany Hall political machine. His relish for the give-and-take of city streets is apparent in his response to a heckler during the campaign. When the heckler shouted, "Tell them all you know, Al. It won't take long!" Smith unflinchingly retorted, "I'll tell them all we both know, and it won't take any longer!"

Smith was the first Roman Catholic to run for president on a major party ticket. His religion enhanced his appeal among urban ethnics (including women), who were voting in increasing numbers, but anti-Catholic sentiments lost him southern and rural votes. Smith had compiled a strong record on Progressive reform and civil rights during his governorship, but his campaign failed to build a coalition of farmers and city dwellers because he stressed issues unlikely to unite these groups, particularly his opposition to prohibition.

Hoover, who emphasized national prosperity under Republican administrations, won the popular vote by 21 million to 15 million and the electoral vote by 444 to 87. Smith's candidacy nevertheless had beneficial effects on the Democratic Party. By luring millions of foreign-stock voters to the polls, he carried the nation's twelve largest cities, which formerly had given majorities to Republican candidates. For the next forty years, the Democratic Party solidified this urban base, which in conjunction with its traditional strength in the South made the party a formidable force in national elections.

Hoover's Administration At his inaugural, Hoover proclaimed a New Day, "bright with hope." His cabinet, composed mostly of businessmen committed to the existing order, included six millionaires. To the lower ranks of government, Hoover appointed young professionals who agreed with him that a scientific approach could solve national problems. If Hoover was optimistic, so were most Americans. There was widespread belief that success resulted from individual effort and that unemployment and poverty signaled personal weakness. Prevailing opinion also held that fluctuations of the business cycle were natural and therefore not to be tampered with by government.

Stock Market Crash This trust dissolved on October 24, 1929, later known as Black Thursday, when stock market prices suddenly plunged, wiping out $10 billion in value (worth around $100 billion today). Panic selling set in. Prices of many stocks hit record lows; some sellers could find no buyers. Stunned crowds gathered outside the frantic New York Stock Exchange. At noon, leading bankers met at the headquarters of J. P. Morgan and Company. To restore faith, they put up $20 million and ceremoniously began buying stocks. The mood brightened, and some stocks rallied. The bankers, it seemed, had saved the day.

But as news of Black Thursday spread, frightened investors decided to sell stocks rather than risk further losses. On Black Tuesday, October 29, prices plummeted again. Hoover, who had never approved of what he called "the fever of speculation," assured Americans that "the crisis will be over in sixty days." Three months later, he still believed that "the worst is over without a doubt." He shared the popular assumptions that the stock market's ills could be quarantined and that the economy was strong enough to endure until the market righted itself. Instead, the crash ultimately helped to unleash a devastating worldwide depression.

In hindsight, it is evident that the depression began long before the stock market crash. Prosperity in the 1920s was not as widespread as optimists believed. Agriculture had been languishing for decades, and many areas, especially in the South, had been excluded from the bounty of consumer society. Racial minorities suffered from economic as well as social discrimination in both urban and rural settings. Industries such as mining and textiles failed to sustain profits throughout most of the decade, and even the high-flying automotive and household goods industries had been stagnant since 1926. The fever of speculation that concerned Hoover included rash investment in California and Florida real estate, as well as in the stock market, and masked much of what was unhealthy in the national economy.

Declining Demand

More generally, the economic weakness that underlay the Great Depression had several interrelated causes. One was declining demand. Since mid-1928, demand for new housing had faltered, leading to declining sales of building materials and unemployment among construction workers. Growth industries, such as automobiles and electric appliances, had been able to expand as long as consumers bought their products. Expansion, however, could not continue unabated. When demand leveled off, factory owners had to cut production and pare work forces. Retailers had amassed large inventories that were going unsold and, in turn, they started ordering less from manufacturers. Farm prices continued to sag, leaving farmers with less income to purchase new machinery and goods. As wages and employment fell, families could not afford things they needed and wanted. Thus, by 1929, a sizable population of underconsumers was causing serious repercussions.

Underconsumption also resulted from widening divisions in income distribution. As the rich grew richer, middle- and lower-income Americans made modest gains at best. Although average per capita disposable income (income after taxes) rose about 9 percent between 1920 and 1929, income of the wealthiest 1 percent rose 75 percent, accounting for most of the general increase. Much of this money went for stock market speculation, not consumer goods.

Corporate Debt and Stock Market Speculation

Furthermore, in their eagerness to boost profits, many businesses overloaded themselves with debt. To obtain loans, they misrepresented their assets in ways that hid their inability to repay if forced to do so. Such practices, overlooked by lending agencies, put the nation's banking system on a precarious footing. When one part of the edifice collapsed, the entire structure crumbled.

Risky stock market speculation also precipitated the depression. Individuals and corporations had bought millions of stock shares on margin, meaning that they invested by placing a down payment of only a fraction of a stock's actual price and then used stocks they had bought, but not fully paid for, as collateral for more stock purchases. When stock prices stopped rising, investors tried to minimize losses by selling holdings they had bought on margin. But numerous investors selling at the same time caused prices to plunge. As stock values crumbled, brokers demanded full payment for stocks bought on margin. Investors attempted to comply by withdrawing savings from banks or selling stocks at a loss for whatever they could get. Cash-short bankers pressured businesses to pay back their loans, tightening the vise further. The more obligations went unmet, the more the system tottered. Inevitably, banks and investment companies collapsed.

Economic Troubles Abroad; Federal Failures at Home

International economic conditions also contributed to the depression. During the First World War and postwar reconstruction, Americans loaned billions of dollars to European nations. By the late 1920s, however, American investors were keeping their money at home, investing instead in the stock market. Europeans, unable to borrow more funds and unable to sell goods in the American market because of high tariffs, began to buy less from the United States. Moreover, the Allied nations depended on German war reparations to pay their own war debts to the United States, and the German government depended on American bank loans to pay those reparations. When the crash choked off American loans, Germany could not meet obligations to the Allies, and in turn the Allies were unable to pay war debts to the United States. The western economy ground to a halt.

Federal policies also underlay the crisis. The government refrained from regulating speculation and only occasionally scolded undisciplined bankers and businesspeople. In keeping with its support of business expansion, the Federal Reserve Board pursued easy credit policies, charging low discount rates (interest on its loans to member banks) even though such loans were financing the speculative mania.

Partly because of optimism and partly because of the relatively unsophisticated state of economic analysis, neither experts nor people on the street realized what really had happened in 1929. Conventional wisdom, based on experiences from previous depressions, held that little could be done to correct economic downturns; they simply had to run their course. So in 1929, people waited for the tailspin to ease, never realizing that the "new era" had come to an end and that the economy, politics, and society would have to be rebuilt.

SUMMARY

Two critical events, the end of the First World War and beginning of the Great Depression, marked the boundaries of the 1920s. In the war's aftermath, traditional customs and values weakened as women and men sought new forms of self-expression and gratification. A host of effects from modern science and technology—automobiles, electric appliances, and mass media, especially radio—touched the lives of rich and poor alike. Sports and movies made entertainment more accessible. Moreover, the decade's freewheeling consumerism enabled ordinary Americans to emulate wealthier people not only by purchasing more but also by trying to get rich through stock market speculation. The depression that followed the stock market crash stifled these habits, at least for a while.

Beneath the "new era" lurked two important phenomena rooted in previous eras. One was the continued prejudice and ethnic tensions that had long tainted the American dream. As Klansmen and immigration restrictionists made their voices heard, they encouraged discrimination against racial minorities and slurs against supposedly inferior ethnic groups. Meanwhile, the distinguishing forces of twentieth-century life—technological change, bureaucratization, mass culture, and growth of the middle class—accelerated, making the decade truly "new." Both phenomena would recur as major themes in the nation's history for the rest of the twentieth century.

25

▼

The Great Depression and the New Deal 1929–1941

HOOVER AND HARD TIMES, 1929–1933

By the early 1930s, as the depression continued to deepen, tens of millions of Americans were desperately poor. In the cities, hungry men and women lined up at soup kitchens. People survived on potatoes, crackers, or dandelion greens; some scratched through garbage cans for bits of food. In West Virginia and Kentucky, hunger was so widespread—and resources so limited—that the American Friends Service Committee distributed food only to those who were at least 10 percent below the normal weight for their height. In November 1932, *The Nation* told its readers that one-sixth of the American population risked starvation over the coming winter. Social workers in New York reported there was "no food at all" in the homes of many of the city's black children. In Albany, New York, a ten-year-old girl died of starvation in her elementary school classroom.

Families, unable to pay rent, were evicted. The new homeless poured into shantytowns, called "Hoovervilles" in ironic tribute to the formerly popular president. Over a million men took to the road or the rails in desperate search of any sort of work. Teenage boys and girls (**the latter called "sisters of the road") also left destitute** families to strike out on their own. With uncertain futures, many young couples delayed marriage; the average age at marriage rose by more than two years during the 1930s. Married people put off having children, and in 1933 the birth rate sank below replacement rates. (Sales of condoms—at $1 per dozen—did not

CHRONOLOGY

1929	Stock market crash (October); Great Depression begins
1930	Hawley-Smoot Tariff raises rates on imports
1931	"Scottsboro Boys" arrested in Alabama
1932	Banks fail throughout nation
	Bonus Army marches on Washington
	Hoover's Reconstruction Finance Corporation tries to stabilize banks, insurance companies, railroads
	Roosevelt elected president
1933	13 million Americans unemployed
	"First Hundred Days" of Roosevelt administration offer major legislation for economic recovery and poor relief
	National bank holiday halts run on banks
	Agricultural Adjustment Act (AAA) encourages decreased farm production
	National Industrial Recovery Act (NIRA) attempts to spur industrial growth
	Tennessee Valley Authority (TVA) established
1934	Long starts Share Our Wealth Society
	Townsend proposes old-age pension plan
	Indian Reorganization (Wheeler-Howard) Act restores lands to tribal ownership
1935	National Labor Relations (Wagner) Act guarantees workers' right to unionize
	Social Security Act establishes insurance for the aged, the unemployed, and needy children
	Works Progress Administration (WPA) creates jobs in public works projects
	Revenue (Wealth Tax) Act raises taxes on business and the wealthy
1936	9 million Americans unemployed
	United Auto Workers win sit-down strike against General Motors
1937	Roosevelt's court-packing plan fails
	Memorial Day massacre of striking steelworkers
	"Roosevelt recession" begins
1938	10.4 million Americans unemployed
	80 million movie tickets sold each week
1939	Marian Anderson performs at Lincoln Memorial
	Social Security amendments add benefits for spouses and widows

fall during the depression.) More than a quarter of women who were between the ages of twenty and thirty during the Great Depression never had children.

Farmers and Industrial Workers

Farmers were hit especially hard by the economic crisis. The agricultural sector, which employed almost one-quarter of American workers, had never shared in the good times of the 1920s. But as urbanites cut back on spending and foreign competitors dumped agricultural surpluses into the global market, farm prices hit rock bottom. Farmers tried to compensate for lower prices by producing more, thus adding to the surplus and depressing prices even further. By 1932, a bushel of wheat that cost North Dakota farmers 77 cents to produce brought only 33 cents. Throughout the nation, cash-strapped farmers could not pay their property taxes or mortgages. Banks, facing their own ruin, foreclosed. In Mississippi, it was reported in 1932, on a single day in April approximately one-fourth of all the farmland in the state was being auctioned off to meet debts. By the middle of the decade, the ecological crisis of the Dust Bowl would drive thousands of farmers from their land.

Unlike farmers, America's industrial workers had seen a slow but steady rise in their standard of living during the 1920s. In 1929, almost every urban American who wanted a job had one, and workers' spending on consumer goods had bolstered the nation's economic growth. But as Americans had less money to spend, sales of manufactured goods plummeted and factories closed—more than seventy thousand had gone out of business by 1933. As car sales dropped from 4.5 million in 1929 to 1 million in 1933, Ford laid off more than two-thirds of its Detroit workers. The remaining workers at U.S. Steel, America's first billion-dollar corporation, were put on "short hours"; the huge steel company had no full-time workers in 1933. Almost one-quarter of industrial workers were unemployed, and those who managed to hang onto a job saw the average wage fall by almost one-third.

Marginal Workers

For workers on the lowest rungs of the employment ladder, the depression was a crushing blow. In the South, where opportunities were already most limited for African Americans, jobs that many white men had considered below their dignity before the depression—street cleaner, bellhop, garbage collector—seemed suddenly desirable. In 1930, a short-lived fascist-style organization, the Black Shirts, recruited forty thousand members with the slogan "No Jobs for Niggers Until Every White Man Has a Job!" Northern blacks did not fare much better. As industry cut production, African Americans were the first fired. An Urban League survey of 106 cities found black unemployment rates averaged 30 to 60 percent higher than rates for whites. By 1932, African American unemployment reached almost 50 percent.

Mexican Americans and Mexican nationals trying to make a living in the American Southwest also felt the twin impacts of economic depression and racism. Their wages on California farms fell from a miserable 35 cents an hour in 1929 to a cruel 14 cents an hour by 1932. Throughout the Southwest, Anglo-Americans claimed that foreign workers were stealing their jobs. Campaigns against "foreigners" hurt not only Mexican immigrants but also American citizens of Hispanic descent whose families had lived in the Southwest for centuries, long before the land belonged to the United States. In 1931, the Labor Department announced plans to deport illegal immigrants to free jobs for American citizens. This policy fell hardest on people of Mexican origin. Even those who had immigrated legally often lacked full documentation. Officials often ignored the fact that children born in the United States were U.S. citizens. The U.S. government officially deported 82,000 Mexicans between 1929 and 1935, but a much larger number—almost half a million people—repatriated to Mexico during the 1930s. Some left voluntarily, but many were coerced or tricked into believing they had no choice.

Even before the economic crisis, women of all classes and races were barred from many jobs and were paid significantly less than men. As the economy worsened, discrimination increased. Most Americans already believed that men should be breadwinners and women homemakers. With so many men unemployed, it was easy to believe that women who worked took jobs from men. In fact, men laid off from U.S. Steel would not likely have been hired as elementary school teachers, secretaries, "salesgirls," or maids. Nonetheless, when a 1936 Gallup poll asked whether wives should work if their husbands had jobs, 82 percent of the respondents (including 75 percent of the women) answered no. Such beliefs translated into policy. Of fifteen hundred urban school systems surveyed in 1930 and 1931, 77 percent refused to hire married women as teachers, and 63 percent fired female teachers who married while employed.

The depression had a mixed impact on women workers. At first, women lost jobs more quickly than men. Women in low-wage manufacturing jobs were laid off before male employees, who were presumed to be supporting families. Hard times hit domestic workers especially hard, as middleclass families economized by dispensing with household help. Almost one-quarter of women in domestic service—a high percentage of them African American—were unemployed by January 1931. And as jobs disappeared, women of color lost even these poorly paid positions to white women who were newly willing to do domestic labor. Despite discrimination and a poor economy, however, the number of women working outside the home rose during the 1930s. "Women's jobs," such as teaching, clerical work, and switchboard operating, were not hit as hard as "men's jobs" in heavy industry, and women—including married women who previously did not work for wages—increasingly sought employment to keep their families afloat during hard times. Still, by 1940, only 15.2 percent of married women worked outside the home.

Middle-Class Workers and Families

Although unemployment rates climbed to 25 percent, most Americans did not lose their homes or their jobs during the depression. Professional and white-collar workers did not fare as badly as industrial workers and farmers. Many middle-class families, however, while never hungry or homeless, "made do" with less. "Use it up, wear it out, make it do, or do without," the saying went, and middle-class women cut back on household expenses by canning food or making their own clothes. Newspapers offered imaginative suggestions for cooking cheap cuts of meat ("Liverburgers") or for using "extenders," cheap ingredients to make food go further ("Cracker-Stuffed Cabbage"). Although most families' incomes fell, the impact was cushioned by the falling cost of consumer goods, especially food. In early 1933, for example, a café in Omaha offered a ten-course meal, complete with a rose for ladies and a cigar for gentlemen, for 60 cents.

As housewives scrambled to make do, men who could no longer provide well for their families often blamed themselves for their "failures." But even for the relatively affluent, the psychological impact of the depression was inescapable. The human toll of the depression was visible everywhere, and no one took economic security for granted any more. Suffering was never equal, but all Americans had to contend with years of uncertainty and with fears about the future of their family and their nation.

Hoover's Limited Solutions

Although Herbert Hoover, "the Great Engineer," had a reputation as a problem solver, the economic crisis was not easily solved, and no one, including Hoover, really knew what to do. Experts and leaders disagreed about the causes of the depression, and they disagreed about the proper course of action as well. Many prominent business leaders believed that financial panics and depressions, no matter how painful, were part of a natural and ultimately beneficial "business cycle." Economic depressions, according to this theory, brought down inflated prices and cleared the way for real economic growth. As one banker told a Senate committee investigating the rising unemployment rates, "You are always going to have, once in so many years, difficulties in business, times that are prosperous and times that are not prosperous. There is no commission or any brain in the world that can prevent it."

Herbert Hoover disagreed. "The economic fatalist," he said, "believes that these crises are inevitable.... I would remind these pessimists that exactly the same thing was once said of typhoid, cholera, and smallpox." Hoover had great faith in "associationalism": business and professional organizations, coordinated by the federal government, working together to solve the nation's problems. The federal government's role was limited to gathering information and serving as a clearinghouse for ideas and plans that state and local governments, along with private industry, could then choose—voluntarily—to implement.

While many Americans thought that Hoover was doing nothing to fight the economic downturn, in truth he stretched his core beliefs about the proper role of government to their limit. He tried voluntarism, exhortation, and limited government intervention. First, he sought voluntary pledges from hundreds of business groups to keep wages stable and renew economic investment. But when individual businesspeople looked at their own bottom lines, few could live up to those promises.

As unemployment climbed, Hoover continued to encourage voluntary responses to mounting need, creating the President's Organization on Unemployment Relief (POUR) to generate private contributions to aid the destitute. Although 1932 saw record charitable contributions, they were nowhere near adequate. By mid-1932, one-quarter of New York's private charities, funds exhausted, had closed their doors. Atlanta's Central Relief Committee could provide only $1.30 per family per week to those seeking help. State and city officials found their treasuries drying up, too. Hoover, however, held firm. "It is not the function of the government to relieve individuals of their responsibilities to their neighbors," he insisted.

Hoover feared that government "relief" would destroy the spirit of self-reliance among the poor. Thus, he authorized federal funds to feed the drought-stricken livestock of Arkansas farmers but rejected a smaller grant to provide food for impoverished farm families. Many Americans were becoming angry at Hoover's seeming insensitivity. When Hoover, trying to restore confidence to the increasingly anxious nation, said, "What this country needs is a good big laugh…. If someone could get off a good joke every ten days, I think our troubles would be over," the resulting jokes were not exactly what he had in mind. "Business is improving," one man tells another. "Is Hoover dead?" asks his companion. In the two short years since his election, Hoover had become the most hated man in America.

Hoover eventually endorsed limited federal action to combat the economic crisis, but it was much too little. Federal public works projects, such as the Grand Coulee Dam in Washington, created some jobs. The Federal Farm Board, established under the Agricultural Marketing Act of 1929, supported crop prices by lending money to cooperatives to buy crops and keep them off the market. But the board soon ran short of money, and unsold surpluses jammed warehouses.

Hoover also signed into law the Hawley-Smoot Tariff (1930), which was meant to support American farmers and manufacturers by raising import duties on foreign goods to a staggering 40 percent. Instead, it hampered international trade as other nations created their own protective tariffs. And as other nations sold fewer goods to the United States, they had less money to repay their U.S. debts or buy American products. Fearing the collapse of the international monetary system, Hoover in 1931 announced a moratorium on the payment of First World War debts and reparations.

In January 1932, the administration took its most forceful action. The Reconstruction Finance Corporation (RFC) provided federal loans to banks, insurance companies, and railroads, an action Hoover hoped would shore up those industries and halt the disinvestment in the American economy. New York mayor Fiorello LaGuardia called this provision of taxpayers' dollars to private industry "a millionaire's dole." But with the RFC, Hoover had compromised his ideological principles. This was direct government intervention, not "voluntarism." If he would support direct assistance to private industries, why not direct relief to the millions of unemployed?

Protest and Social Unrest

More and more Americans had begun to ask that question. Although most met the crisis with bewilderment or quiet despair, social unrest and violence began to surface as the depression deepened. In scattered incidents, farmers and unemployed workers took direct action against what they saw as the causes of their plight. Others lashed out in anger, scapegoating those even weaker than themselves. Increasing violence raised the specter of popular revolt, and Chicago mayor Anton Cermak told Congress that if the federal government did not send his citizens aid, it would have to send troops instead.

Throughout the nation, tens of thousands of farmers took the law into their own hands. Angry crowds forced auctioneers to accept just a few dollars for foreclosed property, and then returned it to the original owners. Farmers also tried to stop produce from reaching the market. In August 1932, a new group, the Farmers' Holiday Association, encouraged farmers to take a "holiday"—to hold back agricultural products as a way to limit supply and drive prices up. In the Midwest, farmers barricaded roads with spiked logs and telegraph poles to stop other farmers' trucks, and then dumped the contents in roadside ditches. In Iowa, strikers shot four other farmers who tried to run a roadblock.

In the cities, too, protest grew. The most militant actions came from Unemployed Councils, local groups similar to unions for unemployed workers that were created and led by Communist Party members. Communist leaders believed the depression demonstrated capitalism's failure and offered an opportunity for revolution. Few of the quarter-million Americans who joined the local Unemployed Councils sought revolution, but they did demand action. "Fight, Don't Starve," read banners in a Chicago demonstration. Demonstrations often turned ugly. When three thousand members of Detroit Unemployment Councils marched on Ford's River Rouge plant in 1932, Ford security guards opened fire on the crowd, killing four men and wounding fifty. Battles between protesters and police broke out in cities from the East Coast to the West Coast but rarely were covered as national news.

As social unrest spread, so, too, did racial violence. Vigilante committees offered bounties in an attempt to force African American workers off the Illinois Central Railroad's payroll: $25 for maiming and $100 for killing black workers. Ten men were murdered and at least seven more wounded. With the worsening economy, the Ku Klux Klan reemerged, and at least 140 attempted lynchings were recorded between January 1930 and February 1933. In most cases, local authorities were able to prevent the lynchings but white mobs tortured, hanged, and mutilated thirty-eight black men during the early years of the Great Depression. Racial violence was not restricted to the South; lynchings took place in Pennsylvania, Minnesota, Colorado, and Ohio as well.

Bonus Army

The worst public confrontation shook the nation in the summer of 1932. More than fifteen thousand unemployed World War I veterans and their families converged on the nation's capital as Congress debated a bill authorizing immediate payment of cash "bonuses" that veterans had been scheduled to receive in 1945. Calling themselves the Bonus Expeditionary Force, or Bonus Army, they set up a sprawling "Hooverville" shantytown in Anacostia Flats, just across the river from the Capitol. Concerned about the impact on the federal budget, President Hoover opposed the bonus bill, and after much debate the Senate voted it down. "We were heroes in 1917, but we're bums today," one veteran shouted after the Senate vote.

Most of the Bonus Marchers left Washington after this defeat, but several thousand stayed on. Some were simply destitute, with nowhere to go; others stayed to press their case. The president called them "insurrectionists" and set a deadline for their departure. On July 28, Hoover sent in the U.S. Army, led by General Douglas MacArthur. Four infantry companies, four troops of cavalry, a machine gun squadron, and six tanks converged on the veterans and their families. What followed shocked the nation. Men and women were chased down by horsemen; children were teargassed; shacks were set afire. The next day, newspapers carried photographs of U.S. troops attacking their own citizens. Hoover was unrepentant, insisting in a campaign speech, "Thank God we still have a government that knows how to deal with a mob."

While desperation-driven social unrest raised fears of revolution, some saw an even greater danger in the growing disillusionment with democracy itself. As the depression worsened, the appeal of a strong leader—someone who would take decisive action, unencumbered by constitutionally mandated checks and balances—grew. In early 1933, media magnate William Randolph Hearst released the film *Gabriel over the White House*, in which a political hack of a president is possessed by the archangel Gabriel and, divinely inspired, assumes dictatorial powers to end

National Archives

In the summer of 1932, unemployed veterans of the First World War gathered in Washington, D.C. to demand payment of their soldiers' bonuses. After Congress rejected the appeal of the "Bonus Army," some refused to leave and President Hoover sent U.S. Army troops to force them out. Here, police battle Bonus Marchers in July 1932.

the misery of the Great Depression. More significantly, in February 1933, the U.S. Senate passed a resolution calling for newly elected president Franklin D. Roosevelt to assume "unlimited power." The rise to power of Hitler and his National Socialist Party in depression-ravaged Germany was an obvious parallel, adding to the sense of crisis that would come to a head in early 1933.

FRANKLIN D. ROOSEVELT AND THE LAUNCHING OF THE NEW DEAL

In the presidential campaign of 1932, voters were presented with a clear choice. In the face of the Great Depression, incumbent Herbert Hoover held to a platform of limited federal intervention. Democratic challenger Franklin Delano Roosevelt insisted that the federal government had to play a much greater role. He supported direct relief payments for the unemployed, declaring that such governmental aid was not charity but instead "a matter of social duty." He pledged "a new deal for the American people." During the campaign, he was never very explicit about the outlines of his New Deal. His most concrete proposals, in fact, were sometimes contradictory (in a nation without national news media, this was less a problem than it would be today). But all understood that he had committed to use the power of the federal government to combat the economic crisis that was paralyzing the nation.

Voters chose Roosevelt over Hoover overwhelmingly: Roosevelt's 22.8 million popular votes far outdistanced Hoover's 15.8 million. Third-party Socialist candidate Norman Thomas drew nearly 1 million votes.

Franklin Roosevelt, the twentieth-century president most beloved by America's "common people," had been born into a world of old money and upper-class privilege. The talented son of a politically prominent family, he seemed destined for political success. After graduating from Harvard College and Columbia Law School, he had married Eleanor Roosevelt, Theodore Roosevelt's niece and his own fifth cousin, once removed. He served in the New York State legislature; was appointed assistant secretary of the navy by Woodrow Wilson; and at the age of thirty-eight, ran for vice president in 1920 on the Democratic Party's losing ticket.

Then, in 1921, Roosevelt was stricken with polio. For two years he was bedridden, fighting one of the most feared diseases of the early twentieth century. He lost the use of his legs but gained, according to his wife Eleanor, a new strength of character that would serve him well as he reached out to depression-scarred America. As Roosevelt explained it, "If you had spent two years in bed trying to wiggle your big toe, after that anything would seem easy." By 1928, Roosevelt was sufficiently recovered to run for—and win—the governorship of New York and then to accept the Democratic Party's presidential nomination in 1932.

Elected in November 1932, Roosevelt would not take office until March 4, 1933. (The Twentieth Amendment to the Constitution—the so-called Lame Duck Amendment, ratified in 1933—shifted all future inaugurations to January 20.) In this long interregnum, the American banking system reached the verge of collapse.

Banking Crisis   The origins of the banking crisis lay in the flush years of World War I and the 1920s, when American banks made countless risky loans. After real-estate and stock market bubbles burst in 1929 and agricultural prices collapsed, many of these loans went bad. As a result, many banks lacked sufficient funds to cover their customers' deposits. Fearful of losing their savings in a bank collapse, depositors pulled money out of banks and put it into gold or under mattresses. "Bank runs," in which crowds of angry, frightened customers lined up to demand their money, became a common sight in economically ravaged towns throughout the nation.

By the 1932 election, the bank crisis was escalating rapidly. Hoover, the lame-duck president, refused to take action without Roosevelt's support, while Roosevelt called Hoover's request for support "cheeky" and refused to endorse actions he could not control. Meanwhile, the situation worsened. By Roosevelt's inauguration on March 4, every state in the Union had either suspended banking operations or restricted depositors' access to their money. The new president understood that this was more than a test of his administration. The total collapse of the U.S. banking system would threaten the nation's survival.

Roosevelt (who reportedly saw the *film Gabriel over the White House* several times before his inauguration) used his inaugural address to promise the American people decisive action. Standing in a cold rain on the Capitol steps, he vowed to face the crisis "frankly and boldly." The lines we best remember from his speech are words of comfort: "Let me assert my firm belief," the new president told the thousands gathered on the Capitol grounds and the millions gathered around their radios, "that the only thing we have to fear is fear itself—nameless, unreasoning, unjustified terror." But the only loud cheers that day came when Roosevelt invoked "the analogue of war," asserting that, if need be, "I shall ask the Congress for the one remaining instrument to meet the crisis—broad Executive power to wage a war against the emergency, as great as the power that would be given to me if we were in fact invaded by a foreign foe."

The next day Roosevelt, using powers legally granted by the World War I Trading with the Enemy Act, closed the nation's banks for a four-day "holiday" and summoned Congress to an emergency session. He immediately introduced the Emergency Banking Relief Bill, which was passed sight unseen by unanimous House vote, approved 73 to 7 in the Senate, and signed into law the same day. This bill provided federal authority to reopen solvent banks and reorganize the rest, and authorized federal money to shore up private banks. In his inaugural address, Roosevelt had attacked "unscrupulous money changers," and many critics of the failed banking system had hoped he planned to remove the banks from private hands. Instead, as one North Dakota congressman complained, "the President drove the money changers out of the Capitol on March 4th and they were all back on the 9th." Roosevelt's banking policy was much like Hoover's—a fundamentally conservative approach that upheld the status quo.

The banking bill could save the U.S. banking system only if Americans were confident enough to deposit money in the reopened banks. So Roosevelt, in the first of his radio "Fireside Chats," asked the support of the American people. "We have provided the machinery to restore our financial system," he said. "It is up to you to support and make it work." The next morning, when the banks opened their doors, people lined up—but this time, most waited to deposit money. It was an enormous triumph for the new president. It also demonstrated that Roosevelt, though unafraid to take bold action, was not as radical as some wished or as others feared.

First Hundred Days

During the ninety-nine-day-long special session of Congress, dubbed by journalists "The First Hundred Days," the federal government took on dramatically new roles. Roosevelt, aided by a group of advisers—lawyers, university professors, and social workers, who were collectively nicknamed "the Brain Trust"—and by the enormously capable First Lady, set out to revive the American economy. These "New Dealers" had no single, coherent plan, and Roosevelt's economic policies fluctuated between attempts to balance the budget and massive deficit spending (spending more than is taken in in taxes and borrowing the difference). But with a strong mandate for action and the support of a Democrat-controlled Congress, the new administration produced a flood of legislation. The first priority was economic recovery. Two basic strategies emerged during the First Hundred Days. New Dealers experimented with national economic planning, and they created a range of "relief" programs to help those in need.

National Industrial Recovery Act

At the heart of the New Deal experiment in planning were the National Industrial Recovery Act (NIRA) and the Agricultural Adjustment Act (AAA). The NIRA was based on the belief that "destructive competition" had worsened industry's economic woes. Skirting antitrust regulation, the NIRA authorized competing businesses to cooperate in crafting industrywide codes. Thus, automobile manufacturers, for example, would cooperate to limit production, establish industrywide prices, and set workers' wages. Competition among manufacturers would no longer drive down prices and wages. With wages and prices stabilized, the theory went, consumer spending would increase, thus allowing industries to rehire workers. Significantly, Section 7(a) guaranteed industrial workers the right to "organize and bargain collectively"—in other words, to unionize.

Individual businesses' participation in this program, administered by the National Recovery Administration (NRA), was voluntary—with one catch. Businesses that adhered to the industrywide codes could display the Blue Eagle, the NRA symbol; the government urged consumers to boycott businesses that did not fly the Blue Eagle. This voluntary program, though larger in scale than any previous government–private sector cooperation, was not very different from Hoover-era "associationalism."

From the beginning, the NRA faced serious problems. As small-business owners had feared, big business easily dominated the NRA-mandated cartels. NRA staff lacked the training and experience to stand up to the representatives of corporate America. The twenty-six-year-old NRA staffer who oversaw the creation of the petroleum industry code was "helped" by twenty highly paid oil industry lawyers. The majority of the 541 codes eventually approved by the NRA reflected the interests of major corporations, not small-business owners, labor, or consumers. Most fundamentally, the NRA did not deliver economic recovery. In 1935, the Supreme Court put an end to the fragile, floundering system. Using an old-fashioned (what Roosevelt called a "horse-and-buggy") definition of interstate commerce, the Supreme Court found that the NRA extended federal power past its constitutional bounds.

Agricultural Adjustment Act   The Agricultural Adjustment Act (AAA) had a more enduring effect on the United States. Establishing a national system of crop controls, the AAA offered subsidies to farmers who agreed to limit production of specific crops. (Overproduction drove crop prices down.) The subsidies, funded by taxing the processors of agricultural goods, were meant to give farmers the same purchasing power they had had during the prosperous period before World War I. But to reduce production in 1933, the nation's farmers agreed to destroy 8.5 million piglets and to plow under crops in the fields. Although limiting production did raise agricultural prices, millions of hungry Americans found it difficult to understand the economic theory behind this waste of food.

Government crop subsidies had unintended consequences: they were a disaster for tenant farmers and sharecroppers. Despite government hopes to the contrary, as landlords cut production they turned tenant farmers off their land. In the South, the number of sharecropper farms dropped by almost one-third between 1930 and 1940 and dispossessed farmers—many of them African American—headed to cities and towns throughout the nation. But the subsidies did help many. In the depression-ravaged Dakotas, for example, government payments accounted for almost three-quarters of the total farm income for 1934.

In 1936, the Supreme Court found that the AAA, like the NRA, was unconstitutional. But the AAA (unlike the NRA) was too popular with its constituency—American farmers—to disappear. The legislation was rewritten to meet the Supreme Court's objections, and farm subsidies continue into the twenty-first century.

Relief Programs   With millions of Americans in desperate poverty, Roosevelt also moved quickly to implement poor relief: $3 billion in federal dollars were allocated in 1935. New Dealers, however—like many other Americans—disapproved of direct relief payments. "Give a man a dole and you save his body and destroy his spirit; give him a job and pay him an assured wage and you save both the body and the spirit," wrote Harry Hopkins, Roosevelt's trusted adviser and head of the president's major relief agency, the Federal Emergency Relief Administration (FERA). Thus New Deal programs emphasized "work relief." By January 1934, the Civil Works Administration had hired 4 million people, most earning $15 a week. And the Civilian Conservation Corps (CCC) paid unmarried young men (young women were not eligible) $1 a day to do hard outdoor labor: building dams and reservoirs, creating trails in national parks. The program was segregated by race but brought together young men from very different backgrounds. By 1942, the CCC had employed 2.5 million men, including 80,000 Native Americans who worked on western Indian reservations.

Work relief programs rarely addressed the needs of poor women. Mothers of young children were usually classified as "unemployable" and were offered relief instead of jobs. But as historian Linda Gordon explains, "mother's-aid" grants were pitifully small compared to wages in federal works programs. In North Carolina, for example, they were one-sixth. While federal relief programs rejected the poor-law tradition that distinguished between the "deserving" and the "undeserving" poor, local officials often did not. "The investigators, they were like detectives," complained one woman who had requested relief. And journalist Lorena Hickok reported to Harry Hopkins that "a woman who isn't a good housekeeper is apt to have a pretty rough time of it. And heaven help the family in which there is any 'moral problem.' "

The Public Works Administration (PWA), created by Title II of the National Industrial Recovery Act, poured money into major construction projects, providing employment for men in the construction industry and building trades and pumping federal money into the economy. Congress appropriated $3.3 billion—or 165% of federal revenues for that year—for PWA projects in 1933. While creating jobs and priming the economy with federal money were crucial goals, New Deal public works programs also promoted economic development by building infrastructure throughout the nation, especially in underdeveloped regions. PWA workers built the Triborough Bridge in New York City, but also the Grand River Dam in Oklahoma, school buildings in almost half of the nation's counties, and the vast majority of all new sewer systems created during the depression years.

The special session of Congress adjourned on June 16, 1933. In just over three months, Roosevelt had delivered fifteen messages to Congress proposing major legislation, and Congress had passed fifteen significant laws (see Table 25.1). The United States had rebounded from near collapse. As columnist Walter Lippmann wrote, at the time of Roosevelt's inauguration, the country was a collection of "disorderly panic-stricken mobs and factions. In the hundred days from March to June we became again an organized nation confident of our power to provide for our own security and to control our own destiny." Throughout the remainder of 1933 and the spring and summer of 1934, more New Deal bills became law. And as New Deal programs were implemented, unemployment fell steadily from 13 million in 1933 to 9 million in 1936. Farm prices rose, along with wages and salaries, and business failures abated (see Figure 25.1).

TABLE 25.1 | NEW DEAL ACHIEVEMENTS

Year	Labor	Agriculture and Environment	Business and Industrial Recovery	Relief	Reform
1933	Section 7(a) of NIRA	Agricultural Adjustment Act Farm Credit Act	Emergency Banking Relief Act Economy Act Beer-Wine Revenue Act Banking Act of 1933 (guaranteed deposits) National Industrial Recovery Act	Civilian Conservation Corps Federal Emergency Relief Act Home Owners Refinancing Act Public Works Administration Civil Works Administration	TVA Federal Securities Act
1934	National Labor Relations Board	Taylor Grazing Act			Securities Exchange Act
1935	National Labor Relations (Wagner) Act	Resettlement Administration Rural Electrification Administration		Works Progress Administration National Youth Administration	Social Security Act Public Utility Holding Company Act Revenue Act (wealth tax)
1937		Farm Security Administration		National Housing Act	
1938	Fair Labor Standards Act	Agricultural Adjustment Act of 1938			

FIGURE 25.1 The Economy Before and After the New Deal, 1929–1941

The New Deal reduced bank closings, business failures, and unemployment, and it increased farm prices, wages, and salaries. Some of the nation's most persistent economic problems, however, did not disappear until the advent of the Second World War.

© Cengage Learning

POLITICAL PRESSURE AND THE SECOND NEW DEAL

Roosevelt's New Deal had enjoyed unprecedented popular and congressional support, but that would not last. The seeming unity of the First Hundred Days masked deep divides within the nation, and once the immediate crisis was averted, the struggle over solutions began in earnest. As some tried to stop the expansion of government power, others pushed for increased governmental action to combat continuing poverty and inequality. Pressure came from all directions as the president considered the next phase of New Deal action.

Business Opposition As the economy partially recovered, many wealthy business leaders began to publicly criticize the New Deal. They condemned government regulation and taxation as well as the use of deficit financing for relief and public works. In 1934, leaders of several major corporations joined with former presidential candidate Al Smith and disaffected conservative Democrats to establish the American Liberty League. This group mounted a highly visible campaign against New Deal "radicalism." In an attempt to turn southern whites against the New Deal and so splinter the Democratic Party, the Liberty League also secretly channeled funds to a racist group in the South, which tried to foster protest by circulating pictures of the First Lady with African Americans.

Demagogues and Populists While many prominent business leaders fought the New Deal, other Americans (sometimes called "populists") thought the government favored business too much and paid too little attention to the needs of the common people. Unemployment had decreased—but 9 million people were still without work. In 1934, a wave of strikes hit the nation, affecting 1.5 million workers. In 1935, enormous dust storms enveloped the southern plains, killing livestock and driving families from their land. Millions of Americans still suffered. As their dissatisfaction mounted, so, too, did the appeal of various demagogues, who played to the prejudices and unreasoning passions of the people.

Father Charles Coughlin, a Roman Catholic priest whose weekly radio sermons reached up to 30 million listeners, spoke to those who felt they had lost control of their lives to distant elites and impersonal forces. Increasingly anti–New Deal, he was also increasingly anti-Semitic, telling his listeners that an international conspiracy of Jewish bankers caused their problems.

Another challenge came from Dr. Francis E. Townsend, a public health officer in Long Beach, California, who was thrown out of work at age sixty-seven with only $100 in savings. His situation was not unusual. With social welfare left to the states, only about 400,000 of the 6.6 million elderly Americans received any sort of state-supplied pension. And as employment and savings disappeared with the depression, many older people fell into desperate poverty. Townsend proposed that Americans over the age of sixty should receive a government pension of $200 a month, financed by a new "transaction" (sales) tax. In fact, Townsend's plan was fiscally impossible (almost three-quarters of working Americans earned $200 a month or less) and profoundly regressive (because sales tax rates are the same for everyone, they take a larger share of income from those who earn least). Thus, Townsend actually sought a massive transfer of income from the working poor to the nonworking elderly. Nonetheless, 20 million Americans, or 1 in 5 adults—concerned about the plight of the elderly and not about details of funding—signed petitions supporting this plan.

Then there was Huey Long, perhaps the most successful populist demagogue in American history. Long was elected governor of Louisiana in 1928 with the slogan "Every Man a King, But No One Wears a Crown." As a U.S. senator, Long initially supported the New Deal but soon decided that Roosevelt had fallen captive to big business. Long countered in 1934 with the Share Our Wealth Society, advocating the seizure (by taxation) of all income exceeding $1 million a year and of wealth in excess of $5 million per family. From these funds, the government would provide each American family an annual income of $2,000 and a one-time homestead allowance of $5,000. (Long's plan was fiscally impossible but definitely not regressive.) By mid-1935, Long's movement claimed 7 million members, and few doubted that he aspired to the presidency. But Long was killed by a bodyguard's bullet during an assassination attempt in September 1935.

Left-Wing Critics

The political left also gained ground as hard times continued. Socialists and communists alike criticized the New Deal for trying to save capitalism instead of working to lessen the inequality of power and wealth in American society. In California, muckraker and socialist Upton Sinclair won the Democratic gubernatorial nomination in 1934 with the slogan "End Poverty in California." That year in Wisconsin, the left-wing Progressive Party provided seven of the state's ten representatives to Congress, as voters reelected Robert La Follette to the Senate and gave his brother Philip the state governorship. Even the U.S. Communist Party found new support as it campaigned for social welfare and relief. Changing its strategy to disclaim any intention of overthrowing the U.S. government, the party proclaimed that "Communism Is Twentieth Century Americanism" and began to cooperate with left-wing labor unions, student groups, and writers' organizations in a "Popular Front" against fascism abroad and racism at home. In the late 1920s, focusing on the plight of African Americans, it established the League of Struggle for Negro Rights to fight lynching, and from 1931 on provided critical legal and financial support to the "Scottsboro Boys," who were falsely accused of raping two white women in Alabama. As one black worker who became a communist organizer in Alabama explained, the Communist Party "fought selflessly and tirelessly to undo the wrongs perpetrated upon my race. Here was no dilly-dallying, no pussyfooting on the question of full equality of the Negro people." In 1938, at its high point for the decade, the party had fifty-five thousand members.

Shaping the Second New Deal

It was not only external critics who pushed Roosevelt to focus on social justice. His administration—largely due to Eleanor Roosevelt's influence—included many progressive activists. Frances Perkins, America's first woman cabinet member, came from a social work background, as did Roosevelt's close adviser Harold Ickes. A group of women social reformers who coalesced around the First Lady became important figures in government and in the Democratic Party. And African Americans had an unprecedented voice in this White House. By 1936, at least fifty black Americans held relatively important positions in New Deal agencies and cabinet-level departments. Journalists called these officials—who met on Friday evenings at the home of Mary McLeod Bethune, a distinguished educator who served as Director of Negro Affairs for the National Youth Administration—the "black cabinet." Finally, Eleanor Roosevelt herself worked tirelessly to put social justice issues at the center of the New Deal agenda.

As Roosevelt faced the election of 1936, he understood that he had to appeal to Americans who had seemingly contradictory desires. Those who had been hit hard by the depression looked to the New Deal for help and for social justice. If that help was not forthcoming, Roosevelt would lose their support. Other Americans—not the poorest, but those with a tenuous hold on the middle class—were afraid of the continued chaos and disorder. They wanted security and stability. Still others, with more to lose, were frightened by the populist promises of people like Long and Coughlin. They wanted the New Deal to preserve American capitalism. With these lessons in mind, Roosevelt took the initiative once more.

During the period historians call the Second New Deal, Roosevelt introduced a range of progressive programs aimed at providing, as he said in a 1935 address to Congress, "greater security for the average man than he has ever known before in the history of America." The first triumph of the Second New Deal was an innocuous-sounding but momentous law that Roosevelt called "the Big Bill." The Emergency Relief Appropriation Act provided $4 billion in new deficit spending, primarily to create massive public works programs for the jobless. It also established the Resettlement Administration, which resettled destitute families and organized rural homestead communities and suburban greenbelt towns for low-income workers; the Rural Electrification Administration, which brought electricity to isolated rural areas; and the National Youth Administration, which sponsored work-relief programs for young adults and part-time jobs for students.

Works Progress Administration   The largest and best-known program funded by the Emergency Relief Appropriation Act was the Works Progress Administration (WPA), later renamed the Work Projects Administration. The WPA employed more than 8.5 million people who built 650,000 miles of highways and roads and 125,000 public buildings, as well as bridges, reservoirs, irrigation systems, sewage treatment plants, parks, playgrounds, and swimming pools throughout the nation. Critics labeled these projects "boondoggles" or argued that they were simply to buy political favor. But WPA projects helped local communities: WPA workers built or renovated schools and hospitals, operated nurseries for preschool children, and taught 1.5 million adults to read and write.

The WPA also employed artists, musicians, writers, and actors for a wide range of cultural programs. The WPA's Federal Theater Project brought vaudeville, circuses, and theater, including African American and Yiddish plays, to cities and towns across the country. Its Arts Project hired painters and sculptors to teach their crafts in rural schools and commissioned artists to decorate post office walls with murals depicting ordinary life in America past and present. The Federal Music Project employed fifteen thousand musicians in government-sponsored orchestras and collected folk songs from around the nation. Perhaps the most ambitious of the New Deal's cultural programs was the WPA's Federal Writers' Project (FWP), which hired talented authors, such as John Steinbeck and Richard Wright. FWP writers created guidebooks for every state and territory, and they wrote about the plain people of the United States. More than two thousand elderly men and women who had been freed from slavery by the Civil War told their stories to FWP writers, who collected these "slave narratives," life stories of sharecroppers and textile workers that were published as *These Are Our Lives* (1939). These and other WPA arts projects were controversial, for many of the WPA artists, musicians, actors, and writers sympathized with the political struggles of workers and farmers. Critics assailed them as left-wing propaganda, and in fact some of these artists were communists. However, the goal of this "Popular Front" culture was not to overthrow the government, but to recover a tradition of American radicalism through remembering, and celebrating artistically, the lives and labor of America's plain folk.

Social Security Act

Big Bill programs and agencies were part of a short-term "emergency" strategy meant to address the immediate needs of the nation. Roosevelt's long-term strategy centered around the second major piece of Second New Deal legislation, the Social Security Act. The Social Security Act created, for the first time, a federal system to provide for the social welfare of American citizens. Its key provision was a federal pension system in which eligible workers paid mandatory Social Security taxes on their wages and their employers contributed an equivalent amount; these workers then received federal retirement benefits. The Social Security Act also created several welfare programs, including a cooperative federal-state system of unemployment compensation and Aid to Dependent Children (later renamed Aid to Families with Dependent Children, AFDC) for needy children in families without fathers present. Over the course of the twentieth century, benefits provided through the Social Security system would save tens of millions of Americans, especially the elderly, from poverty and despair.

Compared with the national systems of social security already in place in most western European nations, the U.S. Social Security system was fairly conservative. First, the government did not pay for old-age benefits; workers and their bosses did. Second, the tax was regressive in that the more workers earned, the less they were taxed proportionally. Finally, the law did not cover agricultural labor, domestic service, and "casual labor not in the course of the employer's trade or business" (for example, janitorial work at a hospital). Thus, a disproportionately high number of people of color, who worked as farm laborers, as domestic servants, and in service jobs in hospitals and restaurants, received no benefits. The act also excluded public-sector employees, so that many teachers, nurses, librarians, and social workers, the majority of whom were women, went uncovered. (Although the original Social Security Act provided no retirement benefits for spouses or widows of covered workers, Congress added these benefits in 1939.) Despite these limitations, the Social Security Act was a highly significant development. With its passage, the federal government took some responsibility for the economic security of the aged, the temporarily unemployed, dependent children, and people with disabilities.

Roosevelt's Populist Strategies As the election of 1936 approached, Roosevelt adopted the populist language of his critics. He made scathing attacks on big business. Denouncing "entrenched greed" and the "unjust concentration of wealth and power," he proposed that government should "cut the giants down to size" through antitrust suits and heavy corporate taxes. He also supported the Wealth Tax Act, which some critics saw as the president's attempt to "steal Huey Long's thunder." The tax act helped achieve a slight redistribution of income by raising the income taxes of the wealthy (see Figure 25.2). It also imposed a new tax on business profits and increased taxes on inheritances, large gifts, and profits from the sale of property.

In November 1936, Roosevelt won the presidency by a landslide, defeating Republican nominee Governor Alf Landon of Kansas by a ratio of 27.8 to 16.7 million votes. The Democrats also won huge majorities in the House and Senate. The Democratic victory was so overwhelming that some worried the two-party system might collapse. In fact, Roosevelt and the Democrats had forged a powerful "New Deal coalition." This new alliance pulled together groups from very different backgrounds and with different interests: the urban working class (especially immigrants

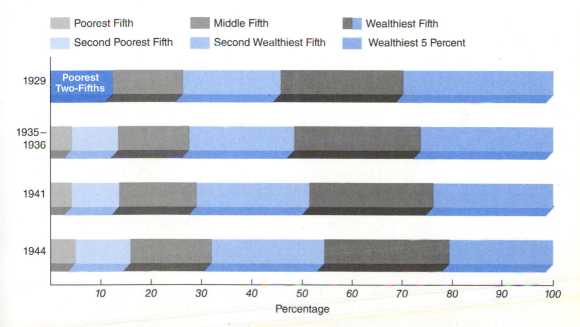

FIGURE 25.2 Distribution of Total Family Income Among the American People, 1929–1944 (percentage)

Although the New Deal provided economic relief to the American people, it did not, as its critics so often charged, significantly redistribute income downward from the rich to the poor.

Source: Adapted from U.S. Bureau of the Census, *Historical Statistics of the United States, Colonial Times to 1970.* Bicentennial Edition, Washington, D.C.: U.S. Government Printing Office, 1975, page 301.

from southern and eastern Europe and their sons and daughters), organized labor, the eleven states of the Confederacy (the "Solid South"), and northern blacks. By this time, the African American population in northern cities was large enough to constitute voting blocs, and New Deal benefits drew them away from the Republican Party, which they had long supported as the party of Lincoln. This New Deal coalition gave the Democratic Party dominance in the two-party system and ensured that Democrats would occupy the White House for most of the next thirty years.

LABOR

During the worst years of the depression, American workers continued to organize and to struggle for the rights of labor. Management, however, resisted unionization vigorously. Many employers refused to recognize unions, and some hired armed thugs to intimidate workers. One business publication declared that "a few hundred funerals will have a quieting influence." As employers refused to negotiate with union representatives, workers walked off the job. Employers tried to replace striking workers with strikebreakers—and workers tried to keep the strikebreakers from crossing their picket lines. The situation often turned violent. Local police or National Guard troops frequently intervened on the side of management, smashing workers' picket lines. As strikes spread throughout the nation, violence erupted in the steel, automobile, and textile industries; among lumber workers in the Pacific Northwest; and among teamsters in the Midwest. In 1934, police met a longshoremen's strike with violence on the docks of San Francisco; 2 union members were killed, and workers' anger spread to other industries. Eventually 130,000 workers joined the general strike.

Workers pushed the Roosevelt administration for support, which came in the 1935 National Labor Relations (Wagner) Act. This act guaranteed workers the right to organize unions and to bargain collectively. It outlawed "unfair labor practices," such as firing workers who joined unions; prohibited management from sponsoring company unions; and required employers to bargain with labor's elected union representatives to set wages, hours, and working conditions. Critical for its success, the Wagner Act created a mechanism for enforcement: the National Labor Relations Board (NLRB). Although labor-management conflict continued, by the end of the decade the NLRB played a key role in mediating disputes. With federal protection, union membership grew. Organizers in the coalfields told miners that "President Roosevelt wants you to join the union," and join they did—along with workers in dozens of industries. In 1929 union membership stood at 3.6 million; in mid-1938 it surpassed 7 million.

The Wagner Act further alienated business leaders from the New Deal. "No Obedience," proclaimed an editorial in a leading business magazine. The business-sponsored Liberty League insisted—incorrectly—that the Supreme Court would soon find the Wagner Act unconstitutional.

Rivalry Between Craft and Industrial Unions   Conflict existed not only between labor and management, but also within the labor movement itself. The rapid growth and increasing militancy of the movement exacerbated an existing division between "craft" and "industrial" unions in the United States. Craft unions represented labor's elite: the skilled workers in a particular trade, such as carpentry. Industrial unions represented all the workers, skilled and unskilled, in a given industry such as automobile manufacture. In the 1930s, it was the industrial unions that had grown dramatically.

Craft unions dominated the American Federation of Labor, the powerful umbrella organization for specific unions. Most AFL leaders offered little support for industrial organizing. Many looked down on the industrial workers, disproportionately immigrants from southern and eastern Europe—"the rubbish at labor's door," in the words of the Teamsters' president. Skilled workers had economic interests different from those of the great mass of unskilled workers, and more conservative craft unionists were often alarmed at what they saw as the radicalism of industrial unions.

In 1935, the industrial unionists made their move. John L. Lewis, head of the United Mine Workers and the nation's most prominent labor leader, resigned as vice president of the AFL. He and other industrial unionists created the Committee for Industrial Organization (CIO); the AFL responded by suspending all CIO unions. In 1938, the slightly renamed Congress of Industrial Organizations had 3.7 million members, slightly more than the AFL's 3.4 million. Unlike the AFL, the CIO included women and people of color in its membership. Union membership gave these "marginal" workers greater employment security and the benefits of collective bargaining.

Sit-Down Strikes

The most decisive labor conflict of the decade came in late 1936, when the United Auto Workers (UAW), an industrial union, demanded recognition from General Motors (GM), Chrysler, and Ford. When GM refused, UAW organizers responded with a relatively new tactic: a "sit-down strike." On December 30, 1936, workers at the Fisher Body plant in Flint, Michigan, went on strike *inside* the Fisher One factory. They refused to leave the building, thus immobilizing a key part of the GM production system. GM tried to force the workers out by turning off the heat. When police attempted to take back the plant, strikers hurled steel bolts, coffee mugs, and bottles. The police tried tear gas. Strikers turned the plant's water hoses on the police.

As the sit-down strike spread to adjacent plants, auto production plummeted. General Motors obtained a court order to evacuate the plant, but the strikers stood firm, risking imprisonment and fines. In a critical decision, Michigan's governor refused to send in the National Guard to clear workers from the buildings. After forty-four days, the UAW triumphed. GM agreed to recognize the union, and Chrysler quickly followed. Ford held out until 1941.

Memorial Day Massacre

On the heels of this triumph, however, came a grim reminder of the costs of labor's struggle. On Memorial Day 1937, a group of picnicking workers and their families marched toward the Republic Steel plant in Chicago, intending to show support for strikers on a picket line in front of the plant. Police blocked their route and ordered them to disperse. One of the marchers threw something at the police, and the police attacked. Ten men were killed, seven of them shot in the back. Thirty marchers were wounded, including a woman and three children. Many Americans, fed up with labor strife and violence, showed little sympathy for the workers. The antilabor *Chicago Tribune* blamed the marchers and praised police for repelling "a trained military unit of a revolutionary body."

At great cost, organized labor made great gains during the 1930s. Gradually violence receded, as the National Labor Relations Board proved effective in mediating disputes. And unionized workers—about 23 percent of the nonagricultural work force—saw their standard of living rise. By 1941, the average steelworker could afford to buy a new coat for himself and his wife every six years and, every other year, a pair of shoes for each of his children.

FEDERAL POWER AND THE NATIONALIZATION OF CULTURE

In the 1930s, national culture, politics, and policies played an increasingly important role in the lives of Americans from different regions, classes, and ethnic backgrounds, as the reach of the national mass media grew and the power of the federal government expanded. During the decade-long economic crisis, political power moved from the state and local level to the White House and Congress. Individual Americans, in new ways, found their lives bound up with the federal government. In 1930, with the single exception of the post office, Americans had little direct contact with the federal government. By the end of the 1930s, almost 35 percent of the population had received some sort of federal government benefit, whether crop subsidies through the federal AAA or a WPA job or relief payments through FERA. As political analyst Michael Barone argues, "The New Deal changed American life by changing the relationship between Americans and their government." Americans in the 1930s began to look to the federal government to play a major and active role in the life of the nation.

New Deal in the West The New Deal changed the American West more than any other region, as federally sponsored construction of dams and other public works projects reshaped the region's economy and environment. During the 1930s, the federal Bureau of Reclamation, an obscure agency created by the Newlands Reclamation Act of 1902 to provide irrigation for small farms and ranches, expanded its mandate dramatically to build large multipurpose dams that controlled entire river systems. The Central Valley Project dammed the Sacramento River and its tributaries. The Boulder Dam (later renamed for Herbert Hoover) harnessed the Colorado River, providing water to southern California municipalities and using hydroelectric power to produce electricity for Los Angeles and southern Arizona. The water from these dams opened new areas to agriculture and allowed western cities to expand; the cheap electricity they produced attracted industry to the region. Large factory farms consolidated their hold in the region with water from these massive projects, which were paid for by taxpayers across the nation and by regional consumers of municipal water and electricity. These federally managed projects also gave the federal government an unprecedented role in the West. Especially after the completion of Washington State's Grand Coulee Dam in 1941, the federal government controlled both a great

The Women's Emergency Brigade and General Motors Sit–Down Strike

During the 1937 sit-down strike by automobile workers in Flint, Michigan, a women's "emergency brigade" of wives, daughters, sisters, and sweethearts demonstrated daily at the plant. When police tried to force the men out of Chevrolet Plant No. 9 by filling it with tear gas, the women used clubs to smash the plant's windows and let in fresh air. Sixteen people were injured that day in the riot between police and strikers. The following day the Women's Emergency Brigade marched again. Using this photograph as visual evidence, how did these women attempt to demonstrate the respectability and mainstream nature of their protest? How does that message fit with the clubs several still carry?

© Bettmann/Corbis

Gerenda Johnson, wife of a striker, leads a march past the GM Chevrolet small parts plant on the day following a violent conflict between police and strikers.

deal of water and hydroelectric power in the region. And in the West, control of water meant control over the region's future.

The federal government also brought millions of acres of western land under its control in the 1930s. Attempting to combat the environmental disaster of the Dust Bowl and to keep crop and livestock prices from falling further, federal programs worked to limit agricultural production. To reduce pressure on the land from over-grazing, the federal government bought 8 million cattle from farmers in a six-month period in 1934–1935 and transported the healthy cattle out of the region. In 1934, the Taylor Grazing Act imposed new restrictions on ranchers' use of public lands for grazing stock. Federal stock reduction programs probably saved the western cattle industry, but they destroyed the traditional economy of the Navajos by forcing them to reduce the size of sheep herds on their federally protected reservation lands. The large farms and ranches of the West benefited immensely from federal subsidies and crop supports through the AAA, but such programs also increased federal government control in the region. As western historian Richard White argues, by the end of the 1930s, "federal bureaucracies were quite literally remaking the American West."

New Deal for Native Americans

New federal activism extended to the West's people as well. Over the past several decades, federal policy toward Native Americans, especially those on western Indian reservations, had been disastrous. The Bureau of Indian Affairs (BIA) was riddled with corruption; in its attempts to "assimilate" Native Americans, it had separated children from their parents, suppressed native languages, and outlawed tribal religious practices. Such BIA-enforced assimilation was not successful. Division of tribal lands had failed to promote individual land ownership—almost half of those living on reservations in 1933 owned no land. In the early 1930s, Native Americans were the poorest group in the nation, plagued by epidemics and malnutrition, with an infant mortality rate twice that of white Americans.

In 1933, Roosevelt named one of the BIA's most vocal critics to head the agency. John Collier, founder of the American Indian Defense Agency, meant to completely reverse the course of America's Indian policy, and his initiatives had many positive results. The Indian Reorganization Act (1934) went a long way toward ending the forced assimilation of native peoples and restoring Indian lands to tribal ownership. It also gave federal recognition to tribal governments. Indian tribes had regained their status as semisovereign nations, guaranteed "internal sovereignty" in all matters not specifically limited by acts of Congress.

Not all Indian peoples supported the IRA. Some saw it as a "back-to-the-blanket" measure based on romantic notions of "authentic" Indian culture. The tribal government structure specified by the IRA was culturally alien—and quite perplexing—to tribes such as the Papagos, whose language had no word for "representative." The Navajo nation also refused to ratify the IRA; in a terrible case of bad timing, the vote took place during the federally mandated destruction of Navajo sheep herds. Eventually, however, 181 tribes organized under the IRA. Collier had succeeded in reversing some of the destructive policies of the past, and the IRA laid the groundwork for future economic development and limited political autonomy among native peoples.

New Deal in the South   New Dealers did not set out to transform the American West, but they did intend to transform the American South. Well before the Great Depression, the South was mired in widespread and debilitating poverty. In 1929, the South's per capita income of $365 per year was less than half of the West's $921. More than half of the region's farm families were tenants or sharecroppers with no land of their own. "Sickness, misery, and unnecessary death," in the words of a contemporary study, plagued the southern poor. Almost 15 percent of South Carolina's people could not read or write.

Roosevelt, who sought a cure for his polio in the pools of Warm Springs, Georgia, had seen southern poverty firsthand and understood its human costs. But in describing the South as "the Nation's No. 1 economic problem" in 1938, he was referring to the economic theory that underlay many New Deal programs. As long as its people were too poor to participate in the nation's mass consumer economy, the South would be a drag on national economic recovery.

The largest federal intervention in the South was the Tennessee Valley Authority (TVA), authorized by Congress during Roosevelt's First Hundred Days. The TVA was created to develop a water and hydroelectric power project similar to the multipurpose dams of the West; dams would not only control flooding but also produce electric power for the region (see Map 25.1). However, confronted with the poverty and hopelessness of the Tennessee River Valley region (which included parts of Virginia, North Carolina, Tennessee, Georgia, Alabama, Mississippi, and Kentucky), the TVA quickly extended its focus. Through the TVA, the federal government promoted economic development, helped bring electricity to rural areas, restored fields worn out from overuse, and fought the curse of malaria.

Although it benefited many poor southerners, over time the TVA proved to be a monumental environmental disaster. TVA strip mining caused soil erosion. Its coal-burning generators released sulfur oxides, which combined with water vapor to produce acid rain. Above all, the TVA degraded the water by dumping untreated sewage, toxic chemicals, and metal pollutants from strip mining into streams and rivers.

During the 1930s, the Roosevelt administration faced a very difficult political situation in the South. The southern senators whose support Roosevelt so desperately needed benefited from the flow of federal dollars to their states. But they were also suspicious of federal intervention and determined to preserve states' rights. Especially when federal action threatened the South's racial hierarchy, they resisted passionately. As the nation's poorest and least educated region, the South would not easily be integrated into the national culture and economy. But New Deal programs began that process and in so doing improved the lives of at least some of the region's people.

Mass Media and Popular Culture   It was not only federal government programs that broke down regional boundaries and fostered national connections during the 1930s. The national mass medium of radio helped millions survive hard times, and America's national popular culture played a critical role in the life of Americans throughout the 1930s.

The sound of the radio filled the days and nights of the depression era. Manufacturers rushed to produce cheaper models, and by 1937 Americans were buying radios at the rate of twenty-eight a minute. By the end of the decade, 27.5 million households owned radios, and families listened on average five hours a day. Roosevelt understood the importance of the radio in American life, going directly to the American people with radio "Fireside Chats" throughout his presidency. Americans, in fact, put him eleventh in a ranking of America's top "radio personalities" in 1938.

The radio offered Americans many things. In a time of uncertainty, radio gave citizens immediate access—as never before—to the political news of the day and to the actual voices of their elected leaders. During hard times, radio offered escape: for children, the adventures of *Flash Gordon* and *Jack Armstrong, The All-American* Boy; for housewives, new soap operas, such as *The Romance of Helen Trent* and *Young Widder Brown*. Entire families gathered to listen to the comedy of ex-vaudevillians Jack Benny, George Burns, and Gracie Allen.

Radio also gave people a chance to participate—however vicariously—in events they could never have experienced before: listeners were carried to New York City

MAP 25.1 The Tennessee Valley Authority

To control flooding and generate electricity, the Tennessee Valley Authority constructed dams along the Tennessee River and its tributaries from Paducah, Kentucky, to Knoxville, Tennessee.

for performances of the Metropolitan Opera on Saturday afternoons, to the Moana Hotel on the beach at Waikiki through the live broadcast of *Hawaii Calls*, to major league baseball games (begun by the St. Louis Cardinals in 1935) in distant cities. Millions shared the horror of the kidnapping of aviator Charles Lindbergh's son in 1932; black Americans in the urban North and rural South experienced the triumphs of African American boxer Joe Louis ("the Brown Bomber"). Radio lessened the isolation of individuals and communities. It helped create a more homogeneous mass culture, as people throughout the nation listened to the same programs, but by offering a set of shared experiences, it also lessened the gulfs among Americans from different regions and class backgrounds.

The shared popular culture of 1930s America also centered on Hollywood movies. The film industry suffered in the initial years of the depression—almost one-third of all movie theaters closed, and ticket prices fell from 30 to 20 cents—but it rebounded after 1933. In a nation of fewer than 130 million people, between 80 and 90 million movie tickets were sold each week by the mid-1930s. Film's power to influence American attitudes was clearly demonstrated when sales of undershirts plummeted after Clark Gable took off his shirt to reveal a bare chest in It *Happened One Night*. As the depression continued, many Americans sought escape from grim realities at the movies. Comedies were especially popular, from the slapstick of the Marx Brothers to the sophisticated banter of *My Man Godfrey* or *It Happened One Night*. However, the appeal of upbeat movies was in the context of economic hard times. The song "Who's Afraid of the Big Bad Wolf?" from Disney's *Three Little Pigs* was a big hit in 1933—as the economy hit bottom.

Yet as a cycle of gangster movies (including *Little Caesar* and *Scarface*) drew crowds in the early 1930s, many Americans worried about the effect of such films. Crime seemed to be glamorized, no matter that the gangster hero always met death or destruction. Faced with a boycott organized by the Roman Catholic Legion of Decency, in 1934 the film industry established a production code that would determine what American film audiences saw—and did not see—for decades. "The vulgar, the cheap, and the tawdry is out," pledged the head of the Production Code Administration. "There is no room on the screen at any time for pictures which offend against common decency."

Finally, in an unintended consequence, federal policies intended to channel jobs to male heads of households strengthened the power of national popular culture. During Roosevelt's first two years in office, 1.5 million youths lost jobs; many young people who would have gone to work at the age of fourteen in better times decided to stay in school. By the end of the decade, three-quarters of American youth went to high school—up from one-half in 1920—and graduation rates doubled. School was free, classrooms were warm, and education seemed to promise a better future. The exuberant, fad-driven peer cultures that had developed in 1920s high schools and colleges were no more, but consumer-oriented youth culture had not died out. And as more young people went to high school, more participated in that national youth culture. Increasingly, young people listened to the same music. More than ever before, they adopted the same styles of clothing, of dance, of speech. Paradoxically, the hard times of the depression did not destroy youth culture; instead, they caused youth culture to spread more widely among America's young.

THE LIMITS OF THE NEW DEAL

Roosevelt began his second term with great optimism and a strong mandate for reform. Almost immediately, however, the president's own actions undermined his New Deal agenda. Labor strife and racial issues divided the American people. As fascism spread in Europe, the world inched toward war, and domestic initiatives lost ground to foreign affairs and defense. By the end of 1938, New Deal reform had ground to a halt, but it had already had a profound impact on the United States.

Court-Packing Plan   Following his landslide electoral victory in 1936, Roosevelt set out to safeguard his progressive agenda. The greatest danger he saw was from the U.S. Supreme Court. In ruling unconstitutional both the National Industrial Recovery Act (in 1935) and the Agricultural Adjustment Act (in 1936), the Court rejected not only specific provisions of hastily drafted New Deal legislation but also the expansion of presidential and federal power such legislation entailed. Only three of the nine justices were consistently sympathetic to New Deal "emergency" measures, and Roosevelt was convinced the Court would invalidate most of the Second New Deal legislation. Citing the advanced age and heavy workload of the nine justices, he asked Congress for authority to appoint up to six new justices to the Supreme Court. But in an era that had seen the rise to power of Hitler, Mussolini, and Stalin, many Americans saw Roosevelt's plan as an attack on constitutional government. Even those sympathetic to the New Deal worried about politicizing the Court. "Assuming, which is not at all impossible," wrote prominent journalist William Allen White, "a reactionary president, as charming, as eloquent and as irresistible as Roosevelt, with power to change the court, and we should be in the devil's own fix." Congress rebelled, and Roosevelt experienced his first major congressional defeat.

The episode had a final, ironic twist. During the long public debate over court packing, the ideological center of the Supreme Court shifted. Key swing-vote justices began to vote in favor of liberal, pro–New Deal rulings. In short order, the Court upheld both the Wagner Act (*NLRB v. Jones & Laughlin Steel Corp.*), ruling that Congress's power to regulate interstate commerce also involved the power to regulate the production of goods for interstate commerce, and the Social Security Act. Moreover, a new judicial pension program encouraged older judges to retire, and the president appointed seven new associate justices in the next four years, including such notables as Hugo Black, Felix Frankfurter, and William O. Douglas. In the end, Roosevelt got what he wanted from the Supreme Court, but the court-packing plan damaged his political credibility.

Roosevelt Recession   Another New Deal setback was the renewed economic recession of 1937–1939, sometimes called the Roosevelt recession. Despite his use of deficit spending, Roosevelt had never abandoned his commitment to a balanced budget. In 1937, confident that the depression had largely been cured, he began to cut back government spending. At the same time, the Federal Reserve Board, concerned about a 3.6 percent inflation rate, tightened credit. The two actions sent the economy into a tailspin: unemployment climbed from 7.7 million in 1937 to 10.4 million in 1938. Soon Roosevelt resumed deficit financing.

The New Deal was in trouble in 1937 and 1938, and New Dealers struggled over the direction of liberal reform. Some urged vigorous trustbusting; others advocated the resurrection of national economic planning as it had existed under the National Recovery Administration. But in the end, Roosevelt rejected these alternatives and chose deficit financing as a means of stimulating consumer demand and creating jobs. And in 1939, with conflict over the world war that had begun in Europe commanding more and more of the nation's attention, the New Deal came to an end. Roosevelt sacrificed further domestic reforms in return for conservative support for his programs of military rearmament and preparedness.

Election of 1940

No president had ever served more than two terms, and many Americans speculated about whether Franklin Roosevelt would run for a third term in 1940. Roosevelt seemed undecided until that spring, when Adolf Hitler's military advances in Europe apparently convinced him to stay on. Roosevelt headed off the predictable attacks from his opponent, Republican Wendell Willkie, by expanding military and naval contracts and thus reducing unemployment. Roosevelt also promised Americans, "Your boys are not going to be sent into any foreign wars."

Roosevelt did not win this election in a landslide, as he had in 1936. But the New Deal coalition held. Once again Roosevelt won in the cities, supported by blue-collar workers, ethnic Americans, and African Americans. He also carried every state in the South. Although New Deal reform was over at home, Roosevelt was still riding a wave of public approval.

Race and the Limits of the New Deal

While the New Deal directly touched the lives of a great many Americans, not all benefited equally. More than anything else, differences were based on race. The New Deal fell short of equality for people of color for two major reasons.

First was the relationship between local and national power. National programs were implemented at the local level, and where local custom conflicted with national intent, as in the South and West, local custom won. In the South, African Americans received lower relief payments than whites and were paid lower wages in WPA jobs. The situation was similar in the Southwest. In Tucson, Arizona, for example, Federal Emergency Relief Agency officials divided applicants into four groups—Anglos, Mexican Americans, Mexican immigrants, and Indians—and allocated relief payments in descending order.

Such discriminatory practices were rooted not only in racism but also in the economic interests of whites/Anglos. The majority of African American and Mexican American workers were paid so poorly that they *earned* less than impoverished whites got for "relief." Why would these workers take low-paying private jobs if government relief or government work programs provided more income? Local communities understood that federal programs threatened a political, social, and economic system based on racial hierarchies.

The case of the Scottsboro Boys illustrates the power of racism in the conflict between local and national power in 1930s America. One night in March 1931, a fight broke out between groups of young black and white "hobos" on a Southern Railroad freight train as it passed through Alabama. The black youths won the fight and tossed the whites off the train. Not long afterward, a posse stopped the train, arrested the black youths, and threw them in the Scottsboro, Alabama, jail. The posse also discovered two white women "riding the rails," who claimed that the young men had raped them. Word spread, and the youths were barely saved from a lynch mob. Medical evidence later showed that the women were lying. But within two weeks, eight of the so-called Scottsboro Boys were convicted of rape by all-white juries and sentenced to death. The ninth, a boy of thirteen, was saved from the death penalty by one vote. The case—so clearly a product of southern racism—became a cause célèbre, both in the nation and, through the efforts of the Communist Party, around the world.

The Supreme Court intervened, ruling that Alabama deprived black defendants of equal protection under the law by systematically excluding African Americans from juries and that the defendants had been denied counsel. Alabama, however, staged new trials. Five of the young men were convicted (four would be paroled by 1950, and one escaped from prison). Despite federal action through the Supreme Court, Alabama prevailed. Southern resistance to federal intervention—centered around issues of race—would not yield easily to federal power.

Second, the gains made by people of color under the New Deal were limited by the political realities of southern resistance. Roosevelt needed the support of southern Democrats to pass his legislative program, and they were willing to hold him hostage over race. For example, in 1938 southern Democrats blocked an antilynching bill with a six-week-long filibuster in the Senate. Roosevelt refused to use his political capital to break the filibuster and pass the bill. Politically, he had much to lose and little to gain. He knew that blacks would not desert the Democratic Party, but without southern senators, his legislative agenda was dead. Roosevelt wanted all Americans to enjoy the benefits of democracy, but he had no strong commitment to the cause of civil rights. As the NAACP's Roy Wilkins put it, "Mr. Roosevelt was no friend of the Negro. He wasn't an enemy, but he wasn't a friend."

African American Support

Why, then, did African Americans support Roosevelt and the New Deal? Because despite discriminatory policies, the New Deal helped African Americans. By the end of the 1930s, almost one-third of African American households survived on income from a WPA job. African Americans held some significant positions in the Roosevelt administration. Finally, there was the First Lady. When the acclaimed black contralto Marian Anderson was barred from performing in Washington's Constitution Hall by its owners, the Daughters of the American Revolution, Eleanor Roosevelt arranged for Anderson to sing at the Lincoln Memorial on Easter Sunday 1939. Such public commitment to racial equality was enormously important to African American citizens.

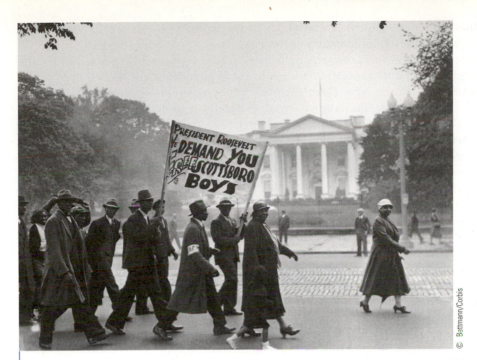

© Bettmann/Corbis

Marchers in Washington, D.C., demand freedom for the Scottsboro Boys, young African American men who were falsely accused and convicted of raping two white women in Alabama in 1931. This 1933 march was organized by the International Labor Defense, the legal arm of the Communist Party of the United States of America, which waged a strong campaign on behalf of the nine young men.

Despite widespread support for Roosevelt and the New Deal, many African Americans were well aware of the limits of New Deal reform. Some concluded that they could depend only on themselves and organized self-help and direct-action movements. In 1934, black tenant farmers and sharecroppers joined with poor whites to form the Southern Tenant Farmers' Union. In the North, the militant Harlem Tenants League fought rent increases and evictions, and African American consumers began to boycott white merchants who refused to hire blacks as clerks. Their slogan was "Don't Buy Where You Can't Work." And the Brotherhood of Sleeping Car Porters, under the astute leadership of A. Philip Randolph, fought for the rights of black workers. Such actions, along with the limited benefits of New Deal programs, helped to improve the lives of black Americans during the 1930s.

An Assessment of the New Deal   Any analysis of the New Deal must begin with Franklin Delano Roosevelt himself. Assessments of Roosevelt varied widely during his presidency: he was passionately hated and just as passionately loved. Roosevelt personified the presidency for the American people. When he spoke directly to Americans in his Fireside Chats, hundreds of thousands wrote to him, sharing their problems, asking for his help, offering their advice.

Eleanor Roosevelt, the nation's First Lady, played a crucial and unprecedented role in the Roosevelt administration. As First Lady, she worked tirelessly for social justice and human rights, bringing reformers, trade unionists, and advocates for the rights of women and African Americans to the White House. Described by some as the conscience of the New Deal, she took public positions—especially on African American civil rights—far more progressive than those of her husband's administration. In some ways she served as a lightning rod, deflecting conservative criticism from her husband to herself. But her public stances also cemented the allegiance of other groups, African Americans in particular, to the New Deal.

Most historians and political scientists consider Franklin Roosevelt a truly great president, citing his courage and buoyant self-confidence, his willingness to experiment, and his capacity to inspire the nation during the most somber days of the depression. Some, who see the New Deal as a squandered opportunity for true political and economic change, charge that Roosevelt lacked vision and courage. They judge Roosevelt by goals that were not his own: Roosevelt was a pragmatist whose goal was to preserve the system. But even scholars who criticize Roosevelt's performance agree that he transformed the presidency. "Only Washington, who made the office, and Jackson, who remade it, did more than Roosevelt to raise it to its present condition of strength, dignity, and independence," claims political scientist Clinton Rossiter. Some find this transformation troubling, tracing the roots of "the imperial presidency" to the Roosevelt administration.

During his more than twelve years in office, Roosevelt strengthened not only the presidency but also the federal government. In the past, the federal government had exercised little control over the economy. Through New Deal programs, the government greatly added to its regulatory responsibilities, including overseeing the nation's financial systems. For the first time, the federal government assumed a responsibility to offer relief to the jobless and the needy, and for the first time it used deficit spending to stimulate the economy. Millions of Americans benefited from government programs that are still operating today. The New Deal laid the foundation of the Social Security system on which subsequent presidential administrations would build.

New Deal programs pumped money into the economy and saved millions of Americans from hunger and misery. However, as late as 1939, more than 10 million men and women were still jobless, and the nation's unemployment rate stood at 19 percent. In the end, it was not the New Deal, but massive government spending during the Second World War that brought full economic recovery. In 1941, as a result of mobilization for war, unemployment declined to 10 percent, and in 1944, at the height of the war, only 1 percent of the labor force was jobless. World War II, not the New Deal, would reinvigorate the American economy.

SUMMARY

In the 1930s, a major economic crisis threatened the future of the nation. By 1933, almost one-quarter of America's workers were unemployed. Millions of people did not have enough to eat or adequate places to live. Herbert Hoover, elected president in 1928, believed that government should play only a limited role in managing and regulating the nation's economy. He tried to solve the nation's economic problems through "associationalism," a voluntary partnership of businesses and the federal government. In the 1932 presidential election, voters turned to the candidate who promised them a "New Deal." President Franklin Delano Roosevelt acted decisively to stabilize America's capitalist system and then worked to ameliorate its harshest impacts on the nation's people.

The New Deal was a liberal reform program that developed within the parameters of America's capitalist and democratic system. Most fundamentally, it expanded the role and power of the federal government. Because of New Deal reforms, banks, utilities, stock markets, farms, and most businesses operated in accord with rules set by the federal government. The federal government guaranteed workers' right to join unions without fear of employer reprisals, and federal law required employers to negotiate with workers' unions to set wages, hours, and working conditions. Many unemployed workers, elderly and disabled Americans, and dependent children were protected by a national welfare system administered through the federal government. And the president, through the power of the mass media and his own charisma, became an important presence in the lives of ordinary Americans.

The New Deal faced challenges from many directions. As the depression wore on, populist demagogues blamed scapegoats or offered overly simple explanations for the plight of the American people. Business leaders attacked the New Deal for its new regulation of business and its support of organized labor. As the federal government expanded its role throughout the nation, tensions between national and local authority sometimes flared up, and differences in regional ways of life and in social and economic structures presented challenges to national policymakers. Both the West and the South were transformed by federal government action, but citizens of both regions were suspicious of federal intervention, and white southerners strongly resisted any attempt to challenge the racial system of Jim Crow. The political realities of a fragile New Deal coalition and strong opposition shaped—and limited—New Deal programs of the 1930s and the social welfare systems with which Americans still live today.

It was the economic boom created by America's entry into World War II, not the New Deal, that ended the Great Depression. However, New Deal programs helped many of America's people live better, more secure lives. And the New Deal fundamentally changed the way that the U.S. government would deal with future economic downturns and with the needs of its citizens in good times and in bad.

26

THE UNITED STATES IN A TROUBLED WORLD 1920–1941

SEARCHING FOR PEACE AND ORDER IN THE 1920S

The First World War left Europe in a shambles. Between 1914 and 1921, Europe suffered tens of millions of casualties from world war, civil wars, massacres, epidemics, and famine. Germany and France both lost 10 percent of their workers. Crops, livestock, factories, trains, forests, bridges—little was spared. The American Relief Administration and private charities delivered food to needy Europeans, including Russians wracked by famine in 1921 and 1922. Americans hoped not only to feed desperate Europeans but also to dampen any appeal political radicalism might have for them. As Secretary of State Charles Evans Hughes put it in the early 1920s, "There will be no permanent peace unless economic satisfactions are enjoyed." Hughes and other leaders expected American economic expansion to promote international stability—that is, out of economic prosperity would spring a world free from ideological extremes, revolution, arms races, aggression, and war.

Collective security, as envisioned by Woodrow Wilson, elicited far less enthusiasm from Hughes and other Republican leaders. Senator Henry Cabot Lodge gloated in 1920 that "we have destroyed Mr. Wilson's League of Nations and ... we have torn up Wilsonism by the roots." Not quite. The Geneva-headquartered League of Nations, envisioned as a peacemaker, did prove feeble, not just because the United States did not join, but also because members failed to utilize the new organization to settle important disputes. Still, starting in the mid-1920s, American officials participated discreetly in League meetings on public health, prostitution, drug and arms trafficking, counterfeiting of currency, and other questions.

CHRONOLOGY

1921–22	Washington Conference limits naval arms
	Rockefeller Foundation begins battle against yellow fever in Latin America
1922	Mussolini comes to power in Italy
1924	Dawes Plan eases German reparations
1928	Kellogg-Briand Pact outlaws war
1929	Great Depression begins
	Young Plan reduces German reparations
1930	Hawley-Smoot Tariff raises duties
1931	Japan seizes Manchuria
1933	Adolf Hitler becomes chancellor of Germany
	United States extends diplomatic recognition to Soviet Union
	United States announces Good Neighbor policy for Latin America
1934	Fulgencio Batista comes to power in Cuba
1935	Italy invades Ethiopia
	Congress passes first Neutrality Act
1936	Germany reoccupies Rhineland
	Spanish Civil War breaks out
1937	Sino-Japanese War breaks out
	Roosevelt makes "quarantine speech" against aggressors
1938	Mexico nationalizes American-owned oil companies
	Munich Conference grants part of Czechoslovakia to Germany
1939	Germany and Soviet Union sign nonaggression pact
	Germany invades Poland; Second World War begins
1940	Germany invades Denmark, Norway, Belgium, the Netherlands, and France
	Selective Training and Service Act starts first U.S. peacetime draft
1941	Lend-Lease Act gives aid to Allies
	Germany attacks Soviet Union
	United States freezes Japanese assets
	Roosevelt and Churchill sign Atlantic Charter
	Japanese flotilla attacks Pearl Harbor, Hawai'i; United States enters Second World War

American jurists served on the Permanent Court of International Justice (World Court), though the United States also refused to join that League body. The Rockefeller Foundation, meanwhile, donated $100,000 a year to the League to support its work in public health.

Peace Groups   Wilson's legacy was felt in other ways as well. In the United States, peace societies worked for international stability, many of them keeping alive the Wilsonian preference for a world body. During the interwar years, peace groups, such as the Fellowship of Reconciliation and the National Council for Prevention of War, drew widespread public support. Women peace advocates gravitated to several of their own organizations because they lacked influence in the male-dominated groups and because of the popular assumption that women—as life givers and nurturing mothers—had a unique aversion to violence and war. Carrie Chapman Catt's moderate National Conference on the Cure and Cause of War, formed in 1924, and the more radical U.S. section of the Women's International League for Peace and Freedom (WILPF), organized in 1915 under the leadership of Jane Addams and Emily Greene Balch, became the largest women's peace groups. When Addams won the Nobel Peace Prize in 1931, she transferred her award money to the League of Nations.

Most peace groups pointed to the carnage of the First World War and the futility of war as a solution to international problems, but they differed over strategies to ensure world order. Some urged cooperation with the League of Nations and the World Court. Others championed the arbitration of disputes, disarmament and arms reduction, the outlawing of war, and strict neutrality during wars. The WILPF called for an end to U.S. economic imperialism, which, the organization claimed, compelled the United States to intervene militarily in Latin America to protect U.S. business interests. The Women's Peace Union (organized in 1921) lobbied for a constitutional amendment to require a national referendum on a declaration of war. The Carnegie Endowment for International Peace (founded in 1910) promoted peace education through publications. Quakers, YMCA officials, and Social Gospel clergy in 1917 created the American Friends Service Committee to identify pacifist alternatives to warmaking. All in all, peaceseekers believed that their various reform activities could and must deliver a world without war.

Washington Naval Conference   Peace advocates influenced Warren G. Harding's administration to convene the Washington Naval Conference of November 1921–February 1922. Delegates from Britain, Japan, France, Italy, China, Portugal, Belgium, and the Netherlands joined a U.S. team led by Secretary of State Charles Evans Hughes to discuss limits on naval armaments. Britain, the United States, and Japan were facing a naval arms race whose huge military spending endangered economic rehabilitation. American leaders also worried that an expansionist Japan, with the world's third largest navy, would overtake the United States, ranked second behind Britain.

Hughes opened the conference by making a stunning announcement: he proposed to achieve real disarmament by offering to scrap thirty major U.S. ships, totaling 846,000 tons. He then turned to the shocked British and Japanese delegations and urged them to do away with somewhat smaller amounts. The final limit, Hughes declared, should be 500,000 tons each for the Americans and the British; 300,000 tons for the Japanese; and 175,000 tons each for the French and the Italians (that is, a ratio of 5:3:1.75). These totals were agreed to in the Five-Power Treaty, which also set a ten-year moratorium on the construction of capital ships (battleships and aircraft carriers). The governments also pledged not to build new fortifications in their Pacific possessions (such as the Philippines).

Next, the Nine-Power Treaty reaffirmed the Open Door in China, recognizing Chinese sovereignty. Finally, in the Four-Power Treaty, the United States, Britain, Japan, and France agreed to respect one another's Pacific possessions. The three treaties did not limit submarines, destroyers, or cruisers, nor did they provide enforcement powers for the Open Door declaration. Still, the conference was a major achievement for Hughes. He achieved genuine arms limitation and at the same time improved America's strategic position vis-à-vis Japan in the Pacific.

Kellogg-Briand Pact   Peace advocates also welcomed the Locarno Pact of 1925, a set of agreements among European nations that sought to reduce tensions between Germany and France, and the Kellogg-Briand Pact of 1928. In the latter document, named for its chief promoters, U.S. secretary of state Frank B. Kellogg and French premier Aristide Briand, sixty-two nations agreed to "condemn recourse to war for the solution of international controversies, and renounce it as an instrument of national policy." The accord passed the Senate 85 to 1, but many lawmakers considered it little more than a statement of moral preference because it lacked enforcement provisions. Although weak—skeptics called it a mere "international kiss"—the Kellogg-Briand Pact reflected popular opinion that war was barbaric and wasteful, and the agreement stimulated serious public discussion of peace and war. But arms limitations, peace pacts, and efforts by peace groups and international institutions all failed to muzzle the dogs of war, which fed on the economic troubles that upended world order.

THE WORLD ECONOMY, CULTURAL EXPANSION, AND GREAT DEPRESSION

While Europe struggled to recover from the ravages of the First World War, the international economy wobbled and then, in the early 1930s, collapsed. The Great Depression set off a political chain reaction that carried the world to war. Cordell Hull, secretary of state under President Franklin D. Roosevelt from 1933 to 1944, often pointed out that political extremism and militarism sprang from maimed economies. "We cannot have a peaceful world," he warned, "until we rebuild the international economic structure." Hull proved right.

Economic and Cultural Expansion   For leaders like Hughes and Hull, who believed that economic expansion by the United States would stabilize world politics, America's prominent position in the international economy seemed opportune. Because of World War I, the United States became a creditor nation and the financial capital of the world (see Figure 26.1). From 1914 to 1930, private investments abroad grew fivefold, to more than $17 billion. By the late 1920s, the United States produced nearly half of the world's industrial goods and ranked first among exporters ($5.2 billion worth of shipments in 1929). For example, General Electric invested heavily in Germany,

American companies began to exploit Venezuela's rich petroleum resources, and U.S. firms began to challenge British control of oil resources in the Middle East. Britain and Germany lost ground to American businesses in Latin America, where Standard Oil operated in eight nations and where the United Fruit Company became a huge landowner.

America's economic prominence facilitated the export of American culture. Hollywood movies saturated the global market and stimulated interest in American ways and products. In Britain, where U.S. silent and talkie films dominated, one woman from a mining town recalled seeing on the screen "all these marvelous [American] film stars. Everything was bright. I just wanted to go there and be like them." Although some foreigners warned against Americanization, others aped U.S. mass-production methods and emphasis on efficiency and modernization. Coca-Cola opened a bottling plant in Essen, Germany; Ford built an automobile assembly plant in Cologne; and General Motors built one for trucks near Berlin. German writer Hans Joachim claimed that this cultural adoption might help deliver a peaceful, democratic world because "our interest in elevators, radio towers, and jazz was ... an attitude that wanted to convert the flame thrower into a vacuum cleaner."

Germans marveled at Henry Ford's economic success and industrial techniques ("Fordismus"), buying out copies of his translated autobiography, *My Life and Work* (1922). In the 1930s, Nazi leader Adolf Hitler sent German car designers to Detroit before he launched the Volkswagen. Further advertising the American capitalist model were the Phelps-Stokes Fund, exporting to black Africa Booker T. Washington's Tuskegee philosophy of education, and the Rockefeller Foundation, battling diseases in Latin America and Africa, supporting colleges to train doctors in Lebanon and China, and funding medical research and nurses' training in Europe.

The U.S. government assisted this cultural and economic expansion. The Webb-Pomerene Act (1918) excluded from antitrust prosecution those combinations set up for export trade, the Edge Act (1919) permitted American banks to open foreign-branch banks, and the overseas offices of the Department of Commerce gathered and disseminated valuable market information. The federal government also stimulated foreign loans by American investors, discouraging those that might be used for military purposes. U.S. government support for the expansion of the telecommunications industry helped International Telegraph and Telephone (IT&T), Radio Corporation of America (RCA), and the Associated Press (AP) become international giants by 1930. The U.S. Navy's cooperation with Juan Trippe's Pan American Airways helped its "flying boats" reach Asia.

Europeans watched American economic expansion with wariness. Even as they snapped up copies of Ford's autobiography, many old-world elites worried that the populist consumerism that he and other U.S. industrialists championed portended social upheaval and the withering of established habits. As a result, the prospect of mass consumerism became a politically charged class issue. When the French Popular Front government in the 1930s sought to raise the purchasing power of workers through wage increases and a shorter workweek, the notion was condemned by conservatives for its radicalism and revolutionary spirit—a spirit that in the United States had generated a consumption-led boom in goods and services in the 1920s.

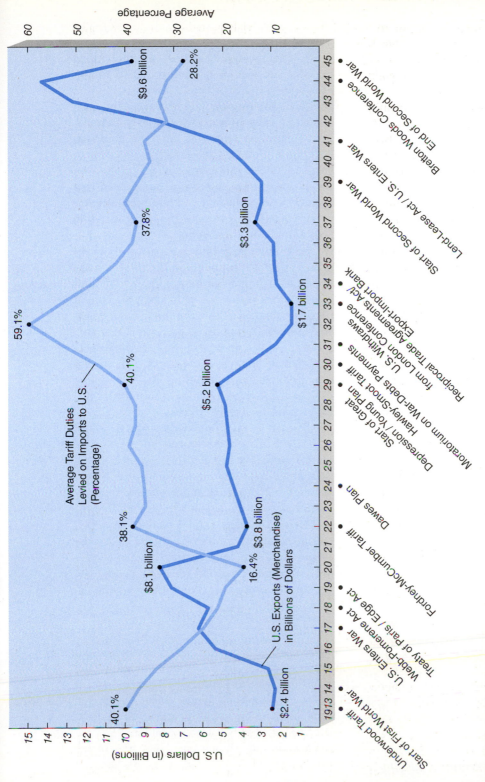

FIGURE 26.1 The United States in the World Economy

In the 1920s and 1930s, global depression and war scuttled the United States' hope for a stable economic order. This graph suggests, moreover, that high American tariffs meant lower exports, further impeding world trade. The Reciprocal Trade Agreements program initiated in the early 1930s was designed to ease tariff wars with other nations.

Source: U.S. Bureau of the Census, *Historical Statistics of the United States, Colonial Times to 1970* (Washington, D.C., 1975).

War Debts and German Reparations

Some Europeans also branded the United States stingy for its handling of World War I debts and reparations. Twenty-eight nations became entangled in the web of inter-Allied government debts, which totaled $26.5 billion ($9.6 billion of them owed to the U.S. government). Europeans owed private American creditors another $3 billion. Europeans urged Americans to erase the government debts as a magnanimous contribution to the war effort. During the war, they angrily charged, Europe had bled while America profited. "There is only one way we could be worse with the Europeans," remarked the humorist Will Rogers, "and that is to have helped them out in two wars instead of one." American leaders insisted on repayment, some pointing out that the victorious European nations had gained vast territory and resources as war spoils. Senator George Norris of Nebraska, emphasizing domestic priorities, declared that the United States could build highways in "every county seat" if only the Europeans would pay their debts.

The debts question became linked to Germany's $33 billion reparations bill—an amount some believed Germany had the capacity but not the willingness to pay. In any case, hobbled by inflation and economic disorder, Germany began to default on its payments. To keep the nation afloat and to forestall the radicalism that might thrive on economic troubles, American bankers loaned millions of dollars. A triangular relationship developed: American investors' money flowed to Germany, Germany paid reparations to the Allies, and the Allies then paid some of their debts to the United States. The American-crafted Dawes Plan of 1924 greased the financial tracks by reducing Germany's annual payments, extending the repayment period, and providing still more loans. The United States also gradually scaled down Allied obligations, cutting the debt by half during the 1920s.

But everything hinged on continued German borrowing in the United States, and in 1928 and 1929 American lending abroad dropped sharply in the face of more lucrative opportunities in the stock market at home. The U.S.-negotiated Young Plan of 1929, which reduced Germany's reparations, salvaged little as the world economy sputtered and collapsed following the stock market crash that autumn. That same year, Britain rejected an offer from President Herbert Hoover to trade its total debt for British Honduras (Belize), Bermuda, and Trinidad. By 1931, when Hoover declared a moratorium on payments, the Allies had paid back only $2.6 billion. Staggered by the Great Depression—an international catastrophe—they defaulted on the rest. Annoyed with Europe, Congress in 1934 passed the Johnson Act, which forbade U.S. government loans to foreign governments in default on debts owed to the United States.

Decline in Trade

As the depression deepened, tariff wars revealed a reinvigorated economic nationalism. By 1932, some twenty-five nations had retaliated against rising American tariffs (created in the Fordney-McCumber Act of 1922 and the Hawley-Smoot Act of 1930) by imposing higher rates on foreign imports. From 1929 to 1933, world trade declined in value by some 40 percent. Exports of American merchandise slumped from $5.2 billion to $1.7 billion.

Who was responsible for the worldwide economic cataclysm? There was blame enough to go around. The United States might have lowered its tariffs so that

Europeans could sell their goods in the American market and thus earn dollars to pay off their debts. Americans also might have worked for a comprehensive, multinational settlement of the war debts issue. Instead, at the London Conference in 1933, President Roosevelt barred U.S. cooperation in international currency stabilization. Vengeful Europeans might have trimmed Germany's huge indemnity. The Germans might have borrowed less from abroad and taxed themselves more. The Soviets might have agreed to pay rather than repudiate Russia's $4 billion debt.

For Secretary of State Hull, finding a way out of the crisis depended on reviving world trade. Increased trade, he insisted, would not only help the United States pull itself out of the economic doldrums but also boost the chances for global peace. Calling the protective tariff the "king of evils," he successfully pressed Congress to pass the Reciprocal Trade Agreements Act in 1934. This important legislation empowered the president to reduce U.S. tariffs by as much as 50 percent through special agreements with foreign countries. The central feature of the act was the most-favored-nation principle, whereby the United States was entitled to the lowest tariff rate set by any nation with which it had an agreement. If, for example, Belgium and the United States granted each other most-favored-nation status, and Belgium then negotiated an agreement with Germany that reduced the Belgian tariff on German typewriters, American typewriters would receive the same low rate.

In 1934, Hull also helped create the Export-Import Bank, a government agency that provided loans to foreigners for the purchase of American goods. The bank stimulated trade and became a diplomatic weapon, allowing the United States to exact concessions through the approval or denial of loans. But in the short term, Hull's ambitious programs—examples of America's independent internationalism—brought only mixed results.

U.S. Recognition of the Soviet Union

Economic imperatives also lay behind another major policy decision in these years: the move by the Roosevelt administration to extend diplomatic recognition to the Soviet Union. Throughout the 1920s, the Republicans had refused to open diplomatic relations with the Soviet government, which had failed to pay $600 million for confiscated American-owned property and had repudiated preexisting Russian debts. To many Americans, the communists ranked as godless, radical malcontents bent on destroying the American way of life through world revolution. Nonetheless, in the late 1920s, U.S. businesses such as General Electric and International Harvester entered the Soviet marketplace, and Henry Ford signed a contract to build an automobile plant there. By 1930, the Soviet Union had become the largest buyer of American farm and industrial equipment.

Upon entering the White House, Roosevelt concluded that nonrecognition had failed to alter the Soviet system, and he speculated that closer Soviet-American relations might help the economy and also deter Japanese expansion. In 1933, Roosevelt granted U.S. diplomatic recognition to the Soviet Union in return for Soviet agreement to discuss the debts question and to grant Americans in the Soviet Union religious freedom and legal rights.

American and Russian laborers fraternize during the building of the Henry Ford plant at Nizhny Novgorod, Soviet Union, in November 1930. This factory, scheduled to turn out 30,000 cars a year, was one of numerous American businesses entering the Soviet marketplace in this period. Others included Westinghouse, Caterpillar, John Deere, American Express, and RCA.

© Bettmann/Corbis

U.S. DOMINANCE IN LATIN AMERICA

One of the assumptions behind Hughes's Washington Treaty system of 1921–1922 was that certain powers would be responsible for maintaining order in their regions—Japan in East Asia, for example, and the United States in Latin America. Through the Platt Amendment, the Roosevelt Corollary, the Panama Canal, military intervention, and economic preeminence the United States had thrown an imperial net over Latin America in the early twentieth century. U.S. dominance in the hemisphere grew apace after the First World War. A prominent State Department officer patronizingly remarked that Latin Americans were incapable of political progress because of their "low racial quality." They were, however, "very easy people to deal with if properly managed."

And managed they were. American-made schools, roads, telephones, and irrigation systems dotted Caribbean and Central American nations. American "money doctors" in Colombia and Peru helped reform tariff and tax laws, and invited U.S. companies to build public works. Washington forced private high-interest loans on the Dominican Republic and Haiti as ways to wield influence there. In El Salvador, Honduras, and Costa Rica, the State Department pressed governments to silence anti-imperialist intellectuals. For a time, Republican administrations curtailed U.S. military intervention in the hemisphere, withdrawing troops from the Dominican Republic (1924) and Nicaragua (1925) that had been committed in the previous decade. But the marines returned to Nicaragua in 1926 to end fighting between conservative and liberal Nicaraguans and to protect American property. In Haiti, the U.S. troop commitment made under Woodrow Wilson in 1915 lasted until 1934, with the soldiers there to keep pro-Washington governments in power. All the while, U.S. authorities maintained Puerto Rico as a colony (see Map 26.1).

American Economic Muscle

By 1929, direct American investments in Latin America (excluding bonds and securities) totaled $3.5 billion, and U.S. exports dominated the trade of the area. Country after country experienced the repercussions of U.S. economic and political decisions. For example, the price that Americans set for Chilean copper determined the health of Chile's economy. North American oil executives bribed Venezuelan politicians for tax breaks.

Latin American nationalists protested that their resources were being drained away as profits for U.S. companies, leaving too many nations in a disadvantageous position. In 1928, at the Havana Inter-American conference, U.S. officials unsuccessfully tried to kill a resolution stating that "no state has a right to intervene in the internal affairs of another." Two years later, a prominent Chilean newspaper warned that the American "Colossus" had "financial might" without "equal in history" and that its aim was "Americas for the Americans—of the North." In the United States, Senator William Borah of Idaho urged that Latin Americans be granted the right of self-determination, letting them decide their own futures. Some Americans also became troubled by the double standard that prevailed. Hoover's secretary of state, Henry L. Stimson, acknowledged the problem in 1932 when he was protesting Japanese incursions in China: "If we landed a single soldier among those South Americans now … it would put me absolutely in the wrong in China, where Japan has done all this monstrous work under the guise of protecting her nationals with a landing force."

Good Neighbor Policy

Renouncing unpopular military intervention, the United States shifted to other methods to maintain its influence in Latin America: Pan-Americanism (a concept dating back some fifty years, which aimed to bring about closer ties between North and South America), support for strong local leaders, the training of national guards, economic and cultural penetration, Export-Import Bank loans, financial supervision, and political subversion. Although this general approach predated his presidency, Franklin Roosevelt gave it a name in 1933: the Good Neighbor policy. It meant that the United States would be less blatant in its domination—less willing to defend exploitative business practices, less eager to launch military expeditions, and less reluctant to consult with Latin Americans.

"Give them a share," Roosevelt said, as he took several measures to show he meant business. Most notably, he ordered home the U.S. military forces that had been stationed in Haiti (since 1915) and Nicaragua (since 1912, with a hiatus in 1925–1926), and he restored some sovereignty to Panama and increased that nation's income from the canal. Such acts greatly enhanced Roosevelt's popularity in Latin America, and his image was further boosted when, in a series of

MAP 26.1 The United States and Latin America Between the Wars

The United States often intervened in other nations to maintain its hegemonic power in Latin America, where nationalists resented outside meddling in their sovereign affairs. The Good Neighbor policy decreased U.S. military interventions, but U.S. economic interests remained strong in the hemisphere.

pan-American conferences, he joined in pledging that no nation in the hemisphere would intervene in the "internal or external affairs" of any other.

Here Roosevelt promised more than he was prepared to deliver. His administration continued to support and bolster dictators in the region, believing they would promote stability and preserve U.S. economic interests. ("He may be an S.O.B.," Roosevelt supposedly remarked of the Dominican Republic's ruthless leader Rafael Leonidas Trujillo, "but he is our S.O.B.") And when a revolution brought a radical government to power in Cuba in 1933, FDR proved unwilling to let the matter be. Although he refrained from sending U.S. ground troops to Cuba, he instructed the American ambassador in Havana to work with conservative Cubans to replace the new government with a regime more friendly to U.S. interests. With Washington's support, army sergeant Fulgencio Batista took power in 1934.

During the Batista era, which lasted until Fidel Castro dethroned Batista in 1959, Cuba attracted and protected U.S. investments while it aligned itself with U.S. foreign policy goals. In return, the United States provided military aid and Export-Import Bank loans, abrogated the unpopular Platt Amendment, and gave Cuban sugar a favored position in the U.S. market. Cuba became further incorporated into the North American consumer culture, and American tourists flocked to Havana's nightlife of rum, rhumba, prostitution, and gambling. Nationalistic Cubans protested that their nation had become a mere extension—a dependency—of the United States.

Clash with Mexican Nationalism   In Mexico, Roosevelt again showed a level of restraint that his predecessors had lacked. Since Woodrow Wilson sent troops to Mexico in 1914 and again in 1916, U.S.-Mexican relations had endured several difficult periods as the two governments wrangled over the rights of U.S. economic interests. Still, throughout the post–World War I period the United States stood as Mexico's chief trading partner, accounting for 61 percent of Mexico's imports and taking 52 percent of its exports in 1934. That year, however, a new government under Lázaro Cárdenas pledged "Mexico for the Mexicans" and promptly strengthened trade unions so they could strike against foreign corporations.

In 1937 workers struck foreign oil companies for higher wages and recognition, but the companies, including Standard Oil, rejected union appeals, hoping to send a message across the hemisphere that economic nationalism could never succeed. In a statement of economic independence the following year, the Cárdenas government boldly expropriated the property of all foreign-owned petroleum companies, calculating that the approaching war in Europe would restrain the United States from attacking Mexico. The United States countered by reducing purchases of Mexican silver and promoting a multinational business boycott against the nation. But Roosevelt rejected appeals from some business leaders that he intervene militarily and instead decided to compromise, in part because he feared that the Mexicans would increase oil sales to Germany and Japan. Negotiations were long and difficult, but in 1942 an agreement was reached whereby the United States conceded that Mexico owned its raw materials and could treat them as it saw fit, and Mexico compensated the companies for their lost property.

All in all, then, under Roosevelt the Good Neighbor policy can be said to have gone a considerable distance toward living up to its name—or at least the United States was now a Markedly Better Neighbor. Even as it remained the dominant power in the hemisphere, its newfound restraint created hopes among Latin Americans that a new era had dawned. Yet the more sober-minded nationalists in the region knew that Washington might be acting differently were it not for the deepening tensions in Europe and Asia. These threats created a sense that all the nations in the Western Hemisphere should stand together.

The Course to War in Europe

The main threat came from a revitalized Germany. On March 5, 1933, one day after the inauguration of Franklin Roosevelt, Germany's parliament granted dictatorial powers to the new chancellor, Adolf Hitler, leader of the Nazi Party. The act marked the culmination of a stunning rise to power for Hitler, whose Nazis very likely would have remained a fringe party had the Great Depression not hit Germany with such force. Production plummeted 40 percent, and unemployment ballooned to 6 million, meaning that two workers out of five did not have jobs. Together with a disintegrating banking system, which robbed millions of their savings, as well as widespread resentment among Germans over the Versailles peace settlement, the plummeting employment figures brought mass discontent to the country. While the communists preached a workers' revolution, German business executives and property owners threw their support behind Hitler and the Nazis, many of them believing they could manipulate him once he had thwarted the communists. They were wrong.

Like Benito Mussolini, who had gained control of Italy in 1922, Hitler was a fascist. Fascism (called Nazism, or National Socialism, in Germany) was a collection of ideas and prejudices that celebrated supremacy of the state over the individual; of dictatorship over democracy; of authoritarianism over freedom of speech; of a regulated, state-oriented economy over a free-market economy; and of militarism and war over peace. The Nazis vowed not only to revive German economic and military strength but also to cripple communism and "purify" the German "race" by destroying Jews and other people, such as homosexuals and Gypsies, whom Hitler disparaged as inferiors. The Nuremberg Laws of 1935 stripped Jews of citizenship and outlawed intermarriage with Germans. Teachers, doctors, and other professionals could not practice their craft, and half of all German Jews were without work.

German Aggression Under Hitler　Determined to get Germany out from under the Versailles treaty system, Hitler withdrew Germany from the League of Nations, ended reparations payments, and began to rearm. While secretly laying plans for the conquest of neighboring states, he watched admiringly as Mussolini's troops invaded the African nation of Ethiopia in 1935. The next year, Hitler ordered his own goose-stepping troopers into the Rhineland, an area that the Versailles treaty had demilitarized. When Germany's timid neighbor France did not resist this act, Hitler crowed, "The world belongs to the man with guts!"

Soon the aggressors joined hands. In 1936, Italy and Germany formed an alliance called the Rome-Berlin Axis. Shortly thereafter, Germany and Japan united against the Soviet Union in the Anti-Comintern Pact. To these events Britain and France responded with a policy of appeasement, hoping to curb Hitler's expansionist appetite by permitting him a few territorial nibbles. The policy of appeasing Hitler, though not altogether unreasonable in terms of what could be known at the time, proved disastrous, for the hate-filled German leader continually raised his demands.

Hitler also made his presence felt in Spain, where a civil war broke out in 1936. Beginning in July, the Loyalists defended Spain's elected republican government against Francisco Franco's fascist movement. The U.S. government was officially neutral, but about three thousand American volunteers, known as the Abraham Lincoln Battalion of the "International Brigades," joined the fight on the side of the Loyalist republicans, which also had the backing of the Soviet Union. Many American Catholics, meanwhile, believed Franco would promote social stability and therefore should be supported, a view also held by some State Department officials. Hitler and Mussolini sent military aid to Franco, who won in 1939, tightening the grip of fascism on the European continent.

Early in 1938, Hitler once again tested the limits of European tolerance when he sent soldiers into Austria to annex the nation of his birth. Then, in September, he seized the largely German-speaking Sudeten region of Czechoslovakia. Appeasement reached its apex that month when France and Britain, without consulting the Czechs, agreed at Munich to allow Hitler this territorial bite, in exchange for a pledge that he would not take more. British prime minister Neville Chamberlain returned home to proclaim "peace in our time," confident that Hitler was satiated. In March 1939, Hitler swallowed the rest of Czechoslovakia (see Map 26.3).

Isolationist Views in the United States   Americans had watched this buildup of tension in Europe with apprehension. Many sought to distance themselves from the tumult by embracing isolationism, whose key elements were abhorrence of war and fervent opposition to U.S. alliances with other nations. Americans had learned powerful negative lessons from the First World War: that war damages reform movements, undermines civil liberties, dangerously expands federal and presidential power, disrupts the economy, and accentuates racial and class tensions. A 1937 Gallup poll found that nearly two-thirds of the respondents thought U.S. participation in World War I had been a mistake.

Conservative isolationists feared higher taxes and increased executive power if the nation went to war again. Liberal isolationists worried that domestic problems might go unresolved as the nation spent more on the military. Many isolationists predicted that, in attempting to spread democracy abroad or to police the world, Americans would lose their freedoms at home. The vast majority of isolationists opposed fascism and condemned aggression, but they did not think the United States should have to do what Europeans themselves refused to do: block Hitler. Isolationist sentiment was strongest in the Midwest and among anti-British ethnic groups, especially Americans of German or Irish descent, but it was a nationwide phenomenon that cut across socioeconomic, ethnic, party, and sectional lines, and it attracted a majority of the American people.

Nye Committee Hearings   Some isolationists charged that corporate "merchants of death" had promoted war and were assisting the aggressors. A congressional committee headed by Senator Gerald P. Nye held hearings from 1934 to 1936 on the role of business and financiers in the U.S. decision to enter the First World War. The Nye committee did not prove that American munitions makers had dragged the nation into that war, but it did uncover evidence that corporations practicing "rotten commercialism" had bribed foreign politicians to bolster arms sales in the 1920s and 1930s and had lobbied against arms control.

Isolationists grew suspicious of American business ties with Nazi Germany and fascist Italy that might endanger U.S. neutrality. Twenty-six of the top one hundred American corporations, including DuPont, Standard Oil, and General Motors, had contractual agreements in 1937 with German firms. And after Italy attacked Ethiopia in 1935, American petroleum, copper, scrap iron, and steel exports to Italy increased substantially, despite Roosevelt's call for a moral embargo on such commerce. A Dow Chemical official stated, "We do not inquire into the uses of the products. We are interested in selling them." Not all American executives thought this way. The Wall Street law firm of Sullivan and Cromwell, for example, severed lucrative ties with Germany to protest the Nazi persecution of Jews.

Reflecting the popular desire for distance from Europe's disputes, Roosevelt signed a series of neutrality acts. Congress sought to protect the nation by outlawing the kinds of contacts that had compromised U.S. neutrality during World War I. The Neutrality Act of 1935 prohibited arms shipments to either side in a war, once the president had declared the existence of belligerency. Roosevelt had wanted the authority to name the aggressor and apply an arms embargo against it alone, but Congress would not grant the president such discretionary power. The Neutrality Act of 1936 forbade loans to belligerents. After a joint resolution in 1937 declared the United States neutral in the Spanish Civil War, Roosevelt embargoed arms shipments to both sides. The Neutrality Act of 1937 introduced the cash-and-carry principle: warring nations wishing to trade with the United States would have to pay cash for their nonmilitary purchases and carry the goods from U.S. ports in their own ships. The act also forbade Americans from traveling on the ships of belligerent nations.

Roosevelt's Evolving Views   President Roosevelt shared isolationist views in the early 1930s. Although prior to World War I he was an expansionist and interventionist like his older cousin Theodore, during the interwar period FDR talked less about preparedness and more about disarmament and the horrors of war, less about policing the world and more about handling problems at home. In a passionate speech delivered in August 1936 at Chautauqua, New York, Roosevelt expressed prevailing isolationist opinion and made a pitch for the pacifist vote in the upcoming election: "I have seen war.... I have seen blood running from the wounded. I have seen men coughing out their gassed lungs.... I have seen the agony of mothers and wives. I hate war." The United States, he promised, would remain unentangled in the European conflict. During the crisis over Czechoslovakia in 1938, Roosevelt endorsed appeasement and greeted the Munich accord with a "universal sense of relief."

All the while, Roosevelt grew troubled by the arrogant behavior of Germany, Italy, and Japan—aggressors that he tagged the "three bandit nations." He condemned the Nazi persecution of the Jews and Japan's expansionist actions in East Asia. Privately he chastised the British and French for failing to collar Hitler. Yet he himself also moved cautiously in confronting the German leader. In November 1938, Hitler launched *Kristallnacht* (or "Crystal Night," so named for the shattered glass that littered the streets after the attack on Jewish synagogues, businesses, and homes) and sent tens of thousands of Jews to concentration camps. Roosevelt expressed his shock, recalled the U.S. ambassador to Germany, and allowed fifteen thousand refugees on visitor permits to remain longer in the United States. But he would not do more, such as break trade relations with Hitler or push Congress to loosen tough immigration laws enacted in the 1920s. Congress, for its part, rejected all measures, including a bill to admit twenty thousand children under the age of fourteen. Motivated by economic concerns and widespread anti-Semitism, more than 80 percent of Americans supported Congress's decision to uphold immigration restrictions.

Even the tragic voyage of the St. Louis did not change government policy. The vessel left Hamburg in mid-1939 carrying 930 desperate Jewish refugees who lacked proper immigration documents. Denied entry to Havana, the *St. Louis* headed for Miami, where Coast Guard cutters prevented it from docking. The ship was forced to return to Europe. Some of those refugees took shelter in countries that later were overrun by Hitler's legions. "The cruise of the *St. Louis*," wrote the *New York Times*, "cries to high heaven of man's inhumanity to man."

Quietly, though, Roosevelt had begun moving to ready the country for war. In early 1938, he successfully pressured the House of Representatives to defeat a constitutional amendment proposed by Indiana Democrat Louis Ludlow to require a majority vote in a national referendum before a congressional declaration of war could go into effect (unless the United States were attacked). Later that year, in the wake of the Munich crisis, Roosevelt asked Congress for funds to build up the air force, which he believed essential to deter aggression. In January 1939, the president secretly decided to sell bombers to France, saying privately that "our frontier is on the Rhine." Although the more than five hundred combat planes delivered to France did not deter war, French orders spurred growth of the U.S. aircraft industry.

For Roosevelt and for other Western leaders, Hitler's swallowing of the whole of Czechoslovakia in March 1939 proved a turning point, forcing them to face a stark new reality. Until now, they had been able to explain away Hitler's actions by saying he was only trying to reunite German-speaking peoples. That argument no longer worked. Leaders in Paris and London realized that, if the German leader was to be stopped, it would have to be by force. When Hitler began eyeing his neighbor Poland, London and Paris announced they would stand by the Poles. Undaunted, Berlin signed a nonaggression pact with Moscow in August 1939. Soviet leader Joseph Stalin believed that the West's appeasement of Hitler had left him no choice but to cut a deal with Berlin. But Stalin also coveted territory: a top-secret protocol attached to the pact carved eastern Europe into German and Soviet zones, and permitted the Soviets to grab the eastern half of Poland and the three Baltic states of Lithuania, Estonia, and Latvia, formerly part of the Russian Empire.

German leader Adolf Hitler (1889–1945) is surrounded in this propagandistic painting by images that came to symbolize hate, genocide, and war: Nazi flags with emblems of the swastika, the iron cross on the dictator's pocket, Nazi troops in loyal salute. The anti-Semitic Hitler denounced the United States as a "Jewish rubbish heap" of "inferiority and decadence" that was "incapable of conducting war."

U.S. Army Center of Military History

Poland and the Outbreak of World War II

In the early morning hours of September 1, German tank columns rolled into Poland. German fighting planes covered the advance, thereby launching a new type of warfare, the *blitzkrieg* (lightning war)—highly mobile land forces and armor combined with tactical aircraft. Within forty-eight hours, Britain and France responded by declaring war on Germany. "It's come at last," Franklin Roosevelt murmured. "God help us all."

When Europe descended into the abyss of war in September 1939, Roosevelt declared neutrality and pressed for repeal of the arms embargo. Isolationist senator Arthur Vandenberg of Michigan roared back that the United States could not be "an arsenal for one belligerent without becoming a target for the other." After much debate, however, Congress in November lifted the embargo on contraband and approved cash-and-carry exports of arms. Using "methods short of war," Roosevelt thus began to aid the Allies. Hitler sneered that a "half Judaized ... half Negrified" United States was "incapable of conducting war."

JAPAN, CHINA, AND A NEW ORDER IN ASIA

While Europe succumbed to political turmoil and war, Asia suffered the aggressive march of Japan. The United States had interests at stake in Asia: the Philippines and Pacific islands, religious missions, trade and investments, and the Open Door in

China. In traditional missionary fashion, Americans also believed that they were China's special friend and protector. "With God's help," Senator Kenneth Wherry of Nebraska once proclaimed, "we will lift Shanghai up and up, ever up, until it is just like Kansas City." Pearl Buck's bestselling novel *The Good Earth* (1931), made into a widely distributed film six years later, countered prevailing images of the very different—and thus deviant—"heathen Chinee" by representing the Chinese as noble, persevering peasants. The daughter of Presbyterian missionaries, Buck helped shift negative American images of China to positive ones. By contrast, the aggressive Japan loomed as a threat to American attitudes and interests. The Tokyo government seemed bent on subjugating China and unhinging the Open Door doctrine of equal trade and investment opportunity.

The Chinese themselves were uneasy about the U.S. presence in Asia. Like the Japanese, they wished to reduce the influence of westerners. The Chinese Revolution of 1911 still rumbled in the 1920s, as antiforeign riots damaged U.S. property and imperiled American missionaries. Chinese nationalists criticized Americans for the imperialist practice of extraterritoriality (the exemption from Chinese legal jurisdiction of foreigners accused of crimes), and they demanded an end to this affront to Chinese sovereignty.

Jiang Jieshi

In the late 1920s, civil war broke out in China when Jiang Jieshi (Chiang Kai-shek) ousted Mao Zedong and his communist followers from the ruling Guomindang Party. Americans applauded this display of anti-Bolshevism and Jiang's conversion to Christianity in 1930. Jiang's new wife, Soong Meiling, also won their hearts. American-educated, Madame Jiang spoke flawless English, dressed in western fashion, and cultivated ties with prominent Americans. Warming to Jiang, U.S. officials abandoned one imperial vestige by signing a treaty in 1928 restoring control of tariffs to the Chinese.

The Japanese grew increasingly suspicious of U.S. ties with China. In the early twentieth century, Japanese-American relations steadily deteriorated as Japan gained influence in Manchuria, Shandong, and Korea. The Japanese sought not only to oust western imperialists from Asia but also to dominate Asian territories that produced the raw materials their import-dependent island nation required. The Japanese also resented the discriminatory immigration law of 1924, which excluded them from emigrating to the United States and declared they were "aliens ineligible to citizenship." Secretary Hughes urged Congress not to pass the act; when it rejected his counsel, he sadly called the law "a lasting injury" to Japanese-American relations. Despite the Washington Conference treaties, naval competition continued, and there was also rivalry in the commercial arena. In the United States, the importation of inexpensive Japanese goods, especially textiles, spawned "Buy America" campaigns and boycotts.

Manchurian Crisis

Relations further soured in 1931 after the Japanese military seized Manchuria from China (see Map 26.2), weakened by civil war and unable to resist. Larger than Texas, Manchuria served Japan both as a buffer against the Soviets and as a vital source of coal, iron, timber, and food. More than half of Japan's foreign investments rested in Manchuria. "We are seeking room that will let us breathe," said a Japanese politician, arguing

MAP 26.2 Japanese Expansion Before Pearl Harbor

The Japanese quest for predominance began at the turn of the century and intensified in the 1930s. China suffered the most at the hands of Tokyo's military. Vulnerable U.S. possessions in Asia and the Pacific proved no obstacle to Japan's ambitions for a Greater East Asia Co-Prosperity Sphere.

that his heavily populated island nation (65 million people in an area slightly smaller than California) needed to expand in order to survive. Although the seizure of Manchuria violated the Nine-Power Treaty and the Kellogg-Briand Pact, the United States did not have the power to compel Japanese withdrawal, and the League of Nations did little but condemn the Tokyo government. The American response came as a moral lecture known as the Stimson Doctrine: the United States would not recognize any impairment of China's sovereignty or of the Open Door policy, Secretary Stimson declared in 1932. He himself later described his policy as largely "bluff."

Japan continued to pressure China. In mid-1937, owing to Japanese provocation, the Sino-Japanese War erupted. Japanese forces seized Beijing and cities along the coast. The gruesome bombing of Shanghai intensified anti-Japanese sentiment in the United States. Senator Norris, an isolationist who moved further away from isolationism with each Japanese thrust, condemned the Japanese as "disgraceful, ignoble, barbarous, and cruel, even beyond the power of language to describe." In an effort to help China by permitting it to buy American arms, Roosevelt refused to declare the existence of war, thus avoiding activation of the Neutrality Acts.

Roosevelt's Quarantine Speech
In a speech denouncing the aggressors on October 5, 1937, the president called for a "quarantine" to curb the "epidemic of world lawlessness." People who thought Washington had been too gentle with Japan cheered. Isolationists warned that the president was edging toward war. On December 12, Japanese aircraft sank the American gunboat *Panay*, an escort for Standard Oil Company tankers on the Yangtze River. Two American sailors died during the attack. Roosevelt was much relieved when Tokyo apologized and offered to pay for damages.

Japan's declaration of a "New Order" in Asia, in the words of one American official, "banged, barred, and bolted" the Open Door. Alarmed, the Roosevelt administration during the late 1930s gave loans and sold military equipment to Jiang's Chinese government. Secretary Hull declared a moral embargo on the shipment of airplanes to Japan. Meanwhile, the U.S. Navy continued to grow, aided by a billion-dollar congressional appropriation in 1938. In mid-1939, the United States abrogated its trade treaty with Tokyo, yet Americans continued to ship oil, cotton, and machinery to Japan. The administration hesitated to initiate economic sanctions because such pressure might spark a Japanese-American war at a time when Germany posed a more serious threat and the United States was unprepared for war. When war broke out in Europe in the late summer of 1939, Japanese-American relations were stalemated.

U.S. ENTRY INTO WORLD WAR II

A stalemate was just fine with many Americans if it served to keep the United States out of war. But how long could the country stay out? Roosevelt remarked in 1939 that the United States could not "draw a line of defense around this country and live completely and solely to ourselves." Thomas Jefferson had tried that with his 1807 embargo—"the damned thing didn't work," and "we got into the War of 1812." America, the president insisted, could not insulate itself from world war. Polls showed that Americans strongly favored the Allies and that most supported aid to Britain and France, but the great majority emphatically wanted the United States to remain at peace. Troubled by this conflicting advice—oppose Hitler, aid the Allies, but stay out of the war—the president gradually moved the nation from neutrality to undeclared war against Germany and then, after the Japanese attack on Pearl Harbor, to full-scale war itself.

Because the stakes were so high, Americans vigorously debated the direction of their foreign policy from 1939 through 1941. Unprecedented numbers of Americans spoke out on foreign affairs and joined organizations that addressed the issues. Spine-chilling events and the widespread use of radio, the nation's chief source of news, helped stimulate this high level of public interest. So did ethnic affiliations with the various belligerents and victims of aggression. The American Legion, the League of Women Voters, labor unions, and local chapters of the Committee to Defend America by Aiding the Allies and of the isolationist America First Committee (both organized in 1940) provided outlets for citizen participation in the national debate. African American churches organized anti-Italian boycotts to protest Mussolini's pummeling of Ethiopia.

In March 1940, the Soviet Union invaded Finland. In April, Germany conquered Denmark and Norway (see Map 26.3). "The small countries are smashed up, one by one, like matchwood," sighed Winston Churchill, who became Britain's prime minister on May 10, 1940, the day Germany attacked Belgium, the Netherlands, and France. German divisions ultimately pushed French and British forces back to the English Channel. At Dunkirk, France, between May 26 and June 6, more than 300,000 Allied soldiers frantically escaped to Britain on a flotilla of small boats. The Germans occupied Paris a week later. A new French government located in the town of Vichy decided to collaborate with the conquering Nazis and, on June 22, surrendered France to Berlin. With France knocked out of the war, the German Luftwaffe (air force) launched massive bombing raids against Great Britain in preparation for a full-scale invasion. Stunned Americans asked whether Washington or New York could be the Luftwaffe's next target.

Alarmed by the swift defeat of one European nation after another, Americans gradually shed their isolationist sentiment. Some liberals left the isolationist fold; it became more and more the province of conservatives. Emotions ran high. Roosevelt

MAP 26.3 The German Advance

Hitler's drive to dominate Europe pushed German troops deep into France and the Soviet Union. Great Britain took a beating but held on with the help of American economic and military aid before the United States entered the Second World War in late 1941.

called the isolationists "ostriches" and charged that some were pro-Nazi subversives. Assuring Americans that New Deal reforms would not have to be sacrificed to achieve military preparedness, the president began to aid the beleaguered Allies to prevent the fall of Britain. In May 1940, he ordered the sale of old surplus military equipment to Britain and France. In July, he cultivated bipartisan support by naming Republicans Henry L. Stimson and Frank Knox, ardent backers of aid to the Allies, secretaries of war and the navy, respectively. In September, by executive agreement, the president traded fifty over-age American destroyers for leases to eight British military bases, including Newfoundland, Bermuda, and Jamaica.

First Peacetime Military Draft Two weeks later, Roosevelt signed into law the hotly debated and narrowly passed Selective Training and Service Act, the first peacetime military draft in American history. The act called for the registration of all men between the ages of twenty-one and thirty-five. Soon more than 16 million men had signed up, and draft notices began to be delivered. Meanwhile, Roosevelt won reelection in November 1940 with promises of peace: "Your boys are not going to be sent into any foreign wars." Republican candidate Wendell Willkie, who in the emerging spirit of bipartisanship had not made an issue of foreign policy, snapped, "That hypocritical son of a bitch! This is going to beat me!" And it did.

Roosevelt claimed that the United States could stay out of the war by enabling the British to win. The United States, he said, must become the "great arsenal of democracy." In January 1941, Congress debated the president's Lend-Lease bill. Because Britain was broke, the president explained, the United States should lend rather than sell weapons, much as a neighbor lends a garden hose to fight a fire. Most lawmakers needed little persuasion. In March 1941, with pro-British sentiment running high, the House passed the Lend-Lease Act by 317 votes to 71; the Senate followed with a 60-to-31 tally. The initial appropriation was $7 billion, but by the end of the war the amount had reached $50 billion, more than $31 billion of it for Britain.

To ensure the safe delivery of Lend-Lease goods, Roosevelt ordered the U.S. Navy to patrol halfway across the Atlantic, and he sent American troops to Greenland. In July, arguing that Iceland was also essential to the defense of the Western Hemisphere, the president dispatched marines there. He also sent Lend-Lease aid to the Soviet Union, which Hitler had attacked in June (thereby shattering the 1939 Nazi-Soviet nonaggression pact). If the Soviets could hold off two hundred German divisions in the east, Roosevelt calculated, Britain would gain some breathing room. Churchill, who had long thundered against communists, now applauded aid to the Soviets: "If Hitler invaded Hell, I would make at least a favorable reference to the Devil in the House of Commons."

Atlantic Charter In August 1941, Churchill and Roosevelt met for four days on a British battleship off the coast of Newfoundland. They got along well, trading naval stories and enjoying the fact that Churchill was half American (his mother was from New York). The two leaders issued the Atlantic Charter, a set of war aims reminiscent of Wilsonianism: collective security, disarmament, self-determination, economic cooperation, and freedom of the seas.

Radio News

In radio's early years, stations broadcast little news. Network executives believed their job was to entertain Americans and that current affairs should be left to newspapers. Yet radio could do something that no previous medium of communication could do: it could report not merely what had happened, but what was happening as it happened.

Franklin Roosevelt was among the first to grasp radio's potential in this regard. As governor of New York, he occasionally went on the air, and after becoming president, he commenced his Fireside Chats. With a voice perfectly suited to the medium, he reassured Americans suffering through the depression that, although current conditions were grim, the government was working hard to help them. So successful were these broadcasts that, in the words of one journalist, "The President has only to look toward a radio to bring Congress to terms."

Across the Atlantic, another leader also understood well the power of radio. Adolf Hitler determined early that he would use German radio to carry speeches directly to the people. His message: Germany had been wronged by enemies abroad and by Marxists and Jews at home. But the Nazis under Hitler's direction would lead the country back to its former greatness. As "Sieg Heil!" thundered over the airwaves, millions of Germans came to see Hitler as their salvation.

In 1938, as events in Europe reached a crisis, American radio networks increased their news coverage. When Hitler annexed Austria in March, NBC and CBS broke into scheduled programs to deliver news bulletins. Then, on the evening of Saturday, March 13, CBS went its rival one better by broadcasting the first international news roundup, a half-hour show featuring live reports on the annexation from the major capitals of Europe. A new era in American radio was born. In the words of author Joseph Persico, what made the broadcast revolutionary "was the listener's sensation of being on the scene" in far-off Europe.

When leaders from France and Britain met with Hitler in Munich later that year, millions of Americans listened with rapt attention to live radio updates. Correspondents soon became well known, none more so than Edward R. Murrow of CBS. During the Nazi air blitz of London in 1940–1941, Murrow's rich, understated, nicotine-scorched voice kept Americans spellbound. "This—is London," he would begin each broadcast, then proceed to give graphic accounts that tried, as he put it, to "report suffering to people [Americans] who have not suffered."

Murrow was resolutely pro-Allies, and there is little doubt his reports strengthened the interventionist voices in Washington by emphasizing Winston Churchill's greatness and England's bravery. More than that, though, radio reports from Europe made Americans feel more closely linked than before to people living thousands of miles and an ocean away. As American writer Archibald MacLeish said of Murrow's broadcasts, "Without rhetoric, without dramatics, without more emotion than needed be, you destroyed the superstition of distance and of time."

Churchill later recalled that the president told him in Newfoundland that he could not ask Congress for a declaration of war against Germany, but "he would wage war" and "become more and more provocative."

Within days, German and American ships came into direct contact in the Atlantic. On September 4, a German submarine launched torpedoes at (but did

President Franklin D. Roosevelt (left) and British prime minister Winston Churchill (1874–1965) confer on board a ship near Newfoundland during their summit meeting of August 1941. During the conference, they signed the Atlantic Charter. On his return to Great Britain, Churchill told his advisers that Roosevelt had promised to "wage war" against Germany and do "everything" to "force an incident."

not hit) the American destroyer *Greer.* Henceforth, Roosevelt said, the U.S. Navy would have authority to fire first when under threat. He also announced a policy that he already had promised Churchill in private: American warships would convoy British merchant ships across the ocean. Thus, the United States entered into an undeclared naval war with Germany. When in early October a German submarine torpedoed the U.S. destroyer *Kearny* off the coast of Iceland, the president announced that "the shooting has started. And history has recorded who fired the first shot." Later that month, when the destroyer *Reuben James* went down with the loss of more than one hundred American lives, Congress scrapped the cash-and-carry policy and further revised the Neutrality Acts to permit transport of munitions to Britain on armed American merchant ships. The United States was edging very close to being a belligerent.

U.S. Demands on Japan

It seems ironic, therefore, that the Second World War came to the United States by way of Asia. Roosevelt had wanted to avoid war with Japan in order to concentrate American resources on the defeat of Germany. In September 1940, after Germany, Italy, and Japan had signed the Tripartite Pact (to form the Axis powers), Roosevelt slapped an embargo on shipments of aviation fuel and scrap metal to Japan. Because the president believed the Japanese would consider a cutoff of oil a life-or-death matter, he did not embargo that vital commodity. But after Japanese troops occupied French Indochina in July 1941, Washington froze Japanese assets in the United States, virtually ending trade (including oil) with Japan. "The oil gauge and the clock stood side by side" for Japan, wrote one observer.

Tokyo recommended a summit meeting between President Roosevelt and Prime Minister Prince Konoye, but the United States rejected the idea. American officials insisted that the Japanese first agree to respect China's sovereignty and territorial integrity and to honor the Open Door policy—in short, to get out of China. According to polls taken in the fall of 1941, the American people seemed willing to risk war with Japan to thwart further aggression. For Roosevelt, Europe still claimed first priority, but he supported Secretary Hull's hard-line policy against Japan's pursuit of the Greater East Asia Co-Prosperity Sphere—the name Tokyo gave to the vast Asian region it intended to dominate.

Roosevelt told his advisers to string out ongoing Japanese-American talks to gain time—time to fortify the Philippines and check the fascists in Europe. By breaking the Japanese diplomatic code and deciphering intercepted messages through Operation MAGIC, American officials learned that Tokyo's patience with diplomacy was fast dissipating. In late November, the Japanese rejected American demands that they withdraw from Indochina. An intercepted message that American experts decoded on December 3 instructed the Japanese embassy in Washington to burn codes and destroy cipher machines—a step suggesting that war was coming.

Surprise Attack on Pearl Harbor   The Japanese plotted a daring raid on Pearl Harbor in Hawai'i. An armada of sixty Japanese ships, with a core of six carriers bearing 360 airplanes, crossed 3,000 miles of the Pacific Ocean. To avoid detection, every ship maintained radio silence. In the early morning of December 7, some 230 miles northwest of Honolulu, the carriers unleashed their planes, each stamped with a red sun representing the Japanese flag. They swept down on the unsuspecting American naval base and nearby airfields, dropping torpedoes and bombs and strafing buildings.

The battleship USS *Arizona* fell victim to a Japanese bomb that ignited explosives below deck, killing more than 1,000 sailors. The USS *Nevada* tried to escape the inferno by heading out to sea, but a second wave of aerial attackers struck the ship. Altogether the invaders sank or damaged eight battleships and many smaller vessels, and smashed more than 160 aircraft on the ground. Huddled in an air-raid shelter, sixteen-year-old Mary Ann Ramsey watched the injured come in "with filthy black oil covering shredded flesh. With the first sailor, so horribly burned, personal fear left me; he brought me the full tragedy of the day." A total of 2,403 died; 1,178 were wounded. By chance, three aircraft carriers at sea escaped the disaster. The Pearl Harbor tragedy, from the perspective of the war's outcome, amounted to a military inconvenience more than a disaster.

Explaining Pearl Harbor How could the stunning attack on Pearl Harbor have happened? After all, American cryptanalysts had broken the Japanese diplomatic code. Although the intercepted Japanese messages told policymakers that war lay ahead, the intercepts never revealed naval or military plans and never mentioned Pearl Harbor specifically. Roosevelt did not, as some critics charged, conspire to leave the fleet vulnerable to attack so that the United States could enter the Second World War through the "back door" of Asia. The base at Pearl Harbor was not on red alert because a message sent from Washington warning of the imminence of war had been too casually transmitted by a slow method and had arrived too late. Base commanders were too relaxed, believing Hawai'i too far from Japan to be a target for all-out attack. Like Roosevelt's advisers, they expected an assault on British Malaya, Thailand, or the Philippines (see Map 26.2). The Pearl Harbor calamity stemmed from mistakes and insufficient information, not from conspiracy.

On December 8, referring to the previous day as "a date which will live in infamy," Roosevelt asked Congress for a declaration of war against Japan. He noted that the Japanese had also, almost simultaneously, attacked Malaya, Hong Kong, Guam, the Philippines, Wake, and Midway, and he expressed the prevailing sense of revenge when he vowed that Americans would never forget "the character of the onslaught against us." A unanimous vote in the Senate and a 388-to-1 vote in the House thrust America into war. Representative Jeannette Rankin of Montana voted no, repeating her vote against entry into the First World War. Britain declared war on Japan, but the Soviet Union did not. Three days later, Germany and Italy, honoring the Tripartite Pact they had signed with Japan in September 1940, declared war against the United States. "Hitler's fate was sealed," Churchill later wrote. "Mussolini's fate was sealed. As for the Japanese, they would be ground to powder.... I went to bed and slept the sleep of the saved and thankful."

A fundamental clash of systems explains why war came. Germany and Japan preferred a world divided into closed spheres of influence. The United States sought a liberal capitalist world order in which all nations enjoyed freedom of trade and investment. American principles manifested respect for human rights; fascists in Europe and militarists in Asia defiantly trampled such rights. The United States prided itself on its democratic system; Germany and Japan embraced authoritarian regimes backed by the military. When the United States protested against German and Japanese expansion, Berlin and Tokyo charged that Washington was applying a double standard, conveniently ignoring its own sphere of influence in Latin America and its own history of military and economic aggrandizement. Americans rejected such comparisons and claimed that their expansionism had benefited not just themselves but the rest of the world. So many incompatible objectives and outlooks obstructed diplomacy and made war likely.

Avoidable War? Likely, but perhaps not inevitable. At least with respect to the Japanese, there is the tantalizing question of whether a more flexible American negotiating posture in the fall of 1941 might have averted a U.S.-Japanese war. Privately, after all, American planners admitted they were largely powerless to affect Japan's moves in China; they further conceded among themselves that any Japanese withdrawal from China would take many months to carry out. So why the public insistence that Japan had to get out, and get out now? Why not assent, grudgingly, to the Japanese presence in China and also reopen at least limited trade with the Tokyo government, in order to forestall further Japanese expansion in Southeast Asia? Such a policy would have delayed any showdown with Japan, allowed continued concentration on the European war, and also given Washington more time to rearm. Writes historian David M. Kennedy, "Whether under those circumstances a Japanese-American war might have been avoided altogether is among the weightiest of might-have-beens, with implications for the nature and timing of America's struggle against Hitler and for the shape of postwar Europe as well as Asia." It was not to be, though, and the United States now prepared to wage war in two theaters half a world apart.

SUMMARY

In the 1920s and 1930s, Americans proved unable to create a peaceful and prosperous world order. The Washington Conference treaties failed to curb a naval arms race or to protect China, and both the Dawes Plan and the Kellogg-Briand Pact proved ineffective. Philanthropic activities fell short of need, and the process of cultural Americanization provided no panacea. In the era of the Great Depression, U.S. trade policies, shifting from protectionist tariffs to reciprocal trade agreements, only minimally improved American or international commerce. Recognition of the Soviet Union barely improved relations. Most ominous of all, the aggressors Germany and Japan ignored repeated U.S. protests, from the Stimson Doctrine onward; as the 1930s progressed, the United States became more entangled in the crises in Europe and Asia. Even where American power and policies seemed to work to satisfy Good Neighbor goals—in Latin America—nationalist resentments simmered and Mexico challenged U.S. dominance.

During the late 1930s and early 1940s, President Roosevelt hesitantly but steadily moved the United States from neutrality to aid for the Allies, to belligerency, and finally to a declaration of war after the attack on Pearl Harbor. Congress gradually revised and retired the Neutrality Acts in the face of growing danger and receding isolationism. Independent internationalism and economic and nonmilitary means to peace gave way to alliance building and war.

The Second World War offered yet another opportunity for Americans to set things right in the world. As publisher Henry Luce wrote in *American Century* (1941), the United States must "exert upon the world the full impact of our influence, for such purposes as we see fit and by such means as we see fit." As they had so many times before, Americans flocked to the colors. Isolationists joined the president in spirited calls for victory. "We are going to win the war, and we are going to win the peace that follows," Roosevelt predicted.

27

THE SECOND WORLD WAR AT
HOME AND ABROAD 1941–1945

CHAPTER OUTLINE

- The United States at War • The Production Front and American Workers
- Life on the Home Front • *VISUALIZING THE PAST* *Portraying the Enemy* • The
Limits of American Ideals • Life in the Military • Winning the War • Summary

THE UNITED STATES AT WAR

As Japanese bombs fell in the U.S. territory of Hawai'i, American antiwar sentiment evaporated. Franklin Roosevelt summoned the nation to war with Japan on December 8, proclaiming that "the American people in their righteous might will win through to absolute victory." When Germany formally declared war on the United States three days later, America joined British and Soviet Allied nations in the ongoing war against the Axis powers of Japan, Germany, and Italy. The American public's shift from caution—even isolationism—to fervent support for war was sudden and dramatic. Some former critics of intervention, seeking a persuasive explanation, turned to the popular children's story *Ferdinand the Bull*. Ferdinand, though huge and powerful, just liked to "sit and smell the flowers"—until the day he was stung by a bee. It was a comforting tale, but inaccurate. As the world went to war, the United States had not been, like Ferdinand, just "smell[ing] the flowers." America's embargo of shipments to Japan and refusal to accept Japan's expansionist policies had brought the two nations to the brink of war, and the United States was deeply involved in an undeclared naval war with Germany well before Japan's attack on Pearl Harbor. By December 1941, Roosevelt had long since instituted an unprecedented peacetime draft, created war mobilization agencies, and commissioned war plans for simultaneous struggle in Europe and the Pacific. America's entry into World War II was not a surprise.

A Nation Unprepared

Nonetheless, the nation was not ready for war. Throughout the 1930s, military funding had been a low priority. In September 1939 (when Hitler invaded Poland and began the Second

CHRONOLOGY

1941   Japan attacks Pearl Harbor

United States enters World War II

1942   War Production Board created to oversee conversion to military production

Allies losing war in Pacific to Japan; U.S. victory at Battle of Midway in June is turning point

Office of Price Administration creates rationing system for food and consumer goods

United States pursues "Europe First" war policy; Allies reject Stalin's demands for a second front and invade North Africa

West Coast Japanese Americans relocated to internment camps

Manhattan Project set up to create atomic bomb

Congress of Racial Equality established

1943   Soviet army defeats German troops at Stalingrad

Congress passes War Labor Disputes (Smith-Connally) Act following coal miners' strike

"Zoot suit riots" in Los Angeles; race riots break out in Detroit, Harlem, and other cities

Allies invade Italy

Roosevelt, Churchill, and Stalin meet at Teheran Conference

1944   Allied troops land at Normandy on D-Day, June 6

Roosevelt elected to fourth term as president

United States retakes Philippines

1945   Roosevelt, Stalin, and Churchill meet at Yalta Conference

British and U.S. forces firebomb Dresden, Germany

Battles of Iwo Jima and Okinawa result in heavy Japanese and American losses

Roosevelt dies; Truman becomes president

Germany surrenders; Allied forces liberate Nazi death camps

Potsdam Conference calls for Japan's "unconditional surrender"

United States uses atomic bombs on Hiroshima and Nagasaki

Japan surrenders

World War), the U.S. Army ranked forty-fifth in size among the world's armies and could fully equip only one-third of its 227,000 men. A peacetime draft instituted in 1940 expanded the U.S. military to 2 million men, but Roosevelt's 1941 survey of war preparedness, the "Victory Plan," estimated that the United States could not be ready to fight before June 1943.

In December 1941, U.S. victory must have seemed unlikely. In Europe, the Allies were losing the war (see Map 26.3). Hitler had claimed Austria, Czechoslovakia, Poland, the Netherlands, Denmark, and Norway. Romania was lost, then Greece and Bulgaria. France had fallen in 1940. Britain fought on, but German planes rained bombs on London. More than 3 million soldiers under German command had penetrated deep into the Soviet Union and Africa. German U-boats controlled the Atlantic from the Arctic to the Caribbean. Within months of America's entry into the war, German submarines sank 216 vessels—some so close to American shores that people could see the glow of burning ships.

War in the Pacific   In the Pacific, the war was largely America's to fight. The Soviets had not declared war on Japan, and although British troops protected Great Britain's Asian colonies, there were too few to make much difference. By late spring of 1942, Japan had captured most of the European colonial possessions in Southeast Asia: the Dutch East Indies (Indonesia); French Indochina (Vietnam); and the British colonies of Malaya, Burma, Western New Guinea, Hong Kong, and Singapore. In the American Philippines, the struggle went on longer, but also in vain. The Japanese attacked the Philippines hours after their success at Pearl Harbor and, finding the entire force of B-17 bombers sitting on the airfields, destroyed U.S. air capability in the region. American and Filipino troops retreated to the Bataan Peninsula, hoping to hold the main island, Luzon, but Japanese forces were superior. In March 1942, under orders from Roosevelt, General Douglas MacArthur, the commander of U.S. forces in the Far East, departed the Philippines for Australia, proclaiming, "I shall return."

Left behind were almost eighty thousand American and Filipino troops. Starving and weakened by disease, they held on for almost another month before surrendering. Those who survived long enough to surrender faced worse horror. The Japanese troops, lacking supplies themselves, were unprepared to deal with such a large number of prisoners, and most believed the prisoners had forfeited honorable treatment by surrendering. In what came to be known as the Bataan Death March, the Japanese force-marched their captives to prison camps 80 miles away. Guards denied the prisoners food and water and bayoneted or beat to death those who fell behind. As many as ten thousand Filipinos and six hundred Americans died on the march. Filipino civilians suffered horribly. Tens of thousands of refugees and prisoners of war died under Japanese occupation.

As losses mounted, the United States began to strike back. On April 18, sixteen American B-25s appeared in the skies over Japan. The Doolittle raid (named after the mission's leader) did little harm to Japan, but it had an enormous psychological impact on Japanese leaders. The image of American bombers over Japan's home islands pushed Japanese commander Yamamoto to bold action. Instead of consolidating control close to home, Yamamoto concluded, Japan must move quickly to lure the weakened United States into a "decisive battle." The target was Midway—two tiny islands about 1,000 miles northwest of Honolulu, where the U.S. Navy had a base. If Japan could take Midway—not implausible, given Japan's string of victories—it would have a secure defensive perimeter far from the home islands (see Map 27.3). By using Guam, the Philippines, and perhaps even Australia as hostages, Japan believed, it could negotiate a favorable peace agreement with the United States.

MAP 27.1 The Allies on the Offensive in Europe, 1942–1945

The United States pursued a "Europe First" policy: first defeat Germany, then focus on Japan. American military efforts began in North Africa in late 1942 and ended in Germany in 1945 on May 8 (V-E Day).

General Yamamoto did not know that America's MAGIC code-breaking machines could decipher Japanese messages. This time, surprise was on the side of the United States, as the Japanese fleet found the U.S. Navy and its carrier-based dive bombers lying in wait. The Battle of Midway in June 1942 was a turning point in the Pacific war. Japanese strategists had hoped that the United States, discouraged by Japan's early victories, would withdraw and leave Japan to control the Pacific. That outcome was no longer a possibility. Now Japan was on the defensive.

"Europe First" Strategy   Despite the importance of these early Pacific battles, America's war strategy was "Europe First." Germany, American war planners recognized, was a greater danger to the United States than Japan. If Germany conquered the Soviet Union, they believed, it might directly threaten the United States. Roosevelt also feared that the Soviet Union, suffering almost unimaginable losses as its military battled Hitler's invading army, might pursue a separate peace with Germany and so undo the Allied coalition. Therefore, the United States would work first with Britain and the USSR to defeat Germany, then deal with an isolated Japan.

British prime minister Winston Churchill and Soviet premier Joseph Stalin disagreed vehemently, however, over how to wage the war against Germany. By late 1941, before the fierce Russian winter stalled their onslaught, German troops had nearly reached Moscow and Leningrad (present-day St. Petersburg) and had slashed deeply into Ukraine, taking Kiev. Over a million Soviet soldiers had died defending their country. Stalin pressed for British and American troops to attack Germany from the west, through France, to draw German troops away from the Soviet front. Roosevelt believed "with heart and *mind*" that Stalin was right and promised to open a "second front" to Germany's west before the end of 1942. Churchill, however, blocked this plan. He had not forgotten Stalin's nonaggression pact with Hitler. More fundamentally, in large part because of experience with the agonies of prolonged trench warfare in World War I, British military commanders did not want a large-scale invasion of Europe. Churchill wanted to win control of the North Atlantic shipping lanes first and promoted air attacks on Germany. He also pushed for a smaller, safer attack on Axis positions in North Africa; halting the Germans there would protect British imperial possessions in the Mediterranean and the oil-rich Middle East.

Against his advisers' recommendation, Roosevelt accepted Churchill's plan. The U.S. military was not yet ready for a major campaign, and Roosevelt needed to show the American public some success in the European war. Thus, instead of coming to the rescue of the USSR, the British and Americans made a joint landing in North Africa in November 1942. American troops, facing relatively light resistance, won quick victories in Algeria and Morocco. In Egypt, the British confronted General Erwin Rommel and his Afrika Korps in a struggle for control of the Suez Canal and the Middle East oil fields. Rommel's army, trapped between British and American troops, surrendered after six months. And in Russia, against all odds, the Soviet army hung on, fighting block by block for control of Stalingrad in the deadly cold, to defeat the German Sixth Army in early 1943. Stalingrad, like Midway, was a major turning point in the war. By the spring of 1943, Germany, like Japan, was on the defensive. But relations among the Allies remained precarious. The Soviet Union had lost 1.1 million men in the Battle of Stalingrad. The United States and Britain, however, continued to resist Stalin's demand that they immediately open a second front. The death toll, already in the millions, continued to mount.

THE PRODUCTION FRONT AND AMERICAN WORKERS

In late December 1940—almost a year before the United States entered the war—Franklin Roosevelt pledged that America would serve as the world's "great arsenal of democracy," making the machines that would win the war for the Allies. After Pearl Harbor, U.S. strategy remained much the same. The United States would prevail through a "crushing superiority of equipment," Roosevelt told Congress. Although the war would be fought on the battlefields of Europe and the Pacific, the nation's strategic advantage lay on the "production front" at home.

Goals for military production were staggering. In 1940, with war looming, American factories had built only 3,807 airplanes. Following Pearl Harbor, Roosevelt asked for 60,000 aircraft in 1942 and double that number in 1943. Plans called for the manufacture of 16 million tons of shipping and 120,000 tanks. The military needed supplies to train and equip a force that would grow to almost 16 million men. Thus, for the duration of the war, military production took precedence over the manufacture of civilian goods. Automobile plants built tanks and airplanes instead of cars; dress factories sewed military uniforms. The War Production Board, established by Roosevelt in early 1942, had the enormous task of allocating resources and coordinating production among thousands of independent factories.

Businesses, Universities, and the War Effort

During the war, American businesses overwhelmingly cooperated with government war-production plans. Patriotism was one reason, but generous incentives were another. Major American industries had at first resisted government pressure to shift to military production. In 1940, as the United States produced armaments for the Allies, the American economy began to recover from the depression. Rising consumer spending built industrial confidence. Auto manufacturers, for example, expected to sell 4 million cars in 1941, a more than 25 percent increase over 1939. The massive retooling necessary to produce planes or tanks instead of cars would be enormously expensive and leave manufacturers totally dependent on a single client—the federal government. Moreover, many major industrialists, such as General Motors head Alfred Sloan, remained suspicious of Roosevelt and what they saw as his antibusiness policies.

Government, however, met business more than halfway. The federal government paid for expensive retooling and factory expansions; it guaranteed profits by allowing corporations to charge the government for production costs plus a fixed profit; it created generous tax write-offs and exemptions from antitrust laws. War mobilization did not require America's businesses to sacrifice profits. Instead, corporations doubled their net profits between 1939 and 1943. As Secretary of War Henry Stimson explained, when a "capitalist country" goes to war, it must "let business make money out of the process or business won't work."

Most military contracts went to America's largest corporations, which had the facilities and experience to guarantee rapid, efficient production. From mid-1940 through September 1944, the government awarded contracts totaling $175 billion, with about two-thirds going to the top hundred corporations. General Motors alone received 8 percent of the total. This approach made sense for a nation that wanted enormous quantities of war goods manufactured in the shortest possible time; most small businesses just did not have the necessary capacity. However, wartime government contracts further consolidated American manufacturing in the hands of a few giant corporations.

Manhattan Project

Wartime needs also created a new relationship between science and the U.S. military. Millions of dollars went to fund research programs at America's largest universities: $117 million to Massachusetts Institute of Technology alone. Such federally sponsored research programs developed new technologies of warfare, such as vastly improved radar systems and the proximity fuse. The most important government-sponsored scientific research program was the Manhattan Project, a $2 billion secret effort to build an atomic bomb. Roosevelt had been convinced by scientists fleeing the Nazis in 1939 that Germany was working to create an atomic weapon, and he resolved to beat them at their own efforts. The Manhattan Project achieved the world's first sustained nuclear chain reaction in 1942 at the University of Chicago, and in 1943 the federal government set up a secret community for atomic scientists and their families at Los Alamos, New Mexico. In this remote, sparsely populated, and beautiful setting, some of America's most talented scientists worked with Jewish refugees from Nazi Germany to develop the weapon that would change the world.

New Opportunities for Workers

America's new defense factories, running around the clock, required millions of workers. At first, workers were plentiful: 9 million Americans were still unemployed in 1940 when war mobilization began, and 3 million remained without work in December 1941. But during the war, the armed forces took almost 16 million men out of the potential civilian labor pool, forcing industry to look elsewhere for workers. Women, African Americans, Mexican Americans, poor whites from the isolated mountain hollows of Appalachia and the tenant farms of the Deep South—all streamed into jobs in defense plants.

In some cases, federal action eased their path. In 1941, as the federal government poured billions of dollars into war industries, many industries refused to hire African Americans. "The Negro will be considered only as janitors and other similar capacities," one executive notified black applicants. A. Philip Randolph, head of the Brotherhood of Sleeping Car Porters, proposed a march on Washington, D.C., to demand equal access to defense industry jobs. Roosevelt, fearing that the march might provoke race riots and that communists might infiltrate the movement, offered the March on Washington movement a deal. In exchange for canceling the march, the president issued Executive Order No. 8802, which prohibited discrimination in war industries and government jobs. The Fair Employment Practices Committee (FEPC) was established to ensure that its provisions were respected. Although enforcement was uneven, hundreds of thousands of black Americans migrated from the South to the industrial cities of the North and West on the strength of this official guarantee of job equality.

Mexican workers also filled wartime jobs in the United States. Although the U.S. government had deported Mexicans as unemployment rose during the Great Depression, about 200,000 Mexican farm workers, or *braceros*, were offered short-term contracts to fill agricultural jobs left vacant as Americans sought well-paid war work. Mexican and Mexican American workers alike faced discrimination and segregation, but they seized the economic opportunities newly available to them. In 1941, not a single Mexican American worked in the Los Angeles shipyards; by 1944, 17,000 were employed there.

Women at Work

Early in the war production boom, employers insisted that women were not suited for industrial jobs. But as labor shortages began to threaten the war effort, employers did an about-face. "Almost overnight," said Mary Anderson, head of the Women's Bureau of the Department of Labor, "women were reclassified by industrialists from a marginal to a basic labor supply for munitions making." Posters and billboards urged women to "Do the Job HE Left Behind." The government's War Manpower Commission glorified the invented worker "Rosie the Riveter," who was featured on posters, in magazines, and in the recruiting jingle "Rosie's got a boyfriend, Charlie / Charlie, he's a marine / Rosie is protecting Charlie / Working overtime on the riveting machine."

Rosie the Riveter was an inspiring image, but she did not accurately represent women in the American work force. Only 16 percent of women workers held jobs in defense plants, and only 4.4 percent of "skilled" jobs (such as riveting) were held by women. Nonetheless, during the war years, more than 6 million women entered the labor force, and the number of working women increased by 57 percent. More than 400,000 African American women left domestic service for higher-paying industrial jobs, often with union benefits. Seven million women moved to war-production areas, such as southern California, home of both shipyards and aircraft factories. And the majority of women workers who did not hold war-production jobs—whether they took traditional "women's jobs" as clerical workers or filled traditionally male jobs as bus drivers or even "lumberjills," as men left for military service or better-paid factory jobs—kept the American economy going and freed other workers for the demanding work in war-production plants.

Workers in defense plants were often expected to work ten days for every day off or to accept difficult night shifts. Recognizing the importance of keeping people on the job, both businesses and the federal government provided workers new forms of support. The West Coast Kaiser shipyards offered not only high pay, but also childcare, subsidized housing, and healthcare: the Kaiser Permanente Medical Care Program, a forerunner of the health maintenance organization (HMO), supplied medical care to workers for a weekly payroll deduction of 50 cents. The federal government also funded childcare centers and before- and after-school programs. At its peak, 130,000 preschoolers and 320,000 school-age children were enrolled in federally sponsored childcare.

Organized Labor During Wartime   Because industrial production was key to America's war strategy, the federal government attempted to make sure that labor strikes, so common in the 1930s, would not interrupt production. Less than a week after Pearl Harbor, a White House labor-management conference agreed to a no-strike/no-lockout pledge. In 1942, Roosevelt created the National War Labor Board (NWLB) to settle labor disputes. The NWLB forged a temporary compromise between labor union demands for a "closed shop," in which only union members could work, and management's desire for "open" shops. Workers could not be required to join a union, but unions could enroll as many members as possible. Between 1940 and 1945, union membership ballooned from 8.5 million to 14.75 million.

However, the government did not hesitate to restrict union power if it threatened war production. When coal miners in the United Mine Workers union went on strike in 1943, following an attempt by the NWLB to limit wage increases to a cost-of-living adjustment, lack of coal halted railroads and shut down steel mills.

Few Americans supported this strike. An air force pilot said, "I'd just as soon shoot down one of those strikers as shoot down Japs—they're doing as much to lose the war for us." As antilabor sentiment grew, Congress passed the War Labor Disputes (Smith-Connally) Act. This act gave the president authority to seize and operate any strike-bound plant deemed necessary to the national security, but it also contained broad, punitive provisions that created criminal penalties for leading strikes and tried to constrain union power by prohibiting contributions to political campaigns during time of war.

Success on the Production Front   For close to four years, American factories operated twenty-four hours a day, seven days a week, fighting the war on the production front. Between 1940 and 1945, American factories turned out roughly 300,000 airplanes, 102,000 armored vehicles, 77,000 ships, 20 million small arms, 40 billion bullets, and 6 million tons of bombs. By war's end, the United States was producing 40 percent of the world's weaponry. This amazing feat depended on transforming formerly skilled work in industries like shipbuilding into an assembly-line process of mass production. Henry Ford, now seventy-eight years old, created a massive bomber plant on farmland along Willow Run Creek not far from Detroit. Willow Run's assembly lines, almost a mile long, turned out B-24 Liberator bombers at the rate of one an hour. On the West Coast, William Kaiser used mass-production techniques to cut construction time for Liberty ships—the huge, 440-foot-long cargo ships that transported the tanks and guns and bullets overseas—from 355 to 56 days. (As a publicity stunt, Kaiser's Richmond shipyard, near San Francisco, built one Liberty ship in 4 days, 15 hours, and 26 minutes.) The ships were not well made; welded hulls sometimes split in rough seas, and one ship foundered while still docked at the pier. However, as the United States struggled to produce cargo ships faster than German U-boats could sink them, speed of production counted for more than quality.

A visitor to the Willow Run plant described "the roar of the machinery, the special din of the riveting gun absolutely deafening nearby, the throbbing crash of the giant metal presses … the far-reaching line of half-born skyships growing wings under swarms of workers." His words reveal the might of American industry but also offer a glimpse of the experience of workers, who did dirty, repetitive, and physically exhausting work day after day "for the duration." Although American propaganda during the war badly overstated the contributions of well-paid war workers as being equal to those of men in combat, 102,000 men and women were killed doing war production work during the first two years of the war and more than 350,000 were seriously injured.

LIFE ON THE HOME FRONT

The United States was the only major combatant in World War II that did not experience warfare directly (Hawai'i was a U.S. territory and the Philippines a U.S. possession, but neither was part of the nation proper). Americans worried about loved ones fighting in distant places; they grieved over the loss of sons and brothers and fathers and husbands and friends. Their lives were disrupted. But the United States, protected by two oceans from its enemies, was spared the war that other nations experienced. Bombs did not fall on American cities; invading armies did not burn and rape and kill. Instead, war mobilization ended the Great Depression and brought prosperity. American civilians experienced the paradox of good times amid global conflagration.

Supporting the War Effort   Although the war was distant, it was a constant presence in the lives of Americans on "the home front." Civilians supported the war effort in many ways, though Americans were never so unified or committed to shared sacrifice as the images of "the greatest generation" that were widespread in popular history and popular culture in the early twenty-first century suggest. During the war, however, families planted 20 million "victory gardens" to free up food supplies for the armed forces. Housewives saved fat from cooking and returned it to butchers, for cooking fat yielded glycerin to make black powder used in shells or bullets. Children collected scrap metal, aware that the iron in one old shovel blade was enough for four hand grenades and that every tin can helped make a tank or Liberty ship.

Many consumer goods were rationed or unavailable. To save wool for military use, the War Production Board directed that men's suits would have narrow lapels, shorter jackets, and no vests or pant cuffs. Bathing suits, the WPB specified, must shrink by 10 percent. When silk and nylon were diverted from stockings to parachutes, women used makeup on their legs and drew in the "stocking" seam with eyebrow pencil. The Office of Price Administration (OPA), created by Congress in 1942, established a nationwide rationing system for such consumer goods as sugar, coffee, and gasoline. By early 1943, the OPA had instituted a point system for rationing food. Feeding a family required complex calculations. Every citizen— regardless of age—received two ration books each month. Blue stamps were for canned fruits and vegetables; red for meat, fish, and dairy. To buy a pound of meat, for example, consumers had to pay its cost in dollars and in points. With only 48 blue points and 64 red points per person per month, in September 1944 a small bottle of ketchup "cost" 20 blue points, while "creamery butter" cost 20 red points and sirloin steak 13 red points a pound. Pork shoulder, however, required only dollars. Sugar was tightly rationed, and people saved for months to make a birthday cake or holiday dessert. A black market existed, but most Americans understood that sugar produced alcohol for weapons manufacture and meat went to feed "our boys" overseas.

Propaganda and Popular Culture   Despite near-unanimous support for the war, government leaders worried that, over time, public willingness to sacrifice might lag. In 1942, Roosevelt created the Office of War Information (OWI), which took charge of domestic propaganda and hired Hollywood filmmakers and New York copywriters to sell the war at home. OWI posters exhorted Americans to save and sacrifice, and reminded them to watch what they said, for "loose lips sink ships."

Popular culture also reinforced wartime messages. A *Saturday Evening Post* advertisement for vacuum cleaners (unavailable for the duration) urged women war workers to fight "for freedom and all that means to women everywhere. You're

VISUALIZING THE PAST

Portraying the Enemy

Racial stereotyping affected how both the Americans and the Japanese waged war. The Americans badly underestimated the Japanese, leaving themselves open for the surprise attack on Pearl Harbor and American forces in the Philippines. And the Japanese, believing Americans were barbarians who lacked a sense of honor, mistakenly expected that the United States would withdraw from East Asia once confronted with Japanese power and determination. This cover for *Collier's* magazine, appearing shortly after the first anniversary of Japan's attack on Pearl Harbor, shows some of the most extreme racial imagery of the war, but it was scarcely alone. How is Japan portrayed here? How might the fact that Japan had launched an immensely successful surprise attack on the United States have shaped this image, or Americans' reactions to it?

American propaganda caricatured all the Axis powers, but the Japanese were most likely to be portrayed as subhuman.

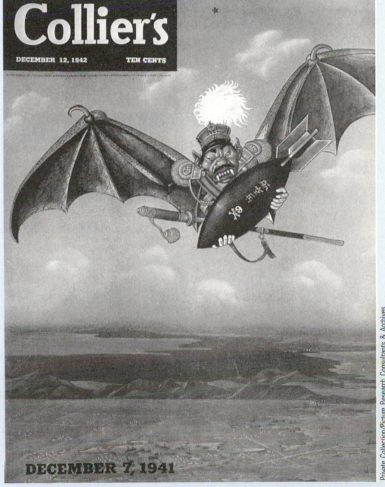

fighting for a little house of your own, and a husband to meet every night at the door. You're fighting for the right to bring up your children without the shadow of fear." Popular songs urged Americans to "Remember December 7th" or to "Accentuate the Positive." Others made fun of America's enemies ("You're a sap, Mr. Jap / You make a Yankee cranky / You're a sap, Mr. Jap / Uncle Sam is gonna spanky") or, like "Cleanin' My Rifle (and Dreamin' of You)," dealt with the hardship of wartime separation.

Movies drew 90 million viewers a week in 1944—out of a total population of 132 million. During the war "Draftee Duck" joined the army, chickens produced for the war effort at "Flockheed," and audiences sang along with an animated version of the song "Der Fuehrer's Face" ("When der fuehrer says we is de master race/We heil (pffft) heil (pffft) right in Der Fuehrer's Face") in pre-film cartoons. For the most part, Hollywood tried to meet Eleanor Roosevelt's challenge to "Keep 'em laughing." *A WAVE, a WAC, and a Marine* promised "no battle scenes, no message, just barrels of fun and jive to make you happy you're alive." Others, such as *Bataan* or *Wake Island*, portrayed actual—if sanitized—events in the war. Even at the most frivolous comedies, however, the war was always present. Theaters held "plasma premieres," offering free admission to those who donated a half-pint of blood to the Red Cross. Audiences rose to sing "The Star Spangled Banner," then watched newsreels featuring carefully censored footage of recent combat before the feature film began. On D-Day, June 6, 1944, as Allied troops landed at Normandy, theater managers across the nation led audiences in the Lord's Prayer or the Twenty-third Psalm ("The Lord is my shepherd … "). It was in movie theaters that Americans saw the horror of Nazi death camps in May 1945. The Universal newsreel narrator ordered audiences, "Don't turn away. Look."

Wartime Prosperity

The war demanded sacrifices from Americans, but it also rewarded them with new highs in personal income. Between 1939 and the end of the war, per capita income rose from $691 to $1,515. Wages and salaries increased more than 135 percent from 1940 to 1945. OPA-administered price controls kept inflation down so that wage increases did not disappear to higher costs. And with little to buy, savings rose.

Fighting World War II cost the United States approximately $304 billion (more than $3 trillion in today's dollars). Instead of financing the war primarily through taxation, the government relied on deficit spending, borrowing money in the form of war bonds sold to patriotic citizens and financial institutions. The national debt skyrocketed, from $49 billion in 1941 to $259 billion in 1945 (and was not paid off until 1970). However, wartime revenue acts increased the number of Americans paying personal income tax from 4 million to 42.6 million—at rates ranging from 6 to 94 percent—and introduced a new system in which employers "withheld" taxes from employee paychecks. For the first time, individual Americans paid more in taxes than corporations.

A Nation in Motion

Despite hardships and fears, the war offered home-front Americans new opportunities, and millions of Americans took them. More than 15 million civilians moved during the

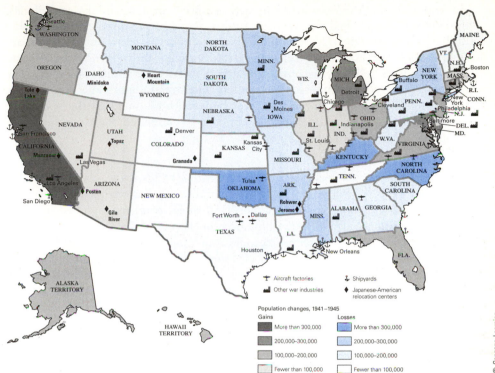

MAP 27.2 A Nation on the Move, 1940–1950

American migration during the 1940s was the largest on record to that time. The farm population dropped dramatically as men, women, and children moved to war-production areas and to army and navy bases, particularly on the West Coast. Well over 30 million Americans (civilian and military) migrated during the war. Many returned to their rural homes after the war, but 12 million migrants stayed in their new locations. Notice the population increases on the West Coast as well as in the Southwest and Florida.

war (see Map 27.2). More than half moved to another state, and half that number moved to another region. Seven hundred thousand black Americans left the South during the war years; in 1943, ten thousand black migrants poured into Los Angeles every month. People who had never traveled farther than the next county found themselves on the other side of the country—or of the world. People moved for defense jobs or to be close to loved ones at stateside military postings. Southerners moved north, northerners moved south, and 1.5 million people moved to California.

The rapid influx of war workers to major cities and small towns strained community resources. Migrants crowded into substandard housing—even woodsheds, tents, or cellars—and into trailer parks without adequate sanitary facilities. Disease spread: scabies and ringworm, polio, tuberculosis. Many long-term residents found the newcomers—especially the unmarried male war workers—a rough bunch. In the small town of Lawrence, Kansas, civic leaders bragged of the economic boost a new war plant gave the town but fretted over the appearance of bars, "dirty windowed dispensaries" that sold alcohol to the war workers.

In and around Detroit, where car factories now produced tanks and planes, established residents called war workers freshly arrived from southern Appalachia "hillbillies" and "white trash." A new joke circulated: "How many states are there in the Union? Forty-five. Tennessee and Kentucky moved to Michigan, and Michigan went to hell." Many of these migrants knew little about urban life. One young man from rural Tennessee, unfamiliar with traffic lights and street signs, navigated by counting the number of trees between his home and the war plant where he worked. Some Appalachian "trailer-ites" appalled their neighbors by building outdoor privies or burying garbage in their yards.

Racial Conflicts   As people from different backgrounds confronted one another under difficult conditions, tensions rose. Widespread racism made things worse. In 1943, almost 250 racial conflicts exploded in forty-seven cities. Outright racial warfare bloodied the streets of Detroit in June. White mobs, undeterred by police, roamed the city attacking blacks. Blacks hurled rocks at police and dragged white passengers off streetcars. At the end of thirty hours of rioting, twenty-five blacks and nine whites lay dead. Surveying the damage, an elderly black woman said, "There ain't no North anymore. Everything now is South."

The heightened racial and ethnic tensions of wartime also led to riots in Los Angeles in 1943. Young Mexican American gang members, or *pachucos*, had adopted the zoot suit: a long jacket with wide padded shoulders, loose pants "pegged" below the knee, a wide-brimmed hat, and dangling watch chain. With cloth rationed, wearing pants requiring five yards of fabric was a political statement, and some young men wore the zoot suit as a purposeful rejection of wartime ideals of service and sacrifice. Although in fact a high percentage of Mexican Americans served in the armed forces, many white servicemen believed otherwise. Racial tensions were not far from the surface in overcrowded L.A., and rumors that pachucos had attacked white sailors quickly led to violence. For four days, mobs of white men—mainly soldiers and sailors—roamed the streets attacking zoot-suiters and stripping them of their clothes. The city of Los Angeles outlawed zoot suits and arrested men who wore them. The "zoot suit riots" ended only when naval personnel were removed from the city.

Families in Wartime   The dislocations of war also had profound impacts on the nation's families. Despite policies that exempted married men and fathers from the draft during most of the war, almost 3 million families were broken up. Young children grew up not knowing their fathers. The divorce rate of 16 per 1,000 marriages in 1940 almost doubled to 27 per 1,000 in 1944. At the same time, hundreds of thousands of men and women were getting married. The number of marriages rose from 73 per 1,000 unmarried women in 1939 to 93 in 1942. Some couples scrambled to get married before the man was sent overseas; others sought military deferments. The birth rate climbed as well: 2.4 million babies were born in 1939 and 3.1 million in 1943. Many were "goodbye babies," conceived to guarantee the continuation of the family if the father died in war.

On college campuses, some virtually stripped of male students, women complained, along with the song lyrics, "There is no available male." But other young women found an abundance of male company, sparking concern about wartime threats to sexual morality. *Youth in Crisis*, a 1943 newsreel, featured a girl with "experience far beyond her age" necking with a soldier on the street. These "victory girls" or "cuddle bunnies" were said to support the war effort by giving their all to men in uniform. Many young men and women, caught up in the emotional intensity of war, behaved as they never would in peacetime. Often that meant hasty marriages to virtual strangers, especially if a baby was on the way. Despite changes in behavior, taboos against unwed motherhood remained strong, and only 1 percent of births during the war were to unmarried women. Wartime mobility also increased opportunities for same-sex relationships, and gay communities grew in such cities as San Francisco.

In many ways, the war reinforced traditional gender roles that had been weakened during the depression, when many men lost the role of breadwinner. Now men defended their nation while women "kept the home fires burning." Some women took "men's jobs," but most understood that they were "for the duration"—the home-front equivalent to men's wartime military service. Even so, women who worked were frequently blamed for neglecting their children and creating an "epidemic" of juvenile delinquency—evidenced by the "victory girl." Nonetheless, millions of women took on new responsibilities in wartime, whether on the factory floor or within their family. Many husbands returned to find that the lives of their wives and children seemed complete without them, and some women realized how much they had enjoyed their greater freedom and independence.

THE LIMITS OF AMERICAN IDEALS

During the war, the U.S. government worked hard to explain to its citizens the reasons for their sacrifices. In 1941, Roosevelt had pledged America to defend "four essential human freedoms"—freedom of speech, freedom of religion, freedom from want, and freedom from fear—and government-sponsored films contrasted democracy and totalitarianism, freedom and fascism, equality and oppression.

Despite such confident proclamations, as America fought the totalitarian regimes of the Axis powers, the nation confronted questions with no easy answers: What limits on civil liberties were justified in the interest of national security? How freely could information flow to the nation's citizens without revealing military secrets to the enemy and costing American lives? How could the United States protect itself against the threat of spies or saboteurs, especially from German, Italian, or Japanese citizens living in the United States? And what about America's ongoing domestic problems—particularly the problem of race? Could the nation address its own citizens' demands for reform as it fought the war against the Axis? The answers to these questions often revealed tensions between the nation's democratic claims and its wartime practices.

For the most part, America handled the issue of civil liberties well. American leaders embraced a "strategy of truth," declaring that citizens of a democratic nation required a truthful accounting of the war's progress. However, the government closely controlled information about military matters. Censorship was serious business, as even seemingly unimportant details might tip off enemies about troop movements or invasion plans: radio stations were forbidden to broadcast weather reports—or even to mention weather conditions—leaving residents without warning of impending storms and sportscasters with no way to explain why play had been suspended or games had been called. During the war, government-created propaganda sometimes dehumanized the enemy, most especially the Japanese. Nonetheless, the American government resorted to hate mongering much less frequently than during the First World War.

More complex was the question of how to handle dissent and how to guard against the possibility that enemy agents were operating within the nation's borders. The Alien Registration (Smith) Act, passed in 1940, made it unlawful to advocate the overthrow of the U.S. government by force or violence, or to join any organization that did so. After Pearl Harbor, the government used this authority to take thousands of Germans, Italians, and other Europeans into custody as suspected spies and potential traitors. During the war, the government interned 14,426 Europeans in Enemy Alien Camps. Fearing subversion, the government also prohibited ten thousand Italian Americans from living or working in restricted zones along the California coast, including San Francisco and Monterey Bay.

Internment of Japanese Americans

In March 1942, Roosevelt ordered that all 112,000 foreign-born Japanese and Japanese Americans living in California, Oregon, and the state of Washington (the vast majority of the mainland population) be removed from the West Coast to "relocation centers" for the duration of the war. Each of the Italian and German nationals interned by the U.S. government faced specific, individual charges. That was not the case for Japanese nationals and Japanese Americans. They were imprisoned as a group, under suspicion solely because they were of Japanese descent.

American anger at Japan's "sneak attack" on Pearl Harbor fueled the calls for internment, as did fears that West Coast cities might yet come under enemy attack. Long-standing racism was evident, as the chief of the Western Defense Command warned, "The Japanese race is an enemy race." Finally, people in economic competition with Japanese Americans strongly supported internment. Although Japanese nationals were forbidden to gain U.S. citizenship or own property, American-born Nissei (second generation) and Sansei (third generation), all U.S. citizens, were increasingly successful in business and agriculture. The eviction order forced Japanese Americans to sell property valued at $500 million for a fraction of its worth. West Coast Japanese Americans also lost their positions in the truck-garden, floral, and fishing industries.

The internees were sent to camps carved out of tax-delinquent land in Arkansas's Mississippi River floodplain, to the intermountain terrain of Wyoming and the desert of western Arizona, and to other arid and desolate spots in the West. The camps were bleak and demoralizing. Behind barbed wire stood tarpapered wooden barracks where entire families lived in a single room furnished only with cots, blankets, and a single bare light bulb. Most had no running water. Toilets and dining and bathing facilities were communal; privacy was almost nonexistent. In such difficult circumstances, people nonetheless attempted to sustain community life, setting up consumer cooperatives and sports leagues (one Arkansas baseball team called itself the Chiggers), and for many, maintaining Buddhist worship in the face of pressure to adopt Christian beliefs.

Betrayed by their government, many internees were profoundly ambivalent about their loyalty to the United States. Some sought legal remedy, but the Supreme Court upheld the government's action in Korematsu v. U.S. (1944). Almost one-quarter of all adults in one Arkansas camp, when asked if they would "swear unqualified allegiance to the United States," answered "no" or expressed some reservation. And almost 6,000 of the 120,000 internees renounced U.S. citizenship and demanded to be sent to Japan. Others sought to demonstrate their loyalty. The all–Japanese American 442nd Regimental Combat Team, drawn heavily from young men in internment camps, was the most decorated unit of its size. Suffering heavy casualties in Italy and France, members of the 442nd were awarded a Congressional Medal of Honor, 47 Distinguished Service Crosses, 350 Silver Stars, and more than 3,600 Purple Hearts. In 1988, Congress issued a public apology and largely symbolic payment of $20,000 to each of the 60,000 surviving Japanese American internees.

African Americans and "Double V"

As America mobilized for war, some African American leaders attempted to force the nation to confront the uncomfortable parallels between the racist doctrines of the Nazis and the persistence of Jim Crow segregation in the United States. Proclaiming a "Double V" campaign (victory at home and abroad), groups such as the National Association for the Advancement of Colored People (NAACP) hoped to "persuade, embarrass, compel and shame our government and our nation … into a more enlightened attitude toward a tenth of its people." Membership in civil rights organizations soared. The NAACP, 50,000 strong in 1940, had 450,000 members by 1946. And in 1942 civil rights activists, influenced by the philosophy of India's Mohandas Gandhi, founded the Congress of Racial Equality (CORE), which stressed "nonviolent direct action" and staged sit-ins to desegregate restaurants and movie theaters in Chicago and Washington, D.C.

Military service was a key issue for African Americans, who understood the traditional link between the duty to defend one's country and the rights of full citizenship. But the U.S. military remained segregated by race and strongly resisted efforts to use black units as combat troops. As late as 1943, less than 6 percent of the armed forces were African American, compared with more than 10 percent of the population. The marines at first refused to accept African Americans at all, and the navy approximated segregation by assigning black men to service positions in which they would rarely interact with nonblacks as equals or superiors.

A Segregated Military

Why did the United States fight a war for democracy with a segregated military? The U.S. military understood that its sole priority was to stop the Axis and win the war, and the federal government and War Department decided that the midst of world war was no time to try to integrate the armed forces. The majority of Americans

During World War II, for the first time, the War Department sanctioned the training and use of African American pilots. These members of the Ninety-ninth Pursuit Squadron—known as "Tuskegee Airmen" because they trained at Alabama's all-black Tuskegee Institute— joined combat over North Africa in June 1943. Like most African American units in the racially segregated armed forces, the men of the Ninety-ninth Pursuit Squadron were under the command of white officers.

National Archives

(approximately 89 percent of Americans were white) opposed integration, many of them vehemently. As a sign of how deeply racist beliefs penetrated the United States, the Red Cross segregated blood plasma during the war. In most southern states, racial segregation was not simply custom; it was the law. Integration of military installations and training camps, the majority of which were in the South, would have provoked a crisis as federal power contradicted state law. Pointing to outbreaks of racial violence in southern training camps as evidence, government and military officials argued that wartime integration would almost certainly provoke even more racial violence, create disorder within the military, and hinder America's war effort. Such resistance might have been short-term, but the War Department did not take that chance. Justifying its decision, the War Department argued that it could not "act outside the law, nor contrary to the will of the majority of the citizens of the Nation." General George C. Marshall, Army Chief of Staff, proclaimed that it was not the job of the army to "solve a social problem that has perplexed the American people throughout the history of this nation…. The army is not a sociological laboratory." Hopes for racial justice, so long deferred, were another casualty of the war.

Despite such discrimination, many African Americans stood up for their rights. Lt. Jackie Robinson refused to move to the back of the bus while training at the army's Camp Hood, Texas, in 1944—and faced court-martial, even though military regulations forbade racial discrimination on military vehicles, regardless of local law or custom. Black sailors disobeyed orders to return to work after surviving an explosion that destroyed two ships, killed 320 men, and shattered windows 35 miles away—an explosion caused by the navy practice of assigning men who were completely untrained in handling high explosives to load bombs from the munitions depot at Port Chicago, near San Francisco, onto Liberty ships. When they were court-martialed for mutiny, future Supreme Court justice and chief counsel for the NAACP Thurgood Marshall asked why only black sailors did this work. He proclaimed, "This is not fifty men on trial for mutiny. This is the Navy on trial for its whole vicious policy toward Negroes."

As the war wore on, African American servicemen did fight on the front lines, and fought well. The Marine Corps commandant in the Pacific proclaimed that "Negro Marines are no longer on trial. They are Marines, period." The "Tuskegee Airmen," pilots trained at the Tuskegee Institute in Alabama, saw heroic service in all-black units, such as the Ninety-ninth Pursuit Squadron, which won eighty Distinguished Flying Crosses. After the war, African Americans—as some white Americans had feared—called on their wartime service to claim the full rights of citizenship. African Americans' wartime experiences were mixed, but the war was a turning point in the movement for equal rights.

America and the Holocaust   America's inaction in the face of what we now call the Holocaust is a tragic failure, though the consequences are clearer in retrospect than they were at the time. As the United States turned away refugees on the *St. Louis* in early 1939 and refused to relax its immigration quotas to admit European Jews and others fleeing Hitler's Germany, almost no one foresaw that the future would bring death camps like Auschwitz or Treblinka. Americans knew they were turning away people fleeing dire persecution, and while anti-Semitism played a significant role in that decision, it was not unusual to refuse those seeking refuge, especially in the midst of a major economic crisis that seemed to be worsening.

As early as 1942, American newspapers reported the "mass slaughter" of Jews and other "undesirables" (Gypsies, homosexuals, the physically and mentally handicapped) under Hitler. Many Americans, having been taken in by manufactured atrocity tales during World War I, wrongly discounted these stories. But Roosevelt knew about the existence of Nazi death camps capable of killing up to two thousand people an hour using the gas Zyklon-B.

In 1943, British and American representatives met in Bermuda to discuss the situation but took no concrete action. Many Allied officials, though horrified, saw Hitler's "Final Solution" as just one part of a larger, worldwide holocaust in which tens of millions were dying. Appalled by the reluctance to act, Secretary of the Treasury Henry Morgenthau Jr. charged that the State Department's foot dragging made the United States an accessory to murder. "The matter of rescuing the Jews from extermination is a trust too great to remain in the hands of men who are indifferent, callous, and perhaps even hostile," he wrote bitterly in 1944. Later that year, stirred by Morgenthau's well-documented plea, Roosevelt created the War Refugee Board, which set up refugee camps in Europe and played a crucial role in saving 200,000 Jews from death. But, lamented one American official, "by that time it was too damned late to do too much." By war's end, the Nazis had systematically murdered almost 11 million people.

LIFE IN THE MILITARY

More than 15 million men and approximately 350,000 women served in the U.S. armed forces during World War II. Eighteen percent of American families had a father, son, or brother in the armed forces. Some of these men (and all of the women) volunteered, eager to defend their nation. But most who served—more than 10 million—were draftees. By presidential order, the military stopped accepting volunteers in December 1942. Faced with the challenge of filling a broad range of military positions while maintaining war production and the civilian economy, the Selective Service system and the new War Manpower Commission attempted to centralize control over the allocation of manpower. Their efforts were often defeated as tensions between local and national control remained strong throughout the war. Most Americans, however, believed that the draft operated fairly. Compared with the Civil War and the Vietnam War, the draft reached broadly and mostly equitably through the American population during World War II.

Selective Service   The Selective Service Act did allow deferments, but they did not disproportionately benefit the well-to-do. Almost 10,000 Princeton students or alumni served—as did all 4 of Franklin and Eleanor Roosevelt's sons—while throughout the nation judges offered minor criminal offenders the choice of the military or jail. The small number of college deferments was more than balanced by deferments for a long list of "critical occupations," including not only war industry workers but also almost 2 million agricultural workers. Most exemptions from military service were for men deemed physically or mentally unqualified to serve. Army physicians discovered what a toll the depression had taken on the nation's youth as draftees arrived with rotted teeth and deteriorated eyesight—signs of malnutrition. Army dentists pulled 15 million teeth and fitted men with dentures; optometrists prescribed 2.5 million pairs of glasses. Hundreds of thousands of men with venereal diseases were cured by sulfa drugs, developed in 1942. Military examiners also found evidence of the impact of racism and poverty. Half of African American draftees had no schooling beyond the sixth grade, and up to one-third were functionally illiterate. Forty-six percent of African Americans and almost one-third of European-Americans called for the draft were classified "4-F"—unfit for service.

Nonetheless, almost 12 percent of America's total population served in the military. Regiments were created rapidly, throwing together men from very different backgrounds. Regional differences were profound, and northerners and southerners often—literally—could not understand one another. Ethnic differences complicated things further. Although African Americans and Japanese Americans served in their own separate units, Hispanics, Native Americans, and Chinese Americans served in "white" units. Furthermore, the differences among "whites"—the "Italian" kid from Brooklyn and the one from rural Mississippi (or rural Montana)—were profound. The result was often tension, but many Americans became less prejudiced and less provincial as they served with men unlike themselves.

Fighting the War   Although military service was widespread, the burdens of combat were not equally shared. Although women served their nation honorably and often courageously, women's roles in the U.S. military were much more re-stricted than in the British or Soviet militaries, where women served as anti-aircraft gunners and in other combat-related positions. U.S. women served as nurses, in communications offices, and as typists or cooks. The recruiting slogan for the WACs (Women's Army Corps) was "Release a Man for Combat." However, most men in the armed forces never saw combat either; one-quarter never left the United States. The United States had the lowest "teeth-to-tail" ratio of any of the combatants, with each combat soldier backed up by eight or more support personnel. Japan's ratio was almost one to one. One-third of U.S. military personnel served in clerical positions, filled mainly by well-educated men. African Americans, though assigned dirty and dangerous tasks, were largely kept from combat service. In World War II, lower-class, less-educated white men bore the brunt of the fighting.

For those who fought, combat in World War II was as horrible as anything humans have experienced. Home-front audiences for the war films Hollywood churned out saw men die bravely, shot cleanly through the heart and comforted by their buddies in their last moments. What men experienced was carnage. Less than 10 percent of casualties were caused by bullets. Most men were killed or wounded by mortars, bombs, or grenades. Seventy-five thousand American men remained missing in action at the end of the war, blown into fragments of flesh too small to identify. Combat meant days and weeks of unrelenting rain in malarial jungles, sliding down a mud-slicked hill to land in a pile of putrid corpses. It meant drowning in the waters of the frigid North Atlantic amid burning wreckage of a torpedoed ship. It meant using flamethrowers that burned at 2,000 degrees Fahrenheit on other human beings. It meant being violently ill on a landing craft steering through floating body parts of those who had attempted the landing first, knowing that if you tripped you would likely drown under the 68-pound weight of your pack, and that if you made it ashore you would likely be blown apart by artillery shells. Service was "for the duration" of the war. Only death, serious injury, or victory offered release. In this hard world, men fought to victory.

In forty-five months of war, close to 300,000 American servicemen died in combat. Almost 1 million American troops were wounded, half of them seriously. Medical advances, such as the development of penicillin and the use of blood plasma to prevent shock, helped wounded men survive—but many never fully recovered from those wounds. Between 20 and 30 percent of combat casualties were psychoneurotic, as men were pushed past the limits of endurance. The federal government strictly censored images of American combat deaths for most of the war, consigning them to a secret file known as "the chamber of horrors." Americans at home rarely understood what combat had been like, and many men, upon return, never talked about their experiences in the war.

WINNING THE WAR

Axis hopes for victory depended on a short war. Leaders in Germany and Japan knew that, if the United States had time to fully mobilize, flooding the theaters of war with armaments and reinforcing Allied troops with fresh, trained men, the war was lost. However, powerful factions in the Japanese military and German leadership believed that the United States would concede if it met with early, decisive defeats. As Hitler, blinded by racial arrogance, had stated shortly after declaring war on the United States, "I don't see much future for the Americans.... It's a decayed country.... American society [is] half Judaized, and the other half Negrified. How can one expect a State like that to hold together." By mid-1942, the Axis powers understood that they had underestimated not only American resolve but also the willingness of other Allies to sacrifice unimaginable numbers of their citizens to stop the Axis advance (see Map 27.1). The chance of an Axis victory grew increasingly slim as the months passed, but though the outcome was virtually certain after spring 1943, two years of bloody fighting lay ahead.

Tensions Among the Allies   As the war continued, the Allies concentrated on defeating the aggressors, but their suspicions of one another undermined cooperation. The Soviets continued to press Britain and the United States to open a second front to the west of Germany and so draw German troops away from the USSR. The United States and Britain, however, continued to delay. Stalin was not mollified by the massive "thousand-bomber" raids on Germany begun by Britain's Royal Air Force in 1942, nor by the Allied invasion of Italy in the summer of 1943. With the alliance badly strained, Roosevelt sought reconciliation through personal diplomacy. The three Allied leaders met in Tehran, Iran, in December 1943. Stalin dismissed Churchill's repetitious justifications for further delaying a second front that would draw German troops away from the Soviet Union. Roosevelt had had enough, too; he also rejected Churchill's proposal for another peripheral attack, this time through the Balkans to Vienna. The three finally agreed to launch Operation Overlord—the cross-channel invasion of France—in early 1944. And the Soviet Union promised to aid the Allies against Japan once Germany was defeated.

War in Europe   The second front opened in the dark morning hours of June 6, 1944: D-Day. In the largest amphibious landing in history, more than 140,000 Allied troops under the command of American general Dwight D. Eisenhower scrambled ashore at Normandy, France. Thousands of ships ferried the men within one hundred yards of the sandy beaches. Landing craft and soldiers immediately encountered the enemy; they triggered mines and were pinned down by fire from cliffside pillboxes. Meanwhile, 15,500 Allied airborne troops, along with thousands of dummies meant to confuse the German defense, dropped from aircraft. Although heavy aerial and naval bombardment and the clandestine work of saboteurs had softened the German defenses, the fighting was ferocious.

By late July, 1.4 million Allied troops were fighting in France. They spread across the countryside, liberating France and Belgium by the end of August but leaving a path of devastation in their wake. Allied bombing, one British soldier wrote, left villages appearing "dead, mutilated and smothered, a gigantic sightless rubble heap so confounded by devastation as to suggest an Apocalypse." Almost 37,000 Allied troops died in that struggle, and up to 20,000 French civilians were killed. In September, the Allies pushed into Germany. German armored divisions counterattacked in Belgium's Ardennes Forest in December, hoping to push on to Antwerp to halt the flow of Allied supplies through that Belgian port. After weeks of heavy fighting in what has come to be called the Battle of the Bulge—because of a "bulge" 60 miles deep and 40 miles wide where German troops had pushed back the Allied line—the Allies gained control in late January 1945.

By that point, "strategic" bombing (though not nearly as precise as was publicly claimed) had destroyed Germany's war-production capacity and devastated its economy. In early 1945, the British and Americans began "morale" bombing, killing tens of thousands of civilians in aerial attacks on Berlin and then Dresden. Meanwhile, battle-hardened Soviet troops marched through Poland and cut a path to Berlin. American forces crossed the Rhine River in March 1945 and captured the heavily industrial Ruhr valley. Several units peeled off to enter Austria and Czechoslovakia, where they met up with Soviet soldiers.

Robert Capa/Magnum Photos, Inc.

U.S. troops land at Normandy during the D-Day invasion on June 6, 1944. Men drowned as they lost their footing in the rough surf and were pulled under by the weight of their 68-pound packs; others were torn by artillery or machine gun fire from German gun batteries on the cliffs that rose steeply from the beaches. About 2,500 Allied troops died in the D-Day invasion. Together, Allied and German troops suffered more than 450,000 casualties (killed, missing, or wounded) during the Battle of Normandy, which lasted until the end of August.

Yalta Conference   Even as Allied forces faced the last, desperate resistance from German troops in the Battle of the Bulge, Allied leaders began planning the peace. In early 1945, Franklin Roosevelt, by this time very ill, called for a summit meeting to discuss a host of political questions— including what to do with Germany. The three Allied leaders met at Yalta, in the Russian Crimea, in February 1945. Each had definite goals for the shape of the postwar world. Britain, its formerly powerful empire now vulnerable and shrinking, sought to protect its colonial possessions and to limit Soviet power. The Soviet Union, with 21 million dead, wanted Germany to pay reparations to fund its massive rebuilding effort. The Soviets hoped to expand their sphere of influence throughout eastern Europe and to guarantee their national security; Germany, Stalin insisted, must be permanently weakened. Two German invasions in a quarter-century were more than enough.

The United States, like the other powers, hoped to expand its influence and to control the peace. To that end, Roosevelt lobbied for the United Nations Organization, approved in principle the previous year at Dumbarton Oaks in Washington, D.C., through which the United States hoped to exercise influence. The lessons of World War I also shaped American proposals; seeking long-term peace and stability, the United States hoped to avoid the debts-reparations fiasco that had plagued Europe after the First World War. U.S. goals included self-determination for liberated peoples; gradual and orderly decolonization; and management of world affairs by what Roosevelt had once called the Four Policemen: the Soviet Union, Great Britain, the United States, and China. (Roosevelt hoped China might help stabilize Asia after the war; the United States abolished the Chinese Exclusion Act in 1943 in an attempt to consolidate ties between the two nations.) The United States was also determined to limit Soviet influence in the postwar world. Obviously, there was much about which to disagree.

Military positions at the time of the Yalta conference helped shape the negotiations. Soviet troops occupied eastern European nations they had liberated, including Poland, where Moscow had installed a pro-Soviet regime despite a British-supported Polish government-in-exile in London. With Soviet troops in place in eastern Europe, Britain and the United States were limited in what they could negotiate regarding these lands. As for Germany, the Big Three agreed that some eastern German territory would be transferred to Poland and the remainder divided into four zones—the fourth zone to be administered by France, which Britain had pressed to be included in plans for postwar control of Germany, so as to reduce the Soviet zone from one-third to one-quarter. Berlin, within the Soviet zone, would also be divided among the four victors. Yalta marked the high point of the Grand Alliance; in the tradition of diplomatic give-and-take, each of the Allies came away with something it wanted. In exchange for U.S. promises to support Soviet claims on territory lost to Japan in the Russo-Japanese War of 1904–1905, Stalin agreed to sign a treaty of friendship with Jiang Jieshi (Chiang Kai-shek), America's ally in China, rather than with the communist Mao Zedong (Mao Tse-tung), and to declare war on Japan two or three months after Hitler's defeat.

Harry Truman   Franklin D. Roosevelt, reelected to an unprecedented fourth term in November 1944, did not live to see the war's end. He died on April 12, and Vice President Harry S Truman became president and

MAP 27.3 The Pacific War

The strategy of the United States was to "island-hop"—from Hawai'i in 1942 to Iwo Jima and Okinawa in 1945. Naval battles were also decisive, notably the Battles of the Coral Sea and Midway in 1942. The war in the Pacific ended with Japan's surrender on August 15, 1945 (V-J Day).

commander-in-chief. Truman, a senator from Missouri who had replaced former vice president Henry Wallace as Roosevelt's running mate in 1944, was inexperienced in foreign policy. He was not even informed about the top-secret atomic weapons project until after he became president. The day after Roosevelt's death, Truman sought out old friends, Democrats and Republicans, in Congress, to ask their help in this "terrible job." Shortly afterward, he told reporters, "Boys, if you ever pray, pray for me now. I don't know whether you fellows ever had a load of hay fall on you, but when they told me yesterday what had happened, I felt like the moon, the stars, and all the planets had fallen on me." Eighteen days into Truman's presidency, Adolf Hitler killed himself in a bunker in bomb-ravaged Berlin. On May 8, Germany surrendered.

As the great powers jockeyed for influence after Germany's surrender, the Grand Alliance began to crumble. At the Potsdam Conference in mid-July, Truman—a novice at international diplomacy—was less patient with the Soviets than Roosevelt had been. And Truman learned during the conference that a test of the new atomic weapon had been successful. The United States, possessing such a weapon, no longer needed the Soviet Union's help in fighting the Pacific war. Roosevelt had secretly promised Stalin territory from Japan's wartime holdings in exchange for help in defeating Japan; the bomb made those concessions unnecessary. The Allies did agree that Japan must surrender unconditionally. But with the defeat of Hitler and the end of the European war, the wartime bonds among the Allies were strained to breaking.

War in the Pacific

In the Pacific, the war continued. Since halting the Japanese advance in the Battle of Midway in June 1942, American strategy had been to "island-hop" toward Japan, skipping the most strongly fortified islands whenever possible and taking the weaker ones, aiming to strand the Japanese armies on their island outposts. To cut off supplies being shipped from Japan's home islands, Americans also targeted the Japanese merchant marine. Allied and Japanese forces fought savagely for control of tiny specks of land scattered throughout the Pacific. By 1944, Allied troops—from the United States, Britain, Australia, and New Zealand—had secured the Solomon, Gilbert, Marshall, and Mariana Islands. General Douglas MacArthur landed at Leyte to retake the Philippines for the United States in October 1944.

In February 1945, while the Big Three were meeting at Yalta, U.S. and Japanese troops battled for Iwo Jima, an island less than 5 miles long, located about 700 miles south of Tokyo. Twenty-one thousand Japanese defenders occupied the island's high ground. Hidden in a network of caves, trenches, and underground tunnels, they were protected from the aerial bombardment that U.S. forces used to clear the way for an amphibious landing. The stark volcanic island offered no cover, and marines were slaughtered as they came ashore. For twenty days, U.S. forces fought their way, yard by yard, up Mount Suribachi, the highest and most heavily fortified point on Iwo Jima. The struggle for Iwo Jima cost the lives of 6,821 Americans and more than 20,000 Japanese—some of whom committed suicide rather than surrender. Only 200 Japanese survived.

A month later, American troops landed on Okinawa, an island in the Ryukyus chain at the southern tip of Japan, from which Allied forces planned to invade the main Japanese islands. Fighting raged for two months; death was everywhere. The monsoon rains began in May, turning battlefields into seas of mud filled with decaying corpses. The supporting fleet endured waves of mass kamikaze (suicide) attacks, in which Japanese pilots intentionally crashed bomb-laden planes into American ships. Almost 5,000 seamen perished in these attacks. On Okinawa, 7,374 American soldiers and marines died in battle. Almost the entire Japanese garrison of 100,000 was killed. More than one-quarter of Okinawa's people, or approximately 80,000 civilians, perished as the two powers struggled over their island.

Bombing of Japan

Even with American forces entrenched just 350 miles from Japan's main islands, Japanese leaders still refused to admit defeat. A powerful military faction was determined to preserve the emperor's sovereignty and to avoid the humiliation of an unconditional surrender. They hung on even while American bombers leveled their cities. On the night of March 9, 1945, 333 American B-29 Superfortresses dropped a mixture of explosives and incendiary devices on a 4-by-3-mile area of Tokyo. Attempting to demonstrate the strategic value of airpower, they created a firestorm, a blaze so fierce that it sucked all the oxygen from the air, creating hurricane-force winds and growing so hot it could melt concrete and steel. Almost 100,000 people were incinerated, suffocated, or boiled to death in canals where they had taken refuge from the fire. Over the following five months, American bombers attacked sixty-six Japanese cities, leaving 8 million people homeless, killing almost 900,000.

Japan, at the same time, was attempting to bomb the U.S. mainland. Thousands of bomb-bearing high-altitude balloons, constructed out of rice paper and potato-flour paste by schoolgirls, were launched into the jet stream. Those that did reach the United States fell on unpopulated areas, occasionally starting forest fires. The only mainland U.S. casualties in the war were five children and an adult on a Sunday school picnic in Oregon who accidentally detonated a balloon bomb that they found in the underbrush. As General Yamamoto had realized at the war's beginning, American resources would far outlast Japan's.

Early in the summer of 1945, Japan began to send out peace feelers through the Soviets. Japan was not, however, willing to accept the "unconditional surrender" terms on which the Allied leaders had agreed at Potsdam, and Truman and his advisers chose not to pursue a negotiated peace. By this time, U.S. troops were mobilizing for an invasion of the Japanese home islands. The experiences of Iwo Jima and Okinawa weighed heavily in the planning; Japanese troops had fought on, well past any hope of victory, and death tolls for Japanese and American troops alike had been enormous. News of the success of the Manhattan Project offered another option, and President Truman took it. Using atomic bombs on Japan, Truman believed, would end the war quickly and save American lives.

Historians still debate Truman's decision to use the atomic bomb. Why would he not negotiate surrender terms? Was Japan on the verge of an unconditional surrender, as some argue? Or was the antisurrender faction of Japanese military leaders strong enough to prevail? Truman knew the bomb could give the United States both real and psychological power in negotiating the peace; how much did his desire to demonstrate the bomb's power to the Soviet Union, or to prevent the Soviets from playing a major role in the last stages of the Pacific war, influence his decision? Did racism or a desire for retaliation play a role? How large were the projected casualty figures for invasion on which Truman based his decision, and were they accurate? No matter the answers to these ongoing debates, bombing (whether conventional or atomic) fit the established U.S. strategy of using machines rather than men whenever possible.

The decision to use the bomb did not seem as momentous to Truman as it does in retrospect. The moral line had already been crossed, as the move to wholesale bombing of civilian populations continued throughout the war: The Japanese had bombed the Chinese city of Shanghai in 1937. Germans had "terror-bombed" Warsaw, Rotterdam, and London. British and American bombers had purposely created firestorms in German cities; on a single night in February 1945, 225,000 people perished in the bombing of Dresden. The American bombing of Japanese cities—accomplished with conventional weapons—had already killed close to a million people and destroyed 56 square miles of Tokyo alone. What distinguished the atomic bombs from conventional bombs was their power and their efficiency—not that they killed huge numbers of innocent civilians in unspeakably awful ways.

On July 26, 1945, the Allies delivered an ultimatum to Japan: promising that the Japanese people would not be "enslaved," the Potsdam Declaration called for the Japanese to surrender unconditionally or face "prompt and utter destruction." Tokyo radio announced that the government would respond with *mokusatsu* (literally, "kill with silence," or ignore the ultimatum). On August 6, 1945, a B-29 bomber named after the pilot's mother, the *Enola Gay*, dropped an atomic bomb above the city of Hiroshima. A flash of dazzling light shot across the sky; then a huge, purplish mushroom cloud boiled forty thousand feet into the atmosphere. Much of the city was leveled by the blast. The bomb ignited a firestorm, and thousands who survived the initial blast burned to death. Approximately 130,000 people were killed. Tens of thousands more would suffer the effects of radiation poisoning.

American planes continued their devastating conventional bombing. On August 8, the Soviet Union declared war on Japan. On August 9, a second American atomic bomb fell on Nagasaki, killing at least 60,000 people. Five days later, on August 14, Japan surrendered. Recent histories argue that the Soviet declaration of war played a much more significant role in Japan's decision to surrender than America's use of atomic weapons. In the end, the Allies promised that the Japanese emperor could remain as the nation's titular head. Formal surrender ceremonies were held September 2 aboard the battleship *Missouri* in Tokyo Bay. The Second World War was over.

SUMMARY

Hitler once prophesied, "We may be destroyed, but if we are, we shall drag a world with us—a world in flames." In that, at least, Hitler was right. World War II devastated much of the globe. In Asia and in Europe, ghostlike people wandered through rubble, searching desperately for food. One out of nine people in the Soviet Union had perished: a total of at least 21 million civilian and military war dead. The Chinese calculated their war losses at 10 million; the Germans and Austrians at 6 million; the Japanese at 2.5 million. Up to 1 million died of famine in Japanese-controlled Indochina. Almost 11 million people had been systematically murdered in Nazi death camps. Across the globe, the Second World War killed at least 55 million people.

Waging war required the cooperation of Allied nations with very different goals and interests. Tensions among them remained high throughout the war, as the United States and Britain resisted Stalin's demands that they open a second front to draw German soldiers away from the Soviet Union. The United States, meanwhile, was fighting a brutal war in the Pacific, pushing Japanese forces back toward their home islands. By the time Japan surrendered in August 1945, the strains between the Soviet Union and its English-speaking Allies made postwar peace and stability unlikely.

American men and machines were a critical part of the Allied war effort. Although Americans did not join in the perfect unity and shared sacrifice suggested by current descriptions of "the greatest generation," American servicemen covered the globe, from the Arctic to the tropics. And on the home front, Americans worked around the clock to make the weapons that would win the war. Although they made sacrifices during the war—including almost 300,000 who gave their lives— many Americans found that the war had changed their lives for the better. Mobilization for war ended the Great Depression, reducing unemployment practically to zero. War jobs demanded workers, and Americans moved in huge numbers to war-production centers. The influx of workers strained the resources of existing communities and sometimes led to social friction and even violence. But many Americans—African Americans, Mexican Americans, women, poor whites from the South— found new opportunities for employment in well-paid war jobs.

The federal government, in order to manage the nation's war efforts, became a stronger presence in the lives of individual Americans—regulating business and employment; overseeing military conscription, training, and deployment; and even controlling what people could buy to eat or to wear. The Second World War was a powerful engine of social change.

Americans emerged from World War II fully confident that theirs was the greatest country in the world. It was certainly the most powerful. At war's end, only the United States had the capital and economic resources to spur international recovery; only the United States was more prosperous and more secure than when war began. In the coming struggle to fashion a new world out of the ashes of the old, soon to be called the Cold War, the United States held a commanding position. For better or worse—and clearly there were elements of each—the Second World War was a turning point in the nation's history.

28

THE COLD WAR AND AMERICAN GLOBALISM 1945–1961

CHAPTER OUTLINE

• From Allies to Adversaries • Containment in Action • The Cold War in Asia • The Korean War • *LINKS TO THE WORLD The People-to-People Campaign* • Unrelenting Cold War • The Struggle for the Third World • Summary

---

FROM ALLIES TO ADVERSARIES

The Second World War had a deeply unsettling effect on the international system. At its end, Germany was in ruins. Great Britain was badly overstrained and exhausted; France, having endured five years of Nazi occupation, was rent by internal division. Italy also emerged drastically weakened and, in Asia, Japan was decimated and under occupation and China was headed toward a renewed civil war. Throughout Europe and Asia, factories, transportation, and communications links had been reduced to rubble. Agricultural production plummeted, and displaced persons wandered about in search of food and family. How would the devastated economic world be pieced back together? The United States and the Soviet Union, though allies in the war, offered very different answers and models. The collapse of Germany and Japan, moreover, had created power vacuums that drew the two major powers into collision as they sought influence in countries where the Axis aggressors had once held sway. And the political turmoil that many nations experienced after the war also spurred Soviet-American competition. For example, in Greece and China, where civil wars raged between leftists and conservative regimes, the two powers supported different sides.

Decolonization   The international system also experienced instability because empires were disintegrating, creating the new Third World. Financial constraints and nationalist rebellions forced the imperial states to set their colonies free. Britain exited India (and Pakistan) in 1947 and Burma and Sri Lanka

CHRONOLOGY

1945	Roosevelt dies; Truman becomes president
	Atomic bombings of Japan
1946	Kennan's "long telegram" criticizes USSR
	Vietnamese war against France erupts
1947	Truman Doctrine seeks aid for Greece and Turkey
	Marshall offers Europe economic assistance
	National Security Act reorganizes government
1948	Communists take power in Czechoslovakia
	Truman recognizes Israel
	United States organizes Berlin airlift
1949	NATO founded as anti-Soviet alliance
	Soviet Union explodes atomic bomb
	Mao's communists win power in China
1950	NSC-68 recommends major military buildup
	Korean War starts in June; China enters in fall
1951	United States signs Mutual Security Treaty with Japan
1953	Eisenhower becomes president
	Stalin dies
	United States helps restore shah to power in Iran
	Korean War ends
1954	Geneva accords partition Vietnam
	CIA-led coup overthrows Arbenz in Guatemala
1955	Soviets create Warsaw Pact
1956	Soviets crush uprising in Hungary
	Suez crisis sparks war in Middle East
1957	Soviets fire first ICBM and launch *Sputnik*
1958	U.S. troops land in Lebanon
	Berlin crisis
1959	Castro ousts Batista in Cuba
1960	Eighteen African colonies become independent
	Vietcong organized in South Vietnam

(Ceylon) in 1948. The Philippines gained independence from the United States in 1946. After four years of battling nationalists in Indonesia, the Dutch left in 1949. In the Middle East, Lebanon (1943), Syria (1946), and Jordan (1946) gained independence, while in Palestine British officials faced growing pressure from Zionists intent on creating a Jewish homeland and from Arab leaders opposed to the prospect. In Iraq, too, nationalist agitation increased against the British-installed government. Washington and Moscow paid close attention to this anticolonial ferment, seeing these new or emerging Third World states as potential allies that might provide military bases, resources, and markets. Not all new nations were willing to play along; some chose nonalignment in the Cold War. "We do not intend to be the playthings of others," declared India's leader, Jawaharlal Nehru.

Stalin's Aims   Driven by different ideologies and different economic and strategic needs in this volatile international climate, the United States and the Soviet Union assessed their most pressing tasks in very different terms. The Soviets, though committed to seeking ultimate victory over the capitalist countries, were most concerned about preventing another invasion of their homeland. It was a territory much less secure than the United States, for reasons both geographic and historical. Its land mass was huge—three times as large as that of the United States—but it had only 10,000 miles of seacoast, much of which was under ice for a large part of the year. Russian leaders both before and after the revolution had made increased maritime access a chief foreign policy aim.

What is more, the geographical frontiers of the USSR were hard to defend. Siberia, vital for its mineral resources, lay 6,000 miles east of Moscow and was vulnerable to encroachment by Japan and China. In the west, the border with Poland had generated violent clashes ever since World War I, and eastern Europe had been the launching pad for Hitler's invasion in 1941: the resulting war cost the lives of 25 million Russians and caused massive physical destruction. Henceforth, Soviet leaders determined, they could have no dangers along their western borders.

Overall, however, Soviet territorial objectives were limited. Although many Americans were quick to compare Stalin to Hitler, Stalin did not have the Nazi leader's grandiose plans for world hegemony. In general, his aims resembled those of the czars before him: he wanted to push the USSR's borders to include the Baltic states of Estonia, Latvia, and Lithuania, as well as the eastern part of prewar Poland. Fearful of a revived Germany, he sought to ensure pro-Soviet governments in eastern Europe. To the south, Stalin wanted to have a presence in northern Iran, and he pressed the Turks to grant him naval bases and free access out of the Black Sea. Economically, the Soviet government promoted economic independence more than trade with other countries; suspicious of their European neighbors, they did not promote rapid rebuilding of the war-ravaged economies of the region or, more generally, expanded world trade.

U.S. Economic   The leadership in the United States, by contrast, came out of
and Strategic   the war highly confident about the immediate security of the
Needs   country's borders. Separated from the other world powers by
two vast oceans, the American home base had been virtually immune from attack during the fighting—only an occasional shell from a submarine or a hostile balloon reached the shores of the continental United States. American casualties were fewer than those of any of the other major combatants— hugely so in comparison with the Soviet Union. With its fixed capital intact, its resources more plentiful than ever, and in lone possession of the atomic bomb, the United States was the strongest power in the world at war's end.

Yet this was no time for complacency, Washington officials reminded one another. Some other power—almost certainly the USSR—could take advantage of the political and economic instability in war-torn Europe and Asia, and eventually seize control of these areas, with dire implications for America's physical and economic security. To prevent this outcome, officials in Washington sought forward bases overseas, in order to keep an airborne enemy at bay. To further enhance U.S. security, American planners, in direct contrast to their Soviet counterparts, sought the quick reconstruction of nations—including the former enemies Germany and Japan—and a world economy based on free trade. Such a system, they reasoned, was essential to preserve America's economic well-being.

The Soviets, on the other hand, refused to join the new World Bank and International Monetary Fund (IMF), created at the July 1944 Bretton Woods Conference by forty-four nations to stabilize trade and finance. They held that the United States dominated both institutions and used them to promote private investment and open international commerce, which Moscow saw as capitalist tools of exploitation. With the United States as its largest donor, the World Bank opened its doors in 1945 and began to make loans to help members finance reconstruction projects; the IMF, also heavily backed by the United States, helped members meet their balance-of-payments problems through currency loans.

Stalin and Truman

The personalities of the two countries' leaders also mattered. Joseph Stalin, though hostile to the western powers and capable of utter ruthlessness against his own people (his periodic purges since the 1930s had taken the lives of millions), had no wish for an immediate war. With the huge Russian losses in World War II, he was all too aware of his country's weakness vis-à-vis the United States. For a time at least, he appears to have believed he could achieve his aspirations peacefully, through continued cooperation with the Americans and the British. Over the long term, though, he envisaged more conflict. Stalin believed that Germany and Japan would rise again to threaten the USSR, probably by the 1960s, and his suspicion of the other capitalist powers knew no bounds. Many have concluded that Stalin was clinically paranoid: the first to do so, a leading Russian neuropathologist in 1927, died a few days later! As historian David Reynolds has noted, this paranoia, coupled with Stalin's xenophobia (fear of anything foreign) and his Marxist-Leninist ideology, created in the Soviet leader a mental map of "them" versus "us" that decisively influenced his approach to world affairs.

Harry Truman had none of Stalin's capacity for deception or ruthlessness, but to a lesser degree he, too, was prone to a "them" versus "us" world-view. Truman often glossed over nuances, ambiguities, and counterevidence; he preferred the simple answer stated in either/or terms. As Winston Churchill, who admired Truman's decisiveness, once observed, the president "takes no notice of delicate ground, he just plants his foot firmly on it." Truman constantly exaggerated, as when he declared in his undelivered farewell address that he had "knocked the socks off the communists" in Korea. Shortly after Roosevelt's death in early 1945, Truman met the Soviet commissar of foreign affairs, V. M. Molotov, at the White House. When the president sharply protested that the Soviets were not fulfilling the Yalta agreement on Poland, Molotov stormed out. Truman had self-consciously developed what he called his "tough method," and he bragged after the encounter that "I gave it to him straight one-two to the jaw." Truman's display of toughness became a trademark of American Cold War diplomacy.

The Beginning of the Cold War   At what point did the Cold War actually begin? No precise start date can be given. The origins must be thought of as a process, one that arguably began in 1917 with the Bolshevik Revolution and the western powers' hostile response, but in a more meaningful sense began in mid-1945, as World War II drew to a close. By the spring of 1947, certainly, the struggle had begun.

One of the first Soviet-American clashes came in Poland in 1945, when the Soviets refused to allow the Polish government-in-exile in London to be a part of the communist government that Moscow sponsored. The Soviets also snuffed out civil liberties in the former Nazi satellite of Romania, justifying their actions by pointing to what they claimed was an equivalent U.S. manipulation of Italy. Moscow initially allowed free elections in Hungary and Czechoslovakia, but as the Cold War accelerated and U.S. influence in Europe expanded, the Soviets encouraged communist coups in Hungary (1947) and Czechoslovakia (1948). Yugoslavia stood as a unique case: its independent communist government, led by Josip Broz Tito, successfully broke with Stalin in 1948.

To defend their actions, Moscow officials pointed out that the United States was reviving their traditional enemy, Germany. Twice in the lifetime of Soviet leaders Germany had wrought enormous suffering on Russia, and Stalin and his associates were determined to prevent a third occurrence. The Soviets also protested that the United States was meddling in eastern Europe. They cited clandestine American meetings with anti-Soviet groups, repeated calls for elections likely to produce anti-Soviet regimes, and the use of loans to gain political influence (financial diplomacy). Moscow charged that the United States was pursuing a double standard—intervening in the affairs of eastern Europe but demanding that the Soviet Union stay out of Latin America and Asia. Americans called for free elections in the Soviet sphere, Moscow noted, but not in the U.S. sphere in Latin America, where several military dictatorships ruled.

Atomic Diplomacy   The atomic bomb also divided the two major powers. The Soviets believed that the United States was practicing "atomic diplomacy"—maintaining a nuclear monopoly to scare the Soviets into diplomatic concessions. Secretary of State James F. Byrnes thought that the atomic bomb gave the United States bargaining power and could serve as a deterrent to Soviet expansion, but Secretary of War Henry L. Stimson thought otherwise in 1945. If Americans continued to have "this weapon rather ostentatiously on our hip," he warned Truman, the Soviets' "suspicions and their distrust of our purposes and motives will increase."

In this atmosphere of suspicion and distrust, Truman refused to turn over the weapon to an international control authority. In 1946, he backed the Baruch Plan, named after its author, financier Bernard Baruch. Largely a propaganda ploy, this

On March 5, 1946, former British prime minister Winston S. Churchill (1874–1965) delivered a speech, which he intended for a worldwide audience, at Westminster College in Fulton, Missouri. President Harry S. Truman (right) had encouraged Churchill (seated) to speak on two themes: the need to block Soviet expansion and the need to form an Anglo-American partnership. Always eloquent and provocative, Churchill denounced the Soviets for drawing an "iron curtain" across eastern Europe. This speech became one of the landmark statements of the Cold War.

Harry S Truman Library

proposal provided for U.S. abandonment of its atomic monopoly only after the world's fissionable materials were brought under the authority of an international agency. The Soviets retorted that this plan would require them to shut down their atomic-bomb development project while the United States continued its own. Washington and Moscow soon became locked in an expensive and frightening nuclear arms race.

By the middle of 1946, the wartime Grand Alliance was but a fading memory; that year, Soviets and Americans clashed on every front. When the United States turned down a Soviet request for a reconstruction loan but gave a loan to Britain, Moscow upbraided Washington for using its dollars to manipulate foreign governments. The two Cold War powers also backed different groups in Iran, where the United States helped bring the pro-West shah to the throne. Unable to agree on the unification of Germany, the former allies built up their zones independently.

Warnings from Kennan and Churchill

After Stalin gave a speech in February 1946 that depicted the world as threatened by capitalist acquisitiveness, the American chargé d'affaires in Moscow, George F. Kennan, sent a pessimistic "long telegram" to Washington. Kennan asserted that Soviet fanaticism made even a temporary understanding impossible. His widely circulated report fed a growing belief among American officials that only toughness would work with the Soviets. The following month, Winston Churchill delivered a stirring speech in Fulton, Missouri. The former British prime minister warned that a Soviet-erected "iron curtain" had cut off eastern European countries from the West. With an approving Truman sitting on the stage, Churchill called for Anglo-American partnership to resist the new menace.

The growing Soviet-American tensions had major implications for the functioning of the United Nations. The delegates who gathered in San Francisco in April 1945 to sign the U.N. charter had agreed on an organization that would include a General Assembly of all member states, as well as a smaller Security Council that would take the lead on issues of peace and security. Five great powers were given permanent seats on the council—the United States, the Soviet Union, Great Britain, China, and France. These permanent members could not prohibit discussion of any issue, but they could exercise a veto against any proposed action. To be effective on the major issues of war and peace, therefore, the U.N. needed great-power cooperation of the type that had existed in wartime but was a distant memory by mid-1946. Of the fifty-one founding states, twenty-two came from the Americas and another fifteen from Europe, which in effect gave the United States a large majority in the assembly. In retaliation, Moscow began to exercise its veto in the Security Council.

Some high-level U.S. officials were dismayed by the administration's harsh anti-Soviet posture. Secretary of Commerce Henry A. Wallace, who had been Roosevelt's vice president before Truman, charged that Truman's get-tough policy was substituting atomic and economic coercion for diplomacy. Wallace told a Madison Square Garden audience in September 1946 that "getting tough never brought anything real and lasting—whether for schoolyard bullies or businessmen or world powers. The tougher we get, the tougher the Russians will get." Truman soon fired Wallace from the cabinet, blasting him privately as "a real Commy and a dangerous man" and boasting that he, Truman, had now "run the crackpots out of the Democratic Party."

Truman Doctrine   East-West tensions escalated further in early 1947, when the British requested American help in Greece to defend their conservative client-government (a government dependent on the economic or military support of a more powerful country) in a civil war against leftists. In his March 12, 1947, speech to Congress, Truman requested $400 million in aid to Greece and Turkey. He had a selling job to do. The Republican Eightieth Congress wanted less, not more, spending; many of its members had little respect for the Democratic president whose administration the voters had repudiated in the 1946 elections by giving the GOP ("Grand Old Party," the Republican Party) majorities in both houses of Congress. Republican senator Arthur Vandenberg of Michigan, a bipartisan leader who backed Truman's request, bluntly told the president that he would have to "scare hell out of the American people" to gain congressional approval.

With that advice in mind, the president delivered a speech laced with alarmist language intended to stake out the American role in the postwar world. Truman claimed that communism, feeding on economic dislocations, imperiled the world. "If Greece should fall under the control of an armed minority," he gravely concluded in an early version of the domino theory, "the effect upon its neighbor, Turkey, would be immediate and serious. Confusion and disorder might well spread throughout the entire Middle East." Truman articulated what became known as the Truman Doctrine: "I believe that it must be the policy of the United States to support free peoples who are resisting attempted subjugation by armed minorities or by outside pressures."

Critics correctly pointed out that the Soviet Union was little involved in the Greek civil war, that the communists in Greece were more pro-Tito than pro-Stalin, and that the resistance movement had noncommunist as well as communist members. Nor was the Soviet Union threatening Turkey at the time. Others suggested that such aid should be channeled through the United Nations. Truman countered that, should communists gain control of Greece, they might open the door to Soviet power in the Mediterranean. After much debate, the Senate approved Truman's request by 67 to 23 votes. Using U.S. dollars and military advisers, the Greek government defeated the insurgents in 1949, and Turkey became a staunch U.S. ally on the Soviets' border.

Inevitable Cold War?   In the months after Truman's speech, the term *Cold War* slipped into the lexicon as a description of the Soviet-American relationship. Less than two years had passed since the glorious victory over the Axis powers, and the two Grand Alliance members now found themselves locked in a tense struggle for world dominance. It would last almost half a century. Could the confrontation have been avoided? Not altogether, it seems clear. Even before World War II had ended, perceptive observers anticipated that the United States and the USSR would seek to fill the power vacuum that would exist after the armistice, and that friction would result. The two countries had a history of hostility and tension, and both were militarily powerful. Most of all, the two nations were divided by sharply differing political economies with widely divergent needs and by a deep ideological chasm. Some kind of confrontation was destined to occur.

It is far less clear that the conflict had to result in a Cold War. The "cold peace" that had prevailed from the revolution in 1917 through World War II could conceivably have been maintained into the postwar years as well. Neither side's leadership wanted war. Both hoped—at least in the initial months—that a spirit of cooperation could be maintained. The Cold War resulted from decisions by individual human beings who might well have chosen differently, who might have done more, for example, to maintain diplomatic dialogue, to seek negotiated solutions to complex international problems. For decades, many Americans would wonder if the high price they were paying for victory in the superpower confrontation was necessary.

CONTAINMENT IN ACTION

Having committed themselves to countering Soviet and communist expansion, the Truman team had to figure out just how to fight the Cold War. The policy they chose, containment, was in place before the term was coined. George Kennan, having moved from the U.S. embassy in Moscow to the State Department in Washington, published an influential statement of the containment doctrine. Writing as "Mr. X" in the July 1947 issue of the magazine *Foreign Affairs*, Kennan advocated a "policy of firm containment, designed to confront the Russians with unalterable counterforce at every point where they show signs of encroaching upon the interests of a peaceful and stable world." Such counterforce, Kennan argued, would check Soviet expansion and eventually foster a "mellowing" of Soviet behavior. Along with the Truman Doctrine, Kennan's "X" article became a key manifesto of Cold War policy.

Lippmann's Critique   The veteran journalist Walter Lippmann took issue with the containment doctrine in his slim but powerful book *The Cold War* (1947), calling it a "strategic monstrosity" that failed to distinguish between areas vital and peripheral to U.S. security. If American leaders defined every place on earth as strategically important, Lippmann reasoned, the nation's patience and resources soon would be drained. Nor did Lippmann share Truman's conviction that the Soviet Union was plotting to take over the world. The president, he asserted, put too little emphasis on diplomacy. Ironically, Kennan himself agreed with much of Lippmann's critique, and he soon began to distance himself from the doctrine he had helped to create.

Invoking the containment doctrine, the United States in 1947 and 1948 began to build an international economic and defensive network to protect American prosperity and security, and to advance U.S. hegemony. In western Europe, the region of primary concern, American diplomats pursued a range of objectives, including economic reconstruction and fostering a political environment friendly to the United States. They sought the ouster of communists from governments, as occurred in 1947 in France and Italy, and blockage of "third force" or neutralist tendencies. To maintain political stability in key capitals, U.S. officials worked to keep the decolonization of European empires orderly. In Germany, they advocated the unification of the western zones. At the same time, American culture—consumer goods, music, consumption ethic, and production techniques—permeated European societies. Some Europeans resisted Americanization, but transatlantic ties strengthened.

Marshall Plan   The first instrument designed to achieve U.S. goals in western Europe was the Marshall Plan. European nations, still reeling economically and unstable politically, lacked the dollars to buy vital American-made goods. Americans, who had already spent billions of dollars on European relief and recovery by 1947, remembered all too well the troubles of the 1930s: global depression, political extremism, and war born of economic discontent. Such cataclysms could not be allowed to happen again; communism must not replace fascism. Western Europe, said one State Department diplomat, was "the keystone in the arch which supports the kind of a world which we have to have in order to conduct our lives."

In June 1947, Secretary of State George C. Marshall announced that the United States would finance a massive European recovery program. Launched in 1948, the Marshall Plan sent $12.4 billion to western Europe before the program ended in 1951 (see Map 28.1). To stimulate business at home, the legislation required that

© Cengage Learning

MAP 28.1 Divided Europe

After the Second World War, Europe broke into two competing camps. When the United States launched the Marshall Plan in 1948, the Soviet Union countered with its own economic plan the following year. When the United States created NATO in 1949, the Soviet Union answered with the Warsaw Pact in 1955. On the whole, these two camps held firm until the late 1980s.

Within the map:

ATLANTIC OCEAN

Reykjavik · ICELAND

💲 Participants in the Marshall Plan

Member of NATO, formed in 1949

Member of COMECON, formed in 1949, and the Warsaw Pact, organized in 1955

NORTHERN IRELAND
IRELAND · Dublin
UNITED KINGDOM
London ·

NORWAY · Oslo
SWEDEN · Stockholm
FINLAND · Helsinki
Moscow ·

North Sea

DENMARK · Copenhagen

NETHERLANDS · Amsterdam
BELGIUM · Brussels
LUX. · Luxembourg
Bonn · WEST GERMANY

West Berlin · Berlin · East Berlin
EAST GERMANY
Prague · CZECHOSLOVAKIA

Baltic Sea

UNION OF SOVIET SOCIALIST REPUBLICS

Exploded first atomic bomb, 1949

Warsaw · POLAND

Communist coup, 1948

FRANCE · Paris

SWITZ. · Bern
AUSTRIA · Vienna
Zones of occupation ended, 1955
Joined NATO, 1955

HUNGARY · Budapest
ROMANIA · Bucharest
Black Sea

YUGOSLAVIA · Belgrade
BULGARIA · Sofia

ITALY · Rome

ALBANIA · Tirana
GREECE · Athens
Joined NATO, 1952

TURKEY · Ankara
Joined NATO, 1952

Cyprus

Mediterranean Sea

PORTUGAL · Lisbon
SPAIN · Madrid
Joined NATO, 1982

Exploded first atomic bomb, 1960
Withdrew from NATO, 1966

Berlin blockade, 1948–1949

0   250   500 Miles
0   250   500 Kilometers

843

Europeans spend the foreign-aid dollars in the United States on American-made products. The Marshall Plan proved a mixed success; some scholars today even argue that Europe could have revived without it. The program caused inflation, failed to solve a balance-of-payments problem, took only tentative steps toward economic integration, and further divided Europe between "East" and "West." But the program spurred impressive western European industrial production and investment and started the region toward self-sustaining economic growth. From the American perspective, moreover, the plan succeeded because it helped contain communism.

National   To streamline the administration of U.S. defense, Truman
Security Act   worked with Congress on the National Security Act of July
1947. The act created the Office of Secretary of Defense (which became the Department of Defense two years later) to oversee all branches of the armed services, the National Security Council (NSC) of high-level officials to advise the president, and the Central Intelligence Agency (CIA) to conduct spy operations and information gathering overseas. By the early 1950s, the CIA had become a significant element in national security policy and had expanded its functions to include covert (secret) operations aimed at overthrowing unfriendly foreign leaders and, as a high-ranking American official put it, a "Department of Dirty Tricks" to stir up economic trouble in "the camp of the enemy." Taken together, the components of the National Security Act gave the president increased powers with which to conduct foreign policy.

In the wake of the Marshall Plan and the National Security Act, Stalin hardened his Cold War posture. He forbade communist satellite governments in eastern Europe to accept Marshall Plan aid and ordered communist parties in western Europe to work to thwart the plan. He also created the Cominform, an organization designed to coordinate communist activities around the world. It was a classic example of what historian Herbert Butterfield called the "security dilemma": whereas American planners saw the Marshall Plan as helping their European friends achieve security against a potential Soviet threat, in Stalin's mind it raised anew the specter of capitalist penetration. He responded by tightening his grip on eastern Europe—most notably, he engineered a coup in Czechoslovakia in February 1948 that ensured full Soviet control of the country—which in turn created more anxiety in the United States. In this way, the U.S.-Soviet relationship became a downward spiral that seemed to gain in velocity with each passing month.

Berlin Blockade   The German problem remained especially intractable. In June
and Airlift   1948, the Americans, French, and British agreed to fuse their
German zones, including their three sectors of Berlin. They sought to integrate West Germany (the Federal Republic of Germany) into the western European economy, complete with a reformed German currency. Fearing a resurgent Germany tied to the American Cold War camp, the Soviets cut off western land access to the jointly occupied city of Berlin, located well inside the Soviet zone. In response to this bold move, President Truman ordered a massive airlift of food, fuel, and other supplies to Berlin. Their spoiling effort blunted, the Soviets finally

lifted the blockade in May 1949 and founded the German Democratic Republic, or East Germany.

The successful airlift was a big victory for Harry Truman, and it may have saved his political career: he surprised pundits by narrowly defeating Republican Thomas E. Dewey in the presidential election that occurred in the middle of the crisis in November 1948. Safely elected, Truman took the major step of formalizing what was already in essence a military alliance among the United States, Canada, and the nations of western Europe. In April 1949, twelve nations signed a mutual defense treaty, agreeing that an attack on any one of them would be considered an attack on all, and establishing the North Atlantic Treaty Organization (NATO; see Map 28.1).

The treaty aroused considerable domestic debate, for not since 1778 had the United States entered a formal European military alliance, and some critics, such as Senator Robert A. Taft, Republican of Ohio, claimed that NATO would provoke rather than deter war. Other critics argued that the Soviet threat was political, not military. Administration officials themselves did not anticipate a Soviet military thrust against western Europe, but they responded that, should the Soviets ever probe westward, NATO would function as a "tripwire," bringing the full force of the United States to bear on the Soviet Union. Truman officials also hoped that NATO would keep western Europeans from embracing communism or even neutralism in the Cold War. The Senate ratified the treaty by 82 votes to 13, and the United States soon began to spend billions of dollars under the Mutual Defense Assistance Act.

By the summer of 1949, Truman and his advisers were basking in the successes of their foreign policy. Containment was working splendidly, they and many outside observers had concluded. West Germany was on the road to recovery. The Berlin blockade had been defeated, and NATO had been formed. In western Europe, the threat posed by communist parties seemed lessened. True, there was trouble in China, where the communists under Mao Zedong were winning that country's civil war. But that struggle would likely wax and wane for years or even decades to come, and besides, Truman could not be held responsible for events there. Just possibly, some dared to think, Harry Truman was on his way to winning the Cold War.

Twin Shocks   Then, suddenly, in late September, came the "twin shocks," two momentous developments that made Americans feel in even greater danger than ever before—two decades later, they were still dealing with the reverberations. First, an American reconnaissance aircraft detected unusually high radioactivity in the atmosphere. The news stunned U.S. officials: the Soviets had exploded an atomic device. With the American nuclear monopoly erased, western Europe seemed more vulnerable. At the same time, the communists in China completed their conquest—the end came more quickly than many expected. Now the world's largest and most populous countries were ruled by communists, and one of them had the atomic bomb. The bipartisan foreign policy of 1945–1948 broke down, as Republicans, bitter over Truman's reelection, declared that traitors in America must have given Stalin the bomb and allowed China to be "lost."

Rejecting calls by Kennan and others for high-level negotiations, Truman in early 1950 gave the go-ahead to begin production of a hydrogen bomb, the

"Super," and ordered his national security team to undertake a thorough review of policy. Kennan bemoaned the militarization of the Cold War and was replaced at the State Department by Paul Nitze. The National Security Council delivered to the president in April 1950 a significant top-secret document labeled NSC-68. Predicting continued tension with expansionistic communists all over the world and describing "a shrinking world of polarized power," the report, whose primary author was Nitze, appealed for a much enlarged military budget and the mobilization of public opinion to support such an increase. The Cold War was about to become a vastly more expensive, more far-reaching affair.

THE COLD WAR IN ASIA

Although Europe was the principal battleground in the early Cold War, Asia gradually became ensnared in the conflict as well. Indeed, it was in Asia that the consequences of an expansive containment doctrine would exact its heaviest price on the United States, in the form of large-scale and bloody wars in Korea and Vietnam. Though always less important to both superpowers than Europe, Asia would be the continent where the Cold War most often turned hot.

From the start, Japan was crucial to U.S. strategy. Much to Stalin's dismay, the United States monopolized Japan's reconstruction through a military occupation directed by General Douglas MacArthur, who envisioned turning the Pacific Ocean into "an Anglo-Saxon lake." Truman did not like "Mr. Prima Donna, Brass Hat" MacArthur, but the general initiated "a democratic revolution from above," as the Japanese called it, that reflected Washington's wishes. MacArthur wrote a democratic constitution, gave women voting rights, revitalized the economy, and destroyed the nation's weapons. U.S. authorities also helped Americanize Japan through censorship; films that hinted at criticism of the United States (for the destruction of Hiroshima, for example) or that depicted traditional Japanese customs, such as suicide, arranged marriages, and swordplay, were banned. In 1951, the United States and Japan signed a separate peace that restored Japan's sovereignty and ended the occupation. A Mutual Security Treaty that year provided for the stationing of U.S. forces on Japanese soil, including a base on Okinawa.

Chinese Civil War   The administration had less success in China. The United States had long backed the Nationalists of Jiang Jieshi (Chiang Kai-shek) against Mao Zedong's communists. But after the Second World War, Generalissimo Jiang became an unreliable partner who rejected U.S. advice. His government had become corrupt, inefficient, and out of touch with discontented peasants, whom the communists enlisted with promises of land reform. Jiang also subverted American efforts to negotiate a cease-fire and a coalition government. "We picked a bad horse," Truman admitted, privately denouncing the Nationalists as "grafters and crooks." Still, seeing Jiang as the only alternative to Mao, Truman backed him to the end.

American officials divided on the question of whether Mao was a puppet of the Soviet Union. Some considered him an Asian Tito—communist but independent—but most believed him to be part of an international communist movement that might give the Soviets a springboard into Asia. Thus, when the Chinese communists made secret overtures to the United States to begin diplomatic talks in 1945 and again in 1949, American officials rebuffed them. Mao decided to "lean" to the Soviet side in the Cold War. Because China always maintained a fierce independence that rankled the Soviets, before long a Sino-Soviet schism opened. Indeed, Mao deeply resented the Soviets' refusal to aid the communists during the civil war.

Then came Mao's victory in September 1949. Jiang fled to the island of Formosa (Taiwan), and in Beijing (formerly Peking) Mao proclaimed the People's Republic of China (PRC). Truman hesitated to extend diplomatic recognition to the new government, even after the British prime minister asked him, "Are we to cut ourselves off from all contact with one-sixth of the inhabitants of the world?" U.S. officials became alarmed by the 1950 Sino-Soviet treaty of friendship and by the harassment of Americans and their property in China. Truman also chose nonrecognition because a vocal group of Republican critics, the so-called China lobby, was winning headlines by asking the question "Who lost China?" The publisher Henry Luce, Senator William Knowland of California, and Representative Walter Judd of Minnesota pinned Jiang's defeat on Truman. The president stoutly answered that the self-defeating Jiang, despite billions of dollars in American aid, had proven a poor instrument of the containment doctrine. The administration nonetheless took the politically safe route and rejected recognition. (Not until 1979 did official Sino-American relations resume.)

Vietnam's Quest for Independence   Mao's victory in China drew urgent American attention to Indochina, the southeast Asian peninsula that had been held by France for the better part of a century. The Japanese had wrested control over Indochina during World War II, but even then Vietnamese nationalists dedicated to independence grew in strength. One leading nationalist, Ho Chi Minh, hoped to use Japan's defeat to assert Vietnamese independence, and he asked for U.S. support. American officials had few kind things to say about French colonial policy, and many were pessimistic that France could achieve a military solution to the conflict. Nevertheless, they rejected Ho's appeals in favor of a restoration of French rule, mostly to ensure France's cooperation in the emerging Soviet-American confrontation. In addition, the Truman administration was wary of Ho Chi Minh's communist politics. Ho, the State Department declared, was an "agent of international communism" who, it was assumed, would assist Soviet and, after 1949, Chinese expansionism. Overlooking the native roots of the nationalist rebellion against French colonialism, and the tenacious Vietnamese resistance to foreign intruders, Washington officials interpreted events in Indochina through a Cold War lens.

Even so, when war between the Vietminh and France broke out in 1946, the United States initially took a hands-off approach. But when Jiang's regime collapsed in China three years later, the Truman administration made two crucial decisions—both of them in early 1950, before the Korean War. First, in February, Washington recognized the French puppet government of Bao Dai, an intelligent but lazy former emperor who had collaborated with the French and Japanese. In the eyes of many Vietnamese, the United States thus became in essence a colonial power, an ally of the hated French. Second, in May, the administration agreed to send weapons and other assistance to sustain the French in Indochina. From 1945 to 1954, the United States gave $2 billion of the $5 billion that France spent to keep Vietnam within its empire—to no avail (see Chapters 30 and 31). How Vietnam ultimately became the site of a major American war, and how the world's most powerful nation failed to subdue a peasant people who suffered enormous losses, is one of the most remarkable and tragic stories of modern U.S. history.

THE KOREAN WAR

Before Vietnam, however, the United States would fight another large-scale military conflict, in Korea. In the early morning of June 25, 1950, a large military force of the Democratic People's Republic of Korea (North Korea) moved across the 38th parallel into the Republic of Korea (South Korea). Colonized by Japan since 1910, Korea had been divided in two by the victorious powers after Japan's defeat in 1945. Although the Soviets had armed the North and the Americans had armed the South (U.S. aid had reached $100 million a year), the Korean War began as a civil war. Virtually from the moment of the division, the two parts had been skirmishing along their supposedly temporary border while antigovernment (and anti-U.S.) guerrilla fighting flared in the South.

Both the North's communist leader, Kim Il Sung, and the South's president, Syngman Rhee, sought to reunify their nation. Kim's military in particular gained

© Bettmann/Corbis

Soldiers from Company D First Marine Division, mounted on a M-26 tank, spearhead a patrol in search of guerrillas during the Korean War.

strength when tens of thousands of battle-tested Koreans returned home in 1949 after serving in Mao's army. Displaying the Cold War mentality of the time, however, President Truman claimed that the Soviets had masterminded the North Korean attack. "Communism was acting in Korea just as Hitler, Mussolini, and the Japanese had acted," he said, recalling Axis aggression.

Actually, Kim had to press a doubting Joseph Stalin, who only reluctantly approved the attack after Kim predicted an easy, early victory and after Mao backed Kim. Whatever Stalin's reasoning, his support for Kim's venture remained lukewarm. When the U.N. Security Council voted to defend South Korea against the invasion from the north, the Soviet representative was not even present to veto the resolution because the Soviets were boycotting the United Nations to protest its refusal to grant membership to the People's Republic of China. During the war, Moscow gave limited aid to North Korea and China, which grew angry at Stalin for reneging on promised Soviet airpower. Stalin, all too aware of his strategic inferiority vis-à-vis the United States, did not want to be dragged into a costly war.

U.S. Forces Intervene   The president first ordered General Douglas MacArthur to send arms and troops to South Korea. He did not seek congressional approval—he and his aides feared that lawmakers would initiate a lengthy debate—and thereby set the precedent of waging war on executive authority alone. Worried that Mao might use the occasion to take Formosa, Truman also directed the Seventh Fleet to patrol the waters between the Chinese mainland and Jiang's sanctuary on Formosa, thus inserting the United States again into Chinese politics. After the Security Council voted to assist South Korea, MacArthur became commander of U.N. forces in Korea. Sixteen nations contributed troops to the U.N. command, but 40 percent were South Korean and about 50 percent American. In the war's early weeks, North Korean tanks and superior firepower sent the South Korean army into chaotic retreat. The first American soldiers, taking heavy casualties, could not stop the North Korean advance. Within weeks, the South Koreans and Americans had been pushed into the tiny Pusan perimeter at the tip of South Korea.

General MacArthur planned a daring operation: an amphibious landing at heavily fortified Inchon, several hundred miles behind North Korean lines. After U.S. guns and bombs pounded Inchon, marines sprinted ashore on September 15, 1950. The operation was a brilliant success, and the troops soon liberated the South Korean capital of Seoul and pushed the North Koreans back to the 38th parallel. Even before Inchon, Truman had redefined the U.S. war goal, changing it from the containment of North Korea to the reunification of Korea by force. Communism not only would be stopped; it would be rolled back.

Chinese Entry into the War   In September, Truman authorized U.N. forces to cross the 38th parallel. These troops drove deep into North Korea, and American aircraft began strikes against bridges on the Yalu River, the border between North Korea and China. The Chinese watched warily, fearing that the Americans would next stab at the People's Republic. Mao publicly warned that China could not permit the bombing of its transportation links with Korea and would not accept the annihilation of North Korea itself.

MacArthur shrugged off the warnings, and Washington officials agreed with the strong-willed general, drawing further confidence from the fact that, as MacArthur had predicted, the Soviets were not preparing for war.

MacArthur was right about the Soviets, but wrong about the Chinese. Mao, concluding that the "Americans would run more rampant" unless stopped, on October 25 sent Chinese soldiers into the war near the Yalu. Perhaps to lure American forces into a trap or to signal willingness to begin negotiations, they pulled back after a brief and successful offensive against South Korean troops. Then, after MacArthur sent the U.S. Eighth Army northward, tens of thousands of Chinese troops counterattacked on November 26, surprising American forces and driving them pell-mell southward. One U.S. officer termed it "a sight that hasn't been seen for hundreds of years: the men of a whole United States Army fleeing from a battlefield, abandoning their wounded, running for their lives."

Truman's Firing of MacArthur By early 1951, the front had stabilized around the 38th parallel. A stalemate set in. Both Washington and Moscow welcomed negotiations, but MacArthur had other ideas. The theatrical general recklessly called for an attack on China and for Jiang's return to the mainland. Now was the time, he insisted, to smash communism by destroying its Asian flank. Denouncing the concept of limited war (war without nuclear weapons, confined to one place), MacArthur hinted that the president was practicing appeasement. In April, backed by the Joint Chiefs of Staff (the heads of the various armed services), Truman fired MacArthur. The general, who had not set foot in the United States for more than a decade, returned home a hero, with ticker-tape parades and cheers on the lecture circuit. Truman's popularity sagged, but he weathered scattered demands for his impeachment.

Armistice talks began in July 1951, but the fighting and dying went on for two more years. The most contentious point in the negotiations was the fate of prisoners of war (POWs). Defying the Geneva Prisoners of War Convention (1949), U.S. officials announced that only those North Korean and Chinese POWs who wished to go home would be returned. Responding to the American statement that there would be no forced repatriation, the North Koreans denounced forced retention. Both sides undertook "reeducation" or "brainwashing" programs to persuade POWs to resist repatriation.

Peace Agreement As the POW issue stalled negotiations, U.S. officials made deliberately vague public statements about using atomic weapons in Korea. American bombers obliterated dams (whose rushing waters then destroyed rice fields), factories, airfields, and bridges in North Korea. Casualties on all sides mounted. Not until July 1953 was an armistice signed. Stalin's death in March and the advent of new leaders in both Moscow and Washington helped ease the way to a settlement that all sides welcomed. The combatants agreed to hand over the POW question to a special panel of neutral nations, which later gave prisoners their choice of staying or leaving. (In the end, 70,000 of about 100,000 North Korean and 5,600 of 20,700 Chinese POWs elected to return home; 21 American and 325 South Korean POWs of some 11,000 decided to stay in North Korea.) The North Korean–South Korean borderline was set near the 38th parallel, the prewar boundary, and a demilitarized zone was created between the two Koreas.

American casualties totaled 54,246 dead and 103,284 wounded. Close to 5 million Asians died in the war: 2 million North Korean civilians and 500,000 soldiers; 1 million South Korean civilians and 100,000 soldiers; and at least 1 million Chinese soldiers—ranking Korea as one of the costliest wars of the twentieth century.

Consequences of the War   The Korean War carried major domestic political consequences. The failure to achieve victory and the public's impatience with a stalemated war undoubtedly helped to elect Republican Dwight Eisenhower to the presidency in 1952, as the former general promised to "go to Korea" to end the war. The powers of the presidency grew as Congress repeatedly deferred to Truman. The president had never asked Congress for a declaration of war, believing that, as commander-in-chief, he had the authority to send troops wherever he wished. He saw no need to consult Congress—except when he wanted the $69.5 billion Korean War bill paid. In addition, the war, which occurred in the midst of the "who lost China?" debate, inflamed party politics in the United States. Republican lawmakers, including Wisconsin senator Joseph McCarthy, accused Truman and Secretary of State Dean Acheson of being "soft on communism" in failing first to prevent, and then to go all-out to win, the war; their verbal attacks strengthened the administration's determination to take an uncompromising position in the negotiations.

The impact on foreign policy was even greater. The Sino-American hostility generated by the war ensured that there would be no U.S. reconciliation with the Beijing government and that South Korea and Formosa would become major recipients of American foreign aid. The alliance with Japan strengthened as the island's economy boomed after filling large procurement orders from the United States. Australia and New Zealand joined the United States in a mutual defense agreement, the ANZUS Treaty (1951). The U.S. Army sent four divisions to Europe, and the administration initiated plans to rearm West Germany. The Korean War also persuaded Truman to do what he had been unwilling to do before the outbreak of hostilities—approve NSC-68. Indeed, the military budget shot up from $14 billion in 1949 to $44 billion in 1953; it remained between $35 billion and $44 billion a year throughout the 1950s. The Soviet Union sought to match this military buildup, and the result was a major arms race between the two nations. In sum, Truman's legacy was a highly militarized U.S. foreign policy active on a global scale.

UNRELENTING COLD WAR

The new foreign policy team of President Eisenhower and Secretary of State John Foster Dulles largely sustained Truman's Cold War policies. Both brought abundant experience in foreign affairs to their posts. Eisenhower had lived and traveled in Europe, Asia, and Latin America and, as a general during the Second World War, had negotiated with world leaders. After the war, he had served as army chief of staff and NATO supreme commander. Dulles had been closely involved with U.S. diplomacy since the first decade of the century. "Foster has been studying to be secretary of state since he was five years old," Eisenhower observed. He relied heavily on Dulles to be his emissary abroad. The secretary of state spent so much time traveling to world capitals that critics exclaimed, "Don't do something, Foster, just stand there!"

Eisenhower and Dulles accepted the Cold War consensus about the threat of communism and the need for global vigilance. Although Democrats promoted an image of Eisenhower as a bumbling, passive, aging hero, deferring most foreign policy matters to Dulles, the president in fact commanded the policymaking process and on occasion tamed the more hawkish proposals of Dulles and Vice President Richard Nixon. Even so, the secretary of state's influence was vast. Few Cold Warriors rivaled Dulles's impassioned anticommunism, often expressed in biblical terms. Though polished and articulate, he impressed people as arrogant, stubborn, and hectoring—and averse to compromise, an essential ingredient in successful diplomacy. Behind closed doors Dulles could show a different side, one considerably more flexible and pragmatic, but there is little evidence that he saw much utility in negotiations, at least where communists were involved. His assertion that neutrality was an "immoral and short-sighted conception" did not sit well with Third World leaders, who resented being told they had to choose between East and West.

"Massive Retaliation"

Dulles said that he considered containment too defensive a stance toward communism. He called instead for "liberation," although he never explained precisely how the countries of eastern Europe could be freed from Soviet control. "Massive retaliation" was the administration's plan for the nuclear obliteration of the Soviet state or its assumed client, the People's Republic of China, if either one took aggressive actions. Eisenhower said that it "simply means the ability to blow hell out of them in a hurry if they start anything." The ability of the United States to make such a threat was thought to provide "deterrence," the prevention of hostile Soviet behavior.

In their "New Look" for the American military, Eisenhower and Dulles emphasized airpower and nuclear weaponry. The president's preference for heavy weapons stemmed in part from his desire to trim the federal budget ("more bang for the buck," as the saying went). Galvanized by the successful test of the world's first hydrogen bomb in November 1952, Eisenhower oversaw a massive stockpiling of nuclear weapons—from 1,200 at the start of his presidency to 22,229 at the end. Backed by its huge military arsenal, the United States could practice "brinkmanship": not backing down in a crisis, even if it meant taking the nation to the brink of war. Eisenhower also popularized the "domino theory": that small, weak, neighboring nations would fall to communism like a row of dominoes if they were not propped up by the United States.

CIA as Foreign Policy Instrument

Eisenhower increasingly utilized the Central Intelligence Agency as an instrument of foreign policy. Headed by Allen Dulles, brother of the secretary of state, the CIA put foreign leaders (such as King Hussein of Jordan) on its payroll; subsidized foreign labor unions, newspapers, and political parties (such as the conservative Liberal Democratic Party of Japan); planted false stories in newspapers through its "disinformation" projects; and trained foreign military officers in counterrevolutionary methods. It hired American journalists and professors, secretly funded the National Student Association to spur contacts with foreign student leaders, used business executives as "fronts," and conducted experiments on unsuspecting Americans to determine the effects of "mind control" drugs (the MKULTRA program). The CIA also launched covert operations (including assassination schemes) to subvert or destroy governments in the Third World. The CIA helped overthrow the governments of Iran (1953) and Guatemala (1954) but failed in attempts to topple regimes in Indonesia (1958) and Cuba (1961).

The CIA and other components of the American intelligence community followed the principle of plausible deniability: covert operations should be conducted in such a way, and the decisions that launched them concealed so well, that the president could deny any knowledge of them. Thus, President Eisenhower disavowed any U.S. role in Guatemala, even though he had ordered the operation. He and his successor, John F. Kennedy, also denied that they had instructed the CIA to assassinate Cuba's Fidel Castro, whose regime after 1959 became stridently anti-American.

Nuclear Buildup

It did not take leaders in Moscow long to become aware of Eisenhower's expanded use of covert action as well as his stockpiling of nuclear weapons. They increased their own intelligence activity and tested their first H-bomb in 1953. Four years later, they shocked Americans by firing the world's first intercontinental ballistic missile (ICBM) and then propelling the satellite *Sputnik* into orbit in outer space. Americans felt more vulnerable to air attack and inferior in rocket technology, even though in 1957 the United States had 2,460 strategic weapons and a nuclear stockpile of 5,543, compared with the Soviet Union's 102 and 650. As President Eisenhower said, "If we were to release our nuclear stockpile on the Soviet Union, the main danger would arise not from retaliation but from fallout in the earth's atmosphere." The administration enlarged its fleet of long-range bombers (B-52s) and deployed intermediate-range missiles in Europe, targeted against the Soviet Union. At the end of 1960, the United States began adding Polaris missile-bearing submarines to its navy. To foster future technological advancement, the National Aeronautics and Space Administration (NASA) was created in 1958.

Overall, though, Eisenhower sought to avoid any kind of military confrontation with the Soviet Union and China; notwithstanding Dulles's tough talk of "liberation" and "massive retaliation," the administration was content to follow Truman's lead and emphasize the *containment* of communism. Eisenhower rejected opportunities to use nuclear weapons, and he proved more reluctant than many other Cold War presidents to send American soldiers into battle. He preferred to fight the Soviets at the level of propaganda. Convinced that the struggle against Moscow would in large measure be decided in the arena of international public opinion, he wanted to win the "hearts and minds" of people overseas. The "People-to-People" campaign, launched in 1956, sought to use ordinary Americans and nongovernmental organizations to enhance the international image of the United States and its people.

LINKS TO THE WORLD

The People–to–People Campaign

Not long after the start of the Cold War, U.S. officials determined that the Soviet-American confrontation was as much psychological and ideological as military and economic. One result was the People-to-People campaign, a state-private venture initiated by the United States Information Agency (USIA) in 1956, which aimed to win the "hearts and minds" of people around the world. In this program, American propaganda experts sought to channel the energies of ordinary Americans, businesses, civic organizations, labor groups, and women's clubs to promote confidence abroad in the basic goodness of the American people and, by extension, their government. In addition, the campaign was designed to raise morale at home by giving Americans a sense of personal participation in the Cold War struggle. The People-to-People campaign, one USIA pamphlet said, made "every man an ambassador."

Campaign activities resembled the home-front mobilization efforts of World War II. If, during the war, Americans were exhorted by the Office of War Information to purchase war bonds, now they were told that $30 could send a ninety-nine-volume portable library of American books to schools and libraries overseas. Publishers donated magazines and books for free distribution to foreign countries—*Woman's Day*, for example, volunteered six thousand copies of the magazine per month. People-to-People committees organized sister-city affiliations and "pen-pal" letter exchanges, hosted exchange students, and organized traveling "People-to-People delegations" representing their various communities.

The travelers were urged to behave like goodwill ambassadors when abroad and to "help overcome any feeling that America is a land that thinks money can buy everything." They were to "appreciate [foreigners'] manners and customs, not to insist on imitations of the American way of doing things."

To extol everyday life in the United States, Camp Fire Girls in more than three thousand communities took photographs on the theme "This is our home. This is how we live. These are my People." The photographs, assembled in albums, were sent to girls in Latin America, Africa, Asia, and the Middle East. The Hobbies Committee, meanwhile, connected people with interests in radio, photography, coins, stamps, and horticulture. One group represented dog owners, in the belief that "dogs make good ambassadors and are capable of hurdling the barriers of language and ideologies in the quest for peace."

Just what effect the People-to-People campaign had on foreign images of the United States is hard to say. The persistence to this day of the widespread impression that Americans are a provincial, materialistic people suggests that skepticism is in order. But alongside this negative image is a more positive one that sees Americans as admirably open, friendly, optimistic, and pragmatic; if the campaign did not erase the former impression, it may have helped foster the latter. Whatever role the People-to-People campaign played in the larger Cold War struggle, it certainly achieved one of its chief objectives: to link ordinary Americans more closely to people in other parts of the world.

In the same way, American cultural exchanges and participation in trade fairs in the Eisenhower years were used to create a favorable atmosphere abroad for U.S. political, economic, and military policies. Sometimes, the propaganda war was waged on the Soviets' own turf. In 1959, Vice President Richard Nixon traveled to Moscow to open an American products fair. In the display of a modern American kitchen, part of a model six-room ranch-style house, Nixon extolled capitalist consumerism, while Soviet premier Nikita Khrushchev, Stalin's successor, touted the merits of communism. The encounter became famous as the "kitchen debate."

Rebellion in Hungary   Eisenhower showed his restraint in 1956 when turmoil rocked parts of eastern Europe. In February, Khrushchev called for "peaceful coexistence" between capitalists and communists, denounced Stalin, and suggested that Moscow would tolerate different brands of communism. Revolts against Soviet power promptly erupted in Poland and Hungary, testing Khrushchev's new permissiveness. After a new Hungarian government in 1956 announced its withdrawal from the Warsaw Pact (the Soviet military alliance formed in 1955 with communist countries of eastern Europe), Soviet troops and tanks battled students and workers in the streets of Budapest and crushed the rebellion.

Although the Eisenhower administration's propaganda had been encouraging liberation efforts, U.S. officials found themselves unable to aid the rebels without igniting a world war. They stood by, promising only to welcome Hungarian immigrants in greater numbers than American quota laws allowed. Even so, the West could have reaped some propaganda advantage from this display of Soviet brute force had not British, French, and Israeli troops—U.S. allies—invaded Egypt during the Suez crisis just before the Soviets smashed the Hungarian uprising.

Hardly had the turmoil subsided when the divided city of Berlin once again became a Cold War flash point. The Soviets railed against the placement in West Germany of American bombers capable of carrying nuclear warheads, and they complained that West Berlin had become an escape route for disaffected East Germans. In 1958, Khrushchev announced that the Soviet Union would recognize East German control of all of Berlin unless the United States and its allies began talks on German reunification and rearmament. The United States refused to give up its hold on West Berlin or to break West German ties with NATO. Khrushchev backed away from his ultimatum but promised to press the issue again.

U-2 Incident   Khrushchev hoped to do just that at a summit meeting planned for Paris in mid-1960. But two weeks before the conference, on May 1, a U-2 spy plane carrying high-powered cameras crashed 1,200 miles inside the Soviet Union. Moscow claimed credit for shooting down the plane, which the Soviets put on display along with Francis Gary Powers, the captured CIA pilot, and the pictures he had been snapping of Soviet military sites. Khrushchev demanded an apology for the U.S. violation of Soviet airspace. When Washington refused, the Soviets walked out of the Paris summit—"a graveyard of lost opportunities," as a Soviet official put it.

While sparring over Europe, both sides kept a wary eye on the People's Republic of China, which denounced the Soviet call for peaceful coexistence. Despite evidence of a widening Sino-Soviet split, most American officials still treated communism as a monolithic world movement. The isolation separating Beijing and

Washington stymied communication and made continued conflict between China and the United States likely. In 1954, in a dispute over some miniscule islands off the Chinese coast—Mazu (Matsu) and the chain known as Jinmen (Quemoy)—the United States and the People's Republic of China lurched toward the brink. Taiwan's Jiang Jieshi held these islands and hoped to use them as a launching point for the counterrevolution on the mainland. Communist China's guns bombarded the islands in 1954. Thinking that U.S. credibility was at stake, Eisenhower decided to defend the outposts; he even hinted that he might use nuclear weapons. Why massive retaliation over such an insignificant issue? "Let's keep the Reds guessing," advised John Foster Dulles. "But what if they guessed wrong?" critics replied.

Formosa Resolution   In early 1955, Congress passed the Formosa Resolution, authorizing the president to deploy American forces to defend Formosa and adjoining islands. In so doing, Congress formally surrendered to the president what it had informally given up at the time of the Korea decision in 1950: the constitutional power to declare war. Although the crisis passed in April 1955, war loomed again in 1958 over Jinmen and Mazu. But this time, after Washington strongly cautioned him not to use force against the mainland, Jiang withdrew some troops from the islands. China then relaxed its bombardments. One consequence accelerated the arms race: Eisenhower's nuclear threats persuaded the Chinese that they, too, needed nuclear arms. In 1964, China exploded its first nuclear bomb.

THE STRUGGLE FOR THE THIRD WORLD

Like Truman before him and all Cold War presidents after him, Eisenhower worried most about the fate of western Europe. Over time, however, his administration focused more and more attention on the threat of communist expansion in Africa, Asia, Latin America, and the Middle East. In much of the Third World, the process of decolonization that began during the First World War accelerated after the Second World War, when the economically wracked imperial countries proved incapable of resisting their colonies' demands for freedom. A cavalcade of new nations cast off their colonial bonds (see Map 28.2). In 1960 alone, eighteen new African nations did so. From 1943 to 1994, a total of 125 countries became independent (the figure includes the former Soviet republics that departed the USSR in 1991). The emergence of so many new states in the 1940s and after, and the instability associated with the transfer of authority, shook the foundations of the international system. Power was redistributed, creating "near chaos," said one U.S. government report. In the traditional U.S. sphere of influence, Latin America, nationalists once again challenged Washington's dominance.

Interests in the Third World   By the late 1940s, when Cold War lines were drawn fairly tightly in Europe, Soviet-American rivalry shifted increasingly to the Third World. Much was at stake. The new nations could buy American goods and technology, supply strategic raw materials, and invite investments (more than one-third of America's private foreign investments were in

© Cengage Learning

MAP 28.2 The Rise of the Third World: Newly Independent Nations Since 1943

Accelerated by the Second World War, decolonization liberated many peoples from imperial rule. New nations emerged in the postwar international system dominated by the Cold War rivalry of the United States and the Soviet Union. Many newly independent states became targets of great-power intrigue but chose nonalignment in the Cold War.

Third World countries in 1959). And they could build cultural ties with the United States. Both great powers, moreover, looked to these new states for votes in the United Nations and sought sites within their borders for military and intelligence bases. But often poor and unstable—and rife with tribal, ethnic, and class rivalries—many new nations sought to end the economic, military, and cultural hegemony of the West. Many learned to play off the two superpowers against each other to garner more aid and arms. U.S. interventions—military and otherwise—in the Third World, American leaders believed, became necessary to impress Moscow with Washington's might and to resolve and counter the nationalism and radical anticapitalist social change that threatened American strategic and economic interests.

To thwart nationalist, radical, and communist challenges, the United States directed massive resources—foreign aid, propaganda, development projects—toward the Third World. By 1961, more than 90 percent of U.S. foreign aid was going to developing nations. Washington also allied with native elites and with undemocratic but anticommunist regimes, meddled in civil wars, and unleashed CIA covert operations. These American interventions often generated resentment among the local populace. When some of the larger Third World states—notably India, Ghana, Egypt, and Indonesia—refused to take sides in the Cold War, Secretary of State Dulles declared that neutralism was a step on the road to communism. Both he and Eisenhower insisted that every nation should take a side in the life-and-death Cold War struggle.

American leaders argued that technologically "backward" Third World countries needed western-induced capitalist development and modernization in order to enjoy economic growth, social harmony, and political moderation. Often these U.S. officials also ascribed stereotyped race-, age-, and gender-based characteristics to Third World peoples, seeing them as dependent, emotional, and irrational, and therefore dependent on the fatherly tutelage of the United States. Cubans, CIA director Allen Dulles told the National Security Council in early 1959, "had to be treated more or less like children. They had to be led rather than rebuffed. If they were rebuffed, like children, they were capable of almost anything."

At other times, American officials used gendered language, suggesting that Third World countries were weak women—passive and servile, unable to resist the menacing appeals of communists and neutralists. In speaking of India, for example—a neutralist nation that Americans deemed effeminate and submissive—Eisenhower condescendingly described it as a place where "emotion rather than reason seems to dictate policy."

Racism and Segregation as U.S. Handicaps   Race attitudes and segregation practices in the United States especially influenced U.S. relations with Third World countries. In 1955, G. L. Mehta, the Indian ambassador to the United States, was refused service in the whites-only section of a restaurant at Houston International Airport. The insult stung deeply, as did many similar indignities experienced by other Third World diplomats. Fearing damaged relations with India, a large nation whose allegiance the United States sought in the Cold War, John Foster Dulles apologized to Mehta. The secretary thought racial segregation in the United States was a "major international hazard," spoiling American efforts to win friends in Third World countries and giving the Soviets a propaganda advantage. American practices and ideals did not align.

Thus, when the U.S. attorney general appealed to the Supreme Court to strike down segregation in public schools, he underlined that the humiliation of dark-skinned diplomats "furnished grist for the Communist propaganda mills." When the Court announced its *Brown* decision in 1954, the government quickly broadcast news of the desegregation order around the world in thirty-five languages on its Voice of America overseas radio network. But the problem did not go away. For example, after the 1957 Little Rock crisis, Dulles remarked that racial bigotry was "ruining our foreign policy. The effect of this in Asia and Africa will be worse for us than Hungary was for the Russians." Still, when an office of the Department of State decided to counter Soviet propaganda by creating for the 1958 World's Fair in Brussels an exhibit titled "The Unfinished Work"—on race relations in the United States and strides taken toward desegregation—southern conservatives kicked up such a furor that the Eisenhower administration closed the display.

American hostility toward revolution also obstructed the quest for influence in the Third World. In the twentieth century, the United States openly opposed revolutions in Mexico, China, Russia, Cuba, Vietnam, Nicaragua, and Iran, among other nations. Americans celebrated the Spirit of '76 but grew intolerant of revolutionary disorder because many Third World revolutions arose against America's Cold War allies and threatened American investments, markets, and military bases. Preferring, like most other great powers in history, to maintain the status quo, the United States usually supported its European allies or the conservative, propertied classes in the Third World. In 1960, for example, when forty-three African and Asian states sponsored a U.N. resolution endorsing decolonization, the United States abstained from the vote.

Development and Modernization

Yet the American approach also had its element of idealism. Believing that Third World peoples craved modernization and that the American economic model of private enterprise and cooperation among business, labor, and government was best for them, American policymakers launched various "development" projects. Such projects held out the promise of sustained economic growth, prosperity, and stability, which the benefactors hoped would undermine radicalism. In the 1950s, the Carnegie, Ford, and Rockefeller Foundations worked with the U.S. Agency for International Development (AID) to sponsor a Green Revolution, a dramatic increase in agricultural production—for example, by the use of hybrid seeds. The Rockefeller Foundation supported foreign universities' efforts to train national leaders committed to nonradical development; from 1958 to 1969, the philanthropic agency spent $25 million in Nigeria. Before Dean Rusk became secretary of state in 1961, he served as president of the Rockefeller Foundation.

To persuade Third World peoples to abandon radical doctrines and neutralism, American leaders, often in cooperation with the business-sponsored Advertising Council, directed propaganda at developing nations. The United States Information Agency (USIA), founded in 1953, used films, radio broadcasts, the magazine *Free World*, exhibitions, exchange programs, and libraries (in 162 cities worldwide by 1961) to trumpet the theme of "People's Capitalism." Citing America's economic success—contrasted with "slave-labor" conditions in the Soviet Union—the message showcased well-paid American workers, political democracy, and religious freedom. To counter ugly pictures of segregation and white attacks on African Americans and civil rights activists in the South, the USIA applauded success stories of individual African Americans, such as boxers Floyd Patterson and Sugar Ray Robinson. In 1960 alone, some 13.8 million people visited U.S. pavilions abroad, including 1 million at the consumer-products exhibit "Tradeways to Peace and Prosperity" in Damascus, Syria.

Undoubtedly, the American way of life had appeal for some Third World peoples. They, too, wanted to enjoy American consumer goods, rock music, economic status, and educational opportunities. Hollywood movies offered enticing glimpses of middle-class materialism, and U.S. films dominated many overseas markets. Blue jeans, advertising billboards, and soft drinks flooded foreign societies. But if foreigners often envied Americans, they also resented them for having so much and wasting so much and for allowing their corporations to extract such high profits from overseas. Americans often received blame for the persistent poverty of the developing world, even though the leaders of those nations made decisions that hindered their own progress such as pouring millions of dollars into their militaries while their people needed food. Nonetheless, anti-American resentments could be measured in the late 1950s in attacks on USIA libraries in Calcutta, India; Beirut, Lebanon; and Bogotá, Colombia.

Intervention in Guatemala   When the more benign techniques of containment—aid, trade, cultural relations—proved insufficient to get Third World nations to line up on the American side in the Cold War, the Eisenhower administration often showed a willingness to press harder, by covert or overt means. Guatemala was an early test case. In 1951, leftist Jacobo Arbenz Guzmán was elected president of Guatemala, a poor country whose largest landowner was the American-owned United Fruit Company. United Fruit was an economic power throughout Latin America, where it owned 3 million acres of land and operated railroads, ports, ships, and telecommunications facilities. To fulfill his promise of land reform, Arbenz expropriated United Fruit's uncultivated land and offered compensation. The company dismissed the offer and charged that Arbenz posed a communist threat—a charge that CIA officials had already floated because Arbenz employed some communists in his government. The CIA began a secret plot to overthrow Arbenz. He turned to Moscow for military aid, thus reinforcing American suspicions. The CIA airlifted arms into Guatemala, dropping them at United Fruit facilities, and in mid-1954, CIA-supported Guatemalans struck from Honduras. U.S. planes bombed the capital city, and the invaders drove Arbenz from power. The new pro-American regime returned United Fruit's land, but an ensuing civil war staggered the Central American nation for decades.

The Cuban Revolution and Fidel Castro   Eisenhower also watched with apprehension as turmoil gripped Cuba in the late 1950s. In early 1959, Fidel Castro's rebels, or *barbudos* ("bearded ones"), driven by profound anti-American nationalism, ousted Fulgencio Batista, a long-time U.S. ally who had welcomed North American investors, U.S. military advisers, and tourists to the Caribbean island. Batista's corrupt, dictatorial regime had helped turn Havana into a haven for gambling and prostitution run by organized crime.

Robert Capa/Magnum Photos, Inc.

In the years 1948–1950, hundreds of thousands of Jewish refugees arrived in the state of Israel. Legendary war photographer Robert Capa snapped this picture of refugees arriving on a boat in Haifa in 1949. A few years later, while on assignment for Life *magazine, Capa would be killed by a land mine in Indochina.*

Cubans had resented U.S. domination ever since the early twentieth century, when the Platt Amendment had compromised their independence. Curbing U.S. influence became a rallying cry of the Cuban revolution, all the more so after the CIA conspired secretly but futilely to block Castro's rise to power in 1958. From the start, Castro sought to roll back the influence of American business, which had invested some $1 billion on the island, and to break the U.S. grasp on Cuban trade.

Castro's increasing authoritarianism, anti-Yankee declarations, and growing popularity in the hemisphere alarmed Washington. In early 1960, after Cuba signed a trade treaty with the Soviet Union, Eisenhower ordered the CIA to organize an invasion force of Cuban exiles to overthrow the Castro government. The agency also began to plot an assassination of the Cuban leader. When the president drastically cut U.S. purchases of Cuban sugar, Castro seized all North American–owned companies that had not yet been nationalized. Threatened by U.S. decisions designed to bring him and his revolution down, Castro appealed to the Soviet Union, which offered loans and expanded trade. Just before leaving office in early 1961, Eisenhower broke diplomatic relations with Cuba and advised president-elect John F. Kennedy to advance plans for the invasion, which came—and failed—in early 1961.

Arab-Israeli Conflict   In the Middle East, meanwhile, the Eisenhower administration confronted challenges posed by ongoing tensions between Arabs and Jews, and by nationalist leaders in Iran and Egypt. Prior to the end of World War II, only France and Britain among the great powers had been much concerned with this region of the world; they had effectively dominated the area during the prior three decades. But the dissolution of empires and the rise of Cold War tensions drew Washington into the region, as did the deepening tensions in British-held Palestine. From 1945 to 1947, Britain tried to enlist U.S. officials in the effort to find a solution to the vexing question of how to split Palestine between the Arabs and Jews who lived there. The Truman administration rejected London's solicitations, and the British, despairing at the violence between Arabs and Jews and at the rising number of British deaths, in 1947 turned the issue over to the United Nations, which voted to partition Palestine into separate Arab and Jewish states. Arab leaders opposed the decision, but in May 1948 Jewish leaders announced the creation of Israel.

The United States, which had lobbied hard to secure the U.N. vote, extended recognition to the new state mere minutes after the act of foundation. A moral conviction that Jews deserved a homeland after the suffering of the Holocaust, and that Zionism was a worthy movement that would create a democratic Israel, influenced Truman's decision, as did the belief that Jewish votes might swing some states to the Democrats in the 1948 election. These beliefs trumped some senior officials' concerns that Arab oil producers might turn against the United States and that close Soviet-Israeli ties could turn Israel into a pro-Soviet bastion in the Middle East. The Soviet Union did promptly recognize the new nation, but Israeli leaders kept Moscow at arm's length, in part because they had more pressing concerns. Palestinian Arabs, displaced from land they considered theirs, joined with Israel's Arab neighbors to make immediate war on the new state. The Israelis stopped the offensive in bloody fighting over the next six months until a U.N.-backed truce was called.

In the years thereafter, American policy in the Middle East centered on ensuring Israel's survival and cementing ties with Arab oil producers. U.S. oil holdings were extensive: American companies produced about half of the region's petroleum in the 1950s. Eisenhower consequently sought to avoid actions that might alienate Arab states, such as drawing too close to Israel, and he cultivated close relations with oil-rich Iran. Its ruling shah had granted American oil companies a 40 percent interest in a new petroleum consortium in return for CIA help in the successful overthrow, in 1953, of his rival, Mohammed Mossadegh, who had attempted to nationalize foreign oil interests. Nor was it only about petroleum: Iran's position on the Soviet border made the shah a particularly valuable friend.

American officials faced a more formidable foe in Egypt, in the form of Gamal Abdul Nasser, a towering figure in a pan-Arabic movement to reduce western interests in the Middle East. Nasser vowed to expel the British from the Suez Canal and the Israelis from Palestine. The United States wished neither to anger the Arabs, for fear of losing valuable oil supplies, nor to alienate its ally Israel, which was supported at home by politically active American Jews. But when Nasser declared neutrality in the Cold War, Dulles lost patience.

Suez Crisis

In 1956, the United States abruptly reneged on its offer to Egypt to help finance the Aswan Dam, a project to provide inexpensive electricity and water for thirsty Nile valley farmland. Secretary Dulles's blunt economic pressure backfired, for Nasser responded by nationalizing the

British-owned Suez Canal, intending to use its profits to build the dam. At a mass rally in Alexandria, Nasser expressed the profound nationalism typical of Third World peoples shedding an imperial past: "Tonight our Egyptian canal will be run by Egyptians. Egyptians!" Fully 75 percent of western Europe's oil came from the Middle East, most of it transported through the Suez Canal. Fearing an interruption in this vital trade, the British and French conspired with Israel to bring down Nasser. On October 29, 1956, the Israelis invaded Suez, joined two days later by British and French forces.

Eisenhower fumed. America's allies had not consulted him, and the attack had shifted attention from Soviet intervention in Hungary. The president also feared that the invasion would cause Nasser to seek help from the Soviets, inviting them into the Middle East. Eisenhower sternly demanded that London, Paris, and Tel Aviv pull their troops out, and they did. Egypt took possession of the canal, the Soviets built the Aswan Dam, and Nasser became a hero to Third World peoples. French and British influence in the region declined sharply. To counter Nasser, the United States determined to "build up" as an "Arab rival" the conservative King Ibn Saud of Saudi Arabia. Although the monarch renewed America's lease of an air base, few Arabs respected the notoriously corrupt Saud.

Eisenhower Doctrine

U.S. officials worried that a "vacuum" existed in the Middle East—and that the Soviets might fill it. Nasserites insisted that there was no vacuum but rather a growing Arab nationalism that provided the best defense against communism. In an effort to improve the deteriorating western position in the Middle East and to protect American interests there, the president proclaimed the Eisenhower Doctrine in 1957. The United States would intervene in the Middle East, he declared, if any government threatened by a communist takeover asked for help. In 1958, fourteen thousand American troops scrambled ashore in Lebanon to quell an internal political dispute that Washington feared might be exploited by pro-Nasser groups or communists. Concentrating the troops in the area of Beirut, Eisenhower said their mission was "not primarily to fight" but merely to show the flag. The restrained use of U.S. military power served to defuse the crisis, as Lebanese officials agreed to work for a peaceful transition to a new leadership. In Dulles's view, the intervention also served to "reassure many small nations that they could call on us in a time of crisis."

Cold War concerns also drove Eisenhower's policy toward Vietnam, where nationalists battled the French for independence. Despite a substantial U.S. aid program initiated under Truman, the French lost steadily to the Vietminh. Finally, in early 1954, Ho's forces surrounded the French fortress at Dienbienphu in northwest Vietnam. Although some of Eisenhower's advisers recommended a massive American air strike against Vietminh positions, perhaps even using tactical atomic weapons, the president moved cautiously. The United States had been advising and bankrolling the French, but it had not committed its own forces to the war. If American airpower did not save the French, would ground troops be required next, and in hostile terrain? As one high-level doubter remarked, "One cannot go over Niagara Falls in a barrel only slightly."

Worrying aloud about a communist victory, Eisenhower pressed the British to help form a coalition to address the Indochinese crisis, but they refused. At home, influential members of Congress—including Lyndon Baines Johnson of Texas, who as president would wage large-scale war in Vietnam—told Eisenhower they wanted "no more Koreas" and warned him against any U.S. military commitment, especially in the absence of cooperation from America's allies. Some felt very uneasy about supporting colonialism. The issue became moot on May 7, when the weary French defenders at Dienbienphu surrendered.

Geneva Accords on Vietnam   Peace talks, already under way in Geneva, brought Cold War and nationalist contenders together—the United States, the Soviet Union, Britain, the People's Republic of China, Laos, Cambodia, and the competing Vietnamese regimes of Bao Dai and Ho Chi Minh. John Foster Dulles, a reluctant participant, feared the communists would get the better of any agreement, yet in the end the Vietminh received less than their dominant military position suggested they should. The 1954 Geneva accords, signed by France and Ho's Democratic Republic of Vietnam, temporarily divided Vietnam at the 17th parallel; Ho's government was confined to the North, Bao Dai's to the South. Only after pressure from the Chinese and the Soviets, who feared U.S. intervention in Vietnam without an agreement, did Ho's government agree to this compromise. The 17th parallel was meant to serve as a military truce line, not a national boundary; the country was scheduled to be reunified after national elections in 1956. Meanwhile, neither North nor South was to join a military alliance or permit foreign military bases on its soil.

Confident that the Geneva agreements ultimately would mean communist victory, the United States from an early point set about trying to undermine them. Soon after the conference, a CIA team entered Vietnam and undertook secret operations against the North, including commando raids across the 17th parallel. In the South, the United States helped Ngo Dinh Diem push Bao Dai aside and inaugurate the Republic of Vietnam. A Catholic in a Buddhist nation, Diem was a dedicated nationalist and anticommunist, but he had little mass support. He staged a fraudulent election in South Vietnam that gave him 99 percent of the vote (in Saigon, he received 200,000 more votes than there were registered voters). When Ho and some in the world community pressed for national elections in keeping with the Geneva agreements, Diem and Eisenhower refused, fearing that the popular Vietminh leader would win. From 1955 to 1961, the Diem government received more than $1 billion in American aid, most of it military. American advisers organized and trained Diem's army, and American agriculturalists worked to improve crops. Diem's Saigon regime became dependent on the United States for its very existence, and the culture of South Vietnam became increasingly Americanized.

National Liberation Front   Diem proved a difficult ally. He acted dictatorially, abolishing village elections and appointing to public office people beholden to him. He threw dissenters in jail and shut down newspapers that criticized his regime. When U.S. officials periodically urged him to implement meaningful land reform, he blithely ignored them. Noncommunists and communists alike began to strike back at Diem's repressive government. In Hanoi,

Ho's government initially focused on solidifying its control on the North, but in the late 1950s it began to send aid to southern insurgents, who embarked on a program of terror, assassinating hundreds of Diem's village officials. In late 1960, southern communists, acting at the direction of Hanoi, organized the National Liberation Front (NLF), known as the Vietcong. The Vietcong in turn attracted other anti-Diem groups in the South. And the Eisenhower administration, all too aware of Diem's shortcomings and his unwillingness to follow American advice, continued to affirm its commitment to the preservation of an independent, noncommunist South Vietnam.

SUMMARY

The United States emerged from the Second World War as the preeminent world power. Confident in the nation's immediate physical security, Washington officials nevertheless worried that the unstable international system, an unfriendly Soviet Union, and the decolonizing Third World could upset American plans for the postwar peace. Locked with the Soviet Union in a "Cold War," U.S. leaders marshaled their nation's superior resources to influence and cajole other countries. Foreign economic aid, atomic diplomacy, military alliances, client states, covert operations, interventions, propaganda, cultural infiltration—these and more became the instruments for waging the Cold War, a war that began as a conflict over the future of Europe but soon spread to encompass the globe.

America's claim to international leadership was welcomed by many in western Europe and elsewhere who feared Stalin's intentions and those of his successors in the Soviet Union. The reconstruction of former enemies Japan and (West) Germany helped those nations recover swiftly and become staunch members of the western alliance. But U.S. policy also sparked resistance. Communist countries condemned financial and atomic diplomacy, while Third World nations, many of them newly independent, sought to undermine America's European allies and sometimes identified the United States as an imperial coconspirator. On occasion, even America's allies bristled at a United States that boldly proclaimed itself economic master and global policeman, and haughtily touted its hegemonic status.

At home, liberal and radical critics protested that Presidents Truman and Eisenhower exaggerated the communist threat, wasting U.S. assets on immoral foreign ventures; crippled legitimate nationalist aspirations; and displayed racial bias. Still, these presidents and their successors held firm to the mission of creating a nonradical, capitalist, free-trade international order in the mold of domestic America. Determined to contain Soviet expansion, fearful of domestic charges of being "soft on communism," they worked to enlarge the U.S. sphere of influence and shape the world. In their years of nurturing allies and applying the containment doctrine worldwide, Truman and Eisenhower held the line—against the Soviet Union and the People's Republic of China, and against nonalignment, communism, nationalism, and revolution everywhere. One consequence was a dramatic increase in presidential power in the realm of foreign affairs—what the historian Arthur M. Schlesinger Jr. called "the Imperial Presidency"—as Congress ceded constitutional power.

Putting itself at odds with many in the Third World, the United States usually stood with its European allies to slow decolonization and to preach evolution rather than revolution. The globalist perspective of the United States prompted Americans to interpret many troubles in the developing world as Cold War conflicts, inspired if not directed by Soviet-backed communists. The intensity of the Cold War obscured for Americans the indigenous roots of most Third World troubles, as the wars in Korea and Vietnam attested. Nor could the United States abide developing nations' drive for economic independence—for gaining control of their own raw materials and economies. Deeply intertwined in the global economy as importer, exporter, and investor, the United States read challenges from this "periphery" as threats to the American standard of living and a way of life characterized by private enterprise. The Third World, in short, challenged U.S. strategic power by forming a third force in the Cold War, and it challenged American economic power by seeking a new economic order of shared interests. Overall, the rise of the Third World introduced new actors to the world stage, challenging the bipolarity of the international system and diffusing power.

All the while, the threat of nuclear war unsettled Americans and foreigners alike. In the film *Godzilla* (1956), a prehistoric monster, revived by atomic bomb tests, rampages through Tokyo. Stanley Kramer's popular but disturbing movie *On the Beach* (1959), based on Nevil Shute's bestselling 1957 novel, depicts a nuclear holocaust in which the last humans on earth choose to swallow government-issued poison tablets so that they can die before H-bomb radiation sickness kills them. Such doomsday or Armageddon attitudes contrasted sharply with official U.S. government assurances that Americans would survive a nuclear war. In *On the Beach*, a dying wife asks her husband, "Couldn't anyone have stopped it?" His answer: "Some kinds of silliness you just can't stop." Eisenhower did not halt it, even though he told Khrushchev in 1959 that "we really should come to some sort of agreement in order to stop this fruitless, really wasteful rivalry."

29

▼

AMERICA AT MIDCENTURY 1945–1960

SHAPING POSTWAR AMERICA

As Americans celebrated the end of World War II and mourned those who would never return, many feared the challenges that lay ahead. The nation had to reintegrate war veterans into civilian society and find places for young families to live. It had to transform a wartime economy to peacetime functions. And it had to contend with the domestic implications of the Cold War and the new global balance of power. Though unemployment rose and a wave of strikes rocked the nation in the immediate aftermath of the war, the economy soon flourished. This strong economy, along with new federal programs, transformed the shape of American society.

The Veterans Return

In 1945, as Germany and then Japan surrendered, the United States faced a new challenge: demobilizing almost 15 million servicemen. Seeking fairness, authorities decided not to demobilize unit by unit, but instead on an individual basis. Each man received a "service score" based on length of time in military service, time overseas, and time in combat—plus the number of his children. Men with the highest scores went home first; those with the lowest numbers were finally demobilized in June 1947.

Veterans' homecomings were often joyful, but in general, Americans were anxious about veterans' return. In one midwestern small town, elected officials estimated that 20 percent of returning veterans would be "debauched and wild," and that many were likely "deadbeats" who "expect too much." Such concerns were so widespread that *Time* magazine, in mid-1945, reassured readers that "the returned overseas soldier is no nerve-shattered civilian-hater who will explode into violent action if he does not get all he thinks he deserves."

CHRONOLOGY

1945	World War II ends
1946	Marriage and birth rates skyrocket
	2.2 million veterans seek higher education
	More than 5 million U.S. workers go on strike
1947	Taft-Hartley Act limits power of unions
	Truman orders loyalty investigation of 3 million government employees
	Mass-production techniques used to build Levittown houses
1948	Truman issues executive order desegregating armed forces and federal government
	Truman elected president
1949	Soviet Union explodes atomic bomb
1950	Korean War begins
	McCarthy alleges communists in government
	"Treaty of Detroit" creates model for new labor-management relations
1951	Race riots in Cicero, Illinois, as white residents oppose residential integration
1952	Eisenhower elected president
1953	Korean War ends
	Congress adopts termination policy for Native American tribes
	Rosenbergs executed as atomic spies
1954	*Brown v. Board of Education* decision reverses "separate but equal" doctrine
	Senate condemns McCarthy
1955	Montgomery bus boycott begins
1956	Highway Act launches interstate highway system
	Eisenhower reelected
	Elvis Presley appears on *Ed Sullivan Show*
1957	King elected first president of Southern Christian Leadership Conference
	School desegregation crisis in Little Rock, Arkansas
	Congress passes Civil Rights Act
	Soviet Union launches *Sputnik*
1958	Congress passes National Defense Education Act
1959	Alaska and Hawai'i become forty-ninth and fiftieth states

Most men found their way—but it was not always easy. Many veterans returned to wives whose lives had gone on without them, to children they barely knew, to a world grown unfamiliar. Some had serious physical injuries. Almost half a million veterans were diagnosed with neuropsychiatric disabilities, and the National Mental Health Act of 1946 passed, in large part, because of awareness of the psychological toll of war on America's veterans. In 1946, Americans flocked to the movie *The Best Years of Our Lives*, which won seven academy awards for its depiction of three veterans struggling to adjust to the world to which they had returned.

Americans also worried about the economic impact of demobilization. As the end of the war approached and the American war machine slowed, factories had begun to lay off workers. Ten days after the Allied victory over Japan, 1.8 million people nationwide received pink slips, and 640,000 filed for unemployment compensation. How was the shrinking job base to absorb millions of returning veterans?

The GI Bill

Though the federal government had done little to prepare for U.S. entry into World War II, it had begun planning for demobilization even while some of the war's most difficult battles lay ahead. In the spring of 1944—a year before V-E Day—Congress unanimously passed the Servicemen's Readjustment Act, known as the GI Bill of Rights. The GI Bill showed the nation's gratitude to the men who fought, but it also attempted to keep the flood of demobilized veterans (almost all of them male) from swamping the U.S. economy. Unemployment benefits, meant to stagger veterans' entry into the civilian job market, were paid to approximately half of all veterans. The GI Bill also provided low-interest loans to buy a house or start a business, and—perhaps most significantly—stipends to cover the cost of college or technical school tuition and living expenses.

Although the GI Bill applied equally to all veterans, regardless of race or gender, so long as they were not less-than-honorably discharged, congressional wrangling and the lobbying of the American Legion put its administration into the Veteran's Administration, a federal agency that lacked the capacity to manage such a vast program. Thus, implementation fell to state and local agencies, allowing racial discrimination. And because men and women charged with homosexuality were not honorably discharged, they also forfeited benefits given to others with whom they had served.

Nonetheless, the GI Bill offered new opportunities to many, and as individuals grasped these opportunities they changed their own lives and the shape of American society. Almost half of returning veterans used GI education benefits, which cost the nation more than the postwar Marshall Plan. Sub-college programs drew 5.6 million veterans, while 2.2 attended college, graduate, or professional school. In 1947, about two-thirds of America's college students were veterans. Enrollment swelled at Syracuse University, tripling in a single year. Admissions quotas meant to limit the number of Jewish students largely disappeared, and while racial segregation persisted, the capacity and size of Negro colleges increased. Facing the influx of nontraditional students, University of Chicago president Robert Maynard Hutchins protested that the GI Bill would turn universities into "educational hobo jungles," but the flood of students and federal dollars into the nation's colleges and universities created a golden age for higher education, and the resulting increase in well-educated or technically trained workers benefitted the American economy.

Education obtained through the GI Bill created social mobility: children of barely literate menial laborers became white-collar professionals. And postwar universities, like the military, brought together people from vastly different backgrounds. The GI Bill fostered the emergence of a national middle-class culture, for as colleges exposed people to new ideas and to new experiences, their students tended to become less provincial, less rooted in ethnic or regional cultures.

Economic Growth

American concerns that economic depression would return with war's end proved unfounded. The first year of adjustment to a peacetime economy was difficult, but the economy recovered quickly, fueled by consumer spending. Although Americans had brought home steady paychecks during the war, there was little on which to spend them. No new cars, for example, had been built since 1942. Americans had saved their money for four years, and they were ready to buy. Companies like General Motors, which flouted conventional wisdom about a coming depression and expanded its operations just after the war, found millions of eager customers. And because most other factories around the world were in ruins, U.S. corporations expanded their global dominance. Farming was also revolutionized. New machines, such as crop dusting planes and mechanical cotton, tobacco, and grape pickers, along with increased use of fertilizers and pesticides greatly increased the total value of farm output, as the productivity of farm labor tripled. The potential for profit drew large investors, and the average size of farms increased from 195 to 306 acres.

Baby Boom

During the Great Depression, young people had delayed marriage, and America's birth rate had plummeted. Marriage and birth rates began to rise as war brought economic recovery. But the end of the war brought a boom. In 1946, the U.S. marriage rate was higher than that of any record-keeping nation (except Hungary) in the history of the twentieth century. The birth rate soared, reversing the downward trend of the past 150 years. "Take the 3,548,000 babies born in 1950," wrote Sylvia F. Porter in her syndicated newspaper column. "Bundle them into a batch, bounce them all over the bountiful land that is America. What do you get?" Porter's answer: "Boom. The biggest, boomiest boom ever known in history. Just imagine how much these extra people, these new markets, will absorb—in food, clothing, in gadgets, in housing, in services. Our factories must expand just to keep pace." Although the baby boom peaked in 1957, more than 4 million babies were born every year until 1965 (see Fugure 29.1). As this vast cohort grew older, it had successive impacts on housing; nursery schools, grade schools, and high schools; fads and popular music; colleges and universities; the job market; and retirement funds, including Social Security.

Where were all these baby-boom families to live? Scarcely any new housing had been built since the 1920s. Almost 2 million families were doubled up with relatives in 1948; 50,000 people were living in Quonset huts, and in Chicago housing was so tight that 250 used trolley cars were sold as homes.

Suburbanization   A combination of market forces, government actions, and individual decisions solved the housing crisis and, in so doing, changed the way large numbers of Americans lived. In the postwar years, white Americans moved to the suburbs. Their reasons varied. Some moved to escape the crowds and noise of the city. People from rural areas moved closer to city jobs. Some white families moved out of urban neighborhoods because African American families were moving in. Many new suburbanites wanted more political influence and more control over their children's education. Most who moved to the suburbs, however, simply wanted to own their own home—and suburban developments were where the affordable housing was. Although suburban development predated World War II, the massive migration of 18 million Americans to the suburbs from cities, small towns, and farms between 1950 and 1960 was on a wholly different scale (see Table 29.1).

In the years following World War II, suburban developers applied techniques of mass production to create acres of modest suburban houses in what had recently been pastures and fields. In 1947, builder William Levitt adapted Henry Ford's assembly-line methods to revolutionize home building. By 1949, instead of 4 or 5 custom homes per year, Levitt's company built 180 houses a week. They were very basic—four and a half rooms on a 60-by-100-foot lot, all with identical floorplans—the Model Ts of houses. But the same floorplan could be disguised by four different exteriors, and by rotating seven paint colors Levitt guaranteed that only 1 in every 28 houses would be identical. In the Levittown on Long Island, a tree was planted every 28 feet (two and a half trees per house). The basic house, appliances included, sold for $7,990. Other homebuilders quickly adopted Levitt's techniques.

Suburban development could never have happened on such a large scale, however, without federal policies that encouraged it. Federal Housing Administration (FHA) mortgage insurance made low-interest GI mortgages and loans possible. New highways also promoted suburban development. Congress authorized construction of a 37,000-mile chain of highways in 1947 and in 1956 passed the Highway Act to create a 42,500-mile interstate highway system. Intended to facilitate commerce and rapid mobilization of the military in case of a threat to national security, these highways also allowed workers to live farther and farther from their jobs in central cities.

TABLE 29.1 | GEOGRAPHIC DISTRIBUTION OF THE U.S. POPULATION, 1930–1970 (IN PERCENTAGES)

Year	Central Cities	Suburbs	Rural Areas and Small Towns
1930	31.8	18.0	50.2
1940	31.6	19.5	48.9
1950	32.3	23.8	43.9
1960	32.6	30.7	36.7
1970	31.4	37.6	31.0

Source: Adapted from U.S. Bureau of the Census, *Decennial Censuses, 1930–1970* (Washington, D.C.: U.S. Government Printing Office).

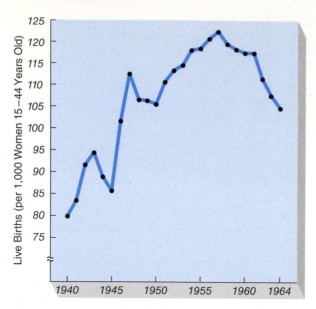

FIGURE 29.1 Birth Rate, 1945–1964

The birth rate began to rise in 1942 and 1943, but it skyrocketed during the postwar years beginning in 1946, reaching its peak in 1957. From 1954 to 1964, the United States recorded more than 4 million births every year.

Source: Adapted from U.S. Bureau of the Census, *Historical Statistics of the United States, Colonial Times to 1970,* Bicentennial Edition (Washington, D.C.: U.S. Government Printing Office, 1975), p. 49.

Inequality in Benefits   Postwar federal programs did not benefit all Americans equally. First, federal policies often assisted men at the expense of women. The federal Selective Service Act guaranteed veterans (overwhelmingly men) priority in postwar employment over the war workers who had replaced them. As industry laid off civilian workers to make room for veterans, women lost their jobs at a rate 75 percent higher than men. Many women stayed in the work force but were pushed into less well-paying jobs. Universities made room for veterans on the GI Bill by excluding qualified women students; a much smaller percentage of college degrees went to women after the war than before.

Inequities were also based on race. Like European American veterans, African American, Native American, Mexican American, and Asian American veterans received educational benefits and hiring preference in civil service jobs following the war. But war workers from these groups were among the first laid off as factories made room for white, male veterans. Federal housing policies also exacerbated racial inequality. Federal loan officers and bankers often labeled African American or racially mixed neighborhoods "high risk" for lending, denying mortgages to members of racial minorities regardless of individual creditworthiness. This practice, called "redlining" because such neighborhoods were outlined in red on lenders' maps, kept African Americans and many Hispanics from buying into the great economic explosion of the postwar era. White families who bought homes with federally guaranteed mortgages saw their small investments grow dramatically over the years. Discriminatory policies denied most African Americans and other people of color that opportunity.

DOMESTIC POLITICS IN THE COLD WAR ERA

Although the major social and economic transformations of the postwar era were due in great part to federal policies and programs, domestic politics were not at the forefront of American life. Foreign affairs were usually paramount, as Democratic president Harry Truman and Republican president Dwight D. Eisenhower both faced significant challenges in the expanding Cold War. Domestically, Truman attempted to build on the New Deal's liberal agenda, while Eisenhower called for balanced budgets and business-friendly policies. But neither administration approached the level of political and legislative activism of the 1930s New Deal.

Harry S. Truman and Postwar Liberalism

Harry Truman, the plain-spoken former haberdasher from Missouri, had never expected to be president. In 1944, when Franklin Roosevelt asked him to join the Democratic ticket as the vice-presidential candidate, he almost refused. Roosevelt, the master politician, played hardball. "If he wants to break up the Democratic Party in the middle of the war, that's his responsibility," the president said flatly. "Oh shit," said Truman, "if that's the situation, I'll have to say yes." But the president, with his hands full as America entered its fourth year of war, had little time for his new vice president and left Truman in the dark about everything from the Manhattan Project to plans for postwar domestic policy. When Roosevelt died, suddenly, in April 1945, Truman was unprepared to take his place.

Truman stepped forward, however, placing a sign on his desk that proclaimed, "The Buck Stops Here." Most of Truman's presidency focused on foreign relations, as he led the nation through the last months of World War II and into the new Cold War with the Soviet Union. Domestically, he oversaw the process of reconversion from war to peace and attempted to keep a liberal agenda—the legacy of Roosevelt's New Deal—alive.

In his 1944 State of the Union address, President Roosevelt had offered Americans a "Second Bill of Rights": the right to employment, healthcare, education, food, and housing. This declaration of government responsibility for the welfare of the nation and its citizens was the cornerstone of postwar liberalism. Truman's legislative program sought to maintain the federal government's active role in guaranteeing social welfare, promoting social justice, managing the economy, and regulating the power of business corporations. Truman proposed an increase in the minimum wage and national housing legislation offering loans for mortgages, and he supported the Full Employment Act, introduced by congressional Democrats in the winter of 1945, which guaranteed work to all who were able and willing, through public-sector employment if necessary.

To pay for his proposed social welfare programs, Truman gambled that full employment would generate sufficient tax revenue and that consumer spending would fuel economic growth. The gamble on economic growth paid off, but Truman quickly learned the limits of his political influence. The conservative co-alition of Republicans and southern Democrats that had stalled Roosevelt's New Deal legislation in the late 1930s was even less inclined to support Truman. Congress refused to raise the minimum wage and gutted the Full Employment Act. By the time Truman signed it into law in early 1946, key provisions regard-ing guaranteed work had virtually disappeared. But the act did reaffirm the fed-eral government's responsibility for managing the economy and created a Council of Economic Advisers to help the president prevent economic downturns.

Postwar Strikes and the Taft-Hartley Act   The difficulties of converting to a peacetime economy helped to undermine Truman's domestic influence. More than 5 million workers walked off the job in the year following Japan's surrender as the end of wartime price controls sent inflation skyrocketing and people struggled to feed their families. Unions shut down the coal, automobile, steel, and electric industries, and halted railroad and maritime transportation. The strikes were so disruptive that Americans began hoarding food and gasoline.

By the spring of 1946, Americans were losing patience with the strikes and with the Democratic administration, which they saw as partly responsible. When unions threatened a national railway strike, President Truman made a dramatic appearance before a joint session of Congress. If strikers in an industry deemed vital to national security refused a presidential order to return to work, he announced, he would ask Congress to immediately draft into the armed forces "all workers who are on strike against their government." The Democratic Party, Truman made clear, would not offer unlimited support to organized labor.

Making the most of public anger at the strikes, in 1947 a group of pro-business Republicans and their conservative Democratic allies worked to restrict the power of labor unions. The Taft-Hartley Act allowed states to adopt right-to-work legisla-tion that outlawed "closed shops," in which all workers were required to join the union if a majority of their number favored a union shop. The law also mandated an eighty-day cooling-off period before unions initiated strikes that imperiled na-tional security. These restrictions limited unions' ability to expand their member-ship, especially in the South and West, where states passed right-to-work laws. Although Truman had used the power of the presidency to avert a national railroad strike, he did not support such limits on union power. But Congress passed the Taft-Hartley Act over Truman's veto.

As Truman presided over the rocky transition from a wartime to a peacetime economy, he had to deal with massive inflation (briefly hitting 35 percent), shortages of consumer goods, and the wave of postwar strikes that slowed produc-tion of eagerly awaited consumer goods and drove prices up further. With powerful congressional opposition, he had little chance of major legislative accomplishments. But his inexperience had contributed to the political impasse. "To err is Truman," people began to joke. Truman's approval rating plunged from 87 percent in late 1945 to 32 percent in 1946.

1948 Election   By 1948, it seemed that Republicans would win the White House in November. A confident Republican Party nominated Thomas Dewey, the man Roosevelt had defeated in 1944, as its presidential candidate. The Republicans were counting on schisms in the Democratic Party to give them victory. Former New Dealer Henry A. Wallace was running on the Progressive Party ticket advocating friendly relations with the Soviet Union, racial desegregation, and nationalization of basic industries. And when the Democratic Party adopted a pro–civil rights plank in 1948, a group of white southerners had created the States' Rights Democratic Party (the Dixiecrats), which nominated the fiercely segregationist governor Strom Thurmond of South Carolina. If Wallace's candidacy did not destroy Truman's chances, experts said, the Dixiecrats certainly would.

Truman, however, refused to give up. He resorted to red-baiting, denouncing "Henry Wallace and his communists" at every opportunity. He also sought support from African American voters in northern cities, becoming the first presidential candidate to campaign in Harlem. In the end, Truman prevailed. Most Democrats saw Truman—in contrast to Thurmond or Wallace—as an appealing moderate. African American voters made the difference, giving Truman the electoral votes of key northern states. Roosevelt's New Deal coalition—African Americans, union members, northern urban voters, and most southern whites—had endured.

Truman's Fair Deal   Truman began his new term brimming with confidence. It was time, he believed, for government to fulfill its responsibility to provide economic security for the poor and the elderly. As he worked on his 1949 State of the Union message, he penciled in his intentions: "I expect to give every segment of our population a fair deal." Truman, unlike Roosevelt, pushed forward legislation to support the civil rights of African Americans, including the antilynching bill that Roosevelt had given only lukewarm support. He proposed a national health insurance program and federal aid for education. Once again, however, little of Truman's legislative agenda came to fruition. A filibuster by southern conservatives in Congress destroyed his civil rights legislation, the American Medical Association denounced his health insurance plan as "socialized medicine," and the Roman Catholic Church opposed aid to education because it would not include parochial schools.

When the postwar peace proved short-lived and Truman ordered troops to Korea in June 1950, many reservists and national guardsmen resented being called to active duty. Inflation began to rise as people, remembering the shortages of the last war, tried to stockpile sugar, coffee, and canned goods. Charges of influence peddling by some of Truman's cronies, along with the unpopular war, pushed the president's public approval rating to an all-time low of 23 percent in 1951, where it stayed for a year.

Eisenhower's Dynamic Conservatism   "It's Time for a Change" was the Republican presidential campaign slogan in 1952, and voters agreed, especially when the Republican candidate was General Dwight D. Eisenhower. Americans hoped that the immensely popular

World War II hero could end the Korean War. And Eisenhower appealed to moderates in both parties (in fact, the Democrats had tried to recruit him as their presidential candidate).

With a Republican in the White House for the first time in twenty years, conservatives hoped to roll back such New Deal liberal programs as the mandatory Social Security system. Eisenhower, however, had no such intention. As a moderate Republican, Eisenhower embraced an approach he called "dynamic conservatism": being "conservative when it comes to money and liberal when it comes to human beings." On the liberal side, in 1954 Eisenhower signed legislation that raised Social Security benefits and added 7.5 million workers, mostly self-employed farmers, to the Social Security rolls. The Eisenhower administration also increased funding for education—though increases were motivated by Cold War fears, not liberal principles. In 1957, when the Soviet Union successfully launched *Sputnik*—the first earth-orbiting satellite—and America's first satellite exploded seconds after liftoff, politicians and policymakers worried about the nation's scientific vulnerability. The resulting National Defense Education Act (NDEA) funded elementary and high-school programs in mathematics, foreign languages, and the sciences and offered fellowships and loans to college students. This Cold War attempt to win the "battle of brainpower" increased the educational opportunities available to young Americans.

Growth of the Military-Industrial Complex   Overall, however, Eisenhower's administration was unabashedly fiscally conservative and pro-business. The president tried to reduce federal spending and to balance the budget. However, faced with three recessions (in 1953–1954, 1957–1958, and 1960–1961) and the tremendous cost of America's global activities, Eisenhower steadily turned to deficit spending. In 1959, federal expenditures climbed to $92 billion, about half of which went to support a large standing military of 3.5 million men and to develop new weapons for the ongoing Cold War.

Eisenhower, however, feared the impact of such developments. In his farewell address to the nation in early 1961, the outgoing president condemned this new "conjunction of an immense military establishment and a large arms industry" and warned that its "total influence—economic, political, even spiritual"—threatened the nation's democratic process. Eisenhower, the former five-star general and war hero, urged Americans to "guard against ... the military-industrial complex."

During Eisenhower's presidency, both liberal Democrats and moderate Republicans occupied what historian Arthur M. Schlesinger Jr. called "the vital center." And with the Cold War between the United States and the Soviet Union portrayed as a battle between good and evil, a struggle for the future of the world, criticism of American society seemed suspect—even unpatriotic. British journalist Godfrey Hodgson described this time as an era of "consensus," when Americans were "confident to the verge of complacency about the perfectibility of American society, anxious to the point of paranoia about the threat of communism."

COLD WAR FEARS AND ANTICOMMUNISM

International relations had a profound influence on America's domestic politics in the years following World War II. Americans were frightened by the Cold War tensions between the United States and the Soviet Union—and there were legitimate reasons for fear. Reasonable fears, however, spilled over into anticommunist demagoguery and witch hunts. Fear allowed the trampling of civil liberties, the suppression of dissent, and the persecution of thousands of innocent Americans.

Anticommunism was not new in American society. A Red Scare had swept the nation following the Russian Revolution of 1917, and opponents of America's labor movement had used charges of communism to block unionization through the 1930s. Many saw the Soviet Union's virtual takeover of eastern Europe in the late 1940s as an alarming parallel to Nazi Germany's takeover of neighboring states. People remembered the failure of "appeasement" at Munich and worried that the United States was "too soft" in its policy toward the Soviet Union.

Espionage and Nuclear Fears   In addition, top U.S. government officials knew that the Soviet Union was spying on the United States (the United States also had spies within the Soviet Union). A top-secret project, code-named "Venona," decrypted almost three thousand Soviet telegraphic cables that proved Soviet spies had infiltrated U.S. government agencies and nuclear programs. Intelligence officials resolved to prosecute Soviet spies, but they kept their evidence from the American public so that the Soviets would not realize their codes had been compromised.

Fear of nuclear war also contributed to American anticommunism. For four years, the United States alone possessed what seemed the ultimate weapon, but in 1949 the Soviet Union exploded its own atomic device. President Truman, initiating a national atomic civil defense program shortly thereafter, told Americans, "I cannot tell you when or where the attack will come or that it will come at all. I can only remind you that we must be ready when it does come." Children practiced "duck-and-cover" positions in their school classrooms, learning how to shield their faces from the atomic flash and flying debris in the event of an attack. *Life* magazine featured backyard fallout shelters. As the stakes of the global struggle increased, Americans worried that the United States was newly vulnerable to attack on its own soil.

Politics of Anticommunism   At the height of the Cold War, American leaders, including Presidents Truman and Eisenhower, did not always draw a sufficient line between prudent attempts to prevent Soviet spies from infiltrating important government agencies and anticommunist scaremongering for political gain. Truman purposely invoked "the communist threat" to gain support for aid to Greece and Turkey in 1947. Republican politicians "red-baited" Democratic opponents, eventually targeting the Truman administration as a whole. In 1947, President Truman ordered investigations into the loyalty of more than 3 million U.S. government employees. As anticommunist hysteria grew, the government began discharging people deemed "security risks," among them alcoholics, homosexuals, and debtors thought susceptible to blackmail. In most cases, there was no evidence of disloyalty.

Leading the anticommunist crusade was the House Un-American Activities Committee (popularly known as HUAC). Created in 1938 to investigate "subversive and un-American propaganda," the viciously anti–New Deal committee had lost credibility then by charging that film stars—including eight-year-old Shirley Temple—were dupes of the Communist Party. In 1947, in a shameless publicity-grabbing tactic, HUAC attacked Hollywood again, using Federal Bureau of Investigation (FBI) files and the testimony of people like Screen Actors Guild president Ronald Reagan (who was also a secret informant for the FBI, complete with code name). Members of a group of screenwriters and directors known as the "Hollywood Ten" were sent to prison for contempt of Congress when they refused to "name names" of suspected communists for HUAC. At least a dozen other Hollywood figures committed suicide. Studios panicked and blacklisted hundreds of actors, screenwriters, directors, even makeup artists who were suspected of communist affiliations. With no evidence of wrongdoing, these men and women had their careers—and sometimes their lives—ruined.

McCarthyism and the Growing "Witch Hunt"   University professors became targets of the growing "witch hunt" in 1949, when HUAC demanded lists of the textbooks used in courses at eighty-one universities. When the board of regents at the University of California, Berkeley, instituted a loyalty oath for faculty, firing twenty-six who resisted on principle, protests from faculty members across the nation forced the regents to back down. But many professors, afraid of the reach of HUAC, began to downplay controversial material in their courses. In the labor movement, the CIO expelled eleven unions, with more than 900,000 members, for alleged communist domination. The red panic reached its nadir in February 1950, when a relatively obscure U.S. senator came before an audience in Wheeling, West Virginia, to charge that the U.S. State Department was "thoroughly infested with Communists." Republican senator Joseph R. McCarthy of Wisconsin was not an especially credible source. He made charges and then retracted them, claiming first that there were 205 communists in the State Department, then 57, then 81. He had a severe drinking problem; downing a water glass full of Scotch in a single gulp, he would follow it with a quarter-pound stick of butter, hoping to counteract the effects of the liquor. He had a record of dishonesty as a lawyer and judge in his hometown of Appleton, Wisconsin. But McCarthy crystallized the anxieties many felt as they faced a new and difficult era in American life, and the anticommunist excesses of this era came to be known as McCarthyism.

With HUAC and McCarthy on the attack, Americans began pointing accusing fingers at one another. The anticommunist crusade was embraced by labor union officials, religious leaders, and the media, as well as by politicians. A bootblack at the Pentagon was questioned by the FBI seventy times because he had given $10 during the 1930s to a defense fund for the Scottsboro Boys, who had been represented by an attorney from the Communist Party. Women in New York who lobbied for the continuation of wartime daycare programs were denounced as

Senator Joseph McCarthy's downfall came in 1954 during the televised Army-McCarthy hearings, when army counsel Joseph Welsh (left) confronted McCarthy on national TV.

communists by the *New York World Telegram.* "Reds, phonies, and parlor pinks," in Truman's words, seemed to lurk everywhere.

Anticommunism in Congress   In such a climate, most public figures found it too risky to stand up against McCarthyist tactics. And most Democrats did support the domestic Cold War and its anticommunist actions. In 1950, with bipartisan support, Congress passed the Internal Security (McCarran) Act, which required members of "Communist-front" organizations to register with the government and prohibited them from holding government jobs or traveling abroad. In 1954, the Senate unanimously passed the Communist Control Act (there were two dissenting votes in the House), which effectively made membership in the Communist Party illegal. Its chief sponsor, Democratic senator Hubert H. Humphrey of Minnesota, told his colleagues just before he cast his vote, "We have closed all of the doors. The rats will not get out of the trap."

The anticommunist fervor was fueled by spectacular and controversial trials of Americans accused of passing secrets to the Soviet Union. In 1948, Congressman Richard Nixon of California, a member of HUAC, was propelled onto the national stage when he accused former State Department official Alger Hiss of espionage. In 1950, Hiss was convicted of lying about his contacts with Soviet agents. That same year, Ethel and Julius Rosenberg were arrested for passing atomic secrets to the Soviets; they were found guilty of treason and executed in 1953. For decades, many historians believed that the Rosenbergs were primarily victims of a witch hunt. In fact, there was strong evidence of Julius Rosenberg's guilt in cables decrypted at the time (as well as evidence that Ethel Rosenberg was less involved than had been charged), but this evidence was not presented at their trial for reasons of national security. The cables remained top secret until 1995, when a Clinton administration initiative opened the files to historians.

Waning of the Red Scare   Some of the worst excesses of Cold War anticommunism waned when Senator McCarthy was discredited on national television in 1954. McCarthy himself was a master at using the press, making sensational accusations—front-page material—just before reporters' deadlines. When the evidence did not pan out or McCarthy's charges proved untrue, retractions appeared in the back pages of the newspapers. Even journalists who knew McCarthy was unreliable continued to report his charges. Sensational stories sell papers, and McCarthy became a celebrity.

But McCarthy badly misunderstood the power of television. His crucial mistake was taking on the U.S. Army in front of millions of television viewers. At issue was the senator's wild accusation that the army was shielding and promoting communists; he cited the case of one army dentist. The so-called Army-McCarthy hearings, held by a Senate subcommittee in 1954, became a showcase for the senator's abusive treatment of witnesses. McCarthy, apparently drunk, alternately ranted and slurred his words. Finally, after he maligned a young lawyer who was not even involved in the hearings, army counsel Joseph Welch protested, "Have you no sense of decency, sir?" The gallery erupted in applause, and McCarthy's career as a witch-hunter was over. In December 1954, the Senate voted to "condemn" McCarthy for sullying the dignity of the Senate. He remained a senator, but exhaustion and alcohol took their toll, and he died in 1957 at the age of forty-eight. With McCarthy discredited, the most virulent strand of anticommunism had run its course. However, the use of fear tactics for political gain, and the narrowing of American freedoms and liberties, were chilling domestic legacies of the Cold War.

THE STRUGGLE FOR CIVIL RIGHTS

The Cold War—at home and abroad—also shaped African American struggles for social justice and the nation's responses to them. As the Soviet Union was quick to point out, the United States could hardly pose as the leader of the free world or condemn the denial of human rights in eastern Europe and the Soviet Union if it practiced segregation at home. Nor could the United States convince new African and Asian nations of its dedication to human rights if African Americans were subjected to segregation, discrimination, disfranchisement, and racial violence. Some African American leaders, in fact, understood their struggle for equal rights in the United States as part of a larger, international movement. To win the support of nonaligned nations, the United States would have to live up to its own ideals. At the same time, many Americans viewed social criticism of any kind as a Soviet-inspired attempt to weaken the United States in the ongoing Cold

War. The Federal Bureau of Investigation and local law enforcement agencies commonly used such anticommunist fears to justify attacks on civil rights activists. In this heated environment, African Americans struggled to seize the political initiative.

Growing Black Political Power   Americans had seen the Second World War as a struggle for democracy and against hatred. African Americans who had helped win the war were determined that their lives in postwar America would be better because of their sacrifices. Moreover, politicians like Harry Truman were beginning to pay attention to black aspirations, especially as black voters in some urban-industrial states began to strongly influence the political balance of power.

President Truman had compelling political reasons for supporting African American civil rights. But he also felt a moral obligation to do something, for he genuinely believed it was only fair that every American, regardless of race, should enjoy the full rights of citizenship. Truman was disturbed by a resurgence of racial terrorism, as a revived Ku Klux Klan was burning crosses and murdering blacks who sought civil rights and racial justice in the aftermath of World War II. But what really horrified Truman was the report that police in Aiken, South Carolina, had gouged out the eyes of a black sergeant just three hours after he had been discharged from the army. Several weeks after this atrocity, in December 1946, Truman signed an executive order establishing the President's Committee on Civil Rights. The committee's report, *To Secure These Rights*, would become the civil rights movement agenda for the next twenty years. It called for antilynching and antisegregation legislation and for laws guaranteeing voting rights and equal employment opportunity. For the first time since Reconstruction, a president had acknowledged the federal government's responsibility to protect blacks and to strive for racial equality.

Truman took this responsibility seriously, and in 1948 he issued two executive orders declaring an end to racial discrimination in the federal government. One proclaimed a policy of "fair employment throughout the federal establishment" and created the Employment Board of the Civil Service Commission to hear charges of discrimination. The other ordered the racial desegregation of the armed forces and appointed a committee to oversee this process. Despite strong opposition to desegregation within the military, segregated units were being phased out by the beginning of the Korean War.

Such actions were possible in part because of changing social attitudes and experiences in postwar America. A new and visible black middle class was emerging, composed of college-educated activists, war veterans, and union workers. White awareness of social injustice had been increased by Gunnar Myrdal's social science study *An American Dilemma* (1944) and by Richard Wright's novel *Native Son* (1940) and autobiography *Black Boy* (1945). Blacks and whites also worked together in CIO unions and service organizations, such as the National Council of Churches. In 1947, a black baseball player, Jackie Robinson, broke the major league color barrier and electrified Brooklyn Dodgers fans with his spectacular hitting and base running.

Supreme Court Victories and School Desegregation

African Americans were successfully challenging racial discrimination both in the courts and in state and local legislatures. Northern state legislatures, in response to pressure by civil rights activists, passed a variety of measures prohibiting employment discrimination in the 1940s and 1950s. National successes came through the Supreme Court. During the 1940s, Thurgood Marshall, head of the NAACP's Legal Defense and Educational Fund and his colleagues carried forward the plan devised by Charles Hamilton Houston to destroy the separate-but-equal doctrine established in *Plessy v. Ferguson* (1896) by insisting on its literal interpretation. In higher education, the NAACP calculated, the cost of true equality in racially separate schools would be prohibitive. "You can't build a cyclotron for one student," the president of the University of Oklahoma acknowledged. As a result of NAACP lawsuits, African American students won admission to professional and graduate schools at several formerly segregated state universities. The NAACP also won major victories through the Supreme Court in *Smith v. Allwright* (1944), which outlawed the whites-only primaries held by the Democratic Party in some southern states; *Morgan v. Virginia* (1946), which struck down segregation in interstate bus transportation; and *Shelley v. Kraemer* (1948), in which the Court held that racially restrictive covenants (private agreements among white homeowners not to sell to blacks) could not legally be enforced.

Even so, segregation was still standard practice in the 1950s, and blacks continued to suffer disfranchisement, job discrimination, and violence, including the 1951 bombing murder of the Florida state director of the NAACP and his wife. But in 1954, the NAACP won a historic victory that stunned the white South and energized African Americans to challenge segregation on several fronts. *Brown v. Board of Education of Topeka*, which Thurgood Marshall argued before the high court, incorporated school desegregation cases from several states. The Court's unanimous decision was written by Chief Justice Earl Warren, who, as California's attorney general, had pushed for the internment of Japanese Americans during World War II and had come to regret that action. The Court concluded that "in the field of public education the doctrine of 'separate but equal' has no place. Separate educational facilities are inherently unequal." But the ruling that overturned *Plessy v. Ferguson* did not demand immediate compliance. A year later, the Court finally ordered school desegregation, but only "with all deliberate speed."

Montgomery Bus Boycott

By the mid-1950s, African Americans were engaged in a grassroots struggle for civil rights in both the North and the South, though southern struggles drew the most national attention. In 1955, Rosa Parks, a department store seamstress and long-time NAACP activist, was arrested when she refused to give up her seat to a white man on a public bus in Montgomery, Alabama. Her arrest gave local black women's organizations and civil rights groups a cause around which to organize a boycott of the city's bus system. They selected Martin Luther King Jr., a recently ordained minister who had just arrived in Montgomery, as their leader. King launched the boycott with a moving speech, declaring, "If we are wrong, the Constitution is wrong. If we are wrong, God Almighty is wrong. If we are wrong, Jesus of Nazareth was merely a utopian dreamer.... If we are wrong, justice is a lie."

Martin Luther King Jr. was a twenty-six-year-old Baptist minister with a recent Ph.D. from Boston University. Committed to the transforming potential of Christian love and schooled in the teachings of India's leader Mohandas K. Gandhi, King believed in nonviolent protest and civil disobedience. By refusing to obey unjust and racist laws, he hoped to focus the nation's attention on the immorality of Jim Crow. King persisted in this struggle even as opponents bombed his house and he was jailed for "conspiring" to boycott.

During the year-long Montgomery bus boycott, blacks young and old rallied in their churches, sang hymns, and prayed that the nation would awaken to the evils of segregation and racial discrimination. They maintained their boycott through heavy rains and the steamy heat of summer, often walking miles a day. One elderly black woman, offered a ride to work by a white reporter, told him, "No, my feets is tired, but my soul is rested." With the bus company near bankruptcy and downtown merchants suffering from declining sales, city officials adopted harassment tactics to bring an end to the boycott. But the black people of Montgomery persevered. Thirteen months after the boycott began, the Supreme Court declared Alabama's bus segregation laws unconstitutional.

White Resistance

As the civil rights movement won significant victories, white reactions varied. Some communities in border states like Kansas and Maryland quietly implemented the school desegregation order, and many southern moderates advocated a gradual rollback of segregation. But others urged defiance. The Klan experienced another resurgence, and white violence against blacks increased. In August 1955, white men in Mississippi beat, mutilated, and murdered Emmett Till, a fourteen-year-old from Chicago, because they took offense at the way he spoke to a white woman; an all-white jury took only 67 minutes to acquit those charged with the crime. Business and professional people created White Citizens' Councils for the express purpose of resisting the school desegregation order. Known familiarly as "uptown Ku Klux Klans," the councils brought their economic power to bear against black civil rights activists. In keeping with the program of "massive resistance" proposed by Virginia's U.S. senator, Harry F. Byrd Sr., they pushed through state laws that provided private-school tuition for white children who left public schools to avoid integration and, in Virginia, refused state funding to integrated schools. When FBI director J. Edgar Hoover briefed President Eisenhower on southern racial tensions in 1956, he warned of communist influences among the civil rights activists and even suggested that, if the Citizens' Councils did not worsen the racial situation, their actions might "control the rising tension."

White resistance to civil rights also gained strength in large northern cities. Chicago's African American population had increased from 275,000 in 1940 to 800,000 in 1960. These newcomers found good jobs in industry, and their increased numbers gave them political power. But they faced racism and segregation in the North as well. In 1951 in Cicero, a town adjoining Chicago, several thousand whites who were determined to keep blacks from moving into their

© Bettmann/Corbis

For leading the movement to gain equality for blacks riding city buses in Montgomery, Alabama, Martin Luther King Jr. (1929–1968) and other African Americans, including twenty-three other ministers, were indicted by an all-white jury for violating an old law banning boycotts. In late March 1956, King was convicted and fined $500. A crowd of well-wishers cheered a smiling King (here with his wife, Coretta) outside the courthouse, where King proudly declared, "The protest goes on!" King's arrest and conviction made the bus boycott front-page news across America.

neighborhood provoked a race riot. Whites welcomed a black family to a Columbus, Ohio, suburb by burning a cross on their front lawn. So racially divided was Chicago that the U.S. Commission on Civil Rights in 1959 described it as "the most residentially segregated city in the nation." Detroit and other northern cities were not far behind. And because children attended neighborhood schools, education in the North was in fact often segregated as well, though not by law, as it had been in the South.

Federal Authority and States' Rights   Unlike Truman, President Eisenhower wanted to avoid taking action on civil rights. Although he disapproved of racial segregation, Eisenhower objected to "compulsory federal law" as a solution, for he believed that race relations would improve "only if [desegregation] starts locally." He also feared that rapid desegregation under his administration would jeopardize Republican inroads in the South. Thus, Eisenhower did not state forthrightly that the federal government would enforce the *Brown* decision as the nation's law. In short, instead of leading, he spoke ambiguously and thereby tacitly encouraged white resistance. In 1956, 101 congressmen and senators from eleven southern states, all Democrats, issued "The Southern Manifesto." This document condemned the *Brown* decision as an "unwarranted exercise of power by the Court," which violated the principle of states' rights, and commended those states that sought to "resist forced integration by any lawful means."

Events in Little Rock, Arkansas, forced the president to act. In September 1957, Arkansas governor Orval E. Faubus defied a court-supported desegregation plan for Little Rock's Central High School. Faubus went on television the night before school began and told Arkansans that "blood would run in the streets" if black students tried to enter the high school the next day. On the second day of school, eight black teenagers tried to enter Central High, but they were turned away by Arkansas National Guard troops the governor had deployed to block their entrance. The ninth student, separated from the others, was surrounded by jeering whites and narrowly escaped the mob with the help of a sympathetic white woman.

It was more than two weeks after school began that the "Little Rock Nine" first entered Central High—and then only because a federal judge intervened. As an angry crowd surrounded the school and television broadcast the scene to the nation and the world, Eisenhower decided to nationalize the Arkansas National Guard (placing it under federal, not state, control) and dispatch one thousand army paratroopers to Little Rock. Troops guarded the students for the rest of the year. Eisenhower's use of federal power in Little Rock was a critical step in America's struggle over racial equality, for he had directly confronted the conflict between federal authority and states' rights. However, state power triumphed the following year, when Faubus closed all public high schools in Little Rock rather than desegregate them.

Nonetheless, federal action continued. In 1957, Congress passed the first Civil Rights Act since Reconstruction, creating the United States Commission on Civil Rights to investigate systemic discrimination, such as in voting. Although this measure, like a voting rights act passed three years later, was not fully effective, it was another federal recognition of the centrality of civil rights. Most important, however, was the growing strength of a new, grassroots civil rights activism. In 1957, Martin Luther King Jr. became the first president of the Southern Christian Leadership Conference (SCLC), organized to coordinate civil rights activities. With the success in Montgomery and the gains won through the Supreme Court and the Truman administration, African Americans were poised to launch a major national movement for civil rights in the years to come.

CREATING A MIDDLE-CLASS NATION

Even as African Americans encountered massive resistance in their struggles for civil rights during the 1950s, in other ways the United States was becoming a more inclusive society. More Americans than ever before participated in a broad middle-class and suburban culture, and divisions among Americans based on class, ethnicity, religion, and regional identity became less important. National prosperity offered ever greater numbers of Americans material comfort and economic security through entrance into an economic middle class. Old European ethnic identities were fading, as an ever smaller percentage of America's people were first- or second-generation immigrants.

In the new suburbs, people from different backgrounds worked together to create communities and build schools, churches, and other institutions. Middle-class Americans increasingly looked to powerful national media rather than to regional or ethnic traditions for advice on matters ranging from how to celebrate Thanksgiving to what car to buy to how to raise children. New opportunities for consumption—whether the fads of a powerful teenage culture or the suburban ranch-style house—also tied together Americans from different backgrounds. In the postwar years, a new middle-class way of life was transforming the United States.

Prosperity for More Americans   During the 1950s, strong economic growth made more Americans than ever before economically comfortable and secure. This economic boom was driven by consumer spending, as Americans eagerly bought consumer goods that had not been available during the war, and industries expanded production to meet consumer demand. Government spending was also important. As the Cold War deepened, the government poured money into defense industries, creating jobs and stimulating the economy.

Cold War military and aerospace spending changed American society and culture in unintended ways. The professional middle class grew because the government's weapons development and space programs required highly educated scientists, engineers, and other white-collar workers. And as universities received billions of dollars to fund such research, they grew rapidly and expanded their roles in American life. Government-funded research focused on military weapon systems and the space race, but it had broader results, as well: the transistor, invented during the 1950s, made possible both the computer revolution and the transistor radio, without which 1950s youth culture would have looked very different.

A new era of labor relations also helped bring economic prosperity to more Americans. By 1950, labor and management created a new, more stable relationship. In peaceful negotiations, the United Auto Workers (UAW) and General Motors led the way for other corporations in providing workers with health insurance, pension plans, and guaranteed cost-of-living adjustments, or COLAs, to protect wages from inflation. The 1950 agreement that *Fortune* magazine called "The Treaty of Detroit" gave GM's workers a five-year contract, with regular wage increases tied to corporate productivity. This was a turning point for the labor movement. In exchange for wages and benefits, organized labor gave up its demands for greater control in corporate affairs. And with wage increases tied to corporate productivity, labor cast its lot with management: workplace stability and efficiency, not strikes, would bring higher wages. During the 1950s, wages and benefits often rivaled those of college-educated professionals and propelled union families into the ranks of the economic middle class.

Sunbelt and Economic Growth   Just as labor agreements helped create prosperity for union members and their families, government policies helped bring the nation's poorest region into the American economic mainstream. In the 1930s, Roosevelt had called the South "the nation's No. 1 economic problem." During World War II, new defense industry plants and military training camps channeled federal money to the region, stimulating economic growth. In the postwar era, huge levels of defense spending, especially for the nation's aerospace industry, continued to shift economic development from the Northeast and Midwest to the South and Southwest—the Sunbelt (see Map 29.1). Government actions—including generous tax breaks for oil companies, siting of military bases, and awarding of defense and aerospace contracts—were crucial to the region's new prosperity.

The Sunbelt's spectacular growth was also due to agribusiness, the oil industry, real-estate development, and recreation. Sunbelt states aggressively—and successfully—sought foreign investment. Industry was drawn to the South by right-to-work laws, which outlawed closed shops, and by low taxes and low heating bills. The development of air conditioning was also crucial, for it made bearable even the hottest summer days. Houston, Phoenix, Los Angeles, San Diego, Dallas, and Miami all boomed; the population of Houston, a center of the aerospace industry and also of oil and petrochemical production, more than tripled between 1940 and 1960. California absorbed no less than one-fifth of the nation's entire population increase in the 1950s. By 1963, it was the most populous state in the Union.

A New Middle-Class Culture   By the 1950s, it seemed that America was becoming a middle-class nation. Unionized blue-collar workers gained middle-class incomes, and veterans with GI Bill college educations swelled the growing managerial and professional class. In 1956, for the first time, the United States had more white-collar than blue-collar workers, and in 1957 there were 61 percent more salaried middle-class workers than just a decade earlier. Also for the first time, a majority of families—60 percent—had incomes in the middle-class range (approximately $3,000 to $9,000 a year in the mid-1950s).

However, middle-class identity was not simply a matter of economics. Half of teenagers whose fathers did unskilled menial labor or whose mothers had only a sixth-grade education, a major 1952 survey discovered, believed their family was "middle class" (not working class or lower class). Paradoxically, the strength of unions in the postwar era contributed to a decline in working-class identity: as large numbers of blue-collar workers participated fully in the suburban middle-class culture, the lines separating working class and middle class seemed less important. Increasingly, a family's standard of living mattered more than what sort of work made the standard of living possible. People of color did not share equally in America's postwar prosperity and were usually invisible in American representations of "the good life." However, many middle-income African Americans, Latinos, and Asian Americans did participate in the broad middle-class culture.

Whiteness and National Culture   The emergence of a national middle-class culture was possible in part because America's population was more homogeneous in the 1950s than before or since. In the nineteenth and early twentieth centuries, the United States had restricted or prohibited immigration from Asia, Africa, and Latin America while accepting millions of Europeans to America's shores. This large-scale European immigration had been shut off in the 1920s, so that by 1960 only 5.7 percent of Americans were foreign-born

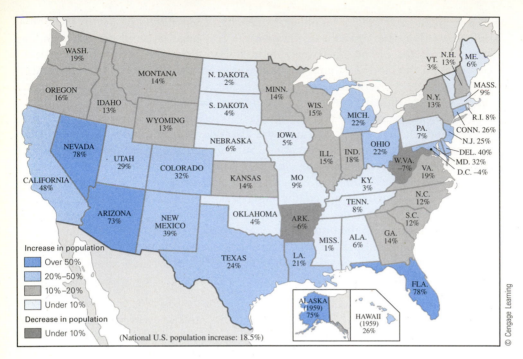

MAP 29.1 Rise of the Sunbelt, 1950–1960

The years after the Second World War saw a continuation of the migration of Americans to the Sunbelt states of the Southwest and the West Coast.

(compared with approximately 15 percent in 1910 and 13 percent in 2010). In 1950, 88 percent of Americans were of European ancestry (compared with 69 percent in 2000), 10 percent of the population was African American, 2 percent was Hispanic, and Native Americans and Asian Americans each accounted for about one-fifth of 1 percent. But almost all European-Americans were at least a generation removed from immigration. Instead of "Italians" or "Russians" or "Jews," they were increasingly likely to describe themselves as "white." In 1959, the addition of two new states, Alaska and Hawai'i, brought more people of native, Asian, or Pacific origin to the U.S. population.

Although the new suburbs were peopled mostly by white families, these suburbs were usually more diverse than the communities from which their residents had come. America's small towns and urban ethnic enclaves were quite homogeneous and usually intolerant of difference and of challenges to traditional ways. In the suburbs, people from different backgrounds came together: migrants from the city and the country; from different regions of the nation, different ethnic cultures, and different religious backgrounds. It was in the suburbs, paradoxically, that many people encountered different customs and beliefs. But as they joined with neighbors to forge new communities, the new suburbanites frequently adopted the norms of the developing national middle class. They traded the provincial homogeneity of specific ethnic or regional cultures for a new sort of homogeneity: a national middle-class culture.

Television

Because many white Americans were new to the middle class, they were uncertain about what behaviors were proper and expected of them. They found instruction, in part, in the national mass media. Women's magazines helped housewives replace the ethnic and regional dishes with which they had grown up with "American" recipes created from national brand-name products—such as casseroles made with Campbell's Cream of Mushroom soup. Television also fostered America's shared national culture and taught Americans how to be middle class. Although television sets cost about $300—the equivalent of $2,000 today—almost half of American homes had TVs by 1953. Television ownership rose to 90 percent by 1960, when more American households had a television set than a washing machine or an electric iron.

On television, suburban families like the Andersons (*Father Knows Best*) and the Cleavers (*Leave It to Beaver*) ate dinner at a properly set dining room table. The mothers were always well groomed; June Cleaver did housework in a carefully ironed dress. When children faced moral dilemmas, parents gently but firmly guided them toward correct decisions. Every crisis was resolved through paternal wisdom—and a little humor. In these families, no one ever yelled or hit. These popular family situation comedies portrayed and reinforced the suburban middle-class ideal that so many American families sought.

The "middle-classness" of television programming was due in part to the economics of the television industry. Advertising paid for television programming, and the corporations that bought advertising did not want to offend potential consumers. Thus, although African American musician Nat King Cole drew millions of viewers to his NBC television show, it never found a sponsor. National corporations were afraid that being linked to a black performer like Cole would hurt their sales among whites—especially in the South. Because African Americans made up only about 10 percent of the population and many had little disposable income, they had little power in this economics-driven system. The *Nat King Cole Show* was canceled within a year; it was a decade before the networks again tried to anchor a show around a black performer.

Television's reach extended beyond the suburbs. People from the inner cities and from isolated rural areas also watched family sitcoms or laughed at the antics of Milton Berle and Lucille Ball. With only network television available—ABC, CBS, and NBC (and, until 1956, DuMont)—at any one time 70 percent or more of all viewers might be watching the same popular program. (In the early twenty-first century, the most popular shows might attract 12 percent of the viewing audience.) Television gave Americans a shared set of experiences; it also helped create a more homogeneous, white-focused, middle-class culture.

Consumer Culture

Linked by a shared national culture, Americans also found common ground in a new abundance of consumer goods. After decades of scarcity, Americans had what seemed a dazzling array of consumer goods from which to choose, and they embraced them with unmatched exuberance. Even the most utilitarian objects got two-tone paint jobs or rocket-ship details; there was an optimism and vulgar joy in the popularity of turquoise refrigerators, furniture shaped like boomerangs, and cars designed to resemble fighter jets. In this consumer society, people used consumer choices to express their personal identity and to claim status within the broad boundaries of the middle class. Cars more than anything else embodied the consumer fantasies and exuberance of newly prosperous Americans. Expensive Cadillacs were the first to develop tail fins, and fins soon soared from midrange Chevys, Fords, and Plymouths as well. Americans spent $65 billion on automobiles in 1955—a figure equivalent to almost 20 percent of the gross national product. To pay for all those cars—and for suburban houses with modern appliances—America's consumer debt rose from $5.7 billion in 1945 to $58 billion in 1961.

Religion   In the same years, Americans turned in unprecedented numbers to organized religion. Membership (primarily in mainline Christian churches) doubled between the end of World War II and the beginning of the 1960s. The uncertainties of the nuclear age likely contributed to the resurgence of religion, and some Americans may have sought spiritual consolation in the wake of the immensely destructive world war. The increasingly important national mass media played a role, as preachers like Billy Graham created national congregations from television audiences, preaching a message that combined the promise of salvation with Cold War patriotism. But along with religious teachings, local churches and synagogues offered new suburbanites a sense of community. They welcomed newcomers, celebrated life's rituals, and supported the sick and the bereaved who were often far from their extended families and old communities. It is difficult to measure the depth of religious belief in postwar America, but church fellowship halls were near the center of the new postwar middle-class culture.

Men, Women, and Youth at Midcentury

Most of all, Americans pursued "the good life" and sought refuge from the tensions of the Cold War world through their homes and families. Having survived the Great Depression and a world war, many sought fulfillment in private life rather than public engagement; they saw their commitment to home and family as an expression of faith in the future. However, despite the real satisfactions that many Americans found in family life, both men and women found their life choices limited by powerful social pressures to conform to narrowly defined gender roles.

Marriage and Families   During the 1950s, few Americans remained single, and most people married very young. By 1959, almost half of American brides had yet to reach their nineteenth birthday; their husbands were usually only a year or so older. This trend toward early marriage was endorsed by experts and approved by most parents, in part as a way to prevent premarital sex. As Americans accepted psychotherapeutic insights in the years following the war, they worried not only that premarital sex might leave the young woman pregnant or ruin her "reputation," but also that the experience could so damage her psychologically that she could never adjust to "normal" marital relations. One popular women's magazine argued, "When two people are ready for sexual intercourse at the fully human level they are ready for marriage.... Not to do so is moral cowardice. And society has no right to stand in their way."

Many young couples—still teenagers—found autonomy and freedom from parental authority by marrying and setting up their own household. Most newlyweds quickly had babies—an average of three—completing their family while still in their twenties. Birth control (condoms and diaphragms) was widely available and widely used, for most couples planned the size of their family. But almost all married couples, regardless of race or class, wanted a large family. Two children were the American ideal in 1940; by 1960, most couples wanted four. And though many families looked nothing like television's June, Ward, Wally, and Beaver Cleaver, 88 percent of children under eighteen lived with two parents (in 2008, the figure was 70 percent). Fewer children were born outside marriage then; only 3.9 percent of births were to unmarried women in 1950 (compared with more than one-third of births in 2000). Divorce rates were also lower. As late as 1960, there were only 9 divorces per 1,000 married couples.

Gender Roles in 1950s Families

In these 1950s families, men and women usually took distinct and different roles, with male breadwinners and female homemakers. This division of labor, contemporary commentators insisted, was based on the timeless and essential differences between the sexes. In fact, the economic and social structure and the cultural values of postwar American society largely determined what choices were available to American men and women.

During the 1950s, it was possible for many families to live in modest middle-class comfort on one (male) salary. There were strong incentives for women to stay at home, especially while children were young. Good childcare was rarely available, and fewer families lived close to the grandparents or other relatives who had traditionally helped with the children. A new cohort of childcare experts, including Dr. Spock, whose 1946 *Baby and Child Care* sold millions of copies, insisted that a mother's full-time attention was necessary for her children's well-being. Because of hiring discrimination, women who could afford to stay home often did not find the jobs available to them attractive enough to justify a double shift, with paid employment simply added to their responsibilities for cooking and housework. Many women thus chose to devote their considerable energies to family life. America's schools and religious institutions also benefited immensely from their volunteer labor.

Women and Work

A great number of women, however, found that their lives did not completely match the ideal of 1950s family life. Suburban domesticity left many women feeling isolated, cut off from the larger world of experiences their husbands still inhabited. The popular belief that one should find complete emotional satisfaction in private life put unrealistic pressures on marriages and family relationships. And finally, despite near-universal celebration of women's domestic roles, many women found themselves managing both job and family responsibilities (see Figure 29.2). Twice as many women were employed in 1960 as in 1940, including 39 percent of women with children between the ages of six and seventeen. A majority of these women worked part-time for some specific family goal: a new car, college tuition for the children. They did not see these jobs as violating their primary role as housewife; these jobs were in service to the family, not a means to independence from it.

Whether she worked to supplement a middle-class income, to feed her children, or to support herself, however, a woman faced discrimination in the world of work. Want ads were divided into "Help Wanted—Male" and "Help Wanted—Female" categories. Female full-time workers earned, on average, just 60 percent of what male full-time workers were paid and were restricted to less well-paid "female" fields, as maids, secretaries, teachers, and nurses. Women with exceptional talent or ambition often found their aspirations blocked. A popular book, *Modern Woman: The Lost Sex*, explained that ambitious women and "feminists" suffered from "penis envy." Textbooks for college psychology and sociology courses warned women not to "compete" with men; magazine articles described "career women" as a "third sex." Medical schools commonly limited the admission of women to 5 percent of each class. In 1960, less than 4 percent of lawyers and judges were female. When future Supreme Court Justice Ruth Bader Ginsburg graduated at the top of her Columbia Law School class in 1959, she could not find a job.

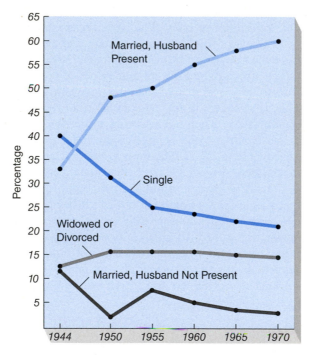

FIGURE 29.2 Marital Distribution of the Female Labor Force, 1944–1970

The composition of the female labor force changed dramatically from 1944 to 1970. In 1944, 41 percent of women in the labor force were single; in 1970, only 22 percent were single. During the same years, the percentage of the female labor force who had a husband in the home jumped from 34 to 59. The percentage who were widowed or divorced remained about the same from 1944 to 1970.

Source: Adapted from U.S. Bureau of the Census, *Historical Statistics of the United States, Colonial Times to 1970, Bicentennial Edition* (Washington, D.C.: U.S. Government Printing Office, 1975), p. 133.

"Crisis of Masculinity"   While academics and mass media critics alike stressed the importance of "proper" female roles, they devoted equal attention to the plight of the American male. American men faced a "crisis of masculinity," proclaimed the nation's mass-circulation magazines, quoting an array of psychological experts. In a bestselling book, sociologist William H. Whyte explained that postwar corporate employees had become "organization men," succeeding through cooperation and conformity, not through individual initiative and risk. Women, too, were blamed for men's crisis: women's "natural" desire for security and comfort, experts insisted, was stifling men's natural instinct for adventure. Some even linked concerns about masculinity to the Cold War, arguing that, unless America's men recovered masculinity diminished by white-collar work or a suburban, family-centered existence, the nation's future was at risk. At the same time, however, men who did not conform to current standards of male responsibility—husband, father, breadwinner—were forcefully condemned, sometimes in the same magazines that preached the crisis of masculinity. One influential book advocated mandatory psychotherapy for men who reached thirty without having married; such single men were open to charges of "emotional immaturity" or "latent homosexuality."

Sexuality   Sexuality was complicated terrain in postwar America. Only heterosexual intercourse within marriage was deemed socially acceptable, and consequences for sexual misconduct could be severe. Women who became pregnant outside marriage were often ostracized by friends and family, and expelled from schools or colleges. Homosexuality was grounds for dismissal from a job, expulsion from college, even jail. At the same time, a great many Americans were breaking the sexual rules of the era. In his major works on human sexuality, *Sexual Behavior in the Human Male* (1948) and *Sexual Behavior in the Human Female* (1953), Dr. Alfred Kinsey, director of the Institute for Sex Research at Indiana University, informed Americans that, despite the fact that more than 80 percent of his female sample disapproved of premarital sex on "moral grounds," half of these women had had premarital sex. He also reported that at least 37 percent of American men had had "some homosexual experience." Americans made bestsellers of Kinsey's dry, quantitative studies—as many rushed to condemn him. One congressman charged Kinsey with "hurling the insult of the century against our mothers, wives, daughters and sisters"; the *Chicago Tribune* called him a "menace to society." Although Kinsey's population samples did not provide a completely accurate picture of American sexual behavior, his findings made many Americans aware that they were not alone in breaking certain rules.

Another challenge to the sexual rules of 1950s America came from Hugh Hefner, who launched *Playboy* magazine in 1953. Within three years, the magazine had a circulation of 1 million. Hefner saw *Playboy* as an attack on America's "ferocious anti-sexuality [and] dark antieroticism" and his nude "playmates" as a means for men to combat what he considered the increasingly "blurred distinctions between the sexes" in a family-centered suburban culture.

Youth Culture   As children grew up in relative stability and prosperity, a distinctive "youth culture" developed. Youth culture was really a set of subcultures; the culture of white, middle-class, suburban youth was not the same as that of black, urban teens or even of the white working class. Youth culture was, however, distinct from the culture of adults. Its customs and rituals were created within peer groups and shaped by national media—teen magazines, movies, radio, advertising, music—targeted toward this huge potential audience.

The sheer numbers of "baby boom" youth made them a force in American society. People sometimes described the baby-boom generation as "a pig in a python," and as this group moved from childhood to youth, communities successively built elementary schools, junior high schools, and high schools. America's corporations quickly learned the power of youth, as children's fads launched multimillion-dollar industries. Slinky, selling for a dollar, began loping down people's stairs in 1947; Mr. Potato Head—probably the first toy advertised on television—had $4 million in sales in 1952. In the mid-1950s, when Walt Disney's television show *Disneyland* featured Davy Crockett, "King of the Wild Frontier," every child in America (and more than a few adults) just *had* to have a coonskin cap. When the price of raccoon fur skyrocketed from 25 cents to $8 a pound, many children had to make do with a Davy Crockett lunchbox or toothbrush instead. As these baby-boom children grew up, their buying power shaped American popular culture.

By 1960, America's 18 million teenagers were spending $10 billion a year. Seventy-two percent of movie tickets in the 1950s were sold to teenagers, and Hollywood catered to this audience with films that ranged from forgettable B-movies like *The Cool and the Crazy* and *Senior Prom* to controversial and influential movies, such as James Dean's *Rebel Without a Cause*. Adults worried that teens would be drawn to romantic images of delinquency in *Rebel Without a Cause*, and teenage boys did copy Dean's rebellious look. The film, however, blamed parents for teenage confusion, drawing heavily on popular psychological theories about sexuality and the "crisis of masculinity." "What can you do when you have to be a man?" James Dean's character implored his father.

Movies helped shape teen fads and fashions, but nothing defined youth culture as much as its music. Young Americans were electrified by the driving energy and beat of Bill Haley and the Comets, Chuck Berry, Little Richard, and Buddy Holly. Elvis Presley's 1956 appearance on TV's *Ed Sullivan Show* touched off a frenzy of teen adulation—and a flood of letters from parents scandalized by his "gyrations." As one reviewer noted, "When Presley executes his bumps and grinds, it must be remembered that even the 12-year-old's curiosity may be overstimulated." Although few white musicians acknowledged the debt, the roots of rock 'n roll lay in African American rhythm and blues. The raw energy and sometimes sexually suggestive lyrics of early rock music faded as the music industry sought white performers, like Pat Boone, to do blander, more acceptable "cover" versions of music by black artists.

The distinct youth culture that developed in the 1950s made many adults uneasy. Parents worried that the common practice of "going steady" made it more likely that teens would "go too far" sexually. Juvenile delinquency was a major concern. Crime rates for young people had risen dramatically in the years following World War II, but much was "status" crime—curfew violations, sexual experimentation, underage drinking—activities that were criminal because of the person's age,

Elvis Presley "gyrates" during a live performance in 1956. Many adults were horrified ("sexhibitionist," Time magazine sneered), but Elvis was selling $75,000 worth of records a day in April 1956.

Picture Research Consultants & Archives

not because of the action itself. Congress held extensive hearings on juvenile delinquency, with experts testifying to the corrupting power of youth-oriented popular culture, comic books in particular. In 1955, *Life* magazine reported, "Some American parents, without quite knowing what it is their kids are up to, are worried that it's something they shouldn't be." Most youthful behavior, however—from going steady to fads in music and dress—fit squarely into the consumer culture that youth shared with their parents. "Rebellious youth" rarely questioned the logic of postwar American culture.

Challenges to Middle-Class Culture

Despite the growing reach and power of this middle-class culture, there were pockets of cultural dissent. Beat (a word that suggested both "down and out" and "beatific") writers rejected both middle-class social decorum and contemporary literary conventions. Jack Kerouac, author of *On the Road*, traced his inspiration to "weariness with all forms of the modern industrial state." The Beat Generation embraced spontaneity in their art, in their lives sought freedom from the demands of everyday life, and enjoyed a more open sexuality and drug use. Perhaps the most significant beat work was Allen Ginsberg's angry, incantational poem "Howl" (1956), the subject of an obscenity trial whose verdict opened American publishing to a much broader range of works. The mainstream press made fun of the beats, dubbing them and their followers "beatniks" (after *Sputnik*, suggesting their un-Americanness). Although they attracted little attention in the 1950s, they laid the groundwork for the 1960s counterculture.

THE LIMITS OF THE MIDDLE-CLASS NATION

During the 1950s, America's popular culture and mass media celebrated the opportunities available to the nation's people. At the same time, a host of influential critics rushed to condemn the new middle-class culture as a wasteland of conformity, homogeneity, and ugly consumerism.

Critics of Conformity   These critics were not lone figures crying out in the wilderness. Americans, obsessed with self-criticism even as most participated wholeheartedly in the celebratory "consensus" culture of their age, rushed to buy books like John Keats's *The Crack in the Picture Window* (1957), which portrayed three families—the "Drones," the "Amiables," and the "Fecunds"—who lived in identical suburban tract houses "vomited" up by developers and sacrificed their remaining individuality in the quest for consumer goods. Some of the most popular fiction of the postwar era, such as J. D. Salinger's *The Catcher in the Rye* and Norman Mailer's *The Naked and the Dead*, was profoundly critical of American society. Americans even made bestsellers of difficult academic works, such as David Riesman's *The Lonely Crowd* (1950) and William H. Whyte's *The Organization Man* (1955), both of which criticized the rise of conformity in American life. Versions of these critiques also appeared in mass-circulation magazines like *Ladies' Home Journal* and *Reader's Digest*. Steeped in such cultural criticism, many Americans even understood *Invasion of the Body Snatchers*—a 1956 film in which zombielike aliens grown in huge pods gradually replace a town's human inhabitants—as criticism of suburban conformity and the bland homogeneity of postwar culture.

Most of these critics were attempting to understand large-scale and significant changes in American society. Americans were contending with some loss of autonomy in work as large corporations replaced smaller businesses; they experienced the homogenizing force of mass production and a national consumer culture; they saw distinctions among ethnic groups and even among socioeconomic classes decline in importance. Many wanted to understand these social dislocations better. Critics of the new culture, however, were often elitist and antidemocratic. Many saw only bland conformity and sterility in the emerging middle-class suburban culture and so missed something important. Identical houses did not produce identical souls; instead, inexpensive suburban housing gave healthier, and perhaps happier, lives to millions who had grown up in dank, dark tenements or ramshackle farmhouses without indoor plumbing. In retrospect, however, other criticisms are obvious.

Environmental Degradation   First, the new consumer culture encouraged wasteful habits and harmed the environment. *Business Week* noted during the 1950s that corporations need not rely on "planned obsolescence," purposely designing a product to wear out so that consumers would have to replace it. Americans replaced products because they were "out of date," not because they did not work, and automakers, encouraging the trend, revamped designs every year. New and inexpensive plastic products and detergents made consumers' lives easier—but were not biodegradable. And America's new consumer society used an ever larger share of the world's resources. By the 1960s, the United States, with only 5 percent of the world's population, consumed more than one-third of its goods and services.

The rapid economic growth that made the middle-class consumer culture possible exacted environmental costs. Steel mills, coal-powered generators, and internal-combustion car engines burning lead-based gasoline polluted the atmosphere and imperiled people's health. As suburbanites commuted greater distances to their jobs, and neighborhoods were built without public transportation or shopping within walking distance of people's homes, Americans relied on private automobiles, consuming the nonrenewable resources of oil and gasoline, and filling cities and suburbs with smog. Vast quantities of water were diverted from lakes and rivers to meet the needs of America's burgeoning Sunbelt cities, including the swimming pools and golf courses that dotted parched Arizona and southern California.

Defense contractors and farmers were among the country's worst polluters. Refuse from nuclear weapons facilities at Hanford, Washington, and at Colorado's Rocky Flats arsenal poisoned soil and water resources for years. Agriculture began employing massive amounts of pesticides and other chemicals. DDT, a chemical used on Pacific islands during the war to kill mosquitoes and lice, was used widely in the United States from 1945 until after 1962, when wildlife biologist Rachel Carson specifically indicted DDT for the deaths of mammals, birds, and fish in her bestselling book *Silent Spring*.

In the midst of prosperity, few understood the consequences of the economic transformation taking place. The nation was moving toward a postindustrial economy in which providing goods and services to consumers was more important than producing goods. Therefore, though union members prospered during the 1950s, union membership grew slowly—because most new jobs were being created not in heavy industries that hired blue-collar workers but in the union-resistant white-collar service trades. Technological advances increased productivity, as automated electronic processes replaced slower mechanical ones—but they pushed people out of relatively well-paid blue-collar jobs into the growing and less well-paid service sector.

Continuing Racism

Largely oblivious to the environmental degradation and work-sector shifts that accompanied economic growth and consumerism, the new middle-class culture also largely ignored those who did not belong to its ranks. Race remained a major dividing line in American society, even as fewer Americans were excluded because of ethnic identity. Racial discrimination stood unchallenged in most of 1950s America. Suburbs, both North and South, were almost always racially segregated. Many white Americans had little or no contact in their daily lives with people of different races—not only because of residential segregation but also because the relatively small populations of nonwhite Americans were not dispersed equally throughout the nation. In 1960, there were 68

LINKS TO THE WORLD

Barbie

Barbie, the "all-American doll," is—like many Americans—an immigrant. Although Barbie was introduced in 1959 by the American toy company Mattel, her origins lie in Germany, where she went by the name Lilli.

As many mothers at the time suspected, noting the new doll's figure (equivalent to 39-21-31 in human proportions), Barbie's background was not completely respectable. The German Lilli doll was a toy for adult men, not little girls. She was based on a character that cartoonist Reinhard Beuthien drew to fill some empty space in the June 24, 1952, edition of the German tabloid *Das Bild*. The cartoon was meant to appear just once, but Lilli was so popular that she became a regular feature. Soon Lilli appeared in three-dimensional form as *Bild* Lilli, an eleven-and-a-half-inch-tall blonde doll—with the figure Barbie would make famous. Dressed in a variety of sexy outfits, Lilli was sold in tobacco shops and bars as a "novelty gift" for men.

Lilli came to America with Ruth Handler, one of the founders and codirectors of the Mattel toy company. In a time when girls were given baby dolls, Handler imagined a grown-up doll that girls could dress as they did their paper dolls. When she glimpsed Lilli while on vacation in Europe, Handler bought three—and gave one to her daughter Barbara, after whom Lilli would be renamed. Mattel bought the rights to Lilli (the doll and the cartoon, which Mattel quietly retired) and unveiled Barbie in March 1959. Despite mothers' hesitations about buying a doll that looked like Barbie, within the year Mattel had sold 351,000 Barbies at $3 each (or about $17 in 2000 dollars). The billionth Barbie was sold in 1997.

Within the United States, Barbie has been controversial—at least among adults. Some have worried that Barbie's wildly unrealistic figure fosters girls' dissatisfaction with their own body—a serious problem in a culture plagued with eating disorders. Others claim that, despite Barbie's 1980s "Girls Can Do Anything" makeover, Barbie represents a model of empty-headed femininity, focused on endless consumption. And many have criticized the ways in which blonde, blue-eyed Barbie failed to represent the diversity of America's people, especially as Mattel's early attempts at racial and ethnic diversity (such as "Colored Francie," introduced in 1967) created dolls with the same Caucasian features as the original Barbie, except with darker skin coloring and hair.

In recent years, Barbie has played a role in important international issues. In 2002, international labor-rights groups called for a boycott of Barbie. They cited studies showing that half of all Barbies are made by exploited young women workers in mainland China: of the $10 retail cost of an average Barbie, Chinese factories receive only 35 cents per doll to pay for all their costs, including labor. Barbie has also played a role in international relations. Saudi Arabia banned sales of Barbie in 2003, arguing that her skimpy outfits and the values she represents are not suitable for a Muslim nation. (A Syrian company now manufactures the very popular "Fulla," who, though with the same proportions as Barbie, comes with an abaya and a pink felt prayer mat.) And a poll found that, following the beginning of the United States' war in Iraq, people in other nations said they were less likely to buy Barbie because she was so closely identified with America.

Even so, the eleven-and-a-half-inch doll remains popular throughout the world, sold in more than 150 countries. Today, the average American girl has ten Barbies—and the typical German girl owns five. Over the years, for better or worse, Barbie has continued to link the United States and the rest of the world.

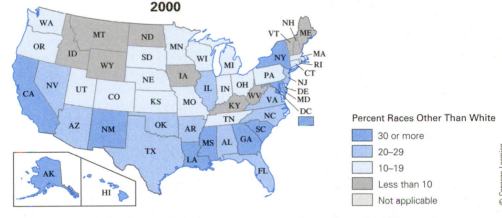

MAP 29.2 Racial Composition of the United States, 1950 and 2000

Compared with present-day America, most states were fairly racially homogeneous in 1950. The exception was the Deep South, where most African Americans still lived.

Source: Adapted from "Demographic Trends in the Twentieth Century," U.S. Census Bureau; www.census.gov/population/www/censusdata/hiscendata.html.

people of Chinese descent and 519 African Americans living in Vermont; 181 Native Americans lived in West Virginia; and Mississippi had just 178 Japanese American residents. Most white Americans in the 1950s—especially those outside the South, where there was a large African American population—gave little thought to race. They did not think of the emerging middle-class culture as "white," but as "American," marginalizing people of color in image as in reality (see Map 29.2).

The new middle-class culture was also indifferent to the plight of the poor. In an age of abundance, more than one in five Americans lived in poverty. One-fifth of the poor were people of color, including almost half of the nation's African American population and more than half of all Native Americans. Two-thirds of the poor lived in households headed by a person with an eighth-grade education or less, one-fourth in households headed by a single woman. More than one-third of the poor were under age eighteen; one-fourth were over age sixty-five. Social Security payments helped the elderly, but many retirees were not yet covered, and medical costs drove many older Americans into poverty. Few of these people had much reason for hope.

Poverty in an Age of Abundance   As millions of Americans (most of them white) were settling in the suburbs, the poor were ever more concentrated in the inner cities. African American migrants from the South were joined by poor whites from the southern Appalachians, many of whom moved to Chicago, Cincinnati, Baltimore, and Detroit. Meanwhile, Latin Americans were arriving in growing numbers from Mexico, the Dominican Republic, Colombia, Ecuador, and Cuba. According to the 1960 census, over a half-million Mexican Americans had migrated to the barrios of the Los Angeles–Long Beach area since 1940. And New York City's Puerto Rican population exploded from 70,000 in 1940 to 613,000 in 1960.

All of these newcomers to the cities came seeking better lives and greater opportunities. Because of the strong economy and low unemployment rate, many did gain a higher standard of living. But discrimination limited their advances, and they endured crowded and decrepit housing and poor schools. In addition, the federal programs that helped middle-class Americans sometimes made the lives of the poor worse. For example, the National Housing Act of 1949, passed to make available "a decent home … for every American family," provided for "urban redevelopment." Redevelopment meant slum clearance. Many poor people lost what housing they had as entire neighborhoods were leveled and replaced with luxury high-rise buildings, parking lots, and even highways.

Rural poverty was a long-standing problem in America, but the growth of large agribusinesses pushed more tenant farmers and owners of small farms off the land. From 1945 to 1961, the nation's farm population declined from 24.4 million to 14.8 million. When the harvesting of cotton in the South was mechanized in the 1940s and 1950s, more than 4 million people were displaced. Southern tobacco growers dismissed their tenant farmers, bought tractors to plow the land, and hired migratory workers to harvest the crops. Many of these displaced farmers traded southern rural poverty for northern urban poverty. And in the West and Southwest, Mexican citizens continued to serve as cheap migrant labor under the *bracero* program. Almost 1 million Mexican workers came legally to the United States in 1959; many more were undocumented workers. Entire families labored, enduring conditions little better than in the Great Depression.

Native Americans were America's poorest people, with an average annual income barely half that of the poverty level. Conditions for native peoples were made worse by a federal policy implemented during the Eisenhower administration: termination. Termination reversed the Indian Reorganization Act of 1934, allowing Indians to terminate their tribal status and so remove reservation lands from federal protection that prohibited their sale. Sixty-one tribes were terminated between 1954 and 1960. Termination could take place only with a tribe's agreement, but pressure was sometimes intense—especially when reservation land was rich in natural resources. The Klamaths of Oregon, for example, lived on a reservation rich in ponderosa pine, which lumber interests coveted. Enticed by cash payments, almost four-fifths of the Klamaths accepted termination and voted to sell their shares of the forest land. With termination, their way of life collapsed. Many Indians left reservation land for the city, joining the influx of other poor Americans seeking jobs and new lives. By the time termination was halted in the 1960s, observers compared the situation of Native Americans to the devastation their forebears had endured in the nineteenth century. Like most of the poor, these Americans were invisible to the growing middle class in the suburbs.

Overall, Americans who had lived through the devastation of the Great Depression and World War II enjoyed the relative prosperity and economic security of the postwar era. But those who had made it to the comfortable middle class often ignored the plight of those left behind. It would be their children—the generation of the baby boom, many reared in suburban comfort—who would see racism, poverty, and the self-satisfaction of postwar suburban culture as a failure of American ideals.

SUMMARY

As the experiences of economic depression and world war receded, Americans worked to create good lives for themselves and their families. People married and had children in record numbers. Millions of veterans used the GI Bill to attend college, buy homes, and start businesses. Although American leaders feared that the nation would lapse back into economic depression after wartime government spending ended, consumer spending brought economic growth. The sustained economic growth of the postwar era lifted a majority of Americans into an expanding middle class.

The Cold War presidencies of Truman and Eisenhower focused on international relations and a global struggle against communism, rather than on domestic politics. Within the United States, Cold War fears provoked an extreme anticommunism that stifled political dissent and diminished Americans' civil liberties and freedoms.

The continuing African American struggle for civil rights drew national attention during the Montgomery bus boycott, reminding whites that not all Americans enjoyed equality. African Americans won important victories in the Supreme Court, including the landmark decision in *Brown v. Board of Education*, and both Truman and Eisenhower used federal power to guarantee the rights of black Americans. With these victories, a national civil rights movement began to coalesce, and racial tensions within the nation increased.

Despite continued racial divisions, the United States became in many ways a more inclusive nation in the 1950s, as a majority of Americans participated in a national, consumer-oriented, middle-class culture. This culture largely ignored the poverty that remained in the nation's cities and rural areas, and contributed to rapidly increasing economic degradation. But for the growing number of middle-class Americans who, for the first time, lived in modest material comfort, the American dream seemed a reality.

30

THE TUMULTUOUS SIXTIES
1960–1968

KENNEDY AND THE COLD WAR

President John F. Kennedy was, as writer Norman Mailer observed, "our leading man." Young, handsome, and vigorous, the new chief executive was the first president born in the twentieth century. Kennedy had a genuinely inquiring mind, and as a patron of the arts he brought wit and sophistication to the White House. He was born to wealth and politics: his Irish American grandfather had been mayor of Boston, and his millionaire father, Joseph P. Kennedy, had served as ambassador to Great Britain. In 1946, the young Kennedy, having returned from the Second World War a naval hero (the boat he commanded had been rammed and sunk by a Japanese destroyer in 1943, and Kennedy had saved his crew), continued the family tradition by campaigning to represent Boston in the U.S. House of Representatives. He won easily, served three terms in the House, and in 1952 was elected to the Senate.

John Fitzgerald Kennedy   As a Democrat, Kennedy inherited the New Deal commitment to America's social welfare system. He generally cast liberal votes in line with the pro-labor sentiments of his low-income, blue-collar constituents. But he avoided controversial issues, such as civil rights and the censure of Joseph McCarthy. Kennedy won a Pulitzer Prize for his *Profiles in Courage* (1956), a study of politicians who had acted on principle, but he shaded the truth when he claimed sole authorship of the book, which had been written largely by aide Theodore Sorensen (though based on more than one hundred pages of notes dictated by Kennedy). In foreign policy,

CHRONOLOGY

1960	Sit-ins begin in Greensboro
	Birth-control pill approved
	John F. Kennedy elected president
	Young Americans for Freedom write Sharon Statement
1961	Freedom Rides protest segregation in transportation
1962	Students for a Democratic Society issues Port Huron Statement
	Cuban missile crisis courts nuclear war
1963	Civil rights March on Washington for Jobs and Freedom draws more than 250,000
	South Vietnamese leader Diem assassinated following U.S.-sanctioned coup d'état
	John F. Kennedy assassinated; Lyndon B. Johnson becomes president
1964	Civil Rights Act passed by Congress
	Race riots break out in first of the "long, hot summers"
	Gulf of Tonkin Resolution passed by Congress
	Free Speech Movement begins at University of California, Berkeley
	Lyndon B. Johnson elected president
1965	Lyndon Johnson launches Great Society programs
	United States commits ground troops to Vietnam and initiates bombing campaign
	Voting Rights Act outlaws practices preventing most African Americans from voting in southern states
	Immigration and Nationality Act lowers barriers to immigration from Asia and Latin America
	Malcolm X assassinated
1966	National Organization for Women founded
1967	"Summer of love" in San Francisco's Haight-Ashbury district
	Race riots erupt in Newark, Detroit, and other cities
1968	Tet Offensive deepens fear of losing war in Vietnam
	Martin Luther King Jr. assassinated
	Robert Kennedy assassinated
	Violence erupts at Democratic National Convention
	Richard Nixon elected president

Senator Kennedy endorsed the Cold War policy of containment, and his interest in world affairs deepened as the 1950s progressed. His record as a legislator was not impressive, but he enjoyed an enthusiastic following, especially after his landslide reelection to the Senate in 1958.

Kennedy and his handlers worked hard to cultivate an image of him as a happy and healthy family man. To some extent, it was a ruse. He was a chronic woman-izer, and his liaisons continued even after he married Jacqueline Bouvier in 1953. Nor was he the picture of physical vitality that his war-hero status and youthful handsomeness seemed to project. As a child, he had almost died of scarlet fever, and he spent large portions of his early years in bed, suffering from one ailment after another. He developed severe back problems, made worse by his fighting experience in World War II. After the war, Kennedy was diagnosed with Addison's disease, an adrenalin deficiency that required daily injections of cortisone in order to be contained. At the time, the disease was thought to be terminal; though Ken-nedy survived, he was often in acute pain. As president, he would require plenty of bed rest and frequent therapeutic swims in the White House pool.

Election of 1960   Kennedy's rhetoric and style captured the imagination of many Americans. Yet his election victory over Republican Richard Nixon in 1960 was extraordinarily narrow—118,000 votes out of nearly 69 million cast. Kennedy achieved only mixed success in the South, but he ran well in the Northeast and Midwest. His Roman Catholic faith hurt him in some states, where voters feared he would take direction from the pope, but helped in states with large Catholic populations. As the sitting vice president, Nixon was saddled with the handicaps of incumbency; he had to answer for sagging economic figures and the Soviet downing of a U-2 spy plane. Nixon also looked disagreeable on TV; in televised debates against the telegenic Kennedy, he looked alternately ner-vous and surly, and the camera made him appear unshaven. Perhaps worse, Eisenhower gave Nixon only a tepid endorsement. Asked to list Nixon's signifi-cant decisions as vice president, Eisenhower replied, "If you give me a week, I might think of one."

In a departure from the Eisenhower administration's staid, conservative image, the new president surrounded himself with mostly young advisers of intellectual verve, who proclaimed that they had fresh ideas for invigorating the nation; writer David Halberstam called them "the best and the brightest." Secretary of Defense Robert McNamara (age forty-four) had been an assistant professor at Harvard at twenty-four and later the whiz-kid president of the Ford Motor Company. Kenne-dy's special assistant for national security affairs, McGeorge Bundy (age forty-one) had become a Harvard dean at thirty-four with only a bachelor's degree. Secretary of State Dean Rusk, the old man in the group at fifty-two, had been a Rhodes scholar in his youth. Kennedy himself was only forty-three, and his brother Robert, the attorney general, was thirty-five.

It was no accident that most of these "best and brightest" operated in the realm of foreign policy. From the start, Kennedy gave top priority to waging the Cold War. In the campaign, he had criticized Eisenhower's foreign policy as unimagina-tive, accusing him of missing chances to reduce the threat of nuclear war with the Soviet Union and of weakening America's standing in the Third World. Kennedy and his advisers exuded confidence that they would change things. As national security adviser McGeorge Bundy put it, "The United States is the engine of man-kind, and the rest of the world is the caboose." Kennedy's inaugural address suggested no halfway measures: "Let every nation know that we shall pay any price, bear any burden, meet any hardship, support any friend, oppose any foe to assure the survival and the success of liberty."

Nation Building in the Third World   In reality, Kennedy in office would not be prepared to pay any price or bear any burden in the struggle against communism. He came to understand, sooner than many of his advisers, that there were limits to American power abroad; overall, he showed himself to be cautious and pragmatic in foreign policy. More than his predecessor, he proved willing to initiate dialog with the Soviets, sometimes using his brother Robert as a secret back channel to Moscow. Yet Kennedy also sought victory in the Cold War. After Soviet leader Nikita Khrushchev endorsed "wars of national liberation," such as the one in Vietnam, Kennedy called for "peaceful revolution" based on the concept of nation building. The administration set out to help developing nations through the early stages of nationhood with aid programs aimed at improving agriculture, transportation, and communications. Kennedy thus oversaw the creation of the multibillion-dollar Alliance for Progress in 1961 to spur economic development in Latin America. In the same year, he also created the Peace Corps, dispatching thousands of American teachers, agricultural specialists, and health workers, many of them right out of college, to assist authorities in developing nations.

Cynics then and later dismissed the Alliance and the Peace Corps as Cold War tools by which Kennedy sought to counter anti-Americanism and defeat communism in the developing world. The programs did have those aims, but both were also born of genuine humanitarianism. The Peace Corps in particular embodied both the idealistic, can-do spirit of the 1960s and Americans' long pursuit of moral leadership in the world. "More than any other entity," historian Elizabeth Cobbs Hoffman has written, "the Peace Corps broached an age-old dilemma of U.S. foreign policy: how to reconcile the imperatives and temptations of power politics with the ideals of freedom and self-determination for all nations."

It was one thing to broach the dilemma, and quite another to resolve it. Kennedy and his aides considered themselves supportive of social revolution in the Third World, but they could not imagine the legitimacy of communist involvement in any such uprising, or that developing countries might wish to be neutral in the East-West struggle. In addition to largely benevolent programs like the Peace Corps, therefore, the administration also relied on the more insidious concept of counterinsurgency to defeat revolutionaries who challenged pro-American Third World governments. American military and technical advisers trained native troops and police forces to quell unrest.

Nation building and counterinsurgency encountered numerous problems. The Alliance for Progress was only partly successful; infant mortality rates improved, but Latin American economies registered unimpressive growth rates, and class divisions continued to widen, exacerbating political unrest. Americans assumed that the U.S. model of capitalism and representative government could be transferred successfully to foreign cultures. Although many foreign peoples welcomed U.S. economic assistance and craved American material culture, they resented intereference by outsiders. And because aid was usually transmitted through a self-interested elite, it often failed to reach the very poor.

Soviet-American Tensions   Nor did the new president have success in relations with the Soviet Union. A summit meeting with Soviet leader Nikita Khrushchev in Vienna in June 1961 went poorly, with the two leaders disagreeing over the preconditions for peace and stability in the world. Consequently, the administration's first year witnessed little movement on controlling the nuclear arms race or even on getting a superpower ban on testing nuclear weapons in the atmosphere or underground. The latter objective mattered a great deal to Kennedy, who saw a test ban as a prerequisite to preventing additional nations from getting the terrifying weapon. Instead, both superpowers continued testing and accelerated their arms production. In 1961, the U.S. military budget shot up 15 percent; by mid-1964, U.S. nuclear weapons had increased by 150 percent. Government advice to citizens to build fallout shelters in their backyards intensified public fear of devastating war.

If war occurred, many believed it would be over the persistent problem of Berlin. In mid-1961, Khrushchev ratcheted up the tension by demanding an end to western occupation of West Berlin and a reunification of East and West Germany. Kennedy replied that the United States would stand by its commitment to West Berlin and West Germany. In August, the Soviets—at the urging of the East German regime—erected a concrete and barbed-wire barricade across the divided city to halt the exodus of East Germans into the more prosperous and politically free West Berlin. The Berlin Wall inspired protests throughout the noncommunist world, but Kennedy privately sighed that "a wall is a hell of a lot better than a war." The ugly barrier shut off the flow of refugees, and the crisis passed.

Bay of Pigs Invasion   Yet Kennedy knew that Khrushchev would continue to press for advantage in various parts of the globe. The president was particularly rankled by the growing Soviet assistance to the Cuban government of Fidel Castro. Kennedy once acknowledged that most American allies thought the United States had a "fixation" with Cuba; whether true of the country as a whole, he himself certainly did. The Eisenhower administration had contested the Cuban revolution and bequeathed to the Kennedy administration a partially developed CIA plan to overthrow Fidel Castro: CIA-trained Cuban exiles would land and secure a beachhead; the Cuban people would rise up against Castro and welcome a new government brought in from the United States.

Kennedy approved the plan, and the attack took place on April 17, 1961, as twelve hundred exiles landed at the swampy Bay of Pigs in Cuba. But no discontented Cubans were there to greet them, only troops loyal to the Castro government. The invaders were quickly surrounded and captured. Kennedy had tried to keep the U.S. participation in the operation hidden—for this reason, he refused to provide air cover for the attackers—but the CIA's role swiftly became public. Anti-American sentiment shot up throughout Latin America. Castro, concluding that the United States would not take defeat well and might launch another invasion, looked even more toward the Soviet Union for a military and economic lifeline.

© Bettmann/Corbis

Reporters take pictures of President Kennedy behind his desk, after he signed the arms embargo against Cuba.

Embarrassed by the Bay of Pigs fiasco, Kennedy vowed to bring Castro down. The CIA soon hatched a project called Operation Mongoose to disrupt the island's trade, support raids on Cuba from Miami, and plot to kill Castro. The agency's assassination schemes included providing Castro with cigars laced with explosives and deadly poison, and an attempt to harpoon him while he was snorkeling at a Caribbean resort. The United States also tightened its economic blockade and undertook military maneuvers in the Caribbean. The Joint Chiefs of Staff sketched plans to spark a rebellion in Cuba that would be followed by an invasion of U.S. troops. "If I had been in Moscow or Havana at that time," defense secretary Robert McNamara later remarked, "I would have believed the Americans were preparing for an invasion."

Cuban Missile Crisis McNamara knew whereof he spoke, for both Castro and Khrushchev believed an invasion was coming. This was one reason for the Soviet leader's risky decision in 1962 to secretly deploy nuclear missiles in Cuba: he hoped the presence of such weapons on the island would deter any attack. But Khrushchev also had other motives. Installing atomic weaponry in Cuba would instantly improve the Soviet position in the nuclear balance of power, he believed, and might also force Kennedy to resolve the German problem once and for all. Khrushchev still wanted to oust the West from Berlin, and he also worried that Washington might provide West Germany with nuclear weapons. What better way to prevent such a move than to put Soviet missiles just 90 miles off the coast of Florida? With Castro's support, Khrushchev moved to install the weapons. The world soon faced brinkmanship at its most frightening.

In mid-October 1962, a U-2 plane flying over Cuba photographed the missile sites. The president immediately organized a special Executive Committee (ExComm) of advisers to find a way to force the missiles and their nuclear warheads out of Cuba. Options that the ExComm considered ranged from full-scale invasion to limited bombing to quiet diplomacy. McNamara proposed the formula that the president ultimately accepted: a naval quarantine of Cuba.

Kennedy addressed the nation on television on October 22 and demanded that the Soviets retreat. U.S. warships began crisscrossing the Caribbean, while B-52s with nuclear bombs took to the skies. Khrushchev replied that the missiles would be withdrawn if the United States pledged never to attack Cuba. And he added that American Jupiter missiles aimed at the Soviet Union must be removed from Turkey. Edgy advisers predicted war, and for several days the world teetered on the brink of disaster. Then, on October 28, came a compromise. The United States promised not to invade Cuba, secretly pledging to withdraw the Jupiters from Turkey in exchange for the withdrawal of Soviet offensive forces from Cuba. Fearing accidents or some provocative action by Castro that might start a "real fire," Khrushchev decided to settle without consulting the Cubans. The missiles were removed from the island.

Many observers then and later called it Kennedy's finest hour. Tapes of the ExComm meetings recorded during the crisis reveal a deeply engaged, calmly authoritative commander-in-chief, committed to removing the missiles peacefully if possible. Critics claim that Kennedy helped cause the crisis in the first place with his anti-Cuban projects; some contend that quiet diplomacy could have achieved the same result, without the extraordinary tension. Other skeptics assert that Kennedy rejected a diplomatic solution because he feared the Republicans would ride the missiles to victory in the upcoming midterm elections. Still, it cannot be denied that the president handled the crisis skillfully, exercising both restraint and flexibility. At this most tense moment of the Cold War, Kennedy had proven equal to the task.

The Cuban missile crisis was a watershed in the Soviet-American relationship. Both Kennedy and Khrushchev acted with greater prudence in its aftermath, taking determined steps toward improved bilateral relations. Much of the hostility drained out of the relationship. In June 1963, Kennedy spoke in conciliatory terms during a commencement address at American University, urging cautious Soviet-American steps toward disarmament. In August, the adversaries signed a treaty banning nuclear tests in the atmosphere, the oceans, and outer space. They also installed a coded wire-telegraph "hot line" staffed around the clock by translators and technicians, to allow near-instant communication between the capitals. Both sides refrained from further confrontation in Berlin.

Individually, these steps were small, but together they reversed the trend of the previous years and began to build much-needed mutual trust. One could even argue that, by the autumn of 1963, the Cold War in Europe was drawing to a close. Both sides, it seemed, were prepared to accept the status quo of a divided continent and a fortified border. At the same time, though, the arms race continued and in some respects accelerated, and the superpower competition in the Third World showed little sign of cooling down.

MARCHING FOR FREEDOM

From the beginning of his presidency, John Kennedy believed that the Cold War was the most important issue facing the American people. But in the early 1960s, young civil rights activists—building on a decades-long struggle—seized the national stage and demanded that the force of the federal government be mobilized behind them. They won victories in their struggle for racial justice, but their gains were paid for in blood.

Students and the Movement   A Woolworth's lunch counter sit-in begun by four freshmen from North Carolina A&T marked a turning point in the African American struggle for civil rights. In 1960, six years after the Brown decision had declared "separate but equal" unconstitutional, only 10 percent of southern public schools had begun desegregation. Fewer than one in four adult black Americans in the South had access to the voting booth, and water fountains in public places were still labeled "White Only" and "Colored Only." But one year after the young men had sat down at the Woolworth's all-white lunch counter in Greensboro, more than seventy thousand Americans—most of them college students—had participated in the sit-in movement. City by city, they challenged Jim Crow segregation at lunch counters in the South and protested at the northern branches of national chains that practiced segregation in their southern stores.

The young people who created the Student Nonviolent Coordinating Committee (SNCC) in the spring of 1960 to help coordinate the sit-in movement were, like Martin Luther King Jr., committed to nonviolence. In the years to come, such young people would risk their lives in the struggle for social justice.

Freedom Rides and Voter Registration   On May 4, 1961, thirteen members of the Congress of Racial Equality (CORE), a nonviolent civil rights organization formed during World War II, purchased bus tickets in Washington, D.C., for a 1,500-mile trip through the South to New Orleans. This racially integrated group, calling themselves Freedom Riders, meant to demonstrate that, despite Supreme Court rulings ordering the desegregation of interstate buses and bus stations, Jim Crow still ruled in the South. These men and women knew they were risking their lives, and some suffered injuries from which they never recovered. One bus was firebombed outside Anniston, Alabama. Riders were badly beaten in Birmingham. In Montgomery, after reinforcements replaced the injured, a mob of more than a thousand whites attacked riders on another bus with baseball bats and steel bars. Police were nowhere to be seen; Montgomery's police commissioner declared, "We have no intention of standing guard for a bunch of troublemakers coming into our city."

News of the violent attacks made headlines around the world. In the Soviet Union, commentators pointed out the "savage nature of American freedom and democracy." One southern business leader, in Tokyo to promote Birmingham as a site for international business development, saw Japanese interest evaporate when photographs of the Birmingham attacks appeared in Tokyo newspapers.

In America, the violence—reported by the national news media—forced many to confront the reality of racial discrimination and hatred in their nation. Middle- and upper-class white southerners had participated in the "massive resistance" to integration following the *Brown* decision, and many white southerners, even racial moderates, remained highly suspicious of interference by the "Yankee" federal government almost a century after the Civil War. The Freedom Rides made some think differently. The *Atlanta Journal* editorialized: "[I]t is time for the decent people ... to muzzle the jackals." The national and international outcry pushed a reluctant President Kennedy to act. In a direct challenge to southern doctrines of states' rights, Kennedy sent federal marshals to Alabama to safeguard the Freedom Riders and their supporters. At the same time, bowing to white southern pressure, he allowed the Freedom Riders to be arrested in Mississippi.

While some activists pursued these "direct action" tactics, others worked to build black political power in the South. Beginning in 1961, thousands of SNCC volunteers, many of them high school and college students, risked their lives walking the dusty back roads of Mississippi and Georgia, encouraging African Americans to register to vote. Some SNCC volunteers were white, and some were from the North, but many were black southerners, and many were from low-income families. These volunteers understood from experience how racism, power-lessness, and poverty intersected in the lives of African Americans.

Kennedy and Civil Rights   President Kennedy was generally sympathetic—though not terribly committed—to the civil rights movement, and he realized that racial oppression hurt the United States in the Cold War struggle for international opinion. However, like Franklin D. Roosevelt, he also understood that if he alienated conservative southern Democrats in Congress, his legislative programs would founder. Thus, he appointed five die-hard segregationists to the federal bench in the Deep South and delayed issuing an executive order forbidding segregation in federally subsidized housing (a pledge made in the 1960 campaign) until late 1962. Furthermore, he allowed FBI director J. Edgar Hoover to harass Martin Luther King and other civil rights leaders, using wiretaps and surveillance to gather personal information and circulating rumors of communist connections and of personal improprieties in efforts to discredit their leadership.

But grassroots civil rights activism—and the violence of white mobs—relentlessly forced Kennedy's hand. In September 1962, the president ordered 500 U.S. marshals to protect James Meredith, the first African American student to attend the University of Mississippi. In response, thousands of whites attacked the marshals with guns, gasoline bombs, bricks, and pipes. The mob killed two men and seriously wounded 160 federal marshals. The marshals did not back down, nor did James Meredith. He broke the color line at "Ole Miss."

Birmingham and the Children's Crusade   In 1961, the Freedom Riders had captured the attention of the nation and the larger Cold War world, and forced the hand of the president. Martin Luther King Jr., having risen through the Montgomery bus boycott to leadership in the

VISUALIZING THE PAST

"Project C" and National Opinion

This photograph of a police dog attacking a 17-year-old demonstrator during a civil rights march in Birmingham, Alabama, appeared on the front page of the *New York Times* on May 4, 1963, just above a second photograph of a fireman spraying a group that included three teenage girls with a high pressure fire hose. The following day President Kennedy discussed this photo in a meeting in the White House. Some historians argue that photographs not only document history, they make it. Is that statement true in this case? How does this photograph fit into Martin Luther King's plans for "Project C"? What difference might it make that the *New York Times* editors chose to run this photograph rather than one of the many others taken that day?

AP Photo/Bill Hudson

Mass media coverage helped galvanize public opinion in support of civil rights protesters.

movement, understood the implications of these events. He and his allies, still committed to principles of nonviolence, concluded that the only way to move to the next stage of the struggle for civil rights was to provoke a crisis that would attract national and international attention, and create pressure for further change.

King and his Southern Christian Leadership Conference (SCLC) began to plan a 1963 campaign in one of the most violently racist cities in America: Birmingham, Alabama. Fully aware that their nonviolent protests would draw violent response, they called their plan Project C—for "confrontation." King wanted all Americans to see the racist hate and violence that marred their nation.

Through most of April 1963, nonviolent protests in Birmingham led to hundreds of arrests. Then, on May 2, in a highly controversial action, King and the parents of Birmingham raised the stakes. They put children, some as young as six, on the front lines of protest. As about a thousand black children marched for civil rights, police commissioner Eugene "Bull" Connor ordered his police to train "monitor" water guns—powerful enough to strip bark from a tree at 100 feet—on them. The water guns mowed the children down, and then police loosed attack dogs. As footage played on the evening news, the nation watched with horror. President Kennedy, once again, was pushed into action. He demanded that Birmingham's white business and political elite negotiate a settlement. Under pressure, they agreed. The Birmingham movement had won a concrete victory. Even more, activists had pushed civil rights to the fore of President Kennedy's political agenda.

"Segregation Forever!"   The Kennedy administration also confronted the defiant governor of Alabama, George C. Wallace. On June 11, Wallace fulfilled a promise to "bar the schoolhouse door" himself to prevent the desegregation of the University of Alabama. Hearing echoes of Wallace's January 1963 inaugural pledge "Segregation now, segregation tomorrow, segregation forever!" and facing a nation rocked by hundreds of civil rights protests, many of them met with white mob violence, Kennedy committed the power of the federal government to guarantee racial justice—even over the opposition of individual states. The next evening, June 12, in a televised address, Kennedy told the American people, "Now the time has come for this nation to fulfill its promise." A few hours later, thirty-seven-year-old civil rights leader Medgar Evers was murdered—in front of his children—in his driveway in Jackson, Mississippi. The next week, the president asked Congress to pass a comprehensive civil rights bill that would end legal discrimination on the basis of race in the entire United States.

March on Washington   On August 28, 1963, a quarter-million Americans gathered in the steamy heat on the Washington Mall. They came from all over America to show Congress their support for Kennedy's civil rights bill; many also wanted federal action to guarantee work opportunities. Behind the scenes, organizers from the major civil rights groups— SCLC, CORE, SNCC, the NAACP, the Urban League, and A. Philip Randolph's Brotherhood of Sleeping Car Porters—grappled with growing tensions within the movement. SNCC activists saw Kennedy's proposed legislation as too little, too late, and wanted radical action. King and other older leaders counseled the virtues of moderation. The movement was beginning to splinter.

Those divisions were not completely hidden. SNCC's John Lewis told the assembled crowd that SNCC members had come to the march "with a great sense of misgiving" and asked, "Where is the political party that will make it unnecessary to march on Washington?" What most Americans saw, however, was a celebration of unity. Black and white celebrities joined hands; folk singers sang songs of freedom. Television networks cut away from afternoon soap operas as Martin Luther King Jr., in southern-preacher cadences, prophesied a day when "all God's children, black men and white men, Jews and Gentiles, Protestants and Catholics, will be able to join hands and sing in the words of the old Negro spiritual, Free at last! Free at last! Thank God Almighty, we are free at last!" The 1963 March on Washington for Jobs and Freedom was a moment of triumph, powerfully demonstrating to the nation the determination of its African American citizens to secure equality and justice. But the struggle was far from over. Just days later, white supremacists bombed the Sixteenth Street Baptist Church in Birmingham, killing four black girls.

Freedom Summer   In the face of violence, the struggle for racial justice continued. During the summer of 1964, more than one thousand white students joined the voter mobilization project in Mississippi. These workers formed Freedom Schools, teaching literacy and constitutional rights, and helped organize the Mississippi Freedom Democratic Party as an alternative to the regular, white-only Democratic Party. Key SNCC organizers also believed that large numbers of white volunteers would focus national attention on Mississippi repression and violence. Not all went smoothly: local black activists were sometimes frustrated when well-educated white volunteers stepped into decision-making roles, and tensions over interracial sexual relationships complicated an already difficult situation. Far worse, project workers were arrested over a thousand times and were shot at, bombed, and beaten. On June 21, local black activist James Cheney and two white volunteers, Michael Schwerner and Andrew Goodman, were murdered by a Klan mob. Four days later, before their bodies had been found, Walter Cronkite told the nightly news audience that all of America was watching Mississippi. CBS played footage of black and white workers holding hands, singing "We Shall Overcome." That summer, black and white activists risked their lives together, challenging the racial caste system of the Deep South.

LIBERALISM AND THE GREAT SOCIETY

By 1963, with civil rights at the top of his domestic agenda, Kennedy seemed to be taking a new path. Campaigning in 1960, he had promised to lead Americans into a "New Frontier," a society in which the federal government would work to eradicate poverty, restore the nation's cities, guarantee healthcare to the elderly, and provide decent schools for all America's children. But few of Kennedy's domestic initiatives were passed into law, in part because Kennedy did not use his political capital to support them. Lacking a popular mandate in the 1960 election, fearful of alienating southern Democrats in Congress, and without a strong vision of domestic reform, Kennedy let his administration's social policy agenda languish.

Instead, Kennedy focused on less controversial attempts to fine-tune the American economy, believing that continued economic growth and prosperity would solve America's social problems. Kennedy's vision was perhaps best realized in America's space program. As the Soviets drew ahead in the Cold War space race, Kennedy vowed in 1961 to put a man on the moon before decade's end. With billions in new funding, the National Aeronautics and Space Administration (NASA) began the Apollo program. And in February 1962, astronaut John Glenn orbited the earth in the space capsule *Friendship 7*.

Kennedy Assassination

The nation would not learn what sort of president John Kennedy might have become. On November 22, 1963, Kennedy visited Texas, the home state of his vice president, Lyndon Johnson. In Dallas, riding with his wife, Jackie, in an open-top limousine, Kennedy was cheered by thousands of people lining the motorcade's route. Suddenly, shots rang out. The president crumpled, shot in the head. Tears ran down the cheeks of CBS anchorman Walter Cronkite as he told the nation their president was dead. The word spread quickly, in whispered messages to classroom teachers, by somber announcements in factories and offices, through the stunned faces of people on the street.

That same day, police captured a suspect: Lee Harvey Oswald, a former U.S. marine (dishonorably discharged) who had once attempted to gain Soviet citizenship. Just two days later, in full view of millions of TV viewers, Oswald himself was shot dead by shady nightclub owner Jack Ruby. Americans, already in shock, were baffled. What was Ruby's motive? Was he silencing Oswald to prevent him from implicating others? The seven-member Warren Commission, headed by U.S. Supreme Court Chief Justice Earl Warren, concluded that Oswald had acted alone. For four days, the tragedy played uninterrupted on American television. Millions of Americans watched their president's funeral: the brave young widow behind a black veil; a riderless horse; three-year-old "John-John" saluting his father's casket. In one awful moment in Dallas, the reality of the Kennedy presidency had been transformed into myth, the man into martyr. People would remember Kennedy less for any specific accomplishment than for his youthful enthusiasm, his inspirational rhetoric, and the romance he brought to American political life. In a peculiar way, he accomplished more in death than in life. In the postassassination atmosphere of grief and remorse, Lyndon Johnson, sworn in as president aboard *Air Force One*, invoked Kennedy's memory to push through the most ambitious program of legislation since the New Deal.

Johnson and the Great Society

The new president was a big and passionate man, different from his predecessor in almost every respect. While Kennedy had been raised to wealth and privilege and was educated at Harvard, Johnson had grown up in modest circumstances in the Texas hill country and was graduated from Southwest Texas State Teachers' College. He was as earthy as Kennedy was elegant, prone to colorful curses, and willing to use his physical size to his advantage. Advisers and aides reported that he expected them to follow him into the bathroom and conduct business while he showered or used the toilet. But Johnson had been in national politics most of his adult life. He filled an empty congressional seat from Texas in 1937, and as Senate majority leader from 1954 to 1960, he had learned how to manipulate people and wield power to achieve his ends. Now, as president, he used these political skills in an attempt to unite and reassure the nation. "Let us here highly resolve," he told a joint session of Congress five days after the assassination, "that John Fitzgerald Kennedy did not live—or die—in vain."

Johnson, a liberal in the style of Franklin D. Roosevelt, believed that the federal government must work actively to improve the lives of Americans. In a 1964 commencement address at the University of Michigan, he described his vision of a nation built on "abundance and liberty for all ... demand[ing] an end to poverty and racial injustice ... where every child can find knowledge to enrich his mind and to enlarge his talents ... where every man can renew contact with nature ... where men are more concerned with the quality of their goals than the quantity of their goods." Johnson called this vision "The Great Society."

Civil Rights Act   Johnson made civil rights his top legislative priority, and in July he signed into law the Civil Rights Act of 1964. This legislation ended *legal* discrimination on the basis of race, color, religion, national origin, in federal programs, voting, employment, and public accommodation; sex discrimination in employment was also banned. The original bill did not include sex discrimination; that provision was introduced by a southern congressman who hoped it would engender so much opposition that the bill as a whole would fail. However, when a bipartisan group of women members of the House of Representatives took up the cause, the bill was passed—with sex as a protected category. Significantly, the Civil Rights Act of 1964 created mechanisms for enforcement, giving the government authority to withhold federal funds from public agencies or federal contractors that discriminated and establishing the Equal Employment Opportunity Commission (EEOC) to investigate and judge claims of job discrimination. However, the EEOC paid little attention to sex discrimination, and in response, in 1966 supporters of women's equality formed the National Organization for Women (NOW). It would be one element in a broad movement for women's rights and equality that would take off in the next decade.

Many Americans did not believe it was the federal government's job to end racial discrimination or to fight poverty. Many white southerners resented federal intervention in what they considered local customs; many white northerners were angry about the violent uprisings in urban ghettos during the summer of 1964. And throughout the nation, millions of conservative Americans believed that since the New Deal, the federal government had been overstepping its constitutional boundaries. They sought a return to local control and states' rights in the face of growing federal power. In the 1964 election, this conservative vision was championed by the Republican candidate, Arizona senator Barry Goldwater.

Election of 1964   Goldwater had not only voted against the 1964 Civil Rights Act; he also opposed the national Social Security system. Like many conservatives, he believed that individual *liberty*, not equality, was the most important American value. Goldwater's calls for "law and order" drew cheers from voters. He also believed that the United States needed a more powerful national military to fight communism; in campaign speeches he suggested that the United States should use tactical nuclear weapons against its enemies. "Extremism in the defense of liberty is no vice," he told delegates at the 1964 Republican National Convention.

Goldwater's campaign slogan, "In your heart you know he's right," was turned against him by Lyndon Johnson's supporters: "In your heart you know he's right … far right," one punned. Another version warned of Goldwater's willingness to use nuclear weapons: "In your heart you know he might." Johnson campaigned on his record, with an unemployment rate under 4 percent and economic growth at better than 6 percent. But he knew that his support of civil rights had broken apart the New Deal coalition. Shortly after signing the Civil Rights Act of 1964, he told an aide, "I think we just delivered the south to the Republican Party for my lifetime and yours."

The tension between Johnson's support of civil rights and his need for southern Democratic support came to a head at the 1964 Democratic National Convention. Two delegations had arrived from Mississippi, each demanding to be seated. The Democratic Party's official delegation was exclusively white; the Mississippi Freedom Democratic Party (MFDP) sent a racially mixed delegation to represent a state in which discriminatory literacy tests and violence disenfranchised its black citizens. The white representatives from southern states threatened to stage a public walkout if the MFDP delegates were seated. MFDP delegate Fannie Lou Hamer offered powerful testimony to the convention's credentials committee, concluding, "[If] the Freedom Party is not seated now, I question America." Johnson tried to engineer a compromise, but the MFDP had no interest in political deals. "We didn't come all this way for no two seats," Hamer said, and the delegation walked out.

Johnson lost the MFDP, and he also lost the Deep South—the first Democrat since the Civil War to do so. Yet he won the election by a landslide, and American voters also gave him the most liberal Congress in American history. With the mandate provided by a record 61.1 percent of the popular vote, Johnson launched his Great Society. Congress responded to Johnson's election with the most sweeping reform legislation since 1935.

Civil rights remained a critical issue. In late 1964, the SCLC put voting rights at the top of its agenda. Martin Luther King Jr. and other leaders turned to Selma, Alabama—a town with a history of vicious response to civil rights protest—seeking another public confrontation that would mobilize national support and federal action. That confrontation came on March 6, when state troopers turned electric cattle prods, chains, and tear gas against peaceful marchers as they crossed the Edmund Pettus Bridge on the way to Montgomery. On March 15, the president addressed Congress and the nation, offering full support for a second monumental civil rights bill, the Voting Rights Act. This act outlawed practices that had prevented most black citizens in the Deep South from voting and provided for federal oversight of elections in districts where there was evidence of past discrimination (see Map 30.1). Within two years, the percentage of African Americans registered to vote in Mississippi jumped from 7 percent to almost 60 percent. Black elected officials became increasingly common in southern states over the following decade.

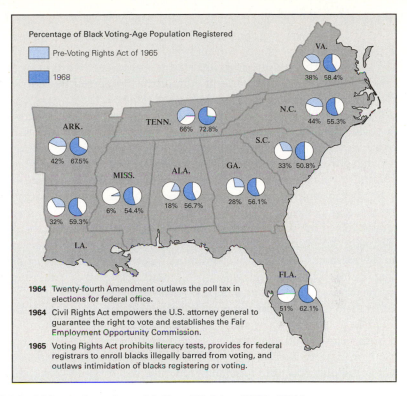

Percentage of Black Voting-Age Population Registered

☐ Pre-Voting Rights Act of 1965

■ 1968

VA.
38% 58.4%

ARK.
42% 67.5%

TENN.
66% 72.8%

N.C.
44% 55.3%

S.C.
33% 50.8%

MISS.
32% 59.3%

ALA.
6% 54.4%

GA.
18% 56.7% 28% 56.1%

LA.

FLA.
51% 62.1%

1964 Twenty-fourth Amendment outlaws the poll tax in elections for federal office.

1964 Civil Rights Act empowers the U.S. attorney general to guarantee the right to vote and establishes the Fair Employment Opportunity Commission.

1965 Voting Rights Act prohibits literacy tests, provides for federal registrars to enroll blacks illegally barred from voting, and outlaws intimidation of blacks registering or voting.

MAP 30.1 African American Voting Rights, 1960–1971

After passage of the 1965 Voting Rights Act, African American registration skyrocketed in Mississippi and Alabama, and rose substantially in other southern states.

Source: Harold W. Stanley, *Voter Mobilization and the Politics of Race: The South and Universal Suffrage, 1952–1984.* Praeger Publishers, p. 97. Copyright 1987 by Greenwood Publishing Group. Reproduced with permission of Greenwood Publishing Group, Inc., Westport, CT.

Improving American Life   Seeking to improve the quality of American life, the Johnson administration established new student loan and grant programs to help low- and moderate-income Americans attend college, and created the National Endowment for the Arts and the National Endowment for the Humanities. The Immigration Act of 1965 ended the racially based quotas that had shaped American immigration policy for decades. And Johnson supported important consumer protection legislation, including the 1966 National Traffic and Motor Vehicle Safety Act, which was inspired by Ralph Nader's expos of the automobile industry, *Unsafe at Any Speed* (1965).

Environmentalists found an ally in the Johnson administration as well. First Lady Claudia Alta Taylor Johnson (known to all as "Lady Bird") successfully pushed for legislation to restrict the billboards and junkyards that had sprung up along the nation's new interstate highway system. Johnson signed "preservation" legislation to protect America's remaining wilderness and supported laws addressing environmental pollution.

War on Poverty   At the heart of Johnson's Great Society was the War on Poverty. Johnson and other liberals believed that, in a time of great economic affluence, the nation had the resources for programs that could end "poverty, ignorance and hunger as intractable, permanent features of American society." Beginning in 1964, the Johnson administration passed more than a score of major legislative acts meant to do so (see Table 30.1).

Johnson's goal, in his words, was "to offer the forgotten fifth of our people opportunity, not doles." Thus, many new laws focused on increasing opportunity. Billions of federal dollars were channeled to municipalities and school districts to improve opportunities for the poverty-stricken, from preschoolers (Head Start) to high schoolers (Upward Bound) to young adults (Job Corps). The Model Cities program offered federal funds to upgrade employment, housing, education, and health in targeted urban neighborhoods, and Community Action Programs involved poor Americans in creating local grassroots antipoverty programs for their own communities.

The Johnson administration also tried to ensure basic economic safeguards, expanding the existing Food Stamp program and earmarking billions of dollars for constructing public housing and subsidizing rents. Two new federal programs guaranteed healthcare for specific groups of Americans: Medicare for those sixty-five and older, and Medicaid for the poor. Finally, Aid to Families with Dependent Children (AFDC), the basic welfare program created during the New Deal, expanded both benefits and eligibility.

The War on Poverty was controversial from its beginnings. Leftists believed the government was doing too little to change fundamental structural inequality. Conservatives argued that Great Society programs created dependency among America's poor. Policy analysts noted that specific programs were ill conceived and badly implemented. Even supporters acknowledged that programs were vastly underfunded and marred by political compromises. Responding to criticisms, Joseph Califano, one of the "generals" in the War on Poverty, claimed, "Whatever historians of the Great Society say twenty years later, they must admit we tried, and I believe they will conclude that America is a better place because we did."

Decades later, most historians judge the War on Poverty a mixed success. War on Poverty programs improved the quality of housing, healthcare, and nutrition available to the nation's poor. Between 1965 and 1970, federal spending for Social Security, healthcare, welfare, and education more than doubled, and the trend continued into the next decade. By 1975, for instance, the number of eligible Americans receiving food stamps had increased from 600,000 (in 1965) to 17 million. Poverty among the elderly fell from about 40 percent in 1960 to 16 percent in 1974, due largely to increased Social Security benefits and to Medicare. The War on Poverty undoubtedly improved the quality of life for many low-income Americans (see Figure 30.1).

But War on Poverty programs less successfully addressed the root causes of poverty. Neither the Job Corps nor Community Action Programs showed significant results. Economic growth, not Johnson administration policies, was primarily responsible for the dramatic decrease in government-measured poverty during the 1960s— from 22.4 percent of Americans in 1959 to 11 percent in 1973. And one structural determinant of poverty remained unchanged: 11 million Americans in female-headed households remained poor at the end of the decade—the same number as in 1963.

TABLE 30.1 | GREAT SOCIETY ACHIEVEMENTS, 1964–1966

	1964	1965	1966

Civil Rights	Civil Rights Act
	Equal Employment
	  Commission
	Twenty-fourth
	  Amendment
		Voting Rights Act	

War on Poverty	Economic
	  Opportunity Act
	Office of Economic
	  Opportunity
	Job Corps
	Legal Services for the
	  Poor
	VISTA
			Model Cities

Education		Elementary and
		  Secondary Education
		  Act
		Head Start
		Upward Bound	

Environment		Water Quality Act Air Quality Act	Clean Water Restoration Act

New Government
  Agencies
		Department of Housing
		  and Urban
		  Development
		National Endowments
		  for the Arts and
		  Humanities
			Department of
			  Transportation

Other		Medicare and
		  Medicaid
		Immigration and
		  Nationality Act	

Note: The Great Society of the mid-1960s saw the biggest burst of reform legislation since the New Deal of the 1930s.

Political compromises that shaped Great Society programs also created long-term problems. For example, Congress accommodated the interests of doctors and hospitals in its Medicare legislation by allowing federal reimbursements of hospitals' "reasonable costs" and doctors' "reasonable charges" in treating elderly patients. With no incentives for doctors or hospitals to hold prices down, the cost of healthcare rose dramatically. National healthcare expenditures as a percentage of the gross national product rose by almost 44 percent from 1960 to 1971. Johnson's Great Society was not an unqualified success, but it was a moment in which many Americans believed they could solve the problems of poverty and disease and discrimination—and that it was necessary to try.

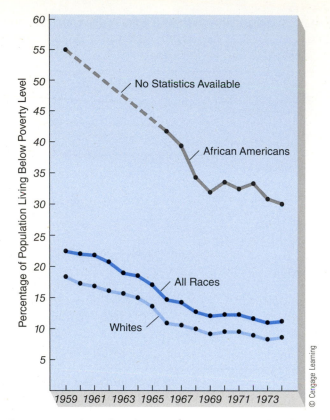

FIGURE 30.1 Poverty in America for Whites, African Americans, and All Races, 1959–1974

Because of rising levels of economic prosperity, combined with the impact of Great Society programs, the percentage of Americans living in poverty in 1974 was half as high as in 1959. African Americans still were far more likely than white Americans to be poor. In 1959, more than half of all blacks (55.1 percent) were poor; in 1974, the figure remained high (30.3 percent). The government did not record data on African American poverty for the years 1960 through 1965.

JOHNSON AND VIETNAM

Johnson's domestic ambitions were threatened from an early point by turmoil overseas. In foreign policy, he held firmly to ideas about U.S. superiority and the menace of communism. He saw the world in simple, bipolar terms—them against us—and he saw a lot of "them." But, mostly, he preferred not to see the world beyond America's shores at all. International affairs had never much interested him, and he had little appreciation for foreign cultures. Once, on a visit to Thailand while vice president, he flew into a rage when an aide gently advised him that the Thai people recoil from physical contact with strangers. Dammit, Johnson exploded, he shook hands with people everywhere, and they loved it. At the Taj Mahal in India, Johnson tested the monument's echo with a Texas cowboy yell. And on a trip to

Senegal, he ordered that an American bed, a special showerhead, and cases of Cutty Sark be sent along with him. "Foreigners," Johnson quipped early in his administration, only half-jokingly, "are not like the folks I am used to."

Kennedy's Legacy in Vietnam

Yet Johnson knew from the start that foreign policy, especially regarding Vietnam, would demand a good deal of his attention. Since the late 1950s, hostilities in Vietnam had increased, as Ho Chi Minh's North assisted the Vietcong guerrillas in the South to advance the reunification of the country under a communist government. President Kennedy had stepped up aid dollars to the Diem regime in Saigon, increased the airdropping of raiding teams into North Vietnam, and launched crop destruction by herbicides to starve the Vietcong and expose their hiding places. Kennedy also strengthened the U.S. military presence in South Vietnam, to the point that by 1963 more than sixteen thousand military advisers were in the country, some authorized to take part in combat alongside the U.S.-equipped Army of the Republic of Vietnam (ARVN).

Meanwhile, opposition to Diem's repressive regime increased, and not just by communists. Peasants objected to programs that removed them from their villages for their own safety, and Buddhist monks, protesting the Roman Catholic Diem's religious persecution, poured gasoline over their robes and ignited themselves in the streets of Saigon. Although Diem was personally honest, he countenanced corruption in his government and concentrated power in the hands of family and friends. He jailed critics to silence them. Eventually U.S. officials, with Kennedy's approval, encouraged ambitious South Vietnamese generals to remove Diem. On November 1, 1963, the generals struck, murdering Diem. Just a few weeks later, Kennedy himself was assassinated.

The timing of Kennedy's murder ensured that Vietnam would be the most controversial aspect of his legacy. Just what would have happened in Southeast Asia had Kennedy returned from Texas alive can never be known, of course, and the speculation is made more difficult by his contradictory record on the conflict. He expanded U.S. involvement and approved a coup against Diem, but despite the urgings of top advisers he refused to commit American ground forces to the struggle. Over time, he became increasingly skeptical about South Vietnam's prospects and hinted that he would end the American commitment after winning reelection in 1964. Some authors have gone further and argued that he was ending U.S. involvement even at the time of his death, but the evidence for this claim is thin. More likely, Kennedy arrived in Dallas that fateful day still uncertain about how to solve the Vietnam problem, postponing the truly difficult choices until later.

Tonkin Gulf Incident and Resolution

Lyndon Johnson viewed his Vietnam options through the lens of the impending 1964 election. He wanted to do nothing that could complicate his aim of winning the presidency in his own right, and that meant keeping Vietnam on the back burner. Yet Johnson also sought victory, or at least that he would not lose the war, which in practice amounted to the same thing. As a result, throughout 1964 the administration secretly laid plans to expand the war to North Vietnam and never seriously considered negotiating a settlement.

In early August 1964, an incident in the Gulf of Tonkin, off the coast of North Vietnam, drew Johnson's involvement (see Map 30.2). Twice in three days, U.S. destroyers reported coming under attack from North Vietnamese patrol boats. Despite a lack of evidence that the second attack occurred, Johnson ordered retaliatory air strikes against selected North Vietnamese patrol boat bases and an oil depot. He also directed aides to rework a long-existing congressional resolution on the use of force. By a vote of 416 to 0 in the House and 88 to 2 in the Senate, Congress quickly passed the Gulf of Tonkin Resolution, which gave the president the authority to "take all necessary measures to repel any armed attack against the forces of the United States and to prevent further aggression." In so doing, Congress essentially surrendered its warmaking powers to the executive branch. The resolution, Secretary of Defense McNamara later noted, served "to open the floodgates."

Decision for Escalation   President Johnson, delighted with the broad authority the resolution gave him, used a different metaphor. "Like grandma's nightshirt," he quipped, "it covered everything." He also appreciated what the Gulf of Tonkin affair did for his political standing— his public approval ratings went up dramatically, and his show of force effectively removed Vietnam as a campaign issue for GOP presidential nominee Barry Goldwater. On the ground in South Vietnam, however, the outlook remained grim in the final weeks of 1964, as the Vietcong continued to make gains. U.S. officials responded by laying secret plans for an escalation of American involvement.

In February 1965, in response to Vietcong attacks on American installations in South Vietnam that killed thirty-two Americans, Johnson ordered Operation Rolling Thunder, a bombing program planned the previous fall, which continued, more or less uninterrupted, until October 1968. Then, on March 8, the first U.S. combat battalions came ashore near Danang. The North Vietnamese, however, would not give up. They hid in shelters and rebuilt roads and bridges with a perseverance that frustrated and awed American decision makers. They also increased infiltration into the South. In Saigon, meanwhile, coups and countercoups by self-serving military leaders undermined U.S. efforts to turn the war effort around. "I don't think we ought to take this government seriously," Ambassador Henry Cabot Lodge told a White House meeting. "There is simply no one who can do anything."

In July 1965, Johnson convened a series of high-level discussions about U.S. policy in the war. Although these deliberations had about them the character of a charade—Johnson wanted history to record that he agonized over a choice he had in fact already made—they did confirm that the American commitment would be more or less open-ended. On July 28, Johnson publicly announced a significant troop increase, disclosing that others would follow. By the end of 1965, more than 180,000 U.S. ground troops were in South Vietnam. In 1966, the figure climbed to 385,000. In 1967 alone, U.S. warplanes flew 108,000 sorties and dropped 226,000 tons of bombs on North Vietnam. In 1968, U.S. troop strength reached 536,100. Each American escalation brought not victory, but a new North Vietnamese

MAP 30.2 Southeast Asia and the Vietnam War

To prevent communists from coming to power in Vietnam, Cambodia, and Laos in the 1960s, the United States intervened massively in Southeast Asia. The interventions failed, and the remaining American troops made a hasty exit from Vietnam in 1975, when the victorious Vietcong and North Vietnamese took Saigon and renamed it Ho Chi Minh City.

escalation. The Soviet Union and China responded to the stepped-up U.S. involve-ment by increasing their material assistance to the Hanoi government.

Opposition to Americanization   The initiation of Rolling Thunder and the U.S. troop com-mitment "Americanized" the war. What could have been seen as a civil war between North and South, or a a war of national reunification, was now clearly an American war against the communist Hanoi government. This "Americanization" of the war in Vietnam came despite deep misgivings on the part of influential and informed voices at home and abroad. In the key months of decision, Democratic leaders in the Senate, major newspapers such as the *New York Times* and the *Wall Street Journal*, and prominent colum-nists like Walter Lippmann warned against deepening involvement. So did some within the administration, including Vice President Hubert H. Humphrey and Undersecretary of State George W. Ball. Abroad, virtually all of America's allies—including France, Britain, Canada, and Japan—cautioned against escalation and urged a political settlement, on the grounds that no military solution favorable to the United States was possible. Remarkably, top U.S. officials themselves shared this pessimism. Most of them knew that the odds of success were not great. They certainly hoped that the new measures would cause Hanoi to end the insurgency in the South, but it cannot be said they were confident.

Why, then, did America's leaders choose war? At stake was "credibility." They feared that, if the United States failed to prevail in Vietnam, friends and foes around the world would find American power less credible. The Soviets and Chinese would be emboldened to challenge U.S. interests elsewhere in the world, and allied govern-ments might conclude that they could not depend on Washington. For at least some key players, too, including the president himself, domestic political credibility and personal credibility were also on the line. Johnson worried that failure in Vietnam would harm his domestic agenda; even more, he feared the personal humiliation that he imagined would inevitably accompany a defeat—and for him, a negotiated withdrawal constituted defeat. As for the stated objective of helping a South Viet-namese ally repulse external aggression, that, too, figured into the equation, but not as much as it would have had the Saigon government—racked with infighting among senior leaders and possessing little popular support—done more to assist in its own defense.

American Soldiers in Vietnam   Even as Johnson Americanized the Vietnam War, he sought to keep the publicity surrounding the action as low as possi-ble. Thus, he rejected the Joint Chiefs' view that U.S. reserve forces should be mobilized and a national emergency declared. This decision not to call up reserve units had a momentous impact on the makeup of the American fighting force sent to Vietnam. It forced the military establishment to rely more heavily on the draft, which in turn meant that Vietnam became a young man's war—the average age of soldiers was twenty-two, as com-pared with twenty-six in World War II. It also became a war of the poor and the working class. Through the years of heavy escalation (1965–1968), college students could get deferments, as could teachers and engineers. (In 1969, the draft was changed so that some students were called up through a lottery system.) The poorest and least educated young men were less likely to be able to avoid the draft and more likely to volunteer. The armed services recruited hard in poor communities, many of them heavily African American and Latino, advertising the military as an avenue of training and advancement; very often, the pitch worked. Once in uniform, those with fewer skills were far more likely to see combat, and hence to die.

Infantrymen on maneuvers carried heavy rucksacks into thick jungle growth, where every step was precarious. Booby traps and land mines were a constant threat. Insects swarmed, and leeches sucked at weary bodies. Boots and human skin rotted from the rains, which alternated with withering suns. "It was as if the sun and the land itself were in league with the Vietcong," recalled marine officer Philip Caputo in *A Rumor of War* (1977), "wearing us down, driving us mad, killing us." The enemy, meanwhile, was hard to find, often burrowed into elaborate underground tunnels or melded into the population, where any Vietnamese might be a Vietcong.

The American forces fought well, and their entry into the conflict in 1965 helped stave off a South Vietnamese defeat. In that sense, Americanization achieved its most immediate and basic objective. But if the stepped-up fighting that year demonstrated to Hanoi leaders that the war would not swiftly be won, it also showed the same thing to their counterparts in Washington. As the North Vietnamese matched each American escalation with one of their own, the war became a stalemate. The U.S. commander, General William Westmoreland, proved mistaken in his belief that a strategy of attrition represented the key to victory—the enemy had a seemingly endless supply of recruits to throw into battle. Under Westmoreland's strategy, the measure of success became the "body count"—that is, the number of North Vietnamese and Vietcong corpses found after battle. From the start, the counts were subject to manipulation by officers eager to convince superiors of the success of an operation. Worse, the American reliance on massive military and other technology—including carpet bombing, napalm (jellied gasoline), and crop defoliants that destroyed entire forests—alienated many South Vietnamese and brought new recruits to the Vietcong.

Divisions at Home

Increasingly, Americans divided into those who supported the war and those who did not. As television coverage brought the war—its body counts and body bags, its burned villages and weeping refugees—into homes every night, the number of opponents grew. On college campuses, professors and students organized debates and lectures on American policy. Sometimes going around the clock, these intense public discussions became a form of protest, called "teach-ins" after the sit-ins of the civil rights movement. The big campus and street demonstrations were still to come, but pacifist groups, such as the American Friends Service Committee and the Women's International League for Peace and Freedom, organized early protests.

In early 1966, Senator William Fulbright held televised public hearings on whether the national interest was being served by pursuing the war. What exactly was the threat? senators asked. To the surprise of some, George F. Kennan testified that his containment doctrine was meant for Europe, not the volatile environment of Southeast Asia. America's "preoccupation" with Vietnam, Kennan asserted, was undermining its global obligations. Whether many minds were changed by the Fulbright hearings is hard to say, but they constituted the first in-depth national discussion of the U.S. commitment in Vietnam. They provoked Americans to think about the conflict and the nation's role in it. No longer could anyone doubt that there were deep divisions on Vietnam among public officials, or that two of them, Lyndon Johnson and William Fulbright, had broken completely over the war.

Defense secretary Robert McNamara, who despite private misgivings championed the Americanization of the war in 1965, became increasingly troubled by the killing and destructiveness of the bombing. Already in November 1965 he expressed skepticism that victory could ever be achieved, and in the months thereafter he agonized over how the United States looked in the eyes of the world. American credibility, far from being protected by the staunch commitment to the war, was suffering grievous damage, McNamara feared. "The picture of the world's greatest superpower killing or seriously injuring 1,000 noncombatants a week, while trying to pound a tiny backward nation into submission on an issue whose merits are hotly disputed, is not a pretty one," he told Johnson in mid-1967.

But Johnson was in no mood to listen or reconsider. Determined to prevail in Vietnam, he dug in, snapping at "those little shits on the campuses." Although on occasion he halted the bombing to encourage Ho Chi Minh to negotiate (on America's terms), and to disarm critics, such pauses often were accompanied by increases in American troop strength. And the United States sometimes resumed or accelerated the bombing just when a diplomatic breakthrough seemed possible. Hanoi demanded a complete suspension of bombing raids before sitting down at the conference table. And Ho could not accept American terms, which amounted to abandonment of his lifelong dream of an independent, unified Vietnam.

A NATION DIVIDED

As Johnson struggled to overcome an implacable foe in Vietnam, his liberal vision of a Great Society faced challenges at home. The divisions among Americans over policy in Vietnam were only one fissure in a society that was fracturing along many different lines: black and white, youth and age, radical and conservative.

Urban Unrest   Even as the civil rights movement was winning important victories in the mid-1960s, many African Americans had given up on the promise of liberal reform. In 1964, shortly after President Johnson signed the landmark Civil Rights Act, racial violence erupted in northern cities. Angry residents of Harlem took to the streets after a white police officer shot a black teenager. The following summer, in the predominantly black Watts section of Los Angeles, crowds burned, looted, and battled police for five days and nights. The riot, which began when a white police officer attempted to arrest a black resident on suspicion of drunken driving, left thirty-four dead and more than one thousand injured. In July 1967, twenty-six people were killed in street battles between African Americans and police and army troops in Newark, New Jersey. A week later, in Detroit, forty-three died as 3 square miles of the city went up in flames. In 1967 alone, there were 167 violent outbreaks in 128 cities.

The "long, hot summers" of urban unrest in the 1960s differed from almost all previous race riots. Past riots were typically started by whites. Here, black residents exploded in anger and frustration over the conditions of their lives. They looted and burned stores, most of them white-owned. But in the process they devastated their own neighborhoods.

In 1968, the National Advisory Commission on Civil Disorders, chaired by Governor Otto Kerner of Illinois, warned that America was "moving towards two societies, one white, one black—separate and unequal," and blamed white racism for the riots. "What white Americans have never fully understood—but what the Negro can never forget—is that white society is deeply implicated in the ghetto. White institutions created it, white institutions maintain it, and white society condones it," concluded the Kerner Commission. Some white Americans rejected this interpretation. Others, shocked at what appeared to be senseless violence, wondered why African Americans were venting their frustration so destructively just when they were making real progress in the civil rights struggle.

The answer stemmed in part from regional differences. Although the *legal* disenfranchisement and discrimination in the South was a clear focal point for civil rights activism, African Americans outside the South also suffered racial discrimination. Increasingly concentrated in the deteriorating ghettos of inner cities, most African Americans lived in societies as segregated as any in the Deep South. They faced discrimination in housing, in the availability of credit and mortgages, and in employment. The median income of northern blacks was little more than half that of northern whites, and their unemployment rate was twice as high. Many northern blacks had given up on the civil rights movement, and few believed that Great Society liberalism would solve their plight.

Black Power   In this climate, a new voice urged blacks to seize their freedom "by any means necessary." Malcolm X, a onetime pimp and street hustler who had converted while in prison to the Nation of Islam faith, offered African Americans a new direction of leadership. Members of the Nation of Islam, commonly known as Black Muslims, espoused black pride and separatism from white society. Their faith, combining elements of traditional Islam with a belief that whites were subhuman "devils" whose race would soon be destroyed, also emphasized the importance of sobriety, thrift, and social responsibility. By the early 1960s, Malcolm X had become the Black Muslims' chief spokesperson, and his advice was straightforward: "If someone puts a hand on you, send him to the cemetery." But Malcolm X was murdered in early 1965 by members of the Nation of Islam who believed he had betrayed their cause by breaking with the Black Muslims to start his own, more racially tolerant organization. In death, Malcolm X became a powerful symbol of black defiance and self-respect.

A year after Malcolm X's death, Stokely Carmichael, SNCC chairman, denounced "the betrayal of black dreams by white America." To be truly free from white oppression, Carmichael proclaimed, blacks had to "stand up and take over"—to elect black candidates, to organize their own schools, to control their own institutions, to embrace "Black Power." That year, SNCC expelled its white members and repudiated both nonviolence and integration. CORE followed suit in 1967.

The best known black radicals of the era were the Black Panthers, an organization formed in Oakland, California, in 1966. Blending black separatism and revolutionary communism, the Panthers dedicated themselves to destroying both capitalism and "the military arm of our oppressors," the police in the ghettos. In direct contrast to earlier, nonviolent civil rights protesters, who had worn suits and ties or dresses to demonstrate their respectability, male Panthers dressed in commando gear, carried weapons, and talked about killing "pigs"—and did kill eleven officers by 1970. Police responded in kind; most infamously, Chicago police murdered local Panther leader Fred Hampton in his bed. However, the group also worked to improve life in their neighborhoods by instituting free breakfast and healthcare programs for ghetto children, offering courses in African American history, and demanding jobs and decent housing for the poor. The Panthers' platform attracted many young African Americans, while their public embrace of violence frightened many whites. Radicalism, however, was not limited to black nationalist groups. Before the end of the decade, a vocal minority of America's young would join in calls for revolution.

Youth and Politics

By the mid-1960s, 41 percent of the American population was under the age of twenty. These young people spent more time in the world of peer culture than had any previous generation, as three-quarters of them graduated from high school (up from one-fifth in the 1920s) and almost half of them went to college (up from 16 percent in 1940). As this large baby-boom generation came of age, many young people took seriously the idea that they must provide democratic leadership for their nation. Black college students had begun the sit-in movement, infusing new life into the struggle for African American civil rights. Some white college students—from both political left and right—also committed themselves to changing the system.

In the fall of 1960, a group of conservative college students came together at the family estate of William F. Buckley in Sharon, Connecticut, to create Young Americans for Freedom (YAF). Their manifesto, the "Sharon Statement," endorsed Cold War anticommunism and a vision of limited government power directly opposed to New Deal liberalism and its heritage. "In this time of moral and political crises," they wrote, "it is the responsibility of the youth of America to affirm certain eternal truths.... [F]oremost among the transcendent values is the individual's use of his God-given free will." The YAF planned to capture the Republican Party and move it to the political right; Goldwater's selection as the Republican candidate for president in 1964 demonstrated their early success.

At the other end of the political spectrum, an emerging "New Left" soon joined conservative youth in rejecting liberalism. Whereas conservatives believed that liberalism's activist government encroached on individual liberty, these young Americans believed that liberalism was not enough, that it could never offer true democracy and equality to all America's people. At a meeting in Port Huron, Michigan, in 1962, founding members of Students for a Democratic Society (SDS) proclaimed, "We are people of this generation, bred in at least modest comfort, housed now in the universities, looking uncomfortably to the world we inherit." Their "Port Huron Statement" condemned racism, poverty in the midst of plenty, and the Cold War. Calling for "participatory democracy," SDS sought to wrest power from the corporations, the military, and the politicians and return it to "the people."

Free Speech Movement

The first indication of the new power of activist white youth came at the University of California, Berkeley. In the fall of 1964, the university administration banned political activity—including recruiting volunteers for civil rights work in Mississippi—from its traditional place along a university-owned sidewalk bordering the campus. When the administration called police to arrest a CORE worker who defied the order, some four thousand students surrounded the police car. Berkeley graduate student and Mississippi Freedom Summer veteran Mario Savio ignited the movement, telling students, "You've got to put your bodies upon the levers ... [and] you've got to indicate to the people who run it, to the people who own it, that unless you're free, the machine will be prevented from working at all."

Student political groups, left and right, came together to create the Free Speech Movement (FSM). The FSM did win back the right to political speech, but not before state police had arrested almost eight hundred student protesters. Berkeley students took two lessons from the Free Speech Movement. Many saw the administration's actions as a failure of America's democratic promises, and they were radicalized by the experience. But the victory of the FSM also demonstrated to students their potential power. By the end of the decade, the activism born at Berkeley would spread to hundreds of college and university campuses.

Student Activism

Many student protesters in the 1960s sought greater control over their lives as students, demanding more relevant class offerings, more freedom in selecting their courses of study, and a greater voice in the running of universities. A major target of protest was the doctrine of in loco parentis, which until the late 1960s put universities legally "in the place of parents" to their students, allowing control over student behavior that went well beyond the laws of the land. The impact of in loco parentis fell heaviest on women, who were subject to strict curfew regulations called parietals, while men had no such rules. Protesters demanded an end to discrimination on the basis of sex, but rejected in loco parentis for other reasons as well. A group at the University of Kansas demanded that the administration explain how its statement that "college students are assumed to have maturity of judgment necessary for adult responsibility" squared with the minute regulation of students' nonacademic lives. One young man complained that "a high school dropout selling cabbage in a supermarket" had more rights and freedoms than successful university students. Increasingly, students insisted they should be allowed the full rights and responsibilities of citizens in a democratic society.

Youth and the War in Vietnam   It was the war in Vietnam, however, that mobilized a nationwide student movement. Believing that it was the democratic responsibility of citizens to learn about and speak out on issues of vital national importance, university students and faculty held "teach-ins" about U.S. involvement in Vietnam as the war escalated in 1965. Students for a Democratic Society sponsored the first major antiwar march that year, drawing twenty thousand protesters to Washington, D.C. Local SDS chapters grew steadily as opposition to the war increased. On campuses throughout the nation, students adopted tactics developed in the civil rights movement, picketing ROTC buildings and protesting military research and recruiting done on their campuses. However, despite the visibility of campus antiwar protests, most students did not yet oppose the war: in 1967, only 30 percent of male college students declared themselves "doves" on Vietnam, while 67 percent proclaimed themselves "hawks." And many young men were, in fact, in Vietnam fighting the war. But as the war continued to escalate, an increasing number of America's youth came to distrust the government that turned a deaf ear to their protests, as well as the university administrations that seemed more a source of arbitrary authority than of democratic education.

Youth Culture and the Counterculture   But the large baby-boom generation would change the nation's culture more than its politics. Although many young people protested the war and marched for social justice, most did not. The sixties' "youth culture" was never homogeneous. Fraternity and sorority life stayed strong on most campuses, even as radicalism flourished. And although there was some crossover, black, white, and Latino youth had different cultural styles: different music, different clothes, even different versions of a youth dialect often incomprehensible to adults. Nonetheless, as potential consumers, young people as a group exercised tremendous cultural authority. Their music and their styles drove American popular culture in the late 1960s.

The most unifying element of youth culture was the importance placed on music. The Beatles had electrified American teenagers—73 million viewers watched their first television appearance on the *Ed Sullivan Show* in 1964. Bob Dylan promised revolutionary answers in "Blowin' in the Wind"; Janis Joplin brought the sexual power of the blues to white youth; James Brown and Aretha Franklin proclaimed black pride; the psychedelic rock of Jefferson Airplane and the Grateful Dead—along with hallucinogenic drugs—redefined reality. That new reality took brief form in the Woodstock Festival in upstate New York in 1969, as more than 400,000 people reveled in the music and in a world of their own making, living in rain and mud for four days without shelter and without violence.

Some young people hoped to turn youth rebellion into something more than a consumer-based lifestyle, rejecting what they saw as hypocritical middle-class values. They attempted to craft an alternative way of life, or counterculture, liberated from competitive materialism and celebrating the legitimacy of pleasure. "Sex, drugs, and rock 'n' roll" became a mantra of sorts, offering these "hippies," or "freaks," a path to a new consciousness. Many did the hard work of creating communes and intentional communities, whether in cities or in hidden stretches of rural America. Although the New Left criticized the counterculture as apolitical, many freaks did envision revolutionary change. As John Sinclair, manager of the rock band MC5, explained, mind-blowing experiences with sex, drugs, or music were far more likely to change young people's minds than earnest speeches: "Rather than go up there and make some speech about our moral commitment in Vietnam, you just make 'em so freaky they'd never want to go into the army in the first place."

The nascent counterculture had first burst on the national consciousness during the summer of 1967, when tens of thousands of young people poured into the Haight-Ashbury district of San Francisco, the heart of America's psychedelic culture, for the "summer of love." As an older generation of "straight" (or Establishment) Americans watched with horror, white youth came to look—and act—more and more like the counterculture. Coats and ties disappeared, as did stockings—and bras. Young men grew long hair, and parents throughout the nation complained, "You can't tell the boys from the girls." Millions used marijuana or hallucinogenic drugs, read underground newspapers, and thought of themselves as alienated from "straight" culture even though they were attending high school or college and not completely "dropping out" of the Establishment.

Some of the most lasting cultural changes involved attitudes about sex. The mass media were fascinated with "free love," and some people did embrace a truly promiscuous sexuality. More important, however, premarital sex no longer destroyed a woman's "reputation." The birth-control pill, distributed since 1960 and widely available to single women by the late 1960s, greatly lessened the risk of unplanned pregnancy, and venereal diseases were easily cured by a basic course of antibiotics. The number of couples living together—"without benefit of matrimony," as the phrase went at the time—increased 900 percent from 1960 to 1970; many young people no longer tried to hide the fact that they were sexually active. Still, 68 percent of American adults disapproved of premarital sex in 1969.

Adults were baffled and often angered by the behavior of youth. A generation that had grown up in the hard decades of depression and war, many of whom saw middle-class respectability as crucial to success and stability, just did not understand. How could young people put such promising futures at risk by having sex without marriage, taking drugs, or opposing the American government over the war in Vietnam?

1968

By the beginning of 1968, it seemed that the nation was coming apart. Divided over the war in Vietnam, frustrated by the slow pace of social change, or angry over the racial violence that wracked America's cities, Americans looked for solutions as the nation faced the most serious domestic crisis of the postwar era.

The Tet Offensive
The year opened with a major attack in Vietnam. On January 31, 1968, the first day of the Vietnamese New Year (Tet), Vietcong and North Vietnamese forces struck all

across South Vietnam, capturing provincial capitals (see Map 30.2). During the carefully planned offensive, the Saigon airport, the presidential palace, and the ARVN headquarters came under attack. Even the American embassy compound in the city was penetrated by Vietcong soldiers, who occupied its courtyard for six hours. U.S. and South Vietnamese units eventually regained much of the ground they had lost, inflicting heavy casualties and devastating numerous villages.

Although the Tet Offensive did not achieve the resounding battlefield victory that Hanoi strategists had hoped for, the heavy fighting called into question American military leaders' confident predictions in earlier months that the war would soon be won. Had not the Vietcong and North Vietnamese demonstrated that they could strike when and where they wished? If America's airpower, dollars, and half a million troops could not now defeat the Vietcong, could they ever do so? Had the American public been deceived? In February, the highly respected CBS television anchorman Walter Cronkite went to Vietnam to find out. The military brass in Saigon assured him that "we had the enemy just where we wanted him." The newsman recalled, "Tell that to the Marines, I thought—the Marines in the body bags on that helicopter."

Top presidential advisers sounded notes of despair. Clark Clifford, who had succeeded Robert McNamara as secretary of defense, told Johnson that the war—"a sinkhole"—could not be won, even with the 206,000 additional soldiers requested by Westmoreland. Aware that the nation was suffering a financial crisis prompted by rampant deficit spending to sustain the war and other global commitments, they knew that taking the initiative in Vietnam would cost billions more, further derail the budget, panic foreign owners of dollars, and wreck the economy. Clifford heard from his associates in the business community; "These men now feel we are in a hopeless bog," he told the president. To "maintain public support for the war without the support of these men" was impossible.

Johnson's Exit

Controversy over the war split the Democratic Party, just as a presidential election loomed in November. Senator Eugene McCarthy of Minnesota and Robert F. Kennedy (now a senator from New York), both strong opponents of Johnson's war policies, forcefully challenged the president in early primaries. Strained by exhausting sessions with skeptical advisers, troubled by the economic implications of escalation, and sensing that more resources would not bring victory, Johnson changed course. During a March 31 television address, he announced a halt to most of the bombing, asked Hanoi to begin negotiations, and stunned his listeners by withdrawing from the presidential race. He had become a casualty of the war, his presidency doomed by a seemingly interminable struggle 10,000 miles from Washington. Peace talks began in May in Paris, but the war ground on.

Assassinations

Less than a week after Johnson's shocking announcement, Martin Luther King Jr. was murdered in Memphis, where he had traveled to support striking sanitation workers. It is still not clear why James

Lyndon Johnson, 1968. The war in Vietnam gradually destroyed his presidency and divided the nation.

Lyndon B. Johnson Presidential Library

Earl Ray, a white forty-year-old drifter and petty criminal, shot King—or whether he acted alone or as part of a conspiracy. By 1968 King, the senior statesman of the civil rights movement, had become an outspoken critic of the Vietnam War and of American capitalism. Although some Americans hated what he stood for, he was widely respected and honored. Most Americans mourned his death, even as black rage and grief exploded in 130 cities. Once again, ghetto neighborhoods burned; thirty-four blacks and five whites died. The violence provoked a backlash from whites—primarily urban, working-class people who were tired of violence and quickly losing whatever sympathy they might have had for black Americans' increasingly radical demands. In Chicago, Mayor Richard Daley ordered police to shoot rioters.

An already shaken nation watched in disbelief as another leader fell to violence only two months later. Antiwar Democratic presidential candidate Robert Kennedy was shot and killed as he celebrated his victory in the California primary. His assassin, Sirhan Sirhan, an Arab nationalist, targeted Kennedy because of his support for Israel.

Chicago Democratic National Convention

Violence erupted again in August at the Democratic National Convention in Chicago. Thousands of protesters converged on the city: students who'd gone "Clean for Gene," cutting long hair and donning "respectable" clothes to campaign for antiwar candidate Eugene McCarthy; members of America's counterculture drawn by a promise from the anarchist group, the Yippies, of a

"Festival of Life" to counter the "Convention of Death"; members of antiwar groups that ranged from radical to mainstream. Mayor Daley, resolving that no one would disrupt "his" convention, assigned twelve thousand police to twelve-hour shifts and had twelve thousand army troops with bazookas, rifles, and fla-methrowers on call as backup. Police attacked peaceful antiwar protesters and journalists. "The whole world is watching," chanted the protesters, as club-swinging police indiscriminately beat people to the ground, and Americans gathered around their television sets, despairing over the future of their nation.

Global Protest   Although American eyes were focused on the clashes in Chicago, upheavals burst forth around the world that spring and summer. In France, university students protested both rigid academic policies and the Vietnam War. They received support from French workers, who occupied their factories and paralyzed public transport; the turmoil contributed to the collapse of Charles de Gaulle's government the following year. In Italy, Germany, England, Ireland, Sweden, Canada, Mexico, Chile, Japan, and South Korea, students also protested—sometimes violently—against universities, governments, and the Vietnam War. In Czechoslovakia, hundreds of thousands of demonstrators flooded the streets of Prague, demanding democracy and an end to repression by the Soviet-controlled government. This so-called Prague Spring developed into a full-scale national rebellion before being crushed by Soviet tanks.

Why so many uprisings occurred in so many places simultaneously is not altogether clear. Sheer numbers had an impact. The postwar baby boom experienced by many nations produced by the late 1960s a huge mass of teenagers and young adults, many of whom had grown up in relative prosperity, with high expectations for the future. The expanded reach of global media also mattered. Technological advances allowed the nearly instantaneous transmittal of televised images around the world, so protests in one country could readily inspire similar actions in others. Although the worldwide demonstrations might have occurred even without the Vietnam War, television news footage showing the wealthiest and most industrialized nation carpet-bombing a poor and developing one—whose leader was the charismatic revolutionary Ho Chi Minh—surely helped fuel the agitation.

Nixon's Election   The presidential election of 1968, coming at the end of such a difficult year, did little to heal the nation. Democratic nominee Hubert Humphrey, Johnson's vice president, seemed a continuation of the old politics. Republican candidate Richard Nixon, like Goldwater in 1964, called for "law and order"—a phrase some understood as racist code words—to appeal to those who were angry about racial violence and tired of social unrest. Promising to "bring us together," he reached out to those he called "the great, quite forgotten majority—the nonshouters and the nondemonstrators, the millions who ask principally to go their own way in decency and dignity." On Vietnam, Nixon vowed he would "end the war and win the peace." Governor George Wallace of Alabama, who only five years before had vowed, "Segregation forever!" and who proposed using nuclear weapons on Vietnam, ran as a third-party candidate. Wallace carried five southern states, drawing almost 14 percent of the popular vote, and Nixon was elected president with the slimmest of margins. Divisions among Americans deepened.

Yet on Christmas Eve 1968—in a step toward fulfilling the pledge John Kennedy had made at the opening of a tumultuous decade—*Apollo 8* entered lunar orbit. Looking down on a troubled world, the astronauts broadcast photographs of the earth seen from space, a fragile blue orb floating in darkness. As people around the world listened, the astronauts read aloud the opening passages of Genesis, "In the beginning, God created the heaven and the earth ... and God saw that it was good," and many listeners found themselves in tears.

SUMMARY

The 1960s began with high hopes for a more democratic America. Civil rights volunteers, often risking their lives, carried the quest for racial equality to all parts of the nation. Gradually, the nation's leaders put their support behind the movement, and the 1964 Civil Rights Act and the 1965 Voting Rights Act were major landmarks in the quest for a more just society. America was shaken by the assassination of President John Kennedy in 1963, but under President Johnson, the liberal vision of government power used to create a better life for the nation's citizens reached new heights, as a flood of legislation was enacted in hopes of creating a Great Society.

But throughout this period, the nation was troubled by threats to its stability. The Cold War between the United States and the USSR grew in size and scope during the 1960s. The world came close to nuclear war in the 1962 Cuban missile crisis. Cold War geopolitics led the United States to become more and more involved in the ongoing war in Vietnam. Determined not to let Vietnam "fall" to communists, the United States sent military forces to prevent the victory of communist Vietnamese nationalists led by Ho Chi Minh in that nation's civil war. By 1968, there were more than half a million American ground troops in Vietnam. America's war in Vietnam divided the country, undermined Great Society domestic programs, and destroyed the presidency of Lyndon Johnson.

Despite real gains in civil rights and in attempts to promote justice and end poverty, divisions among Americans deepened. Many African Americans turned away from the civil rights movement, seeking more immediate change in their lives. Poor African American neighborhoods burned as violent unrest spread through the nation. Integrationists and civil rights advocates fought both separatist Black Power militants and white segregationists. Vocal young people—and some of their elders—questioned whether democracy truly existed in the United States. Large numbers of the nation's white youth embraced another form of rebellion, claiming membership in a "counterculture" that rejected white middle-class respectability. With great passion, Americans struggled over the future of their nation.

The year 1968 was one of crisis, of assassinations and violence in the streets. The decade that had started with such promise was moving toward its end in fierce political polarization.

31

CONTINUING DIVISIONS AND NEW LIMITS 1969–1980

THE NEW POLITICS OF IDENTITY

The social change movements of the 1960s evolved into new and powerful forms during the 1970s. By the end of the 1960s, as divisions continued to deepen among the American people, movements for social justice and racial equality had become stronger, louder, and often more radical. The civil rights movement, begun in a quest for equal rights and integration, splintered, as many young African Americans turned away from the tactics of nonviolence, rejected integration in favor of separatism, and embraced a distinct African American culture. Mexican Americans and Native Americans, inspired by the civil rights movement to struggle against their own marginalization in American society, had created powerful "Brown Power" and "Red Power" movements by the early 1970s. Like young African Americans, they demanded not only equal rights but also recognition of their distinct cultures. These movements fueled the development of a new "identity politics." Advocates of identity politics believed that differences among American racial and ethnic groups were critically important. Group identity, these Americans argued, must be the basis for political action. And government and social leaders must stop imagining the American public as individuals and instead address the needs of different identity-based groups.

CHRONOLOGY

1969	Stonewall Inn uprising begins gay liberation movement
	Apollo 11 Astronaut Neil Armstrong becomes first person to walk on moon's surface
	National Chicano Liberation Youth Conference held in Denver
	"Indians of All Tribes" occupy Alcatraz Island
	Nixon administration begins affirmative-action plan
1970	United States invades Cambodia
	Students at Kent State and Jackson State Universities shot by National Guard troops
	First Earth Day celebrated
	Environmental Protection Agency created
1971	Pentagon Papers published
1972	Nixon visits China and Soviet Union
	CREEP stages Watergate break-in
	Congress approves ERA and passes Title IX, which creates growth in women's athletics
1973	Peace agreement in Paris ends U.S. involvement in Vietnam
	OPEC increases oil prices, creating U.S. energy crisis
	Roe v. Wade legalizes abortion
	Agnew resigns; Ford named vice president
1974	Nixon resigns under threat of impeachment; Ford becomes president
1975	In deepening economic recession, unemployment hits 8.5 percent
	New York City saved from bankruptcy by federal loan guarantees
	Congress passes Indian Self-Determination and Education Assistance Act in response to Native American activists
1976	Carter elected president
1978	*Regents of the University of California v. Bakke* outlaws quotas but upholds affirmative action
	California voters approve Proposition 13
1979	Three Mile Island nuclear accident raises fears
	Camp David accords signed by Israel and Egypt
	American hostages seized in Iran
	Soviet Union invades Afghanistan
	Consumer debt doubles from 1975 to hit $315 billion

African American Cultural Nationalism

By 1970, most African American activists no longer sought political power and racial justice through the universalist claim of the civil rights movement that "We are all the same but for the color of our skin." Instead, they emphasized the distinctiveness of black culture and society. These ideas attracted a large following, even among older, less radical people. Many black Americans, powerfully disillusioned by the racism that outlasted the end of legal segregation, had come to believe that integration would mean subordination in a white-dominated society that had no respect for their history and cultural traditions.

In the early 1970s, though mainstream groups like the NAACP continued to seek political and social equality through the nation's courts and ballot boxes, many African Americans (like the white youth of the counterculture) looked to culture rather than to narrow political action for social change. Rejecting current European American standards of beauty, young people let their hair grow into "naturals" and "Afros"; they claimed the power of black "soul." Seeking strength in their own histories and cultural heritages, black college students and young faculty members fought successfully to create black studies departments in American universities. African traditions were reclaimed—or sometimes created. The new holiday Kwanzaa, created in 1966 by Maulana Karenga, professor of black studies at California State University, Long Beach, offered celebration of a shared African heritage. Many African Americans found pride in their history and culture; the most radical activists gave up on the notion of a larger "American" culture altogether.

Mexican American Activism   In 1970, the nation's 9 million Mexican Americans (4.3 percent of America's total population) were heavily concentrated in the Southwest and California. Although these Americans were officially classified as white by the federal government— all Hispanics were counted as white in the federal census—discrimination in hiring, pay, housing, schools, and the courts was commonplace. In cities, poor Mexican Americans lived in rundown barrios. In rural areas, poverty was widespread. Almost half of Mexican Americans were functionally illiterate. High school dropout rates were astronomical: in 1974, only 21 percent of Mexican American males graduated high school. Although growing numbers of Mexican Americans were middle class, almost one-quarter of Mexican American families remained below the poverty level. Especially dire was the plight of migrant farm workers.

The national Mexican American movement for social justice began with these migrant workers. From 1965 through 1970, labor organizers César Chávez and Dolores Huerta led migrant workers, the majority of whom were of Mexican ancestry, in a strike (*huelga*) against large grape growers in California's San Joaquin Valley. Grape growers paid workers as little as 10 cents an hour (the minimum wage in 1965 was $1.25) and often lodged them in squalid housing without running water or indoor toilets. A national consumer boycott of table grapes led by Chávez and the AFL-CIO affiliated United Farm Workers (UFW) brought the growers to the bargaining table, and in 1970 the UFW won its fight for better wages and working conditions. The UFW's roots in the Mexican and Mexican American communities were critical to its success. The union resembled nineteenth-century Mexican *mutualistas*, or cooperative associations, as much as it did a traditional American labor union. Its members founded cooperative groceries, a Spanish-language newspaper, and a theater group; they called on the Virgin de Guadalupe for assistance in their struggle.

Chicano Movement

During the same period, more radical struggles were also beginning. In northern New Mexico, Reies Tijerina created the Alianza Federal de Mercedes (Federal Alliance of Grants) to fight for the return of land that the organization claimed belonged to local *hispano* villagers, whose ancestors had occupied the territory before it was claimed by the United States, under the 1848 Treaty of Guadalupe Hidalgo. In Denver, former boxer Rudolfo "Corky" Gonzáles drew Mexican American youth to his "Crusade for Justice"; more than one thousand young people gathered there for the National Chicano Liberation Youth Conference in 1969. They adopted a manifesto, *El Plan Espiritual de Aztlan*, which condemned the "brutal 'Gringo' invasion of our territories" and declared "the Independence of our ... Nation."

These young activists called for the liberation of "La Raza" (from *La Raza de Bronze*, "the brown people") from the oppressive force of American society and culture, not for equal rights through integration. They also rejected a hyphenated "Mexican-American" identity. The "Mexican American," they explained in *El Plan Espiritual de Aztlan*, "lacks respect for his culture and ethnic heritage ... [and] seeks assimilation as a way out of his 'degraded' social status." These young people called themselves "Chicanos" or "Chicanas"—a term drawn from barrio slang and associated with *pachucos*, the hip, rebellious, and sometimes criminal young men who symbolized much of what "respectable" Mexican Americans despised.

Many middle-class Mexican Americans and members of the older generations never embraced the term *Chicano* or the separatist, cultural nationalist agenda of *el movimiento*. Throughout the 1970s, however, younger activists continued to seek "Brown Power" based on a separate and distinct Chicano/Chicana culture. They succeeded in introducing Chicano studies into local high school and college curricula and in creating a strong and unifying sense of cultural identity for Mexican American youth. Some activists made clear political gains as well, founding La Raza Unida (RUP), a Southwest-based political party that registered tens of thousands of voters and won several local elections. The Chicano movement was never as influential nationally as the African American civil rights movement or the Black Power movement. However, it effectively challenged discrimination on the local level and created a basis for political action as the Mexican American (and broader Latino) population of the United States grew dramatically over the following decades.

Native American Activism

Between 1968 and 1975, Native American activists forced American society to hear their demands and to reform U.S. government policies toward native peoples. Like African Americans and Mexican Americans, young Native American activists were greatly influenced by cultural nationalist beliefs. Many young activists, seeking a return to the "old ways," joined with "traditionalists" among their elders to challenge tribal leaders who advocated assimilation and cooperation with federal agencies.

In November 1969, a small group of activists, calling themselves "Indians of All Tribes," occupied Alcatraz Island in San Francisco Bay, demanding that the land be returned to native peoples for an Indian cultural center. The protest,

Calling their movement "Red Power," these American Indian activists dance in 1969 while "reclaiming" Alcatraz Island in San Francisco Bay. Arguing that an 1868 Sioux treaty entitled them to possession of unused federal lands, the group occupied the island until mid-1971.

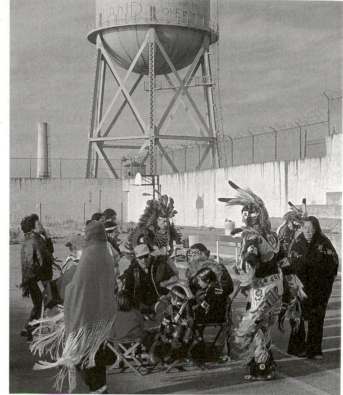

Ralph Crane, Life Magazine, Time, Inc.

which lasted nineteen months and eventually involved more than four hundred people from fifty different tribes, marked the consolidation of a "pan-Indian" approach to activism. Before Alcatraz, protests tended to be reservation based and concerned with specific local issues. Many of the Alcatraz activists were urban Indians, products in part of government policies that led Native Americans to leave reservations and seek jobs in the nation's cities. They were interested in claiming a shared "Indian" identity that transcended tribal differences. Although the protesters did not succeed in reclaiming Alcatraz Island, they drew national attention to their struggle and inspired the growing "Red Power" movement. In 1972, members of the radical American Indian Movement occupied a Bureau of Indian Affairs office in Washington, D.C., and then in 1973 a trading post at Wounded Knee, South Dakota, where U.S. Army troops had massacred three hundred Sioux men, women, and children in 1890.

At the same time, more moderate activists, working through such pan-tribal organizations as the National Congress of American Indians and the Native American Rights Fund, lobbied Congress for greater rights and resources to govern themselves and to strengthen their tribal cultures. In response to those demands, Congress and the federal courts returned millions of acres of land to tribal ownership, and in 1975 Congress passed the Indian Self-Determination and Education Assistance Act. Despite these successes, conditions for most Native Americans remained grim during the 1970s and 1980s: American Indians had a higher rate of tuberculosis, alcoholism, and suicide than any other group. Nine of ten lived in substandard housing, and unemployment rates for Indians were almost 40 percent.

Affirmative Action

As activists from various groups made all Americans increasingly aware of discrimination and inequality, policymakers struggled to frame remedies. As early as 1965, President Johnson had acknowledged the limits of civil rights legislation. "You do not take a person who, for years, has been hobbled by chains and liberate him, bring him up to the starting line of a race and then say, 'you are free to compete with all the others,'" Johnson told an audience at Howard University, "and still justly believe that you have been completely fair." In this speech, Johnson called for "not just legal equality ... but equality as a fact and equality as a result." Here Johnson joined his belief that the federal government must help *individuals* attain the skills necessary to compete in American society to a new concept: equality could be measured by *group* outcomes or results.

Practical issues also contributed to the shift in emphasis from individual opportunity to group outcomes. The 1964 Civil Rights Act had outlawed discrimination but seemingly had stipulated that action could be taken only when an employer "intentionally engaged" in discrimination against an individual. This individual, case-by-case approach to equal rights created a nightmare for the Equal Employment Opportunity Commission (EEOC). The tens of thousands of cases filed suggested a pervasive pattern of racial and sexual discrimination in American education and employment, but each required proof of "intentional" actions against an individual. Some people were beginning to argue that it was possible, instead, to prove discrimination by "results"—by the relative number of African Americans or women, for example, an employer had hired or promoted.

In 1969, the Nixon administration implemented the first major government affirmative-action program to promote "equality of results." The Philadelphia Plan (so called because it targeted government contracts in that city) required businesses contracting with the federal government to show (in the words of President Nixon) "affirmative action to meet the goals of increasing minority employment" and set specific numerical "goals," or quotas, for employers. Affirmative action for women and members of racial and ethnic minorities was soon required by all major government contracts, and many large corporations and educational institutions began their own programs.

Supporters saw affirmative action as a remedy for the lasting effects of past discrimination. Critics (some of whom were supporters of racial and sexual equality) argued that attempts to create proportional representation for women and minorities meant discrimination against other individuals who had not created past discrimination, and that group-based remedies violated the principle that individuals should be judged on their own merits. As affirmative-action programs began to have an impact in hiring and university admissions, bringing members of underrepresented groups into college classrooms, law firms, schoolrooms, construction companies, police stations, and firehouses nationwide, a deepening recession made jobs scarce. Thus, increasing the number of minorities and women hired often meant reducing the number of white men. White working-class men were most adversely affected by the policy, and many resented it.

THE WOMEN'S MOVEMENT AND GAY LIBERATION

During the 1950s, even as more and more women joined the paid work force and participated in the political life of the nation, American society and culture emphasized women's private roles as wives and mothers. The women's movement that had won American women the vote in the 1920s had all but disappeared. But during the 1960s, a "second wave" of the American women's movement emerged, and by the 1970s mainstream and radical activists waged a multifront battle for "women's liberation."

In 1963, the surprise popularity of Betty Friedan's *The Feminine Mystique* signaled there was ample fuel for a revived women's movement. Writing as a housewife and mother (though she had a long history of political activism as well), Friedan described "the problem with no name," the dissatisfaction of educated, middle-class wives and mothers like herself, who—looking at their nice homes and families—wondered guiltily if that was all there was to life. This "problem" was not new; the vague sense of dissatisfaction plaguing housewives had been a staple topic for women's magazines in the 1950s. But Friedan, instead of blaming individual women for failing to adapt to women's proper role, blamed the role itself and the society that created it.

Liberal and Radical Feminism   The organized, liberal wing of the women's movement emerged in 1966, with the founding of the National Organization for Women (NOW). NOW, made up primarily of educated, professional women, was a traditional lobbying group; its goal was to pressure the EEOC to enforce the 1964 Civil Rights Act. Racial discrimination was the EEOC's focus, and discrimination on the basis of sex was such a low priority that the topic could be treated as a joke. When a reporter asked EEOC chair Franklin Roosevelt Jr., "What about sex?" Roosevelt laughed, "Don't get me started. I'm all for it." Women who faced workplace discrimination were not amused by such comments, and by 1970, NOW had one hundred chapters with more than three thousand members nationwide.

Another strand of the women's movement developed from the nation's increasingly radical movements for social change and justice. Many women, as they worked for civil rights or against the war in Vietnam, found themselves treated as second-class citizens—making coffee, not policy. As they analyzed inequality in America's social and political structure, these young women began to discuss their own oppression, and the oppression of all women, in American society. In 1968, a group of women gathered outside the Miss America Pageant in Atlantic City to protest the "degrading mindless-boob girlie symbol" represented by the beauty pageant. Although nothing was burned, the pejorative 1970s term for feminists, "bra-burners," came from this event, in which women threw items of "enslavement" (girdles, high heels, curlers, and bras) into a "Freedom Trashcan."

The feminism embraced by these young activists and others who challenged women's oppression was never a single, coherent set of beliefs. Some argued that the world should be governed by peaceful, noncompetitive values, which they believed were intrinsically female; others claimed that society imposed gender roles and that there were no innate differences between men and women. Most radical feminists, however, practiced what they called "personal politics." They believed, as feminist author Charlotte Bunch explained, that "there is no private domain of a person's life that is not political, and there is no political issue that is not ultimately personal." Some of these young women began to meet in "consciousness-raising" groups to discuss how, in their personal, everyday lives, women were subordinated by men and by a patriarchal society. In the early 1970s, women throughout the nation came together, in suburban kitchens, college dorm rooms, and churches or synagogues, to create their own consciousness-raising groups, exploring topics such as power relationships in romance and marriage, sexuality, abortion, healthcare, work, and family.

Accomplishments of the Women's Movement During the 1970s, the diverse groups that made up the women's movement claimed significant achievements. Feminists worked for reforms that touched all aspects of American life: the right of a married woman to obtain credit in her own name; the right of an unmarried woman to obtain birth control; the right of women to serve on juries; the end of sex-segregated help wanted ads. They sought to change attitudes about rape and procedures for dealing with rape victims, such as the claim by a psychiatrist at the University of Kansas student health center in 1970: "A woman sometimes plays a big part in provoking her attacker by ... her overall attitude and appearance." But by the end of the decade, activists working on the state and local level had established rape crisis centers, educated local police and hospital officials about procedures for protecting survivors of rape, and even changed laws.

As most of the medical establishment paid little attention to women's desires to understand—and take control of—their own sexual and reproductive health, the Boston Women's Health Collective published *Our Bodies, Ourselves* in 1971 (the original edition sold more than 3 million copies). And women who sought the right to safe and legal abortions won a major victory in 1973 when the Supreme Court, in a 7-to-2 decision on *Roe v. Wade*, ruled that privacy rights protected a woman's choice to end a pregnancy.

NOW and many other women's organizations worked together to promote an Equal Rights Amendment that would end all discriminatory treatment on the basis of sex, the same amendment first proposed by the National Woman's Party in the 1920s. On March 22, 1972, Senate Republicans and Democrats joined to approve the amendment, which stated simply that "equality of rights under the law shall not be denied or abridged by the United States or by any State on account of sex," by a vote of 82 to 8. By the end of the year, 22 states (of the 38 necessary to amend the Constitution) had ratified the ERA. Also in 1972, Congress passed Title IX of the Higher Education Act, which prevented federal funds from going to any college or university that discriminated against women. As a result, universities began to channel money to women's athletics, and women's participation in sports boomed.

Women's applications to graduate programs also boomed. In 1970, only 8.4 percent of medical school graduates and 5.4 percent of law school graduates were women. By 1979, 23 percent of the graduating class of America's medical schools was female, and 28.5 percent of new lawyers were women. Women made up a greater proportion of the armed forces, increasing from 1.3 to 7.6 percent of enlisted ranks personnel between 1971 and 1979. In 1976, women were first admitted to the nation's military academies, intensifying a debate about the proper roles of women in the military. Women also increased their roles in religious organizations, and some denominations began to ordain women. Colleges and universities established women's studies departments; by 1980, more than thirty thousand college courses focused on the study of women or gender.

Opposition to the Women's Movement   The women's movement encompassed a broad range of women, but it was met by powerful opposition, much of it from women. Many women believed that middle-class feminists did not understand the realities of their world. They had no desire to be "equal" if that meant giving up traditional gender roles in marriage or going out to work at low-wage, physically exhausting jobs. African American women and Latinas, many of whom had been active in movements for the liberation of their peoples and some of whom had helped create second-wave feminism, often came to regard feminism as a "white" movement that ignored their cultural traditions and needs; some believed the women's movement diverted time and energy away from the fight for racial equality.

Organized opposition to feminism came primarily from conservative, often religiously motivated men and women. As one conservative Christian writer claimed, "The Bible clearly states that the wife is to submit to her husband's leadership ... just as she would to Christ her Lord." Such beliefs, along with fears about changing gender roles and expectations, fueled the STOP-ERA movement led by Phyllis Schlafly, a lawyer and prominent conservative political activist. Schlafly argued that ERA supporters were "a bunch of bitter women seeking a constitutional cure for their personal problems." She attacked the women's movement as "a total assault on the role of the American woman as wife and mother, and on the family as the basic unit of society." Schlafly and her supporters argued that the ERA would foster federal intervention in personal life, decriminalize rape, force Americans to use unisex toilets, and make women subject to the military draft.

Many women saw feminism as an attack on the choices they had made and felt that by opposing the ERA they were defending their traditional roles. In fighting the ERA, tens of thousands of women became politically experienced; they fed a growing grassroots conservative movement that would come into its own in the 1980s. By the mid-1970s, the STOP-ERA movement had stalled the Equal Rights Amendment. Despite Congress's extension of the ratification deadline, the amendment would fall three states short of ratification and expire in 1982.

Gay Liberation   In the early 1970s, gay men and lesbians faced widespread discrimination. Consensual sexual intercourse between people of the same sex was illegal in almost every state, and until 1973 homosexuality was labeled a mental disorder by the American Psychiatric Association. Homosexual couples did not receive partnership benefits, such as health insurance; they could not adopt children. The issue of gay and lesbian rights divided even progressive organizations: in 1970, the New York City chapter of NOW expelled its lesbian officers. Gay men and lesbians, unlike most members of racial minorities, could conceal the identity that made them vulnerable to discrimination and harassment. Remaining "in the closet" offered individuals some protection against widespread discrimination, but that option also made it very difficult to organize a political movement. There were small "homophile" organizations, such as the Mattachine Society (named for the Société Mattachine, a medieval musical organization whose members performed in masks, to evoke the "masked" lives of gay Americans) and the Daughters of Bilitis (after a work of love poems between women), which had worked for gay rights since the 1950s. But the symbolic beginning of the gay liberation movement came on June 28, 1969, when New York City police raided the Stonewall Inn, a gay bar in Greenwich Village, for violating the New York City law that made it illegal for more than three homosexual patrons to occupy a bar at the same time. That night, for the first time, patrons stood up to the police. As word spread through New York's gay community, hundreds more joined the confrontation. The next morning, New Yorkers found a new slogan spray-painted on neighborhood walls: "Gay Power."

Inspired by the Stonewall riot, some men and women worked openly and militantly for gay rights. They focused on a dual agenda: legal equality and the promotion of Gay Pride. In a version of the identity politics adopted by racial and ethnic communities, some rejected the notion of fitting into straight (heterosexual) culture and helped create distinctive gay communities. By 1973, there were about eight hundred gay organizations in the United States. Centered in big cities and on college campuses, most organizations tried to create supportive environments for gay men and lesbians to come "out of the closet." Once "out," they could use their numbers ("We are everywhere" was a popular slogan) to push for political reform, such as nondiscrimination statutes similar to those that protected women and racial minority groups. By the end of the decade, gay men and lesbians were a public political force in cities including New York, Miami, and San Francisco, and played an increasingly visible role in the social and political life of the nation.

The End in Vietnam

Of all the divisions in American politics and society at the end of the 1960s, none was as pervasive as that over the war in Vietnam. "I'm not going to end up like LBJ," Richard Nixon vowed after winning the 1968 presidential election, recalling that the war had destroyed Johnson's political career. "I'm going to stop that war. Fast." But he did not. He understood that the conflict was generating deep divisions at home and hurting the nation's image abroad, yet—like officials in the Johnson administration—he feared that a precipitous withdrawal would harm American credibility on the world stage as well as his own domestic standing. Anxious to get American troops out of Vietnam, Nixon was at the same time no less committed than his predecessors to preserving an independent, noncommunist South Vietnam. To accomplish these aims, he set upon a policy that at once contracted and expanded the war.

Invasion of Cambodia   A centerpiece of Nixon's policy was "Vietnamization"—the building up of South Vietnamese forces to replace U.S. forces. Nixon hoped that such a policy would quiet domestic opposition and advance the peace talks under way in Paris since May 1968. Accordingly, the president began to withdraw American troops from Vietnam, decreasing their number from 543,000 in the spring of 1969 to 156,800 by the end of 1971, and to 60,000 by the fall of 1972. Vietnamization did help limit domestic dissent, but it did nothing to end the stalemate in the Paris negotiations. Even as he embarked on this troop withdrawal, therefore, Nixon intensified the bombing of North Vietnam and enemy supply depots in neighboring Cambodia, hoping to pound Hanoi into concessions.

The bombing of neutral Cambodia commenced in March 1969. Over the next fourteen months, B-52 pilots flew 3,600 missions and dropped over 100,000 tons of bombs on that country. At first, the administration went to great lengths to keep the bombing campaign secret. When the North Vietnamese refused to buckle, Nixon turned up the heat: in April 1970, South Vietnamese and U.S. forces invaded Cambodia in search of arms depots and North Vietnamese army sanctuaries. The president announced publicly that he would not allow "the world's most powerful nation" to act "like a pitiful, helpless giant."

Protests and Counter demonstrations   Instantly, the antiwar movement rose up, as students on about 450 college campuses went out on strike and hundreds of thousands of demonstrators gathered in various cities to protest the administration's policies. The crisis atmosphere intensified further on May 4, when National Guardsmen in Ohio fired into a crowd of students at Kent State University, killing 4 young people and wounding 11. Ten days later, police and state highway patrolmen armed with automatic weapons blasted a women's dormitory at Jackson State, a historically black university in Mississippi, killing 2 students and wounding 9 others. The police claimed they had been shot at, but no evidence of sniping could be found. In Congress, where opposition to the war had been building over the previous months, Nixon's widening of the war sparked outrage, and in June the Senate terminated the Tonkin Gulf Resolution of 1964. After two months, U.S. troops withdrew from Cambodia, having accomplished little.

Americans still, however, remained divided on the war. Although a majority told pollsters they thought the original U.S. troop commitment to Vietnam to have been a mistake, 50 percent said they believed Nixon's claim that the Cambodia invasion would shorten the war. Angered by the sight of demonstrating college students, many voiced support for the president and the war effort. In Washington, an "Honor America Day" program attracted more than 200,000 people who heard Billy Graham and Bob Hope laud administration policy. Nevertheless, though Nixon welcomed these expressions of support, the tumult over the invasion served to reduce his options on the war. Henceforth, solid majorities could be expected to oppose any new missions for U.S. ground troops in Southeast Asia.

Nixon's troubles at home mounted in June 1971, when the *New York Times* began to publish the Pentagon Papers, the top-secret official study of U.S. decisions in the Vietnam War. Nixon secured an injunction to prevent publication, but the Supreme Court overturned the order. Americans learned from this study that political and military leaders frequently had lied to the public about their aims and strategies in Southeast Asia.

Morale Problems in the Military

Equally troubling, to both opponents and supporters of the war, was the growing evidence of decay within the armed forces. Morale and discipline among troops had been on the decline even before Nixon took office, and there were growing reports of drug addiction, desertion, racial discord, even the murder of unpopular officers by enlisted men (a practice called "fragging"). Stories of atrocities committed by U.S. troops also began to make their way home. The court-martial and conviction in 1971 of Lieutenant William Calley, who was charged with overseeing the killing of more than three hundred unarmed South Vietnamese civilians in the hamlet of My Lai in 1968, got particular attention. An army photographer captured the horror in graphic pictures. For many, the massacre signified the dehumanizing impact of the war on those who fought it.

Paris Peace Accords

The Nixon administration, meanwhile, stepped up its efforts to pressure Hanoi into a settlement. Johnson had lacked the will to "go to the brink." Nixon told Kissinger, "I have the will in spades." When the North Vietnamese launched a major offensive across the border into South Vietnam in March 1972, Nixon responded with a massive aerial onslaught against North Vietnam. In December 1972, after an apparent peace agreement collapsed when the South Vietnamese refused to moderate their position, the United States launched a massive air strike on the North—the so-called Christmas bombing.

A diplomatic agreement was, however, close. Months earlier, Kissinger and his North Vietnamese counterpart in the negotiations, Le Duc Tho, had resolved many of the outstanding issues. Most notably, Kissinger agreed that North Vietnamese troops could remain in the South after the settlement, while Tho abandoned Hanoi's insistence that the Saigon government of Nguyen Van Thieu be removed. Nixon had instructed Kissinger to make concessions because the president was eager to improve relations with the Soviet Union and China, to win back the allegiance of America's allies, and to restore stability at home. On January 27, 1973, Kissinger and Le Duc Tho signed a cease-fire agreement in Paris, and Nixon compelled a reluctant Thieu to accept it by threatening to cut off U.S. aid while at the same time promising to defend the South if the North violated the agreement. In the accord, the United States promised to withdraw all of its troops within sixty days. North Vietnamese troops would be allowed to stay in South Vietnam, and a coalition government that included the Vietcong eventually would be formed in the South.

VISUALIZING THE PAST

The Image of War

The Vietnam War has been called the first "television war." More than ever before (or arguably since) news clips and photos brought Americans and others around the world face-to-face with the fighting and its victims. On June 8, 1972, as children and their families fled the village of Trang Bang, their bodies seared by napalm, Huynh Cong "Nick" Ut took this iconic photograph that became an antiwar rallying point and symbol of hope. The girl in the center, Phan Thi Kim Phuc, survived the attack but had to endure fourteen months of painful rehabilitation to treat the third-degree burns that covered more than half of her body. Kim later became a Canadian citizen and a Goodwill Ambassador for the United Nations Educational, Scientific and Cultural Organization (UNESCO). Some analysts have argued that a single image can become the voice of popular protest; others say that even indelible images such as this one cannot have that power. What do you think?

AP Images/Huynh Cong "Nick" Ut

The United States pulled its troops out of Vietnam, leaving behind some military advisers. Soon, both North and South violated the cease-fire, and full-scale war erupted once more. The feeble South Vietnamese government, despite holding a clear superiority in the number of tanks and combat-ready troops, could not hold out. Just before its surrender, hundreds of Americans and Vietnamese who had worked for them were hastily evacuated from Saigon. On April 29, 1975, the South Vietnamese government collapsed, and Vietnam was reunified under a communist government based in Hanoi. Shortly thereafter, Saigon was renamed Ho Chi Minh City for the persevering patriot who had died in 1969.

Costs of the Vietnam War

The overall costs of the war were immense. More than 58,000 Americans and between 1.5 and 2 million Vietnamese had died. Civilian deaths in Cambodia and Laos numbered in the hundreds of thousands. The war cost the United States at least $170 billion, and billions more would be paid out in veterans' benefits. The vast sums spent on the war became unavailable for investment in domestic programs. Instead, the nation suffered inflation and retreat from reform, as well as political schism and abuses of executive power. The war also delayed accommodation with the Soviet Union and the People's Republic of China, fueled friction with allies, and alienated Third World nations.

In 1975, communists assumed control and formed repressive governments in Vietnam, Cambodia, and Laos, but beyond Indochina the domino effect once predicted by U.S. officials never occurred. Acute hunger afflicted the people of those devastated lands. Soon refugees—"boat people"—crowded aboard unsafe vessels in an attempt to escape their battered homelands. Many emigrated to the United States, where they were received with mixed feelings by Americans reluctant to be reminded of defeat in Asia. But many Americans faced the fact that the United States, which had relentlessly bombed, burned, and defoliated once-rich agricultural lands, bore considerable responsibility for the plight of the southeast Asian peoples.

Debate over the Lessons of Vietnam

Americans seemed both angry and confused about the nation's war experience. Hawkish observers claimed that America's failure in Vietnam undermined the nation's credibility and tempted enemies to exploit opportunities at the expense of U.S. interests. They pointed to a "Vietnam syndrome"—a resulting American suspicion of foreign entanglements—which they feared would inhibit the future exercise of U.S. power. America lost in Vietnam, they asserted, because Americans had lost their guts at home.

Dovish analysts drew different conclusions, denying that the military had suffered undue restrictions. Some blamed the war on an imperial presidency that had permitted strong-willed men to act without restraint and on a weak Congress that had conceded too much power to the executive branch. Make the president adhere to the checks-and-balances system—make him go to Congress for a declaration of war—these critics counseled, and America would become less interventionist. This view found expression in the War Powers Act of 1973, which sought to limit the president's warmaking freedom. Henceforth, Congress would have to approve any commitment of U.S. forces to combat action lasting more than sixty days. In the same year, the draft (which had been shifted to a lottery system in 1969), came to an end; the U.S. military would henceforth be a volunteer army.

Vietnam
Veterans
Public discussion of the lessons of the Vietnam War was also stimulated by veterans' calls for help in dealing with post-traumatic stress disorder, which afflicted thousands of the 2.8 million Vietnam veterans. Once home, they suffered nightmares and extreme nervousness. Doctors reported that the disorder stemmed primarily from the soldiers' having seen so many children, women, and elderly people killed. Some GIs inadvertently killed these people; some killed them vengefully and later felt guilt. Other veterans heightened public awareness of the war by publicizing their deteriorating health from the effects of the defoliant Agent Orange and other herbicides they had handled or were accidentally sprayed with in Vietnam. The Vietnam Veterans Memorial, erected in Washington, D.C., in 1982, has kept the issue alive, as have many oral history projects of veterans conducted by school and college students in classes to this day.

NIXON, KISSINGER, AND THE WORLD

Even as Nixon and Kissinger tried to achieve victory in Vietnam, they understood that the United States had overreached in the 1960s with a military commitment that had caused massive bloodshed, deep domestic divisions, and economic dislocation. The difficulties of the war signified to them that American power was limited and, in relative terms, in decline. This reality necessitated a new approach to the Cold War, and both moved quickly to reorient American policy. In particular, they believed the United States had to adapt to a new, multipolar international system; no longer could that system be defined simply by the Soviet-American rivalry. Western Europe was becoming a major player in its own right, as was Japan. The Middle East loomed increasingly large, due in large part to America's growing dependence on oil from the region. Above all, Americans had to come to grips with the reality of China by rethinking the policy of hostile isolation followed since the communist takeover in 1949.

They were an unlikely duo—the reclusive, ambitious Californian, born of Quaker parents, and the sociable, dynamic Jewish intellectual who had fled Nazi Germany as a child. Nixon, ten years older, was more or less a career politician, while Kissinger had made his name as a Harvard professor and foreign policy consultant. Whereas Nixon was a staunch Republican, Kissinger had no strong partisan commitments and indeed said disparaging things about Republicans to his Democratic friends. What the two men had in common was a tendency toward paranoia about rivals and a capacity to think in broad conceptual terms about America's place in the world.

Nixon Doctrine
In July 1969, Nixon and Kissinger acknowledged the limits of American power and resources when they announced the Nixon Doctrine. The United States, they said, would continue to provide economic aid to allies in Asia and elsewhere, but these allies should no longer count on American troops. It was an admission that Washington could no longer afford to sustain its many overseas commitments and therefore would have to rely more on regional allies—including, it turned out, many authoritarian regimes—to maintain

an anticommunist world order. Although Nixon did not say so, his doctrine amounted to a partial retreat from the 1947 Truman Doctrine, with its promise to support noncommunist governments facing internal or external threats to their existence.

Détente

If the Nixon Doctrine was one pillar of the new foreign policy, the other was détente: measured cooperation with the Soviets through negotiations within a general environment of rivalry, drawn from the French word for "relaxation." Détente's primary purpose, like that of the containment doctrine it resembled, was to check Soviet expansion and limit the Soviet arms buildup, though now that goal would be accomplished through diplomacy and mutual concessions. The second part of the strategy sought to curb revolution and radicalism in the Third World so as to quash threats to American interests. More specifically, the Cold War and limited wars like that in Vietnam were costing too much; expanded trade with friendlier Soviets and Chinese might reduce the huge U.S. balance-of-payments deficit. And improving relations with both communist giants, at a time when Sino-Soviet tensions were increasing, might exacerbate feuding between the two, weakening communism.

The Soviet Union's leadership had its own reasons for wanting détente. The Cold War was a drain on its resources, too, and by the late 1960s defense needs and consumer demands were increasingly at odds. Improved ties with Washington would also allow the USSR to focus more on its increasingly fractious relations with China and might generate serious progress on outstanding European issues, including the status of Germany and Berlin. Some ideologues in the Moscow leadership remained deeply suspicious of cozying up to the American capitalists, but they did not prevail over advocates of change. Thus, in May 1972, the United States and the USSR agreed in the ABM Treaty (officially the Treaty on the Limitation of Anti-Ballistic Missile Systems) to slow the costly arms race by limiting the construction and deployment of intercontinental ballistic missiles and antiballistic missile defenses.

Opening to China

While cultivating détente with the Soviet Union, the United States took dramatic steps to end more than two decades of Sino-American hostility. The Chinese welcomed the change because they wanted to spur trade and hoped that friendlier Sino-American relations would make their onetime ally and now enemy, the Soviet Union, more cautious. Nixon reasoned the same way: "We're using the Chinese thaw to get the Russians shook." In early 1972, Nixon made a historic trip to "Red China," where he and the venerable Chinese leaders Mao Zedong and Zhou Enlai agreed to disagree on a number of issues, except one: the Soviet Union should not be permitted to make gains in Asia. Sino-American relations improved slightly, and official diplomatic recognition and the exchange of ambassadors came in 1979.

The opening to communist China and the policy of détente with the Soviet Union reflected Nixon's and Kissinger's belief in the importance of maintaining stability among the great powers. In the Third World, too, they sought stability, though there they hoped to get it not by change but by maintaining the status quo. As it happened, events in the Third World would provide the Nixon-Kissinger approach with its greatest test, and not merely because of Vietnam.

Wars in the Middle East
In the Middle East, the situation had grown more volatile in the aftermath of the Arab-Israeli Six-Day War in 1967. In that conflict, Israel had scored victories against Egypt and Syria, seizing the Sinai Peninsula and the Gaza Strip from Egypt, the West Bank and East Jerusalem from Jordan, and the Golan Heights from Syria (see Map 33.1). Instantly, Israel's regional position was transformed, as it gained 28,000 square miles and could henceforth defend itself more easily against invading military forces. But the victory came at a price. Gaza and the West Bank were the ancestral home of hundreds of thousands of Palestinians and the more recent home of additional hundreds of thousands of Palestinian refugees from the 1948 Arab-Israeli conflict (see Chapter 28). Suddenly, Israel found itself governing large numbers of people who wanted nothing more than to see Israel destroyed. When the Israelis began to establish Jewish settlements in their newly won areas, Arab resentment grew even stronger. Terrorists associated with the Palestinian Liberation Organization (PLO) made hit-and-run raids on Jewish settlements, hijacked jetliners, and murdered Israeli athletes at the 1972 Olympic Games in Munich, West Germany. The Israelis retaliated by assassinating PLO leaders.

In October 1973, on the Jewish High Holy Day of Yom Kippur, Egypt and Syria attacked Israel. Their motives were complex, but primarily they sought revenge for the 1967 defeat. Caught by surprise, Israel reeled before launching an effective counteroffensive against Soviet-armed Egyptian forces in the Sinai. In an attempt to punish Americans for their pro-Israel stance, the Organization of Petroleum Exporting Countries (OPEC), a group of mostly Arab nations that had joined together to raise the price of oil, embargoed shipments of oil to the United States and other supporters of Israel. An energy crisis and dramatically higher oil prices rocked the nation. Soon Kissinger arranged a cease-fire in the war, but OPEC did not lift the oil embargo until March 1974. The next year, Kissinger persuaded Egypt and Israel to accept a UN peacekeeping force in the Sinai. But peace did not come to the region, for Palestinians and other Arabs still vowed to destroy Israel, and Israelis insisted on building more Jewish settlements in occupied lands.

Antiradicalism in Latin America and Africa
In Latin America, meanwhile, the Nixon administration sought to preserve stability and to thwart radical leftist challenges to authoritarian rule. In Chile, after voters in 1970 elected a Marxist president, Salvador Allende, the CIA began secret operations to disrupt Chile and encouraged military officers to stage a coup. In 1973, a military junta ousted Allende and installed an authoritarian regime under General Augusto Pinochet. (Allende was subsequently murdered.) Washington publicly denied any role in the affair that implanted iron-fisted tyranny in Chile for two decades.

In Africa as well, Washington preferred the status quo. Nixon backed the white-minority regime in Rhodesia (now Zimbabwe) and activated the CIA in a failed effort to defeat a Soviet- and Cuban-backed faction in newly independent Angola's civil war.

In South Africa, Nixon tolerated the white rulers who imposed the segregationist policy of apartheid on blacks and mixed-race "coloureds" (85 percent of the population), keeping them poor, disfranchised, and ghettoized in prisonlike townships. After the leftist government came to power in Angola, however, Washington took a keener interest in the rest of Africa, building economic ties and sending arms to friendly black nations, such as Kenya and the Congo. The administration also began to distance the United States from the white governments of Rhodesia and South Africa. America had to "prevent the radicalization of Africa," said Kissinger.

PRESIDENTIAL POLITICS AND THE CRISIS OF LEADERSHIP

Richard Nixon took pride in his foreign policy accomplishments, but they were overshadowed by his failures at home. He betrayed the public trust and broke laws, large and small. His misconduct, combined with Americans' growing belief that their leaders had lied to them repeatedly about the war in Vietnam, shook Americans' faith in government. This new mistrust joined with conservatives' traditional suspicion of big, activist government to create a crisis of leadership and undermine liberal policies that had governed the nation since the New Deal, even in the Eisenhower era. The profound suspicion of presidential leadership and government action that enveloped the nation by the end of the Watergate hearings would limit what Gerald Ford and Jimmy Carter, Nixon's successors to the presidency, could accomplish.

Nixon's Domestic Agenda

Richard Nixon was one of America's most complex presidents. Brilliant, driven, politically cunning, able to address changing global realities with creativity—Nixon was also crude, prejudiced against Jews and African Americans, happy to use dirty tricks and the power of the presidency against those he considered his enemies, and driven by a sense of resentment that bordered on paranoia. Despite his tenacity and intelligence, Nixon—the son of a grocer from an agricultural region of southern California—was never accepted by the sophisticated northeastern liberal elite. (After Nixon's election, *Washingtonian* magazine joked that "cottage cheese with ketchup" had replaced elegant desserts at White House dinners.) Nixon loathed the liberal establishment, which loathed him back, and his presidency was driven by that hatred as much as by any strong philosophical commitment to conservative principles.

Nixon's domestic policy initiatives have long confused historians. Much of his agenda was liberal, expanding federal programs to improve society. The Nixon administration pioneered affirmative action. It doubled the budgets of the new National Endowment for the Humanities (NEH) and National Endowment for the Arts (NEA). Nixon supported the ERA, signed major environmental legislation, created the Occupational Safety and Health Administration (OSHA), actively attempted to manage the economy using deficit spending, and even proposed a guaranteed minimum income for all Americans.

At the same time, Nixon pursued a conservative agenda. One of his major legislative goals was "devolution," or shifting federal government authority to states and localities. He promoted revenue-sharing programs that distributed federal funds back to the states to use as they saw fit, thus appealing to those who were angry about, as they saw it, paying high taxes to support liberal "giveaway" programs for poor and minority Americans. As president, Nixon worked to equate the Republican Party with law and order and the Democrats with permissiveness, crime, drugs, radicalism, and the "hippie lifestyle." To capitalize on the backlash against the 1960s movements for social change and consolidate the support of those he called "the silent majority," Nixon fostered division, using his outspoken vice president, Spiro Agnew, to attack war protesters and critics as "naughty children," "effete ... snobs," and "ideological eunuchs." He appointed four conservative justices to the Supreme Court: Warren Burger, Harry Blackmun, Lewis Powell Jr., and William Rehnquist.

With such a confusing record, was Nixon liberal, conservative, or simply pragmatic? The answer is complicated. For example, when the Nixon administration proposed a guaranteed minimum income for all Americans, including the working poor, his larger goal was to dismantle the federal welfare system and destroy its liberal bureaucracy of social workers (no longer necessary under Nixon's model). And though Nixon doubled funding for the NEA, he redirected awards from the northeastern art establishment—the "elite" that he thought of as an enemy—toward local and regional art groups that sponsored popular art forms, such as representational painting or folk music.

In addition, recognizing the possibility of attracting white southerners to the Republican Party, Nixon pursued a highly pragmatic "southern strategy." He nominated two southerners for positions on the Supreme Court—one of whom had a segregationist record—and when Congress declined to confirm either nominee, Nixon protested angrily, saying, "I understand the bitter feelings of millions of Americans who live in the South." After the Supreme Court upheld a school desegregation plan that required a North Carolina school system—still highly segregated fifteen years after the *Brown* decision—to achieve racial integration by removing both black and white children from their neighborhood schools and busing them to schools elsewhere in the county (*Swann v. Charlotte-Mecklenburg*, 1971), Nixon denounced busing as a reckless and extreme remedy. (Neither resistance to busing nor continuing segregation was a purely southern phenomenon, as Boston residents protested—sometimes violently—court-ordered busing to combat school segregation in 1974.)

Enemies and Dirty Tricks   Nixon was almost sure of reelection in 1972. His Democratic opponent was George McGovern, a progressive senator from South Dakota and strong opponent of the Vietnam War. McGovern appealed to the left and essentially wrote off the middle, declaring, "I am not a centrist candidate." Alabama governor George Wallace, running on a third-party ticket, withdrew from the race after an assassination attempt left him paralyzed. The Nixon campaign, however, was taking no chances. On June 17, four months before the election, five men were caught breaking into the Democratic National Committee's offices at the Watergate apartment and office complex in Washington, D.C. The men were associated with the Committee to Re-elect the

President, or CREEP. The break-in got little attention at the time, and Nixon was swept into office in November with 60 percent of the popular vote. McGovern carried only Massachusetts and the District of Columbia. But even as Nixon triumphed, his downfall had begun.

From the beginning of his presidency, Nixon was obsessed with the idea that, in a time of national turmoil, he was surrounded by enemies. He made "enemies lists," hundreds of names long, that included all black members of Congress and the presidents of most Ivy League universities. The Nixon administration worked, in the words of one of its members, to "use the available federal machinery to screw our political enemies." On Nixon's order, his aide Charles Colson (best known for his maxim "When you've got them by the balls, their hearts and minds will follow") formed a secret group called the Plumbers. Their first job was to break into the office of the psychiatrist treating Daniel Ellsberg, a former Pentagon employee who had gone public with the Pentagon Papers, looking for material to discredit him. The Plumbers expanded their "dirty tricks" operations during the 1972 presidential primaries and campaign, bugging phones, infiltrating campaign staffs, even writing and distributing anonymous letters falsely accusing Democratic candidates of sexual misconduct. They had already bugged the Democratic National Committee offices and were going back to plant more surveillance equipment when they were caught by the D.C. police at the Watergate complex.

Watergate Cover-up and Investigation   Nixon was not directly involved in the Watergate break-in. But instead of distancing himself and firing those responsible, he tried to cover it up, ordering the CIA to stop the FBI's investigation, citing reasons of national security. At this point, Nixon had obstructed justice—a felony and, under the Constitution, an impeachable crime—but he had also, it seemed, halted the investigation. However, two young, relatively unknown reporters for the *Washington Post*, Carl Bernstein and Bob Woodward, would not give up on the story. Aided by an anonymous, highly placed government official whom they code-named Deep Throat (the title of a notorious 1972 X-rated film), they began to follow a money trail that led straight to the White House. (W. Mark Felt, who was second-in-command at the FBI in the early 1970s, publicly identified himself as Watergate's Deep Throat in 2005.)

The Watergate cover-up continued to unravel under the scrutiny of both the courts and Congress. From May to August 1973, the Senate held televised public hearings on the Watergate affair. White House Counsel John Dean, fearful that he was being made the fall guy for the entire Watergate fiasco, gave damning testimony. Then, on July 13, a White House aide told the Senate Committee that Nixon regularly recorded his conversations in the Oval Office. These tape recordings were the "smoking gun" that could prove Nixon's direct involvement in the cover-up—but Nixon refused to turn the tapes over to Congress.

Impeachment and Resignation   As Nixon and Congress fought over the tapes, Nixon faced scandals on other fronts. In October 1973, Vice President Spiro Agnew resigned, following charges that he had accepted bribes while governor of Maryland. Following constitutional procedures,

Nixon appointed and Congress approved Michigan's Gerald Ford, the House minority leader, as Agnew's replacement. Meanwhile, Nixon's staff was increasingly concerned about his excessive drinking and seeming mental instability. Then, on October 24, 1973, the House of Representatives began impeachment proceedings against the president.

Under court order, Nixon began to release edited portions of the Oval Office tapes to Congress. Although the first tapes revealed no criminal activity, the public was shocked by Nixon's constant obscenities and racist slurs. Finally, in July 1974, the Supreme Court ruled that Nixon must release all the tapes. Despite "mysterious" erasures on two key tapes, the House Judiciary Committee found evidence to impeach Nixon on three grounds: obstruction of justice, abuse of power, and contempt of Congress. On August 9, 1974, facing certain impeachment and conviction, Richard Nixon became the first president of the United States to resign his office.

The Watergate scandal shook the confidence of American citizens in their government. It also prompted Congress to reevaluate the balance of power between the executive and legislative branches. Beginning in 1973, Congress passed several major bills aimed at restricting presidential power. They included not only the War Powers Act, but also the 1974 Budget and Impoundment Control Act, which made it impossible for the president to disregard congressional spending mandates.

Ford's Presidency

Gerald Ford, the nation's first unelected president, faced a nation awash in cynicism. The presidency was discredited. The economy was in decline. The nation's people were divided. When in one of his first official acts as president, Ford issued a full pardon to Richard Nixon, forestalling any attempts to bring criminal charges, his approval ratings plummeted from 71 to 41 percent. Some suggested, with no evidence, that he had struck some sort of sordid deal with Nixon. Ford insisted, for decades, that he had simply acted in the interest of the nation, but shortly before his death in late 2006 he told a reporter that, though few knew it, he and Nixon had been good friends and "I didn't want to see my real friend have the stigma" of criminal charges.

While Ford was, overall, a decent and honorable man who did his best to end what he called "the long national nightmare," he accomplished little domestically during his two and a half years in office. The Democrats gained a large margin in the 1974 congressional elections and, after Watergate, Congress was willing to exercise its power. Ford almost routinely vetoed its bills—39 in one year—but Congress often overrode his veto. And Ford had become the object of constant mockery. In political cartoons, comedy monologs, and especially on the new hit television show *Saturday Night Live*, he was portrayed as a buffoon and a klutz. When he slipped on the steps exiting *Air Force One*, footage appeared on major newscasts. The irony of portraying Ford—who had turned down a chance to play in the National Football League in order to attend Yale Law School—as physically inept was extraordinary. But as Ford understood, these portrayals began to give the impression that he was a "stumbler," in danger of making blunders of all kinds.

Resigning in disgrace as impeachment for his role in the Watergate cover-up became a certainty, Richard Nixon flashes the "V for victory" sign as he leaves the White House for the last time.

Nixon Presidential Materials Project, National Archives and Record Administration

Ford caught the fallout of disrespect that Nixon's actions had unleashed. No longer would respect for the office of the presidency prevent the mass media from reporting presidential slips, stumbles, frailties, or misconduct. Ford was the first president to discover how much the rules had changed.

Carter as "Outsider" President

Jimmy Carter, who was elected in 1976 by a slim margin, initially benefited from Americans' suspicion of political leadership. Carter was a one-term governor of Georgia, one of the new southern leaders who were committed to racial equality and integration. He had grown up in the rural Georgia town of Plains, where his family owned a peanut farm, graduated from the Naval Academy, then served as an engineer in the navy's nuclear submarine program. Carter, a deeply religious born-again Christian, made a virtue of his lack of political experience. Promising the American people, "I will never lie to you," he emphasized his distance from Washington and the political corruption of recent times.

From his inauguration, when he broke with the convention of a motorcade and walked down Pennsylvania Avenue holding hands with his wife and close adviser, Rosalynn, and their young daughter, Amy, Carter rejected the trappings of the imperial presidency and emphasized his populist, outsider appeal. But the outsider status that gained him the presidency would be one of Carter's major drawbacks as president. Though an astute policymaker, he scorned the deal making that was necessary to pass legislation in Congress.

Carter faced problems that would have challenged any leader: the economy continued to decline, energy shortages had not abated, the American people distrusted their government. More than any other American leader of the post–World War II era, Carter was willing to tell the American people things they did not want to hear. As shortages of natural gas forced schools and businesses to close during the bitterly cold winter of 1977, Carter went on television—wearing a cardigan sweater—to speak to the American people about the new era of limits and called for "sacrifice." Carter put energy conservation measures into effect at the White House and government buildings, and proposed to Congress a detailed energy plan that emphasized conservation. In the defining speech of his presidency, as the nation struggled with a sense of uncertainty and unease, Carter told Americans that the nation suffered from a crisis of the spirit. He talked about the false lures of "self-indulgence and consumption," about "paralysis and stagnation and drift." And he called for a "new commitment to the path of common purpose." But he was unable to offer practical solutions for what was then described as a national malaise.

Carter did score some noteworthy domestic accomplishments. He worked to ease burdensome government regulations without destroying consumer and worker safeguards, and created the Departments of Energy and Education. He also created environmental protections, establishing a $1.6 billion "superfund" to clean up abandoned chemical-waste sites and placing more than 100 million acres of Alaskan land under the federal government's protection as national parks, national forests, and wildlife refuges.

ECONOMIC CRISIS

Americans' loss of confidence in their political leaders was intensified by a growing economic crisis. Since World War II, except for a few brief downturns, prosperity had been a fundamental condition of American life. A steadily rising gross national product, based largely on growing rates of productivity, had propelled large numbers of Americans into the economically comfortable middle class. Prosperity had made possible the great liberal initiatives of the 1960s and improved the lives of America's poor and elderly citizens. But in the early 1970s, that long period of economic expansion and prosperity came to an end. Almost every economic indicator drove home bad news. In 1974 alone, the gross national product dropped 2 full percentage points. Industrial production fell 9 percent. Inflation—the increase in costs of goods and services—skyrocketed, and unemployment grew.

Stagflation and Its Causes   Throughout most of the 1970s, the U.S. economy floundered in a condition that economists dubbed "stagflation": a stagnant economy characterized by high unemployment combined with out-of-control inflation. Stagflation was almost impossible to manage with traditional economic remedies. When the federal government increased spending to stimulate the economy and so reduce unemployment, inflation grew. When the federal government tried to rein in inflation by cutting government spending or tightening the money supply, the recession deepened and unemployment rates skyrocketed.

The causes of the economic crisis were complex. Federal management of the economy was in part to blame: President Johnson had reversed conventional economic wisdom and created inflationary pressure by insisting that the United States could have both "guns and butter," as he waged a very expensive war in Vietnam while greatly expanding domestic spending in his Great Society programs. But fundamental problems also came from America's changing role in the global economy. After World War II, with most leading industrial nations in ruins, the United States had stood alone at the pinnacle of the global economy. But the war-ravaged nations—often with major economic assistance from the United States—rebuilt their productive capacities with new, technologically advanced industrial plants. By the early 1970s, both of America's major wartime adversaries, Japan and Germany, had become major economic powers—and major competitors in global trade. In 1971, for the first time since the end of the nineteenth century, the United States imported more goods than it exported, beginning an era of American trade deficits.

American corporate actions also contributed to the growing trade imbalance. During the years of global dominance, few American companies had reinvested profits in improving production techniques or educating workers. Consequently, American productivity—that is, the average output of goods per hour of labor— had begun to decline. As workers' productivity declined, however, their wages rarely did. The combination of falling productivity and high labor costs meant that American goods became more and more expensive—both for American consumers and for consumers in other nations. Even worse, without significant competition from foreign manufacturers, American companies had allowed the quality of their goods to decline. From 1966 to 1973, for example, American car and truck manufacturers had to recall almost 30 million vehicles because of serious defects.

America's global economic vulnerability was driven home by the energy crisis that began in 1973. Americans had grown up with cheap and abundant energy, and their lifestyles showed it. American passenger cars got an average of 13.4 miles per gallon in 1973, when a gallon of gas cost 38 cents (about $1.40 in 2006 dollars); neither home heating nor household appliances were designed to be energy-efficient. The country, however, depended on imported oil for almost one-third of its energy supply. When OPEC cut off oil shipments to the United States, U.S. oil prices rose 350 percent. The increases reverberated through the economy: heating costs, shipping costs, and manufacturing costs increased, and so did the cost of goods and services. Inflation jumped from 3 percent in early 1973 to 11 percent in 1974. Sales of gas-guzzling American cars plummeted as people rushed to buy energy-efficient subcompacts from Japan and Europe. American car manufacturers, stuck with machinery for producing large cars, were hit hard. GM laid off 6 percent of its domestic work force and put an even larger number on rolling unpaid leaves. As the ailing automobile industry quit buying steel, glass, and rubber, manufacturers of these goods laid off workers, too.

Attempts to Fix the Economy   American political leaders tried desperately to manage the economic crisis, but their actions often exacerbated it instead. As America's rising trade deficit undermined international confidence in the dollar, the Nixon administration ended the dollar's link to the gold standard; free-floating exchange rates increased the price of foreign goods in the United States and stimulated inflation. President Ford created a voluntary program, Whip Inflation Now (complete with red and white "WIN" buttons), in 1974 to encourage grassroots anti-inflation efforts. Following the tenets of monetary theory, which held that, with less money available to "chase" the supply of goods, price increases would gradually slow down, ending the inflationary spiral, Ford curbed federal spending and encouraged the Federal Reserve Board to tighten credit—and prompted the worst recession in forty years. In 1975 unemployment climbed to 8.5 percent.

Carter first attempted to bring unemployment rates down by stimulating the economy, but inflation careened out of control; he then tried to slow the economy down—and prompted a major recession during the election year of 1980. In fact, Carter's larger economic policies, including his 1978 deregulation of airline, trucking, banking, and communications industries, would eventually foster economic growth—but not soon enough. After almost a decade of decline, Americans were losing faith in the American economy and in the ability of their political leaders to manage it.

Impacts of the Economic Crisis   The economic crisis of the 1970s accelerated the nation's transition from an industrial to a service economy. During the 1970s, the American economy "deindustrialized." Automobile companies laid off workers. Massive steel plants shut down, leaving entire communities devastated. Other manufacturing concerns moved overseas, seeking lower labor costs and fewer government regulations. New jobs were created— 27 million of them—but they were overwhelmingly in what economists called the "service sector": retail sales, restaurants, and other service providers. As heavy industries collapsed, formerly highly paid, unionized workers took jobs in the growing but not unionized service sector. These jobs—such as warehouse work or retail sales, for example—paid much lower wages and often lacked healthcare benefits.

Formerly successful blue-collar workers saw their middle-class standards of life slipping away. More married women joined the work force because they had to—though some were drawn by new opportunities. Even in the best of times the economy would have been hard pressed to produce jobs for the millions of baby boomers who joined the labor market in the 1970s. Young people graduating from high school or college in the 1970s, raised with high expectations, suddenly found very limited possibilities—if they found jobs at all.

The economic crisis also helped to shift the economic and population centers of the nation. As the old industrial regions of the North and Midwest went into decline, people fled the "snow belt" or the "rust belt," speeding up the Sunbelt boom already in progress (see Map 31.1). The Sunbelt was where the jobs were. The federal government had invested heavily in the South and West during the postwar era, especially in military and defense industries, and in the infrastructures necessary for them. Never a major center for heavy manufactures, the Sunbelt was primed for the rapid growth of modern industries and services—aerospace, defense, electronics, transportation, research, banking and finance, and leisure. City and

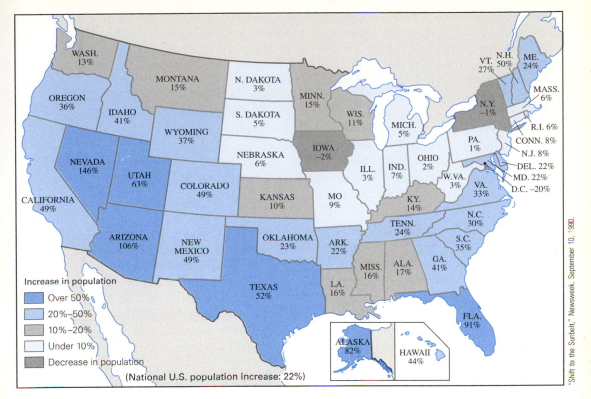

Throughout the 1970s and 1980s, Americans continued to leave economically declining areas of the North and East in pursuit of opportunity in the Sunbelt. States in the Sunbelt and in the West had the largest population increases.

MAP 31.1 The Continued Shift to the Sunbelt in the 1970s and 1980s

state governments competed to lure businesses and investment dollars, in part by preventing the growth of unions. Atlanta, Houston, and other southern cities marketed themselves as cosmopolitan, sophisticated, and racially tolerant; they bought sports teams and built museums.

This population shift south and west, combined with the flight of middle-class taxpayers to the suburbs, created disaster in northern and midwestern cities. New York City, close to financial collapse by late 1975, was saved only when the House and Senate Banking Committees approved federal loan guarantees. Cleveland defaulted on its debts in 1978, the first major city to do so since Detroit declared bankruptcy in 1933.

Tax Revolts   Even as stagflation and Sunbelt growth transformed American politics, a "tax revolt" movement emerged in the rapidly growing American West. In California, inflation had driven property taxes up rapidly, hitting middle-class taxpayers hard. In this era of economic decline and post-Watergate suspicion, angry taxpayers saw government as the problem. Instead of calling for wealthy citizens and major corporations to pay a larger share of taxes, voters rebelled against taxation itself. California's Proposition 13, passed by a landslide in 1978, rolled back property taxes and restricted future increases. Within months of Proposition 13's passage, thirty-seven states cut property taxes, and twenty-eight lowered their state income-tax rates.

The impact of Proposition 13 and similar initiatives was initially cushioned by state budget surpluses, but as those surpluses turned to deficits, states cut services—closing fire stations and public libraries, ending or limiting mental health services and programs for the disabled. Public schools were hit especially hard. The tax revolt movement signaled the growth of a new conservatism; voters who wanted lower taxes and smaller government would help bring Ronald Reagan to the White House in the election of 1980.

Credit and Investment   The runaway inflation of the 1970s also changed how Americans managed their money. Before this era, home mortgages and auto loans were the only kind of major debt most Americans would venture. National credit cards had become common only in the late 1960s, and few Americans—especially those who remembered the Great Depression—were willing to spend money they did not have. In the 1970s, however, thriftiness stopped making sense. Double-digit inflation rates meant double-digit declines in the purchasing power of a dollar. It was economically smarter to buy goods before their prices went up—even if it meant borrowing the money. Because debt was paid off later with devalued dollars, the consumer came out ahead. In 1975, consumer debt hit a high of $167 billion; it almost doubled, to $315 billion, by 1979.

The 1970s were also the decade in which average Americans became investors rather than savers. Throughout the 1970s, because of regulations created during the Great Depression, the interest rates that banks could pay on individual savings accounts were capped. An average savings account bearing 5 percent interest actually *lost* more than 20 percent of its value from 1970 through 1980 because of inflation. That same money, invested at market rates, would have grown dramatically. Fidelity Investments, a mutual fund company, saw a business opportunity: its money market accounts combined many smaller investments to purchase large-denomination Treasury bills and certificates of deposit, thus allowing small investors to get the high interest rates normally available only to major investors. Money flooded out of passbook accounts and into money funds, and money market investments grew from $1.7 billion in 1974 to $200 billion in 1982. At the same time, deregulation of the New York Stock Exchange spawned discount brokerage houses, whose low commission rates made it affordable for middle-class investors to trade stocks.

An Era of Cultural Transformation

The 1970s have been dismissed as a cultural wasteland, an era in which the nation confronted new limits without much passion or creativity. But it was during the 1970s, as Americans struggled with economic recession, governmental betrayal, and social division, that major strands of late-twentieth-century culture were developed or consolidated. The current environmental movement, the growth of technology, the rise of born-again Christianity and a "therapeutic culture," contemporary forms of sexuality and the family, new roles for youth, and America's emphasis on diversity all have roots in this odd decade sandwiched between the political vibrancy of the 1960s and the conservatism of the 1980s.

Environmentalism Just as Americans were forced to confront the end of postwar prosperity, a series of ecological crises drove home the limits on natural resources and the fragility of the environment. In 1969, a major oil spill took place off the coast of Santa Barbara, California; that same year, the polluted Cuyahoga River, flowing through Cleveland, caught fire. Although the energy crisis of the 1970s was due to an oil embargo, not a scarcity of oil, it drove home the real limits of the world's supplies of oil and natural gas. In 1979, human error contributed to a nuclear accident at the Three Mile Island nuclear power plant near Harrisburg, Pennsylvania, and in 1980 President Carter declared a federal emergency at New York State's Love Canal, which had served as a dump site for a local chemical manufacturer, after it was discovered that 30 percent of local residents had suffered chromosome damage. Public activism during the 1970s produced major environmental regulations and initiatives, from the Environmental Protection Agency (EPA), created (under strong public pressure) in 1970 by the Nixon administration, to eighteen major environmental laws enacted by Congress during the decade.

When almost 20 million Americans—half of them schoolchildren—gathered in local communities to celebrate the first Earth Day on April 22, 1970, they signaled the triumph of a relatively new understanding of environmentalism. Traditional concerns about preserving "unspoiled" wilderness had joined with a new focus on "ecology," which stressed the connections between the earth and all living organisms, including humans. Central to this movement was a recognition that the earth's resources were finite and must be both conserved and protected from the consequences of human action, such as pollution. In 1971, biologist Barry Commoner insisted, "The present course of environmental degradation ... is so serious, that, if continued, it will destroy the capability of the environment to support a reasonably civilized human society." Many of those concerned about the strain on earth's resources also identified rapid global population growth as a problem, and state public health offices frequently dispensed contraceptives as a way to stem this new "epidemic."

Technology During these years, Americans became increasingly uneasy about the science and technology that had been one source of America's might. In a triumph of technology, American astronaut Neil Armstrong stepped onto the lunar surface on July 20, 1969, as people worldwide watched the grainy television transmission and heard, indistinctly, his first words—"That's one small step for a man, one giant step for mankind." But the advances that could take a man to the moon seemed unable to cope with earthbound problems of poverty, crime, pollution, and urban decay; and the failure of technological warfare to deliver victory in Vietnam came at the same time antiwar protesters were questioning the morality of using such technology. Some Americans joined a movement for "appropriate technology" and human-scale development, but the nation was profoundly dependent on complex technological systems. And it was during the 1970s that the foundation was laid for America's computer revolution. The integrated circuit was created in 1970, and by 1975 the MITS Altair 8800—operated by toggle switches that entered individual binary numbers, boasting 256 bytes of memory, and requiring about thirty hours to assemble—could be mail-ordered from Albuquerque, New Mexico.

Religion and the Therapeutic Culture   As Americans confronted material limits, they increasingly sought spiritual fulfillment and well-being. Some turned to religion, though not to traditional mainstream Protestantism. Methodist, Presbyterian, and Episcopalian churches all lost members during this era, while membership in evangelical and fundamentalist Christian churches grew dramatically. Protestant evangelicals, professing a personal relationship with their savior, described themselves as "born again" and emphasized the immediate, daily presence of God in their lives. Even some Catholics, such as the Mexican Americans who embraced the *cursillo* movement (a "little course" in faith), sought a more personal relationship with God. Other Americans looked to the variety of beliefs and practices described as "New Age." The New Age movement drew from and often combined versions of nonwestern spiritual and religious practices, including Zen Buddhism, yoga, and shamanism, along with insights from western psychology and a form of spiritually oriented environmentalism. Some desires for spiritual comfort went badly wrong, as when 907 members of the People's Temple, a religious cult led by James Jones, committed "revolutionary suicide" by drinking cyanide-laced Kool-Aid at "Jonestown," the group's compound in Guyana, in 1978.

Also in the 1970s, America saw the full emergence of a "therapeutic" culture. Although some Americans were disgusted with the self-centeredness of the "Me-Decade," bestselling books by therapists and self-help gurus insisted that individual feelings offered the ultimate measure of truth; emotional honesty and self-awareness were social goods surpassing the bonds of community, friendship, or family. Self-help books with titles like *I Ain't Much Baby—But I'm All I've Got*, or *I'm OK—You're OK* (first published in 1967, it became a bestseller in the mid-1970s) made up 15 percent of all bestselling books during the decade.

Sexuality and the Family   One such self-help book was *The Joy of Sex* (1972), which sold 3.8 million copies in two years. Sex became much more visible in America's public culture during the 1970s, as network television loosened its regulation of sexual content. At the beginning of the 1960s, married couples in television shows were required to occupy twin beds; in the 1970s, hit television shows included *Three's Company*, a situation comedy based on the then-scandalous premise that a single man shared an apartment with two beautiful female roommates—and got away with it only by pretending to their suspicious landlord that he was gay. *Charlie's Angels*, another major television hit, capitalized on what people called the "jiggle factor," and displayed (for the time) lots of bare female flesh. A major youth fad of the era was "streaking," running naked through public places. Donna Summers's 1975 disco hit "Love to Love You Baby" contained sixteen minutes of sexual moaning. Discos were sites of sexual display, both for gay men and for macho working class cultures; the hustle (a dance) originated in a Latino section of the Bronx, and the 1977 hit film *Saturday Night Fever* portrayed an Italian-American young man who escaped the confines of his family and the limits of his dead-end job in sexually-charged dance at a Brooklyn disco. And though very few Americans participated in heterosexual orgies at New York City's Plato's Retreat, many knew about them through a *Time* magazine feature story.

Sexual behaviors had also changed. The seventies were the era of singles bars and gay bathhouses, and some Americans led sexual lives virtually unrestrained by the old rules. For most Americans, however, the major changes brought about by the "sexual revolution" were a broader public acceptance of premarital sex and a limited acceptance of homosexuality, especially among more educated Americans. More and more heterosexual young people "lived together" without marriage during the 1970s; the census bureau even coined the term *POSSLQ* ("persons of opposite sex sharing living quarters") to describe the relationship. When First Lady Betty Ford said on *60 Minutes* that she would not be surprised if her then-seventeen-year-old daughter Susan began a sexual relationship, it was clear that much had changed in the course of a decade.

Changes in sexual mores and in the roles possible for women helped to alter the shape of the American family as well. Both men and women married later than in recent decades, and American women had fewer children. By the end of the 1970s, the birth rate had dropped almost 40 percent from its 1957 peak. Almost one-quarter of young single women in 1980 said that they did not plan to have children. And a steadily rising percentage of babies were born to unmarried women, as the number of families headed by never-married women rose 400 percent during the 1970s. The divorce rate also rose, in part because states implemented "no fault" divorce. Although families seemed less stable in the 1970s than in the previous post-war decades, Americans also developed a greater acceptance of various family forms (the blended family of television's *Brady Bunch*, for example), and many young couples sought greater equality between the sexes in romantic relationships or marriages.

Youth

Young people gained new freedoms and responsibilities in American society during the 1970s, but they also confronted economic crisis and social upheaval. In 1971, largely in recognition that the eighteen-year-old men who were eligible for the draft were not eligible to vote, Congress passed and the states quickly ratified the Twenty-sixth Amendment, which guaranteed the right of eighteen-year-olds to vote. In a similar impulse, twenty-nine states lowered their minimum drinking age. Marijuana use skyrocketed, and several states moved toward decriminalization. As young people graduated from high school or college, they were more likely to live with others their own age than with their parents. In the early part of the decade, some young people established communes—both urban and rural—and attempted to create countercultural worlds outside "the system." Later in the decade, a very different group of young people, partly in reaction to a postindustrial landscape of limited opportunity and the seeming impossibility of political change, created the punk movement, which offered new physical and cultural spaces for youth both through music and its do-it-yourself ethic.

Diversity
The racial-justice and identity movements of the late 1960s and 1970s made all Americans more aware of differences among the nation's peoples—an awareness made stronger by the great influx of new immigrants, not from Europe but from Latin America and Asia. It was a challenge, however, to figure out how to acknowledge the new importance of "difference" in public policy. The solution developed in the 1970s was the idea of "diversity." Difference was not a problem but a strength; the nation should not seek policies to diminish differences among its peoples but should instead seek to foster the "diversity" of its schools, workplaces, and public culture.

One major move in this direction came in the 1978 Supreme Court decision *Regents of the University of California v. Bakke.* Allan Bakke, a thirty-three-year-old white man with a strong academic record, had been denied admission to the medical school of the University of California at Davis. Bakke sued, charging that he had been denied "equal protection" of the law because the medical school's affirmative-action program reserved 16 percent of its slots for racial-minority candidates, who were held to lower standards than other applicants. The case set off furious debates nationwide over the legitimacy of affirmative action. In 1978, the Supreme Court, in a split decision, decided in favor of Bakke. Four justices argued that any race-based decision violated the Civil Rights Act of 1964; four saw affirmative-action programs as constitutionally acceptable remedies for past discrimination. The deciding vote, though for Bakke, contained an important qualification. A "diverse student body," Justice Lewis Powell wrote, is "a constitutionally permissible goal for an institution of higher education." To achieve the positive quality of "diversity," educational institutions could take race into account when making decisions about admissions.

RENEWED COLD WAR AND MIDDLE EAST CRISIS

When Jimmy Carter took office in 1977, he asked Americans to put their "inordinate fear of Communism" behind them. With reformist zeal, Carter vowed to reduce the U.S. military presence overseas, to cut back arms sales (which had reached the unprecedented height of $10 billion per year under Nixon), and to slow the nuclear arms race. At the time, more than 400,000 American military personnel were stationed abroad, the United States had military links with ninety-two nations, and the CIA was active on every continent. Carter promised to avoid new Vietnams through an activist preventive diplomacy in the Third World and to give more attention to environmental issues as well as relations between rich and poor nations. He especially determined to improve human rights abroad—the freedom to vote, worship, travel, speak out, and get a fair trial. Like his predecessors, however, Carter identified revolutionary nationalism as a threat to America's prominent global position.

Carter's Divided Administration   Carter spoke and acted inconsistently, in part because in the post-Vietnam years, no consensus existed in foreign policy and in part because his advisers squabbled among themselves. One source of the problem was the stern-faced Zbigniew Brzezinski, a Polish-born political scientist who became Carter's national security adviser. An old-fashioned Cold Warrior, Brzezinski blamed foreign crises on Soviet expansionism. Carter gradually listened more to Brzezinski than to Secretary of State Cyrus Vance, an experienced public servant who advocated quiet diplomacy. Vocal neoconservative intellectuals, such as Norman Podhoretz, editor of *Commentary* magazine, and the Committee on the Present Danger, founded in 1976 by such Cold War hawks as Paul Nitze, who had composed NSC-68 in 1950, criticized Carter for any relaxation of the Cold War and demanded that he jettison détente.

Nitze got his wish. Under Carter détente deteriorated, and the Cold War deepened. But it did not happen right away. Initially, Carter maintained fairly good relations with Moscow and was able to score some foreign policy successes around the world. In Panama, where citizens longed for control over the Canal Zone, which they believed had been wrongfully taken from them in 1903, Carter reenergized negotiations that had begun after anti-American riots in Panama in 1964. The United States signed two treaties with Panama in 1977. One provided for the return of the Canal Zone to Panama in 2000, and the other guaranteed the United States the right to defend the canal after that time. With conservatives denouncing the deal as a sellout, the Senate narrowly endorsed both agreements in 1978. The majority agreed with Carter's argument that relinquishing the canal was the best way to improve U.S. relations with Latin America.

Camp David Accords   Important though it was, the Panama agreement paled next to what must be considered the crowning accomplishment of Carter's presidency: the Camp David accords, the first mediated peace treaty between Israel and an Arab nation. Through tenacious personal diplomacy at a Camp David, Maryland, meeting in September 1978 with Egyptian and Israeli leaders, the president persuaded Israel and Egypt to agree to a peace treaty, gained Israel's promise to withdraw from the Sinai Peninsula, and forged a provisional agreement that provided for continued negotiations on the future status of the Palestinian people living in the occupied territories of Jordan's West Bank and Egypt's Gaza Strip (see Map 33.1). Other Arab states denounced the agreement for not requiring Israel to relinquish all occupied territories and for not guaranteeing a Palestinian homeland. But the accord at least ended warfare along one frontier in that troubled area of the world. On March 26, 1979, Israeli prime minister Menachem Begin and Egyptian president Anwar al-Sadat signed the formal treaty on the White House lawn, with a beaming Carter looking on.

Soviet Invasion of Afghanistan   Carter's moment of diplomatic triumph did not last long, for soon other foreign policy problems pressed in. Relations with Moscow had deteriorated, with U.S. and Soviet officials sparring over the Kremlin's reluctance to lift restrictions on Jewish emigration from the USSR, and over the Soviet decision to deploy new intermediate-range ballistic missiles aimed at western Europe. Then, in December 1979, the Soviets invaded Afghanistan. A remote, mountainous country, Afghanistan had been a source of great-power conflict because of its strategic position. In the nineteenth century, it was the fulcrum of the Great Game, the contest between Britain and Russia for control of Central Asia and India. Following World War II, Afghanistan settled into a pattern of ethnic and factional squabbling; few in the West paid attention until the country spiraled into anarchy in the 1970s. In late 1979, the Red Army bludgeoned its way into Afghanistan to shore up a faltering communist government under siege by Muslim rebels. Moscow officials calculated that they could be in and out of the country before anyone really noticed, including the Americans.

To their dismay, Carter not only noticed but reacted forcefully. He suspended shipments of grain and high-technology equipment to the Soviet Union, withdrew a major new arms control treaty from Senate consideration, and initiated an international boycott of the 1980 Summer Olympics in Moscow. He also secretly authorized the CIA to distribute aid, including arms and military support, to the Mujahidin (Islamic guerillas) fighting the communist government and sanctioned military aid to their backer, Pakistan. Announcing the Carter Doctrine, the president asserted that the United States would intervene, unilaterally and militarily if necessary, should Soviet aggression threaten the petroleum-rich Persian Gulf. This string of measures represented a victory of the hawkish Brzezinski over the pro-détente Vance. Indeed, Carter seemed more ardent than Brzezinski in his denunciations of the Kremlin. He warned aides that the Soviets, unless checked, would likely attack elsewhere in the Middle East, but declassified documents confirm what critics at the time said: that the Soviet invasion was limited in scope and did not presage a push southwest to the Persian Gulf.

Iranian Hostage Crisis   Carter's aggressive rhetoric on Afghanistan may be partly explained by the fact that he simultaneously faced a tough foreign policy test in neighboring Iran. The shah, long the recipient of American favor, had been driven from his throne by a broad coalition of Iranians, many of whom resented that their traditional ways had been dislocated by the shah's attempts at modernization. American analysts failed to perceive the volatility that this dislocation generated and were caught off guard when riots led by anti-American Muslim clerics erupted in late 1978. The shah went into exile, and in April 1979 Islamic revolutionaries, led by the Ayatollah Khomeini, an elderly cleric who denounced the United States as the stronghold of capitalism and western materialism, proclaimed a Shi'ite Islamic Republic. In November, with the exiled shah in the United States for medical treatment, mobs stormed the U.S. embassy in Teheran. They took American personnel as hostages, demanding the return of the shah to stand trial. The Iranians eventually released a few American prisoners, but fifty-two others languished under Iranian guard. They suffered solitary confinement, beatings, and terrifying mock executions.

Unable to gain the hostages' freedom through diplomatic intermediaries, Carter said that he felt "the same kind of impotence that a powerful person feels when his child is kidnapped." He took steps to isolate Iran economically, freezing Iranian assets in the United States. When the hostage takers paraded their blindfolded captives before television cameras, Americans felt taunted and humiliated. In April 1980, frustrated and at a low ebb in public opinion polls, Carter broke diplomatic relations with Iran and ordered a daring rescue mission. But the rescue effort miscarried after equipment failure in the sandy Iranian desert, and during the hasty withdrawal two aircraft collided, killing eight American soldiers. The hostages were not freed until January 1981, after Carter left office and the United States unfroze Iranian assets and promised not to intervene again in Iran's internal affairs.

The Iranian revolution, together with the rise of the Mujahidin in Afghanistan, signified the emergence of Islamic fundamentalism as a force in world affairs. Socialism and capitalism, the great answers that the two superpowers offered to the problems of modernization, had failed to solve the problems in Central Asia and the Middle East, let alone satisfy the passions and expectations they had aroused. Nor had they assuaged deeply held feelings of humiliation generated by centuries of western domination. As a result, Islamic orthodoxy found growing support for its message: that secular leaders such as Nasser in Egypt and the shah in Iran had taken their peoples down the wrong path, necessitating a return to conservative Islamic values and Islamic law. The Iranian revolution in particular expressed a deep and complex mixture of discontent within many Islamic societies.

Rise of Saddam Hussein   U.S. officials took some consolation from the fact that Iran faced growing friction from the avowedly secular government in neighboring Iraq. Ruled by the Ba'athist Party (a secular and quasi-socialist party with branches in several Arab countries), Iraq had already won favor in Washington for its ruthless pursuit and execution of Iraqi communists. When a Ba'athist leader named Saddam Hussein took over as president of Iraq in 1979 and began threatening the Teheran government, U.S. officials were not displeased; to them, Saddam seemed likely to offset the Iranian danger in the Persian Gulf region. As border clashes between Iraqi and Iranian forces escalated in 1980, culminating in the outbreak of large-scale war in September, Washington policymakers took an officially neutral position but soon tilted toward Iraq.

Jimmy Carter's record in foreign affairs sparked considerable criticism from both left and right. He had earned some diplomatic successes in the Middle East, Africa, and Latin America, but the revived Cold War and the prolonged Iranian hostage crisis had hurt the administration politically. Contrary to Carter's goals, more American military personnel were stationed overseas in 1980 than in 1976; the defense budget climbed and sales of arms abroad grew to $15.3 billion in 1980. On human rights, the president proved inconsistent. He practiced a double standard by applying the human-rights test to some nations (the Soviet Union, Argentina, and Chile) but not to U.S. allies (South Korea, the shah's Iran, and the Philippines). Still, if inconsistent, Carter's human-rights policy was not unimportant: he gained the release and saved the lives of some political prisoners, and he popularized and institutionalized concern for human rights around the world. But Carter did not satisfy Americans who wanted a post-Vietnam restoration of the economic dominance and military edge the United States once enjoyed. He lost the 1980 election to the hawkish Ronald Reagan, former Hollywood actor and governor of California.

SUMMARY

The 1970s were a difficult decade for Americans. From the crisis year of 1968 on, it seemed that Americans were ever more polarized—over the war in Vietnam, over the best path to racial equality and equal rights for all Americans, over the meaning of equality, and over the meaning of America itself. As many activists for social justice turned to "cultural nationalism," or group-identity politics, notions of American unity seemed a relic of the past. And though a new women's movement won great victories against sex discrimination, a powerful opposition movement arose in response.

During this era, Americans became increasingly disillusioned with politics and presidential leadership. Richard Nixon's abuses of power in the Watergate scandal and cover–up, combined with growing awareness that the administration had lied to its citizens repeatedly about America's role in Vietnam, produced a profound suspicion of government. A major economic crisis ended the post–World War II expansion that had fueled the growth of the middle class and social reform programs alike, and Americans struggled with the psychological impact of a new age of limits and with the effects of stagflation: rising unemployment rates coupled with high rates of inflation.

Overseas, a string of setbacks—defeat in Vietnam, the oil embargo, and the Iranian hostage crisis—signified the waning of American power during the 1970s. The nation seemed increasingly unable to have its own way on the world stage. Détente with the Soviet Union had flourished for a time, as both superpowers sought to adjust to the new geopolitical realities; however, by 1980 Cold War tensions were again on the rise. But if the nation's most important bilateral relationship remained that with the USSR, an important change, not always perceptible at the time, was under way: more and more, the focus of U.S. foreign policy was on the Middle East.

Plagued by political, economic, and foreign policy crises, America ended the 1970s bruised, battered, and frustrated. The age of liberalism was long over; the elements for a conservative resurgence were in place.

32

CONSERVATISM REVIVED 1980–1992

REAGAN AND THE CONSERVATIVE RESURGENCE

The 1970s had been a hard decade for Americans: defeat in Vietnam; the resignation
of a president in disgrace; the energy crisis; economic "stagflation" and the Iranian
hostage crisis. In the election year of 1980, President Carter's public approval rating
stood at 21 percent, even lower than Richard Nixon's during the depths of Watergate. The nation was divided and dispirited as people who had grown accustomed
to seemingly endless economic growth and unquestioned world power confronted
new limits at home and abroad. The time was ripe for a challenge to Carter's presidential leadership, to the Democratic Party, and to the liberal approaches that had, in
the main, governed the United States since Franklin Roosevelt's New Deal.

Ronald Reagan   In 1980, several conservative Republican politicians entered the
                        presidential race. Foremost among them was Ronald Reagan,
former movie star and two-term governor of California. In the 1940s, as president of
the Screen Actors Guild in Hollywood, Reagan had been a New Deal Democrat. But
in the 1950s, as a corporate spokesman for General Electric, he became increasingly
conservative. In 1964, Reagan's televised speech in support of Republican presidential
candidate Barry Goldwater catapulted him to the forefront of conservative politics.
America, Reagan said, had come to "a time for choosing" between free enterprise and
big government, between individual liberty and "the ant heap of totalitarianism."

The New   Elected governor of California just two years later, Reagan
Conservative   became well known for his right-wing rhetoric: America
Coalition   should "level Vietnam, pave it, paint stripes on it, and
                        make a parking lot out of it," Reagan claimed. And in

CHRONOLOGY

1980	Reagan elected president
1981	AIDS first observed in United States
	Economic problems continue; prime interest rate reaches 21.5 percent
	"Reaganomics" plan of budget and tax cuts approved by Congress
1982	Unemployment reaches 10.8 percent, highest rate since Great Depression
	ERA dies after Stop-ERA campaign prevents ratification in key states
1983	Reagan introduces SDI
	Terrorists kill U.S. marines in Lebanon
	U.S. invasion of Grenada
1984	Reagan aids contras despite congressional ban
	Economic recovery; unemployment rate drops and economy grows without inflation
	Reagan reelected
	Gorbachev promotes reforms in USSR
1986	Iran-contra scandal erupts
1987	Stock market drops 508 points in one day
	Palestinian *intifada* begins
1988	George H. W. Bush elected president
1989	Tiananmen Square massacre in China
	Berlin Wall torn down
	U.S. troops invade Panama
	Gulf between rich and poor at highest point since 1920s
1990	Americans with Disabilities Act passed
	Communist regimes in eastern Europe collapse
	Iraq invades Kuwait
	South Africa begins to dismantle apartheid
1991	Persian Gulf War
	USSR dissolves into independent states
	United States enters recession
1992	Annual federal budget deficit reaches high of $300 billion at end of Bush presidency

1969, when student protesters occupied "People's Park" near the University of California in Berkeley, he threatened a "bloodbath" and dispatched National Guard troops in full riot gear. Reagan was often pragmatic, however, about policy decisions. He denounced welfare but presided over reform of the state's social welfare bureaucracy. And he signed one of the nation's most liberal abortion laws.

In the 1980 election, Reagan, in stark contrast to incumbent Jimmy Carter, offered an optimistic vision for America's future. With his Hollywood charm and strong conservative credentials, he succeeded in forging very different sorts of American conservatives into a new political coalition. Reagan built on a natural constituency of political conservatives. These strong anticommunists wanted to strengthen national defense; they also believed the federal government should play a more limited role in the nation's domestic life and wished to roll back the liberal programs begun under the New Deal in the 1930s and the Great Society in the 1960s. Reagan reached out to less ideologically oriented economic conservatives, promising economic deregulation and tax policies that would benefit corporations, wealthy investors, and entrepreneurs. He also attracted a relatively new cohort of neoconservatives, a small but influential group composed primarily of academics and intellectuals, many of them former Democrats who believed the party had lost its way after Vietnam and who rejected the old conservatism as backward looking. The neoconservatives took particular interest in foreign policy and embraced the Reagan campaign's aggressively anti-Soviet posture.

In a major accomplishment, Reagan managed to unite these political, economic, and neoconservatives with two new constituencies. He tapped into the sentiments that fueled the tax revolt movement of the 1970s, drawing voters from traditionally Democratic constituencies, such as labor unions and urban ethnic groups. Many middle- and working-class whites resented their hard-earned money's going to what they saw as tax-funded welfare for people who did not work; some had reacted angrily to government programs, such as busing children to achieve racial integration of schools, meant to combat racial inequities. Many also thought that Reagan's joke that there was nothing more frightening than finding a government official on the doorstep saying, "I'm from the government and I'm here to help," rang true. These "Reagan Democrats" found the Republican critique of tax-funded social programs and "big government" appealing, even though Reagan's proposed economic policies would benefit the wealthy at their expense.

Finally, in the largest leap, Reagan tied these groups to the religiously based New Right, an increasingly powerful movement of social conservatives, many of them evangelical and born-again Christians, who believed (in Moral Majority founder Jerry Falwell's words) that America's "internal problems are the direct result of her spiritual condition." Reagan, seeking their support, declared: "I want you to know I endorse you and what you are doing."

Reagan's Conservative Agenda
On election day, Reagan claimed victory with 51 percent of the popular vote. Jimmy Carter carried only six states. Reagan's victory in 1980 began more than a decade of Republican power in Washington: Reagan served two terms as president, followed by his vice president, George H. W. Bush, who was elected in 1988. Reagan, as much as any president since Franklin Roosevelt, defined the era over which he presided.

Reagan, as president, was not especially focused on the details of governing or the specifics of policies and programs. When outgoing president Jimmy Carter briefed him on urgent issues of foreign and domestic policy, Reagan listened politely but took not a single note and asked no questions. Critics argued that his lack of knowledge could prove dangerous—as when he insisted that intercontinental ballistic missiles carrying nuclear warheads could be called back once launched, or when he said that "approximately 80 percent of our air pollution stems from hydrocarbons released by vegetation."

But supporters insisted that Reagan was a great president in large part because he focused on the big picture. When he spoke to the American people, he offered what seemed to be simple truths—and he did it with the straightforwardness of a true believer and the warmth and humor of an experienced actor. Although many—even among Reagan supporters—winced at his willingness to reduce complex policy issues to simple (and often misleading) stories, Reagan was to most Americans the "Great Communicator." He won admiration for his courage after he was seriously wounded in an assassination attempt just sixty-nine days into his presidency. Reagan quipped to doctors preparing to remove the bullet lodged near his heart, "I hope you're all Republicans."

Most important, Reagan had a clear vision for America's future. He and his advisers wanted nothing less than to roll back the liberal policies of the past fifty

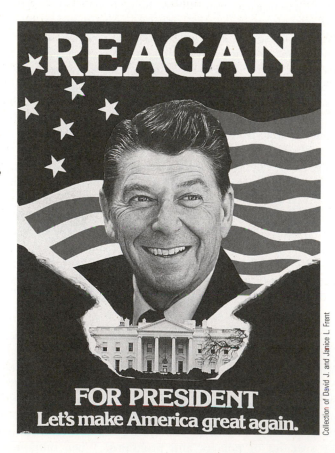

Ronald Reagan, the Republican presidential candidate in 1980, campaigned for "family values," an aggressive anti-Soviet foreign and military policy, and tax cuts. He also exuded optimism and appealed to Americans' patriotism. This poster issued by the Republican National Committee included Reagan's favorite campaign slogan, "Let's make America great again."

Collection of David J. and Janice L. Frent

years that had made government increasingly responsible for the health of the nation's economy and for the social welfare of its citizens. In the words of David Stockman, a Reagan appointee who headed the Office of Management and Budget, the administration meant to "create a minimalist government" and sever "the umbilical cords of dependency that run from Washington to every nook and cranny of the nation."

Attacks on Social Welfare Programs   Reagan, like traditional conservatives, believed America's social problems could not be solved by the federal government. But he also tapped into a broader, and less coherent, backlash against the social policies and programs of the Great Society. Many Americans who struggled to make ends meet during the economic crises of the 1970s and early 1980s resented paying taxes that, they believed, funded government "handouts" to people who did not work. Reagan used existing racial tensions to undermine support for welfare, repeatedly describing a "welfare queen" from Chicago's South Side (a primarily African American area) who had collected welfare checks under eighty different last names and defrauded the government of $150,000 (the actual case involved two aliases and $8,000). In 1981, the administration cut funding for social welfare programs by $25 billion. But "welfare" (Aid to Families with Dependent Children and food stamp programs) was a small part of the budget compared with Social Security and Medicare—social welfare programs that benefited Americans of all income levels, not just the poor. Major budget cuts for these popular, broadly based programs proved impossible. The Reagan administration did shrink the *proportion* of the federal budget devoted to social welfare programs (including Social Security and Medicare) from 28 to 22 percent by the late 1980s—but only because it increased defense spending by $1.2 trillion.

Pro-Business Policies and the Environment   Reagan also attacked federal environmental, health, and safety regulations that he believed reduced business profits and discouraged economic growth. Administration officials claimed that removing the stifling hand of government regulation would restore the energy and creativity of America's free-market system. However, they did not so much end government's role as deploy government power to aid corporate America. The president even appointed opponents of federal regulations to head agencies charged with enforcing them—letting foxes guard the chicken coop, critics charged.

Environmentalists were appalled when Reagan appointed James Watt, a well-known antienvironmentalist, as secretary of the interior. Watt was a leader in the "Sagebrush Rebellion," which sought the return of publicly owned lands in the West, such as national forests, from federal to state control. Land control issues were complicated: the federal government controlled more than half of western lands—including 83 percent of the land in Nevada, 66 percent in Utah, and 50 percent in Wyoming—and many westerners believed that eastern policymakers did not understand the realities of western life. But states' ability to control land within their borders was not the sole issue; Watt and his group wanted to open western public lands to private businesses for logging, mining, and ranching.

Watt also dismissed the need to protect national resources and public wilderness lands for future generations, noting during his 1981 Senate confirmation hearing, "I don't know how many generations we can count on until the Lord returns." As interior secretary, Watt allowed private corporations to acquire oil, mineral, and timber rights to federal lands for minuscule payments. He was forced to resign in 1983 after he dismissively referred to a federal advisory panel as "a black . . . a woman, two Jews, and a cripple." Even before Watt's resignation, his appointment had backfired, as his actions reenergized the nation's environmental movement and even provoked opposition from business leaders who understood that uncontrolled strip-mining and clear-cut logging of western lands could destroy lucrative tourism and recreation industries in western states.

Attacks on Organized Labor   As part of its pro-business agenda, the Reagan administration undercut organized labor's ability to negotiate wages and working conditions. Union power was already waning; labor union membership declined in the 1970s as jobs in heavy industry disappeared, and efforts to unionize the high-growth electronics and service sectors of the economy had not succeeded. Setting the tone for his administration, in August 1981 Reagan intervened in a strike by the Professional Air Traffic Controllers Organization (PATCO). The air traffic controllers—federal employees, for whom striking was illegal—were striking to protest working conditions they believed compromised the safety of American air travel. Only forty-eight hours into the strike, Reagan fired the 11,350 strikers and stipulated that they could never be rehired by the Federal Aviation Administration.

With the support of an anti-union secretary of labor and appointees to the National Labor Relations Board who consistently supported management, businesses took an increasingly hard line with labor during the 1980s. Unions failed to mount an effective opposition, and by 1990 only 12 percent of workers in the private sector were unionized. Yet an estimated 44 percent of union families had voted for Reagan in 1980, drawn to his geniality, espousal of old-fashioned values, and vigorous anticommunist rhetoric.

The New Right   Although much of Reagan's domestic agenda focused on traditional conservative political and economic goals, the New Right and its agenda played an increasingly important role in Reagan-era social policy. It is surprising that the strongly religious New Right was drawn to Reagan, a divorced man without strong ties to religion or, seemingly, his own children. But the non-church-going Reagan lent his support to New Right social issues: he endorsed the anti-abortion cause, and his White House issued a report supporting prayer in public schools.

Reagan's judicial nominations also pleased the religious New Right. Though the Senate, in a bipartisan vote, refused to confirm Supreme Court nominee Robert Bork after eighty-seven hours of antagonistic hearings, Congress eventually confirmed Anthony M. Kennedy instead. Reagan also appointed Anton Scalia, who would become a key conservative force on the Court, and Sandra Day O'Connor (the first woman appointee), and elevated Nixon appointee William Rehnquist to chief justice. In 1986, the increasingly conservative Supreme Court upheld a Georgia law that punished consensual anal or oral sex between men with up to twenty years in jail (*Bowers v. Hardwick*); in 1989, justices ruled that a Missouri law restricting the right to an abortion was constitutional (*Webster v. Reproductive Health Services*), thus encouraging further challenges to *Roe v. Wade*. In federal courts, Justice Department lawyers argued New Right positions on such social issues, and Reagan's 378 appointees to the federal bench usually ruled accordingly. Overall, however, the Reagan administration did not push a conservative social agenda as strongly as some members of the new Republican coalition had hoped.

REAGANOMICS

The centerpiece of Reagan's domestic agenda was the economic program that took his name: Reaganomics. The U.S. economy was in bad shape at the beginning of the 1980s. Stagflation had proved resistant to traditional economic remedies: when the government increased spending to stimulate a stagnant economy, inflation skyrocketed; when it cut spending or tightened the money supply to reduce inflation, the economy plunged deeper into recession and unemployment rates jumped. Everyone agreed that something had to be done to break the cycle, but few thought that government intervention would work. Even some Democrats voiced a "nonideological skepticism about the old, Rooseveltian solutions to social problems."

Reagan offered the American people a simple answer to economic woes. Instead of focusing on the complexities of global competition, deindustrialization, and OPEC's control of oil, Reagan argued that U.S. economic problems were caused by government intrusion in the "free-market" economic system. At fault were intrusive government regulation of business and industry, expensive government social programs that offered "handouts" to nonproductive citizens, high taxes, and deficit spending—in short, government itself. The Reagan administration's economic agenda was closely tied to its larger conservative ideology of limited government: it sought to "unshackle" the free-enterprise system from government regulation and control, to slash spending on social programs, to limit government's use of taxes to redistribute income among the American people, and to balance the budget by reducing the role of the federal government.

Supply-Side Economics Reagan's economic policy was based largely on supply-side economics, the theory that tax cuts (rather than government spending) will create economic growth. Economist Arthur Laffer had proposed one key concept for supply-siders, sketching his soon-to-be-famous Laffer curve on a cocktail napkin for a *Wall Street Journal* writer and President Gerald Ford's chief of staff (and the future vice president) Dick Cheney in 1974. According to Laffer's theory, at some point rising tax rates discourage people from engaging in taxable activities (such as investing their money): if profits from investments simply disappear to taxes, what is the incentive to invest? As people invest less, the economy slows. Even though tax rates remain high, the government collects less in tax revenue because the economy stalls. Cutting taxes, on the other hand, reverses the cycle and increases tax revenues.

Although economists at the time accepted the larger principle behind Laffer's curve, almost none believed that U.S. tax rates approached the point of disincentive. Even conservative economists were highly suspicious of supply-side principles. Reagan and his staff, however—on the basis of the unproven assumption that both corporate and personal tax rates in the United States had reached a level that discouraged investment—sought a massive tax cut. They argued that American corporations and individuals would invest funds freed up by lower tax rates, producing new plants, new jobs, and new products. Economic growth would more than make up for the tax revenues lost. And as prosperity returned, the profits at the top would "trickle down" to the middle classes and even to the poor.

Reagan's economic program was most fully developed by David Stockman, head of the Office of Management and Budget. Stockman proposed a five-year plan to balance the federal budget through economic growth (created by tax cuts) and deep cuts, primarily in social programs. Congress cooperated with a three-year, $750 billion tax cut, at that point the largest ever in American history. Cutting the federal budget, however, proved more difficult. Stockman's plan for balancing the budget assumed $100 billion in cuts from government programs, including Social Security and Medicare—and Congress was not about to cut Social Security and Medicare benefits. Reagan, meanwhile, canceled out gains from domestic spending cuts by dramatically increasing annual defense spending.

Major tax cuts, big increases in defense spending, small cuts in social programs: the numbers did not add up. The annual federal budget deficit exploded—from $59 billion in 1980 to more than $100 billion in 1982 to almost $300 billion by the end of George Bush's presidency in 1992. The federal government borrowed money to make up the difference, transforming the United States from the world's largest creditor nation to its largest debtor. The national debt grew to almost $3 trillion. Because an ever greater share of the federal budget went to pay the interest on this ballooning debt, less was available for federal programs, foreign or domestic.

Harsh Medicine for Inflation

Reaganomics attempted to stimulate the economy—but economic growth would not solve the persistent problem of inflation. Here the Federal Reserve Bank, an autonomous federal agency, stepped in. In 1981, the Federal Reserve Bank raised interest rates for bank loans to an unprecedented 21.5 percent, battling inflation by tightening the money supply and slowing the economy down. The nation plunged into recession. During the last three months of the year, the gross national product (GNP) fell 5 percent, and sales of cars and houses dropped sharply. With declining economic activity, unemployment soared to 8 percent, the highest level in almost six years.

By late 1982, unemployment had reached 10.8 percent, the highest rate since 1940. For African Americans, it was 20 percent. Many of the unemployed were blue-collar workers in ailing "smokestack industries," such as steel and automobiles. Reagan and his advisers promised that consumers would lift the economy out of the recession by spending their tax cuts. But as late as April 1983, unemployment still stood at 10 percent, and people were angry. Jobless steelworkers paraded through McKeesport, Pennsylvania, carrying a coffin that bore the epitaph "American Dream." Agriculture, too, was faltering and near collapse. Farmers suffered not only from falling crop prices due to overproduction, but also from floods, droughts, and burdensome debts that they had incurred at high interest rates. Many lost their property through mortgage foreclosures and farm auctions. Others filed for bankruptcy. As the recession deepened, poverty rose to its highest level since 1965.

It was harsh medicine, but the Federal Reserve Bank's plan to end stagflation worked. High interest rates helped drop inflation from 12 percent in 1980 to less than 7 percent in 1982. The economy also benefited from OPEC's 1981 decision, after eight years of engineering an artificial scarcity, to increase oil production, thus lowering prices. In 1984, the GNP rose 7 percent, the sharpest increase since 1951, and midyear unemployment fell to a four-year low of 7 percent. The economy was booming, but without sparking inflation.

"Morning in America"   By the presidential election of 1984, the recession was only a memory. Reagan got credit for the recovery, though it had little to do with his supply-side policies. In fact, the Democratic candidate, former vice president Walter Mondale, repeatedly hammered at Reagan's economic policies. Insisting that the rapidly growing budget deficit would have dire consequences for the American economy, he said (honestly, but probably not very astutely) that he would raise taxes. And he focused on themes of fairness and compassion; not all Americans, Mondale told the American public, were prospering in Reagan's America. Reagan, in contrast, proclaimed, "It's morning again in America." Television ads showed heartwarming images of American life, as an off-screen narrator told viewers, "Life is better. America is back. And people have a sense of pride they never felt they'd feel again." Reagan won in a landslide, with 59 percent of the vote. Mondale, with running mate Geraldine Ferraro—U.S. congresswoman from New York and the first woman vice-presidential candidate—carried only his home state of Minnesota.

Deregulation   Supply-side economics was not the only policy that transformed America's economy in the 1980s. Deregulation, begun under Jimmy Carter and expanded vastly under Reagan (the *Federal Register*, which contains all federal regulations, shrank from 87,012 pages in 1980 to 47,418 pages in 1986), created new opportunities for American business and industry. The 1978 deregulation of the airline industry lowered ticket prices both short-term and long-term; airline tickets cost almost 45 percent less in the early twenty-first century (in constant dollars) than in 1978. Deregulation of telecommunications industries created serious competition for the giant AT&T, and long-distance calling became inexpensive.

The Reagan administration loosened regulation of the American banking and finance industries and purposely cut the enforcement ability of the Securities and Exchange Commission (SEC), which oversees Wall Street. In the early 1980s, Congress deregulated the nation's savings-and-loan institutions (S&Ls), organizations previously required to invest depositors' savings in thirty-year, fixed-rate mortgages secured by property within a 50-mile radius of the S&L's main office. Stagflation had already left many S&Ls insolvent, but the 1980s legislation created conditions for a collapse. By ending government oversight of investment practices, while guaranteeing to cover losses from bad S&L investments, Congress left no penalties for failure. S&Ls increasingly put depositors' money into high-risk investments and engaged in shady—even criminal—deals.

Junk Bonds and Merger Mania   High-risk investments carried the day on Wall Street as well, as Michael Milken, a reclusive bond trader for the firm Drexel Firestone, pioneered the "junk bond" industry and created wildly lucrative investment possibilities. Milken offered financing to debt-ridden or otherwise weak corporations that could not get traditional, low-interest bank loans to fund expansion, using bond issues that paid investors high interest rates because they were high-risk (thus "junk" bonds). Many of these corporations, Milken realized, were attractive targets for takeover by other corporations or investors—who, in turn, could finance takeovers with junk bonds. Such "predators" could use the first corporation's existing debt as a tax write-off, sell off unprofitable units, and lay off employees to create a more efficient—and thus more profitable—corporation. Investors in the original junk bonds could make huge profits by selling their shares to the corporate raiders.

By the mid-1980s, it was no longer only weak corporations that were targeted for these "hostile takeovers"; hundreds of major corporations—including giants Walt Disney and Conoco—fell prey to merger mania. Profits for investors were staggering, and by 1987 Milken, the guru of junk bonds, was earning $550 million a year—about $1,046 a minute—in salary; counting investment returns, Milken's income was about $1 billion a year.

What were the results of such practices? Heightened competition and corporate downsizing often created more efficient businesses and industries. Deregulation helped smaller and often innovative corporations challenge the virtual monopolies of giant corporations in fields like telecommunications. And through much of the 1980s, following the "Reagan recession," the American economy boomed. Although the stock market plunged 508 points on a single day in October 1987—losing 22.6 percent of its value, or almost double the percentage loss in the crash of 1929—it rebounded quickly. The high-risk boom of the 1980s did, however, have significant costs. Corporate downsizing meant layoffs for white-collar workers and management personnel, many of whom (especially those past middle age) had difficulty finding comparable positions. The wave of mergers and takeovers left American corporations as a whole more burdened by debt than before. It also helped to consolidate sectors of the economy—such as the media—under the control of an ever smaller number of players.

The Rich Get Richer   The high-risk, deregulated boom of the 1980s, furthermore, was rotten with corruption. By the late 1980s, insider trading scandals—in which people used "inside" information about corporations, which was not available to the general public, to make huge

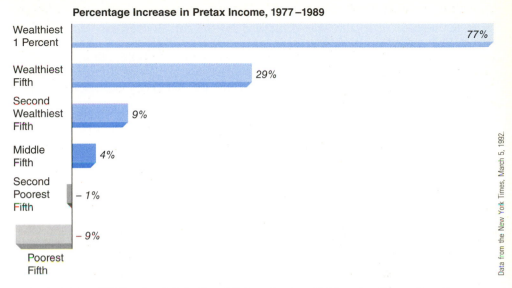

Percentage Increase in Pretax Income, 1977–1989

Wealthiest
1 Percent — 77%

Wealthiest
Fifth — 29%

Second
Wealthiest
Fifth — 9%

Middle
Fifth — 4%

Second
Poorest
Fifth — –1%

Poorest
Fifth — –9%

Data from the New York Times, March 5, 1992.

FIGURE 32.1 While the Rich Got Richer in the 1980s, the Poor Got Poorer

Between 1977 and 1989, the richest 1 percent of American families reaped most of the gains from economic growth. In fact, the average pretax income of families in the top percentage rose 77 percent. At the same time, the typical family saw its income edge up only 4 percent. And the bottom 40 percent of families had actual declines in income.

Source: Data from the *New York Times*, March 5, 1992.

profits trading stocks—rocked financial markets and sent some of the most prominent figures on Wall Street to jail (albeit comfortable, "country club" jails). Savings and loans lost —billions of dollars in bad investments, sometimes turning to fraud to cover them up. Scandal reached all the way to the White House: Vice President Bush's son Neil was involved in shady S&L deals. The Reagan-Bush administration's bailout of the S&L industry cost taxpayers half a trillion dollars.

Finally, during the 1980s, the rich got richer, and the poor got poorer (see Figure 32.1). Merger mania and the financial market bonanza contributed, as the number of Americans reporting an annual income of $500,000 increased tenfold between 1980 and 1989. According to the Economic Policy Institute, the average compensation of a corporate executive officer increased from approximately 35 times an average worker's pay in 1978 to 71 times workers' average pay in 1989 (in 2005 the ratio was 262 to 1). In 1987 the United States had forty-nine billionaires—up from one in 1978. While the number of very wealthy Americans grew, middle-class incomes were stagnant.

Most of the new inequality was due to Reagan's economic policies, which benefited the wealthy at the expense of middle- and lower-income Americans. Reagan's tax policies decreased the "total effective tax rates"—income taxes plus Social Security taxes—for the top 1 percent of American families by 14.4 percent. But they increased tax rates for the poorest 20 percent of families by 16 percent. By 1990, the richest 1 percent of Americans controlled 40 percent of the nation's wealth; fully 80 percent of wealth was controlled by the top 20 percent. Not since the 1920s had America seen such economic inequality.

REAGAN AND THE WORLD

A key element in Reagan's winning strategy in the 1980 election was his forthright call for the United States to assert itself on the world stage. Though lacking a firm grasp of international issues, history, and geography—friends and associates often marveled at his ability to get even elementary facts wrong—Reagan adhered to a few core principles. One was a deep and abiding anticommunism, which had dictated his world-view for decades and which formed the foundation of his presidential campaign. A second was an underlying optimism about the ability of American power and values to bring positive change in the world. Reagan liked to quote Thomas Paine of the American Revolution: "We have it in our power to begin the world over again." Yet Reagan was also a political pragmatist, particularly as time went on and his administration became mired in scandal. Together, these elements help explain both his aggressive anticommunist foreign policy and his willingness to respond positively in his second term to Soviet leader Mikhail Gorbachev's call for "new thinking" in world affairs.

Soviet-American Tension   Initially, toughness vis-à-vis Moscow was the watchword. Embracing the strident anticommunism that characterized U.S. foreign policy in the early Cold War, Reagan and his advisers rejected both the détente of the Nixon years and the Carter administration's focus on extending human rights abroad. Where Nixon and Carter perceived an increasingly multipolar international system, the Reagan team reverted to a bipolar perspective defined by the Soviet-American relationship. Young neoconservatives, such as Richard Perle and Paul Wolfowitz, who held mid-level positions in the administration, provided much of the intellectual ballast and moral fervor for this shift toward confrontation with Moscow.

In his first presidential press conference Reagan described a malevolent Soviet Union, whose leaders thought they had "the right to commit any crime, to lie, to cheat." When Poland's pro-Soviet leaders in 1981 cracked down on an independent labor organization, Solidarity, Washington responded by restricting Soviet-American trade and hurled angry words at Moscow. In March 1983, Reagan told an audience of evangelical Christians in Florida that the Soviets were "the focus of evil in the modern world . . . an evil empire." That same year, Reagan restricted commercial flights to the Soviet Union after a Soviet fighter pilot mistakenly shot down a South Korean commercial jet that had strayed some 300 miles off course into Soviet airspace, killing 269 passengers.

Reagan believed that a substantial military buildup would thwart the Soviet threat and intimidate Moscow. Accordingly, the administration launched the largest peacetime arms buildup in American history, driving up the federal debt. In 1985, when the military budget hit $294.7 billion (a doubling since 1980), the Pentagon spent an average of $28 million an hour. Assigning low priority to arms control talks, Reagan announced in 1983 his desire for a space-based defense shield against incoming ballistic missiles: the Strategic Defense Initiative (SDI). His critics tagged it "Star Wars" and said such a system could never be made to work scientifically—some enemy missiles would always get through the shield. Moreover, the critics warned, SDI would have the effect of elevating the arms race to dangerous new levels. But Reagan was undaunted, and in the years that followed SDI research and development consumed tens of billions of dollars.

Reagan Doctrine   Because he attributed Third World disorders to Soviet intrigue, the president declared the Reagan Doctrine: the United States would openly support anticommunist movements—"freedom fighters"—wherever they were battling the Soviets or Soviet-backed governments. In Afghanistan, the president continued Jimmy Carter's policy of providing covert assistance, through Pakistan, to the Mujahidin rebels in their war against the Soviet occupation. CIA director William J. Casey made numerous trips to Pakistan to coordinate the flow of arms and other assistance. When the Soviets stepped up the war in 1985, the Reagan administration sent more high-tech weapons. Particularly important were the anti-aircraft Stinger missiles. Easily transportable and fired by a single soldier, the Stingers turned the tide in the Afghan war by making Soviet jets and helicopters vulnerable below eleven thousand feet.

The administration also applied the Reagan Doctrine aggressively in the Caribbean and Central America. Senior officials believed that the Soviets and Castro's Cuba were fomenting disorder in the region (see Map 32.1). Accordingly, in October 1983 the president sent U.S. troops into the tiny Caribbean island of Grenada to oust a pro-Marxist government that appeared to be forging ties with Moscow and Havana. In El Salvador, he provided military and economic assistance to a military-dominated government struggling against left-wing revolutionaries. The regime used (or could not control) right-wing death squads. By the end of the decade, they had killed forty thousand dissidents and other citizens, as well as several American missionaries who had been working with landless peasants. By the end of the decade, the United States had spent more than $6 billion there in a counterinsurgency war. In January 1992 the Salvadoran combatants finally negotiated a U.N.-sponsored peace.

Contra War in Nicaragua   The Reagan administration also meddled in the Nicaraguan civil war. In 1979, leftist insurgents in Nicaragua overthrew Anastasio Somoza, a long-time ally of the United States and member of the dictatorial family that had ruled the Central American nation since the mid-1930s. The revolutionaries called themselves Sandinistas in honor of Csar Augusto Sandino—who had headed the nationalistic, anti-imperialist Nicaraguan opposition against U.S. occupation in the 1930s, battled U.S. marines, and was finally assassinated by Somoza henchmen—and they denounced the tradition of

© Cengage Learning

MAP 32.1 The United States in the Caribbean and Central America

The United States has often intervened in the Caribbean and Central America. Geographical proximity, economic stakes, political disputes, security links, trade in illicit drugs, and Cuban leader Fidel Castro's long-time defiance of Washington have kept U.S. eyes fixed on events in the region.

U.S. imperialism in their country. When the Sandinistas aided rebels in El Salvador, bought Soviet weapons, and invited Cubans to work in Nicaragua's hospitals and schools and help reorganize the Nicaraguan army, Reagan officials charged that Nicaragua was becoming a Soviet client. In 1981, the CIA began to train, arm, and direct more than ten thousand counterrevolutionaries, known as contras, to overthrow the Nicaraguan government.

The U.S. interventions in El Salvador and Nicaragua sparked a debate reminiscent of the earlier one over Vietnam. Many Americans, including Democratic leaders in Congress, were skeptical about the communist threat to the region and warned that Nicaragua could become another Vietnam. Congress in 1984 voted to stop U.S. military aid to the contras. Secretly, the Reagan administration lined up other countries, including Saudi Arabia, Panama, and South Korea, to funnel money and weapons to the contras, and in 1985 Reagan imposed an economic embargo against Nicaragua. The president might have opted for a diplomatic solution, but he rejected a plan proposed by Costa Rica's president Oscar Arias Sanchez in 1987 to obtain a cease-fire in Central America through negotiations and cutbacks in military aid to all rebel forces. (Arias won the 1987 Nobel Peace Prize.) Three years later, after Reagan had left office, all of the Central American presidents at last brokered a settlement; in the national election that followed, the Sandinistas lost to a U.S.-funded party. After nearly a decade of civil war, thirty thousand Nicaraguans had died, and the ravaged economy had dwindled to one of the poorest in the hemisphere.

Iran-Contra Scandal

Reagan's obsession with defeating the Sandinistas almost caused his political undoing. In November 1986, it became known that the president's national security adviser, John M. Poindexter, and an aide, marine lieutenant colonel Oliver North, in collusion with CIA director Casey, had covertly sold weapons to Iran as part of a largely unsuccessful attempt to win the release of several Americans being held hostage by Islamic fundamentalist groups in the Middle East. During the same period, Washington had been condemning Iran as a terrorist nation and demanding that America's allies not trade with the Islamic state. Still more damaging was the revelation that money from the Iran arms deal had been illegally diverted to a fund to aid the contras—this after Congress had unambiguously rejected providing such aid. North later admitted he had illegally destroyed government documents and lied to Congress to keep the operation clandestine.

Although Reagan survived the scandal—it remained unclear just what he did and did not know about the operation—his presidency suffered a major blow. His personal popularity declined, and an emboldened Congress began to reassert its authority over foreign affairs. In late 1992, outgoing president George Bush pardoned several former government officials convicted of lying to Congress. Critics smelled a cover-up, for Bush himself, as vice president, had participated in high-level meetings on Iran-contra deals. As for North, his conviction was overturned on a technicality. In view of its deliberate thwarting of congressional authority, the Iran-contra secret network, the scholar William LeoGrande has argued, "posed a greater threat to democracy in the United States than Nicaragua ever did."

U.S. Interests in the Middle East   The Iran-contra scandal also pointed to the increased importance in U.S. foreign policy of the Middle East and terrorism. As before, the United States had as its main goals in the Middle East preserving access to oil and supporting its ally Israel, while at the same time checking Soviet influence in the region. In the 1980s, though, American leaders faced new pressures, in the form of a deepened Israeli-Palestinian conflict and an anti-American and anti-Israeli Islamic fundamentalist movement that began to spread after the ouster of the shah of Iran in 1979.

The 1979 Camp David accords between Israel and Egypt had raised hopes of a lasting settlement involving self-government for the Palestinian Arabs living in the Israeli-occupied Gaza Strip and West Bank. It did not happen, as Israel and the Palestinian Liberation Organization (PLO) remained at odds. In 1982, in retaliation for Palestinian shelling of Israel from Lebanon, Israeli troops invaded Lebanon, reaching the capital, Beirut, and inflicting massive damage. The beleaguered PLO and various Lebanese factions called on Syria to contain the Israelis. Thousands of civilians died in the multifaceted conflict, and a million people became refugees. Reagan made no effort to halt the Israeli offensive, but he agreed to send U.S. marines to Lebanon to join a peacekeeping force. Soon the American troops became embroiled in a war between Christian and Muslim factions, as the latter accused the marines of helping the Christian-dominated government rather than acting as neutral peacekeepers. In October 1983, terrorist bombs demolished a barracks, killing 241 American servicemen. Four months later, Reagan recognized failure and pulled the remaining marines out.

Terrorism   The attack on the marine barracks showed the growing danger of terrorism to the United States and other western countries. In the 1980s, numerous otherwise powerless groups, many of them associated with the Palestinian cause or with Islamic fundamentalism, relied on terrorist acts to further their political aims. Often they targeted American citizens and property, on account of Washington's support of Israel and U.S. involvement in the Lebanese civil war. Of the 690 hijackings, kidnappings, bombings, and shootings around the world in 1985, for example, 217 were against Americans. Most of these actions originated in Iran, Libya, Lebanon, and the Gaza Strip. In June 1985, for example, Shi'ite Muslim terrorists from Lebanon hijacked an American jetliner, killed one passenger, and held thirty-nine Americans hostage for seventeen days. Three years later, a Pan American passenger plane was destroyed over Scotland, probably by pro-Iranian terrorists who concealed the bomb in a cassette player.

Washington, firmly allied with Israel, continued to propose peace plans designed to persuade the Israelis to give back occupied territories and the Arabs to give up attempts to push the Jews out of the Middle East (the "land-for-peace" formula). As the peace process stalled in 1987, Palestinians living in the West Bank began an *intifada* (Arabic for "uprising") against Israeli forces. Israel refused to negotiate, but the United States decided to talk with PLO chief Yasir Arafat after he renounced terrorism and accepted Israel's right to live in peace and security. For the PLO to recognize Israel and, in effect, for the United States to recognize the PLO were major developments in the Arab-Israeli conflict, even as a lasting settlement remained elusive.

In South Africa, too, American diplomacy became more aggressive as the decade progressed. At first, the Reagan administration followed a policy of "constructive engagement"—asking the increasingly isolated government to reform its apartheid system, designed to preserve white supremacy. But many Americans demanded economic sanctions: cutting off imports from South Africa and pressuring some 350 American companies—top among them Texaco, General Motors, Ford, and Goodyear—to cease operations there. Some American cities and states passed divestment laws, withdrawing dollars (such as pension funds used to buy stock) from American companies active in South Africa. Public protest and congressional legislation forced the Reagan administration in 1986 to impose economic restrictions against South Africa. Within two years, about half of the U.S. companies in South Africa had pulled out.

Enter Gorbachev   Many on the right disliked the South Africa sanctions policy—they believed the main black opposition group, the African National Congress (ANC), was dominated by communists, and they doubted the efficacy of sanctions—and the more extreme among them soon found another reason to be disenchanted with Reagan. A new Soviet leader, Mikhail S. Gorbachev, had come to power, and Reagan, his own popularity beginning to sag, showed a newfound willingness to enter negotiations with the "evil empire." Gorbachev called for a friendlier superpower relationship and a new, more cooperative world system. At a 1985 Geneva summit meeting between the two men, Reagan agreed in principle with Gorbachev's contention that strategic weapons should be substantially reduced, and at a 1986 Reykjavik, Iceland, meeting they came very close to a major reduction agreement. SDI, however, stood in the way: Gorbachev insisted that the initiative be shelved, and Reagan refused to part with it, despite continuing scientific objections that the plan would cost billions of dollars and never work.

But Reagan and Gorbachev got along well, despite the language barrier and their differing personalities. Reagan's penchant for telling stories rather than discussing the intricacies of policy did not trouble the detail-oriented Gorbachev. As General Colin Powell commented, though the Soviet leader was far superior to Reagan in mastery of specifics, he never exhibited even a trace of condescension. He understood that Reagan was, as Powell put it, "the embodiment of his people's down-to-earth character, practicality, and optimism." And Reagan toned down his strident anti-Soviet rhetoric, particularly as his more hawkish advisers left the administration in the late 1980s.

Perestroika and Glasnost   The turnaround in Soviet-American relations stemmed more from changes abroad than from Reagan's decisions. As Reagan said near the end of his presidency, he had been "dropped into a grand historical moment." Under the dynamic Gorbachev, a younger generation of Soviet leaders came to power in 1985. They began to modernize the highly bureaucratized, decaying economy through a reform program known as *perestroika* ("restructuring") and to liberalize the authoritarian political system through *glasnost* ("openness"). For these reforms to work, however, Soviet military expenditures had to be reduced and foreign aid decreased.

In 1987, Gorbachev and Reagan signed the Intermediate-Range Nuclear Forces (INF) Treaty banning all land-based intermediate-range nuclear missiles in Europe. Soon began the destruction of 2,800 missiles, including Soviet missiles targeted at western Europe and NATO missiles aimed at the Soviet Union. Gorbachev also unilaterally reduced his nation's armed forces, helped settle regional conflicts, and began the withdrawal of Soviet troops from Afghanistan. After more than forty chilling years, the Cold War was coming to an end.

AMERICAN SOCIETY IN THE 1980S

As the Cold War waned, so, too, did the power of the belief in an America united by a set of shared, middle-class values. Although the ideal of shared values was never a reality, it had exercised a powerful hold in the nation's public culture from World War II well into the 1960s. By the 1980s, after years of social struggle and division, few Americans believed in the reality of that vision; many rejected it as undesirable. And though the 1980s were never as contentious and violent as the era of social protest in the 1960s and early 1970s, deep social and cultural divides existed among Americans. A newly powerful group of Christian conservatives challenged the secular culture of the American majority. A growing class of affluent, well-educated Americans seemed a society apart from the urban poor, and new technologies reshaped both work and leisure.At the same time, immigration was dramatically changing the composition of the American population.

Growth of the Religious Right   As late as 1980, many Americans believed that the 1925 Scopes trial over the teaching of evolution had been the last gasp of fundamentalist Christianity in the United States. They were wrong. Since the 1960s, America's mainline liberal Protestant churches—Episcopalian, Presbyterian, Methodist—had been losing members, while Southern Baptists and other denominations that offered the spiritual experience of being "born again" through belief in Jesus Christ and that accepted the literal truth of the Bible (fundamentalism) had grown rapidly. Fundamentalist preachers reached out to vast audiences through television: by the late 1970s, televangelist Oral Roberts was drawing an audience of 3.9 million. Close to 20 percent of Americans identified themselves as fundamentalist Christians in 1980.

Most fundamentalist Christian churches stayed out of the social and political conflicts of the 1960s and early 1970s, arguing that preaching the "pure saving gospel of Jesus Christ" was more important. But in the late 1970s—motivated by what they saw as the betrayal of God's will in an increasingly permissive American society—some influential preachers began to mobilize their flocks for political struggle. In a "Washington for Jesus" rally in 1980, fundamentalist leader Pat

Robertson told crowds, "We have enough votes to run the country.... And when the people say, 'We've had enough,' we are going to take over." The Moral Majority, founded in 1979 by Jerry Falwell, sought to create a "Christian America," in part by supporting political candidates on the local and national levels. Falwell's defense of socially conservative "family values" and his condemnation of feminism (he called NOW the "National Order of Witches"), homosexuality, pornography, and abortion resonated with many Americans.

Throughout the 1980s, the coalition of conservative Christians known as the New Right waged campaigns against America's secular culture. Rejecting the "multiculturalist" belief that different cultures and lifestyle choices were equally valid, the New Right worked to make "God's law" the basis for American society. Concerned Women for America, founded by Beverly LaHayes in 1979, attempted to have elementary school readers containing "unacceptable" religious beliefs (including excerpts from *The Diary of Anne Frank* and *The Wizard of Oz*) removed from school classrooms, and fundamentalist Christian groups once again began to challenge the teaching of evolutionary theory in public schools. The Reagan administration frequently turned to James Dobson, founder of the conservative Focus on the Family organization, for policy advice.

"Culture Wars"   Although the New Right often found an ally in the Reagan White House, many other Americans vigorously opposed a movement they saw as preaching a doctrine of intolerance and threatening basic freedoms—including freedom of religion for those whose beliefs did not accord with the conservative Christianity of the New Right. In 1982, prominent figures from the fields of business, religion, politics, and entertainment founded People for the American Way to support American civil liberties and freedoms, the separation of church and state, and the values of tolerance and diversity. The struggle between the religious right and their opponents for the future of the nation came to be known as the "culture wars."

It was not only organized groups, however, that opposed the agenda of the religious right. Many beliefs of Christian fundamentalists ran counter to the way most Americans lived—especially when it came to women's roles. By the 1980s, a generation of girls had grown up expecting freedoms and opportunities that their mothers never had. Legislation such as the Civil Rights Act of 1964 and Title IX had opened both academic and athletic programs to girls and women. In 1960, there were thirty-eight male lawyers for every female lawyer in the United States; by 1983, the ratio was 5.5 to 1. By 1985, more than half of married women with children under three worked outside the home—many from economic necessity. The religious right's insistence that women's place was in the home, subordinated to her husband, contradicted not only the gains made toward sexual equality in American society but also the reality of many women's lives.

The New Inequality   As Americans fought the "culture wars" of the 1980s, another major social divide threatened the nation. A 1988 national report on race relations looked back to the 1968

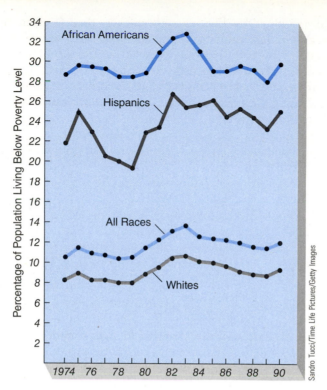

FIGURE 32.2 Poverty in America by Race, 1974–1990

Poverty in America rose in the early 1980s but subsided afterward. Many people of color, however, experienced little relief during the decade. Notice that the percentage of African Americans living below the poverty level was three times higher than that for whites. It was also much higher for Hispanics.

Source: Adapted from U.S. Bureau of the Census, *Statistical Abstract of the United States* (Washington, D.C.: 1992), p. 461.

Kerner Commission report to claim, "America is again becoming two separate societies," white and black. It argued that African Americans endured poverty, segregation, and crime in inner-city ghettos while most whites lived comfortably in suburban enclaves. In fact, America's separate societies of comfort and hardship were not wholly determined by race. The majority of America's poor were white, and the black middle class was strong and expanding. But people of color made up a disproportionate share of America's poor. In 1980, 33 percent of blacks and 26 percent of Latinos lived in poverty, compared with 10 percent of whites (see Figure 32.2).

Reasons for poverty varied. For people of color, the legacies of racism played a role. The changing job structure was partly responsible, as the overall number of well-paid jobs for both skilled and unskilled workers decreased, replaced by lower-paid service jobs. New York alone had 234,000 fewer blue-collar workers in 1980 than at the beginning of the 1970s. In addition, families headed by a single mother were more likely to be poor—five times more likely than families of the same race maintained by a married couple. By 1990, a high rate of unwed pregnancy and a rising divorce rate meant that about one-quarter of all children lived in a household without a father. Racial differences were significant: by 1992, 59 percent of African American children and 17 percent of white children lived in households headed by a single woman, and almost half of black children lived in poverty.

Social Crises in American Cities   As inequality increased, so, too, did social pathology. In impoverished and often hopeless inner-city neighborhoods, violent crime—particularly homicides and gang warfare—grew alarmingly, as did school dropout rates, crime rates, and child abuse. Some people tried to find escape in hard drugs, especially crack, a derivative of cocaine, which first struck New York City's poorest neighborhoods in 1985. Crack's legacy included destroyed families, abused children, and heavily armed teenage drug dealers. Gang shootouts over drugs were deadly: the toll in Los Angeles in 1987 was 387 deaths, more than half of them innocent bystanders. Shocked by the violence, many states instituted mandatory prison sentences for possessing small amounts of crack, making penalties for a gram of crack equivalent to those for 100 grams of cocaine, the drug of choice for more affluent, white Americans during the 1980s. Such policies increased America's prison population almost fourfold from 980 to the mid-1990s, with black and Latino youth arrested in disproportionate numbers. By 2000, young black men were more likely to have been arrested than to have graduated from a four-year college.

Rates of homelessness also grew during the 1980s, in part because of major cuts to low-income housing subsidies. Some of the homeless were impoverished families; many of the people living on the streets had problems with drugs or alcohol. About one-third of the homeless were former psychiatric patients discharged from psychiatric wards in a burst of enthusiasm for "deinstitutionalization." By 1985, 80 percent of the total number of beds in state mental hospitals had been eliminated on the premise that small neighborhood programs would be more responsive to people's needs than large state hospitals. Such local programs failed to materialize. Without adequate medical supervision and medication, many of America's mentally ill citizens wandered the streets.

The AIDS Epidemic   Another social crisis confronting Americans in the 1980s was the global spread of acquired immune deficiency syndrome, or AIDS. Caused by the human immunodeficiency virus (HIV), which attacks cells in the immune system, AIDS leaves its victims susceptible to deadly infections and cancers. The human immunodeficiency virus itself is spread through the exchange of blood or body fluids, often through sexual intercourse or needle sharing by intravenous drug users.

AIDS was first diagnosed in the United States in 1981. Between 1981 and 1988, of the fifty-seven thousand AIDS cases reported, nearly thirty-two thousand resulted in death. Politicians were slow to devote resources to combating AIDS, in part because it was initially perceived as a "gay man's disease" that did not threaten other Americans. "A man reaps what he sows," declared the Reverend

Jerry Falwell of the Moral Majority. AIDS, along with other sexually transmitted diseases, such as genital herpes and chlamydia, ended an era defined by penicillin and "the pill," in which sex was freed from the threat of serious disease or unwanted pregnancy.

New Immigrants from Asia

The divisions affecting American society in the 1980s were complicated by the arrival of new immigrants from regions not formerly strongly represented in the U.S. ethnic mix. Between 1970 and 1990, the United States absorbed more than 13 million new arrivals, most from Latin America and Asia. Before the immigration act reforms of 1965, Americans of Asian ancestry had made up less than 1 percent of the nation's total population; that percentage more than tripled, to almost 3 percent, by 1990.

The composition of this small slice of America's population also changed dramatically. Before 1965, the majority of Asian Americans were of Japanese ancestry (about 52 percent in 1960), followed by Chinese and Filipino. There were only 603 Vietnamese residents of the United States in 1964. By 1990, the United States had absorbed almost 800,000 refugees from Indochina, casualties of the war in Vietnam and surrounding nations. Immigrants flooded in from South Korea, Thailand, India, Pakistan, Bangladesh, Indonesia, Singapore, Laos, Cambodia, and Vietnam. Japanese Americans became a much smaller portion of the Asian American population, at 15 percent surpassed by Chinese and Filipino Americans and rivaled by the Vietnamese.

Immigrants from Asia tended to be either highly skilled or unskilled. Unsettled conditions in the Philippines in the 1970s and 1980s created an exodus of well-educated Filipinos to the United States. India's economy was not able to support its abundance of well-trained physicians and healthcare workers, who increasingly found employment in the United States and elsewhere. Korea, Taiwan, and China also lost skilled and educated workers to the United States. Other immigrants from China, however, had few job skills and spoke little or no English. Large numbers of new immigrants crowded into neighborhoods like New York City's Chinatown, where women worked long hours under terrible conditions in the city's nonunion garment industry. Immigrants from southeast Asia were the most likely to be unskilled and to live in poverty in the United States, though some found opportunities for success.

But even highly educated immigrants often found their options limited. A 1983 study found that Korean immigrants or Korean Americans owned three-quarters of the approximately twelve hundred greengroceries in New York City. Though often cited as a great immigrant success story, Korean greengrocers usually had descended the professional ladder: 78 percent of them had college or professional degrees.

The Growing Latino Population

Although immigration from Asia was high, unprecedented rates of immigration coupled with a high birth rate made Latinos the fastest-growing group of Americans. New immigrants from

Sandro Tucci/Time Life Pictures/Getty Images

Applicants for visas wait in line at the U.S. embassy in New Delhi, India. In 1985, 140,000 people were on the waiting list for one of 20,000 annual immigrant visas. Many poorer nations, such as India, experienced a "brain drain" of highly educated people to the United States and western Europe.

Mexico joined Mexican Americans and other Spanish-surnamed Americans, many of whose families had lived in the United States for generations. In 1970 Latinos comprised 4.5 percent of the nation's population; that percentage jumped to 9 percent by 1990, when one out of three Los Angelenos and Miamians were Hispanic, as were 48 percent of the population of San Antonio and 70 percent of El Paso. Mexican Americans, concentrated in California and the Southwest, made up the majority of this population, but Puerto Ricans, Cubans, Dominicans, and other immigrants from the Caribbean also lived in the United States, clustered principally in East Coast cities.

During the 1980s, people from Guatemala and El Salvador, fled civil war and government violence, and many found their way to the United States. Although the U.S. government commonly refused to grant them political asylum (about 113,000 Cubans received political refugee status during the 1980s, compared with fewer than 1,400 El Salvadorans), a national Sanctuary movement of Christian churches defied the law to protect refugees from deportation back to places where they risked violence or death. Economic troubles in Mexico and throughout Central and South America also produced a flood of a different sort of refugee: undocumented workers who crossed the poorly guarded 2,000-mile border between the United States and Mexico, seeking economic opportunities. Some were sojourners, who moved back and forth across the border. A majority meant to stay. These new Americans created a new hybrid culture that became an important part of the

American mosaic. "We want to be here," explained Daniel Villanueva, a TV executive in Los Angeles, "but without losing our language and our culture. They are a richness, a treasure that we don't care to lose."

The incorporation of so many newcomers into American society was not always easy, as many Americans believed new arrivals threatened their jobs and economic security, and nativist violence and simple bigotry increased. In 1982, twenty-seven-year-old Vincent Chin was beaten to death in Detroit by an unemployed auto worker and his uncle. American auto plants were losing in competition with Japanese imports, and the two men seemingly mistook the Chinese American Chin for Japanese, reportedly shouting at him, "It's because of you little [expletive deleted] that we're out of work." In New York, Philadelphia, and Los Angeles, inner-city African Americans boycotted Korean groceries. Riots broke out in Los Angeles schools between black students and newly arrived Mexicans. In Dade County, Florida, voters passed an antibilingual measure that led to the removal of Spanish-language signs on public transportation, while at the state and national level people debated initiatives declaring English the "official" language of the United States. Public school classrooms, however, struggled with practical issues: in 1992, more than one thousand school districts in the United States enrolled students from at least eight different language groups.

Concerned about the flow of illegal aliens into the United States, Congress passed the Immigration Reform and Control (Simpson-Rodino) Act in 1986. The act's purpose was to discourage illegal immigration by imposing sanctions on employers who hired undocumented workers, but it also provided amnesty to millions who had immigrated illegally before 1982. As immigration continued at a high rate into the 1990s, however, it would further transform the face of America, offering both the richness of diverse cultures and the potential for continued social conflict.

New Ways of Life

Many Americans found their ways of life transformed during the 1980s, in large part due to new technologies and new models of distribution and consumption. American businesses made huge capital investments in technology during the 1980s as computers became increasingly central to the workplace. Such new communications technology made it possible to locate large office parks on the outskirts of cities, where building costs were low; these new workplaces fostered the development of "edge cities" or "technoburbs" filled with residents who lived, worked, and shopped outside the old city centers. New single family homes grew larger and more expensive; the average cost of a new home rose from two and a half times the median household salary in 1980 to more than four times the median salary in 1988, and 42 percent of new homes had three or more bathrooms.

While the very rich embraced ostentation (Donald Trump's $29 million yacht had gold-plated bathroom fixtures) during this decade, people of more modest means also consumed more. Between 1980 and 1988, Wal-mart's sales jumped from $1.6 billion to $20.6 billion. The number of American shopping malls increased by two-thirds during the decade, and supermarkets stocked twice as many different items as they had ten years before. Eating out became common; by the end of the decade McDonald's was serving 17 million people a day, while "nouvelle cuisine" (artfully presented small portions, emphasizing fresh ingredients) appeared in upscale restaurants. The percentage of Americans who are overweight or obese increased dramatically during the 1980s, even as more and more people began to run marathons (or compete in the much more demanding triathlons), tens of millions took aerobics classes or bought actress Jane Fonda's aerobics exercise videos, and the rapidly growing Nike brand launched its new slogan: "Just Do It."

New technology was not restricted to the workplace. Almost half of American families owned some form of home computer by 1990. Cable television expanded the choices offered by broadcast TV; about half of all families subscribed by the middle of the decade. When MTV (Music Television) was launched in 1981, only a few thousand cable subscribers in New Jersey had access, but it quickly grew to a national phenomenon. The first generation of MTV stars included Michael Jackson, whose fourteen-minute "Thriller" video premiered there in 1983, and Madonna, whose creative manipulation of her own image, from "Boy Toy" sexuality to celebration of female empowerment in "Express Yourself," infuriated both sides in the decades's culture wars. Newly affordable VCRs also gave consumers more choice. Movie attendance dropped as Americans rented movies to view at home, and children no longer had to wait for the annual and much-anticipated airing of *Cinderella* or *The Wizard of Oz* on television, but could instead watch *The Muppets Take Manhattan* or a host of other child-focused videos on demand—or as often as parents would allow.

THE END OF THE COLD WAR AND GLOBAL DISORDER

The departure of Ronald Reagan from the presidency coincided with a set of changes in world affairs that would lead in short order to the end of the Cold War and the dawn of a new international system. Reagan's vice president, George Herbert Walker Bush, would become president and oversee the transition. The scion of a Wall Street banker who had been a U.S. senator from Connecticut, Bush had attended an exclusive boarding school and then gone on to Yale. An upper-class, eastern Establishment figure of the type that was becoming increasingly rare in the Republican Party, he had the advantage over his rivals for the presidential nomination in that he had been a loyal vice president. And he possessed a formidable résumé—he had been ambassador to the United Nations, chairman of the Republican Party, special envoy to China, and director of the CIA. He had also been a war hero, flying fifty-eight combat missions in the Pacific in World War II and receiving the Distinguished Flying Cross.

George Herbert Walker Bush Bush entered the 1988 presidential campaign trailing his Democratic opponent, Massachusetts governor Michael Dukakis, by a wide margin. Republican operatives turned that around by waging one of the most negative campaigns in American history. Most notoriously, the Bush camp aired a television commercial featuring a black convicted murderer, Willie Horton, who had terrorized a Maryland couple, raping the woman, while on weekend furlough—a temporary release program begun under Dukakis's Republican predecessor but associated in the ad with the implication that Dukakis was "soft on crime." The Republicans also falsely suggested that Dukakis had a history of psychiatric problems. His patriotism was questioned, as was that of his wife, who was wrongly accused of having burned an American flag while protesting the Vietnam War. These personal attacks generally did not come from Bush himself, but neither did he disavow them. Dukakis, meanwhile, did not engage in personal attacks on Bush but ran an uninspired campaign. On election day, Bush won by 8 percentage points in the popular vote and received 426 electoral votes to Dukakis's 112. The Democrats, however, retained control of both houses of Congress.

From the start, Bush focused most of his attention on foreign policy, but he was by nature cautious and reactive in world affairs, much to the chagrin of neoconservatives, even in the face of huge changes in the international system. Mikhail Gorbachev's reforms in the Soviet Union were now taking on a life of their own, stimulating reforms in eastern Europe that ultimately led to revolution. In 1989, many thousands of people in East Germany, Poland, Hungary, Czechoslovakia, and Romania, longing for personal freedom, startled the world by repudiating their communist governments and staging mass protests against a despised ideology. In November 1989, Germans scaled the Berlin Wall and then tore it down; the following October, the two Germanys reunited after forty-five years of separation. By then, the other communist governments in eastern Europe had either fallen or were about to do so.

Pro-Democracy Movements   Challenges to communist rule in China met with less success. In June 1989, hundreds—perhaps thousands—of unarmed students and other citizens who for weeks had been holding peaceful pro-democracy rallies in Beijing's Tiananmen Square were slaughtered by Chinese armed forces. The Bush administration, anxious to preserve influence in Beijing, did no more than denounce the action, allowing the Chinese government, whose successful economic reforms had won much admiration in the 1980s, to emphatically reject political liberalization.

Elsewhere, however, the forces of democratization proved too powerful to resist. In South Africa, a new government under F. W. de Klerk, responding to increased domestic and international pressure, began a cautious retreat from the apartheid system. In February 1990, de Klerk legalized all political parties in South Africa, including the ANC, and ordered the release of Nelson Mandela, a hero to black South Africans, after a twenty-seven-year imprisonment. Then, in a staged process lasting several years, the government repealed its apartheid laws and opened up the vote to all citizens, regardless of color. Mandela, who became South Africa's first black president in 1994, called the transformation of his country "a small miracle."

**Collapse of
Soviet Power**   In 1990, the Soviet Union itself began to disintegrate. First the Baltic states of Lithuania, Latvia, and Estonia declared independence from Moscow's rule. The following year, the Soviet Union itself ceased to exist, disintegrating into independent successor states—Russia, Ukraine, Tajikistan, and many others. Muscled aside by Russian reformers who thought he was moving too slowly toward democracy and free-market economics, Gorbachev himself lost power. The breakup of the Soviet empire, the dismantling of the Warsaw Pact (the Soviet military alliance formed in 1955 with communist countries of eastern Europe), the repudiation of communism by its own leaders, German reunification, and a significantly reduced risk of nuclear war signaled the end of the Cold War. The Soviet-American rivalry that for half a century had dominated international politics—and circumscribed domestic prospects in both countries—was over.

The United States and its allies had won. The containment policy followed by nine presidents—from Truman through Bush—had many critics over the years, on both the left and the right, but it had succeeded on a most basic level: it had contained communism for four-plus decades without blowing up the world and without obliterating freedom at home. Two systems competed in this East-West confrontation, and that of the West had clearly triumphed—as anyone who experienced life in both a NATO country and a Warsaw Pact nation quickly realized. Next to the glitz and bustle and well-stocked store shelves of the former were the drab housing projects, polluted skies, and scarce consumer goods of the latter. Over time, the Soviet socialist economy proved less and less able to compete with the American free-market one, less and less able to cope with the demands of the Soviet and eastern European citizenry.

Yet the Soviet empire might have hobbled along for years more had it not been for Gorbachev, one of the most influential figures of the twentieth century. His ascension to the top of the Soviet leadership was the single most important event in the final phase of the Cold War, and it is hard to imagine the far-reaching changes of the 1985–1990 period without his influence. Through a series of unexpected overtures and decisions, Gorbachev fundamentally transformed the nature of the superpower relationship in a way that could scarcely have been anticipated a few years before. Ronald Reagan's role was less central but still vitally important, not so much because of his hard-line policies in his first term as because of his later willingness to enter into serious negotiations and to treat Gorbachev more as a partner than as an adversary. George H. W. Bush, too, followed this general approach. In this way, just as personalities mattered in starting the Cold War, so they mattered in ending it.

Costs of Victory   The victory in the Cold War elicited little celebration among Americans. The struggle had exacted a heavy price in money and lives. The confrontation may never have become a hot war on a global level, but the period after 1945 nevertheless witnessed numerous bloody Cold War–related conflicts claiming millions of lives. In the Vietnam War alone, between 1.5 million and 2 million people died, more than 58,000 of them Americans. Military budgets, meanwhile, had eaten up billions upon billions of dollars that could have been allocated to domestic programs. Some Americans wondered whether the steep price had been necessary, whether the communist threat had ever been as grave as officials, from the late 1940s on, had claimed.

Bush proclaimed a "new world order," but for him and his advisers the question was: what happens next? As the Cold War closed, they struggled futilely to describe the dimensions of an international system that they said would be based on democracy, free trade, and the rule of law. The administration signed important arms reduction treaties with the Soviet Union in 1991 and with the postbreakup Russia in 1993, leading to major reductions in nuclear weapons on both sides, but the United States sustained a large defense budget and continued to station large numbers of military forces overseas. As a result, Americans were denied the "peace dividend" that they hoped would reduce taxes and free up funds to address domestic problems.

In Central America, the Bush administration cooled the zeal with which Reagan had meddled because the interventions had largely failed and, with the Cold War over, anticommunism seemed irrelevant. Still, like so many presidents before him, Bush showed no reluctance to intervene forcefully and unilaterally in the region to further U.S. aims. In December 1989, American troops invaded Panama to oust military leader Manuel Noriega. A long-time drug trafficker, Noriega had stayed in Washington's favor in the mid-1980s by providing logistical support for the contras in nearby Nicaragua, but in the early 1990s, exposés of his sordid record, which provoked protests in Panama, changed Bush's mind. Noriega was captured in the invasion and taken to Miami, where, in 1992, he was convicted of drug trafficking and imprisoned. Devastated Panama, meanwhile, became all the more dependent on the United States, which offered little reconstruction aid.

Saddam Hussein's Gamble

The strongest test of Bush's foreign policy came in the Middle East. The Iran-Iraq War had ended inconclusively in August 1988, after eight years of fighting and almost 400,000 dead. The Reagan administration had assisted the Iraqi war effort with weapons and intelligence, as had many other NATO countries. In mid-1990, Iraqi president Saddam Hussein, facing massive war debts and growing domestic discontent, invaded neighboring Kuwait, hoping thereby to enhance his regional power and his oil revenues and shore up domestic support. He counted on Washington to look the other way. Instead, George Bush condemned the invasion and vowed to defend Kuwait. He was outraged by Hussein's act of aggression and also feared that Iraq might threaten U.S. oil supplies, not merely in Kuwait but also in petroleum-rich Saudi Arabia next door.

Within weeks, Bush had convinced virtually every important government, including most of the Arab and Islamic states, to sign on to an economic boycott of Iraq. Then, in Operation Desert Shield, Bush dispatched more than 500,000 U.S. forces to the region, where they were joined by more than 200,000 from the allies. Likening Saddam to Hitler and declaring the moment the first post–Cold War "test of our mettle," Bush rallied a deeply divided Congress to authorize "all necessary means" to oust Iraq from Kuwait (a vote of 250 to 183 in the House and 52 to 47 in the Senate). Although Bush did not invoke the 1973 War Powers Act, numerous observers saw his seeking a congressional resolution of approval as reinforcing the intent of the act. Many Americans believed that economic sanctions imposed on Iraq should be given more time to work, but Bush would not wait. "This will not be another Vietnam," the president said, by which he meant it would not be a lengthy and frustrating affair. Victory would come swiftly and cleanly.

Operation Desert Storm

Operation Desert Storm began on January 16, 1991, with the greatest air armada in history pummeling Iraqi targets. American cruise missiles reinforced round-the-clock bombing raids on Baghdad, Iraq's capital. It was a television war, in which CNN reporters broadcast live from a Baghdad hotel while bombs were falling in the city, and millions of Americans sat transfixed in their living rooms, eyes glued to the TV. In late February, coalition forces under General Norman Schwartzkopf launched a ground war that quickly routed the Iraqis from Kuwait. When the war ended on March 1, at least 40,000 Iraqis had been killed, while the death toll for allied troops stood at 240 (148 of them Americans). Almost one-quarter of the American dead were killed by "friendly fire"—by weapons fired by U.S. or allied troops.

Bush rejected a call from some of his advisers to take Baghdad and topple Hussein's regime. Coalition members would not have agreed to such a plan—it would go beyond the original objective of forcing Iraq out of Kuwait—and it was also not clear who in Iraq would replace the dictator. Some also warned that the drive to Baghdad could bog down, subjecting U.S. forces to a costly and drawn-out campaign. So Saddam Hussein survived in power, though with his authority curtailed. The U.N. maintained an arms and economic embargo, and the Security Council issued Resolution 687, demanding that Iraq provide full disclosure of all aspects of its program to develop weapons of mass destruction and ballistic missiles with a range greater than 150 kilometers. In Resolution 688, the Security Council condemned a brutal crackdown by the Iraqi regime against Kurds in northern Iraq and Shi'ite Muslims in the south and demanded access for humanitarian groups. The United States, Britain, and France seized on Resolution 688 to create a northern "no-fly zone" prohibiting Iraqi aircraft flights. A similar no-fly zone was set up in southern Iraq in 1992 and expanded in 1996.

Although in time some would question President Bush's decision to stop short of Baghdad, initially there were few objections. In the wake of Desert Storm, the president's popularity in the polls soared to 91 percent, beating the previous high of 89 percent set by Harry Truman in June 1945 after the surrender of Germany. Cocky White House advisers thought Bush could ride his popularity right through the 1992 election and beyond. In the afterglow of military victory it seemed a good bet, particularly as Bush could also claim achievements on the domestic front that seemed to affirm his inauguration-day pledge to lead a "kinder, gentler nation."

LINKS TO THE WORLD

CNN

When Ted Turner launched CNN, his Cable News Network, on June 1, 1980, few people took it seriously. CNN, with a staff of three hundred—mostly young, mostly inexperienced—operated out of the basement of a converted country club in Atlanta. Dismissed by critics as the Chicken Noodle Network, CNN was at first best known for its on-air errors, as when a cleaning woman walked onto the set and emptied anchor Bernard Shaw's trash during his live newscast. But by 1992, against all expectations, CNN was seen in more than 150 nations worldwide, and *Time* magazine named Ted Turner its "Man of the Year" for realizing media theorist Marshall McLuhan's vision of the world as a "global village" united by mass media.

Throughout the 1980s, CNN steadily built relations with local news outlets in nations throughout the world. As critical—and sometimes unanticipated—events reshaped the world, CNN reported live from Tiananmen Square and from the Berlin Wall in 1989. Millions watched as CNN reporters broadcast live from Baghdad in the early hours of the Gulf War in 1991. CNN changed not only viewers' experience of these events but diplomacy itself. When the Soviet Union wanted to denounce the 1989 U.S. invasion of Panama, officials called CNN's Moscow bureau instead of the U.S. embassy. During the Gulf War, Saddam Hussein reportedly kept televisions in his bunker tuned to CNN, and U.S. generals relied on its broadcasts to judge the effectiveness of missile attacks. In 1992, President George H. W. Bush noted, "I learn more from CNN than I do from the CIA."

Although Turner's twenty-four-hour news network had a global mission, its American origins were often apparent. During the U.S. invasion of Panama, CNN cautioned correspondents not to refer to the American military forces as "our" troops. Turner himself once sent his staff a memo insisting that anyone who used the word *foreign* instead of *international* would be fined $100. What CNN offered was not so much international news, but a global experience: people throughout the world joined in watching the major moments in contemporary history as they unfolded. America's CNN created new links among the world's people. But as *Time* magazine noted (while praising Turner as the "Prince of the Global Village"), such connections "did not produce instantaneous brotherhood, just a slowly dawning awareness of the implications of a world transfixed by a single TV image."

Domestic Issues   In 1990, for example, Bush had signed the Americans with Disabilities Act. This act, which applied to companies with twenty-five or more employees and covered 87 percent of all wage earners, banned job discrimination against those with disabilities who can, with reasonable accommodation, perform the essential tasks required by the job. It also required that "reasonable accommodations," such as wheelchair ramps, be made available to people with disabilities. Also in 1990, the president, much to the disappointment of

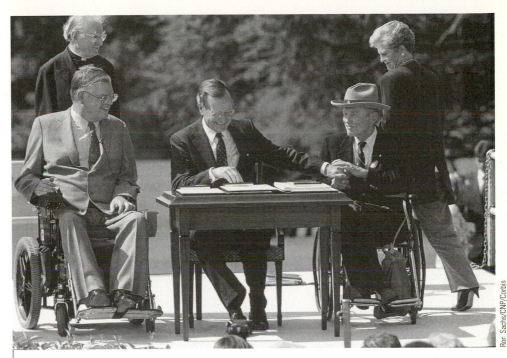

President George Bush signs the Americans with Disabilities Act (ADA) on the White House lawn, July 26, 1990. As he lifted his pen, the president said: "Let the shameful wall of exclusion finally come tumbling down."

conservatives, who opposed increased regulation, signed the Clean Air Act, which sought to reduce acid rain by limiting emissions from factories and automobiles. And in 1991, after many months of contentious debate, Bush and Congress agreed on a civil rights bill to protect against job discrimination.

Yet not long after reaching their historic highs, Bush's poll numbers started falling and kept falling, largely because of the president's ineffectual response to the weakening American economy. He was slow to grasp the implications of the heavy burden of national debt and the massive federal deficit, which had been out of control for nearly a decade. When the nation entered into a full-fledged recession in the months after the Gulf War, Bush did not respond, beyond proclaiming that things were not really that bad. Echoed his treasury secretary Nicholas Brady, "I don't think it's the end of the world even if we have a recession. We'll pull out of it again. It's no big deal."

For millions of ordinary Americans, it was a big deal. Business shrank, despite low interest rates that theoretically should have encouraged investment. Real-estate prices plummeted. American products faced steadily tougher competition from products made overseas, especially in Japan and elsewhere in Asia. As unemployment climbed to 8 percent, consumer confidence sank. By late 1991, fewer than 40 percent of the American people felt comfortable with the way the country was going. Many demanded that the federal government address neglected problems, such as the rising cost of healthcare.

Clarence Thomas Nomination   Bush's credibility was diminished further by confirmation hearings for Clarence Thomas, whom Bush nominated to the Supreme Court in the fall of 1991. The Bush administration hoped that those who opposed the nomination of yet another conservative to the high court might nonetheless support the addition of an African American justice. But in October, Anita Hill, an African American law professor at the University of Oklahoma, charged that Thomas had sexually harassed her when she worked for him during the early 1980s. The Judiciary Committee hearings, carried live on television, turned ugly, and some Republican members suggested that Hill was either lying or mentally ill. Thomas described himself as the "victim" of a "high-tech lynching," and African American groups were passionately divided over the Hill-Thomas testimony. However, Hill's testimony focused the nation's attention on issues of power, gender, sex, and the workplace. And the Senate's confirmation of Thomas, along with the attacks on Hill, angered many, further increasing the gender gap in American politics.

As George H. W. Bush and the Republicans entered the election year of 1992, the glow of military victory in the Gulf War had faded completely.

SUMMARY

When Ronald Reagan left the White House in 1988, succeeded by his vice president, George Bush, the *New York Times* summed up his presidency: "Ronald Reagan leaves no Vietnam War, no Watergate, no hostage crisis. But he leaves huge question marks—and much to do." George H. W. Bush met the foreign policy promises of the 1980s, as the Soviet Union collapsed and America achieved victory in the decades-long Cold War. He also led the United States into war with Iraq—a war that ended in swift and decisive victory but left Saddam Hussein in power.

During the 1980s, the United States moved from deep recession to economic prosperity. However, deep tax cuts and massive increases in defense spending created huge budget deficits, increasing the national debt from $994 billion to more than $2.9 trillion. This enormous debt would limit the options of subsequent presidential administrations. Pro-business policies, such as deregulation, created opportunities for the development of new technologies and prompted economic growth but also opened the door to corruption and fraud. Policies that benefited the wealthy at the expense of middle-class or poor Americans widened the gulf between the rich and everyone else. The social pathologies of drug addiction, crime, and violence grew, especially in the nation's most impoverished areas. The legacies of the 1980s included thousands of children born addicted to crack, who would live the rest of their lives with mental and physical impairments, and prisons that overflowed with young men.

The 1980s also saw the coalescence of the "culture wars" between fundamentalist Christians who sought to "restore" America to God and opponents who championed separation of church and state, and embraced liberal values. The nation shifted politically to the right, though the coalitions of economic and social conservatives that supported Reagan were fragile and did not guarantee continued Republican dominance.

Finally, during the 1980s, the face of America changed. A society that many had thought of as white and black became ever more diverse. The nation's Latino population grew in size and visibility. New immigrants from Asia arrived in large numbers; though still a small part of the population, they would play an increasingly important role in American society. During the Reagan-Bush years, America had become both more divided and more diverse. In the years to come, Americans and their leaders would struggle with the legacies of the "Reagan era."

33

INTO THE GLOBAL MILLENNIUM: AMERICA SINCE 1992

CHAPTER OUTLINE

• Social Strains and New Political Directions • Globalization and Prosperity • 9/11 and the War in Iraq • Domestic Politics in Post-9/11 America • Americans in the First Decade of the New Millennium • *LINKS TO THE WORLD* The "Swine Flu" Pandemic • Summary

---

SOCIAL STRAINS AND NEW POLITICAL DIRECTIONS

Although the 1990s would be remembered as an era of relative peace and prosperity, the decade did not start that way. Scourges of drugs, homelessness, and crime plagued America's cities. Racial tensions had worsened; the gulf between rich and poor had grown more pronounced. The economy, slowing since 1989, had tipped into recession. Public disillusionment with political leaders ran strong. As the 1992 presidential election year began, Americans were frustrated and looking for a change.

Turmoil in L.A.   The racial tensions that troubled the nation erupted in the South Central neighborhood of Los Angeles in 1992. Like most such outbreaks of violence, there was an immediate cause. A jury (with no African American members) had acquitted four white police officers charged with beating a black man, Rodney King, who had fled a pursuing police car at speeds exceeding 110 miles per hour.

The roots of the violence, however, went deeper. Almost one-third of South Central residents lived in poverty—a rate 75 percent higher than for the city as a whole—after well-paid jobs disappeared during the deindustrialization of the 1970s and 1980s. Tensions increased as new immigrants—Latinos from Mexico and Central America, who competed with African American residents for jobs as well as Koreans who established small businesses such as grocery stores—sought a foothold in the area. Outside the legitimate economy, the 40 Crips (an African

CHRONOLOGY

1992   Violence erupts in Los Angeles over Rodney King verdict

Major economic recession

Clinton elected president

1993   Congress approves North American Free Trade Agreement (NAFTA)

1994   Contract with America helps Republicans win majorities in House and Senate

Genocide in Rwanda

U.S. intervention in Haiti

1995   Domestic terrorist bombs Oklahoma City federal building

U.S. diplomats broker peace for Bosnia

1996   Welfare reform bill places time limits on welfare payments

Clinton reelected

1998   House votes to impeach Clinton

1999   Senate acquits Clinton of impeachment charges

NATO bombs Serbia over Kosovo crisis

Antiglobalization demonstrators disrupt World Trade Organization (WTO) meeting in Seattle

2000   Nation records longest economic expansion in its history

Supreme Court settles contested presidential election in favor of Bush

2001   Economy dips into recession; period of low growth and high unemployment begins

Bush becomes president

Al Qaeda terrorists attack World Trade Center and Pentagon

United States attacks Al Qaeda positions in Afghanistan, topples ruling Taliban regime

2003   United States invades Iraq, ousts Saddam Hussein regime

2004   Bush reelected

2005   Hurricane Katrina strikes Gulf Coast

2006   By end of year U.S. deaths in Iraq reach three thousand

Democrats take both houses of Congress in midterm elections

2007   Major economic recession begins in December

2008   Barack Obama elected president

2009   Obama announces increased U.S. military commitment to Afghanistan; U.S. continues troop drawdown in Iraq

American gang) and the 18th Street gang (Latino) struggled over territory as the crack epidemic further decimated the neighborhood and the homicide rate soared. Police tactics had alienated most neighborhood residents, and relations were especially strained between African Americans and the new Korean population, as many African American and Latino residents saw high prices in Korean-owned shops as exploitation, while Korean shopkeepers complained of frequent shoplifting, robberies, even beatings.

The violence in Los Angeles (which the Korean community called Sa-I-Gu, or 4/29, for the date it began) was a multi-ethnic uprising that left at least fifty-three people dead and symbolized, for many, fundamental conflicts at the heart of American society. Economic problems also troubled the nation. The economy had grown slowly or not at all during the Bush administration. The state of California, left in an impossible position by 1978's Proposition 13—the first in a series of "tax revolts" across the nation that had cut property taxes while the population boomed—faced bankruptcy in mid-1992. California was not alone; thirty states were in financial trouble in the early 1990s. Many businesses, deeply burdened with debt, closed down or cut back. Factory employment was at its lowest level since the recession of 1982, and corporate downsizing meant that well-educated white-collar workers were losing jobs as well. In 1991, median household incomes hit the most severe decline since the 1973 recession; in 1992, the number of poor people in America reached the highest level since 1964.

Clinton's Victory   As the American economy suffered, so did President George H. W. Bush's approval rating. Despite the credit Bush gained for foreign policy—the end of the Cold War and the quick victory in the Gulf War—economic woes and a lack of what he once called the "vision thing" left him vulnerable in the 1992 presidential election.

Democratic nominee Bill Clinton, the governor of Arkansas, offered a profound contrast to George Bush. Clinton's campaign headquarters bore signs with the four-word reminder "It's the economy, stupid." In a town hall–format presidential debate, a woman asked how the economic troubles had affected each candidate, and Clinton moved from behind the podium to ask her, "Tell me how it's affected you again? You know people who've lost their jobs and lost their homes?" George Bush was caught on camera looking at his watch.

On election day, Clinton and his running mate, Tennessee Senator Al Gore, swept New England, the West Coast, and much of the industrial Midwest, even making inroads into what had become an almost solidly Republican South and drawing "Reagan Democrats" back to the fold.

Clinton and the "New Democrats"   Bill Clinton was one of the most paradoxical presidents in American history. A journalist described him in a 1996 New York Times article as "one of the biggest, most talented, articulate, intelligent, open, colorful characters ever to inhabit the White House," while noting that Clinton "can also be an undisciplined, fumbling, obtuse, defensive, self-justifying rogue.... He is breathtakingly bright while capable of doing really dumb things." Clinton was a larger-than-life figure, a born politician from a small town called Hope who had wanted to be president most of his life. In college at Georgetown University in Washington, D.C., during the 1960s he had protested the Vietnam War and (like many of his generation) had maneuvered to keep himself from being sent to Vietnam. Clinton had won a Rhodes scholarship to Oxford, earned his law degree from Yale, and returned to his home state of Arkansas, where he was elected governor in 1978 at the age of thirty-two. Bill Clinton's wife, Hillary Rodham Clinton, was the first First Lady to have a significant career of her own during her married life; they had met when they were both law students at Yale, where Hillary Rodham had made Law Review (an honor not shared by her husband).

Politically, Bill Clinton was a "new Democrat." He, along with other members of the new Democratic Leadership Council, advocated a more centrist—though still socially progressive—position for the Democratic Party. Clinton and his colleagues asked whether large government bureaucracies were still appropriate tools for addressing social problems in modern America. They emphasized private-sector economic development rather than public jobs programs, focusing on job training and other policies that they believed would promote opportunity, not dependency. They championed a global outlook in both foreign policy and economic development. Finally, they emphasized an ethic of "mutual responsibility" and "inclusiveness."

Clinton plunged into an ambitious program of reform and revitalization, beginning with his goal of appointing a cabinet that "looks like America" in all its diversity. But almost immediately he ran into trouble. Republicans, determined not to allow Clinton the traditional "honeymoon" period, maneuvered him into attempting to fulfill a campaign pledge to end the ban on gays in the military before he had secured congressional or widespread military support. Amid great public controversy, Clinton finally accepted a "don't ask, don't tell" compromise that alienated liberals, conservatives, the gay community, and the military.

Clinton's major goal was to make healthcare affordable and accessible for all Americans, including the millions who had no insurance coverage. But special interests mobilized in opposition: the insurance industry worried about lost profits; the business community feared higher taxes to support the uninsured; the medical community was concerned about more regulation, lower government reimbursement rates, and reduced healthcare quality. The administration's healthcare task force, cochaired by Hillary Rodham Clinton, could not create a political coalition strong enough to defeat these forces. Within a year, the centerpiece of Clinton's fledgling presidency had failed.

"Republican Revolution" and Political Compromise   With Clinton beleaguered, new-style Republicans seized the chance to challenge the new Democrat. In September 1994, shortly before the midterm congressional elections, more than three hundred Republican candidates for the House of Representatives endorsed the "Contract with America." Developed under the leadership of Georgia congressman Newt Gingrich, the

"Contract" promised "the end of government that is too big, too intrusive, and too easy with the public's money [and] the beginning of a Congress that respects the values and shares the faith of the American family." It called for a balanced-budget amendment to the Constitution, reduction of the capital gains tax, a two-year limit on welfare payments (while making unmarried mothers under eighteen ineligible), and increased defense spending.

In the midterm elections, the Republican Party mobilized socially conservative voters to score a major victory. Republicans took control of both houses of Congress for the first time since 1954 and made huge gains in state legislatures and governorships. Ideological passions ran high, and many Republicans believed their ongoing attempts to weaken federal power and to dismantle the welfare state would now succeed.

The Republicans of the 104th Congress, however, miscalculated. Although many Americans applauded the idea of cutting government spending, they opposed cuts to most specific programs, including Medicare and Medicaid, education and college loans, highway construction, farm subsidies, veterans' benefits, and Social Security. Republicans made a bigger mistake when they issued President Clinton an ultimatum on the federal budget. Clinton refused to accept their terms, Republicans refused to pass a continuing resolution to provide interim funding, and the government was forced to suspend all nonessential action during the winter of 1995–1996. An angry public blamed the Republicans.

Such struggles showed Clinton's resolve, but they also led him to make compromises that moved American politics to the right. For example, he signed the 1996 Personal Responsibility and Work Opportunity Act, a welfare reform measure mandating that heads of families on welfare must find work within two years (though states could exempt up to 20 percent of recipients), limiting welfare benefits to five years over an individual's lifetime, and making many legal immigrants ineligible. The Telecommunications Act of 1996, signed by Clinton, reduced diversity in America's media by permitting companies to own more television and radio stations.

Clinton and Gore were reelected in 1996 (defeating Republican Bob Dole and Reform Party candidate Ross Perot), in part because Clinton stole some of the conservatives' thunder. He declared that "the era of big government is over" and invoked family values, a centerpiece of the Republican campaign. Sometimes Clinton's actions were true compromises with conservative interests; other times he attempted to reclaim issues from the conservatives, as when he redefined family values as "fighting for the family-leave law or the assault-weapons ban or . . . trying to keep tobacco out of the hands of kids."

Clinton's legislative accomplishments during his two terms in office were modest but included programs that made life easier for American families. The Family and Medical Leave Act guaranteed 91 million workers the right to take time off to care for ailing relatives or newborn children. The Health Insurance Portability and Accountability Act ensured that, when Americans changed jobs, they would not lose health insurance because of preexisting medical conditions. Government became more efficient: the federal government operated with 365,000 fewer employees by the end of Clinton's term, and Vice President Gore led an initiative that eliminated sixteen thousand pages of federal regulations.

Clinton created national parks and monuments that protected 3.2 million acres of American land and made unprecedented progress cleaning up toxic waste dumps throughout the nation. Perhaps more than anything else, however, the 1990s will be remembered as an era of prosperity and economic growth.

Political Partisanship and Scandal   Despite widespread economic security and Clinton's moves toward the political center, the battles in American politics were divisive and often ugly during the Clinton era as the political right attacked Clinton with a vehemence not seen since Franklin Roosevelt's New Deal. Hillary Clinton was a frequent target; when she told a hostile interviewer during her husband's first presidential campaign, "I suppose I could have stayed home and baked cookies and had teas. But what I decided to do was pursue my profession, which I entered before my husband was in public life," the New York Post called her "a buffoon, an insult to most women." And as rumors of scandal plagued the White House, an independent counsel's office headed by Kenneth Starr, a conservative Republican and former judge, would spend $72 million investigating allegations of wrongdoing by Hillary and Bill Clinton. Starr, who was appointed by a judicial board independent from the Justice Department, was originally charged with investigating Whitewater, a 1970s Arkansas real-estate deal in which the Clintons had invested. Though he turned up no evidence of wrongdoing in Whitewater, Starr expanded the range of his investigation and offered proof that Clinton had lied to a grand jury when he testified that he had not engaged in sexual relations with twenty-two-year-old White House intern Monica Lewinsky.

In a 445-page report to Congress, Starr outlined eleven possible grounds for impeachment of the president, accusing Clinton of lying under oath, obstruction of justice, witness tampering, and abuse of power. In December 1998, the House of Representatives, voting largely along party lines, concluded that the president had committed perjury in his grand jury testimony and that he had obstructed justice. Clinton became the second president—and the first in 130 years—to face a trial in the Senate, which has the constitutional responsibility to decide (by two-thirds vote) whether to remove a president from office.

But the American people did not want Clinton removed from office. Polls showed that large majorities approved of the president's job performance, even as many condemned his personal behavior. And many did not believe his actions rose to the level of "high crimes and misdemeanors" (normally acts such as treason) required by the Constitution as grounds for impeachment. The Republican-controlled Senate, responding at least in part to popular opinion, did not convict Clinton of the charges.

Politics, the Media, and Celebrity Culture   Clinton, of course, bears responsibility for his own actions. However, how those actions became grounds for impeachment, with the explicit sexual details contained in the Starr Report circulated by Internet around the world, is part of a larger story. Clinton was not the first president to engage in illicit sex. President John F. Kennedy, among others, had numerous and well-known sexual affairs, including one with a nineteen-year-old intern. But after the Watergate scandals of the early 1970s, the mass media were no longer willing to turn a blind eye to presidential misconduct. The fiercely competitive twenty-four-hour news networks that began with CNN in 1980 relied on scandal, spectacle, and crisis to lure viewers. Public officials also contributed to the blurring of lines between public and private, celebrity and statesman. Clinton, for example, had appeared on MTV during his first campaign and answered a question about his preference in underwear (boxers).

The partisan political wars of the 1990s created a take-no-prisoners climate in which no politician's missteps would be overlooked. As fallout from the Clinton impeachment, both Republican Speaker of the House Newt Gingrich and his successor, Robert Livingston, resigned when faced with evidence of their own extramarital affairs. Finally, as former Clinton aide Sidney Blumenthal writes, the impeachment struggle was about more than presidential perjury and sexual infidelity. It was part of the "culture wars" that divided the American people: "a monumental battle over very large political questions about the Constitution, about cultural mores and the position of women in American society, and about the character of the American people. It was, ultimately, a struggle about the identity of the country."

Violence and Anger in American Society   A political extremism that existed well beyond the bounds of Washington politics exploded into view on April 19, 1995, when 168 children, women, and men were killed in a powerful bomb blast that destroyed the nine-story Alfred P. Murrah Federal Building in downtown Oklahoma City. At first, many thought the bomb had come from abroad, perhaps set off by Middle Eastern terrorists. But a charred piece of truck axle located two blocks from the explosion, with the vehicle identification number still legible, led investigators to Timothy McVeigh, a native-born white American and a veteran of the Persian Gulf War. McVeigh was seeking revenge for the deaths of members of the Branch Davidian religious sect, whom he believed the FBI had deliberately slaughtered in a standoff over firearms charges on that date two years before in Waco, Texas.

In the months that followed, reporters and government investigators discovered networks of militias, tax resisters, and various white-supremacist groups throughout the nation. These groups were united by distrust of the federal government. Many saw federal gun control laws, such as the Brady Bill, signed into law in 1993, as a dangerous usurpation of citizens' right to bear arms. Members of these groups believed that the federal government was controlled by "sinister forces," including Zionists, cultural elitists, Queen Elizabeth, and the United Nations. After McVeigh's act of domestic terrorism these groups lost members but also turned to the new Internet to spread their beliefs.

Other forms of violence also haunted America. On April 20, 1999, eighteen-year-old Eric Harris and seventeen-year-old Dylan Klebold opened fire on classmates and teachers at Columbine High School in Littleton, Colorado, killing thirteen before turning their guns on themselves. No clear reason why two academically successful students in a middle-class suburb would commit mass

On April 20, 1999, students evacuated Columbine High School in Littleton, Colorado, after two schoolmates went on a shooting rampage, killing twelve students and a teacher before killing themselves.

Adapted from Dow Jones & Company.

murder ever emerged. And the Columbine massacre was not an isolated event: students in Paducah, Kentucky; Springfield, Oregon; and Jonesboro, Arkansas, massacred classmates.

Finally, two hate crimes shocked the nation in the late 1990s. James Byrd Jr., a forty-nine-year-old black man, was murdered by three white supremacists who dragged him for miles by a chain from the back of a pickup truck in Jasper, Texas, in 1998. Later that year, Matthew Shepherd, a gay college student, died after being beaten unconscious and left tied to a wooden fence in freezing weather outside Laramie, Wyoming. His killers said they were "humiliated" when he flirted with them at a bar. Some argued that these murders demonstrated the strength of racism and homophobia in American society, while others saw the horror that most Americans expressed at these murders as a sign of positive change.

Clinton's Diplomacy

Still, it remained true that the United States occupied a uniquely powerful position on the world stage. The demise of the Soviet Union had created a one-superpower world, in which the United States stood far above other powers in political, military, and economic might. Yet in his first term Clinton was more wary in traditional aspects of foreign policy—great-power diplomacy, arms control, regional disputes—than in facilitating American cultural and trade expansion. He was deeply suspicious of foreign military involvements. The Vietnam debacle had taught him that the American public had limited patience for wars lacking clear-cut national interest, a lesson he found confirmed by George Bush's failure to gain lasting political strength from the Gulf War victory.

This mistrust of foreign interventions was cemented for Clinton by the difficulties he inherited from Bush in Somalia. In 1992, Bush had sent U.S. marines to the East African nation as part of a U.N. effort to ensure that humanitarian supplies reached starving Somalis. But in summer 1993, when Americans came under deadly attack from forces loyal to a local warlord, Clinton withdrew U.S. troops. And he did not intervene in Rwanda, where in 1994 the majority Hutus butchered 800,000 of the minority Tutsis in a brutal civil war.

Balkan Crisis   That Somalia and Rwanda were on the policy agenda at all testified to the growing importance of humanitarian concerns in post–Cold War U.S. policy. Many administration officials argued for using America's power to contain ethnic hatreds, support human rights, and promote democracy worldwide. The notion faced a severe test in the Balkans, which erupted in a series of ethnic wars. Bosnian Muslims, Serbs, and Croats were soon killing one another by the tens of thousands. Clinton talked tough against Serbian aggression and atrocities in Bosnia-Herzegovina, especially the Serbs' "ethnic cleansing" of Muslims through massacres and rape camps. He occasionally ordered air strikes, but he primarily emphasized diplomacy. In late 1995, American diplomats brokered a fragile peace.

But Yugoslav president Slobodan Milosevic continued the anti-Muslim and anti-Croat fervor. When Serb forces moved to violently rid Serbia's southern province of Kosovo of its majority ethnic Albanians, Clinton was pressed to intervene. Initially he was reluctant; the ghosts of Vietnam were ever present in Oval Office deliberations. But reports of Serbian atrocities and a major refugee crisis stirred world opinion and pressed Clinton to intervene. In 1999, U.S.-led NATO forces launched a massive aerial bombardment of Serbia. Milosevic withdrew from Kosovo, where U.S. troops joined a U.N. peacekeeping force. That same year, the International War Crimes Tribunal indicted Milosevic and his top aides for atrocities.

Agreements in the Middle East   In the Middle East, Clinton took an active role in trying to bring the PLO and Israel together to settle their differences. In September 1993, the PLO's Yasir Arafat and Israel's prime minister, Yitzhak Rabin, signed an agreement at the White House for Palestinian self-rule in the Gaza Strip and the West Bank's Jericho. The following year Israel signed a peace accord with Jordan, further reducing the chances of another full-scale Arab-Israeli war. Radical anti-Arafat Palestinians, however, continued terrorist attacks on

Israelis, while extremist Israelis killed Palestinians and, in November 1995, Rabin himself. Only after American-conducted negotiations and renewed violence in the West Bank did Israel agree in early 1997 to withdraw its forces from the Palestinian city of Hebron. Thereafter, the peace process alternately sagged and spurted.

The same could be said of international efforts to protect the environment, which gathered pace in the 1990s. The George H. W. Bush administration had opposed many provisions of the 1992 Rio de Janeiro Treaty protecting the diversity of plant and animal species, and resisted stricter rules to reduce global warming. Clinton, urged on by Vice President Al Gore, signed the 1997 Kyoto protocol, which aimed to combat emissions of carbon dioxide and other gases that most scientists believe trap heat in the atmosphere. The treaty required the United States to reduce its emissions by 2012 to 7 percent below its 1990 levels. But facing strong congressional opposition, Clinton never submitted the protocol for ratification to the Republican-controlled Senate.

Bin Laden and Al Qaeda   Meanwhile, the administration was increasingly concerned about the threat to U.S. interests by Islamic fundamentalism. In particular, senior officials worried about the rise of Al Qaeda (Arabic for "the base"), an international terrorist network led by Osama bin Laden, which was dedicated to purging Muslim countries of what it saw as the profane influence of the West and installing fundamentalist Islamic regimes.

The son of a Yemen-born construction tycoon in Saudi Arabia, bin Laden had supported the Afghan Mujahidin in their struggle against Soviet occupation. He then founded Al Qaeda and financed terrorist projects with his substantial inheritance. U.S. officials grew more concerned, particularly as bin Laden focused on American targets. In 1995, a car bomb in Riyadh killed 7 people, 5 of them Americans. In 1998, simultaneous bombings at the American embassies in Kenya and Tanzania killed 224 people, including 12 Americans. In Yemen in 2000, a boat laden with explosives hit the destroyer USS Cole, killing 17 American sailors. Although bin Laden masterminded and financed these attacks, he eluded U.S. attempts to apprehend him. In 1998, Clinton approved a plan to assassinate bin Laden at an Al Qaeda camp in Afghanistan, but the attempt failed.

GLOBALIZATION AND PROSPERITY

Despite conflicts abroad and partisan struggles in Washington, the majority of Americans experienced the late 1990s as a time of unprecedented peace and prosperity, fueled by the dizzying rise of the stock market. Between 1991 and 1999, the Dow Jones Industrial Average climbed from 3,169 to a high of 11,497 (see Figure 33.1). The booming market benefited the middle class and the wealthy, as mutual funds, 401(k) plans, and other new investment vehicles drew a majority of Americans into the stock market. In 1952, only 4 percent of American households owned stocks; by 2000, almost 60 percent did.

At the end of the 1990s, the unemployment rate stood at 4.3 percent—the lowest peacetime rate since 1957. That made it easier to implement welfare reform, and

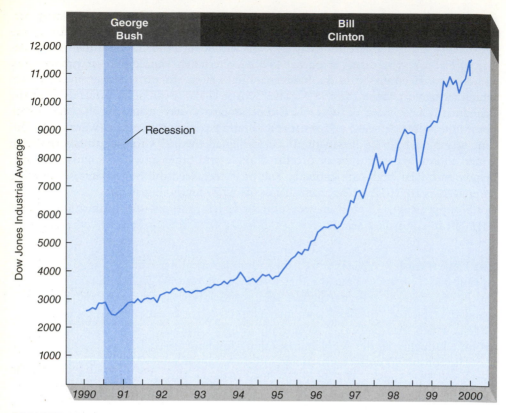

FIGURE 33.1 The American Stock Market

This graph of the Dow Jones Industrial Average, climbing steadily in the bull market of the 1990s, illustrates the great economic expansion of the decade.

Source: Adapted from Dow Jones & Company.

welfare rolls declined 50 percent. Both the richest 5 percent and the least well-off 20 percent of American households saw their incomes rise almost 25 percent. But that translated to an average gain of $50,000 for the top 5 percent and only $2,880 for the bottom 20 percent, further widening the gap between rich and poor. Still, by decade's end, more than two-thirds of Americans were homeowners— the highest percentage in history.

Just how much credit Clinton deserved for the improved economy is debatable. Presidents typically get too much blame when the economy struggles and too much credit when times are good. The roots of the 1990s boom were in the 1970s, when American corporations began investing in new technologies, retooling plants to become more energy-efficient, and cutting labor costs. Specifically, companies reduced the influence of organized labor by moving operations to the union-weak South and West and to countries such as China and Mexico, where labor was cheap and pollution controls were lax.

Digital Revolution   Even more important than the restructuring of existing corporations was the emergence of a powerful new sector of the economy associated with digital technology. The rapid development of what came to be called "information technology"—computers, fax machines, cell phones, and the Internet—had a huge economic impact in the 1980s and 1990s. New companies and industries sprang up, many headquartered in the "Silicon Valley" near San Francisco. By the second half of the 1990s, the Forbes list of the 400 richest Americans featured high-tech leaders such as Microsoft's Bill Gates, who became the wealthiest person in the world with worth approaching $100 billion, as his company produced the operating software for most personal computers. The high-tech industry had considerable spillover effects, generating improved productivity, new jobs, and sustained economic growth.

The heart of this technological revolution was the microprocessor. Introduced in 1970 by Intel, the microprocessor miniaturized the central processing unit of a computer, meaning small machines could now perform calculations previously requiring large machines. Computing chores that took a week in the early 1970s took one minute by 2000; the cost of storing one megabyte of information, or enough for a 320-page book, fell from more than $5,000 in 1975 to 17 cents in 1999. The implications for business were enormous.

Analysts dubbed this technology-driven sector "The New Economy," and it would have emerged no matter who was in the White House. Yet Clinton and his advisers had some responsibility for the dramatic upturn. With the U.S. budget deficit topping $500 billion, they made the politically risky move of abandoning the middle-class tax cut and making deficit reduction a top priority. White House officials rightly concluded that, if the deficit could be brought under control, interest rates would drop and the economy would rebound. And that is what happened. The budget deficit decreased (by 1997, it had been erased), which lowered interest rates, which boosted investment. Stock prices soared, and the gross national product rose by an average of 3.5 to 4 percent annually.

Globalization of Business   Clinton perceived early on that the technology revolution would shrink the world and make it more interconnected. He was convinced that, with the demise of Soviet communism, capitalism—or at least the introduction of market forces, freer trade, and deregulation—was spreading around the globe.

Globalization was not a new phenomenon—it had been under way for a century—but now it had unprecedented momentum. Journalist Thomas L. Friedman asserted that the post–Cold War world was "the age of globalization," characterized by the integration of markets, finance, and technologies. U.S. officials lowered trade and investment barriers, completing the North American Free Trade Agreement (NAFTA) with Canada and Mexico in 1993, and in 1994 concluding the Uruguay Round of the General Agreement on Tariffs and Trade (GATT), which lowered tariffs for the seventy member nations that accounted for about 80 percent of world trade. The administration also endorsed the 1995 creation of the World Trade Organization (WTO), to administer and enforce agreements made at the Uruguay Round. Finally, the president formed a National Economic Council to promote trade missions around the world.

Multinational corporations were the hallmark of this global economy. By 2000, there were 63,000 parent companies worldwide and 690,000 foreign affiliates. Some, such as Nike and Gap, Inc., subcontracted production of certain merchandise to whichever developing countries had the lowest labor costs. Such arrangements created a "new international division of labor" and generated a boom in world exports, which, at $5.4 trillion in 1998, had doubled in two decades. U.S. exports reached $680 billion in 1998, but imports rose even higher, to $907 billion (for a trade deficit of $227 billion). Sometimes the multinationals directly affected foreign policy, as when Clinton in 1995 extended full diplomatic recognition to Vietnam partly in response to pressure from such corporations as Coca-Cola, Citigroup, General Motors, and United Airlines, which wanted to enter that emerging market.

Critics of Globalization

While the administration promoted open markets, labor unions argued that free-trade agreements exacerbated the trade deficit and exported American jobs. Average real wages for American workers declined steadily after 1973, from $320 per week to $260 by the mid-1990s. Other critics maintained that globalization widened the gap between rich and poor countries, creating a mass of "slave laborers" in poor countries working under conditions that would never be tolerated in the West. Environmentalists charged that globalization also exported pollution to countries unprepared to deal with. Still other critics warned about the power of multinational corporations and the global financial markets over traditional cultures.

Antiglobalization fervor reached a peak in the fall of 1999, when thousands of protesters disrupted a WTO meeting in Seattle. In the months that followed, there were sizable protests at meetings of the International Monetary Fund (IMF), which controls international credit and exchange rates, and the World Bank, which issues funds for development projects in numerous countries. In July 2001, fifty thousand demonstrators protested an IMF and World Bank meeting in Genoa Italy.

Target: McDonald's

Activists also targeted corporations, such as the Gap, Starbucks, Nike, and, especially, McDonald's, which by 1995 was serving 30 million customers daily in twenty thousand franchises in over one hundred countries. Critics assailed the company's slaughterhouse techniques, alleged exploitation of workers, its high-fat menu, and its role in creating an increasingly homogeneous and sterile world culture. For six years starting in 1996, McDonald's endured hundreds of often-violent protests, including bombings in Rome, Prague, London, Macao, Rio de Janeiro, and Jakarta.

Others decried the violence and the underlying arguments of the antiglobalization campaigners. True, some economists acknowledged, statistics showed that global inequality had grown in recent years. But if one included quality-of-life measurements, such as literacy and health, global inequality had actually declined. Some studies found that wage and job losses for U.S. workers were caused not primarily by globalization factors, such as imports, production outsourcing, and immigration, but by technological change that made production more efficient.

Other researchers saw no evidence that governments' sovereignty had been seriously compromised or that there was a "race to the bottom" in environmental standards from globalization.

As for creating a homogeneous global culture, McDonald's, others said, tailored its menu and operating practices to local tastes. And although American movies, TV programs, music, computer software, and other "intellectual property" often dominated world markets, foreign competition also made itself felt in America. Millions of American children were gripped by the Japanese fad Pokemon, and satellite television established a worldwide following for European soccer teams. An influx of foreign players added to the international appeal of both the National Basketball Association and Major League Baseball, while in the National Hockey League some 20 percent of players by the late 1990s hailed from Europe.

The Bush-Gore Race   The strong economy seemingly put Vice President Al Gore in a strong position to win the 2000 presidential election. But Gore failed to inspire voters. Earnest and highly intelligent, with a sparkling resumé that included service in Vietnam and six terms in Congress, he appeared to many to be a well-informed policy wonk rather than a charismatic leader.

Gore's Republican opponent was best known nationally as the son of George H. W. Bush, the forty-first president of the United States. An indifferent student, George W. Bush had graduated from Yale in 1968 and pulled strings to jump ahead of a one-and-a-half-year waiting list for the Texas Air National Guard, thus avoiding service in Vietnam. After a difficult period, which included a rocky career in the oil business, Bush's fortunes improved while his father was president, and in 1994 he was elected to the first of two terms as governor of Texas.

The Contested Election of 2000   On election day, Al Gore narrowly won the popular vote. But he did not win the presidency. It all came down to Florida (where Bush's brother Jeb was governor) and its twenty-five electoral votes. According to the initial tally, Bush narrowly edged Gore out in Florida, but by so close a margin that a recount was legally required. Charges and countercharges flew. In several heavily African American counties, tens of thousands of votes were not counted because voters failed to fully dislodge the "chads," or small perforated squares, when punching the old-fashioned paper ballots. Lawyers struggled over whether "hanging chads" (partially detached) and "pregnant chads" (punched but not detached) were sufficient signs of voter intent. In Palm Beach County, many elderly Jewish residents were confused by a poorly designed ballot. Thinking they were selecting Gore, they voted instead for the allegedly anti-Semitic Pat Buchanan. After thirty-six days of confusion, with court cases at the state and federal levels, the Supreme Court voted 5 to 4 along narrowly partisan lines to end the recount process. Florida's electoral votes—and the presidency—went to George Bush. Struggles over the election outcome further polarized the nation, and as Bush waited for the January inaugural, critics and comics began referring to him as the "president select."

In view of the close election and bitter Florida controversy, many believed that Bush would govern from the center. Some also thought that he was philosophically centrist, as his father had been, and that he had moved to the right only to ensure turnout among conservative evangelical Christians, who made up an increasingly large part of the Republican base. From the administration's first days, however, Bush governed from the right, arguably further to the right than any administration of modern times. As the head of the Heritage Foundation, a conservative Washington think tank, enthused, the new team was "more Reaganite than the Reagan administration."

9/11 AND THE WAR IN IRAQ

In international affairs, the administration charted a unilateralist course. Given America's preponderant power, senior Bush officials reasoned, it did not need other countries' help. Accordingly, Bush withdrew the United States from the 1972 Anti-Ballistic Missile Treaty with Russia to develop a National Missile Defense system (forbidden under the treaty) broadly similar to Reagan's "Star Wars." The White House also renounced the 1997 Kyoto protocol on controlling global warming and opposed a carefully negotiated protocol to strengthen the 1972 Biological and Toxin Weapons Convention. These decisions and the administration's hands-off policy toward the Israeli-Palestinian peace process caused consternation in Europe.

9/11   Then came September 11. On that sunny Tuesday morning, nineteen hijackers seized control of four commercial jets departing from East Coast airports. At 8:46 A.M. one plane crashed into the 110-story North Tower of the World Trade Center in New York City. At 9:03 A.M., a second plane flew into the South Tower. In less than two hours, both buildings collapsed, killing thousands of office workers, firefighters, and police officers. At 9:43, the third plane crashed into the Pentagon, leaving a huge hole in its west side. The fourth plane was also headed toward Washington, but several passengers—learning of the World Trade Center attacks through cell-phone conversations—stormed the cockpit; in the ensuing scuffle, the plane crashed in Somerset County, Pennsylvania, killing all aboard.

More than three thousand people died, making this the deadliest act of terrorism in history. Not since the Japanese assault on Pearl Harbor in 1941 had the United States experienced such a devastating attack on its soil. The hijackers—fifteen Saudi Arabians, two Emiratis, one Lebanese, and, leading them, an Egyptian—had ties to Al Qaeda, Osama bin Laden's radical Islamic organization. Some officials in the Clinton and Bush administrations had warned that an Al Qaeda attack was inevitable, but neither administration made counterterrorism a foreign policy priority.

Afghanistan War   In an instant, counterterrorism was priority number one. President Bush responded quickly with large-scale military force. Al Qaeda operated out of Afghanistan with the blessing of the ruling Taliban, a repressive Islamic fundamentalist group that had gained power in 1996.

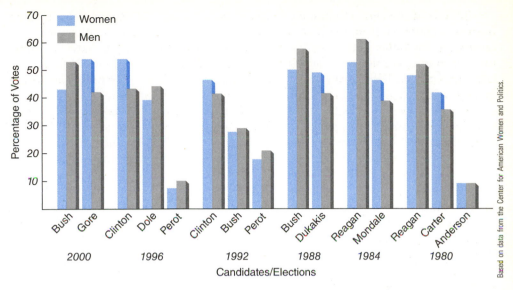

Based on data from the Center for American Women and Politics.

FIGURE 33.2 The Gender Gap in American Presidential Elections

The gender gap, or the difference in voting patterns between men and women, was first identified in 1980 by National Organization for Women president Eleanor Smeal and has been recognized as an important force in American politics ever since. In virtually every presidential election portrayed here, greater percentages of women (no matter their race or ethnicity, income, level of education, or marital status) than men voted for the Democratic candidate.

Source: Based on data from the Center for American Women and Politics.

In early October, the United States launched a sustained bombing campaign against Taliban and Al Qaeda positions, and sent special operations forces to help a resistance organization in northern Afghanistan. Within two months, the Taliban was driven from power, although bin Laden and top Taliban leaders eluded capture.

As administration officials acknowledged, the swift military victory did not end the terrorist threat. Bush spoke of a long struggle against evil forces, in which the nations of the world were either with the United States or against it. Some questioned whether a "war on terrorism" could ever be won in a meaningful sense, given that the foe was a nonstate actor weak in the traditional measures of power—territory and governmental power—and with little to lose. Most Americans, however, were ready to believe. Stunned by September 11, they experienced a renewed sense of national unity and pride. Flag sales soared, and Bush's approval ratings skyrocketed. Citizenship applications from immigrants rose dramatically.

PATRIOT Act   But the new patriotism had a dark side. Congress passed the USA PATRIOT Act (Uniting and Strengthening America by Providing Appropriate Tools Required to Intercept and Obstruct Terrorism), making it easier for law enforcement to conduct searches, wiretap telephones, and obtain electronic records on individuals. Attorney General John Ashcroft approved giving FBI agents new powers to monitor the Internet, mosques, and rallies. Civil libertarians charged that the Justice Department had overstepped, and some judges ruled against the tactics. Yet according to a June 2002 Gallup poll, 80 percent of Americans were willing to exchange some freedoms for security.

In surveys weeks after the attacks, 71 percent said that they felt depressed, and one-third had trouble sleeping. Yet people continued shopping in malls, visiting amusement parks, and working in skyscrapers. Although airline bookings dropped significantly in the early weeks (causing severe economic problems for many airlines), people still took to the skies. In Washington, the partisanship that had all but disappeared after 9/11 returned, as Democrats and Republicans sparred over judicial appointments, energy policy, and the proposed new Department of Homeland Security. Approved by Congress in November 2002, the department incorporated parts of eight cabinet departments and twenty-two agencies to coordinate intelligence and defense against terrorism.

Economic Uncertainty

Economically, the months before September 11 witnessed a collapse of the "dot-coms," Internet companies that were the darlings of Wall Street in the 1990s. In 2001, some five hundred dot-coms declared bankruptcy or closed. There were other economic warning signs as well, notably a meager 0.2 percent growth rate in goods and services for the second quarter of 2001—the slowest growth in eight years. Corporate revenues were also down.

Economic concerns deepened after 9/11 with a four-day closing of Wall Street and a subsequent sharp drop in stock prices. The week after the markets reopened, the Dow Jones Industrial Average plunged 14.26 percent—the fourth largest weekly drop in percentage terms since 1900. The markets eventually rebounded, but questions remained about the economy's overall health. Such was Bush's political strength after 9/11, however, that neither this economic uncertainty nor the failure to capture Osama bin Laden and top Taliban leaders dented his popularity. In the 2002 midterm elections, Republicans retook the Senate and increased their majority in the House.

International Responses

Overseas, the president's standing was not nearly so high. Immediately after September 11, there was an outpouring of support from people everywhere. "We are all Americans now," said the French newspaper Le Monde after the attacks. Moments of silence in honor of the victims were held in many countries, and governments worldwide announced they would work with Washington against terrorism. But within a year, attitudes changed dramatically. Bush's bellicose stance and good-versus-evil terminology had put off many foreign observers from the start, but they initially swallowed their objections. When the president hinted that America might unilaterally strike Saddam Hussein's Iraq or deal forcefully with North Korea or Iran—the three countries of Bush's "axis of evil"—many allied governments strongly objected.

At issue was not merely the prospect of an American attack on one of these countries but the underlying rationale that would accompany it. Bush and other top officials argued that in an age of terrorism, the United States would not wait for a potential security threat to become real; henceforth, it would strike first. Americans, Bush declared, had to be "ready for preemptive action when necessary to defend our liberty and to defend our lives." Critics, among them many world leaders, called it recklessly aggressive and contrary to international law, and they wondered what would happen if dictators around the world claimed the same right of preemption.

But Bush was determined, particularly on Iraq. Several of his top advisers, including Secretary of Defense Donald Rumsfeld and Vice President Dick Cheney, had wanted to oust Saddam Hussein for years, indeed since the end of the Gulf War in 1991. After the Twin Towers fell, they folded Iraq into the larger war on terrorism—even though counterterrorism experts saw no link between Saddam and Al Qaeda. For a time, Secretary of State Colin Powell, the first African American in that post, kept the focus on Afghanistan, but gradually the thinking in the White House shifted. In November 2001, Bush ordered the Pentagon to initiate war planning for Iraq; by spring 2002, a secret consensus was reached: Saddam Hussein would be removed by force.

Why Iraq?

In September 2002, Bush challenged the United Nations to enforce its resolutions against Iraq, or the United States would act on its own. In subsequent weeks, he and his aides offered shifting reasons for getting tough with Iraq. They said Saddam was a major threat to the United States and its allies, a leader who possessed and would use banned biological and chemical "weapons of mass destruction" (WMDs) and who sought to acquire nuclear weapons. They claimed, contrary to their own intelligence estimates, that he had ties to Al Qaeda and could be linked to the 9/11 attacks. They said that he brutalized his own people and generated regional instability with his tyrannous rule.

Beneath the surface lurked other motivations. Neocon-servatives saw in Iraq a chance to use U.S. power to reshape the region in America's image, to oppose tyranny and spread democracy. Ousting Saddam, they said, would enhance the security of Israel, America's key Middle East ally, and likely start a chain reaction that would extend democracy throughout the region. White House political strategists, meanwhile, believed a swift removal of a hated dictator would cement Republican domination in Washington and virtually assure Bush's reelection. Finally, Bush wanted to prevent an Iraq armed with WMDs from destabilizing an oil-rich region.

Congressional Approval

Like his father in 1991, Bush claimed he did not need congressional authorization for military action against Iraq; also like his father, he nevertheless sought it. In early October 2002, the House of Representatives voted 296 to 133 and the Senate 77 to 23 to authorize force against Iraq. Many who voted in favor were unwilling to defy a president so close to a midterm election, even though they opposed military action without U.N. sanction. Critics complained that the president had not presented evidence that Saddam Hussein constituted an imminent threat or was connected to the 9/11 attacks. Bush switched to a less hawkish stance, and in early November, the U.N. Security Council unanimously approved Resolution 1441, imposing rigorous new arms inspections on Iraq.

Behind the scenes, though, the Security Council was divided over the next move. In late January 2003, the weapons inspector's report castigated Iraq for failing to complete "the disarmament that was demanded of it" but also said it was too soon to tell whether inspections would succeed. Whereas U.S. and British officials said the time for diplomacy was up, France, Russia, and China called for more inspections. As the U.N. debate continued, and as massive antiwar demonstrations took place around the world, Bush sent about 250,000 soldiers to the region. Britain sent about 45,000 troops.

Fall of Baghdad   In late February, the United States floated a draft resolution to the U.N. that proposed issuing an ultimatum to Iraq, but only three of the fifteen Security Council members affirmed support. Bush abandoned the resolution and all further diplomatic efforts on March 17, when he ordered Saddam Hussein to leave Iraq within forty-eight hours or face an attack. Saddam ignored the ultimatum, and on March 19 the United States and Britain launched an aerial bombardment of Baghdad and other areas. A ground invasion followed (see Map 33.1). The Iraqis initially offered stiff resistance, but on April 9, Baghdad fell.

Thus, when violence and lawlessness soon erupted, American planners seemed powerless to respond. The plight of ordinary Iraqis deteriorated as the occupation authority proved unable to maintain order. In Baghdad, electricity worked only a few hours each day, and telephone service was nonexistent. Decisions by the Coalition Governing Council (CPA), headed by Ambassador Paul Bremer, made matters worse—notably Bremer's move in May to disband the Iraqi army, which left tens of thousands of men, angry and armed, out of work. A multisided insurgency of Saddam loyalists, Iraqi nationalists of various stripes, and foreign Islamic revolutionaries took shape; soon, U.S. occupying forces faced frequent ambushes and hit-and-run attacks. By October 2003, more troops had died from these attacks than had perished in the initial invasion.

The mounting chaos in Iraq and the failure to find weapons of mass destruction had critics questioning the war's validity. The much-derided sanctions and U.N. inspections, it was now clear, had in fact been successful in rendering Saddam a largely toothless tyrant, with a hollow military and no chemical or biological weapons. Prewar claims of a "rush to war" resounded again. Even defenders of the invasion castigated the administration for its failure to anticipate the occupation problems. In spring 2004, graphic photos showing Iraqi detainees being abused by American guards at Abu Ghraib prison were broadcast worldwide, generating international condemnation.

Election of 2004   President Bush, facing reelection that fall, expressed disgust at the Abu Ghraib images and fended off charges that he and his top aides knew of and condoned the abuse. The White House also made much of the dissolution of the CPA in late June and the transfer of sovereignty to an

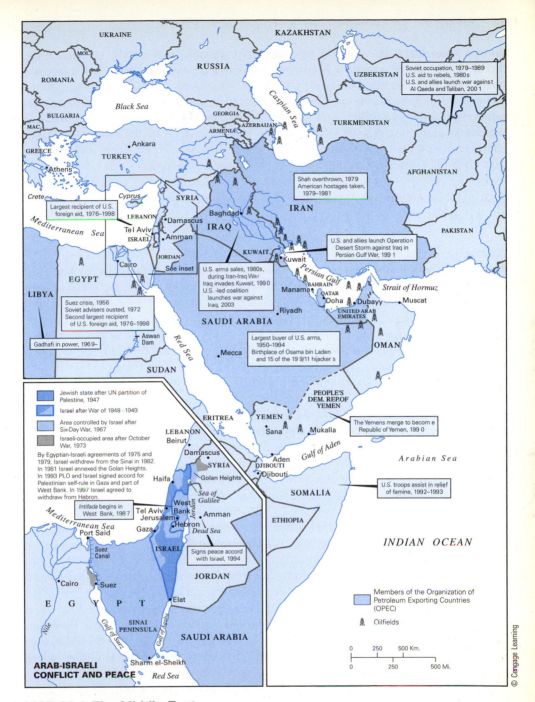

MAP 33.1 The Middle East

Extremely volatile and often at war, the nations of the Middle East maintained precarious relations with the United States. To protect its interests, the United States extended large amounts of economic and military aid, and sold huge quantities of weapons to the area. At times, Washington ordered U.S. troops to the region. The Arab-Israeli dispute particularly upended order, although the peace process moved forward intermittently.

interim Iraqi government—developments, it predicted, that would soon take the steam out of the insurgency. Many were skeptical, but voters that fall were prepared to give Bush the benefit of the doubt. His Democratic opponent, Senator John Kerry of Massachusetts, a Vietnam veteran who had reluctantly voted for the Iraq resolution in October 2001, had difficulty finding his campaign footing and never articulated a clear alternative strategy on the war. With the electorate deeply split, Bush won reelection with 51 percent of the popular vote to Kerry's 48 percent. The GOP also increased its majorities in the House and Senate.

America Isolated   Internationally, too, Bush faced criticism, not only on account of Iraq and Abu Ghraib, but also because of his administration's lack of engagement in the Israeli-Palestinian dispute and seeming disdain for diplomacy generally. The White House, critics said, rightly sought to prevent North Korea and Iran from joining the nuclear club but seemed incapable of working imaginatively and multilaterally to make it happen. In Europe, Bush continued to be depicted as a gun-slinging cowboy whose moralistic rhetoric and aggressive policies threatened world peace. According to a Pew survey in June 2006, the percentage of the public expressing confidence in Bush's leadership in international affairs had fallen to 30 in Britain, 25 in Germany, 15 in France, and 7 in Spain.

Iraq, though, remained the chief problem. The bill for the Iraq war now exceeded $1 billion per week. In March 2005, the American war dead reached 1,500; in December 2006, it reached 3,000. Meanwhile, estimates of Iraqi civilian deaths since the invasion ranged by mid-2006 from 60,000 to 655,000. These Iraqi casualties resulted from insurgent suicide attacks and U.S. bombing of suspected insurgent hideouts, as well as from increasing sectarian violence between Sunnis and Shi'ites.

The Bush administration denied that Iraq had degenerated into civil war or that the struggle had become a Vietnam-like quagmire, but it seemed uncertain about how to end the fighting. In Congress and the press, calls for withdrawal from Iraq multiplied, but skeptics cautioned it could make things worse, triggering sectarian bloodshed and a collapse of the Baghdad government. The power and regional influence of neighboring Iran would increase, and American credibility would be undermined throughout the Middle East. Some commentators instead called for an increase of U.S. forces in Iraq, and Bush heeded their advice. The "surge" of 2007 contributed to a drastic reduction in violence, as commanders shifted the focus to a counterinsurgency strategy emphasizing protection of the population. But the surge did not achieve meaningful results in its second goal: promoting political reconciliation among the competing factions in Iraq. That objective remained elusive when Bush left office in early 2009.

Domestic Politics in Post–9/11 America

While the Bush administration focused on what Bush had labeled "the global war on terrorism" (or GWOT), it also pursued domestic goals. The centerpiece of the Bush domestic agenda, achieved before the attacks of 9/11, was a $1.3 trillion tax cut—the largest in U.S. history. As Bush intended, this tax cut wiped out the $200 billion budget surplus he had inherited from the Clinton administration.

The Presidency of George W. Bush

Throughout his years as president, George W. Bush embraced conservative ideals, though sometimes in ways that seemed paradoxical. Much of his agenda fit smoothly with conservative principles. Religious conservatives were pleased by the newly prominent role of religion in the political process. The president spoke frequently of his faith; Bush's attorney general, John Ashcroft, a Pentecostal Christian who had stated, prior to his confirmation, that America had "no king but Jesus," held prayer meetings at 8 A.M. every morning in the Justice Department. And Bush appointed the medical director of a Christian pregnancy-counseling center whose website claimed that the "distribution of birth control is demeaning to women, degrading of human sexuality and adverse to human health and happiness" to head the nation's federal family planning program.

Bush was also a strong advocate of economic deregulation. His administration dismantled environmental restrictions on the oil, timber, and mining industries, and as Wall Street developed an incredible array of new and risky financial instruments, he maintained a full hands-off approach to regulation. While his plan to partially privatize the Social Security system failed, as did his efforts at comprehensive immigration reform, Bush did reshape the Supreme Court. Fifty-year-old conservative U.S. Circuit Court judge John Roberts was confirmed as chief justice following the death of Chief Justice William Renquist at age eighty, and another strong conservative, fifty-five-year-old Samuel Alito, became junior associate justice following the resignation of Sandra Day O'Connor, who had often voted with the more liberal faction of the court.

At the same time, Bush often turned to a form of "big government" conservatism. While Ronald Reagan had tried to abolish the federal Department of Education, Bush dramatically increased the federal government's role in public education through his "No Child Left Behind" initiative. Meant to fix a "broken system of education that dismisses certain children and classes of children as unteachable," the legislation linked federal funding to state action: in order to receive federal dollars for education, states were required to set "high standards" for all students, evaluating them through a series of standardized tests that would hold failing schools accountable. And while conservatives traditionally argued that the federal government was not responsible for the medical care of the nation's citizens, the Bush administration created an enormously expensive new entitlement program that covered prescription drugs for American seniors, regardless of income, under Medicare.

Hurricane Katrina

Although Bush won the presidential election in 2004, growing perceptions of administrative incompetence began to undermine the American people's confidence in the president and his administration. In late August 2005, a major hurricane hit the U.S. Gulf Coast and New Orleans. Hurricane Katrina destroyed the levees that kept low-lying parts of New Orleans from being swamped by water from Lake Pontchartrain and surrounding canals. Floodwater covered 80 percent of New Orleans, and more than eighteen hundred people died in the storm and the floods that followed.

Tens of thousands of people who lacked the resources to flee New Orleans sought shelter at the Superdome. Supplies of food and water quickly ran low, and toilets backed up; people wrapped the dead in blankets and waited for rescue. Those outside the Gulf region, watching the suffering crowd of mainly poor, black New Orleanians stranded at the Superdome, began a soul-searching conversation about what Democratic party leader Howard Dean called the "ugly truth": that poverty remains linked to race in this nation. Quickly, however, public attention shifted to charges of administrative mismanagement—at local, state, and federal levels—and to the seeming indifference of the president. "Nothing about the President's demeanor yesterday," concluded the New York Times shortly after the hurricane, "which seemed casual to the point of carelessness—suggested he understood the depth of the current crisis."

Economic Recession   But much larger troubles were brewing: American home prices—a huge "housing bubble"—were on the verge of collapse.
Following the beginnings of deregulation in the financial markets during the 1980s, financial institutions had sought new ways to expand their market and their profits. They began experimenting with "subprime" mortgages for people who, in previous years, would not have qualified for credit. For example, "NINA" loans went to home buyers with "No Income, No Assets." By 2006, one-fifth of all home loans were subprime. As more Americans bought homes, increased demand kept housing prices rising. In 2000, a median-priced house "cost" three full years of a (median-earning) family's income. At the height of the bubble in 2006, it cost 4.6 years of work. This was good news for lenders: because housing prices kept going up, they saw little risk. If a family defaulted on their mortgage and lost their house, the property could be sold for more—sometimes much more—than the mortgage was worth. Wall Street firms saw an opportunity for rapid short-term profit. They began buying up mortgages, bundling them together, good and bad, into multibillion dollar packages to sell to investors. These mortgage-backed securities were complex and difficult to value—but deregulation let large financial institutions get away with very risky practices.

This unstable structure began to fail in 2007, as more and more borrowers began to default on their mortgages. People tried to escape unaffordable mortgages by selling their houses, but housing prices dropped rapidly. Increasingly, mortgages were larger than the declining value of houses. And the huge financial institutions who had gambled on mortgage-backed securities did not have enough capital to sustain such losses. America's major financial institutions—indeed, key banks around the world—were on the verge of collapse.

The U.S. economy depends on the availability of credit—for business loans, car loans, home loans, credit cards. This crisis paralyzed the credit markets. Businesses couldn't get the loans they needed to buy raw materials or inventory; consumers couldn't get the credit they needed to buy large items, such as cars. And many Americans were already deeply in debt. They had taken out home equity loans against the rising value of their houses; they owed money on several credit cards. In 1981, families saved more than 10 percent of their post-tax income; in 2005, the average family spent more than it earned—and for those under thirty-five, the savings rate was minus 16 percent. As credit tightened, people bought less. Businesses began laying off workers, and the unemployment rate began to climb. Those who were unemployed or worried about their jobs spent less money, and the cycle continued. The Bush administration attempted to prevent the collapse of the financial system by bailing out some of America's largest banks and credit providers—those that were deemed "too big too fail." The Troubled Asset Relief Program (TARP) eventually provided $700 billion in loans to failing institutions, but as "main street" recovered more slowly than "Wall Street," many Americans were angry that tax dollars had gone to rescue wealthy bankers.

Election of 2008   The presidential election of 2008 was shaped by the growing worldwide economic crisis, as Americans worried about the economy and Bush's approval rating fell to 27 percent, but it was also the most dramatic contest in decades. The hard-fought Democratic primary pitted New York senator Hillary Clinton against Illinois senator Barack Obama, forcing Americans to confront the meaning of race and gender in American politics and society. Obama, who won the Democratic nomination, ran against John McCain, the senior senator from Arizona. McCain, an independent-minded and sometimes explosive Vietnam veteran who had survived five years in a P.O.W. camp, had a reputation for honesty and plain-spokenness, but he never drew enthusiastic support from the more socially conservative wing of the Republican Party. Obama, in contrast, mobilized the grassroots: young people, African Americans, people who had never voted before. More than any previous candidate, he used new technology to reach out to voters. People contributed millions of dollars through his web site, much of it in small amounts, and a home-made music video of "Obama Girl" singing about her crush on Obama went viral on YouTube early in the campaign.

McCain gained support from socially conservative Republicans when he named Alaska governor Sarah Palin as his running mate. Palin drew huge crowds, but appeared unprepared and largely ignorant of key national and international issues. Comedienne Tina Fey adopted Palin's own words (and garbled syntax) to create popular Saturday Night Live parodies, and critics, charging that McCain had chosen Palin simply to gain a short-term political advantage, argued that McCain had shown a failure of judgment that could be disastrous in the presidency. But the economy was the deciding factor in the 2008 election. McCain's claim, in the midst of Wall Street's meltdown in September 2008, that "the fundamentals of our economy are strong" backfired. Americans found Obama's calm and deliberate presence a better bet for dealing with the economic crisis, and gave him victory in November.

Barack Obama   Barack Hussein Obama, the nation's forty-fourth president, was born in Hawai'i in 1961. His mother was a young white woman from Kansas, his father a Kenyan graduate student at the University of Hawai'i. (The couple divorced when their child was two years old and each married again, giving Barack both African and Indonesian half-siblings.) Obama spent part of his childhood in Indonesia with his mother, attended high school in Hawai'i, and moved to the U.S. mainland for college. After graduating from

© Bettmann/Corbis

More than 75,000 people gathered in Chicago's Grant Park to celebrate Barack Obama's election on November 4, 2008.

Harvard Law School, where he served as president of the Harvard Law Review, Obama moved to Chicago, the city in which he had worked as a community organizer. There he met and married fellow Harvard Law graduate Michelle Robinson and worked as a civil rights lawyer and as a law professor at the University of Chicago before entering state politics in 1997. Obama caught the nation's attention when he delivered the keynote speech at the 2004 Democratic national convention; within three years, as a first-term senator, he was running for the presidency.

Obama was an inspirational speaker who offered messages of "hope" and "change." Supporters were passionate about him, expecting in some cases that he would almost miraculously solve the nation's problems and bring bipartisan harmony to a deeply divided Congress. Obama began his presidency with big ideas and ambitious goals. He vowed to pass a comprehensive healthcare reform bill within the year, but he also had to confront his inheritance: two unresolved wars, a massive federal deficit, and a major recession that threatened to spin into a global meltdown. In February 2009, Obama signed legislation creating a $787 billion economic stimulus package in an attempt to jumpstart the economy, and supported expanding TARP and bailing out auto giants GM and Chrysler, which were both on the verge of failing. The economy began a slow recovery in 2009, but unemployment rates remained high. In late 2009, the official employment rate (counting only those who actively sought work in the past four weeks) was 10.2 percent, but 17.5 percent of those who wished to work were either jobless or underemployed. One in eight Americans received food stamps from the government, and Walmart pointed to evidence of hard times: a big jump in the purchase of kitchen storage containers for leftovers.

Fierce partisan bickering continued in Washington, stalling progress on healthcare reform and job creation. Some commentators saw the gridlock as proof that the United States had become ungovernable, its leaders unable to adequately address long-term social and economic challenges; others countered that the system was designed by the Founders to function in precisely this way—slowly and cautiously. Although Congress did finally pass a healthcare bill in March 2010, not a single Republican in the House of Representatives voted for it.

In foreign affairs, Obama had more latitude, as presidents typically do. In Iraq, U.S. casualty figures continued to decline in 2009, and Obama stuck to a timeline for withdrawal that would have all combat forces out of the country by August 2010. In Afghanistan, however, the worsening security situation moved American policy in the opposite direction. Following lengthy deliberation in the fall of 2009, Obama announced that he would boost U.S. troop numbers in Afghanistan by about 30,000, bringing the total to 100,000. To allay concerns that an eight-year-old war would stretch on indefinitely, the president simultaneously declared that the United States would begin withdrawing its forces in 2011. Critics were unmoved, questioning the strategic logic of the escalation and calling Afghanistan "Obama's War."

AMERICANS IN THE FIRST DECADE OF THE NEW MILLENNIUM

At the beginning of the twenty-first century, the United States is a nation of extraordinary diversity. For much of the twentieth century, however, it had seemed that the United States was moving in the opposite direction. Very few immigrants had been allowed into the United States from the 1920s through 1965. New technologies, such as radio and television, had a homogenizing effect at first, for these mass media were dependent on reaching the broadest possible audience—a mass market. Although local and ethnic traditions persisted, more and more Americans participated in a shared mass culture. During the last third of the twentieth century, however, those homogenizing trends were reversed. Immigration reform in the mid-1960s opened American borders to large numbers of people from a wider variety of nations than ever before. New technologies—the Internet, and cable and satellite television, with their proliferation of channels—replaced mass markets with niche markets. Everything from television shows to cosmetics to cars could be targeted toward specific groups defined by age, ethnicity, class, gender, or lifestyle choices. These changes did not simply make American society more fragmented. Instead, they helped to make Americans' understandings of identity more fluid and more complex.

Race and Ethnicity in Recent America   In the 2000 U.S. government census, for the first time Americans were allowed to identify themselves as belonging to more than one race. New census categories recognized that notions of biological "race" were problematic. Why could a white woman bear a "black" child when a black woman could not bear a white child? The change also acknowledged the growing number of Americans born to parents of different racial backgrounds, as American mixed-race and mixed-ethnicity marriages grew from less than 1 percent in 1970 to 8 percent in 2008. Critics, however, worried that, because census data are used to gather information about social conditions in the United States and as a basis for allocating resources, the new "multiracial" option would reduce the visibility and clout of minority groups. Thus the federal government counted those who identified both as white and as members of a racial or ethnic minority as belonging to the minority group. Under this system, the official population of some groups increased: more Americans than ever before, for example, identified themselves as at least partly Native American. Others rejected racial and ethnic categories altogether: 20 million people identified themselves simply as "American," up more than 50 percent since 1990.

On October 17, 2006, the United States officially passed the 300 million population mark (it hit 100 million in 1915 and 200 million in 1967), and its people were more diverse than at any time in the past. During the 1990s, the population of people of color grew twelve times as fast as the white population, fueled by both immigration and birth rates. In 2003, Latinos moved past African Americans to become the second largest ethnic or racial group in the nation (after non-Hispanic whites), making the United States the fifth largest "Latino" country in

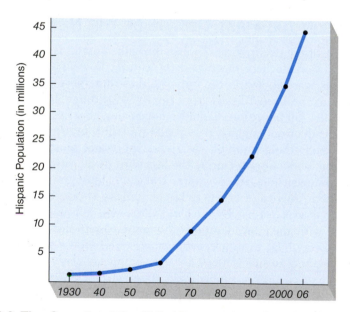

FIGURE 33.3 The Growth of the U.S. Hispanic Population

"Hispanic" combines people from a wide variety of national origins or ancestries—including all the nations of Central and South America, Mexico, Cuba, Puerto Rico, the Dominican Republic, Spain—as well as those who identify as Californio, Tejano, Nuevo Mexicano, and Mestizo.

Source: Adapted from the U.S. Department of Commerce, Economics and Statistics Information, Bureau of the Census, 1993 report "We, the American ... Hispanics"; also recent Census Bureau figures for the Hispanic population.

world (see Figure 33.3). Immigration from Asia also remained high, and in 2007, 5 percent of the U.S. population was Asian or Asian American. Most of this immigration is legal, but in 2005 an estimated 11.1 million people were in the United States without official documentation, up from 3 million in 1980. Undocumented workers made up almost 5 percent of the U.S. labor force in 2005, including 20 percent of computer hardware engineers and almost 30 percent of roofers and agricultural workers.

These rapid demographic changes have altered the face of America. At a Dairy Queen in the far southern suburbs of Atlanta, 6 miles from the Gone with the Wind Historical District, teenage children of immigrants from India and Pakistan serve Blizzards and Brownie Earthquakes. In the small town of Ligonier, Indiana, the formerly empty main street now boasts three Mexican restaurants and a Mexican western-wear shop; Mexican immigrants drawn in the 1990s by plentiful industrial jobs cross paths with the newest immigrants, Yemenis, some in traditional dress, and with Amish families in horse-drawn buggies.

Although many of America's schools and neighborhoods remain racially segregated and public debates about the consequences of illegal immigration are heated, American popular culture has embraced the influences of this new multiethnic population. Economics were important: the buying power of the growing Latino population exceeded $798 billion in 2006, and average income for Asian American households topped that for all other groups. But American audiences also crossed racial and ethnic lines as, for example, African American rap and hip-hop attracted large followings of white young men.

The Changing American Family

Americans were divided over the meaning of other changes as well—especially the changing shape of American families. The median age at marriage continued to rise, reaching 28.1 for men and 25.9 for women in 2009 (for women who pursued graduate degrees, the median age at first marriage was almost thirty). The number of people living together without marriage also increased. In 2006, when households composed of married couples slipped below 50 percent for the first time, unmarried, opposite-sex partners made up about 5 percent of households, and same-sex couples accounted for slightly less than 1 percent. One-third of female-partner households and one-fifth of male-partner households had children, and in 2002 the American Academy of Pediatrics endorsed adoption by gay couples. A vocal antigay movement coexisted with rising support for the legal equality of gay, lesbian, transgendered, and bisexual Americans. Although the federal Defense of Marriage Act, passed by Congress in 1996, defined marriage as "only" a union between one man and one woman, many states and private corporations extend domestic partner benefits to gay couples, and same-sex marriages are legally performed in several states.

The birth rate to unmarried women increased significantly in the early twenty-first century, rising to four of every ten babies in 2007. (In Sweden, the rate was 55 percent; in Japan, 2 percent.) In the majority of married-couple families with children under eighteen, both parents held jobs. Although almost one-third of families with children had only one parent present—usually the mother—children also lived in blended

LINKS TO THE WORLD

The "Swine Flu" Pandemic

When United flight 803 from Washington, D.C., landed at Tokyo's Narita airport on May 20, 2009, Japanese health officials boarded the plane. Garbed in respirator masks, goggles, and disposable scrubs, they used thermal scanners to check passengers for elevated temperatures. Passengers waited anxiously as officials interviewed each person on board, aware that, if any symptoms or suspicious travel patterns were discovered, the entire plane might be quarantined. Japan had already closed its borders to all travelers from Mexico, where the H1N1 "swine flu" virus had emerged about three weeks earlier. Mexico took extraordinary actions, closing schools and businesses and drawing on public health expertise from around the world. Nevertheless the H1N1 virus had, by mid-May, already spread to more than twenty-two countries. It was much too late to stem the spread of swine flu by isolating travelers from its country of origin.

Soon after a series of deaths in Mexico in late April, the World Health Organization had raised its alert level to stage 5, signaling that officials expected the virus to create the first major flu pandemic in more than forty years. Articles in the world media reminded readers of the flu pandemic of 1918 while emphasizing how much had changed. International air travel had brought the world into much closer contact. Health analysts made clear that the "right" pathogen, if it emerged in

the "right" place, might spread throughout the world in the space of a day, well before anyone was conscious of the threat it posed.

On the other hand, global connections also offered new tools to combat pandemics: global surveillance of disease, though not equally well-developed or dependable in all countries, might head off developing health threats. Individual nations and global organizations pool expertise as they develop vaccines and techniques to cope with pandemics, should one emerge. Because of lessons learned during the 2003 SARS outbreak, Hong Kong provided a model to the rest of the world with its plans for the prevention and management of major outbreaks of infectious disease. Finally, some believe that a global culture where borders present little barrier may facilitate the growth of global immunities to infectious diseases.

People around the world were relieved when the swine flu, after the initial deaths in Mexico, turned out to be no more deadly than a usual flu season. In previous years, SARS (severe, acute respiratory syndrome) and the H5N1 "bird flu" had also failed to develop into major worldwide heath threats. But the World Health Organization and the U.S. Center for Disease Control cautioned that the emergence of a major pandemic was simply a matter of time. "We live in one world, with one health," observed a UN official. In the era of

---

families created by second marriages or moved back and forth between households of parents who had joint custody. Based on current statistical analysis, for couples who married in the mid-1990s the woman's level of education was the clearest predictor of divorce: if the woman graduated from a four-year college, the couple had a 25 percent likelihood of divorce; if she had not, the rate jumped to 50 percent.

globalization, diseases do not stop at borders or respect wealth and power, and the links between Americans and the rest of the world's peoples cannot be denied.

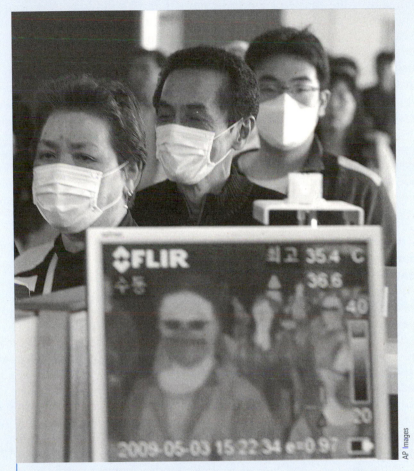

As the H1N1 virus—"swine flu"—spread rapidly in the spring of 2009, nations around the world attempted to prevent the spread of infection. Here, thermal cameras check the body temperatures of passengers arriving at Incheon International Airport in South Korea.

In 2006, the leading edge of the baby-boom generation turned 60; the median age of the American population was 36.7 in 2008, up from 29.5 in 1967. Although baby boomers are not aging in the same manner as their parents and grandparents—"Sixty is the new forty," the saying goes—the large and growing proportion of older people will have a major impact on American society. As life expectancy increases, the growing number of elderly Americans will put enormous pressure on the nation's healthcare system and family structure—who will care for people when they can no longer live independently?—and strain the Social Security and Medicare systems.

Other health issues have become increasingly important as well. In a rapid change over the course of a decade, more than two-thirds of American adults are now overweight or obese—conditions linked to hypertension, cardiovascular disease, and diabetes. In 1995, no state had an adult obesity rate that hit 20 percent. By 2009, only Colorado fell below that 20 percent mark, and Louisiana, Mississippi, West Virginia, and Tennessee topped 30 percent. Childhood obesity rates are worse, exceeding 30 percent in twenty-nine states, with Mississippi rapidly approaching 50 percent. On the other hand, cigarette smoking continues a slow but steady decline. Slightly less than one-fifth of American adults smoked in 2008, down from about one-third of adults in 1980 and from 42 percent in 1965. Approximately 440,000 people die each year from illness caused by smoking, and medical costs and lost productivity total about $157 billion a year. With clearer understanding of the danger of second-hand smoke, local governments have increasingly banned smoking in public spaces, including restaurants and bars.

Medicine, Science, and Religion   As scientists and medical researchers continue to struggle to find cures for devastating diseases like cancer and AIDS, rapid advances in the field of biogenetics offer great new possibilities and, for many Americans, raise ethical or philosophical conundrums. During in vitro fertilizations—in which sperm and egg combine in a sterile dish and the fertilized egg or eggs are then transferred to the uterus—five- or six-cell blastocytes are formed by the initial division of fertilized eggs. These blastocytes contain stem cells, unspecialized cells that can be induced to become cells with specialized functions. For example, stem cells might become insulin-producing cells of the pancreas, and thus a cure for diabetes; or they might become dopamine-producing neurons, offering therapy for Parkinson's disease, a progressive disorder of the nervous system affecting over 1 million Americans. President Bush in 2001 called embryonic stem cell research "the leading edge of a series of moral hazards," because extracting stem cells destroys the blastocyte's "potential for life," and limited federally funded research to the existing seventy-eight stem cell lines, the majority of which turned out not to be viable for research. However, the majority of Americans support stem cell research, believing (along with Nancy Reagan, whose husband and former U.S. president Ronald Reagan suffered from Alzheimer's disease) that the moral good of curing diseases that devastate the lives of many men, women, and children outweighs the moral good of preserving the potential life of blastocytes. In early 2009, President Obama signed an executive order ending the Bush restrictions, a move that signaled a significant shift in approach to scientific issues.

At the same time, many Americans see a fundamental conflict between religious belief and scientific study. Fundamentalist Christians have struggled to prevent the teaching of evolution in the nation's science classes or to introduce parallel instruction of biblical "creationism" or theories of "intelligent design," which hold that an intelligent creator lies behind the development of life on earth. The percentage of Americans who accept the scientific evidence for evolution is lower than that in any other major nation in the world, with the sole exception of Turkey.

Century of Change

The twentieth century had seen more momentous change than any previous century—change that brought enormous benefits to human beings, change that threatened the very existence of the human species. Research in the physical and biological sciences had provided insight into the structure of matter and of the universe. Technology—the application of science—had made startling advances that benefited Americans in nearly every aspect of life: better health, more wealth, more mobility, less drudgery, greater access to information.

Through these advances, Americans at the start of the new century were more connected to the rest of humankind than ever before. This interconnection was perhaps the most powerful product of globalization. A commodities trader in Chicago in February 2010 could send a text message to her fiancé in Tokyo while she spoke on the phone to a trader in Frankfurt and emailed another one in Bombay, and kept one eye on NBC's live coverage of the Winter Olympics; within a minute or two, she could receive a reply from her fiancé saying that he missed her, too. If she felt sufficiently lovesick, she could board an airplane and be in Japan the following day.

The world had shrunk to the size of an airplane ticket. In 1955, 51 million people a year traveled by plane. By the turn of the century, 1.6 billion were airborne every year, and 530 million—or about 1.5 million each day—crossed international borders. This permeability of national boundaries brought many benefits, as did the integration of markets and the global spread of information that occurred alongside it.

Globalization and World Health

But there was a flip side to this growing connectivity, which even advocates of globalization perceived. The rapid increase in international air travel was a particularly potent force for the dissemination of global disease, as flying made it possible for people to reach the other side of the world in far less time than the incubation period for many ailments. Environmental degradation also created major global health threats. In 2003, the World Health Organization (WHO) estimated that nearly one-quarter of the global burden of disease and injury was related to environmental disruption and decline. For example, some 90 percent of diarrheal diseases (such as cholera), which were killing 3 million people a year, resulted from contaminated water. WHO also pointed to globalization and environmental disruption as contributing to the fact that, in the final two decades of the twentieth century, more than thirty infectious diseases were identified in humans for the first time—including AIDS, Ebola virus, hantavirus, and hepatitis C and E. Environmentalists, meanwhile, insisted that the growing interaction of national economies was having a deleterious impact on the ecosystem through climate change, ozone depletion, hazardous waste, and damage to fisheries.

Confronting Terrorism In military and diplomatic terms, though, 9/11 made a deep and lasting impression. The attacks that day brought home what Americans had only dimly perceived before then: that globalization had shrunk the natural buffers that distance and two oceans provided the United States. Al Qaeda, it was clear, had used the increasingly open, integrated, globalized world to give itself new power and reach. It had shown that small cells of terrorists could become true transnational threats—thriving around the world without any single state sponsor or home base. According to American intelligence, Al Qaeda operated in more than ninety countries—including the United States.

How would one go about vanquishing such a foe? Was a decisive victory even possible? These remained open questions nine years after the World Trade Center collapsed. Unchallenged militarily and seeing no rival great power, the United States felt few constraints about intervening in Afghanistan and then Iraq, but the problems in both countries showed that it could take scant comfort from this superiority. It continued to spend colossal sums on its military, more indeed than the rest of the world combined. (Including the supplemental appropriations for Iraq and Afghanistan, the Pentagon in 2010 spent more than $680 billion, or roughly $77 million per hour.) America had taken on military commitments all over the globe, from the Balkans and Iraq to Afghanistan and Korea. Its armed forces looked colossal, but its obligations looked even larger.

SUMMARY

The 1990s were, for most Americans, good times. A digitized revolution in communications and information—as fundamental as the revolution brought about by electricity and the combustion engine a century earlier, or the steam engine a century before that—was generating prosperity and transforming life in America and around the globe. The longest economic expansion in American history—from 1991 to 2001—meant that most Americans who wanted jobs had them, that the stock market boomed, that the nation had a budget surplus instead of a deficit, and that more Americans than ever before owned their own homes. And America was not only prosperous; it was powerful. With the Soviet Union gone and no other formidable rival on the horizon, the United States stood as the world's lone superpower, its economic and military power daunting to friend and foe alike.

Although America seemed at the apex of power and prosperity, unsettling events troubled the nation, abroad and at home. Just minutes before midnight on December 31, 1999, President Clinton called on the American people not to fear the future, but to "welcome it, create it, and embrace it." The challenges of the future would be greater than Americans imagined as they welcomed the new millennium that night. In 2000, the contested presidential election was decided by the Supreme Court in a partisan 5-to-4 vote; in 2001 the ten-year economic expansion came to an end.

Then, on September 11 of that year, radical Islamic terrorists attacked the World Trade Center and the Pentagon, killing thousands and altering many aspects of American life. The new president, George W. Bush, declared a "war on terrorism," one with both foreign and domestic components. While U.S. air and ground forces went after targets in Afghanistan, Congress moved to create the Department of

Homeland Security and passed the PATRIOT Act, expanding the federal government's powers of surveillance. In March 2003, Bush took the nation into war in Iraq, not expecting the full-blown insurgency that followed. Bush won reelection in 2004, but his fortunes soon waned. The combination of two costly wars abroad and a severe economic crisis at home paved the way for Barack Obama's historic election in 2008.

The world that Americans found in the first decade of the twenty-first century was much different from the one they had looked forward to with confidence and high hopes as they celebrated the coming of the new millennium on New Year's Eve 1999. The horror of the terror attacks of September 11, 2001, shook America to its core. Then came two lengthy and inconclusive wars, to be followed in turn by the most severe economic downturn since the Great Depression. By decade's end, Americans were deeply divided over how to respond to the nation's problems. To some, the obstacles seemed impossibly daunting. Yet the American people had faced difficult times before in their history; each time, they had proved their resilience and weathered the storm. As a new decade dawned, Americans continued to struggle over foreign and domestic policy priorities, over the direction of their nation, with the passion and commitment that keeps democracy alive.

Appendix A: The Declaration of Independence

THE UNANIMOUS DECLARATION OF THE THIRTEEN UNITED STATES OF AMERICA

When in the Course of human events it becomes necessary for one people to dissolve the political bands which have connected them with another, and to assume among the Powers of the earth, the separate and equal station to which the Laws of Nature and of Nature's God entitle them, a decent respect to the opinions of mankind requires that they should declare the causes which impel them to the separation.

We hold these truths to be self-evident, that all men are created equal, that they are endowed by their Creator with certain unalienable Rights, that among these are Life, Liberty and the pursuit of Happiness. That to secure these rights, Governments are instituted among Men, deriving their just Powers from the consent of the governed. That whenever any Form of Government becomes destructive of these ends, it is the Right of the People to alter or to abolish it, and to institute new Government, laying its foundation on such principles and organizing its Powers in such form, as to them shall seem most likely to effect their Safety and Happiness. Prudence, indeed, will dictate that Governments long established should not be changed for light and transient causes; and accordingly all experience hath shewn, that mankind are more disposed to suffer, while evils are sufferable, than to right themselves by abolishing the forms to which they are accustomed. But when a long train of abuses and usurpations, pursuing invariably the same Object evinces a design to reduce them under absolute Despotism, it is their right, it is their duty, to throw off such Government, and to provide new Guards for their future security. Such has been the patient sufferance of these Colonies; and such is now the necessity which constrains them to alter their former Systems of Government. The history of the present King of Great Britain is a history of repeated injuries and usurpations, all having in direct object the establishment of an absolute Tyranny over these States. To prove this, let Facts be submitted to a candid world.

He has refused his Assent to Laws, the most wholesome and necessary for the public good.

He has forbidden his Governors to pass Laws of immediate and pressing importance, unless suspended in their operation till his Assent should be obtained; and when so suspended, he has utterly neglected to attend to them.

Text is reprinted from the facsimile of the engrossed copy in the National Archives. The original spelling, capitalization, and punctuation have been retained. Paragraphing has been added.

He has refused to pass other Laws for the accommodation of large districts of people, unless those people would relinquish the right of Representation in the Legislature, a right inestimable to them and formidable to tyrants only.

He has called together legislative bodies at places unusual, uncomfortable, and distant from the depository of their Public Records, for the sole Purpose of fatiguing them into compliance with his measures.

He has dissolved Representative Houses repeatedly, for opposing with manly firmness his invasions on the rights of the People.

He has refused for a long time, after such dissolutions, to cause others to be elected; whereby the Legislative Powers, incapable of Annihilation, have returned to the People at large for their exercise; the State remaining in the mean time exposed to all the dangers of invasion from without, and convulsions within.

He has endeavoured to prevent the Population of these States; for that purpose obstructing the Laws for Naturalization of Foreigners; refusing to pass others to encourage their migrations hither, and raising the conditions of new Appropriations of Lands.

He has obstructed the Administration of Justice, by refusing his Assent to Laws for establishing Judiciary Powers.

He has made Judges dependent on his Will alone, for the tenure of their offices, and the amount and payment of their salaries.

He has erected a multitude of New Offices, and sent hither swarms of Officers to harass our People, and eat out their substance.

He has kept among us, in times of peace, Standing Armies without the Consent of our legislatures.

He has affected to render the Military independent of and superior to the Civil Power.

He has combined with others to subject us to a jurisdiction foreign to our constitution, and unacknowledged by our laws; giving his Assent to their Acts of pretended Legislation:

For Quartering large bodies of armed troops among us:

For protecting them, by a mock Trial, from Punishment for any Murders which they should commit on the Inhabitants of these States:

For cutting off our Trade with all parts of the world:

For imposing Taxes on us without our Consent:

For depriving us in many cases, of the benefits of Trial by Jury:

For transporting us beyond Seas to be tried for pretended offences:

For abolishing the free System of English Laws in a neighbouring Province, establishing therein an Arbitrary government, and enlarging its Boundaries so as to render it at once an example and fit instrument for introducing the same absolute rule into these Colonies:

For taking away our Charters, abolishing our most valuable Laws, and altering fundamentally the Forms of our Governments:

For suspending our own Legislatures, and declaring themselves invested with Power to legislate for us in all cases whatsoever.

He has abdicated Government here, by declaring us out of his Protection, and waging War against us.

He has plundered our seas, ravaged our Coasts, burnt our towns, and destroyed the lives of our people.

He is at this time transporting large Armies of foreign Mercenaries to compleat the works of death, desolation and tyranny, already begun with circumstances of Cruelty and perfidy scarcely paralleled in the most barbarous ages, and totally unworthy the Head of a civilized nation.

He has constrained our fellow Citizens taken Captive on the high Seas to bear Arms against their Country, to become the executioners of their friends and Brethren, or to fall themselves by their Hands.

He has excited domestic insurrections amongst us, and has endeavoured to bring on the inhabitants of our frontiers, the merciless Indian Savages, whose known rule of warfare, is an undistinguished destruction of all ages, sexes and conditions.

In every stage of these Oppressions We have Petitioned for Redress in the most humble terms: Our repeated Petitions have been answered only by repeated injury. A Prince, whose character is thus marked by every act which may define a Tyrant, is unfit to be the ruler of a free People.

Nor have We been wanting in attentions to our British brethren. We have warned them from time to time of attempts by their legislature to extend an unwarrantable jurisdiction over us. We have reminded them of the circumstances of our emigration and settlement here. We have appealed to their native justice and magnanimity, and we have conjured them by the ties of our common kindred to disavow the usurpations, which, would inevitably interrupt our connections and correspondence. They too have been deaf to the voice of justice and of consanguinity. We must, therefore, acquiesce in the necessity, which denounces our Separation, and hold them, as we hold the rest of mankind, Enemies in War, in Peace Friends.

We, therefore, the Representatives of the United States of America, in General Congress, Assembled, appealing to the Supreme Judge of the world for the rectitude of our intentions, do, in the Name, and by Authority of the good People of these Colonies, solemnly publish and declare, That these United Colonies are, and of Right ought to be Free and Independent States; that they are Absolved from all Allegiance to the British Crown, and that all political connection between them and the State of Great Britain, is and ought to be totally dissolved; and that, as Free and Independent States, they have full Power to levy War, conclude Peace, contract Alliances, establish Commerce, and to do all other Acts and Things which Independent States may of right do. And for the support of this Declaration, with a firm reliance on the protection of divine Providence, we mutually pledge to each other our Lives, our Fortunes and our sacred Honor.

Appendix B: The Constitution of the United States of America

We the People of the United States, in Order to form a more perfect Union, establish Justice, insure domestic Tranquility, provide for the common defence, promote the general Welfare, and secure the Blessings of Liberty to ourselves and our Posterity, do ordain and establish this Constitution for the United States of America.

ARTICLE I

Section 1 All legislative Powers herein granted shall be vested in a Congress of the United States, which shall consist of a Senate and House of Representatives.

Section 2 The House of Representatives shall be composed of Members chosen every second Year by the People of the several States, and the Electors in each State shall have the Qualifications requisite for Electors of the most numerous Branch of the State Legislature.

No Person shall be a Representative who shall not have attained to the Age of twenty five Years, and been seven Years a Citizen of the United States, and who shall not, when elected, be an Inhabitant of that State in which he shall be chosen.

Representatives and direct Taxes[1] shall be apportioned among the several States which may be included within this Union, according to their respective Numbers, which shall be determined by adding to the whole Number of free Persons, including those bound to Service for a Term of Years, and excluding Indians not taxed, three fifths of all other Persons.[2] The actual Enumeration shall be made within three Years after the first Meeting of the Congress of the United States, and within every subsequent Term of ten Years, in such Manner as they shall by Law direct. The Number of Representatives shall not exceed one for every thirty Thousand, but each State shall have at Least one Representative; and until such enumeration shall be made, the State of New Hampshire shall be entitled to chuse three; Massachusetts eight; Rhode Island and Providence Plantations one; Connecticut five; New York six; New Jersey four; Pennsylvania eight; Delaware one; Maryland six; Virginia ten; North Carolina five; South Carolina five; and Georgia three.

When vacancies happen in the Representation from any State, the Executive Authority thereof shall issue Writs of Election to fill such Vacancies.

The House of Representatives shall chuse their Speaker and other Officers; and shall have the sole Power of Impeachment.

Text is from the engrossed copy in the National Archives. Original spelling, capitalization, and punctuation have been retained.

Section 3   The Senate of the United States shall be composed of two Senators from each State, chosen by the Legislature thereof, for six Years; and each Senator shall have one Vote.[3]

Immediately after they shall be assembled in Consequence of the first Election, they shall be divided as equally as may be into three Classes. The Seats of the Senators of the first Class shall be vacated at the Expiration of the second Year, of the second Class at the Expiration of the fourth Year, and of the third Class at the Expiration of the sixth Year, so that one third may be chosen every second Year; and if Vacancies happen by Resignation, or otherwise, during the Recess of the Legislature of any State, the Executive thereof may make temporary Appointments until the next Meeting of the Legislature, which shall then fill such Vacancies.[4]

No Person shall be a Senator who shall not have attained to the Age of thirty Years, and been nine Years a Citizen of the United States, and who shall not, when elected, be an Inhabitant of that State for which he shall be chosen.

The Vice President of the United States shall be President of the Senate, but shall have no Vote, unless they be equally divided.

The Senate shall chuse their other Officers, and also a President pro tempore, in the Absence of the Vice President, or when he shall exercise the Office of President of the United States.

The Senate shall have the sole Power to try all Impeachments. When sitting for that Purpose, they shall be on Oath or Affirmation. When the President of the United States is tried, the Chief Justice shall preside: And no Person shall be convicted without the Concurrence of two thirds of the Members present.

Judgment in Cases of Impeachment shall not extend further than to removal from Office, and disqualification to hold and enjoy any Office of honor, Trust or Profit under the United States: but the Party convicted shall nevertheless be liable and subject to Indictment, Trial, Judgment and Punishment, according to Law.

Section 4   The Times, Places and Manner of holding Elections for Senators and Representatives, shall be prescribed in each State by the Legislature thereof, but the Congress may at any time by Law make or alter such Regulation, except as to the Places of chusing Senators.

The Congress shall assemble at least once in every Year, and such Meeting shall be on the first Monday in December, unless they shall by Law appoint a different Day.[5]

Section 5   Each House shall be the Judge of the Elections, Returns and Qualifications of its own Members, and a Majority of each shall constitute a Quorum to do Business; but a smaller Number may adjourn from day to day, and may be authorized to compel the Attendance of absent Members, in such Manner, and under such Penalties as each House may provide.

Each House may determine the Rules of its Proceedings, punish its Members for disorderly Behaviour, and, with the Concurrence of two thirds, expel a Member.

Each House shall keep a Journal of its Proceedings, and from time to time publish the same, excepting such Parts as may in their Judgment require Secrecy; and the Yeas and Nays of the Members of either House on any question shall, at the Desire of one fifth of those Present, be entered on the Journal.

Neither House, during the Session of Congress, shall, without the Consent of the other, adjourn for more than three days, nor to any other Place than that in which the two Houses shall be sitting.

Section 6   The Senators and Representatives shall receive a Compensation for their Services, to be ascertained by Law, and paid out of the Treasury of the United States. They shall in all Cases, except Treason, Felony and Breach of the Peace, be privileged from Arrest during their Attendance at the Session of their respective Houses, and in going to and returning from the same; and for any Speech or Debate in either House, they shall not be questioned in any other Place.

No Senator or Representative shall, during the Time for which he was elected, be appointed to any civil Office under the Authority of the United States, which shall have been created, or the Emoluments whereof shall have been encreased during such time; and no Person holding any Office under the United States, shall be a Member of either House during his Continuance in Office.

Section 7   All Bills for raising Revenue shall originate in the House of Representatives; but the Senate may propose or concur with Amendments as on other Bills.

Every Bill which shall have passed the House of Representatives and the Senate shall, before it become a Law, be presented to the President of the United States; If he approve he shall sign it, but if not he shall return it, with his Objections to that House in which it shall have originated, who shall enter the Objections at large on their Journal, and proceed to reconsider it. If after such Reconsideration two thirds of that House shall agree to pass the Bill, it shall be sent, together with the Objections, to the other House, by which it shall likewise be reconsidered, and if approved by two thirds of that House, it shall become a Law. But in all such Cases the Votes of both Houses shall be determined by yeas and Nays, and the Names of the Persons voting for and against the Bill shall be entered on the Journal of each House respectively. If any Bill shall not be returned by the President within ten Days (Sundays excepted) after it shall have been presented to him, the Same shall be a Law, in like Manner as if he had signed it, unless the Congress by their Adjournment prevent its Return, in which Case it shall not be a Law.

Every Order, Resolution, or Vote to which the Concurrence of the Senate and House of Representatives may be necessary (except on a question of Adjournment) shall be presented to the President of the United States; and before the Same shall take Effect, shall be approved by him, or being disapproved by him shall be repassed by two thirds of the Senate and House of Representatives, according to the Rules and Limitations prescribed in the Case of a Bill.

Section 8   The Congress shall have power To lay and collect Taxes, Duties, Imposts and Excises, to pay the Debts and provide for the common Defence and general Welfare of the United States; but all Duties, Imposts and Excises shall be uniform throughout the United States;

To borrow Money on the credit of the United States;

To regulate Commerce with foreign Nations, and among the several States, and with the Indian Tribes;

To establish an uniform Rule of Naturalization, and uniform Laws on the subject of Bankruptcies throughout the United States;

To coin Money, regulate the Value thereof, and of foreign Coin, and fix the Standard of Weights and Measures;

To provide for the Punishment of counterfeiting the Securities and current Coin of the United States;

To establish Post Offices and post Roads;

To promote the Progress of Science and useful Arts, by securing for limited Times to Authors and Inventors the exclusive Right to their respective Writings and Discoveries;

To constitute Tribunals inferior to the supreme Court;

To define and punish Piracies and Felonies committed on the high Seas, and Offences against the Law of Nations;

To declare War, grant Letters of Marque and Reprisal, and make Rules concerning Captures on Land and Water;

To raise and support Armies, but no Appropriation of Money to that Use shall be for a longer Term than two Years;

To provide and maintain a Navy;

To make Rules for the Government and Regulation of the land and naval Forces;

To provide for calling forth the Militia to execute the Laws of the Union, suppress Insurrections and repel Invasions;

To provide for organizing, arming, and disciplining, the Militia, and for governing such Part of them as may be employed in the Service of the United States, reserving to the States respectively, the Appointment of the Officers, and the Authority of training the Militia according to the discipline prescribed by Congress;

To exercise exclusive Legislation in all Cases whatsoever, over such District (not exceeding ten Miles square) as may, by Cession of particular States, and the Acceptance of Congress, become the Seat of the Government of the United States, and to exercise like Authority over all Places purchased by the Consent of the Legislature of the State in which the Same shall be, for the Erection of Forts, Magazines, Arsenals, dock-Yards, and other needful Buildings;—And

To make all Laws which shall be necessary and proper for carrying into Execution the foregoing Powers, and all other Powers vested by this Constitution in the Government of the United States, or in any Department or Officer thereof.

Section 9   The Migration or Importation of such Persons as any of the States now existing shall think proper to admit, shall not be prohibited by the Congress prior to the Year one thousand eight hundred and eight, but a Tax or duty may be imposed on such Importation, not exceeding ten dollars for each Person.

The Privilege of the Writ of Habeas Corpus shall not be suspended, unless when in Cases of Rebellion or Invasion the public Safety may require it.

No Bill of Attainder or ex post facto Law shall be passed.

No Capitation, or other direct, Tax shall be laid, unless in Proportion to the Census or Enumeration herein before directed to be taken.

No Tax or Duty shall be laid on Articles exported from any State.

No Preference shall be given by any Regulation of Commerce or Revenue to the Ports of one State over those of another: nor shall Vessels bound to, or from, one State, be obliged to enter, clear, or pay Duties in another.

No Money shall be drawn from the Treasury, but in Consequence of Appropriations made by Law, and a regular Statement and Account of the Receipts and Expenditures of all public Money shall be published from time to time.

No Title of Nobility shall be granted by the United States: And no Person holding any Office of Profit or Trust under them, shall, without the Consent of the Congress, accept of any present, Emolument, Office, or Title, of any kind whatever, from any King, Prince, or foreign State.

Section 10   No State shall enter into any Treaty, Alliance, or Confederation; grant Letters of Marque and Reprisal; coin Money; emit Bills of Credit; make any Thing but gold and silver Coin a Tender in Payment of Debts; pass any Bill of Attainder, ex post facto Law, or Law impairing the Obligation of Contracts, or grant any Title of Nobility.

No State shall, without the Consent of the Congress, lay any Imposts or Duties on Imports or Exports, except what may be absolutely necessary for executing its inspection Laws: and the net Produce of all Duties and Imposts, laid by any State on Imports or Exports, shall be for the Use of the Treasury of the United States; and all such Laws shall be subject to the Revision and Controul of the Congress.

No State shall, without the Consent of Congress, lay any Duty of Tonnage, keep Troops, or Ships of War in time of Peace, enter into any Agreement or Compact with another State, or with a foreign Power, or engage in War, unless actually invaded, or in such imminent Danger as will not admit of delay.

ARTICLE II

Section 1   The executive Power shall be vested in a President of the United States of America. He shall hold his Office during the Term of four Years, and, together with the Vice President, chosen for the same Term, be elected, as follows:

Each State shall appoint, in such Manner as the Legislature thereof may direct, a Number of Electors, equal to the whole Number of Senators and Representatives to which the State may be entitled in the Congress: but no Senator or Representative, or Person holding an Office of Trust or Profit under the United States, shall be appointed an Elector.

The Electors shall meet in their respective States, and vote by Ballot for two Persons, of whom one at least shall not be an Inhabitant of the same State with themselves. And they shall make a List of all the Persons voted for, and of the Number of Votes for each; which List they shall sign and certify, and transmit sealed to the Seat of the Government of the United States, directed to the President of the Senate. The President of the Senate shall, in the Presence of the Senate and House of Representatives, open all the Certificates, and the Votes shall then be counted. The Person having the greatest Number of Votes shall be the President, if such Number be a Majority of the whole Number of Electors appointed; and if there be more than one who have such Majority, and have an equal Number of Votes, then the House of Representatives shall immediately chuse by Ballot one of them for President; and if no Person have a Majority, then from the five highest on the List the said House shall in like Manner chuse the President. But in chusing the President, the Votes shall be taken by States, the Representation from each State having one Vote; A quorum for this Purpose shall consist of a Member or Members from two thirds of the States, and a Majority of all the States shall be necessary to a Choice. In every Case, after the Choice of the President, the Person having the greatest Number of Votes of the Electors shall be the Vice President. But if there should remain two or more who have equal Votes, the Senate shall chuse from them by Ballot the Vice President.[6]

The Congress may determine the Time of chusing the Electors, and the Day on which they shall give their Votes; which Day shall be the same throughout the United States.

No Person except a natural born Citizen, or a Citizen of the United States, at the time of the Adoption of this Constitution, shall be eligible to the Office of President, neither shall any Person be eligible to that Office who shall not have attained to the Age of thirty five Years, and been fourteen Years a Resident within the United States.

In Case of the Removal of the President from Office, or of his Death, Resignation, or Inability to discharge the Powers and Duties of the said Office, the Same shall devolve on the Vice President, and the Congress may by Law provide for the Case of Removal, Death, Resignation or Inability, both of the President and Vice President, declaring what Officer shall then act as President, and such Officer shall act accordingly, until the Disability be removed, or a President shall be elected.[7]

The President shall, at stated Times, receive for his Services, a Compensation, which shall neither be encreased nor diminished during the Period for which he shall have been elected, and he shall not receive within that Period any other Emolument from the United States, or any of them.

Before he enter on the Execution of his Office, he shall take the following Oath or Affirmation:—"I do solemnly swear (or affirm) that I will faithfully execute the Office of President of the United States, and will to the best of my Ability, preserve, protect and defend the Constitution of the United States."

Section 2   The President shall be Commander in Chief of the Army and Navy of the United States, and of the Militia of the several States, when called into the actual Service of the United States; he may require the Opinion, in writing, of the principal Officer in each of the executive Departments, upon any Subject relating to the Duties of their respective Offices, and he shall have Power to grant Reprieves and Pardons for Offences against the United States, except in Cases of Impeachment.

He shall have Power, by and with the Advice and Consent of the Senate, to make Treaties, provided two thirds of the Senators present concur; and he shall nominate, and by and with the Advice and Consent of the Senate, shall appoint

Ambassadors, other public Ministers and Consuls, Judges of the supreme Court, and all other Officers of the United States, whose Appointments are not herein otherwise provided for, and which shall be established by Law; but the Congress may by Law vest the Appointment of such inferior Officers, as they think proper, in the President alone, in the Courts of Law, or in the Heads of Departments.

The President shall have Power to fill up all Vacancies that may happen during the Recess of the Senate, by granting Commissions which shall expire at the End of their next Session.

Section 3   He shall from time to time give the Congress Information of the State of the Union, and recommend to their Consideration such Measures as he shall judge necessary and expedient; he may, on extraordinary Occasions, convene both Houses, or either of them, and in Case of Disagreement between them, with Respect to the Time of Adjournment, he may adjourn them to such Time as he shall think proper; he shall receive Ambassadors and other public Ministers; he shall take Care that the Laws be faithfully executed, and shall Commission all the Officers of the United States.

Section 4   The President, Vice President and all civil Officers of the United States, shall be removed from Office on Impeachment for, and Conviction of, Treason, Bribery, or other high Crimes and Misdemeanors.

ARTICLE III

Section 1   The judicial Power of the United States, shall be vested in one supreme Court, and in such inferior Courts as the Congress may from time to time ordain and establish. The Judges, both of the supreme and inferior Courts, shall hold their Offices during good Behaviour, and shall, at stated Times, receive for their Services, a Compensation, which shall not be diminished during their Continuance in Office.

Section 2   The judicial Power shall extend to all Cases, in Law and Equity, arising under this Constitution, the Laws of the United States, and Treaties made, or which shall be made, under their Authority;—to all Cases affecting Ambassadors, other public Ministers and Consuls;—to all Cases of admiralty and maritime Jurisdiction;—to Controversies to which the United States shall be a Party;—to Controversies between two or more States;—between a State and Citizens of another State;[8]—between Citizens of different States,—between Citizens of the same State claiming Lands under Grants of different States, and between a State, or the Citizens thereof, and foreign States, Citizens or Subjects.

In all Cases affecting Ambassadors, other public Ministers and Consuls, and those in which a State shall be Party, the supreme Court shall have original Jurisdiction. In all the other Cases before mentioned, the supreme Court shall have appellate Jurisdiction, both as to Law and Fact, with such Exceptions, and under such Regulations as the Congress shall make.

The Trial of all Crimes, except in Cases of Impeachment, shall be by Jury; and such Trial shall be held in the State where the said Crimes shall have been committed; but when not committed within any State, the Trial shall be at such Place or Places as the Congress may by Law have directed.

Section 3   Treason against the United States, shall consist only in levying War against them, or in adhering to their Enemies, giving them Aid and Comfort. No Person shall be convicted of Treason unless on the Testimony of two Witnesses to the same overt Act, or on Confession in open Court.

The Congress shall have Power to declare the Punishment of Treason, but no Attainder of Treason shall work Corruption of Blood, or Forfeiture except during the Life of the Person attainted.

ARTICLE IV

Section 1   Full Faith and Credit shall be given in each State to the public Acts, Records, and judicial Proceedings of every other State. And the Congress may by general Laws prescribe the Manner in which such Acts, Records and Proceedings shall be proved, and the Effect thereof.

Section 2   The Citizens of each State shall be entitled to all Privileges and Immunities of Citizens in the several States.

A Person charged in any State with Treason, Felony, or other Crime, who shall flee from Justice, and be found in another State, shall on Demand of the executive Authority of the State from which he fled, be delivered up, to be removed to the State having Jurisdiction of the Crime.

No Person held to Service or Labour in one State, under the Laws thereof, escaping into another, shall, in Consequence of any Law or Regulation therein, be discharged from such Service or Labour, but shall be delivered up on Claim of the Party to whom such Service or Labour may be due.

Section 3   New States may be admitted by the Congress into this Union; but no new State shall be formed or erected within the Jurisdiction of any other State, nor any State be formed by the Junction of two or more States, or Parts of States, without the Consent of the Legislatures of the States concerned as well as of the Congress.

The Congress shall have Power to dispose of and make all needful Rules and Regulations respecting the Territory or other Property belonging to the United States; and nothing in this Constitution shall be so construed as to Prejudice any Claims of the United States, or of any particular State.

Section 4   The United States shall guarantee to every State in this Union a Republican Form of Government, and shall protect each of them against Invasion; and on Application of the Legislature, or of the Executive (when the Legislature cannot be convened) against domestic Violence.

ARTICLE V

The Congress, whenever two thirds of both Houses shall deem it necessary, shall propose Amendments to this Constitution, or, on the Application of the Legislatures of two thirds of the several States, shall call a Convention for proposing Amendments, which, in either Case, shall be valid to all Intents and Purposes, as Part of this Constitution, when ratified by the Legislatures of three fourths of the several States, or by Conventions in three fourths thereof, as the one or the other Mode of Ratification may be proposed by the Congress; Provided that no Amendment which may be made prior to the Year One thousand eight hundred and eight shall in any Manner affect the first and fourth Clauses in the Ninth Section of the first Article; and that no State, without its Consent, shall be deprived of its equal Suffrage in the Senate.

ARTICLE VI

All Debts contracted and Engagements entered into, before the Adoption of this Constitution, shall be as valid against the United States under this Constitution, as under the Confederation.

This Constitution, and the Laws of the United States which shall be made in Pursuance thereof; and all Treaties made, or which shall be made, under the Authority of the United States, shall be the supreme Law of the Land; and the Judges in every State shall be bound thereby, any Thing in the Constitution or Laws of any State to the Contrary notwithstanding.

The Senators and Representatives before mentioned, and the Members of the several State Legislatures, and all executive and judicial Officers, both of the United States and of the several States, shall be bound by Oath or Affirmation, to support this Constitution; but no religious Test shall ever be required as a Qualification to any Office or public Trust under the United States.

ARTICLE VII

The Ratification of the Conventions of nine States, shall be sufficient for the Establishment of this Constitution between the States so ratifying the Same.

Done in Convention by the Unanimous Consent of the States present the Seventeenth Day of September in the Year of our Lord one thousand seven hundred and Eighty seven and of the Independence of the United States of America the Twelfth. In witness whereof We have hereunto subscribed our Names,

Articles in Addition to, and Amendment of, the Constitution of the United States of America, Proposed by Congress, and Ratified by the Legislatures of the Several States, Pursuant to the Fifth Article of the Original Constitution.

AMENDMENT I[9]

Congress shall make no law respecting an establishment of religion, or prohibiting the free exercise there-of; or abridging the freedom of speech, or of the press; or the right of the people peaceably to assemble, and to petition the Government for a redress of grievances.

AMENDMENT II

A well regulated Militia, being necessary to the security of a free State, the right of the people to keep and bear Arms shall not be infringed.

AMENDMENT III

No Soldier shall, in time of peace, be quartered in any house, without the consent of the Owner, nor in time of war, but in a manner to be prescribed by law.

AMENDMENT IV

The right of the people to be secure in their persons, houses, papers, and effects, against unreasonable searches and seizures, shall not be violated, and no Warrants shall issue, but upon probable cause, supported by Oath or affirmation, and particularly describing the place to be searched, and the persons or things to be seized.

AMENDMENT V

No person shall be held to answer for a capital or otherwise infamous crime, unless on a presentment or indictment of a Grand Jury, except in cases arising in the land or naval forces, or in the Militia, when in actual service in time of War or public danger; nor shall any person be subject for the same offence to be twice put in jeopardy of life or limb; nor shall be compelled in any criminal case to be a witness against himself, nor be deprived of life, liberty, or property, without due process of law; nor shall private property be taken for public use, without just compensation.

AMENDMENT VI

In all criminal prosecutions, the accused shall enjoy the right to a speedy and public trial, by an impartial jury of the State and district wherein the crime shall have been committed, which district shall have been previously ascertained by law, and to be informed of the nature and cause of the accusation; to be confronted with the witnesses against him; to have compulsory process for obtaining witnesses in his favor, and to have the Assistance of Counsel for his defence.

AMENDMENT VII

In suits at common law, where the value in controversy shall exceed twenty dollars, the right of trial by jury shall be preserved, and no fact tried by a jury, shall be otherwise reexamined in any Court of the United States, than according to the rules of the common law.

AMENDMENT VIII

Excessive bail shall not be required, nor excessive fines imposed, nor cruel and unusual punishments inflicted.

AMENDMENT IX

The enumeration in the Constitution, of certain rights, shall not be construed to deny or disparage others retained by the people.

AMENDMENT X

The powers not delegated to the United States by the Constitution; nor prohibited by it to the States, are reserved to the States respectively, or to the people.

AMENDMENT XI[10]

The Judicial power of the United States shall not be construed to extend to any suit in law or equity, commenced or prosecuted against one of the United States by Citizens of another State, or by Citizens or Subjects of any Foreign State.

AMENDMENT XII[11]

The Electors shall meet in their respective States and vote by ballot for President and Vice-President, one of whom, at least, shall not be an inhabitant of the same State with themselves; they shall name in their ballots the person voted for as President, and in distinct ballots the person voted for as Vice-President, and they shall make distinct lists of all persons voted for as President, and of all persons voted for as Vice-President, and of the number of votes for each, which lists they shall sign and certify, and transmit sealed to the seat of the government of the United States, directed to the President of the Senate;—The President of the Senate shall, in the presence of the Senate and House of Representatives, open all the certificates and the votes shall then be counted;—The person having the greatest number of votes for President, shall be the President, if such number be a majority of the whole number of Electors appointed; and if no person have such majority, then from the persons having the highest numbers not exceeding three on the list of those voted for as President, the House of Representatives shall choose immediately, by ballot, the President. But in choosing the President, the votes shall be taken by states, the representation from each state having one vote; a quorum for this purpose shall consist of a member or members from two-thirds of the states, and a majority of all the states shall be necessary to a choice. And if the House of Representatives shall not choose a President whenever the right of choice shall devolve upon them, before the fourth day of March next following, then the Vice-President shall act as President, as in the case of the death or other constitutional disability of the President.—The person having the greatest number of votes as Vice-President, shall be the Vice-President, if such number be a majority of the whole number of Electors appointed, and if no person have a majority, then from the two highest numbers on the list, the Senate shall choose the Vice-President; a quorum for the purpose shall consist of two-thirds of the whole number of Senators, and a majority of the whole number shall be necessary to a choice. But no person constitutionally ineligible to the office of President shall be eligible to that of Vice-President of the United States.

AMENDMENT XIII[12]

Section 1   Neither slavery nor involuntary servitude, except as a punishment for crime whereof the party shall have been duly convicted, shall exist within the United States, or any place subject to their jurisdiction.

Section 2   Congress shall have power to enforce this article by appropriate legislation.

AMENDMENT XIV[13]

Section 1   All persons born or naturalized in the United States, and subject to the jurisdiction thereof, are citizens of the United States and of the State wherein they reside. No State shall make or enforce any law which shall abridge the privileges or immunities of citizens of the United States; nor shall any State deprive any person of life, liberty, or property, without due process of law; nor deny to any person within its jurisdiction the equal protection of the laws.

Section 2   Representatives shall be apportioned among the several States according to their respective numbers, counting the whole number of persons in each State, excluding Indians not taxed. But when the right to vote at any election for the choice of electors for President and Vice-President of the United States, Representatives in Congress, the Executive and Judicial officers of a State, or the members of the Legislature thereof, is denied to any of the male inhabitants of such State, being twenty-one years of age, and citizens of the United States, or in any way abridged, except for participation in rebellion, or other crime, the basis of representation therein shall be reduced in the proportion which the number of such male citizens shall bear to the whole number of male citizens twenty-one years of age in such State.

Section 3   No person shall be a Senator or Representative in Congress, or elector of President and Vice-President, or hold any office, civil or military, under the United States, or under any State, who, having previously taken an oath, as a member of Congress, or as an officer of the United States, or as a member of any State legislature, or as an executive or judicial officer of any State, to support the Constitution of the United States, shall have engaged in insurrection or rebellion against the same, or given aid or comfort to the enemies thereof. But Congress may by a vote of two-thirds of each House, remove such disability.

Section 4   The validity of the public debt of the United States, authorized by law, including debts incurred for payment of pensions and bounties for services in suppressing insurrection or rebellion, shall not be questioned. But neither the United States nor any State shall assume or pay any debt or obligation incurred in aid of insurrection or rebellion against the United States, or any claim for the loss or emancipation of any slave; but all such debts, obligations, and claims shall be held illegal and void.

Section 5 The Congress shall have the power to enforce, by appropriate legislation, the provisions of this article.

AMENDMENT XV[14]

Section 1 The right of citizens of the United States to vote shall not be denied or abridged by the United States or by any State on account of race, color, or previous conditions of servitude—

Section 2 The Congress shall have power to enforce this article by appropriate legislation.

AMENDMENT XVI[15]

The Congress shall have power to lay and collect taxes on incomes, from whatever source derived, without apportionment among the several States, and without regard to any census or enumeration.

AMENDMENT XVII[16]

The Senate of the United States shall be composed of two Senators from each State, elected by the people thereof, for six years; and each Senator shall have one vote. The electors in each State shall have the qualifications requisite for electors of the most numerous branch of the State legislatures.

When vacancies happen in the representation of any State in the Senate, the executive authority of such State shall issue writs of election to fill such vacancies: *Provided,* That the legislature of any State may empower the executive thereof to make temporary appointments until the people fill the vacancies by election as the legislature may direct.

This amendment shall not be so construed as to affect the election or term of any Senator chosen before it becomes valid as part of the Constitution.

AMENDMENT XVIII[17]

Section 1 After one year from the ratification of this article the manufacture, sale, or transportation of intoxicating liquors within, the importation thereof into, or the exportation thereof from the United States and all territory subject to the jurisdiction thereof for beverage purposes is hereby prohibited.

Section 2 The Congress and the several States shall have concurrent power to enforce this article by appropriate legislation.

Section 3 This article shall be inoperative unless it shall have been ratified as an amendment to the Constitution by the legislatures of the several States, as provided in the Constitution, within seven years from the date of the submission hereof to the States by the Congress.

AMENDMENT XIX[18]

Section 1   The right of citizens of the United States to vote shall not be denied or abridged by the United States or by any State on account of sex.

Congress shall have power to enforce this article by appropriate legislation.

AMENDMENT XX[19]

Section 1   The terms of the President and Vice-President shall end at noon on the 20th day of January, and the terms of Senators and Representatives at noon on the 3rd day of January, of the years in which such terms would have ended if this article had not been ratified; and the terms of their successors shall then begin.

Section 2   The Congress shall assemble at least once in every year, and such meeting shall begin at noon on the 3rd day of January, unless they shall by law appoint a different day.

Section 3   If, at the time fixed for the beginning of the term of the President, the President elect shall have died, the Vice-President elect shall become President. If a President shall not have been chosen before the time fixed for the beginning of his term, or if the President elect shall have failed to qualify, then the Vice-President elect shall act as President until a President shall have qualified; and the Congress may by law provide for the case wherein neither a President elect nor a Vice-President elect shall have qualified, declaring who shall then act as President, or the manner in which one who is to act shall be selected, and such person shall act accordingly until a President or Vice-President shall have qualified.

Section 4   The Congress may by law provide for the case of the death of any of the persons from whom the House of Representatives may choose a President whenever the right of choice shall have devolved upon them, and for the case of the death of any of the persons from whom the Senate may choose a Vice-President whenever the right of choice shall have devolved upon them.

Section 5   Sections 1 and 2 shall take effect on the 15th day of October following the ratification of this article.

Section 6   This article shall be inoperative unless it shall have been ratified as an amendment to the Constitution by the legislatures of three-fourths of the several States within seven years from the date of its submission.

AMENDMENT XXI[20]

Section 1   The eighteenth article of amendment to the Constitution of the United States is hereby repealed.

Section 2   The transportation or importation into any State, Territory, or possession of the United States for delivery or use therein of intoxicating liquors, in violation of the laws thereof, is hereby prohibited.

Section 3   This article shall be inoperative unless it shall have been ratified as an amendment to the Constitution by conventions in the several States, as provided in the Constitution, within seven years from the date of the submission hereof to the States by the Congress.

AMENDMENT XXII[21]

No person shall be elected to the office of the President more than twice, and no person who has held the office of President, or acted as President, for more than two years of a term to which some other person was elected President shall be electesd to the office of the President more than once.

But this Article shall not apply to any person holding the office of President when this Article was proposed by the Congress, and shall not prevent any person who may be holding the office of President, or acting as President, during the term within which this Article becomes operative from holding the office of President or acting as President during the remainder of such term.

AMENDMENT XXIII[22]

Section 1   The District constituting the seat of Government of the United States shall appoint in such manner as the Congress may direct:

A number of electors of President and Vice President equal to the whole number of Senators and Representatives in Congress to which the District would be entitled if it were a State, but in no event more than the least populous State; they shall be in addition to those appointed by the States, but they shall be considered, for the purposes of the election of President and Vice President, to be electors appointed by the State; and they shall meet in the District and perform such duties as provided by the twelfth article of amendment.

Section 2   The Congress shall have power to enforce this article by appropriate legislation.

AMENDMENT XXIV[23]

Section 1   The right of citizens of the United States to vote in any primary or other election for President or Vice President, or for Senator or Representative in Congress, shall not be denied or abridged by the United States or any State by reason of failure to pay any poll tax or other tax.

Section 2   The Congress shall have power to enforce this article by appropriate legislation.

Amendment XXV[24]

Section 1   In case of the removal of the President from office or of his death or resignation, the Vice President shall become President.

Section 2   Whenever there is a vacancy in the office of the Vice President, the President shall nominate a Vice President who shall take office upon confirmation by a majority vote of both Houses of Congress.

Section 3   Whenever the President transmits to the President pro tempore of the Senate and the Speaker of the House of Representatives his written declaration that he is unable to discharge the powers and duties of his office, and until he transmits them a written declaration to the contrary, such powers and duties shall be discharged by the Vice President as Acting President.

Section 4   Whenever the Vice President and a majority of either the principal officers of the executive department or of such other body as Congress may by law provide, transmit to the President pro tempore of the Senate and the Speaker of the House of Representatives their written declaration that the President is unable to discharge the powers and duties of his office, the Vice President shall immediately assume the powers and duties of the office of Acting President

Thereafter, when the President transmits to the President pro tempore of the Senate and the Speaker of the House of Representatives his written declaration that no inability exists, he shall resume the powers and duties of his office unless the Vice President and a majority of either the principal officers of the executive department or of such other body as Congress may by law provide, transmit within four days to the President pro tempore of the Senate and the Speaker of the House of Representatives their written declaration that the President is unable to discharge the powers and duties of his office. Thereupon Congress shall decide the issue, assembling within forty-eight hours for that purpose if not in session. If the Congress, within twenty-one days after receipt of the latter written declaration, or, if Congress is not in session, within twenty-one days after Congress is required to assemble, determines by two-thirds vote of both Houses that the President is unable to discharge the powers and duties of his office, the Vice-President shall continue to discharge the same as Acting President; otherwise, the President shall resume the powers and duties of his office.

Amendment XXVI[25]

Section 1   The right of citizens of the United States, who are eighteen years of age or older, to vote shall not be denied or abridged by the United States or by any State on account of age.

Section 2   The Congress shall have power to enforce this article by appropriate legislation.

AMENDMENT XXVII[26]

No law, varying the compensation for the service of the Senators and Representatives, shall take effect, until an election of Representatives shall have intervened.

NOTES

1. Modified by the Sixteenth Amendment.
2. Replaced by the Fourteenth Amendment.
3. Superseded by the Seventeenth Amendment.
4. Modified by the Seventeenth Amendment.
5. Superseded by the Twentieth Amendment.
6. Superseded by the Twelfth Amendment.
7. Modified by the Twenty-fifth Amendment.
8. Modified by the Eleventh Amendment.
9. The first ten amendments were passed by Congress September 25, 1789. They were ratified by three-fourths of the states December 15, 1791.
10. Passed March 4, 1794. Ratified January 23, 1795.
11. Passed December 9, 1803. Ratified June 15, 1804.
12. Passed January 31, 1865. Ratified December 6, 1865.
13. Passed June 13, 1866. Ratified July 9, 1868.
14. Passed February 26, 1869. Ratified February 2, 1870.
15. Passed July 12, 1909. Ratified February 3, 1913.
16. Passed May 13, 1912. Ratified April 8, 1913.
17. Passed December 18, 1917. Ratified January 16, 1919.
18. Passed June 4, 1919. Ratified August 18, 1920.
19. Passed March 2, 1932. Ratified January 23, 1933.
20. Passed February 20, 1933. Ratified December 5, 1933.
21. Passed March 12, 1947. Ratified March 1, 1951.
22. Passed June 16, 1960. Ratified April 3, 1961.
23. Passed August 27, 1962. Ratified January 23, 1964.
24. Passed July 6, 1965. Ratified February 11, 1967.
25. Passed March 23, 1971. Ratified July 5, 1971.
26. Passed September 25, 1789. Ratified May 7, 1992.

Index